BIOFEEDBACK
and SELF-CONTROL
1975/76

EDITORS

BIOFEEDBACK
and SELF-CONTROL
1975/76

*an Aldine Annual on the
regulation of bodily processes
and consciousness*

ALDINE PUBLISHING COMPANY
Chicago

First published 1976 by
Aldine Publishing Company
529 South Wabash Avenue
Chicago, Illinois 60605

ISBN 0-202-25110-1 clothbound edition
Library of Congress Catalog Number 74-151109

Printed in the United States of America

CONTENTS

Preface   xi
Introduction. Self-Control: Temperature Biofeedback,
Hypnosis, Yoga, and Relaxation   xiii

I. GENERAL ARTICLES AND OVERVIEWS

1. *A Cognitively Oriented Psychologist Looks at Biofeedback*
   RICHARD S. LAZARUS   3
2. *Biofeedback, Self-Regulation, and the Patterning of*
   Physiological Processes
   GARY E. SCHWARTZ   12
3. *Biological Awareness as a State of Consciousness*
   BARBARA B. BROWN   34

II. MEDITATION AND YOGA

4. *Psychophysiological Correlates of Meditation*
   ROBERT L. WOOLFOLK   51
5. *Biofeedback and Meditation in the Treatment of Psychiatric*
   Illnesses
   BERNARD C. GLUECK AND CHARLES F. STROEBEL   58
6. *Sleep During Transcendental Meditation*
   ROBERT R. PAGANO, RICHARD M. ROSE, ROBERT M. STIVERS,
   AND STEPHEN WARRENBURG   78
7. *Transcendental Meditation and Asthma*
   ARCHIE F. WILSON, RONALD HONSBERGER, JOHN T. CHIU,
   AND HAROLD S. NOVEY   83
8. *Twelve-Month Follow-Up of Yoga and Biofeedback in the*
   Management of Hypertension
   CHANDRA PATEL   90

III. HYPNOSIS, SUGGESTION, AND AUTOGENIC TRAINING

9. *Responding to "Hypnotic" Suggestions: An Introspective Report*
   T. X. BARBER   96
10. *Hypnotic Suggestions for Blister Formation: Subjective and Physiological Effects*
    R. F. Q. JOHNSON AND T. X. BARBER   116
11. *The Influence of Presleep Suggestions on Dream Content*
    PRISCILLA CAMPBELL WALKER AND R. F. Q. JOHNSON   125
12. *Hypnosis and Biofeedback in the Treatment of Migraine Headache*
    THEODORE ANDREYCHUK AND CHRISTIAN SKRIVER   134
13. *Self-Regulation of Pain: The Use of Alpha-Feedback and Hypnotic Training for the Control of Chronic Pain*
    RONALD MELZACK AND CAMPBELL PERRY   147
14. *Visceral Responses to Opposite Types of Autogenic-Training Imagery*
    DAVID A. BLIZARD, PATRICIA COWINGS, AND NEAL E. MILLER   165

IV. EMG FEEDBACK, HEADACHES, AND RELAXATION

15. *Differential Effectiveness of Electromyographic Feedback, Verbal Relaxation Instructions and Medication Placebo*
    DANIEL J. COX, ANDREW FREUNDLICH, AND ROBERT G. MEYER   175
16. *Electromyographic Biofeedback and Relaxation Instructions in the Treatment of Muscle Contraction Headaches*
    STEPHEN N. HAYNES, PHILIP GRIFFIN, DEAN MOONEY, AND MARIO PARISE   182
17. *Relaxation Training and Biofeedback in the Reduction of Frontalis Muscle Tension*
    STEPHEN N. HAYNES, DIANNE MOSELEY, AND WILLIAM T. McGOWAN   189
18. *Continuous Biofeedback and Discrete Posttrial Verbal Feedback in Frontalis Muscle Relaxation Training*
    ROBERT A. KINSMAN, KATY O'BANION, SHARON ROBINSON, AND HERMAN STAUDENMAYER   195
19. *Electromyographic Feedback as a Relaxation Technique*
    ROBERT D. COURSEY   201
20. *An Experimental Test of Assumptions Relating to the Use of Electromyographic Biofeedback as a General Relaxation Technique*
    A. BARNEY ALEXANDER   211

21. *Effects of Various Forms of Relaxation Training on Physiological and Self-Report Measures of Relaxation*
RICHARD H. REINKING AND MARILYN L. KOHL   218

V. EEG ALPHA

22. *Autoregulation of the EEG Alpha Rhythm: A Program for the Study of Consciousness*
JOE KAMIYA   227
23. *Subjective Aspects of Alpha Enhancement*
T. A. TRAVIS, C. Y. KONDO, AND J. R. KNOTT   237
24. *Expectation Effects in Alpha Wave Control*
RONALD S. VALLE AND JOHN M. LEVINE   242
25. *Occipital Alpha and the Attributes of the "Alpha Experience"*
WILLIAM B. PLOTKIN AND ROBIN COHEN   246
26. *Alpha Feedback and Relaxation: A Cautionary Note*
ELIZABETH GRYNOL AND JOHN JAMIESON   252
27. *Relationships Among EEG Alpha Frequency, Reaction Time, and Age: A Biofeedback Study*
DIANA S. WOODRUFF   254
28. *Effects of Self-Enhanced EEG Alpha on Performance and Mood After Two Nights of Sleep Loss*
DAVID J. HORD, MARY L. TRACY, A. LUBIN, AND L. C. JOHNSON   263
29. *Alpha Activity: The Influence of Unpatterned Light Input and Auditory Feedback*
GARY BRIDGWATER, CLIFFORD J. SHERRY, AND THADDEUS J. MARCZYNSKI   269

VI. TEMPERATURE CONTROL

30. *Individual Differences and Autonomic Control: Absorption, Hypnotic Susceptibility, and the Unilateral Control of Skin Temperature*
ALAN H. ROBERTS, J. SCHULER, J. R. BACON, R. L. ZIMMERMAN, AND R. PATTERSON   281
31. *Conditioning Changes in Differential Skin Temperature*
FRANCIS J. KEEFE   288

VII. CARDIOVASCULAR CONTROL

32. *Role of Feedback in Voluntary Control of Heart Rate*
STEPHEN B. MANUCK, ROBERT W. LEVENSON, JAMES J. HINRICHSEN, AND STEVEN L. GRYLL   297

33. *Psychological and Physiological Variables Associated with Large Magnitude Voluntary Heart Rate Changes*
JOSEPH H. STEPHENS, ALAN H. HARRIS, JOSEPH V. BRADY, AND JOHN W. SHAFFER   303

34. *Voluntary Control and Reactivity of Human Heart Rate*
IRIS R. BELL AND GARY E. SCHWARTZ   310

35. *Heart Rate Perception and Heart Rate Control*
RICHARD A. McFARLAND   320

36. *Heart Rate Regulation with Success and Failure Signals*
CAMIL BOUCHARD AND JOHN A. CORSON   324

37. *Differential Effects of Heart Rate Modification Training on College Students, Older Males, and Patients with Ischemic Heart Disease*
PETER J. LANG, WILLIAM G. TROYER, JR., CRAIG T. TWENTYMAN, AND ROBERT J. GATCHEL   330

38. *Evaluation of an Intra-Cardiac Limit of Learned Heart Rate Control*
THEODORE WEISS AND BERNARD T. ENGEL   346

39. *Frequency of Feedback and Learned Heart Rate Control*
ROBERT J. GATCHEL   349

40. *Systolic Blood Pressure and Heart Rate Changes During Three Sessions Involving Biofeedback or No Feedback*
STEVEN G. FEY AND ERNEST LINDHOLM   360

41. *Clinical Applications of Biofeedback: Voluntary Control of Heart Rate, Rhythm, and Blood Pressure*
NEAL E. MILLER   367

42. *The Effects of Muscle Relaxation on Blood Pressure of Essential Hypertensives*
JAMES E. SHOEMAKER AND DONALD L. TASTO   378

43. *Learned Control of Blood Pressure in Patients with High Blood Pressure*
DONALD A. KRISTT AND BERNARD T. ENGEL   393

44. *Psychotherapeutic Control of Hypertension*
RICHARD A. STONE AND JAMES DE LEO   402

45. *Relationship Between Essential Hypertension and Cognitive Functioning: Effects of Biofeedback*
HERBERT GOLDMAN, KENNETH M. KLEINMAN, MURIEL Y. SNOW, DONALD R. BIDUS, AND BERNARD KOROL   407

46. *Instrumental Blood Pressure Conditioning in Out-Patient Hypertensives*
S. THOMAS ELDER AND NANCY K. EUSTIS   412

47. *A Simple Feedback System for the Treatment of Elevated Blood Pressure*
EDWARD B. BLANCHARD, LARRY D. YOUNG, AND MARY RUTH HAYNES   417

VIII. EPILEPSY

48. *Reduction of Seizures and Normalization of the EEG in a Severe Epileptic Following Sensorimotor Biofeedback Training: Preliminary Study*
WILLIAM W. FINLEY, HOYT A. SMITH, AND MURRAY D. ETHERTON   425

49. *Biofeedback in Epileptics: Equivocal Relationship of Reinforced EEG Frequency to Seizure Reduction*
BONNIE J. KAPLAN   440

50. *Comments on "Biofeedback in Epileptics: Equivocal Relationship of Reinforced EEG Frequency to Seizure Reduction" by Bonnie J. Kaplan*
HENRI GASTAUT   448

51. *Reply to Professor Gastaut's Comments on "Biofeedback in Epileptics"*
BONNIE J. KAPLAN   450

52. *Firing Patterns of Epileptic and Normal Neurons in the Chronic Alumina Focus in Undrugged Monkeys During Different Behavioral States*
ALLEN R. WYLER, EBERHARD E. FETZ, AND ARTHUR A. WARD, JR.   451

IX. BIOFEEDBACK IN REHABILITATION

53. *Sensory Feedback Therapy as a Modality of Treatment in Central Nervous Systems Disorders of Voluntary Movement*
JOSEPH BRUDNY, JULIUS KOREIN, LUCIE LEVIDOW, BRUCE B. GRYNBAUM, ABRAHAM LIEBERMAN, AND LAWRENCE W. FRIEDMANN   473

54. *Assessment of an Audio-Visual Feedback Device Used in Motor Training*
C. G. KUKULKA AND J. V. BASMAJIAN   480

55. *A Preliminary Report on Biofeedback Training for Early Finger Joint Mobilization*
C. G. KUKULKA, D. MIKE BROWN, AND J. V. BASMAJIAN   495

56. *Biofeedback Treatment of Foot-Drop After Stroke Compared with Standard Rehabilitation Technique: Effects on Voluntary Control and Strength*
J. V. BASMAJIAN, C. G. KUKULKA, M. G. NARAYAN, AND K. TAKEBE   498

X. OTHER APPLICATIONS OF BIOFEEDBACK AND OPERANT CONDITIONING

57. *Voluntary Control of Penile Tumescence*
RAYMOND C. ROSEN, DAVID SHAPIRO, AND GARY E.
SCHWARTZ   507
58. *Modification of Human Acid Secretion with Operant-Conditioning Procedures*
WILLIAM W. WHITEHEAD, PIERRE F. RENAULT, AND ISRAEL
GOLDIAMOND   512
59. *A Biofeedback Treatment for Stuttering*
RICHMOND HANNA, FRANZ WILFLING, AND BRENT MCNEILL   521
60. *On Voluntary Ocular Accommodation*
ROBERT R. PROVINE AND JAY M. ENOCH   526
61. *Biofeedback and Reinforcement to Increase Heterosexual Arousal in Homosexuals*
DAVID H. BARLOW, W. STEWART AGRAS, GENE G. ABEL,
EDWARD B. BLANCHARD, AND LARRY D. YOUNG   529
62. *Behaviorally Conditioned Immunosuppression*
ROBERT ADER AND NICHOLAS COHEN   536
63. *Food-Reinforced Inhibition of Conditioned Salivation in Dogs*
M. M. SHAPIRO AND DENNIS L. HERENDEEN   543

XI. BIOFEEDBACK INSTRUMENTS

64. *Of Bread, Circuses, and Alpha Machines*
ROBERT L. SCHWITZGEBEL AND JOHN D. RUGH   551
65. *Biofeedback Instrumentation: Soldering Closed the Loop*
DAVID A. PASKEWITZ   558
66. *Buying Biofeedback*
DANIEL A. GIRDANO   566

Name Index   573
Subject Index   577

PREFACE

This volume of *Biofeedback and Self-Control,* like its predecessors, presents an authoritative selection of the most important work on the subject that appeared in the last year. The criteria of selection are those of the scholars making up the Editorial Board, whose interests reflect the several main trends in this field of study as well as its general scope and breadth.

The final selection and organization of material to be published is each year made by a member of the Editorial Board, who also presents an overview of work and trends in the field. Theodore X. Barber, Director of Research at Medfield State Hospital, Medfield, Massachusetts, assumed these responsibilities for the current volume, and his Introduction follows. In this, as in previous volumes, several papers appear that were originally published prior to the specific period that the Annual covers but that the Editors regard as exceptionally important. We gratefully acknowledge the cooperation of the various authors, journals, and organizations and publishers who granted their permission to reprint the selections in this volume. Each selection is reproduced exactly as it originally appeared in order to publish each year's Annual as soon as possible. The editors will greatly appreciate comments and suggestions from readers to help make these volumes a more valuable reference work.

INTRODUCTION
Self-Control: Temperature Biofeedback, Hypnosis, Yoga, and Relaxation

Although biofeedback refers to specific procedures which show individuals how their bodily functions are varying from moment-to-moment, the term is at times used in a shorthand way to refer to a much broader area of inquiry. The larger area, which has been labeled as biofeedback and *self-control,* refers not only to biofeedback in the strict sense but also to a series of other endeavors— e.g., hypnosis, autogenic training, yoga, and meditation—which include techniques that can alter psychophysiological functions. For instance, although it has been recently demonstrated that biofeedback is useful in learning to raise or lower skin temperature, earlier studies had shown that some individuals who were trained in hypnosis, autosuggestions (autogenic training), hatha yoga, or meditation could also produce localized alterations in temperature. In brief, biofeedback techniques are useful in learning to control a wide variety of psychophysiological processes but similar results have been produced by other methods. These considerations raise a series of interesting and important questions. Which of the techniques are most effective? Is one technique more effective in producing one kind of desired outcome whereas another technique is more effective in producing another kind of outcome? For example, it may be that hypnotic suggestions are more effective in producing a generalized elevation in skin temperature (due to generalized relaxation) whereas temperature biofeedback is more effective in producing a localized elevation in skin temperature (due to localized control of blood flow). Are the effects of these various techniques mediated by the same factors? Can these various techniques be combined in several ways so that the combination is more useful than any one technique taken alone?

Several of the above questions will be discussed in the first section of this introduction which pertains to the control of skin temperature. Subsequent sections will discuss self-control and hypnosis, self-control and yoga, and relaxation and biofeedback.

CONTROL OF SKIN TEMPERATURE

The overlap among the various fields of endeavor mentioned above—"hypnotic" suggestions, autogenic training, yoga, and biofeedback—can be seen clearly in the studies from each of these areas which attempted to demonstrate that individuals can learn to control their skin temperature. Let us look at the studies from each area.

Direct Suggestions and "Hypnotic" Suggestions

In an early study Hadfield (1920) demonstrated that it is possible to produce dramatic changes in the temperature of the skin by direct suggestions. Hadfield worked with one subject. Before the experiment the subject had exercised vigorously and the temperature of both her hands had reached 95° F. Hadfield then suggested to the subject that her right hand was becoming cold. Within half an hour, the temperature of the subject's right palm fell to 68° while the temperature of her left palm remained at 94°. Next the subject was given the suggestion that her right hand was becoming warm. The temperature of the right hand rose within twenty minutes to 94°. Although this subject had previously participated in hypnotic experiments and was judged to be a very good hypnotic subject, Hadfield insisted that he did not "hypnotize" her in this experiment and that the changes in her hand temperature occurred when she was entirely in the "waking condition."

McDowell (1959) reported similar results with a "hypnotized" subject. He suggested to this good hypnotic subject that his leg was immersed in warm water. In response to the suggestion the subject showed vasodilation and an increase in the skin temperature of the leg. Previously, Menzies (1941) had discovered that some individuals show localized vasodilation and a concomitant rise in skin temperature when they are asked to recall earlier experiences involving warmth of the limb; also, Menzies found that some subjects show localized vasoconstriction with a concomitant drop in skin temperature when asked to recall prior experiences involving cold.

A more recent study (Maslach, Marshall, & Zimbardo, 1972) similarly showed that some subjects can use self-suggestions to raise and also lower their skin temperature. The three subjects who participated in this investigation had received training in relaxing, in concentrating, in imagining vividly, and in dissociating themselves from specific stimulating events, that is, they had received training in "hypnosis." In the experimental session, each subject was first exposed to a hypnotic induction procedure that focused on deep relaxation. Each subject was then asked to make one hand hot and the other hand cold. Several images were suggested that might be useful in changing the temperature of the hands and each subject was also encouraged to give himself suggestions and to generate his own imagery. All three subjects succeeded in lowering the temperature of one hand (by about 2° to 7° C) and two of the three also succeeded in raising the temperature of the other hand (by about 2° C). When the subjects raised and lowered their hand temperature, they were typically imagining that one hand was becoming red with anger while the other was becoming white with fear or that one hand was in a bucket of ice water while the other hand was under a heat lamp (Zimbardo *et al.*, 1970). It appeared that the training in relaxing, concentrating, imagining, and dissociating was important in enabling the subjects to alter their skin temperature. Subjects in a non-hypnotic control group who had not received this training did not succeed in altering the temperature of their hands.

Autogenic Training

Research utilizing autogenic training has yielded results harmonious with those described above.

Autogenic training was developed in Germany by J. H. Schultz after he had worked rather extensively with "hypnosis." Schultz removed the traditional "hypnotic induction" components from the situation and focused on self-suggestions given by the client to himself; the role of the "hypnotist" or leader became similar to that of a teacher or guide. When undergoing autogenic training the client is given practice in responding to suggestions that he gives to himself. The self-suggestions include, for example, "My right arm is heavy," "My left hand is warm," "My heartbeat is calm and regular," and "My forehead is cool."

Schultz and other investigators carried out many studies to assess the physiological effects of the self-suggestions used in autogenic training. For instance, in an early study, Schultz (1926) found that about 80 percent of relaxed subjects who were asked to imagine that their hand was exposed to heat showed a rise of about 2° C in the surface temperature of the hand.

More recently, a group of workers in Japan (Harano, Ogawa & Naruse, 1965) asked clients who were undergoing autogenic training to repeat to themselves the self-suggestion, "My arms are warm." When repeating this suggestion to themselves, they generally exhibited several interrelated changes in the arms—an increase in the feeling of warmth, an increase in the surface temperature, and an increase in blood volume.

Other studies from the area of autogenic training also indicate that self-suggestions of warmth in a limb are associated with a rise in temperature of the limb (Luthe, 1970, pp. 50-57).

Hatha Yoga

It has also been demonstrated that at least some individuals who have undergone extensive training in hatha yoga are able voluntarily to raise and lower their skin temperature.

About fifteen years ago an American research team (Wenger & Bagchi, 1961) traveled to India to study the psychophysiological effects of yoga training. They found one yogi who was able to raise his forehead temperature and produce perspiration from the forehead within ten minutes after he began meditating. The American researchers provided the following background data:

This man had spent part of two winters in caves in the Himalayas. During such periods, usually alone and unclad except for an animal skin, much of the time was spent in meditation . . . The cold distracted him, and his teacher advised him to concentrate on *warmth* and to visualize himself in extremely high temperature situations . . . He reported gradual success *after about six months of practice.* Later he found that in a moderate climate the same practices produced not only increased sensations of warmth but perspiration [p. 313].

More recently, Green *et al.* (1970) noted that Swami Rama was able voluntarily to produce a temperature difference of 2-7° F on two sides of his palm. One side of the palm (the thenar eminence) became reddish and warm while the other side of the palm (the hypethenar eminence) became gray and cold.

Biofeedback

Earlier reports (e.g., Roberts, Kewman, & Macdonald, 1973; Sargent, Green & Walters, 1973; Taub & Emurian, 1972) and more recent reports by Keefe (article 31) and Roberts *et al.* (article 30) indicate that individuals can raise and also lower the temperature of a limb when they are given temperature biofeedback together with instructions to raise or lower the limb temperature.

In the study by Roberts *et al.* (article 30) seven excellent hypnotic subjects and seven poor hypnotic subjects were exposed to biofeedback of their hand temperature while receiving instructions to raise the temperature of one hand and to lower the temperature of the other. The subjects generally learned to alter their skin temperature and the magnitude of the effect was not especially small—more than half of the subjects were able to change their hand temperature by at least 1° C. The excellent hypnotic subjects did not perform differently than the poor hypnotic subjects; in the same amount of time both groups learned to control hand temperature to about the same degree.

The most impressive studies with temperature biofeedback have been carried out by Taub and his coworkers. Taub and Emurian (1972) set out to train subjects to control the temperature of an index finger. In four 15-minute training sessions, in which variations in temperature were indicated by the brightness of a light, 19 of 20 subjects showed control of temperature;·on the average these 19 subjects could increase and also decrease the finger temperature by about 2.5° F. After additional training, the subjects were able to raise and to lower finger temperature as easily without biofeedback as with it and they retained the ability to vary the temperature when retested after an interval of four to five months.

Subsequent work by the same investigators (Taub, in press) showed that after learning to raise and lower skin temperature, some subjects: (a) could easily display changes of 8° to 15° F in 15 minutes; (b) could maintain a considerable increase in peripheral temperature for about 45 minutes while performing a concurrent task; and (c) could maintain a warm skin when subjected to cold stress.

General Considerations

In summary, in a series of studies subjects were either instructed to recall previous experiences of cold or warmth, or were given direct suggestions that a limb was becoming cold or warm, or were instructed under "hypnosis" to raise or lower their skin temperature. Each of these instructions or suggestions was effective in increasing or decreasing the temperature of the skin. However, similar changes in the temperature of a limb have been observed when clients undergoing autogenic training have given themselves suggestions that a limb is warm. Also, a few individuals trained in hatha yoga have demonstrated remarkable control over skin temperature. More recently, biofeedback techniques have been shown to be markedly effective in helping individuals learn to alter skin temperature.

It thus appears that a variety of techniques are useful in teaching temperature control and that further research is needed to ascertain how the techniques can be most effectively combined. As Taub (in press) has pointed out, if unequivocal self-regulation of temperature through control of blood flow is achieved, it could have a wide variety of very useful practical applications such as treatment of migraine headaches and Raynaud's disease, protection against cold injury, production of temporary sterility by elevation of scrotal temperature, reduction of edema and pain following tissue damage, reduction in size of tumors by reducing blood flow and concomitant nutrition to the area of the tumor, and promotion of wound healing by increasing blood flow to the affected area.

Further studies are also needed to determine how the effect is mediated. It appears possible that techniques such as "hypnosis" or autogenic training may give rise to a generalized relaxation which is associated with increased warmth in the hands. On the other hand, individuals who are trained in hatha yoga may control skin temperature by contracting and relaxing muscles which indirectly increase or decrease blood flow to the area.

Although it appears that skin temperature control may at times be an indirect result of changes in arousal and at other times an indirect result of localized contraction and relaxation of specific muscles, there is also evidence indicating that when temperature control is achieved with the help of biofeedback the subject may have learned to exert a direct effect on blood flow. For instance, Taub and Emurian (in press) presented evidence suggesting that in their biofeedback investigations the control of skin temperature was due to a direct effect on volume blood flow and was not mediated by muscular activity. For instance, they noted that: (a) electromyographic recordings from the trained forearm were not correlated with the observed changes in temperature; (b) careful observation of subjects failed to reveal movements or isometric muscular contractions during the temperature regulation; (c) subjects who did perform maneuvers involving muscular contractions showed very small changes in skin temperature; and (d) the temperature regulation was limited to a precise locus —it was *not* diffuse as might be expected if muscular contraction and relaxation were responsible for the temperature change.

Further studies are also needed to clarify why some individuals are more proficient than others in learning temperature control. Roberts *et al*. (article 30) hypothesize that subjects who learn to control skin temperature most quickly show more "confidence or belief in the phenomena or in their own ability" and that confidence may be mediated in part by "experimenter-subject interactions as well as by early success or failure experiences" [p. 278]. More broadly, Roberts *et al*., hypothesize that the individual differences are due to "psycho-physiological variables such as autonomic responsivity or lability, inter-personal variables such as attitude toward and relationship to experimenter, and attitudinal and motivational variables such as confidence . . ." [p. 278].

Taub (in press) has presented data in line with the contention that the experimenter-subject interaction may play an important role. He reported that an experimenter who adopted an impersonal attitude toward the subjects and who was not convinced of the feasibility of temperature control was able to train only about 9 percent of his subjects whereas experimenters who did not doubt the feasibility of the task and who communicated their confidence were successful in training at least 80 percent of their subjects.

SELF-CONTROL AND "HYPNOSIS"

Research in "hypnosis" has flourished during the past two decades. During this time it has become increasingly clear that a wide variety of bodily functions can be influenced by suggestions or instructions given with or without hypnotic induction procedures. Investigators in this area appear to be reaching a con-sensus that suggestions are effective in altering psychophysiological processes when the subject imagines with and thinks along with the themes that are sug-gested (Spanos & Barber, 1974). Some individuals are ready and willing, without any special preliminaries, to think with and to imagine those things that are suggested; they do not require a "hypnotic induction procedure" or other special preparation in order to accept the suggestions. Other individuals seem to need special encouragement or task motivational instructions in order to think with the suggestions, and still others find it easier to think with sugges-tions when they have been exposed to relaxation procedures or "hypnotic in-duction procedures" (Barber, Spanos, & Chaves, 1974).

Control of Pain

During recent years evidence has been accumulating that tolerance of pain can be increased and the discomfort due to noxious stimulation can be reduced by suggestions or instructions given with and also without "hypnotic induction procedures" (Barber, 1970, Chap. 5; Chaves & Barber, 1974; Hilgard & Hil-gard, 1975; Meichenbaum & Turk, 1976). When instructions or suggestions increase pain tolerance, it is not especially important whether or not the subject has been "hypnotized"; far more important are such factors as the subject's general responsiveness to pain, the way the suggestions or instructions are worded, and whether the subject thinks with (instead of covertly contradicting) those things that are suggested (Barber, 1969b, Chap. 7). Even Ernest Hilgard, who has been one of the most vocal defenders of the traditional notions regarding "hypnosis," has drastically revised his contentions during recent years and now agrees with Barber, Sarbin, and others that "hypnosis" is not an important factor when suggestions are effective in reducing reactions to pain. Hilgard (1975) now writes that, "It does not matter very much whether the suggestions for pain reduction are given in the nonhypnotic state or after hypnotic induction, so that the results are more attributable to individual differences in responsiveness to suggestions than to hypnosis as such" [p. 29].

The experimental studies in this area have shown that several types of suggestions or instructions are effective in increasing pain tolerance or reducing pain reactivity. These include, for example, (a) instructions to think about pleasant events when exposed to the pain-producing stimulus (Barber & Hahn, 1962; Chaves & Barber, 1974); (b) suggestions that the part of the body that is exposed to pain stimulation is becoming numb and insensitive (Barber, 1969a; Barber & Hahn, 1962; Evans & Paul, 1970; Spanos, Barber, & Lang, 1974); (c) instructions to verbalize positive self-statements about the pain (Meichenbaum & Turk, 1976); (d) suggestions to "dissociate" one's self from the painful body part, etc. (Hilgard & Hilgard, 1975).

Some of the aforementioned suggestions or instructions are also used by individuals who "naturally" tolerate noxious stimulation without discomfort. For instance, one such individual (Jack Schwartz) used the "dissociation" technique when he pushed a large steel needle deep into his biceps; he stated immediately afterward that he maintained a state of "detachment" and he did not perceive himself as sticking a needle through his arm but as sticking a needle "through *an* arm" (Pelletier, 1974; Green & Green, 1973). We can also hypothesize that similar self-suggestions or self-talk may be used by yogis when they are able to keep their hand in ice water without showing signs of discomfort and while continuing to maintain alpha activity on the EEG (Anand, Chhina, & Singh, 1961a).

Control of Skin Reactions

Remarkable control over skin responses has been repeatedly demonstrated in "hypnosis" situations. Although the crucial variable has often been labeled as "hypnosis," the evidence indicates that the critical mediating variable can be more appropriately conceptualized as acceptance of, involvement in, or belief in the suggestions. For instance, Ikemi and Nakagawa (1962) worked with 13 subjects who were allergic to the leaves of two trees found in Japan. Five of the subjects were exposed to a hypnotic induction procedure and, when their eyes were closed, they were told that they were being touched by the allergy-producing leaves when they were actually touched by leaves from a harmless tree. The remaining eight subjects were assigned to a control treatment; these subjects were blindfolded and were also touched by harmless leaves and told they were being stimulated by the allergy-producing leaves. When thus led to believe that they were being stimulated by the allergy-producing leaves, the *harmless* leaves produced a slight to marked degree of the skin allergic response—e.g., flushing, erythema, and papules—in *all* of the hypnotic subjects and *all* of the control subjects. The experimental procedure was also reversed and all subjects were told that they were being touched with the leaves of a harmless tree while they were actually touched with the allergy-producing leaves. When thus led to believe that the allergy-producing leaves were harmless, four of the five hypnotic subjects and seven of the eight control subjects did not show the expected allergic response.

In brief, the results presented by Ikemi and Nakagawa indicate that in allergic individuals: (a) the allergic response can be inhibited when the individual is led to believe that the allergy-producing substance is harmless; (b) some aspects of the allergic response can be produced by a harmless substance when the individual is led to believe it is an allergy-producing substance; (c) formal hypnotic induction procedures are not necessary or especially useful in producing these effects; and (d) it appears that the mediating variable that is critical in producing these effects is the subjects' belief that the allergy-producing substance is actually a harmless substance and, vice versa, that a harmless substance will give rise to the allergic response.

Other dramatic effects on the skin have also been demonstrated. For instance, a rare skin ailment, fishskin disease (congenital ichthyosiform erythrodermia of Brocq) has been alleviated by suggestions that the skin will improve first in one area and then in another (Mason, 1952; Wink, 1961). A recent study by Johnson and Barber included in this volume (article 10) and another recent study by the same investigators (Johnson & Barber, 1976) have confirmed earlier reports (Barber, 1970, Chap. 4) that: (a) suggestions intended to produce skin blisters are at times followed by localized cutaneous alterations; and (b) suggestions that warts will go away are at times associated with the disappearance of warts.

Improving Nearsighted Vision

A series of studies (Graham & Leibowitz, 1972; Harwood, 1970, 1971; Kelley, 1958) have shown that visual acuity can be heightened in myopic individuals by suggestions to imagine something pleasant and by suggestions to relax the muscles around the eyes. These studies are also notable in that both "hypnotized" myopic subjects and "nonhypnotized" myopic subjects showed about the same degree of improved visual acuity in response to the suggestions. In fact, almost all of the nearsighted subjects showed some degree of enhanced visual acuity and some subjects at some times showed a marked degree of improvement. For instance, in one of these studies (Kelley, 1958) the overall average improvement in both the "hypnotized" subjects and the "nonhypnotized" subjects was equivalent to the difference between 20/50 and 20/20 acuity. In other studies (Harwood, 1970, 1971) the myopic subjects showed an average enhancement of about 15 percent in visual acuity, but some subjects at times manifested markedly improved vision since they perceived targets that were half the size of those they could normally perceive.

Further studies are needed to specify the most efficient procedures for improving vision in myopes. It appears likely that biofeedback techniques can be utilized to inform the myope of small changes in his refractive error and that the biofeedback techniques can be usefully combined with suggestions for improved vision (Lanyon & Giddings, 1974).

Control of Dreams

Studies from the "hypnosis" area have also shown that individuals can learn self-control of dreaming. For instance, the review by Walker and Johnson (article 11) indicates that individuals should be able to dream at night on specific topics by telling themselves repeatedly before they go to sleep that they shall dream on a particular topic. Similarly, it can be hypothesized from the available data (Tart, 1963) that sleepers can become aware that they are dreaming and can awaken at the beginning or end of a dream by giving themselves suggestions before they go to sleep that they will be aware that they are dreaming and will be able to awaken at the beginning or end of the dream.

UNDERESTIMATION OF NORMAL CAPABILITIES

As implied above, workers in "hypnosis" are realizing that they may have underestimated the abilities and potentialities of normal individuals. A rather large number of recent experimental studies have demonstrated, that non-hypnotized subjects are able to perform in the same way as "hypnotized" subjects in controlling pain, in experiencing age regression, and in manifesting a high level of strength, endurance, learning proficiency, etc. (Barber, 1969b, 1970; Barber & Ham, 1974; Barber, Spanos, & Chaves, 1974). Earlier investigators in this area had generally underestimated the capabilities of normal individuals or control subjects, not because they had tested their capabilities and found them wanting, but because they had *not* evaluated the capabilities of the normal subjects when special efforts were made to motivate them for maximal performance (Barber, 1969b).

The kind of underestimation of normal capabilities that occurred in the "hypnosis" area has also been present during recent years in the biofeedback area. For instance, some years ago several research reports demonstrated that "deeply hypnotized" subjects showed an increase in heart rate when given the suggestion that the heart was accelerating. Although these results seemed dramatic, it was nevertheless pointed out at that time (Barber, 1961) that several dozen documented cases existed of individuals who could accelerate and also decelerate their heart whenever they desired to do so. Similar events have occurred recently in the area of biofeedback. Although a number of studies were published in which subjects who received cardiac biofeedback learned to accelerate the heart, the reports by Manuck *et al.* (article 32), Bell and Schwartz (article 34), and Stephens *et al.* (article 33) indicate that subjects can do about as well when they are simply asked to increase their heart rate or pulse.

Along similar lines, Redmond *et al,* (1974) asked subjects to try to raise and also to lower their blood pressure. The subjects were able to alter their blood pressure up and down about the same degree as had been observed in the studies which used biofeedback of blood pressure. When the subjects raised blood pressure, they reported that they imagined stimulating activities, and when they lowered blood pressure they imagined relaxing activities.

In brief, although control over heart rate and blood pressure can be produced by biofeedback training, the same degree of control can be observed when subjects are directly asked to produce the effects. However, it also appears that in many instances biofeedback may be helpful in producing phenomena which can also be produced without biofeedback in a somewhat weaker form. For instance, Rosen *et al.* (article 57) found that some degree of penile tumescence was produced voluntarily by a control group of male subjects who were asked directly to produce an erection. However, a somewhat greater degree of erection was observed in the experimental subjects who were given biofeedback together with monetary rewards for increases in penile diameter.

In summary, it appears that in at least two areas covered in these Aldine annuals—"hypnosis" and biofeedback—investigators have underestimated the degree untrained individuals can alter physiological functions when they are directly asked to do so. This conclusion has implications for understanding human potentialities (we have greater potentials for psychophysiological control than we commonly assume). It also has implications for the conduct of research in these areas (control subjects should be used who are told directly that they are expected to alter the physiological function that is being studied).

SELF-CONTROL AND YOGA

The increasing interest in self-control has revived interest in the feats attributed to yogis. Anecdotal reports concerning the psychophysiological capabilities of yogis do not seem as surprising now as they did just a few years ago. For instance, the recent study by Rosen, Shapiro, and Schwartz (article 57), which showed that unselected male subjects can voluntarily produce a degree of penile tumescence, lends some credence to the following anecdotal report presented by Arthur Koestler (1960):

> I must mention in this context a report given to me by an eminent Bombay psychiatrist who had watched, and photographed, a Yogi showman attaching with a string a twenty-pound weight to the tip of his penis, and lifting it by producing an erection in front of the audience [pp. 117-118].

Relatively recent studies with individuals who are highly trained in hatha yoga have yielded data such as the following:

1. After awakening from a period of deep sleep, as indicated by delta waves on the EEG, Swami Rama accurately reported what had been occurring around him during the period that he was asleep (Green, Green, & Walters, 1971). Cross-validation of these results would necessitate a revision of our notions about delta wave sleep; despite our traditional belief that only a very small amount of awareness can be present during deep sleep, it appears that one can be rather well aware of one's surroundings while manifesting a deep sleep pattern—delta waves—on the EEG.

2. When attempting to stop his heart, Swami Rama produced atrial flutter at the rate of 300 beats per minute for a period of 17 seconds (Green, Ferguson, Green, & Walters, 1970). Although he did not actually stop the heart, he produced a very striking and unusual change in heart function—the heart was apparently firing "at its maximum rate without blood either filling the chambers properly or the valves working properly" (Green, Green, & Walters, 1971, p. 5). Since Swami Rama had *learned* to affect his heart in this unusual way, presumably others can also learn to affect the functioning of the heart.

3. Anand, Chhina, and Singh (1961b) reported that a trained yogi was able to stay in an air-tight box for 10 hours as compared to about 7 hours and 4 hours for two control subjects. The important finding in this study, however, was not that the yogi remained in the box longer than the controls but that he was able to reduce markedly his oxygen consumption. During the time the yogi was in the air-tight box his oxygen consumption averaged 13.3 liters per hour as compared to his basal rate of 19.5 liters per hour. While in the box, the oxygen consumption of one of the control subjects was more than his basal requirements and the other control subject did not show any significant change from his normal basal oxygen requirement.

4. In 1970 the same investigators—B. K. Anand and G. S. Chhina—replicated their earlier findings with the same yogi. In this more recent study, which is described by Calder (1970, pp. 85-88), the yogi stayed in the air-tight box for about 5½ hours. During most of this period the yogi's oxygen consumption was about half his basal requirement and during the third hour of his stay in the box it fell to about one-fourth of his basal oxygen requirement. In fact, after 3½ hours in the air-tight box, the yogi had reduced his oxygen consumption to 4.4 liters per hour as compared to his basal rate of 19.4 liters per hour. Since oxygen consumption (reflecting metabolic rate) depends on the tone of the skeletal muscles and the activities of the organs of the body, these studies indicate that the yogi was able to achieve not only a super-relaxation of his skeletal muscles but was also able to drastically reduce the activity of his internal organs. Since the yogi had presumably *learned* how to reduce his metabolic rate drastically, it appears probable that some if not many other individuals also have the potential for learning how to drastically alter the functioning of their body.

RELAXATION AND BIOFEEDBACK

The concept of relaxation continues to become more and more closely intertwined with the concept of biofeedback. Relaxation is both an independent variable and a dependent variable in research on EEG alpha biofeedback and in EMG *frontalis* biofeedback. Relaxation is also an important antecedent variable in the biofeedback-assisted reduction of tension headaches, hypertension, and insomnia. Let us look briefly at some of the recent biofeedback studies which underscore the importance of relaxation.

In a series of investigations included in earlier issues of these Aldine Annuals, Budzynski, Stoyva, and their coworkers (1970, 1973) demonstrated that

EMG *frontalis* muscle biofeedback together with home practice in relaxation is generally effective in alleviating tension headaches. Although there are many complexities to be considered in these studies, it appears that the training in relaxation was the crucial variable in helping the patients. If the EMG *frontalis* biofeedback played any role at all, it apparently did so only to the extent that it helped the headache sufferers in learning to relax.

Along similiar lines, Raskin *et al.* (1973) showed that training in relaxation (assisted by EMG *frontalis* biofeedback) was useful with chronically anxious patients in alleviating tension headaches and insomnia. Again, it appears that the relaxation training was the important antecedent variable and that the EMG biofeedback, at best, played an ancillary role in helping the patients to relax.

Training in relaxation also appears to have been the critical variable in helping the migraine sufferers who participated in the study by Sargent, Green, and Walters (1973). Similarly, Haynes, Griffin, Mooney, and Parise (article 16) and Cox, Freundlich, and Meyer (article 15) have demonstrated that relaxation instructions are effective in reducing tension headaches.

Relaxation also appears to play an important role in the reduction of hypertension. Shoemaker and Tasto (article 42) found that relaxation lowered the blood pressure of essential hypertensives to within a normal range. The investigation by Patel (article 8) also indicates that training in relaxation is a useful technique for the reduction of hypertension.

Further studies are needed to compare the effects of various types of relaxation procedures on various types of ailments. A variety of techniques and methods are available for producing relaxation: the techniques of progressive relaxation as originally delineated by Jacobson or as abbreviated and modified by Wolpe; the lengthy techniques of autogenic training as developed by Schultz and Luthe; brief techniques for self-suggested relaxation ("I'm becoming calm . . . relaxed . . . tranquil . . . at peace . . ."); brief or lengthy suggestions of relaxation given by an experimenter or by a hypnotist; the technique of transcendental meditation, etc. Which of these techniques are generally most effective in producing relaxation? Are some of the techniques more effective with some types of subjects or some types of patients? Are some of these relaxation techniques more effective than others in treating certain kinds of ailments? Is it possible to combine facets from each of the techniques to construct a more effective relaxation-treatment package?

Although most of the above questions have not as yet been addressed by researchers, a number of studies have been conducted recently which compared the effects of two or more relaxation procedures. For instance, Haynes, Moseley, and McGowan (article 17) found that suggestions of relaxation were as effective as EMG *frontalis* biofeedback and more effective than Jacobson-like "progressive relaxation" instructions in producing relaxation (denoted by reduction in *frontalis* muscle tension). Along similar lines, the paper by Reinking and Kohl (article 21) indicates that EMG feedback from the *frontalis* muscle may be more efficient than the Jacobson-Wolpe progressive relaxation instructions in teaching relaxation. Although Coursey (article 19) also reconfirmed that EMG biofeedback is an effective means of reducing muscle tension, Alexander (article 20) showed that heightened feelings of relaxation can be produced as effectively by simple instructions to relax. We can expect that further research will clarify the effectiveness of the various techniques and, as Coursey (article 19) has pointed out, will ask the more sophisticated question: "What sort of relaxation technique is effective with what sort of people with what sort of problems in conjunction with what other procedures?"

We might also expect that ongoing research in this area will arrive at a more sophisticated concept of relaxation. The concept of *relaxation* is multidimensional and is often used ambiguously. In biofeedback studies, relaxation has been defined operationally by: (a) reduction of action potentials from the *frontalis* muscles; (b) reduction of tension in various other muscles; and (c) subject's report that he feels relaxed. Each of these and other means of indexing relaxation have problems and lead to complex questions, such as: To what extent does reduction of tension in the *frontalis* muscle correlate with reduction of tension in other muscles? To what extent does reduced tension in various muscles correlate with subjects' reports of relaxation? Is it possible for an individual to relax his muscles while he thinks about events that are anxiety-provoking? If a subject is able to relax many muscles while he is worrying or thinking about events that make him anxious, is he to be considered as relaxed? Should relaxation be considered a total organismic response that involves calm thoughts, relaxed muscles, and a reduced level of activity of all the internal organs? If so, how do we conceptualize relaxation in a monistic framework that does not separate the functioning of the muscles and internal organs from emotions and cognitive processes?

ADDITIONAL HIGHLIGHTS

Each volume of these Aldine Annuals has included ground-breaking papers that have had wide repercussions. The present volume also includes many seminal papers. In addition to several that have already been mentioned in this Introduction, I expect that the following three additional papers will also have broad repercussions and will be widely cited.

1. The provocative paper on transcendental meditation by Pagano *et al.* (article 6) challenges the widely-publicized conclusions previously reported by Wallace, Benson, and Wilson (1971) and by Wallace and Benson (1972). Contrary to the earlier findings, the recent study indicates that: (a) when experienced meditators are practicing transcendental meditation they are asleep a substantial proportion of the time, that is, they show sleep stages 2, 3, or 4 on the EEG about 40 percent of the time while meditating; (b) the conclusion indicated by the EEG records is confirmed by the experienced meditators' subjective reports—they state that at times they were asleep; and (c) since various states of consciousness are observed during meditation, it is clear that transcendental meditation is not spent in a unique, wakeful, hypometabolic state.

2. The misleading nature of the conclusions drawn from the early work with alpha biofeedback is indicated again by Plotkin and Cohen (article 25). These investigators reconfirmed that: (a) occipital alpha is directly related to oculo-motor processing; (b) alpha feedback training *per se* does *not* produce tranquility or relaxation; and (c) "the major contribution that alpha feedback makes to the attainment of meditative-like experiences is the supply of a setting which is conducive to the *natural self*-inducement of such states."

3. An earlier study (Welgan, 1974) suggested that it may be possible to bring gastric secretions under voluntary control with the help of biofeedback. This conjecture has been confirmed by Whitehead, Renault, and Goldiamond (article 58) who showed that biofeedback procedures (together with money reinforcers) are effective in teaching control of gastric pH. The implications of these results for both the production and alleviation of duodenal ulcers is obvious.

THEODORE XENOPHON BARBER

REFERENCES

Anand, B. K., Chhina, G. S., and Singh, B. Some aspects of electroencephalographic studies in yogis. *Electroencephalography and Clinical Neurophysiology*, 1961, *13*, 452-456. (a) (Reprinted in *Biofeedback & Self-Control: An Aldine Reader*, article 63)

Anand, B. K., Chhina, G. S., and Singh, B. Studies on Shri Ramanand Yogi during his stay in an air-tight box. *Indian Journal of Medical Research*, 1961, *49*, 82-89. (b)

Barber, T. X. Physiological effects of "hypnosis." *Psychological Bulletin*, 1961, *58*, 390-419.

Barber, T. X. Effects of hypnotic induction, suggestions of anesthesia, and distraction on subjective and physiological responses to pain. Paper presented at the annual meeting of the Eastern Psychological Association, Philadelphia, April 10, 1969. (a)

Barber, T. X. *Hypnosis: A Scientific Approach*. New York: Van Nostrand Reinhold, 1969. (b)

Barber, T. X. *LSD, Marihuana, Yoga and Hypnosis*. Chicago: Aldine, 1970.

Barber, T. X., and Hahn, K. W., Jr. Physiological and subjective responses to pain producing stimulation under hypnotically-suggested and waking-imagined "analgesia." *Journal of Abnormal and Social Psychology*, 1962, *65*, 411-418.

Barber, T. X., and Ham, M. W. *Hypnotic Phenomena*. Morristown, N.J.: General Learning Press, 1974.

Barber, T. X., Spanos, N. P., and Chaves, J. F. *Hypnosis, Imagination, and Human Potentialities*. Elmsford, New York: Pergamon, 1974.

Budzynski, T., Stoyva, J., and Adler, C. Feedback-induced muscle relaxation: Application to tension headache. *Journal of Behavior Therapy and Experimental Psychiatry*, 1970, *1*, 205-211. (Reprinted in *Biofeedback & Self-Control: 1970*, article 31)

Budzynski, T. H., Stoyva, J. M., Adler, C. S., and Mullaney, D. J. EMG biofeedback and tension headache: A controlled outcome study. *Psychosomatic Medicine*, 1973, *35*, 484-496. (Reprinted in *Biofeedback & Self-Control: 1973*, article 19)

Calder, N. *The Mind of Man*. New York: Viking Press, 1970.

Chaves, J. F., and Barber, T. X. Cognitive strategies, experimenter modeling, and expectation in the attenuation of pain. *Journal of Abnormal Psychology*, 1974, *83*, 356-363.

Evans, M. B., and Paul, G. L. Effects of hypnotically suggested analgesia on physiological and subjective responses to cold stress. *Journal of Consulting and Clinical Psychology*, 1970, *35*, 362-371. (Reprinted in *Biofeedback & Self-Control: 1971*, article 29)

Graham, C., and Leibowitz, H. W. The effect of suggestion on visual acuity. *International Journal of Clinical and Experimental Hypnosis*, 1972, *20*, 169-186. (Reprinted in *Biofeedback & Self-Control: 1972*, article 31)

Green, E. E., Ferguson, D. W., Green, A. M., and Walters, E. D. Preliminary report on Voluntary Controls Project: Swami Rama. Topeka, Kansas: Research Dept., Menninger Foundation, 1970.

Green, E. E., and Green, A. M. Regulating our mind-body processes. Topeka, Kansas: Research Dept., Menninger Foundation, 1973.

Green, E. E., Green, A. M., and Walters, E. D. Biofeedback for mind-body self-regulation: Healing and creativity. Topeka, Kansas: Research Dept., Menninger Foundation, 1971.

Hadfield, J. A. The influence of suggestion on body temperature. *Lancet*, 1920, *2*, 68-69.

Harano, K., Ogawa, K., and Naruse, G. A study of plethysmography and skin temperature during active concentration and autogenic exercise. In W. Luthe (Ed.) *Autogenic Training*. New York: Grune & Stratton, 1965, pp. 55-58.

Harwood, L. W. Changes in visual acuity in myopic subjects during hypnosis. Paper presented at the annual meeting of the American Academy of Optometry, Miami, December 13, 1970.

Harwood, L. R. Changes in visual acuity in myopic subjects which are similar to those in hypnotized myopic subjects. Paper presented at the annual meeting of the American Academy of Optometry, Toronto, 1971.

Hilgard, E. R. Hypnosis. *Annual Review of Psychology*, 1975, *26*, 19-44.

Hilgard, E. R., and Hilgard, J. R. *Hypnosis in the Relief of Pain*. Los Altos, Calif.: William Kaufmann, 1975.

Ikemi, Y., and Nakagawa, S. A psychosomatic study of contagious dermatitis. *Kyushu Journal of Medical Science*, 1962, *13*, 335-350.

Johnson, R. F. Q., and Barber, T. X. Hypnotic and non-hypnotic suggestions for wart removal: An empirical exploration. Medfield, Mass.: Medfield Foundation, 1976.

Kelley, C. R. Psychological factors in myopia. Doctoral dissertation, New School for Social Research, 1958.

Koestler, A. *The Lotus and the Robot*. New York: Harper & Row, 1960.

Lanyon, R. I., and Giddings, J. W. Psychological approaches to myopia: A review. *American Journal of Optometry and Physiological Optics*, 1974, *51*, 271-281.

Luthe, W. *Autogenic Therapy. Volume IV. Research and Theory*. New York: Grune & Stratton, 1970.

Maslach, C., Marshall, G., and Zimbardo, P. Hypnotic control of peripheral skin temperature. *Psychophysiology*, 1972, *9*, 600-605. (Reprinted in *Biofeedback & Self-Control: 1972*, article 32)

Mason, A. A. A case of congenital ichthyosiform erythrodermia of Brocq treated by hypnosis. *British Medical Journal*, 1952, *2*, 422-423.

McDowell, M. Hypnosis in dermatology. In J. M. Schneck (Ed.) *Hypnosis in Modern Medicine*. (2nd ed.) Springfield, Ill.: Charles C. Thomas, 1959, pp. 101-115.

Meichenbaum, D. and Turk, D. The cognitive-behavioral management of anxiety, anger and pain. In P. Davidson (Ed.) *Behavioral Management of Anxiety, Depression and Pain*. New York: Brunner/Mazel, 1976.

Menzies, R. Further studies of conditioned vasomotor responses in human subjects. *Journal of Experimental Psychology*, 1941, *29*, 457-482.

Pelletier, K. R. Neurophysiological parameters of alpha, theta, and cardiovascular control. Paper presented at Western Psychological Association meeting, San Francisco, April 24-27, 1974.

Raskin, M., Johnson, G., Rondestvedt, J. W. Chronic anxiety treated by feedback-induced muscle relaxation: A pilot study. *Archives of General Psychiatry*, 1973, *28*, 263-266. (Reprinted in *Biofeedback & Self-Control: 1973*, article 22)

Redmond, D. P., Gaylor, M.S., McDonald, R. H., Jr., and Shapiro, A. P. Blood pressure and heart-rate response to verbal instruction and relaxation in hypertension. *Psychosomatic Medicine*, 1974, *36*, 285-297.

Roberts, A. H., Kewman, D. G., and MacDonald, H. Voluntary control of skin temperature: Unilateral changes using hypnosis and feedback. *Journal of Abnormal Psychology*, 1973, *82*, 163-168. (Reprinted in *Biofeedback & Self-Control: 1973*, article 1)

Sargent, J. D., Green, E. E., and Walters, E. D. Preliminary report on the use of autogenic feedback training in the treatment of migraine and tension headaches. *Psychosomatic Medicine*, 1973, *35*, 129-135. (Reprinted in *Biofeedback & Self-Control: 1973*, article 21)

Schultz, J. H. Ueber selbsttätige (autogene) Umstellungen der Wärmestrahlung der Menschlichen Haut im Autosuggestiven Training. *Deutsche medizinische Wochenschrift*, 1926, *14*, 571-572.

Spanos, N. P., and Barber, T. X. Toward a convergence in hypnosis research. *American Psychologist,* 1974, *29,* 500-511. (Reprinted in *Biofeedback & Self-Control: 1974,* article 43)

Spanos, N. P., Barber, T. X., and Lang, G. Cognition and self-control: Cognitive control of painful sensory input. In H. London and R. E. Nisbett (Eds.) *Thought and Feeling: Cognitive Alteration of Feeling States.* Chicago: Aldine, 1974, pp. 141-158.

Tart, C. T. Effects of posthypnotic suggestion on the process of dreaming. Doctoral dissertation, University of North Carolina, 1963.

Taub, E. Self-regulation of human tissue temperature. In G. E. Schwartz and J. Beatty (Eds.), *Biofeedback: Theory and Research.* New York: Academic Press, in press.

Taub, E., and Emurian, C. Autoregulation of skin temperature using a variable intensity feedback light. Paper presented at annual meeting of Biofeedback Research Society, Boston, 1972. (Reprinted in *Biofeedback & Self-Control: 1972,* article 37)

Taub, E., and Emurian, C. S. Feedback aided self-regulation of skin temperature with a single feedback locus: 1. Acquisition and reversal training. *Biofeedback and Self-Regulation,* in press.

Wallace, R. K., and Benson, H. The physiology of meditation. *Scientific American,* 1972, *226,* No. 2. (Reprinted in *Biofeedback & Self-Control: 1972,* article 28).

Wallace, R. K., Benson, H., and Wilson, A. F. A wakeful hypometabolic physiologic state. *American Journal of Physiology,* 1971, *221,* 795-799. (Reprinted in *Biofeedback & Self-Control: 1971,* article 7).

Welgan, P. R. Learned control of gastric acid secretions in ulcer patients. *Psychosomatic Medicine,* 1974, *36,* 411-419. (Reprinted in *Biofeedback & Self Control: 1974,* article 40)

Wenger, M. A., and Bagchi, B. K. Studies of autonomic functions in practitioners of Yoga in India. *Behavioral Science,* 1961, *6,* 312-323.

Wink, C.A.S. Congenital ichthyosiform erythrodermia treated by hypnosis: Report of two cases. *British Medical Journal,* 1961, *2,* 741-743.

Zimbardo, P. G. Maslach, C., and Marshall, G. Hypnosis and the psychology of cognitive and behavioral control. Department of Psychology, Stanford University, 1970.

I

GENERAL ARTICLES AND OVERVIEWS

A Cognitively Oriented Psychologist Looks at Biofeedback

1

Richard S. Lazarus

Feedback is without a doubt one of the most profound and unifying concepts in all the behavioral sciences. It is fundamental in biological adaptation, being the basis of natural selection and evolution. Feedback from the environment about the consequences of one's acts provides the rewards and punishments that are in part responsible for learning. Maintenance of homeostasis and the neurohumoral regulation of behavior also operate through feedback loops; the brain is, among other things, a great feedback or servomechanism system. Social psychology too makes use of feedback principles in viewing the interaction of persons—social reactions feed back and modify the behavior of each party to a social interaction. Biofeedback is a special case, referring to information the person receives about his bodily processes. Whether and how this information may be used to regulate such processes is not yet fully understood.

Current research in biofeedback brings together under a single rubric a group of psychologists with very diverse objectives and interests. For some, the fundamental issue of such research is whether or not visceral reactions can be controlled through a "pure" process of operant conditioning, pure in the sense that it is said not to depend on any of several types of mediation, including extraneous cues, per-

ceptual or cognitive processes, internal muscular or respiratory ones, and so on. You realize I have in mind here the recent debate between Katkin and Murray (1968) and Crider, Schwartz, and Shnidman (1969). For still others, a key virtue of biofeedback consists of the practical possibilities it affords for the amelioration of diseases of adaptation, for example, tension headaches, hypertension, and so on (Schwartz, 1973). There is still some uncertainty about the practical potential of biofeedback procedures in the control of autonomic end-organ responses, as evidenced by Blanchard and Young's (1973) review of such work with cardiovascular measures; recent research on alpha rhythm by Lynch, Paskewitz, and Orne (1974); and an article by Miller (in press). However, my purpose is not to rehash such issues, nor to review biofeedback research or its use in clinical practice. Rather, I want to embed biofeedback research and clinical practice in what I see as a larger context, namely, adaptation and emotion. Many of the points I make here are much in accord with the valuable comments and analyses made recently by Schwartz (1973), though I was not aware of his article when I prepared this paper.

Biofeedback processes are important for three main reasons: First, the recognition that bodily processes can be volitionally regulated, even if only to a small extent, is a corrective to the partially erroneous classical position in which voluntary regulation was opposed to involuntary or autonomic regulation (Schwartz, 1973). I shall say no more about this here. Second, biofeedback seems to offer an informational aid to the person in his

The article is based on an invited address presented at the annual meeting of the Biofeedback Research Society at Colorado Springs, Colorado, February 15, 1974.

Requests for reprints should be sent to Richard S. Lazarus, Department of Psychology, 3210 Tolman Hall, University of California, Berkeley, California 94720.

quest for the self-regulation of his bodily processes, particularly those that get in the way of successful behavioral adaptation or result in "diseases of adaptation." Third, biofeedback research could throw light on important theoretical and practical questions about the diverse psychological processes by which people regulate their emotional lives and how well these processes work.

In this article, there are three main, interrelated themes: (a) The somatic reactions with which biofeedback deals are really part of a much broader set of issues, namely, those related to the stress emotions and their role in human adaptation; (b) emotional processes and their self-regulation are products of mediating cognitive appraisals about the significance of an event for a person's well-being; and (c) the control of somatic processes is an integral aspect of emotional states and their self-regulation. Indeed, this self-regulation is going on all the time in day-to-day living and is accomplished through a variety of mechanisms whose workings, determinants, and consequences are badly in need of understanding. The first theme is merely an obvious assertion that requires no further elaboration, while the second and third have to do with the nature of emotions and their regulation, and hence form the crux of the argument in the remainder of the article.

Cognitive Processes and Emotion

If indeed the somatic reactions dealt with in biofeedback research and therapy are aspects of emotion and adaptation, then we must consider what an emotional state is and how it is brought about and regulated. From my theoretical perspective (Lazarus, 1966, 1968; Lazarus, Averill, & Opton, 1970), the various emotions arise from and reflect the nature of a person's or animal's ongoing adaptive commerce or transactions with his environment. Each of us has special personality attributes (e.g., motives, belief systems, and competencies to cope with environmental pressures) that shape our reactions and the way we interpret and arrange these transactions.

I define and analyze emotion as a complex disturbance that includes three main components: subjective affect, physiological changes related to species-specific forms of mobilization for adaptive action, and action impulses having both instrumental and expressive qualities. The somatic disturbance arises from the impulse to act that, in part, defines biologically the particular emotion. The quality and intensity of the emotion and its action impulse all depend on a particular kind of cognitive appraisal of the present or anticipated significance of the transaction for the person's well-being. Four kinds of appraisal are critical to the emotional response, namely, that the transaction is damaging, threatening (implying the likelihood of future damage), productive of positive well-being, or challenging (implying the likelihood of overcoming obstacles in the pursuit of something). In lower animals, such as those studied by Tinbergen, the evaluative or appraisal feature of the emotion-eliciting perception is very concrete, simple, and built into the nervous system. In higher animals, such as man, symbolic thought processes and learning play a predominant role.

The historically oriented reader will recognize that this viewpoint is a specific version of numerous earlier and current attempts to develop a meta-theory of psychological activity and behavior in cognitive-phenomenological terms. It contains recognizable elements of William James for whom emotion involved an evaluative perception, the field theoretical approach of Lewin, and the more recent cognitive outlooks of theoreticians such as Tolman, Heider, Murray, Rotter, and a current group of attribution theorists such as Weiner (1972). Thus, cognitive approaches are certainly not new. Bolles (1974), in summarizing the historical trend of cognitive viewpoints, points out that psychology has always been more or less cognitive in outlook. It has only rather recently turned to mechanistic philosophy, and for only a brief interlude in the overall history of the field. Bolles thinks that psychology has begun to turn around from its brief flirtation with a mechanistic approach to behavior and that it has returned to a cognitive orientation.

In regard specifically to emotion, a cognitive-phenomenological approach was evident in the earlier writings on stress of Grinker and Spiegel (1945) in which the term *appraisal* appeared, though somewhat unsystematically, and in the more recent writings of Arnold (1960), who used the term quite systematically in her analysis of emotion. The relatively recent resurgence of cognitive approaches to emotion is also illustrated by the Loyola Symposium on Feelings and Emotions (see Arnold, 1970), a follow-up of two earlier ones, the Wittenberg Symposium in 1927 and the Mooseheart Symposium in 1948, which were clearly dominated by a mechanistic orientation.

One way to highlight the importance of cognitive appraisal in the mediation of emotional states is to point to a contrast between Hans Selye, with his *general adaptation syndrome*, on the one hand, and John Mason and me, on the other. Selye argued that the general adaptation syndrome is a universal biological defensive reaction aroused by any physically noxious agent. Mason (1971), also an endocrinologist, pointed out, however, that the endocrine response to stressor conditions is constantly being affected by cognitive processes. To express this mediation of the physiological response, Mason used the compound term *psychoendocrinology*. Mason and I have gone even further in this direction, both having suggested (Lazarus, 1966; Mason, 1971) that the essential mediator of the general adaptation syndrome may indeed be cognitive. In effect, the pituitary-adrenal cortical response to disturbed commerce with the environment may require that the animal or person somehow recognize his plight. Any animal that has sustained an injury is apt to sense that he is in trouble; and if he doesn't, there will be no general adaptation syndrome. In research on the general adaptation syndrome, cognitive mediation has almost never been ruled out. Thus, one could argue with some justification that this cognitive appraisal of harm via cerebrally controlled processes is necessary to initiate the body's defensive adrenal cortical response.

An animal that is unconscious can sustain bodily harm without the psychoendocrine mechanisms of the general adaptation syndrome becoming active. Data from Symington, Currie, Curran, and Davidson (1955), for example, suggest that unconsciousness and anesthesia eliminate the adrenal effects of physiological stress. It was observed that patients who were dying from injury or disease showed a normal adrenal cortical condition as assessed during autopsy as long as they have remained unconscious during the period of the fatal condition. In contrast, patients who were conscious during the periods of the fatal disease process and died did show adrenal cortical changes. Also relevant, Gray, Ramsey, Villarreal, and Krakaner (1956) showed that general anesthesia, by itself, does not produce a significant adrenal reaction. These studies raise the question of whether it is the psychological significance of the injury rather than the physiologically noxious effects of that injury that produces the adrenal cortical changes associated with stress.

In his recent book, *Stress without Distress*, Selye (1974) now seems to have changed his generalist, noncognitive position somewhat by suggesting that only certain kinds of stress, for example, the stress of frustration or failure, are harmful, but other kinds of stress, such as the joyful pursuit of one's occupation, are benign or even beneficial. This seems to limit the general adaptation syndrome, or at least its damaging features, to certain kinds of transactions, and gives to mediating psychological processes an essential role. Similarly, Rahe (1964), who had once emphasized that all life changes demanding adaptive effort contributed to illness regardless of whether they were regarded as positive or negative, now considers it important to consider psychological defenses and coping activities as mediators of somatic illness. There seems to be a widespread movement toward the position that cognitive processes intervening between the person's adaptive transactions with the environment and the emotional reaction (including its somatic consequences) are important determinants, though the empirical case for this position still remains somewhat uncertain.

In arguing that such a view is relevant to the biofeedback context, let me take a somewhat different tack and consider the point made recently by Janis (Note 1) that the interpersonal features of biofeedback research and therapy situations are primary sources of the mediating psychological processes responsible for successful training in the control of bodily reactions, in contrast with the conditioning paradigm variables that some biofeedback researchers think are sufficient (see also Morris & Suckerman, 1974a, 1974b). Janis quoted (see Jonas, 1972) a young woman who had undergone an arduous 10-week training period during which she succeeded temporarily in lowering her diastolic blood pressure from 97 to about 80. She stated:

I always depend very heavily on Barry Dworkin's [her trainer] encouragement and on his personality. I think he could be an Olympic Coach. He not only seems aware of my general condition but he is never satisfied with less than my best, and I can't fool him. I feel we are friends and allies—it's really as though *we* were lowering my pressure.

In this case, one mediator of the self-control processes appears to be the quality and significance to the subject of the relationship with the therapist, a relationship that sustains her in the arduous training program and without which the self-control might have been impossible. If we can accept the statements of the young woman at face value, we must look at the components of this relationship and their determinants to understand adequately the way biofeedback procedures work, and perhaps to arrange for something to take their place outside the laboratory situation for generalization to occur. I am saying two things here: First, we cannot in our thinking isolate the somatic disturbances and their self-regulation in biofeedback from the larger context of the person's adaptive commerce with his environment. Second, this adaptive commerce is constantly being mediated by social and psychological processes.

A comparable point is implied in Marston and Feldman's (1972) analysis of the concept of self-control in the context of behavior modification

Although seeming to identify themselves as behavior modifiers, they made use of mediating psychological processes in discussing the acquisition of self-control as a two-stage process. Initially, there is the development of a general cognitive set in which the person comes to value the inhibition of the impulse and commits himself to the effort. The authors used the expression *executive response* in referring to this cognitive set. The person is described as making a commitment and evaluating the chances of success and the relative importance of the desired change against the effort required. There are surely individual differences in the motivation to do this and in the relative costs and benefits as evaluated by the person. There follow attempts by the person, with or without therapeutic guidance, to arrange the environmental contingencies that presumably will aid in overcoming the bad habit or impulse. Why not recognize at the outset that in the biofeedback situation, just as in any other situation of learning and performing, there is an active, striving, evaluating person at the helm struggling to do something for which information about his own success can be enormously useful in increasing his chances of ultimate mastery or self-control?

From this standpoint, we have a great need for an adequate transactional language to describe individual differences in the way a person relates psychologically to the environment. I have constructed a simple hypothetical example. Consider two different persons who perceive that they are facing a demand, or the juxtaposition of several demands, which seems to them to be at the borderline or beyond their capacity to master—too much is expected of them. As a result of their individual histories and particular personalities, Person A feels that failure of mastery reflects his own inadequacy, while Person B, by contrast, feels the same inadequacy but interprets the situation as one in which people are constantly trying to use or abuse him. Both experience similar degrees of anticipatory stress and are mobilized to cope with the problem. Prior to the confrontation that will reveal the success or failure of mastery, both experience anxiety, an anticipatory emotion in the context of appraised threat. In Person A, the anxiety is mixed, perhaps with anticipatory depression, while in Person B, the anxiety is mixed with external blaming and anger. Following confrontation in which, let us say, both perform badly, Person A experiences mainly loss and depression, while Person B experiences mainly anger and resentment. A similar set of overwhelming demands have been construed or appraised quite differently because of different personality dispositions. If these persons do well

in the confrontation, both may experience elation because they have overcome the difficulty, depending on whether the explanation of the success is luck or their own perseverance and skill; for example, see Weiner's (1974) attribution theory approach to achievement motivation. In any case, such subtle differences in appraisal of a stressful commerce with the environment underly variations among individuals in the severity (and possibly the pattern) of bodily reactions, the intensity and chronicity of the accompanying emotion, the quality of the effects experienced, and the types of solutions for which they opt, including seeking, accepting, and using clinical help. I don't think such personality-based variations can be ignored in biofeedback therapy settings or in any other kind, and in research on how such therapy works. As Schwartz (1973) put it:

> biofeedback should be viewed as but one approach to the treatment of the "total person," realizing that to "cure" a problem such as hypertension will require more than just the patient consciously attempting to lower his pressure. (p. 670)

The Self-Regulation of Emotion

What about the third theme, concerning self-regulation? Emotion is not a constant thing, but it ebbs and flows and changes over time, as the nature of the adaptive commerce and the information about it changes. Anger suddenly melts and changes to guilt, depression, and love; anxiety changes to euphoria; guilt changes to anger. Rarely are strong emotional states so simple that they have only one quality; more often, emotions involve complex combinations of affect, each deriving from multiple elements of cognitive appraisal—some even ambivalent—to be found in any complex human transaction with the environment. These shifts in intensity and quality over time reflect perceived and appraised changes in the person's relationship with the environment, based in part on feedback from the situation and from his own reactions. In the stress emotions, the changes reflect, in part, the person's constant efforts to master the interchange by overcoming the damage, by postponing or preventing the danger, or by tolerating it. Thus, expectations and discoveries about his power to deal with the environment and master danger are a constantly changing factor, and sometimes a stable determinant, of whether he will feel threatened, for instance, or challenged by what happens.

This latter theme is especially important for an understanding of emotional processes, and for the link between biofeedback and the study of emotion, because it places emphasis on coping processes as a central feature of the emotional state. We are, of course, sometimes accidentally confronted by a situation having major relevance for our welfare; but we also do a great deal of active regulating of our emotional reactions. To some extent, the person selects the environment to which he must respond; he shapes his commerce with it, he plans, chooses, avoids, tolerates, postpones, escapes, demolishes, and manipulates his attention, and he also deceives himself about what is happening, as much as possible casting the relationship in ways that fit his needs and premises about himself in the world. In regulating his emotional life, he is also thereby regulating the bodily reactions that are an integral part of any emotional state.

The idea of coping is hardly new. It has a considerable recent history, largely clinical in focus, although as will be seen shortly coping processes have usually been treated as consequences of an emotion rather than playing the causal role I give to them. The Freudian conception of anxiety, for example, emphasized not only its cue function but also its control by ego-defensive operations, and it helped establish a tradition of study of coping processes in adaptive functioning. It would not be fruitful here to try to summarize this history of ideas about the relationships between coping processes and emotional states. Suffice it to say now that my basic position is that we cannot hope to understand the emotions unless we also take into account the coping activities that affect them.

There are countless observations of the important role that coping or self-regulatory processes play. In a previous discussion of these (Lazarus, in press), I cited both everyday-life anecdotal examples, such as the management of grief, the escalation of discouragement of a love relationship, being a good loser; and formal research examples, such as field studies of combat stress, the psychoendocrine research of the Bethesda group on parents of children dying of leukemia, and research from my own laboratory (Koriat, Melkman, Averill, & Lazarus, 1972) dealing with the self-control of emotional states. There is insufficient time here to do full justice to the problem, but it will be useful to illustrate with some examples below.

COPING AS A CAUSAL FACTOR IN EMOTION

There would be little argument that people are capable of inhibiting emotional behaviors such as avoidance and aggression, or the behavioral expression of emotions such as grief, love, depression, and joy. I am saying, of course, more than this; namely, that intrapsychic forms of coping such as detachment and denial are also capable of modify-

ing, eliminating, or changing the emotion itself, including its subjective affect and bodily changes. When successful, these mechanisms not only affect the visible signs of emotion but also dampen or eliminate the entire emotional syndrome. Thus, in the well-known NIH studies of parents with children dying of leukemia (Wolff, Friedman, Hofer, & Mason, 1964), by denying the fatal significance of their child's illness the NIH parents no longer felt as threatened, and in consequence they exhibited lower levels of adrenal cortical stress hormones than those parents who acknowledged the tragic implications.

Moreover, by successfully distancing themselves from the emotional features of an autopsy, the medical students observed by Lief and Fox (1963) not only behaved unemotionally but in all likelihood, if the appropriate measurements had been made, would have been shown to react with little or no affect and without the bodily disturbances that are an integral part of stress emotion. Lief and Fox (1963) conducted extensive interviews with medical students witnessing for the first time a medical autopsy. Most such students, who are probably self-selected to a high degree, achieve detachment from the experience, though there are some failures too. Certain features of the procedure itself and of the institutionalized behavior of the participants, probably evolved out of the wisdom of long professional experience, provide great help to the student in the process of achieving detachment. During the autopsy, for example, the room is immaculate and brightly lit, and the task is approached with seriousness, skill, and a professional air facilitating a clinical and impersonal attitude toward death. Certain parts of the body are kept covered, particularly the face and genitalia; and the hands, which are so strongly connected with human, personal qualities, are usually not dissected. Once the vital organs are removed, the body is taken from the room, bringing the autopsy down to isolated tissues that are more easily depersonalized. Students avoid talking about the autopsy; and when they do, the discussion is impersonal and stylized. Finally, whereas in laboratory dissection humor appears to be a widespread and effective emotional control device, it is absent in the autopsy room, perhaps because the death has been too recent and joking would appear too insensitive. One senses here the process of struggling to achieve a proper balance between feeling things and looking at them objectively, in short, an effort to regulate a common and expected emotional reaction in which detachment or distancing is the mode of coping. We also recognize that some individuals in medicine and nursing overdo the coping strategy of detachment or dehumanization and appear to their patients as cold and indifferent.

Moreover, much coping activity is anticipatory; that is, the person expects a future harmful confrontation, such as failing an examination, performing in public, or confronting a flood, tornado, or a personal criticism, and this leads him to prepare against the future possibility of harm. To the extent that he prepares effectively, overcoming or avoiding the danger before it materializes or being better able to function adequately in the anticipated confrontation, he thereby changes the nature of the ultimate transaction, along with the emotions that might have been experienced in the absence of such anticipatory coping. Overcoming the danger before it materializes can lead to exhilaration rather than fear, grief, depression, or whatever, depending upon the nature of the harm or loss that might have been experienced and the appraisal of the reasons for success.

You will note that this analysis reverses the usual wisdom that coping always follows emotion (or is caused by it) and suggests that coping can precede emotion and influence its form or intensity. In fact, my general position requires the assertion that coping never follows emotion in anything but a temporal sense, a stance in direct opposition to the long-standing and traditional view that emotions (such as anxiety) serve as drives or motives for adaptive behavior (Lazarus, 1968). The exception to this is when the person is trying to regulate the bodily state directly; but more about this in a moment.

Unfortunately, the psychology of coping is largely descriptive in nature, rather than systematic and predictive. People use a wide variety of coping processes, depending on their personal characteristics, the nature of the environmental demands and contingencies, and how these are appraised. They engage in a variety of preparatory activities. For example, they may worry without taking adequate steps to increase their effectiveness in confrontation; they reduce intense arousal by periodic disengagements from stressful transactions; they take tranquilizers to lower excessive levels of arousal; they use antispasmodics to quiet their bowels; they practice positive mental attitudes; they try to tell themselves that the problem will work itself out or that there is really no problem; they seek support from loved ones or those they trust; they try this or that stress-preventative fad or fashion, such as transcendental meditation, psychotherapy, relaxation, hypnosis, and yoga; they direct their attention away from the source of threat and toward benign or escapist literature or movies; they cope with loss ultimately by giving up what was previously a central portion of their psychological domain. However, we still know extremely little about the conditions, both within the person and in the stimulus configuration, that led to one or another coping process, about the relative effectiveness of such diverse coping processes in regulating emotional states, or about the comparative costs or maladaptive consequences of each form of coping.

A TYPOLOGY OF SELF-REGULATION

My earlier comment about attempts directly to regulate bodily reactions draws an implicit distinction between two kinds of emotion-regulatory or coping processes, a distinction others too have made (cf. Mechanic, 1962). One type, which might properly be called *direct action*, concerns behavioral efforts by the person to deal with the problem generating the stress emotion in the first place. Whether the person attacks or avoids the harmful agency, or engages in some preparatory activity, the focus of the coping effort is on preventing or extricating himself from the plight in which he finds himself. The other type, which might be called *palliation* of emotion, is focused on reducing the visceral or motor disturbances that are a feature of the stress emotion generated by troubled commerce with the environment. Palliation includes both intrapsychic defensive modes and somatically oriented ones such as muscle-relaxant drugs and narcotics.

Thus, if a student who is facing an important and very threatening examination spends the anticipatory interval reading relevant books and articles, rehearsing his understanding of the subject matter with other students or teachers, trying to guess or find out the questions that will be asked, and so on, he is engaged in direct-action forms of coping with the problem, whether he does this effectively or ineffectively. He is attempting to alter his basic relationship with the environment, or, put differently, to change the nature of his troubled commerce with it. To the extent that such activity leads to a more benign appraisal of the potential outcome of the examination, for example, by giving him a sense of preparedness and mastery, the emotional reaction attendant on the threatening character of the situation for him is to some extent short-circuited. Anxiety is also reduced, along with its bodily concomitants, and he is better able to sleep, think, draw upon his knowledge in the examination, etc.

On the other hand, if the same student uses tranquilizers, drinks to control his disturbed bodily state, takes sleeping pills, engages in muscle relaxation, deceives himself into believing he has nothing to be concerned about, diverts his attention for a time, or tries other techniques designed to quiet his heightened arousal, he is employing palliative modes to control the emotional response itself rather than to cope actively with the environmental transaction that generated the arousal in the first place. He is dealing with the somatic reaction rather than its cause. In all likelihood, the rules by which these two divergent kinds of processes operate are quite different.

I do not intend any derogation of this latter "symptom"-oriented or peripheral approach. We all use a variety of coping devices, including palliation, and these often help greatly. Sometimes they are the only ones available, perhaps because the tendency to appraise certain situations as threatening is very deep-rooted in the person, or the source of threat is unknown to him and hence fairly refractory to change. In the case of inevitable harms such as death or imminent surgery, there is little concrete that he can do to alter his plight. Moreover, as in the handling of test anxiety, sometimes effective action in the problem-oriented sense is severely impaired by the emotion itself, as when the person finds he cannot think clearly about his problem and prepare adequately in the face of the interfering effects. Under such conditions, reducing the anxiety or the correlates of anxiety by *any* means available may serve to facilitate adaptive coping. Moreover, in chronic or repeated situations of threat, even merely lowering debilitating arousal may swing the balance of the approach–avoidance conflict in favor of approach and commitment and away from avoidance and disengagement, and this may make possible the attainment of goals of great importance.

The palliative form of control that aims at reducing somatic turmoil rather than at resolving its psychodynamic origins is the arena into which biofeedback research and its use in therapy fall. I would argue that those who want to rule out cognitive or other mediators in biofeedback research miss the central point in the self-regulation of emotion. Not only does such an effort greatly narrow the scope of such self-regulation, but it minimizes the complexity of the problem and the diverse patterns by which it typically operates in all our lives. We need to have more knowledge of the myriad forms of self-regulation that are available and serviceable to given kinds of people and in given types of situations in managing their emotional lives (see also Schwartz, 1973). As my opening statements suggest, a major virtue of the biofeedback movement lies in the opportunity it provides to test some of our ideas about the coping

processes used by people and about those that are capable of influencing the emotional response.

What actually mediates biofeedback effects themselves is still an open question. One possibility is that the relaxation process could serve as a means of attention deployment (Budzynski, Stoyva, Adler, & Mullaney, 1973). The person learns to focus his attention on relaxing his muscles, and his attention is turned away from the stress-producing sources of the tension from which the headaches are indirectly derived. Or alternatively, such training might induce a relaxed psychological state that is incompatible with the tension, a mechanism that has been suggested by Wolpe (1958) and by Mendelsohn (1962). Or it might merely create a physiological state (muscle relaxation) that is itself incompatible with the physiological headache mechanism. If these processes could be shown to generalize to situations outside the laboratory, they might provide a powerful tool of therapy as well as research into the efficacy of various mediating self-regulatory processes.

Some of my own research (Koriat et al., 1972), in fact, has emphasized the cognitive mediators regulating autonomic nervous system activity while subjects watched a stressful movie. We asked subjects to watch the film while adopting two different attitudes, one to involve themselves more fully in the stressful episodes and the other to detach or distance themselves. Evidence that our subjects were capable of such self-control of emotional states came from autonomic as well as self-report measures. This research was also designed to discover the cognitive processes producing altered emotional arousal, though it might well have been improved by the use of biofeedback procedures to aid subjects in assessing how well they were succeeding in involving or detaching themselves from the stressful scenes. We found that certain strategies were reportedly widely used to achieve detachment, while others predominated in the effort to create emotional involvement. But we could not adequately test the effectiveness of these strategies.

COPING AND ENVIRONMENTAL INTERACTIONS

An important qualification should be made here. We should not expect given self-regulating strategies to be effective in every context of adaptive commerce. Rather, depending on the environmental demands and options open to the person, some strategies should be serviceable and others not. For example, Cohen and Lazarus (1973) found that patients who approached surgery with avoidant strategies, that is, those who did not want to know about their illness and the nature of the surgery, showed a more rapid and smoother post-surgical recovery than did patients adopting a vigilant strategy. It was speculated that vigilance might actually be a handicap for the surgical patient because there was nothing constructive he could really do in the postoperative recuperation period except simply to ignore or deny the sources of threat and pain. Trying postoperatively to pay attention vigilantly to every possible cue of danger or sign of discomfort resulted in a longer and more complicated recovery, and this appeared to be maladaptive in this situation.

However, a very different strategy seems called for in the stressful context studied by Reuven Gal (Note 2), namely, seasickness among Israeli navy personnel. Holding constant the degree of sea-sickness, it was found that sailors who had the trait or disposition of coping in an active, purposive, and vigilant fashion despite their sickness functioned much better at their normal jobs. Forgetting for a moment several possible sources of confounding, such as the measures of coping (trait versus state) and the type of population, the juxtaposition of these two studies points up the potential interaction that might exist between type of coping and the nature of the environmental demands. Moreover, such research also points up another one of the major gaps in theory and research in the biofeedback arena, namely, the absence of evident interest in individual differences. Biofeedback procedures even when oriented to therapy seem generally to be approached normatively rather than ipsatively to assess the contribution of situations and individual differences in personality to the results. Depending on preferred coping styles and patterns of belief and expectation and on the nature of the situational demands, individuals should differ greatly in their capacity to profit from particular biofeedback procedures and to acquire control over their bodily reactions (see also Schwartz, 1973, p. 672).

Concluding Comment

We are a long way from understanding the modes of self-regulation of emotion that are available to individuals and serviceable in any given environmental context. Indeed, this seems to me to be one of psychology's most important issues, and the biofeedback arena offers unparalleled opportunities to tackle it. I am convinced that self-regulation of emotion is a perfectly normal part of everyday living and does not emerge only in the biofeedback laboratory. We need to know more about these modes of self-regulation, their efficacy, and the rules of their operation, and biofeedback studies could provide a powerful tool to resolve these basic issues. I believe that such research will go further if it is approached within the larger context of emotion and adaptation and oriented to the wide variety of mediators that affect the reaction pattern, rather than being treated as a special or unique kind of process limited to the biofeedback laboratory.

REFERENCE NOTES

1. Janis, I. L. *Preventing dehumanization: Some comments on Howard Leventhal's analysis.* Unpublished manuscript. (Available from Yale University, Department of Psychology.)

2, Gal, R. *Coping processes under seasickness conditions.* Manuscript submitted for publication, 1975.

REFERENCES

Arnold, M. B. *Emotion and personality.* New York: Columbia University Press, 1960.

Arnold, M. B. (Ed.). *Feelings and emotions.* New York: Academic Press, 1970.

Blanchard, E. B., & Young, L. D. Self-control of cardiac functioning: A promise yet unfulfilled. *Psychological Bulletin,* 1973, *79,* 145–163.

Bolles, R. C. Cognition and motivation: Some historical trends. In B. Weiner (Ed.), *Cognitive views of human motivation.* New York: Academic Press, 1974.

Budzynski, T. H., Stoyva, J. M., Adler, C. S., & Mullaney, D. J. EMG biofeedback and tension headache: A controlled outcome study. *Psychosomatic Medicine,* 1973, *35,* 484–496.

Cohen, F., & Lazarus, R. S. Active coping processes, coping dispositions, and recovery from surgery. *Psychosomatic Medicine,* 1973, *35,* 375–389.

Crider, A., Schwartz, G., & Shnidman, S. On the criteria for instrumental autonomic conditioning: A reply to Katkin and Murray. *Psychological Bulletin,* 1969, *71,* 455–461.

Gray, S. J., Ramsey, C. S., Villarreal, R., & Krakaner, L. J. Adrenal influences upon the stomach and the gastric response to stress. In H. Selye & G. Hensen (Eds.), *Fifth Annual Report on Stress, 1955–1956.* New York: MD Publications, 1956.

Grinker, R. R., & Spiegel, J. P. *Men under stress.* New York: McGraw-Hill, 1945.

Jonas, G. Profiles: Visceral learning I. (On Neal E. Miller.) *New Yorker*, August 19, 1972, pp. 34–36+.

Katkin, E. S., & Murray, E. N. Instrumental conditioning of autonomically mediated behavior: Theoretical and methodological issues. *Psychological Bulletin*, 1968, 70, 52–68.

Koriat, A., Melkman, R., Averill, J. R., & Lazarus, R. S. The self-control of emotional reactions to a stressful film. *Journal of Personality*, 1972, 40, 601–619.

Lazarus, R. S. *Psychological stress and the coping process.* New York: McGraw-Hill, 1966.

Lazarus, R. S. Emotions and adaptation: Conceptual and empirical relations. In E. J. Arnold (Ed.), *Nebraska Symposium on Motivation* (Vol. 16). Lincoln: University of Nebraska Press, 1968.

Lazarus, R. S. The self-regulation of emotion. In L. Levi (Ed.), *Parameters of emotion.* New York: Raven Press, in press.

Lazarus, R. S., Averill, J. R., & Opton, E. M., Jr. Towards a cognitive theory of emotion. In M. B. Arnold (Ed.), *Feelings and emotions.* New York: Academic Press, 1970.

Lief, H. I., & Fox, R. S. Training for "detached concern" in medical students. In H. I. Lief, V. F. Lief, & N. R. Lief (Eds.), *The psychological basis of medical practice.* New York: Harper & Row, 1963.

Lynch, J. J., Paskewitz, D. A., & Orne, M. T. Some factors in the feedback control of human alpha rhythm. *Psychosomatic Medicine*, 1974, 36, 399–410.

Marston, A. R., & Feldman, S. E. Toward the use of self-control in behavior modification. *Journal of Consulting and Clinical Psychology*, 1972, 39, 429–433.

Mason, J. W. A re-evaluation of the concept of 'non-specificity' in stress theory. *Journal of Psychiatric Research*, 1971, 8, 323–333.

Mechanic, D. *Students under stress.* New York: The Free Press of Glencoe, 1962.

Mendelsohn, G. A. The competition of affective response in human subjects. *Journal of Abnormal and Social Psychology*, 1962, 65, 26–31.

Miller, N. E. Critical issues in the therapeutic application of biofeedback. In G. E. Schwartz & J. Beatty (Eds.), *Biofeedback: Theory and research.* New York: Academic Press, in press.

Morris, R. J., & Suckerman, K. R. The importance of the therapeutic relationship in systematic desensitization. *Journal of Consulting and Clinical Psychology*, 1974, 42, 148. (a)

Morris, R. J., & Suckerman, K. R. Therapist warmth as a factor in automated systematic densensitization. *Journal of Consulting and Clinical Psychology*, 1974, 42, 244–250. (b)

Rahe, R. H. The pathway between subjects' recent life changes and their near-future illness reports: Representative results and methodological issues. In B. S. Dohrenwend & B. P. Dohrenwend (Eds.), *Stressful life events: Their nature and effects.* New York: Wiley, 1974.

Schwartz, G. E. Biofeedback as therapy: Some theoretical and practical issues. *American Psychologist*, 1973, 28, 666–673.

Selye, H. *Stress without distress.* Philadelphia, Pa.: J. B. Lippincott, 1974.

Symington, T., Currie, A. R., Curran, R. S., & Davidson, J. N. The reaction of the adrenal cortex in conditions of stress. In *Ciba Foundations Colloquia on Endocrinology* (Vol. 8). *The human adrenal cortex.* Boston: Little, Brown, 1955.

Weiner, B. *Theories of motivation.* Chicago: Markham, 1972.

Weiner, B. An attributional interpretation of expectancy-value theory. In B. Weiner (Ed.), *Cognitive views of human motivation.* New York: Academic Press, 1974.

Wolff, C. T., Friedman, S. B., Hofer, M. A., & Mason, J. W. Relationship between psychological defenses and mean urinary 17-hydroxycorticosteroid excretion rates: Parts I and II. *Psychosomatic Medicine*, 1964, 26, 576–609.

Wolpe, J. *Psychotherapy by reciprocal inhibition.* Stanford, Calif.: Stanford University Press, 1958.

Biofeedback, Self-Regulation, and the Patterning of Physiological Processes

2

Gary E. Schwartz

By training subjects to control voluntarily combinations of visceral, neural, and motor responses, it is possible to assess linkages between physiological responses and their relationship to human consciousness

Although we do not usually think about it, we are constantly regulating complex patterns of neural and visceral processes in our dynamic interchange with our environment. How often do we ponder the multiplicity of biological processes we must voluntarily orchestrate in order to perform an everyday act like writing a sentence? Not very often; for we usually direct our attention to the goal of our actions rather than reflecting upon the pattern of interacting processes we generate to produce the desired behavior. But if a skill is unique or unexpected—like the feats of bodily or cognitive self-regulation long claimed by certain yogis and meditators, and more recently demon-

Gary E. Schwartz received his Ph.D. in 1971 from Harvard University, where he is currently Assistant Professor of Personality Psychology in the Department of Psychology and Social Relations. His teaching and research interests center on psychophysiology, consciousness and self-regulation, and biological foundations of personality and psychopathology. He is also Chief of the Clinical Psychophysiology Unit at the Erich Lindemann Mental Health Center, Massachusetts General Hospital, where he directs clinical research on self-regulation and patterning of physiological processes in affec- *tive and psychosomatic disorders. In 1972 he received the Young Psychologist Award from the American Psychological Association, and he served in 1973–74 as president of the Biofeedback Research Society. He is the senior editor of the forthcoming volumes* Biofeedback: Theory and Research *(Academic Press) and* Consciousness and Self-Regulation: Advances in Research *(Plenum Press), and is at work on a new textbook on the biological bases of personality. Address: Department of Psychology and Social Relations, Harvard University, 1544 William James Hall, Cambridge, MA 02138.*

Reprinted by permission from *American Scientist,* journal of Sigma Xi, The Scientific Research Society of North America, 1975, Vol. 63, 314-324.

strated with biofeedback, our fascination with the nature of the processes involved is rekindled.

It has been found that, if humans and lower animals are provided with (1) new information in the form of biofeedback for internal responses such as heart rate, blood pressure, and electrical activity of the brain, and (2) incentives or rewards for changing or controlling the feedback, they can learn to control voluntarily the physiological responses associated with the feedback. Biofeedback research has raised the question whether responses once considered to be involuntary may be controlled consciously (Miller 1969). It has also stimulated interest in the use of self-regulation techniques in both clinical treatment and in research which seeks to determine the limits of self-control.

Despite the abundance of research in this area (see Barber et al. 1971; Kamiya et al. 1971; Stoyva et al. 1972; Shapiro et al. 1973; Miller et al. 1974), there has been little effort to explain exactly how self-regulation develops or what are the underlying psychobiological mechanisms and constraints (Miller 1974). Most research treats only single responses or response systems and fails to address the more normal but complex phenomenon of the voluntary coordination of multiple physiological processes. Drawing upon research conducted by my colleagues and students over the past six years, I will describe in this paper experiments using biofeedback procedures to teach voluntary control of combinations of responses, and then relate our findings to the broader question of the biocognitive mechanisms involved. This includes our research on the

regulation of imagery and emotion and its clinical application to elucidating the mechanisms underlying relaxation, meditation, and other self-regulation therapies. Biofeedback and related cognitive procedures provide a unique and powerful research tool for investigating both the interrelationships among physiological systems and their constraints in the intact human and the role of patterns of physiological responses in the generation of subjective experience (Schwartz 1974, in press).

I hope that this paper will also help to dispel some of the prevailing popular notions about biofeedback. Unfortunately, research on biofeedback and on related cognitive self-regulation procedures such as meditation is tainted by simplistic and at times wild speculation by scientists and journalists alike. It is understandable how research that challenges our basic conception of man's biological structure and psychological capabilities can stimulate novel ideas about basic research and clinical issues, but such theorizing has alienated an important segment of the scientific community. One area of controversy involves the application of visceral self-regulation to psychosomatic disorders; another is the application of brain wave biofeedback to bring about altered states of consciousness. At one extreme are those who argue that biofeedback can enable us to control literally any aspect of our biology at will; at the other extreme are a growing number who dismiss biofeedback as a useless gimmick. I suggest that neither of these extremes is appropriate and that current research on biofeedback from a pattern perspective not only expands our understanding of human self-regulation but helps us to recognize its limitations.

Specificity and the brain

The capacity of the human brain to regulate various dynamic patterns of neural, skeletal, and visceral responses grows out of its extraordinary capacity for response specificity. In this respect the brain is a highly efficient organ, for under most circumstances it is capable of recruiting and coordinating only those sensory, visceral, and motor processes needed to perform a given task. Biofeedback procedures have been applied to the voluntary control of individual skeletal muscles, and Basmajian (1972) has shown that subjects can learn to control individual motor units within a specific muscle when given feedback and reward for activity of the designated unit. He finds that, early in training, adjacent motor units in the muscle are also activated, but as the subject practices controlling the feedback, the irrelevant units drop out. At a more general level, Germana (1968) illustrates how, as subjects learn a variety of cognitive and motor tasks, initial learning is accompanied by increases in multiple responses including heart rate, sweat gland activity, and muscle tension over much of the body. However, as the subject masters the specific task, activation peaking occurs, and the various physiological responses return to levels adjusted to maintaining effective performance. In both of these examples, learned specificity grows out of more general physiological arousal.

The motor system is a good model for conceptualizing the self-regulation of autonomic and electrocortical responses, because it highlights the principle that learning typically progresses from more general arousal to greater response specificity with training. Cardiovascular biofeedback researchers such as Lang (1974) and Brener (1974) have recently begun to emphasize specificity of motor skill learning and its interaction with biofeedback. In my laboratory we have applied to heart rate control. Fleishman's (1966) model for understanding the acquisition of autonomic skills. Fleishman describes five basic components of complex motor skills: strength, endurance, steadiness, control precision, and reaction time. With few exceptions, biofeedback research has used a combination of the strength and endurance paradigms—the subject's task being to increase or decrease the frequency or amplitude of the response as much as possible and sustain the effect for some period of time (e.g. a minute). Schwartz, Vogler, and Young (in press) have developed a different autonomic skill —a cardiac reaction-time paradigm—in which the subject's primary task is to raise (or lower) his heart rate as quickly as possible at the onset of the trial, briefly holding control for 3 consecutive seconds. On the basis of the motor skills literature, we predicted that specificity of cardiac skill learning would show little transfer of training between the strength-endurance and the reaction-time skills. Our experiment bore out the prediction.

This finding of specificity of skill learning *within a single autonomic response* underscores the power of biofeedback procedures to tap specific capabilities for learned self-regulation normally not exercised by human beings. The study may be taken as one model for studying the similarities and differences between specific motor and visceral self-regulatory processes. However, the specific-skills approach to biofeedback leads us away from rather than toward the major concern of this paper—the nature of self-regulation of combinations of responses. We did not recognize the full importance of learned specificity with biofeedback until we were confronted with selective voluntary control of systolic blood pressure versus heart rate; this discovery prompted the development of pattern biofeedback procedures.

Systolic pressure and heart rate control

One of the most convincing, but initially surprising, illustrations of the specificity of human self-regulation in the autonomic nervous system emerged in our early studies on the self-regulation of systolic blood pressure and heart rate (Shapiro et al. 1969; Shapiro, Tursky, and Schwartz 1970a, 1970b). In the first two experiments, subjects were given binary (on/off) feedback (a light and tone) at each heart beat when systolic blood pressure was either higher or lower than the median blood pressure for a 50-beat trial (Tursky, Shapiro, and Schwartz 1972). Subjects were instructed to make the feedback light and tone occur as often as possible; however, they were not told the nature of the response or the direction in which it was to change. As an added incentive, subjects were shown bonus slides after every 20 feedback stimuli (in the early studies, the all-male subjects were

shown pictures of nude females; later, a variety of rewards including travel slides and monetary bonuses were added). The results of both experiments showed that, in a single experimental session, subjects could exert relative self-control over their blood pressure and that these changes were independent of heart rate.

In the third experiment, the procedure was reversed; subjects were given feedback and reward for raising and lowering heart rate while systolic blood pressure was monitored; here subjects showed relative self-control of heart rate independent of blood pressure. As we discovered from postexperimental questionnaires, the essentially *uninstructed* subjects did not report using consistent cognitive or somatic strategies; for example, those who decreased their blood pressure or heart rate did not use relaxing imagery more frequently than those who increased these responses.

Given the complex physiological constraints between these two responses (heart rate, in addition to stroke volume and peripheral resistance, can act as a physical determinant of blood pressure), the ease and speed with which specificity was learned was surprising. The biofeedback results seemed to be pointing to something specific about the behavioral relationship (presumed but not explicitly measured) between the two responses (Schwartz 1972).

If systolic blood pressure and heart rate were so related over time that increases in one were always associated with increases in the other, then when an experimenter gave feedback and reward for one, he would unwittingly provide it for the other as well. Therefore, we would expect that both functions should be learned simultaneously and in the same direction. But if these two functions were so related that when one increased, the other simultaneously decreased, then if feedback and reward were given for one, the other would simultaneously receive the opposite inducement. Both functions should again be learned, only now in opposite directions. However, since neither of these findings was empirically obtained in our prior research, it would follow that systolic blood pressure and heart rate must be so related that binary feedback for one causes simultaneous *random* feedback for the other.

If this were so, how could a subject be taught to control both processes? One approach might be to give the feedback and reward only when the desired *pattern* of responses occurs. In theory, it should be possible to teach a person to integrate his systolic blood pressure and heart rate voluntarily (make both functions increase or decrease together) or differentiate them (make them go in opposite directions) by providing feedback and reward for the desired pattern. The required procedure for tracking, in real time, patterns of phasic and tonic changes in both systems was developed based on the binary feedback model that detected at each heart beat whether blood pressure and heart rate were in one of the 4 possible states: $BP^{up}HR^{up}$, $BP^{up}HR_{down}$, $BP_{down}HR^{up}$, or $BP_{down}HR_{down}$ (Schwartz, Shapiro, and Tursky 1971).

If behavior operated without physiological constraints, a straight be-

havioral analysis of the feedback-response relationship could alone predict learned patterning. But these predictions would fail to the extent that biological constraints are operative. This realization led to the hypothesis that, by determining the ease with which subjects could learn both to integrate and to differentiate various combinations of physiological responses, it would be possible to uncover and assess natural biological relationships in the intact human (Schwartz 1972). Quite unexpectedly, the pattern biofeedback procedure was found to be a far more sensitive indicator of underlying constraints than the single-system biofeedback procedure.

We next performed an experiment using binary feedback and instructions like those of the initial studies, but with four groups of subjects, each of which received biofeedback for one of the four possible BP–HR patterns (Schwartz 1972). Analysis of the resting frequency of the BP–HR patterns indicated that each occurred spontaneously about 25% of the time; this supported the initial prediction that systolic BP and HR are phasically unrelated, at least from the point of view of a simple binary feedback system. However, as can be seen in Figure 1, pattern feedback uncovers strong constraints between the systems that were not exposed with single-system training.

When subjects were required to produce an integration pattern ($BP^{up}HR^{up}$ or $BP_{down}HR_{down}$) they showed simultaneous control of both blood pressure and heart rate in the same direction. This is in contrast to the previous findings,

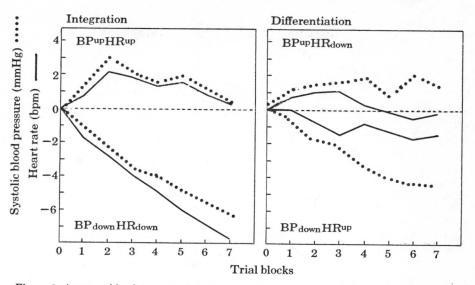

Figure 1. A strong blood pressure–heart rate (BP–HR) integration constraint emerges with pattern biofeedback. In one experiment, each of 4 groups of subjects received biofeedback for one of the 4 possible BP or HR patterns. Simultaneous control of systolic blood pressure (*dots*) and heart rate (*black*) was achieved rapidly when subjects were required to integrate these functions (raising or lowering them together) (*left*).

When subjects were required to differentiate the two—to make blood pressure change in the opposite direction from heart rate—only moderate control was attained (*right*). Curves represent the mean of 10 subjects, 5 trials each, set to zero by the pre-experimental baseline values; beats per minute and millimeters of mercury are therefore on the same axis. (From Schwartz 1972.)

which showed specific control of one response without simultaneous changes in the other. More important, however, is that feedback for the integration patterns produces more rapid learning and somewhat larger changes than biofeedback for the single systems alone! The findings for the differentiation conditions bore out this conclusion. Although the curves suggest that some BP$_{down}$HR^{up} and BP^{up}HR$_{down}$ control was achieved, the magnitude of control was substantially less than that obtained for integration control.

An additional finding of particular importance to the pattern concept

was that when subjects were taught to lower *both* functions simultaneously (as opposed to lowering either function alone), they began spontaneously and consistently to report feelings of relaxation and calmness, a subjective state we would expect to be associated with more diffuse physiological relaxation. If we recall that these subjects were told nothing about the precise meaning of the feedback, this finding becomes even more significant. In the attempt to understand and extend biofeedback techniques to patterns of responses, the research uncovers new information about the nature of the physiological systems and constraints and their relation to subjective experience.

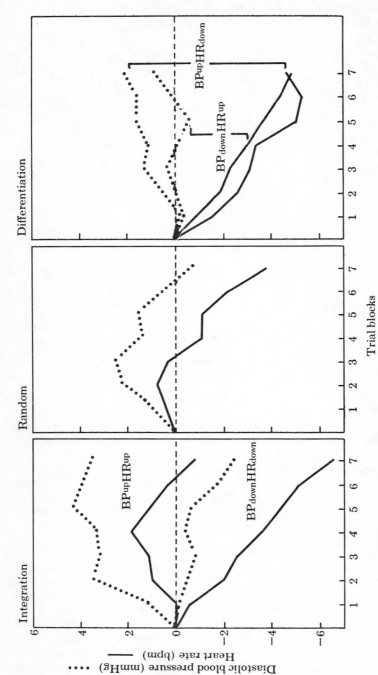

Figure 2. In order to assess accurately a subject's ability to regulate patterns of internal responses, the results for feedback groups must often be compared with results obtained for groups given random biofeedback. In this experiment, in the random condition (center), diastolic blood pressure (dots) and heart rate (black) not only do not remain constant over a session but change at different rates. Subjects required to integrate BP and HR (left) were able to do so rapidly; but subjects required to differentiate the two responses (right) showed no ability to separate them beyond their normal divergence in the random condition. Curves represent the mean of 10 subjects, 5 trials each, set to zero by the pre-experimental baseline values; beats per minute and millimeters of mercury are therefore on the same axis. (From Schwartz 1974.)

Diastolic pressure and heart rate control

Shapiro, Schwartz, and Tursky (1972) observed that, when uninstructed subjects were given direct binary feedback and reward for *diastolic* as opposed to systolic blood pressure, some covariance of heart rate control also occurred. An important finding was that the learned changes in diastolic blood pressure emerged earlier in the session than those for heart rate, and the magnitude of the heart rate change was smaller than that previously observed for direct heart rate biofeedback.

On the basis of these observations, we predicted that diastolic blood pressure and heart rate must be partially (but not completely) phasically integrated. Consequently, biofeedback for the pressure would result in partial (but not complete) feedback for comparable heart rate changes as well; this would explain why some learning of heart rate control occurred with diastolic pressure biofeedback. Analysis of the resting BP–HR patterns confirmed that the two responses changed spontaneously in the same direction about two-thirds of the time. In light of this apparent phasic constraint, we predicted that subjects should be readily able to integrate their diastolic blood pressure and heart rate at will, but they would find it extremely difficult to differentiate them. We performed an experiment modeled after the previously described (Schwartz 1972) pattern experiment but added a fifth group as a control, to be given random feedback and reward (Schwartz, Shapi-

ro, and Tursky 1972). The results are shown in Figure 2.

The curves for random feedback reveal that the baselines for diastolic blood pressure and heart rate not only do not remain constant over the session but change at relatively different rates (HR lower than BP). Thus, to assess learning over time accurately, self-regulation must be measured vis-à-vis the changing baselines that are exposed, for example, by comparison with a random feedback control group (Crider, Schwartz, and Shnidman 1969). Note that for integration feedback, rapid learning of both diastolic pressure and heart rate occurs; again, the rate of growth in learning is greater than that obtained for single-system biofeedback. This finding is contrasted with the results for the two differentiation conditions, which show essentially no evidence of separation beyond that occurring with random feedback.

These data support the notion that the resting phasic relationship observed between diastolic blood pressure and heart rate reflects a biological constraint. However, it should be emphasized that a simple correlation of two responses over time does not necessarily indicate a causal relationship between them. A causal relationship can be proved only by determining the ease with which the two responses can be separated—for example, using the self-regulation pattern strategy described here. Further, an accurate assessment of the degree to which such relationships are fixed requires additional sessions of training. Unfortunately, with the exception of the experiment to be described below, multisession pattern studies have not yet been reported.

EEG and heart rate control

If pattern biofeedback training can be used effectively to study relationships *within* the autonomic nervous system, then perhaps the pattern approach may have more general use in investigating integrations and constraints across sensory, visceral, and motor systems (Schwartz 1974; Black 1974). My laboratory has recently been using the pattern biofeedback approach to examine the role of cortical processes in the self-regulation of autonomic activity. At the outset, it became clear that it would be desirable to teach an individual rapidly to regulate, on command, a host of different patterns of EEG and autonomic activity, so as to reduce problems of intersubject variability and to enable us to assess the stability of constraints over time.

Learning to perform a dual task —for example, rubbing the stomach with one hand and patting the head with the other—can be difficult. One way to achieve a patterned skill is to practice each response alone and then coordinate the two. This training strategy is valuable for a number of reasons. Unlike the direct pattern feedback approach, which requires digital logic or computer facilities to quantify complex patterns on-line to provide feedback (we currently use a PDP11 system for measuring multiple responses on-line), the coordination approach requires simple biofeedback equipment. Separate portable devices for different responses can be used to train combinations of responses outside the laboratory. In addition, this procedure stimulates the subject to develop self-control naturally. He is allowed to experiment at his own pace in learning what strategies are effective for increasing and decreasing the feedback (Engel 1972), and the "free play" periods interspersed with test trials make the task both more challenging and more rewarding.

Previous single-system studies have suggested that, while heart rate control has no appreciable effect on EEG from the occipital region (Schwartz, Shaw, and Shapiro 1972), self-regulation of occipital alpha may have a small effect on heart rate (Beatty and Kornfeld 1973). Occipital alpha is an EEG wave of 8–13 hz recorded from the back of the head. It is most prevalent in the typical subject when he is relaxed, with eyes closed.

In a series of studies, we have examined both single-system and pattern training for occipital alpha and heart rate using the coordination training procedure (Hassett and Schwartz, in press). In one experiment, 12 subjects were studied over two sessions, receiving single-system training for EEG alpha from the right occipital region and heart rate in Session 1, and coordination training with simultaneous biofeedback for the two systems in Session 2. The results showed that subjects were able to produce on command, within specific limits, all eight patterns of occipital alpha and heart rate.

More interesting, however, was the consistency of the alpha–heart rate constraints. The results showed that occipital alpha regulation influenced heart rate, while the opposite was not the case. This effect was especially evident in the pattern conditions, where heart rate control was actually enhanced

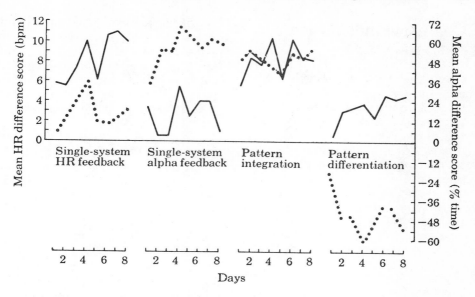

Figure 3. Studies of relationships between cortical processes and autonomic activity reveal an apparent one-way constraint of occipital alpha (an EEG wave of 8-13 hz; dots) and heart rate (*black*). The results for one subject in a series of 8-day tests are shown here. The subject achieved very specific control in the single-system response tests, and when instructed to integrate the two responses, he was able to do so fairly successfully. But instructions to differentiate them resulted in reduced heart rate control with slightly enhanced alpha control. The consistency with which this constraint is found during pattern regulation suggests that occipital alpha may influence heart rate, but not vice versa. (From Hassett and Schwartz, in press.)

when alpha was simultaneously self-regulated in an arousal pattern (e.g. $HR^{up}alpha^{off}$). Conversely, differentiation of heart rate and alpha led to an impairment of heart rate regulation, compared to single-system heart rate control. These results were maintained even when subjects were tested after training without feedback.

Three subjects have been run for 8 training sessions, and the results, especially for the pattern conditions, are quite consistent from day to day. A particularly good self-regulation subject, showing exceptional specificity during single-system control in both responses over the 8 days, is shown in Figure 3. Whereas during integration he produced substantial regulation of both responses, during differentiation he showed reduced heart rate control and slightly enhanced alpha control (but in the opposite direction, as expected). The consistency of this pattern effect with repeated training and testing makes the concept of a one-way occipital alpha–heart rate constraint more compelling. When two of the subjects were posttested, in a ninth session 7 months after the training sessions, self-regulation of the patterns was retained, as was the alpha–heart rate constraint.

Cognitive mechanisms in pattern control

Given that subjects can learn with the aid of pattern biofeedback training to regulate combinations of autonomic and brain wave activity, the next question is, How do they do it? We might begin by asking them—and this leads us to the question of the relationship between cognitive strategies and the control of particular patterns of physiological activity. Can cognitive processes elicit or "mediate" patterned physiological changes?

The idea that cognition was an epiphenomenon, either unimportant or downright interfering, was long held by strict behaviorists and is still in vogue in some quarters. Katkin and Murray (1968) went so far as to conclude that, in order to demonstrate true instrumental conditioning of an autonomic response in humans, it would be necessary for the subjects to be paralyzed by curare (to remove overt skeletal mediators) and to be rendered unconscious (to eliminate cognitive mediators)! In reply to this article, Crider, Schwartz, and Shnidman (1969) pointed out that there was surprisingly little experimental data from which to argue that cognitive events could influence discrete physiological responses in the first place. More recently, Kimmel (1974) in an evaluation of the blood pressure–heart rate pattern findings, stated that "mediationists may also have to become cognitive contortionists to deal with data such as these." However, data and theory have made substantial progress over the past six years, and Kimmel's conclusion needs to be qualified.

Carefully controlled studies have demonstrated that cognitive activity *can* elicit physiological responses (McGuigan and Schoonover 1973). Self-induced affective thoughts can themselves elicit increases in heart rate (Schwartz 1971). In another experiment (Schwartz and Higgins 1971), generating a verbal image (silently thinking the word "stop") at the end of a 5-second light elicited anticipatory time-locked changes in heart rate comparable to those observed when subjects performed a simple task (pushing a button). As shown in Figure 4, fast button-presses are *preceded* by a cardiac deceleration that reaches its trough sooner than if button-presses are made deliberately slow; the identical, although slightly attenuated, anticipatory heart rate curves are generated when the same paced task is performed cognitively with no obvious overt response. In other words, thoughts can act as both "stimuli" and "responses" with predictable physiological consequences.

The question remains whether there is any evidence that classes of cognitive events can elicit specific *patterns* of physiological responses corresponding to those regulated through biofeedback. And if so, are we therefore justified in concluding that the strategies reflect underlying neural mechanisms involved in regulating the physiological changes? In the clinical area, in a series of classic studies in the 1950s (reviewed by Graham 1972), Graham and his associates demonstrated that various psychosomatic disorders were associated with definable attitudes in patients. For example, hypertensive patients reported feeling threatened with

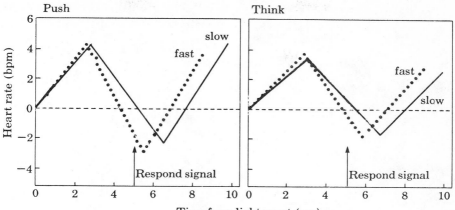

Figure 4. Studies have shown that cognitive activity can elicit physiological responses. In one study, silently thinking the word "stop" at the end of a 5-second warning light produced (*right*) changes in heart rate comparable to those elicited when subjects responded overtly to the signal by pushing a button (*left*). In both cases, fast responses to the signal (*dotted curves*) are preceded by a slowing down of heart beat that reaches its trough sooner than if the same task is performed slowly (*black curves*). Curves represent mean heart rate values at critical points in the trial for 20 subjects. (From Schwartz and Higgins 1971.)

harm and having to be ready for anything. Further, when such attitudes were suggested to normal subjects under hypnosis, the suggestion elicited measurable changes that mimicked the patterns originally observed in the patients. It is unfortunate that these early studies have not been followed up, for current advances in psychophysiology and neuropsychology provide a framework in which such findings can be understood.

Patterns of facial muscle activity

Drawing on Darwin's early observations of emotion in lower animals and man (1872), Ekman, Friesen, and Ellsworth (1972) and Izard (1971) have provided experimental data indicating that specific facial expressions reflect distinct emo-

tions which are innate and universal, although their overt manifestation can be regulated to some extent. Of particular importance for the self-regulation pattern concept is Izard's neurophysiological theory of emotion, which postulates that discrete patterns of facial and postural muscle activity are processed in parallel and integrated by the brain and, in fact, make up a significant component of the conscious experience of emotion.

We have recently extended this concept to self-regulated imagery, demonstrating that small but discrete patterns of facial muscle activity are reliably generated when a person simply thinks about prior emotional experiences (Schwartz et al. 1974a, b; in press a, b). Electrodes are placed over carefully selected muscles, and low levels of electromyographic (EMG) activity

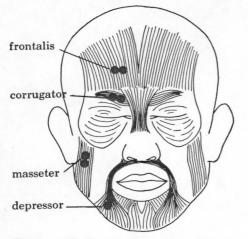

frontalis

corrugator

masseter

depressor

Figure 5. Emotional states are associated with identifiable covert facial expressions that may not be readily discernible to either the casual observer or the subject himself. The expressions may be monitored by recording and quantifying electromyographic (EMG) activity by means of electrodes placed over specific muscles. The muscles involved and the positioning of the electrodes are shown here. (From Schwartz et al. 1974b.)

are recorded and quantified (Fig. 5).

In one experiment 12 normal subjects were requested to generate happy, sad, or angry imagery while EMG from the corrugator, frontalis, depressor, and masseter muscle regions was continuously monitored (Schwartz et al. 1974b). The results showed that the self-induced emotional states were associated with identifiable "covert" facial expressions not typically noticeable by either the casual observer or the subject himself. As seen in Figure 6, "happy" imagery in normal subjects is associated with decreases in corrugator EMG below resting levels, while "sad" imagery produces increases in corrugator EMG. On the other hand, "angry" (more than "sad") imagery elicits

reliable activity over the depressor region of the mouth.

It is interesting to note the similarity in the normal subjects' "happy" and "typical day" graphs in Figure 6. Asked to think about a "typical day," normal subjects generated an EMG pattern very like the happiness pattern. Another comparison of interest is between the normal results and those obtained from 12 subjects who were clinically depressed. In the depressed state people characteristically feel sad, blue, and often angry. At the same time, they feel incapable of making themselves feel happy—that is, of regulating a happy state. The EMG patterns for the four imagery conditions provide objective support for this generalization. While depressed subjects produce EMG patterns comparable to those of normal subjects for sadness and anger, they show attenuated EMG patterns for the self-induced happy condition. And when depressed subjects are asked to think about a typical day, the resulting EMG pattern is one of sadness.

The ability of affective imagery to produce discrete muscular patterns supports the view that specific self-induced cognitive states can generate discrete bodily patterns, and that these heretofore unnoticed somatic patterns may serve as a major physiological mechanism allowing imagery to elicit the subjective feelings associated with different emotions. In other words, a self-regulated internal feedback loop may be created, when the particular "thought" triggers a specific *pattern* of peripheral physiological activity which is then itself reprocessed by the brain, contributing to the unique "feeling" state associ-

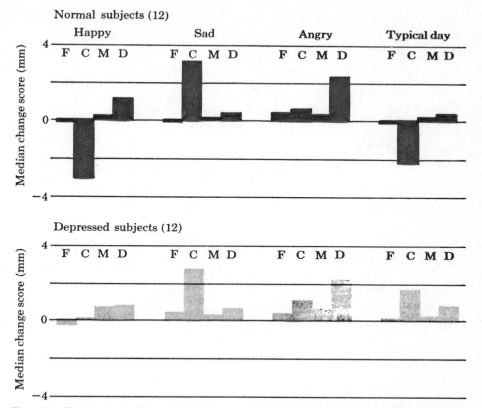

Figure 6. Changes in facial muscle tension (EMG) were monitored for 12 normal subjects (*black bars*) and 12 depressed subjects (*grey bars*) who were instructed to generate imagery for happiness, sadness, anger, and a "typical day." The muscle regions monitored, the frontalis (F), corrugator (C), masseter (M), and depressor (D), are shown in Figure 5. For the normal subjects, the 3 classes of affective imagery elicit different EMG patterns, while the "typical day" imagery produces a miniature "happy" pattern. The depressed subjects show strong EMG patterns for sad and angry imagery, but they are less able to generate a "happy" image pattern; for them the "typical day" EMG pattern is one of sadness. The data represent integrated EMG, with 1 mm = 45 microvolts/30 sec. (From Schwartz et al. 1974b.)

ated with the image. The EMG findings for depressed subjects indicate that a person's ability to regulate patterns of physiological activity by means of imagery depends in part on his emotional state.

Patterns of hemispheric asymmetry

Another important illustration of how self-regulated cognitive processes can be associated with discrete patterns of physiological activity has emerged recently from studies of hemispheric asymmetry and human behavior. By means of a variety of EEG and behavioral indices, it has been found that cognitive tasks requiring verbal or sequential processes are associated with activity in the left hemisphere of the brain (in the normal right-handed subject), while tasks requiring spatial, musical, or simultaneous processes tend to be associated with activation of the right hemisphere (Galin and Ornstein 1972; Kinsbourne 1972; Kimura 1973).

If the pattern perspective on self-regulated physiological activity can be generalized, then, on the basis of the analogy with tasks requiring dual motor skills, self-regulated patterns of cognitive and affective processes may be considered complex neuropsychological skills with associated physiological response patterns. For example, Schwartz, Davidson, Maer, and Bromfeld (1974) have observed that speaking the lyrics to a familiar song in a monotone produces relative activation of the EEG (alpha^{off}) over the left hemisphere, while whistling the song produces relative activation of the EEG over the right hemisphere. We would hypothesize that singing, a dual skill pattern, is a complex task involving, at least initially, activation and coordination of both hemispheres. The EEG data bear this out.

Similarly, we have found that the nonverbal component of emotion (like music, which long has been used as a stimulus for influencing mood) involves the right hemisphere. Questions involving both verbal (left hemisphere) and emotional (right hemisphere) processes (e.g. What is the primary difference in the meaning of the words "anger" and "hate?") accordingly elicit evidence of dual hemispheric activation. Questions that involve both spatial (right hemisphere) and emotional (right hemisphere) processes (e.g. Picture your father's face—what emotion first strikes you?) elicit evidence of accentuated right hemispheric activation.

The hemispheric asymmetry data are important because they lead us to dissect complex self-regulated cognitive tasks or "states" into components that make neuropsychological sense. Once the basic processes have been isolated, we can investigate how the components can be voluntarily combined into more complex gestalts with their associated physiological pattern correlates. Subjects may then be trained with biofeedback to regulate specific patterns of EEG activity across the hemispheres and to relate these physiological states to specific underlying cognitive and affective experiences.

Cognitive and somatic patterning

As compelling as these data are, are we justified in concluding that *all* physiological self-regulation has a discrete or identifiable cognitive referent? Clearly, regulation of specific muscles or patterns of motor behavior is not necessarily associated with specific cognitive referents (if asked How do you move your arm? most people cannot tell you). Similarly, control of individual physiological responses may not typically have identifiable subjective states. But we can hypothesize that certain self-regulated *patterns* of sensory-autonomic-motor activity do have strong subjective referents, and when a person generates those subjective experiences, he is also regulating their associated physiological patterns.

Humans, unfortunately, are not very good at observing and categorizing internal sensations. Therefore we must avoid taking subjects' reports at face value and must place such reports in a neuropsychological framework if we are to understand them. When subjects are simply *instructed,* without feedback, to "control and raise your heart rate" when one light comes on and to "control and lower your heart rate" when another light comes on, the typical subject almost immediately produces up-minus-down differences in heart rate on the order of 8 beats per minute (Bell and Schwartz, in press).

When these instructed subjects are asked later to list what kinds of thoughts they used, they report generating angry, aggressive, tense, or sexual fantasies while raising heart rate, and quiet, relaxing fantasies while lowering it. This consistency in subjective strategy is very different from that observed in the previous single-system studies, where subjects were not so instructed. Instructions lead subjects to draw immediately on previously learned cognitive strategies; the few data on this suggest that such instructions actually elicit patterns of autonomic arousal out of which specificity can grow with biofeedback training (Klinge 1972; Brener 1974).

But to what extent are these cognitive images the sole mechanism eliciting the observed heart rate changes? If subjects were directly instructed to "make yourselves aroused by thinking arousing thoughts," this should presumably elicit large heart rate changes, comparable to those observed with "control and raise" instructions. But this hypothesis does not take into account that one of the major physiological determinants of heart rate is somatic activity and associated metabolic demands (Obrist et al. 1974). Obrist and his colleagues have shown that, as subjects are given, via instructions, more and more freedom to move around and use their muscles in the heart rate biofeedback situation, larger and larger heart rate increases are observed.

In light of these findings, Bell and Schwartz (1973) predicted that simple instructions to "think arousing thoughts," without mentioning control of heart rate, would not generate large heart rate increases in comparison to "control and raise" instructions. We hypothesized that the "think" instructions would lead subjects to direct so much of their attention to the generation of imagery per se that this would produce a relative inhibition of general body movement; on the other hand, the "control" instructions would lead the subjects actively to generate subtle movement commands in concert with the imagery, even though they might not be aware of it. When this experiment was performed, our prediction was confirmed. Apparently there is a major difference between *having* a fantasy and *acting* upon it.

We are only beginning to accumulate data on combinations of cognitive and somatic mechanisms in biofeedback, and many questions remain. Recording discrete patterns of physiological activity selected because of their neuropsychological association with the processes under study is a fruitful direction in which to move. One strategy is to look at patterns of cortical activity generated when subjects are instructed to use various strategies to regulate a given response (or pattern of responses) with biofeedback. Neyers and Schwartz (MS in preparation) have recently found that when subjects are instructed to use muscle tension and relaxation as the main strategy to regulate their heart rate with biofeedback, associated EEG activation (alpha^{off}) can be found over the left sensory motor area (Sterman 1973) but not over the left occipital area, which is involved with visual processes (Mulholland 1973). But when subjects are instructed to regulate their heart rate by "thinking arousing thoughts," the sensory motor EEG differences over the left hemisphere are attenuated or disappear.

In our laboratory we are currently using pattern biofeedback training to assess the degree of self-regulated integration and differentiation that can be achieved between heart rate and these two different cortical EEG sites. If heart rate–sensory motor EEG pattern regulation shows enhanced integration and restricted differentiation compared to heart rate–occipital alpha EEG, this finding will provide further evidence of a cardiosomatic constraint at the level of the brain (Obrist et al. 1974). We are also investigating the possibility that the "thinking arousing thoughts" strategy, in light of our previous hemispheric asymmetry data, may involve right rather than left hemispheric sensory-motor sites.

Researchers interested in the mechanisms by which people learn to control specific functions or patterns of functions have an obvious interest in assessing cognitive correlates. However, this requires the

use of sophisticated cognitive paradigms and neuropsychological strategies on a par with the methodology already developed for physiological recording and feedback displays. Such cognitive approaches are available (e.g. Luria 1973) and may be combined with the biofeedback paradigm. In addition, biofeedback may be used as the independent variable in investigating the physiology of subjective experience. By training uninstructed subjects to control patterns of physiological activity, it is possible to study how patterns of physiological responses combine to elicit unique subjective states. Here, pattern biofeedback is used as an objective research tool for investigating the psychobiology of human consciousness.

Meditation and patterns of relaxation

One aspect of our self-regulation pattern approach with direct clinical applications involves physiological states produced by meditation and other relaxation procedures. Wallace and Benson (1972) have described a "hypometabolic" state produced by transcendental meditation—a simple, passive procedure in which the subject silently repeats to himself a Sanskrit word, or mantra. During meditation, decreases occur in many responses, including heart rate, blood pressure, sweat gland activity, respiration rate, EEG frequencies (to alpha/theta ranges), level of lactate acid in the blood, and measures of body metabolism. Although the EEG patterns superficially represent a drowsy or Stage 1 sleep pattern, and the decreases in metabolism appear equal to, if not greater than, those occurring during sleep, the meditator claims to feel awake and alert.

Recently, Benson and his colleagues have described this pattern as reflecting a more centrally integrated "relaxation response" (Benson, Beary, and Carol 1974), opposite to the fight-or-flight response originally described by Cannon (1936). Claiming that it is an innate, integrated neurophysiological pattern, they show that when subjects regulate a simple pattern of attention and cognition, attending passively to their breathing and saying the word "one" after each breath—an American analogue of certain Zen procedures—marked decreases in metabolism are obtained (Beary and Benson 1974).

Stimulated by such findings, many biofeedback researchers formulated the following hypothesis: since low-frequency EEG occurs in passive meditation, and subjects can learn with biofeedback to regulate such EEG patterns, then biofeedback for these changes will lead to deep relaxation—an "instant, electronic yoga." The major fallacy in this logic is that single-system biofeedback training is prone to emphasize specificity, not patterns. As mentioned earlier, consistent reports of subjective relaxation emerged when uninstructed subjects were lowering a *pattern* of low blood pressure and low heart rate ($BP_{down}HR_{down}$); decreases in either one alone did not produce this result (Schwartz 1972). Similarly, when subjects regulate patterns of occipital alpha and heart rate (Hassett and Schwartz, in press), they report that $HR_{down}alpha_{on}$ is quite relaxing. In fact, one of the subjects run for 8 sessions found this particular pattern so rewarding that she continued to practice it outside the laboratory as a means of producing relaxation. Deep physiological relaxation is not simply low frontalis muscle activity, or low heart rate, or occipital alpha, or slow breathing, but rather the combination of such changes.

Individuals differ in their patterns of response to stress (Lacey 1967), and the systems or combinations of systems associated with deep relaxation also depend on the individual. If subjects are trained with biofeedback to decrease their heart rate voluntarily in anticipation of receiving a noxious stimulus, the pain is experienced as less intense. However, this effect occurs primarily in subjects who report experiencing cardiac symptoms in normal stress situations (Sirota, Schwartz, and Shapiro 1974).

Patterns in meditation are likely to be even more complex than currently acknowledged. In *Psychophysiology of Zen,* Hirai (1974) provides physiological data from Japanese subjects and argues for the concept of a state of "relaxed awareness." Similarly, in the U.S., Goleman and Schwartz (MS) have found evidence that a major effect of transcendental meditation is the generation of a unique and somewhat paradoxical pattern of cortical and limbic arousal, roughly equivalent to the differential subjective experiences of perception versus emotion. We hypothesize that passive meditation practices can lead to *heightened cortical arousibility* plus *decreased limbic arousibility at the same time,* experienced as heightened perceptual awareness and simultaneously reduced emotional arousal and stress.

If this conclusion is generally correct, several important issues arise: Is it possible, using biofeedback techniques, to mimic this psychophysiological state? What combination of responses and biofeedback training procedures would be necessary to match the pattern of physiological changes that occur naturally during meditation? And if it is possible, is it worth the effort?

My own response is divided according to the needs of basic research versus clinical applications. The pattern biofeedback approach provides a new research procedure for investigating how patterns of physiological systems combine to produce unique subjective gestalts and behavioral correlates; at this level, the approach promises to be quite fruitful. However, if the physiological patterns produced by meditation or other relaxation techniques are of therapeutic value (e.g. for reducing overall limbic stress and its many expressions in diseases; Selye 1973), then they should be induced and practiced using the nonelectronic, easily portable, and generalizable machinery of our own biocognitive system.

When we consider the phenomenon of relaxation still more broadly, it becomes clear that various patterns of cognitive, attentional, and somatic strategies can be brought into play, and that different relaxation procedures emphasize the regulation of *different combinations* of processes. Davidson and Schwartz (in press) have outlined how relaxation paradigms utilize different combinations of strategies, which will be reflected in different patterns of physiological responses. Similarly, it is possible to classify various kinds of anxiety, involving combinations of cognitive, visceral, and somatic components. The most effective relaxation procedure may depend on the type of anxiety the person is experiencing at the time.

Take for example a case of high cognitive–low somatic anxiety, in which a person, although physically exhausted, is unable to fall asleep because his mind is racing with disturbing images and thoughts. The age-old treatment for this pattern of anxiety is to visualize sheep and count them—a cognitive self-regulation procedure that may be effective because it blocks both unwanted visual (right hemisphere) and verbal (left hemisphere) images at the same time.

Another pattern is exemplified by the person who feels somatically tense and jittery, but can point to no particular cause for his anxiety (no specific images come to mind). For such cases of low cognitive–high somatic anxiety, effective "relaxation" strategies include jogging, gardening, or other self-generated somatic activities that serve to block the undesirable somatic state and use up some of the unwanted metabolism at the same time, thereby producing fatigue.

The pattern orientation to anxiety assessment and relaxation treatment is not unlike Lazarus's (1973) concept of multimodality therapy, which seeks to classify for the individual the patterns of responses that need to be modified and treat them either singly or in combination, recognizing that the selected treatment for one component will not necessarily lead to reductions in others. Similar applications of the pattern approach to biofeedback therapy are described elsewhere (Schwartz, in press).

Pattern biofeedback and emergent property

One major thesis that has slowly emerged from biofeedback research is that patterns of physiological processes can be both generated and processed by the brain, producing unique cross-system interactions and perceptual gestalts that make up a significant component of human behavior and subjective experience. The concept of pattern refers not simply to viewing, in isolation, combinations of physiological responses, but rather goes beyond the individual responses making up the pattern to recognize the novel, interactive, or emergent property that patterns can acquire. Simply stated, the whole can be qualitatively different from the sum of its parts, and yet be dependent upon the organization of its parts for its unique properties. This phenomenon is seen at all levels of physics and chemistry and extends through biology and neuropsychology (Weiss 1969).

The concept of emergent property is what I wish to emphasize in patterning. Although it is not new, with few exceptions it is still ignored. Neuropsychologists concerned with the biology of consciousness employ the same idea when they speak of cell assemblies (Hebb 1974), neural engrams (John 1972), holograms (Pribram 1971), dynamic neural patterns (Sperry 1969), or functional systems (Luria 1973). Emotion was described by William James (1890) as the perception of patterns of autonomic consequences of action. More recent researchers, such as Schachter and Singer (1962), have added cognitive processes to autonomic arousal as an integral part of this pattern. Today, theorists like Izard (1971) stress the interaction of combinations of neurophysiological systems, including discrete patterns of postural and facial muscle activity, as the mechanism underlying the emergent experience of emotion.

Research on biofeedback and the regulation of combinations of responses extends this basic concept of patterning by providing a new paradigm for investigating physiological relationships in the intact human. Self-regulation as a general research strategy is useful because it enables researchers to isolate component parts of systems and then examine how they combine to produce unique physiological and associated subjective states. Our laboratory has shown that the regulation of patterns of responses can produce effects that are different from those observed when single functions are regulated. As I have illustrated, this simple principle proves to have important basic as well as clinical ramifications.

It is not inconceivable, however, that the act of regulating a pattern of responses will have consequences somewhat different from those found when a similar pattern is elicited by other means. If future research proves this to be true, it would limit the general applicability of the approach. On the other hand, such a finding could provide a further key to the nature of the self-regulation process itself.

References

Barber, T. X., L. V. DiCara, J. Kamiya, N. E. Miller, D. Shapiro, and J. Stoyva, eds. 1971. *Biofeedback and Self-Control, 1970: An Aldine Annual on the Regulation of Bodily Processes and Consciousness.* Chicago: Aldine-Atherton.

Basmajian, J. V. 1972. Electromyography comes of age. *Science* 176:603–09.

Beary, J. F., and H. Benson, with H. P. Klemchuk. 1974. A simple psychophysiologic technique which elicits the hypometabolic changes of the relaxation response. *Psychosomatic Med.* 36: 115–20.

Beatty, J., and C. Kornfeld. 1973. Relative independence of conditioned EEG changes from cardiac and respiratory activity. *Physiology and Behavior* 9:773–36.

Bell, I., and G. E. Schwartz. 1973. Cognitive and somatic mechanisms in the voluntary control of human heart rate. In Shapiro et al., eds., *Biofeedback and Self-Control, 1972.*

Bell, I. R., and G. E. Schwartz. In press. Voluntary control and reactivity of human heart rate. *Psychophysiology.*

Benson, H., J. F. Beary, and M. P. Carol. 1974. The relaxation response. *Psychiatry* 37:37–46.

Black, A. H. 1974. Operant autonomic conditioning: The analysis of response mechanisms. In P. A. Obrist, A. H. Black, J. Brener and L. V. DiCara, eds., *Cardiovascular Psychophysiology.* Chicago: Aldine.

Brener, J. 1974. A general model of voluntary control applied to the phenomena of learned cardiovascular change. In Obrist et al., eds., *Cardiovascular Psychophysiology.*

Cannon, W. B. 1936. *Bodily Changes in Pain, Hunger, Fear, and Rage.* N.Y.: Appleton-Century.

Crider, A., G. E. Schwartz, and S. R. Shnidman. 1969. On the criteria for instrumental autonomic conditioning: A reply to Katkin and Murray. *Psychological Bull.* 71:455–61.

Darwin, C. 1872. *The Expression of the Emotions in Man and Animals.* London: John Murray.

Davidson, R. J., and G. E. Schwartz. In press. Psychobiology of relaxation and related states: A multi-process theory. In D. Mostofsky, ed., *Behavior Control and Modification of Physiological Activity.* Englewood Cliffs: Prentice-Hall.

Ekman, P., W. V. Friesen, and P. Ellsworth. 1972. *Emotion in the Human Face.* N.Y.: Pergamon.

Engel, B. T. 1972. Operant conditioning of cardiac function: A status report. *Psychophysiology* 9: 161–77.

Fleishman, E. A. 1966. Human abilities and the acquisition of skill. In E. A. Bilodeau, ed., *Acquisition of Skill.* N.Y.: Academic Press.

Galin, D., and R. Ornstein. 1972. Lateral specialization of cognitive mode: An EEG study. *Psychophysiology* 9:412–18.

Germana, J. 1968. The psychophysiological correlates of conditioned response formation. *Psychological Bull.* 70:105–14.

Goleman, D. J., and G. E. Schwartz. MS. Fractionation of skin conductance level and responses in meditators and controls: A dual component theory.

Graham, D. T. 1972. Psychosomatic medicine. In N. S. Greenfield and R. A. Sternbach, eds., *Handbook of Psychophysiology.* N.Y.: Holt, Rinehart and Winston.

Hassett, J., and G. E. Schwartz. In press. Relationships between heart rate and occipital alpha: A biofeedback approach. *Psychophysiology* (abstract).

Hebb, D. O. 1974. What psychology is about. *Am. Psychologist* 29:71–79.

Hirai, T. 1974. *Psychophysiology of Zen.* Tokyo: Igaku Shoin.

Izard, C. E. 1971. *The Face of Emotion.* N.Y.: Appleton-Century-Crofts.

James, W. 1890. *Principles of Psychology.* N.Y.: Holt.

John, E. R. 1972. Switchboard versus statistical theories of learning and memory. *Science* 177: 850–64.

Kamiya, J., L. V. DiCara, T. X. Barber, N. E. Miller, D. Shapiro, and J. Stoyva, eds. 1971. *Biofeedback and Self-Control: An Aldine Reader on the Regulation of Bodily Processes and Consciousness.* Chicago: Aldine-Atherton.

Katkin, E. S., and E. N. Murray. 1968. Instrumental conditioning of automatically mediated behavior: Theoretical and methodological issues. *Psychological Bull.* 70:52–68.

Kimmel, H. D. 1974. Instrumental conditioning of autonomically mediated responses in human beings. *Am. Psychologist* 29:325–35.

Kimura, D. 1973. The asymmetry of the human brain. *Sci. Am.* 228(3):70–80.

Kinsbourne, M. 1972. Eye and head turning indicates cerebral lateralization. *Science* 176:539–41.

Klinge, V. 1972. Effects of exteroceptive feedback and instructions on control of spontaneous galvanic skin response. *Psychophysiology* 9:305–17.

Lacey, J. 1967. Somatic response patterning and stress: Some revisions of activation theory. In M. Appley and R. Trumbull, eds., *Psychological Stress.* N.Y.: Appleton-Century-Crofts.

Lang, P. J. 1974. Learned control of human heart rate in a computer-directed environment. In Obrist et al., eds., *Cardiovascular Psychophysiology.*

Lazarus, A. A. 1973. Multimodal behavior therapy: Treating the "Basic Id." *J. Nervous and Mental Disease* 156:404–11.

Luria, A. R. 1973. *The Working Brain: An Introduction to Neuropsychology.* N.Y.: Basic Books.

McGuigan, F. J., and R. A. Schoonover, eds. 1973. *The Psychophysiology of Thinking.* N.Y.: Academic Press.

Miller, N. E. 1969. Learning of visceral and glandular responses. *Science* 163:434–45.

————. 1974. Introduction: Current issues and key problems. In Miller et al., eds., *Biofeedback and Self-Control 1973*.

————, T. X. Barber, L. V. DiCara, J. Kamiya, D. Shapiro, and J. Stoyva, eds. 1974. *Biofeedback and Self-Control 1973: An Aldine Annual on the Regulation of Bodily Processes and Consciousness*. Chicago: Aldine.

Mulholland, T. 1973. Objective EEG methods for studying covert shifts of visual attention. In McGuigan and Schoonover, eds., *The Psychophysiology of Thinking*.

Neyers, M. A. and G. E. Schwartz. In prep. Patterning of sensory-motor and occipital alpha in the self-regulation of heart rate.

Obrist, P. A., J. L. Howard, J. E. Lawler, R. A. Galosy, K. A. Meyers, and C. J. Gaebelein. 1974. The cardiac-somatic interaction. In Obrist et al., eds., *Cardiovascular Psychophysiology*.

Pribram, K. H. 1971. *Languages of the Brain: Experimental Paradoxes and Principles in Neuropsychology*. Englewood Cliffs: Prentice Hall.

Schachter, S., and J. E. Singer. 1962. Cognitive, social and physiological determinants of emotional state. *Psychological Rev.* 69:379–99.

Schwartz, G. E. 1971. Cardiac responses to self-induced thoughts. *Psychophysiology* 8:462–67.

————. 1972. Voluntary control of human cardiovascular integration and differentiation through feedback and reward. *Science* 175:90–93.

————. 1973. Biofeedback as therapy: Some theoretical and practical issues. *Am. Psychologist* 666–73.

————. 1974. Toward a theory of voluntary control of response patterns in the cardiovascular system. In Obrist et al., eds., *Cardiovascular Psychophysiology*.

————. In press. Self-regulation response patterning: Implications for psychophysiological research and therapy. *Biofeedback and Self-Regulation*.

————, R. Davidson, F. Maer, and E. Bromfield. 1974. Patterns of hemispheric dominance during musical, emotional, verbal, and spatial tasks. *Psychophysiology* 11:227 (abstract).

————, P. L. Fair, P. S. Greenberg. M. Freedman, and J. L. Klerman. 1974a. Facial electromyography in assessment of emotion. *Psychophysiology* 11:237 (abstract).

————, P. L. Fair, P. S. Greenberg, M. R. Mandel, and J. L. Klerman. 1974b. Facial expression and depression: An electromyographic study. *Psychosomatic Med.* 36:458 (abstract).

————, P. L. Fair, P. S. Greenberg, J. M. Foran, and G. L. Klerman. In press a. Self-generated affective imagery elicits discrete patterns of facial muscle activity. *Psychophysiology* (abstract).

————, P. L. Fair, P. S. Greenberg, M. R. Mandel, and G. L. Klerman. In press b. Facial expression and depression II: An electromyographic study. *Psychosomatic Med.* (abstract).

————, and J. D. Higgins. 1971. Cardiac activity preparatory to overt and covert behavior.

Science 173:1144–46.

————, D. Shapiro, and B. Tursky. 1971. Learned control of cardiovascular integration in man through operant conditioning. *Psychosomatic Med.* 33:57–62.

————, D. Shapiro, and B. Tursky. 1972. Self-control of patterns of human diastolic blood pressure and heart rate through feedback and reward. *Psychophysiology* 9:270 (abstract).

————, G. Shaw, and D. Shapiro. 1972. Specificity of alpha and heart rate control through feedback. *Psychophysiology* 9:269 (abstract).

————, J. Vogler, and L. Young. In press. Heart rate self-regulation as skill learning: Strength endurance versus cardiac reaction time. *Psychophysiology* (abstract).

Selye, H. 1973. The evolution of the stress concept. *Am. Sci.* 61:692–99.

Shapiro, D., T. X. Barber, L. V. DiCara, J. Kamiya, N. E. Miller, and J. Stoyva, eds. 1973. *Biofeedback and Self-Control 1972: An Aldine Annual on the Regulation of Bodily Processes and Consciousness*. Chicago: Aldine.

————, G. E. Schwartz, and B. Tursky. 1972. Control of diastolic blood pressure in man by feedback and reinforcement. *Psychophysiology* 9: 296–304.

————, B. Tursky, E. Gershon, and M. Stern. 1969. Effects of feedback and reinforcement on the control of human systolic blood pressure. *Science* 163:588–89.

————, B. Tursky, and G. E. Schwartz. 1970a. Control of blood pressure in man by operant conditioning. *Circ. Res.* 26: supp. 1; 127:I-27–I-32.

————, B. Tursky, and G. E. Schwartz. 1970b. Differentiation of heart rate and blood pressure in man by operant conditioning. *Psychosomatic Med.* 32:417–23.

Sirota, A. D., G. E. Schwartz, and D. Shapiro. 1974. Voluntary control of human heart rate: Effects on reactions to aversive stimuli. *J. Abnormal Psychology* 83:261–67.

Sperry, R. W. 1969. A modified concept of consciousness. *Psychological Rev.* 76:532–36.

Sterman, M. B. 1973. Neurophysiologic and clinical studies of sensorimotor EEG biofeedback training: Some effects on epilepsy. *Seminars in Psychiatry* 5:507–24.

Stoyva, J., T. X. Barber, L. V. DiCara, J. Kamiya, N. E. Miller, and D. Shapiro, eds. 1972. *Biofeedback and Self-Control 1971: An Aldine Annual on the Regulation of Bodily Processes and Consciousness*. Chicago: Aldine-Atherton.

Tursky, B., D. Shapiro, and G. E. Schwartz. 1972. Automated constant cuff pressure system to measure average systolic and diastolic blood pressure in man. *IEEE Transactions on Biomedical Engineering* 19:271–75.

Wallace, R. K., and H. Benson. 1972. The physiology of meditation. *Sci. Am.* 226(2):84–91.

Weiss, P. A. 1969. The living system: Determinism stratified. In A. Koestler and J. R. Smythies, eds., *Beyond Reductionism: New Perspectives in the Life Sciences*. Boston: Beacon Press.

Biological Awareness as a State of Consciousness

3

Barbara B. Brown

The past few years have seen a dynamic transition in the thinking of scientists concerned with mind and consciousness. Exciting, innovative approaches to the mind-body mystery have sprung up in every mind science discipline, and the analysis of new data about interactions between mental and biological processes is stimulating new perspectives on that unique property of human beings called consciousness.

Subconscious processes,[1] generally interpreted as all activity of mind not recognized in conscious awareness, have been documented to possess extra-ordinary complexity, depth of informational resources, associative and integrative mechanisms, mechanisms for evaluation and judgment of integrated data, and a remarkable facility for direction and efficiency of action. The broad scope of these activities and the effective but parsimonious execution of subconscious functions strongly imply a systematic arrangement with dis-criminable levels of organization. This essay is based on a concept of con-sciousness that considers three levels: conscious awareness, and subconscious processes having at least two aspects (one confirmed to the subjective appreciation of biological information and the second concerned with the association, integration and evaluation of information).

What follows is an argument to support the concept of independent "sub-jectively appreciated" mental processes, and particularly the identification and characterization of those subjectively appreciated mental processes perceiving

---

[1] Although "unconscious" is traditionally preferable in psychoanalytic theory, the prefix "un" connotes absence of consciousness whereas the prefix "sub" connotes below or beneath. Perhaps "para" would be a more apt descriptor, but would be even more confusing to introduce at this time. This essay will therefore use subconscious activity as synonomous with the unconscious.

and expressing biological information that is otherwise inexpressible. It is the product of this latter activity that may represent an independent state of consciousness that I will call *biological awareness*. I will describe evidence indicating that this state—although the mental processes which mediate it do not directly communicate with conscious awareness—performs a vital role in the internal communication between physiologic and other subconscious processes concerned with the association, evaluation and integration of information. I propose that the latter be termed the *integrative subconscious.*

In this discussion the qualifier "subjectively appreciated" is employed in its most fundamental sense, i.e., referring to information perceivable exclusively to the individual. These internally generated perceptions are considered as distinct from "objectively appreciated" perceptions which become characterized in mutual agreement by approximating apparent correspondences of internal events to events external to individual consciousness. By this definition, "subjectively appreciated" consciousness is comprised of all internally derived sensations and percepts, as well as subjective mental activity which process perceptual and cognitive data independently of conscious awareness and direction.

Thus the concept of the biological awareness aspect of subjectively appreciated consciousness may be described as an internal recognition and awareness of the entire range of biological events in the body by mental processes capable of communicating the information so recognized to "integrative subconscious" processes which facilitate association, integration and evaluation of biological awareness with other perceptual and cognitive information. It is the integrative subconscious processes that assess the significance of biological awareness relevant to other perceptual and cognitive information and select appropriate biological expression. The integrative subconscious processes also communicate a synthesis of the information to conscious awareness.

The Definition Dilemma

Probably more than for any other subject, there is a lack of consensus about the substance and mechanisms of consciousness. This is a disadvantage to critical analysis of the subject and particularly when attempting to define a previously undescribed state of consciousness. The disparity of information and concepts about consciousness and the mind (brain) make it difficult to organize the material and logic needed to support new concepts. The effect of this is that the kinetic energy of unavoidably incomplete organization of ideas and data outweighs the potential energy of new concepts, and consequently obscures what might be significant new information and the development of ideas. One part of this predicament is a reflection, a datum, which expresses the absence of unifying concepts of consciousness and the mind and brain.

Because there are many diverse concepts of consciousness, there is a need for meaningful qualifiers of the consciousness set. The need to qualify consciousness descriptively does not appear to have a high priority in discussions of either the characteristics or mechanisms of consciousness. From this one might conclude that there is either broad consensus of the meaning of the concept or that bases for concepts of consciousness are so elusive and disparate that qualifiers about different states of consciousness are more confusing than helpful. A review of concepts reveals that they derive from bodies of knowledge that are essentially separately organized and documented, with little if any concurrence. One may find reasonably acceptable hypotheses from physical, experiential, sociologic or philosophic points of view, yet none of these defines nor qualifies consciousness satisfactorily for all points of view. This suggests either information voids or inadequate communication among bodies of information.

One of the information voids is that of experiential information. Except for certain philosophic considerations, usable (i.e., consensual) information about the experiential is generally inferred from objectively perceived[2] information (that which can be communicated), not from subjectively appreciated perceptions (essentially inexpressible). The present discussion attempts to examine the characteristics of a subset of consciousness that is primarily *subjectively* perceived and to cite the implications which can be deduced from this process of silent perception.

The first difficulty for a discussion of this kind is the virtual absence of definitions, or indeed for any real consensus about levels, states, mechanisms or the nature of consciousness. A second complication for a discussion of subjectively appreciated consciousness is that nowhere has background information from human psychophysiologic studies been consolidated or synthesized for consideration about the mind–body relationship. And finally, many of the supporting data are of such recent origin that they have not yet been incorporated into more structured hypotheses of the consciousness–brain relationship.

For the past several years I have been reviewing new data on the psycho-physiology of consciousness and have become aware of a perspective on consciousness and the mind–body problem which as yet eludes interpretation by the classical approaches, i.e., from the standpoint of either the observer or the observed. My thoughts and conclusions are in process . . . somewhat analogous to a process that would occur following the opening of a Pandora's box of biological events that put to question certain fundamental considerations of the mind–body problem. These events, whose implications may bring a new

---

[2] Regardless of whether the perception arises from external or internal sources, the objectivity occurs through a communicated agreement about the characterization and significance of the perception.

perspective to concepts of consciousness, are those which can be deducted from the biofeedback phenomenon.

Although the explosive publicity about biofeedback has engendered un- qualified enthusiasm among many psychologists, it has been received with somewhat less enthusiasm by physiologists. This may be due chiefly to the failure of psychology to attend to the physiologic implications of both the methodology and interpretations of psychophysiologic research. Therefore, I will review some of the compelling biologic support to establish the role of higher mental processes in the biofeedback phenomenon and how these considerations lead to the idea of purely subjectively appreciated brain processes.

Although evidence for the independence of a subjectively appreciated consciousness and its aspect of a biological subconscious is most striking in the biofeedback process, there is a wealth of unorganized evidence from both earlier and concurrent research. Evidence deduced from a variety of unrelated studies will be cited first, concluding with an analysis of the biofeedback phenomenon as experimental evidence for a subjectively appreciated set of brain processes having the capability to affect or direct itself and its own biologic mechanisms without external physical intervention, which thus may be considered to function with some degree of apparent independence of its substrate.[3]

The Effect of Cognitive Information on Biologic Activity

While it is well-known and there is reasonable scientific evidence that cognitive information (words, ideas, attitudes) affects underlying physiologic activities, much prevailing scientific opinion tends to attribute such physiologic effects more to automatic, autonomic responses than to non-aware but reasoning mental activity. The present examples from bio-psychologic research are cited to indicate the alternative explanation: that complex high level mental activity operates efficiently and effectively via subconscious mechanisms.

---

[3] This concept of subjective activity is not unlike that expressed by Sperry [1], that "subjective experiences in the form of emergent phenomena actively govern the flow pattern of neural excitation." Additional quotations from the same paper clarify Sperry's concept: "describing consciousness as a dynamic property of cerebral excitation that is inseparately tied to, and a direct property of, the brain process, and not a disembodied or supernatural agent;" "there has been general agreement that subjective epiphenomena do not act back upon, or in any way influence, the brain's physical activity. The present view contends, in contradiction, that the conscious phenomena as direct emergent properties of the cerebral activity do interact with and casually determine the brain process." "The present view differs (from the identity theory) in postulating that the phenomena of subjective experience as pattern properties are distinct, different from, and more than the neural activities of which they are composed. It may be noted further that the same conscious effect in the present view can be produced by different neural events on different occasions in different neural contexts provided the critical operational result at the holistic functional level is the same."

One of the first intriguing studies of the human potential to direct non-consciously his own quite specific biological activity was reported more than 35 years ago [2]. The significance of this study remained unrecognized for several decades while experimental psychologists were in the throes of conditioning theory and behaviorism which asserted that behavior consisted mainly of responses to external stimuli. In the study noted, normal individuals were trained to produce a change in skin electrical activity in response to the words "electric shock" by giving a mild electric shock to the fingers a few seconds later. The experiment then proceeded to substitute the *words* "electric shock" for the real electric shock, and further, to precede these words by the words "green light." The subjects quickly transferred the skin electrical change to the mere words "green light" when said a few seconds before the words "electric shock." The subjects received no information about their skin electrical activity other than being advised *when* they produced a change satisfactory to the researchers. When the words "electric shock" were omitted after the words "green light," the subjects quickly failed to produce a skin electrical change. Moreover, when a real green light and a real electric shock were used in a duplicate experiment, the learning to transfer the skin response was much less than when verbal stimuli were used.

The situation of the experiment was essentially a "cognitive" one, i.e., the subjects were given minimal information and they were expected not only to deduce the significance or application of the information, but also to provide a specific and appropriate body response to that information. The cognitive information consisted of (a) being told that they had made a body response recorded through electrodes on their hand, and (b) instructions to make the same body response when they heard certain words. One can deduce that the subjects were, in some way, able to first recognize and then associate a particular biological state with the information that they had biologically responded satisfactorily, and then were further able to transfer this particular state of biologic activity to the words used by the researchers precisely when instructed to do so. Since the subjects were not informed either that they were *expected* to transfer the body response to the words "green light" or that they were successful in this, it can only be assumed that they interpreted the highly limited circumstances of the situation, consciously or subconsciously, and performed via a body change which could be recorded through the finger electrodes. At no time was there information available for conscious recognition, thus there appears to be implicated a process of logical subconscious processing of information, presumably stemming from private assessment of differences in specific body activities during different conditions of the experiment. This assessment suggests that mental processes are capable of interpreting differences in specific body activities under quite specific sets of circumstances and it is for this reason that I propose that the basis of this capability be called "biological awareness."

The hypothesis is that there are mind-brain processes which are capable of discriminating specific attributes of biological activity, and that these constitute a form of consciousness capable of independent operation with respect to organizing relationships between mind and body. In the case of the experiment above, this biological awareness appears to have been internally communicated to and associated with the mental activity which assessed the conditions.and instructions of the experiment. Over time this association of information became isolated to the specific circumstances of the experiment such that the information derived from biological awareness was used to initiate a change in body activity.

To summarize, the specific "cognitive" situation was that there was an implicit command to do something, and that "something" was limited to changing some body process. The critical part of the process was the transfer of information contained in the events of the experiment (including the prior implicit affirmation—but no explicit information—of what comprised a successful response) to the brain mechanisms which direct changes in body activities. The process implies biologically appreciated, non-consciously aware mental associations capable of directly and effectively discriminating and directing physiologic activity.

Evidential Indications from Various Unrelated Psychophysiologic Phenomena

Experiments with subliminal perception directly support the above conclusion. Numerous studies have been conducted which contrast body responses to words having emotional content and those without emotional significance. Heart rate, skin electrical activity, blood pressure and brain waves all change significantly when emotion producing words are presented to subjects at a level of stimulus intensity below that which allows conscious recognition of the words or symbols, the *significance* of the words therefore has been recognized, associated, evaluated and acted upon, all on a level below (or parallel to) that of conscious awareness. While this phenomenon has been generally interpreted as indicating an activity of subconscious processes, I propose that the actual mechanism is biological awareness operating via the rich non-linear neuronal networks of the brain to monitor the relative state of each physiologic system. Information is thus available for communication with other networks which transmit information both from memory stores and sensory perception as well as available for communication with the linear neuronal systems, i.e., the primary nervous pathways used to convey information to organs to effect appropriate responses.

Other evidence lies in universal observations. In hypnosis, for example, when a subject is deeply hypnotized and is instructed not to bleed to a pin prick or during surgery, he does not bleed [5]. Whatever the mechanism, it is apparent that it is a mental rather than a physical process. It is mental activity that directs physiologic processes to mobilize "automatic," "involuntary" activity in a way that is contrary to normal biologic responses (i.e., normally one bleeds after vascular injury). While suggestions to perform a specific physiologic function are received via the mechanisms of consciousness, the accomplishment of the feat is *not* recognized in conscious awareness, nor is the *mode* of execution of the feat recognized despite the obvious intentionality and voluntariness of the act. These events imply the existence of mental processes capable of mobilizing, integrating and directing informational forces with remarkable specificity operating efficiently and effectively on levels below (or parallel to) conscious awareness. From these processes one might deduce that one portion of non-conscious activity functions to appraise the biological situation, e.g., the vascular activity at the wound site, whereas a different function of the non-conscious mental activity integrates the biological information with the cognitive appraisal of the hypnotic suggestions. It would seem parsimonious for biological information to be monitored and assessed for qualities of dynamics, status and location *prior* to a central integrative action which organizes and discriminates the significance of data from other sources (other perceptual data and other subjective information such as intent, instructions, motivation, etc.).

Alternative perspectives or reinterpretations of other types of experimental observations can also provide support for an independently functioning subjectively appreciated biological subconscious.

There is, for example, a criticism that biofeedback may not differ from the essentials of conditioned learning because the process can be effected in lower animals via conditioning techniques. One answer to this is that it has never been demonstrated that animals are not subjectively aware, just as human beings may be, and animals may accomplish learning by similar mechanisms. One has only to take a leaf from the natural scientist's notebook to conclude that animals display a keen awareness of internal body processes, much more than do human beings. For example, many of the so-called instinctual actions of animals, such as eating grasses for an upset stomach, or kitty's insisting upon a clean toilet, may also represent a keen awareness of internal melieu. There are also the experiments of DiCara and Miller in conditioning rats to change heart rate under curare [6]. Their success in training rats to change heart rate could as well indicate the influence of internal awareness as it does effectiveness of rewards (intrinsic to operant conditioning); not enough experiments have been done to conclude one way or the other. Parenthetically, though, prejudice favors the opinion that animals have no such internal awareness.

Further, in the DiCara and Miller experiments, the direction of learned heart rate changes under curare exerted a profound influence on the animals' subsequent behavior and ability to learn other tasks [7]. Rats who learned to slow their hearts became more tranquil and relaxed and also learned subsequent tasks more efficiently; while rats who had learned to increase heart rates learned subsequent tasks poorly and moreover many became frantic, exhausted and died. While there are several neurophysiologic answers possible, it is also possible that disruption of a normal internal awareness and organized subjective information in the adverse direction may account for the deterioration in both mental and physical health.

Evidence from newer, sophisticated studies can be found in a recent publication by Fetz and Finnochio [8]. Monkeys were trained by a combination of conditioning and biofeedback techniques to effect a series of sophisticated patterned, coordinated muscle actions, including isometric contractions of single muscles among those required for the pattern. It was found, by monitoring selected cortical cells, that a single cortical cell may relate to both the production of a learned coordinated muscle movement and to each of the muscles involved when insolated from the pattern, and furthermore that the *same* cortical cell apparently could selectively abstain its involvement in the action of selected muscles of the coordinated effort while still being critical to the action of another muscle of that pattern.

If the temporarily related responses of cortex and muscle could imply a causal relationship, then the implications of this study are enormous. They suggest that a single cortical cell may have the capability to determine its output for several options selectively. This in turn may indicate how subjectively appreciated information (gained from proprioception and from associations during training) in some way influences cellular discriminations. The study suggests that a single cortical cell may selectively be involved in the actions of one or many effectors, and can control its own excitant and inhibitory effects, possibly by feedback mechanisms.

THE EVIDENCE FROM BIOFEEDBACK

Since the vast amount of information about the biofeedback phenomenon has not yet been pulled together into any unifying concept, a brief discussion of both some observable characteristics of the process and some deductions which can be made about events occurring within the process are necessary in order to discuss implications of the process. Certain characteristics of the system appear to constitute "new" (or rediscovered) information and warrant consideration in formulations about the mind-body problem. Some of the "new" knowledge may be simply new perspectives or old phenomena which examination of the "newly discovered" phenomenon has crystallized. In general, the new information accumulating from biofeedback studies appears to support and to extend the concept of a biologic consciousness as an entity derived from and functionally tied to physiologic activity, but with capabilities distinct from the direct products of that activity, and which feed back as part of a self-regulatory system.

Briefly, in the biofeedback process, psychobiologic information, in symbolic form, is fed back to the generator of the concrete forms and logic of that same psychobiologic information. The mechanics and significance of biologic feedback control systems are considered elsewhere. In this discussion emphasis is on the unique nature of the process and the implications about consciousness which stem from observations of the phenomenon.

An important element of biofeedback has been a recognition that intention (the will) appears to possess the capability for functioning as an activity of brain function that can organize, integrate and direct the physical processes of the body with molecular specificity. And, more often than not, intention operates in the absence of conscious awareness. These conclusions are based upon the synthesis of results from hundreds of studies on biofeedback and related phenomena. I will give several examples from the recent scientific literature on biofeedback which illustrate the ability of mental processes to direct the activity of specific biological functions, often when there is minimal possibility for conscious appreciation of cognitive information.

There is some misunderstanding about various aspects of the biofeedback process because the phenomenon evolved partially via conditioning theory. In reality the biofeedback process is more effective and efficient in the absence of these constraints. Moreover, in retrospect, much of the experimental base for conditioning theory can be viewed as essentially a biofeedback process (e.g., influence of information contained in set and setting, in the conditioning stimulus, in the absence of signal, etc.).

In the conditioning-free biofeedback process, a representation of a simple monitor of a complex physiologic function provides information to the individual about the functioning of a system. By means of either direct or indirect instructions, direction of the effect is specified and accomplished without conscious awareness. A non-aware cognitive process appears to recognize both the significance of the abstraction of a physiologic activity and the mechanism by which selective alteration of the biologic process can be directed. The role of information is crucial to the biofeedback process. The more information, whether conceptual, environmental or biological, the more efficient is the process, presumably because communication about internal events is facilitated below the level of conscious awareness. Moreover, in the biofeedback process, the way in which biologic information is perceived is shifted to a fuller representation of the time dimension of physiologic processes, hence it simultaneously utilizes temporarily distributed information as events occur within the spaces of the body.

In biofeedback the biological information can be represented as a mechanical symbol of the information or, in fact, *any* kind of information that is linked, however indirectly, to a biological activity.

In some experiments biofeedback information is in the form of a perceptually recognizable symbol (such as visual or auditory signals) of the biologic activity. An experiment of this type is that in which EEG alpha activity was fed back to the subjects in the form of a blue light signal [9]. Subjects were informed only that this indicated some kind of brain wave activity, and their instructions were to find some mental means to keep the light on for periods as long as possible. Subjects learn this task with remarkable rapidity (this type of experiment has been repeated ad nauseum). Again, the individual is provided only with an artificial symbol of his biologic activity.

The sequence of events deduced to occur in this experiment has a striking similarity to those which may be deduced from numerous experiments in which experimental subjects are simply requested to change a specific biologic activity voluntarily [10]. The events are also similar to those deduced to occur in the non biofeedback augmented learning or "conditioning" of skin electrical activity by verbal stimuli.

COMPLETELY INTERNALIZED VOLUNTARY CONTROL OVER INTERNAL BIOLOGIC ACTIVITY

Although for many practical purposes and in the laboratory the biofeedback process appears to rely on an element external to the internal circuitry, there is support for the contention that the process is fundamentally a completely internal process. First, the phenomenon may be equally well demonstrated using instructions only [11]. Also, normally, the process rapidly becomes independent of the external conditions when these are used. Moreover, many individuals have developed auto-control over internal physiologic events in the absence of external assistance (heart rate, temperature, pain, resorption of urine, etc.), and some individuals in other cultures regularly develop such auto–control without external aids. The essential difference between biofeed-back–augmented and non-augmented voluntary control over internal events is that with biofeedback the process is not only highly efficient, but proceeds without conscious awareness.

In some visceral learning experiments a minimum amount of cognitive information is given in the form of a feedback symbol while in other experiments the subjects are deliberately misinformed about the meaning of the signal which is actually feeding back biological information. Learned control occurs, but less efficiently, less rapidly and less satisfactorily than when cognitive information about the process is supplied.

Recent heart rate biofeedback experiments further reveal the ability of non-aware mental function to process information efficiently and effectively and with definitive focus [12]. For example, in several experiments subjects were confronted with red and green lights which were associated with the sounding of high and low tones, and were told that when the different colors appeared to try by "mental means" to produce high or low tones. They were not told that the tones were their actual heart rates. The subjects learned quite rapidly to shift their heart rates between fast and slow to make high or low tone appropriate to the light signals. In this case, in order to perform correctly, the subjects had to have made some association between heart rate and pitch of the tones, and then to discriminate quickly and precisely between two physiologic states.

Presently several investigators have either maximized the amount of information given to their subjects about what physiologic task they wanted them to do, or others simply have given verbal instructions to change a certain physiologic activity [10, 11]. Many researchers have now reported that simply asking subjects to increase or decrease heart rate resulted in quite large changes—more than in many biofeedback studies. Of course, it should be remembered that heart rate is one physiologic activity with a fairly obvious ability to be appreciated as a subjective feeling. Nonetheless, the question has simply not been asked before: please change your heart rate. The remarkable results have several implications: first, that given a chance, human beings can develop a body of subjectively appreciated information specifically related to a particular physiologic activity; and second, they can then employ the information to direct that activity in a specific manner and accomplish an effect on a non-aware level of mental function.

Many other examples of internally generated alterations of physiologic processes via mental activity are accumulating. Although these rely chiefly on normally operating physiologic feedback systems, current emphasis is on the cognitive (subjectively or objectively appreciated) direction of biologic activity. The central mechanisms are illustrated in these examples: when filaments of the nerve to the trapezius muscle of the shoulder were sutured to remnants of the facial nerve distal to where it had been severed, feedback procedures resulted in recovery of completely normal facial muscle activity [13]. The implication is that voluntary control can be dissociated and redirected with remarkable specificity by intention only. In another example, learned control over EEG alpha activity has revealed dissociation between the usual accompaniments of different brain wave conditions, i.e., problem solving and memory search could occur during a steady alpha state of relaxed wakefulness previously believed to preclude the simultaneous processes of intellection and relaxation [14].

Consciousness and the Biofeedback Process

The last example is a striking one of the existence of an inexpressible intelligence. Basmajian and others have demonstrated that the visual or auditory display of motor unit activity to the generator of such activity, along with instructions to alter the symbol of that activity, results in rapid accomplishment of the instructions to isolate and to control voluntarily one or several such motor units [15-17]. The process occurs in the absence of conscious awareness and, indeed, may be inhibited by conscious influences. Finally, the process becomes stable and can be reproduced in the absence of the external monitors.

This example of the biofeedback process can be rephrased in terms of the conditions and events which comprise the process. First, sets of concepts are presented to the conscious mind: abstract symbols of complex, spatiotemporal biologic activity; instructions; and surrounding attitudes. Second, the conceptual information appears to be utilized to produce an effective and ordered alteration of biologic function compatible with projections of the concepts (i.e., one might deduce that the conceptual information contained in the symbols, instructions, and attitudes and that information derived from subjectively identified and perceived mind–body relationships is integrated, evaluated and productively directed to discriminate more and more finely the direction of the intent to alter body function). Third, implementation of the intent is not conceptualized in terms of conscious awareness of mental activity. Fourth, signs of the mental activity are communicated via alterations of physiologic activity.

One very basic and obvious question that the biofeedback process raises concerns the mechanism by which individuals accomplish sophisticated and skilled actions not previously known or experienced, i.e., how individuals use symbolic and abstract information about interior processes not only to mobilize, direct and control a single neuronal pathway, normally functioning cooperatively with many other similar neuronal routes, but also to suppress the others simultaneously and selectively. Basmajian has called it will power, as have others when referring to voluntary control over atrial fibrillation.

The type of awareness which develops in the biofeedback process is one generally described by, "I know that I am doing this, but I do not know how I am doing it." This appears to represent an internally derived, non-verbalizable awareness of biologic states having the distinctive properties that the *biologic awareness* is neither communicable by ordinary means nor predominantly influenced by consensual consciousness. Thus the two subsets of consciousness may be distinguishable: subjectively appreciated and objectively appreciated.

As noted earlier, one concept of brain function which may apply to this situation suggests that sequential, *linear* neuronal transmission of information may account for conscious thought since conscious thought processes are essentially linear, and that the vast paralleling networks of *non-linear* connections provide a rich network of information transfer possibilities since these are essentially incapable of linear output to the normal outputs of conscious thought, and thus may subserve mental activity in a way which is subjectively appreciated only.

The most important result of the process is that for the first time we have reached a point where we are able to manipulate non-consciously perceived mental activity.

Summary

Events in the biofeedback process can be summarized as: (1) Abstract, symbolic information is directly and intentionally used by a form of consciousness to direct alterations in mind–body function. (2) The process takes place in the absence of conscious awareness of the biologic functioning. (3) Specific relationships between subjectively appreciated mental and body functions are manipulated. (4) An integration of conceptual information and non-aware recognition of internal events results in alteration of physiologic processes on all levels of physical activity. (5) The expression of the phenomenon constitutes a formerly unrecognized mode of communication.

Some deductions from these characteristic events may be: (1) The process defines subsets of the mind–body relationship. (2) A "specific" mind–body relationship is identified and isolated. (3) The process defines a distinctive subset of consciousness: subjectively appreciated mental activity which is not incompatible with objectively appreciated mental activity. (4) The integration process is efficient to the concept and directs its own result via a complex organization of spatio-temporally distributed information (i.e., there is correspondence between the concept and the integration of it with non-aware recognition. (5) The concept of auto-control of internal states allows implementation of that control. (6) The observer *is* the observed.

Speculations: The complex interplay of a rapidly accelerating exchange of information and shifting attitudes also provides the base for both expanding concepts of consciousness and penetrating the boundaries of convention physical-world relationships. The apparent dependence of the biofeedback phenomenon upon the subjective appreciation of mental activity stimulates a wide range of speculations. For example: (1) To what degree do objectively and subjectively derived mental activities differ? (2) What are the effects of one type of consciousness on the other? Do they have mutually excitant and/or inhibitory properties? (3) Do the two types of mental activity differ in their mode of operation? (4) Can the events in the biofeedback process unify objective and subjective characterizations of consciousness? (5) Does the isolation of a subjectively perceived consciousness reflect a new or undiscovered, or evolving process of mind? (6) Does the intentional aspect identify a set of consciousness or an independent derivative of neuronal activity? (7) Does internally perceived awareness reflect the physical order and reality of nature more accurately than consensual consciousness?

REFERENCES

1. Sperry, R.W. An objective approach to subjective experiences: further explanation of a hypothesis. *Psychol. Rev.* 77:585–590, 1970.
2. Cook, S. & Harris, R.E. The verbal conditioning of the galvanic skin reflex. *J. Exp. Psychol.* 21:202–210, 1937.

3. Dixon, N.F. & Lear, T.E. Electroencephalograph correlates of threshold regulation. *Nature* 198:870–872, 1963.
4. Schwartz, G.E. Cardiac responses to self-induced thoughts. *Psychophysiology* 8:462–467, 1971.
5. Barber, T.X. Physiological effects of "hypnotic suggestions": a critical review of recent research (1960–1964). *Psychol. Bull.* 63:201, 1965.
6. DiCara, L.V. & Miller, N.E. Long term retention of instrumentally learned heart-rate changes in the curarized rat. *Comm. Behav. Biol.* 2:19–23, 1968.
7. DiCara, L.V. & Miller, N.E. Heart-rate learning in the noncurarized state, transfer to the curarized state, and subsequent retraining in the non-curarized state. *Psychol Behav.* 4:621–624, 1969.
8. Fetz, E.E. & Finocchio, D.V. Operant conditioning of specific patterns of neural and muscular activity. *Science* 174:431, 1971.
9. Brown, B.B. Recognition of aspects of consciousness through association with EEG alpha activity represented by a light signal. *Psychophysiology* 6:442–452, 1970.
10. Headrick, M.W., Feather, B.W. & Wells, D.T. Unidirectional and large magnitude heart rate changes with augmented sensory feedback. *Psychophysiology* 8:132–142, 1971.
11. Stephens, J.H., Harris, A.H. & Brady, J.V. Large magnitude heart rate changes in subjects instructed to change their heart rates and given interoceptive feedback. *Psychophysiology* 9:283–285, 1972.
12. Brener, J. & Hothersall, D. Heart rate control under conditions of augmented sensory feedback. *Psychophysiology* 3:23–28, 1966.
13. Booker, H.E., Rubow, R.T. & Coleman, P.J. Simplified feedback in neuromuscular retraining: An automated approach using electromyographic signals. *Arch. Phys. Med.* 50:621–625, 1969.
14. Brown, B.B. Awareness of EEG-subjective activity relationships detected within a closed feedback system. *Psychophysiology* 7:451–464, 1970.
15. Basmajian, J.V. Control and training of individual motor units. *Science* 141:440–441, 1963.
16. Basmajian, J.V. Electromyography comes of age. The conscious control of individual motor units in man may be used to improve his physical performance. *Science* 176:603–609, 1972.
17. Petajan, J.H. & Phillip, B.A. Frequency control of motor unit action potentials. *Electroenceph. Clin. Neurophysiol.* 27:66–72, 1969.

II

MEDITATION AND YOGA

Psychophysiological Correlates of Meditation 4

Robert L. Woolfolk

● **The scientific research that has investigated the physiological changes associated with meditation as it is practiced by adherents of Indian Yoga, Transcendental Meditation, and Zen Buddhism has not yielded a thoroughly consistent, easily replicable pattern of responses. The majority of studies show meditation to be a wakeful state accompanied by a lowering of cortical and autonomic arousal. The investigations of Zen and Transcendental Meditation have thus far produced the most consistent findings.**

Additional research into the mechanisms underlying the phenomena of meditation will require a shifting from old to new methodological perspectives that allow for adequate experimental control and the testing of theoretically relevant hypotheses.

(Arch Gen Psychiatry 32:1326-1333, 1975)

For many centuries, individuals in the East have practiced different forms of meditation and alleged salutary effects on physical and psychological functioning. Numerous similarities have been noted among methods of meditation and such Western therapeutic devices as progressive relaxation and autogenic training.[1] Meditation has been successfully substituted for relaxation as a counter-conditioning agent in systematic desensitization[2] and has been theorized to operate as a kind of "global desensitization procedure."[3] As an adjunct to psychotherapy, meditation has been employed with neurotic populations[4] and with inpatient groups classified as psychotic.[5] The practice of meditation has been found to be associated with lowered trait anxiety,[6] decreased drug abuse,[7,8] and gains on a measure of self-actualization.[9,10] Some research has shown that regular practice of meditation can lead to improvement in bronchial asthma[11] and decreased systolic blood pressure in hypertensive patients.[12]

The evidence cited above is largely suggestive, some arising from uncontrolled research and some based on conclusions from paper-and-pencil psychometric data rather than more salient behavioral or physiological data.

Accepted for publication Jan 3, 1975.

From the Department of Psychology, University College, Rutgers University, New Brunswick, NJ.

Reprints not available.

Clinical outcome studies can suggest that *something* involved in the rather complex "package" of training in and practice of meditation (usually Transcendental Meditation) may possibly produce therapeutic benefits. But what remains unknown is *which* aspects of the package are the active ingredients and *what* mechanisms underlie their purported efficacy. The increasingly widespread use of meditation procedures requires both an adequate scientific understanding of these phenomena as well as controlled studies of efficacy. This review, in bringing together the basic psychophysiological research on meditation, will attempt to clarify what is known about the effects of meditation, to indicate what sorts of questions are as yet unanswered, and to specify methods for obtaining answers to those questions. It does not specifically focus on the issues of methodology relating to efficacy.

The search for psychophysiological correlates of meditation has centered essentially on three groups: Yogis and students of Yoga in India, adherents of Transcendental Meditation in the United States, and practitioners of Zen Buddhism in Japan. These studies have typically measured various physiological indexes (electroencephalogram [EEG], galvanic skin response [GSR]) of individuals "accomplished" at meditation and have made comparisons either with control groups or in a within-subject design. What actually has been investigated is the effects of some rather specific meditative procedures practiced by individuals within a complex framework of philosophical commitment and social influence. The experimental designs reviewed do not allow us to draw inferences concerning the relative effects of these technical and "extratechnical" factors. Thus, the findings reported here pertain to the effects of very complex sets of independent variables, rather than the influences of variables specifiable and manipulatable under normal laboratory conditions.

YOGA

Yoga has been an integral feature of the Hindu culture for over 2,000 years. The term itself refers to the set of practices and beliefs whose goal is the attainment of *samadhi*, or "union" with the "Universal Self." The different sects of Yoga vary greatly in their use of such tech-

Table 1.—Summary of Studies of Indian Yogic Meditation

References	Experience of Meditators	Changes During Meditation*	Type of Design	Quality of Control Procedures
Das & Gastaut[13]	Highly experienced	Faster EEG, increase in HR	Within-subject	Poor, measurements taken in field under highly variable conditions
Anand et al[14]	Highly experienced	Faster EEG, decrease in O_2 consumption, decrease in HR	Within-subject	Excellent, laboratory study
Bagchi & Wegner[15]	Highly experienced	No change in EEG, increase in SR level, no change in HR, no change in BP	Within-subject	Poor, measurements taken in field under highly variable conditions
Kasamatsu et al[18]	Highly experienced	Slower EEG	Within-subject	Adequate, laboratory study, meditation period too short
Anand et al[19]	Highly experienced	Slower EEG	Within-subject	Excellent, laboratory conditions
Wegner & Bagchi[20]	Moderately experienced	Decrease in SR level, decrease in respiration rate, increase in HR, increase in BP	Within-subject	Poor, initial readings not comparable before meditation & relaxation periods
Karambelkar et al[21]	Moderately experienced	No change in SR level, increase in O_2 consumption, no change in HR, no change in BP	Between-subjects	Poor, no control over duration of meditation, sketchy reporting

* Electroencephalogram indicated by EEG; heart rate, HR; oxygen, O_2; skin resistance, SR; and blood pressure, BP.

niques as physical postures (*asana*), breath control (*pranayama*), fixed attention on an idea or image (*dharana*), and extended contemplation or meditation (*dhyana*). Sects also vary in their degree of mysticism from Hatha Yoga, which primarily emphasizes different bodily postures and exercises as a means of achieving physical health and psychological well-being, to the esoteric schools and their decidedly more spiritual orientations. These divergences in belief and practice are, in all likelihood, responsible for the dissimilarity of findings produced by the following research into the physiological correlates of Indian Yoga (see Table 1).

Electrocortical Activity

Das and Gastaut[10] measured the EEGs of seven practitioners of Yoga during 20 meditative sessions. During meditation, high-frequency electrocortical activity replaced slower premeditation rhythms and remained until meditation was terminated. The one subject who reported achieving *samadhi* evidenced considerable increases in the amplitude of the beta waves recorded during this state. During this period, his EEG was not affected by the presentation of auditory or visual stimulation, indicating an insensibility to external events. In research that examined the responses of a highly regarded Indian Yogi during two periods of prolonged meditation in an airtight box, Anand et al[14] also found meditation to be associated with beta activity. Prior to his entry into the box, the EEG of the subject showed a predominance of alpha waves. This pattern was quickly replaced by higher-frequency beta activity with occasional runs of alpha waves interspersed, suggestive of drowsiness or light sleep. Bagchi and Wegner[15] found no change in the EEG patterns of 14 Yogis when comparisons were made between readings taken during meditation and readings taken during control periods of quiet rest in the lotus position. Although the predominant electrocortical activity observed during meditation was in the alpha frequency range, this was also the case during control periods. An increase in the slower frequencies that some writers[15–17] have considered to be a defining characteristic of meditation was not observed. In the following two studies on Indian Yoga, however, this slowing of the EEG was demonstrated. Kasamatsu et al[18] compared the EEGs taken during meditation of an experienced Yogi and a control subject whose resting EEG was similar to that of the Yogi. After

eight minutes the Yogi demonstrated a substantial increase in alpha activity, while the pattern of the resting control remained unchanged. There was no blocking of the meditator's alpha rhythm on the sudden presentation of auditory stimuli.

In a well-controlled study, Anand et al[19] made within-subject comparisons of the electrocortical activity of four experienced Yogis during rest and during meditation. All the subjects displayed considerable alpha activity during periods of rest. This activity became more prominent and increased in amplitude during meditation. Two Yogis were exposed to auditory, haptic, and visual stimuli before and during meditation. During the control period, all stimulation blocked the alpha rhythm, converting it to low-voltage fast activity. This blocking pattern failed to habituate on repetition of the same stimuli. When the Yogis were in meditation, however, no blocking of the alpha rhythm occurred. Failure of alpha blocking to habituate has been hypothesized to reflect both heightened perceptual sensitivity and some degree of cortical excitation.[17]

Electrodermal Activity

Bagchi and Wegner[15] found that palmar skin resistance (SR) increased during meditation, with a median increase of 56% during control periods. When these same authors[20] compared the responses of four Yoga students during meditation in the lotus position with responses from an equivalent period of reclining relaxation, SR was found to be greater during meditation.

The interpretation of this last finding is unclear not only because of the postural differences but also because the conditions were not comparable with respect to initial readings. The picture regarding Indian Yogic meditation and electrodermal activity is also complicated by a third study that found no consistent differences between two practitioners of Yoga and two control subjects on measures of SR.[21] In considering this finding, criticism must be directed both at the small sample size for a between-subjects design and the lack of clarity of the authors' report, from which it is not clear whether the Yogis were involved in meditation throughout the entire experiment.

Respiration

Bagchi and Wegner[15] found that during meditation the rate of respiration tended to decline relative to levels set

Table 2.—Summary of Studies of Transcendental Meditation

References	Experience of Meditators	Changes During Meditation*	Type of Design	Quality of Control Procedures
Wallace[22]	Moderately experienced	Slower EEG, increase in SR level, decrease in O$_2$ consumption, decrease in HR	Within-subject	Excellent, laboratory study, statistical comparisons made
Wallace et al[23]	Moderately experienced	Slower EEG, increase in SR level, decrease in O$_2$ consumption, decrease in BP	Within-subject	Excellent, laboratory study, statistical comparisons made
Schwartz[24]	Moderately experienced	Slower EEG, increase in SR level (these changes not significantly from those found in controls)	Between-subjects	Excellent, laboratory study, statistical comparisons made, appropriate control group
Banquet[25]	Moderately experienced	Slower EEG (stages I & II), in some individuals faster EEG observed during third stage	Within-subject	Excellent, laboratory study, statistical comparisons made
Orme-Johnson[26]	Moderately experienced	Galvanic skin response more stable	Between-subjects	Excellent, laboratory study, statistical comparisons made, appropriate control group
Allison[30]	Not reported	Decrease in rate of respiration	Within-subject	Adequate, laboratory study, sketchy reporting

* See footnote to Table 1.

during control periods. Wegner and Bagchi[20] found the rate of respiration to be slower during meditation than during reclining relaxation. The Anand et al[14] study found dramatic decreases in oxygen consumption during meditation in an airtight box, while a study that attempted to replicate these results[21] found that the oxygen consumption of Yogis, relative to basal levels, was greater than that of controls exposed to the same environment.

Cardiovascular Responses

Das and Gastaut[18] found that heart rate increased during meditation. Their findings were supported by Wegner and Bagchi[20] who recorded faster heart rate and higher systolic and diastolic blood pressure during meditation. Anand et al[14] observed a decrease in heart rate during meditation, while two studies[15,21] failed to find meditation associated with consistent changes in any cardiovascular response.

Despite the presence of many obvious inconsistencies, one clear commonality does emerge from the research on physiological concomitants of Indian Yogic meditation. The failure of meditator's EEGs to be affected by sensory input was a clear finding in three studies.[15,18,19] This evidence suggests that a "turning off" of awareness or a "shutting down" of input processing occurred in these subjects. Methodologically speaking, the research on Yoga leaves much to be desired. Many of the studies were conducted in the field under adverse circumstances. Yogis willing to submit to psychophysiological measurement often were not readily available. Thus, consequent small numbers and the considerable variability among subjects likely contributed to the incompatible findings reported. Some Yoga states[14,15,20] are associated with patterns of electrocortical excitation, while others[15,18,19] produce a predominance of slow wave activity. Findings with respect to other variables, eg, heart rate, show a similar inconsistency. These divergences, in large part, result from the lack of uniformity both among the experimental procedures employed and in the goals, beliefs, and practices of Indian Yoga.

TRANSCENDENTAL MEDITATION

A variety of Yoga known as Transcendental Meditation (TM) was adapted from the Indian Yogic tradition by the Maharishi Mahesh Yogi. As an object of scientific study, it offers many advantages over more traditional forms of Yoga. It is a much less rigorous and demanding discipline, apparently easily learned, and widely practiced in the United States. Essentially, it is a streamlined form of Mantram Yoga in which practitioners meditate in any comfortable position on a specific *mantram*, or set of words. Meditators, in two daily 20-minute sessions, silently repeat the words of a particular mantram again and again throughout each session, returning focus to the words whenever attention wanders.

Although less esoteric than its Hindu precursors, TM is not without its own brand of arcane practices that include delivery of an "individualized" secret mantram to every student. The additional presence of philosophical teachings and strong expectations of salutary derivative effects precludes drawing any inferences from the following research (see Table 2) concerning effects of the meditative techniques per se.

Electrocortical Activity

Wallace[22] recorded the EEGs of 15 college-aged students of TM during meditation and made within-subjects comparisons with base lines taken during periods of quiet rest. The EEGs of subjects showed that alpha activity present prior to meditation increased in regularity and amplitude. Some of the subjects demonstrated periods of low-voltage theta wave predominance. In most subjects, alpha activity was blocked by both auditory and visual stimuli. This blocking failed to habituate on repeated presentation of the stimuli.

A similar pattern of electrocortical activity was observed in the 36 meditators studies by Wallace et al.[23] The EEG pattern during TM showed increases in alpha activity. In some subjects, the increases in alpha activity were accompanied by occasional trains of theta waves.

Schwartz[24] reported two experiments that obtained results that can be interpreted as being at variance with those of Wallace and his co-workers. First, occipital alpha activity was recorded from 12 experienced meditators during three brief meditations separated by brief periods of relaxation with eyes open. The investigation employed a control group matched on age and sex who relaxed with eyes closed during the meditation periods. Increases in alpha activity were recorded for both groups during periods when eyes were closed relative to times when eyes were open. However, alpha activity declined during the periods of meditation, the decrease in alpha being somewhat less for the meditators. An interesting finding reported was what appeared to be a postmeditation "cortical sensitization effect." Although pre-experimental measurements of both groups taken with eyes open disclosed more alpha activity in meditator's EEGs, during the post-meditation phase meditators evidenced less alpha activity than did the controls. In a second experiment that attempted to replicate this effect, Schwartz[24] recorded the EEGs of 16 meditators during one 22-minute meditation session. The findings were consistent with those of the earlier experiment. When compared with data from the control group, the electrocortical readings did suggest a sensitization effect in meditators following meditation.

A recent study of electrocortical activity during TM[25] found for all meditators an initial slowing of the EEG, indicative of lowered cortical arousal. Alpha activity present at the beginning of meditation became predominant, yielding to a dominant theta pattern as the meditation progressed. However, subsequent to the period of theta predominance, some subjects displayed a pattern of generalized fast beta frequencies similar to those recorded by Das and Gastaut.[14] As in this earlier research on Indian Yoga, these periods of beta activity were associated with subjects' reports of very deep meditation. In response to click-and-flash stimulation, alpha activity, when present, was usually not blocked; but the theta pattern was blocked by stimuli. The beta activity associated with "profound meditation" was not affected by auditory or visual stimulation.

Electrodermal Activity

Wallace[22] reported a substantial increase in palmar SR during TM. This increase was not sustained in the rest period following meditation. Wallace et al[23] observed a substantial increase of approximately 60% during meditation. Schwartz[24] reported very slight increases in SR during meditation. However, increases in SR observed in meditators were comparable to those found in a group of matched controls who rested with eyes closed. Following meditation, SR levels fell below those of controls, suggesting heightened arousal in the meditators following meditation.

Orme-Johnson[20] reported two studies that sought to determine if stability of SR results from the practice of TM. Fluctuations in SR have been associated in the literature both with individual stress levels and with various environmental stressors.[27-29] In the first study, GSR habituation to noxious tones was observed in eight practitioners of TM and eight controls after both groups had been instructed to relax in a comfortable sitting position. It was found that GSR habituated faster for meditators than for controls. In a subsequent test of GSR stability, meditators made fewer spontaneous GSR fluctuations during meditation than did controls during an equal period of rest.

In the second experiment, which attempted to control for differences between individuals who chose to learn TM and randomly selected controls, Orme-Johnson studied spontaneous GSR in eight meditators and eight nonmeditators who planned to begin TM training in two weeks. The findings of the earlier study were replicated. The GSR of meditators was demonstrated to be more stable during meditation than that of the resting controls. Some support of Wallace's findings was generated in that a substantial decrease of basal SR was observed for meditators during meditation but not found in the resting controls.

Respiration

Allison,[30] in a one-subject study, found that the subject's rate of respiration during meditation decreased by approximately 50% relative to a base rate achieved while the subject watched television. Breathing became somewhat shallower, returning to control levels during the period following meditation. Wallace[22] observed that for his subjects, oxygen consumption showed a mean decrease of 20%, rising to control levels following meditation. Wallace et al[23] reported measures of respiration on five meditators that indicated a decrease in both rate of respiration and in oxygen consumption during meditation.

Cardiovascular Responses

Wallace and his co-workers,[22,23] to my knowledge, are the only investigators to have reported cardiovascular data on TM. They reported a decrease in heart rate during TM and no substantial change in systolic or diastolic blood pressure.

When compared to the variegated corpus of Indian Yoga, the methods of TM are highly consistent. As one might expect, the data on physiological concomitants also evidence greater consistency. All studies that measured rate of respiration found decreases on this variable during TM. All studies showed initial increases in alpha activity during meditation, with other frequencies often appearing during the latter stages of a meditation period. In some cases theta rhythms were observed,[22,12] while in one study,[25] beta frequencies were recorded. In Schwartz studies,[24] equipment settings did not allow a determination of which frequencies increased as alpha diminished.

During TM there appears to be both an increase and stabilization of SR, although Schwartz[24] demonstrated only minimal changes in GSR. Procedural differences involving sequencing and duration of meditation and control periods may account for some of the disparity in the data. However, Schwartz[24] suggests that the differences in findings may have stemmed from the fact that Wallace et al[22,23] maintained a personal relationship with their subjects and were able to put them at ease, allowing them to attain a deeper and more natural state of meditation. As support for this contention that situational factors may interact with meditation procedures, Schwartz[24] presents some compelling evidence. Skin resistances of 30 meditators and 30 nonmeditators were compared as they anticipated the viewing of a stressful film. Meditators showed a mean *decrease* in SR while meditating. This decrease was greater than that observed in the controls who simply rested. These findings serve again to highlight the necessity for rigorous experimental controls. The pattern or hypometabolism seen in some studies may indeed be an elusive one, obtained with great difficulty under less than optimum experimental conditions.

ZEN

Zazen, or Zen meditation is an integral part of both the Soto and Rinzai sects of Zen Buddhism. It is the primary method by which the enlightened or transcendent state known as *satori* is achieved. The practice of Zazen itself is much more highly standardized than are the various Yogic techniques of meditation. Zazen is practiced in the lotus or half-lotus position with eyes open. An initiate begins by focusing all attention on his breathing. After some period of time, when he has learned to rivet attention on the process of breathing, the student is given a *koan*, or riddle to meditate on. The aim is not for the student to generate a solution through rational proceses, but rather to provide a more difficult exercise in concentration. Serious practitioners of Zen lead very austere and disciplined lives, no small part of which is the attempt to emulate the style and attitudes of the Zen master.

Physiological studies of Zen meditation suggest that it may be a state quite similar to that achieved through forms of Yogic meditation (see Table 3).

References	Experience of Meditators	Changes During Meditation*	Type of Design	Quality of Control Procedures
Kasamatsu et at[18]	Highly experienced	Slower EEG	Within-subject	Adequate, laboratory study, meditation period too short
Kasamatsu & Hirai[31]	Moderately experienced & highly recommended	Slower EEG	Within-subject	Excellent, laboratory conditions
Akishige[32]	Highly experienced	Slower EEG, galvanic skin response more stable, decrease in O$_2$ consumption, decrease in respiration rate	Within-subject	Excellent, laboratory conditions
Hirai[33]	Highly experienced	Slower EEG, decrease in respiration rate	Within-subject	Adequate, laboratory conditions
Sugi & Akutsu[34]	Highly experienced	Decrease in O$_2$ consumption	Within-subject	Excellent, laboratory conditions
Goyeche et al[35]	Minimally experienced	Decrease in respiration rate, decrease in HR	Within-subject	Excellent, laboratory conditions, order of meditation & control periods randomized

Table 3.—Summary of Studies of Zen Meditation

* See footnote to Table 1.

Electrocortical Activity

Kasamatsu et al[18] report substantial increases in alpha activity during the Zazen of an experienced practitioner of Zen. These changes were analogous to changes in the EEG of a Yogi who meditated under the same conditions. Blocking of alpha activity by external stimuli was not observed. Kasamatsu and Hirai,[31] in a rather intensive study, measured the electrocortical activity of 48 priests and disciples during Zazen. All subjects showed an increase in alpha activity immediately subsequent to beginning meditation. Less experienced subjects tended to maintain high-amplitude alpha throughout the meditative session, whereas the EEGs of those with more years in Zen training showed rhythmical theta wave patterns during latter stages of Zazen. Whether or not these differences are the result of their greater experience itself or other differences between subjects, eg, age, is not clear. These findings are consistent with those of Akishige[32] and Hirai[33] who found a similar slowing of the EEG during Zazen. Kasamatsu and Hirai[31] observed that both alpha and theta activity were blocked by the presentation of auditory stimuli. This blocking failed to habituate. In control subjects habituation of alpha occurred quite rapidly.

Electrodermal Activity

In his study of experienced practitioners of Zen, Akishige[32] reports a decrease in spontaneous skin conductance responses during Zazen. This tendency for GSR to stabilize was similar to that reported in research on TM.[20]

Respiration

Sugi and Akutsu[34] observed a 20% decrease in oxygen consumption associated with the meditation of ten Zen monks with many years of experience. Hirai[33] discovered that the respiratory rate decreased during Zazen. Still more studies of skilled practitioners of Zen[32] showed both a decrease of oxygen consumption and rate of respiration. In another study,[35] the rate of respiration associated with Zen meditation was found to be slower than during control periods.

Cardiovascular Responses

Goyeche and others[35] compared Zen meditation with relaxation. In their within-subject design the order of treatment was randomly assigned to each of the eight subjects. It was found that heart rate decreased during Zen meditation.

The available research on Zen shows a pattern of physiological correlates that are analogous to those reported in some of the studies of Indian Yogic meditation and TM.

Oxygen consumption, rate of respiration, and frequency of electrocortical activity were all found to diminish during Zazen. The observed changes were in the direction of hypometabolism and suggest a lowered state of arousal of the autonomic and central nervous systems.

COMMENT

The studies reported thus far have sought to bring the precision of laboratory measurement to bear on the study of individuals schooled in various meditation techniques. In these studies, relatively great control was exercised over the selection and collection of dependent measures. These were not, however, investigations of the influences of easily specified and highly refined independent variables. The inference of precise causal relationships is not possible from the data.

From the perspective of one seeking scientific understanding of the mechanisms that underlie the various forms of meditation, the research reviewed is only suggestive. Findings reflect the influences of very complex sets of social, cognitive, perceptual, and physiological variables. New methodologies will be required to specify and tease out the effects of these variables. The early research does suggest three areas whose exploration might provide us with added refinement of variables and tentative hypotheses concerning the relationships of these variables. These areas are the phenomenological reports of meditators, the techniques of meditation themselves, and the physiological correlates.

An examination of phenomenology is of great potential import. For example, if some technique of meditation consistently produced reports of pleasurable affect from all who used it, the technique would be of great interest for this reason alone. However, all the severe problems of introspective research that caused scientific inquiry to turn away from subjective data are present in the research on meditation. These problems are particularly acute in the study of disciplines whose vocabularies are highly esoteric and mystical. The variability of practices within the sects and practitioners of Indian Yoga leave the investigator in a quandary when attempting to understand such issues as the difference between a period of meditation that yields *samadhi* and one in which the experience approximates but does not achieve the sought-after state. Although *samadhi* is universally described by terms such as "transcendence" and "bliss" and characterized as a "turning off" of the external world, one Yogi shows cortical excitation in very "deep" meditation while another clearly evidences greater synchronization and slowing of the EEG. Thus consistent reports of the phenomenology of meditation may simply reflect similarly shaped verbal sets, rather than any regularities along other dimensions.

On conducting an inspection of the meditative techniques themselves employed by the different disciplines, we find many interesting similarities. Virtually all forms of meditation require physical immobility. All require some form of perceptual concentration. This concentration may be on an object, idea, image, or mantram, as in many forms of Yoga. In Zazen, attention is focused on the breathing or on a *koan*. The net result of this concentration of awareness is a limitation of one or more of the visual, auditory, or haptic sensory modes to a single invariate stimulus configuration.

When we turn to the physiological data of the research literature on meditation in a search for commonalities, we find what seems to be a somewhat inconsistent picture. Studies have thus far failed to verify an easily replicable, special "state" of meditation with physiological concomitants that are consistent across the various esoteric traditions. This is not surprising in view of the fact that extra-technical factors inherent in the training of meditators and laboratory situational factors have tended to be quite diverse. These problems are particularly evident in studies of Indian Yoga, while the research on TM and Zen has yielded a much more consistent picture. This research indicates meditation to be associated with a slowing and increased synchronization of electrocortical rhythms, an increased or more stable SR, and slower rate of respiration. These changes are all in the direction of lowered arousal and suggest a diminishing of energy metabolism. The results of several studies, however, demonstrate a profile unlike that arising from simple relaxation. For example, Banquet[25] found high-frequency electrocortical activity to be evidenced by some meditators during the latter stages of a meditative period. It should also be recalled that the majority of studies used control periods of nonmeditative rest in comparison with meditation and found differences between the two conditions. Several authors[17,31] have concluded that the failure of habituation of blocking of alpha activity by sensory input indicates some substantial degree of cortical excitation to be present during meditation. This dishabituation, however, is not consistent across all studies. For example, Anand et al[19] found that, in Yogis, alpha blocking failed to habituate in control periods, but that during meditation sensory input did not alter their subjects' EEGs. Naranjo and Ornstein[16] have suggested that the data on alpha blocking reflect:

... two basic types of meditation exercises ... those which "turn off" input processing for a period of time to achieve an *after-effect* of "opening up" of awareness, and those which consist of the active practice of "opening up" during the period of the exercise.[16(p198)]

Any future investigations that attempt to ascertain what, if any, are the effects of the meditative procedures removed from their religious contexts will likely begin to grapple with the question of underlying mechanisms. Two theories have thus far been put forth that address this issue.

Kasamatsu and Hirai[21] noted similarities between the EEG of Zen meditation and that produced by other situations that reduce the consumption of oxygen. When air is breathed at high altitudes under reduced pressure, oxygen intake is lowered and an increase of alpha activity is observed.[36] Watanabe et al[37] proposed the reduction of oxygen consumption common to all forms of meditation to be the single most important factor in producing the physiological changes associated with meditation. The potential utility of this theory is very great as it is quite amenable to empirical confirmation. Its fundamental proposition could be tested quite easily by holding oxygen consump-

tion constant across meditative and control sessions by use of a breathing apparatus that would allow the experimenter to systematically vary the oxygen-nitrogen mixture. If changes associated with meditation do not occur when oxygen consumption is held constant, then powerful support for the theory is generated. Conversely, if psychophysiological correlates of meditation are observed, it would suggest a role of limited importance for anoxia in the production of meditative phenomena. It should be noted that there is evidence indicating that for Zen meditation the observed reduction in respiratory rate per se does not account for decreases in oxygen consumption.[34] The oxygen consumption of controls who had assumed meditative postures *increased* slightly when breathing frequencies were lowered to levels found in Zazen.

Deikman[38,39] and Ornstein[40] have proposed that similarities existing among the correlates of different types of meditation are due to their common procedural feature, the focusing of perception on invariate sources of stimulation. Ornstein contends that the central nervous system is so constructed that concentration of awareness on an unchanging stimulus produces a cessation of awareness of the external world. This theory finds some support in the experimental literature. Cohen[41] studied the effects of an unchanging, homogeneous visual field of low illumination (*Ganzfeld*) on perception. Five of 16 subjects reported a total "cessation" of visual experience:

This was a unique experience which involved a complete disappearance of the sense of vision for short periods of time, and not simply the presence of a dark, undifferentiated visual field.[41(p407)]

In a subsequent experiment the phenomenon was replicated.[42] Bursts of alpha activity were associated with visual cessation, and subjects whose EEGs showed high levels of alpha activity were more likely to experience the visual termination. Cohen hypothesized that perceptual mechanisms may have evolved to process differentiated fields and that unchanging stimulation may cause a temporary disruption of these mechanisms.

Lehmann et al[43] produced a "stabilized" image on subjects' retinas by means of a tiny projector mounted on a contact lens. Subjects reported disappearance of the image after a few seconds of continuous viewing. The authors reported that electrocortical activity was low-voltage beta during periods of visibility as contrasted with predominant alpha after a fading out of the image.

These studies do suggest that restriction and repetition of sensory input may be a very important ingredient in meditative procedures. This perceptual theory of meditation is likely to prove of great heuristic value for the more carefully controlled studies required to demonstrate what are the contributions of technical factors to the correlative phenomena of meditation. More specifically, to pursue its implications investigators would attempt to isolate the effects on psychophysiological variables of stimulus consistency across one or more modes of sensation.

The methodologies of such studies would of necessity require better control over the influences of independent variables than has been exercised in the research on the esoteric schools of meditation. For the major task of any future research on meditation is that of developing experimental designs enabling the teasing out of variables active in producing the effects associated with the meditative practices of the mystical traditions. The study of individuals who meditate in conjunction with religious practices is highly inappropriate because of the impossibility of separating the effects of techniques per se from the multiple additional factors comprising the context within which the techniques are practiced. Furthermore, the use of such individuals often requires relationships of a more personal nature between subjects and experimenters (resulting from the exigencies of recruitment and preparation of subjects) than is optimal in research seeking to limit uncontrolled sources of variation.

When naïve subjects are employed and specific, repeatable procedures tested, the important questions are more readily answered. The effects of various techniques potentially can be examined without the contaminating influence of expectations and demand characteristics. Furthermore, these extratechnical factors can be experimentally manipulated while techniques are held constant to permit systematic investigation of set and setting variables.

These recommended changes in methodology are necessary not only to achieve a scientifically acceptable explanation of meditation, but also if effective meditative procedures are likely ever to achieve appropriate clinical availability. All who have investigated this area believe that meditation may be, at the very least, of great potential utility to members of stressful, high-speed Western societies. The average citizen has not the time to study for years in Japan or India, nor often the inclination to become an acolyte of the Maharishi. As long as the mechanisms that underlie meditation remain shrouded in mystery, whatever benefits it may hold will be for most of us unrealized.

CONCLUSIONS

Various practices of Yoga, Zen Buddhism, and other esoteric disciplines share the common label "meditation."

Scientific investigation of these practices has failed to demonstrate an integrated, clearly defined set of responses common to all forms of meditation. The studies of Zen and TM have thus far yielded the most consistent pattern of responses associated with meditation. The pattern most frequently observed is indicative of a reduction in arousal and a slowing of energy metabolism. However, some Yoga states have been found to be associated with electrocortical excitation and increases in oxygen consumption.

Although the preponderance of evidence on the various forms of meditation suggests that meditative procedures can produce under some circumstances a lowering of cortical and autonomic arousal, variables of set and setting have been shown to determine to some extent the kind of state produced. The research thus far has not generated an adequate scientific understanding of the specific independent variables and causal relationships that account for meditative phenomena. This is largely because research has thus far investigated the effects of rather specific techniques practiced within a complex framework of expectation, philosophical belief, and social influence. To develop acceptable scientific explanations of meditative phenomena, future research must address itself to the development of new methodologies that allow for the systematic isolation and investigation of technical and extratechnical factors that are active in producing psychophysiological change.

References

1. Benson H, Beary JF, Carol MP: The relaxation response. *Psychiatry* 37:37-46, 1974.
2. Boudreau L: Transcendental Meditation and Yoga as reciprocal inhibitors. *J Behav Ther Exp Psychiatry* 3:97-98, 1972.
3. Coleman D: Meditation as a meta-therapy: Hypotheses toward a proposed fifth state of consciousness. *J Transpers Psychol* 3:1-25, 1971.
4. Carrington P, Ephron HS: Meditation as an adjunct to psychotherapy, in Arieti S, Chrzanowski G (eds): *New Dimensions in Psychiatry: A World View.* New York, John Wiley & Sons Inc, 1975.
5. Glueck B: Current research on Transcendental Meditation. Read at the Rensselaer Polytechnic Institute, Hartford, Conn, 1973.
6. Nidich S, Seeman W, Siebert M: Influence of Transcendental Meditation on state anxiety. *J Clin Consult Psychol*, to be published.
7. Benson H, Wallace RK: Decreased drug abuse with Transcendental Meditation: A study of 1,862 subjects, in Arafonetis CJD (ed): *Drug Abuse: Proceedings of the International Conference.* Philadelphia, Lea & Febiger, 1972, pp 369-376.
8. Shafii M, Lavely R, Jaffe R: Meditation and marijuana. *Am J Psychiatry* 131:60-63, 1974.
9. Seeman W, Nidich S, Banta T: Influence of Transcendental Meditation on a measure of self-actualization. *J Counsel Psychol* 19:184-187, 1972.
10. Nidich S, Seeman W, Dreskin T: Influence of Transcendental Meditation: A replication. *J Counsel Psychol* 20:565-566, 1973.
11. Wilson AF, Honsberger R: The effects of Transcendental Meditation upon bronchial asthma. *Clin Res* 21:278, 1973.
12. Benson H, Rosner BA, Marzetta BR: Decreased systolic blood pressure in hypertensive subjects who practiced meditation. *J Clin Invest* 52:8a, 1973.
13. Das NN, Gastaut H: Variations de l'activité electrique due cerveau, du coeur et des muscles squelettiques au cours de la meditation et de l'extase Yogique. *Electroencephalogr Clin Neurophysiol Suppl* 6:211-219, 1955.
14. Anand BK, Chhina GS, Singh B: Studies on Shri Ramanand Yogi during his stay in an air-tight box. *Indian J Med Res* 49:82-89, 1961.
15. Bagchi BK, Wenger MA: Electrophysiological correlates of some Yogi exercises. *Electroencephalogr Clin Neurophysiol Suppl* 7:132-149, 1957.
16. Naranjo C, Ornstein R: *On the Psychology of Meditation.* New York, The Viking Press, 1971.
17. Gellhorn E, Kiely WF: Mystical states of consciousness: Neurophysiological and clinical aspects. *J Nerv Ment Dis* 154:399-405, 1972.
18. Kasamatsu A, Okuma T, Takenaka S, et al: The EEG of Zen and Yoga practitioners. *Electroencephalogr Clin Neurophysiol Suppl* 9:51-52, 1957.
19. Anand BK, Chhina GS, Singh B: Some aspects of electroencephalographic studies in Yogis. *Electroencephalogr Clin Neurophysiol* 13:452-456, 1961.
20. Wenger MA, Bagchi BK: Studies of autonomic functions in practitioners of Yoga in India. *Behav Sci* 6:312-323, 1961.
21. Karambelkar PV, Vinekar SL, Bhole MV: Studies on human subjects staying in an air-tight pit. *Indian J Med Res* 56:1282-1288, 1968.

22. Wallace RK: Physiological effects of Transcendental Meditation. *Science* 167:1751-1754, 1970.
23. Wallace RK, Benson H, Wilson AF: A wakeful hypometabolic physiological state. *Am J Physiol* 221:795-799, 1971.
24. Schwartz GE: Pros and cons of meditation: Current findings on physiology and anxiety, self-control, drug abuse and creativity. Read before the 81st annual convention of the American Psychological Association, Montreal, 1973.
25. Banquet JP: Spectral analysis of the EEG in meditation. *Electroencephalogr Clin Neurophysiol* 35:143-151, 1973.
26. Orme-Johnson DW: Autonomic stability and Transcendental Meditation. *Psychosom Med* 35:341-349, 1973.
27. Mundy-Castle AC, McKiever BL: The psychophysiological significance of the galvanic skin response. *J Exp Psychol* 46:15-24, 1953.
28. Katkin ES: Relationship between manifest anxiety and two indices of autonomic response to stress. *J Pers Soc Psychol* 2:324-333, 1965.
29. Katkin ES, McCubbin RJ: Habituation of the orienting response as a function of individual differences in anxiety and autonomic lability. *J Abnorm Psychol* 74:54-60, 1969.
30. Allison J: Respiration changes during Transcendental Meditation. *Lancet* 1:833-834, 1970.
31. Kasamatsu A, Hirai T: An electroencephalographic study on the Zen meditation (Zazen). *Psychologia* 12:205-225, 1969.
32. Akishige Y: A historical survey of the psychological studies in Zen. *Kyushu Psychol Stud* 11:1-56, 1968.
33. Hirai T: Electroencephalographic study on the Zen Meditation. *Psychiatr Neurol Japon* 62:76-105, 1960.
34. Sugi Y, Akutsu K: Studies on respiration and energy-metabolism during sitting in Zazen. *Res J Physiol* El 12:190-206, 1968.
35. Goyeche JRM, Chihara T, Shimizu H: Two concentration methods: A preliminary comparison. *Psychologia* 15:110-111, 1972.
36. Gibbs FA, Williams D, Gibbs EL: Modification of the cortical frequency spectrum by changes in CO_2, blood sugar, and O_2. *J Neurophysiol* 3:49-58, 1940.
37. Watanabe T, Shapiro D, Schwartz GE: Meditation as an anoxic state: A critical review and theory. *Psychophysiologia* 9:279, 1972.
38. Deikman AJ: Experimental meditation. *J Nerv Ment Dis* 136:329-343, 1963.
39. Deikman AJ: Implications of experimental meditation. *J Nerv Ment Dis* 142:101-116, 1966.
40. Ornstein R: *The Psychology of Consciousness.* San Francisco, WH Freeman, 1972.
41. Cohen W: Spatial and textural characteristics of the Ganzfeld. *Am J Psychol* 70:403-410, 1957.
42. Cohen W, Cadwallader TC: Cessation of visual experience under prolonged uniform visual stimulation. *Am Psychol* 13:410, 1958.
43. Lehmann D, Beeler GW, Fender DH: EEG responses during the observation of stabilized and normal retinal images. *Electroencephalogr Clin Neurophysiol* 22:136-142, 1967.

Biofeedback and Meditation in 5 the Treatment of Psychiatric Illnesses

Bernard C. Glueck and Charles F. Stroebel

HOMO SAPIENS SURVIVES, and is able to perform the incredibly complex activities demanded by Western society in part because of elegantly sophisticated biofeedback mechanisms built into his anatomy and physiology. The ability to stand on two feet and to locomote requires kinesthetic and proprioceptive feedback signals from the muscles, joints, tendons, etc. that provide instantaneous information about the position of the limbs and the tension or relaxation of the musculature required to overcome gravitational pull. Another example, part of the standard neurologic examination, is the ability, with eyes closed, to bring the extended index finger around to touch the tip of the nose. A few moments consideration will indicate the tremendous complexity of the feedback signals involved in this apparently simple task.

Until recently psychologists taught that it was impossible to condition the autonomic nervous system, smooth muscles, and glands by other than classic Pavlovian techniques. This was in contrast to the very complex types of operant conditioning procedures employed in the animal laboratory which enabled investigators to teach a wide range of mammals intricate skeletal muscle performance tasks. In 1960, Kimmel and Hill[1] demonstrated the possibility of instrumental conditioning of the galvanic skin response (GSR). Since then, there have been reports of learned control of a wide range of autonomic nervous system responses, including the GSR,[2,3] heart rate,[4,5] blood pressure,[6] vasomotor responses,[7,8] salivation,[9] and the relaxation of striated muscle.[10]

From the Institute of Living, Hartford, Conn.

Bernard C. Glueck, M.D.: *Director of Research;* Charles F. Stroebel, M.D., Ph.D.: *Director, Psychophysiology Laboratory and Clinic, Institute of Living, Hartford, Conn.*

© *1975 by Grune & Stratton, Inc.*

Reprinted by permission from *Comprehensive Psychiatry*, 1975, Vol. 16, No. 4, 303-321.

The use of biofeedback techniques requires the application of relatively ordinary technical procedures for a revolutionary purpose: Allowing persons to monitor and alter their normally unconscious physiologic responses to the daily adaptational tasks, in order to help themselves achieve and maintain physical and emotional well-being. The use of these techniques has made it possible for individuals to learn to control physiologic functions that had previously been considered inaccessible to voluntary self-control. In fact, these functions have been found to be surprisingly responsive to self-alteration through biofeedback training. The premise of such training is that, if an organism is placed in a closed biofeedback loop and provided with information about one or more of its bodily processes, such as brain wave activity, it can actually learn to control the specific function or functions.

For example, EEG biofeedback is the feeding back of his own brain wave patterns to the subject, i.e., in alpha biofeedback, brain waves in the 8- to 13-Hz region. A common feedback mechanism employs a tone which increases in frequency when alpha waves are not being produced. Attempts to correlate specific EEG frequencies with a subjective state of mind have been somewhat conflicting. However, most subjects report positive kinds of feelings, such as relaxed, floating, peaceful, very pleasant, and free from anxiety as the main subjective awareness at the time that alpha frequencies are occurring. An occasional subject may report some feeling of discomfort from the detachment of dissociative feelings that arise at this time.[11-13]

EEG patterns during passive meditation states also generally show an increase in the densities of alpha rhythms, particularly in the occipital areas, with a tendency toward a slowing of the alpha frequency, a gradual sweeping forward toward the frontal areas of the dominant alpha frequencies, and an occasional appearance of trains of theta waves, especially in the frontal leads.[14]

What might be termed the relaxed alpha state, marked by a predominance of alpha density in the EEG, whether achieved through EEG biofeedback, passive meditation, autogenic training, or naturally as the hypnogogic or hypnopompic transitions between waking and sleeping, is clearly incompatible with the fight or flight emergency response to stress.[15] Because many psychiatric patients activate the emergency response system at inappropriate times and with inappropriate or misperceived stimuli, speculation has been widespread that training in self-recognition and voluntary control of the alpha state would be a useful adjunct in the treatment of emotional disorder. Would one alpha-state relaxation technique be preferable over others for patients with different psychiatric conditions?

In 1972 we began a study to answer this question, comparing autogenic training, alpha EEG biofeedback, and a passive meditation technique as treatment adjuncts with a variety of psychiatric conditions in an inpatient setting where average length of stay is 5.5 months.

After investigating a number of meditation techniques, we decided specifically to evaluate Transcendental Meditation (TM) as our passive meditation procedure for the following reasons: The technique is standardized, with a large cadre of trained instructors available in most locales (hence, replication of the instruction and basic technique should pose no problems); the technique is simple, requiring 4–6 hr of verbal instruction and practice and is entirely mental, not requiring physical exercise, special diets, or other ascetic demands; and published studies[16,17] had already documented physiologic changes consistent with the relaxation response. Very briefly, TM is a mantra-type passive-relaxation technique that was introduced to the Western world in its present form by Maharishi Mahesh Yogi. The technique is quite simple, consisting of sitting comfortably, with eyes closed, for 20 min twice a day, and thinking to oneself a Sanskrit sound, a mantra, that has been given to the meditator by a teacher of the technique.*

In the summer of 1971 we ran extensive psychophysiologic studies on a number of subjects who were TM meditators of from 6 months to 4 years experience. Several of these individuals had been through the more intensive training process involved in becoming teachers of TM. These were all individuals under the age of 30, and all were males. Without exception, they showed significant amounts of spontaneous alpha on the EEG, and showed considerable ability to control alpha density, being able to turn alpha on and off on request without the assistance of a biofeedback signal. In addition, two of the subjects who had been meditating longer periods of time showed frequent epochs of slower wave production in the theta range, with occasional delta density uncorrelated with eye movements. A number of the physiologic changes described by Wallace,[16,17] e.g., slowing of the heart rate, slowing of respiration, and an increase in the galvanic skin resistance (GSR), were replicated in our studies, with the most consistent finding being a universal increase in the GSR in all subjects (up to 30% increase over baseline), although we never saw the extreme changes described by Wallace in his original studies (up to 400%).

The subjective reports of these meditators were generally positive, the meditational state being described as a special kind of free-floating attentional state that is essentially nonverbal and nonconceptual in nature, a state of restful alertness. All of these skilled meditators reported a marked reduction in their levels of anxiety and tension subsequent to starting regular daily meditation.

As a result of these findings, we began a series of experiments designed to test the biofeedback hypothesis; namely, that if we could train volunteer subjects to produce increased alpha densities in their EEGs we would help them toward a less tense and anxious general level of adaptation. The subjects were all volunteers, mainly college students and other young adults. The ability of these subjects to produce spontaneous alpha, particularly from the occipital areas, simply by sitting relaxed and closing the eyes varied considerably. It seemed to be related to the amount of psychopathology present in an individual as described on a self-report, the Minnesota Multiphasic Personality Inventory (MMPI), and on evaluation by two psychiatrist-observers during the course of the study.

In general, the higher the level of psychopathology, the greater the difficulty experienced by the subject in producing spontaneous alpha rhythms during eyes-closed control sessions. This same general pattern followed through during the

---

*For a more detailed description see Robins and Fisher, *Tranquility without Pills*,[18] or Forem, *Transcendental Meditation: Maharishi Mahesh Yogi and the Science of Creative Intelligence*.[19]

biofeedback conditioning, with those subjects who produced the greatest amount of spontaneous alpha seeming to show a more rapid development of good control in turning alpha on or off on demand, frequently achieving maximum performance by the tenth training session. In contrast, three of the subjects who had the greatest amount of psychopathology experienced great difficulty in controlling their alpha frequencies and never really approached consistent performance over the entire 20 training trials.

The subjective reports of the alpha subjects during the alpha-on condition were generally feelings of well-being. However, a few of the subjects reported some discomfort, especially a feeling of lightheadedness or dizziness immediately after the sessions, which persisted for an hour or two.

A third approach to providing the increased general relaxation of the alpha state is the method originally described as autogenic training by Luthe[20] and more recently as formalized by Wolpe and Lazarus[21] as part of the general relaxation training used in their reciprocal-inhibition treatment. Similar claims of reductions in the general levels of anxiety and tension have been made for this approach, which consists in gradually attempting to relax the voluntary musculature in a progressive fashion, starting with the toes and feet and sweeping upward to involve the whole body.

In the summer of 1972 we designed a research project to test the relative efficacy of these three types of general relaxation techniques in psychiatric inpatients at the Institute of Living. Our reasons for utilizing three comparison groups were based upon the obvious impossibility of designing a blind study utilizing intervention techniques that demanded specific behavior activity obvious to everyone. A second important limitation was our inability to use the kind of strict controls of other treatment variables that would be preferred in a tight research design, since this would involve withholding other known effective treatment techniques in order to test the efficacy of these three unknown intervention modalities.

Patients were evaluated before beginning the study on the following psychophysiologic measures: EEG recordings from eight leads, the right and left frontal, parietal, temporal, and occipital areas;* respiration, as recorded by a nasal thermistor; eye movements from bilateral leads over the external canthus; EKG from right and left wrist leads; and silver–silver chloride electrodes for measurement of skin conductance between the middle finger and wrist of the subject's right hand.

Measures of the patient's behavioral state and level of psychopathology were obtained by a self-report, the Minnesota Multiphasic Personality Inventory (MMPI), standardized descriptors of behavior obtained by the research psychiatrist and research staff utilizing the Minnesota Hartford Personality Assay (MHPA), and the automated daily nursing notes in use at the Institute of Living,

---

*International electrode placements: Fp1, left frontal; Fp2, right frontal; T3, left mid-temporal; T4, right mid-temporal; O1, left occipital; O2, right occipital; P3, left parietal; P4, right parietal; A1, left ear (is used for ground). Reference electrodes are placed on the mastoid bone behind each ear, R1 and R2.

which give daily quantified measures of levels of acceptable behavior, anxiety, depression, antisocial behavior, disorganization, etc., as observed by nursing personnel on the patient's unit. These evaluations were repeated at intervals during the 16 weeks of the study.

In an attempt to equalize the amount of individual and group attention being given to the patients in the project, determined primarily by the amount of time spent by the TM instructors with the patients learning to meditate, we expected patients in all three groups to spend up to 20 min twice a day, which is the usual routine for the meditators, practicing their technique, and also to meet weekly as a group, since this was also part of the plan for the meditators.

Two groups of 6 patients each were started in the autogenic training to produce general relaxation. For the first 2–3 weeks the novelty of the activity held their attention. However, it was rapidly apparent that they were not experiencing much in the way of a positive kind of subjective experience from the relaxation attempts and began to find the relaxation exercises quite boring. As a result, by their fourth week in the project all of these patients had asked to stop, with some asking to switch to one of the other two experimental groups.

The patients assigned to the EEG alpha biofeedback training were able to learn some control of alpha density after 15 training sessions. They had considerable difficulty, however, in applying this training when they were not getting the biofeedback signals. This appeared to be related to an inadequate set of cues that would indicate to them when they were in the alpha state. For a number of patients in the alpha biofeedback group, the attempts to produce alpha resulted in an increase in tension and anxiety because of the uncertainty about the results and did little to promote the relaxation and tranquility that were the primary goals of the technique. We therefore terminated the alpha EEG biofeedback phase of the project after 26 patients had been through this type of biofeedback training.

Recently, other investigators, especially Green[22] at the Menninger Clinic, have reported that their subjects can learn effective control of alpha EEG and theta EEG densities if the biofeedback training is continued for a period of up to 4 months. Further investigation of this possibility certainly is necessary, but an argument against this would be the impracticality of this approach, which requires 1 hour a day of subject time 5 days a week for a period of 4 months, and which also ties up the rather expensive polygraph-computer equipment, for a relatively small number of patients, over this long period of time. In contrast to this, learning TM is a relatively simple matter that can be done quite easily and that requires no special equipment of any sort to learn.

The third experimental group consisted of patients who were taught to meditate using the TM technique. We decided to use a somewhat different procedure with our psychiatric patients from that followed in the usual course of instruction to the general public. Since, on occasion, individuals do experience considerable distress, both psychological and physical, during the early stages of meditation, usually stemming from a misunderstanding of the instructions or a misuse of the technique, we felt that our psychiatric patients might need a longer and more continuous follow-up period than is ordinarily given in order to learn to meditate properly. As a result we established a policy of daily checking of the meditation process by the teacher during the first 3 weeks, meeting once a week as a group, and individually on the other days. We believe that this precautionary measure has enabled us to avoid any serious psychological or physiologic upset in most of our patients that might have been a consequence of starting to meditate. One indication that this in fact has been the case is the relatively low attrition rate in the patients who learned to meditate. Of the 187 patients who were taught TM in the hospital, 33 patients (17%) stopped meditating regularly, that is, at least once a day, during the first weeks after learning the technique. However, 21 of these patients did meditate occasionally and were quite cooperative in continuing with the data collection for the research project. Only 12 patients (6%) both stopped meditating entirely and refused further data collection in the project.

The loss of the two comparison groups, the alpha EEG biofeedback group and the autogenic training group, created a problem in evaluating the results obtained by the patients who were practicing TM, for the reasons discussed above. In an effort to provide a comparison group, we have matched each patient in the experimental group with a "twin" in the general population of the hospital. This matching was done on the basis of sex, age within 3 years, and similarity of self-description on the MMPI, as indicated by a statistical analysis of the profile type. Some of the outcome data that follow are based on a comparison between these two groups and the full hospital population. In addition, for the experimental group, their previous behaviors in the hospital, as indicated by the nursing-notes factor scores and the medications utilized, provide a useful comparison of the patients' progress in the hospital before and after starting TM, permitting analysis by crossover design.

The results that follow must be considered tentative, since they involve less than one-half of the total number of patients who will eventually be studied in the project. In addition, full analysis of all of the data that have been collected is still in progress, especially much of the psychophysiologic data. We are also attempting to follow the patients for at least 1 year, and preferably 2 years, after they leave the hospital. This follow-up has just begun and will, of course, be one of the critical factors in determining the long-term effectiveness of TM intervention with these patients.

The first patients were started in the TM project in September of 1972. Through November 1, 1974, 116 patients were started in the study. Ninety-six patients have completed more than 8 weeks of data collection in the study, 83 have been discharged, 13 remain in hospital after completing the study, and 20 are currently active in the study. Seventy additional patients were taught TM, but since they were to be discharged from the hospital within a few weeks or did not complete 8 weeks of data collection, they have not been included in the various analyses of outcome, since even though they had begun to meditate, blind evaluation of any improvement or worsening in their condition could be attributed to variables other than TM.

Some indication of the acceptance of TM in the hospital might be gathered from the fact that, in addition to randomly selected patients, we have been running a waiting list for the project of from 17 to 25 patients; these patients have

	TM	Hospital
Recovered and much improved	0 / 38 E / 30	0 24.4 (153) / E / 32
Moderately improved	28 / 24	21.4 (134) / 25
Slightly improved and unimproved	6 / 18	29.9 (187) / 18

Fig. 1. Outcome measure: TM (patients in project more than 8 weeks) discharges versus hospital discharges, 1972–1973. x^2 = 19.69; $p < 0.001$; df = 2.

	TM (Observed)	Match (Expected)
Recovered and much improved	38	25
Moderately improved	28	32
Slightly improved and unimproved	6	15

Fig. 2. Outcome measure: TM (patients in project more than 8 weeks) versus matched comparison group condition on discharge; x^2 = 28.42; $p = 0.001$; df = 2.

either been referred by their treating psychiatrist or have heard about the TM study and have asked their therapist about starting in the project and have received his approval. The delay in starting these patients is due to the rather extensive work-up required in order to collect data for the study before the patient can start meditating.

One criterion of the effectiveness of any intervention, even though it is a rather crude global judgment, is the condition on discharge from the hospital. An evaluation of the condition on discharge was condensed into three levels; recovered and much improved, moderately improved, and slightly improved or unimproved. Fifty-four TM patients who had completed more than 8 weeks in the study before discharge have been matched with a comparison twin. They showed a greater level of improvement than the improvement rates for all hospital discharges in the 1972–73 year. The difference is significant at better than the 0.001 level (x^2 = 19.69 [2 df]) (Fig. 1). Similar differences in levels of improvement are seen when the TM patients are compared with the matched twin comparison group, the TM patients showing a higher level of recovery than their twins. This difference is significant at the 0.001 level (x^2 = 28.42 [2 df]) (Fig. 2). When the

	Group	Hospital
Recovered and much improved	0 / 25 E / 24	0 24.4 (153) / E / 25
Moderately improved	32 / 26	21.4 (134) / 27
Slightly improved and unimproved	15 / 22	29.9 (187) / 23

Fig. 3. Outcome measure: Matched comparison group versus hospital discharges, 1972–1973; x^2 = 6.97; $p = 0.05$; df = 2.

twin comparison group members are evaluated against the total hospital discharges, they show a slightly better rate of recovery than the total hospital group. The difference here is significant at the 0.05 level (χ^2 = 6.97 [2 df]) (Fig. 3).

Additional data showing differences in the experimental and comparison groups of patients will be published in subsequent papers. Among these are total amounts of psychotropic and sedative drugs used by the patients in the two groups during the course of their hospital stay and levels of pathology, utilizing the MMPI, and calculating a pathology score for each profile using multiple regression weights. Since the comparison group was not a control group, we do not have any psychophysiologic evaluations on this group of patients. However, certain characteristics of the changes observed in the experimental group are worthy of description at this time.

The most consistent finding across all of the psychophysiologic variables was an increase in skin resistance (GSR) that was seen in all of the TM patients at every session where this was monitored. The consistency of this finding was quite surprising, since one would expect some variability, even in the same patient, with evaluations on a number of occasions in the course of 12–16 weeks.

A second finding is a rather consistent change in the EEG record as analyzed by a power-spectrum analysis. The increased amounts of alpha-wave production found in our TM subjects, and found in other laboratories studying trained yogis and Zen masters, have been described above. While there was considerable variability among our patients in their ability to produce alpha EEG during the control session, most began to show significant increases in the density and duration of alpha wave production as they began to meditate. While this would appear to be an important finding, correlated perhaps with the subjects' reports of increased feelings of tranquility and inner calm, we have been more impressed by the appearance of rather unique patterns of alpha wave production that appear to involve the entire dominant hemisphere within a few minutes of starting to meditate, and that spread quite rapidly to the opposite hemisphere. This same phenomenon has been described by Banquet,[14] who studied experienced meditators, mainly teachers of the TM technique, while working at the Stanley Cobb Laboratories for Psychiatric Research, Massachusetts General Hospital. We have been very intrigued by this finding and are currently in the process of evaluating all of the records on our meditating patients to see how consistently, and at what point in time, these episodes of synchronous alpha-wave patterns occur.

One of the critical questions raised by our inability to control other treatment interventions in our research design is the issue of whether the improvement seen in the meditating patients, at least as judged by their condition on discharge, is related to the TM intervention or to some other combination of factors. The differences seen in level of recovery between the TM group and their comparison "twins," who, on self-description at least, have essentially the same kind and amount of pathology, and who had fairly similar treatment patterns in the hospital, would tend to argue toward the importance of TM in explaining the difference in levels of improvement.

Crossover analysis of longitudinal measures of level of pathology for each

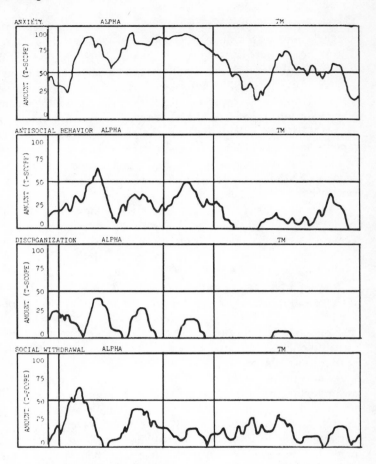

Fig. 4. Daily nursing-note T scores for patient receiving both alpha biofeedback training and Transcendental Meditation

patient, as judged by factor scores obtained from automated nursing notes, as well as by the patients' self-evaluation (MMPI), tend to support this conclusion. Figures 4 and 5 show the changes on some of the nursing-notes factors after the start of TM in 2 patients selected at random. An example of the type of self-evaluation change is shown in Fig. 6, where a succession of self-evaluations, utilizing the MMPI, indicates that this patient reported a fairly consistent drop in the level of symptoms while involved in the TM study.

We have been attempting to follow our discharged patients at fairly frequent intervals in an effort to gage the longer term effects of the meditation experience following discharge from the hospital. Our initial inquiries have been concerned primarily with the extent to which these patients continue to meditate after leaving the hospital environment, which was very supportive in encouraging them to continue regular meditation. By June 1, 1974, 110 first-contact letters were sent to patients who had been discharged from the hospital prior to March 1, 1974. We had received replies from 77 patients through July 15, 1974, a rather high response rate compared to other follow-up studies, both in this hospital and in other institutions. Thirty-two patients reported that they were meditating

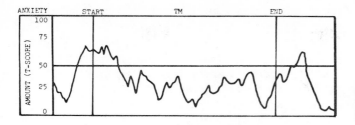

Fig. 5. Daily nursing-note anxiety rating on Transcendental Meditation patient.

regularly, that is, at least once daily, while another 20 patients reported that they were meditating less often than once daily but with plans to continue with the meditation. Twenty-five patients, or 32% of the group, reported that they had stopped meditating. One potentially very important difference in the behavior of the regular meditators compared to those who had stopped meditation was the use of the local TM centers in their home communities by the regular meditators, whereas only three of the nonmeditators had been in contact with the local center. This appears to be a significant finding, since the narrative comments on

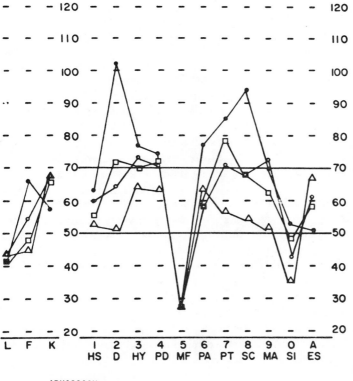

Fig. 6. Self-description on the MMPI by patient shown in Fig. 5.

the questionnaires indicate that a sizable number of patients had stopped meditating because they were confused about the correct practice of the meditation technique, or were having upsetting experiences, or felt they could not find the time. This is not a unique finding with meditation; it applies to every treatment modality. Psychiatric patients are notorious for their inability to continue to follow a prescribed treatment plan after leaving the hospital. We are attempting to improve on our instructions at the time of discharge and believe that we may be able to help more of our discharged patients to continue using the meditation technique by more precise instructions about referral to the TM centers in their local communities.

On the positive side, many of the patients who were continuing to meditate regularly seemed to feel that TM had been a valuable addition to their pattern of living, frequently far beyond their initial expectations, and they have expressed their gratitude for being allowed to participate in the research project.

The problem of fitting the twice-daily meditation period into their usual routine is not unique to psychiatric patients, since, while there are no accurate figures that can be cited, there are a number of reports of a comparably high dropout rate among TM meditators in the general population. This has been commented on rather extensively by Dr. Otis,[23] who speculates about some of the reasons why this may happen. We have also seen the same sort of phenomenon in patients who have learned specific biofeedback techniques, such as hand warming for control of their migraine headaches. In the face of their complete relief, in some instances, from the excruciating pain and disability of their migraine headaches, some of these patients have stopped doing the daily 20 min of hand warming that had relieved them of their symptoms and are very surprised and unhappy when their migraine attacks return.

A similar pattern is also seen in many psychiatric patients who leave the hospital on a psychotropic medication regimen that has relieved their overt symptoms. Despite this relief, they stop taking their medication, which often results in relapse, with recurrence of symptoms and frequently rehospitalization, in anywhere from 3 weeks to 3 months after they have stopped the medication.

It may well be, as Dr. Otis[23] suggests, that many individuals simply cannot tolerate the relative freedom from discomfort that these various techniques provide. Formulations about the masochistic personality,[24] or the pain-dependent individual,[25] would tend to document the fact that, for a number of individuals, a life free from some sort of discomfort is quite impossible, unless, of course, their basic personality characteristics can be modified and new patterns of adaptation developed, usually through long-term psychotherapeutic intervention.

When we turn to an evaluation of the phenomena observed during the process of TM meditation, there are a number of striking findings that seem to be unique to this particular technique. The changes in the EEG patterns appear more consistently, with greater rapidity, and to a greater degree in TM meditators than in individuals using other types of meditation and in nonmeditating resting subjects. Some of the other psychophysiologic changes, such as the GSR, tend to follow a similar pattern. However, the most impressive findings appear to be in the EEG. Experienced TM meditators, i.e., 6 months or more of meditation experience, characteristically show a high density of alpha brain-wave production. As they begin to meditate, that is, start thinking the mantra, the alpha density rapidly increases and appears to sweep forward to involve the entire dominant cerebral hemisphere. Within a relatively short period of time, frequently no more than 1 or 2 min, the opposite hemisphere also shows the predominant alpha rhythm. This phenomenon has been described by a number of laboratories, and, at this point, would appear to be a characteristic of passive, TM-type meditation. In addition, as the meditation continues, trains of theta-wave (4–7-Hz) activity appear, and there may be a fairly rhythmic appearance of highly synchronous alpha (8–13-Hz) activity intermixed with theta and alternating with periods of very low voltage, high-frequency activity in the beta range (20–35-Hz). At the same time, the GSR tends to increase as the skin of the fingers becomes less moist, heart rate drops a few beats, respiration drops, and changes occur in the O_2, CO_2, and lactic acid concentrations of the blood that have been interpreted as indicating a rapid reduction in metabolic rate.[16,17,26]

In addition to the relative constancy of these findings, we have been very impressed by the rapidity with which these changes appear after the individual starts meditating. Even in the inexperienced psychiatric patient we have observed many of these changes occurring to some degree with the very first meditation, frequently within the first 4 or 5 min.

In two recent articles Benson[27,28] has described a modification of the TM technique that he has been using with hypertensive patients. Instead of learning the meditation procedure from a TM teacher, Benson has his patients sit quietly in a chair, eyes closed, and gets them to try progressively to relax the various muscle groups and then to breathe slowly and rhythmically and think to themselves a word or phrase of their own choosing. In other words, he is using essentially the same technique, with the exception that the mantra is chosen by the individual, rather than chosen for him (presumably on the basis of a number of rules) by the TM teacher. Benson insists that he gets the same kind of "general relaxation response," as he has designated the syndrome seen, as with individuals who were doing TM-type meditation. However, he did not measure the EEG in his patients.

We have looked at a number of individuals who were doing their own variants of meditation, usually a mantra-type meditation, and we do indeed find that they have many changes similar to those seen with the TM meditator. However, these tend to be less consistent and, in terms of the EEG, appear to involve primarily the posterior cortical areas, rarely involving the frontal areas and rarely involving the opposite hemisphere. Also, the density of the alpha waves produced is considerably less than that of those seen with TM-type meditation. The differences between these various techniques need to be studied further, since all of them have been used from time to time to achieve the same general goal, namely a state of nirvana, samahdi, or satori, depending upon the particular religious and/or philosophic context in which the meditation technique is usually employed. To date, as observed in our laboratory, the TM-type meditation would seem to produce a maximum effect more rapidly than any of the other techniques.

Maharishi and his followers insist that the mantra is the critical factor in the technique, and we tend to agree with this. Unfortunately, they are inclined to make a rather considerable mystery about the process of choosing the correct mantra for a given individual. This has been a source of a good deal of frustration for most investigators, who feel that they are dealing with a completely unknown quantity in terms of the choice of mantra.

Since we agree that the mantra seems to be the key factor in achieving the kinds of psychophysiologic changes observed, we have formulated the concept that the mantra represents a rather powerful input stimulus to the central nervous system, most likely the limbic circuitry. We have been informed that analysis of the resonance frequencies of a number of mantras gives a value of 6-7-Hz, which is in the high-theta EEG range and also approximates the optimal processing of the basic language unit, the phoneme, by the auditory system.[29] Our current speculation goes as follows: Since the mantra is a series of sounds, the formation of the thought mantra, e.g., Oom, which is a common, well-known mantra, probably takes place, according to most neurophysiologists, in the ideational speech area in the temporal lobe. Penfield[30] has mapped three areas involved in the ideational elaboration of speech—a large area in the posterior temporal lobe, an area in the posterior-inferior parietal region, and a small area in the posterior part of the third frontal convolution anterior to the motor-voice control area. Penfield claims that the second two areas both can be destroyed and speech will return, so that the posterior temporal speech area is the fundamental locus for the formation of words. Penfield states that the ideational mechanism of speech is organized for function in one hemisphere only, usually the dominant hemisphere. Therefore, if we are thinking a mantra, we are introducing a rather significant stimulus in the temporal lobe and probably directly into the series of cell clusters and fibre tracts that have come to be known as the limbic system. Since limbic-system activity is fairly well accepted today as the origin of much emotionally based behavior, and since an increasing excitation in the limbic system through a series of feedback stimulatory mechanisms has been postulated to explain disturbed behavior, we are theorizing that introducing a driving mechanism with a dominant frequency of 6-7-Hz may act, with considerable rapidity, to dampen the limbic-system activity and produce a relative quiescence in this critical subcortical area.

Since there are extensive connections running from the thalamic structures to the cortex, quieting the limbic-system activity might allow for the inhibition of cortical activation, with the disappearance of the usual range of frequencies and amplitudes ordinarily seen coming from the cortex, and with the imposition of the basic resting or idling rhythms as shown by the appearance of very dense, high-amplitude, alpha-wave production.

Similarly, since the autonomic nervous system is controlled to a considerable extent by stimuli arising in the midbrain, the rapid changes observed in the peripheral autonomic nervous system, such as the GSR changes and the change in respiratory rate, heart rate, etc., could be explained by the quieting of the limbic system activity.

Presumably, in sleep, limbic-system activity diminishes, mediated perhaps by the reticular activating system. One of the theories about the appearance of dreams, especially about the ideational content in dreams, has to do with an increasing access to the nondominant hemisphere, where presumably repressed memories are stored. The weakening of the repression barrier that occurs in sleep and in other altered states of consciousness, such as free association during the process of psychoanalytic therapy, *may* be produced in a relatively simple fashion during TM meditation. This would offer an explanation of a phenomenon that has been reported by a number of investigators, and which we have seen repeatedly in our patients. During meditation, thoughts and ideas may appear that are ordinarily repressed, such as intense hostile-aggressive drives, murderous impulses, and, occasionally, libidinal ideation. An impressive aspect of this phenomenon is that, during the meditation, the intense emotional affect that would ordinarily accompany this ideation, e.g., when obtained by free association, seems to be markedly reduced or almost absent.

Our speculation is that, during meditation, the limbic-system activities are diminished sufficiently to permit the regulatory mechanisms for transmission of signals between the hemispheres, via the commissures and corpus callosum, to respond to this more muted, tranquil state of the limbic system by opening up the pathways. This allows a freer interchange of information between the hemispheres that ordinarily does not occur during the fully alert waking state when attention is directed at sensory input. In our experience, and that of other therapists, this seems to allow significant repressed material to come into conscious awareness relatively rapidly and comfortably, material that might otherwise not be available, or might take long periods of intensive psychotherapy to reach. The apparent splitting of ideation and affect that the meditational state produces, we feel, may be primarily responsible for this. This phenomenon has been used to advantage by a number of our therapists to assist the psychotherapeutic process. In our experience this has permitted a much more rapid recovery of significant repressed material than might otherwise have been the case. This has also been reported in detail by Carrington and Ephron,[31] who have been using TM as a specific adjunct to the treatment of their psychotherapeutic and psychoanalytic patients.

While the above comments indicate a potentially very useful role for TM in assisting in the psychotherapeutic process, there are two possible negative consequences of the phenomenon described above. It is our speculation that a major reason for individuals stopping TM meditation may be the appearance of these rather primitive, very distressing thoughts and ideas. For the average individual who starts to meditate and suddenly begins to experience very intense hostile-aggressive impulses or intense sexual ideation that he finds quite frightening, a natural reaction would be to seriously question whether the meditation was causing some disorganization of the personality, or, more colloquially, "driving me crazy." Since most of the TM instructors are rather youthful and there is no consistent follow-up procedure (although increasingly this is being urged), individuals experiencing these kinds of phenomena may find it very difficult to understand them and to utilize them constructively without explanation and support. We feel that the natural consequence, more often than not, is for the individual to conclude that TM not only is not helping but is actually harmful and to stop meditating.

A second consequence may be an extension of the above, that is, the precipitation of an overt psychotic episode. This has occurred in a relatively few instances of which we are aware, usually in individuals with a previous history of psychiatric disorder who have not followed the rules about frequency and duration of meditation. In general they have medi*ated more than twice a day, and for longer periods than the usual 20 min.

An interesting contrast with the meditation results can be highlighted by returning to results with alpha EEG biofeedback training with psychiatric inpatients. Each patient received 20 1-hr sessions of alpha biofeedback with gradual weaning from the instrumentation beginning with the 15th hr. Most patients were able to learn discriminative control of alpha density by the end of training and reported very positive feelings of general relaxation while immersed in the demand characteristics of the laboratory environment.[32] However, follow-up evaluation 4 weeks after training indicated poor persistence of this relaxation effect, even though patients had been encouraged to practice each day on their own. Schizophrenic patients ($N = 6$) were able to learn discriminative control of alpha density, but tended to react to the alpha-on state with a "So what?" attitude. Four patients diagnosed with obsessive-compulsive neurosis had great difficulty in acquiring discriminative control, but did report some benefit from the feeling of "passively letting go" when they eventually became infuriated with the task and suddenly experienced an increase in feedback when they "just simply gave up." Significant clinical improvement from this experience only occurred in 1 of the 4 patients. In general this did not prove to be an effective means for improving these patients' ability to relax, nor did it have a significant impact on their anxiety symptoms.

In contrast to the disappointment with the alpha EEG biofeedback technique, we have found quite the opposite to be the case when "specific-type" biofeedback techniques were used with patients experiencing psychosomatic symptoms. These specific-type techniques include a variety of procedures used to regulate, or lower, the activation of a target-organ system that presents clinically as a psychosomatic symptom. As in the general type of biofeedback, voluntary control in the specific biofeedback situation also involves a kind of passive volition but permits a much greater degree of mental activity and attention to external cues. Hence these procedures can more easily be incorporated into a behavioral therapy desensitization framework. The types of biofeedback and the syndromes for which they are utilized are listed in Table 1. Our research and clinical activities have been directed toward the relief of migraine headache, tension headache, muscular back pain, insomnia, Raynaud's disease, and the irritable colon syndrome.

Results in our initial studies on patients with migraine (vascular) headache, where a thermal biofeedback technique that enhances peripheral vasodilation and central vasoconstriction was used, proved sufficiently successful in relieving the headache symptoms in 70%–80% of our patients that we now have established a new outpatient clinical service for the treatment of these conditions. In the

Table 1. Types of Biofeedback

General	Specific
(Objective: Relaxation and lowering of tension)	(Objective: To regulate or lower the activation of a target organ system)

EEG alpha
EEG theta
Frontalis EMG
	Thermal— Migraine headache
	          Raynaud's disease
	          Hypertension
	Neck EMG—Tension headache
	Back EMG—Muscular back pain
	pH— Gastric ulcer
	Pressure— Irritable colon
	          Blood pressure
	          Ulcerative colitis
	EKG— Cardiac dysrhythmias

thermal biofeedback training, thermistors are placed on the patient's forehead and the middle finger of the right hand (Fig. 7).[33,34] The patient is told to try to warm his hand and cool his forehead. Any changes in temperature between these two areas are indicated on a dial marked in degrees or can also be indicated by means of a tone. As in the alpha EEG biofeedback, the instrument is usually set

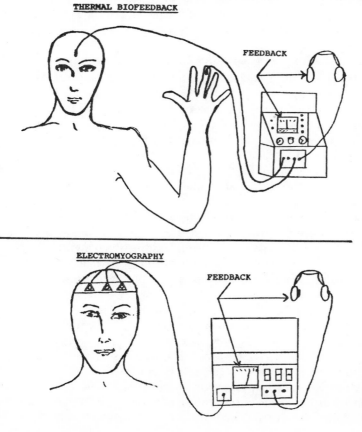

THERMAL BIOFEEDBACK

FEEDBACK

ELECTROMYOGRAPHY

FEEDBACK

Fig. 7. Schematic representation of thermal and EMG feedback.

so that as the hand is warmed the tone becomes lower in pitch and volume. Autogenic instructions are suggested to the patient to help him achieve the temperature changes, such as: "Try to think of your hand as being hot, heavy, and filling with blood," or "Think of your forehead being cooled by a cool breeze." The majority of our patients find some means for shifting the temperature differential in the appropriate direction by the end of the first training session. Our pattern has been two 1-hr training sessions a week for six to eight sessions. For most of the patients, by the fourth or fifth session good control of the temperature differential is achieved, with differences between the finger and forehead running quite commonly at 10° F and, in some patients, as high as 20° F. The patients are encouraged to try to practice the hand warming once a day for 20 min or so on their own and are also given instructions regarding possible dietary factors that may trigger a migraine attack.

Patients with muscular-contraction (tension) headache[10] are given a different type of biofeedback training. Electrodes are placed on the frontalis muscle with the firing of the muscle spindles as the feedback signal. This again can be displayed on a dial or, more commonly, converted to an audible sound (Fig. 7). The patient is asked to relax the muscles of the forehead and scalp and recognizes when this is happening by a drop in the volume and frequency of the sounds made by the muscle firing. A similar type of feedback from the neck musculature can also be used if the primary focus of the tension appears to be in the neck and posterior scalp muscles.

We have developed a number of tapes that carry various suggestions about the biofeedback techniques and also suggestions about increasing the general relaxation response that some of the patients find quite helpful. It appears that, after 3–4 months of practicing the specific biofeedback technique, either the hand warming or the muscle relaxation, or both (in mixed vascular-muscular headache patients), there tends to be a generalized spreading of the relaxation produced in the musculature in the head to the entire body, so that a generalized feeling of warmth and relaxed comfort may be achieved. Similarly, the relaxation of the scalp and neck muscles seems to spread so that the striated muscle throughout the body becomes more relaxed.

We concur with Miller that "Biofeedback should be well worth trying on any symptom, functional or organic, that is under neural control, that can be continuously monitored by modern instrumentation, and for which a given direction of change is clearly indicated medically ... for example, cardiac arrhythmias, spastic colitis, and asthma, and those cases of high blood pressure that are not essential compensation for kidney damage."[35]

Miller's stature as a leading psychobiologist gave credibility to biofeedback and its medical potential. The mass media, and not a few scientists, began to serve biofeedback up as the new magic-bullet cure for all ills. Dozens of firms began to capitalize on this publicity by producing inexpensive over-the-counter feedback boxes. However, unpredictably, reports began emanating from Miller's laboratory that the exciting early work with operant autonomic control under curare could not be replicated. Whereas the earlier studies actually demonstrated faster acquisition of control under the curare state (explanation: muscle movement apparently interfered with visceral learning) and transfer of control to the noncurare state, studies since 1970 have demonstrated very little acquired control of variables such as heart rate under the curare condition. A number of explanations for the replication failure have been advanced, e.g., the usual pharmaceutical supplier of curare changed sources in 1969. It is conceivable that the curare agent available since then is less pure with some antihomeostatic effect that alters learning.

Despite the replication failure under curare, evidence for the active principle of biofeedback (i.e., acquiring voluntary control of autonomic and neural responses) remains convincing in animal studies without curare and is affirmative, although not conclusive, in human studies.[10,36,37] Biofeedback, specifically directed, may be the treatment of choice for many psychosomatic symptoms, since it emphasizes the responsibility of the patient himself in regulating the inappropriate activation of the target organ in question when confronted by stress. Symptom reduction tends to reinforce and encourage regular practice of the biofeedback technique, an inducement that does not occur in use of biofeedback for general relaxation; this rationale may explain the poor persistence of alpha training in our experiments.

In conclusion, we have described four different attempts at solving the problem posed for many individuals in our "hyper" Western culture, namely, too much emergency response too much of the time, frequently on minimal stimulation. If this can be characterized as the general stress syndrome, described so well by Hans Selye,[15] then it may very well be appropriate to try to describe the conditions we are attempting to produce in our patients as the "general relaxation response," a term suggested by Benson.[27,28] We are convinced that there are a number of potential avenues that can be used to achieve this goal. The problem for the clinician is the proper choice of the most appropriate technique for the particular patient and the problems that he presents.

In our experience, the most appropriate technique to use with psychiatric patients, in an attempt to produce an increase in the generalized relaxation response, appears to be a mantra-type passive meditation, Transcendental Meditation. This technique was learned readily by our psychiatric patients. It appeared to hold their interest over a considerable period of time, in contrast to autogenic training and alpha EEG biofeedback training. It also appears to add a significant positive therapeutic dimension to the overall hospital treatment program.

In sharp contrast to the difficulties experienced by our patients in utilizing alpha EEG biofeedback for generalized relaxation, we have described the successful application of specific biofeedback conditioning utilizing thermal and muscle-tension feedback signals for the treatment of patients with vascular headaches, muscle contraction headaches, and Raynaud's disease. The emphasis on the patient's ability for self-regulation of the somatic symptoms and the prompt symptom reduction appears to reinforce and encourage regular practice of the specific biofeedback techniques, an inducement that apparently does not occur in the use of biofeedback general relaxation. This appears to be a critical difference in the two types of biofeedback training and adds additional emphasis to our conclusion that the various types of biofeedback and general relaxation techniques must be carefully tailored to the needs of the individual patient. None of these techniques is universally effective, and all require careful diagnostic appraisal of the patient's condition and a decision by clinicians skilled in the application of these techniques about the specific modality or modalities to be used.

REFERENCES

1. Kimmel E, Hill R: Operant conditioning of the GSR. Psychol Rep 7:555-562, 1960

2. Shapiro D, Crider A, Tursky B: Differentiation of an autonomic response through operant reinforcement. Psychosom Med 1:147-148, 1964.

3. Fowler R, Kimmel H: Operant conditioning of GSR. J Exp Psychol 63:536-567, 1962

4. Engel B, Chism R: Operant conditioning of heart rate speeding. Psychophysiology 3:418 426, 1967

5. Engel B, Hansen S: Operant conditioning of heart rate slowing. Psychophysiology 3:563 567, 1966

6. DiCara L, Miller N: Instrumental learning of systolic blood pressure responses by curarized rats: Dissociation of cardiac and vascular changes. Psychosom Med 30:489 494, 1968c

7. DiCara L, Miller N: Instrumental learning of peripheral vasomotor responses by curarized rat. Commun Behav Biol 1(A):209-212, 1968a

8. DiCara L, Miller N: Instrumental learning of vasomotor responses by rats: Learning to respond differentially in two ears. Science 159:1485 1486, 1968b

9. Delse C, Feather R: The effect of augmented sensory feedback on control of salivation. Psychophysiology 5:15-21, 1968

10. Budzynski T, Stoyva J, Adler C: Feedback induced muscle relaxation: Application to tension headache. J. Behav Exp Psychiatry 1:205, 1970

11. Brown B: Recognition of aspects of consciousness through association with EEG alpha activity represented by a light signal. Psychophysiology 6:442, 1970

12. Lynch JJ, Paskewitz DA: On the mechanisms of the feedback control of human brain wave activity, in Biofeedback and Self Control. Chicago, Aldine, 1971

13. Stroebel CF, Glueck BC: Biofeedback treatment in medicine and psychiatry: An ultimate placebo? Semin Psychiatr 5:379 393, 1973

14. Banquet JP: Spectral analysis of the EEG in meditation. Electroencephalogr Clin Neurophysiol 35:143 151, 1973

15. Selye H: The Physiology and Pathology of Exposure to Stress. Montreal, Acta, 1950

16. Wallace RK: Physiological Effects of Transcendental Meditation: A Proposed Fourth State of Consciousness. PhD thesis, Physiology Department, University of California, Los Angeles, 1970 (available from MIU Press)

17. Wallace RK: Physiological effects of transcendental meditation. Science 167:1751 1754, 1970

18. Robins J, Fisher D: Tranquility without Pills. New York, Peter H. Widen, 1972

19. Forem J: Transcendental Meditation: Maharishi Mahesh Yogi and The Science of Creative Intelligence, New York, EP Dutton, 1973

20. Luthe WL, Schultz J: Autogenic Therapy, II Medical Applications. New York, Grune & Stratton, 1969

21. Wolpe J: Psychotherapy by Reciprocal Inhibition. Stanford, Stanford University Press, 1958

22. Green EE: personal communication, 1974

23. Otis L: If well integrated but anxious, try TM. Psychology Today 7:45 46, 1974

24. Freud S: Psycho-analytic notes on an autobiographical account of a case of paranoia (Dementia Paranoides), in Strachey J (tr): Standard Edition of the Complete Psychological Works of Sigmund Freud. London, Hogarth, 1958

25. Rado S: Adaptational Psychodynamics; Motivation and Control. New York, Science House, 1969

26. Wallace RK, Benson H, Wilson AF: A wakeful hypometabolic physiologic state. Am J Physiol 221:795 799, 1971

27. Beary JF, Benson H: A simple psychophysiologic technique which elicits the hypometabolic change in the relaxation response. Psychosom Med 36:115 120, 1974

28. Benson H, Beary JF, Carol MP: The relaxation response. Psychiatry 37:37 46, 1974

29. Lenneberg EH: Biological Foundation of Language. New York, John Wiley & Sons, 1967

30. Penfield W, Roberts L: Speech and Brain

Mechanisms. Princeton, Princeton University Press, 1959

31. Carrington P, Ephron HS: Meditation as an adjunct to psychotherapy, in Arieti S, Chrzanowski G (eds): The World Biennial of Psychotherapy and Psychiatry. New York, John Wiley & Sons (in press)

32. Orne MT: On the social psychology of the psychological experiment: With particular reference to demand characteristics and their implications. Am Psychol 17:776, 1962

33. Sargent J, Green E, Walters E: Preliminary report on the use of autogenic feedback training in the treatment of migraine and tension headaches. Psychosom Med 35:129 135, 1973

34. Sargent J, Walters E, Green E: Psychosomatic self-regulation of migraine headaches. Semin Psychiatry 5:415 428, 1973

35. Miller NE: Learning of visceral and glandular responses. Science 163:434, 1969

36. Green EE, Green AM, Walters ED: Voluntary control of inner states: Psychological and physiological. J Transper Psychol 2:1, 1970

37. Shapiro D, Schwartz GE: Biofeedback and visceral learning clinical applications. Semin Psychiatry 4:171 184, 1972

Sleep During Transcendental Meditation

6

Robert R. Pagano, Richard M. Rose, Robert M. Stivers, and Stephen Warrenburg

Abstract. *Five experienced practitioners of transcendental meditation spent appreciable parts of meditation sessions in sleep stages 2, 3, and 4. Time spent in each sleep stage varied both between sessions for a given subject and between subjects. In addition, we compare electroencephalogram records made during meditation with those made during naps taken at the same time of day. The range of states observed during meditation does not support the view that meditation produces a single, unique state of consciousness.*

In 1970, Wallace reported several physiological changes observed during transcendental meditation (TM) (*1*). His results were replicated and extended by Wallace, Benson, and Wilson (*2*) and they were subsequently made available to a wider audience (*3*). They found, in meditating subjects, reduced oxygen consumption, increased skin resistance, increased alpha activity in the electroencephalogram (EEG), decreased heart rate, and decreased blood lactate. Although many of these changes take place in ordinary relaxed wakefulness and in sleep, Wallace and his co-workers postulated that, during most of the meditation period, experienced practitioners of TM enter a single, unique state of consciousness, a "wakeful hypometabolic state," that differs from ordinary relaxed or sleep states.

The Stanford Research Institute estimates that, from a few hundred in 1965, the number of practitioners of TM has increased to more than 240,000 as of June 1973. Estimates from the TM organization indicate that this number now exceeds 900,000 (*4*). The findings of Wallace and his co-workers are often cited to prospective meditators and may have played an important role in producing this increase.

We have found that meditators spend considerable time in sleep stages 2, 3, and 4 during meditation; their subjective reports of sleep confirm our analysis of the EEG records. Further, our data suggest that the meditation period is not spent in a single, unique, wakeful, hypometabolic state.

The five subjects we observed had at least 2.5 years of experience with TM, and four of them were teachers of the technique. All were male Caucasians between the ages of 20 and 30, accustomed to meditating for 40-minute periods twice each day, and not in the habit of napping. Subjects reported, on the average, 7.8 hours of sleep per night.

Psychophysiological measures were made on each subject during ten sessions, each of which lasted 40 minutes. During five of these sessions, the subjects were asked to meditate in their accustomed sitting position, and in the other five sessions, they were asked to nap lying down on a bed. The first nap and the first meditation were scheduled on the first observation day. The data collected on this day are not included for analysis here because initial unfamiliarity with the laboratory situation produces atypical sleeping patterns (5). On eight subsequent days, subjects were asked either to meditate or to nap. These sessions were all conducted in the afternoon within 2 hours of the same time each day. The order in which the two types of sessions were scheduled followed an irregular pattern, and subjects were not told whether they would be asked to meditate or to nap on a particular day until they arrived in the laboratory. If a subject reported that his previous night's sleep was more than 30 minutes shorter than normal, he did not take part on that day. Subjects were asked not to consume food, coffee, or tea for at least 2 hours before each session.

At the beginning of each session, electrodes were applied so that occipital, central, and frontal EEG responses, eye movements, submental (below the chin) muscle potentials, and skin resistance level could be measured (6). The subject then moved to the room where he was to meditate or nap. A 45-db white noise partially masked any disturbance from the adjoining apparatus room (7). The room in which the subject sat during meditation was dimly illuminated, but the room was dark when the subject lay down to nap. Once the recording was proceeding smoothly, the subject was asked to relax for 5 minutes with his eyes closed, and then a signal was given to begin meditation or napping. After 40 minutes, an identical signal required the subject to stop meditating or napping and to relax with his eyes closed for an additional 5 minutes before leaving the recording room. At the end of the session, the subject filled out a questionnaire on his subjective impressions of what had transpired and stated whether he had slept or become drowsy during the meditation or nap.

Table 1. Percentage of time spent in stages 2, 3, or 4 during each session.

Subject	Meditation session				Nap session			
	1	2	3	4	1	2	3	4
1	51	90	59	78	37	41	59	62
2	0	0	0	26	78	92	79	58
3	49	0	0	78	86	31	83	89
4	0	90	59	74	18	38	95	88
5	37	0	86	31	95	95	93	78

Table 2. Percentage of time spent in each stage, averaged over sessions.*

Subject	Meditation				Nap			
	W	1	2	3, 4	W	1	2	3, 4
1	19	12	42	27	32	17	40	10
2	44	46	6	0	7	14	62	14
3	53	15	16	15	15	12	31	41
4	37	6	28	27	31	8	51	9
5	43	17	23	15	1	7	54	36

*These percentages do not sum to 100 because some epochs were scored as movement time.

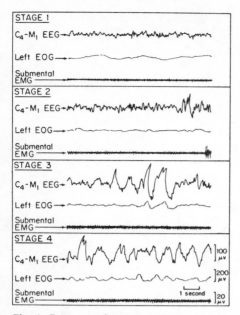

Fig. 1. Representative records from subject 5 during a meditation session. The time scale and channel gain are shown on the stage 4 record.

The most striking feature of our data is that meditators spent appreciable amounts of time in EEG sleep stages 2, 3, and 4 while they were meditating (Fig. 1). Averaged over meditation sessions, we found that 39 percent of the time was spent in wakefulness (stage W), 19 percent in stage 1, 23 percent in stage 2, and 17 percent in stages 3 or 4. More than a quarter of the meditation time was spent in stages 2, 3, or 4 in 13 out of the 20 meditation sessions (Table 1). It is customary to identify stages 2, 3, and 4 as sleep and stage 1 as drowsiness (8); according to these conventional designations, our subjects were asleep during, on the average, 40 percent of their meditation time.

Meditation might produce a dissociation between the EEG and consciousness that would permit a subject to be awake even though his EEG record indicated sleep (9). However, this does not appear to have occurred in our study, because our subjects reported having slept in 12 of the 13 medi-

tation sessions in which patterns of stages 2, 3, or 4 appeared. In addition, they reported feeling drowsy in 18 of the 19 sessions during which they spent more than 30 seconds in stage 1. The consistency of the reports with the EEG rcords indicates that the conventional EEG criteria defining sleep and drowsiness were applicable.

No rapid eye movement (REM) sleep was observed during either the meditations or the naps. This is probably because we conducted all sessions during the afternoon and limited each session to a length of 40 minutes; REM sleep does not normally occur during the first 40 minutes of an afternoon nap (10).

Although meditation in a laboratory might lead to a state different from that outside the laboratory, our subjects' ratings of their meditations indicated that in 7 of the 13 sessions in which stage 2 was observed, the subject rated his meditation as typical rather than atypical. Further, on a 7-point scale from 7 (very deep) to 1 (very light), the modal depth of meditation was 5, and there was no significant correlation between reported depth of meditation and the amount of time asleep. Thus, in several meditations described as typical and relatively deep, considerable amounts of sleep occurred. This corroborates reports that we have received from these and other meditators that they occasionally fall asleep while meditating in their normal settings.

If TM produces the wakeful state described by Wallace (1), one would expect to find less sleep during meditation than during a nap period. An analysis of variance of time spent in sleep stages 2, 3, or 4 revealed no significant differences between meditation and nap sessions ($F = 3.2$, $P > .1$). Because we obtained repeated measures over sessions for each subject, we also carried out individual t-tests on each subject's data. Only in subject 2 was there a significant difference ($t = 7.3$, $P < .01$) indicating fewer EEG sleep patterns during meditations than during naps. Because of the high variability in the states observed, we caution against the conclusion that meditation and napping produce identical distributions of EEG stages.

One of the striking features of our data was the variability in the time spent in the various EEG stages both for a single subject (from meditation to meditation) and between subjects (Tables 1 and 2). For example, subject 2 slept in only one of his four meditations, whereas subject 1 slept more than half the time in each of his four meditations. Subjects 3, 4, and 5 each had at least one meditation in which they did not sleep at all and another in which they slept for more than three-fourths of the session. What emerges from these EEG findings is that meditation is an activity that gives rise to quite different states both from day to day and from meditator to meditator.

Our data differ from the EEG responses reported by Wallace (1). Only 4 of his 15 subjects occasionally evidenced drowsiness, and he states, "The EEG pattern during meditation clearly distinguishes this state from the sleeping state. There are no slow (delta) waves or sleep spindles, but alpha-wave activity predominates." Several factors may account for the differences between Wallace's data and ours. He reported on records from just one session per subject, presumably the first experience for the subject in the laboratory. In addition, many of his subjects meditated while breathing through a mouthpiece or with arterial cannulae or rectal thermometers in place (1, 2). Both of these factors would probably tend to activate the EEG more

than would be expected in a normal meditation session outside the laboratory.

Wallace's subjects meditated for 20 to 30 minutes, whereas our sessions lasted 40 minutes; it could be argued that sleep was more likely to occur in our longer sessions. But when we examined the data from the first 20 minutes of each of our subject's meditations, the discrepancies remained: In the first 20 minutes, an average of 42.5 percent of the time was spent in sleep stages 2, 3, and 4.

In three other studies EEG responses were recorded during transcendental meditation: Younger et al. report that advanced meditators spent 41 percent of their meditations in sleep stages 1 and 2 (11); Wada and Hamm also found sleep stages 1 and 2 in the EEG records of both experienced and inexperienced meditators (12); Banquet recorded EEG responses during meditation but did not present an analysis by sleep stage (13). He did, however, mention the presence of "short bursts of large amplitude delta waves identical to those of sleep stage 4."

The results of Younger et al., of Wada and Hamm, and of this experiment raise the question of whether the beneficial effects reported for meditation (14) are due to the sleep that occurs during meditation or to some other feature of that process.

Robert R. Pagano, Richard M. Rose
Robert M. Stivers
Stephen Warrenburg

Department of Psychology, University of Washington, Seattle 98195

References and Notes

1. R. K. Wallace, Science 167, 1751 (1970).
2. _____, H. Benson, A. F. Wilson, Am. J. Physiol. 221, 795 (1971).
3. R. K. Wallace and H. Benson, Sci. Am. 226 (No. 2), 84 (1972).
4. D. P. Kanellakos and J. S. Lukas, The Psychobiology of Transcendental Meditation: A Literature Review (Stanford Research Institute, Menlo Park, 1973), p. iii; Fundamentals of Progress: Scientific Research on Transcendental Meditation (Maharishi International Univ. Press, New York, 1975).
5. See, for example, H. W. Agnew, Jr., W. B. Webb, R. L. Williams, Psychophysiology 2, 263 (1966).
6. Electrodes for the EEG were placed according to the international 10-20 system, and recordings were taken between each of leads O_2, C_4, and F, and a reference electrode on the opposite mastoid. A Beckman Dynograph (type RM) was used to record the data, and the records were scored according to the criteria of Rechtschaffen and Kales [A. Rechtschaffen and A. Kales, Eds., A Manual of Standardized Terminology, Techniques, and Scoring System for Sleep Stages of Human Sub-

jects (Public Health Service Publ. No. 204, Government Printing Office, Washington, D.C., 1968), pp. 8–15]. The scorers had no knowledge of the condition under which a record was made; the agreement between the two scorers averaged 93 percent.

7. In order to make additional comparisons between meditation and naps beyond those that we report here, a 45-db, 600-hertz tone of 0.5-second duration was presented on an irregular schedule averaging one presentation per minute. This tone was found to evoke EEG responses without disturbing the course of meditation, as judged by pilot subjects. In this report we present only the sleep stage and sleep report data. The galvanic skin responses and the responses to the tone have not yet been analyzed.

8. F. Snyder and J. Scott, in *Handbook of Psychophysiology*, N. S. Greenfield and R. A. Sternback, Eds. (Holt, Rinehart & Winston, New York, 1972), p. 645.

9. E. Green, in *Biofeedback and Self-Control 1972*, D. Shapiro *et al.*, Eds. (Aldine, Chicago, 1973), p. 164; A. Jus and K. Jus, in *Proceedings of the Third International Congress of Psychiatry*, B. Stoukis, Ed. (Montreal, 1961), pp. 473–482.

10. L. Maron, A. Rechtschaffen, E. A. Wolpert, *Arch. Gen. Psychiatry* **11**, 503 (1964); S. A. Lewis, *Br. J. Psychiatry* **115**, 107 (1969); I. Karacan, W. W. Finley, R. L. Williams, C. J. Hursch, *Biol. Psychiatry* **2**, 261 (1970).

11. J. Younger, W. Adriance, R. Berger, *Percept. Mot. Skills* **40**, 953 (1975).

12. J. A. Wada and A. E. Hamm, paper presented at the 27th annual meeting, American EEG Society, Boston, Mass., 15 and 16 June 1973.

13. J. P. Banquet, *Electroencephalogr. Clin. Neurophysiol.* **35**, 143 (1973).

14. See, for example, H. Benson and R. K. Wallace [in *Drug Abuse: Proceedings of the International Conference*, C. J. D. Zarafonetis, Ed. (Lea & Febiger, Philadelphia, 1972), p. 369]; S. Nidlich, W. Seeman, T. Dreskin [*J. Couns. Psychol.* **20**, 565 (1973)]; and J. Robbins and D. Fisher [*Tranquility Without Pills* (Wyden, New York, 1972)].

15. We thank A. Lubin, G. Chatrian, D. Barash, and A. Marlatt for constructive comments. We thank the Student International Meditation Society Seattle Center for their cooperation in helping us locate subjects.

17 June 1975; revised 12 November 1975.

Transcendental Meditation 7
and Asthma

Archie F. Wilson, Ronald Honsberger, John T. Chiu, and Harold S. Novey

Abstract. A 6-month study with crossover at 3 months was designed to evaluate the possible beneficial effects of transcendental meditation upon bronchial asthma. 21 patients kept daily diaries of symptoms and medications and answered questionnaires at the end of the study and 6 months later. Other measurements included physician evaluation, pulmonary function testing, and galvanic skin resistance. The results indicated that transcendental meditation is a useful adjunct in treating asthma.

Key Words
Transcendental meditation
Asthma
Galvanic skin resistance
Questionnaire
Airway resistance
Symptoms

Introduction

Bronchial asthma is a multifactorial disease in which environmental, infectious, allergic and psychologic elements are of varying etiologic importance [1]. The potential significance of psychological factors has been suggested by personality and emotional questionnaires [2], psychiatric interviews [3], and hypnotic induction and relief of bronchospasm [4]. However, specific psychological intervention in treating of asthma has been infrequent [5].

During investigation of the physiology of transcendental meditation (TM), health questionnaires answered by some practitioners of this easily learned and simple technique indicated apparent beneficial effects of TM

Reprinted by permission from *Respiration*, Vol. 32, 74-80, (Karger, Basel, 1975)

upon asthma [6]. Therefore, to evaluate the therapeutic potential of TM, we undertook an investigation of the prospective effects of TM upon a group of patients with bronchial asthma but with neither obvious psychological problems nor previous experience with TM.

Method

The study encompassed 6 months – October 17, 1971, to April 9, 1972. Following two 2-hour introductory sessions, the patients were divided by random lot into two groups. Group A was taught the practice of TM and meditated for 20–30 min twice daily during the initial 3 months. Group B was given the book, *Science of Being and Art of Living* by MAHARISHI MAHESH YOGI [7] to read for the same period of time; this book does not describe the practice of TM. After 3 months the groups exchanged functions, i.e. group A was requested to cease meditating and begin reading, while group B was instructed in the practice of TM and began meditating.

Patients with stable asthma under the care of a practicing allergist for at least 1 year and receiving essentially the same medication for 3 months were selected for study. Further criteria for selection included demonstration of reversible airways obstruction and lack of complicating cardiac, pulmonary, or psychiatric disease. No age limits were placed, and the ages ranged from 14 to 57. Of the 26 patients who were female and 11 male. Because of the ethnic make-up of the suburban private were female and 11 male. Because of the ethnic makeup of the suburban private practices of the participating allergists, all subjects were Caucasian. The allergists were not told into which group their patients had been placed until after final evaluation was completed.

Measurements were of several types: questionnaires, daily diaries, physician evaluation, pulmonary function testing, and galvanic skin resistance (GSR). The patients kept a daily diary which was collected weekly. They scored their symptoms on a 0–5 severity scale and recorded duration of symptoms. From this data a duration-severity symptom score was developed [8]. Medication was also recorded daily [8]. At 6 months (immediately following conclusion of the study) and 12 months (6 months after conclusion of study) a questionnaire was sent to the patients requesting evaluation of TM usefulness. Similarly, immediately following the conclusion of the study, the attending physicians were asked to compare the clinical condition of their patients between the two periods of the study. Pulmonary function testing was done at '0' (immediately prior to study), 3 months (time of crossover), and 6 months (immediately after study). At '0' spirometry, peak flow rate, body plethysmography, and single-breath carbon monoxide diffusing capacity were measured. At 3 and 6 months, only spirometry and body plethysmography measurements were performed. GSR was measured once in each subject (while they were practicing TM to ascertain whether they were probably meditating); a characteristic increase of skin resistance had been noted earlier [9]. Statistical significance was determined from Student's t test utilizing paired data.

Results

Four of the 25 patients who entered the initial phase of this study, either withdrew or did not faithfully record their daily symptom scores. Therefore, 21 patients finished the study, of whom 10 were in group A (5 male, 5 female) while 11 were in group B (4 male, 7 female).

The plan of the study was to have two parallel groups with crossover at the midpoint and differing only in the experimental parameter of TM. Unfortunately, it was extremely difficult to insure that patients who meditated initially (group A) ceased the practice of TM during the last 3 months of the study. Five of the 10 patients in this group spontaneously admitted to continuing meditation at least occasionally; the others were not questioned. Therefore, the second period of group A was a somewhat inadequate control.

The normalized symptom duration-severity index results are shown in figure 1. Normalization was accomplished by dividing the weekly sum of the individual duration-severity scores by that of the first week and multiplying by 100. It may be seen that group A (who meditated first) had a marked worsening of symptoms at the third week and then progressively improved until crossover between the 12th and 13th weeks. During the 'nonmeditation' second period the symptoms of group A continued at a low level (as noted above, at least 50% of these subjects continued to meditate at least sporadically). Group B symptom scores ranged around the initial values at the outset but declined somewhat during the final weeks of the initial period except for a peak at the tenth week. Subsequently, during the second or meditation period, symptom scores continued to decline so that at the 24th week the two groups had almost identical symptom indices; as was previously noted with group A, a brief worsening of symptoms occurred at the third week after beginning TM. Medication scores did not change significantly or noticeably between groups or between periods.

Pulmonary function results are indicated in table I. As compared to initial values recorded prior to the onset of either meditation or reading, significant improvement of forced expiratory volume in 1 sec (FEV_1), peak expiratory flow rate (PEFR), and airway resistance (R_{AW}) was noted in group A (TM first) immediately following the TM period. Subsequently, following the 3-month reading period, values returned toward control levels. In group B (read first), no significant changes occurred during the initial reading period, though some improvement was noted.

Table I. Changes in pulmonary function during study

	FEV$_1$, l	PEFR, l/min	R$_{AW}$, cm H$_2$O/l/sec
Group A			
control	2.09 ± 0.20	377 ± 28	5.63 ± 1.40
TM	2.33 ± 0.19[1]	423 ± 20[1]	2.90 ± 0.57[1]
read	2.10 ± 0.25	399 ± 31	4.44 ± 0.90
Group B			
control	1.90 ± 0.23	321 ± 30	4.51 ± 0.72
read	2.14 ± 0.26	349 ± 37	3.75 ± 0.55
TM	2.04 ± 0.24	316 ± 37	2.67 ± 0.45[1]

Values are mean ±SEM.
[1] Significant change (p < 0.05).

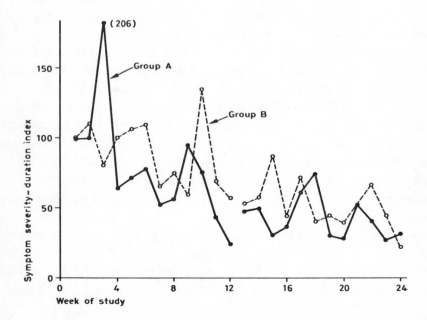

Fig. 1. Symptom severity-duration index throughout the course of the study. Group A meditated during weeks 1–12, and group B meditated from start of week 13 to end of week 24.

Table II. Questionnaire answers

	Yes		No	
	6 months[1]	12 months[2]	6 months[1]	12 months[2]
Patients				
TM beneficial for asthma?	11	10	7	7
TM useful?	15	14	3	3
Meditating still?	15	14	3	3
Physicians[3]				
Less asthma during TM period as compared to the reading period?	12	–	5	–

[1] 6 months (conclusion of study).
[2] 12 months (6 months after conclusion of study).
[3] Four subjects evaluated by physicians as unchanged.

Following TM, however, significant improvement of R_{AW} only occurred; a reduction of R_{AW} was noted in 94% of subjects of both groups following the TM period when compared to control. FEV_1 and PEFR did not change significantly in group B. Single breath diffusing capacity for carbon monoxide, which was measured only prior to the study, was normal or elevated in all patients; this is characteristic of asthma patients and excludes the presence of significant emphysema.

GSR demonstrated a characteristic increase during TM with a marked fall immediately thereafter in 15 of the 19 subjects in whom it was measured. It is of interest that 2 of the 4 subjects who did not show the characteristic GSR response had discontinued the practice and the other 2 were irregular in utilizing TM 6 months after the study (table II).

Two questionnaires were submitted to the subjects and one to their physicians (table II). At 6 months (conclusion of study) 11 of the 18 responders thought that TM had helped their asthma; 15 subjects thought that TM was useful in other ways and continued to mediate. At 12 months (6 months after conclusion of the study) the results were similar for the 17 responders. The physician evaluation was similar to that of their patients.

Discussion

It would appear that TM is a useful adjunct in treating asthma based upon the following observations: reduction in symptom severity-duration index (fig. 1); improvement of pulmonary function abnormalities, particularly R$_{AW}$ (table I); subject and physician evaluation (table II). The fact that the total medication used by the patients did not change between groups or periods emphasizes the supportive rather than curative role of TM in the therapy of asthma. On the other hand, 3 of the 5 patients who were taking prednisone at the beginning of the study had stopped by the end of the study. Patients apparently enjoyed the practice of TM, even in instances where they (and their physicians) were not impressed with beneficial effects on TM upon asthma (table II).

Transcendental meditation is an easily learned technique which produces immediate and pronounced changes in cardiopulmonary and metabolic parameters including reduction of oxygen consumption, carbon dioxide elimination, respiratory rate, minute ventilation, arterial pH, blood lactate and heart rate; GSR uniformly increases, and arterial blood pressure does not change acutely [9]. Another interesting change is increase in the relative intensity of α-wave activity, which might relate to the reported feeling of well-being [9]. Recently, evidence has been accumulated that TM may produce a long-term reduction in blood pressure [10].

The exact mechanism(s) underlying the beneficial effects of TM upon asthma are speculative. They might include (1) reduction of psychological stress [5], (2) reduction of bronchomotor tone via reflex or chemical factors [11], (3) reduction in minute ventilation, i.e. decreased need for oxygen delivery and carbon dioxide elimination. Our data do not allow choice between these or other possibilities. Similarly, the worsening of symptoms at the third week following the beginning of the practice of TM (fig. 1) is speculative as to whether it is psychological or physiological in origin.

It would seem that, before therapeutic recommendations can be made, these studies should be extended further with a larger number of patients who preferably have had previous psychological evaluation and are investigated over a longer period of time. It would seem likely that individual patients may experience dramatic lessening of symptoms, as was true of several of our patients. Clearly, crossover from meditation to a control period is unlikely to be successful, and other means of ensuring adequate control, such as a parallel group, should be considered.

References

1 HOWELL, J. B. L.: Asthma: A clinical view; in PORTER and BIRCH Identification of Asthma, pp. 151–160 (Churchill Livingstone, Edinburgh 1971).

2 AITKEN, R. C. B.; ZEALLEY, A. K., and ROSENTHAL, S. V.: Psychological and physiological measures of emotion in chronic asthmatic subjects. J. psychosom. Res. *13:* 289–297 (1969).

3 KELLY, E. and ZELLER, A.: Asthma and the psychiatrist. J. psychosom. Res. *13:* 377–395 (1969).

4 SMITH, M. M.; COLEBATCH, H. J. H., and CLARKE, P. S.: Increase and decrease in pulmonary resistance with hypnotic suggestion in asthma. Amer. Rev. resp. Dis. *102:* 236–242 (1970).

5 MOORE, N.: Behaviour therapy in bronchial asthma. A controlled study. J. psychosom. Res. *9:* 257–268 (1965).

6 WALLACE, R. K.: thesis, University of California, Los Angeles (1970).

7 YOGI, M. M.: The science of being and art of living, pp. 50–59 (International SRM Publ., London 1966).

8 CHEN, J. L.; MOORE, N.; NORMAN, P. S., and VEN METRE, T. E., jr.: Disodium cromoglycate, a new compound for the prevention of exacerbation of asthma. J. Allergy *43:* 89–100 (1969).

9 WALLACE, R. K.; BENSON, H., and WILSON, A. F.: A wakeful hypometabolic physiologic state. Amer. J. Physiol. *221:* 795–800 (1971).

10 BENSON, H. and WALLACE, R. K.: Decreased blood pressure in hypertensive subjects who practiced meditation. Circulation *46:* 130 (1972).

11 COREY, P.: Personal commun.

Request reprints from: ARCHIE F. WILSON, MD, Ph.D, Department of Medicine, University of California, *Irvine, CA 92664* (USA)

Twelve-Month Follow-Up of 8
Yoga and Biofeedback in the
Management of Hypertension

Chandra Patel

Summary Twenty hypertensive patients treated by psychophysical relaxation exercises were followed up monthly for 12 months. Age and sex matched hypertensive controls were similarly followed up for 9 months. Statistically significant reductions in blood-pressure (B.P.) and antihypertensive drug requirements were satisfactorily maintained in the treatment group. Mere repetition of B.P. measurements and increased medical attention did not in themselves reduce B.P. significantly in control patients.

Introduction

AFTER a preliminary investigation had established that psychophysical relaxation exercise based on yogic principles and reinforced by bio-feedback instruments could produce a statistically significant reduction in high blood-pressure (B.P.),[1] a further trial was set up with age and sex matched controls, so that the effect of increased medical attention and repeated B.P. measurements could be eliminated. I report a 12-month follow-up in the treatment and control groups.

Reprinted by permission from *Lancet*, 1975, i, 62.

TABLE I—TRIAL PATIENTS AND CONTROLS

	Trial	Controls
Total	20	20
Males	9	9
Females	11	11
Average age (yr.)	57·35	57·2
Average duration of hypertension (yr.)	6·8	7·05
No. on antihypertensive drugs ..	19	18
Original systolic B.P. before drug treatment (mm. Hg [mean±S.D.])	201·5± 24·2	197±31·8
Original diastolic B.P. before drug treatment (mm. Hg [mean±S.D.])	121·8± 12·4	115±17·8

Patients

Twenty hypertensive patients treated by the new therapy were compared with twenty age and sex matched hypertensive controls from the same general practice. To eliminate any bias in selection, patients of the same age and sex whose names began with the same or nearest alphabetical letter were chosen as controls. If a patient of the same age was not found then a patient born in the following or preceding year was sought. Details of the patients and controls are given in table I.

Methods

Patients were asked if they would cooperate in research on high blood-pressure which would involve coming to the surgery over a period of 3 months three times a week for half an hour of relaxation training. Appointments were given to suit individual circumstances, but once an appointment time was fixed it was kept for all the sessions. History taking, investigations, number of attendances, time spent at each session, and procedure for B.P. measurements were kept the same in the controls as in the treatment group, but instead of being trained in relaxation the control patients were asked to rest on the couch.

The treatment patients were followed up monthly for 12 months. The control group patients were followed up similarly for 9 months after the initial 3 months of control study. Their B.P. was taken while standing, sitting, and supine on arrival only. No more training sessions were given during the follow-up period, although patients in the treatment group were encouraged to continue practice in relaxation and meditation. Drug dosage was only adjusted to keep the B.P. within a satisfactory range.

Results

The results in the control patients were analysed and those of the treatment patients were reanalysed by a statistician. To eliminate any unconscious bias in the previous analysis [1] the mean of eighteen B.P. measurements taken during the first 3 sessions of the relaxation training was taken as a " pretrial " baseline B.P. and an average of twenty-four measurements taken during the last 4 sessions as the " end of trial " B.P. Similar criteria were applied in the analysis of data from the control group (table II).

In the treatment group the average systolic pressure at the end of the training period was reduced by $20\cdot4\pm11\cdot4$ mm. Hg (mean difference $\pm$ S.D.), while the diastolic pressure was reduced by $14\cdot2\pm7\cdot5$ mm. Hg ($P<0\cdot001$). The total drug requirement in twelve patients fell by an average of $41\cdot9\%$ (range 33–100%).[1] In the control group systolic B.P. was reduced by $0\cdot5\pm14\cdot5$ and diastolic B.P. by $2\cdot1\pm6\cdot2$ mm. Hg. Their drug requirement remained unchanged.

During follow-up B.P.s were taken " on arrival " only. The patients did not have their half-hour of relaxation or rest as described above (table III). When

TABLE II—ALTERATION IN B.P. OVER THE 3 MONTHS OF RELAXATION TRAINING

—	Treatment group	Control group
" Pretrial " B.P.*:		
Mean systolic±s.d.	$159\cdot1\pm15\cdot9$	$163\cdot1\pm20\cdot9$
Mean diastolic±s.d.	$100\cdot1\pm12\cdot8$	$99\cdot1\pm12\cdot8$
" End of trial " B.P.†:		
Mean systolic ±s.d.	$138\cdot7\pm16\cdot0$	$162\cdot6\pm24\cdot4$
Mean diastolic±s.d.	$85\cdot9\pm8\cdot7$	$97\cdot0\pm12\cdot0$
Difference:		
Systolic±s.d.	$20\cdot4\pm11\cdot4$	$0\cdot5\pm14\cdot5$
Diastolic±s.d.	$14\cdot2\pm7\cdot5$	$2\cdot1\pm6\cdot2$
Paired t *test:*		
Systolic	$7\cdot75$	$0\cdot15$
Diastolic	$8\cdot50$	$1\cdot52$
P	$<0\cdot001$	$>0\cdot1$

* Mean of 18 B.P. measurements taken during the first 3 sessions of relaxation training.

† Mean of 24 B.P. measurements taken during the last 4 sessions of relaxation training.

TABLE III—FOLLOW-UP RESULTS

—	Treatment group	Control group
End of trial arrival B.P.:		
Systolic±s.d.	144·6±11·0	167·7±9·73
Diastolic±s.d.	86·0±5·74	97·1±6·54
3-mo. follow-up:		
Systolic±s.d.	143·9±13·38	167·6±8·08
Diastolic±s.d.	84·0±3·84	97·4±7·73
6-mo. follow-up:		
Systolic±s.d.	146·7±10·72	164·1±15·0
Diastolic±s.d.	88·3±6·84	97·3±8·02
12* and 9† mo. follow-up:		
Systolic±s.d.	144·4±9·83	163·6±9·42
Diastolic±s.d.	86·7±3·33	98·1±7·83
P	>0·01	>0·1

* Treatment group.   † Control group.

these follow-up B.P.s are compared with average " end of trial " pressures found on arrival at the surgery, the maintenance of the reduction in B.P. is very satisfactory.

In the first 3 months the drugs in one patient in the treatment group were further reduced (clonidine was reduced to 0·3 mg. in patient 10), making the total drug reduction 42·9%. In the second 3 months, however, another patient's drug requirement increased, making the total drug reduction 40·2% (methyldopa was increased to 250 mg. daily in patient 11). In the control group the drug requirement increased by 5·5% in the first 3 months of the follow-up period.

Discussion

The results in control patients show that merely repeating B.P. measurements and increasing medical attention does not reduce blood-pressure in long-established cases of hypertension, although there is often some ·initial reduction in blood-pressure in new cases of hypertension because of emotional desensitisation—i.e., patients get used to the physician and the procedure.

Although the programme worked out during follow-up was quite effective in reducing B.P., some patients found it difficult to discipline themselves to 20 minutes of regular relaxation and meditation twice or even once a day during the follow-up period. Since relief in terms of symptoms is almost non-existent in hypertensive patients, the motivation to continue this time-consuming discipline is often not strong enough. Methods had to be found to incorporate relaxation and meditation in their daily activities—e.g., red traffic lights and ringing telephones and door bells served as signals to quickly check for tension and relaxation. This has been found to be an effective substitute for regular practice.

Placebos can reduce high B.P.[2-6] In a double-blind study of patients whose initial B.P.s were more than 200/120 mm. Hg, both guanethidine (average dose 60 mg. per day) and oral placebo produced comparable and statistically significant reductions in B.P. over a 12-week period.[7] The average decreases in the placebo group were 25 and 12 mm. Hg for the systolic and diastolic B.P.s, respectively. These results show that people can reduce their B.P. without the help of active drugs, and the higher the initial B.P. the bigger the drop.[7] The term placebo often implies that the beneficial effect is only transient and that it is possibly due to a favourable doctor/patient relationship. However, in my study, the beneficial effect in the treatment group has lasted for as long as one year and is still continuing. The doctor/patient relationship was exactly the same for both the groups and hence the mechanism of the therapeutic effect must be different.

If the patient can follow a suitable programme of relaxation, it is not only possible to reduce the resting B.P. and anti-hypertensive-drug requirement but also the magnitude and duration of the rises in B.P. associated with everyday emotional stresses.[8]

Evidence in laboratory animals suggests that reduction in proprioception lowers the sympathetic responsiveness of the hypothalamus and vice versa.[9-12] The rise in B.P. is a part of the sympathetic response. B.P. was reduced in hypertensive patients by profound relaxation of muscles with considerable reduction in electromyographic activity.[13,14] Meditation was associated with reduced oxygen consumption, carbon-dioxide elimination, respiratory-rate, and minute ventilation, without any change in the respiratory quotient.[15,16] Cardiac output and heart-rate were also reduced and B.P. remained low throughout in normotensive people, whereas B.P. gradually decreased in hypertensive people.[17] There was a four-fold increase in the electrical resistance of the skin,[15] while alpha and theta waves predominated in the electroencephalogram (E.E.G.).[18] It has been suggested [19] that E.E.G. pattern of meditators demonstrates not only increased parasympathetic predominance but also concomitant relatively weak sympathetic discharge which prevents the E.E.G. pattern of alpha dominance from passing into a state of sleep. Wallace and Benson [15] described this as a " wakeful hypometabolic state ". This relaxation response [20,21] seems to be the reverse of the " fight or flight " response, and regular elicitation of this relaxation response [20,21] may not only reduce the high blood-pressure but may also maintain the reduction. Brod [22] demonstrated that the hæmo-dynamic pattern in patients with essential hypertension under resting conditions is similar to that found in normotensive people in response to emotional stress.

It is postulated that reduction in B.P. is brought about by a lower sympathetic tone, which is maintained by altered habitual interaction with the environment.

I thank Dr Khosla for statistical help, Professor Pilkington for helpful suggestions in preparing this paper, and my partners and staff for their cooperation during this study.

This work was supported by a grant from the South-West Thames Regional Health Authority.

REFERENCES

1. Patel, C. H. *Lancet,* 1973, ii, 1053.
2. Pickering, T. *ibid.* p. 1440.
3. Miller, N. E. *in* Biofeedback and Self-control (edited by N. E. Miller, T. X. Barber, L. V. Dicara, J. Kamiya, D. Shapiro, and J. Stoyva); p. 11. Chicago, 1973.
4. Althausen, T. L., Kerr, W. J., Burnett, T. C. *Am. J. med. Sci.* 1929, **177,** 398.
5. Althausen, T. L., Kerr, W. J. *ibid.* p. 470.
6. Ayman, D. *J. Am. med. Ass.* 1930, **95,** 246.
7. Grenfell, R. F., Brigg, A. H., Holland, W. C. *Sth. med. J. Nashville,* 1963, **56,** 1410.
8. Patel, C. H. *Clin. Sci. molec. Med.* (in the press).

9. Gellhorn, E. *Psychol. Rev.* 1964, **71**, 457.
10. Bernhaut, M., Gellhorn, E., Rasmussen, A. T. *J. Neurophysiol.* 1953, **16**, 21.
11. Gellhorn, E. *Electroenceph. clin. Neurophysiol.* 1958, **10**, 697.
12. Hodes, R. *ibid.* 1962, **14**, 220.
13. Jacobson, E. Progressive Relaxation. Chicago, 1938.
14. Love, W. A., Jr., Montgomery, D. D., Moeller, T. A. Proceedings of the Biofeedback Research Society Meeting, p. 34. Colorado Springs, 1974.
15. Wallace, R. K., Benson, H. *Scient. Am.* 1972, **226**, 84.
16. Allison, J. *Lancet*, 1970, i, 833.
17. Benson, H., Rosner, B. A., Marzetta, B., Klemchuk, H. M. *ibid.* 1974, i, 289.
18. Banquet, J. P. *Electroenceph. clin. Neurophysiol.* 1973, **35**, 143.
19. Gellhorn, E., Kiely, W. F. *J. nerv. ment. Dis.* 1972, **154**, 399.
20. Wolpe, J. Psychotherapy by Reciprocal Inhibition. Stanford, 1958.
21. Breary, J. F., Benson, H., Klemchuk, H. P. *Psychosom. Med.* 1974, **36**, 115.
22. Brod, J. *Lancet*, 1960, ii, 773.

III

HYPNOSIS, SUGGESTION, AND AUTOGENIC TRAINING

Responding to "Hypnotic" Suggestions: An Introspective Report

9

T. X. Barber

The author first presents an introspective report which describes some of his attitudes, motivations, and expectancies and ongoing thought processes while he is responding to 'hypnotic' suggestions. The introspective report indicates that (a) suggested effects are experienced when a person thinks with and imaginatively focuses on those things that are suggested and (b) a person imaginatively focuses on the suggestions when he sees the test situation as useful and worthwhile and when he wants to and expects to experience those things that are suggested. It is then argued that the responsive subject in a hypnotic situation differs in every important respect from the sleepwalker and closely resembles the person who is involved in reading an interesting novel or in observing an interesting motion picture. Finally, the author outlines a course, now being developed, that aims to teach individuals how to respond to suggestions.

Behavioral scientists try to maintain an objective stance with regard to their areas of inquiry. In attempting to remain objective, they rarely serve as experimental subjects and, in those rare cases in which they take the role of a subject, they usually do not write about their personal experiences. Specifically, in the area of hypnotism, investigators report how their subjects respond to 'hypnotic' suggestions but they rarely·if ever report how they themselves

respond. Although objective data are necessary, I, nevertheless, believe that the different viewpoints toward hypnotism could be better understood if the researchers in this area would describe their own experiences.

With the above considerations in mind, I shall present an introspective report describing and interpreting my personal experiences while I am responding to suggestions. This personal report may help to illustrate some of the major aspects of the theory that I and my co-workers have presented elsewhere (Barber, 1972; Barber & DeMoor, 1972; Barber & Ham, 1974; Barber, Spanos, & Chaves, 1974) and may also show how the theory is harmonious with my own experiences. Of course, this personal report, in the same way as any in-

[1] Work on this paper was supported by a research grant (MH 21294) from the National Institute of Mental Health. Copyright © 1975 by Michael H. Siegel and H. Philip Zeigler. From the forthcoming book entitled *Psychology from the Inside Out* edited by Michael H. Siegel and H. Philip Zeigler soon to be published by Harper & Row, Publishers, Inc.

trospective report, fails to convey the full flavor of the experiences. Furthermore, this rather matter-of-fact report from a 'sophisticated' or knowledgeable subject lacks the emotional involvement and elaborate descriptions that are proffered by some responsive subjects. However, since it includes more introspections than are usually provided by subjects concerning underlying attitudinal, motivational, and expectancy factors and ongoing cognitive processes, it should be helpful in illustrating my viewpoint toward 'hypnosis' which emphasizes the importance of these kinds of factors and processes.[2]

AN INTROSPECTIVE REPORT

An experimenter[3] enters my office and asks me if I am willing to participate as a pilot subject in an experiment involving responses to suggestions. I agree to participate.[4]

Hand Rigidity

The experimenter begins by asking me to clasp my hands together tightly with fingers interlaced. He then states, "Your hands are hard, solid, rigid. They are very rigid and solid. They are two pieces of steel that are welded together. They are rigid, solid, stuck together." He continues with these kinds of suggestions for about 30 seconds and finally states, "Try to take your hands apart. Notice that the harder you try, the more difficult it becomes. Try to take them apart; you can't."

---

[2] I do not know of any other present-day investigator in this area who has presented his own personal report. Our understanding of hypnotism might be enhanced if other investigators, especially those who adhere to the traditional 'hypnotic trance' viewpoint, would present their own introspective reports describing, to the best of their ability, their underlying attitudes, motivations, and expectancies and their ongoing thought processes while they are responding to 'hypnotic' suggestions.

[3] Dr. R. F. Q. Johnson.

[4] This is not the first time I have taken the role of a subject in an experiment involving suggestions (or 'hypnosis'). I have presented one of my earlier introspective reports elsewhere (Barber, 1972).

If the experimenter had given these suggestions to me five or six years ago, I would have felt that it was somehow 'improper' for me to respond to the suggestions (negative 'attitude'), I would have wanted to be 'non-suggestible' (negative 'motivation'), and I would have believed that it was impossible for my hands to become 'stuck together' (negative 'expectancy'). Consequently, I would not have squeezed my hands together tightly, I would not have focused on the rigidity in my hands and on the idea that they were stuck together, and I would have taken them apart without difficulty.

During the past five or six years, while conducting many studies in this area, I have slowly changed my own attitudes, motivations, and expectancies toward responding to suggestions. At the present time, I see this type of test situation as a valuable and useful experience (positive 'attitude'), I want to experience those things that are suggested (positive 'motivation'), and I believe or expect that I, and also other investigators, can experience the suggested effects (positive 'expectancy') if we temporarily put aside critical or analytical thoughts such as "It's impossible for my hands to become stuck together." Since I have positive attitudes, motivations, and expectancies, I cooperate and 'think with' or 'imagine' those things that are suggested. When the experimenter first asks me to hold my hands together tightly, I clasp them very tightly. I then let myself think and imagine that my hands are rigid and that they are two pieces of metal that are solidly stuck together. While thinking with the suggestions that my hands are welded pieces of metal, I do not have negative feelings such as "My hands cannot become rigid." When the experimenter states, "Try to take them apart. Notice that the harder you try the more difficult it becomes", I continue to focus my thoughts on the rigidity in the hands and to imagine that they are made of welded metal. I pull on the hands but they feel very rigid, like a solid piece of metal. I exert more effort, I am aware that the hands are red and sore, but they do not come apart. Finally, the experimenter states, "Now relax your hands. You can now easily unclasp them." After I relax the hands, I have a feeling of pleasant surprise to see how easily they now come apart.

Age Regression

The experimenter next asks me to close my eyes (presumably to remove distractions) and then gives a series of suggestions along the following lines: "Time is going back . . . You are six years old. You are six years old and you are sitting in your first grade classroom."

Since I feel that age regression is a worthwhile experience, and since I want to and expect to experience it, I have no reason to contradict his suggestions. There is simply no reason to think about the fact that I am an adult. On the contrary, I think with the suggestions and I imagine and feel myself as small and as six years old. For a few moments, as I begin to feel myself back at the earlier time, I also have a feeling that the ongoing suggestions of the experimenter are bothersome and distracting. However, the experimenter soon stops talking and my thoughts focus on the idea that I am six years old. I feel myself as small and my hands feel tiny and I see myself in the second grade classroom. (I presume that I had the fleeting thought that I was in the second grade when I was six years old.) I then find myself sitting behind a brown desk and I notice the knife-marks, the round inkwell, and the large yellow pencil on the desk-top. I 'touch' the chewing-gum on the bottom of the desk and I 'smell' the paste in the room. I look around the room and I notice five large windows and a cloak room and I 'see' the teacher and children interacting. I then 'see' the teacher leave the room, and as soon as she leaves, I wrestle with another boy who sits next to me. The teacher returns and makes me stay in the corner. I feel myself standing there and I feel the need to turn around and look at the others in the class.

Afterwards, when the experiment is over, I report that I felt I was six years old and that I was in the second grade. I go on to describe in detail the events that I re-experienced and how I felt that I 'saw' once again and knew the names of children whom I had not thought about in many years.

Anesthesia

The experimenter next asks me to open my eyes and to "come back to the present" and then gives suggestions of anesthesia as follows:

"Lift your right hand two inches above the desk. Imagine Novocain being injected into the hand. The Novocain is beginning to move into the little finger. You begin to feel small changes in the little finger as the Novocain starts to move in. The little finger is beginning to feel a little different, a little numb. Now the Novocain is beginning to move into the second finger. It too feels a little different, it's beginning to feel a little numb and insensitive. Now you notice the Novocain moving into the third finger . . . now the fourth finger . . . now into the thumb. Now you feel the Novocain in all of the fingers. They feel more and more numb, more and more insensitive. Dull, numb, and insensitive. More and more numb, losing all feelings and sensations. Now rub the fingers with the other hand and notice how they feel rubbery, as if they have lost all feelings and sensations. Pinch the fingers now with your other hand and notice how they feel dull, numb, and insensitive."

After a brief pause, the experimenter concludes, "All right now, your hand is normal again — it is no longer numb. It is normal again."

I think with and I focus imaginatively on the ideas that are suggested. I imagine Novocain being injected into the hand and beginning to move into the little finger. As soon as I begin focusing my attention on the little finger it seems to 'stand off' from the rest of the hand and I feel as if there are small 'sensations' in it that resemble those experienced when Novocain is just beginning to take effect. I then focus on the second finger and think with the suggestion that it is beginning to feel a little different and this finger also seems to be 'set off' from the remainder of the hand and to feel somewhat numb. I continue to think with the suggestions as they are given, I imagine Novocain moving into each of the other fingers and I find it very interesting that each finger in turn seems to feel as if Novocain is moving into it. I also imaginatively elaborate the suggestions, for instance, as I look at the fingers, I think of them as made of wax, then as made of rubber, and then as 'things' sitting 'out there' by themselves, as not belonging to me. After a while the experimenter asks me to pinch the fingers with the other hand. As I pinch each finger, I continue imagining that it has been injected with Novocain and I find that I am not feeling the pinches — the fingers feel rubbery and 'dead.' Afterwards, when the experimenter asks me if I felt the pinches I state that the fingers felt rubbery and insensitive and that I did not feel them.

Auditory Hallucination

The experimenter tells me to close my eyes again and then states, "You are at a large concert hall. You see the orchestra on the stage. The conductor raises his baton and you hear the orchestra begin to play."

I think with the suggestions and I visualize a previous time when I was at a concert. I 'see' the concert hall and the orchestra in front of me. When the music begins, however, I am surprised to 'hear' a soprano singing *Amazing Grace* and even more surprised to feel that I am listening to my radio. I do not care about this transformation of locus; instead, I listen to the penetrating tones and word of the song and I feel the same way when I, many times previously, had heard *Amazing Grace* on the FM station — each tone exquisite, penetrating, vibrating throughout my body.

Later, I describe to the experimenter how I 'transported' myself from the situation in which I was observing the orchestra to one in which I was listening to the radio and I state that *Amazing Grace* was intense,

penetrating, and even had a tinge of sexual arousal.

Relaxation, Drowsiness, Sleep and Hypnosis

The experimenter next states, "Keep your eyes closed. Feel yourself lying on a large cottony, cushiony cloud. The cloud is made of cotton and you are sinking into it. Soft, quiet, peaceful, and relaxed. Floating easily and gently. You feel a soft breeze and the warm sun. Becoming more and more relaxed, lazy, comfortable, peaceful . . . So relaxed . . . drowsy . . . drowsier and drowsier . . . comfortable, laxy, relaxed . . . drowsy and sleepy . . . drowsier and drowsier . . . sleepier and sleepier . . . So drowsy, so sleepy, going into a hypnotic trance . . . a deep trance, a deep hypnotic trance."

In tune with the words of the experimenter, I think with the themes of the suggestions. I imagine that I am floating on a cloud made of cotton and I 'feel' the warm sun and the breeze touching my body. As I think with the themes of the suggestions, my arms begin to feel limp, my legs loosen, and I feel my head dropping. For a few moments, I become aware that my head is bent forward on my chest, my arms are hanging loosely, and I am breathing very slowly. As I continue thinking with the ongoing suggestions, I feel tranquil and I catch a fleeting thought that it would be so nice to be able to lie down and go to sleep. Somewhat later, I feel very detached and 'away from things'. Towards the end of these suggestions, I feel as if my body has become weightless and as if I am alone and floating very peacefully.

Post-Experimental ('Post-Hypnotic') Behavior

The experimenter next asks me to open my eyes. For a few moments after I open them I feel that the experimenter is far away and my surroundings seem dreamlike. This feeling of detachment and tranquility disappears, however, as the experimenter states, "An interesting thing will occur when the experiment is over. When I click my finger, you will cough automatically.'' He reinforces the suggestion by repeating that I will cough when he clicks.

When the experimenter states that the experiment is over and then clicks his fingers, I find myself clearing my throat and I feel as if the 'cough' came 'by itself' — involuntarily. Apparently, I thought with this suggestion in the same way I had thought with the preceding ones. I did not seem to say to myself, "I will not (or cannot) cough when he clicks." Instead, it seems that I expected that I would cough and I expected that it would feel automatic.

Looking Back Restrospectively

The reader should note that I generally experienced a series of suggested effects — hand rigidity, age regression, anesthesia, and auditory hallucination — *before* the experimener told me that I was becoming relaxed, drowsy, sleepy, and was entering a hypnotic trance. Was I 'hypnotized' or in a 'hypnotic trance' when I was responding to these suggestions? When I try to answer this question introspectively, I find that it is not especially meaningful. I felt that I simply let myself think with and imaginatively focus on those things that were suggested. Looking back retrospectively, I can also make the following interpretations concerning some of the effects that I experienced:

Hand rigidity. I can see now that I produced a strong feeling of rigidity in my hands when I clasped them together tightly and contracted the muscles. Consequently, when I was thinking with and imaginatively elaborating the suggestions, I was focusing on the rigidity that was already present. Also, retrospectively, I can see that in order to have unclasped my hands, when the experimenter said "Try, you can't", I would have had to shift my underlying attitudes and motivations from very positive to very negative. Instead of focusing my thoughts on the rigidity, I would have had to say to myself something like, "That is absurd. Of course, I can take my hands apart." Fur-

thermore, to have unclasped my hands, it would have been necessary to remove the muscular contractions by relaxing my hands. However, I had no reason to contradict the suggestions and to relax my hands. Since my underlying attitudes, motivations, and expectancies were quite positive — I perceived the situation as one in which I would have worthwhile experience and I wanted and expected to experience the suggested effects —, I continued to think of my hands as rigid and to maintain the muscular contractions which prevented me from unclasping my hands.

Age regression. Retrospectively, it seems that it was very easy to focus on the idea that I was a child. I had no reason to say to myself that I was actually an adult and that I was in an experimental situation. As I let my thoughts go with the idea of being a child, I 'recreated' scenes of childhood. When the experimenter stated that I was six years of age and that I was in the first grade classroom, I 'felt' myself sitting in the second grade classroom. (I presume I had a fleeting thought that I was in the second grade when I was six years old.) I did not 'care' about this contradiction. Although I was thinking and imagining with the *themes* of the suggestions, the particular details did not matter. In the same way as many other responsive subjects, I was carrying out 'goal-directed imagining', that is, I was imagining a situation (the second grade) which was in harmony with the goal of the suggestions even though I was not literally following the suggestion (that I was in the first grade) (Spanos, 1971; Spanos & Barber, 1972). Retrospectively, I 'felt' small, I 'reexperienced' sitting in the second grade classroom and I felt as if I was again experiencing the same emotions that I had felt when the teacher caught me wrestling with another boy and when I was standing in the corner facing the wall.

Anesthesia. Looking back, it seems that the suggestions of anesthesia began when the experimenter asked me to lift my hand above the desk. When the fingers are not touching and moving across an object, they 'naturally' do not seem sensitive. I could easily interpret this actual fact — 'not seeming sensitive' — as meaning that the fingers were becoming insensitive. Also, by focusing my attention on each finger, while the hand was sitting relaxed above the desk, I could discriminate slight 'sensations' which could easily be interpreted as the kind of feelings which one observes when Novocain is beginning to take effect. When I rubbed the fingers and also when I pinched the fingers, they felt rubbery and insensitive. However, when I rub and pinch the fingers now, the feeling of rubberiness and insensitivity is there in a minimal way. It seems, retrospectively, that during the experiment I was magnifying the feelings of insensitivity which are normally present in the fingers when the hand is relaxed and the fingers are not touching anything or being moved across a surface.

When the experimenter stated, "All right now, your hand is normal again — it is no longer numb", I can see now, retrospectively, that the hand did not feel 'normal' immediately; it felt 'normal' only when I moved the fingers a second or two later. In other words, it appears that the feeling of insensitivity is based, in part, on the fact that one is focusing on fingers that are not being moved and if the fingers are in movement it would be much more difficult to experience the suggested insensitivity.

Auditory hallucination. Looking back, it seems that the experimenter's suggestions induced me to 'hear' the music 'in my head' and to feel as if the 'internal music' was coming from outside of me. Although the experimenter suggested that I was at a concert hall, I found it more congruent with my previous experience to 'transport' myself to a room in which I was listening to an FM radio and hearing the exquisite notes of *Amazing Grace*. In the same way as many responsive subjects, the details of the suggestions were not important to me. I was engaged in 'goal-directed imagining', that is, I was imagining a situation which was harmonious with the goals of the suggestions even though I was not imagining what the experimenter had literally suggested. Although responding to this

type of suggestions may seem very difficult to some readers, I believe most of us can think about and imaginatively focus on a previous time when we heard music that was especially moving. While focusing on such a previously-experienced situation, we will naturally 'hear' the music 'in our head' and, if we do not have or if we put aside a critical attitude, negative thoughts, such as "I am not actually hearing anything", will not arise. In fact, the act of focusing on 'imagined' music or on 'music in our head' is difficult to distinguish subjectively from the act of listening to actual music.

Suggestions of relaxation, drowsiness, sleep, and hypnosis. Retrospectively, it seems that I responded to this set of suggestions for the same reasons that I responded to the preceding suggestions. Since I had positive attitudes, motivations, and expectancies toward the test situation, I thought with and imaginatively focused on the ongoing suggestions and I felt relaxed, drowsy, and then passive and detached.

It should be noted that the suggestions of relaxation, drowsiness, sleep, and hypnosis were given towards the end of the experimental session that was described above. However, such suggestions are usually given at the beginning of the experiment and it is commonly assumed that (a) a subject who responds to suggestions for relaxation, drowsiness, sleep, and hypnosis enters a 'hypnotic trance' and (b) the 'hypnotic trance' gives rise to a high level of responsiveness to subsequent suggestions for limb rigidity, age regression, anesthesia, etc. However, if the suggestions of relaxation, drowsiness, sleep, and hypnosis are placed toward the end of the session, they can be seen to be another set of suggestions to which the subject may or may not respond. If the subject responds to the suggestions of relaxation, drowsiness, sleep, and hypnosis, he does so for the same reasons that he responded to the preceding test suggestions — he has positive attitudes, motivations, and expectancies toward the test situation and, consequently, thinks with the suggestions and imagines the suggested effects. Let me clarify this further by describing two common events that involve similar processes.

ANALOGIES: READING A NOVEL AND WATCHING A MOVIE[5]

It seems to me that the processes involved in responding to suggestions are similar to those that are present when I am reading an interesting novel or am watching a motion picture or stage play. Let me describe each of these analogies in turn.

When I am reading an interesting novel, I think with and vividly imagine the communications from the printed page. To the extent that I become involved in my imaginings, I do not have contradictory thoughts such as "This is only a novel", or, "This is only make-believe." Instead, I experience a variety of emotions while empathizing and 'living with' the character. At times I experience sadness and tears may cover my face. At times I may smile to myself and I may laugh aloud. Along similar lines, Shor (1970) has previously pointed out that, when reading a novel, some individuals "think the thoughts in the story and they feel the emotions". Shor labeled this behavior as the *book reading fantasy* and noted the following relevant characteristics:

. . . the reader creates the fantasy for his own purposes, to satisfy his own motives. The fantasy is not implanted in the mind by the words in the book. The reader is not forced to create the fantasy by the inexorable "suggestive" power of the words. The words do not express themselves with the reader's will held in abeyance. The reader is not too much asleep to control his own mind. He is not an automaton obeying the commands of his master. The words in the book have no ideomotor powers in their own right except insofar as the reader deliberately gives them expression. The reader is deliberately using the words in the book for his own ends [p. 93].

[5] This section on analogies, and the next two sections (on the sleepwalker and on training in human potentialities) are adapted from material that I wrote for a recent book (Barber, Spanos, & Chaves, 1974). I am indebted to Pergamon Press for permission to use the material and to Drs. Spanos and Chaves for critically evaluating the original manuscript.

It seems to me that the processes involved in responding to suggestions also resemble those present when I have a variety of emotional experiences while observing a motion picture or a stage play. At a movie, I think with the communications from the screen. As I become imaginatively involved in the action, I do not have negative thoughts such as, "These are only actors", "This is just a story that someone made up", or "This is just a series of lights playing upon a screen." Since I think with the communications, I feel, emote, and experience in line with the intentions of the writer of the screen-play — I feel sad, I weep, I emphathize, I feel happy, I laugh, etc. I think with the communications because I am attending the performance in order to have new experiences. My *attitude* toward the movie is that it is interesting and worthwhile to feel sad, to feel happy, to empathize, and to have the other thoughts, feelings, and emotions that the actors are attempting to communicate. Furthermore, I both *desire* and *expect* that the actors will arouse in me new thoughts and emotions. It is misleading to claim that I am having intense experiences and emotions as I observe the movie because I have entered a 'hypnotic trance'. I have intense experiences while observing a movie and I have intense experiences when I am responding to suggestions because in both cases, I have positive attitudes, motivations, and expectancies toward the situation and I think with and imaginatively focus on the communications.

When I am observing a movie and also when I am responding to suggestions I am thinking with and imaginatively focusing on the communications that I receive. However, I am being exposed to different kinds of communications in these situations. The communications from the movie are intended to elicit certain kinds of thoughts, emotions, and experiences — to feel excited or shocked, to empathize, to laugh or to cry, and to feel happy or sad. The communications from the experimenter are intended to elicit somewhat different types of thoughts, emotions, and experiences — to feel that an arm is light and is rising, to experience oneself as a child, to vividly imagine (or 'hallucinate') an orchestra playing, etc. When I am responding to suggestions I have different experiences than when I am observing a movie, *not because I am in a different 'state of consciousness', but because I am receiving different communications.*

It should also be noted that an individual who is in a motion picture audience may have negative attitudes, motivations, and expectancies toward the performance and may fail to experience the emotions which the actors are attempting to communicate. He may be attending the movie theater unwillingly and may be uninterested in having new experiences. He may not especially desire and may not expect to feel happy, sad, shocked, excited, or empathic. Given these kinds of attitudes, motivations, and expectancies, this member of the audience may say to himself that this is just a movie and he is just watching actors perform their roles. If he observes the movie in this uninvolved and distant manner, he will be continually aware that he is in an audience and that he is observing a deliberately contrived performance. He will not think with and imaginatively focus on the communications, and he will not laugh, feel sad, empathize or, more generally, think, feel, emote, and experience in line with the communications from the screen. I believe such an individual closely resembles the subject who is unresponsive to suggestions. Both have negative attitudes, motivations, and expectancies toward the situation which prevent them from thinking with and imaginatively focusing on the communications.

THE TRADITIONAL ANALOGY: THE SLEEPWALKER

The analogies which I presented above are drastically different from the traditional analogy which views the responsive subject in a hypnotic situation as similar, in many respects, to the sleepwalker. As Hilgard (1969) pointed out, "Hypnosis is com- monly considered to be a 'state' perhaps resembling the state in which the sleepwalker finds himself, hence the term 'somnambulist' as applied to the deeply hypnotized person." I believe that the sleepwalker analogy is incorrect and misleading. Let me try to clarify my belief by first describing the characteristics of the sleepwalker and then those of the responsive hypnotic subject.

A series of recent studies (Jacobson, Kales, Lehmann, Zweizig, 1965; Kales, Jacobson, Paulson, Kales, & Walter, 1966; Pai, 1946) indicate that the sleepwalker manifests the following four sets of characteristics:

First, when the sleepwalker arises from his bed at night, the electroencephalogram (EEG) shows that he is sleeping (stages 3 or 4 of sleep). When the sleepwalking episode is brief in duration, the EEG shows that the sleepwalker remains asleep. However, during longer sleepwalking episodes, the EEG shows that the sleepwalker enters light sleep or very relaxed wakefulness.

Second, the sleepwalker shows rigid or shuffling movements, a drastically reduced awareness of his surroundings, a fixed focus of attention, a low level of motor skill, and a blank stare. The sleepwalker rarely replies when someone speaks to him. To get his attention, it is usually necessary to continue talking to him or to interrupt his movements. When the sleepwalker does reply, he tends to mumble or to speak in a vague or detached manner.

Third, when the sleepwalker is told to wake up, he does not awaken. Persistent measures are needed to awaken him. For example, it may be necessary to shake him or to repeat his name over and over, each time more loudly.

Finally, when the sleepwalker is awakened in the morning, or if he is awakened during his sleepwalking, he shows no indication of remembering the episode.

A subject who is said to be 'hypnotized' is often termed a 'somnambulist' with the clear implication that he resembles the sleepwalker. Laymen have commonly assumed that the responsive hypnotic subject resembles the sleepwalker in that he is 'half asleep', has a low level of awareness, is detached from his surroundings, has a fixed focus of attention, and shows amnesia on awakening. I believe these assumptions are fallacious. It seems to me that the so-called 'hypnotized' subject differs from the sleepwalker in every important respect.

First, the EEG of the 'hypnotized' subject does not remotely resemble the EEG of the sleepwalker. Judging from EEG criteria, the sleepwalker is typically asleep whereas the subject who is said to be 'hypnotized' is awake. More specifically, responsive hypnotic subjects do not show changes on the EEG that might clearly distinguish them from subjects who are said to be 'awake'. The EEG of the so-called 'hypnotized' subject varies continually, in the same way as in any 'normally awake' person, with whatever instructions or suggestions he is given or with whatever activities he is engaged in (Barber, 1961; Chertok & Kramarz, 1959).[6]

Second, some so-called 'hypnotized' subjects may seem to resemble the sleepwalker in that they show a fixed focus of attention, a blank stare, a rigid facial expression, a lack of spontaneity, and a dis-

inclination to talk. However, in the hypnotic subject, but *not* in the sleepwalker, these kinds of characteristics have been produced by suggestions to become relaxed, drowsy, and sleepy and they can be easily removed by suggestions, for example, by suggestions to be alert.

Third, although the sleepwalker does not awaken when he is simply told to do so, practically all subjects who are said to be 'hypnotized' open their eyes and 'awaken' when they are simply told, "The experiment is over" or "Wake up."[7]

Fourth, sleepwalkers do not remember their sleepwalking. In contrast, if suggestions for amnesia are not given during the hypnotic session, practically all hypnotic subjects remember the events that occurred (Barber & Calverley, 1966; Hilgard, 1966).[8] In addition, it appears that *no* subject has ever forgotten the events occur-

---

[6] Other physiological measures also vary in 'hypnotized' subjects in the same way as in control 'awake' subjects. Depending on the instructions or suggestions that the subject receives, both the 'hypnotized' subject and the 'waking control' subject at times show high levels and at times medium or low levels of heart rate, blood pressure, skin resistance, basal metabolic rate, respiration, peripheral blood flow, blood clotting time, oral temperature, and so forth (Barber, 1961, 1965, 1970; Crasilneck & Hall, 1959; Levitt & Brady, 1963; Sarbin, 1956; Sarbin & Slagle, 1972; Timney & Barber, 1969). Furthermore, when specific types of suggestions (for example, suggestions of anesthesia) produce physiological changes in subjects who are said to be 'hypnotized', the suggestions also produce very similar physiological changes in control subjects who are said to be 'awake' (Barber, 1961, 1965). For instance, in both 'hypnotized' subjects and in control subjects, suggestions of anesthesia or analgesia at times reduce respiratory and electromyographic responses to noxious stimulation (Barber & Hahn, 1962).

[7] In very rare cases, a 'hypnotized' subject does not open his eyes when told that the experiment is over. These rare cases are due to such reasons as the following: The subject may have actually fallen asleep, or he may not have fallen asleep but he (a) wants to remain a little longer in a relaxed or passive condition, (b) has been given a posthypnotic suggestion that he does not want to carry out, (c) is purposively resisting the hypnotist, (d) is testing the hypnotist's ability to control him, (e) is manifesting spite towards the hypnotist, or (f) is attempting to frighten the hypnotist by refusing to 'awaken' (Weitzenhoffer, 1957, pp. 226–229; Williams, 1953).

[8] In rare instances, 'hypnotized' subjects who are *not* given suggestions for amnesia state postexperimentally that they do not remember what occurred during the session. There are several reasons for viewing this apparent amnesia not as a spontaneous occurrence but as due to explicit or implicit suggestions: (a) In many of these cases, the subject had received suggestions for amnesia in a previous hypnotic session and may have generalized the suggestions for amnesia to apply to subsequent sessions as well. (b) Suggestions to sleep were administered during the hypnotic session. Since sleep is followed by amnesia, the suggestions to sleep included the implicit suggestion that the subject is expected to show amnesia on 'awakening'. (c) A substantial proportion of present-day subjects believe that 'hypnotized' persons manifest amnesia (London, 1961) and that they will be considered 'poor' subjects, the experimenter will be disappointed, and the experiment may be 'spoiled' if they state postexperimentally that they remember what occurred.

ring during a hypnotic session when he was told, during the session, that he should remember the events (Barber, 1962; Orne, 1966; Watkins, 1966).

In brief, I believe that subjects who are said to be 'hypnotized' differ from the sleepwalker in every important respect. It seems to me that it is erroneous and misleading to view the responsive subject in a hypnotic situation as resembling the sleepwalker.

RECAPITULATION

Let me restate a theme that underlies the preceding discussion. It has been traditionally assumed that individuals experience suggested age regression, anesthesia, auditory hallucination, etc., when they have been 'hypnotized' or placed in a 'hypnotic trance'. My viewpoint, which regards the concept of 'hypnotized' or 'hypnotic trance' as misleading, allows for a broader conception of the capabilities and potentialities of normal human beings. My viewpoint postulates that: (a) Age regression, anesthesia, and other phenomena that have been traditionally subsumed under the term 'hypnotism' are elicited when an individual thinks and imagines with the suggestions for age regression, anesthesia, etc. (b) A large proportion of individuals have the potential to think and imagine with the themes of the suggestions. However, (c) the potential often remains dormant until the individual has positive attitudes, motivations, and expectancies toward the situation. Let me now present some methods that might prove useful for producing the necessary attitudes, motivations, and expectancies and that might also directly help individuals to think and imagine with the themes of suggestions.

TRAINING IN HUMAN POTENTIALITIES

Since 1969, while conducting group workshops and also while working with a small number of individual subjects, I have been developing a course that I have labeled as *Training in Human Potentialities*. Although the course has not as yet

been finalized and only some parts of the course have been evaluated (Chaves & Barber, 1974; Comins, Fullam, & Barber, 1973), there are two reasons why I believe it is worthwhile to outline it here: (a) The outline should illustrate in a concrete manner how some of the principles presented in this article can be applied and (b) other investigators may see the procedures as useful and may proceed to evaluate them experimentally.[9]

Defining the Situation

I typically define the situation as one which the subject will learn to fulfill his own potentialities. I tell the subject that I can help him learn how to focus his thoughts, how to recall useful material by vividly imagining a previous situation, how to improve his learning proficiency, how to control pain, and how to control his bodily processes by first learning to control his mental processes. I emphasize to the subject that the training he receives in the experimental situation should prove useful in his daily life.

Learning to Control Pain

Although I can begin the training course in various ways, I usually begin by trying to teach the subject how to control pain. I tell him that he will first learn to tolerate a normally painful stimulus and not be bothered by it at all. I also explain to him that the learning will be useful in a wide va-

---

[9] Kinney (1969), Sachs (1971), and Diamond (1972) have also recently presented methods for training subjects to become more responsive to 'hypnotic' suggestions. The training procedure that I am presenting in this section differs in several important respects and was developed independently from those presented by Kinney, Sachs, and Diamond. However, the methods I am using also have several features in common with those developed by other investigators. These various methods for training subjects are discussed together elsewhere (Barber, Spanos, & Chaves, 1974, Chap. 11).

riety of situations in which he normally experiences pain. For instance, I might state, "It should be useful not only in overcoming the pains and discomforts of daily life but also in dentistry and [for female subjects] during childbirth. Once you have learned how to control pain, you may be able to transfer or extrapolate what you have learned to other situations in your life in which anxiety, distress, or fear are present."

I then expose the subject for a period of one minute to the Forgione-Barber (1971) pain stimulator which brings a weight to bear on the bony part of a finger. Next, I tell the subject that he can control the pain produced by the weight by keeping his mind on other things during the stimulation and also by imagining vividly that the stimulated finger is dull, numb, or insensitive.

Next, I model for the subject. I show him how I can control pain by utilizing the two techniques mentioned above. I place the weight on my own finger and then I state, "I am going to think of other things. I am not going to let myself think of the heavy weight on my finger." While the weight remains on my finger, I verbalize aloud some of the things I am thinking about, for example, "I am thinking back to last summer when I was on the beach . . . I am sitting on the hot sand . . . The sun is hot but pleasant . . . As I enter the water, I find it is comfortably cool . . . In the distance I see an airplane slowly moving overhead . . .". I continue for several minutes verbalizing some of the things I am thinking and visualizing, while the weight remains on my finger and I show no signs of pain or distress.

I then state, "I will now try to think of the finger as numb and insensitive . . . I am imagining that Novocain has been injected into the finger . . . I am thinking of the Novocain spreading slowly throughout the finger and it is becoming dull, numb, like a piece of rubber . . . I am imagining that the finger is just a piece of matter — a lump of matter without feelings or sensations . . ." For several minutes I continue imagining numbness and insensitivity, I verbalize my thoughts aloud, and I manifest no signs of pain or distress.

Finally, I remove the weight from my finger and I tell the subject that he can control pain by using the same procedures. I ask him to try, to the best of his ability, to think and imagine in the way I have just demonstrated. The heavy weight is then placed on the subject's finger and he practices carrying out the processes of trying to think of other things and then trying to imagine that the finger has become insensitive. Although some subjects find it difficult to think and imagine in this way, other subjects are able to do it rather easily and they succeed in tolerating the pain-producing stimulus.

In further development of this course, I hope to delineate other techniques that subjects can use to control pain. Some techniques that might prove useful include thinking and imagining that the stimulated body part is just a 'thing' that is not actually part of oneself, and thinking of the sensations, not as 'pain,' but as a variety of unusual sensations with their own unique properties. Also, in further development of the course, I expect to give subjects additional practice in tolerating pain produced by other kinds of stimuli, for instance, pain produced by immersion of a limb in ice water and pain produced by blocking off the blood supply to an arm by means of a tourniquet. When a subject has learned to control pain in the laboratory, I shall attempt to determine if his learning can be transferred to a situation outside of the laboratory. For instance, I shall ask the subject to try to undergo his next dental appointment without Novocain and to try to utilize what he has learned in the laboratory; for example, to try to think of other things during the dentistry or to try to imagine that Novocain has been injected and that his teeth and gums have become insensitive. As I develop the training course, I also hope to find methods that subjects can use to transfer what they have learned to other situations in their daily life that involve anxiety or pain.

Learning to Experience a Variety of Phenomena

Although I typically begin the course by trying to teach the subject to tolerate pain, I can also begin in other ways; for example, by first trying to teach the subject how to experience a variety of effects that have been traditionally associated with suggestions and hypnotism.

In teaching the subject to experience a variety of interesting phenomena, I use procedures that are similar to those that were described above. I first tell the subject that he can fulfill his potentialities by learning to control his thinking and imagining. I then state that he will receive practice in focusing his thinking and imagining on the idea that one arm is very heavy and rigid, the other arm is very light and is rising, his body is rigid and immoveable, he feels very thirsty, etc. I then model for the subject, verbalizing aloud how I am experiencing one of these phenomena, such as arm heaviness and rigidity, by thinking and imagining that my arm is heavy and rigid. I may also explain to the subject that when I think and vividly imagine that my arm is rigid, the muscles of my arm naturally contract; the contraction of the muscles makes my arm feel heavy and rigid; then by keeping my thoughts on the induced heaviness and rigidity, my arm can feel exceedingly heavy and rigid.

After the subject has attempted to carry out the same kind of cognitive processes, I interview him to determine to what extent he was able to concentrate on the idea of heaviness or rigidity. If the subject reports that negative thoughts intruded, for example, the thought that "My arm cannot become heavy and rigid," I tell him to try it again while trying to imagine more vividly and that, if he concentrates on imagining, the negative thoughts will disappear.

The same procedures are used to teach the subject to experience other phenomena such as arm levitation, body immobility, thirst hallucination, amnesia, age-regression, and relaxation. Let me describe how the general procedures are applied to the latter two phenomena — age regression and relaxation.

Experiencing Age Regression

I tell the subject that he can heighten his recall of earlier events by vividly imagining a past time. I also give several examples of how this technique is useful in daily life. For instance, I tell the subject that when he is taking an examination and he wishes to recall material that he learned previously, he can heighten his recall by imagining and clearly visualizing the concrete situation in which he originally learned the material. I then state: "I will show you how to re-experience a past time. In a moment, I will close my eyes so that I can remove distractions. Then, I will tell myself that I am ten years of age and I will imagine and visualize that I am in the fourth grade classroom. I will then concentrate my thinking and imagining on the idea that I am ten years old and, when I succeed in concentrating my thinking and imagining around this idea, thoughts that I am an adult in an experimental situation will not arise. Once I begin clearly visualizing the fourth grade, I will let my imagination 'move' and I will let myself 'go with' the events that I imagine."

I then close my eyes. After a few minutes I open them, I state that I felt I was ten years old, and I describe how I experienced myself, the teacher, and the students in the classroom.

I then tell the subject: "In a minute I will ask you to close your eyes and to think back to the time you were ten years old. Imagine that you are sitting in the classroom. Concentrate your thinking and imagining on the idea that you are in the classroom, feel yourself in that situation, and then let your imagination 'move'. As you let the teacher, the students, and yourself interact and 'come alive', thoughts about your being an adult in an experimental situation, will disappear."

The subject is then given practice in experiencing himself as ten years old. Subsequently, he is given further practice in experiencing various other age levels.

Experiencing Relaxation

I introduce the training in relaxation by speaking to the subject along the following lines:

"Most individuals are so busy living their daily lives that they rarely, if ever, allow themselves to experience total relaxation. In fact, it is questionable whether most individuals know how to relax. This is unfortunate because the ability to relax completely is very useful in our daily lives. Once we have learned to relax, we are able to remain calm and at ease in many situations that normally produce anxiety or tension. For instance, many individuals become tense or anxious when they meet new people, when they are in a strange or new situation, and when they feel that they are being judged by others. Also, individuals who are alcoholics, or who are obese, or who cannot quit smoking become tense and anxious when they have not had alcohol, or food, or a cigarette for a period of time. Some individuals also have specific kinds of fears; for instance, fear of riding in an airplane, fear of heights, or fear of narrow spaces. If these individuals could learn how to relax, they could control their anxiety, tension, or fear. An important fact that has been emphasized by behavior therapists is that anxiety and tension are incompatible with physical and mental relaxation. If a person lets himself relax, he can control or block the anxiety, tension, or fear. In fact, many of the useful effects that are attributed to yoga, hypnosis, Zen, and transcendental meditation appear to be due to the relaxation that is produced by each of these techniques."

I next state that I will now model for the subject, showing him how to relax. I introduce the modeling demonstration as follows:

"I will now show you how to relax. To get rid of distractions, I will first close my eyes. Then I will think to myself that I am becoming very relaxed. I will tell myself that my arms are relaxing, my legs are relaxing, my eyes are relaxing, all parts of my body are relaxing. I will then imagine that I am floating on a soft cloud and that my body feels very, very relaxed. I will continue telling myself that I am completely relaxed and I will imagine scenes, such as floating softly on smooth water, which will make me feel more and more relaxed."

I then model for the subject, demonstrating how to relax. After a few minutes, I open my eyes, report what I was thinking and imagining during the period of relaxation, and then ask the subject to try relaxing in the same way. I may give the subject several practice trials during the session, asking him to relax for longer and longer periods of time. Before the subject leaves, I usually ask him to continue practicing the relaxation technique at home and to try to use what he has learned about relaxation in his daily life whenever he begins to feel anxious or tense.

Experimental Evaluation

The effectiveness of parts of the above course of training have been evaluated experimentally. In one recent experiment (Comins, Fullam, & Barber, 1973), the experimenter modeled for one group of subjects, showing them (a) how he thought and imagined those things that he suggested aloud to himself (arm heaviness, arm levitation, hand clasp, and thirst 'hallucination') and (b) how he, consequently, experienced an involuntary lowering and rising of his arm, and inability to unclasp his hands, and extreme thirst. The subjects who had observed the experimenter responding to the suggestions were then tested on the Barber Suggestibility Scale. Their scores on the scale were compared with the scores of two random groups of subjects: a control group that had not received any instructions and a hypnotic induction group that had been exposed to repeated suggestions of relaxation, drowsiness, and hypnotic sleep. Subjects who had observed the experimenter model were markedly more responsive than the control subjects to the test-suggestions of the Barber Suggestibility Scale and they were as responsive as the subjects who had been exposed to the standardized hypnotic induction procedure.

In a second evaluative study (Chaves & Barber, 1974), 120 subjects were first exposed to a pain pretest (a heavy weight was applied to a finger for two minutes). Before receiving the pain stimulus a second time (post-test), some of the subjects were told to imagine pleasant events during the pain stimulation, others were told to imagine that the finger was insensitive, and the remaining subjects were used as controls. With regard to the subjects who were told to imagine, half were and half were not exposed to experimenter modeling. Those who were exposed to experimenter modeling observed how the experimenter could tolerate the pain when he imagined pleasant events or imagined that his finger was insensitive. Overall, subjects who were told to imagine pleasant events or to imagine that the finger was insensitive reported less pain than the control subjects. Also, the experimenter modeling procedure was effective in producing a further reduction in pain in subjects who reported a high level of pain during the pretest and who were asked to imagine pleasant events during the post-test.

Although the above two studies evaluated the effects of the experimenter modeling procedure, they did not define the situation to the subjects as one in which they could learn to fulfill their potentialities. Further studies are planned to test the separate and combined effects of (a) experimenter modeling and (b) defining the situation as training in human potentialities.

SUMMARY

In the first part of this article I presented an introspective report describing and interpreting some of my underlying attitudes, motivations, and expectancies and ongoing thought processes while I was responding to suggestions. This introspective report was presented in order (a) to illustrate some of the major facets of the theory of 'hypnosis' that I have presented elsewhere and (b) to show that although the theory was originally derived from experimental studies (Barber, 1969, 1970, 1972; Barber & DeMoor, 1972; Barber & Ham, 1974; Barber, Spanos, & Chaves, 1974), it is also harmonious with my own personal experiences.

The underlying contentions were that (a) suggested effects are experienced when a subject thinks with and imaginatively focuses on those things that are suggested and (b) a subject imaginatively focuses on the suggestions when he has positive attitudes, motivations, and expectancies toward the test situation — when he sees the test situation as useful and worthwhile, and when he wants to and expects to experience those things that are suggested.

In the second part of the article the processes involved in responding to suggestions were compared with those found when an individual is experiencing sadness, happiness, empathy, excitement, shock, and a variety of other emotions as he reads an interesting novel or observes a motion picture. In each of these instances — when responding to suggestions, reading a novel, or observing a movie — the individual who has positive attitudes, motivations, and expectancies toward the situation, thinks with and imaginatively focuses on the communications he is receiving.

The analogies presented in this article, which viewed the person who is responding to suggestions as resembling the person who is reading an interesting novel or is observing an interesting motion picture, are drastically different from the traditional analogy which views the responsive subject in a hypnotic situation as similar, in many respects, to the sleepwalker. The latter analogy was analyzed in the third part of the article and was shown to be misleading — the responsive subject in a hypnotic situation differs in every important respect from the sleepwalker.

In the final part of the article I outlined a course, now being developed, that aims to teach individuals how to respond to self-suggestions and also to suggestions given by another person. Since learning to respond to suggestions enables the individual to broaden his capabilities, for example, it enables the individual to control pain and to reexperience previous events, the situation is defined to the subject as *Training in Human Potentialities*. An important feature of this course is that I model for the subject. I demonstrate how I can control pain by thinking and imagining that my finger is insensitive, how I can experience age regression by thinking and imagining that I am a child, how I can relax by thinking and imagining that I am floating on a cloud, etc.

After I demonstrate how I go about having each experience, I ask the subject to try to think and imagine in the same way and I then give him practice in having the experience. Two recent experimental studies indicated that this experimenter modeling procedure is a useful technique for teaching subjects how to respond to suggestions. Further studies are planned that will also evaluate the effectiveness of other aspects of the training course, for example, the effectiveness of defining the situation to the subject as 'training in human potentialities.'

REFERENCES

BARBER, T. X. Physiological effects of "hypnosis." *Psychological Bulletin*, 1961, 58, 390–419.

BARBER, T. X. Toward a theory of hypnosis: Posthypnotic behavior. *Archives of General Psychiatry*, 1962, 7, 321–342.

BARBER, T. X. Physiological effects of "hypnotic suggestions:" A critical review of recent research (1960–64). *Psychological Bulletin*, 1965, 63, 201–222.

BARBER, T. X. *Hypnosis: A scientific approach.* New York: Van Nostrand Reinhold, 1969.

BARBER, T. X. *LSD, marihuana, yoga, and hypnosis.* Chicago: Aldine, 1970.

BARBER, T. X. Suggested ("hypnotic") behavior: The trance paradigm versus an alternative paradigm. In E. Fromm and R. E. Shor (Eds.) *Hypnosis: Research Developments and Perspectives.* Chicago: Aldine-Atherton, 1972. Pp. 115–182.

BARBER, T. X., & CALVERLEY, D. S. Toward a theory of "hypnotic" behavior: Experimental analyses of suggested amnesia. *Journal of Abnormal Psychology*, 1966, 71, 95–107.

BARBER, T. X., & DeMOOR, W. A theory of hypnotic induction procedures. *American Journal of Clinical Hypnosis*, 1972, 15, 112–135.

BARBER, T. X., & HAHN, K. W., JR. Physiological and subjective responses to pain producing stimulation under hypnotically-suggested and waking-imagined "analgesia". *Journal of Abnormal and Social Psychology*, 1962, 65, 411–418.

BARBER, T. X., SPANOS, N. P., & CHAVES, J. F. *Hypnosis, imagination, and human potentialities.* Elmsford, New York: Pergamon, 1974.

CHAVES, J. F., & BARBER, T. X. Cognitive strategies, experimenter modeling, and expectation in the attenuation of pain. *Journal of Abnormal Psychology*, 1974, 83, 356–363.

CHERTOK, L., & KRAMARZ, P. Hypnosis, sleep, and electro-encephalography. *Journal of Nervous and Mental Disease*, 1959, 128, 227–238.

COMINS, J., FULLAM, F., & BARBER, T. X. Experimenter modeling, demands for honesty, and response to "hypnotic" suggestions. Medfield, Mass.: Medfield Foundation, 1973.

CRASILNECK, H. B., & HALL, J. A. Physiological changes associated with hypnosis: A review of the literature since 1948. *International Journal of Clinical and Experimental Hypnosis*, 1959, 7, 9–50.

DIAMOND, M. J. The use of observationally-presented information to modify hypnotic susceptibility. *Journal of Abnormal Psychology*, 1972, 79, 174–180.

FORGIONE, A. G., & BARBER, T. X. A strain gauge pain stimulator. *Psychophysiology*, 1971, 8, 102–106.

HILGARD, E. R. Posthypnotic amnesia: Experiments and theory. *International Journal of Clinical and Experimental Hypnosis*, 1966, 14, 104–111.

HILGARD, E. R. Altered states of awareness. *Journal of Nervous and Mental Disease*, 1969, 149, 68–79. (a) [Reprinted in T. X. Barber *et al.* (eds.) *Biofeedback and Self-Control: An Aldine Reader.* Chicago: Aldine-Atherton, 1971. Pp. 763–774.]

JACOBSON, A., KALES, A., LEHMANN, D., & ZWEIZIG, J. R. Somnambulism: All-night electro-encephalographic studies. *Science*, 1965, 148, 975–977.

KALES, A., JACOBSON, A., PAULSON, M. J., KALES, J. D., & WALTER, R. D. Somnambulism: Psychophysiological correlates. I. All-night EEG studies. *Archives of General Psychiatry*, 1966, 14, 586–594.

KINNEY, J. C. M. Modification of hypnotic susceptibility. Doctoral dissertation, Stanford University,

1969. Ann Arbor, Michigan: University Microfilms, 70–10, 476.

LEVITT, E. E., & BRADY, J. P. Psychophysiology of hypnosis. In J. M. Schneck (Ed.) *Hypnosis in Modern Medicine*. (3rd Ed.) Springfield, Ill.: C. C Thomas, 1963. Pp. 314–362.

LONDON, P. Subject characteristics in hypnosis research: I. A survey of experience, interest, and opinion. *International Journal of Clinical and Experimental Hypnosis*, 1961, 9, 151–161.

ORNE, M. T. On the mechanism of posthypnotic amnesia. *International Journal of Clinical and Experimental Hypnosis*, 1966, 14, 121–134.

PAI, M. N. Sleep-walking and sleep activities. *Journal of Mental Science*, 1946, 92, 756–783.

SACHS, L. B. Construing hypnosis as modifiable behavior. In A. Jacobs and L. B. Sachs (Eds.) *The Psychology of Private Events*. New York: Academic Press, 1971. Pp. 61–75.

SARBIN, T. R. Physiological effects of hypnotic stimulation. In R. M. Dorcus (Ed.) *Hypnosis and its Therapeutic Applications*. New York: McGraw-Hill, 1956. Chap. 4.

SARBIN, T. R., & SLAGLE, R. W. Hypnosis and psychophysiological outcomes. In E. Fromm and R. E. Shor (Eds.) *Hypnosis: Research Developments and Perspectives*, Chicago: Aldine-Atherton, 1972. Pp. 185–214.

SHOR, R. E. The three-factor theory of hypnosis as applied to the book-reading fantasy and to the concept of suggestion. *International Journal of Clinical and Experimental Hypnosis*, 1970, 18, 89–98.

SPANOS, N. P. Goal-directed phantasy and the performance of hypnotic test suggestions. *Psychiatry*, 1971, 34, 86–96.

SPANOS, N. P., & BARBER, T. X. Cognitive activity during "hypnotic" suggestibility: Goal-directed fantasy and the experience of non-volition. *Journal of Personality*, 1972, 40, 510–524.

TIMNEY, B. N., & BARBER, T. X. Hypnotic induction and oral temperature. *International Journal of Clinical and Experimental Hypnosis*, 1969, 17, 121–132.

WATKINS, J. G. Symposium on posthypnotic amnesia: Discussion. *International Journal of Clinical and Experimental Hypnosis*, 1966, 14, 139–149.

WEITZENHOFFER, A. M. *General techniques of hypnotism*. New York: Grune & Stratton, 1957.

WILLIAMS, G. W. Difficulty in dehypnotizing. *Journal of Clinical and Experimental Hypnosis*, 1953, 1, 3–12.

Hypnotic Suggestions for Blister Formation: Subjective and Physiological Effects

10

R. F. Q. Johnson and T. X. Barber

The influence of hypnotic suggestions for blister formation on subsequent physiological and subjective responses was investigated. After the administration of a formal hypnotic induction procedure, each of 40 adult subjects was given (a) the suggestion that the back of one hand had been burned accidentally and (b) repeated suggestions that a blister was forming there. Although no blisters were evident as a result of this procedure, two of the subjects exhibited skin changes. Localized inflammation and swelling of the skin observed in one subject was attributed to self-injury. Localized inflammation observed in the other subject was interpreted as having a possible relationship to a genuine skin injury that the subject had suffered in the past. It was suggested that future research focus on the assessment of subjects with either (a) highly sensitive skin, or (b) a previous history of skin injury relevant to blister formation.

More than a dozen studies have ostensibly shown that localized blisters can be produced by verbal suggestions given to hypnotized subjects (Borelli, 1953; Doswald & Kreibich, 1906; Foachon, 1886; Hadfield, 1917; Heller & Schultz, 1909; Jendrassik, 1888; Krafft-Ebing, 1889; Podiapolski, 1909; Rybalkin, 1890; Schindler, 1927; Smirnoff, 1912; Ullman, 1947; Wells, 1944; Wetterstrand, 1915). In general, this purported relationship between blister formation and hypnotic suggestion has been accepted by recent writers (Brown, 1974; Waters, 1971; Weil, 1972) and has even been incorporated into introductory textbooks on psychology (cf CRM, 1972; McConnell, 1974). Consider the following:

. . . a demonstration . . . has been made again and again in hypnotic subjects — one whose significance has been badly missed for decades by medical scientists. If a subject in a good trance is touched by a finger represented to him as a piece of hot metal, an authentic blister will develop at the point of contact. The blister is real [Weil, 1972, p. 160].

and,

[1] This study was supported by a grant (MH21294) from the National Institute of Mental Health. We are indebted to Joseph Albert, M.D. for serving as medical consultant to this project. In additon, we thank Shirley R. Aleo, John F. Chaves, Martin W. Ham, and Nicholas P. Spanos for helpful comments on earlier drafts of the paper.

[2] Requests for reprints should be sent to Dr. R.F.Q. Johnson, The Medfield Foundation, Medfield, Massachusetts 02052.

The power of the mind over the body can produce effects which seem almost magical.

Consider: a subject in hypnotic trance is told that his arm will be touched with a red-hot rod — the experimenter then touches him lightly with a pencil. What happens? A heat blister appears; it is exactly the same sort of blister that would have appeared had the subject actually been burned [Waters, 1971, p. 31].

Nevertheless, investigators who have critically reviewed this phenomenon (Barber. 1961; Hull, 1933; Pattie, 1941; Paul. 1963; Sarbin, 1956; Weitzenhoffer, 1953) agree that all reports to date should be viewed only as pilot studies. They point out that, although it may be physiologically possible for localized blisters to be produced by hypnotic suggestion, most of the supporting evidence has been gathered under severely limited conditions.

Some of the problems characteristic of past investigations can be illustrated by briefly describing a study presented by Ullman (1947). Ullman's subject had previously been cured of hysterical blindness and had previously shown herpetic blisters after hypnotic stimulation. This subject was hypnotized and induced to recall a battle in which he had recently participated. He was then given the suggestion that a small particle of molten shell fragment had glanced off the dorsum of his hand. At this point in the procedure, the experimenter brushed the hand with a small flat file to add emphasis to the suggestion. Pallor followed immediately in the circumscribed area. After about 20 minutes a narrow red margin was evident about the area of pallor and after one hour the beginning of a blister was noticeable. The subject was then dismissed and returned approximately four hours later; at this time a full blister about one centimeter in diameter was evident. The subject was not observed during the intervening period.

Regardless of the particular procedure used, virtually all past studies are subject to the following limitations:

1. Adequate precautions were not taken to insure that the blister was not formed by the subject injuring himself. Even when care was taken in past studies to cover the test site with a bandage, subjects were found who tried to form a blister by irritating the skin through the bandage.

2. Subjects were often exposed to some sort of mechanical stimulation at the target site (e.g., the stroke of a file, the pressing of a coin against the skin), allowing for the possibility that any observed skin change could be a result of mechanical stimulation, or contact dermatitis.

3. The subjects were often highly hypnotizable, or "somnambulistic," individuals. Thus, no assessment was made of medium and low hypnotizable subjects' responses to suggestions for blister formation.

4. With few exceptions, the subjects possessed a high level of skin sensitivity, or had a history of hives, eczema, hysterical ecchymoses, etc. Thus, no assessment was made of relative skin sensitivity and its relationship to response to suggestions for blister formation.

5. With one exception (Doswald & Kreibich, 1906), all reports have involved the examination of only one subject or patient, thus making the findings even more difficult to generalize.

The purpose of the present investigation was to attempt to produce localized, nonherpetic blisters by means of hypnotic suggestions, while at the same time controlling for the limitations of prior investigations. During the present study: (a) The experimenter directly observed the subject, and thereby controlled for the possibility that a blister may have been formed by self-injurious behavior. (b) In order to control for extraneous effects, such as mechanical stimulation and bias, an analogous skin area on the body was monitored along with thes test site. Except for the suggestions that a blister would from at the site, the control site was treated exactly the same as the test site; in addition, the experimenter was kept blind as to the identity of the test site until the experiment was over. (c) In order to assess the influence of varying levels of hypnotizability, all subjects were evaluated on a standard scale of hypnotizability. (d) In order to assess the influence of varying levels of skin sensitivity, a dermatological history and a test for dermographism was completed for each subject. (e) Lastly, in order to assess the various possible skin changes that might occur as a result of the suggestions, notations were made not only of blisters but also of erythema, wheals, and changes in skin temperature at both the test and control sites.

METHOD

Subjects

Forty-eight student nurses were asked to participate in a "study involving hypnosis and dermatology," for which they would each be paid $4.00. Forty, or 84%, of these nurses volunteered (39 females and 1 male). None had had prior experience with hypnotic procedures. During a pretest session, all 40 subjects (a) were administered the Harvard Group Scale of Hypnotic Susceptibility: Form A (Shor & Orne, 1962), (b) were asked to fill out a dermatological history questionnaire, and (c) were administered the clinical test for dermographism (Lewis, 1927). The mean score on the Harvard Group Scale was 7.1, with a range of 1-12; only one subject demonstrated the full triple response (dermographism); and 19 of the 40 subjects had at some time in the past been professionally treated and/or diagnosed for a skin ailment.

Procedure

The procedure was the same for all subjects; each subject came to the laboratory for an individual test session with the experimenter (RFQJ). At the beginning of the test session, the subject was fully informed of the nature of the study, with particular emphasis placed upon the fact that it involved the production of a skin blister by hypnotic techniques. In order to familiarize the subject with the nature of the suggestion to be used, she was asked to read a brief passage from Weil (1972, Pp. 160–161) which was quoted in part in the introduction to this paper. At this point, the protocol called for the dismissal of any subject who showed gross signs of nervousness or doubt concerning participation in the study; however, since none behaved in this manner, none was dismissed. After being made fully aware of the nature of the study, the subject was asked to read and to sign an informed consent agreement.

Assignment of the skin area to be tested. The subject was then told that the test site was to be the dorsum of one of her hands, and that only she would know during the test which hand it was; the experimenter was to remain "blind" concerning the identity of the skin area to be tested. The subject was given a "secret envelope" which she was told to open and to read. The "secret envelope" contained a note informing the subject which hand was to be considered the "test hand" (*i.e.*, the hand eventually to serve as the site for the suggestions for blister formation). The envelopes had been prepared beforehand and placed in a random order, half of them indicating that the test hand would be the nondominant hand. The experimenter remained blind as to the identity of the test hand until the test session was over.

Equipment. Life-size color photographs were then made of the dorsum of each hand by means of a Polaroid CU-5 laboratory camera. After photographs were made, thermistors were attached (with hypoallergenic Dermicel tape) to the dorsum of each hand. Temperature readings accurate to 0.1°C were made from a Yellow Springs telethermometer Model 46 TUC. Room temperature was monitored on a separate channel; during the study room temperature ranged between 21° and 27°C, but never varied more than 2°C during any one particular session. The subject was then asked to lie down on a couch for the remainder of the test session.

Hypnotic induction and suggestion for blister formation. The experimenter then administered a formal hypnotic induction procedure (adapted from Barber, 1969), consisting of repeated suggestions of relaxation, drowsiness, sleep, and "hypnosis." This was immediately followed by a series of three "warm-up" test suggestions (arm lowering, arm levitation, and thirst hallucination) derived from the Barber Suggestibility Scale (Barber, 1969). At this point, initial temperature readings were made, with four more readings being made at five minute intervals during the remaining 20 minutes of the session. The suggestion for blister formation was then begun. The subject was given the suggestion that she was in her kitchen at home, that it was morning, and that bacon was being cooked in a red hot frying pan. It was then suggested that she was burned on the back of her test hand, when she accidentally touched the frying pan. Excerpts from the suggestion include:

. . . the red hot frying pan touches the back of your test hand, right where the temperature sensing device is . . . the frying pan burns the back of your hand. Concentrate on the sharp, burning pain there . . . You move away from the frying pan now . . . But you can still feel the burning sensation . . . Soon a blister will form there — right where the temperature sensing device is . . . A blister is forming there.

Assessment of blister hallucination and blister formation. This suggestion was administered for five minutes, whereupon the subject was asked to report whether or not she felt the blister forming (blister hallucination). The experimenter then continued to administer the blister suggestion for another five minutes, whereupon the subject was again asked if she felt the blister forming. At the conclusion of an additional 10 minutes of suggestions for blister formation (20 minutes of suggestions for blister formation in all), the thermistors were removed and both hands were examined for any visible skin changes. The experimenter then told the subject:

I will now count backwards from five to one; when I reach one, you will be wide awake, refreshed, and your test hand will be normal again, just like the other one. No more pain, no more burning, . . . Completely normal again . . . Five, four, three, two, *one!* Wide awake! Fully awake!

Judgment of being hypnotized. At this point, prior to being permitted to view the backs of her own hands, the subject was given a formal questionnaire on which she was asked to report whether or not she felt

she had been hypnotized during the test session.

Photographs were then taken of the dorsum of each hand, the subject was told not to tell others that the study concerned the production of a skin blister, and lastly the subject was asked to return on the following day for a final set of photographs and for her pay.

On the following day, the subject's hands were examined for any indication of skin reaction (blister, wheal, inflammation, etc.). Photographs were again taken, and the subject was paid and dismissed. If the subject did show a reaction at this session, she was extensively interviewed in order to ascertain what may have caused the reaction (particularly, self-injurious behavior), and she was followed closely until the skin reaction disappeared.

RESULTS

Physiological Effects: Visible Skin Changes

Of the 40 subjects, none exhibited a fully developed blister. Two of the subjects, however, did demonstrate visible skin changes.

S-2 showed no visible skin reaction during the test session. However, upon returning 24 hours later (for her pay and a final set of photographs), the dorsum of her test hand (dominant-left) was inflamed and slightly swollen. She reported that the skin at the test site had been "itching" ever since the test session and that she had been scratching it in order to relieve the itch. The test site was bandaged, and S-2 was told that the itching would probably go away within 24 hours. Upon returning three days later (She could not come back sooner because she was leaving town for two days.), she reported that the itching had gone away within the ensuing 24 hours, as the experimenter had suggested. Her test hand no longer presented any inflammation or swelling. During the entire 4 days the control hand exhibited no visible skin reaction. S-2 had passed 11 of the 12 items on the Harvard Group Scale of Hypnotic Susceptibility, rated herself as being hypnotized during the test session, reported that she felt the blister forming on the back of her test hand, and reported on the dermatological history questionnaire that she had been successfully treated for plantar warts five years earlier. During the test session, each hand dropped 0.2°C.

S-11 showed inflammation at and around the test site during the final 15 minutes that the verbal suggestions for blister formation were being administered. The inflammation was bright red, formed an irregular pattern over the dorsum of the test hand (non-dominant-left), and covered approximately 75% of the area including part of the index finger to the first knuckle. The boundary between the inflamed and uninflamed portions was sharp and easily visible to both the experimenter and the subject. The inflammation disappeared within three minutes of the completion of the suggestion for blister formation. The control hand exhibited no visible skin change. S-11 passed 5 of the 12 items on the Harvard Group Scale of Hypnotic Susceptibility, rated herself as being hypnotized during the session, reported that she felt the blister forming, and reported no prior history of being treated for a skin ailment. S-11 did report, however, that she had been burned by hot grease on that very spot six years earlier and that the outline of the inflammation coincided with the burned area as she recalled it. During the 20-minute verbal suggestion for blister formation the temperature of her test hand dropped 0.2°C, while the temperature of her control hand dropped 0.5°C.

The remaining 38 subjects exhibited no visible skin reaction at the test site either during the test session or at the 24-hour follow-up session.

Physiological Effects: Temperature Changes

The mean change in temperature of the test hand and the mean change in temperature of the control hand from just before the administration of the suggestion to five, 10, 15, and 20 minutes (completion) later are presented in Table 1 for all subjects. The results of an analysis of variance of these

TABLE 1

MEAN CHANGE IN SKIN TEMPERATURE (°C) DURING THE 20 MINUTES OF SUGGESTIONS FOR BLISTER FORMATION

Mean Change After:	Test Hand	Control Hand
5 minutes	+ .08	+ .10
10 minutes	+ .26	+ .31
15 minutes	+ .50	+ .41
20 minutes	+ .59	+ .55

data showed that, while the temperature of both hands increased over time ($F = 10.94$, $df = 3/117, p < .001$,) the test hand did not differ from the control hand with respect to this temperature change ($F < 1$). In addition, no statistically significant differences were found between the temperature change of the test hand and the temperature change of the control hand when the data were analyzed separately for (a) only those subjects who rated themselves as having been hypnotized during the test session, (b) only those subjects who scored above the median - 7 - on the Harvard Group Scale of Hypnotic Susceptibility, (c) only those subjects who reported feeling a blister forming (blister hallucination), and (d) only those subjects who reported a history of having been treated and/or diagnosed for a skin ailment. Even when the data were analyzed separately for only those subjects who *simultaneously* scored above the median on the Harvard Group Scale, rated themselves as being hypnotized during the test session, and reported feeling a blister forming, *no* temperature differences were found between the test hand and the control hand ($N = 12$, eight of whom had been professionally treated or diagnosed for a skin ailment at least once in the past).

Subjective Effects: Blister Hallucination

Eighteen of the 40 subjects reported upon the first inquiry that they felt the blister forming on the back of the test hand. After an additional five minutes of suggestions that the blister was forming, nine more subjects reported that they felt the blister forming on the back of the test hand. The remaining 13 subjects did not report at any time that they felt a blister forming on the back of the test hand. The two subjects who did demonstrate some visible skin reaction at the test site, S-2 and S-11, were among the 18 subjects who reported upon the first inquiry that they felt a blister forming on the back of the test hand.

Subjective Effects: Report of Being Hypnotized

At the immediate close of the hypnosis part of the test session, each subject was asked to state whether or not she had been hypnotized. Twenty-seven of the 40 subjects reported that they had been hypnotized during the test session. The two subjects who had demonstrated a visible skin reaction to the suggestion for blister formation, S-2 and S-11, were among those subjects who reported that they had been hypnotized. A point-biserial correlation coefficient between this self report of being hypnotized and each subject's score of the Harvard Group Scale of Hypnotic Susceptibility was significant: $r_{pb} = .38$, $p < .01$.

DISCUSSION

Most prior studies which have reported successful attempts to produce blister formation by hypnotic suggeston did not control for the possibility that subsequent blister formation may have been due to self-injurious behavior, a preexisting labile skin condition, extraneous mechanical stimulation at the test site, contact dermatitis, etc. (Barber, 1961; Paul, 1963). The present investigation is the first attempt to produce blister formation by hypnotic suggestion, while at the same time controlling for the major limitaitons of past studies.

The results of the present investigation were that the administration of hypnotic suggestions for blister formation did *not* produce blisters. Since inflammation under normal conditions is often associated with a rise in skin temperature (Lewis, 1927), it was expected that there may at least be

some systematic changes in skin temperature at the test site (which differed from changes at the control site) that would indicate a preliminary stage of inflammation. However, *no* such systematic changes in skin temperature were observed for the group. One might argue that not enough good hypnotic subjects were included, and therefore any positive response to the suggestion for blister formation by the good hypnotic subjects may have been obscured by the analysis. However, even when separate analyses were performed on those 12 subjects who *simultaneously* (a) had scored above the median on the Harvard Group Scale of Hypnotic Susceptibility, (b) had reported that they were hypnotized during the test session, and (c) had reported that they felt a blister forming at the test site (blister hallucination), no systematic changes in skin temperature at the test site were found that differed from temperature changes at the control site.

Only two subjects, S-2 and S-11, exhibited visible skin changes at the target site. The reactions of these subjects, however, did not appear to be solely due to the administration of verbal suggestions for blister formation in a hypnotic setting. Let us now turn our discussion to possible explanations for the responses of these two subjects.

The Role of Self-Injurious Behavior

As has been noted by previous writers (Barber, 1961; Pattie, 1941; Paul, 1963; Weitzenhoffer, 1953), self-injurious behavior, as the cause of any skin change subsequent to suggestions for blister formation, is to be considered a possibility if the subject is permitted to remain unobserved during the test. In the present study S-2 was the only subject who showed any swelling at the target site, and she did so only after being left unobserved for 24 hours. That the inflammation and swelling was caused by self-injurious behavior rather than the hypnotic suggestions *per se* was made obvious when the subject reported that she had been scratching the skin at the test site during those 24 hours.

In the present study it is possible that if the subject had scratched the skin any more vigorously or any more frequently than she actually did, a blister might have formed at the test site (Lewis, 1927). Past and future studies which permit the subject to be left unobserved, even if for only a very brief period of time, must remain open to the possibility that any inflammation, swelling, or blistering of the skin may be due to self-injurious behavior (and not necessarily due to hypnotic suggestions for blister formation). Wolberg (1948,1972), for example, once suggested to a hypnotic subject that hives would develop on the forearms. Although no hives were observed, the subject did demonstrate a "markedly irritated skin" several days later. The subject denied that he had in any way irritated the skin. However, during a subsequent hypnotic session, the subject confided that he had taken a walk in the woods, "picked poison ivy and rubbed it vigorously on the inner surfaces of his arms [1972, p. 126]."

The Role of Prior Skin Injuries

S-11 was the only other subject to demonstrate a visible skin reaction at the test site. Unlike S-2, however, S-11 exhibited a visible skin reaction *prior* to any opportunity for self-injury. Therefore, (a) since the skin reaction occurred while she was being observed, and (b) since her control hand was treated in exactly the same manner as the test hand, the possibilities that the skin reaction was due to self-injurious behavior, extraneous mechanical stimulation by the experimenter, or contact dermatitis due to the presence of the tape and/or the thermistor can be excluded.

In an attempt to explain blister formation by hypnotic suggestion, Weitzenhoffer (1953) has made two points: First, he has noted that tissue damage is not a necessary condition for blister formation. Reports in the literature (Brandt, 1950; Graff & Wallerstein, 1954; Moody, 1946, 1948) indicate that skin changes may result when an individual recalls an emotional experience in which dermatological changes (including wheals and blisters) occurred. Second,

Weitzenhoffer has noted that vasomotor responses can be conditioned. Menzies (1937, 1941) has reported the conditioning of vasomotor responses to a variety of stimuli in human subjects. In fact, he reported the apparent conditioning of vasodilation to "imagining extreme heat" at a skin area which had previously undergone extreme heat. Weitzenhoffer has suggested that,

blister formation as a result of suggestion is probably a conditioned response, in which the re-experiencing of sensory or other elements associated on past occasions with situations causing blisters brings about reflexedly the somatic changes that were once associated with the same elements [1953, p. 296].

Furthermore, Weitzenhoffer has proposed two requirements for blister formation by suggestion:

First, for the suggestion to be effective the subject must have previously experienced traumatic situations leading to blister formation. Second the success of the experiment would depend considerably on the subject's re-experiencing vividly such a past experience, or at least some of the elements involved in it [1953, p. 298].

It will be noted that S-11 fulfilled both of Weitzenhoffer's requirements for positive response to suggestions for blister formation. She not only reported that six years earlier she had been burned by hot grease *at the test site*, but she also reported that she felt the blister forming (blister hallucination) and that many of the suggested elements were the same as those that had existed when she had been burned six years earlier (*i.e.*, both the original burn and the suggested burn included either actual or imaginal elements involving an accident in the kitchen in which the subject is burned while cooking). Weitzenhoffer's proposed explanation for blister formation by suggestion receives some support as a result of these observations. Clearly, further research is warranted.

Suggestions for Further Research

Blister formation subsequent to suggestions for its occurrence was not observed in this study. However, the possibility that blister formation *may* at times occur subsequent to its suggestion is not excluded. The results of the present investigation suggest two lines of research be pursued.

Assess subjects with high skin sensitivity. One possible explanation for the failure to obtain blister formation is that, in spite of the fact that one-half of the subjects had a prior history of professional treatment for various skin disorders, none of the subjects had highly sensitive skin (Beahrs, Harris, & Hilgard, 1970). Only one of our subjects displayed dermographism, and none had a dermatological history indicating high skin sensitivity, such as hysterical ecchymoses, hysterical anesthesia, "delicate skin," etc. Most subjects who were reported to have responded positively in past studies did have such a history (Hadfield, 1917; Krafft-Ebing, 1889; Rybalkin, 1890; Schindler, 1927; Ullman, 1947; Wetterstrand, 1915). One possibility for future research includes a study comparing the responses of normal subjects with the responses of subjects with high skin sensitivity. More specifically, the present study could be repeated with the addition of a second group of subjects for comparison; this second group of subjects would consist of patients from a dermatology clinic who have been preselected for high skin sensitivity.

Assess subjects who have previously experienced relevant skin injuries. Another line of investigation pertains to the possibility that Weitzenhoffer's (1953) explanation of blister formation by suggestion is correct. A study could be conducted in which Weitzenhoffer's requirements for positive response are fulfilled. Specifically, the present study could be repeated using only subjects who (a) have experienced a traumatic situation leading to a blister and (b) report re-experiencing vividly such a past experience during the suggestion for blister formation. This investigation could be accomplished in one of two ways. First, a study could be conducted similar to the present one, with the exception that only subjects are tested who at one time in the *natural situation* had a skin injury that involved blister formation. The experimenter would obtain details pertinent to the time, place, and situation (accidental, criminal, etc.) in which the injury occurred, and then incorporate these details into the suggestion for blister formation. An alternative method would involve the experimental production of a blister *in the laboratory* (*e.g.*, by means of radiant heat from a Hardy-Wolff-Goodell dolorimeter) and the subsequent vivid recall of the injury after the blister healed. Although this latter method requires that some serious ethical problems first be resolved, it does offer the advantage of control over the magnitude of the initial skin injury, the precise amount of stimulus energy required to produce it, and the conditions under which it occurred.

Lastly, if the formation of blisters were to be observed during one of these suggested studies, parametric studies would then be required in order to determine the necessary and sufficient conditions for blister formation by verbal suggestion. This would include determining the necessity of using hypnotic techniques when administering the suggestions for blister formation; past studies have indicated that the administration of a hypnotic induction procedure prior to the verbal suggestion for blister formation may *not* be required (Barber, 1961; Pattie, 1941; Paul, 1963; Schindler, 1927).

REFERENCES

BARBER, T. X. Physiological effects of "hypnosis." *Psychological Bulletin*, 1961, 58. 390–419.

BARBER, T. X. *Hypnosis: A scientific approach.* New York: Van Nostrand Reinhold, 1969.

BEAHRS, J. O., HARRIS, D. R., & HILGARD, E. R. Failure to alter skin inflammation by hypnotic suggestion in five subjects with normal skin reactivity. *Psychosomatic Medicine*, 1970, 32, 627–631.

BORELLI, S. Psychische Einflusse und reactive Hauterscheinungen. *Munchener Medizinische Wochenschrift*, 1953, 95, 1078–1082.

BRANDT, B. A tentative classification of psychological factors in the etiology of skin diseases. *Journal of Investigative Dermatology*, 1950, 14, 81–90.

BROWN, R. *New mind, new body; biofeedback: New directions for the mind.* New York: Harper & Row, 1974.

CRM. *Psychology today: An introduction. (2nd Ed.)* Del Mar, California: CRM Books, 1972.

DOSWALD, D. C. & KREIBICH, K. Zur Frage der posthypnotischen Hautphanomene. *Monatschefte Fuer Praktische Dermatologie*, 1906, 43, 634–640.

FOCACHON, 1886. In H. Bernheim. *Hypnosis and suggestion in psychotherapy.* New York: Jason Aronson, Inc., 1973 (translated from the second edition published in 1886). Pp. 75–77.

GRAFF, N. I. & WALLERSTEIN, R. S. Unusual wheal reaction in a tattoo. *Psychosomatic Medicine*, 1954, 16, 505–515.

HADFIELD, J. A. The influence of suggestion on body temperature. *Lancet*, 1917, 2, 678–679.

HELPER, F. & SCHULTZ, J. H. Ueber einen Fall hypnotisch erzeuter Blasenbildung. *Munchener Medizinische Wochenschrift*, 1909, 56, 2112.

HULL, C. L. *Hypnosis and suggestibility: An experimental approach.* New York: Appleton-Century-Crofts, 1933.

JENDRASSIK, E. Einiges uber suggestion. *Neurologisches Zentralblatt*, 1888, 7, 281–283, 321–330.

KRAFT-EBING, R. VON. *Eine experimentelle Studie auf dem Gebiete des Hypnotismus.* (2nd Edition) Stuttgart: 1889. Pp. 26–27, 58–59.

LEWIS, T. *The blood vessels of the human skin and their responses.* London: Shaw, 1927.

MCCONNELL, J. V. *Understanding human behavior.* New York: Holt, Rinehart, and Winston, 1974.

MENZIES, R. Conditioned vasomotor responses in human subjects. *Journal of Psychology*, 1937, 4, 75–120.

MENZIES, R. Further studies of conditioned vasomotor responses in human subjects. *Journal of Experimental Psychology*, 1941, 29, 457–482.

MOODY, R. L. Bodily changes during abreaction. *Lancet*, 1946, 2, 934–935.

MOODY, R. L. Bodily changes during abreaction. *Lancet*, 1948, 1, 964.

PATTIE, F. A., JR. The production of blisters by hypnotic suggestion: A review. *Journal of Abnormal and Social Psychology*, 1941, 36, 62–72.

PAUL, G. L. The production of blisters by hypnotic suggestion: Another look. *Psychosomatic Medicine*, 1963, 25, 233–244.

PODIAPOLSKI, P. P. [Vasomotor disturbances produced by hypnotic suggestion.] *Zhurnal Neuropatologii i Psikhiatrii*, 1909, 9, 101–109.

RYBALKIN, J. Brulure du second degree provoquee par suggestion. *Revue de Hypnotisme et de la Psychologie Physiologique*, 1890, 4, 361–362.

SARBIN, T. R. Physiological effects of hypnotic stimulation. In Dorcus, R. M. *Hypnosis and its therapeutic applications.* New York: McGraw-Hill, 1956.

SCHINDLER, R. *Nervensystem und spontane Blutange*, Berlin: Karger, 1927.

SHOR, R. E. & ORNE, E. C. *Harvard group scale of hypnotic susceptibility: Form A.* Palo Alto, California: Consulting Psychologists Press, 1962.

SMIRNOFF, D. Zur Frage der durch hypnotische Suggestion hervorgerufenen vasomotorischen Storungen. *Zeitschrift fuer Psychotherapie und Medizinische Psychologie*, 1912, 4, 171–175.

ULLMAN, M. Herpes simplex and second degree burn induced under hypnosis. *American Journal of Psychiatry*, 1947, 103, 828–830.

WATERS, T. A. *Psychologistics: An operating manual for the mind.* New York: Random House, 1971.

WEIL, A. *The natural mind.* Boston: Houghton Mifflin, 1972.

WEITZENHOFFER, A. *Hypnotism: An objective study in suggestibility.* New York: Wiley, 1953.

WELLS, W. R. The hypnotic treatment of the major symptoms of hysteria: A case study. *Journal of Psychology*, 1944, 77, 269–297.

WETTERSTRAND, 1915. In S. Alrutz, Die suggestive Vesikation. *Journal Fuer Psychologie und Neurologie*, 1915, 21, 1–10.

WOLBERG, L. R. *Medical hypnosis.* New York: Grune & Stratton, 1948.

WOLBERG, L. R. *Hypnosis: Is it for you?* New York: Harcourt, Brace, & Jovanovich, 1972.

The Influence of Presleep Suggestions on Dream Content

11

Priscilla Campbell Walker
and R. F. Q. Johnson

Both experimental and clinical data have indicated that with some subjects the administration of presleep suggestions to dream on a specific topic can influence the content of nocturnal dreams. This relationship has been found to occur regardless of whether or not the dream reports are solicited upon awakening in the morning, upon awakening from rapid eye movement (REM) sleep, or upon awakening from nonrapid eye movement (NREM) sleep. Adequate specification of the relationship between presleep suggestions and dream content has been hindered by a variety of methodological problems, such as inadequate assessment techniques, dream reports of questionable validity, and the confounding of suggested effects with other effects. Failure to recognize that there are nocturnal mental activities other than the dream has also impeded progress. Promising directions for future research are discussed.

During the past 80 years, researchers have made sporadic attempts to assess the influence of presleep suggestions to dream about a specific topic (Barber & Calverley, 1962; Barber, Walker, & Hahn, 1973; Fisher, 1953; Nachmansohn, 1925; Newman, Katz, & Rubenstein, 1960; Schroetter, 1911; Stoyva, 1961; Tart, 1964; Tart & Dick, 1970; Titchener, 1895). Typically, the subject is told that if he tries to the best of his ability he will be able to dream on a preselected topic. The subject often receives no further instructions concerning exactly how he is to

accomplish this task. He is awakened during the night or on the following morning and is asked to report the content of his dreams. On the basis of such studies, claims have been made that the administration of presleep suggestions to dream on a specific topic increases the probability that the subject will dream on that topic.

Following a review of the available data, the methodological problems associated with this area of research are discussed. Although recognition of these methodological shortcomings severely limits the generalizability of past research, it suggests promising directions for future research.

EFFECTS OF PRESLEEP SUGGESTIONS ON THE CONTENT OF DREAMS

Studies on the effects of presleep suggestions to dream on a specific topic can be divided into two groups. One group consists of studies in which the individual is asked

[1] Writing of this paper was supported in part by Grant MH 21294 from the National Institute of Mental Health. The authors are indebted to T. X. Barber for valuable comments on earlier drafts of this article.

[2] Requests for reprints should be sent to R. F. Q. Johnson, Medfield Foundation, Medfield, Massachusetts 02052.

to report the content of his dream upon awakening in the morning. The other group consists of studies in which dream reports are solicited from the individual during the night. Each group is discussed in turn.

Studies Using Morning Recall

In 1911, Schroetter reported that he was able to influence dream content by "hypnotic suggestion." [3] Two female subjects were hypnotized, given suggestions to dream on a specific topic, dehypnotized, and then, on the following morning, asked to report the content of their dreams. The subjects successfully responded on four separate occasions. For example, prior to sleep, Schroetter suggested to one subject that the size of objects would be abnormally small in the first part of her dream and abnormally large in the second part. On the next day the subject reported that she had been small enough to crawl through the eye of a needle at the beginning of her dream and that she had been extremely large, as if magnified by a magnifying glass, during the second part of her dream. Making use of a similar hypnotic procedure, Nachmansohn (1925) also reported the successful response by hypnotized female subjects to presleep suggestions to dream on a specific topic. [4]

More recently, Fisher (1953) presented data to indicate that presleep suggestions need not be preceded by a hypnotic induction procedure in order to be effective. Fisher solicited dream reports from: (a) five subjects who were personal friends of his and who had been given a total of six dream suggestions in nonexperimental settings; (b) one hypnotic subject who had received 21 dream suggestions; and (c) six psychoanalytic patients who, on separate occasions, had received a total of 95 suggestions to dream on specific topics. As a control, the six psychoanalytic patients were asked to

give a total of 60 dream reports on mornings when they had not been given any prior dream suggestions. The proportion of dreams that were clearly related to the specified topic was 33% for the personal friends, 14% for the hypnotic subject, 12% for the psychoanalytic patients on experimental days, and 3% for the psychoanalytic patients on control days. Fisher concluded that regardless of the presence or absence of the hypnotic trance, the interpersonal relationship between the experimenter and the subject plays an important role in the response to dream suggestions. Fisher's experiment is limited by the fact that it was not performed in a rigorous fashion; as has been pointed out by Barber (1962), only one hypnotic subject was used, the suggested dream topic varied with each presentation, and the data were not treated statistically.

Nevertheless a subsequent study by Barber and Calverley (1962) did provide support for Fisher's (1953) findings. In their experiment, 6 hypnotic subjects and 11 nonhypnotic subjects were administered presleep suggestions to dream about riding a bicycle. A separate group of 35 control subjects, who had received neither a hypnotic induction nor suggestions to dream on a particular topic, were asked to record any dreams that occurred during the next night. Data analysis showed that the presleep suggestion influenced the dream reports of the hypnotic subjects and the nonhypnotic subjects to an equal degree. In agreement with Fisher, Barber and Calverley concluded that (a) the administration of presleep suggestions to dream on a specific topic is effective with some subjects in influencing nocturnal dream content, and (b) the administration of a hypnotic induction procedure is not a necessary condition for subjects to respond to presleep suggestions to dream on a specific topic.

A serendipitous finding in another study has indicated that aspects of the experimental situation other than presleep suggestions may affect nocturnal dream content. While carrying out a series of attempts to influence the night dreams of one hypnotic subject, Newman, Katz, and Rubenstein (1960) found that oftentimes the dreams of their subject included elements of the hypnotic test situation itself—the furniture in the experimental room, the hypnotist, the building, and so forth. Similar findings have been found in

---

[3] Throughout this article, hypnotic suggestion refers to a suggestion that has been preceded by the administration of a "hypnotic induction procedure," (i.e., suggestions that the subject is becoming more and more relaxed, drowsy, sleepy, and is entering a hypnotic state.)

[4] Three early writings concerning attempts to influence dream content are not reviewed here because one was a novel (Van Eeden, 1909), one was a diary (Hervey de Saint-Denis, 1867), and the other was unclear as to procedure (Titchener, 1895).

subsequent investigations (Bertini, Lewis, & Witkin, 1964; Witkin & Lewis, 1965).

In brief, studies that use morning recall as a method for soliciting dream reports indicate that (*a*) with some subjects, the administration of presleep suggestions to dream on a specific topic can influence the contents of nocturnal dreams; (*b*) the hypnotic induction procedure is not a necessary antecedent condition for dream suggestions to be effective; and (*c*) the experimental setting itself and the interpersonal relationship between the experimenter and the subject may play important roles in effecting changes in dream reports.

Studies Using Night Recall

Data from several recent investigations indicate that nocturnal dreams chiefly occur when the subject shows rapid eye movement (REM) together with a Stage 1 electroencephalographic (EEG) pattern (Dement & Kleitman, 1957a, 1957b). The probability that a subject will recall a dream when awakened from Stage 1 REM sleep is approximately 84%, whereas by the morning-recall method the probability is approximately 37.5% (cf. Webb, 1973, pp. 734–748).[5] In addition, the typical subject exhibits an average of four to six Stage 1 REM periods per night. Thus by soliciting dream reports from subjects who are awakened from Stage 1 REM, researchers are able to study more directly the effects of suggestions on dream content.

Next follows a discussion of those studies in which the effects of presleep suggestions

---

[5] Originally researchers of sleep and dreaming (Dement & Kleitman, 1957a, 1957b) found that when awakened from REM, subjects would report approximately 84% of the time that they were dreaming or that they had just finished a dream. When the subject was awakened from NREM, the incidence of dream recall was originally reported to be approximately 7%. Subsequent research has shown that recall of NREM mental activity can range from 23% to 74% (Foulkes, 1967), whereas Stage 1 REM recall of mental activity can range from 60% to 88% (Hartmann, 1967). Although it was at one time thought that dreams were associated only with REM, it is now clear that dream reports are also associated with NREM. The exact nature of the difference (if there is a difference) between REM and NREM mental activity remains an unresolved issue (cf. Stoyva & Kamiya, 1968; Webb, 1973).

were examined by means of the night-recall method (Barber et al., 1973; Stoyva, 1961; Tart, 1964; Tart & Dick, 1970). In each of these studies, the subjects were given presleep suggestions to dream on a specified topic and then were awakened at REM periods during the night and asked to give dream reports. In some of these studies, the subjects were also awakened during nonrapid eye movement (NREM) periods; the results of the solicitations of NREM dream reports (which are usually reported to be more like thoughts than dreams) are also discussed.

In 1961, Stoyva reported a study of 16 highly hypnotizable subjects. Each subject was administered presleep suggestions on six or more experimental nights. Sometimes the presleep suggestions were given in conjunction with a standard hypnotic induction procedure and sometimes they were not. Subjects reported dreams on the suggested topic under both the hypnotic and the nonhypnotic conditions. When they had received the hypnotic treatment, however, a larger proportion of the subjects (44%) reported frequent dreaming on the suggested topic than when they had received the nonhypnotic treatment (25%). Stoyva concluded that the hypnotic trance is not necessary to produce dreaming in accordance with presleep suggestions but that the use of hypnosis appears to increase the probability that the subject will dream in accordance with the topic suggested. An important additional finding was that Stage 1 REM dreaming was not the only nocturnal mental activity affected by the presleep suggestions; awakenings at Stages 2, 3, and 4 also yielded dreams on the suggested topic.

A confounding variable in Stoyva's study has been pointed out by Barber et al. (1973). Specifically, the presleep suggestions with hypnosis were given in a repeated and emphatic manner, whereas the presleep suggestions without hypnosis were given in a simple "by the way," nonemphatic manner. Consequently, based on Stoyva's data alone, it is highly questionable whether presleep suggestions with hypnosis are more effective than presleep suggestions without hypnosis.

Data from two subsequent studies (Tart, 1964; Tart & Dick, 1970) also indicated that presleep suggestions given in conjunction with a hypnotic induction procedure can increase the probability of dreaming on a selected topic. More importantly, attempts were made in both of these studies to assess quantitatively the extent to which each individual's dream was influenced by the presleeep suggestion. This was done by counting the number of elements from the suggested topic that appeared in each dream. In both studies, it was found that although a minimum of 50% of the subjects dreamed on the suggested topic, only a few of the potential number of elements were present in each dream. Unfortunately neither study made use of an independent control group consisting of nonhypnotic subjects who received suggestions to dream on a specified topic.

In the most recent study under review, Barber et al. (1973) examined the effects of hypnotic induction and wording of presleep suggestions by means of a 2 × 3 factorial experiment. Half of the subjects (77 randomly selected females) were exposed to a hypnotic induction procedure and half were not. In addition, all subjects were given either authoritative suggestions, permissive suggestions, or no suggestions to think and dream on a specific topic (the death of President Kennedy). The authoritative suggestion included phrases such as, "You will think about and dream about the death of President Kennedy," whereas the permissive suggestion included phrases such as, "I want you to try very hard and to the very best of your ability to think about and dream about the death of President Kennedy. Please try." The subjects were awakened at sleep onset, at REM, and at least once 45 minutes after REM (NREM). Upon being awakened, each subject was asked (a) to state in detail anything that had been going through her mind just prior to waking, (b) if it was a dream or a thought, and (c) whether she had been asleep or awake.

The complex results of this study were as follows: Both hypnotic and nonhypnotic subjects who received presleep suggestions to think and dream about the death of President Kennedy thought and dreamed about the topic more often than did the control subjects (who never thought or dreamed about the topic). With respect to dreams, presleep suggestions were found to alter dream content in 25% of the subjects, regardless of whether or not they had received a hypnotic induction procedure. Also, there was a significant interaction between hypnotic induction and types of suggestions such that the presleep sugges-

tions had the greatest effect on dreams when given authoritatively to hypnotic subjects and when given permissively to nonhypnotic subjects. With respect to thoughts, presleep suggestions were found to alter thought content in 42% of the subjects regardless of whether or not they had received a hypnotic induction procedure. Also, with respect to thoughts, there was no significant interaction between hypnotic induction and type of suggestion; the hypnotic induction procedure alone, however, was more effective than no induction in increasing the number of suggested elements in the thoughts. In other words, the results of the Barber et al. study indicate that (a) presleep suggestions exert an effect not only on nocturnal dreaming but also on nocturnal thinking, (b) presleep suggestions exert an effect not only on subjects who have been exposed to a hypnotic induction procedure but also on those who have not; (c) with respect to their influence on dream reports, certain types of suggestions are more effective with hypnotic subjects, and others are more effective with nonhypnotic subjects; and (d) hypnotic subjects think about the suggested topic more often than do nonhypnotic subjects.

In brief, the results of studies using night recall of dreams indicate that (a) presleep suggestions to dream on a certain topic can influence nocturnal dream content, as reported by subjects who are awakened from Stage 1 REM sleep; (b) presleep suggestions can also influence nocturnal dream content, as reported by subjects who are awakened from NREM sleep; (c) even though there is conflicting evidence with respect to whether or not the hypnotic induction procedure facilitates response to dream suggestions, it is clear that the hypnotic induction procedure is not a necessary antecedent condition; (d) presleep suggestions to dream on a certain topic apparently affect nocturnal thoughts and dreams in different ways; and (e) subtle variables, such as the wording and phrasing of the presleep suggestions, may play a significant role in whether or not dream content is influenced.

METHODOLOGICAL PROBLEMS

It is clear from this brief review that, regardless of the method of data collection (morning recall or night recall), the administration of presleep suggestions to dream on a specific topic produces an effect on dream content. It is also clear that this relationship is not a simple one. As research has progressed, an awareness of methodological problems has increased. The following discussion of some of these methodological problems offers clues to some promising directions for future research.

Differentiation of Nocturnal Mental Activities

Recent research in the general area of sleep and dreams has indicated that a wide variety of mental activities occurs during sleep. Series of unconnected visual images and short dreamlike segments of visual imagery have been reported at sleep onset (Foulkes, 1962; Vogel, Barrowclough, & Giesler, 1972); both brief and extended dreams, or connected visual sequences, have been reported to occur throughout the night (Foulkes, 1962; Foulkes & Vogel, 1965); and a thinking type of activity, wherein the subject reports imageless mental activity that he feels he is directing, has been described as occurring both during REM and NREM sleep (Goodenough, Lewis, Shapiro, Jaret, & Sleser, 1965). Consequently, past research on the effects of presleep suggestions has been limited because most researchers have focused solely on the subject's dream reports. This is not to say that mental activities other than dreams have been totally disregarded by researchers in this area. On the contrary, Barber et al. (1973) have shown that subjects confidently discriminate between nocturnal thoughts and nocturnal dreams and that presleep suggestions are related to each of these mental activities in different ways. In addition, both Stoyva (1961) and Barber et al. have reported that presleep suggestions can affect NREM mental activity in Stages 2, 3, and 4.

Findings such as these emphasize the importance of conducting more intensive investigations that both differentiate the various types of mental activity and follow these mental activities throughout the night. Prior to the inception of programmatic studies of the effects of presleep suggestions on nocturnal mental activity, researchers should endeavor to standardize the criteria for distinguishing between a dream and a thought. In the Barber et al. study, the subject was permitted to make the distinction—this may or may not be the most desirable procedure. An alternate solution would be to permit either the subject or an independent judge to rate the reported mental activities along several dimensions, such as thoughtlike, dreamlike, vividness, bizarreness, degree of self-control, and so forth. With this latter solution, a description could be made of the subject's nocturnal mental activity without restricting the subject to only the two categories of dreams and thoughts.

In any event, it is clear that failure to differentiate types of nocturnal mental activity and failure to monitor that activity during NREM periods lead to the omission of data that have already proven to be useful in tracing the effects of presleep suggestions.

Validity of the Subject's Dream Report

In each of the studies reviewed in this article, the main dependent variable has been the subject's verbal or written recollection of his nocturnal dreams or thoughts. Because much research has indicated that personal reports of past events are subject to distortion due to normal "forgetting processes" (cf. Bartlett, 1932; McGeoch, 1942; Slamecka, 1967), one must consider the validity of such dream reports. Images and thoughts experienced during sleep are difficult for the subject to "catch," even if he is questioned immediately after being awakened. Many subjects have reported the frustrating experience of remembering a dream or thought only to have it suddenly disappear.

In addition, the personal testimony of individuals can be distorted by bias, as has been pointed out by recent writers (cf. Barber, 1973; Rosenthal, 1966). Barber (1962) has suggested the possibility that in order to comply with the wishes of the experimenter or therapist, some subjects may purposely construct, or make up, their dreams. This possibility is not so remote because in both the Fisher (1953) and the Barber and Calverley (1962) studies some subjects (both hypnotic and nonhypnotic) reported that they would awaken frequently during the night and have thoughts about the suggestions that they had been given.

Witkin (1969) suggested that in order to increase the accuracy of dream reports, the subject should be trained in dream reporting. Training would involve telling the subject ahead of time that he would be asked to give certain basic information concerning his nocturnal mental activities. This information would include not only a detailed account of his dream content but also an account of his feelings during the dream and his emotional reaction to the dream. Such a procedure would permit the experimenter to ask questions concerning omitted material without suggesting to the subject that he is more interested in some aspects of his report than in others. It would also indicate specific gaps or omissions in dream reports.

The adoption of the night-recall method was an advancement over the morning-recall method for soliciting dream reports. It avoided the problems involved when the subject had to remember dream contents that occurred several hours prior to waking in the morning. Nevertheless, it is clear that in the future increased efforts must be made to obtain even more accurate reports of nocturnal dreams and thoughts.

Even with the night-recall method, there remain many opportunities for error in the subject's verbal report. Successful response to suggestions to dream on a specific topic may be construed as involving a six-step process: (*a*) The experimenter must correctly present the suggestion to the subject; (*b*) the subject must perceive the suggestion accurately; (*c*) he must retain the suggestion at least until sleep onset; (*d*) the suggestion must somehow act to influence the content of dreams during the night; (*e*) the subject must retain the dream content until it is requested by the experimenter; and (*f*) he must be able to recall and report the content of his dreams accurately when requested by the experimenter. Valuable information would be gained if future research were aimed at evaluating the effects of variations in procedure at each of these six steps. For example, requiring a subject to repeat to the experimenter the presleep suggestion that he has received would aid in determining if the subject has accurately perceived the presleep suggestion. Measuring the time interval between the administration of the presleep suggestion and the time of sleep onset would aid in determining the effect of length of retention time on dream content. And so on. Experiments such as these would yield valuable information concerning the complex process required in order for presleep suggestions to affect the content of nocturnal dreams and thoughts.

Assessing the Effect of the Presleep Suggestion

In response to the suggestion, "Dream all night about rowing a boat," a subject in Stoyva's (1961) study replied, " I dreamt I threw a pebble into a pool of water." The subject was subsequently given one-half point on a zero-to-one point scale. How much can the content of a subject's report vary from the suggested topic and still be considered a successful response to the presleep suggestion?

Past scoring systems used for assessing the effect of presleep suggestions have been designed to measure only direct effects. This has been accomplished either by counting the number of elements in the dream report that are identical to the specific topic suggested or by rating the overall similarity between the theme of the suggested topic and the theme of the subsequent dream report. Thus there is no way for possible distortion or or symbolization (cf. Kramer, 1969) to be evaluated by the present scoring systems. In order to correct for his deficiency, Witkin (1969) has suggested that the aid of the dreamer be solicited. Witkin contended that in order to best understand the nature of the dream, it is necessary to know the dreamer's associations to his dreams as well as something about the background of these associations. A careful inquiry performed jointly by the experimenter and the subject into the content of the dream would be helpful. In addition, emphasis would be placed on the subject's associations concerning the dream because these may help clarify the meaning of the dream.

The problem one must face in deciding whether or not a dream has been influenced by a presleep suggestion remains a difficult one. An open attitude toward the possibility of finding suggested effects embedded within distorted dreams, as well as a more extensive use of the subject's personal background and feelings toward the dream topic, may prove to be important factors in solving this problem.

Separation of Suggested Effects from Other Effects

Often the effects of presleep suggestions have been confounded with the effects of other stimuli. This point was made obvious in the study by Newman et al. (1960) wherein the subject's dream content was strongly influenced by the specific characteristics of the setting (i.e., the experimental room, the hypnotist, the furniture, and so forth). In order to assess the main effects of presleep suggestions, these and other extraneous stimuli must be adequately controlled. For example, there are variables that, depending on the way they are presented, may or may not enhance responsiveness to presleep suggestions. Even though it is now accepted that the hypnotic induction procedure is not a necessary antecedent condition for successful response to presleep suggestions, there is still some question as to whether or not it raises response to presleep suggestions above that level found under nonhypnotic conditions. Because the administration of a hypnotic induction procedure has often been incorporated into procedures designed to influence dreams, an evaluation of its relative effect on dream content is of prime importance.

Another variable to be controlled is the exact wording of the presleep suggestion. Because empirical investigation (Barber et al., 1973) has shown that permissive suggestions work best with nonhypnotic subjects (and authoritative suggestions work best with hypnotic subjects), further investigation into the complex effects of the wording, phrasing, and tone of presleep suggestions is warranted.

Other variables that merit evaluation include: (*a*) the length of the presleep suggestion, in total number of words, which has varied from only a few words (e.g., Stoyva, 1961) to many (e.g., Tart & Dick, 1970); (*b*) the emotional tone of the suggested dream content, which has varied from the fear of personal harm (Tart, 1964) to a charming narrative about a leisurely stroll through the forest (Tart & Dick, 1970); (*c*) the frequency of the suggested dream, because some investigators (Barber et al., 1973; Stoyva, 1961; Tart & Dick, 1970) have asked their subjects to dream on the suggested topic in every dream during the night and others (Tart, 1964) have not; and (*d*) amnesia for the suggested topic, because some investigators (Stoyva, 1961; Tart, 1964) have suggested amnesia for the presleep suggestions and others (Barber et al., 1973; Tart & Dick, 1970) have not. Systematically varying these variables and making controlled comparisons of the effects would be of great value in the effort to delineate the precise relationship between presleep suggestions and dream content.

The Influence of Subject Characteristics

It is not known why some subjects' nocturnal dreams and thoughts are more easily influenced by presleep suggestions than are others'. The only subject variable to be assessed has been hypnotizability (Stoyva, 1961; Tart, 1964; Tart & Dick, 1970). Tart and Dick (1970) reported a "somewhat positive" relationship between hypnotizability and the presence of the suggested topic in dream contents. However, because they used only subjects scoring high on hypnotizability, the relationship did not necessarily apply to subjects scoring low or medium on this measure. Indeed, Barber et al. (1973), who included subjects scoring low, medium, and high on hypnotizability, found that hypnotizability was not related to the presence of the suggested topic in dreams and thoughts. The relationship between hypnotizability and responsiveness to presleep suggestions is ambiguous. Research aimed at replicating prior studies is needed to determine whether high hypnotizability does or does not facilitate the effects of presleep suggestions on dream content.

In addition to hypnotizability, standard personality characteristics should be investigated. Also, as pointed out by Barber et al., dream-related characteristics, such as frequency of dream recall and vividness of dream recall, may be of particular interest. A subject who spends much time thinking about his dreams and whose dreams occupy an important place in his life may be more susceptible to the influence of presleep suggestions than the subject who rarely remembers his dreams and/or views them as chance happenings.

CONCLUSIONS

1. With some patients and experimental subjects, the administration of presleep suggestions to dream on specific topics can influence the content of nocturnal dreams. This relationship has been found to occur regardless of whether or not the dream reports are solicited upon awakening in the morning, upon awakening from REM sleep, or upon awakening from NREM sleep.

2. Even though historically the prior administration of a hypnotic induction procedure has been considered to be an important part of the presleep suggestion procedure, it is clear that the hypnotic induction procedure is not a necessary antecedent condition for a subject's successful response to presleep suggestions. Whether or not it enhances response has yet to be determined.

3. Further investigation of subtle variables is needed. These include the exact wording and phrasing of the presleep suggestion, the tone in which it is administered, the interpersonal relationship between the experimenter and the subject (or therapist and patient), and the setting (laboratory, office, home) in which the suggestions are administered and in which the dream reports are solicited.

4. The extent of the effectiveness of presleep suggestions on dream content is a question for future research to determine. The major implication of the methodological problems discussed in this review is that research

strategies will have to be expanded in order to account for the numerous variables involved. Specifically, subjects should be taught to describe and differentiate between types of nocturnal mental activities; they should be awakened and asked for dream reports at times other than REM periods; they should be taught to give more complete reports of the nature of their experiences; more information should be gathered from the subject following these reports; controls should be used to clarify the effects of stimuli other than the presleep suggestions themselves; and subject characteristics other than hypnotizability should be assessed.

Information gained through intensive research on the presleep suggestion will be of considerable value both to the researcher and to the therapist. It will not only aid in the more accurate interpretation of the causes of dream behavior, but it will also aid in the determination of the effect of suggested cognitive manipulations on dream behavior.

REFERENCES

BARBER, T. X. Toward a theory of "hypnotic" behavior: The "hypnotically induced dream." *Journal of Nervous and Mental Disease,* 1962, **135,** 206–221.

BARBER, T. X. Pitfalls in research: Nine investigator and experimenter effects. In R. M. W. Travers (Ed.), *Second handbook of research on teaching.* Chicago: Rand McNally, 1973.

BARBER, T. X., & CALVERLEY, D. S. "Hypnotic behavior" as a function of task motivation. *Journal of Psychology,* 1962, **54,** 363–389.

BARBER, T. X., WALKER, P. C., & HAHN, K. W., JR. Effects of hypnotic induction and suggestions on nocturnal dreaming and thinking. *Journal of Abnormal Psychology,* 1973, **82,** 414–427.

BARTLETT, F. C. *Remembering.* London: Cambridge University Press, 1932.

BERTINI, M., LEWIS, H. B., & WITKIN, H. A. Some preliminary observations with an experimental procedure for the study of hypnagogic and related phenomena. *Archivio di Psicologia Neurologia e Psichiatria,* 1964, **6,** 493–534.

DEMENT, W., & KLEITMAN, N. Cyclic variations in EEG during sleep and their relation to eye movements, body motility, and dreaming. *Electroencephalography and Clinical Neurophysiology,* 1957, **9,** 673–690. (a)

DEMENT, W., & KLEITMAN, N. The relation of eye movements during sleep to dream activity: An objective method for the study of dreaming. *Journal of Experimental Psychology,* 1957, **53,** 339–346. (b)

FISHER, C. Studies on the nature of suggestion: Part 1. Experimental induction of dreams by direct suggestion. *Journal of the American Psychoanalytic Association,* 1953, **1,** 222–255.

FOULKES, D. NREM mentation. *Experimental Neurology,* 1967, Supplement 4, 28–38.

FOULKES, D., & VOGEL, G. Mental activity at sleep onset. *Journal of Abnormal Psychology,* 1965, **70,** 231–243.

FOULKES, W. D. Dream reports from different stages of sleep. *Journal of Abnormal and Social Psychology,* 1962, **65,** 14–25.

GOODENOUGH, D. R., LEWIS, H. B., SHAPIRO, A., JARET, L., & SLESER, I. Dream reporting following abrupt and gradual awakenings from different types of sleep. *Journal of Personality and Social Psychology,* 1965, **2,** 170–179.

HARTMANN, E. L. *The biology of dreaming.* Springfield, Ill.: Charles C Thomas, 1967.

HERVEY DE SAINT-DENIS, M. J. L. *Les rêves et les moyens de les diriger.* Paris: Amyot, 1867.

KRAMER, M. *Dream psychology and the new biology*

of dreaming. Springfield, Ill.: Charles C Thomas, 1969.

McGeoch, J. A. *The psychology of human learning.* New York: Longmans, Green, 1942.

Nachmansohn, M. Ueber Experimentell Erzeugte Traeume nebst Kritischen Memerkungen ueber die Psychoanalytische Methodik. *Zeitschrift Neurologie und Psychiatrie,* 1925, **98,** 556–586. In *Organization and pathology of thought.* (Trans. by D. Rapaport) New York: Columbia University Press, 1951.

Newman, R., Katz, J., & Rubenstein, R. The experimental situation as a determinant of hypnotic dreams. *Psychiatry,* 1960, **23,** 63–73.

Rosenthal, R. *Experimenter effects in behavioral research.* New York: Appelton-Century-Crofts, 1966.

Schroetter, K. Experimentelle Traueme. *Zentralblatt für Psychoanalyse,* 1911, **2,** 638–648. In *Organization and pathology of thought.* (Trans. by D. Rapaport) New York: Columbia University Press, 1951.

Slamecka, N. J. (Ed.) *Human learning and memory.* New York: Oxford, 1967.

Stoyva, J. The effects of suggested dreams on the length of rapid eye movement periods. Unpublished doctoral dissertation, University of Chicago, 1961.

Stoyva, J., & Kamiya, J. Electrophysiological studies of dreaming as the prototype of a new strategy in the study of consciousness. *Psychological Review,* 1968, **75,** 192–205.

Tart, C. T. A comparison of suggested dreams occurring in hypnosis and sleep. *International Journal of Clinical and Experimental Hypnosis,* 1964, **12,** 263–289.

Tart C. T., & Dick, L. Conscious control of dreaming: I. The posthypnotic dream. *Journal of Abnormal Psychology,* 1970, **76,** 304–315.

Titchener, E. B. Taste dreams. *American Journal of Psychology,* 1895, **6,** 505–509.

Van Eeden, F. *De Nachtbruid* (1909). [*The bride of dreams.*] New York and London: Mitchell Kennerley, 1913.

Vogel, G. W., Barrowclough, B., & Giesler, D. D. Limited discriminability of REM and sleep onset reports and its psychiatric implications. *Archives of General Psychiatry,* 1972, **26,** 449–455.

Webb, W. B. Sleep and dreams. In B. B. Wolman (Ed.), *Handbook of general psychology.* Englewood Cliffs, N.J.: Prentice-Hall, 1973.

Witkin, H. A. Influencing dream content. In M. Kramer (Ed.), *Dream psychology and the new biology of dreaming.* Springfield, Ill.: Charles C Thomas, 1969.

Witkin, H. A., & Lewis, H. The relationship of experimentally induced presleep experiences to dreams: A report on method and preliminary findings. *Journal of the American Psychoanalytic Association,* 1965, **13,** 819–849.

Hypnosis and Biofeedback in the Treatment of Migraine Headache

12

Theodore Andreychuk and Christian Skriver

Abstract: A study was made to explore the effects of subject-hypnotizability in response to 3 treatment procedures applied to 33 migraine headache sufferers. These treatment procedures included biofeedback training for hand-warming, biofeedback training for alpha enhancement, and training for self-hypnosis. The Hypnotic Induction Profile (HIP) of Spiegel & Bridger (1970) was given to each S to determine degree of hypnotizability and the MMPI was administered to all Ss. All 3 treatment groups showed significant reductions in headache rates and there were no significant differences between groups. Cutting across treatment groups, high hypnotizable Ss ($N = 15$) showed significant reductions in headache rates when compared with low hypnotizable Ss ($N = 13$). There was no correlation between HIP scores and the hysteria scale of the MMPI.

Much interest has been generated in the last few years in the use of biofeedback procedures to bring about voluntary control of autonomic functions—something that had previously been thought to be impossible. Starting with the work of Miller (1969) and DiCara (1970) with animals and that of Kamiya (1969), Shapiro and Schwartz (1972), Schwartz (1973), and Stoyva and Budzynski (1973) with humans, considerable advances have been made with respect to both methodological and technical problems. Growing consideration is being given to the possible applications of these procedures to human problems, particularly those involving psychosomatic illnesses. Many researchers are

[1] Reprint requests should be addressed to Theodore Andreychuk, Department of Psychology, Texas Tech University, Lubbock, Texas 79409.

becoming increasingly involved in attempts to cope with these problems as attested to by the increasing number of published reports in the professional literature.

The basic principle underlying the biofeedback paradigm is quite simple, employing instrumental learning as its central feature. The individual is placed in a closed feedback system where he is continuously provided with information concerning the bodily function or functions which E is interested in altering (Davidson & Krippner, 1972). When S is successful, he receives reinforcement—either as simple satisfaction knowing that he is obtaining positive results or in a more tangible form such as monetary reward.

Much of the research which has been done has concerned itself with the types of bodily responses that are easily subjected to measurement such as heart rate, blood pressure, GSR, and skin temperature. It has been demonstrated rather clearly that changes in these functions can be brought about even when S is not aware of which function is being altered or in what direction it is being changed (Schwartz, 1973). It might appear that there is a direct relationship between the experimental treatment and the change in function and that there is no need to be concerned with any intervening or mediating factors such as client–expectations. However, when one is dealing with illness or disease entities, the problem becomes much more complicated. It is not usually possible to conceal the true purpose of the study from S particularly when the researcher calls for volunteers with a specific type of disease entity, nor is it always feasible to establish a control group, especially when the study will be extended over a lengthy period of time. It is therefore important in such cases that E not be too hasty in drawing his conclusions lest he overlook placebo effects which might be in operation. Shapiro and Schwartz (1972) and Schwartz (1973) refer to this problem very pointedly and suggest that in clinical research it might at times even be very desirable to utilize the patient's expectations for maximum effect.

Sargent, Green, and Walters (1973) combined the use of autogenic traning (Schultz & Luthe, 1969) with biofeedback techniques in order to observe the effects of this approach in the amelioration of migraine headaches. Of the 20 Ss in this study who were diagnosed as suffering from migraine headaches, there was a clear agreement among the investigators that 12 of them were improved and 3 were not improved. Also included in the study were 4 Ss suffering from tension headaches; 2 were judged to be improved and 2 unimproved. The assumption in this study was that it was the combination of relaxation and handwarming which produced the generally positive results. Since this hypothesis seemed to be derived specifically from the investigators' interpretation of the mechanics of the migraine headache, it was not clear how improvement in the tension headaches could be accounted for, unless it was assumed that the relaxation alone was sufficient to produce this effect. No mention was made about the possible effect of subject–expectations in this study.

When we deal with the role of expectancy in its relation to the placebo effect it seems that the suggestibility of research Ss becomes an important issue. Spiegel and Shainess (1963) classified personality types along a continuum of hypnotizability, with a hysteria type being identified as the most hypnotizable. This type of individual is characterized by "the proneness to accept without much critical appraisal the direct or indirect guidance and influence of the therapist [p. 486]." They concluded that with the hysteric S "Direct symptom removal or alteration by hypnosis is useful because of this, as is Christian Science, religious conversions, and the indirect influence so well illustrated by the placebo effect [p. 487]." There is little if any evidence as to the direct effect of suggestibility on the results of biofeedback studies.

The present study was an attempt to demonstrate that hypnotizability plays an important role in producing symptom changes in biofeedback research with psychosomatic illnesses. Migraine headache was the focus of the research project. It was hypothesized (a) that migraine sufferers would show significant degrees of improvement regardless of the treatment method employed and that there would be no significant differences in improvement between treatments; (b) that the more hypnotizable Ss would how greater improvement across treatments than would the less hypnotizable Ss; and (c) that there would be a correlation between hypnotizability and hysteric personality characteristics.

METHOD

Subjects

The sample was selected from a group of migraine headache sufferers who volunteered to participate as the result of publicity about the project in the local news media. From an original group of about 50 volunteers, 33 Ss were selected for inclusion in the study. The 17 volunteers who were not selected were ruled out because their headaches were clearly not migraine, or because their headaches were so infrequent that it would not have been possible to develop comparative data within the time period allotted for the study. Each prospective S was briefly interviewed by the principal investigator and responded to a headache questionnaire.

Eleven Ss were randomly assigned to each of three treatment conditions. The time limitations imposed upon this particular study did not make it possible to utilize a non-treatment control group, which would have necessitated some follow-up treatment for this group. While this would have been a desirable procedure, it was not felt to be an insurmountable obstacle. [Findings in other studies (e.g., Stoyva & Budzynski, 1974) tend to show that no-treatment controls typically reveal no significant symptom changes when compared with treatment groups, although a study reported by Budzynski, Stoyva, Adler, and Mullaney (1973) pointed out that 25% of their Ss showed temporary reductions of their headaches before EMG training began. However, these latter Ss, which were not included in their main study, were not selected as controls but were selected out because of a low baseline headache index. Their regular control group showed no decrease of headaches over the time period of the study.] The three treatment groups included a hypnosis group (H), a hand-temperature group (T), and an alpha-enhancement group (A). The H group was specifically selected as a type of control group since there was no biofeedback involved. The T group was included because of positive results with this type of treatment previously reported (Sargent et al., 1973). The A group treatment had no known relationship to migraine headache but it was suspected that an effect might also manifest itself in such a group.

Apparatus and Test Instruments

Prior to the beginning of the treatment programs, each S was asked to maintain a daily headache record on a form which was adapted for this purpose from one used by Budzynski, Stoyva, and Adler (1970). The form was constructed so that a clear picture could be obtained both of the onset and duration of the headache, as well as its intensity, on an hour–to–hour basis. This procedure was then continued for the duration of the treatment program. Thus, a Headache Index (HI) was compiled for the 6–week period prior to the treatment program and also for the last 5 weeks during treatment. This was computed by multiplying the number of hours duration by the severity of the headache rated on a 5–point scale, summing these figures each week, and computing the average weekly rating for each period.

During the initial waiting period, each S was asked to take the Minnesota Multiphasic Personality Inventory (MMPI) Form R (Hathaway &McKinney, 1966). The scores on the Hysteria scale were of primary interest but other scores were also examined.

Each S was also given the Hypnotic Induction Profile, Eye-Roll

Hand Levitation Method (HIP) developed by Spiegel and Bridger (1970). This is an empirically derived scale which enables one to obtain a very quick estimate of hypnotic susceptibility through a standardized induction procedure which takes about 10 minutes. The procedure enables the operator to objectively derive a profile score which ranges from 0-5. There are no published reliability data on this scale although the evidence seems to support a fairly high degree of inter-scorer reliability.[2] The assumption was made that the higher the degree of hypnotic susceptiility, the more suggestible S would be.

In the T group the technique for biofeedback training involved the use of a Temperature Feedback Meter.[3] The output was programmed into a PDP-8/e computer and a 100 Hz tone was sounded whenever the hand temperature was rising.

The Aquarius Brain Wave Analyzer[4] was used for the treatment group which was being trained for the enhancement of alpha brain wave production. In this treatment the 8–13 cycle frequency range was utilized in the feedback sessions and presented to Ss in the form of a 1000 Hz signal.

Procedure

All treatments were administered in a pleasant, 4 × 8 foot, sound-attenuating cubicle. Very dim, indirect lighting was utilized. A ceiling exhaust fan provided cooling and ventilation as well as a background hum which obscured any transient sounds which may have been otherwise audible in the cubicle.

At the time of the initial interview, each prospective S was given a statement to read. This basic statement briefly described the timetable of the study and what would be expected of Ss. No details were provided about the nature of the treatments except to say that Ss would be assigned to a treatment procedure at a later date. The Ss were told that each of the treatments held considerable promise for being helpful and that if they had any doubts about being able to complete the program they should, in all fairness to the study, not start. At this time, and throughout the course of the study, all Ss were constantly encouraged to develop as high a degree of positive expectation toward success as possible.

Following the initial record–keeping period, each S was randomly

[2] Spiegel, personal communication, August 1973.

[3] Obtainable from Scott Behavioral Electronics, Inc., Box 3306, Lawrence, Kansas 66044.

[4] Obtainable from Aquarius Electronics, Box 627, Mendocino, California 95460.

assigned to one of the three treatment groups. The treatments were approximately 45 minutes in length and were regularly scheduled for each S, once a week for a period of 10 weeks. Throughout the treatment sessions each group was given maximum encouragement to do well and to attend regularly. During the first session, each S listened to a tape which explained the treatment procedure and the rationale behind it.

The H group listened to the preliminary instruction and was then immediately given the step by step procedure for inducing self-hypnosis. The procedure involved relaxation instruction, visual imagery, verbal reinforcers, and direct suggestions for dealing with pain. Each S listened to the hypnosis tape twice in each 45-minute period.

In the T group, following the preliminary taped instruction in the first session, tapes employing autogenic relaxation instructions were played. The S then concentrated on producing and maintaining the audio signal which was activated each time hand temperature went up. Practice sessions lasted about 15 minutes at a time with a short rest period between.

The A group received similar preliminary instructions in the first session followed by appropriate relaxation instruction. EEG readings were obtained through bi-polar measurement from electrodes placed on the right and left occipital areas using the right ear as a common ground. Practice periods were of approximately 15 minutes in duration, and two periods were utilized in each session with a rest in between.

The Ss in each group were urged to practice at least twice each day between sessions at the laboratory. The headache chart was used to indicate the time of day at which each practice session occurred. These data were not used for research purposes but the procedure was maintained as a motivating device to encourage practice. Each time S came to the laboratory his chart was reviewed with him in order to check the accuracy of record keeping but also to impress upon him the importance of this procedure.

RESULTS

At the beginning of the study, 11 Ss were assigned to each of the three treatment groups. There was a slight attrition for various reasons, so that at the conclusion of the study there were 10 Ss (2 males and 8 females) remaining in the H group and 9 Ss each in the T (1 male and 8 females) and A (1 male and 8 females) groups.

A mean Headache Index (HI) score was computed for each S for the 6 weeks preceding treatment (pre-treatment) and for the last 5 weeks

TABLE 1

NUMBERS OF HIGH AND LOW SUGGESTIBLE Ss IN EACH TREATMENT CONDITION

Treatment	High Hypnotizable	Low Hypnotizable	Total
Alpha	3	6	9
Temperature	7	2	9
Hypnosis	5	5	10
Totals	15	13	28

(treatment) of the 10–week treatment period. From these figures, percent–improvement scores were calculated for each treatment group.

A comparison of pre-treatment and treatment HI scores was made within each of the three groups. A t test for correlated samples showed significant improvement in HI means in all three groups. The obtained t ratios of 2.57, 3.01, and 2.87 were significant at the .025, .01, and .025 levels of confidence for the alpha, temperature, and hypnosis groups respectively.

A t test for independent samples was also used to compare the mean percent–improvement scores for each pair of treatment groups. The obtained t values of 1.19 for A-T groups, .91 for A-H groups, and .62 for T-H groups were not significant.[5]

The Hypnotic Induction Profile (HIP) was utilized to obtain hypnotic susceptibility scores for each S. The pattern of scores permitted a breakdown of Ss into two groups. There were 15 Ss in the high hypnotizable group (scores of 2 and above) and 13 Ss in the low hypnotizable group. Both of these groups were scattered across all three treatment procedures in the proportions indicated in Table 1.

The mean percent–improvement scores for the high and low HIP groups were 71.3% and 41.4% respectively ($t = 2.05$, $p < .05$, one tailed test). The high HIP Ss as a group responded better to treatment regardless of what the treatment was than did the low suggestible Ss.

A series of t tests was also computed to see if there were any differences between mean percent–improvement scores of high and low HIP

[5] While some record was maintained of medications used by Ss during the study, no attempt was made to make statistical comparisons between groups because of the wide diversity and dosages of medications used. A partial list of medications used by Ss during the study includes the following: Excedrin, Aspirin, Anacin, etc.; Darvon; Bellergal Spacetabs; Synalgos D. C.; Tylenol; Demerol; Perodan; Talwin; Valium; Cafergot; Pariactin; Dramamine; Teractin; and Fiorinal. An examination of the data, however, revealed that there was a definite pattern of reduction of drug use which accompanied improvement in HI scores.

TABLE 2

HEADACHE INDEX (HI) MEANS AND PERCENT–IMPROVEMENT SCORES FOR
LOW AND HIGH HIP GROUPS IN EACH TREATMENT

Treatment	Hypnotizability	Pre-treatment HI Means	Post-treatment HI Means	% Improvement
Alpha	High	88.1	29.1	66.9
	Low	66.3	46.0	30.6
Temperature	High	156.0	26.2	83.2
	Low	48.4	16.7	65.7
Hypnosis	High	114.2	69.8	38.8
	Low	60.7	40.4	33.4

scorers within each treatment group. (See Table 2 for a summary of this data.) The obtained t values of 1.53, 1.80, and 1.28 for the A, T, and H groups were significant at about the .08, .07, and .15 levels of confidence. In view of the fact that the composite high and low HIP groups were significantly different in mean–improvement scores, this finding can probably be attributed to the fact that the number of Ss in the within treatment breakdown was too small.

A correlational analysis showed no relationship between Hysteria on the MMPI and hypnotizability using HIP scores. Correlations between HIP scores and other MMPI scales were also insignificant. A fairly high correlation, .48, was found between HIP and pre-treatment HI scores.

Biofeedback research often suggests that initial symptom severity is related to improvement after treatment. Since initial symptom severity (pre-treatment HI) and hypnotizability (HIP scores) showed some correlation in this study it was necessary to investigate the function of this relationship in the treatment outcome. Thus, Ss were divided into two groups according to their pre-treatment HI scores, namely a high HI group and a low HI group with 14 Ss in each group. A t test for comparing the pre-treatment scores of these groups was significant at the .001 level showing a considerable difference between them. A comparison of these two groups in regard to percent–improvement scores however, showed no significant difference ($t = .78$). This demonstrates that in this study it was the responsiveness of Ss to the various treatments employed rather than initial symptom severity which is related to treatment outcomes.

DISCUSSION

The three different treatment groups all showed significant degrees of improvement, and there were no significant differences in improvement between any of the treatment groups. The T group showed a higher percent–improvement rate than the A and H groups, although this was not statistically significant. This trend however, might seem to indicate an advantage for this type of treatment, thus supporting the findings in the Sargent et al. (1973) study that handwarming was related to reduction of headaches. A closer examination of the data however, reveals that the T group had a higher proportion of high HIP Ss, 7 out of 9; than the H group, 5 out of 10; or the A group, 3 out of 9. Since the high HIP group as a whole showed significantly greater improvement scores over the low HIP group, this could explain the advantage for the T group, even though the within treatment comparisons barely missed significance as explained above. The trend is clearly in support of the position that more suggestible Ss are apt to respond favorably to treatment situations where they have high expectations of being helped than are low suggestible Ss, producing what is often referred to as the placebo effect. In short, the particular biofeedback treatments were not necessarily the relevant variables in producing these effects. It is obvious however, that more research with larger numbers of Ss is required before firm conclusions may be drawn.

The conclusion that suggestibility was the primary variable influencing the results of this study might be challenged on the grounds that each of the treatments also focused considerable emphasis on relaxation and that this may have been the crucial variable involved. There is no denying that relaxation can and does have a therapeutic benefit in many types of disorders. However, the fact that the high HIP Ss showed a significantly greater percent–improvement rate than the low HIP Ss would support a placebo explanation. There is the possibility of course, that high HIP Ss can learn to relax to a greater degree than low HIP Ss and that is why they showed greater improvement rates. It may be supposed that relaxation is one of the mediating variables which produces the placebo effect. However, many past placebo studies with positive results, notably drug studies, have not utilized relaxation as part of the procedure. The specific responses which go into producing such effects have not as yet been defined and this presents a very fertile field of inquiry for the future.

The finding of a fairly high correlation between pre-treatment HI scores and hypnotizability would seem to be related to the fact that once a person focuses on a particular physical symptom as a way of responding to stressful life situations, he tends to produce that symptom in proportion to his responsivity to his life situation and to his experience of stress within this situation. Accordingly, the more highly suggestible *S* experiencing such stress would tend to produce more headaches, but likewise would respond more favorably to a treatment situation wherein he had high expectations of obtaining relief. This seemed to be the case in this study.

The finding that there was no correlation between hypnotizability and scores on the hysteria scale of the MMPI was not necessarily surprising. Dahlstrom and Welsh (1960) reported several studies which seem to support such a relationship. Other studies however, (Hilgard, 1965) have not found such a relationship. Spiegel and Shainess (1963) proposed a classificatory scheme whereby individuals who make the best hypnotic *S*s are described as being hysteric personality types. However, Spiegel and Shainess also pointed out that their hysteric personality type was not to be construed as the kind which produces transient symptoms (which is what the MMPI scale may measure), but rather as a type of "massive hysteria" which endows one with a "quality of *gullibility* that allows individuals of this type to abandon almost in totality a current MBC [Myth-Belief Constellation] in favor of a 'new' formulation which may be forcefully and appropriately presented them [p. 483]." It may very well be that the characteristics measured by Spiegel's HIP and those measured by the MMPI Hysteria Scale deal with different dimensions of hysteria so that no relationship is apparent. It is of interest to note, however, that the 24 female *S*s as a whole showed a mean score of 69 on the hysteria scale which was the highest for any of the scales on the MMPI. The 4 males were somewhat below this.

The results of this study indicate the necessity for exercising care in formulating conclusions about the outcome of biofeedback research. This is particularly true in respect to research dealing with psychosomatic illnesses where the specificity of mediating variables is difficult to define. This should in no way discourage researchers and clinicians from utilizing techniques which show promise in the alleviation of symptoms. The caution is directed mainly against drawing hasty and unwarranted conclusions where such variables as the placebo effect may be in operation. A more important finding, however, is the need to consider and account for the role of suggestibility in any studies where mediating variables such as subject–expectations come into play.

REFERENCES

BUDZYNSKI, T. H., STOYVA, J., & ADLER, C. Feedback-induced muscle relaxation: Application to tension headache. *J. behav. Ther. exp. Psychiat.*, 1970, *1*, 205–211.

BUDZYNSKI, T. H., STOYVA, J. M., ADLER, C. S., & MULLANEY, D. J. EMG biofeedback and tension headache: A controlled outcome study. *Psychosom. Med.*, 1973, *35*, 484–496.

DAHLSTROM, W. G., & WELSH, G. S. *An MMPI handbook: A guide to use in clinical practice and research.* Minneapolis: Univer. of Minnesota Press, 1960.

DAVIDSON, R., & KRIPPNER, S. Biofeedback research: The data and their implications. In J. Stoyva, T. X. Barber, L. V. DiCara, J. Kamiya, N. E. Miller, & D. Shapiro (Eds.), *Biofeedback & self-control, 1971.* Chicago: Aldine-Atherton, 1972. Pp. 3–34.

DICARA, L. V. Learning in the autonomic nervous system. *Sci. Amer.*, 1970, *222*(1), 30–39.

HATHAWAY, S. R., & McKINNEY, J. C. *Minnesota Multiphasic Personality Inventory, Form R.* New York: Psychological Corp., 1966.

HILGARD, E. R. *Hypnotic susceptibility.* New York: Harcourt, Brace & World, 1965.

KAMIYA, J. Operant control of the EEG alpha rhythm and some of its reported effects on consciousness. In C. E. Tart (Ed.), *Altered states of consciousness: A book of readings.* New York: Wiley, 1969. Pp. 507–517.

MILLER, N. E. Learning of visceral and glandular responses. *Science*, 1969, *163*, 434–445.

SARGENT, J. D., GREEN, E. E., & WALTERS, E. D. Preliminary report on the use of autogenic feedback training in the treatment of migraine and tension headaches. *Psychosom. Med.*, 1973, *35*, 129–135.

SCHULTZ, H. A., & LUTHE, W. *Autogenic therapy: A psychophysiologic approach to psychotherapy.* New York: Grune & Stratton, 1959.

SCHWARTZ, G. E. Biofeedback as therapy: Some theoretical and practical issues. *Amer. Psychologist*, 1973, *28*, 666–673.

SHAPIRO, D., & SCHWARTZ, G. E. Biofeedback and visceral learning: Clinical applications. *Semin. Psychiat.*, 1972, *4*, 171–184.

SPIEGEL, H., & BRIDGER, A. A. *Manual for Hypnotic Induction Profile: Eye-roll levitation method.* New York: Soni Medica, 1970.

SPIEGEL, H., & SHAINESS, N. Operational spectrum of psychotherapeutic process. *Arch. gen. Psychiat.*, 1963, *9*, 477–488.

STOYVA, J., & BUDZYNSKI, T. H. Cultivated low arousal—An antistress response? In L. V. DiCara (Ed.), *Recent advances in limbic and autonomic nervous system research.* New York: Plenum, 1974. Pp. 369–394.

Hypnose und Biofeedback in der Migränebehandlung

Theodore Andreychuk und Christian Skriver

Abstrakt: In einem Studium, das der Erforschung der Hypnotisierbarkeitseffekte eines Subjektes in der Reaktion auf 3 Behandlungsweisen diente, wurden diese bei 33 unter Migräne Leidenden angewandt. Diese Behandlungsverfahren schlossen Biofeedbacktraining im Erwär-

men der Hände und in der Verstärkung der Alphawellen ein, sowie ein Training in Selbsthypnose. Das Hypnose-Induktions-Profil (HIP) von Spiegel & Bridger (1970) wurde bei jeder *Vp.* gebraucht, um das Grad der Hypnotisierbarkeit zu bestimmen. Ausserdem wurden alle *Vpn.* mit dem MMPI (Minnesota-Multiphasen-Persönlichkeits-Inventar) gemessen. Bei allen 3 Behandlungsgruppen zeigten sich bedeutende Reduktionen in der Kopfschmerzrate, jedoch bestanden zwischen den Gruppen keine bedeutenden Unterschiede. Ein Durchschnitt durch die Behandlungsgruppen zeigte, dass hoch-hypnotisierbare *Vpn.* (*N* = 15) eine bedeutende Reduktion in der Kopfschmerzrate aufwiesen, wenn man sie mit den schwach-hypnotisierbaren *Vpn.* (*N* = 13) verglich. Es bestand keine Korrelation zwischen den an dem HIP gemessenen Ergebnissen und der Skala für Hysterie bei dem MMPI.

L'hypnose et la rétroaction biologique dans le traitement de la migraine

Theodore Andreychuk et Christian Skriver

Résumé: Exploration des effets du degré de susceptibilité hypnotique sur la réponse à 3 méthodes de traitement de patients migraineux. Ces méthodes de traitement comprennent un entraînement, par rétroaction biologique, au réchauffement des mains, un entraînement destiné à augmenter le rythme alpha par rétroaction biologique, et un entraînement à l'auto-hypnose. Le profil d'induction hypnotique (HIP) de Spiegel et Bridger (1970) est administré individuellement à chaque *S* dans le but de déterminer son niveau de susceptibilité hypnotique. Le MMPI est aussi administré à tous les *Ss*. On observe des réductions significatives des taux de céphalée dans les 3 groupes traités, et il n'y a pas de différence significative entre les groupes. Par ailleurs, indépendamment des traitements, la réduction des taux de céphalée est significativement plus grande chez les *Ss* de susceptibilité hypnotique élevée que chez les *Ss* de susceptibilité faible. Il n'y a pas de corrélation entre les scores du HIP et l'échelle d'hystérie du MMPI.

Hipnosis y biorretroacción en el tratamiento de la jaqueca

Theodore Andreychuk y Christian Skriver

Resumen: Se realizó un estudio para explorar los efectos de la susceptibilidad hipnótica del sujeto sobre la respuesta a 3 tipos de tratamiento aplicados a 33 sujetos que sufrían de jaqueca. Dichos tratamientos constaban de entrenamiento en el calentamiento de las manos y en la elevación del ritmo alfa, por biorretroacción, y entrenamiento en auto-hipnosis. El Perfil de Inducción Hipnótica (HIP: *Hypnotic Induction Profile*) de Spiegel & Bridger (1970) fue administrado a cada uno de los *Ss* con el fin de determinar el grado de susceptibilidad hipnótica; todos los *Ss* fueron sometidos al MMPI. Los 3 grupos de tratamiento acusan reducciones significativas de los índices de jaqueca, no encontrándose diferencias significativas entre ellos. La comparación global intergrupo muestra que los Ss altamente hipnotizables ($N = 15$) experimentan reducciones significativas de los índices de jaqueca, con respecto a los Ss poco hipnotizables ($N = 13$). No hay correlación entre las puntuaciones del HIP y la escala de histeria del MMPI.

Self-Regulation of Pain: 13
The Use of Alpha-Feedback and Hypnotic Training for the Control of Chronic Pain

Ronald Melzack and Campbell Perry

Patients suffering chronic pain of pathological origin received alpha-feedback training methods in association with prior hypnotic training. Changes in the intensity and quality of pain were measured with the McGill Pain Questionnaire. The combined procedures produced a substantial decrease in pain (by 33% or greater) in 58% of the patients during the training sessions. Both the sensory and affective dimensions of the pain were diminished. The EEG records indicated that the majority of patients learned to increase their alpha output during the training sessions. In contrast, patients who received the alpha training alone reported no decreases in pain even though they showed increases in alpha output. Patients who received hypnotic training alone also produced increased EEG alpha during the training sessions and showed substantial (though not statistically significant) decreases in pain. The results demonstrate that chronic, pathological pain can be reduced in a significant number of patients by means of a *combination* of alpha-feedback training, hypnotic training, and placebo effects. It is concluded, however, that the contribution of the alpha training procedure to pain relief is not due to increased EEG alpha as such but, rather, to the distraction of attention, suggestion, relaxation, and sense of control over pain which are an integral part of the procedure.

[1] Supported by the Advanced Research Projects Agency of the Department of Defense and monitored by the Office of Naval Research under Contract No. N00014-70-C-0350. We are grateful to Elliott Dainow and Stephen Southmayd for their outstanding assistance in carrying out these studies. We also appreciate the technical assistance of Mary Ellen Jeans, Jacques Perras, Paul Taenzer and Joseph Vanagas, and the generous cooperation of Dr. Maurice Dongier at the Allan Memorial Institute, McGill University, and Dr. Serge Bikadoroff at the Lethbridge Rehabilitation Center, Montreal.

Reprinted by permission from *Experimental Neurology*, 1975, Vol. 46, 452-469.

INTRODUCTION

There is convincing evidence that pain perception is not simply a function of amount of physical damage alone. Rather, it is also determined by expectation, suggestion, level of anxiety, the meaning of the situation in which injury occurs, competing sensory stimuli and other psychological variables (9). It is therefore apparent that brain activities subserving these psychological processes play an essential role in determining the quality and intensity of perceived pain.

Alpha-feedback training methods (7) appear to provide an effective technique for the self-regulation of pain. Gannon and Sternbach (3) found that a subject who received prolonged alpha training was able to delay onset of migraine headaches by self-induction of an "alpha state," but was not able to modify the pain once it was underway. These observations are suggestive, and it is clear that a thorough study is needed. It is also apparent that alpha training can provide a "handle" on the general phenomenon of psychological (or cognitive) control of pain. Four variables, at least, can contribute to pain relief in the alpha-training procedure:

(a) Distraction of attention from a painful body site is known to be a mechanism of pain control in a variety of situations (14). Alpha training could teach people to distract themselves from pain by directing attention to different inner feelings and to a feedback signal (during training) which, because of its intermittent nature, is attention-demanding.

(b) Suggestion is known to affect pain experience (8). If alpha training is given with strong suggestion that the procedure will effectively diminish pain, these suggestive effects could be maximized by the use of hypnotic training procedures.

(c) The relaxation that accompanies an "alpha state" can produce a decrease in sensory inputs, such as those from muscles and viscera, which would reduce the general arousal level. This, in turn, would also lower the person's anxiety level (6), thereby diminishing the level of perceived pain (5).

(d) Finally, the development of a sense of control over pain is known to diminish the level of perceived pain (13). The knowledge that one is able to do something about pain, which is inherent in the alpha-training procedure, can bring about a marked reduction in the anxiety associated with pain and, therefore, in the pain itself (5).

The purpose of this study was to determine whether alpha training provides a suitable method for the control of pain of pathological origin. Our strategy has been to utilize alpha training in combination with hypnotic training and suggestion as a method of pain autoregulation, and to determine the relative contributions of each.

METHODS

Subjects. Twenty-four patients, six males and 18 females, ranging in age from 28–70 yr (mean age of 48 yr), served as subjects in the experiment. They were outpatients who sought pain relief at two Montreal hospitals and were referred to this study by medical colleagues after consultation regarding their suitability. The pain syndromes and number of patients treated in each group are the following: back pain (10); peripheral nerve injury (4); cancer pain (3); arthritis (2); phantom limb and stump pain (2); post-traumatic pain (2); head pain (1).

The subjects were chosen on the basis of several criteria: (a) They suffered chronic pain of known somatic pathological origin, verified by thorough medical examination; many had persistent pain despite disc surgery, neurosurgical root or cord sections, or one or more standard physiotherapeutic methods. (b) They had continuous, unremitting pain, although it fluctuated in intensity. (c) The pain did not diminish significantly when the patient merely lay down and rested; indeed, many subjects stated that their pain often became worse when they were in a reclining position. (d) The subjects had to be English-speaking and demonstrate that they could understand and answer a Pain Questionnaire. (e) The patients had a normal EEG. (f) The pain could not be blocked completely by any analgesic or other drugs that they were taking. Patients that did not meet these criteria were rejected as prospective subjects. The subjects were randomly assigned to one of three groups: Group I ($N = 12$) received hynpotic training plus alpha training; Group II ($N = 6$) received hypnotic training alone; Group III ($N = 6$) received alpha training alone.

Hypnotic Training. These instructions consisted of a sequence of items. They began with a set of extensive relaxation techniques, in which attention was focussed upon relaxing each successive muscle group in turn and upon controlled breathing (6). They were followed by an adaptation of Hartland's Ego Strengthening Techniques (4) in which emphasis was placed upon feeling stronger and healthier, greater alertness and energy, less fatigue, less discouragement, a feeling of greater tranquility and of being able to overcome things that are ordinarily upsetting and worrying. The final portion consisted of suggestions that dealt with being able to think more clearly, to concentrate, to remember things, to be emotionally more calm, to be less tense both emotionally and physically, to be more self-confident and independent, and to be less fearful of failure. The duration of these instructions, which were specially prepared and taped for this study, was about 20 min. [2]

[2] Copies of the hypnotic training tape are available at cost from Dr. Campbell Perry, Sir George Williams University, Montreal.

Alpha Training. The instructions for alpha training consisted of strong, explicit suggestion that the alpha training would enable the subject to achieve control over pain. The subject was told that he would hear music when he produced alpha, and his aim should be to produce as much alpha as possible, thus keeping the music on; by this means he would learn to achieve a state that would enable him to control pain. The music feedback consisted of Bach flute music rearranged with a slight jazz beat. [3] This music was chosen because it was found to appeal to all who listened to it, regardless of musical tastes. All but the first few subjects received cassettes of the music to play at home to help them practice the alpha training between sessions.

Apparatus. The experiment was carried out in a shielded, sound-proof room which was furnished to resemble a comfortable sitting-room. After the electrodes were attached to the occipital and frontal scalp, the subjects lay on a comfortable reclining chair. EEG recordings were made using a Grass Model 8 Polygraph situated in an adjacent room. Specially constructed EEG integrators were used, with variable "windows" and digital read-out devices that registered the percentage of alpha for successive 100 second blocks. A Uher tape recorder was used to transmit the taped instructions or the music into the experimental room through a loudspeaker behind the subject's head. The room was dimly lit, yet there was enough light for the experimenter to observe the subject periodically via closed circuit television.

Procedure. All subjects, regardless of group, were told that they would be taught a technique, using electroencephalographic records, that would enable them to enter a "state" in which they would be better able to control their pain. For Groups I (alpha training plus Hypnotic training) and III (alpha training alone) this state was described as an "alpha state," while for Group II (hypnotic training alone) it was represented as an "hypnotic state."

The training methods consisted of the following component procedures (which are described below in detail): Baseline sessions; Training sessions (hypnotic training and/or alpha training); Practice sessions. Table 1 shows the sequence of these component procedures for each of the three groups. The sessions were scheduled at a rate of two or three per week, depending on the subject's available time.

Baseline Sessions. There were two baseline sessions of approximately 1 hr each. During the first of these, the subjects were given, for about 30 min, a thorough description of the methods and aims of the study, and strong

---

[3] The recording used was: *Moe Kaufman Plays Bach*; GRT Recording Co., Record #9230-1008.

TABLE 1

TRAINING PROCEDURES FOR THE SELF-REGULATION OF PAIN

Group	Type of session	No. of sessions
Group I	Baseline	2
	Hypnotic training	2
	Hypnotic training plus Alpha training	2
	Alpha training	6
	Practice	2
Group II	Baseline	2
	Hypnotic training	4
	Practice	2
Group III	Baseline	2
	Alpha training	8
	Practice	2

assurances that the procedure would diminish their pain. Their EEG was then recorded in the apparatus for 30 min. The second baseline session consisted of a shorter instruction period followed by the EEG recording period. Pain Questionnaires were administered before and after each session. These sessions provided baseline EEG data, against which later alpha levels could be compared. It was apparent from the Pain Questionnaires that many of the subjects felt better to some degree after the baseline sessions. Presumably this was because they had received strong suggestion that their pain would be relieved by the procedures, because they had obtained a sympathetic hearing of their pain problem, and because they were able to relax in a reclining chair with their eyes closed for a prolonged period of time. These sessions, then, should be considered as baseline-placebo sessions for pain control.

Training Sessions. Each subject, on each training session, received the following: Pain Questionnaire; fitting of electrodes to the frontal and occipital scalp; first sessional baseline recording (10 min); the hypnotic instructions (20 min) and /or the alpha-feedback training (20 min) appropriate to the group; second sessional baseline recording (10 min); practice alpha-on without feedback (5 min; the subject was told to produce as much alpha as possible) and practice alpha-off (5 min; the subject was told to produce as little alpha as possible); removal of the electrodes; Pain Questionnaire. The duration of each training session, including Questionnaires, was approximately 2 hr for Group I and 1.0–1.5 hr for Groups II and III,

Group I received both the hypnotic training and the alpha training, whereas Groups II and III received portions of the same training procedures. Subjects in Group II listened to the taped recording of the hypnotic training instructions, and were told that these procedures would enable them to achieve control over their pain. They were also told that the EEG provides an index of relaxation, and that their EEG was being monitored to see how well they were doing. Subjects in Group III received alpha training with the instruction that learning to increase the amount of alpha would enable them to control their pain. Groups II and III received the same number of sessions of hypnotic instruction or alpha training as Group I (see Table 1), since the study sought to control for type of "treatment" rather than total number of sessions *per se.*

Practice Sessions. Finally, for two sessions, the patients were told to practice the techniques they had learned in the training sessions in order to reduce their pain without benefit of feedback. As in all other sessions, the subjects were given a Pain Questionnaire at the beginning and end of each session.

Five subjects in Group I and one subject in Group III left the study before the training sessions were completed or before the practice sessions were begun. They left because of previously scheduled operations, illness, or the promise of immediate total pain relief by a local acupuncturist. If subjects left before completion of the training sessions, the data on the last two days of training or the mean data for all training days were used in the data analyses. This occurred only in subjects in Group I; one subject left after 7 training sessions, and three left after eight sessions. Subjects who did not participate in the practice sessions were excluded from the data analyses of the practice sessions only.

Pain Measurement. The McGill Pain Questionnaire (11, 12) was used to measure the quality and intensity of pain perceived by the subject. The portion of the questionnaire relevant for this study is the list of words that describes the qualitative dimensions of pain. The classes and subclasses that comprise the qualitative "Pain Descriptor" list are shown in Table 2.

The McGill Pain Questionnaire has been shown (11) to provide valid, reliable scores which reflect the quality and intensity of clinical pain experienced by patients. The *Pain Rating Index* consists of the sum of the rank values of all the qualitative words chosen in selected subclasses. Thus the Pain Rating Index scores can be computed separately for the sensory or affective dimensions of pain, or for all the subclasses together. The latter score has been shown (11) to correlate highly with the intensity values designated on a 1–5 ordinal scale, but it is more sensitive to subtle, qualitative changes in perceived pain. Since the Pain Questionnaire was ad-

TABLE 2

CLASSES AND SUBCLASSES OF PAIN DESCRIPTORS

Classes subclasses	Pain descriptors	Rank value	Classes subclasses	Pain descriptors	Rank value
Sensory			Affective		
Temporal	Flickering	1	Tension	Tiring	1
	Quivering	2		Exhausting	2
	Pulsing	3			
	Throbbing	4	Autonomic	Sickening	1
	Beating	5		Suffocating	2
	Pounding	6			
			Fear	Fearful	1
Spatial	Jumping	1		Frightful	2
	Flashing	2		Terrifying	3
	Shooting	3			
			Punishment	Punishing	1
Punctate	Pricking	1		Gruelling	2
pressure	Boring	2		Cruel	3
	Drilling	3		Vicious	4
	Stabbing	4		Killing	5
	Lancinating	5			
			Affective-evaluative-sensory:		
Incisive	Sharp	1	sensory:	Wretched	1
pressure	Cutting	2	miscellaneous	Blinding	2
	Lacerating	3			
Constrictive	Pinching	1	Evaluative	Annoying	1
pressure	Pressing	2		Troublesome	2
	Gnawing	3		Miserable	3
	Cramping	4		Intense	4
	Crushing	5		Unbearable	5
Traction	Tugging	1	Supplementary		
pressure	Pulling	2	Sensory:	Spreading	1
	Wrenching	3	spatial-pressure	Radiating	2
				Penetrating	3
Thermal	Hot	1		Piercing	4
	Burning	2			
	Scalding	3	Sensory:	Tight	1
	Searing	4	pressure-dullness	Numb	2
				Drawing	3
Brightness	Tingling	1		Squeezing	4
	Itchy	2		Tearing	5
	Smarting	3			
	Stinging	4	Sensory:	Cool	1
			thermal	Cold	2
				Freezing	3

TABLE 2—*Continued*

Dullness	Dull	1			
	Score	2			
	Hurting	3	Affective	Nagging	1
	Aching	4		Nauseating	2
	Heavy	5		Agonizing	3
				Dreadful	4
Sensory:	Tender	1		Torturing	5
miscellaneous	Taut	2			
	Rasping	3			
	Splitting	4			

ministered at the beginning and end of each session, it was possible to determine the differences between the pre- and post-session Pain Rating Index scores. These differences thus represent measures of pain relief produced by the procedures presented during each session.

In addition to the Pain Questionnaire data, tape-recorded information was obtained in the course of conversation at the beginning and end of each session. This information was concerned with each subject's general activity level, drug intake, and overall mood and response to treatment.

Alpha Measurement. The occipital EEG was used for feedback and data analysis in all subjects. The EEG alpha data consisted of the % alpha in 100-sec blocks during each entire session. The 100-sec block which showed the highest % alpha was taken as an index of the % alpha output during each part of the procedure. It was found that the high point within a section of the procedure was highly correlated with the average alpha during the entire session, and thus appears to be a valid measure of overall alpha activity. The 100-sec block was chosen as the index of alpha output in order to eliminate artifacts from the computation, such as subjects dozing off for short periods.

In a preliminary study, verbal feedback of the % alpha emitted by the subject was provided every 5 min. Most subjects, however, complained that the interruption was disruptive and they reported difficulty resuming the "alpha state" or concentrating on the hypnotic instructions. They stated, moreover, that the % alpha meant little to them. Consequently, verbal feedback of % alpha was not given during the main study. The music feedback itself, plus assurances from the experimenter that they were progressing well, proved to be sufficient.

Because some subjects increased their % alpha output per session at a rapid rate, it was necessary, following the procedures of other investigators (3), to narrow their trigger "window" for the feedback period on subsequent sessions. This was done once only and it had the effect of challenging them to work harder to achieve maximum alpha output. It produced the problem, however, of comparing alpha output during the feedback periods at different sessions recorded at different trigger levels. This was overcome by using a correction factor which was based on a comparison of the percentages of alpha output during two successive 100-sec blocks, one with the old trigger level and the other with the new one.

RESULTS

Pain Questionnaire Data. The Pain Questionnaire was administered at the beginning and end of each baseline, training and practice session. The data are summarized in Tables 3 and 4.

Table 3 shows the mean percent decreases in the various Pain Rating Index scores for the baseline and all training Sessions for Groups I, II and III. It is apparent that the training procedures used in Group I produced larger mean decreases in Pain Rating Index scores than those produced during baseline-placebo sessions. Sign tests show that the p values are statistically significant for all Pain Rating Index scores. In contrast, the hypnotic training alone (Group II) and the alpha training alone (Group III) failed to produce changes that are statistically larger than those produced during the baseline sessions.

The largest net percent change on any measure was the decrease in the affective dimension of pain in Group I, although there were smaller, significant decreases in the sensory dimension and in the overall Pain Rating Index based on all words. It should be noted that the decreases based on all words during baseline sessions for Groups I, II and III vary from 16% (Group I) to 10% (Group III). In order to rule out the possibility of experimenter bias in the allocation of subjects to any particular group, the percent decreases during the baseline sessions for all three groups were compared. No significant differences between groups were found.

For convenience, Table 3 does not include data comparing pain decreases during the final practice sessions with those during the initial baseline sessions. In all cases, these levels fell below statistical significance. Nevertheless, the percentages of subjects who achieved pain decreases during practice sessions (Table 4) were impressive, although not statistically significant.

Table 4 shows the mean percent decreases in the Pain Rating Index based on pre- and post-session Questionnaires during the last two training sessions. This analysis was carried out to evaluate improvement toward the end of the series of training sessions, where the effects of training could

TABLE 3

MEAN PERCENT (%) DECREASES IN THE PAIN RATING INDEX BASED ON PRE- AND POST-SESSION PAIN QUESTIONNAIRES PRESENTED DURING THE BASELINE (B) AND ALL TRAINING (T) SESSIONS FOR GROUPS I, II, AND III

Category of Pain Rating Index	Group I—hypnotic training plus alpha training (N = 12)			Group II—hypnotic training alone (N = 6)			Group III—alpha training alone (N = 6)		
	Baseline (B)	Training (T)	p $T > B$	Baseline (B)	Training (T)	p $T > B$	Baseline (B)	Training (T)	p $T > B$
Sensory									
Mean[a]	14%	33%	0.02	11%	21%	NS[b]	10%	12%	NS
Range[a]	$(33^- - 70^+\%)$	$(3^+ - 77^+\%)$		$(12^- - 45^+\%)$	$(19^- - 53\%)$		$(0 - 15^+\%)$	$(2^+ - 30^+\%)$	
Affective									
Mean[a]	8%	48%	0.03	29%	32%	NS	18%	15%	NS
Range[a]	$(200^- - 100^+\%)$	$(13^+ - 86^+\%)$		$(12^- - 80^+\%)$	$(13^- - 75\%)$		$(0 - 60^+\%)$	$(0 - 57\%)$	
All Descriptors									
Mean[a]	16%	34%	0.02	14%	23%	NS	10%	9%	NS
Range[a]	$(28^- - 81^+\%)$	$(9^+ - 67^+\%)$		$(17^- - 57^+\%)$	$(20^- - 55\%)$		$(4^+ - 30^+\%)$	$(9^- - 23^+\%)$	

[a] A minus sign represents a pain increase.

[b] NS: not statistically significant.

TABLE 4

MEAN PERCENT (%) DECREASES IN THE PAIN RATING INDEX BASED ON PRE- AND POST-SESSION PAIN QUESTIONNAIRES PRESENTED DURING THE BASELINE (B), THE LAST TWO TRAINING (T), AND THE PRACTICE (P) SESSIONS FOR GROUPS I, II, AND III

	Group I—hypnotic training plus alpha training			Group II—hypnotic training alone			Group III—alpha training alone		
	Baseline (B)	Training (T)	Practice (P)	Baseline (B)	Training (T)	Practice (P)	Baseline (B)	Training (T)	Practice (P)
All descriptors									
Mean[a]	16%	36%	36%	14%	22%	45%	10%	-4%	17%
Range[a]	$(28^- - 81^+\%)$	$(20^- - 75^-\%)$	$(3^+ - 83^+\%)$	$(0 - 57^+\%)$	$(39^- - 57^+\%)$	$(12^+ - 100^+\%)$	$(5^+ - 30^+\%)$	$(40^- - 12^+\%)$	$(20^- - 54^+\%)$
% Subjects reporting pain decrease >33%	25%	58%	57%	17%	50%	60%	0%	0%	33%
p value, $T > B$		0.03			NS			NS	
p value, $P > B$			NS[b]			NS			NS

[a] A minus sign represents a pain increase.
[b] NS: not statistically significant.

be expected to be optimal. Statistical analysis of the differences between the baseline and the last two training sessions, using the t test, shows that significant decreases in pain were produced only in Group I. Further analysis of the data (Table 4) indicates that 58% of the subjects in Group I experienced a decrease in pain of 33% or more during the last two training sessions, while 50% of the subjects in Group II and none of the subjects in Group III showed comparable levels of pain decrease.

The placebo effects—such as relaxation, suggestion, and the anticipation of pain relief—provided by the baseline sessions indicate the extent to which these effects contribute to the pain relief produced by the training procedures. The net differences between training and baseline sessions in the percentages of subjects who showed a pain decrease of 33% or more is 33% for Groups I and II, with mean decreases in the Pain Rating Index of 20% and 8% respectively. None of the subjects in Group III showed a pain decrease greater than 33% and, indeed, there was a slight increase in the mean PRI for the group. A subject-by-subject analysis of the differences between training and baseline sessions further indicates the powerful contribution of placebo effects to the overall effects of the training procedures. In Group I, 25% showed a net pain decrease of 33% or more, and 50% showed a net decrease of 20% or more. For Group II, the percentages of subjects who showed net decreases larger than 33% and 20% are 17% and 50% respectively. None of the subjects in Group III showed a net pain decrease greater than 20%.

Seven subjects in Group I carried out the practice sessions after completion of the training sessions. Four of the seven subjects (57%) showed a pain decrease of 33% or greater, compared with three out of five subjects (60%) in Group II who achieved comparable pain reduction. Compared to baseline-placebo sessions, however, only two subjects in Group I (29%), and two subjects in Group II (40%) showed more than 33% pain reduction. One subject in Group III (17%) showed more than 33% pain reduction compared to baseline sessions.

All the data, taken together, show that, for Group I, significantly greater decreases in all Pain Rating Index scores were produced during training sessions than during baseline sessions. Although none of the mean percent changes in pain produced in Groups II and III were large enough to achieve statistical significance, it is noteworthy that the effects were larger in Group II (hypnotic training alone) than in Group III (alpha training alone). Furthermore, almost identical percentages of the subjects in Group II as in Group I showed a pain reduction of 33% or more. Indeed, there was no significant difference between Groups I and II in terms of the number of subjects who diminished their pain by 33% or more, whereas

TABLE 5

PERCENTAGE (%) OF SUBJECTS SHOWING INCREASES IN EEG ALPHA
RHYTHM AND MEAN PERCENT ALPHA INCREASES ACROSS THE
BASELINE AND LAST TWO TRAINING SESSIONS, AND
WITHIN THE LAST TWO TRAINING SESSIONS

	Group I— hypnotic training plus alpha training	Group II— hypnotic training alone	Group III— alpha training alone
Across sessions			
Alpha-feedback period > baseline sessions			
% Subjects	82%	60%	50%
Mean Increase	13%	14%	13%
Range	2%–37%	6%–25%	4%–17%
Practice-on period > baseline sessions			
% Subjects	88%	80%	33%
Mean Increase	23%	11%	13%
Range	9%–39%	5%–32%	8%–22%
Within Training Sessions			
Alpha-feedback period > first sessional baseline			
% Subjects	27%	60%	100%
Mean	15%	14%	13%
Range	5%–21%	1%–25%	5%–21%
Second sessional baseline > first sessional baseline			
% Subjects	36%	50%	83%
Mean	10%	13%	16%
Range	3%–16%	8%–18%	8%–33%
Practice-on period > first sessional baseline			
% Subjects	50%	40%	83%
Mean	8%	13%	18%
Range	3%–20%	5%–21%	10%–23%
Practice-on > practice-off			
% Subjects	88%	80%	50%
Mean	8%	9%	9%
Range	1%–31%	7%–10%	7%–12%

the data show that subjects in both groups learned to increase their EEG
alpha output. A relevant observation here is that the subjects in Group I
showed a higher percent alpha on the last two sessional baselines compared

Group III achieved less pain reduction than either of the other two groups (Fisher Exact Probability test; $p = 0.05$).

Alpha Training. Analysis of the EEG alpha data for the last two training sessions shows that the subjects in Groups I and III learned to increase their EEG alpha output. However, the data (Table 5) reveal a surprising difference. The EEG alpha data may be compared across sessions (comparison of Training with Baseline sessions), or within sessions (comparison of the Training and the first Baseline periods of each session). It is apparent, in Table 5, that Group I shows larger increases in EEG alpha output in cross-session comparisons, while Group III shows larger increases in within-session comparisons. Since both methods of analysis are valid, with the baseline sessions, while subjects in Group III showed a decreased percent alpha when the same comparison was made. Although the subjects in Group II did not receive alpha training, the increases in percent alpha while they practiced the hypnotic-training procedure are shown in Table 5 and indicate that they increased their EEG alpha output to levels that compare favorably with the subjects that actually received alpha training.

In a portion of the training procedure, the subjects were asked to practice alpha or hypnotic training in the absence of feedback (Pr-on). Of 18 subjects in the three groups who provided reliable, artifact-free data, 13 produced increased alpha, four produced less alpha, and one showed no change. Using a sign test, the effect is significant at the 0.025 level. A further analysis is the comparison between Pr-on and Pr-off (the subjects were asked *not* to produce alpha). For this comparison, serial effects were avoided by reversing the order of Pr-on and Pro-off from one session to the next. In Group I, the subjects produced more alpha during the Pr-on than during the Pr-off condition; although the net difference is small, it is consistent ($p = 0.025$). The difference is not significant in Group III.

While the data indicate that increases in alpha occurred in the majority of subjects, from small to substantial amounts, the fact that Group II (hypnotic training alone) showed comparable alpha increases suggests that these alpha increases can be obtained by means other than alpha training.

Duration of Relief. An important feature of the effect of the treatment is that the duration of relief outlasted each training session by several hours (1–4 hr) in seven of the 12 subjects, and by 15–30 min in three. The subjects also reported even longer indirect changes. Several indicated that they slept better, were happier, and went to parties or met friends which they had not done for years. There appeared to be a carry-over effect as a result of the procedure: pain relief for several hours in some; a happier, more confident mood in others.

Drug Intake. Nine of the subjects in Group I took large quantities of analgesic drugs. On their own initiative, during the training sessions, three of these subjects decreased their drug intake by 30%, and one by 50%. Two others reported that they decreased their drug intake but could not provide a definite figure. Three subjects reported no change in drug intake.

Interview Follow-Up Data. Eleven subjects, distributed through the three groups, were interviewed 4–6 mo after completion of training. It was found that all those who obtained relief in the training sessions continued to practice hypnotic training or alpha training regularly or from time to time when their pain became unbearable. They further reported that they were able to reduce the pain to bearable levels by means of the procedures. Many of these subjects kept their cassettes of the music tapes, and stated that they utilized them as part of their home practice to control their pain.

DISCUSSION

The data show that alpha training can produce a marked reduction in severe clinical pain, but only if it is accompanied by hypnotic training, which emphasizes "ego-strengthening" and "progressive-relaxation" techniques, and by placebo effects, which include distraction, suggestion, and the diminished anxiety due to anticipation of pain relief. No one of these contributions, taken alone, produces a significant effect. All three together provide a useful method of pain control in patients suffering severe pain which cannot be brought under control by other methods. The effect of the combined procedures is impressive: a substantial number of patients (58%) reported a significant reduction in pain (by 33% or greater). The alpha training alone had the smallest effect on the pain. The hypnotic suggestion had a larger effect, although it was not statistically significant. The effects with both procedures are statistically significant compared to the baseline-placebo effects. The effect of all three contributions (alpha training and hypnotic training, plus placebo effects) may be considered to be sufficiently large to comprise a useful clinical tool when other conventional procedures fail. An important additional observation is the fact that about half the subjects that received the combined procedures reduced their drug intake by substantial amounts during the training sessions.

Two points merit special consideration. First, three workman-compensation cases were included in Group I, and all three showed a resistance to admitting being helped. The magnitudes of the pain decreases during training sessions in these patients were among the lowest in the entire group. The proportion of people helped by the procedure, therefore, might be even higher than that indicated by the data, although 58% nevertheless remains a substantial proportion. Secondly, a decrease in pain by 33% represents a considerable success in view of the nature of the pain suffered by these patients. The majority had severe, chronic pain for years that was not diminished by several operations, neurosurgery on the spinal roots or spinal cord, prolonged physiotherapy, psychotherapy, or drugs. A decrease by 33%, therefore, is a substantial improvement in cases that had in many instances been labelled as hopeless.

It is reasonable to assume, on the basis of the data, that the alpha-feedback training procedure plays a role in the control of pain. However, the data indicate that the increase in EEG alpha is not the critical variable in pain relief; all three groups showed comparable increases in EEG alpha during the training sessions, but Groups I and II showed substantial pain relief while Group III did not. It is concluded, therefore, that the contribution of the alpha training procedure to pain relief is *not* due to increased EEG alpha as such but, rather, to the distraction of attention, suggestion, relaxation, and sense of control over pain which are an integral part of the procedure.

The data show that the practice sessions, in which the subjects attempted to diminish their pain without alpha-feedback or the hypnotic training tape, failed to provide relief at statistically significant levels, although 57% of the subjects in Group I and 60% of those in Group II were able to reduce their pain by 33% or more. While these percentages are impressive, the fact that statistical significance was not achieved further indicates the importance of *all the contributions of the training procedures in combination* in producing substantial pain relief.

The powerful contribution of the placebo effects, demonstrated in the comparisons between the training and baseline-placebo sessions, is not surprising. Approximately half of the effectiveness of powerful analgesic compounds—ranging from aspirin to morphine—are known (1, 2) to be attributable to placebo effects. Evans (2) has shown that a placebo's effectiveness is directly proportional to the apparent effectiveness of the active analgesic agent that doctor and patient believe they are using. The present study suggests that this relationship between placebo and pharmacological analgesic also holds true for other pain-relieving methods such as the combination of alpha-feedback and hypnotic training.

The magnitude of the contribution of the hypnotic-training procedure developed for this study is strikingly high. Although the effects did not achieve statistical significance, it is apparent that the hypnotic training comprises a major contribution to the pain relief. Group II (hypnotic training alone) does not differ statistically from Group I in terms of the proportion of subjects that achieve substantial pain relief, but both differ significantly from Group III (alpha training alone). This result needs to be taken in conjunction with the finding that only subjects in Group I showed a mean percent decrease during training sessions that significantly exceeded the amount of pain relief achieved during baseline-placebo sessions. These two sets of data suggest that both techniques help a substantial number of subjects to reduce pain but that alpha training with hypnotic training leads to quantitatively greater pain decreases. The number of hours spent in training to reduce pain does not appear to be the crucial variable that determines the amounts of pain relief obtained in the present study, since the hypnosis-alone group did substantially better than the alpha-alone group even though the latter group received approximately twice as many hours in training.

The data show that Group I exhibits larger alpha increases when compared to the baseline sessions (across sessions), while Group III exhibits larger increases when compared to the sessional baseline segment (*within sessions*). It is possible that Group I subjects achieved significant degrees of pain relief so that, by the last two training sessions, they began the sessions in a relaxed state, anticipating relief, and therefore already producing considerable alpha. During subsequent training, they learned to raise the alpha to some extent, but it was not significantly higher than the sessional baseline levels although it was very much higher than the alpha levels in the first baseline sessions. Group III subjects, on the other hand, achieved little or no pain relief, and anticipated little relief at the beginning of the last two training sessions. Their alpha level was in fact lower than the initial baseline levels when their anticipation of relief was high. During training, therefore, they learned to raise their alpha levels well above the sessional baselines, but the final level achieved was not sufficiently higher than the initial baseline sessions. This speculation does not explain every detail of the alpha increases that were produced, but it suggests in a broad way why different results are obtained using across-session and within-session analyses.

This study resembles an earlier study by Melzack, Weisz and Sprague (13) which showed that intense auditory input together with strong suggestion that it diminishes pain produced significant increases in pain tolerance levels; in contrast, the auditory input alone or the strong suggestion alone had no effect. This in no way diminishes the importance of the auditory input. Rather it indicates that it must be accompanied by other contributions if it is to have an effect on pain. Similarly, the alpha-feedback contribution to the pain relief observed in Group I is not diminished in importance by the fact that hypnotic training may have to accompany it in order to reduce chronic pain.

It is clear that the effects of the combined procedures are not obtained in all patients, and the degree of pain relief is variable. It is important, nevertheless, to recognize that *some* people have achieved substantial pain relief which, though not total, is sufficient to make life more bearable, more productive, and happier. It is a fundamental fact in the field of pain that some patients will suffer pain for the rest of their lives. In such cases, the most effective therapy may be to teach them to live with their pain, to carry on productive lives in spite of it (10). In the present study, it is clear that alpha training alone has little effect on pain but has substantial effects when it is combined with hypnotic training and placebo contributions. The three contributions in combination may have dramatic effects in some patients. One effect does not detract from the others. Instead the data show that multiple approaches are more effective than each alone in treating pain which, it is now known (9), has multiple, interacting determinants.

REFERENCES

1. BEECHER, H. K. 1959. "Measurement of Subjective Responses: Quantitative Effects of Drugs." Oxford Univ. Press, New York.
2. EVANS, F. J. 1974. The placebo response in pain reduction, pp. 289–296. *In* "Advances in Neurology, Vol. 4: International Symposium on Pain." J. J. Bonica [Ed.]. Raven Press, New York.
3. GANNON, L., and R. A. STERNBACH. 1971. Alpha enhancement as a treatment for pain: a case study. *J. Behav. Ther. Exp. Psychiat.* 2: 209–213.
4. HARTLAND, J. 1971. Further observations on the use of ego-strengthening techniques. *Amer. J. Clin. Hypnosis* 14: 1–8.
5. HILL, H. E., C. H. KORNETSKY, H. G. FLANARY, and A. WIKLER. 1952. Effects of anxiety and morphine on discrimination of intensities of painful stimuli. *J. Clin. Invest.* 31: 473–480.
6. JACOBSON, E. 1938. "Progressive Relaxation." Chicago Univ. Press, Chicago.
7. KAMIYA, J. 1972. Conscious control of brain waves. *In* "Readings in Psychology Today." CRM Books, Del Mar, Cal.
8. McGLASHAN, T. H., F. J. EVANS, and M. T. ORNE. 1969. The nature of hypnotic analgesia and placebo response to experimental pain. *Psychosom. Med.* 31: 227–246.
9. MELZACK, R. 1973. "The Puzzle of Pain." Basic Books, New York.
10. MELZACK, R. 1974. Psychological concepts and methods for the control of pain, pp. 275–280. *In* "Advances in Neurology, Vol. 4: International Symposium on Pain." J. J. Bonica [Ed.]. Raven Press, New York.
11. MELZACK, R. 1975. A questionnarie for the measurement of pain. In preparation.
12. MELZACK, R., and W. S. TORGERSON. 1971. On the language of pain. *Anesthesiology* 34: 50–59.
13. MELZACK, R., A. Z. WEISZ, and L. T. SPRAGUE. 1963. Stratagems for controlling pain: contributions of auditory stimulation and suggestion. *Exp. Neurol.* 8: 239–247.
14. MORGENSTERN, F. S. 1964. The effects of sensory input and concentration on post-amputation phantom limb. pain. *J. Neurol. Neurosurg. Psychiatry* 27: 58–65.

Visceral Responses to 14
Opposite Types of
Autogenic-Training Imagery

David A. Blizard, Patricia Cowings,
and Neal E. Miller

The purpose of this experiment was to test whether suggestions of imagery of the type used in autogenic training have specific effects on autonomic responses. In order to control for the effort involved in imagery and to determine the specificity of the effect, opposite types of imagery were used: (a) hands warm and heavy, and (b) hands cool and light. Nine subjects were trained for six daily sessions. Within each day 16 stimulus presentations were made, equally balanced between the two types of imagery. Heart rate, respiration rate, and EEG in the alpha frequency were recorded throughout all sessions. The 'cool' instruction reliably increased heart rate and respiration above pre-stimulus baselines; the 'warm' instruction resulted in statistically insignificant changes in the opposite direction. Large, consistent individual differences in autonomic response were found.

1. Introduction

Several procedures have been used to enable individuals to control their visceral responses. Among these techniques are hypnosis (Maslach, Marshall, and Zimbardo, 1972), biofeedback procedures (Brener and Hothersall, 1966), transcendental meditation (Wallace, 1970), the use of simple instructions (Bergman and Johnson, 1972), and the employment of a somatic response linked in some way to the visceral event (Sroufe, 1971).

In the present experiment we wished to assess the effects of the elicitation of simple images, such as those used during autogenic training (Schultz and Luthe, 1959). Autogenic training is a relaxation technique developed for the

*Now at Department of Neurology, New York University Medical Center, New York, N.Y. 10016, U.S.A.
†Now at Ames Research Center, Neurosciences Branch, Moffett Field, California 94040, U.S.A.
‡Requests for reprints should be addressed to this author.

Reprinted by permission from *Biological Psychology*, 1975, Vol. 3, 49-55.

treatment of a wide variety of psychological and somatic illnesses. It is reported to have therapeutic effects on visceral function, although most observations that have been held to support this claim could be attributed to placebo or other effects just as much as to the application of autogenic imagery (Luthe, 1970).

The reasons for performing the experiment were twofold. First, for therapeutic purposes we wanted to find the conditions most suited to obtaining large autonomic changes. Secondly, autogenic training has not been adequately evaluated as a technique since many of the findings related to it could be ascribed to placebo effects. In this experiment we included a standard autogenic exercise (hand-warming) and also an organ-specific exercise (hand-cooling) to see if differences in response to such procedures could be found. By the use of the organ-specific exercise it was intended to control for placebo effects and effects of distraction in producing autonomic changes.

2. Methods

Nine male and female subjects were used; ages ranged from 17 to 32 years. They were respondents to a newspaper advertisement and were accepted if they had no history of cardiac or respiratory disorder. They received $2.50/hr as payment for participation in the study.

2.1. Apparatus

The various physiological measures were recorded on a Grass model 7 polygraph. Respiration was measured by means of a pneumograph. Heart rate was recorded from Beckman silver chloride electrodes. The output of the electrocardiogram (ECG) amplifier operated a cardiotachometer which provided input to a print-out counter that printed out heart rate at 1 min intervals in phase with the experimental instructions outlined below.

Raw electroencephalogram (EEG) deriving from needle electrodes in 0–0 coordinates was filtered at alpha frequency (8–13 Hz) and subjected to d.c. integration. The integrated signal, which fluctuated in accordance with variations in the amount of alpha present in the EEG, operated a switch when it exceeded a predetermined d.c. voltage. When this voltage was exceeded, counts were accumulated at the rate of three per second on the print-out counter.

2.2. Procedure

On the first day of training, the subject was seated alone in a darkened, quiet room, the physiological transducers were attached while methods of measurement were explained to him. He was asked to sit comfortably with his eyes closed and without moving, as this would interfere with measurements being taken. All further instructions were delivered to the subject through headphones.

As an induction procedure in the first part of each autogenic training session, each subject was initially taught the first two standard exercises of autogenic training, 'heaviness' and 'warmth'. The subject received suggestions designed to make him feel more relaxed by passive means. He was told that he would learn to influence the temperature of his hands and thereby influence his blood pressure. He was told to focus his attention (to the exclusion of all other intervening thoughts) on the particular limb that he would affect by self-suggestion. This procedure is called 'making mental contact' and is recommended by Schultz and Luthe (1969).

When the subject reported that he experienced little difficulty in focusing attention, the standard exercise was carried out as follows: 'To help you relax further, in a few minutes from now (when the green light comes on), imagine that your right arm is heavy. Repeat over and over to yourself in a continuous verbal stream, "My right arm is heavy, my right arm is heavy". This is *passive*, not *active* concentration. You don't *make* it happen, you let go and *let* it happen.' When the subject reported experiencing a sensation of heaviness in the relevant limb, this suggestion was modified by the addition of the second standard exercise, 'warmth'. The suggestion then became, 'My right arm is heavy and warm.'

The induction procedure lasted several minutes, after which the subject was told to relax for 4 min before the start of the experiment proper. Then suggestions of 'warm and heavy' (the standard autogenic procedure, hereinafter called warm) or of 'cool and light' (the organ-specific autogenic procedure, hereinafter called cool) were made to the subject at regular intervals. The organ-specific procedure consisted of an opposite set of instructions, i.e. the subject was asked to cool a limb and given suggestions that it was light rather than heavy. This task was described as requiring an active rather than a passive frame of mind. Each subject was required to warm or to cool his right or left hand for 1 min periods that were separated by 1 min rest intervals. The instructions appropriate for each autogenic phase were introduced verbally by the experimenter in the last 10 sec of each rest period. Sixteen stimulus periods, equally divided between warm and cool and between right and left hands, were included in the experiment on each day; they were presented randomly with the restriction that stimuli to each limb were given two consecutive trials, as follows: warm right hand; rest; warm right hand; rest; cool left hand; rest; cool left hand; rest; warm left hand; rest; warm left hand; rest; etc. Thus, a subject was given four training sessions on each hand with both warm and cool instructions during each daily session. Six consecutive days of training were given to each subject.

It should be pointed out that, although temperature would appear to have been the most suitable physiological candidate for study considering the nature of the instructions (warm and cool), nevertheless our primary therapeutic interest was in the control of heart rate.

3. Results

To evaluate the effects of autogenic training, all physiological responses were averaged over consecutive 60 sec periods, enabling pre-stimulus levels of heart rate and respiration rate to be compared with their respective levels during the 60 sec warm and cool trials.

3.1. Heart rate

Figure 1 shows that for the mean of all subjects on all experimental days the response to the cool instruction was an increase in heart rate of 4 beat/min, and that to the warm instruction was a decrease of 0.5 beat/min. A dependent t-test for the difference between these two changes showed that it was highly reliable ($t = 6.17$, df $= 8$, $p < 0.01$). Considering the two changes separately, the increase to the cool instruction was highly reliable ($t = 6.17$, df $= 8$, $p < 0.01$), but the response to the warm instruction was not reliable.

Using the mean daily change from pre-stimulus baseline heart-rate level within each subject as the unit of analysis, six out of nine subjects exhibited a significant increase in heart rate after the cool instruction, the probabilities being $p < 0.01$ for five of them and <0.05 for the other one. In response to the warm instruction, two subjects showed reliable decreases ($p < 0.05$); the remaining seven showed no reliable changes. Inspection of the daily records showed that the changes occurred on the first day's trials; no consistent trend of improvement was noted; the changes on the last day were not reliably different from those on the first day.

Further analysis showed consistent individual differences in the per-

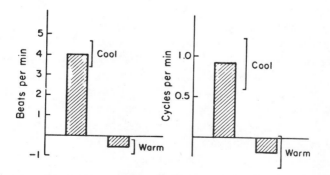

Fig. 1. Mean change in heart rate (left) and respiration (right) following the instructions for imagery of 'warm and heavy' versus 'cool and light'. The results represent the mean change from the pre-experimental baseline in all subjects over all sessions.

formance of the different subjects. The difference between the response to the warm and to the cool instructions on odd trials was reliably correlated with that on even trials ($r = 0.91$, $p < 0.01$). For responses to the cool instruction, the odd–even reliability was 0.88 ($p < 0.01$); to the warm instruction, it was less reliable ($r = 0.69$, $p = < 0.05$).

3.2. Respiration

Figure 1 shows for the mean of all subjects on all experimental days that the response to the cool instruction was an increase in respiratory rate of 0.92 cyc/min, whereas that to the warm instruction was a slight decrease. A dependent t-test for the difference between these two changes showed that it was statistically reliable ($t = 2.99$, df $= 8$, $p < 0.02$). Considering the two changes separately, the increase to the cool instruction was reliable ($t = 2.79$, df $= 8$, $p < 0.05$). No statistically significant change occurred to the warm instruction. Individual differences in respiratory response were consistent following the cool instruction. The product–moment correlation comparing odd and even trial responses was $r = 0.74$ ($p < 0.01$). The respiratory responses following the warm instruction were not significantly correlated.

Because a correlation exists between cardiovascular and respiratory responses, we studied the relationship between cardiovascular and respiratory responses during the warm and cool trials. In this analysis, correlations were positive on both warm and cool trials but not statistically significant.

3.3. Alpha response

Changes in EEG alpha amplitude and frequency exhibited wide variability. No significant differences in response to the warm and cool instructions were found.

3.4. Finger temperature

As a change in temperature would appear to be the most likely result of the autogenic exercises, this was assessed by evaluating changes in temperature of the index finger of the left hand during training sessions which were continued after this experiment was concluded. Both the direction and degree of change were taken into account in this analysis by sampling temperature at two specified points during the last 10 sec of the rest period and the last 10 sec of the warm or cool periods. Two measures were taken in each instance, 2.5 and 7.5 sec after the start of the sampling interval. There was some indication that temperature was more likely to show a decrease during the cool period than to increase or show no change. This was not the case during the warm period, when decreases or increases in finger temperature were equally likely. Despite the trends in the expected direction in the cool phase, no significant difference was found in a comparison of the responses to warm versus cool, nor did the responses to cool achieve reliability.

4. Discussion

This experiment shows that instructions for a specific type of imagery can change the cardiovascular responses of human subjects. In order to control for the effort involved in the imagery, the effects of two opposite types – 'cool and light' versus 'warm and heavy' – were contrasted. The increases produced by cool were large and reliable, whereas the decreases produced by warm were small and unreliable. This difference in effectiveness of the two types of imagery may have been because the effort of producing the imagery produced an increase which summated with the effect of cool but counteracted the effect of warm, and/or it may have been because the baseline of the subjects at the end of their rest periods was probably much nearer the lower than the upper limit of their range. In any event, the results agree with the general trend of literature, which is that increases are easier to produce than decreases, and may even involve different mechanisms (Engel, 1972).

There were large and consistent differences in individual subjects as far as cardiovascular response was concerned. Such differences have been reported by other experimenters (Stephens, Harris, and Brady, 1972). The present differences appeared at the very beginning of the experiment; there was little evidence of progressive change.

The principal findings of this experiment are that an organ-specific autogenic exercise (cool) increases heart rate, while the standard autogenic exercise (warm) had no reliable effect. In apparent contrast, previous work, largely of a clinical nature relating to the effects of autogenic training (Luthe, 1970), reported that decreases in cardiac rate generally followed the heaviness exercise, although 'paradoxical' increases were sometimes found. These clinical findings and those relating to individual differences in the present experiment may complement each other in that one explanation of diverse clinical findings relating to the influence of the heaviness exercise may represent further documentation of the pronounced individual differences in psychophysiological response found in the present study.

The fact that reliable increases in heart rate can be produced both by simple images *and*, as previous work has demonstrated, by biofeedback may suggest a mechanism for the explanation of the results of experiments using feedback to exert control over the cardiovascular system. That is, that cardiac changes in visceral control studies are produced by the evocation of images like the successful one used in this study (Murray and Katkin, 1968).

In this experiment, instruction for different types of imagery evoked different changes in the subjects' respiration. It is conceivable that the respiratory differences were the primary ones and that the differences in heart rate were mediated by peripheral changes in relevant parameters (Katkin and Murray, 1968). Another possibility is that these two changes were parallel effects of some central response (Freyschuss, 1970; Goesling and Brener, 1972).

The ideomotor theory of voluntary activity would lead one to expect that the imagery of the kinesthesis of a visceral response would tend to produce that response (Miller, 1969), but in this case the effects of the imagery seem to be considerably more indirect. In any event, the results of this experiment encourage the idea that the use of imagery, and perhaps even specific training in imagery, may be useful as one means of helping to gain control over autonomically mediated responses (Miller and Dworkin, 1974).

Acknowledgements
This work was supported by grants MH 13189, MH 19183, and GM 01789 from the National Institutes of Health, and U 2355 from the Health Research Council of the City of New York.

References
Bergman, J. S. and Johnson, H. J. (1972). Sources of information which affect training and raising of heart rate. *Psychophysiology*, 9, 30–49.
Brener, J. and Hothersall, D. (1966). Heart-rate control under conditions of augmented sensory feedback. *Psychophysiology*, 3, 23–28.
Engel, B. T. (1972). Operant conditioning of cardiac function: A status report. *Psychophysiology*, 9, 161–177.
Freyschuss, U. (1970). Cardiovascular adjustment to somatomotor activation. *Acta Physiologica Scandinavica*, Suppl. 342.
Goesling, W. J. and Brener, J. (1972). Effects of activity and immobility conditioning upon subsequent heart-rate conditioning in curarized rats. *Journal of Comparative and Physiological Psychology*, 81, 311–317.
Katkin, E. S. and Murray, E. N. (1968). Instrumental conditioning of autonomically mediated behavior: Theoretical and methodological issues. *Psychological Bulletin*, 70, 52–68.
Luthe, W. (1970). *Autogenic Therapy, Vol. 4: Research and Theory*. Grune and Stratton: New York.
Maslach, C., Marshall, G. and Zimbardo, P. G. (1972). Hypnotic control of peripheral skin temperature: A case report. *Psychophysiology*, 9, 600–605.
Miller, N. E. (1969). Learning of visceral and glandular responses. *Science*, 163, 434–445.
Miller, N. E. and Dworkin, B. R. (1974). Visceral learning: Recent difficulties with curarized rats and significant problems for human research. In: Obrist, P. A. et al. (Eds.) *Cardiovascular Psychophysiology*. Aldine: Chicago, 312–331.
Murray, E. N. and Katkin, E. S. (1968). Comment on two recent reports of operant heart rate conditioning. *Psychophysiology*, 5, 192–195.

Schultz, J. H. and Luthe, W. (1959). *Autogenic Training*. Grune and Stratton: New York.

Schultz, J. H. and Luthe, W. (1969). *Autogenic Therapy, Vol. 1: Autogenic Methods*. Grune and Stratton: New York.

Sroufe, L. A. (1971). Effects of depth and rate of breathing on heart rate and heart rate variability. *Psychophysiology*, **8**, 648–655.

Stephens, J. H., Harris, A. H. and Brady, J. V. (1972). Large magnitude heart rate changes in subjects instructed to change their heart rates and given exteroceptive feedback. *Psychophysiology*, **9**, 283–285.

Wallace, R. K. (1970). Physiological effects of transcendental meditation. *Science*, **167**, 1751–1754.

IV

EMG FEEDBACK, HEADACHES, AND RELAXATION

Differential Effectiveness of Electromyographic Feedback, Verbal Relaxation Instructions and Medication Placebo

15

Daniel J. Cox, Andrew Freundlich, and Robert G. Meyer

Twenty-seven adults from the general population with chronic tension headaches were divided into three groups. Nine were assigned to auditory electromyograph (EMG) feedback, 9 to progressive relaxation instructions, and 9 to placebo treatment. Subjects came for 2 weeks of pre- and posttreatment assessment, with 4 intervening weeks of treatment. Measures were taken on headache frequency, intensity and duration, frontalis EMG recordings, medication intake, locus of control, and additional psychosomatic complaints. Comparison of postassessment and 4-month follow-up data indicated that biofeedback and verbal relaxation instructions were equally superior to the medicine placebo on all measured variables in the direction of clinical improvement, except for shifts in locus of control. All groups experienced equally significant shifts toward internality.

Survey data (Waters, & O'Connor, 1971; Wolff, 1972) indicate that between 50% and 70% of adults experience headaches, 40% of which are tension or muscle-contraction headaches (Kashiwagi, McClure, & Wetzel, 1972). Tension headaches are characterized by bilateral tightening sensations originating usually in the frontal or suboccipital region and are directly related to excessive and sustained contraction in scalp and/or neck muscles. Despite this high frequency of occurrence and the known mechanism of pain, traditional treatment has been restricted to symptomatic medication, for example, tranquilizers, muscle relaxants, and analgesics, or individual psychotherapy.

Recently, the self-control technique of electromyograph (EMG) biofeedback (Budzyn-

ski, Stoyva, Adler, & Mullaney, 1973; Wickramasekera, 1972) has been used in the successful training of headache victims in relaxation of relevant muscular structures for prevention of muscle-contraction headaches. However, a review by Blanchard, Young, and Jackson (1974) pointed out that biofeedback research concerning tension headaches "confirms the efficacy of the combination of feedback and home practice in relaxation; their designs do not make it possible to isolate the effects of biofeedback alone" (p. 578). The question is whether home practice of relaxation instructions is sufficient to achieve similar therapeutic effects repeatedly demonstrated by electronically sophisticated biofeedback techniques.

McKenzie, Ehrisman, Montgomery, and Barnes (1974) and Wickramasekera (1973) have combined relaxation instructions and biofeedback in the successful treatment of tension headaches. Tasto and Hinkle (1973)

Requests for reprints should be sent to Daniel J. Cox, Department of Psychology, University of Louisville, Louisville, Kentucky 40208.

and Fichtler and Zimmerman (1973) have demonstrated that verbal relaxation instructions alone can produce significant reductions in headache activity. Jacobson (1935) indicated that progressive relaxation training is capable of lowering muscle activity and suggests its use in the treatment of tension headaches. In a detailed case study, Jacobson (1970) demonstrates the effective application of relaxation training in the remediation of chronic headaches. However, all of these studies were deficient in adequate controls and comparisons to answer the question of differential treatment effectiveness. This study attempts to address the question of whether biofeedback training itself makes a significant contribution to the treatment of tension headaches.

METHOD

Subjects

A newspaper article generated 93 respondents. Of these, 27 were selected who most closely fit the following criteria: experienced headaches of a steady bilateral pain originating in the frontal or suboccipital region, occurred three or more times a week, and had no organic basis according to family physician. The 27 subjects consisted of 7 males and 20 females, whose age ranged from 16 to 64 years with an average age of 39. Mean duration of headache history was 11 years, ranging from 1 to 39 years.

Procedure

During the first 2 weeks, subjects came for individual weekly pretreatment assessment. The first meeting involved signing a treatment contract, making a $20 refundable deposit, obtaining family physician's approval, recording frontalis EMG following a 20-minute rest period, and administration of the Nowicki-Strickland Locus of Control Scale (Nowicki & Duke, Note 1) and the Psychosomatic Checklist. The Psychosomatic Checklist, developed for this study, lists 18 common psychosomatic complaints, each of which is given a rating by the subject on intensity and frequency. During the following week, and all subsequent weeks, subjects filled out a daily Headache Data Sheet recording intensity and duration of each headache experienced, circumstances surrounding headache onset and how it was responded to, and medication taken. The second pretreatment session included recording frontalis EMG, as did all following sessions, and a review of Headache Data Sheets. Subjects were assigned to a treatment group at the third session, with groups equated for headache frequency and locus of control scores.

Biofeedback group. Biofeedback subjects came twice weekly for eight hourly treatment sessions. Auditory analogue EMG feedback was given for 30 minutes a session. Feedback was generated from frontalis EMG monitored by three disk electrodes placed across the forehead (Budzynski et al., 1973),

which was amplified and rectified allowing average peak-to-peak voltage readings over a 1-sec interval.[1] Subjects were instructed to use cue-controlled breathing (Russell & Sipich, 1974) immediately following 30 min of feedback. Subjects accomplished this by maintaining their relaxed condition and focusing on their natural rhythmic breathing while simultaneously using the covert self-instruction, "relax."

Reduction of EMG was progressively shaped and auditory feedback systematically faded out during training. Shaping was accomplished by gradually increasing feedback gain, or sensitivity, requiring progressively lower levels of EMG to maintain low auditory feedback signals. Intervals of no feedback were introduced as subjects gained greater control of their frontalis activity in an effort to fade out feedback dependency. To further facilitate generalizing the training effect, subjects practiced relaxation in techniques learned during feedback twice daily and used cue-control breathing prior to each meal. All home practice was recorded (Tasto & Hinkle, 1973). After the third feedback session, biofeedback subjects were instructed to begin applying their relaxing skills at the first sign of a headache onset.

Verbal relaxation instruction group. Bernstein and Borkovec's (1973) procedure was used in training relaxation. The first three of the eight twice-weekly treatment sessions were concerned with tightening and relaxing 16 muscle groups. The subsequent five sessions dealt with progressively reducing the operated muscle groups until subjects only recalled feelings of relaxation and used cue-control breathing, thus eliminating the need for any vigorous exercises. Identical to biofeedback subjects, relaxation subjects engaged in cue-control self-instruction following their relaxation exercise, practiced their relaxation exercises and cued breathing at home, and began to implement their relaxation skills at initial signs of a headache following the third treatment session.

Medication placebo group. These subjects received a green and white glucose capsule administered during weekly individual hourly sessions. They were told that it was a peripheral-acting time-release muscle relaxant known to be effective.

Sessions of the 2-week posttreatment assessment, as well as the 2 weeks of follow-up occurring 4 months later, were identical to pretreatment sessions for all subjects. The Nowicki-Strickland and the Psychosomatic Checklist scales were administered during the second week of both evaluation periods.

RESULTS

Analysis of covariance (Winer, 1971) was used to analyze posttreatment levels of headache activity and frontalis EMG since it controls for group differences in pretreatment levels. The dimension of headache activity analyzed was an H_D conversion (Budzynski et al., 1973) in which hours of headache activity were weighed by intensity of head-

---

[1] For a detailed description of the EMG biofeedback unit, contact Electronic Systems, Development Corporation, P.O. Box 18223, Louisville, Kentucky.

TABLE 1

CRITICAL VALUES FROM THE COMPARISON OF TREATMENT EFFECTIVENESS

Comparison	Biofeedback vs. vs. placebo	Verbal instructions vs. placebo	Biofeedback vs. verbal instructions
Posttreatment			
H_D scores			
F	5.73**	2.95*	.81
df	1, 23	1, 23	2, 23
Frontalis EMG			
F	41.12****	33.31****	1.69
df	1, 23	1, 23	1, 23
Medication reduction			
U	21	21	39
df	9, 9	9, 9	9, 9
Psychosomatic Checklist reduction			
U	4.0****	4.5****	39.5
df	9, 9	9, 9	9, 9
Locus of control changes			
U	28	28	30
df	9, 9	9, 9	9, 9
Follow-up			
H_D scores			
F	10.10****	10.96***	.03
df	1, 20	1, 20	1, 20
Frontalis EMG			
F	3.52*	8.60***	.21
df	1, 20	1, 20	1, 20
Medication reduction			
U	15**	15**	39
df	8, 8	8, 8	8, 8
Psychosomatic Checklist reduction			
U	15**	13**	9*
df	8, 8	8, 8	8, 8
Locus of control changes			
U	28	22	30
df	8, 8	8, 8	8, 8

* $p < .10$.
** $p < .05$.
*** $p < .01$.
**** $p < .001$.

ache pain.[2] Using pretreatment data as the covariant, an overall F of 2.86 ($df = 2, 23$, $p < .10$) was obtained. Since the trend was in the predicted direction, an a priori comparison of weighted means (Winer, 1971, p. 785) was carried out. Table 1 shows biofeedback superior to placebo ($p < .05$) and equivalent to relaxation, whereas relaxation subjects show a trend ($p < .10$) over placebo. This is further substantiated by inspection of Figure 1 in which biofeedback and relaxation subjects show a progressively parallel improvement rate over weeks and the placebo profile exhibits no such trend. Virtually identical results and treatment trends were obtained when analyzing unweighted hours of headache activity (Cox, 1974).

When comparing posttreatment frontalis EMG taken after a 20-minute rest interval, an overall F of 3.88 ($df = 2, 23$, $p < .05$) was observed. As seen in Table 1, a comparison of adjusted means shows that biofeedback ($p < .001$) and relaxation ($p < .001$) were superior to placebo. Biofeedback and relaxation did not differ.

Secondary effects of treatment were analyzed in terms of medication intake and additional psychosomatic complaint reductions. A Kruskal-Wallis analysis of variance yielded an H of 5.90 ($df = 2$, $p < .05$) when comparing prereduction and postreduction of psy-

---

[2] $H_D = \Sigma (I:D)/24$ where headache intensity (I), as indicated on a 5-point scale, is multiplied by the hours of headache duration (D); these products being summed for each day and divided by 24, yielding an hourly weighted average of headache activity.

chosomatic complaints. Again Table 1 shows that biofeedback ($p < .001$) and relaxation ($p < .001$) were superior to placebo and equivalent to one another as analyzed by the Mann-Whitney U test. Similarly, reduction in units of medication taken was found to be differentially effected, H (2) $= 14.77$, $p < .001$, with biofeedback producing significantly greater medication reduction than placebo ($p < .05$) and equivalent reductions to relaxation, whereas relaxation was superior to placebo ($p < .05$). Group means and standard deviations of these measures are given in Table 2.

Shifts in locus of control scores as a function of treatment were similar for all groups, as seen in Table 1. Chi-square analysis demonstrated significant pre–post shifts toward internality for biofeedback, χ^2 (1) $= 7.08$, $p < .01$, relaxation, χ^2 (1) $= 6.00$, $p < .05$, and placebo, χ^2 (1) $= 6.00$, $p < .05$. There was no significant correlation between initial locus of control scores and amount of headache reduction.

Follow-Up Data

As displayed in Figure 1 and Table 2, treatment effectiveness of biofeedback and relaxation training continued to improve for the eight available subjects in each treatment at a 4-month follow-up. This is substantiated by an overall analysis of covariance F of 4.62 ($df = 2$, 23, $p < .05$) showing biofeedback and relaxation equivalently superior to placebo (see a priori F values in Table 1). This analysis was done by comparing the H_D follow-up data of treatment groups to posttreatment data of placebo. Placebo follow-up data were contaminated by the fact that two of the women had quit their stress-related jobs, another had sought relaxation training at the clinic, one had gotten a divorce, a fifth subject was in the hospital at the time, and a sixth man was undergoing twice-weekly chiropractic massages for his headaches. All this had taken place during the 4-month interim, whereas no such changes were noted with the treatment subjects as evaluated by questionnaire.

Covariance analysis of EMG data was significant, $F(2, 23) = 5.61$, $p < .05$, with the results in Table 1 suggesting that relaxation effects were more reliable than biofeedback.

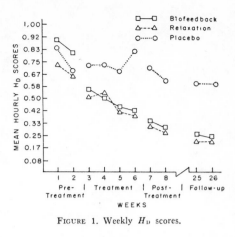

FIGURE 1. Weekly H_D scores.

Psychosomatic complaints and medication intake reduction held stable as can be seen in Table 1.

DISCUSSION

EMG feedback and relaxation instructions were found to be equally superior treatments to medication placebo in reducing headache activity and frontalis EMG. These procedures were also similarly effective in producing reductions of medication intake and ancillary psychosomatic complaints. Even though the relaxation instructions did not significantly differ from placebo on reduction of headache activity at posttreatment, the continually improving profile of relaxation in Figure 1, contrasted to placebo and the clinically significant data presented in Table 3 indicate that relaxation instruction is a superior technique after only 4 weeks of treatment. This treatment effectiveness is further substantiated by placebo subjects' consistent reports of seeking alternative forms of headache relief during the 4 months following treatment, whereas no such reports were received from treatment subjects. This is not a reaction to being in a "placebo group," since the subjects were never informed that they were receiving an inert drug until after the follow-up assessment.

Reduction in medication is not surprising since with fewer headaches there should be less need for medication. This, along with the stable reduction of ancillary psychosomatic complaints, was also reported by Budzynski et al. (1973). However, in contrast to Budzynski's finding of an r of .90 between re-

TABLE 2

MEANS AND STANDARD DEVIATIONS OF DEPENDENT MEASURES AT PREASSESSMENT, POSTASSESSMENT
AND FOLLOW-UP ASSESSMENT FOR ALL TREATMENT GROUPS

Measure	Biofeedback		Relaxation		Placebo	
	M	SD	M	SD	M	SD
H_D score						
Pre	1.69	1.14	1.35	.57	1.55	1.05
Post	.63	.77	.63	.54	1.25	.73
Follow-up	.60	.85	.46	.53	.90	.70
Improvement[a]	63%		53%		19%	
Headache frequency per week						
Pre	18.4	8.9	16.6	4.1	17.8	9.8
Post	9.1	12.4	7.9	4.0	13.9	11.4
Follow-up	7.8	12.8	8.0	6.3	14.4	13.6
Improvement	51%		52%		23%	
Hours of headaches per week						
Pre	94.7	62.0	79.7	35.4	84.4	54.4
Post	33.0	37.3	37.2	27.0	68.3	67.6
Follow-up	31.3	41.2	28.4	30.0	37.6	27.7
Improvement	65%		53%		19%	
Medication per week						
Pre	34.2	32.0	28.1	17.8	34.4	39.4
Post	14.1	26.8	11.3	11.6	33.0	42.3
Follow-up	8.5	11.6	7.0	9.1	37.4	54.8
Improvement	59%		60%		−14%	
Locus of control scores						
Pre	9.9	4.6	10.7	5.9	10.4	4.4
Post	6.8	3.1	8.9	6.9	8.7	3.2
Follow-up	7.4	3.7	8.5	6.1	11.6	3.3
Improvement	24%		17%		16%	
Psychosomatic Checklist scores						
Pre	31.9	18.3	18.9	8.2	26.9	20.2
Post	13.1	13.0	9.9	8.4	20.1	15.1
Follow-up	16.5	16.4	11.6	7.2	26.4	19.1
Improvement	58%		48%		23%	

[a] Percentage of improvement from preassessment to postassessment.

duction of headache activity and reduction of frontalis EMG, the same correlation in the present study yielded an r of .42. In other words, reduction in EMG only accounted for 18% of the variance in treatment effect. The difference in these two findings is possibly a consequence of EMG sampling; whereas Budzynski et al.'s EMG readings were taken during feedback sessions, relevant EMG readings in the present analysis were recorded during 2 weeks of pretreatment and posttreatment when no feedback or training was offered.

This low correlation raises the question of what else accounts for the treatment effect besides the sampled EMG reduction. It is proposed that successful treatment is de-

pendent on four steps: (a) learning EMG reduction in treatment; (b) increased relaxation throughout daily activities; (c) recognizing early onset of a headache; and (d) adequate, early application of relaxation skills. Budzynski et al.'s procedure focused on feedback training and application and was thus concerned with a and d, whereas the present study additionally required subjects to use their relaxation skills, in the form of cue-controlled breathing, daily prior to each meal, and to record and examine conditions in which headaches arose. Hence, this study also focused on Steps b and c. The effect of incorporating additional skills in the treatment paradigm allows additional techniques

TABLE 3

FREQUENCY DISTRIBUTION OF (SUBJECTS') IMPROVEMENT ON H_D SCORES AT POSTTREATMENT
AND FOLLOW-UP, RELATIVE TO PRETREATMENT LEVELS

Range of % improvement	Biofeedback		Relaxation		Placebo	
	Posttreatment	Follow-up	Posttreatment	Follow-up	Posttreatment	Follow-up
0–24	1	1	2	0	4	4
25–49	0	0	3	1	3	1
50–74	5	2	2	3	1	2
75–100	3	5	2	4	1	1

to contribute to the treatment effect. This multidimensional approach achieved similar therapeutic effects in 8 hours of treatment to Budzynski's 16 hours of treatment. However, the specific relevance of this additional focus needs further research to delineate its treatment contribution.

In considering Table 3, the range of variance is observed to be large in all groups. Initial locus of control scores were anticipated to account for some of this variance, but its low correlation with percentage of reduction in H_D indicates the poor predictability of this instrument. The Nowicki-Strickland Locus of Control Scale is primarily concerned with perceived control of social interactions. Possibly, an instrument constructed to measure perception of intrapersonal self-control, specifically on a physiological dimension, would have a greater predictive value. It is apparent that additional subject dimensions should be investigated to allow greater prediction of treatment responsiveness and to permit individual tailoring of a therapeutic procedure. Subsequent research at the clinic suggests that subject variables, such as extreme obsessive-compulsive characteristics, may interfere with the effective use of biofeedback techniques; that is, excessive concern with auditory feedback may produce an interfering performance anxiety. For such subjects, a relaxation procedure absent of an overt achievement criterion, such as verbal relaxation training, may be the treatment of choice. Investigation of such a hypothesis is presently being conducted.

Recent research (Shoemaker & Tasto, 1975) supplements the present study's findings of equivalent effectiveness for a biofeedback technique and relaxation instructions in the treatment of the psychosomatic complaint essential hypertension. We also concur with their conclusion that optimal results may be obtained by combining biofeedback techniques and relaxation instructions or by using different types of biofeedback techniques.

In using intervention techniques such as EMG feedback and relaxation instructions in treatment of headaches, one must be sure that the headache source is a high level of neuromuscular activity. Additionally, it should be investigated whether maintenance of headaches is not being contributed to by secondary gains or resulting from a modeling effect. Given these precautions, either relaxation technique is a justified intervention.

REFERENCE NOTE

1. Nowicki, S., & Duke, M. *A locus of control scale for adults: An alternative to the Rotter.* Unpublished manuscript, Emory University, 1972.

REFERENCES

Bernstein, D. A., & Borkovec, T. D. *Progressive relaxation training: A manual for the helping professions.* Chicago: Research Press, 1973.

Blanchard, E. B., Young, L. C., & Jackson. Clinical applications of biofeedback training. *Archives of General Psychiatry,* 1974, *30,* 573–589.

Budzynski, T. H., Stoyva, J. M., Adler, C. S., & Mullaney, D. J. EMG biofeedback and tension headaches: A controlled outcome study. *Seminars Psychiatry,* 1973, *5,* 387–410.

Cox, D. J. *Differential effectiveness of EMG feedback, verbal relaxation instructions and medication placebo with muscle contraction headaches* (master's thesis, University of Louisville, 1974), University Microfilms No. 31RB2.

Fichtler, H., & Zimmerman, R. R. Changes in reported pain from tension headaches. *Perceptual and Motor Skills,* 1973, *36,* 712.

Jacobson, E. *Progressive relaxation.* Chicago: University of Chicago Press, 1935.

Jacobson, E. *Modern treatment of tense patients.* Springfield, Ill.: Charles C Thomas, 1970.

Kashiwagi, T., McClure, J. N., & Wetzel, R. D. Headache and psychiatric disorders. *Diseases of the Nervous System,* 1972, *33,* 659–663.

McKenzie, R. E., Ehrisman, W. J., Montgomery, P. S., & Barnes, R. H. The treatment of headache by means of electroencephalographic biofeedback. *Headache,* 1974, *13,* 164–172.

Russell, R. K., & Sipich, J. R. Treatment of test anxiety by cue-control relaxation. *Behavior Therapy,* 1974, *5,* 673–676.

Shoemaker, J. E., & Tasto, D. L. The effects of muscle relaxation on blood pressure of essential hypertensives. *Behaviour Research and Therapy,* 1975, *13,* 29–43.

Tasto, D. L., & Hinkle, J. E. Muscle relaxation treatment for tension headaches. *Behaviour Research and Therapy,* 1973, *11,* 347–349.

Waters, W. E., & O'Connor, P. J. Epidemiology of headaches and migraine in women. *Journal of Neurology, Neurosurgery, and Psychiatry,* 1971, *34,* 148–155.

Wickramasekera, I. Electromyographic feedback training and tension headaches: Preliminary observations. *American Journal of Clinical Hypnosis,* 1972, *15,* 83–85.

Wickramasekera, I. The application of verbal instructions and EMG feedback training to the management of tension headaches—preliminary observations. *Headache,* 1973, *13,* 74–76.

Winer, R. J. *Statistical principles in experimental design.* New York: McGraw-Hill, 1971.

Wolff, R. *Headaches and other head pains.* New York: Oxford University Press, 1972.

Electromyographic 16
Biofeedback and Relaxation
Instructions in the Treatment of
Muscle Contraction Headaches

Stephen N. Haynes, Philip Griffin,
Dean Mooney, and Mario Parise

To assess the comparative effectiveness of relaxation instructions and frontalis electromyographic (EMG) biofeedback in the treatment of muscle-contraction (tension) headaches, 21 volunteers were assigned to either a relaxation training group, a biofeedback group or a no-treatment control group. Each group met for six 1/2-hr sessions. The EMG biofeedback and the relaxation instructions resulted in significant decreases in reported headache activity. Both procedures were significantly more effective than the control procedure, but did not differ significantly from each other in effectiveness. The effectiveness of the two experimental procedures was maintained at follow-up. Frontalis EMG levels were higher during sessions in which a headache was reported than in sessions when no headache was reported. The importance of individual differences is emphasized.

Historically, the analysis and treatment of psychophysiological disorders has been based upon a psychodynamic or medical model (Alexander, 1950). Recently, however, numerous investigations concerning both etiology and intervention procedures with psychophysiological disorders are being derived from behavioral frameworks (Stoyva & Budzynski, 1973). The use of behavioral intervention procedures with these disorders is based upon the supposition that they are physiological responses which covary with specific environmental situations and are amenable, therefore, to modification through application of such procedures.

In biofeedback procedures, an individual receives information (e.g., variable frequency tone, points, light signals) about the functioning of a

The authors express their appreciation to Benjamin Lahey and Jack Wackwitz for their help in preparation of this manuscript. Requests for reprints may be addressed to Stephen N. Haynes, Department of Psychology, University of South Carolina, Columbia, SC 29208.

Reprinted by permission from *Behavior Therapy*, 1975, Vol. 6, No. 5, 672-678.

physiological response which allows him to monitor and subsequently, gain some degree of control over that response (Miller, 1969; DiCara, 1970). Biofeedback procedures have been used to successfully treat various psychophysiological disorders (Shapiro & Schwartz, 1972; Weiss & Engel, 1971).

Muscle-contraction headache (tension headache) is a familiar psychophysiological disorder apparently caused by sustained contraction of the muscles of the head and neck (Wolff, 1963). If this hypothesis is valid, procedures which reduce muscle tension of the head and neck should result in a decrease in measures of headache activity.

Budzynski, Stoyva, and Adler (1970), and Budzynski, Stoyva, Adler, and Mullaney (1973) employed frontalis muscle biofeedback and relaxation practice at home with several muscle-contraction headache patients and found a significant decrease in measures of headache activity when compared to individuals undergoing control procedures. While this well-controlled study provided evidence supporting the effectiveness of a treatment package including biofeedback in the treatment of muscle-contraction headaches, it did not allow for the assessment of the comparative effectiveness of the therapy components. Relaxation instructions have been shown to result in decreased levels of muscle tension (Haynes, Moseley & McGowan, 1975) and might be expected also to result in a decrease in measures of headache activity.

The function of the present study was to assess the comparative effectiveness of frontalis electromyographic (EMG) biofeedback and relaxation instructions in decreasing measures of muscle-contraction headache activity.

METHOD

Subjects

Twenty-one university students (7 males, 14 females; average age of 20.9 yr) who responded to advertisements in the campus newspaper and to classroom announcements concerning an experimental treatment program for tension headaches. All volunteers were interviewed for diagnostic purposes and to inform them of the program requirements. Twenty-one subjects demonstrating distinct, frequently occurring "tension-headache" syndromes were selected from 34 applicants. All but two had consulted a physician about their headaches. The subjects were completely naive as to the treatment procedures to be employed. An average headache history of 5.2 yr was reported.

Setting and Apparatus

All treatment sessions occurred in a 10 × 7 ft. (3.1 × 2.1 m) environmentally controlled, sound attenuated room. The experimenter sat in an adjacent room separated from the subject by a one-way mirror. All instructions were on audio tape. Subject–experimenter contact was minimal and primarily confined to placement and removal of electrodes.

A model PA-2 Bioelectric Information Feedback System (BIFS)[1] was used to monitor EMG level and provide a variable frequency tone through a headset. The pitch of the tone varied directly with the relative level of EMG activity. (Instrumentation and procedures are more fully explained in Budzynski, 1969.)

Measurement of Headache and EMG Activity

Each subject maintained a "headache data sheet" on which he rated the occurrence and intensity of his headaches on an 11 point scale (0—no headache, 10—very severe headache) every 2 hr from 10:00 AM through 10:00 PM.

Frontalis EMG activity was monitored throughout each training session. The frontalis muscle was selected because of its sensitivity, correlation with other physiological systems, and possible function in the etiology of muscle-contraction headaches (Stoyva & Budzynski, 1973). Frontalis muscle tension data consisted of EMG levels from a series of 64-sec integrated trials with a 20-sec intertrial interval.

Experimental Design and Procedures

Each subject monitored his headache activity following the initial interview 2 wk prior to the first treatment session. In addition to providing baseline data, this phase also helped assess and control for the reactive effects of self-observation.

Following the 2-wk self-observation phase, subjects were randomly assigned to either a biofeedback group ($N = 8$), relaxation-instructions group ($N = 8$), or a no-treatment group ($N = 5$). Subjects continued to monitor their headache activity throughout the experimental phase. Training sessions occurred twice a week for 3 wk (except for expected variations due to uncontrollable factors). Upon entering the experimental room for the training session, subjects were seated in a reclining chair, their forehead scrubbed with acetone, electrodes placed over the frontalis muscles (Budzynski, 1969), and earphones over their ears. The experimenter then left the room and played taped instructions which told the subject to remain as still as possible until further instructions. Baseline EMG activity was then assessed for 9.8 min prior to any experimental instructions.

Following the baseline phase, each subject received taped instructions appropriate to his group assignment. Subjects in the biofeedback group were told to become as relaxed as possible and that they would hear a tone to assist them in relaxing. The function of the tone was then described in detail. Subjects in the relaxation-instructions group were told to become as relaxed as possible and that they would receive instructions to help them relax. Taped relaxation instructions then began. Subjects in the control group were told to become as relaxed as possible, but received no further intervention procedure. This treatment phase of each session lasted for 19.6 min (20.3 min for the relaxation-instructions group).[2] At the end of the experimental phase, each subject received a taped message that he was learning how to relax and that he should employ what he was learning to prevent or terminate his headaches. The experimenter then removed the electrodes, and the session was terminated. Subjects monitored their headache activity for 1 wk following treatment, and were phoned 5–7 mo later for follow-up.

[1] Biofeedback Systems, Inc., Boulder, CO 80302

[2] Previous research (Haynes, Moseley, & McGowan, 1974) demonstrated that 20 min of these specific instructions resulted in a significant decrease in frontalis EMG level. A transcript of the relaxation instructions is available upon request.

TABLE 1

Self-Report of Headache Frequency, Duration, Intensity and Index Overall Activity (Weekly Averages) during Baseline, Post-Treatment and Follow-Up as a Function of Treatment Procedure

| | Baseline | | | | Treatment phase | | | | | | | |
| | | | | | Posttreatment | | | | Follow-up | | | |
Group	Frequency	Duration	Intensity	Headache index	Frequency	Duration	Intensity	Headache Index	Frequency	Duration	Intensity	Headache index
Relaxation instructions	5.2	5.7	3.6	102.3	1.4	3.6	2.0	18.6	0.3	0.4	2.0	0.5
Biofeedback	5.5	4.7	3.4	82.1	1.5	2.9	1.7	20.9	1.2	2.3	4.1	11.4
Control	6.1	2.5	4.2	68.7	5.5	3.1	4.0	87.8	4.7	1.7	6.0	48.3

RESULTS

The index of overall headache activity (Table 1), an additive function calculated by summing the headache ratings each day with weekly averages, reflects frequency, intensity, and duration.

A repeated-measures analysis of variance (Winer, 1962) on pre- and post-treatment measures revealed that there are significant differences between treatment groups on measures of reported headache frequency ($F(2,18) = 4.14$, $p < .05$), and in overall reported headache activity ($F(2,18) = 6.17$, $p < .01$).

There was no significant pretreatment–posttreatment difference between the groups on measures of reported headaches duration ($F(2/18) = 1.05$, N.S.) or in reported headache intensity ($F(2/18) = 1.11$, N.S.). There was no significant difference between groups on any pre-treatment baseline measure.

Posthoc Neuman Keuls analysis comparing pretreatment and post-treatment reports of the three groups revealed: (1) biofeedback ($q(3,18) = 7.7$, $p < .01$) and relaxation instructions ($q(2,18) = 7.9$, $p < .01$) were both significantly more effective than the control procedure in reducing reports of headache frequency, (2) biofeedback ($q(3,18) = 5.86$, $p < .01$) and relaxation instructions ($q(2,18) = 6.06$, $p < .01$) were both significantly more effective than the control procedure in reducing the index of overall reported headache activity, and (3) biofeedback and relaxation instructions did not differ significantly from

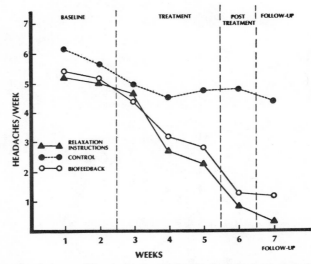

FIG. 1.   Mean headache rate (headaches/week) for the 2-wk pretreatment phase, the wk following treatment, and at follow-up as a function of intervention procedure.

each other in their effect on reported headache frequency or overall headache activity.

Inspection of Fig. 1 reveals a dramatic decrease in reported headache frequency associated with biofeedback and relaxation-instruction procedures.

Five subjects (two Biofeedback, two relaxation instruction, and one control) could not be located at follow-up, precluding statistical analysis of the follow-up.

An analysis of baseline EMG activity for subjects who reported a headache during the training session compared to baseline EMG activity of the same subjects when they reported no headache revealed that reported tension headaches were associated with elevated frontalis EMG activity. An average integrated baseline EMG level of (5.37 mV/min) was found for subjects when they reported a headache compared to a level of (4.19 mV/min) for the same subjects when they reported no headache. A t-test for correlated data revealed a significant difference $(t(9) = 2.48, p < .05)$.

DISCUSSION

Frontalis electromyographic biofeedback and relaxation instructions resulted in significant decreases in reported headache frequency and overall headache activity. Both intervention procedures were significantly more effective than a no-treatment control procedure. Improvement was found to be maintained at follow-up.

It should be noted that an earlier study (Haynes, Moseley, & McGowan, 1975) indicated that commonly used methods of relaxation training are differentially effective in reducing EMG activity. It is impossible, therefore, to assume that relaxation procedures other than the one used here would be effective in the treatment of muscle contraction headaches.

Subjects demonstrated a higher average frontalis EMG when they reported having a headache during the session than when they reported having no headache. Several subjects, however, did not demonstrate this relationship between headache occurrence and EMG level. Assuming the absence of procedural or instrumentation errors, several interpretations are possible: (1) The headaches of these individuals did not have a muscular-contraction etiology, (2) The headache was a function of increased muscular contraction in another part of the head (e.g., neck) and was not reflected in elevated frontalis muscle tension, and (3) Self-report varied as a function of other unidentified variables (e.g., perceived demands in the experiment, stressful life experiences).

In a previous unpublished study, the frontalis EMG level of subjects who reported frequent tension headaches was significantly above that of a group of subjects who reported few or no tension headaches. The resting frontalis integrated EMG level was 3.42 mV/min for subjects who reported few or no tension headaches compared to 5.26 for subjects who reported frequent tension headaches. Closer inspection of the data, however reveals interesting individual differences. Some individuals with extremely high frontalis EMG levels reported few or no tension headaches. Others with relatively low frontalis EMG levels reported frequent tension headaches. These findings underline the need for additional assessment of individual differences in psychophysiological disorders.

Particular care must be exercise in the design of intervention outcome studies involving self-report measures to minimize the sensitivity of the data to suggestion, demand characteristics, or placebo effects. In the present study, attempts were made to minimize these sources of bias by (1) including a 2-week self-observation period to control for the reactive effects of self-observation, (2) standardizing, as well as possible, demand and expectation variables across all three groups, (3) relying on self-report of behavior (e.g., headache ratings) rather than self-report of behavior change (e.g., improvement), and (4) minimizing response bias by using data sheets to record headache activity rather than plotted graphs (cf Budzynski, et al. 1973).

REFERENCES

Alexander, F. *Psychosomatic medicine.* New York: Norton, 1950.

Budzynski, T. H. *Feedback-induced muscle relaxation and activation level.* Unpublished doctoral dissertation. University of Colorado, 1969.

Budzynski, T. H., and Stoyva, J. M. An instrument for producing deep muscle relaxation by means of analog information feedback. *Journal of Applied Behavior Analysis,* 1969, **2**, 231–237.

Budzynski, T. H., Stoyva, J. M., and Adler, C. S. Feedback induced muscle relaxation: Application to tension headaches. *Behavior Therapy and Experimental Psychiatry,* 1970, **1**, 205–211.

Budzynski, T. H., Stoyva, J. M., Adler, C. S., and Mullaney, D. J. EMG biofeedback and tension headache: A controlled outcome study. *Psychosomatic Medicine,* 1973, **35**, 484–496.

DiCara, L. V. Learning in the autonomic nervous system. *Scientific American,* 1970, **222**, 30–39.

Haynes, S., Moseley, D., and McGowan, W. T. The comparative effectiveness of EMG biofeedback and relaxation instructions. *Psychophysiology,* 1975 (in press).

Miller, N. E. Learning of visceral and glandular responses. *Science,* 1969, **163**, 434–445.

Shapiro, D., and Schwartz, G. E. Biofeedback and visceral learning: Clinical applications. *Seminars in Psychiatry,* 1972, **4**, 171–184.

Stoyva, J. M. and Budzynski, T. H. Cultivated low arousal—An anti-stress response? In L. V. DiCara (Ed.), *Recent advances in limbic and autonomic nervous system research.* New York: Plenum, 1973.

Weiss, T., and Engel, B. T. Operant conditioning of heart rate in patients with premature ventricular contractions. *Psychosomatic Medicine,* 1971, **33**, 301–321.

Winer, B. J. *Statistical principles in experimental design.* New York: McGraw-Hill, 1962.

Wolff, H. G. *Headache and other head pain.* New York: Oxford University Press, 1963.

Relaxation Training and 17 Biofeedback in the Reduction of Frontalis Muscle Tension

Stephen N. Haynes, Dianne Moseley, and William T. McGowan

ABSTRACT

To assess the comparative effectiveness of frontalis electromygraphic (EMG) biofeedback and relaxation instructions in reducing frontalis EMG levels, 101 male and female university students were randomly assigned to one of the following groups: 1) frontalis EMG biofeedback (variable frequency auditory feedback), 2) passive relaxation instructions (instructions to attend to and relax muscles), 3) active relaxation instructions (tensing and relaxing exercises), 4) false feedback, and 5) no treatment control. In a one-session design, subjects receiving biofeedback and passive relaxation instructions demonstrated the greatest decrement in frontalis EMG level. The relationships between decrements in frontalis EMG level and sex, baseline EMG, and manifest anxiety are discussed.

DESCRIPTORS: Biofeedback, Relaxation training, Electromyography.

Muscle relaxation has been an important component in systematic desensitization (Lang, 1969; Mathews, 1971; Paul, 1966) and has been used as the primary treatment modality for various psychophysiological and stress-related disorders such as anxiety neurosis (Jacobson, 1970; Raskin, Johnson, & Rondestveldt, 1973), asthma (Davis, Saunders, Creer, & Chai, 1973; Alexander, 1972), tension headache (Stoyva & Budzynski, 1974), insomnia (Kahn, Baker, & Weiss, 1968; Geer & Katkin, 1966), and hypertension (Luthe, 1963; Moeller & Love, 1973). The hypothesized function of muscle relaxation in desensitization is to facilitate reciprocal inhibition—the treatment paradigm upon which desensitization was originally based (Wolpe, 1969). Theoretically, deep

The authors would like to express their appreciation to Mervyn K. Wagner, Martha Bays, and Diane Follingstad for their help in preparation of this manuscript.

The author's address is: Stephen N. Haynes, Department of Psychology, University of South Carolina, Columbia, SC 29208.

muscle relaxation inhibits physiological arousal to imagined feared stimuli and thereby reduces verbal and behavioral concomitants of anxiety. In the treatment of psychophysiological and other stress-related disorders, relaxation presumably reduces the individual's physiological response to stress and may, therefore, lead to symptom diminution.

Research on the role of relaxation in desensitization has had variable results with some studies finding that relaxation facilitated desensitization (Grings & Uno, 1968; Lehrer, 1972; Davison, 1968; Paul, 1969; Van Egeren, Feather, & Hein, 1971; Wolpe & Flood, 1970) and others finding that relaxation did not have a facilitating effect on desensitization (Bellack, 1973; Marshall & Strawbridge, 1972; Folkins, Lawson, Opton, & Lazarus, 1968; Rachman, 1968; Rimm, 1970; Vodde & Gilner, 1971; Waters, McDonald, & Koresko, 1972). Most of the reports on the use of muscle relaxation in the treatment of psychophysiological disorders have suggested that relaxation has potential therapeutic benefit but were conducted without the benefit of appropriate control groups. Because many and diverse training methods are used and the outcome of behavior research and treatment programs involving relaxation is a function of the effectiveness of the particular relaxation technique used, it is important to assess the relative effects of the various methods of relaxation training commonly reported in the literature.

Several studies have assessed and compared the physiological effects of various relaxation training methods. Lader and Mathews (1970) found that one session of Jacobson's relaxation instructions (Jacobson, 1938, 1970) did not result in decreases in physiological indices of activation. Barber and Hahn (1963) were unable to find decrements in physiological indices of activation after hypnotic suggestions of relaxation when compared to a control condition in which subjects were merely told to sit quietly. That relaxation training can result in significantly decreased levels of physiological arousal has been demonstrated by Mathews and Gelder (1969), Lehrer (1972), and Riddick and Meyer (1973). Relaxation training based on autogenic training methods (Luthe, 1963), has also been shown to result in reduced physiological indices of arousal (Geissman & Noel, 1961; Jus & Jus, 1969). It can be concluded from the above studies that some but not other methods of relaxation training have been effective in reducing physiological indices of arousal with the samples involved. Research comparing methods of inducing deep muscle relaxation, however, has not been conducted.

Biofeedback techniques offer a promising new method of producing deep levels of muscular relaxation in an efficient manner. In biofeedback procedures, information concerning some aspect of their physiological functioning is presented to the individual in analogue form. For example, a person may hear a tone which varies in pitch as a function of his level of muscle tension (electromyographic (EMG) feedback). By receiving immediate feedback concerning his level of muscle tension, he may quickly learn to voluntarily produce deep levels of muscular relaxation. Biofeedback-facilitated relaxation has been used with apparent success in studies by Stoyva and Budzynski (1974), Budzynski and Stoyva (1969), Davis et al. (1973), Moeller and Love (1973), and Green, Walters, Green, and Murphy (1969).

This study was designed to compare the effects of EMG biofeedback with the more commonly used verbal relaxation instructions in reducing frontalis muscle tension.

Method

Subjects and Procedure

Subjects were 101 male and female university students, average age 18.9 yrs, from introductory psychology classes. Subjects volunteered to participate in an experiment on "Relaxation and Muscle Tension" to fulfill course requirements for research participation. Each volunteer was assigned randomly to one of three experimental or two control groups; assignments were balanced for time-of-day of session to randomize diurnal physiological variability.

Each subject was brought into a small testing room and administered the Manifest Anxiety Scale (MAS, Taylor, 1953). He then entered a $3.1m \times 2.2m$ temperature and humidity controlled, sound attenuated room and was seated in a comfortable reclining chair. His forehead was scrubbed with acetone prior to the placement of electrodes to measure frontalis muscle activity (EMG activity from muscle groups adjacent to the frontalis also influence readings from the electrode placement). Standard frontalis electrode placement suggested by Venables and Martin (1967) was used.

Earphones were placed over the subject's ears. While electrodes and earphones were being attached, taped instructions were played explaining the function of the electrodes and earphones. There was no verbal interaction between the subject and the experimenter. The subject was then instructed to close his eyes, remain as still as possible, and wait for further instructions. After the experimenter left the room, a 5.6 min baseline period ensued.[1] The function of this phase was to reduce EMG variability and to generate baseline data with which to assess the effectiveness of the treatment conditions.

Following the baseline phase all subjects heard taped instructions explaining that their task was to become as relaxed as possible. The tapes for the various groups were identical except for the specific instructions about how to relax. Following the instructions, a 20-min experimental phase ensued structured according to the group assignment of the subject.[2]

Groups

Feedback. Subjects (12 males, 10 females) received auditory biofeedback about their level of frontalis muscle tension. Through earphones, they heard a tone which varied directly with changes in their EMG level. The tone decreased in pitch as they became more relaxed and increased in pitch as their EMG level increased. Subjects were instructed to relax by lowering the tone. The experimenter could control the tone pitch at any level of EMG activity. As a subject reduced his EMG activity and lowered the pitch of the tone, the experimenter increased the pitch to the middle of the frequency range. To lower the tone again, the subject was required to relax further. The pitch was increased contingent on 15 sec of steady low tone. Therefore, subjects were "shaped" into lower levels of muscle activity.

Relaxation A.[3] Subjects (9 males, 9 females) heard taped relaxation instructions of the kind frequently used in abbreviated relaxation training (Wolpe, 1969). They were instructed to attend to various muscle groups and to passively allow them to become relaxed. The tape was made by a clinical psychologist experienced in behavior therapy and in the use of this type of relaxation instructions. Instructions began with suggestions to attend to and relax specific muscle groups (hand,

---

[1]Previous pilot testing indicated that, although adaptation continues for a period of time, significant decreases in EMG level for most subjects are confined to the first 5 min of a baseline phase.

[2]Previous pilot testing indicated that maximal effects of relaxation training within this experimental situation are approximated after 20 min. After 20 min relaxation continues but at a slower rate.

[3]Complete transcripts of the relaxation instructions are available upon request.

forearm, biceps, triceps, shoulder, back, etc.) and ended with suggestions of total body relaxation.

Relaxation B.[3] Subjects (11 males, 11 females) heard taped relaxation instructions of the kind advocated by Jacobson (1938, 1970) and frequently used in relaxation training by behavior therapists. This tape was made by another clinical psychologist experienced in behavior therapy and in the use of this type of relaxation instructions. This method consisted of alternate muscular tensing and relaxing exercises. As in Relaxation A, attention initially focused on specific muscle groups and ended with the suggestions of total body relaxation (last 3 min).

False Feedback. Subjects (11 males, 11 females) received instructions identical to those in the "Feedback" group but heard a noncontingent tone. The variable frequency tone was varied randomly via a manual override control and was not a function of the subject's level of relaxation or tension. The function of this group was to control for placebo effect, any relaxing effects of the tone itself, and the effect of monotonous stimuli. Rachman (1968) has suggested that "mental relaxation" produced by "monotonous" stimuli is responsible for the effects of relaxation.

Control. As in the other groups, subjects (8 males, 9 females) were told to become as relaxed as possible but received no relaxation instructions or auditory stimuli of any kind during the experimental period. The function of this group was to control for the effect of the initial suggestion to relax and for the time-related effect of merely sitting quietly.

Data and Apparatus

The frontalis muscle (forehead) was chosen to assess EMG activity because it is suitable for standardization of electrode placement and previous research has suggested that it may be correlated with muscle tension levels in other areas of the body and with other indices of autonomic arousal such as heart rate and skin resistance (Jacobson, 1970; Stoyva & Budzynski, 1974; Sainsbury & Gibson, 1954; Budzynski, 1969). In addition to being a sensitive indicator of varying levels of physiological arousal, the frontalis muscle is one of the most difficult muscles to relax (Stoyva & Budzynski, 1974; Balshan, 1962).

Data collection on frontalis muscle tension began as soon as the experimenter left the testing room and consisted of 64-sec integrated EMG measurements with 20-sec intertrial intervals (Budzynski & Stoyva, 1969). The integrated EMG data was converted to mV/min for chart and table presentations. Additional information concerning the principles and methods of electromyography is available in Goldstein (1972). A Bioelectric Information Feedback System[4] was used for the integrated measurement and to provide the analogue feedback. An earlier model of this system was described by Budzynski and Stoyva (1969).

Results

Because physiological responses are often a function of baseline level (Sternbach, 1966), baseline EMG measures of the 5 groups were compared. Separate ANOVAs were conducted on average baseline, level in the last baseline phase, and change in EMG level during the baseline phase (1st–4th baseline period). There were no reliable between groups baseline effects, $F_{(4/96)}=1.38$, 1.02, and .73, respectively.[5]

[4]Bio-Feedback Systems, Inc., 2736 47th St., Boulder, Colorado, 80301.

[5]The .05 rejection region was adopted in all statistical comparisons.

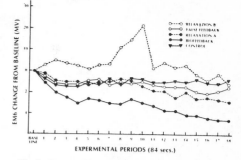

Fig. 1. Average EMG changes during the experimental phase for each group.

Plotted in Fig. 1 are average EMG changes during the experimental phase for each group. EMG changes were calculated by subtracting the EMG reading of each of the 18 experimental periods from the average of the 4 baseline periods. Inspection of Fig. 1 reveals that subjects receiving biofeedback demonstrated the greatest and most rapid reduction in EMG level. Not unexpectedly, the Relaxation B procedure, involving tensing and relaxing exercises, produced an initial increase in EMG level followed by a decrease toward the end when suggestions of body relaxation were given. The peak in EMG level for Relaxation B was associated with tensing the facial and forehead muscles.

To assess differences between the five procedures in their effect on EMG level, a change score was calculated for each subject by subtracting the EMG level in the last experimental period from the average of the 4 baseline periods. Because changes in EMG were found to be highly correlated with initial baseline level, $r(100)=.57$, the comparative effectiveness of the various procedures was assessed by an analysis of covariance (based on multiple regression methods) on change score with baseline level as the covariate. This analysis demonstrated that there were significant differences between the procedures in their ability to affect change in EMG level, $F(4/95)=7.34$. Baseline and experimental EMG averages are presented in Table 1. A post-hoc comparison between the procedures using Duncan's analysis is presented in Table 2. Inspection of Table 2 reveals that biofeedback was the most effective procedure in reducing EMG level although the difference between biofeedback and Relaxation A was not reliable. Relaxation A was significantly more effective than the Control or Relaxation B procedures but did not differ significantly from False Feedback. Relaxation B and control were not differentially effective in reducing EMG level.

To assess whether or not significant changes in EMG level resulted from each of the procedures, an *A*-test (McGuigan, 1968) was conducted. The

TABLE 1

EMG averages for the five relaxation procedures

Groups	EMG Levels (mV/min)				
	Baseline Average (4 Periods)	Experimental Average (Last 4 Periods)	Change Baseline (Baseline−Experimental)	Last Period	Lowest Level During Experimental Phase
Biofeedback	7.98	3.70	4.26	3.48	2.68
Relaxation A	6.50	3.82	2.68	3.58	2.84
Relaxation B	7.26	7.04	.22	6.00	3.54
False Feedback	5.66	3.82	2.24	4.04	2.32
Control	6.56	5.38	1.16	5.60	3.30

TABLE 2

Mean change scores for treatment methods (mV/min)

Biofeedback	Relax A	False	Relax B	Control
4.50	2.92	1.62	1.26	.96

Note.—Duncan's test ranges underlined, $p < .05$.

A-test is computationally simpler and more stringent than the conventionally used t-test. Results of this analysis indicated that Biofeedback, $A(21) = .068$, and Relaxation A, $A(17) = .094$, resulted in significant EMG changes (baseline average − last experimental), and that the other procedures did not result in a statistically significant change in EMG level.

Manifest anxiety was found to be significantly correlated with baseline EMG average, $r(100) = .20$, and average of the last 4 experimental periods; $r(100) = .17$, indicating that individuals with elevated MAS scores demonstrated greater resting physiological arousal as measured by EMG level and did not lower their EMG to as low a level as individuals with lower MAS scores. MAS was unrelated to any other experimental or baseline measure. There was an inverse correlation between age and average baseline level, $r(100) = -.26$, and the average of the last 4 experimental periods, $r(100) = -.21$, indicating that younger individuals demonstrated greater resting physiological arousal as measured by EMG level and did not lower their EMG to as low a level as older individuals. There were no significant correlations between sex and any measure of baseline or experimental EMG level. An independent correlational analysis with the biofeedback group revealed a strong association between baseline level and change during the experimental period, $r(100) = .71$, but not between sex ($r = .07$), age ($= .02$), or anxiety ($r = -.16$).

Discussion

In the present study, electromyographic biofeedback was an effective method of facilitating muscle relaxation, as indicated by reduction in frontalis EMG activity. Biofeedback was significantly more effective in reducing EMG levels than two control procedures or an active relaxation procedure involving tensing-relaxing exercises commonly used in behavior therapy. Although biofeedback was more effective than passive relaxation procedures, the difference did not reach statistical significance. Not only did biofeedback produce lower levels of frontalis EMG activity, it lowered EMG activity faster than the other methods of relaxation training. The effectiveness and efficiency of biofeedback suggests that it may be useful in desensitization and other behavior therapies relying on muscle relaxation. If the effectiveness of a particular behavior therapy is a function of muscle relaxation, EMG biofeedback would be expected to have a facilitative effect. The potential usefulness of biofeedback in behavior therapy is enhanced because of the availability to the behavior therapist of a quantitative index of muscle activity and the immediate feedback provided to the therapist concerning the physiological activity and reactivity of the patient during relaxation training and desensitization.

Passive relaxation (Relaxation A) also proved to be effective in reducing frontalis EMG levels. The greater effectiveness of passive relaxation training when compared to relaxation training involving alternate tensing and relaxing exercises suggests that the tensing exercise may be unnecessary in relaxation training. Because the relaxation instructions were administered by different behavior therapists, however, it is difficult to generalize from these results to these types of relaxation instructions. Both therapists, however, were very experienced in using their respective type of relaxation instructions and believed it to be effective in producing muscle relaxation. The design provided, therefore, a strong test for the comparative effectiveness of biofeedback. The demonstrated degree of muscle relaxation produced by biofeedback and Relaxation A provide a good basis from which to compare other relaxation training methods.

The false-feedback condition was designed to control for possible relaxation-facilitating effects of a variable frequency tone. It is possible that "yoked" feedback from a subject who successfully reduced his EMG levels would provide a stronger control from which to assess the biofeedback procedures.

Because of the theoretical and practical importance of assessing the function of muscular relaxation in systematic desensitization, care must be taken to ensure that the methods to produce muscular relaxation used in these studies have the desired effect. Many studies designed to assess the role of muscular relaxation in desensitization (Bellack, 1973; Marshall & Strawbridge, 1972; Rimm & Medeiros, 1970; Vodde & Gilner, 1971) did not, in fact, demonstrate that their relaxation training procedures resulted in muscular relaxation. Without this demonstration, these studies are impossible to interpret.

The efficacy of EMG biofeedback and, to a lesser extent, passive relaxation instructions was demonstrated in this single-session design but generalization of these findings across time and other dependent variables remains to be demonstrated.

The effect of the various procedures on the subjects' degree of "learned control" over frontalis EMG activity in other trials or situations remains to be assessed.

Generalization is particularly important when considering applications of these techniques to behavior therapy. Although covariance between frontalis EMG activity and EMG activity in other skeletal muscle groups and other physiological indices of arousal has been suggested in previous research (Stoyva & Budzynski, 1974), this relationship remains to be demonstrated and the effect of the procedures used in the present study on other indices of physiological activity can only tentatively be inferred. It is possible that the various procedures differ in their effects on measures other than frontalis EMG and that different results would have been obtained from the analysis of other indices of physiological activity.

The ultimate criterion upon which to assess differential effectiveness must be overt behavior change. Clinical assessment of the differential effectiveness of these methods of inducing relaxation might be carried out by reference to behavioral criteria such as approach to a feared stimulus (a frequently used method in systematic desensitization research) or reduction in the occurrence of stress-related symptoms (e.g., frequency of tension headaches) as a result of method of relaxation training.

REFERENCES

Alexander, A. B. Systematic relaxation and flow rates in asthmatic children: Relationship to emotional precipitants and anxiety. *Journal of Psychosomatic Research*, 1972, *12*, 405–410.

Balshan, I. B. Muscle tension and personality in women. *Archives of General Psychiatry*, 1962, 7, 436–448.

Barber, T. X., & Hahn, K. W. Hypnotic induction and "relaxation." *Archives of General Psychiatry*, 1963, *8*, 295–300.

Bellack, A. Reciprocal inhibition of a laboratory conditioned fear. *Behavior Research & Therapy*, 1973, *11*, 11–18.

Budzynski, T. H. Feedback-induced muscle relaxation and activation level. Unpublished doctoral dissertation, University of Colorado, 1969.

Budzynski, T. H., & Stoyva, J. M. An instrument for producing deep muscle relaxation by means of analogue information feedback. *Journal of Applied Behavior Analysis*, 1969, *2*, 231–237.

Davis, M., Saunders, D., Creer, T., & Chai, H. Relaxation training facilitated by biofeedback apparatus as a supplemental treatment in bronchial asthma. *Journal of Psychosomatic Research*, 1973, *17*, 121–128.

Davison, G. C. Systematic desensitization as a counterconditioning process. *Journal of Abnormal Psychology*, 1968, *73*, 91–99.

Folkins, C. H., Lawson, K. D., Opton, E. M., & Lazarus, R. S. Desensitization and the experimental reduction of threat. *Journal of Abnormal Psychology*, 1968, *73*, 100–113.

Geer, J. H., & Katkin, E. S. Treatment of insomnia using a variant of systematic desensitization: A case report. *Journal of Abnormal Psychology*, 1966, *71*, 101–104.

Geissman, P., & Noel, C. EEG study with frequency analysis and polygraphy of autogenic training. *Proceedings of the 3rd World Congress of Psychiatry*, 1961, *3*, 468–472.

Goldstein, I. B. Electromyography: A measure of skeletal muscle response. In N. S. Greenfield & R. A. Sternbach (Eds.), *Handbook of psychophysiology*. New York: Holt, Rinehart and Winston, Inc. 1972. Pp. 329–366.

Green, E. E., Walters, E. D., Green, A. M., & Murphy, G. Feedback technique for deep relaxation. *Psychophysiology*, 1969, *6*, 371–377.

Grings, W. W., & Uno, T. Counterconditioning: Fear and relaxation. *Psychophysiology*, 1968, *4*, 479–485.

Jacobson, E. *Progressive relaxation*. Chicago: University of Chicago Press, 1938.

Jacobson, E. *Modern treatment of tense patients*. Springfield, Ill.: Charles C Thomas, 1970.

Jus, A., & Jus, K. Some remarks on "passive" concentration and on autogenic shift. In L. Chertok (Ed.), *Psychophysiolog-*

ical mechanisms of hypnosis. Berlin: Springer-Verlag, 1969.

Kahn, M., Baker, B., & Weiss, J. M. Treatment of insomnia by relaxation training. *Journal of Abnormal Psychology,* 1968, *73,* 556–558.

Lader, M. H., & Mathews, A. M. Comparison of methods of relaxation using physiological measures. *Behavior Research & Therapy,* 1970, *8,* 331–337.

Lang, P. J. The mechanics of desensitization and the laboratory study of human fear. In C. M. Franks (Ed.), *Behavior therapy, status and appraisal.* New York: McGraw Hill, 1969. Pp. 160–191.

Lehrer, P. M. Physiological effects of relaxation in a double blind analogue of desensitization. *Behavior Therapy,* 1972, *3,* 193–208.

Luthe, W. Autogenic training: Method, research and application in medicine. *American Journal of Psychotherapy,* 1963, *17,* 174–185.

Marshall, W. L., & Strawbridge, H. The role of mental relaxation in experimental desensitization. *Behavior Research & Therapy,* 1972, *10,* 355–366.

Mathews, A. Psychophysiological approaches to the investigation of desensitization and related procedures. *Psychological Bulletin,* 1971, *76,* 73–91.

Mathews, A. M., & Gelder, M. G. Psycho-physiological investigations of brief relaxation training. *Journal of Psychosomatic Research,* 1969, *13,* 1–12.

McGuigan, F. S. *Experimental psychology: A methodological approach.* Englewood Cliffs, N.J.: Prentice Hall, 1968.

Moeller, T. A., & Love, W. A., Jr. A method to reduce arterial hypertension through muscular relaxation: A technical report. *The Journal of Biofeedback,* 1973, *1,* 37–43.

Paul, G. L. *Insight vs. desensitization in psychotherapy: An experiment in anxiety reduction.* Stanford: Stanford University Press, 1966.

Paul, G. L. Inhibition of physiological response to stressful imagery by relaxation training and hypnotically suggested relaxation. *Behavior Research & Therapy,* 1969, *7,* 249–256.

Rachman, S. The role of muscular relaxation in desensitization therapy. *Behavior Research & Therapy,* 1968, *6,* 159–166.

Raskin, M., Johnson, G., & Rondestvedt, J. Chronic anxiety treated by feedback induced muscle relaxation. *Archives of General Psychiatry,* 1973, *28,* 263–267.

Riddick, C., & Meyer, R. G. The efficacy of automated relaxation training with response contingent feedback. *Behavior Therapy,* 1973, *4,* 331–337.

Rimm, E. C., & Medeiros, D. C. The role of muscle relaxation in participant modeling. *Behavior Research & Therapy,* 1970, *8,* 127–132.

Sainsbury, P., & Gibson, J. F. Symptoms of anxiety and tension and the accompanying physiological changes in the muscular system. *Journal of Neurology, Neurosurgery & Psychiatry,* 1954, *17,* 216.

Sternbach, R. A. *Principles of psychophysiology.* New York: Academic Press, 1966.

Stoyva, J., & Budzynski, T. Cultivated low arousal—an antistress response? In L. V. DiCara (Ed.), *Limbic and autonomic nervous systems research.* New York: Plenum, 1974. Pp. 370–394.

Taylor, J. A. A personality scale of manifest anxiety. *Journal of Abnormal & Social Psychology,* 1953, *48,* 285–292.

Van Egeren, L. F., Feather, B. W., & Hein, P. L. Desensitization of phobias: Some psychophysiological propositions. *Psychophysiology,* 1971, *8,* 213–228.

Venables, P. H., & Martin, I. (Eds.) *A manual of psychophysiological methods.* New York: John Wiley & Sons, 1967.

Vodde, T. W., & Gilner, F. H. The effects of exposure to fear stimuli on fear reduction. *Behavior Research & Therapy,* 1971, *9,* 169–175.

Waters, W. F., McDonald, D. G., & Koresko, R. L. Psychophysiological responses during analogue systematic desensitization and non-relaxation control procedures. *Behavior Research & Therapy,* 1972, *10,* 318–393.

Wolpe, J. *The practice of behavior therapy.* New York: Pergamon Press, 1969.

Wolpe, J., & Flood, J. The effect of relaxation on the galvanic skin response to repeated phobic stimuli in ascending order. *Journal of Behavior Therapy & Experimental Psychiatry,* 1970, *1,* 195–200.

Continuous Biofeedback and Discrete Posttrial Verbal Feedback in Frontalis Muscle Relaxation Training

18

Robert A. Kinsman, Katy O'Banion, Sharon Robinson, and Herman Staudenmayer

ABSTRACT

During training to relax the *frontalis* muscle, continuous biofeedback (BF) was compared to discrete verbal feedback (VF) delivered immediately after each trial. Both feedback modalities were based on *frontalis* electromyographic (EMG) activity. Training consisted of 3 consecutive daily sessions each comprised of 3 baseline (nonfeedback) trials followed by 10 training trials of 128 sec. The presence or absence of the two informationally positive feedback modalities were combined factorially to define four training conditions: BF + VF, NO BF + VF, BF + NO VF, and NO BF + NO VF.

Results indicated that while VF alone facilitated muscle relaxation, BF was clearly prepotent in effecting consistent decreases in EMG activity both across trials and days of training. Additionally, the facilitating effect of BF transferred to nonfeedback trials while VF did not affect performance on nonfeedback trials. Finally, accuracy of self-evaluations of performance on a trial by trial basis was markedly improved by BF, while VF improved accuracy only for trials having a very large absolute difference between levels of EMG activity. Ss receiving no feedback neither reduced muscle tension during training nor were able to evaluate their performance accurately even when large absolute differences occurred between trials in *frontalis* EMG activity.

DESCRIPTORS: Biofeedback, Verbal feedback, *Frontalis* muscle relaxation training, EMG.

Until recently. subjective report has been the only measure of skeletal muscle relaxation commonly used. Experience has indicated that such subjective evaluation is not always a reliable indication of the level of muscle tension (Matus, 1972). Following the development of biofeedback techniques based on bioelectric activity within single motor units (Basmajian, 1963; Simard & Basmajian, 1967), a new training procedure for

The authors would like to thank Drs. David Wm. Shucard. Thomas Budzynski, and Irwin Matus for their constructive comments.

This research was supported in part by NIH Grants 1 R01 MH24222-01 and AI-10398.

Address requests for reprints to: Robert A. Kinsman, Ph.D.. Psychophysiology Research Laboratories, Department of Behavioral Sciences, National Jewish Hospital and Research Center, 3800 East Colfax Avenue, Denver, Colorado 80206.

deep relaxation of muscle *groups* applicable to Wolpe's (1958) systematic desensitization has become available. This technique also provides an objective measure of muscle tension.

Budzynski and Stoyva (1969) have described such a biofeedback instrument employed to record and train muscle relaxation with continuous biofeedback (BF). During the training procedure the subject monitors an explicit cue — a light, tone, or series of clicks — which changes continuously and is correlated with electromyographic (EMG) activity recorded from a selected, specific muscle group. With this procedure, subjects are reportedly able to reach low levels of muscle tension (relaxation) within a few sessions (e.g., Budzynski & Stoyva, 1969, 1973). compared to the relatively lengthy training required for other techniques such as autogenic training (Schultz & Luthe, 1958) or progressive relaxation (Jacobsen, 1938). A crucial test for the effectiveness of BF training would be to compare it to other conditions of feedback that supply positive information to the subject regarding his level of relaxation. While Budzynski and Stoyva (1969) have demonstrated that BF facilitates relaxation as compared to training conditions involving either no information feedback, a constant level of a pseudo-feedback signal, or presentation of biofeedback from yoked controls, these control conditions have been either informationally empty, as in the case of no informative feedback and constant pseudo-feedback signals, or potentially misleading as in the case of yoked controls.

The purpose of this study is to compare BF relaxation training directly to an alternative feedback procedure which is clearly informationally positive.

By using a trial by trial training procedure with relatively brief trial durations rather than longer continuous training sessions, an alternative informationally positive feedback modality becomes readily available. After each trial, the subject can be told whether he relaxed more or less than on the preceding trial as indexed by his level of EMG activity during the trial periods. Such a procedure that uses discrete verbal information feedback (VF) meets the requirement of being informationally positive and, additionally, is similar to those procedures widely used in studies of skill acquisition (e.g., Bilodeau, 1969; Taylor & Noble, 1962).

Presumably, BF derives its effectiveness by making ambiguous internal cues explicit, providing accurate information about changes in the target response, e.g., muscle tension, during training so that instrumental control of the response is facilitated. VF based on EMG activity also provides knowledge about changes in muscle tension, although from one discrete time interval to another. However, BF should provide more precise information than VF about muscle tension levels for at least two reasons: First, BF is continuous and presented immediately during the trial period; and, second, BF provides information about the absolute level of muscle tension whereas VF supplies only information about muscle tension relative to the previous trial. It is therefore predicted that, although both BF and VF will facilitate relaxation, BF will be more effective because it should provide more complete and immediate information about muscle tension.

A second aspect of the study will investigate the effects of both BF and VF training on the ability of the subject to evaluate his performance from one trial period to the next (i.e., "guess") accurately. Kamiya (1969) has described application of a similar procedure in evaluating effects of training on the control of brain waves. Again, BF should produce more accurate evaluations since this modality provides more precise information than VF.

Method

Subjects

The Ss were 64 male volunteers, ranging in age from 18 to 31, and paid at the rate of $5/hour for a total of 3 hourly sessions.

Apparatus

The apparatus to deliver BF was a Bioelectric Information Feedback System (BIFS; Biofeedback Systems, Inc., Boulder, Colorado) which has been described in detail elsewhere (Budzynski & Stoyva, 1969). Bipolar surface electrodes (E & M Company, Houston, Texas) for the BIFS were mounted in a special headband which permitted consistent positioning of the electrodes over the same site on the *frontalis* muscle group of the forehead. The conducting medium was Beckman electrode paste. Before positioning the electrodes on the *frontalis*, the forehead was scrubbed with fine grade Brasivol to obtain an electrode resistance of less than 10,000 ohms.

The BIFS is an EMG feedback system which monitors EMG activity in the range of 95 Hz to 1K Hz. While the low frequency cut off may eliminate some of the EMG signal, it is used to eliminate any artifacts from other bioelectric sources below 95 Hz (e.g., EKG). The integrated muscle action potential is converted to a BF signal which continuously tracks changes in the level of EMG activity. The BF signal, a continuous stream of clicks, was presented to S through earphones. Preliminary adjustment in the noise cancellation circuit of the BIFS was made to deliver approximately 2 clicks/sec when no EMG activity was present. One click, corresponding to one EMG count, was delivered each time the half-wave rectified EMG signal attained an integrated value of .169 μV-sec.[1] A nixie-tube readout panel on the BIFS monitor indicated the integrated EMG activity in equivalent sinusoidal peak-to-peak μV-min for each trial period. For Ss receiving NO BF, a simple electronic circuit was designed to present clicks at the slow, constant rate of 2 clicks/sec while permitting the EMG level to be monitored on each trial.

The equipment was housed in a quiet room below ground level which provided minimal interference from acoustical and electrical noise. The room was equipped with a reclining couch and a hospital screen to separate S from the BIFS control station.

Procedure

All Ss participated in 3 1-hr sessions held during the mornings of 3 consecutive days. Each of the 3 sessions consisted of 3 baseline trials without feedback followed

---

[1]The gain of the preamplifier of the Bioelectric Information Feedback System (BIFS) used in this study was lowered by 43% of the standard settings commonly used for units now in production. Each individual EMG count corresponded to 1 BF click delivered to S and was delivered each time the half-wave rectified EMG signal attained an integrated value of .169 μV-sec. The EMG counts for each 128 sec trial in this study were converted to μV-min by multiplying the counts by .169 and dividing by 60.

by 10 training trials. All trials were 128 sec in length separated by a 40-sec intertrial period during which no measurement was taken. Immediately preceding the first session, Ss were given 5 min of muscle tensing and relaxing exercises adapted from Jacobsen (1938) and given a brief explanation of the study and the use of the BIFS equipment. The S was instructed to remove his shoes and lie on the couch with his arms at his sides and his eyes closed. Following this, E affixed the electrodes to S's forehead. All Ss were told that they should relax their whole body, but especially their forehead and that the object was to attain as deep a level of relaxation as possible.

To provide a clear distinction between trials, S was told at the start of each trial: "Tense your forehead" and immediately thereafter to "Relax." The remainder of the intertrial period followed so that measurement of the EMG began approximately 40 sec after the instruction to relax and continued for a full 128 sec trial period.

Additional instructions were presented according to the condition to which S was assigned: Ss in the BF conditions were told they would hear a series of clicks, the rate of which would be determined by the level of muscle tension of their forehead. These Ss were instructed to use the BF clicks as a guide for relaxation and to "not try to control the clicks, but let the clicks be a guide for your level of relaxation." Ss in the NO BF conditions were simply told they would hear a slow but continuous series of clicks which would not change but "would provide something relaxing to attend to" during each session. Ss in the VF conditions were told that E would report immediately after each trial whether S relaxed more or became more tense than on the immediately preceding trial. If S relaxed more, E would say "Down" and if S became more tense E would say "Up." Ss in the NO VF conditions received no additional instructions.

One-half of the Ss in each condition were required to guess immediately after each trial whether they relaxed more or became more tense than on the immediately preceding trial. Guesses, made before presentation of VF, were given by saying "Down" if S thought he relaxed more and "Up" if more tense than on the previous trial.

Design

The design of the study was a $2 \times 2 \times 2 \times 3 \times 10$ factorial with repeated measures on the last 2 factors. The factors were BF (Presented or Not Presented), VF (Presented or Not Presented), Guess (Required or Not Required), Days (1st, 2nd, 3rd), and Trials (1 to 10). This produced a total of 8 independent cells in the design. The criterion measure was the average muscle action potential in μV measured peak-to-peak obtained during each trial period. Separate analyses were performed for the baseline trials. Noise levels, obtained during each test session using three 6.8K resistors in a delta arrangement simulating a zero EMG source impedance, were subtracted from each S's EMG levels for each trial. All analyses reported use the corrected EMG levels for each trial period.

Results

EMG Levels at Baseline

The mean EMG values for the feedback conditions during the baseline (nonfeedback) trials for 3 days of training are presented in Table 1. To determine if there were differences between groups attributable to the two kinds of reinforcement, a $2 \times 2 \times 2 \times 3 \times 3$ factorial analysis of variance

TABLE 1

Integrated EMG values in equivalent sinusoidal peak-to-peak μV-min during baseline trials

Feedback Conditions	EMG Values			
	1	2	3	Condition Means
BF + VF	2.04	1.58	1.58	1.73
BF + NO VF	2.34	1.65	1.87	1.95
BF Mean	2.19	1.61	1.72	1.84
NO BF + VF	2.81	2.37	2.52	2.57
NO BF + NO VF	1.99	2.32	2.52	2.18
NO BF Mean	2.40	2.34	2.37	2.37
Daily Means	2.29	1.98	2.05	

Note. — All values are corrected for noise levels.

(ANOVA) with the last 2 variables as repeated measures was performed for BF (Presented or Not Presented), VF (Presented or Not Presented), Guess (Required or Not Required), and 3 Days, and 3 Trials. Results indicated that BF Ss had a significantly lower overall baseline EMG value than NO BF Ss $(F(1/56) = 6.81, p < .05)$, while no differences occurred attributable to VF $(F(1/56) = 0.17, p > .5)$. The BF $\times$ Days interaction was also significant $(F(2/112) = 3.10, p < .05)$. Individual comparisons of means by t-test indicated that while BF and NO BF Ss did not differ on Day 1 $(t(190) = 1.32, p < .1)$, BF Ss had lower EMG values on Day 2 $(t(190) = 4.49, p < .01)$ and Day 3 $(t(190) = 3.58, p < .01)$ than did the NO BF Ss, probably as a consequence of the intervening training. However, since the groups did not differ at the outset of training, i.e., Day 1 baseline, they were regarded as initially well matched for the subsequent analyses.

EMG Levels During Training

Data from the experimental trials (1–10) for the 3 days were also analyzed by ANOVA using three different dependent measures: 1) raw score EMGs, 2) difference from Day 1 baseline, and 3) percentage of Day 1 baseline. Significant results for all three measures were essentially identical. Results are presented only for percentage of Day 1 baseline since this gives the most readily understandable measure of change while also taking individual differences on initial values into consideration.

A $2 \times 2 \times 2 \times 2 \times 3 \times 10$ factorial ANOVA, with 4 Ss per cell and the last 2 variables repeated measures, was performed for BF (Presented or Not Presented), VF (Presented or Not Presented), Guess (Required or Not Required), 2 Experimenters, 3

Days, and 10 Training Trials. Two main effects were significant: BF $(F(1/48) = 15.44$, $p < .001)$, indicating that, on an overall basis, Ss receiving BF were able to lower their EMG more than Ss receiving NO BF; and Trials $(F(9/432) = 8.17$, $p < .001)$, indicating a general improvement in lowering EMG from the first to the tenth trial.

Two first order interactions were also significant: BF × Days $(F(2/96) = 3.07$, $p < .05)$ and VF × Days $(F(2/96) = 6.08$, $p < .01)$. BF Ss showed a relatively large drop from baseline (100%) on the Day 1 training trials (to 71.5%) that continued on Day 2 (62.8%) and on Day 3 (58.4%). In contrast, NO BF Ss showed almost no drop from baseline on Day 1 (to 93.9%) and Day 2 (94.1%) and baseline performance on Day 3 (101.2%). VF Ss showed a moderate drop on Day 1 (to 88.7%) which increased and stabilized on Day 2 (to 72.7%) and Day 3 (72.8%), though not reaching the level of the BF Ss. Lastly, the NO VF Ss showed a relatively large drop on Day 1 (to 76.7%) but moved closer to baseline performance on Day 2 (84.2%) and Day 3 (86.8%). In sum, while reduction of EMG activity is facilitated by VF, the effect is not as substantial as with BF.

Let us turn now to the combined effects of BF and VF. The second order interaction of BF × VF × Days was significant $(F(2/96) = 5.45$, $p < .005)$. The results are schematically summarized in Fig. 1. Overall percentage of baseline EMG across all 3 days is lowest for BF + NO VF Ss (68.9%, 60.6%, and 56.8%, respectively), slightly higher for BF + VF Ss (74.1%, 65.0%, and 60.1%, respectively), much higher for NO BF + VF Ss (103.4%, 80.4%, and 85.5%), and highest for NO BF + NO VF Ss (84.4%, 107.7%, and 116.8%). Ss with BF, receiving either VF or NO VF, decreased their EMG levels steadily across Days with the largest decrease on Day

1. Ss with neither form of feedback, i.e., neither BF nor VF, increased EMG steadily across days. Ss with VF but NO BF showed an initial substantial decrease but no consistent trend across days of training. The data indicate that VF is nonsalient information when given along with BF since the effect of BF overrides VF. However, when NO BF was given, VF became salient information which had a facilitating effect on performance, although not approaching the effect of BF.

Finally, the third order interaction of BF × VF × Days × Trials was significant $(F(18/864) = 1.64$, $p < .05)$. The performance of those Ss receiving BF improved both over Days and over Trials while performance of those Ss receiving NO BF either remained stable (with VF) or deteriorated somewhat (with NO VF) both over Days and over Trials.

Guessing Performance

The ability to guess whether the amount of relaxation as measured by EMG activity was higher or lower on any trial in comparison to the previous trial was analyzed separately for the BF and VF conditions. The first point to be made is that these Ss had some ability to judge relaxation without any feedback at all. The overall probability of guessing correctly (P(c)) was above the chance level (.5) for Ss receiving BF (P(c) = .72, $Z = 9.13$, $p < .01$); as well as for Ss receiving NO BF (P(c) = .60, $Z = 4.35$, $p < .01$); likewise, Ss receiving VF (P(c) = .67, $Z = 7.04$, $p < .01$) as well as Ss receiving NO VF (P(c) = .64, $Z = 6.10$, $p < .01$) guessed correctly more often than expected by chance alone. While Ss could guess above chance, overall guessing performance of Ss receiving BF was superior to those receiving NO BF ($Z = 5.43$, $p < .01$). However, the overall guessing performance of Ss receiving VF was statistically no better than that of Ss receiving NO VF ($Z = 1.34$, $p > .1$).

To evaluate guessing performance in relation to the absolute number of EMG counts (where 1 count = 1 click in the BF signal during a 128 sec trial period) between trials, the differences in EMG counts were classified into 4 separate intervals based upon the absolute difference in the number of EMG counts between adjacent trials: the first interval ranged from 1 to 40 counts, the second from 41 to 80 counts, the third from 81 to 160 counts, while the fourth interval contained all differences greater than 160 counts. P(c) for each of the interval categories for the BF feedback comparisons is presented in Fig. 2A and for VF feedback

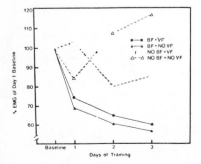

Fig. 1. Percent EMG of Day 1 baseline across days of training.

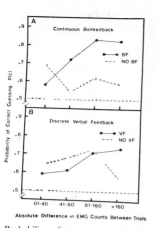

Fig. 2. Probability of correct guessing (P(c)) as a function of the absolute difference in EMG counts between adjacent trials.

comparisons in Fig. 2B. Data presented are average values for Ss grouped across both levels of the feedback modality (Presented and Not Presented) which is excluded from the comparison. Pairwise comparisons for each of the intervals between Ss receiving BF and Ss receiving NO BF showed that Ss with BF performed statistically better on the second ($z = 3.50$, $p < .01$), third ($z = 4.81$, $p < .01$), and fourth ($z = 6.53$, $p < .01$) intervals while Ss with NO BF performed somewhat better on the first interval ($z = -2.55$, $p < .05$). Comparisons between Ss receiving VF and NO VF showed only the guessing performance for the fourth category, containing trials having the largest EMG differences, to be significant ($z = 4.10$, $p < .01$), with Ss receiving VF guessing more accurately. Since the data for VF Ss were grouped across levels of the BF factor, the P(c) for both VF and NO VF is generally inflated by inclusion of Ss receiving BF.

These findings suggest that the ability to evaluate the relative level of relaxation is facilitated by BF, but only when differences in the biofeedback signal become discriminable. Knowledge of relative relaxation may also be facilitated by VF, but only when differences in the EMG levels between trials are very large.

Discussion

During relaxation training, Ss receiving BF improved considerably and consistently throughout the experiment in their ability to reduce EMG activity or relax the *frontalis* muscle. The Ss receiving NO BF improved moderately when given VF, while those given no feedback at all became more tense

throughout the experiment. The prepotency of BF clearly indicates that it produces superior ability to relax compared to an alternative, positive feedback modality, namely VF. For Ss receiving BF, there is also evidence that learning to relax during training transfers to situations where no feedback is provided. Thus, after the first training day, Ss receiving BF achieved lower levels of *frontalis* muscle tension during the baseline (nonfeedback) trials as compared to Ss who received NO BF training. Since the VF used in this study is not necessarily related to other established relaxation training techniques, it would be of interest to compare BF relaxation training to alternative modes of training commonly used in clinical practice, e.g., those involving adaptations of Jacobsen's progressive relaxation.

The results of the guessing performance data indicate that Ss could guess above chance level about their relative level of relaxation from trial to trial even without any feedback. However, guessing performance was significantly augmented with the addition of BF even for relatively small differences in EMG counts between trials, i.e., 41-80 counts corresponding to differences in integrated EMG ranging from $6.92 - 13.52$ μV-sec. In contrast, the addition of VF improved guessing at only the largest interval for differences in EMG counts between adjacent 128 sec trials, i.e., above 160 counts, corresponding to differences in integrated EMG of more than 27.04 μV-sec.

The evidence clearly demonstrates the facilitating effect of BF over VF and suggests that it provides, as expected, additional information used by S to evaluate his level of relaxation.

One aspect of this study that warrants further investigation is the difference in ability to guess correctly when the EMG activity is more as opposed to less than the previous trial. It is possible that Ss receiving BF developed a behavioral strategy to say "down" more often than "up" when guessing. Since BF leads to generally steady decreases in EMG levels from trial to trial, this strategy would maximize P(c). If this strategy is used, P(c) for Ss who lower their EMG across trials could be inflated for a reason other than their ability to judge absolute differences in relaxation from trial to trial.

There are several ways to separate the effects on P(c) of such a maximizing response strategy from information provided by BF. For one, P(c) could be calculated separately for those trials when EMG activity increased or decreased. To the extent that a maximizing strategy was being used, P(c) for trials on which EMG decreased (P(c) *down*) would be expected to approach unity while P(c) for trials on which EMG increased (P(c) *up*) would approach zero. In the current data, there is the definite suggestion that such a trend exists: overall P(c) *down* for BF Ss was .85, while P(c) *up* was .58. Further comparisons indicate that even for the P(c) *up*, BF provides substantial information provided the absolute difference between trials is more than 27.04 μV-sec. These observations should be regarded as preliminary since it would be desirable to increase the number of Ss who guessed in order to obtain more accurate estimates of P(c) *down* and

P(c) *up* in the different conditions. Additionally, to separate the effect of EMG performance from P(c), Ss could be divided into "good," "medium," and "poor" performers as defined by their ability to lower EMG activity over trials. If a maximizing strategy were used, the difference between P(c) *down* and P(c) *up* would be expected to be greatest for "good" performers since they would likely have more trials in sequence for which EMG decreases. While at this point there is evidence for use of a maximizing strategy in guessing, evidence also indicates that BF provides information Ss use to evaluate their level of relaxation during training.

REFERENCES

Basmajian, J. V. Control and training of individual motor units. *Science*, 1963, *141*, 440–441.

Bilodeau, I. McD. Information feedback. In E. A. Bilodeau & I. McD. Bilodeau (Eds.), *Principles of skill acquisition*. New York: Academic Press, 1969. Pp. 255–285.

Budzynski, T. H., & Stoyva, J. M. An instrument for producing deep muscle relaxation by means of analog information feedback. *Journal of Applied Behavioral Analysis*, 1969, *2*, 231–237.

Budzynski, T. H., & Stoyva, J. M. Biofeedback techniques in behavior therapy. In D. Shapiro, T. X. Barber, L. V. DiCara, J. Kamiya, N. E. Miller, & J. Stoyva (Eds.), *Biofeedback and self-control: 1972*. Chicago: Aldine Publishing Company, 1973. Pp. 437–459.

Jacobsen, E. *Progressive relaxation*. Chicago: University of Chicago Press, 1938.

Kamiya, J. Operant control of the EEG alpha rhythm

and some of its reported effects on consciousness. In C. Tart (Ed.), *Altered states of consciousness*, New York: John Wiley & Sons, Inc., 1969. Pp. 507–517.

Matus, I. Internal awareness, muscle sense and muscle relaxation in bioelectric information feedback training. Unpublished doctoral dissertation, University of Denver, 1972.

Schultz, J. H., & Luthe, W. *Autogenic training: A psychophysiologic approach in psychotherapy*. New York: Grune and Stratton, 1958.

Simard, T. G., & Basmajian, J. V. Methods in training the conscious control of motor units. *Archives of Physical Medicine & Rehabilitation*, 1967, *48*, 12–19.

Taylor, A., & Noble, C. E. Acquisition and extinction phenomena in human trial-and-error learning under different schedules of reinforcing feedback. *Perceptual & Motor Skills*, 1962, *15*, 31–44.

Wolpe, J. *Psychotherapy by reciprocal inhibition*. Stanford: Stanford University Press, 1958.

Electromyograph Feedback as a Relaxation Technique

19

Robert D. Coursey

This study compared an electromyograph (EMG) feedback group of 10 normal undergraduate males with two control conditions of 10 subjects each. One control group was told to relax but given no specific instructions nor feedback, only a constant tone. The second control group was given instructions about relaxation, a constant tone but no feedback. The feedback group received variable-tone feedback from the frontalis muscle. Every subject had one baseline session and seven 21-minute practice sessions over a 2-week period. Planned comparisons showed that the feedback group achieved significantly lower EMG scores than the two control groups, which did not significantly differ between themselves. Measures of subjective anxiety showed significant decreases between the beginning and end of each session for all three groups, but only one of the six measures of state anxiety favored the feedback group over the controls. No differences between groups emerged on measures of trait anxiety.

The use of biofeedback as a therapeutic technique seems to be mushrooming (Gaarder, 1971), and the feedback of electromyograph (EMG) recordings is likewise expanding. Two general uses for EMG feedback have emerged so far. The first is its utility in enhancing the control of voluntary muscles where that control has either not been developed (Scully & Basmajian, 1969) or where it is diminished through dysfunction (Harrison & Connolly, 1971). The second area consists of attempts at achieving low levels of muscle tension (Green, Walters, Green, & Murphy, 1969) with patients who experience chronic tension headaches (Budzynski, Stoyva, & Adler, 1970; Wickramasekera, 1972) and chronic anxiety (Raskin, Johnson, Rondestvedt, 1973). Other possible uses include the treatment of bronchial asthma (Davis, Saunders, Creer & Chai, 1973), insomnia (Raskin et al., 1973), or any disorder that is associated with muscle tension.

Most of the work has been in case studies using 5–10 subjects. Moreover, few basic methodological studies have been reported concerning EMG feedback as a relaxation procedure. From these few studies it is still not clear whether EMG feedback is more effec-

Thanks are extended to P. Starr, E. Dannemiller, M. Jason, R. Blackman, K. Layton, and R. Ashburner who helped run the experiment and analyze the data; to Barry Smith for reading and commenting on the manuscript; and to John Holmgren for statistical advice.

This research was supported by grants from the General Research Board of the University of Maryland and the University of Maryland Computer Science Center.

Requests for reprints should be sent to Robert D. Coursey, Department of Psychology, University of Maryland, College Park, Maryland 20742.

tive in relieving muscle tension than other methods of relaxation, nor is it clear how the subject uses the biofeedback. Two methodological studies have thus far been reported. Budzynski and Stoyva (1969) compared 5 subjects in a feedback group, 5 subjects who were told that a constant tone would help them relax, and 5 subjects who were simply told to relax as deeply as possible. By the fifth session, there was an overall significant effect between the three groups. However, specific differences between each of the three groups were not tested for significance. Although the EMG feedback group achieved the lowest mean, the significant overall difference was probably a function of the constant-tone control group whose scores increased by 28% over the five sessions, while the scores for the other two groups dropped.

A second study is the doctoral dissertation of Cleaves (1970). He compared four groups of 20 females each (EMG with auditory feedback, EMG with visual feedback, verbal relaxation training using a combination of Jacobsonian and autogenic methods, and a control group without training). Only one 2-hour practice session was provided. Tension reduction during training and at a 1-week follow-up produced similar results: Overall differences emerged due to significantly poorer scores of the no-training group, but no differences were found among the three training groups.

Neither study presented any data on whether the subjects experienced increased subjective relaxation with decreased levels of EMG, nor did they explore the manner in which the subjects made use of the EMG feedback. The present study was an attempt to begin exploration of these areas.

Although it is clear from previous studies (Budzynski & Stoyva, 1969; Cleaves, 1970) that a person in an EMG biofeedback situation does become muscularly less tense across trials within a session and across sessions, it is not clear that this is the result of biofeedback itself. In order to demonstrate that EMG biofeedback is an effective means of reducing muscle tension, several alternative explanations need to be ruled out. The first explanation might be that the lower levels of muscle tension are simply the result of assuming a comfortable position, becoming familiarized with the experimental research conditions, listening to a soothing low tone, and relaxing by whatever means one

normally uses. This was the first control group, "relax only." Although this explanation was considered in previous studies, no measures of subjective relaxation were taken, and it may well be that what a subject defines as a state of relaxation is not a correlate of low muscle tension but some mental state that he achieves by his own relaxation methods.

A second mechanism was suggested by interviews with previous EMG feedback clients: The subject generates cognitive instructions to himself about what might relax him, then tries them out using the EMG feedback as a criterion. If this self-instruction is the essential element of the EMG feedback procedure and if most subjects are essentially alike, then a more efficient and inexpensive method of achieving relaxation would be simply to instruct subjects on how to relax directly. Therefore, a set of instructions was generated from the reports of the pilot subjects about what helped them achieve a low level of muscle tension during feedback. This constituted the second control group, "cognitive instructions."

The answers to a number of other questions were also sought: Does the subjective sense of relaxation differ for these different methods of muscle tension reduction? If so, does feedback from the frontalis muscle result in a sense of relaxation for body parts other than the forehead? Does biofeedback result in a clearer sense for the subject of what the "relaxed state" feels like than when he achieves relaxation by some other means?

METHOD

Selection of Subjects

Subjects were drawn from a large introductory psychology course. Only males participated since all six experimenters were men and Cleaves (1970) suggested that his heterosexual conditions tended to provoke erotic fantasies in his subjects during the training. A preexperimental interview was conducted to screen subjects for major psychiatric disorders, to determine whether the subjects were facing any major tension-producing problems, to estimate tension level via behavioral signs using the McReynolds Anxiety Behavior Checklist (McReynolds, 1965), and to screen subjects for prior training in relaxation such as yoga or transcendental meditation. Subjects were also screened for breathing problems such as colds, hay fever, postnasal drip, as well as for constant nappers. Only those subjects not on medication were used, and all subjects were requested to refrain from the use of marijuana and other drugs for the 2 weeks of the experiment. Thirty subjects, 10 in each of the three conditions, were scheduled at times that they were not normally drowsy and during a period when they were not facing special academic pressure such as exams and papers.

Conditions

The 10 subjects in the EMG feedback condition received the muscle-tension feedback via a variable tone (130–650 Hz). These variable tones, as well as constant tones for the other two groups, were delivered over earphones and were matched for decibel levels (approximately 55 db.). Subjects in all three conditions were told that the experiment was concerned with ways of achieving relaxation and that during the sessions they were to relax as much as possible. In addition, instructions for the feedback group included the following statements:

You have been connected to a machine which measures muscle tension. This machine then transforms your muscle tension into a tone, so that the more relaxed you are, the lower the tone. Your job, then, is to lower the tone you hear as much as possible by relaxing. The more you relax, the lower the tone will be. As you learn to relax more deeply we may have to change the pitch of the tone between sessions in order to give you the middle range.

Instructions for all three groups were delivered via a tape recorder and repeated before each session. All subjects were asked not to practice relaxation between sessions.

Group 2, relaxation only, was told that they had "been connected to a machine which measures muscle tension" (the EMG without the feedback). They were also told: "In addition, you will receive a tone to help mask out noises. Your job is to relax as much as possible, using whatever means you find helpful."

The cognitive instructions group was also told that they were connected to a machine measuring muscle tension and would receive a tone to help mask out noises. They were also told:

From our previous work we have found that the following procedures generally produce the most relaxation. Close your eyes. Try not to blink, swallow, or move your face, but let it feel heavy and sagging. Let the jaw drop and leave the mouth open. Breathe deeply and rhythmically. Try to settle into a day-dreamy type of state.

Course of Training

Five male experimenters were trained to run the experiment with the author. They were assigned on the basis of their own schedules. Consequently, 2–4 experimenters helped in attaching electrodes, monitoring for sleep, and recording results for each subject.

Relaxation training consisted of one habituation-baseline session, six training sessions, and a final testing session that was similar to the training sessions. Each session was on a different day, and all eight sessions fell within a 2-week period. The number of sessions were based on pilot work suggesting that normals reached a minimal tension baseline after approximately five sessions. Each training session consisted of 15 64-sec trials, with 20-sec intertrial intervals. The EMG measure for each session consisted of the total EMG

score derived from adding the EMG scores for the 15 trials. The division into 15 trials was for recording purposes only; subjects received continuous tones during the entire 21 min. Pilot work had suggested that sessions longer than 21 min resulted in the subjects becoming restless. The habituation session consisted of 17 trials of constant tone for all three groups, with the exception of the feedback group which received variable feedback for the last 2 trials.

Since deep relaxation is often the prelude to sleep, it was necessary to prevent the subjects from falling asleep. Consequently, the experimenter monitored each subject's electroencephalogram (EEG) for signs of sleep as well as watched for behavioral signs of sleep. When the subject showed signs of sleep, he was given a mild stimulus (a light touch on the back of his left hand) to which he responded if he was awake by raising his index finger. If the subject was alseep, several more taps invariably aroused him out of light sleep.

Room and Instruments

Subjects lay on an analyst-type couch in a semi-reclining position. During the trials the room was dimly lit, well-insulated from outside noises, with air conditioning and equipment hum further dampening the sounds within the room.

The instrument used to record EMG and to transform the muscle tension level into a variable audio-feedback (130–650 Hz) was the Model B-1 Bio-Electric Information Feedback System, produced by Biofeedback Systems, Inc. The EMG reading was proportional to the area under the curve of half-wave rectified input voltage versus time. The readout was directly in peak-to-peak microvolt minutes.

Stainless-steel surface electrodes were placed at Fp 1 and Fp 2 (International 10-20 Electrode Placement), which would primarily measure frontalis muscle activity. Resistance between any pair of the three electrodes was always below a maximum of 10,000 Ω. This was achieved by cleaning the forehead with an abrasive cleanser (Brasivol) and using Beckman electrode paste. The frontalis muscle was chosen since it is less affected by posture and gravity than most other muscles. In addition, the frontalis muscle is difficult to relax voluntarily (Weddell, Feinstein, & Pattle, 1944) and frequently remains tense in anxious subjects (Malmo & Smith, 1955; Smith, 1973). The tone was adjusted between sessions so that feedback subjects achieved the lower tones (below 345 Hz) about 80% of the time (Budzynski et al., 1970). To monitor for sleep, a Grass EEG preamplifier (Model 5P5) was used with a dc driver amplifier (Model 5B).

Since it sometimes happens that a sharp noise, cough, sneeze, or other extraexperimental factor can grossly interfere with baseline readings, the following conservative rule was adopted: If a subject's EMG total increased threefold over the previous session and was three times the mean for his other seven sessions, that mean was substituted in place of the higher score. Out of 240 sessions, the rule was invoked four times for four different subjects: subjects in the EMG and cognitive instructions conditions during Session 4 and the relax-only and cognitive conditions in Session 8.

Subjective Measures

A variety of self-report measures were collected.

TABLE 1

PREEXPERIMENTAL MEASURES

Measure	EMG feedback		Relaxation only		Cognitive		F
	M	SD	M	SD	M	SD	(2, 27)
EMG	97.90	33.77	96.91	65.72	96.93	44.82	0.00
Mooney Problem Checklist							
Checked	40.64	26.56	36.40	22.36	35.90	30.78	.10
Circled	12.64	13.90	10.30	9.75	5.90	5.95	1.09
TMAS	17.91	9.40	17.80	8.46	15.60	6.83	.25
No. methods for relaxing	2.45	1.44	1.70	1.06	1.80	1.32	1.08
How easy to relax (1–9)[a]	4.55	1.69	5.20	1.69	4.80	1.40	.44
How easy to fall asleep during the day (1–9)[b]	4.27	1.79	5.20	1.75	4.10	1.37	1.29
McReynold's Anxiety Behavior Checklist	1.09	1.14	1.40	1.35	.90	.74	.52

Note. The scores reported are μV-min totals for 15 64-sec trials (16 min).
[a] 1 = relax deeply and fully within seconds; 9 = Am tense most of the time. It takes a long time to unwind.
[b] 1 = Extremely easy; 9 = extremely difficult.

Before and after the experiment, trait anxiety was measured by assessing the sources of anxiety using the Mooney Problem Checklist (Mooney & Gordon, 1950) and by assessing the symptoms of anxiety with the Taylor Manifest Anxiety Scale (TMAS; Taylor, 1953). Before and after each session, the subject's emotional state was measured by the Nowlis Mood Adjective Check List (MACL; Nowlis & Nowlis, 1956) and his subjective experience of tension by Mattsson's Anxiety Scale (Mattsson, 1960). A preexperimental questionnaire investigated the number of ways the subject had for relaxing and how easy he found it to relax or fall asleep. The postexperimental questionnaire sought to discover whether the subject had a better sense of the relaxed state, whether his ability to relax quickly and deeply had subjectively increased, and whether he discovered any new methods of relaxing during the course of the experiment.

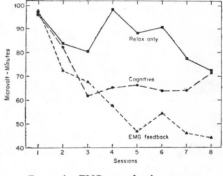

FIGURE 1.   EMG scores for three groups.

RESULTS

Preexperimental Measures

Table 1 presents the anxiety–relaxation measures taken prior to the experiment. As can be seen, there were no significant differences between the groups on any of the measures.

Training

Figure 1 presents the corrected EMG means for each session for each condition. Because we wished to investigate whether the EMG group's progressively lower levels of muscle tension across the training sessions were significantly better than those achieved by the two control groups, a two-way analysis of variance was performed (three conditions × eight ses-

sions), and the linear trend across the Sessions ×Group interaction was examined. The important question was not whether any of the differences between groups was significant but whether the feedback group differed from each of the control groups. This can be most powerfully established by two planned orthogonal comparisons: First, the mean EMG scores for the feedback group must differ significantly from the average of the means of the two control groups; second, the means of the two control groups must not significantly differ from one another. If these two conditions are met, then it can logically be concluded that the feedback group significantly differs from each control group.

Table 2 presents the results of the analysis.

The slope of the feedback group across sessions was −6.65, whereas the slope for the relax control group was −2.17 and that of the cognitive instructions group was −3.09. As can be seen from Table 2, the EMG slope does significantly differ from the average of the two control groups, $F = 5.63$, $p < .05$, and the slopes of the two control groups do not significantly differ between themselves ($F = .24$).

A simple analysis of Session 8 alone, using the two planned comparisons strategy, yields similar results. The feedback mean significantly differed from the average of the means of the two control groups, $F(1, 27) = 4.29$, $p < .05$, and the means of the two control groups did not significantly differ, $F(1, 27) = 0.00$. Although Session 8 has two corrected scores, the same analysis of Session 7 alone, in which no corrected scores are used, produced similar significant results, $F(1, 27) = 4.39$, $p < .05$, and for the comparison between controls, $F(1, 27) = .98$.

Subjective Measures

Table 3 presents the means and standard deviations for the state measures (Nowlis' MACL and Mattsson's Anxiety Scale) taken before and after each session. For convenience, only those scores for Sessions 1 (baseline) and 8 are reported.

Three-way analyses of variance were performed on each of the subscale scores (eight sessions × pre–post × three conditions), and these results are presented in Table 4. Of most

interest are the differences in subjective feelings after the last training session (postscores of Session 8). Using the same planned-comparison strategy, again only one instance was found in which the feedback group reported a more relaxed state than the two control groups. For MACL Fatigue, the F ratio for the comparison between EMG and the mean of the two control groups was 4.01 ($df = 1, 432$, $p < .05$), whereas the comparison between relax only and cognitive instruction yielded an F of .27 (*ns*).

Although there were few individual differences between the EMG and the control groups, inspection of the complete analyses of variance in Table 4 shows that there are highly significant differences in mood for all groups between the beginning and end of each training session in the direction of greater relaxation

TABLE 2

TWO-WAY ANALYSIS OF VARIANCE WITH PLANNED COMPARISONS ON THE GROUP × SESSION LINEAR TREND

Source	SS	df	F
Between groups	25,577.0	2	2.02
Error (within groups)	170,927.0	27	
Sessions	27,181.0	7	5.42*
Linear trend	19,855.3	1	24.82**
Groups × Sessions	12,385.0	14	
Linear trend	4,694.1	2	
EMG vs. relaxation + cognitive	4,501.1	1	5.63*
Relax vs. cognitive	193.0	1	.24
Error (within-groups × sessions)	135,495.0	189	
Linear trend error	21,599.8	27	
Total	371,565.0	239	

* $p < .05$.
** $p < .01$.

TABLE 3

MEANS AND STANDARD DEVIATIONS FOR STATE MEASURES FROM SESSIONS 1 TO 8

		Preexperiment						Postexperiment					
		EMG		Relaxation		Cognitive		EMG		Relaxation		Cognitive	
Scale	Session	M	SD	M	SD	M	SD	M	SD	M	SD	M	SD
						Nowlis MACL							
Aggression (0–18)	1	1.20	3.16	1.00	2.16	.50	1.08	.30	.67	.20	.63	.30	.95
	8	.70	1.57	.40	.52	.60	.97	.20	.63	.30	.67	.20	.42
Anxiety (0–16)	1	2.30	1.95	3.20	2.74	1.70	2.11	.30	.67	.40	.97	.40	.70
	8	1.30	1.64	1.00	1.25	1.60	2.27	2.20	2.15	.80	1.32	.70	1.25
Fatigue (0–26)	1	.70	1.06	.60	1.08	1.60	1.58	4.30	5.21	3.90	2.60	2.10	2.51
	8	1.20	2.15	.80	1.14	1.00	1.94	1.40	2.12	2.00	2.75	2.60	4.12
Vigor (0–18)	1	2.30	2.50	2.70	2.00	1.40	1.51	.70	1.89	.70	1.89	.30	.48
	8	2.10	2.56	1.50	1.08	1.60	1.65	.80	1.03	.90	1.73		
Peaceful (0–6)	1	.70	1.06	1.20	1.23	1.00	1.25	2.00	1.94	2.90	1.79	1.60	1.84
	8	.30	.48	1.20	1.14	.30	.67	1.90	2.23	1.40	1.35	1.50	1.84
						Mattsson's Anxiety (6–36)							
	1	17.80	4.61	18.30	7.12	19.10	5.15	12.20	5.20	11.80	4.42	15.80	3.89
	8	14.90	5.13	15.00	5.10	15.40	5.97	10.00	3.74	12.10	6.35	14.00	3.89

TABLE 4

Results of Three-Way Analysis of Variance
for Subjective Mood Measures

	F		
Scale	8 sessions[a]	Pre–post[b]	3 groups[c]
Mattsson's Anxiety	1.65	63.17**	.95
Nowlis MACL			
Aggression	.89	21.75**	.14
Anxiety	.57	35.31**	.14
Fatigue	1.11	19.13**	.47
Vigor	1.00	21.61**	.57
Peaceful	3.17*	38.19**	1.02

[a] $df = 7, 189$.
[b] $df = 1, 27$.
[c] $df = 2, 27$.
* $p < .01$.
** $p < .001$.

(less aggressive feelings and lowered anxiety and vigor, as well as increased feelings of fatigue and peace). However, there was only one significant trend over sessions for all subjects to increase in relaxation (MACL, peaceful); and no interaction effects for any of the analyses were found except for MACL Anxiety, in which the Pre–Post × Sessions interaction was significant, $F(7, 189) = 3.18$, $p < .01$. Table 5 presents the postexperimental measures on trait anxiety (the Mooney Problem Check List and the TMAS), as well as measures

aimed at assessing the subjects' sense of whether their awareness of the relaxed state had expanded and whether their ability to relax quickly and deeply had grown. Two-way analyses of variance (three conditions × pre–post experiment) were run for the Mooney Problem Check List and the TMAS and one-way analyses of variance for the postexperimental questionnaire. Planned comparisons between feedback versus the mean of the control groups for the postexperimental Taylor and Mooney scales showed no differences. Planned comparisons did reveal that the feedback group reported gaining more of a sense of what the relaxed state feels like than the control groups combined, $F(1, 27) = 4.61$, $p < .05$; F for relax-only versus cognitive groups = 0.00, and felt that they could relax more quickly, $F(1, 27) = 4.17$, $p < .05$; whereas for the relax versus cognitive instructions groups, $F(1, 27) = .81$. However, the feedback group did not differ from the combined control groups on reported ability to relax deeply or on the number of articulated ways of achieving relaxation.

Looking at other aspects of the analyses, the experimental conditions did not affect the measures of trait anxiety, except the mean TMAS scores for all three groups did increase from 17.33 preexperiment to 19.37 postexperiment, which was significant at $p < .10$. No interaction effects were significant.

TABLE 5

Postexperimental Subjective Measures

Scales	EMG feedback		Relaxation only		Cognitive		F	
	M	SD	M	SD	M	SD	3 groups	Pre– post
Mooney Problem Checklist								
Checked only	43.91	27.98	37.30	37.05	48.30	46.74	.13[a]	1.44[b]
Circled	7.18	7.88	10.90	14.00	5.20	8.73	.96[a]	.90[b]
TMAS	19.64	7.65	20.00	7.02	17.40	7.28	.52[a]	3.55[b]
Now have a better sense of what relaxed state feels like. (1 = very much; 4 = no)[c]	1.45	.52	2.10	.88	2.10	.87	2.50*	
Ability to relax quickly (1 = very much improved; 4 = has decreased)[c]	1.36	.50	1.80	.92	2.10	.74	2.69*	
Ability to relax deeply (1 = has grown very much; 4 = cannot relax as deeply)[c]	1.82	.40	1.80	.79	2.50	.53	4.65**	
Discovered new methods to relax[c]	1.27	1.01	.80	.92	1.40	1.17	.93	

[a] $df = 2, 27$.
[b] $df = 1, 27$.
[c] Subjects were asked to compare after the experiment with their ability prior to experiment ($df = 2, 27$).
* $p < .10$.
** $p < .05$.

Since the focus of the training for the feedback and cognitive conditions was on the forehead region, the question arose whether feelings of relaxation might generalize from the forehead to the rest of the body. Each subject was asked to attend to different parts of his body (feet, hands, face, forehead, etc.) and rate on a 9-point scale (1 = deeply relaxed, 9 = extremely tense) how relaxed each part of his body was. This questionnaire was administered before Session 1 and after Session 8. Two-way analyses of variance (three conditions × pre–post experiment) were run for each part of the body. Planned comparisons between the feedback group and the mean of the two control groups on postexperiment means yielded no significant differences. However, for all three groups four body parts became subjectively less tense after relaxation training. As might be expected, these parts were in the upper bodily area (hands, upper arms, face, and forehead); F ratios for pre–post $(1, 27)$ = 6.51, 6.29, 6.24, 5.92, respectively, all ps < .025.

DISCUSSION

The results of this study showed rather clearly that EMG feedback is more effective in lowering tension in a specific muscle throughout training than either simple verbal instructions or the reduction achieved by the subject's own unaided efforts. To insure the validity of these results, we checked a number of alternative explanations and possible artifacts. These data are presented in Table 6.

The first explanation was that subjects in the control conditions, having no variable feedback, might fall asleep more often and be awakened more often, and this arousal might cause higher EMG levels. However, Table 6 shows that the number of times the subjects were touched to be awakened did not significantly differ among the conditions.

A second explanation suggests that EMG feedback simply serves to suppress occasional restless muscle movements such as eye and eyelid movement, coughs, swallows, or other bodily movements—all of which strongly affect EMG recordings from the forehead. None of the measures of these artifacts, however, showed significant differences (see Table 6), although the feedback group generally had the fewest movement artifacts.

A number of other possible artifacts were tested, and it was discovered that no differences emerged. Among these possible methodological problems were the following: (a) There were no significant differences in mean EMG scores among the six therapists (mean EMG scores per session ranged from 75.12 μV-min. to 89.95), $F(5, 234)$ = .35. (b) No differences in EMG scores were found across the 6 weeks of the experiment. (c) The number of therapist experimenters who worked with each subject did not differ across conditions, nor did the differing number of therapists per subject affect the subject's EMG scores.

Furthermore, the control groups were developed to test some major alternative interpretations of the feedback phenomenon. The fact that the feedback condition was significantly more effective than the relaxation-only condition suggests that EMG feedback consists of more than just the subject growing increasingly comfortable with the experimental situation while using his own methods of relaxation, although this process in itself does tend to

TABLE 6

EXPERIMENTAL ARTIFACTS

Measure	Feedback		Relaxation only		Cognitive		F	H[a]
	M	SD	M	SD	M	SD		
Touches per subject	3.64	3.31	5.40	6.48	7.70	6.10	1.33	
No. coughs, swallows, etc., per subject	4.27	5.14	5.10	7.89	5.60	4.23	.20	
No. body movements per subject	3.82	4.21	12.20	14.87	10.70	9.15		3.48
No. eye movements	3.36	3.42	6.30	5.92	1.40	2.06		5.32*
Total no. movements per subject	11.46	8.92	24.40	23.50	17.60	13.47		1.64

Note. For F ratio, df = 2, 27; for H, df = 2.
[a] Kruskal-Wallis used because of significant differences in the variance.
* p < .10.

lower muscle tension some (from 96.91 μV-min to 72.43). Use of the cognitive-instruction control group suggests that the feedback process is more than a cognitive process of figuring out what strategies cause the tone to fall and the tension to decrease, even though this, too, seems to be a component in the tension-reduction process. Further substantiation that self-instruction is not the major mechanism is the fact that the feedback group was not able to verbalize the means of achieving lower tension any better than the control groups. Achieving reduced levels of muscular tension, then, may be like achieving any other motor skill: Although aspects of reducing muscle tension may consist of self-instruction, much of the tension reduction is accomplished in a nonverbal manner. If such a motor skills model is adopted to understand EMG feedback, then the general failure to find differences in consciously experienced feelings of relaxation between the feedback and control groups makes more sense.

Although EMG feedback did serve to reduce muscle tension when compared with the two control groups, it does not appear to be a very powerful technique when used by itself. For instance, in Session 8, only about 12% of the variance (Hays, 1963, p. 381) in EMG scores was accounted for by the experimental conditions. This was true in spite of the fact that the experiment was set up to optimize the possibility of finding some differences. For instance, the dependent measure was the EMG on the same muscle that had received six training sessions; and the dependent measure of EMG level for the test session (Session 8) was taken while the EMG group was actually receiving feedback. (In this preliminary study the short- or long-term ability of subjects to achieve and maintain their levels of deep relaxation after feedback training was not considered.) Moreover, only one of the eight subjective measures of relaxation revealed any differences among the three groups.

On the other hand, only normal volunteers whose muscle tension and anxiety were initially quite low participated in this study. For instance, Table 3 reveals that the means for the subjective state measures are generally within the lowest decile of the scale. The small effects for both EMG and subjective measures may be the result of their already being near some basal level. Those subjects who had higher initial EMG baselines achieved greater reduc-

tions in tension than those subjects with lower levels.

Another possible limitation of EMG feedback is its failure to generalize relaxation across parts of the body. The questionnaire data showed that only the upper body parts (face, forehead, upper arms, and hands) increased in subjective sense of relaxation; and a study by Alexander and Hanson (Note 1) found no EMG generalization across muscles after five 20-minute training sessions. The reason may be that the popularly used frontalis muscle does not correlate with a general muscle tension factor that Balshan (1962) found when he factor analyzed 16 muscle groups. An integrated recording of multiple muscle groups would probably solve this aspect of the generalization problem.

In addition to the difficulties in generalizing relaxation across parts of the body, this study also raises questions about generalization across time. Strong differences appeared between the beginning and end of each session for all groups on state measures, but no differences emerged for the trait measures; indeed, there seemed to be a borderline significant increase in anxiety scores. This increase in scale scores might be the result of prolonged attention to tension–relaxation feelings. Such a sensitization effect, if replicated, could prove quite useful clinically since many tense patients are often unaware of their tension much of the time. Of course, seven training sessions within a 2-week period is probably too short a time to substantially change the subjects' levels of trait anxiety, and the results from other short-term studies confirm this (Stoudenmire, 1972). However, even researchers with long-term relaxation training have had mixed results, generally finding that EMG feedback training did not generalize outside the laboratory (Budzynski et al., 1970; Raskin et al., 1973; LeBoeuf, Note 2).

This difficulty in changing anxiety levels through EMG feedback raises the fundamental question of whether EMG tension as measured from the frontalis muscle correlates with the subjective experience of anxiety. To establish the relationship for trait anxiety, the scores for all 30 subjects on the TMAS taken just prior to the experiment were correlated with their baseline EMG scores (Session 1); the correlation was significant ($r = .385$, $p < .05$). However, EMG change scores between Sessions 1 and 8 did not significantly correlate with change scores for the pre–post Taylor measures ($r = .228$). For state anxiety, we calculated intraindividual correlations using Mattsson's prescores and postscores for all eight sessions with the first and last $2\frac{1}{2}$ minutes of EMG recordings (Trials 1, 2, 14, and 15) for all eight sessions. The mean intraindividual correlation for all 30 subjects (using Fisher's r-to-z transformation) was .19. For the subjects in the feedback condition who heard their EMG level, the mean correlation was .34; for the relaxation-only condition the mean correlation was .14, and for the cognitive instruction group, .08. In general, then, for the normal young adult male, muscle tension is probably only one small element contributing to the subjective sense of anxiety.

The difficulties of generalizing across muscle groups, situations, and time, and from muscle tension to subjective anxiety may simply be due to the fact that feedback researchers have not yet developed generalization techniques. For instance, the subject's focus of attention during feedback training has thus far generally been on controlling the feedback itself rather than on the anxiety-producing stimuli as in systematic desensitization. But a procedure that emphasizes the feedback rather than the stimulus situation is not likely to generalize much outside the laboratory.

A final and quite intriguing question concerns the extent to which subjects in the feedback condition actually use the feedback. My experience has been that subjects use the feedback in earlier and more active attempts to lower their EMG levels but often discover that they achieve their deepest levels of relaxation when they stop trying so hard, adopt a more passive stance, often indulge in hypnogogic imagery or drifting, and essentially abandon the task of lowering the pitch. Indeed, subjective reports from this experiment indicate that the amount of time subjects attended to the feedback decreased over sessions. This may expose a weakness of the EMG feedback technology and a peculiarly Western-world paradox inherent in such methods, namely, the belief that one should actively work in conjunction with a machine to achieve control over a passive, control-abandoning, non-goal-directed, noneffortful state. For chronically tense subjects, the EMG technique may well emphasize an active intervention strategy that tense patients already overuse. It is often this strategy that the subject must learn to set aside, at least for periods of relaxation. In such cases, EMG feedback as a general relaxation technique may be self-defeating. This is not to question its value for affecting a specific muscle group or for rehabilitation purposes, but as a method for lowering trait anxiety in the obsessive, hard-driving, high-tension neurotic, it may not be the technique of choice.

However, these speculations do not empirically establish the relative merits of EMG feedback as a relaxation technique over other methods such as transcendental meditation, autogenic training, or Jacobson's methods. Nor do we have much evidence of its ability to reduce chronic tension in various psychopathological states. We should arrive fairly soon at the point of asking the more sophisticated question: What sort of relaxation technique is effective with what sort of people with what sort of problems in conjunction with what other procedures?

REFERENCE NOTES

1. Alexander, B., & Hanson, D. *An experimental test of assumptions relating to the use of EMG biofeedback as a general relaxation training technique.* Paper presented at the meeting of the Biofeedback Research Society, Colorado Springs, February 1974.

2. LeBoeuf, A. *The importance of individual differences in the treatment of chronic anxiety by EMG feedback techniques.* Paper presented at the meeting of the Biofeedback Research Society, Colorado Springs, February 1974.

REFERENCES

Balshan, L. Muscle tension and personality in women. *Archives of General Psychiatry*, 1962, 7, 436–448.

Budzynski, T., & Stoyva, J. An instrument for producing deep muscle relaxation by means of analog information feedback. *Journal of Applied Behavioral Analysis*, 1969, 2, 231–237.

Budzynski, T., Stoyva, J., & Adler, C. Feedback-induced muscle relaxation: Application to tension headache. *Journal of Behavior Therapy and Experimental Psychiatry*, 1970, 1, 205–211.

Cleaves, C. *The control of muscle tension through psychophysiological information feedback.* Unpublished doctoral dissertation, George Washington University, 197 .

Davis, M., Saunders, D., Creer, T., & Chai, H. Relaxation training facilitated by biofeedback apparatus as a supplemental treatment in bronchial asthma. *Journal of Psychosomatic Research*, 1973, *17*, 121–128.

Gaarder, K. Control of states of consciousness. *Archives of General Psychiatry*, 1971, *25*, 429–441.

Green, E., Walters, E., Green, A., & Murphy, G. Feedback technique for deep relaxation. *Psychophysiology*, 1969, *6*, 371–377.

Harrison, A., & Connolly, K. The conscious control of fine levels of neuromuscular firing in spastic and normal subjects. *Developmental Medicine and Child Neurology*, 1971, *13*, 762–771.

Hays, W. *Statistics for psychologists.* New York: Holt, Rinehart & Winston, 1963.

Malmo, R., & Smith, A. Forehead tension and motor irregularities in psychoneurotic patients under stress. *Journal of Personality*, 1955, *23*, 391–406.

Mattsson, P. Communicated anxiety in a two-person situation. *Journal of Consulting Psychology*, 1960, *24*, 488–495.

McReynolds, P. On the assessment of anxiety: I. By a behavior checklist. *Psychological Reports*, 1965, *16*, 805–808.

Mooney, R., & Gordon, L. *The Mooney Problem Check List Manual.* New York: Psychological Corporation, 1950.

Nowlis, V., & Nowlis, H. The description and analysis of mood. *Annals of the New York Academy of Sciences*, 1956, *65*, 345–355.

Raskin, M., Johnson, G., & Rondestvedt, J. Chronic anxiety treated by feedback-induced muscle relaxation. *Archives of General Psychiatry*, 1973, *28*, 263–267.

Scully, H., & Basmajian, J. Motor-unit training and influence of manual skill. *Psychophysiology*, 1969, *5*, 625–632.

Smith, R. Frontalis muscle tension and personality. *Psychophysiology*, 1973, *10*, 311–312.

Stoudenmire, J. Effects of muscle relaxation training on state and trait anxiety in introverts and extraverts. *Journal of Personality and Social Psychology*, 1972, *24*, 273–275.

Taylor, J. A personality scale of manifest anxiety. *Journal of Abnormal and Social Psychology*, 1953, *48*, 285–290.

Weddell, G., Feinstein, B., & Pattle, R. The electrical activity of voluntary muscle in man under normal and pathological conditions. *Brain*, 1944, *67*, 178–257.

Wickramasekera, I. Electromyographic feedback training and tension headache: Preliminary observations. *American Journal of Clinical Hypnosis*, 1972, *15*, 83–85.

An Experimental Test of **20**
Assumptions Relating to the Use of
Electromyographic Biofeedback as
a General Relaxation Technique

A. Barney Alexander

ABSTRACT

Twenty-eight normal adults participated in an experimental test of two assumptions underlying the use of electromyographic (EMG) biofeedback as a general relaxation training technique: (1) that trained EMG reduction in one muscle generalizes to untrained muscles; and (2) that subjective feelings of relaxation are related to EMG reduction. An experimental group received 5 sessions, during the middle 3 of which EMG biofeedback training was offered on the frontalis muscle. Throughout all sessions, EMG recordings were also taken from the forearm and lower leg, and ratings of subjective relaxation feelings were obtained at regular intervals. A control group, matched with the experimental group on baseline frontalis EMG, received 5 similar sessions without feedback. Employing a maximum p of .05, the results revealed no evidence of generalization of EMG reduction from the frontalis to the untrained sites, nor any tendency for successful frontalis EMG reduction to result in increased feelings of relaxation beyond what was obtainable from relaxing without the benefit of training. The results were interpreted as suggesting that EMG biofeedback cannot yet be accepted as a viable general relaxation training technique.

DESCRIPTORS: Electromyography, Biofeedback, Relaxation training.

In their review of the clinical applications of biofeedback training, Blanchard and Young (1974) sum up the area of EMG (electromyographic) applications thusly: "The work on the application of EMG feedback training to clinical problems is the oldest and the soundest work in the biofeedback

This research was supported in part by grants from the National Heart and Lung Institute (#HL-15620) and the National Institute of Mental Health (#MH-19884).

The author gratefully acknowledges the assistance of Donald G. Hanson and Pamela W. Holland during the data analysis and preparation of this manuscript.

Preliminary reports of portions of this research were presented at the Thirteenth Annual Meeting of the Society for Psychophysiological Research in Galveston, Texas, October 1973, and the Annual Meeting of the Biofeedback Research Society in Colorado Springs, February 1974.

Address requests for reprints to: A. Barney Alexander, The National Asthma Center, 1999 Julian Street, Denver, Colorado 80204.

area [p. 579]." It is clear, however, that the justification of this claim is due mainly to the strength of the work in muscular rehabilitation and elimination of subvocalization during reading. While these latter applications have not received widespread attention, two other areas have generated considerable enthusiasm among clinicians generally: EMG biofeedback as a treatment for tension headache and as a general relaxation technique. Summing up the status of these applications, Blanchard and Young concluded that "in the treatment of tension headaches ... the question remains as to the therapeutic contribution of EMG feedback [and] there is no clear-cut evidence to support the efficacy of EMG feedback training to teach relaxation either as an intermediary to some other therapeutic endeavor or as the basic training itself [p. 579]." Alexander, French, and Goodman (1975) echoed this sentiment. Despite such cautious assessments, and to a large extent prior to their publication, the apparent successes with tension headache, the easy extrapolation to EMG biofeedback of claims regarding the beneficial clinical effects of profound muscular relaxation using techniques such as Jacobson's (1938) progressive relaxation training, and anecdotal reports (e.g. Budzynski & Stoyva, 1972) that successful frontalis training led to general bodily relaxation, EMG biofeedback training became the leading candidate for an effective, efficient, and quantifiable general relaxation training method. Far outstripping adequate scientific support EMG biofeedback applications, typically employing frontalis training, have proliferated in clinics across the country beyond what can be estimated from the literature. In the main unpublished, these applications have included hypertension, alcoholism, smoking, general and specific anxieties, adjunctive use in treatments such as systematic desensitization, and a whole variety of clinical problems in which psychological or physical "tension" was considered to be the focal point. In one form or another, the therapeutic rationale has been that "relaxation," promoted by the feedback training, was the crucial treatment variable mediating outcome. Among those endeavors which have been conspicuously absent are experimental studies designed to test the validity of the belief that EMG biofeedback is a viable general relaxation training technique.

The most widely employed approach to EMG biofeedback relaxation training has been to offer training on one muscle: the frontalis. Such a procedure has included two notable assumptions, both of which are as yet unsupported experimentally: first, that muscle tension reduction resulting from training of one muscle, such as the frontalis, generalizes to other major muscles without benefit of specific training on those other muscles; or, by logical extension, that training on only one (or maybe a few) key muscles is a sufficient condition for generalized skeletal muscle tension reduction throughout the body; and second, that the subjective experience of becoming or being relaxed is related to trained EMG reduction. The present study was designed as an *initial* test of these two assumptions. Regarding the second assumption, two possible relationships between EMG and feelings of relaxation were considered: (1) changes in reports of relaxation feelings may reliably accompany or correlate with changes in frontalis EMG levels; and (2) frontalis EMG reduction, achieved by training, may produce increased feelings of relaxation. The experiment consisted of a group of subjects who were given feedback training on the frontalis muscle, while recordings were made from two untrained sites, and a control group who had no training while similar recordings were obtained from the same three muscle sites. The control group was included to provide a basis for evaluating the presence of successful frontalis tension reduction in experimental subjects and to provide comparison data on the behavior of

the two untrained sites from subjects who received no frontalis feedback training. All subjects rated their perceptions of changes in the subjective experience of relaxation feelings at regular intervals throughout each session.

Method

Subjects

The subjects were 13 male and 15 female adult volunteers, who were interviewed by the author prior to participation in order to ensure adequate motivation and to eliminate potential subjects who manifested any evidence of significant psychopathology or who reported likely problems related to muscle tension, e.g. tension headache or muscle ache. Ages ranged from 19 to 26 yrs.

Apparatus

EMG activity at the three muscle sites was detected by three separate preamplifiers and processed by a single integrator-feedback unit (Models PA-2 and B-1, respectively, Biofeedback Systems, Boulder, Colorado). Recording bandwidth was set at 95 Hz to 1K Hz. Feedback was provided by the B-1 unit in the form of a continuous series of "clicks" whose frequency varied in proportion to the moment-to-moment level of integrated EMG activity present. Integrated EMG readouts were recorded at the end of each trial from a digital display calibrated in μV-min (referred to the input of the preamplifier). Interval timers controlled both the 30-sec trial duration and the 5-sec intertrial interval.

Differential surface EMG recordings were obtained using the electrode sets supplied with the preamplifiers, which consisted of three stainless-steel "snap" electrodes affixed to a strip of neoprene to standardize electrode spacing. The recording sites were prepared by abrading the skin gently with Brasivol (Stiefel Laboratories, Inc., Oak Hill, New York), and Beckman electrode paste was employed as an electrode-skin interface. The active recording electrodes were placed according to the descriptions by Davis (1952) over three standard sites: (1) the forehead (frontalis muscle); (2) the forearm (extensor muscles located in the dorsal aspect of the left forearm); and (3) the leg (extensor muscles located in the lateral aspect of the left lower leg). The central electrode of each set always served as the reference for recording and was located equidistant from the active electrodes on a line joining their centers.

Prior to each session, the DC resistance was measured between each active electrode and the reference electrode at each recording site. Resistance values in the range of 2KΩ to 10KΩ were judged acceptable. These measures were repeated after each session to verify the adequacy of electrode contact. At the beginning of each session, the subjects were asked to tense each of the relevant muscles several times in order to confirm that the recording equipment was working properly.

All recordings of EMG activity were corrected in the following manner for electrical noise arising in the equipment and recording environment. Before each session, a "dummy load" consisting of a delta configuration of 10KΩ resistors was connected to the active and reference leads of each preamplifier such that 6.7KΩ resistance appeared between any two of these leads. This dummy load was placed on the bed at the approximate subsequent location of that muscle for the subject in the experimental room and connected individually to the inputs of each of the three preamplifiers. Integrated "noise" readings were then collected from the model B-1 over time periods identical to the trial duration. These noise readings were subtracted from the raw EMG readings recorded from each preamplifier throughout the session.

Subjects reclined in a comfortable, supine posture on a bed in a dark, sound-attenuated room adjacent to the control room. A two-way intercom provided communication with the subject, who wore comfortable stereo headphones (Realistic Nova 10) through which EMG feedback was also presented at designated points in the experiment.

Procedure

The experiment consisted of 5 individually conducted sessions on alternate days for each subject. Only one EMG integrator and feedback unit was available. This had two major consequences for the design of the experiment. First, it was necessary to switch sequentially between muscle sites for recording EMG from the separate locations. Second, for experimental subjects it was not possible to record from the two untrained sites during the time feedback training was being given on the frontalis. Hence, each session was divided into a baseline period, consisting of 3 30-sec frontalis recording trials, followed by 4 blocks of 9 30-sec recording trials per block. During training sessions, 2 of the blocks were designated feedback blocks while 2 were designated non-feedback blocks. The interval between blocks was approximately 1 min, which provided the time necessary to obtain subjective report data at the conclusion of each block. During non-feedback blocks, 3 recording trials were obtained on each muscle, while during feedback blocks, all 9 trials yielded frontalis readings only. Both the order of sequencing between muscle sites and the alternation of the 2 feedback and 2 non-feedback blocks per session for experimental subjects were counterbalanced to avoid possible order effects. Following each of the 4 blocks during all 5 sessions, each subject rated the extent to which his subjective experience of relaxation had changed during the immediately preceding block, i.e., the net change perceived between the beginning and end of each block. Two such ratings were obtained on each occasion; one reflecting changes in physical feelings ("how your whole body and muscles feel physically") and the other reflecting changes in mental feelings of relaxation ("feelings of pleasantness, calmness, and lack of mental tension"). The 5-point rating scale ranged from +2 (meaning a large degree of perceived change in the more relaxed direction) through 0 (meaning no change) to −2 (a large decrease in feelings of relaxation). To supply their ratings, the previously-instructed subjects simply called out on command, first the physical, and then the mental rating. These verbal responses (called out as a number, e.g., "plus one") were then repeated by the experimenter to confirm recording accuracy. The block duration of approximately 4.5 min was chosen on the basis of pilot results which indicated the necessity of establishing an interval length that was short enough to reveal phasic shifts in subjective feelings within a session, but not so short as to disrupt the training-relaxation process. The presence of non-feedback blocks afforded the opportunity to obtain subjective ratings which could not be biased by the information available from contemporaneous feedback.

Session 1 was a baseline or no feedback session for both groups. Prior to beginning, the rating scale was explained and then the subjects were told simply to relax the whole body, and especially the relevant muscle sites, as much as they could. Readings were taken on all three muscles during each of the 4 blocks and physical and mental relaxation ratings were obtained at the conclusion of each block as described previously. On the basis of the results from the baseline session, the 28 subjects were divided into two groups of 19 experimental and 9 control subjects on a random basis with the restriction that the baseline session mean frontalis EMG level of the two groups was matched as closely as possible.[1] Subjects in the control group received 4 further sessions identical to the baseline session. Instructions were the same as during the baseline session, but it was reemphasized that the experimenters were studying how people relax and that they should relax as much as possible, especially the muscles at the three recording sites. Experimental subjects received 3 training sessions, consisting of 2 feedback and 2 non-feedback blocks, and a final non-training session identical to the baseline session. During feedback training sessions, the experimental subjects knew that the feedback was coming from the frontalis muscle and were instructed to attempt to relax this muscle as much as possible by lowering the feedback "click" rate. They were told that the experimenters were studying how people relax and that this was a means of attaining a relaxed state of the whole body. It was emphasized that they should try to relax their whole body using the feedback as a guide.

Results

In order to describe the level of EMG characteristic of a particular subject at a given session, the mean of each subject's EMG readings per block for each muscle was first obtained. Then, for each subject, an overall session mean for each muscle was computed from the 4 block means and was employed to describe the EMG level for that session.

The overall EMG results of the experiment are displayed graphically in Fig. 1 as group means. Inspection of this figure suggests that as a whole, the experimental group appeared to evidence reductions in frontalis EMG over sessions, while the control group manifested no change. In contrast, the arm data show increases over sessions for both control and experimental groups, while values for the leg remained at very low levels throughout.

Before attempting to evaluate the evidence regarding either the generalization question or whether trained frontalis EMG reduction results in the subjective experience of relaxation, it must first be demonstrated that the experimental group manifested significant reductions in frontalis EMG over sessions in comparison to the control group, i.e., that there was a training effect. Only then can the correlates of such training be evaluated. Analysis of variance[2] on the data in Fig. 1 revealed that the main effect for frontalis over sessions was not significant but the interaction between groups and sessions was reliable, $F(4/104)=2.66$, $MS_e=1.11$. Simple effects analysis confirmed the significant decrease in frontalis levels for the experimental group alone

---

[1]Originally, it was decided that the subject pool should be divided such that there would be a minimum of 20 subjects in the experimental group. Since it was necessary that all subjects receive the initial session before any subject was assigned to a group, new subjects were accepted, as they became available, until 30 subjects had undergone the initial session. Then, in order to get the study under way, a further decision was made to close admission to the study and proceed with 20 subjects in the experimental group, as planned, and 10 subjects in the control group. Subsequently, 1 subject from each group had to be dropped due to inability to complete the required 4 sessions.

[2]The maximum size of the rejection region used in all statistical tests was .05.

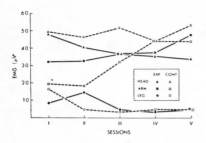

Fig. 1. Experimental and control group mean EMG levels (μV peak-to-peak) over sessions for the three muscle sites.

over sessions, $F(4/104)=5.44$. Hence, it appears that successful frontalis training in the experimental group was attained.

Generalization Data

The analysis of variance on the data displayed in Fig. 1 indicated that the main effect increase over sessions for forearm EMG was significant, $F(4/104)=4.12$, $MS_e=4.75$. However, the interaction between groups and sessions was nonsignificant, which suggests a reliable increase in forearm EMG levels for all subjects, but no significant difference between the groups, despite the apparently different rates of increase for experimentals and controls. For the leg, all F ratios were nonsignificant. A separate two-way analysis of variance with repeated measures on both factors was undertaken specifically to compare the interaction between the head and arm for experimental subjects because these curves are the most important in evaluating the evidence for generalization. The results of this analysis revealed that the interaction between muscle sites and sessions was significant, $F(4/72)=4.10$, $MS_e=2.81$. It also confirmed the reliability of the decrease in frontalis EMG, $F(4/72)=3.66$, $MS_e=1.65$, and indicated that the increase in forearm EMG over sessions for the experimental subjects was significant, $F(4/72)=4.33$. In sum, these analyses seemed to confirm the lack of evidence for generalization in this experiment. However, it could be argued that if the control forearm mean is subtracted from the experimental forearm mean at each session, evidence for generalization could be inferred from the less-steep slope for experimental than control forearm means over sessions. Such a procedure, while it requires some difficult-to-support scaling assumptions, could be said to correct for the difference between experimental and control forearm means during the baseline session. The nonsignificant interaction reported previously between experimental and control subjects and sessions for the forearm data indicated that this procedure was unnecessary.

So far, the data from the experimental group has been viewed as a whole. For evaluation of a question like generalization, it can be persuasively argued that only the data from those subjects who manifest relatively indisputable evidence of a training effect for frontalis EMG reduction should be analyzed for evidence of generalization. Hence, an attempt was made to divide the experimental group into several sub-groups based upon the strength of the evidence that each subject had "learned" frontalis tension reduction. First, slopes for frontalis EMG over sessions were calculated individually for each experimental subject. It was found that 16 subjects had negative slopes while 3 subjects had positive slopes. Next, an F ratio across sessions was calculated for each of these subjects. Referring to the head data on Fig. 2, the 3 subjects in Group 4 all had positive slopes and nonsignificant ($p>.05$) F ratios. Subjects in both Groups 1 and 2 had negative slopes, significant F ratios, and strong linear trends over sessions. However, because the 3 subjects who comprise Group 1 had such high baseline levels they were not considered comparable to Group 2 subjects and, hence, were displayed separately. Group 3 represents the remaining subjects having negative slopes but whose F ratios were either nonsignificant or a marked non-linearity over sessions was present. Within the present experimental sample, it was considered that the 4 subjects in Group 2 met a relatively strong criterion for showing a training effect and were most comparable to the sample as a whole. Analysis of variance for simple effects on these data confirmed the reliability of the decrease for Group 2 over sessions, $F(3/60)=3.153$, $MS_e=0.649$, while the sessions effects for Groups 3 and 4 were nonsignificant. The sessions effect for Group 1 was, of course, highly significant, $F(3/60)=15.159$. Analysis of variance on the forearm data in Fig. 2 revealed no significant effects, including the apparent increase over sessions for Group 2, attesting to the high degree of variability in the arm data.

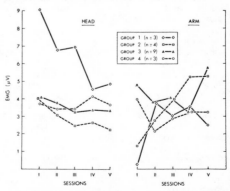

Fig. 2. Head and arm EMG means (μV peak-to-peak) for experimental subjects separated into groups based upon success in frontalis EMG reduction.

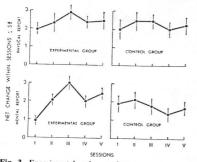

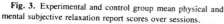

Fig. 3. Experimental and control group mean physical and mental subjective relaxation report scores over sessions.

Subjective Report Data

In order to find out if successful frontalis training leads to the *feeling* of being relaxed, in excess of that attainable by unassisted relaxing in similar circumstances, it was necessary to derive a measure of the total amount of subjectively experienced relaxation over an entire session. To do so, the 4 block ratings were algebraically summed resulting in one session rating each for mental and physical feelings. It can be seen in Fig. 3 that both experimental and control groups reported remarkably similar degrees of *mildly* increased feelings of relaxation. Separate *t*-tests of the subjective relaxation ratings (collapsed across sessions) by both groups showed that the reports differed significantly from zero, which corresponded to a "no change" rating: experimental group physical rating, $t(18)=3.16$; mental rating, $t(18)=11.9$; control group physical rating, $t(8)=18.3$. Analysis of variance revealed no significant differences between experimental and control groups on the physical report data. For mental reports, there were a significant sessions main effect, $F(4/104)=2.84$, and a significant groups-by-sessions interaction, $F(4/104)=3.48$. However, inspection of the data suggested that both of these effects were due almost entirely to the depression of the Session 1 mean in the experimental group. This inference was tested in two ways: first, the two-way analysis of variance was repeated with data from Session 1 eliminated, and no significant effects remained. Second, one-way analyses of variance on the mental report data with Session 1 included showed a significant sessions effect for the experimental group, $F(4/72)=8.27$, but not for the control group. The latter tests were more conservative than simple effects tests derived from the complete two-way analysis of variance because the error mean-squares were larger and the *df* smaller in the one-way analyses. It was therefore concluded that the significant sessions and interaction effects in the two-way analysis could not be attributed to the EMG biofeedback training.

It should be noted that the amount of increase each session, indicated by the means on this figure, is not profound. The greatest amount of change

would be a session score of $+8$ which would result from a maximal rating of $+2$ times 4 rating occasions. Hence, the obtained session means of approximately $+2$ represent an increase of only one-half a scale unit each block for these subjects: a rather small perceived change, falling somewhere between "no change" and a "small amount" in terms of the verbal referents attached to the scale used. Therefore, it would appear that lying comfortably in the darkened experimental room and attempting to relax led to a similar modest degree of feeling relaxed for all subjects but that the successful biofeedback training of the frontalis added no further relaxing influence.

Nevertheless, while a frontalis biofeedback session as a whole seemed to provide no unique relaxing conditions, it was possible that changes in frontalis EMG over shorter periods of time were reliably related to changes in feelings of relaxation within those same shorter periods. To answer this question, a product-moment correlation coefficient was calculated for each subject across all blocks and sessions between the change in EMG and the subjective report for the relevant block. Hence, for each subject there was one correlation coefficient for mental feelings and one for physical feelings reflecting for that subject how closely related his changes in feelings of relaxation were with his changes in frontalis EMG. The mean EMG × mental report r was $+.116$ while the mean EMG × physical report r was $+.13$. The mean correlation between mental and physical reports was $+.513$. For statistical analysis, the distributions of these correlation coefficients were normalized by employing a Fisher r to z transform, and t-tests were employed to see if the mean of each distribution was different from zero. The only significant mean correlation was between mental and physical reports, $t(18)=11.8$. Hence, in these subjects, no tendency was found for changes in EMG, whether or not they resulted from training, to be associated with corresponding changes in relaxation feelings.

As with the generalization data, no tendency was found among the "best" frontalis EMG performers (as defined previously) toward any closer correspondence between frontalis EMG and subjective experience (all r's less than .10). Also, no significant differences between feedback and no-feedback *blocks* were found in any of the EMG or subjective report data, although there was a tendency for frontalis EMG levels to be slightly lower during feedback as opposed to no-feedback blocks.

Discussion

Within the scope of this experiment, no support was found for the assumption that successful lowering of frontalis EMG with biofeedback assistance leads automatically to concomitant reductions of EMG in untrained muscles. Further, there was no support in these data for the claim that frontalis

EMG reduction is either related to or produces general feelings of relaxation. This was the case no matter how the data were viewed. However, while there is little encouragement in these data for the use of frontalis EMG biofeedback training as a method of general relaxation training, the experiment was preliminary in nature, and some important limitations of this study should be pointed out. Regarding the generalization question, only one of the two secondary sites, namely the forearm but not the leg, yielded pertinent data. The tonic baseline levels on the leg were so low in virtually all subjects that it is unlikely that further decreases could take place. This was, of course, not true for the forearm. If future research were to be undertaken on this topic, it would seem advisable, for example, to test additional secondary sites, especially those more closely related to the training sites either functionally or anatomically, or other muscles with tonic levels in the supine subject comparable to the training site. Also, while there is little reason to believe that rotating every 30 sec from one muscle to the next failed to capture the "simultaneous" behavior in these muscles, true simultaneous recording would certainly be the method of choice in this sort of experiment.

There are two important issues concerning the generalization question which were not dealt with in this preliminary investigation. First, we do not as yet know if a generalization effect, or the lack of it, would be transitive, in other words if training one muscle A is found to generalize to muscle B, will training on B generalize to A? It is conceivable that forearm training might generalize to the frontalis. Second, evidence for "generalization" might be sought in other ways, e.g., the training of tension reduction in one muscle facilitating the learning of tension reduction in another, i.e., a transfer of training effect.

Finally, it must be pointed out that to expect a trained reduction in tension in one muscle group to *lead to* the reduction in tension in a second, completely unrelated muscle group may be rather naive, both physiologically and psychologically. While on the one hand, there are numerous examples of both synergistic and antagonistic relationships in the skeletal musculature, these operate largely beyond voluntary control. On the other hand, a remarkable degree of differentiation and capacity for independent action, operating under voluntary control, is also characteristic of the skeletal musculature system. Both of these aspects of the system in part account for, among other things, man's ability to develop fine motor skills. Furthermore, biofeedback training may be considered by its very nature from a psychological point of view, as *highly discriminative* rather than as training designed to promote *generalization*. If, in addition, EMG biofeedback training is conceptualized as a form of motor skill learning, then to expect generalization in the context of the typical frontalis feedback, "relaxation training" procedure is naive at best. Such reasoning could account for both the success of EMG feedback in muscle rehabilitation and the lack of success in the use of one muscle EMG feedback as a "relaxation" training technique.

In considering the results on the relationship of EMG reduction to the subjective experience of relaxation feelings, the use of ratings as employed in the present study can be criticized as relatively insensitive to both the presumed richness of the "relaxation" experience and to the complexities of the interaction between personality variables and the accuracy of verbal report. Nevertheless, in initial investigations, such gross and simple measures are often the only recourse until more knowledge has been accumulated. It also remains possible that a significant relationship between changes in muscle tone and subjective experience might be found in a different population than that employed here. For example, individuals with very high muscle tension levels, or those who evidence some muscular tension related pathology, such as tension headache, or more generally, individuals who are disposed to respond to stress with muscular tension may in fact manifest generalization and subjective effects. While in the present study, the highest baseline subjects failed to manifest these effects, these possibilities remain to be studied.

There is one further caution. In general, the necessary contribution of feedback to the reductions in EMG over sessions in trained subjects reported previously (Budzynski & Stoyva, 1969; Alexander et. al. 1975; Kinsman, O'Banion, Robinson, & Staudenmayer, 1975) has been accepted as adequately demonstrated. Control group EMG behavior in the present study was both highly variable and increased during the last session. It can be questioned just how effectively control subjects in this and previous studies have been motivated to "relax" or decrease muscle tone. The contrast between the performance of trained and control subjects has been, of course, the basis of the acceptance of a real biofeedback training phenomenon. While there is little question that the reputation of biofeedback, the instructions to subjects, and the mere presence of a truly muscle-contingent feedback stimulus have conspired to adequately motivate the subjects receiving training and to bring their behavior under some degree of stimulus control, it would appear to remain an open question whether or not the subjects not receiving training have been motivated sufficiently to perform to their capabilities. Do they experience boredom? Aggravation? If so, they do not constitute an adequate control group.

In conclusion, it is felt that both some hard reconceptualization and much more research needs to be done before EMG feedback training can be accepted as a viable general relaxation training technique, beyond the attainment of, say, relative inactivity in a few muscles.

REFERENCES

Alexander, A. B., French, C. A., & Goodman, N. J. A comparison of auditory and visual feedback in biofeedback assisted muscular relaxation training. *Psychophysiology*, 1975, *12*, 119–123.

Blanchard, E. B., & Young, L. D. Clinical applications of biofeedback training. *Archives of General Psychiatry*, 1974, *30*, 573–589.

Budzynski, T. H., & Stoyva, J. M. An instrument for producing deep relaxation by means of analog information feedback. *Journal of Applied Behavior Analysis*, 1969, *2*, 231–237.

Budzynski, T. H., & Stoyva, J. M. Biofeedback techniques in behavior therapy. In N. Birbaumer (Ed.), *Die bewaltigung von agnst. Birtrage der neurophychologie zur angstforschung. (The making of anxiety. Contributions of neuropsychology to anxiety research.)* Reihe Fortschritte der Klinischen Psychologie, Bd. 4, Munchen Wjen: Verlag Urban & Schwarzenberg, 1972.

Davis, J. F. *Manual of surface electromyography*. Montreal: Laboratory for Psychological Studies, Allan Memorial Institute of Psychiatry, 1952.

Jacobsen, E. *Progressive relaxation*. Chicago: University of Chicago Press, 1938.

Kinsman, R. A., O'Banion, K., Robinson, S., & Staudenmayer, H. Continuous biofeedback and discrete posttrial verbal feedback in frontalis muscle relaxation training. *Psychophysiology*, 1975, *12*, 30–35.

Effects of Various Forms of Relaxation Training on Physiological and Self-Report Measures of Relaxation

21

Richard H. Reinking and Marilyn L. Kohl

This study examined the relative effectiveness of four types of relaxation train-ing using electromyograph (EMG) and self-report measures of relaxation as dependent measures. The four experimental groups were (a) classic Jacobson–Wolpe instructions, (b) EMG feedback, (c) EMG feedback plus Jacobson–Wolpe instructions, and (d) EMG feedback plus a monetary reward. These groups were compared with each other and a no-treatment control group over 3 baseline and 12 training periods. All groups reported increased relaxation, but EMG measures showed that in speed of learning and depth of relaxation the EMG groups were superior to the Jacobson–Wolpe group, and the control group did not master relaxation at all.

Anxiety is a central tenet in most theories of psychopathology, and most theories of psychotherapy agree that anxiety must be dealt with if therapy is to succeed. A number of anxiety treatments stress the importance of relaxation. Although there has been con-siderable debate about the necessity of relaxa-tion per se in psychotherapy (Nawas, Welch, & Fishman, 1970; Rachman, 1968; Stampfl & Levis, 1968; Sue, 1972), most evidence indicates that relaxation is helpful if not absolutely essential, and is especially impor-tant with severe, acute cases (Budzynski & Stoyva, 1972; Farmer & Wright, 1971; Lader & Mathews, 1968; Paul, 1969).

If relaxation is helpful in therapy, it would be important to consider the relative effectiveness of relaxation training methods. Jacobson (1938), Wolpe (1958), Schultz and

Luthe (1959), and Wallace and Benson (1972) all reported physiological and self-report data confirming that their cognitive relaxation procedures produced relaxation and concomitantly reduced anxiety. Budzynski and Stoyva (1969) and Green, Green, and Walters (1970) reported the same effects using biofeedback procedures based on muscle tension and skin temperature recordings. Schwartz (1974) reported similar relaxation effects following biofeedback training to re-duce heart rate and blood pressure. Each of these methods was considered to produce relaxation and reduce anxiety. The hypothesis of this study was that these methods are not equally quick, reliable, and profound in their effects.

Because there has been considerable dis-parity between different measures of anxiety, this study used both physiological and self-report indexes as dependent measures. The self-report index was a subjective rating of experienced tension before and after each relaxation training session. For the physio-

Requests for reprints should be sent to Richard Reinking, Department of Psychology, Washington State University, Pullman, Washington 99163.

logical measure, electromyograph (EMG) recordings of muscle action potential were chosen. Though most theories of therapeutic relaxation focus on sympathetic nervous system patterns, which the EMG only indirectly reflects, EMG records were still chosen for the following reasons. First, EMG and sympathetic activity covary in a variety of situations. There is evidence that the best single correlate of sympathetic arousal is skeletal muscle action potential (Budzynski & Stoyva, 1972; Malmo, 1966), even though measures of sympathetic arousal vary from subject to subject (Cameron, 1944). Second, the training procedures of most relaxation therapies focus primarily on skeletal muscle relaxation, despite their theoretical emphasis on general autonomic system functions. Consequently, the EMG seems a useful dependent measure of tension and a reliable means of judging the relative effectiveness of various relaxation methods. Of the two measures, physiological and self-report, EMG recordings were considered more useful (though not necessarily more valid) because they are less influenced by experimental demand conditions.

This study sought to determine which of a series of relaxation training procedures was most effective in producing a state of relaxation. Two basic procedures were compared: classical Jacobson–Wolpe cognitive training exercises and EMG biofeedback. To evaluate all of the possible interactive parameters, four experimental groups were constructed and compared with each other and a no-treatment control group. The four experimental groups were (a) Jacobson–Wolpe relaxation training, (b) EMG feedback, (c) EMG feedback plus Jacobson–Wolpe relaxation training, and (d) EMG feedback plus a monetary reward for attainment of progressively deeper EMG relaxation. Group d was used because Schwartz and Johnson (1969) noted that feedback alone may not be a sufficient reinforcer to maximize training results. The control group received no training in relaxation procedures, but like the experimental groups it was evaluated using the EMG and self-report measures.

The following hypotheses were tested: (a) All experimental groups should perform better (i.e., learn to relax their muscles more deeply) than the no-training control group. (b) EMG training alone should be better than the combined Jacobson–Wolpe method.

(c) The addition of either cognitive or monetary supports to EMG training should be superior to EMG feedback alone. (d) No distinction should occur between EMG plus relaxation training and EMG plus monetary reward groups.

METHOD

Subjects

The subjects were 50 randomly chosen students enrolled in undergraduate psychology classes. Each subject agreed to complete the entire experiment. If he did not agree to that provision, he was excused before training and randomly replaced by another student. The population ranged in age from 17 to 25 years and contained 31 females and 19 males.

Apparatus

The laboratory contains three rooms: a waiting room and separate rooms for subjects and experimenters. The subject and experimenter rooms were connected by a one-way vision screen and an automatic two-way intercom system. Both rooms were partially shielded from electronic noise and had environmental control systems for light and heat. In addition, all three rooms were soundproofed.

The subject's room contained a bed, an overstuffed recliner chair, an intercom, and the feedback apparatus (electrodes and visual and auditory feedback system). All of the recording equipment was in the experimenter's room. From that room the experimenter could control both the physical and feedback environments for the subject. The EMG was part of an EMG feedback training unit developed by Bio-Feedback Technology (Model B-1). Recording electrodes were Beckman silver–silver chloride units placed in an adjustable headband and were changed regularly.

Procedure

The experiment involved a preliminary adaptation session followed by 15 1-hour sessions. During the adaptation session the subjects were informed of the time constraints of the experiment, were asked to agree to finish the process once begun, and if they consented, were subsequently attached to the EMG. During adaptation each subject also tried both visual and auditory feedback systems, choosing the channel he was most comfortable with. After adaptation the experiment proper began. For all subjects the first three sessions were baseline recording periods. The subjects were told to relax any way they knew how, as deeply as possible. During this period their EMG levels were recorded. Each baseline and experimental session consisted of 15 $\mu V/min$ recordings. Once these recordings were completed, the session was terminated. Before and after each session, the subjects were asked "On a scale of 1 to 10, 10 being as tense as you have ever felt, how tense do you feel now?"

When the three baseline sessions were finished, the subjects were randomly assigned to one of the five groups. The self-report measures continued and EMG level was recorded and averaged as before for all groups. The control group simply continued baseline session procedures. They were told to relax but were given no training or feedback.

Each of the remaining groups then began receiving its own type of relaxation training. The classical relaxation training group began each treatment session by listening to a 12-minute audiotape containing a combination of Jacobson's and Wolpe's instructions focusing on facial relaxation. Once the tape was finished, the subjects were told to practice relaxing while their EMG level was monitored. Then 15 60-sec EMG recording trials ensued, bringing the session to a close.

All EMG feedback training groups received live data on their muscle potential levels. What differentiated these groups was the presence or absence of additional relaxation training supports. The EMG feedback group received no specific instructions concerning how to relax. Rather, they were told only to relax and keep the feedback within a certain range. The EMG feedback plus monetary reinforcement group received the same instructions as the EMG feedback group, except they were also told that they would earn a dollar for each 20% decrease in action potential level, with the preceding session serving as the criterion. The EMG feedback plus relaxation training group began by listening to the Jacobson–Wolpe tape and then practiced the exercises using EMG feedback to tell them how successful their attempts were.

All recordings were from the forehead muscles, primarily the frontalis, using surface electrodes. Once the electrodes were in place, skin resistance was checked. The ohm count had to be less than 10,000 K before the session began. The EMG's data output was in the form of a digital readout expressing the subject's μV/min average over the last 60-sec period. These 60-sec readouts were averaged over the 15 trials of each session, forming one of the dependent measures of this study. Electronic noise was statistically controlled using an average noise count score gathered before and after each session as a correction term.

RESULTS

The independent variable of this study was relaxation training, expressed by comparing the four training groups with each other and a no-training control group. The dependent measures consisted of EMG and self-report assessments of muscle tension levels. Self-report assessment scores ranged from 10 (high tension) to 1 (low tension). From these raw estimates a mean subjective tension score for each session was derived by averaging the before and after estimates. These mean scores were blocked in units of three sessions and evaluated in a 5 × 5 analysis of variance (Winer, 1962) repeated-measures design.

The EMG dependent measures were also analyzed using a 5 × 5 analysis of variance repeated-measures design. Here the basic raw

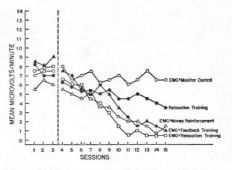

FIGURE 1. Electromyogram (EMG) trends for each group across baseline (Sessions 1–3) and training (Sessions 4–15) periods.

data consisted of average μV/min readings taken every 60 sec during the 20-min training trial. These 15 scores were then averaged to form a tension score per session per subject. The scores were then blocked across three successive sessions to form the final EMG score for each subject in this part of the analysis.

Figure 1 shows the EMG trends for each group across baseline (Sessions 1–3) and training (Sessions 4–15) periods. The analysis of variance data based on this graph show significant effects for conditions ($F = 6.21$, $p < .001$), trials ($F = 27.25$, $p < .001$), and Trials × Conditions ($F = 10.31$, $p < .001$). The conditions factor represents the effects of the four training groups compared against each other and the control group. From these results we can see that the type of training a subject received significantly affected the overall degree of relaxation control a subject acquired. The trials effect represents the influence of practice on relaxation training. The results show that learning to relax is in part a function of practice. But the Trials × Conditions interaction shows that while both practice and type of training influence the course of training, it is the combination of both effects that is most important in predicting the outcome of relaxation training.

Following the analysis of variance of EMG data, a Newman-Keuls post hoc analysis was performed (Winer, 1962). This analysis revealed that none of the groups differed significantly during the baseline period, that the control group's EMG readings did not change significantly across blocks, and that the three EMG groups did not differ significantly in

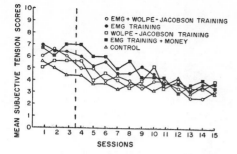

FIGURE 2. Self-report data for each group across sessions. (EMG = electromyograph.)

their relaxation levels during the last two blocks of trials. However, the post hoc analysis did reveal a significant difference between the control, relaxation training, and the three EMG groups across the last two training blocks. While the control group did not change at all, all four training groups improved their relaxation potentials significantly. Furthermore, the three EMG groups were superior to the classical relaxation training group by a wide margin.

Figure 2 shows the self-report data for each group across the same sessions. The analysis of variance reveals significant effects for the trials variable ($F = 7.01$, $p < .001$), showing that practice does influence subjective reports of relaxation. Subsequent analysis revealed that all groups, including the control group, reported an increased ability to relax. There was a slight change favoring the EMG groups but that effect was not significant. Thus, all groups reported a subjective relaxation effect whether or not such an effect actually occurred (in terms of EMG data) or whether or not such change was theoretically expected.

Since most experimental literature dealing with anxiety reports low correlations between physiological and subjective measures of anxiety, many studies use both types of measures when testing a hypothesis on anxiety. As a corollary to this study, the correlations of EMG and self-report measures were computed for the first and last experimental blocks. During the first three sessions, the correlation was comparable with previous reports ($r = .38$). The correlations for the control group remained the same for the last experimental block. However, for all four

treatment groups, this correlation improved to .57 during the last three sessions.

DISCUSSION

The results of this study basically support the hypotheses examined. It is possible to teach people the type of deep muscle relaxation that Jacobson and Wolpe and Schultz, among others, consider therapeutically essential, but some special form of instruction is necessary. A number of procedures can teach this control, but some are more effective than others. In particular, some form of EMG feedback seems to be needed to produce maximum results.

It is important to note that the results of this study do not support the hypothesis concerning the interaction of EMG feedback and other instructional supports. The results reported here show that other procedures accompanying EMG feedback had little additive effect. It may be that the experimental subjects were relatively relaxed before training began. Certainly the results show a floor effect, with all EMG groups approximating and holding for days an EMG level essentially at the tonic level of the forehead muscles. It may be that future studies using populations with higher initial baseline levels may be able to resolve this question.

The effect of relaxation training on this essentially normal population contribute to an important theoretical and clinical debate. The controversy concerning the relative importance of physical relaxation in therapeutic procedures has already been noted. Almost every form of behavior therapy postulates some form of counterconditioning, usually involving physiological variables. Various studies call into question the necessity of physiological relaxation, but these studies in turn have been criticized because of (a) the use of nonpathological populations and (b) uncontrolled demand effects (Budzynski & Stoyva, 1972).

This study cannot resolve the question of whether deep muscle relaxation is either necessary or sufficient in treating neurotic reactions. However, it provides a basis for further criticizing the methodology of most past studies investigating the necessity of relaxation: Did the studies testing the necessity of relaxation training really produce the theoretically required state of deep muscle relaxation? From this study it seems that classic relaxation training programs do help a person relax, but the effect is weak and hard to produce. The classic relaxation group in this study only reduced its muscle tension level by 50% over 12 sessions, while the EMG groups decreased their tension levels by almost 90% during the same period. Research designs using classic measures, especially over short periods, may not in fact have produced sufficient relaxation to adequately test the hypothesis.

Further, it seems legitimate to interpret the analysis of variance of self-report measures as partially reflecting experimental demand effects, which also may have operated in earlier sutdies. The subjects were told that this was an experiment in learning relaxation methods; they seemed to expect increasing relaxation and reported such, even when EMG measures of forehead muscle tension did not show physiological relaxation. It is clear that subjects in conventional research designs relying on self-report measures could well have reported a relaxation effect in which no muscle relaxation existed. However, one qualification is in order. It is possible that subjective reports in the present study accurately reflected whole body relaxation, rather than relaxation of forehead muscles. EMG feedback is remarkably specific (Basmajian, 1967) and the EMG groups may have reduced only forehead tension, relaxing the rest of their bodies no more than did the other groups. Future studies might check this possible differential relaxation by recording from a second site, distant from the training muscles and unrelated to training procedures.

The results of this study also have implications for clinical practice. It is important to professional therapists to produce the effect they assume is beneficial to their clients. If that effect is subjective calm, then the results reported here would indicate that any procedure should work equally well if "sold" as a relaxation procedure. However, the pro-duction of a physiological state of relaxation is a different matter. Simple undirected practice does not seem to work (as reflected by the control group). Classical procedures do work but only marginally, even with normal subjects like these, who still do not approach an absolute level of relaxation. More anxious clients might be expected to have even more difficulty in learning to relax by classical methods. Only the biofeedback procedures worked well both in producing absolute relaxation levels and in doing so in a short period of time.

It is clear that EMG biofeedback is a useful research and clinical tool. It has the potential to help unravel several difficult theoretical and clinical problems. It also may help resolve the longstanding problem of low correlation between subjective and physiological indexes of anxiety. While this problem was not the focus of this study, the results indicate that the correlation between the two measures increases with practice and can approach a respectable level. It may be that the initial low correlation came from subjects making their subjective judgments primarily on the basis of situational variables. But all of the relaxation training methods employed here forced the subjects to focus on internal, physiological cues in judging anxiety. Thus the increasing correlations may show subjects' improving ability to perceive and discriminate the internal cues reflecting autonomic arousal. This is a hypothesis worth pursuing.

Finally, there is one more implication of this study worth considering. Cognitive set and personality factors also may affect relaxation training. Deep muscle relaxation is a skill dependent on perception of minimal body cues. We seldom pay attention to these internal cues, and any factor such as inappropriate attentional set (e.g., Rotter's internal–external locus of control) or anxiety could effectively mask awareness of these cues and thereby slow acquisition rates. The effects of these variables also should be examined in future studies.

REFERENCES

Basmajian, J. *Muscles alive: Their functions revealed by electromyography* (2nd. ed.). Baltimore: Williams & Wilkins, 1967.

Budzynski, T., & Stoyva, J. An instrument for producing deep muscle relaxation by means of analog information feedback. *Journal of Applied Behavior Analysis*, 1969, *2*, 231–237.

Budzynski, T., & Stoyva, J. Biofeedback techniques in behavior therapy. In D. Shapiro (Ed.), *Biofeedback and self-control*. Chicago: Aldine Press, 1972.

Cameron, D. Observations on the patterns of anxiety. *American Journal of Psychiatry*, 1944, *101*, 36.

Farmer, R., & Wright, J. Muscular reactivity and systematic desensitization. *Behavior Therapy*, 1971, *2*, 1–10.

Green, E., Green, A., & Walters, D. Voluntary control of internal states: Psychological and physiological. *Journal of Transpersonal Psychology*, 1970, *1*, 1–26.

Jacobson, E. *Progressive relaxation* (2nd ed.). Chicago: University of Chicago Press, 1938.

Lader, M., & Mathews, A. A physiological model of phobic anxiety and desensitization. *Behaviour Research and Therapy*, 1968, *6*, 411–421.

Malmo, R. Studies of anxiety. In C. D. Spielberger (Ed.). *Anxiety and behavior*. New York: Academic Press, 1966.

Nawas, M. M., Welch, W. V., & Fishman, S. T. The comparative effectiveness of pairing aversive imagery with relaxation, neutral tasks and muscular tension in reducing snake phobia. *Behaviour Research and Therapy*. 1970, *8*, 63–68.

Paul, G. L. Inhibition of physiological response to stressful imagery by relaxation training and hypnotically suggested relaxation. *Behaviour Research and Therapy*, 1969, *7*, 249–256.

Rachman, S. The role of muscular relaxation in desensitization therapy. *Behaviour Research and Therapy*, 1968, *6*, 159–166.

Schultz, J., & Luthe, W. *Autogenic training: A psychophysiological approach to psychotherapy.* New York: Grune & Stratton, 1959.

Schwartz, G. Biofeedback as therapy: Some theoretical and practical issues. *American Psychologist*, 1974, *28*, 666–674.

Schwartz, B., & Johnson, H. Affective visual stimuli as operant reinforcers of the GSR. *Journal of Experimental Psychology*, 1969, *80*, 28–32.

Stampfl, T. G., & Levis, D. J. Essentials of implosive therapy. *Journal of Abnormal Psychology*, 1968, *72*, 496–503.

Sue, D. The role of relaxation in systematic desensitization. *Behaviour Research and Therapy*, 1972, *10*, 153–158.

Wallace, R. K., & Benson, H. The physiology of meditation. *Scientific American*, 1972, *226*, (2), 84–90.

Winer, B. *Statistical principles in experimental design.* New York: McGraw-Hill, 1962.

Wolpe, J. *Psychotherapy by reciprocal inhibition.* Stanford: Stanford University Press, 1958.

V

EEG ALPHA

Autoregulation of the EEG 22 Alpha Rhythm: A Program for the Study of Consciousness

Joe Kamiya

In keeping with the functionalist outlook of contemporary Western psychological research, most studies of the behavior of organisms employ procedures which require the behavior to be externally directed so as to involve the organism in gross interaction with the environment. In contrast, the new studies in trained autoregulation or "biofeedback training" require the organism to produce an internal effect. The methods of experimental control are external, as before, but the goal-directed behavior specified by the experimenter is an internal physiological effect.

The point of departure we have taken in our studies with the new methods is that these trained physiological effects seem to have behavioral properties. At the human level one of these behavioral properties is experiential or subjective concomitants. The fact that humans can compare the effects of the physiological training with other behavioral states, by verbal reports and by other discriminative behaviors, poses interesting questions.

We will describe the various studies we have done to establish that humans can be trained to discriminate and to control the average amplitude of their occipital electroencephalographic alpha rhythms. We will then describe a general methodology which we hope will be fruitful in specifying the dimensions of experiential qualities associated with such trained control.

This investigation was supported in part by a Research Scientists Development Award #MH 38897 from the National Institute of Mental Health, and in part by the Advanced Research Projects Agency of the Department of Defense under contract N-0014-70-C-350 to the San Diego State College Foundation, monitored by the Office of Naval Research.

But first a word of commentary on the concepts that seem to be reflected by the recent surge of interest in this field. What we seem to be witnessing is an increasing convergence of several diverse methodologies, concepts and interests. These include the application of behavioral technology and electronic instrumentation to the historically controversial area of such private internal events as feelings, conscious control, attention, etc. This surge of interest appears to be spurred by studies that show physiological concomitants of Eastern-style meditation practices, by a growing interest in expanded awareness of body and mind through sensitivity training, and by an increasing number of studies relating physiological and pharmacological variables to states of consciousness. The studies of dreaming and of the effects of the hallucinogenic drugs are good examples of these convergent trends.

These trends seem to be signs of progress. First, psychology appears to be getting less stiff about accepting "mentalistic" concepts such as dreaming as reasonable, hypothetical processes to account for the facts of dream-reporting behavior. Second, there appears to be growing recognition of the notion that the body is not only a part of the O side of the Organism-Environment dichotomy, but that it is also a proximal environment in which behaviors can take place (*e.g.*, trained control of peripheral blood flow) and have their effects more centrally (as in headache control) as well as have effects in the more distal environment (as in controlled blushing by actors). The recognition of the body as a discriminable and controllable entity points to its status both as an environment itself and as an interface with the more distal ecology. Biofeedback training seems to me to be especially helpful in emphasizing this unitive concept in which behavior and experience are no longer incompatible, but are instead intrinsic to biological organization.

Clearly, however, the theoretical tools for sharpening our comprehension of the entire range of phenomena are still quite primitive. As a way of helping progress toward the development of a more adequate theory, or at least in pointing out issues that seem to be relevant, the following points may be worthwhile. Initially, we might ask why trained physiological control sometimes, if not always, appears to have behavioral concomitants at all. Whether these concomitants are in the form of observable responses or are restricted to internal experience, why should they ever occur in association with operantly trained physiological activity? Three possible reasons occur to me: First, the same reinforcers that control externally directed behaviors appear to work for training physiological control. Food, water, termination or avoidance of aversive stimuli, and electrical stimulation of brain centers have all been used successfully in training physiological control in animals. For humans, monetary rewards, course credits, and praise or status seem to work for many physiologically defined behaviors as well as for externally oriented behaviors. A consequence of this similarity may be that, at least for the period of the experiment, the functional significance of the arbitrarily chosen physiological change (*e.g.*, a decrease in heart rate) is similar to that of an already-established external operant (*e.g.*, a bar press), since both obtain the same reinforcer (*e.g.*, food). Also, whatever physiological events constitute the process of reinforcement should be similar, whether the specific response is behaviorally or physiologically defined; and they might be expressed as secondary effects in behavior or experience.

Second, whatever the physiological processes underlying responses to discriminative stimuli may be, such processes should have similar effects on behavior if they can be initiated by the organism itself as a result of trained physiological control.

Third, the very physiological processes that are being brought under operant control have evolved phlogenetically, at least in part as mechanisms subserving externally directed behavior. For example, cardiac acceleration assists the organism in stressful emergencies. Animals trained by operant methods under nonstressful conditions to increase heart rate, therefore, might well be expected later to show altered signs of emotional responsiveness in stressful conditions, as in DiCara and Weiss's study (1969).

Although these considerations are couched in the language of external behavior, they can be stated in terms of internal behavior as well. That is, operantly controlled physiological activity can be thought of as behavior itself, albeit purely internal. The subjective concomitants, then, may well be a reflection of internal discriminative activity associated with the behavior, either as mediators or as resultants of the behavior. That is, the internal behavior has stimulus properties that are discriminable.

At any rate, an empirical search for physiological and psychological concomitants seems worthwhile. We turn now to a brief description of work done in our lab along these lines, with feedback training of the EEG.

The first of our studies on the EEG alpha rhythm and consciousness was done in 1958 at the University of Chicago. William Dement had just introduced me to the techniques of EEG recording and dream detection in the sleep laboratory of Professor Nathaniel Kleitman, and there was much talk about dreaming, consciousness, and Stage 1 sleep. Because the waxing and waning alpha rhythm of the subject who had yet to fall asleep fascinated me (and perhaps partly because studying awake subjects was less demanding than studying all-night sleep subjects), I found myself gradually defecting from sleep and dream research.

What I wanted to know about the waxings and wanings of the alpha rhythm was whether they were accompanied by changes in consciousness. A conditioned discrimination was tried in which a bell was rung from time to time, and the subject's task was to guess each time whether or not he had been generating alpha at the moment just before the bell was rung (Kamiya, 1971). The fact that subjects could learn this task was gratifying, not only because of the specific evidence relating alpha to an apparently discriminable state of awareness, but also because the method seemed to provide a promising paradigm for the behavioral study of many other physiological measures.

Retrospective reports by the subjects implicated close-up visual imagery as being associated with the absence of alpha. Since the experiments were conducted with the eyes closed and in total darkness, their imagery was not from actual seeing. The presence of alpha was reported as being associated with less visual imagery, and as being more relaxed, less attentive to anything in particular, and less intense. Quite by accident of experimental whim we found that subjects trained in making these discriminations were, by virtue of the training, able to produce the fluctuations in alpha at our command. Thus, it appeared that discrimination of the internal state of alpha-nonalpha was intimately related to control of the state.

Subsequently, in 1961 in our laboratory at the Langley Porter Neuropsychiatric Institute, we decided to train for alpha control directly, and devised the first of our audio feedback systems for this purpose (Kamiya, 1969). A tone in the subject's room was made to go on (or off) when the amplitude of the filtered, full-wave rectified and smoothed alpha rhythm reached a criterion threshold. When the amplitude fell below this level, the tone went off (or on). Additional feedback was provided in the form of a numerical score shown every 30 sec, indicating the percent of time the tone had been on (or off). The subject's task was to increase the percent of time the tone was on. He sat with his eyes closed in a dark room. The equipment was in an adjacent room.

Most subjects learned quite quickly, within one or two sessions of about 45 minutes each, to suppress alpha significantly. Specific coaching by suggesting close-up visual imagery, and especially instructions to attend to phosphenes, helped subjects to suppress alpha even further. Learning to increase alpha in relation to baseline percentages was more difficult, often requiring four or more sessions to demonstrate such increases. Some subjects failed to reach scores which were consistently higher than baseline scores. All subjects showed a decrease in alpha, relative to pretraining baselines, in the first one or two trials of feedback training to increase their alpha. This decrease was sometimes not fully recovered even after an entire hour of training. The early parts of alpha-increase trials were, therefore, very much as described by Lynch and Paskewitz (1971)—a matter of overcoming the factors that inhibit alpha.

It was found that the training produced a change in alpha during the baseline trials which followed immediately, where no feedback was given and where the subject was instructed to wait quietly with his eyes closed and not try to control his EEG. These were given after every five training trials. If the training trials were *increase* trials, the baseline scores went up by approximately the same amount as did the training scores. If the training trials were *decrease* trials, the baseline scores went down, also to the same degree as the training scores. There thus appeared to be an inertial effect of training trials on the resting baseline scores.

The subjects' feelings during alpha-increase trials were described in general as being relaxed though alert, calm, and sometimes pleasant. The alpha-decrease trials were described as more involved with close-up visual imagery and with more tension, anxiety, and fatigue than the increase trials.

Experiments using an alternating sequence of increase and decrease trial blocks, sandwiched by baseline trials, were more useful in determining the degree of control achieved by subjects. Alternation also permitted a test of the behavior of the baseline scores. The sequence of trial blocks in one study was five 30-sec increase trials, two 30-sec baseline trials and five 30-sec decrease trials. This sequence was repeated over the entire session of about 45 min.

The results were as follows: (1) Both increase and decrease trial scores departed significantly from initial baseline values in the expected direction. (2) Alpha-decrease scores became significant in relation to initial baseline scores more quickly than did increase scores. (3) The basal scores followed the same course as the increase trial scores, and were not distinguishable from them.

Thus, when subjects were allowed to rest between alternations of increase and decrease trial blocks, they clearly behaved like alpha-increase subjects. This result was replicated in additional studies using the same design and the same equipment. Again, Lynch and Paskewitz's interpretation seems, in general, to apply (Lynch and Paskewitz, 1971). However, in subsequent experiments some modifications designed to improve the efficiency of learning resulted in data which throw serious doubt on the interpretation that learning to increase alpha is merely a matter of learning to overcome its inhibitors.

The first modification was a change in the method of feedback. Rather than continue the use of a dichotomous on-off feedback signal triggered by an arbitrary criterion amplitude, we changed to a continuous tone whose loudness varied monotonically with the amplitude of the alpha envelope. This gave a more faithful reproduction of the manner in which trains of alpha activity actually varied in amplitude. Second, we turned to scoring for the time integral of the area under the alpha envelope, thus giving a measure that was proportional to the average amplitude. This measure is especially important for giving appropriate feedback to subjects who appear to level off in alpha production in terms of percentage of alpha time, but who might continue to increase the amplitude of their alpha rhythms. Third, we changed to a 2-minute trial period instead of a 30-second period, thus giving the subjects a greater opportunity to move into a sustained high-amplitude state.

With these modifications in use over the last four years of work, we have consistently found that after about four sessions of training of about 45 minutes each, subjects being trained to increase alpha tend to go above their pretraining baseline levels, as well as above their baseline scores taken during rest periods in the training sessions. This is true whether the training consists of increase trials only, or of alternating blocks of five trials of increase or decrease training. For training subjects to decrease alpha, the earlier method is not appreciably different from the modified methods.

One interpretation of the results is that alpha amplitude increases are learned, much like other skills are learned, and that, if it is a matter of learning to overcome inhibitors, such learning is aided by feedback training. A current study utilizing noncontingent feedback supports this view. However, the results presented so far tend to give an overly simple account of the factors affecting alpha. A persistent and serious problem in the interpretation of alpha amplitude feedback learning presents itself in the following observations.

Alpha-increase trials were interrupted in the middle of the session, and the experimenter entered the subject's room for three or four minutes to ask the subject to relate the states of mind he felt were most conducive to the control of the rhythm. When the training was resumed immediately thereafter, the average amplitude of the subject's alpha was found to be increased in the next one or two trials by considerably more than would occur if the subject were left alone to continue his trials. The gain lasted for only two or three minutes, with the scores then returning to their previous trend of a more gradual increase characteristic of feedback alpha training. More than half of all subjects have shown this effect.

This increase is puzzling. It does not appear to be the result of merely taking a break, for equal periods of time-out without the reporting do not result in an increased alpha level. Neither does such an increase result when the subject is not in the feedback training situation at all, but is merely waiting during a period corresponding to the length of the training period, and is then engaged in conversation for a period equal to the time of interruption of the experimental subjects. This increase is seen even in highly trained subjects.

We seem to be seeing a kind of potentiation of the effect of alpha-increase trials by the self-reporting period. Further studies are needed to determine the component of these periods which is responsible for the increase. Several possibilities need checking, including the possibility that personal contact between experimenter and subject is responsible. Meanwhile, the results serve to remind us that a factor not encompassed by the feedback training method can affect alpha amplitude very substantially. If the increases are being *elicited* by a factor not yet understood, a modification of methodology to include classical conditioning procedures might be useful in augmenting experimental control.

The work described thus far has to do with the control of the average amplitude of the alpha rhythm. We have also observed that subjects can be trained to control alpha frequency (Kamiya, 1969). In this study, an electronic device sent either a high-pitched or low-pitched click into the subject's room, depending on whether the duration of each alpha cycle detected by the circuit was longer or shorter than the median duration of his pretraining alpha cycles. With the aid of these signals, subjects learned to control the predominance of slow waves relative to fast waves.

Theta waves are likewise subject to trained control through the use of feedback devices (Green, 1970; Brown, 1971). In our own laboratory a system for feeding back an auditory signal that was a function of the difference between theta and alpha envelope amplitudes was successfully used in an effort to sharpen the subject's differentiation between theta and alpha. We also found that subjects could control the cross-correlation between simultaneous values of left- and right-side alpha recorded between central and occipital electrodes if they were presented a tone controlled by the fluctuations in the correlation (computed from a moving one-second window).

Finally, following the lead of Galin and Ornstein (1972), we have found that a tone feedback system can be used by subjects to control the asymmetry between the amplitude of the left bipolar occipital-to-central alpha envelope and the amplitude of the right bipolar occipital-to-central alpha envelope. In this system, the asymmetry between the two alpha envelopes is computed by an on-line computer for a half-second moving window by the function (L. ampl − R. ampl)/(L. ampl + R. ampl). Changes in the index are translated into variations in pitch.

The assessment of the subjective experiences associated with control of these EEG parameters of frequency, differences in envelope amplitude, cross-correlation, etc. is, of course, one of our primary aims. It is too early to describe with adequate reliability what the subjective concomitants are. The individual differences in retrospective verbal reports for any one parameter are very large, and within a single subject the reports change over time, in part because precision of control increases with training. What was felt subjectively to be important at one stage is often later considered unimportant, new concepts emerge to abstract the various experiences of the subject in a more general way, and so forth.

The aim of mapping the subjective qualities of controlled physiological activity is difficult to achieve for at least two reasons. First, the physiological response discriminations necessary for the achievement of control are often quite difficult for subjects to acquire. Second, it commonly occurs that simple verbal labels available to the subject are not satisfactory for describing the experiences associated with physiological control. This is not surprising in light of the fact that he has never heard others describe their experiences with feedback. Nor has he ever had others label his specific experience with the feedback task, as he often had other experiences labeled in his childhood (for example, when his mother used the word "hurt" to describe his sensations from a bruise).

It is important to recognize that the natural language of the subject for referring to internal events is perhaps the best medium currently available for assessing his discriminative repertoire for the physiological processes under discussion, and that rating scales, adjective check lists, etc. should be developed to optimize the validity of the verbal data. However, it also seems that the verbal reports in even the most articulate subjects simply do not match the discriminative precision implied by the high degree of control over physiological processes which is frequently seen, or by his capacity to differentiate one feedback task from another.

The aim of determining subjective experiences, fortunately, need not be limited to verbal report methods. In principle, a program of research combining features of both multidimensional psychophysics and operant training of physiological parameters could yield a more rigorous mapping of the subjective qualities of physiological self-control than any method now available. The general approach described below would seem to be required.

First, subjects should be trained to a high degree of control of the physiological measure to strengthen their discriminative grasp of the ability involved.

Second, each subject should be trained over a wide variety of measures. For example, in the EEG field, this would include alpha amplitude, alpha frequency, theta and beta patterns, and left-right and posterior-anterior dominance of each of these. Control of local circulation, EMG at different body sites, respiratory patterns, gastric motility and acidity, and many more measurable processes, singly and in various combinations, would be other examples.

Third, assessment of the behavioral or subjective equivalence of control among all the measures should be undertaken, and matrices of indices comparing each physiological measure with each of the others should be attempted. I can think of three types of these indices:

(a) Ask the subject to provide simple ratings of the degree of similarity of one controlled measure to the others. For example, how similar is alpha to theta, to low EMG at frontalis muscle, to warm hands? Ratings along other dimensions such as *calmness*, etc. might also be tried.

(b) In a detection type of task, ask the subject, upon a signal, to guess which one of each of two parameters is showing the more extreme state at that moment. For instance, ring a bell for either left-side alpha or right-side alpha, and ask the subject to guess which is present. Determination of the frequency with which one parameter is mistaken for another would provide a measure of their stimulus equivalence.

(c) Ask the subject to produce changes in one state. Observe the covariation with the other states as a measure of response equivalence.

Fourth, from such matrices for each subject, the best reference axes (factors) for descriptive purposes should be extracted mathematically, so that any one parameter can be characterized as a combination of "loadings" along such axes.

Fifth, adjectives commonly used to describe experiential states should be matched to these axes.

Such a program would obviously require an effort not realizable within any single laboratory in the foreseeable future, and doubtless would need considerable modification before it could be implemented. But several gains could result:

(1) Currently the choice of physiological parameters as candidates for operant training is highly arbitrary. This is especially true in the field of electroencephalography, where so little is known of the functional significance of the parameters extracted. It is reasonable to expect that the approach outlined would reduce the frequency of blind selection, and provide some guide posts based on knowledge of functionally equivalent parameters.

(2) If individual differences in the axes were low enough, the language of subjective states for specifiable physiological states would be much more precise, and serious comparisons of the distances between points in the subjective space could be attempted.

(3) Exploration of new areas in the subjective space could be tried, partly as a validation of the descriptive system. For example, if particular combinations of values of several physiological measures have never occurred before in the person, training in the production of such

combinations should lead to experiences the subject had not had before, but whose qualities might be predicted in advance.

(4) Characterization of the degree to which different subjects yielded different axes would change many of the all-too-speculative and philosophical disputes concerning the similarity of private experiences among different persons into empirically resolvable disputes.

(5) A most important gain that we can hope for is that the mapping operation described above, or some replacement of it, will help to bridge both the conceptual and the empirical gaps among physiology, behavior, and subjective experience.

REFERENCES

BROWN, 1971.
    Brown, B.B. Awareness of EEG—subject activity relationships detected within a closed feedback system. *Psychophysiology*, 7:451-464, 1971.
DICARA AND WEISS, 1969.
    DiCara, L.V. and Weiss, J.M. Effect of heart-rate learning under curare on subsequent noncurarized avoidance learning. *J. Comp. Physiol. Psychol.*, 69:368-374, 1969.
GALIN AND ORNSTEIN, 1972.
    Galin, D. and Ornstein, R. Lateral specialization of cognitive mode: An EEG study. *Psychophysiology*, 9:412-418, 1972.
GREEN ET AL., 1970.
    Green, E.E., Green, A.M., and Walters, E.D. Voluntary control of internal states: Psychological and physiological. *J. Transpers. Psychol.*, 2:1-26, 1970.
KAMIYA, 1969.
    Kamiya, J. Operant control of the EEG alpha rhythm and some of its reported effects on consciousness. In: *Altered States of Consciousness* (C.T. Tart, Ed.). New York, Wiley, 1969. pp. 507-517.
KAMIYA, 1971.
    Kamiya, J. Conditioned discrimination of the EEG alpha rhythm in humans. Abstract of a paper presented at the Western Psychological Association meeting, 1962. Reprinted in: *Biofeedback and Self-control: A Reader* (T. Barber *et al.*, Eds.). Chicago, Aldine-Atherton, 1971. p. 279.
LYNCH AND PASKEWITZ, 1971.
    Lynch, J.J. and Paskewitz, D.A. On the mechanisms of feedback control of human brain wave activity. *J. Nerv. Ment. Dis.*, 153:205-217, 1971.

Subjective Aspects of 23
Alpha Enhancement
T. A. Travis, C. Y. Kondo, and J. R. Knott

Summary

Early reports on enhancing occipital alpha through feedback noted that subjects reported the experience as being pleasant and relaxing. This paper reports the subjective experiences of 140 subjects who participated in four studies which examined the alpha enhancement phenomenon. Under both eyes-open and eyes-closed conditions, approximately 50 per cent of the subjects reported that alpha enhancement was 'pleasant' and 50 per cent 'unpleasant/neutral'. With eyes-open training conditions, about half the subjects stated that the experience was 'relaxing' and the other half 'not relaxing'. During eyes-closed training, 63 per cent of the subjects noted that enhancing alpha was 'relaxing', while 37 per cent reported that the experience was 'not relaxing'. However, in the last case the circular relationship between increased alpha and deep relaxation may obtain.

INTRODUCTION

The technique of 'biofeedback' consists of presenting information about an internal physiological process to a subject, normally not available to him. The basic hypothesis underlying all research in biofeedback (also a term for 'operant conditioning' or 'instrumental learning') is that once cognizant of an internal physiological state to which he would otherwise have no access the individual can 'learn' to modify or control this process. There are many areas in which research examining this hypothesis and the possible clinical application of this technique is being done. They include cardiovascular (heart rate, blood pressure, arrhythmias); gastrointestinal (gastric motility, oesophageal reflux, faecal incontinence, functional diarrhoea, obesity); striated muscle (silent reading, torticollis, tension headache); electroencephalography (enhancement of specific brain wave patterns, reduction of seizures in epilepsy); and altered states of consciousness (hypnosis, meditation).

The general techniques of biofeedback have been reviewed by Gaarder (1971), and clinical applications using biofeedback have recently been reviewed by Blanchard and Young (1974) and Birk (1973). A series of annual collections of papers covering all aspects of research in this area has been published (Barber et al., 1971; Stoyva et al., 1972; Shapiro et al., 1973; and Miller et al., 1974).

The area of biofeedback which has received widespread popular attention and rather naive acceptance by the public is that of 'alpha conditioning' or 'alpha enhancement training'. Although conditioned suppression of alpha activity had been studied as early as 1941 (Jasper and Shagass; Knott and Henry), it was not until the late 1960's that studies appeared involving conditioned enhancement of alpha. These investigators (Kamiya, 1968; Kamiya, 1969; Nowlis and Kamiya, 1970; Brown, 1970) reported that subjects given training to enhance the abundance of the occipital alpha rhythm reported the experience to be pleasant and relaxing. This reputed positive subjective state associated with the 'alpha experience' has led to speculation that 'alpha enhancement' may have therapeutic value. The present paper presents the subjective reports of subjects who participated in four different alpha enhancement experiments in our laboratory during the past 30 months.

METHODS AND PROCEDURES

Method

Subjects: Subjects were 140 (male, N = 46; female, N = 94) students and employees of the University of Iowa, each of whom participated in one of four alpha enhancement studies. Forty-two subjects had received five 10-minute eyes-open alpha enhancement training sessions in Study I. Thirty-two participants, in Study II, received ten 5-minute eyes-open and ten 5-minute eyes-closed training sessions; sixteen additional subjects received random non-contingent reinforcement (10 trials, each 5 minutes in length). Participants in Study III (N = 30) received ten 5-minute eyes-closed alpha enhancement sessions. In Study IV, half the subjects (N = 10) were trained to enhance and half (N = 10) were trained to suppress alpha, though both groups were told that the former condition obtained. Thirty minutes of eyes-closed practice was given to all 20 subjects.

Apparatus: All subjects were run in a sound-attenuated room, which was dimly lit. The temperature ranged from 73° to 79°F.

Silver-silver-chloride electrodes were applied with collodion-soaked strips of gauze (resistance below 5 kilohms) placed as follows: (1) 2 cm. above the inion (Oz); (2) on the right ear or mastoid; (3) at the vertex (Cz); (4) above and below the right eyes; (5) on the forehead (ground). The following data were monitored: (1) alpha (Oz—ear/mastoid); (2) drowsiness (Cz—ear/mastoid); (3) eye movements (right eye electrodes).

Equipment to accomplish the biofeedback training consisted of the following: (1) a Grass Instrument Co. Model 78 polygraph; (2) a Krohnhite Model 330 band pass filter; (3) a Wavetek Model 136 function generator; (4) a Heathkit Model AA-18 audio amplifier. In general, electroencephalographic activity (EEG) was recorded from the subjects by the Model 78 polygraph with 8–13 Hz activity extracted from it using the Kronhite filter. The alpha was then transformed into a DC potential which reflected the average amplitude of the sinusoidal alpha waveform by means of a Grass Model 7P3 preamplifier. This DC potential was used to control the feedback signal. In some of the experiments, subjects received the feedback signal only when their alpha voltage and amount exceeded some predetermined criterion of performance. No signal was presented when insufficient alpha was being produced (Study I; part of Study II). In other studies (part of Study II; Studies III and IV) subjects heard a tone whose pitch varied directly and continuously with the amount of alpha being emitted. In this case, the DC potential was fed into the Wavetek function generator which modulated the frequency of the feedback signal as the amount of alpha

(and therefore the *level* of the DC potential) varied.

Quantification of alpha was accomplished in two ways. Number of seconds of criterion alpha (i.e. amount of time a pre-determined criterion was equal or exceeded) was timed using electro-mechanical clocks. A second method, using the technique of Knott, McAdam and Grass (1964) used a 7P10 Grass integrator-preamplifier. This unit was set so that it counted an event every time it had integrated 100 uV-seconds of EEG activity. The number of these events together with the time period within which they occurred yielded the average amplitude of the alpha wave for that time period.*

Procedures

As indicated above, in some experiments subjects were trained with their eyes open (EO), in some with their eyes closed (EC), or both. When EO training was examined, subjects rested with their eyes closed; and, when EC training was used, subjects were asked to keep their eyes open between trials. Subjects in Studies I, III and IV were asked to rate the task as pleasant, unpleasant or neutral, and also whether they felt that the 'alpha experience' was relaxing or not relaxing. Subjects in Study II were only asked to relate pleasantness of the task.

Study I: The basic phenomenon of alpha conditioning was examined (Travis, Kondo and Knott, 1974); could subjects, given knowledge of their alpha level, increase the amount of alpha emitted? A visual (blue light) feedback signal was used. Subjects received the feedback signal when they equalled or exceeded a predetermined *criterion alpha*. This was defined as 0·07 to 0·13 seconds of 8–13 Hz activity which was 50 per cent or more of the amplitude of the maximum eyes-closed alpha observed during an initial calibration period. Two control groups were examined, one receiving noncontingent feedback and one receiving no feedback, just sitting quietly. After we had determined to our satisfaction that this was indeed the case, we proceeded in Study II (Travis, Kondo and Knott, 1974) to examine the parameters of the alpha enhancement situation more closely.

Study II: The following questions were examined: (1) Was there a difference between EC and EO training? (2) Could subjects learn the task more efficiently with on/off or continuous feedback? and (3) how good a dependent variable was integrated alpha? The feedback signal was auditory for all subjects, half of the subjects receiving continuous reinforcement and half receiving reinforcement for equalling or exceeding criterion alpha as defined above. Feedback signal for the former group was a tone which varied continuously between 300 and 500 cycles per second, depending on the amplitude and abundance the alpha produced. On the other hand, the group whose feedback was based on criterion alpha heard a 400 cycle tone when they equalled or exceeded criterion.

Control subjects in this study received a random

---

* As an example: 1 event = 100 uV-seconds, if 50 events were marked in 100 seconds, the average amplitude would =

$$\frac{50 \text{ events}}{100 \text{ seconds}} = \frac{100 \text{ uV-sec}}{100 \text{ seconds}} = 50 \text{ uV, average amplitude.}$$

on/off or continuous signal unrelated to alpha output. The control subjects were led to believe that they were participating in an alpha enhancement study and that their reinforcement was in fact relevant.

We found that subjects learned to enhance their alpha output under both eye conditions, but to a greater degree during EO training (since EO alpha levels are very low, this was not surprising). It was also determined that continuous feedback was superior to on/off in producing alpha changes; and, finally, that integrated alpha was a very sensitive measure of changes during alpha enhancement training.

Study III: (Kondo, Travis and Knott, 1974). We looked at the effects of increasing monetary reward on alpha enhancement and found, as expected, that the promise of more money spurred the subjects to greater efforts. These subjects received a continuous frequency modulated tone reinforcement. Subjects experienced ten 5-minute training and five 5-minute no-tone test periods following the training sessions. Four bonus levels were used in this investigation ($0.00, $2.50, $5.00 and $10.00), the criterion for full bonus being production of alpha in each of the last five trials 20 per cent greater than baseline levels.

Study IV: In this study (Kondo, Travis, Knott and Bean, 1975) the subjects received a continuous frequency modulated tone. Half of the subjects heard a tone which *increased* in frequency with increased occipital alpha, while the other half heard a tone which *decreased* in frequency with increases in alpha. Both groups, however, were told that the former condition obtained and that their task was to keep the tone as high as possible. Subjects receiving true feedback produced more alpha than those receiving false.

RESULTS

Study I: EO Alpha Training (5, 10 minute trials) —Table I. Of the 42 subjects, 20 (48 per cent) reported that the 'alpha experience' was pleasant, while 22 subjects (52 per cent) reported that the alpha experience was 'neutral or unpleasant'. Of the 20 subjects who reported that they found the alpha experience to be 'pleasant', only 10 could definitely say that the experience was intrinsically pleasant. The other 10 could not say whether the pleasant feeling they experienced was from the alpha production *per se* or because of the reinforcement received for having succeeded at the task. Again, of the 42 subjects 24 (57 per cent) reported that the 'alpha experience' was relaxing; 18 (43 per cent) of the subjects reported either that the task was demanding or that it was not relaxing.

Study II: EC/EO Alpha Training (10, 5 minute sessions)—Table II. Sixty-three per cent of the patients who received continuous feedback and 38 per cent of those receiving binary feedback during eyes-closed training rated the experience as pleasant. Following eyes-open enhancement training, on the other hand, 27 per cent of those receiving continuous and 50 per cent of those receiving binary feedback reported the alpha experience to be pleasant. It is interesting that 63 per cent of the random continuous feedback control and 50 per cent of the random binary feedback controls also found the experience to be pleasant. No consistent pattern

TABLE I

Subjective reports of subjects who received 5 ten-minute eyes-open training trials (n = 42)

Pleasant	Unpleasant	Neutral	Relaxing	Not relaxing	Intrinsically pleasant
20	2	20	24	18	10

TABLE II

Subjective reports of subjects who received continuous and binary feedback under eyes-open and eyes-closed conditions, and control subjects who received eyes-closed training with random feedback (n = 48)

				Pleasant	Unpleasant	Neutral	Intrinsically pleasant
Eyes closed experiment:							
Binary feedback	..	..	..	6	1	9	5
Continuous feedback	..	..	..	10	1	5	5
Eyes open experiment:							
Binary feedback	..	..	..	8	0	8	7
Continuous feedback	..	..	..	5	0	3	3
Eyes closed control:							
Binary feedback	..	..	..	4	0	4	2
Continuous feedback	..	..	..	6	0	10	4

TABLE III

Subjective reports of subjects who received continuous feedback under three levels of reward (n = 30)

		Pleasant	Unpleasant	Neutral	Relaxing	Not relaxing	Intrinsically pleasant
High S+	..	8	0	2	7	3	7
Medium S+	..	3	0	7	6	4	2
Low S+ ..	..	7	0	3	8	2	5

TABLE IV

Subjective reports of subjects who received true and inverted continuous feedback for 30 minutes (n = 20)

		True feedback	Inverted feedback
Pleasant	..	3	1
Unpleasant	..	3	2
Neutral	..	4	7
Relaxing	..	4	3
Not relaxing	..	6	7

can be discerned in this table concerning possible patterns of responses; i.e. 'pleasant', 'unpleasant' and 'neutral' feelings do not seem to be related to any degree to the kind of the feedback stimulus experienced or the eye condition during training. Further, a fair number of the subjects in all categories noted or felt that the alpha experience was intrinsically pleasant, i.e. was pleasant independent of task success. Performances of subjects who rated a task pleasant and those who rated it unpleasant did not differ in learning alpha.

Study III: EC Alpha Training (10, 5 minute sessions)—Table III. A majority of the groups who received the high and low levels of rewards rated the task as 'pleasant'. There does appear to be a reversal in the medium reward group; no explanation can be offered for this at present.

Study IV: EC Alpha Training (1, 30 minute session)—Table IV. It can be seen that subjective responses of persons who were trying to increase

(true feedback) and of those who were trying to suppress (inverted feedback) alpha production were nearly the same.

All subjects: It can be seen in Table V that approximately half of the subjects who received alpha enhancement under either eye condition rated the task 'pleasant'. On the other hand, more of the subjects who received eyes-closed alpha enhancement found the training relaxing than did subjects who received eyes-open training.

DISCUSSION

The evidence to date suggests that the alpha enhancement task is not as overwhelmingly pleasant, as had been suggested by Nowlis and Kamiya (1970) and Brown (1970). The auditory, eyes-closed enhancement, however, appears in a number of people to be related to relaxation. Although the use of this type of training for therapy would be decidedly premature, it does appear that in some cases relaxation can be increased coincident with 'learned' alpha enhancement. Of course, this may be a circular process, since 'relaxation' with decrease in anxiety and tension leads to an increase in per cent time alpha.

ACKNOWLEDGEMENTS

The research was done at the Department of Psychiatry and EEG and Neurophysiology, College of Medicine, University of Iowa, 500 Newton Road, Iowa City, Iowa 52240. T. A. Travis, M.D. was then Assistant Professor of Psychiatry at the College of Medicine, University of Iowa. This study was supported in full by the Iowa Mental Health Research Fund.

TABLE V

Combined reports of all subjects who have participated in alpha enhancement studies to date

				Pleasant	Unpleasant	Neutral	Intrinsically pleasant
Eyes open (n = 66)	..	..	..	50%	3%	47%	61%
Eyes closed (n = 62)	..	..	..	55%	3%	42%	71%
				Relaxing		Not relaxing	
Eyes open (n = 42)	..	..	..	57%		43%	
Eyes closed (n = 40)	..	..	..	63%		37%	

REFERENCES

BROWN, B. B. (1970) Recognition of aspects of consciousness through association with EEG alpha activity represented by a light signal. *Psychophysiology*, **6**, 442–52.

BARBER, T. X. *et al.* (Editors) (1971) *Biofeedback and Self-Control*. Chicago.

—— (1971) *Biofeedback and Self-Control 1970*. Chicago.

BIRK, L. (1973) *Biofeedback: Behavioral Medicine*. New York.

BLANCHARD, E. B. & YOUNG, L. D. (1974) Clinical application of biofeedback training. *Arch. Men. Psychiat.*, **30**, 573–89.

GAARDER, K. (1971) Control of states of consciousness. *Arch. gen. Psychiat.*, **25**, 429–47.

JASPER, H. & SHAGASS, C. (1974) Conditioning the occipital alpha rhythm in man. *J. eng. Psychol.*, **28**, 373–88.

KAMIYA, J. (1968) Conscious control of brain waves. *Psychology Today*, **1**, 56–60.

—— (1969) Operant control of EEG alpha rhythms and some of its reported effects on consciousness. In *Altered States of Consciousness* (ed. Tart). New York.

KNOTT, J. R. & HENRY, C. E. (1941) The conditioning of the blocking of the alpha rhythm of the human EEG. *J. exp. Psychol.*, **28**, 362–6.

—— MCADAM, D. & GRASS, R. W. (1964) A system for quantification of frequency specific responses in the EEG during classical condition. *EEG clin. Neurophys.*, **17**, 574–7.

KONDO, C. Y., TRAVIS, T. A. & KNOTT, J. R. (1974) The effects of changes in motivation on alpha enhancement. Accepted for publication by *Psychophysiology*.

—— —— —— & BEAN, J. A. Submitted to Biofeedback Research Society Annual Meeting, Monterey, California, 1975.

MILLER, N. E. *et al.* (Editors) (1974) *Biofeedback and Self-Control, 1973*. Chicago.

NOWLIS, D. F. & KAMIYA, J. (1970) The control of electroencephalographic alpha rhythm activity through auditory feedback and the associated mental activity. *Psychophysiology*, **6**, 476–84.

SHAPIRO, D. *et al.* (Editors) (1973) *Biofeedback and Self-Control, 1972*. Chicago.

STOYVA, J. *et al.* (Editors) (1972) *Biofeedback and Self-Control, 1971*. Chicago.

TRAVIS, T. A., KONDO, C. Y. & KNOTT, J. R. (1974) Alpha conditioning: a controlled study. *J. nerv. ment. Dis.*, **158**, 163–73.

—— —— —— (1974) Parameters of eyes-closed alpha enhancement. *Psychophysiology*, **11**, 674–81

Terry A. Travis, M.D., *Associate Professor, Dept. of Psychiatry, Southern Illinois University School of Medicine, Box 3926, Springfield, Illinois 62708*

C. Y. Kondo, M.A., *Dept. of Psychiatry and EEG and Neurophysiology, College of Medicine, University of Iowa, 500 Newton Road, Iowa City, Iowa 52240*

J. R. Knott, Ph.D., *Dept. of Psychiatry and EEG and Neurophysiology, College of Medicine, University of Iowa, 500 Newton Road, Iowa City, Iowa 52240*

Ronald S. Valle and John M. Levine

ABSTRACT

In a study designed to investigate expectation artifact in EEG alpha training, Ss' actual direction of alpha change and expected direction of change were orthogonally manipulated in a 2×2 design. Twenty Ss actually enhanced alpha and 20 actually suppressed alpha (Task manipulation). Within each Task group, 10 Ss were led to believe they enhanced alpha and 10 were told they suppressed alpha (Expectation manipulation). Five high and 5 low alpha baseline Ss were assigned to each of the 4 conditions. Ss participated in 4 alpha training sessions in a dark room, each composed of a 2-min eyes-closed baseline period followed by 20 2-min training periods with a tone indicating S's EEG activity. Results, based on percent alpha change between the baseline period and the final alpha training period in each session, indicated that Ss who believed they enhanced alpha controlled alpha significantly better (more enhancement in the Task Enhancement condition and more suppression in the Task Suppression condition) than Ss who believed they suppressed alpha. Implications of expectation artifact for EEG biofeedback studies were discussed.

DESCRIPTORS: Alpha training, EEG biofeedback, Experimental artifact.

An increasingly popular research topic is the volitional control of electroencephalographic (EEG) alpha wave activity. It has been demonstrated that individuals who are provided with feedback concerning their own alpha activity can learn to alter alpha wave production (Hart, 1968; Kamiya, 1968, 1969). In addition, studies have related alpha wave production to subjective feeling states (Brown, 1971; Nowlis & Kamiya, 1970), Zen meditation (Kasamatsu & Hirai, 1969), hypnotic susceptibility (Engstrom, London, & Hart, 1970; London, Hart, & Leibovitz, 1968; Now-

The authors wish to thank Beau Brinker for designing, constructing, and maintaining the EEG filtering and timing equipment. Thanks are extended to R. Buck, D. De-Good, G. Koeske, and R. Willis for comments and technical assistance during the course of this research. Computer facilities were provided by the University of Pittsburgh Computer Center.

Address requests for reprints to: Ronald S. Valle, Department of Psychology, Duquesne University, Pittsburgh, Pa. 15219.

lis & Rhead, 1968), task performance (Vogel, Broverman, & Klaiber, 1968), and a variety of personality dimensions including activity-passivity, anxiety, and introversion-extraversion.

Recently, investigators have demonstrated the susceptibility of volitional alpha control to artifactual intrusion. According to Kruglanski (1973), " . . . the term artifact refers to a factor producing a spurious relationship between variables, thus leading to invalid inferences in scientific inquiry . . . To constitute an artifact, a variable needs to satisfy two conditions: (*a*) be capable (singularly or in interaction) of influencing the phenomenon under study and (*b*) be systematically associated with some of the experimental treatments or with the background conditions of an experiment (or experiments) [p. 348]." Recent discussions of artifact in contexts other than biofeedback research have mentioned such diverse factors as: S's desire to confirm or disconfirm the experimental hypothesis, S's desire to be evaluated positively, experimenter's expectations and behavior, effects of prior testing, etc. (Rosenthal & Rosnow, 1969; Rosnow & Aiken, 1973; Weber & Cook, 1972). Specifically in regard to alpha training, Hart (1968) showed that increased alpha production typically attributed to EEG feedback is due in part to merely sitting quietly in a darkened room. Moreover, Paskewitz and Orne (1973) recently demonstrated that EEG feedback produces reliable alpha increases only when dim ambient illumination depresses alpha level below that spontaneously emitted under optimal (total darkness) conditions.

In the present study we investigated the impact of another potentially important artifact in alpha control research: S's belief, or expectation, regarding the type of alpha change he is producing (i.e., enhancement vs suppression). Typically, Ss in alpha control studies are given expectations congruent with their actual task (i.e., told they are enhancing alpha in genuine enhancement conditions and suppressing alpha in genuine suppression conditions). However, because popular treatments of brain wave control generally extol subjective states accompanying alpha enhancement but rarely mention, much less make attractive, alpha suppression, volunteer Ss instructed to enhance alpha may become more enthusiastic about their task and work harder than Ss instructed to suppress alpha. If so, Ss' ability to suppress alpha in previous studies may have been underestimated, and alpha suppression might be facilitated by misleading Ss to believe they are actually enhancing alpha. On the other hand, ability to enhance alpha might decrease markedly if Ss are led to believe they are in fact suppressing alpha.

To test these notions, Task and Expectation were varied orthogonally in a 2×2 design. Thus, one-half of the Ss actually enhanced alpha and one-half actually suppressed alpha (Task manipulation). Each Task group was divided into two subgroups; members of one subgroup were led to believe they were enhancing alpha and members of the other subgroup were led to believe they were suppressing alpha (Expectation manipulation).

Method

Subjects

The Ss were 40 unpaid male college students who volunteered for a "brain wave biofeedback" experiment. Ss had no previous biofeedback experience. Interviews conducted prior to the beginning of the study indicated that Ss had little knowledge of, or interest in, the physiological bases of alpha, but expected alpha training to produce relaxation, altered states of consciousness, and general self-improvement.

Procedure and Apparatus

One week after the last of 4 pretest sessions, in which[2] Ss filled out paper-and-pencil personality tests and took the Rod and Frame Test (Witkin, Lewis, Hertzman, Machover, Meissner, & Wapner, 1954), Ss reported individually to the laboratory for an alpha baseline session. The S was seated in a comfortably padded chair in an anechoic chamber (test room) and a standard Grass EEG electrode was placed midline occipital with a right earlobe reference. The EEG signal, after being fed into a differential preamplifier circuit, was fed through a narrow bandpass filter which had frequency corner points of 8.5 and 13.5 Hz with a roll-off of 40 dB ± 3 dB at each corner. This circuitry produced an amplified filtered alpha signal which was recorded on a Beckman Type T polygraph and was used to activate a trigger circuit set at a 10 μV firing level. The trigger circuit activated a digital timer which recorded the number of sec (to the nearest tenth) per 2-min interval in which alpha amplitude exceeded 10 μV. (In subsequent training sessions, filtered alpha above 10 μV was also transmitted as a tone through earphones worn by the S. Tone loudness varied directly as a function of alpha amplitude.) The S was instructed to relax with his eyes closed in the completely darkened test room for 10 min. After 8 min, a 2-min eyes-closed percent time alpha baseline was recorded. The S was then dismissed.

Baselines obtained from the 40 Ss were ordered from high to low. Ss were then divided at the median of the baseline distribution into high and low alpha groups (20 Ss per group).

One week after the baseline session, Ss reported individually for the first of 4 weekly 1-hr alpha training sessions. Ten Ss (5 high alpha baseline and 5 low alpha baseline) were randomly assigned to each of the four conditions (see Table 1). Task instructions manipulated the actual physiological change the S was attempting to produce. In Task Enhancement conditions, Ss were instructed to maximize tone duration and loudness. In Task Suppression conditions, Ss were instructed to minimize tone duration and loudness. Expectation instructions manipulated S's belief about the type of physiological change (i.e., alpha enhancement vs alpha suppression) he was attempting to produce. In Task Enhancement–Expectation Enhancement and Task Suppression–Expectation Suppression conditions, Ss were told that presence of the feedback tone indicated presence of alpha. In Task Enhancement–Expectation Suppression and Task Suppression–Expectation Enhancement conditions, Ss were told that absence of the feedback tone indicated presence of alpha. Thus, Expectation instructions were consistent with Task instructions in the first two conditions and inconsistent with Task instructions in the last two conditions. In order to reduce suspicion regarding subjective experience in the two conditions where Task and Expectation were inconsistent, all Ss were told that

TABLE 1
Summary of experimental design, with abbreviated instructions for each condition

Task	Expectation	
	Enhancement	Suppression
Enhancement	Keep tone on. Tone = alpha.	Keep tone on. No tone = alpha.
Suppression	Keep tone off. No tone = alpha.	Keep tone off. Tone = alpha.

Note. — Apparatus was constructed so that the tone indicated the presence of alpha.

people vary widely in their subjective experiences during alpha training. Finally, Ss were told that, following the fourth alpha training session, they would have an opportunity to suppress alpha if they had participated in the Task Enhancement condition or enhance alpha if they had participated in the Task Suppression condition.

In each of the 4 training sessions, the S was instrumented as in the baseline session and given instructions appropriate to his experimental condition. After the S had sat in the lighted test room with his eyes open for 3 min, a 2-min eyes-open percent time alpha baseline was obtained. The lights in the test room were then turned off and 8 min later a 2-min eyes-closed percent time alpha baseline was obtained. The S was then provided with the feedback tone, and his percent time alpha was recorded on the digital timer in 20 2-min periods, separated by 10-sec intervals. At the end of the session, the experimenter turned on the test room lights, removed the electrodes and earphones, and told the S he was doing "a bit above average" in learning to control alpha. Thirty-four Ss completed 4 training sessions, 5 Ss completed 3 sessions, and 1 S completed 2 sessions.

Results and Discussion

A score reflecting percent alpha change relative to eyes-closed baseline in each of the 4 training sessions was calculated for each S who completed all training sessions. For example, in a given session, a S showing 40 sec of alpha during the 2 min eyes-closed baseline period and 60 sec of alpha during the final 2-min training period would receive a score of 50 percent $((60-40)/40)$. Scores were computed so that (a) positive scores reflected alpha enhancement in the Task Enhancement conditions and suppression in the Task Suppression conditions and (b) negative scores reflected suppression in the Task Enhancement conditions and enhancement in the Task Suppression conditions. Hartley's test (Winer, 1971) conducted on alpha control scores collapsed across training sessions revealed heterogeneity of within-cell variance, F_{max} (4/33) = 13.52. Therefore, scores were subjected to square root transformation (following addition of 150 to each score to produce uniformly positive scores) prior to the analysis of variance. Regarding mean transformed alpha control scores presented below, the larger the score the more Ss behaved in accordance with Task instructions (i.e., enhanced alpha in Task Enhancement conditions and suppressed alpha in Task Suppression conditions).

A $2 \times 2 \times 4$ repeated measures analysis of variance was conducted on mean transformed alpha control scores (between-subjects factors: Task, Expectation; within-subjects factor: Sessions). Only a significant Expectation main effect emerged, $F(1/30)=5.75$, $MS_e=14.83$, $p<.05$. This effect was attributable to higher alpha control in the Expectation Enhancement ($\overline{X} = 13.26$) than in the Expec-

tation Suppression ($\overline{X} = 11.98$) conditions. That is, *regardless* of the direction of alpha change dictated by Task instructions, Ss who thought they were enhancing alpha (Expectation Enhancement) exhibited significantly greater ability to control alpha than did Ss who thought they were suppressing alpha (Expectation Suppression). Thus, Ss in the Task Enhancement–Expectation Enhancement condition ($\overline{X} = 13.91$) *increased* alpha more than Ss in the Task Enhancement–Expectation Suppression condition ($\overline{X} = 11.59$), while Ss in the Task Suppression–Expectation Enhancement condition ($\overline{X} = 12.74$) *decreased* alpha more than Ss in the Task Suppression–Expectation Suppression condition ($\overline{X} = 12.31$).

The present study indicated that whether Ss expected to enhance or suppress alpha had an important effect on their ability to control alpha. This finding was obtained in spite of the fact that Ss were told (a) that people vary widely in their subjective reactions during alpha training and (b) that they would subsequently be allowed to enhance alpha if they had suppressed it or suppress alpha if they had enhanced it.

Present findings have important implications for the interpretation of data obtained in EEG biofeedback studies. First, as demonstrated above, expectations can affect alpha production, per se. As suggested in the Introduction, Ss' motivation is assumed to mediate the relationship between manipulated expectation and alpha production. That is, instructions to enhance alpha are assumed to create greater task motivation than instructions to suppress alpha. In addition, expectations may also influence phenomena (e.g., reported feelings, hypnotic susceptibility) which seem associated with alpha production. Here, it is suggested that Ss' prior beliefs about states accompanying alpha enhancement and suppression may at least partially account for the apparent causal relationship between alpha activity and these associated states. For example, studies report quite different subjective feelings among Ss enhancing vs suppressing alpha, but do not make explicit whether Ss knew the direction of the alpha change they were producing (Brown, 1971; Nowlis & Kamiya, 1970). If Ss' expectations were consistent with task instructions in these studies, reported feelings may have been at least partially attributable to pre-existing beliefs about how alpha enhancement and suppression were "supposed" to feel. Engstrom et al. (1970) found that hypnotic susceptibility (a) was correlated with alpha activity both before and after alpha training and (b) increased as a function of alpha training. It is possible, however, that the apparent functional relationship between alpha activity and hypnotizability was due partially to an expectation artifact, since *S*s were told, prior to training: " . . . that the study involved training in brain wave autocon-trol as a method of improving hypnotic susceptibility [p. 1261]." Regardless of the viability of an expectation interpretation of these particular studies, however, present results clearly indicate that *S*s' expectations warrant consideration in future alpha training studies.

REFERENCES

Brown. B. Awareness of EEG-subjective activity relationships detected within a closed feedback system. *Psychophysiology*, 1971, *7*, 451–464.

Engstrom, D., London, P., & Hart, J. Hypnotic susceptibility increased by EEG alpha training. *Nature*, 1970, *227*, 1261–1262.

Hart, J. Autocontrol of EEG alpha. *Psychophysiology*, 1968, *4*, 506. (Abstract)

Kamiya, J. Conscious control of brain waves. *Psychology Today*, 1968, *1*, 57–60.

Kamiya, J. Operant control of the EEG alpha rhythm and some of its reported effects on consciousness. In C. Tart (Ed.), *Altered states of consciousness*. New York: Wiley, 1969. Pp. 507–517.

Kasamatsu, A., & Hirai, T. An electroencephalographic study on the Zen meditation (Zazen). In C. Tart (Ed.), *Altered states of consciousness*. New York: Wiley, 1969. Pp. 489–501.

Kruglanski, A. Much ado about the "volunteer artifacts." *Journal of Personality & Social Psychology*, 1973, *28*, 348–354.

London, P., Hart, J., & Leibovitz, M. EEG alpha rhythms and susceptibility to hypnosis. *Nature*, 1968, *219*, 71–72.

Nowlis, D., & Kamiya, J. The control of electroencephalographic alpha rhythms through auditory feedback and the associated mental activity. *Psychophysiology*, 1970, *6*, 476–484.

Nowlis, D., & Rhead, J. Relation of eyes-closed resting EEG alpha activity to hypnotic susceptibility. *Perceptual & Motor Skills*, 1968, *27*, 1047–1050.

Paskewitz, D., & Orne, M. Visual effects on alpha feedback training. *Science*, 1973, *181*, 360–363.

Rosenthal, R., & Rosnow, R. (Eds.) *Artifact in behavioral research*. New York: Academic Press, 1969.

Rosnow, R., & Aiken, L. Mediation of artifacts in behavioral research. *Journal of Experimental Social Psychology*, 1973, *9*, 181–201.

Vogel, W., Broverman, D., & Klaiber, E. EEG and mental abilities. *Electroencephalography & Clinical Neurophysiology*, 1968, *24*, 166–175.

Weber, S., & Cook, T. Subject effects in laboratory research: An examination of subject roles, demand characteristics, and valid inference. *Psychological Bulletin*, 1972, *77*, 273–295.

Winer, B. *Statistical principles in experimental design*. New York: McGraw-Hill, 1971.

Witkin, H., Lewis, H., Hertzman, M., Machover, K., Meissner, P., & Wapner, S. *Personality through perception*. New York: Harper, 1954.

Occipital Alpha and the Attributes of the "Alpha Experience" 25

William B. Plotkin and Robin Cohen

ABSTRACT

The present research was designed to study to what extent occipital alpha strength is related to five subjective dimensions that are associated with the "alpha experience." These are (1) the degree of oculomotor processing, (2) the degree of sensory awareness, (3) the degree of body awareness, (4) the deliberateness of thought, and (5) the pleasantness of emotional state. One experimental group of 8 persons was run for each of the above five dimensions. First, while an integrated amplitude measure of occipital alpha strength was recorded, our research participants practiced two "simple awareness techniques" (without feedback) corresponding to the two poles of their group's dimension. Later they were given the task of associating their two "awareness techniques" with occipital alpha strength by means of feedback-augmented alpha enhancement and suppression. The results showed that only the first two dimensions—the degree of oculomotor processing and the degree of sensory awareness—are significantly related to occipital alpha strength. These findings support the notion that the "alpha experience" as a whole is not intrinsically or directly associated with enhanced occipital alpha strength, and that occipital alpha strength is a *direct* function of only oculomotor processing.

DESCRIPTORS: Occipital alpha, "Alpha experience," Alpha feedback, Biofeedback, EEG alpha, Oculomotor system.

The aspect of occipital alpha feedback training that has generated the greatest popular interest is the notion that this training induces a pleasant, quasi-meditational state of consciousness, known as the "alpha experience." Of special interest here is the hypothesis that alpha feedback induces this phenomenological state by increasing the strength of the occipital alpha rhythm, which is purported to be *directly* associated with the "alpha experience." Frequently cited in support of this view are the observations that (1) the EEGs of meditators often

A shorter version of this paper was read at the Sixth Annual Meeting of the Biofeedback Research Society, February 2, 1975, in Monterey, California.

Address requests for reprints to: William B. Plotkin, Sleep Lab, Department of Psychology, University of Colorado, Boulder, Colorado 80302.

show increased alpha strength during meditation (Anand, Chhina, & Singh, 1961; Kasamatsu & Hirai, 1969; Wallace, 1970), and (2) some participants in some biofeedback experiments have reported "alpha experiences" during alpha enhancement training (Brown, 1970; Hart, 1968; Kamiya, 1969; Nowlis & Kamiya, 1970).

However, reports from other laboratories have not always confirmed the findings of a direct and simple relationship between occipital alpha and the "alpha experience" (Beatty, 1972; Lynch & Paskewitz, 1971; Paskewitz & Orne, 1973; Peper, 1971; Peper & Mulholland, 1970; Plotkin, 1976; Regestein, Pegram, Cook, & Bradley, 1974; Walsh, 1974). In our previous study (Plotkin, 1976), which carefully controlled for the effects of different control strategies, suggestion, the presence of light, and physiological feedback itself, we found that very high or enhanced levels of occipital alpha strength were not invariably accompanied by the "alpha experience." In fact, most persons who were not led to expect it, did not have an "alpha experience" during occipital alpha-enhancement feedback. Thus, it is apparent that the "alpha experience" *as a whole* is not directly or intrinsically associated with enhanced occipital alpha strength. However, there are several independent attributes of the "alpha experience," and it is possible that one or more of these attributes *are* related to alpha, even though the "alpha experience" as a whole is not. In fact, this is already known to be the case for two of the attributes, as we shall discuss below.

The five subjective attributes that have been most frequently reported to be aspects of the "alpha experience" are (1) "not-looking" or reduced oculomotor processing, (2) enhanced "internal" awareness or non-sensory awareness, (3) reduced body awareness and relaxation, (4) undirected, free-flowing thought or thoughtlessness—often termed "mental relaxation," and (5) a pleasant emotional state, peacefulness and tranquility. Research reported by Dewan (1967), Mulholland (1968, 1972), Peper (1970, 1971), Peper and Mulholland (1970), and Plotkin (1976) has conclusively demonstrated that the first attribute— reduced oculomotor processing—*is* directly associated with occipital alpha. In addition, Plotkin (1976) found that the second attribute—non-sensory awareness (such as an absorption in thoughts and emotions)—is also reliably associated with occipital alpha. This last association is what would be expected given the close connection between occipital alpha and oculomotor processing: since vision is the dominant sensory modality in humans, it is reasonable that when visual-processing is reduced during alpha-enhancement feedback that there is also reduced sensory awareness in general and often greater attention to thoughts and emotions.

However, it is not yet known to what extent, if at all, each of the latter three attributes are individually related to enhanced occipital alpha strength, an issue which is of great importance since these three attributes contribute much more to the uniqueness of the "alpha experience" than do the first two relatively ordinary attributes. Since our earlier research (Plotkin, 1976) did not deal in detail with the relationship of the "alpha experience" to occipital alpha, we conducted the following experiment in order to specifically explore and compare the individual relationships between occipital alpha strength and each of the five attributes of the "alpha experience." We were interested in determining to what extent, if at all, the latter three attributes were related to alpha as compared to the first two attributes, on the one hand, and to an unrelated (control) attribute, on the other. In addition, we were interested in seeing just how well

the second attribute, non-sensory awareness, was related to occipital alpha, since the exact extent of this relationship was not determined in our previous research.

We began by developing the following list of five subjective dimensions that correspond to the above five attributes of the "alpha experience": (1) the degree of oculomotor processing, (2) the degree of sensory awareness, (3) the degree of body awareness, (4) the deliberateness of thought, and (5) the pleasantness of emotional state. Next we reasoned that if a given subjective dimension is directly or reliably associated with occipital alpha, then we should be able to find measurable differences in occipital alpha strength when persons are in the two subjective states corresponding to the two extreme poles of that dimension. Thus, for example, we should expect to find higher alpha strength when a person is unaware of his body than when he is in a state of heightened body awareness, if it is true that the degree of body awareness is associated with alpha strength. Furthermore, when given alpha-strength feedback, persons should be able to tell us which pole of these subjective dimensions, if either, is related to enhanced alpha and which to suppressed alpha.

Method

Research Participants

Forty-eight undergraduates from the University of Colorado served as research participants in order to partially satisfy the requirements of an introductory psychology course. The following restrictions were used in selection: (1) age range of 18 to 23, (2) no prior biofeedback experience, and (3) resting alpha strength of at least an average of 15 μV peak-to-peak per min with eyes *closed*, since persons with less alpha than this rarely show any alpha control.

The research participants were randomly assigned to the six between-subject conditions (N=8), corresponding to six subjective dimensions (see below), with the stipulation that there were equal numbers of each sex in each condition. No mention was ever made to any participant that the research concerned the study of alpha waves, in order to minimize the possible interfering effects of preconceived notions. Instead, they were simply told that we were "studying the effects on brain waves of practicing simple awareness techniques."

Apparatus

The EEG was recorded by bipolar leads attached to the right occipital and right frontal lobes (O_2 and F_4 of the 10-20 system) with the left mastoid as ground. This electrode placement is the same one that we have previously used (Plotkin, 1976) and was chosen since it generally gave us the occipital alpha recording of highest amplitude. It is also one of the two placements used by Nowlis and Kamiya (1970). Although other occipital alpha researchers have used different placements, we know of no reports of any relevant differences in results when using the O_2–F_4 placement versus other occipital lobe placements such as O_1–O_2 or O_2–C_4 (e.g., Nowlis & Kamiya, 1970).

The EEG was amplified and filtered by a Bio-feedback Systems, Inc. model AT-1. The center frequency of the alpha filter on this unit is 10.0 Hz, with a 3 dB attenuation of 7.5–8.5 Hz and of 11.5–12.5 Hz, and with a 20 dB attenuation of 5.0–7.0

Hz and of 15.0–17.0 Hz. The output of the AT-1 was fed to two locations: an audio feedback generator and a digital quantifier.

The audio feedback was in the form of an intensity-modulated tone appearing over a headphone set. The intensity (volume) of the tone is essentially proportional to the strength of the alpha signal being sensed.

The digital quantifier, model DQ-1, also manufactured by Bio-feedback Systems, Inc., is a variable time base, four-digit accumulating counter. The integration time was set to automatically stop every 2 min, and to reset after about 2 sec. The count accumulated over the 2 min time period is proportional to the area under the curve of alpha strength versus time.

The research participants sat in an upright, comfortable chair which was placed approximately in the center of a 9 ft by 10 ft sound-attenuated and carpeted room. During the entire session the lights were kept at a low, ambient level. This level, intermediate between total darkness and normal room levels, was chosen because light level and the opportunity to "look" are known to have very significant effects on baseline alpha levels, and, therefore, an intermediate light level seemed to offer the greatest generality of results.

Procedure

While the research participant was being prepared for recording, the experimenter attempted to minimize his or her anxiety by engaging in light conversation, by explaining each step in the placement of electrodes, and by giving him or her an opportunity to ask questions. Research participants were never referred to by other than their names, and never as "subjects."

After the recording electrodes were attached, the participant was seated in the experimental room and was read the initial instructions and orientation materials. Then the experimenter returned to the control room and gave the participant 5 min to relax, followed by 2 2-min baseline recording periods (first with eyes open, then with eyes closed).

After the baseline recordings, the experimenter re-entered the participant's room and read him or her the instructions explaining the nature of the task. In the first half of the session, our volunteers were asked to practice "two simple awareness techniques" (without feedback) corresponding to the two poles of their group's dimension, which were explained to them in the following terms, although more elaborately:

(1) the degree of oculomotor processing: "not-looking," defocusing, visual inattentiveness OR "looking," focusing, visual attentiveness.

(2) the degree of sensory awareness: non-sensory awareness of thoughts and feelings OR sensory awareness of the "external" world.

(3) the degree of body awareness: "disembodied" and relaxed OR heightened body awareness.

(4) the deliberateness of thought: undirected, free-flowing, or absent thought OR intense concentration and problem solving.

(5) the pleasantness of emotional state: a pleasant, peaceful state OR negative, unpleasant emotional excitement.

(6) a control dimension, unrelated to both alpha strength and the "alpha experience": attending to and relaxing the left side of the body OR attending to and relaxing the right side.

Each participant alternately practiced his or her two "awareness techniques" for 4 periods each, each period lasting 2 min. The absolute alpha strength for each period was recorded. Persons were asked to keep their eyes open throughout the experimental session in order to guard against drowsiness, and in order to standardize procedure (since eye-closing is known to have large effects on occipital alpha strength).

After these 8 trials, the experimenter returned to the research participant's room and read him or her the instructions for the second half of the session, during which the participant was given auditory feedback. They were told the following before beginning feedback: "The techniques you must use to make the tone louder and softer *are* the awareness techniques you have practiced in the first half of the session. Your task is to determine which technique makes the tone louder and which technique makes the tone softer." Thus, in this study we were not interested in seeing how well our research participants did at alpha control, but rather whether or not they found their group's subjective dimension to be related to alpha strength, and, if so, in which direction. Persons were first given a 2 min "exploratory" feedback period followed by 2 sets of 3 periods, each set containing a 2-min enhancement, rest, and suppression period. They trained with eyes open and a low level of ambient lighting.

At the end of the session, participants were brought back into the control room where they were unwired and asked to fill out a questionnaire on which they listed the strategies they used to increase and decrease the tone volume during the second half of the session.

Results

Divergence Scores

From the first half of the sessions, we had eight absolute alpha-strength scores from each research participant, consisting of four "alpha-experience" (AE) scores and four "non-alpha-experience" (NAE) scores. With the following equation: $(AE_i - NAE_i)/(AE_i + NAE_i)$, where i = trial number, we obtained a set of four divergence scores for each person; the magnitude of each of these scores corresponds to the degree to which the subjective dimension of that person's group was related to alpha strength for that given individual. The denominator corrects for between-subject differences in alpha strength. With these scores a $6 \times 2 \times 4$ ANOVA ($\alpha = .01$) was run, corresponding to the six levels of subjective dimension, the two levels of sex, and the four trials. The main effect of subjective dimension was significant, $F(5/36) = 8.39$. The means were .303 for the oculomotor group, .195 for the sensory-awareness group, .088 for the body-awareness group, .063 for the deliberateness-of-thought group, .049 for the emotional-state group, and .007 for the control group. A Duncan Range Test ($\alpha = .05$) showed that only the first two of these five dimensions of the "alpha experience" were related to alpha strength to a significantly greater degree than the control dimension, which showed virtually no relationship to alpha strength, as suspected. Moreover, the oculomotor group had significantly higher divergence scores than the sensory-awareness group. The divergence scores for the other three groups did not differ significantly from the control group. However, of these three dimensions, the data suggest that the degree of body awareness is associated with occipital alpha strength in most persons to a small degree and in the expected direction. We concluded this for three reasons: (1) When looking at the performance of the individuals in this group, we saw that 5 persons showed moderately to highly positive divergence scores, 3 scored close to zero, while none scored predominantly negative. In contrast, some individuals in the deliberateness-of-thought and emotional-state groups showed negative divergence scores, while others showed positive and neutral scores. (2) The divergence scores for the body-awareness group showed relatively large increases across trials ($-.005$, $.051$, $.151$, $.156$), whereas the scores for the deliberateness-of-thought group ($.062$, $.055$, $.061$, $.077$) and the emotional-state group ($.024$, $.056$, $.071$, $.046$) did not. (3) The data from the second half of the sessions (see below) showed that most of the subjects in the body-awareness group found their "awareness techniques" to be effective in controlling the tone volume (in the appropriate directions), while this was not true for the other two groups. Thus, although the average score of the body-awareness group was not significantly greater than that of the control group, the data may warrant a tentative conclusion of at least a weak relationship between the degree of body awareness and occipital alpha strength. And, as we shall see below, there is some logical support for this conclusion.

The only other significant effect from the ANOVA was the main effect of trial number, $F(3/108)=4.07$, which showed that the divergence scores, across all groups, increased across the first 3 trials ($.082$, $.116$, $.138$, $.135$).

Control Strategies

The above data were supported and extended by the findings from the post-session questionnaires, on which we asked our research participants how they made the tone louder and softer (corresponding to enhanced and suppressed alpha strength, respectively). We told each participant that we wanted to know which control strategies they used regardless of whether or not they employed either of the two "awareness techniques" that they practiced in the first half of the session.

Six out of 8 persons in the oculomotor group reported that they enhanced alpha by "not-looking." The other popular enhance strategy was "thinking" or "reviewing personal memories"—some pleasant, some unpleasant. To suppress alpha, 6 individuals in this group used visual concentration.

In the sensory-awareness group, persons reported that they increased the tone volume by visual blurring or by paying attention to sounds, odors, breathing, or thoughts and emotions. Since visual blurring and paying attention to sounds, odors, and breathing are instances of sensory awareness, we must conclude that sensory awareness is not incompatible with occipital alpha as long as the sensory awareness does not include oculomotor processing (which none of the above do). To suppress alpha, these individuals observed their environment, particularly emphasizing visual attentiveness and focusing.

In the body-awareness group, the most popular enhancement strategy concerned non-sensory awareness, with body relaxation second. To suppress alpha, these individuals reported either heightened body awareness or visual attentiveness.

In the deliberateness-of-thought group, 6 out of 8 persons felt that high tone volumes were related to *directed* thought and that low volumes accompanied free-flowing thought. This is in the opposite direction to what would be expected based on the reported association between occipital alpha and the "alpha experience." However, it turned out that our participants varied as to what they considered "thought" to be. Those who took "thought" to mean exclusively non-sensory awareness found that directed thought and concentration increased the tone volume, and that intense sensory (visual) awareness (which entails no thought or undirected thought for these persons) decreased it. On the other hand, the two persons in this group who took "thought" to *include* observation—or who were in the habit of visually focusing while concentrating or problem solving—reported that directed thought or concentration decreased the volume, and that no thought (which also implicates no sensory awareness for these persons) increased it.

The alpha enhancement reports of all of the 8 persons in the emotional-state group concerned non-sensory states of attending to thoughts and emotions. Four of these persons reported that, during the enhancement trials, attending to unpleasant emotions worked as well as pleasant emotions. Two thought the enhancement strategy was pleasant emotions, one thought it to be exclusively unpleasant states, and the final individual didn't say. In short, our research participants in the emotional-state group all agreed that non-sensory awareness was related to enhanced alpha, but their combined reports make it clear that alpha strength is not related to subjective pleasantness. The two popular suppress strategies in this group were visual attentiveness and "not-thinking" or "blank-mind."

The control dimension seemed to confuse the control group so well that it is hard to see much of any trend in their reports of control strategies. Some attended to the left side to enhance and to the right to suppress (few in this group showed any success at control); some did it the other way around; and others did it both ways. Several made reference to strategies that we can fit with the oculomotor and sensory-awareness dimensions.

Discussion

The data from the first half of the experimental sessions demonstrated that, of the six subjective dimensions studied, only the degree of oculomotor processing and the degree of sensory awareness are significantly related to occipital alpha strength. Alpha strength increases when persons are "not-looking" and when they are engaged in non-sensory awareness (e.g., attending to thoughts and emotions). Moreover, the degree of oculomotor processing was found to be related to alpha strength to a significantly greater degree than the sensory-awareness dimension. The data from the second half of the sessions explicated this finding by demonstrating that some of our participants in the sensory-awareness group paid attention to non-visual sensory modalities—or to the visual modality without actively engaging the oculomotor system (e.g., looking without focusing)—during some of the time that they were engaged in the sensory-awareness pole of their dimension; and sensory awareness will block alpha only when it includes oculomotor processing. In addition, a person who is asked to engage in non-sensory awareness will most likely not reduce oculomotor processing—and thereby enhance alpha—to as great an extent as a person who is specifically asked to refrain from oculomotor activity.

Of the four subjective dimensions that were found to be not significantly related to alpha strength, we did find that the degree of body awareness was *marginally* related to alpha in most of the subjects. Alpha strength was usually somewhat higher when persons were less aware of their bodies. It makes sense that the degree of body awareness would be roughly correlated with alpha strength since an easy way of becoming unaware of one's body is to enter a general non-sensory state of awareness, such as an absorption in thoughts and emotions. And as we have seen, a state of non-sensory awareness is usually characterized by reduced oculomotor processing due to the dominance, in humans, of the visual modality. In a similar way, when one is very aware of body feelings, one may also be engaged in oculomotor processing while looking at some part of the body, or as a component of the general orienting response.

The data from the second half of the sessions showed us that the oculomotor and sensory-awareness groups agreed that the "awareness techniques" which they had practiced in the first half were, in fact, related to alpha strength, and in the expected direction. For the other four groups, a general finding was that many persons discovered, regardless of which "awareness techniques" they had practiced, that the loudness of the feedback tone was a function of the degree of oculomotor activity or the degree of sensory awareness, even though these subjective dimensions had never been mentioned to these individuals. These findings strongly support the notion that reduced oculomotor processing is intrinsically and directly associated with enhanced occipital alpha strength, and that a state of non-sensory awareness is a reliable correlate of reduced oculomotor activity and, thereby, of high alpha strength.

Our research has demonstrated that undirected, free-flowing thought or thoughtlessness, and pleasant emotional states, are in no way *intrinsi-*

cally associated with enhanced occipital alpha strength, and that the degree of body awareness is related to alpha strength only to a small degree. We may speculate that the reports of earlier researchers of close connections between these three subjective attributes and enhanced alpha can be explained by aspects of the biofeedback *setting* other than the effects of feedback itself, such as (1) the expectations of having an "alpha experience" (and/or some kind of generally pleasant experience) whether derived from interaction with the experimenter(s) or from extra-experimental sources (as demonstrated by Walsh, 1974), (2) the mild sensory deprivation resulting from prolonged sitting in a soundproof, darkened room, (3) the sustained attention while constantly monitoring the feedback signal, and (4) the effects of the experience of success at what many research participants consider to be a difficult and unusual task.

As for the generality of the results reported here, it should be noted that, taken most conservatively, this research concerns only the relationship of the "alpha experience" to the specific EEG parameter that we studied—namely, *alpha strength* from a *right occipital-frontal* recording. However, although exact electrode placements among occipital alpha researchers have varied, there is no evidence that the placement makes any difference, relevant to the present research, as long as at least one electrode is over the occiput. Nevertheless, this is a possibility that deserves further exploration. Furthermore, an integrated amplitude measure of strength, as used here, is a more sensitive and accurate measure of alpha changes than other alpha measures (such as probability of occurrence and alpha density) since only the former is sensitive to changes in both abundance and amplitude. At any rate, it is quite possible that reports of other EEG parameters—related or unrelated to ours—that are "directly" associated with the "alpha experience" or similar states have also been affected—to at least some degree—by the above situational variables. Therefore, these variables should always be taken into consideration, or carefully controlled for, in future EEG biofeedback research.

Another essential feature of our procedure was having participants keep their eyes open in a dimly lit room, which allows for visual feedback between the oculomotor system and the environment. Although this is a typical arrangement in alpha feedback research, it should be noted how the results may have been different if participants' eyes were kept closed or if there was no light. Certainly the divergence scores of the oculomotor group would have been lower since these persons would have had a harder time "looking" without any visual feedback from the environment. This of course is the reason why occipital alpha is harder to control with eyes closed and/or no lights (Nowlis & Kamiya, 1970; Paskewitz & Orne, 1973; Plotkin, 1976). For the same reason the scores of the sensory awareness group would have been lower. However, it seems extremely unlikely that closed eyes and/or the absence of light would have made any difference in the performance of the other three groups. Although sitting in a dark room and/or with eyes closed almost always lead to reduced oculomotor processing and often to non-sensory awareness (e.g., daydreaming), these conditions are not intrinsically associated with thoughtlessness, pleasantness, or body unawareness.

In conclusion, the major implication of our results is that the three most definitive attributes of the "alpha experience" (body relaxation, "mental relaxation," and tranquility) are not induced by alpha feedback training *per se*. Thus it appears that the major contribution that alpha feedback makes to

the attainment of meditative-like experiences is the supply of a setting which is conducive to the *natural self*-inducement of such states. Through the alpha feedback research we have seen that some persons will rapidly achieve an "alpha experience" if they are convinced that it is actually being induced by electronic equipment, even when they are, in point of fact, manifesting these psychological changes essentially through the exercise of their own personal powers. We are now engaged in further research to explicitly determine (1) the relevant dispositions and powers of those persons who have "alpha experiences" during occipital alpha feedback, and (2) those aspects of the feedback setting which are most conducive to the occurrence of such experiences.

REFERENCES

Anand, B. K., Chhina, G. S., & Singh, B. Some aspects of electroencephalographic studies in yogis. *Electroencephalography & Clinical Neurophysiology*, 1961, *13*, 452–456.

Beatty, J. Similar effects of feedback signals and instructional information on EEG activity. *Physiology & Behavior*, 1972, *9*, 151–154.

Brown, B. Recognition of aspects of consciousness through association with EEG alpha activity represented by a light signal. *Psychophysiology*, 1970, *6*, 442–452.

Dewan, E. M. Occipital alpha rhythm, eye position, and lens accommodation. *Nature* (London), 1967, *214*, 975–977.

Hart, J. Autocontrol of EEG alpha. *Psychophysiology*, 1968, *4*, 506. (Abstract)

Kamiya, J. Operant control of the EEG alpha rhythm and some of its reported effects on consciousness. In C. T. Tart (Ed.), *Altered states of consciousness*. New York: Wiley, 1969. Pp. 507–517.

Kasamatsu, A., & Hirai, T. An electroencephalographic study on the Zen meditation (Zazen). In C. T. Tart (Ed.), *Altered states of consciousness*. New York: Wiley, 1969. Pp. 489–501.

Lynch, J. J., & Paskewitz, D. A. On the mechanisms of the feedback control of human brain wave activity. *The Journal of Nervous & Mental Disease*, 1971, *153*, 205–217.

Mulholland, T. Feedback electroencephalography. *Activas Nervosa Superior*, 1968, *10*, 410–438.

Mulholland, T. Occipital alpha revisited. *Psychological Bulletin*, 1972, *3*, 176–182.

Nowlis, D. P., & Kamiya, J. The control of electroen-

cephalographic alpha rhythms through auditory feedback and the associated mental activity. *Psychophysiology*, 1970, *6*, 476–484.

Paskewitz, D. A., & Orne, M. T. Visual effects on alpha feedback training. *Science*, 1973, *181*, 360–363.

Peper, E. Feedback regulation of the alpha electroencephalogram activity through control of the internal and external parameters. *Kybernetic*, 1970, *7*, 107–112.

Peper, E. Reduction of efferent motor commands during alpha feedback as a facilitator of EEG alpha and a precondition for changes in consciousness. *Kybernetic*, 1971, *9*, 226–231.

Peper, E., & Mulholland, T. B. Methodological and theoretical problems in the voluntary control of electroencephalographic occipital alpha by the subject. *Kybernetic*, 1970, *7*, 10–13.

Plotkin, W. B. On the self-regulation of the occipital alpha rhythm: Control strategies, states of consciousness, and the role of physiological feedback. *Journal of Experimental Psychology: General*, 1976, in press.

Regestein, Q. R., Pegram, V., Cook, B., & Bradley, D. Alpha rhythm percentage maintained during 4- and 12-hour feedback periods. In N. E. Miller, T. X. Barber, L. V. DiCara, J. Kamiya, D. Shapiro, & J. Stoyva (Eds.), *Biofeedback and self-control, 1973*. Chicago: Aldine-Atherton, 1974. Pp. 155–162.

Wallace, R. K. Physiological effects of transcendental meditation. *Science*, 1970, *167*, 1751–1754.

Walsh, D. H. Interactive effects of alpha feedback and instructional set on subjective state. *Psychophysiology*, 1974, *11*, 428–435.

Alpha Feedback and 26
Relaxation: A Cautionary Note

Elizabeth Grynol and John Jamieson

Increases in EEG alpha-wave production through operant conditioning have been reported to result in pleasant, relaxed states (Kamiya, 1969), raising the possibility of using alpha conditioning for the clinical treatment of anxiety. The present study attempted to demonstrate the relaxing effects of alpha conditioning. Two standardized anxiety measures (Cattell & Scheier, 1963; Spielberger, Gorsuch, & Lushene, 1970) were given to 20 female undergraduates who volunteered for an experiment on alpha conditioning. Ss were given 3 weekly 30-min. training sessions. For 10 Ss a tone sounded when they were in alpha. The other 10 Ss received alternating correct and incorrect feedback (the output of the relay to the tone was reversed every minute). Both groups were told that the tone indicated the time in alpha and were instructed to keep the tone on. A fourth session, serving as an extinction period, was run without auditory feedback. Duration of time in alpha was recorded for each session. Cattell and Scheier's scale was administered before and after the four sessions; the A-State measured relaxation state after each session.

Data indicated that Ss receiving correct feedback learned to increase their alpha time over sessions [Ms (SDs) = 6.35(4.05), 7.87(4.49), 13.49(4.43), 10.59(4.95) min.]; $F_{1,27} = 26.41$ ($p < .01$). The group given alternating false and correct feedback actually decreased their alpha production [Ms (SDs) = 12.70(6.36), 9.85(3.07), 9.75(2.07), 7.79(2.26) min.]; $F_{1,27} = 5.07$ ($p < .05$). There were no differences between the responses of the two groups on either the Cattell and Scheier ($F < 1.0$) or the A-State scale ($F < 1.0$), although over-all decrease in anxiety was shown on the former ($F_{1,18} = 7.17$, $p < .05$) and A-State scale ($F_{1,54} = 6.53$, $p < .05$). These results are consistent with previous work (Kamiya, 1969) demonstrating increased alpha production as a result of conditioning. However, since equally positive psychological benefits were reported by both groups, this study did not show unique benefits of increased alpha production beyond those attributable to a placebo effect. In fact, one control subject reported that it was the most relaxing thing she had ever done! These results indicate that a placebo control definitely should be included in future studies of alpha feedback.

---

[1]This study is based on an Honors thesis submitted by the first author to Lakehead University. Tabled data are available in Document NAPS-02499 from Microfiche Publications, 440 Park Avenue South, New York, N. Y. 10016. Remit $1.50 for microfiche or $5.00 for photocopy.

Reprinted with permission of author and publisher from *Perceptual and Motor Skills*, 1975, Vol. 40, 58.

REFERENCES

CATTELL, R. B., & SCHEIER, I. H. *IPAT Anxiety Scale Questionnaire.* Champaign, Ill.: Institute for Personality & Ability Testing, 1963.

KAMIYA, J. Operant control of EEG alpha rhythm and some of its reported effects on consciousness. In C. Tart (Ed.), *Altered states of consciousness.* New York: Wiley, 1969. Pp. 507-517.

SPIELBERGER, C. D., GORSUCH, R. W., & LUSHENE, R. E. *State-Trait Anxiety Inventory (Form X-1).* Palo Alto, Calif.: Consulting Psychologists Press, 1970.

Diana S. Woodruff

ABSTRACT

To examine the relationship between the frequency of the EEG alpha rhythm and reaction time, the biofeedback technique was used to manipulate brain wave frequency in 10 young and 10 old subjects. Subjects first learned to increase the percent time they spent in their modal brain wave frequency, and then they were trained to increase the percent time they spent in brain wave frequencies 2 Hz faster and 2 Hz slower than their modal frequency. Simple auditory reaction time (RT) was measured during biofeedback immediately after subjects reached a set criterion at each biofeedback task. To control for the effect of biofeedback training on RT, groups of 5 old and 5 young subjects heard a pre-recorded feedback signal which was not contingent upon their brain wave activity. Experimental subjects increased the abundance of alpha activity above baseline levels while control subjects did not. Results indicated that experimental alteration of brain wave frequency affected RT. When the subjects produced fast brain waves their RT was significantly faster than when they produced slow brain waves. Correlations between brain wave period and RT were small. Thus, the data did not provide unequivocal support for the notion that the alpha rhythm serves as a master timing mechanism for behavior, but the relationship between controlled EEG activity and RT was clearly demonstrated.

DESCRIPTORS: Alpha rhythm, Reaction time, Biofeedback, Age, Arousal. (D. Woodruff)

The slowing of response speed with age is a reliable and well-documented phenomenon which most likely occurs beyond young adulthood in all who survive (Birren, 1965). An almost equally well-established change is the slowing of the EEG alpha rhythm with age (see Obrist & Busse, 1965; Thompson & Marsh, 1973 for reviews). The rela-

This report is based on part of a Ph.D. dissertation presented at the University of Southern California where the author was supported by National Institute of Child Health and Human Development Training Grant 157–04. Data were collected at the Long Beach Veterans Administration Hospital. The author gratefully acknowledges Drs. James E. Birren, Gary Galbraith, George Rhodes, and John Rohrbaugh for their technical assistance and their helpful suggestions.

Address requests for reprints to: Diana S. Woodruff, Andrus Gerontology Center, University of Southern California, Los Angeles, California 90007.

tionship between the slowing of response speed and alpha rhythm has been examined by Surwillo, who, in a series of experiments, simultaneously recorded reaction time (RT) and EEG in subjects of varying age. In one sample of 13 subjects ranging in age from 18 to 72, Surwillo (1961) found a rank-order correlation of .81 between period of the alpha rhythm (inverse of alpha frequency) and simple RT to auditory stimuli. Surwillo (1963a) has replicated these results with a sample of 100 subjects, and he also has demonstrated (1963b, 1964a) that the alpha period is related to RT variability and to the latency of choice RTs (and hence presumably to central decision time). On the basis of these results Surwillo has hypothesized that the alpha period represents a fundamental unit of time in the programming of events in the central nervous system.

The possibility that the alpha rhythm reflects

periodicity in the activity of the central nervous system was first considered by Bishop (1933, 1936) and by Jasper (1936), who speculated that alpha rhythm reflects cyclic fluctuations in brain excitability. Such a concept underlies Surwillo's hypothesis (1968) that the EEG alpha rhythm is the master timing unit for behavior. Lindsley (1952) summarized a variety of psychological and neurophysiological research in support of this proposition and suggested that such fluctuations may arise from synchronous and rhythmic metabolic or respiratory activities in large aggregates of cells. Subsequent research (e.g., Andersen & Andersson, 1968; Callaway, 1962; Dustman & Beck, 1965; Frost, 1968) consistently has supported the general notion that the alpha cycle reflects underlying modulations in brain responsiveness.

While a number of differing research approaches have converged to suggest some form of fluctuating excitability evidenced by the alpha rhythm, Surwillo's specific hypothesis, that the alpha cycle is the master timing unit of behavior, has been challenged. Several investigators have failed to replicate Surwillo's (1961, 1963a) results using subjects in younger and narrower age ranges than used by Surwillo. Birren (1965) tested subjects ranging in age from 20 to 30 yrs and Boddy (1971) tested subjects between the ages of 17 and 54, and neither investigator found a significant correlation between alpha period and RT.

Since much of the slowing of the alpha rhythm occurs after the sixth decade (Obrist, 1954, 1963; Obrist & Busse, 1965; Wang & Busse, 1969), Surwillo's samples undoubtedly included a much larger proportion of subjects in which alpha slowing had occurred. Hence, the high inter-individual correlation between alpha period and RT in Surwillo's studies may be attributable at least in part to a third variable (perhaps a health factor such as age changes in the cardiovascular system) which could cause both RT and alpha frequency to slow. To control for this possibility, Surwillo (1963a) statistically partialled out the variance in the RT/alpha period correlation due to age and still obtained a correlation of .78 between alpha period and RT. However, since changes in variables such as health status are not perfectly correlated with chronological age (e.g., Shock, 1962; Timeras, 1972), statistical removal of the variance due to age did not entirely rule out the possibility that changes in the health status in the older subjects were responsible for the high alpha period/RT correlations.

Surwillo's hypothesis implies a causal relationship between alpha period and RT, and correlational evidence does not provide unequivocal support for this hypothesis. More convincing evidence for the hypothesis that alpha frequency determines RT could be derived from a demonstration that experimental alterations in alpha frequency lead to changes in RT. One such experiment has been reported by Surwillo (1964b) who attempted to modify alpha frequency with photic stimulation at rates of 6–15 flashes per sec. The technique proved ineffective since only 5 of the 48 subjects showed evidence of alpha synchronization over more than a restrictively narrow range of photic frequencies. Consequently, the limited results of this study do not convincingly test Surwillo's hypothesis.

Until recently, alternative techniques for manipulating the alpha frequency, and hence for experimentally testing the relationship between alpha frequency and RT, were not available. The newly emergent biofeedback technique, however, provided another means by which alpha frequency could be manipulated. The work of Kamiya (1968, 1969) and others (e.g., Beatty, 1971; Brown, 1970; Bundzen, 1966; Dewan, 1966; Mulholland, 1968; Runnals & Mulholland, 1965) have demonstrated that subjects can increase and decrease the abundance of activity in the EEG band encompassing the alpha rhythm. Furthermore, it has been established that subjects can selectively increase the abundance of EEG activity within narrow frequency bandwidths (Green, Green, & Walters, 1970a, 1970b; Kamiya, 1969). Using a biofeedback technique to manipulate experimentally the frequency of the alpha rhythm, the present experiment was undertaken to examine the relationship between EEG frequency and RT. It was predicted that experimental changes in EEG alpha frequency would lead to changes in RT.

Method

Subjects

Fifteen male subjects between the ages of 18 and 29 yrs (mean age = 23.7) and 15 male subjects in the age range of 60 to 81 yrs (mean age = 72.5) participated in the study. Subjects were asked to volunteer for an experiment dealing with RT and brain waves, and they were randomly assigned to experimental and control groups.

Baseline Session

All volunteers participated in an initial baseline session during which modal EEG frequency and mean RT were determined. During this and all subsequent sessions EEG was recorded on a Beckman Type R Dynograph from a biopolar array of silver/silver-chloride electrodes located at P_3 and O_1 according to the international 10–20 system (Jasper, 1958). The modal EEG frequency was determined during the first 16 min while the subjects sat in a darkened room with their eyes closed. The EEG at an intermediate stage of amplification was passed through the filter portion of an Intelex filter-feedback system, set to a center frequency of 6, 8, 10, or 12 Hz and a bandwidth of ±1 Hz. Four min of EEG was recorded at each center frequency. The time during which the activity at each frequency exceeded a threshold amplitude level was recorded on a Hunter Klockounter, and the frequency at which a subject spent the greatest percent of time was designated the modal frequency for that subject. Modal frequencies ranged from 8 to 11 Hz, and only those subjects with a baseline of 25% time or more in the modal frequency were included in the sample. Four subjects were excluded because they did not meet this criterion.

After modal EEG frequency was determined, simple RT was measured to a click of moderate intensity. The subject was instructed to depress a microswitch with his thumb upon the onset of the click, which was generated by a Grass S-4 stimulator and delivered through earphones at random intervals of approximately 2–5 sec. Reaction time was registered to the nearest msec on a Hunter Klockounter, and pulses synchronous with the stimulus onset and the response were marked on the oscillograph record. Subjects received 20 practice trials, followed by 40 trials on which RT was recorded. During the 40 RT trials EEG was also measured. The event pulses and the EEG were recorded on magnetic tape.

Training Sessions

Ten young and 10 old subjects were randomly selected for the experimental groups and subsequently received EEG feedback training at their modal frequency and at frequencies 2 Hz above and below the mode. Training was accomplished with the Intelex filter-feedback system which incorporated a bandpass filter with available central frequency settings ranging from 1 to 20 Hz and bandwidths from ±0.5 Hz to ±2.0 Hz. In the first training sessions the center frequency of the filter was set at a subject's modal frequency (mode condition) with a bandwidth of ±1.0 Hz. Whenever the subject's EEG activity within this bandwidth exceeded a preselected amplitude threshold, a Mallory sonalert was triggered to deliver a 5000 Hz tone over the subject's earphones. Subjects were instructed to produce and sustain this feedback tone as long as possible. Training progressed in periods lasting 2 min. When a subject reached a criterion of producing modal EEG activity for two-thirds of the time during 3 consecutive 2-min periods, 40 RT trials were administered concurrently with the feedback task. All subjects were able to meet the training criterion for modal frequency within 1 to 10 one-hour training sessions, with the average number of 2-min trials to criterion being 23.0. The criterion of spending two-thirds time in alpha was exceeded by 5 of the 20 experimental subjects during the baseline session, thus training represented an increase in modal alpha output for 15 of the subjects.

An attempt was made to disassociate the feedback signal from the click RT stimulus by presenting the click both in intervals when the feedback signal was on and in intervals when it was off. This procedure was adopted so that the feedback signal would not serve as a warning signal for the RT task and so that the interstimulus interval would be uniform and determined by the experimenter rather than by the subject.

Following the RT session at the modal frequency, feedback training was undertaken at EEG center frequencies of 2 Hz faster (fast condition) and 2 Hz slower (slow condition) than the modal EEG frequency. The training criterion for these conditions was an increase in the EEG activity within the selected frequency range of 33% or more time than the baseline value. Subjects took, on average, 53.8 2-min trials to achieve criterion in the slow condition and 79.5 2-min trials to reach criterion in the fast condition. Upon reaching this criterion, RT was measured in each condition. As in the modal frequency condition, subjects continued to perform the feedback task concurrently with the 40 RT trials. Total time in the experiment for a subject ranged from 2 to 24 one-hour sessions.

The order in which the fast and slow conditions were presented was counterbalanced over subjects so that half the young and half the old subjects were trained in the fast condition first while the other subjects were trained first in the slow condition. Subjects were not informed about the frequency condition in which they were trained, so this information could not affect their RT performance. In order to examine RT practice effects, additional sessions were run after the fast and slow conditions in which RT

was measured during feedback at the modal EEG frequency. Hence, the following two sequences of training and test conditions were used for both young and old subjects: Group I—Mode, Fast, Mode, Slow, Mode; Group II—Mode, Slow, Mode, Fast, Mode.

Control Subjects

The 5 remaining subjects in each age group served as control subjects to test the effect of dummy biofeedback on EEG alpha abundance and frequency and on RT. Each of these control subjects was matched with a different one of the experimental subjects from their respective age group, and were treated exactly as their matched subject except that their brain waves did not control the feedback tone. Instead, the control subjects heard a sequence of tones which had been pre-recorded during the initial modal-frequency training session of an experimental subject. This recorded sequence of tones was repeated for as many sessions as had originally been required for the matched experimental subject to reach training criterion in the mode condition only. Four of the 10 control subjects who had high initial abundance of alpha maintained their high levels thus achieving criterion while the other 6 control subjects declined or maintained baseline alpha levels and did not reach the criterion level. As with the experimental subjects, the control subjects concluded with 40 RT trials presented while they heard the pre-recorded feedback tone. Upon debriefing all control subjects acknowledged a belief that their EEG had controlled the feedback tone.

Control subjects were not continued after the mode condition because the data indicated that the feedback signal did not affect RT and increases in alpha output did not occur in the dummy feedback group. Since brain waves in individual subjects were moved both to faster and slower frequencies, experimental subjects served as their own controls in these conditions.

EEG Frequency Analysis

An EEG frequency score for each RT trial was determined in the following manner. The magnetic tape on which EEG and event pulses had been recorded was played back through the Intelex filter four times: once each with the filter set at center frequencies of 6, 8, 10, and 12 Hz, and the bandpass set at ±1.0 Hz. The continuously variable output from the filter, which was related to the amount of EEG activity within the selected frequency band, was manually measured from an oscillograph record of the filter output. Amplitude measurements were made at points corresponding to the onset of the click RT signals. EEG frequency scores for individual RT trials were computed by weighting each center frequency by the amplitude within its bandwidth and then averaging these values.

Results

To examine the relationship between alpha frequency and RT, the subjects were given training designed to increase the amount of EEG activity within frequency bands encompassing their modal frequency, and at bands slower and faster than their modal frequency. It was anticipated that this training would: 1) lead to changes in EEG alpha frequency, which in turn would; 2) yield changes in RT.

Biofeedback Training of EEG Alpha Frequency

The results of this study confirm previous results indicating that human subjects can successfully learn to increase the abundance of their modal EEG alpha frequency. That this increase in abundance of alpha activity resulted from the biofeedback procedure itself and not from some ancillary factor in the experimental situation is evidenced in the results comparing alpha abundance for the entire modal frequency training period in 5 experimental and matched control subjects, as depicted in Fig. 1. With time, young and old experimental subjects who received biofeedback consistently increased the time in their modal frequency while the control subjects who heard tape recorded "feedback" signals did not. In a $2 \times 2 \times 3 \times 5$ analysis of variance comparing the effects of age, group (experimental vs control), time (first, middle, and last trial), and subjects on seconds in modal alpha frequency, the only significant effect was the Group × Time interaction ($F = 7.94$; $df = 2/18$; $p < .01$). Alpha abundance in the experimental and control groups was not initially different, but the effect of biofeedback conditioning over time differentiated the brain waves of the two groups.

In addition to increasing the alpha activity in their modal EEG frequency, the subjects were able to enhance activity at selected frequencies 2 Hz faster and 2 Hz slower than their modal frequency. Fig. 2 depicts the changes in selected brain wave frequen-

cies for the 10 old and 10 young experimental subjects. Statistical analysis indicated that the biofeedback induced increases in abundance at various alpha frequencies were reliable occurrences. Separate $2 \times 2 \times 10$ analyses of variance comparing the time in alpha for 10 young and 10 old subjects on the first and last 2-min trials of the biofeedback task were carried out for the fast and slow conditions. With biofeedback, there was a significant increase in alpha abundance in both the fast ($F = 8.11$; $df = 1/9$; $p < .02$) and the slow ($F = 99.44$; $df = 1/9$; $p < .001$) conditions. Old and young subjects performed equally well since the effect of age was not significant nor was the Age × Trials interaction.

Several other features of the results of this experiment are apparent in Fig. 2. First, it is clear that alpha abundance is greater at the modal frequency than at frequencies 2 Hz faster or slower than the mode. Even with feedback training, the subjects never attained a level of alpha abundance equal to the output at their modal frequency. Because there is more baseline alpha activity at the modal frequency, there is more alpha activity which can be reinforced. This may be the reason that increasing alpha abundance at the modal frequency is a much easier task and is accomplished more quickly than the tasks of producing more fast or slow brain waves. This is the second feature of the results apparent in Fig. 2. The subjects attained the criterion at the modal frequency (which was higher than the criterion for the fast and slow conditions) in fewer biofeedback trials than they needed to reach criterion in the fast and slow conditions. These results have been discussed in greater detail previously (Woodruff & Birren, 1972).

Changes in RT

Alpha abundance at various brain wave frequencies was manipulated to determine if EEG frequency changes would yield changes in RT. Table 1 presents the mean RT and EEG data for young and old subjects in the three brain wave frequency conditions. A $2 \times 3 \times 10$ analysis of variance comparing the effects of age, brain wave frequency, and subjects on RT was carried out, and a planned comparison was made between fast and slow brain wave frequency conditions to ensure maximum power.[1] RT was significantly faster in the fast than in the slow brain wave frequency condition supporting the hypothesis that brain wave frequency affects RT ($F = 3.97$; $df = 1/36$; $p < .05$). None of the other effects or interactions were statistically significant.

One consequence of the procedure whereby the RT signals were delivered both when the feedback tone was on and when it was off in the various

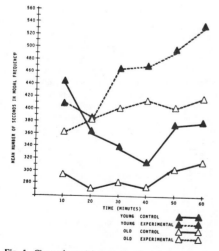

Fig. 1. Change in modal alpha abundance in 5 young and 5 old subjects receiving biofeedback (experimental subjects) or dummy biofeedback (control subjects). The problem of variability in trials to criterion was handled by including alpha abundance on each subject's criterion trial in all subsequent trials. This means of treating data was also used for control subjects.

[1]Since data were originally collected in a $2 \times 2 \times 6 \times 5$ design comparing the effects of age, order, brain wave frequency, and subjects, the final analyses represented a collapse of the order

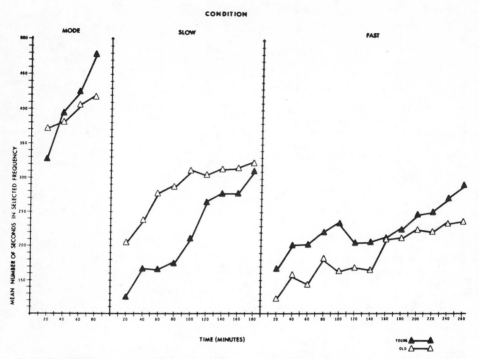

Fig. 2. Change in alpha abundance for 10 young and 10 old experimental subjects receiving biofeedback at three different brain wave frequencies: modal frequency; 2 Hz slower than the mode; 2 Hz faster than the mode. The problem of variability in trials to criterion was handled by including alpha abundance on each subject's criterion trial in all subsequent trials.

frequency conditions was that not all RT trials were collected during the desired EEG frequency for that experimental condition (fast, mode, slow). Thus, when EEG frequency was evaluated for all RT trials

TABLE 1

Mean RT and EEG frequency for young and old subjects in three brain wave biofeedback conditions

Biofeedback Conditions	Young (N=10)		Old (N=10)	
	RT (msec)	EEG (Hz)	RT (msec)	EEG (Hz)
Fast	207.4	9.42	259.4	9.16
Mode	211.9	9.45	280.0	9.07
Slow	214.8	9.31	285.4	9.04

variable and the averaging over the four modal brain wave frequency conditions. These steps were taken to increase the power of the test, and they were justified since preliminary analysis indicated that the effect of order was not statistically significant on either the dependent variable of EEG period ($F = 0.159$; $df = 1/16$; $p < .70$) or RT ($F = 1.55$; $df = 1/16$; $p < .23$). Additionally, there was not a significant RT practice effect since RT was not significantly different in the four modal brain wave frequency conditions ($F = 0.93$; $df = 3/54$; $p < .43$).

in the three brain wave conditions, the EEG frequency differences were small (around a magnitude of 0.1 Hz) and were not significantly different in the fast and slow conditions. For this reason, RT data were selected on the basis of brain wave frequency for those trials in which the subjects were most closely approximating the appropriate EEG frequency. For each subject in the fast, mode, and slow conditions, those 10 trials were selected in which the subject came closest to meeting the respective EEG frequency criterion. If EEG frequency affected RT, then maximizing frequency differences in this manner should result in greater RT differences between the fast and slow brain wave conditions. These data are presented in Fig. 3, in which EEG period (inverse of computed frequency score) and RTs (represented by the dotted lines) are plotted as a function of frequency condition. Separate functions are drawn for young (solid points) and old subjects (open points) and are averaged over all 10 subjects within each experimental group. As predicted, RT and EEG periods were longest in the slow condition and fastest in the fast condition, and the RT differences were greater in these trials selected on the basis of maximizing EEG frequency differences. Individual data were generally consistent with the group averages presented here. In all

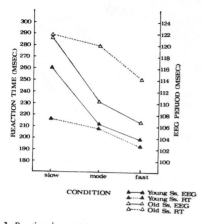

Young Ss, EEG
Young Ss, RT
Old Ss, EEG
Old Ss, RT

Fig. 3. Reaction time and EEG period for young and old experimental subjects in three brain wave frequency conditions.

cases EEG period was shorter in the fast than in the slow condition, and RTs were faster in the fast condition for 9 of the 10 old subjects and 7 of the 10 young subjects.

The significance of the RT effects accompanying these trials selected on the basis of EEG frequency was examined in a $2 \times 3 \times 10$ analysis of variance comparing the effects of age, brain wave frequency condition, and subjects on RT. A planned comparison between fast and slow frequency conditions revealed that RTs were significantly faster in the fast than in the slow condition ($F = 7.49$; $df = 1/36$; $p < .01$). The effect of age and the age by frequency interaction effects were not statistically significant.

The significance of the EEG trends for the selected data was examined in a $2 \times 3 \times 10$ analysis of variance comparing the effects of age, frequency condition, and subjects, with EEG period as the dependent variable. Planned comparisons were made between fast and slow frequency conditions to ensure maximum power. This analysis revealed that EEG period was significantly different in the fast and slow conditions ($F = 116.68$; $df = 1/36$; $p < .001$). Neither the effect of age nor the interaction of age by frequency condition approached statistical significance.

Modifications in RT occurred only when there were training-induced EEG changes. Differences in RT were not significantly different in experimental subjects between the baseline condition when they heard no feedback and the first feedback condition which was at the modal frequency (baseline RT = 219.0 msec, modal RT = 230.4 msec). Moreover, no changes were observed in RTs for control subjects who heard irrelevant feedback signals (baseline RT = 235.5 msec, modal RT = 238.2 msec). Statistical analysis of these data indicated that listening to the feedback tone (which

was providing relevant information about modal EEG frequency for the experimental subjects and was not providing relevant information for the control subjects) did not significantly affect RT. A $2 \times 2 \times 2 \times 5$ analysis of variance comparing the effects of age, baseline vs modal session, relevance of feedback signal, and subjects revealed that these RT differences between baseline and modal sessions were not statistically significant ($F = 2.51$; $df = 1/16$; $p < .13$). Neither was the effect of feedback relevance ($F = 0.15$; $df = 1/16$; $p < .70$) nor any of the interaction effects. The only significant effect was the effect of age ($F = 14.87$; $df = 1/16$; $p < .001$). RTs of old subjects were significantly slower than RTs of young subjects. This pattern of results emphasized the fact that aside from age differences in RT, significant RT changes were associated only with EEG frequency changes achieved through training with relevant feedback.

In an effort to determine if the present results replicated those obtained by Surwillo (1961, 1963a), inter-individual correlations between EEG period and RT were computed for all subjects. Baseline data were used because these data were not subject to any training effects and thus most closely resembled those used by Surwillo. Since the N was relatively small (N=30), a rank-order correlation coefficient was computed. This rank-order correlation between EEG period and RT of .40 was significant at the .05 level of confidence, but was considerably smaller than the rank-order correlation of .81 obtained by Surwillo (1961).

The mean intra-individual correlation between EEG period and RT which was .41 in Surwillo (1963a) was not replicated in the present experiment. Intra-individual Pearson product-moment correlations between EEG period and RT in the baseline session were computed, and these correlations ranged from $-.31$ to $+.35$. Intra-individual correlations were averaged by means of an r to z transformation, and the mean intra-individual correlation between EEG period and RT was 0.018 which was not significantly different from zero.

Intra-individual correlations between EEG period and RT were also computed for each experimental subject in the five EEG frequency conditions involving feedback training (Mode, Fast, Mode, Slow, Mode), as well as the intra-individual EEG period/RT correlations for all 240 RT trials. Most intra-individual correlations between these two variables were low, and they ranged from $+.49$ to $-.40$. These intra-individual correlations were not statistically different in the various EEG frequency conditions ($F = 1.29$; $df = 4/64$; $p < .285$). Hence, although analysis of variance indicated a relationship between EEG frequency and RT in the different brain wave frequency conditions, correlational analysis suggested that the relationship between small fluctuations in alpha period and RT in individual subjects was small or non-existent.

Discussion

Experimental subjects in the present study were able to increase the abundance of alpha activity in their modal frequency and in brain wave frequencies 2 Hz faster and slower than the mode. In view of Orne, Paskewitz, and Lynch's work (Lynch & Paskewitz, 1971; Paskewitz & Orne, 1973), one might ask whether this is due to decreased alpha inhibition. The present data do not permit a test of this question, but the observation of increased output at three different frequencies would suggest that subjects learn to modify brain wave activity rather than merely learning to decrease alpha inhibition.

The results of this experiment indicate that biofeedback manipulation of EEG alpha frequency leads to changes in brain wave frequency and changes in the speed of response in young as well as old individuals. It is not clear from this work, however, that the EEG alpha rhythm serves as the master timing mechanism for behavior. Shifting brain wave frequency within the range of the alpha bandwidth appears to shift RT in most subjects, but the intra-individual correlations between brain wave frequency and RT were too small to suggest a perfect correspondence between alpha period and RT. Several explanations involving either methodological issues or alternatives to an excitability cycle hypothesis could account for this lack of perfect correspondence.

Methodological Issues

One methodological difference between Surwillo (1963a), the present experiment, and Boddy (1971; who failed to replicate Surwillo) involves the technique employed in determining EEG frequency. Surwillo measured the raw complex wave form appearing on the EEG record and calculated the frequency by averaging the lineal width between the waves occurring during the RT period. While Boddy used this same method, he achieved poorer resolution of alpha frequency because he used a slower running speed for the EEG paper output. Tuned filters were used in the present experiment to evaluate EEG frequency, and RT in individual subjects was not correlated with this measure of EEG. By using the spectral measure, it is possible to establish an EEG frequency for all RT trials, whereas Surwillo's method allows for evaluation of frequency only on those RT trials in which there is clearly defined alpha activity. Thus, it may be that alpha frequency is directly related to RT only during those epochs in which the alpha rhythm is clearly defined. Another possibility, suggested by Surwillo (Note 1), is that the spectral measure of EEG confounds amplitude with frequency and is thus not a "pure" frequency measure. This point merits further evaluation which might be accomplished with a period analysis of EEG data collected in the present experiment. Given the possibility that the failure to replicate Surwillo (1963a) in finding significant within subjects correlations between brain wave period and RT might have arisen due to the methodological differences in EEG analyses, these present data do not provide a clear basis on which to refute Surwillo's notion that the alpha rhythm serves as a timing mechanism for behavior. Indeed, manipulation of EEG frequency affected RT, clearly suggesting the existence of a relationship between EEG activity and RT.

The segment of the EEG analyzed in relation to the RT stimulus is a second methodological difference between Surwillo, Boddy, and the present experiment. Surwillo selected the EEG segment between the onset of the stimulus and the initiation of the response for analysis, but Boddy argued that the EEG interval immediately following the stimulus is complexly determined; being composed of background alpha activity, the alpha blocking response, and the sensory evoked potential. To achieve a "purer" estimate of EEG frequency, Boddy measured the activity occurring during the 1-sec interval prior to the RT stimulus. EEG measurements in the present experiment were made at the moment of stimulus onset, but, due to an inherent time lag in the filter device, they were determined by EEG activity immediately preceding the stimulus. That these differences in sampling of EEG segment can account for the differences in results is doubtful, however, since Boddy suggested that it was unlikely that EEG frequency would change dramatically in the time intervals immediately preceding and following stimulus onset. He also demonstrated that auditory evoked potentials to the click RT stimulus were not the source of correlation in Surwillo's experiments (Boddy, 1970, 1971).

A third methodological difference involves the placement of electrodes. In all of the investigations, EEG recording was bipolar, but Surwillo used an occipital-frontal derivation, Boddy used temporal-temporal, occipital-temporal, and occipital-parietal derivations, and the electrode derivation in the present experiment was occipital-parietal. Since the source of alpha activity in all of these electrode derivations (with the exception of Boddy's temporal-temporal recordings) is in the posterior regions, it is unlikely that the choice of electrode sites can account for the discrepant results.

Alternatives to an Excitability Cycle Hypothesis

While Surwillo (1963a, 1968) interpreted his results in terms of an event programming mechanism, Boddy (1971) suggested that level of arousal might also explain the results, and this suggestion receives support from several studies. In a vigilance task Morrell (1966) found that the dominant EEG frequency in the 1-sec interval preceding a signal was related to the speed of response, with brain wave frequencies in the alpha bandwidth associated with faster responses than frequencies in the theta bandwidth. Williams, Granda, Jones, Jones, Lubin, and Armington (1962) tested RT in subjects after prolonged sleep deprivation and found a correlation between brain wave frequency and RT. In these data EEG frequency ranged from theta to the alpha bandwidths, thus probably reflecting shifts in arousal level.

While the brain wave frequency shifts reported in this investigation were well within the alpha range, it is possible that shifts in power from alpha to frequencies either within beta or theta bands occurred. The used of tuned filters for the frequency analysis allows for the possibility that frequency shifts to the theta or beta range spuriously appeared as alterations in alpha rhythm frequency. Major shifts of this sort are known to affect RT.

Thus, in the present experiment shifts induced by biofeedback conditioning to faster and slower frequencies within the alpha bandwidth may also reflect shifts beyond the alpha frequency range and shifts in arousal. This explanation could account for the fact that both RT and EEG were faster in the fast than in the slow brain wave frequency condition, yet intra-individual correlations between EEG period and RT were negligible. Subjects may have learned that they could achieve the EEG training criteria by becoming more aroused and perhaps producing more beta activity when they were attempting to produce fast alpha waves and less aroused and more likely to produce theta activity when they were attempting to produce slow alpha waves.

In summary, biofeedback was used to train young and old subjects to increase the abundance of alpha activity at their modal frequency and at frequencies 2 Hz faster and 2 Hz slower than the mode. Statistically significant increases in alpha abundance above baseline at all three alpha frequency bandwidths were achieved by experimental subjects. Control subjects presented with dummy feedback (in the mode condition only) did not increase alpha output above baseline. RTs of the experimental subjects were significantly faster in the fast than in the slow brain wave condition. Since within subjects correlations between alpha period and RT were negligible, the data did not provide unequivocal support for an excitability cycle hypothesis. It was suggested that shifts in arousal level could account for the relationship between controlled EEG activity and RT.

REFERENCES

Andersen, P., & Andersson, A. *Physiological basis of the alpha rhythm*. New York: Appleton-Century-Crofts, 1968.

Beatty, J. Effects of initial alpha wave abundance and operant training procedures on occipital alpha and beta wave activity. *Psychonomic Science*, 1971, *23*, 197–199.

Birren, J. E. Age changes in speed of behavior: Its central nature and physiological correlates. In A. T. Welford & J. E. Birren (Eds.), *Behavior, aging and the nervous system*. Springfield, Ill.: Charles C Thomas, 1965. Pp. 191–216.

Bishop, G. H. Cyclic changes in excitability of the optic pathway of the rabbit. *American Journal of Physiology*, 1933, *103*, 213–224.

Bishop, G. H. The interpretation of cortical potentials. *Cold Spring Harbor Symposium on Quantitative Biology*, 1936, *4*, 305–319.

Boddy, J. The behavioral significance of some EEG phenomena, Unpublished doctoral dissertation, University of Manchester, England, 1970.

Boddy, J. The relationship of reaction time to brain wave period: A reevaluation. *Electroencephalography & Clinical Neurophysiology*, 1971, *30*, 229–235.

Brown, B. B. Recognition of aspects of consciousness through association with EEG alpha activity represented by a light signal. *Psychophysiology*, 1970, *6*, 442–452.

Bundzen, P. U. Autoregulation of functional state of the brain: An investigation using photostimulation with feedback. *Federal Proceedings Translation Supplement*, 1966, *25*, 551–554.

Callaway, E. Factors influencing the relationship between alpha activity and visual reaction time. *Electroencephalography & Clinical Neurophysiology*, 1962, *14*, 674–682.

Dewan, E. M. Communication by voluntary control of the electroencephalogram. *Proceedings of the Symposium on Biomedical Engineering*, 1966, *1*, 349–351.

Dustman, R. E., & Beck, E. C. Phase of alpha brain waves, reaction time, and visually evoked potentials. *Electroencephalography & Clinical Neurophysiology*, 1965, *18*, 433–440.

Frost, J. D. EEG-intracellular potential relationships in isolated cerebral cortex. *Electroencephalography & Clinical Neurophysiology*, 1968, *24*, 434–443.

Green, E. E., Green, A. M., & Walters, E. D. Self-regulation of internal states. In J. Rose (Ed.), *Progress of cybernetics: Proceedings of the international congress of cybernetics, London, 1969*. London: Gordon & Breach, 1970. (a)

Green, E. E., Green, A. M., & Walters, E. D. Voluntary control of internal states: Psychological and physiological. *Transpersonal Psychology*, 1970, *2*, 1–26. (b)

Jasper, H. H. Cortical excitatory state and synchronism in the control of bioelectric autonomous rhythms. *Cold Spring Harbor Symposium on Quantitative Biology*, 1936, *4*, 320–338.

Jasper, H. H. The ten-twenty electrode system of the International Federation. *Electroencephalography & Clinical Neurophysiology*, 1958, *10*, 371–375.

Kamiya, J. Conscious control of brain waves. *Psychology Today*, 1968, *1*, 56–60.

Kamiya, J. Operant control of EEG alpha rhythm and some of its reported effects on consciousness. In C. T. Tart (Ed.), *Altered states of consciousness*. New York: Wiley, 1969. Pp. 507–517.

Lindsley, D. B. Psychological phenomena and the electroencephalogram. *Electroencephalography & Clinical Neurophysiology*, 1952, *4*, 443–456.

Lynch, J. J., & Paskewitz, D. A. On the mechanisms of the feedback control of human brain wave activity. *Journal of Nervous & Mental Disease*, 1971, *153*, 205–217.

Morrell, L. K. EEG frequency and reaction time—a sequential analysis. *Neuropsychologica,* 1966, *4,* 41–48.

Mulholland, T. Feedback electroencephalography. *Activitas Nervosa Superior,* 1968, *10,* 410–438.

Obrist, W. D. The electroencephalogram of normal aged adults. *Electroencephalography & Clinical Neurophysiology,* 1954, 6, 235–244.

Obrist. W. D. The electroencephalogram of healthy aged males. In J. E. Birren, R. N. Butler, S. W. Greenhouse, L. Sokoloff, & M. R. Yarrow (Eds.), *Human aging: A biological and behavioral study.* Washington, D.C.: U.S. Government Printing Office, 1963. Pp. 76–93.

Obrist. W. D., & Busse. E. W. The electroencephalogram in old age. In W. W. Wilson (Ed.), *Applications of electroencephalography in psychiatry: A symposium.* Durham: Duke University Press, 1965. Pp. 185–205.

Paskewitz, D. A., & Orne, M. T. Visual effects on alpha feedback training. *Science,* 1973, *181,* 361–363.

Runnals, S., & Mulholland, T. Selected demonstrations of voluntary regulations of cortical activation, *Bedford Research,* 1965, *11,* 26.

Shock, N. The physiology of aging. *Scientific American,* 1962. *206,* 100–110.

Surwillo, W. W. Frequency of the "alpha" rhythm, reaction time, and age. *Nature,* 1961, *191,* 823–824.

Surwillo, W. W. The relation of simple response time to brain wave frequency and the effects of age. *Electroencephalography & Clinical Neurophysiology,* 1963, *15,* 105–114. (a)

Surwillo, W. W. The relation of response time variability to age and the influence of brain wave frequency. *Electroencephalography & Clinical Neurophysiology,* 1963, *15.* 1029–1032. (b)

Surwillo, W. W. The relation of decision time to brain wave frequency and to age. *Electroencephalography & Clinical Neurophysiology,* 1964, *16,* 510–514. (a)

Surwillo, W. W. Some observations on the relation of response speed to frequency of photic stimulation under conditions of EEG synchronization. *Electroencephalography & Clinical Neurophysiology,* 1964, *17,* 194–198. (b)

Surwillo, W. W. Timing of behavior in senescence and the role of the central nervous system. In G. A. Talland (Ed.), *Human aging and behavior.* New York: Academic Press, 1968. Pp. 1–35.

Thompson, L. W., & Marsh, G. R. Psychophysiological studies of aging. In C. Eisdorfer & M. P. Lawton (Eds.), *The psychology of adult development and aging.* Washington, D.C.: American Psychological Association, 1973. Pp. 112–148.

Timeras, P. S. *Developmental physiology and aging.* New York: Macmillan, 1972.

Wang, H. W., & Busse, E. W. EEG of healthy old persons—A longitudinal study. 1. Dominant background activity and occipital rhythm. *Journal of Gerontology,* 1969, *24,* 419–426.

Williams, H. L., Granda, A. M., Jones, R. C., ~ubin, A., & Armington, J. C. EEG Frequency and finger pulse volume as predictors of reaction time during sleep loss. *Electroencephalography & Clinical Neurophysiology,* 1962, *14,* 76–80.

Woodruff, D. S., & Birren, J. E. Biofeedback conditioning of the EEG alpha rhythm in young and old subjects. *Proceedings of the 80th Annual Convention of the American Psychological Association,* 1972, 673–674.

REFERENCE NOTE

1. Surwillo. W. W. Personal communication, October, 1972.

Effect of Self-Enhanced EEG Alpha on Performance and Mood After Two Nights of Sleep Loss

28

David J. Hord, Mary L. Tracy, A. Lubin, and L. C. Johnson

ABSTRACT

Can the deleterious effects of acute sleep loss on performance and mood be ameliorated by self-enhanced alpha activity? Fourteen Naval volunteers were divided equally into an experimental (alpha-contingent auditory feedback) group and a yoked control (pseudofeedback) group. All subjects received feedback plus performance and mood tests during 3 baseline days and following 2 days and 2 nights without sleep. Feedback was given for 45 min in the morning and 45 min in the afternoon, preceding performance and mood tests. The self-enhanced alpha (experimental) subjects did produce more alpha than the yoked controls during all feedback sessions except for one pair that was discarded. Of eleven measures that were sensitive to sleep loss, two performance scores and one mood score showed significantly less sleep-loss decrement for the self-enhanced alpha group (at the usual univariate .05 level). Two recall scores and an anxiety score showed more impairment for the self-enhanced alpha group following sleep loss. The differences were not significant, however, by the conservative Dunn-Bonferroni multivariate criterion, so our results are not conclusive.

Alpha enhancement may help maintain performance that requires continuous attention, such as counting and auditory discrimination, but does not ameliorate the sleep-loss effect for anxiety, memory, and addition.

DESCRIPTORS: Alpha feedback, Sleep loss.

The purpose of this experiment was to test the hypothesis that contingent alpha enhancement can reduce the performance decrement and mood change produced by two nights of sleep loss.

Some studies of alpha enhancement have suggested that pleasant feelings of relaxation accompany increases in alpha activity attributable to the presence of alpha-contingent reinforcers (Kamiya, 1969). Others have hinted that alpha enhancement aided task performance (Nowlis & Kamiya, 1970), improved delayed recall (Green, Green, & Walters, 1970), raised the pain threshold (Gannon & Sternbach, 1971), or facilitated ESP (Honorton, Davidson, & Bindler, 1971).

This meager handful of published studies, plus many unpublished informal reports about the beneficial effects of high alpha, was picked up by the popular press. For many laymen, it became a

This research was supported by the Advanced Research Projects Agency of the Department of Defense under Order No. 1596, Program Codes 0D20 and 1D20, and by Department of the Navy, Bureau of Medicine and Surgery, under Task No. M4305.07-3008DAC5. The views and conclusions contained in this document are those of the authors and should not be interpreted as necessarily representing the official policies, either expressed or implied, of the Advanced Research Projects Agency, the Department of the Navy, or the U. S. Government.

The authors thank Paul Naitoh, Marion T. Austin, Don A. Irwin, and Raymond P. Hilbert for help in planning and executing this experiment.

Address requests for reprints to: David J, Hord, Ph.D., Naval Health Research Center, San Diego, California 92152.

proved scientific fact that high alpha universally enhances both work and play (e.g., Howard, 1972). At the present time, there are several commercial companies that sell alpha-feedback devices and/or alpha-learning programs based on the putative beneficial effects of high alpha.

One rather frequent claim is that sustained periods of alpha enhancement can lead to a decreased need for sleep (Regestein, Buckland, & Pegram, 1973). No mechanism has been specified to support this claim. However, one of the first signs of drowsiness, or stage 1 sleep, is the reduction of EEG alpha. Therefore, it could be argued that a subject who sustains high alpha would not show performance lapses due to drowsiness. Since our laboratory has had considerable experience with sleep-loss studies and uses a number of tests known to be very sensitive to one night of sleep loss (Lubin, Moses, Johnson, & Naitoh, 1974; Johnson, Naitoh, Moses, & Lubin, 1974), we had the expertise necessary to test the hypothesis that alpha enhancement can reduce performance decrement and mood change following acute sleep loss. So far as we can ascertain, ours is the first published study which relates objective measures of EEG alpha to objective measures of performance. Beatty, Greenberg, Deibler, and O'Hanlon (1974), however, have reported that EEG theta suppression maintains monitoring efficiency.

Method

Subjects

Fourteen male volunteers were selected from Navy and Marine Corps training facilities on the basis of interviews held with one of the experimenters. Selection was based on the subject's apparent cooperativeness and freedom from unusual sleep habits or disturbances. The age range of the subjects was 18–22 yrs.

General Apparatus

A 12-channel Beckman Type R Dynograph was used to record physiological variables and certain performance variables. Paper speed was 10 mm/sec. Selected channels were amplified and recorded on a Hewlett-Packard Model 3900 Tape Recorder at 1⅞ ips for subsequent computer analysis.

Feedback Signal

Previous work in this laboratory (Hord & Barber, 1971) led to a procedure which allowed the subject to manipulate alpha abundance with a contingent auditory reinforcer. The signal was provided by filtering occipital EEG (O_2 referenced to linked mastoids; 10-20 International Electrode System) with a Kronhite filter centered at 10 Hz with a 24 dB per octave roll off. The resultant wave form was integrated with a laboratory constructed alpha relay (Pasquali, 1969). The output of this alpha relay controlled a BRS Auditory Signal Generator and a Hewlett Packard Model 5321B digital counter which displayed relay-on time. The loudness and pitch of the resulting tone was adjusted to levels that were both comfortable and discernible to the subject. The total number of alpha relay-on min was scored for each session. On the first experimental day, the threshold of the feedback tone was adjusted for each subject to a 50%

alpha-relay-on time under eyes-open no-feedback conditions. This was done on a Tektronix 2A-61 Amplifier intermediate between the 10 Hz filter and the alpha relay. This threshold was held constant for each subject for the entire experiment.

Procedure

The subjects were alternately assigned to an alpha-contingent feedback group (CFB) and a non-contingent, pseudofeedback group (PFB). All subjects underwent a 9-day experimental period consisting of 3 baseline days (B_1, B_2, and B_3), 3 days and 2 nights of sleep loss (SL_1, SL_2, and SL_3), and 3 recovery days (R_1, R_2, and R_3). Feedback and testing were done on all days except SL_1 and SL_2. On the baseline days, day SL_3, and the recovery days, the feedback and testing schedules were as follows:

0700–0845 Breakfast, electrode hook-up.
0845–1015 45 min of auditory feedback (alpha-contingent or pseudo-) preceded and followed by a 9-min rest period. The serial counting task was carried out concurrently with feedback.
1015–1145 Auditory discrimination reaction time task and visual evoked potentials.
1145–1245 Lunch.
1245–1445 Feedback and counting as in the morning.
1445–1530 Wilkinson Addition.
1530–1600 Williams Word Memory, Primary Affect Scale, Lorr-McNair Mood Scale, and Spielberger "State" Anxiety Inventory.

A modified yoked-control design was employed. All CFB subjects were run prior to PFB subjects. The experimental conditions were the same for both groups with one exception: the auditory signals that were generated during the CFB subject's feedback sessions were taped for later playback to the yoked PFB subject during his pseudofeedback sessions. All subjects were told that their brain activity was controlling the tones they heard and were instructed to "keep the tone ON as much as possible while keeping your *eyes open* and refraining from any unnecessary movements." Each of the 45-min feedback sessions was preceded and followed by a 9-min, eyes-open, no-feedback resting condition, at which time the subject's resting alpha level was recorded. During the contingent feedback sessions, the percent tone-on time was displayed every 3 min via closed-circuit television. The subjects were encouraged to keep these values above 50% as much as possible. The same display accompanied taped presentations of auditory feedback to the yoked-control PFB subjects. In this way, there were no true alpha contingencies involved in the feedback paradigm for the PFB group and it can be assumed that no learning took place.

The subjects sat in a semi-reclining position in a sound-attenuated dimly lit room during the feedback sessions and during the auditory discrimination reaction time task. A closed-circuit television monitoring system and ongoing EEG activity from the polygraph were used to observe signs of drowsiness.

Tests

Serial Counting Task. This task has been described by Lubin et al. (1974). During all feedback sessions, subjects counted by pressing nine keys on a response panel, one at a time, in an orderly sequence. When the subject wished to relax for a moment, he signaled by depressing the zero key three times. The score was the number of gaps of 7 sec or more during each of the 45-min feedback sessions. The test was used to monitor arousal during feedback.

Tone-discrimination Task. This task was designed to serve two purposes: (1) to record visual evoked responses as a function of sleep deprivation (these data are not reported here), and (2) to assess the effects of sleep loss on an auditory discrimination reaction time task. Stimuli were presented in the following sequence: A 10-μsec light flash from a Grass Model 2P Photostimulator was presented approximately 25 cm in front of the subject's glabella. Five sec later, the subject was required to discriminate between two tones (either 800 or 1000 Hz) by pressing one of two buttons. Five sec later, another flash would follow, etc. The tone-flash sequence continued for 60 min during which the subject received 360 light flashes and made 360 auditory discrimination responses. The complete series of flashes and tones was presented to the subject by means of punched paper tape read by a Tally Model 1440 B tape reader.

Spielberger "State" Anxiety Inventory. Subjects indicated degree of affect on a list of 20 sentences that described levels of anxiety (Spielberger, 1968). Scores were weighted such that higher levels of anxiety received higher scores.

Wilkinson Addition Test. This is a 45-min pencil-and-paper test which measures speed and accuracy in addition (Wilkinson, 1969). The test was scored for number of problems attempted and percent correct.

Williams Word Memory. This test is designed to evaluate the subject's immediate and long-term recall of lists of 30 commonly used words. Immediately after the presentation of the words, the subject wrote down as many words as he could recall in 10 min. The long-term test was presented 24 hrs after the immediate-recall test during baseline and recovery days. A 72-hr period separated long-term recall from the immediate-recall test between days B_3 and SL_3. The subject was asked to recall as many of the words from the previous list as he could during 10 min (Williams, Gieseking, & Lubin, 1966). The score was the number of words correctly recalled.

Primary Affect Scale. Subjects rated their level of affect on

five variables (Johnson & Myers, Note 1). High scores represented high levels of affect.

Lorr-McNair Mood Scale. This test consists of a list of 52 adjectives, an early version of the McNair, Lorr, and Droppleman (1971) 65-item Profile of Moods (POMS) test. In the present study, a particular set of 19 items was used, called the Positive Mood Scale, that was devised to be maximally sensitive to one night of sleep loss (Lubin et al., 1974).

Results

For purposes of presentation and analysis, scores were grouped into four phases: Baseline (B), Sleep Loss Day 3 (SL_3) following 2 nights of sleep loss, Recovery Day 1 (R_1), and total recovery (REC). The baseline and recovery phases were examined for linear trend to determine the best score to use.

Baseline (B)

The trend analysis was based on the Lyerly (1952) and Lubin (1961) rank-order test, backed by the usual linear contrast. If there was no trend in the 3 baseline days, all three scores were averaged to yield $\bar{B}$. If there was a trend, the difference between B_3 and B_2 was tested by Student's t and the Wilcoxon Signed-Rank Test to see if we could average B_2 and B_3 (Wilcoxon, 1949). Failing this, we used B_3 as our best estimate of the pre-sleep-loss level. Table 1 shows the baseline measure used for each test.

TABLE 1

Sleep loss effects

Tests	Baseline Measure	Within Groups				Between Groups
		Alpha Enhancement CFB (N=6) (SL_3−B)		PFB (N=6) (SL_3−B)		CFB–PFB
		$\bar{X}$	SD	$\bar{X}$	SD	Correlation Ratio
Spielberger "State" Anxiety Inventory	$\bar{B}$	11.7[a]	4.9	6.2[a]	4.4	.29[a]
Primary Affect Scale:						
"Depression"	$\bar{B}$	2.0	3.7	4.5*	5.0	.09
"Arousal"	$\bar{B}$	−5.3	11.2	−10.5*	4.2	.11
Positive Mood Scale	$\bar{B}$	−3.2	7.9	−12.2*	5.1	.38*
Wilkinson Addition:						
Number attempted	B_3	−37.0*	36.0	−72.8	89.0	.08
Percent correct	B_3	−7.5*	3.0	−9.3*	7.0	.03
Williams Word Memory:						
Short-term recall	$(B_1 + B_2)/2$	−3.9*	4.5	−3.4	8.5	.01[a]
Long-term recall	$\bar{B}$	−6.3	1.9	−4.6	3.8	.09[a]
Auditory Discrimination Reaction Time Task:						
Errors of discrimination	$\bar{B}$	33.3*	23.0	74.3*	40.0	.32*
Reaction time	$\bar{B}$	196.0*	65.0	219.4*	136.0	.01
Serial Counting Task:						
Number of gaps during feedback	B_3	10.8*	10.7	38.8*	28.0	.34*

[a] Wrong direction.

*$p < .05$, one-tail.

Recovery (R_1 and REC)

One night of recovery sleep sometimes is not enough to return the subject's performance to baseline levels after 2 nights of sleep loss, so Recovery Day 1 (R_1) was treated as a separate score. A test of the differences between R_2 and R_3 indicated that the scores could be combined to yield a single average score (REC). Student's t-test showed no carry-over of the sleep-loss effect for any test on Day R_1. Therefore, the recovery measures were not used in the analysis.

Feedback and Pseudofeedback

The independent variable was the alpha-relay-on time produced by feedback (for the CFB group) or by pseudofeedback (for the PFB group). Table 2 shows the Relative Percent Alpha (RPA) produced by each subject during all phases of the experiment. The RPA was obtained by comparing the percent relay-on time produced during each 45-min feedback (or pseudofeedback) session with the percent relay-on time produced during the 9-min pre- and post-feedback rest sessions. The computational formula for RPA is:

$$RPA = 100 \, (F-C)/C,$$

where F is the percent time that the alpha relay was on during the feedback session and C is the percent relay-on time produced during the resting conditions. One CFB subject and his yoked PFB control were eliminated due to a *negative* RPA score on all days.

In Table 2, the correlation ratios associated with each phase of the experiment indicate that the CFB group produced significantly higher levels of alpha than did the PFB group. The correlation ratio equals $t^2/(t^2 + n_1 + n_2 - 2)$. Thus, the feedback procedure worked; all CFB subjects increased their alpha during the feedback sessions and the PFB group produced no more alpha than during the rest periods.

Tests

A total of 14 scores were analyzed. Table 1 is a summary of sleep-loss effects within and between groups. Only the eleven scores that showed a significant sleep-loss effect in one or both groups are included. (Within-group analysis of long-term recall on the Williams Word Memory Test was omitted due to the fact that recall was tested over a 24-hr period on baseline and a 72-hr period on SL_3.) Given that a sleep-loss effect could be demonstrated for a variable, the main concern of this study was whether a between-groups difference also existed. When the CFB group showed significantly better performance than the PFB group, this offered support for the hypothesis that self-enhanced alpha can sustain performance during acute sleep loss.

The differences between baseline scores and

TABLE 2

Relative percent alpha (RPA)

Period	Alpha Enhancement CFB Group N=6		PFB Group N=6	
	S	RPA	S	RPA
	01	40	06	17
	02	47	07	−29
(B)	03	43	08	58
Baseline	04	66	09	−36
	05	19	10	13
$\frac{B_1+B_2+B_3}{3}$	12	16	14	8
	$\bar{X}$	38.5	$\bar{X}$	5.2
	SD	18.7	SD	34.2
		CFB vs PFB[a] = .30*		
	01	74	06	9
	02	37	07	−3
(SL_3)	03	46	08	−5
Sleep Loss Day 3	04	61	09	−4
	05	27	10	6
	12	4	14	4
	$\bar{X}$	41.5	$\bar{X}$	1.2
	SD	24.9	SD	5.7
		CFB vs PFB[a] = .60*		
	01	55	06	5
	02	50	07	−39
(R_1)	03	87	08	8
Recovery Day 1	04	69	09	−6
	05	3	10	26
	12	7	14	−1
	$\bar{X}$	45.1	$\bar{X}$	−1.2
	SD	33.8	SD	21.6
		CFB vs PFB[a] = .44*		
	01	229	06	4
	02	27	07	−20
(REC)	03	59	08	10
Total Recovery	04	492	09	−22
	05	33	10	−5
$\frac{R_2+R_3}{2}$	12	28	14	4
	$\bar{X}$	144.6	$\bar{X}$	−4.8
	SD	187.1	SD	13.5
		CFB vs PFB[a] = .27*		

[a]Between-groups correlation ratio.
*$p < .05$.

sleep-loss scores were examined within each group using Student's t test for correlated means, backed by the Wilcoxon Signed-Rank Test. There were a few disparities between the t-test and the Wilcoxon Test, which were resolved by logarithmic transformation of the original scales. This made the differences fit closer to the assumptions of a normal distribution with constant variance. The one-tail .05 level of significance was always used in testing for the effect of sleep loss. The between-group differences (i.e., the effects of alpha enhancement) were assessed by Student's one-tail t-test for independent means, backed by the Wilcoxon Rank-sum Test. A few disagreements were resolved, as before, by logarithmic transformation of the raw scores. The "Between Groups" column in Table 1 gives the results of the Student's t-test. Results are presented in the form of correlation ratios, as before, since they are directly interpretable as the percent of deviance due to the group differences.

Since eleven separate t-tests were made with unknown dependencies between them, the Dunn-Bonferroni criterion ($.05/11 = .004545$) was used to ascertain whether any one of the eleven t ratios was significant (Dunn, 1959). A value of 3.226 was required for an overall .05 level of significance. None of the t values approached this level.

Discussion

The experimental hypothesis was that alpha enhancement, by means of contingent auditory feedback, would reduce the deleterious effects of sleep loss. *The results are inconclusive.* The majority of the eleven measures indicated some reduction of the sleep-loss impairment, and three of them showed a significant ameliorative effect, when judged by the usual univariate .05 level of significance. But none of them met the Dunn-Bonferroni .05 criterion, a conservative multiple comparisons procedure. The multivariate F ratio could not be calculated since the number of measures, eleven, was greater than the within-groups degrees of freedom, $12 - 2 = 10$.

Three of the results were contrary to the hypothesis, indicating that alpha enhancement increased rather than decreased the sleep-loss decrement.

If enhanced alpha helps to maintain performance during sleep loss, then the chief amelioration is on tasks that require some level of continuous sensory-motor activity. Thus, errors of discrimination on the Auditory task indicate sensory discontinuities and lapses on the serial counting task are manifestations of motor discontinuities. In other kinds of tasks, sensory-motor lapses might occur without directly affecting performance such as in the memory test.

Studies using more subjects and more intensive testing are being conducted to resolve the present inconclusive results. Preliminary analysis of the data has *failed* to support the hypothesis that self-enhanced alpha activity will ameliorate sleep-loss effects during a 40-hr period of sustained performance.

Summary and Conclusions

Does self-enhanced high alpha activity sustain performance and mood following 2 nights of sleep loss? Of eleven variables sensitive to sleep loss, an ameliorative effect of high alpha was seen in one mood scale and two performance measures by the usual univariate criterion, but not by the more conservative Dunn-Bonferroni criterion. Errors of discrimination on an auditory discrimination task, gaps on a counting task, and positive mood showed the supposed ameliorative effects of high alpha. However, the high alpha group had a greater increase in anxiety and a greater memory decrement than the pseudofeedback group. Our tentative guess is that continuous attention may be maintained by alpha enhancement during sleep loss, but that anxiety, memory, and addition are certainly not helped.

REFERENCES

Beatty, J., Greenberg, A., Deibler, W. P., & O'Hanlon, J. F. Operant control of occipital theta rhythm affects performance in a radar monitoring task. *Science*, 1974, *183*, 871–873.

Dunn, O. J. Confidence intervals for the means of dependent normally distributed variables. *Journal of the American Statistical Association*, 1959, *54*, 613–621.

Gannon, L., & Sternbach, R. A. Alpha enhancement as a treatment for pain: A case study. *Journal of Behavior Therapy & Experimental Psychiatry*, 1971, *2*, 209–213.

Green, E. E., Green, A. M., & Walters, E. D. Voluntary control of internal states: Psychological and physiological. In T. X. Barber, L. V. DiCara, J. Kamiya, N. E. Miller, D.

Shapiro, & J. Stoyva (Eds.), *Biofeedback and self-control.* Chicago: Aldine-Atherton, 1970. Pp. 3–28.

Honorton, C., Davidson, R., & Bindler, P. Feedback-augmented EEG alpha, shifts in subjective state, and ESP card-guessing performance. *Journal of the American Society for Psychical Research*, 1971, *65*, 308–323.

Hord, D., & Barber, J. Alpha control: Effectiveness of two kinds of feedback. *Psychonomic Science*, 1971, *25*, 151–154.

Howard, J. Flow gently, sweet alpha. *Life*, April 21, 1972.

Johnson, L. C., Naitoh, P., Moses, J. M., & Lubin, A. Interaction of REM deprivation and stage 4 deprivation with total sleep loss: Experiment 2. *Psychophysiology*, 1974, *11*, 147–159.

Kamiya, J. Operant control of the EEG alpha rhythm and some of its reported effects on consciousness. In C. T. Tart (Ed.), *Altered states of consciousness*. New York: Wiley, 1969. Pp. 507–517.

Lubin, A. L'utilisation des correlations par rang pour eprouver une tendance dans un ensemble de moyennes. *Bulletin de Centre d'Etudes et Recherches Psychotechniques*, 1961, *10*, 433–444.

Lubin, A., Moses, J. M., Johnson, L. C., & Naitoh, P. The recuperative effects of REM sleep and stage 4 sleep on human performance after complete sleep loss: Experiment 1. *Psychophysiology*, 1974, *11*, 133–146.

Lyerly, S. B. The average Spearman rank correlation coefficient. *Psychometrika*, 1952, *17*, 421–428.

McNair, D. M., Lorr, M., & Droppleman, L. F. *Manual for the POMS*, San Diego, Ca.: Educational & Industrial Testing Service, 1971.

Nowlis, D. P., & Kamiya, J. The control of electroencephalo-graphic alpha rhythms through auditory feedback and the associated mental activity. *Psychophysiology*, 1970, *6*, 476–484.

Pasquali, E. A relay controlled by alpha rhythm. *Psychophysiology*, 1969, *6*, 207–208.

Regestein, Q. R., Buckland, G. H., & Pegram, G. V. Effect of daytime alpha rhythm maintenance on subsequent sleep. *Psychosomatic Medicine*, 1973, *35*, 415–418.

Spielberger, C. D. *The Spielberger state-trait anxiety inventory*. Palo Alto, CA.: Consulting Psychologists Press, 1968.

Wilcoxon, F. *Some rapid approximate statistical procedures*. New York: American Cyanamid Co., 1949.

Wilkinson, R. T. Sleep deprivation: Performance tests for partial and selective sleep deprivation. In L. E. Abt & B. F. Riess (Eds.), *Progress in clinical psychology*. Vol. 8. New York: Grune & Stratton, 1969. Pp. 28–43.

Williams, H. L., Gieseking, C. F., & Lubin, A. Some effects of sleep loss on memory. *Perceptual & Motor Skills*, 1966, *23*, 1287–1293.

REFERENCE NOTE

1. Johnson, E. III, & Myers, T. I. *The development and use of the Primary Affect Scale (PAS)* (Research Report No. 31). Bethesda, MD: Naval Medical Research Institute, 1967.

Alpha Activity: The 29
Influence of Unpatterned Light
Input and Auditory Feedback

Gary Bridgwater, Clifford J. Sherry, and Thaddeus J. Marczynski

Summary

The electroencephalographic alpha activity was studied in ten non-paid healthy volunteers of either sex, 24-to-27 years of age, under the following experimental conditions: in the dark, in the presence of light of various intensity (1-foot candle, 3-foot candle, and 15-foot candle), with and without alpha contingent auditory feedback. Subjects wore light-diffusing goggles that prevented patterned vision throughout the experimental session.

The diffuse-light input was found to be devoid of any effect on alpha activity in the absence of auditory feedback. However, during the feedback, the light intensity above 1-foot candle had a significant suppressant effect on alpha activity. This phenomenon can be explained by an interaction between these two modalities. The 40-minute feedback training did not enhance the basic capacity of subjects to produce alpha activity above their own baseline level.

Conflicting observations on the effects of auditory feedback on alpha density have been reported by several investigators who used reliable controls prior to, and during the feedback training. Nowlis and Kamiya (10) found an increase in alpha density after 15 minutes of feedback. Strayer (16) showed an increase of alpha production in yoked as well as contingently reinforced subjects. Cleeland (4) found a higher alpha density during the non-contingent, i.e., false feedback, as compared to the contingent feed-

Reprinted with permission from *Life Sciences*, Vol. 16, No. 5, (March 1975), 729-739.

back. Regestein (13), however, was not able to observe any increase in alpha density during the last hour of feedback as compared to the first hour of training.

Adrian (1) showed that the suppressant effect of light on alpha activity is reduced or even abolished when visual input becomes more diffuse and, therefore, the number of foveal fixations is reduced, an observation later corroborated by Gale (5) who found that a decrease in alpha activity is correlated with an increase in stimulus complexity, e.g., with an increasing number of white squares on a black background. These observations (see also Mulholland [9]) support the hypothesis that the volitional acts such as reading, recognizing an object through proper accommodation, convergence, tracking eye movements, and sequences of foveal fixations are responsible for alpha block rather than the light input alone (12).

Paskewitz and Orne (11) found that the suppressant effect of light in subjects with eyes open can be partially overcome by an alpha contingent auditory feedback. In this laboratory, it was found that a threshold input of unpatterned light through translucent "milky" contact lenses is necessary for the occurrence of instrumentally conditioned alpha-like activity over the striate and parastriate cortex of cats despite the fact that these animals have been trained to perform in the dark (7). Moreover, in the dark, electrical stimulation of the optic nerve during operantly conditioned behavior apparently provided a good substitute for the light input since it fully restored the postreinforcement bursts of alpha activity (14). All these observations support the hypothesis that alpha activity depends on recurrent postsynaptic inhibition which requires a threshold input to trigger the phasing mechanism and recruitment of a larger population of neurons (cf. 2 and 7).

In view of the contradictory results, we have decided to reinvestigate, in normal volunteers, the interaction between the auditory feedback and the light input under experimental conditions in which the volitional acts of convergence, accommodation, smooth-pursuit eye movements, and foveal fixations are eliminated by preventing patterned vision through the use of light-diffusing goggles.

Methods and Procedures

The subjects were ten non-paid volunteers, 24-to-27 years of age—six males and four females. They wore light-diffusing goggles that prevented patterned vision throughout the experimental session. The goggles reduced the intensity of light by 1-foot candle. The electroencephalographic (EEG) activity was recorded in the supine position in a sound-attenuating and electrically shielded chamber. A 300-watt incandescent bulb, located 12 feet from the subject's head, provided the ambient light whose intensity could be adjusted from 1-foot candle to 15-foot candle. Two standard Beckman-type electrodes were used over the right occipital lobe for bipolar recording between the vertex and the O2 electrode placement (6).

The EEG activity was amplified and displayed by a Grass polygraph 7P511 amplifier and recorded on a Sony TC-366-A quadradial stereo tape recorder through a Vetter Model 2 FM recording adapter. Using another Grass 7P511 amplifier, the signals were filtered and displayed by a Mentor N-750 amplitude discriminator on a Tektronix Type 565 oscilloscope with a 3A3 dual-trace differential amplifier plug-in unit.

The investigator observed the alpha activity on the EEG paper and the oscilloscope, and, subsequently, adjusted the "window" of the amplitude discriminator to select alpha waves above an arbitrary minimum and below a certain maximum amplitude. The adjustment of the maximum amplitude was helpful in eliminating contaminations from high-amplitude movement artifacts. These settings remained unaltered during the experimental session. Each alpha wave, which satisfied the criteria of amplitude set for each subject (the range used for all subjects was 10-to-23 μV) and frequency (9-to-

10.5 Hz), triggered a standard pulse in the amplitude discriminator, one millisecond in duration and one volt in amplitude. These pulses were amplified and fed to a speaker located 0.5 meters from the subject's head. The audio signal was 10 dB above the background noise of 60 dB. This signal was recorded on a separate channel of the tape recorder and displayed on the EEG paper. After the 80-minute session, the recorded pulses were played back and counted, using a Hewlett-Packard 5212 electronic counter.

As shown in Table 1, the experimental session consisted of a total of eight 10-minute trials. The trials were separated by approximately two-minute rest periods. During the first trial, the subjects were told to keep their eyes closed in the dark (EC-D); during the second and third trials, they were instructed to keep their eyes open in the dark and in the light condition (3-foot candle), respectively.

During the 4th through 7th trials, the subjects received the auditory feedback and various intensities of light (1-foot candle; 3-foot candle; or 15-foot candle; during one trial, the feedback was presented in the dark (D). The sequence of these light conditions during feedback was kept random. The feedback was demonstrated to each subject before the fourth time block by having the subjects produce a burst of alpha by closing their eyes. Subjects were then instructed to maximize alpha production in each feedback trial by trying to keep the speaker clicking as much as possible.

During the last, i.e., the 8th trial, the EEG was recorded without feedback with eyes open and in the presence of light (3-foot candle), i.e., in a condition identical with the Trial 3, prior to the feedback trials.

Results

The number of single cycles of alpha waves recorded from ten subjects during the eight 10-minute time blocks under various conditions: with eyes open (EO) or closed (EC); in the presence of alpha contingent feedback or without feedback; or in the

Discussion

There is a popular belief that the alpha feedback training improves the basic capacity for producing alpha activity in the absence of feedback in a relaxed state. However, we have found that, after a 40-minute feedback training, our subjects were not able to exceed the alpha activity of their own baseline. Thus, our results are in agreement with those of Paskewitz and Orne (11) who could not find any basic enhancement in alpha density even after a much more extensive training.

Our subjects, in contrast to those of Paskewitz and Orne (11), did not show any reduction of alpha activity upon eye opening in the dark in the absence of auditory feedback. If there was any change at all, our subjects showed a tendency toward enhancement, rather than reduction in alpha activity.

The use of goggles that prevented patterned vision has eliminated the normally observed blocking effect of eye opening during the trials prior to the alpha contingent auditory feedback (Trials 2 and 3). Thus, our results agree with the original observation made by Adrian (1) who showed that diffuse light, in contrast to the patterned light, has no suppressant effect on alpha activity. Interestingly enough, however, we have found that diffuse light acquires a significant alpha blocking property during alpha contingent auditory feedback, a phenomenon that can only be explained by an interaction between these two modalities. Apparently, such an interaction requires a certain minimum level of light input since the lowest intensity of light (1-foot candle) had no significant effect.

Since "the main effect" of feedback was found to be not significant in our experimental paradigm, it appears that the suppressant effect of light was brought about by an auditory-induced change in the way the diffuse light is processed by the polymodality systems. It is well-known that many neurons in the visual cortical projections respond in a specific manner to auditory and visual stimuli, and that these neurons can be conditioned to respond with "visual" patterns of discharges to acoustic stimuli and vice versa (cf. Morrell, 8). It is thus possible that the non-suppressant unpatterned light input prior to auditory feedback, after the introduction of a patterned acoustic stimulus, acquires some of the electrophysiologic characteristics of a patterned visual input, thereby becoming inhibitory to alpha activity. Our observation on the acoustic modulation of diffuse light input seems to warrant further investigation on the nature of this interaction.

Paskewitz and Orne (11) found that their subjects with eyes open in ambient light can partially overcome the suppressant effect of light during auditory feedback training as compared to the short rest periods between feedback trials. We do not consider their observations as contradictory to ours because, during the rest periods, the ambient light allowed their subjects to engage in scanning that might have been responsible for alpha suppression. Hence, it may be assumed that their subjects "learned" to overcome the suppressant effect of light during feedback by paying less attention to patterned visual stimuli, rather than learning to respond to the auditory feedback per se.

Acknowledgements

The authors are grateful to Dr. Klaus R. Unna for his encouragement.

References

1. E. D. Adrian and B. H. C. Matthews, Brain 57, 355 (1934).

2. P. Andersen and S. A. Andersen, Physiological Basis of Alpha Rhythm, Appleton-Century-Crofts, New York, 1968.

3. J. V. Bradley, Distribution Free Statistical Tests, Prentice Hall, Englewood Cliffs, New Jersey, 1968.

4. C. S. Cleeland, H. E. Booker and K. Hosokawa, Psychophysiology 8, 262 (1971).

5. A. Gale, B. Christie and V. Penfold, Br. J. Psychol. 62, 527 (1971).

6. H. H. Jasper, EEG Clin. Neurophysiol. 10, 371 (1958).

7. T. J. Marczynski, J. T. Hackett, C. J. Sherry and S. L. Allen, Brain Research 28, 57 (1971).

8. F. Morrell, in: Brain and Human Behavior, A. G. Karczmar and J. C. Eccles (eds), p. 259, Springer-Verlag, New York, 1972.

9. T. Mulholland and S. Runnals, EEG Clin. Neurophysiol. 17, 371 (1964).

10. D. P. Nowlis and J. Kamiya, Psychophysiology 6, 476 (1970).

11. D. A. Paskewitz and M. T. Orne, Science 181, 360 (1973).

12. D. A. Pollen and M. C. Trachtenberg, Brain Research 41, 303 (1972).

13. Q. R. Regestein, G. V. Pegram, B. Cook and D. Bradley, Psychosomatic Med. 35, 215 (1973).

14. J. H. Rick and T. J. Marczynski, Unpublished results.

15. S. Siegel, Nonparametric Statistics for the Behavioral Sciences, McGraw-Hill, New York, 1956.

16. F. Strayer, W. B. Scott and P. Bakan, Canad. J. Psychol. 27, 248 (1973).

VI

TEMPERATURE CONTROL

Individual Differences and 30
Autonomic Control: Absorption, Hypnotic Susceptibility, and the Unilateral Control of Skin Temperature

Alan H. Roberts, J. Schuler, J. R. Bacon, R. L. Zimmerman, and R. Patterson

We proposed to (a) replicate earlier findings that human subjects could voluntarily control peripheral skin temperature, (b) test the hypothesis that hypnotic susceptibility and the capacity for absorbed, imaginative attention will enhance autonomic learning and performance, and (c) demonstrate a learning effect, if one exists. We compared seven subjects who scored high with seven subjects who scored low on both a modified version of the Harvard Group Scale of Hypnotic Susceptibility and the Tellegen Absorption Scale. Auditory feedback was used to train subjects to produce a difference in skin temperature in one hand relative to the other in a direction specified by the experimenter. Large and reliable performance and learning effects were found, but they were unrelated to hypnotic susceptibility or the capacity for absorbed, imaginative attention. Variables that might account for individual differences in learning and performance are discussed.

Although large differences in the ability to learn autonomic control have been noted (cf. Miller, 1974), there have been few attempts to systematically investigate personality traits that might be associated with these individual differences (Roessler, 1972; Wenger, 1966; Bell & Schwartz, Note 1). Historically, the earliest reports of voluntary autonomic control have almost always been related to hypnosis, meditation, altered states of con-

The work reported in this paper was supported, in part, by Social and Rehabilitation Service Research and Training Grant 16-P-56810 and by a Grant-In-Aid from the Graduate School of the University of Minnesota. The authors wish to thank David Lykken, who first suggested the design for this study, and Auke Tellegen for his help, encouragement, and critical comments.

Requests for reprints should be sent to Alan H. Roberts, Box 297 Mayo, University of Minnesota, Minneapolis, Minnesota 55455.

sciousness, or similar phenomena (cf. Dalal & Barber, 1969).

Miller (1969) noted that his laboratory animals that had been paralyzed by curare learned to control normally involuntary functions significantly better than did noncurarized controls. He suggested that it might be worthwhile to try to use hypnotic suggestion to achieve similar results in human subjects. Following his suggestion, Maslach, Marshall, and Zimbardo (1972) presented case reports of three subjects well trained in hypnosis who were able to voluntarily raise or lower the temperature of one hand relative to the other during two or three trial sessions while hypnotized.

Roberts, Kewman, and Macdonald (1973) attempted to replicate the findings of Maslach et al. Because they were unable to demonstrate reliable effects using hypnosis alone, they introduced biofeedback training proce-

TABLE 1

CHARACTERISTICS AND TEST SCORES OF HIGH SUSCEPTIBLE–HIGH ABSORPTION ($n = 7$) AND LOW SUSCEPTIBLE–LOW ABSORPTION ($n = 7$) SUBJECTS

Subject group and number	Sex	Age	Group Scale of Hypnotic Susceptibility	Tellegen Absorption Scale	Performance			Learning		Maximum temperature difference	Maximum of mean temperature differences Sessions 9–16	
					M	SD	p<	Beta	p<	Sessions 9–16	M	SD
High susceptible–high absorption												
1	F	20.0	53.0	12.0	2.17	1.33	.001	.22	.001	4.70	2.53	1.09
2	F	21.0	48.0	12.0	1.42	.60	.001	.08	.01	3.42	1.60	.81
3	M	22.0	52.0	13.0	.57	.96	.05	.13	.01	3.95	1.04	1.08
5	F	20.0	45.0	15.0	.23	.54	.10	.09	.001	1.34	.59	.48
6	M	23.0	47.0	16.0	.18	.41	.10	.04	.05	1.08	.34	.61
9	F	20.0	49.0	14.0	.41	.89	.10	.16	.001	2.90	1.15	.80
13	F	20.0	46.0	13.0	-.26	.30	ns	.01	ns	2.00	-.02	.21
M		20.9	48.6	13.6	.67			.10		2.77	1.03	
SD		1.22	2.99	1.51	.84			.07		1.36	.85	
Low susceptible–low absorption												
4	F	20.0	11.0	-11.0	.43	.45	.001	-.03	ns	2.29	.28	.55
7	M	19.0	-3.0	-11.0	1.76	1.43	.001	.21	.01	5.70	2.32	.67
8	F	28.0	6.0	-12.0	1.19	1.04	.001	.18	.001	3.66	2.17	1.11
10	M	21.0	-4.0	-13.0	.70	.67	.001	-.02	ns	3.69	.51	.72
11	M	19.0	9.0	-11.0	.17	.53	ns	.02	ns	2.26	.58	.76
12	M	19.0	6.0	-21.0	.37	.41	.01	.05	.01	1.82	.62	.58
14	F	28.0	-1.0	-14.0	-.12	.25	ns	.03	.05	.57	-.01	.12
M		22.0	3.4	-13.3	.64			.06		2.86	.92	
SD		4.16	6.02	3.59	.64			.09		1.65	.93	

dures and concluded that some subjects were able to achieve a high degree of voluntary control over the autonomic processes involved in peripheral skin temperature regulation. However, many questions were raised or left unanswered by their study. Even in their group of highly selected, highly talented, highly trained hypnotic subjects, there were large individual differences in ability to learn, rate of learning, and magnitude of control that could be achieved. Further, the manner in which their data were gathered did not permit a clear-cut demonstration of a learning curve, if one existed.

The study by Roberts et al. also confounded the variables of auditory feedback and hypnosis, so it was unclear whether hypnosis was a necessary adjunct to learning or promoted the learning process. They hypothesized that "the *ability* to alter one's state of consciousness (Hilgard, 1969; Tart, 1972), together with associated motivational and training variables, will be among the more critical variables in predicting the ability to control voluntary autonomic processes, while hypnosis per se may not be necessary" (p. 168).

Taub and Emurian (Note 2) report having trained subjects to alternately increase and decrease the skin temperature of the index finger on one hand. However, Lynch, Hama,

Kohn, and Miller (Note 3), in attempting to replicate the findings of Roberts et al. as well as the work of Taub and Emurian, reported reliable findings in only a very few of many subjects they have attempted to train. There is question, therefore, about the replicability of previously reported work in this area, as well as about the variables that may be associated with individual and group differences in the ability to learn skin temperature control.

The purpose of the present study is threefold: (a) to attempt to again demonstrate that human subjects can voluntarily control peripheral skin temperature under stringent laboratory conditions; (b) to test the hypothesis that hypnotic susceptibility and the capacity for absorbed, imaginative attention will enhance autonomic learning; and (c) to demonstrate a learning effect (as differentiated from performance), if one exists.

METHOD

Subjects

A tape-recorded modified version of the Harvard Group Scale of Hypnotic Susceptibility (GSHS) and a 409-item questionnaire containing the Tellegen Absorption Scale (TAS), both described below, were administered to 172 male and 153 female undergraduate students who received course points in psychology for volunteering as experimental subjects.

From these, eight subjects scoring high on both the GSHS and TAS and seven subjects scoring low on both measures were asked to volunteer for biofeedback training, for which they were paid $1 per session and $24 as a bonus if they completed 16 training sessions. Additional money, up to $2 per session, could be earned as reinforcement for learning.[1]

The GSHS, the TAS, and the several hundred other personality test items were administered in groups of 20 to 30 subjects at a time. As part of the instructions, these subjects were routinely told that some of them might be randomly sampled and asked to participate in other experiments. Several months later, the subjects used in this experiment were contacted by phone, told they had been sampled from the subject pool, and were asked to volunteer for an experiment that would require many hours of their time and for which they would be paid. Subjects were not told that our biofeedback experiments were in any way concerned with hypnosis, hypnotic susceptibility, or the absorption variable. Experimenters did not know which subjects were high or low on these variables.

Absorption and hypnotic susceptibility were deliberately confounded in the interest of parsimony. If the two groups of subjects performed or learned differently, it was our intention to later separate the hypnotic susceptibility and absorption variables for additional experimentation. The mean of the high absorption subjects was separated from the mean of the low absorption subjects by over $2\frac{1}{2}$ standard deviations, whereas the means of the high and low hypnotic susceptibility subjects were separated by over 3 standard deviations (see Table 1, where age and sex are also shown).

One of the eight high absorption–high hypnotic susceptibility subjects was later dropped from our data analyses because there was a possibility that he might be malingering. However, this subject completed all 16 training sessions and had his data been included in the analyses it would not have changed our overall conclusions, despite the fact that he was the best performer of all our subjects.

Independent Variables

Group Scale of Hypnotic Susceptibility (GSHS). The GSHS is a tape-recorded modified version of the Harvard Group Scale of Hypnotic Susceptibility (Shor & Orne, 1962) and was used by Tellegen and Atkinson (1974) in their derivation of the TAS. It is described in detail by Roberts and Tellegen (1973). The GSHS is a standard hypnotic induction procedure that may be administered to several individuals simultaneously. Subjects report not only their overt responses to suggestions but also rate how vivid and compelling the subjective experiences were that resulted from the suggestions by filling out a standard rating scale. Behavioral and subjective ratings from this scale correlate over .80 and we used a combined score which has consistent alpha coefficient reliabilities over .80. The mean GSHS score for the initial group of 325 subjects was 26.88 with a standard deviation of 14.09.

---

[1] A detailed explanation of the reinforcement schedule may be obtained by writing the authors.

Group measures of hypnotic susceptibility are not, of course, perfectly correlated with the later administration of individual scales. However, because the reliabilities were more than adequate, we decided to use a group administration to increase the size of the sample. The modifications that were made to improve certain aspects of the scale invalidate its comparison with the Shor and Orne (1963) norms. Researchers interested in normative comparisons should, of course, use the Shor and Orne (1962) scale.

Tellegen Absorption Scale (TAS). The TAS is a 32-item scale developed by Tellegen (Tellegen & Atkinson, 1974) through a series of replicated, cross-validated, factor analytic studies. It has alpha coefficient reliabilities over .80 and consistently correlates about .40 with measures of hypnotic susceptibility. Absorption is interpreted as reflecting a capacity for absorbed attention that fully engages a person's representational resources and results in a full commitment of available perceptual, enactive, imaginative, and ideational resources to a unified representation of the attentional object.

People scoring high on the TAS report a heightened sense of the reality of things they attend to, even if the attentional object is constructed from memory. They are reportedly impervious to normally distracting events. They relate a sense of altered awareness of reality in general and of the self in particular, and they describe a variety of other phenomena that are characteristic of transient, statelike episodes. Tellegen and Atkinson's data strongly support the interpretation that transient, altered-state-of-consciousness episodes can be interpreted as manifestations of absorption as a cognitive motivational trait. They show absorption to be fully independent of stability (ego-resiliency) and introversion–extroversion (ego-control).

The TAS is reported here in standard scores with a mean of 0 and a standard deviation of 10. The correlation between the TAS and the GSHS for our initial 325 subjects was again .40.

Procedure

Each subject received 16 identical, individual 1-hour training sessions. The subject reclined on a hospital bed alone in a semidark, electrically shielded, temperature-controlled room with ambient temperature set at 25° C. The experimenter could observe the subject through a window and two-way communication was conducted via intercom.

Subjects were given no instructions concerning how to mediate temperature control except that they were to use "mental control" rather than muscles or movements. Thermistors were attached to the center of the finger print of the middle finger of each hand and to the anterior aspect of the wrist at the level of the proximal carpal row just medial to the tendon of the palmaris longus.

Skin temperature was measured by Yellow Springs thermilinear components with a Type 709 surface temperature probe. The time constant of the probe in a liquid was 1.1 sec. Electronic circuitry was developed to provide four channels of absolute temperature differences. The output sensitivity of the absolute temperature channels was 100 mV/° C. The temperature difference channels had four sensitivity ranges of 0 to ±1° C, 0 to ±2° C, 0 to ±5° C, and 0 to ±10° C. The full-scale output voltage for each range was ±1 V. The absolute accuracy of the temperature measurements was ±.2° C, which a linearity of ±.05° C.

The output signal from one temperature difference channel, the channel that recorded the temperature difference between the two fingertips, was connected to a combined voltage-controlled frequency and amplitude oscillator. The output from the oscillator was used to produce a tone in a stereo headset that changed in frequency ±200 Hz for a ±1-V input (which corresponds to a full-scale output from the thermistor circuitry) from a center frequency of 350 Hz. The amplitude-modulating characteristics of the oscillator caused the tone to increase in one earphone and simultaneously decrease in the opposite earphone, depending on the sign and magnitude of the input control signal. Thus, as the right finger became warmer relative to the left, the frequency of the tone increased and the tone moved toward the right earphone. As the left finger became warmer relative to the right, the frequency of the tone decreased and it moved toward the left earphone.

The output signals from the thermistor electronic circuitry were recorded on a Sanborn Model 150 recorder. The output signals were also connected to an Analogic Model 2510 3½-digit panelmeter. This allowed absolute temperatures to be read with a resolution of ±.1° C and temperature difference to ±.01° C.

After the thermistors were attached, the experimenter left the room and the subject had 10 min to rest and establish a baseline without feedback. At the end of this period the temperature differences between left and right fingers and between left and right wrists were zeroed manually by the experimenter and the absolute temperature of each finger and wrist was recorded as the baseline for that session. Feedback sensitivity was set at the highest range and the subject was instructed as follows:

For the next several minutes, left hand and finger are cold and right hand and finger are warm. Left is cold and right is warm. Left finger cold, right finger warm. Left cold, right warm. Tone to the right side and up in pitch.

This was followed by 8 min without interruption by the experimenter, and then the instruction was repeated for the opposite hand. This was again followed by 8 min without interruption, another reversal of instruction, and another uninterrupted 8 min. The feedback signal was then turned off and the subject was instructed to rest, relax, equalize the temperature of both hands, and make both hands comfortable. The hand chosen to start each session was randomly assigned to each subject for each session with the restriction that half of the sessions would begin with the left hand and half with the right.

Dependent Variables

Performance. The temperature difference between left and right fingers was adjusted to a zero baseline at the beginning of each session. The differential in degrees Celsius between right finger and left finger was recorded as deviations from this baseline at 1-min intervals for each of the three 8-min trials per session.

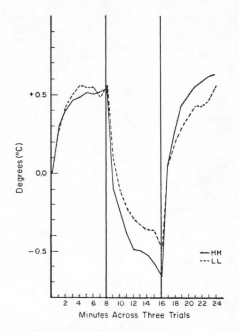

FIGURE 1. Average finger differential of seven high absorption-hypnotic (HH) and seven low absorption-hypnotic (LL) subjects for the last eight sessions.

For each subject for each session the last five readings for each trial were summed. The sums for Trials 1 and 3 were averaged and the sum for Trial 2 was subtracted from their average. If Trials 1 and 3 were left-hand warm trials, the criterion measure was multiplied by −1.

Temperature differences between fingers were also recorded using a zero baseline at the beginning of each trial instead of only at the beginning of each session. Deviations from these baselines were given a positive sign if they were in the requested direction and a negative sign if in the wrong direction. This measure is comparable to the one reported by Roberts et al. (1973) and is used to compute maximum temperature differences and the means of maximum temperature differences achieved by the subjects.

Learning. Learning was defined as sequential change in the direction of requested performance across sessions. The slope (beta) of the regression line of performance, as previously defined, across 16 training sessions was used as a measure of learning. The probability values for individual subjects for the beta coefficients were calculated from the variance about the regression line.

RESULTS

Skin Temperature Changes

Data were analyzed at 1-min intervals. The

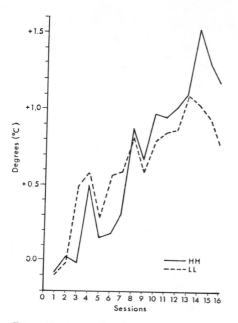

FIGURE 2. Average learning curve for seven high absorption-hypnotic (HH) and seven low absorption-hypnotic (LL) subjects for 16 sessions.

results are summarized in Table 1 for each subject separately and in Figures 1 and 2 for high and low groups separately.

Total group (n = 14) *performance and learning.* Group means of performance were compared against chance deviations that might be expected due to individual differences using the conservative (between-subjects) error variance. Fingertip differential for the total group, averaged across the last eight training sessions, reaches statistically significant levels ($p \leqslant .05$) in the expected direction for each 1-min reading for all trials except the first minute of Trials 2 and 3, which are transitional readings. The total group mean performance is significantly different from zero beyond the .01 level of confidence. The group average of beta coefficients was .08 ($SD = .08$), which is significant at the .01 level of confidence (again using the conservative between-subjects error variance), indicating that the group as a whole showed statistically significant learning effects.

High (n = 7) *versus low* (n = 7) *group performance and learning.* There were no statistically significant differences between high and low subjects on measures of performance (Figure 1) or learning (Figure 2).

Individual performance and learning. Subjects 1 and 2 from the high group and Subjects 7, 8, and 12 from the low group showed high overall performance, which improved significantly across sessions. Subjects 4 and 10 from the low group showed relatively good overall performance but no improvement across the 16 sessions.

Subjects 3, 5, and 9 from the high group showed highly significant improvement in performance across sessions, but only reached stable, significant performance levels late in the 16 sessions. Subjects 6 and 13 of the high group and Subjects 11 and 14 of the low group showed only minimal learning and did not achieve stable temperature control.

Table 1 shows the maximum temperature difference achieved during any one of the last 24 trials by each of the 14 subjects. This measure was derived by rezeroing the baseline for each trial, as described earlier, to make the data comparable to those reported by Roberts et al. (1973). These maximum temperature differences range from .57° C to 5.70° C, with a mean of 2.81 ($SD = 1.45$).

Using these same rezeroed values, the eight minute-by-minute readings were averaged for each subject across the last 24 trials (eight sessions). The maximum of these minute-by-minute mean differences achieved by each subject is also shown in Table 1. They range from −.01° C to 2.53° C, with a mean of .98 ($SD = .86$).

These two sets of data do not differ significantly from similar data derived from the six subjects in the study by Roberts et al. (1973). In that study, the maximum temperature difference achieved during any one of the last nine trials ranged from 1.5° C to 5.6° C, with a mean of 2.78 ($SD = 1.46$). The maximum of the average temperature differences in the earlier study ranged from .18° C to 2.96° C, with a mean of 1.43 ($SD = 1.09$).

Response Patterns

When the absolute temperature of each finger was graphed for each subject separately for each trial, four response patterns could be discerned: (a) the temperature differential went the wrong way, (b) both fingers were heated and cooled together but at different rates, (c) one finger was held constant and the other changed in the correct direction, and (d) the finger temperatures diverged or converged.

Preliminary analyses of the detailed protocols indicate that, during the best sessions, subjects varied temperature in the two hands independently. Early training sessions and all sessions for poor performers were accompanied by high correlations between the absolute temperatures for the two hands.

Sessions in which high performance occurred showed lower correlation between the two hands, frequently near zero or even negative. Learning was also associated with higher correlation between the finger tip differential temperature and the wrist differential, suggesting that control was exercised over fairly large areas of the distal portions of the arms.

DISCUSSION

Some human subjects can learn to voluntarily control peripheral skin temperature. In this respect, the results of this study support the earlier findings of Maslach et al. (1972), who used hypnosis to produce differences between the finger temperatures of two hands; Roberts et al. (1973), who used a combination of hypnosis and biofeedback to train subjects to perform the same task; and Taub and Emurian (Note 2), who trained subjects to alternately increase or decrease the temperature of one hand using biofeedback without hypnosis. Lynch et al. (Note 3), on the other hand, have been able to demonstrate consistent, reliable results in only a few subjects after evaluating a wide variety of subjects under different experimental conditions. There continues to be a need for independent replication using, as a minimum, the kinds of controls described in this study.

There appear to be large individual differences among subjects, and the conditions under which subjects learn or fail to learn autonomic control have not yet been delineated. Earlier studies and lore had implicated hypnosis or related phenomena as possibly being related to autonomic learning and control. The data from this study demonstrate that the trait of hypnotic susceptibility, the capacity for absorbed, imaginative attention, and by inference, hypnosis itself (or other altered states of consciousness) are not necessary conditions for learning autonomic control of the type described in this paper.

The possibility of a low order correlation between either or both of the independent variables and autonomic performance or learning is not ruled out because extreme groups of only seven subjects each were compared. It is also possible that highly talented hypnotic subjects or highly absorbed individuals can learn these kinds of autonomic control without biofeedback procedures.

The subjects in this study did about as well on the average as the 6 highly trained, highly talented hypnotized subjects in the Roberts et al. (1973) study. Only 1 of the 14 subjects in this study (Subject 7) had even been hypnotized prior to participaitng in this experiment.

Because the two extreme groups were used in this study, there is a remaining possibility of a curvilinear relation. Highly susceptible, highly absorbed subjects might conceivably be less aware of the reality of bodily changes than subjects lower on these measures. Middle-range subjects should be tested in future experiments.

Our data demonstrate a clear-cut learning curve for all subjects combined and highly significant learning effects for 8 out of 14 subjects. Further, the magnitude of the effect, averaging one or more degrees Celsius in at least half of the subjects, adds additional support to the idea that voluntary skin temperature control can be learned to a level consistent with possible medical applications. These data also provide additional support for the theoretical issues raised by Miller (1969).

Although instrumentally conditioned or voluntarily emitted skeletal responses cannot be absolutely ruled out as mediators of the temperature changes found in this study, they seem highly unlikely. We have evaluated our subjects with electromyographic tests of the forearms and hands and can detect no muscle movements that can be associated with skin temperature changes. In fact, Subject 15 was eliminated from our study when he could not produce skin temperature changes with the electromyograph hooked up and an observer in the room recording readings.

In an attempt to formulate hypotheses relating to individual differences and learning ability, we have conducted post hoc analyses contrasting our good learners and performers with our poor learners and performers. These include detailed statistical analyses of 14 separate Minnesota Multiphasic Personality Inventory scales, including the ego-strength scale which Roessler (1972) reported to predict autonomic learning ability, and 5 additional scales developed by Tellegen (Tellegen & Atkinson, 1974) representing broad, replicated, largely independent personality dimensions. None of these data show differences between good performers and poor performers or good learners and poor learners.

One post hoc variable that seems promising to explore further is the subjects' confidence or belief in the phenomena or in their own ability. Their confidence seems to predict their performance ability across the entire series of 16 training sessions, as well as on a session-by-session basis, and later studies should employ systematic measures of this variable. Confidence may be partially mediated by experimenter–subject interactions as well as by early success or failure experiences.

We conclude that some subjects can learn some degree of unilateral skin temperature control if they are provided with sufficient training and are sufficiently motivated. We continue to find that there are significant individual differences in learning ability, but that the trait of hypnotic susceptibility and, by inference, the hypnotic state itself, as well as the capacity for absorbed, imaginative involvement, are not *necessary* conditions for learning.

Instead, it seems more likely that psychophysiological variables such as autonomic responsivity or lability, interpersonal variables such as attitude toward and relationship to experimenter, and attitudinal and motivational variables such as confidence are more likely to account for many of the observed differences in learning. Because many of these potential mediators of autonomic conditioning are themselves subject to conditioning or control, considerable potential remains for (a) developing methods of training subjects who appear to be recalcitrant to our present training methods, or (b) increasing abilities in people with small initial talent.

REFERENCE NOTES

1. Bell, I. R., & Schwartz, G. E. *Individual and situational factors in bidirectional voluntary control and reactivity of human heart rate.* Paper presented at the meeting of the Western Psychological Association, Anaheim, California, April 1973.
2. Taub, E., & Emurian, C. *Autoregulation of skin temperature using a variable intensity feedback light.* Paper presented at the annual meeting of the Biofeedback Research Society, Boston, November 1972.
3. Lynch, W. C., Hama, H., Kohn, S., & Miller, N. E. *Instrumental learning of vasomotor responses: A progress report.* Paper presented at the meeting of the Biofeedback Research Society, Colorado Springs, February 1974.

REFERENCES

Dalal, A. S., & Barber, T. X. Yoga, "yogic feats" and hypnosis in the light of empirical research. *Journal of Clinical Hypnosis,* 1969, *11,* 155–166.

Hilgard, E. R. Altered states of awareness. *Journal of Nervous and Mental Diseases,* 1969, *149,* 68–79.

Maslach, C., Marshall, G., & Zimbardo, P. Hypnotic control of peripheral skin temperature: A case report. *Psychophysiology,* 1972, *9,* 600–605.

Miller, N. E. Learning of visceral and glandular responses. *Science,* 1969, *163,* 434–445.

Miller, N. E. Applications of learning and biofeedback to psychiatry and medicine. In A. M. Freedman, H. I. Kaplan, & B. J. Sadock (Eds), *Comprehensive textbook of psychiatry* (2nd ed.). Baltimore: Williams & Wilkins, 1974.

Roberts, A. H., Kewman, D. G., & Macdonald, H. Voluntary control of skin temperature: Unilateral changes using hypnosis and feedback. *Journal of Abnormal Psychology,* 1973, *82,* 163–168.

Roberts, A. H., & Tellegen, A. Ratings of "trust" and hypnotic susceptibility. *The International Journal of Clinical and Experimental Hypnosis,* 1973, *21,* 289–297.

Roessler, R. Personality, psychophysiology, and performance. *Psychophysiology,* 1972, *10,* 315–327.

Shor, R. E., & Orne, E. C. *Harvard Group Scale of Hypnotic Susceptibility.* Palo Alto, Calif.: Consulting Psychologists Press, 1962.

Shor, R. E., & Orne, E. C. Norms on the Harvard Group Scale of Hypnotic Susceptibility, Form A. *International Journal of Clinical and Experimental Hypnosis,* 1963, *11,* 39–47.

Tart, C. T. States of consciousness and state-specific sciences. *Science,* 1972, *176,* 1203–1210.

Tellegen, A., & Atkinson, G. Openness to absorbing and self-altering experiences ("Absorption"), A trait related to hypnotic susceptibility. *Journal of Abnormal Psychology,* 1974, *83,* 268–277.

Wenger, M. A. Studies of autonomic balance: A summary. *Psychophysiology,* 1966, *2,* 173–185.

Conditioning Changes in 31
Differential Skin Temperature

Francis J. Keefe

Summary.—8 male Ss were presented with visual and auditory analog feedback regarding the difference between forehead and finger temperature. 4 Ss were instructed to raise the temperature of their finger in comparison with the forehead, while a second group of 4 Ss was instructed to lower the temperature of their finger in comparison with the temperature of the forehead. After 12 15-min. training sessions all Ss were able to produce changes in differential skin temperature in the specified direction. Differential changes in skin temperature correlated highly with changes in absolute finger temperature. These results are discussed as relevant to the clinical application of skin temperature control.

The recent application of operant conditioning techniques to the modification of autonomic responses has generated considerable interest both in laymen (Stoler, 1974) and scientists (Davidson & Krippner, 1972; Schwartz, 1973). Experiments using such techniques have demonstrated that humans can gain some degree of voluntary control over such "involuntary" functions as heart rate (Engel & Chism, 1967), blood pressure (Shapiro, Tursky, & Schwartz, 1970), and vasomotor responses (Christie & Kotses, 1973).

Autonomic self-control likewise has stimulated keen interest among clinicians. The ability to control peripheral skin temperature appears to be especially helpful in the treatment of certain vascular disorders. For example, Sargent, Green, and Walters (1973) found that pain associated with migraine headache was markedly reduced after 2 to 4 mo. of daily feedback training to increase

[1]Requests for reprints should be sent to Francis J. Keefe, Psychology Dept., Ohio University, Athens, Ohio 45701.

hand, relative to midforehead, skin temperature. Case studies (Peper, 1972; Peper & Grossman, 1974) using similar differential hand-forehead feedback training have also reported successful treatment of patients suffering from Raynaud's disease.

Recently, a number of investigations, conducted under more controlled laboratory conditions, have purported to demonstrate the conditioning of differential skin temperature changes of relatively large magnitude (McDonagh & McGinnis, 1973; Roberts, Kewman, & Macdonald, 1973; Taub & Emurian, 1971, 1972). These studies, however, are open to criticism on several grounds. First, in each study biofeedback training has been used in conjunction with an instructional set, designed to induce skin temperature changes, e.g., autogenic phrases (McDonagh & McGinnis, 1973), hypnotic suggestions (Roberts, *et al.*, 1973), or encouragement to use "thermal imagery" (Taub & Emurian, 1971, 1972). The simultaneous use of such multiple treatment procedures makes it impossible to evaluate whether feedback or the specific instructional sets are responsible for the observed changes in skin temperature. Secondly, with the exception of Roberts, *et al.* (1973), no data have been presented on changes in absolute temperature of each skin site measured during differential temperature training.

The present study attempted to meet the above criticisms. Subjects were given both feedback and response-specific instructions. The response-specific instructions were simple and straightforward. They merely informed *Ss* of the response being monitored and the direction of temperature change desired. The purpose of the study was: (a) to investigate whether *Ss* could produce either increases in differential skin temperature (Increase group) or decreases in differential skin temperature (Decrease group), and (b) to investigate the relationship between over-all changes in differential skin temperature and changes in the absolute temperature of the finger.

METHOD

Subjects

Ss were eight male college students, ages 18 to 21 yr. enrolled in courses in introductory psychology.

Apparatus

Differential skin temperature was recorded on a Varian Model G-14 single channel recorder. Measurements of hand-forehead differential skin temperature were made using two Yellow Springs thermistors and a Biofeedback Technology Model BFT301 feedback thermometer in differential mode. One thermistor was positioned on the right index finger and the other was positioned on the midforehead. The output of the feedback thermometer was used to control continuous auditory and visual feedback delivered to *Ss*. The auditory feedback, presented through headphones, consisted of a soft tone which varied in pitch as a function of the difference between hand and forehead skin temperature. An increase in hand relative to forehead temperature resulted in an increase in tone frequency, while a decrease in hand relative to forehead temperature resulted in a decrease in tone frequency. The visual feedback consisted of a closed-circuit television picture of the center-set meter mounted on the feedback thermometer. A Panasonic Model WV 220P video camera was used to transmit the picture and the feedback was presented to S on a Magnavox 24-in. monitor. Changes in differential skin temperature were indicated on the meter as follows: an increase in hand relative to forehead temperature resulted in deflection of the meter needle from the center to the right, while a decrease in hand relative to forehead temperature resulted in deflection of the meter needle from the center to the left.

Measurements of absolute temperature of the right index finger were recorded by E using the feedback thermometer in absolute mode.

Procedure

Ss were randomly assigned in equal numbers to one of two groups: an Increase group, in which Ss were trained to produce increases in hand relative to forehead temperature, and a Decrease group in which decreases in hand relative to forehead temperature were conditioned. All Ss participated in 12 training sessions on 12 consecutive days. Each session consisted of a 5-min. rest followed by a 10-min. feedback period.

At the start of a session each S was seated in a comfortable chair in a room maintained at 70°F. Thermistors were positioned on the right index finger and midforehead with surgical tape. Increase group Ss were instructed that their task was to raise the temperature of the right hand relative to the temperature of the forehead during the feedback period. They were also informed that when they were successful the pitch of the feedback tone would increase and the needle on the feedback meter would move to the right. Decrease group Ss were told that their task was to lower the temperature of the hand relative to the temperature of the forehead and that success in doing this would be indicated by a decrease in the pitch of the feedback tone and movement of the meter needle to the left. All Ss were instructed to refrain from irregular respiration and unnecessary movement. After reading the instructions, and placing the earphones on S, E entered an adjacent control room, and initiated the training session.

During the 5-min. rest S was given no feedback. The first 2 min. of this period were used for equipment warmup and the last 3 min. were used as a baseline period during which measurements of differential skin temperature were recorded. At the end of the rest period an initial measurement of absolute temperature of the right finger was taken. The differential thermometer was then rebalanced so that the needle was positioned at a zero-center reading, and

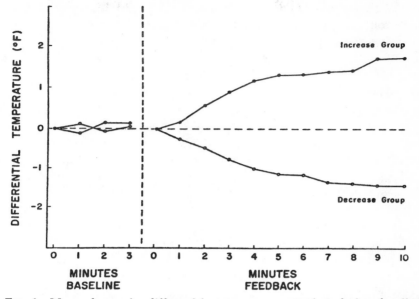

FIG. 1. Mean change in differential temperature occurring during baseline and feedback periods of training Session 12 for Increase and Decrease groups

S was presented with a 10-min. feedback period during which both auditory and visual feedback were presented. At the end of the feedback period a second measurement of absolute finger temperature was taken.

RESULTS[2] AND DISCUSSION

Fig. 1 portrays the mean change in differential skin temperature of *S*s in the Increase and in the Decrease group during the twelfth training session. Inspection clearly suggests that bidirectional changes in differential forehead-hand skin temperature were obtained as a result of feedback training. *S*s in the Increase group showed an average increase in differential skin temperature of up to 1.9°F over the 10-min. feedback period, while *S*s in the Decrease group showed an average decrease of up to 1.5°F over this same period.

Changes in *S*s' differential temperature during the twelfth session were calculated at 1-min. intervals, and an analysis of variance was then computed for the Increase and Decrease groups. Increase and Decrease groups differed significantly ($F_{1,6} = 46.88$, $p < .01$). In addition, the interaction of Groups × Minutes of Feedback ($F_{9,54} = 18.17$, $p < .01$) was significant. *Post hoc* comparisons between the means for the two groups were made for Mins. 1, 3,

[2]Four supplementary tables of more detailed results can be obtained by writing to: Microfiche Publications, 440 Park Ave. S., New York, N. Y. 10016 for Document NAPS-02451. Remit $1.50 for microfiche or $5.00 for photocopy.

5, 7, and 9 of the feedback period by means of Tukey's HSD statistic. The results of these comparisons indicated that there was no statistically significant difference between the performance of the Increase and Decrease groups after one minute of feedback, although significant differences between the two groups occurred after both 3, 5, 7, and 9 min. of feedback.

To analyze variations in absolute skin temperature of the right finger over the feedback period, change scores were computed by subtracting the initial absolute skin temperature reading from the final reading. Over the 10-min. feedback period, Increase group Ss showed an average increase in absolute finger temperature of 1.7°F, whereas Decrease group Ss showed an average decrease of 1.2°F. Furthermore, changes in absolute finger temperature correlated highly ($r = .87$, $p < .01$) with over-all changes in differential skin temperature. Thus, bidirectional changes in absolute finger temperature occurred concurrently with bidirectional changes in differential skin temperature.

Although it was not the original intent of this study to examine the results of early training sessions, it was felt that the progress of Ss should be examined over sessions. Measurements of differential temperature were made for Sessions 4 and 8. Inspection of these data suggested that after four sessions of training, Ss had achieved relatively poor control over differential skin temperature. Ss in the Increase group displayed a decrease in differential skin temperature of 0.2°F after 10 min. of feedback, while Ss of the Decrease group showed a decrease of 0.1°F. However, after eight sessions it was evident that control over differential skin temperature had been developed. Ss of the Increase group showed a mean increase of 0.9°F after 10 min. of feedback, while Ss in the Decrease group showed an average decrease of 1.2°F. These results suggest that extended period of training was needed to condition differential changes in skin temperature using the techniques and population described.

The present study demonstrates that changes in skin temperature can be obtained using feedback and response-specific instructions. Ss clearly responded to instructions to attempt to change skin temperature. Those Ss who were informed that their task was to increase temperature showed significant increases during the final training session. Likewise, Ss who were told that their task was to decrease temperature showed significant decreases during the final training session. These results are consistent with previous research (Bergman & Johnson, 1971), indicating the importance of instructional set in the acquisition of autonomic self-control.

The successful conditioning of changes in skin temperature, without the concurrent use of autogenic phrases or hypnotic suggestions, is a finding of considerable interest. Nevertheless, the simultaneous use of feedback and response-specific instructions leaves the present study open to criticism. The failure to separate experimentally the effects of feedback and instructions leaves several important questions unanswered, e.g., can Ss given instructions to modify skin temperature do so in the absence of response-contingent feedback?, and can Ss who are uninformed that feedback or reinforcement is being provided for changes in skin temperature exert some degree of control over this response? Research designed to answer these questions is presently being conducted.

The additional finding that changes in differential skin temperature are related to changes of large magnitude in absolute temperature of the hand is also noteworthy. Reliability and generality of this finding must be established. In future experiments providing differential feedback on temperature, routine measurements of absolute temperature at each skin site should be made.

REFERENCES

BERGMAN, J. S., & JOHNSON, H. J. The effects of instructional set and autonomic perception on cardiac control. *Psychophysiology*, 1971, 8, 180-190.

CHRISTIE, D. J., & KOTSES, H. Bidirectional operant conditioning of the cephalic vasomotor response. *Journal of Psychosomatic Research*, 1973, 17, 167-170.

DAVIDSON, R., & KRIPPNER, S. Biofeedback research: the data and their implications. In J. Stoyva, T. X. Barber, L. V. DiCara, J. Kamiya, N. E. Miller, & D. Shapiro (Eds.), *Biofeedback and self-control, 1971: an Aldine annual on the regulation of bodily processes and consciousness.* Chicago: Aldine-Atherton, 1972. Pp. 3-34.

ENGEL, B. T., & CHISM, R. A. Operant conditioning of heart rate speeding. *Psychophysiology*, 1967, 3, 418-426.

McDONAGH, J. M., & McGINNIS, M. M. Skin temperature increases as a function of baseline temperature, autogenic suggestion, and biofeedback. Paper presented at annual meeting of the American Psychological Association, Montreal, 1973.

PEPER, E. Case report presented at the annual meeting of the Biofeedback Research Society, Boston, 1972.

PEPER, E., & GROSSMAN, E. Preliminary observations of thermal biofeedback in children with migraines. Paper presented at annual meeting of the Biofeedback Research Society, Colorado Springs, Colorado, 1974.

ROBERTS, A. H., KEWMAN, D. G., & MACDONALD, H. Voluntary control of skin temperature: unilateral changes using hypnosis and feedback. *Journal of Abnormal Psychology*, 1973, 82, 163-168.

SARGENT, J. D., GREEN, E. E., & WALTERS, E. D. Preliminary report on the use of autogenic feedback training in the treatment of migraine and tension headaches. *Psychosomatic Medicine*, 1973, 35, 129-135.

SCHWARTZ, G. E. Biofeedback as therapy: some theoretical and practical issues. *American Psychologist*, 1973, 28, 666-673.

SHAPIRO, D., TURSKY, B., & SCHWARTZ, G. E. Control of blood pressure in man by operant conditioning. *Circulation Research*, 1970, 27 (Supplement 1), 1-27 to 1-32.

STOLER, P. Exploring the frontiers of the mind. *Time*, 1974, 103(2), 50-59.

TAUB, E., & EMURIAN, C. E. Operant control of skin temperature. Paper presented at annual meeting of the Biofeedback Research Society, St. Louis, 1971.

TAUB, E., & EMURIAN, C. E. Self-regulation of skin temperature using a variable intensity light. Paper presented at annual meeting of the Biofeedback Research Society, Boston, 1972.

VII

CARDIOVASCULAR CONTROL

Role of Feedback in 32
Voluntary Control of Heart Rate

Stephen B. Manuck, Robert W. Levenson,
James J. Hinrichsen, and Steven L. Gryll

Summary.—The relative effectiveness of biofeedback techniques on the voluntary control of heart rate was examined by randomly assigning 32 Ss to one of four feedback conditions in a bi-directional heart-rate control task: (1) no feedback, (2) binary feedback—S was signaled when an interbeat interval had changed in the correct direction, (3) "real-time," proportional feedback—S was provided information about the relative duration of successive interbeat intervals, and (4) numerical, proportional feedback—each interbeat interval was represented as a numeral indicating its relationship to pre-trial mean by direction and magnitude. Significant over-all heart-rate changes were evidenced for both increase and decrease directions, but no differences were found between the feedback conditions. While these data suggest that feedback may be a relatively insignificant factor in voluntary heart-rate control, it was recommended that further investigation examine the role of feedback within the context of other training, mediating and motivational variables.

The accumulating literature relating to the ability of human Ss to attain voluntary control of heart rate attributes much of the obtained cardiac control to the employment of heart-rate feedback techniques. These feedback procedures, which signal S when he is changing his heart rate in the instructed direction, have been utilized in studies of heart-rate increases (Bergman & Johnson, 1972; Blanchard, Young, Scott, & Haynes, 1974; Engel & Chism, 1967) and decreases (Engel & Hansen; 1966), as well as investigations of bi-directional changes (Blanchard & Young, 1972; Blanchard, Young, & McLeod, 1972; Brener & Hothersall, 1966, 1967; Brener, Kleinman, & Goesling, 1969; Headrick, Feather, & Wells, 1971; Lang & Twentyman, 1974; Levene, Engel, & Pearson, 1968; Levenson & Strupp, 1972; Levenson, 1974; Ray, 1974; Ray & Lamb, 1974; Stephens, Harris, & Brady, 1972). In general, these investigators have found that with appropriate response contingent feedback, human Ss can readily attain some degree of control over their heart rates. A theoretical extension of this

Reprinted with permission of author and publisher from *Perceptual and Motor Skills*, 1975, Vol. 40, 747-752.

conclusion within an information-theory framework would predict that Ss will attain a greater magnitude of heart-rate change when greater amounts of relevant information (feedback) are provided (Brener, *et al.*, 1969). For example, Lang and Twentyman (1974) have reported that an analog or proportional feedback procedure is superior to simple binary feedback in the production of heart-rate increases.

However, as Bergman and Johnson (1971) point out, experimenters have generally assumed that any obtained heart-rate changes can be attributed to the feedback manipulations, thus ignoring the possibility that Ss could produce successful heart-rate control without feedback. Furthermore, these authors demonstrated significant increases and decreases when Ss were merely instructed to alter heart rate, suggesting that instructional sets, alone, can account for heart-rate changes. In a subsequent study, Bergman and Johnson (1972) found that heart-rate increases were no greater for Ss receiving feedback than for "no-feedback" controls. On the other hand, Blanchard and his associates (Blanchard & Young, 1972; Blanchard, *et al.*, 1974) and Ray (1974) have reported results indicating that feedback may facilitate heart-rate control, especially heart-rate increases, and in an investigation of bi-directional control, Brener, *et al.* (1969) concluded that increasing amounts of feedback produced greater heart-rate changes. Levenson and Strupp (1972), providing Ss with three levels of feedback (no feedback, heart-rate feedback, heart-rate plus respiration-rate feedback), found successful over-all heart-rate control but no significant differences between the three feedback conditions, implying that feedback had no significant effect on heart-rate control. This last result has recently been replicated under more protracted training conditions (Levenson, 1974). Thus, it appears that the current literature is ambiguous concerning the extent to which heart-rate changes in control tasks employing heart-rate contingent feedback can be attributed to the feedback procedures. Moreover, the diversity of feedback techniques, both in terms of modality, i.e., visual or auditory, and level of information, i.e., binary or proportional, further obscures the comparison of relevant studies.

The purpose of the present experiment was to investigate the role of feedback in voluntary heart-rate control by manipulating the level of information that Ss received as feedback. Accordingly, there were four feedback conditions: (1) no feedback, (2) binary feedback—S was signaled when an interbeat interval had changed in the instructed direction, (3) "real time," proportional feedback—S was provided information about the relative duration of successive interbeat intervals, and (4) numerical, proportional feedback—each interbeat interval was represented as a numeral indicating its relationship to pre-trial mean by direction and magnitude. Following Lang and Twentyman (1974), it was predicted that the "proportional" feedback procedures, which provide the greatest amount of information concerning heart-rate control, would yield larger heart-rate changes than the binary feedback condition. Likewise, it was predicted that the no-feedback condition would yield the smallest magnitude of heart-rate changes.

METHOD

Subjects

Ss (16 male, 16 female) were students in introductory psychology courses at Vanderbilt University. They received course credit for their participation.

Apparatus

Heart-rate data were recorded and analyzed on-line using a Grass Model 7 polygraph in conjunction with a Hewlett-Packard 2114A laboratory computer. In addition, the computer operated the three feedback displays: (1) For binary feedback, a signal light was illuminated whenever an interbeat interval deviated from pre-trial baseline mean by at least 30 msec. (2) For "real-time," proportional feedback, the first light of a string of 16 lights was illuminated 350 msec. after the onset of the first R-wave of a given trial. An additional light was illuminated every 60 msec. thereafter until the occurrence of the next R-wave, at which point the display blanked and the procedure started anew. In this manner the number of lights illuminated before blanking was proportional to the length of the interbeat interval. This system was previously utilized by Ray (1974). (3) For numerical, proportional feedback, a display of numerals "2" through "8" was operated such that "5" was equated with an interbeat interval within 30 msec. of the pre-trial baseline mean. Additional increases of 60 msec. in the interbeat interval were associated with successively lower numerals, while similar decreases caused successively higher numerals to light. Feedback of this nature (reported by Levenson & Strupp, 1972) provides S with information as to the directional and magnitudinal relationship between each interbeat interval and the baseline mean.

Procedure

Each S was scheduled for a 1-hr. session and was randomly assigned to one of the four conditions: (1) no feedback, (2) binary feedback, (3) "real-time," proportional feedback, and (4) numerical, proportional feedback. Following a ten-min. adaptation period, tape-recorded instructions were played corresponding to S's feedback condition. Specifically, Ss were told that they were to attempt to increase or decrease their heart rates, as indicated by the instruction light on the feedback-display panel, on successive trials. Between trials, they were simply to relax quietly. Ss were instructed to use "mental" means only in changing their heart rates, and cautioned against changing their respiration or muscle tension. There were 12 heart-rate control trials which each lasted for 100 interbeat intervals (six increase and six decrease trials in randomized order). During the control trials, Ss received feedback or no feedback consistent with their assigned conditions. Baselines of 40 interbeat intervals were taken preceding each heart-rate control trial.

RESULTS

Mean interbeat intervals were calculated for all baseline and heart-rate control periods for each S. These data were subjected to a $4 \times 2 \times 6 \times 2$ (Feedback Condition $\times$ Direction $\times$ Trials $\times$ Periods, i.e., baseline or control) analysis of variance.

The Direction $\times$ Periods interaction ($F_{1,28} = 47.67$, $p < .001$) indicated that Ss were able to produce significant heart-rate changes across feedback conditions and trials. Planned comparisons between baseline and control period means showed that the heart-rate changes were significant in both the increase [$t_{28} = 3.03$, $p < .005$; $M\Delta = -25$ msec. ($+2.6$ bpm)] and decrease [$t_{28} = 3.15$, $p < .005$; $M\Delta = +27$ msec. (-2.6 bpm)] directions. However, the Feedback Condition $\times$ Direction $\times$ Periods interaction was not significant ($F < 1.00$), indicating that the magnitude of the obtained heart-rate changes did not vary as a function of the type of feedback Ss received. Further, the lack of a significant Feedback Condition $\times$ Direction $\times$ Trials $\times$ Periods interaction indicated that Ss in no group produced heart-rate changes of increasing magnitude as the experimental session progressed.

In order to investigate the consistency with which heart-rate changes were produced, the number of "correct" interbeat intervals (defined as a change, in the instructed direction, of at least 30 msec.) per trial were subjected to a $4 \times 2 \times 6$ (Feedback Condition $\times$ Direction $\times$ Trials) analysis of variance. No significant main effects or interactions were obtained, indicating that neither type of feedback nor length of training had an effect on the consistency with which Ss produced heart-rate changes.

Although Ss were not balanced by sex across feedback conditions, a separate analysis showed no over-all sex-related differences in the magnitude of heart-rate control in either the increase or decrease direction.

DISCUSSION

The present findings, while demonstrating significant bi-directional heart-rate changes, do not support the hypothesis that feedback facilitates voluntary heart-rate control. Neither the predicted rank order of feedback conditions nor the general hypothesis that feedback groups would produce greater heart-rate control than Ss receiving no feedback, received support from this investigation.[1] Thus, it may be speculated that the case for feedback assisted heart-rate control has been somewhat overstated in the recent literature. The interpretation and generalizability of these results, however, must be tempered by a number of methodological considerations.

Sample Size

With a between-Ss design, as in the present study, a considerably larger sample size may be necessary to detect small differences in magnitude between

---

[1] It might be argued that Ss in the no-feedback condition did receive some feedback of a covert nature via heart palpitations or pulsations in some part of the body. As feedback, however, this type of information would prove rather insensitive since Ss would need to discriminate very small differences between successive interbeat intervals. In addition, Ss in the present study did not report the presence or use of such "covert" feedback, although this possibility remains an unexplored hypothesis.

feedback and no-feedback conditions. Of course, if very large numbers of Ss are required to demonstrate a minimal effect of feedback, this too would tend to indicate the relative weakness of manipulations.

Length of Training

Effects of feedback may not become manifest in the initial stages of training, but require more extended practice, as suggested by Headrick, et al. (1971). Even though the extent of feedback-training in the present study was sufficient to show significant heart-rate changes, the typical single session design may simply be too short to provide an adequate test of the effects of feedback. This conclusion is supported by the fact that significant effects of feedback have usually been reported only in studies involving more than one experimental session (Blanchard & Young, 1972; Blanchard, et al., 1974; Brener, et al., 1969).

Concomitant Somatic Responses

While the question of respiratory or skeletal mediation of heart-rate control remains unresolved in the literature (Blanchard & Young, 1973), a consideration of this issue suggests a possible interaction between the effects of feedback and mediators, such that muscular and respiratory changes may be prepotent over feedback contingencies when somatic variables are not controlled. Reciprocally, feedback may contribute significantly to heart-rate changes only when the potential effects of the mediators have been minimized or eliminated.

Motivational Variables

A seldom studied factor within the heart-rate control paradigm involves motivational constraints and incentives operating on Ss. With respect to the present investigation, highly motivated Ss, e.g., those receiving performance-contingent monetary rewards, might have made greater use of the feedback than our Ss, who received course credit for their participation.

In summary, the foregoing results indicate the heart-rate-contingent feedback is not a necessary condition for voluntary heart-rate control. While these data also suggest that feedback may not facilitate heart-rate changes, either, it was argued that some effects of feedback might be demonstrated under conditions of increased sample size, protracted training, effective somatic restraint, or heightened motivation of Ss.

REFERENCES

BERGMAN, J. S., & JOHNSON, H. J. The effects of instructional set and autonomic perception on cardiac control. *Psychophysiology*, 1971, 8, 180-190.

BERGMAN, J. S., & JOHNSON, H. J. Sources of information which affect training and raising of heart rate. *Psychophysiology*, 1972, 9, 30-39.

BLANCHARD, E. B., & YOUNG, L. D. Relative efficiency of visual and auditory feedback for self-control of heart rate. *Journal of General Psychology*, 1972, 87, 195-202.

BLANCHARD, E. B., & YOUNG, L. D. Self-control of cardiac functioning: a promise as yet unfulfilled. *Psychological Bulletin*, 1973, 79, 145-163.

BLANCHARD, E. B., YOUNG, L. D., & MCLEOD, P. G. Awareness of heart activity and self-control of heart rate. *Psychophysiology*, 1972, 9, 63-68.

BLANCHARD, E. B., YOUNG, L. D., SCOTT, R. W., & HAYNES, M. R.   Differential effects of feedback and reinforcement in voluntary acceleration of human heart rate.   *Perceptual and Motor Skills*, 1974, 38, 683-691.

BRENER, J., & HOTHERSALL, D. Heart rate control under conditions of augmented sensory feedback. *Psychophysiology*, 1966, 3, 23-28.

BRENER, J., & HOTHERSALL, D. Paced respiration and heart rate control. *Psychophysiology*, 1967, 4, 1-6.

BRENER, J., KLEINMAN, R. A., & GOESLING, W. J. The effects of different exposures to augmented sensory feedback on the control of heart rate. *Psychophysiology*, 1969, 5, 510-516.

ENGEL, B. T., & CHISM, R. A. Operant conditioning of heart rate speeding. *Psychophysiology*, 1967, 4, 418-426.

ENGEL, B. T., & HANSEN, S. P. Operant conditioning of heart rate slowing. *Psychophysiology*, 1966, 3, 176-187.

HEADRICK, M. W., FEATHER, B. W., & WELLS, D. T. Unidirectional and large magnitude heart-rate changes with augmented sensory feedback. *Psychophysiology*, 1971, 8, 132-142.

LANG, P. J., & TWENTYMAN, C. T. Learning to control heart rate; binary vs analog feedback. *Psychophysiology*, 1974, 11, 616-629.

LEVENE, H. I., ENGEL, B. T., & PEARSON, J. A. Differential operant conditioning of heart rate. *Psychosomatic Medicine*, 1968, 30, 837-845.

LEVENSON, R. W. Simultaneous heart rate and respiration rate feedback and the relationship of tidal volume to heart rate control. Unpublished doctoral dissertation, Vanderbilt Univer., 1974.

LEVENSON, R. W., & STRUPP, H. H. Simultaneous feedback and control of heart rate and respiration rate. Presented at the Twelfth Annual Meeting of the Society for Psychophysiological Research, November, 1972.

RAY, W. J. The relationship of locus of control, self-report measures, and feedback to the voluntary control of heart rate. *Psychophysiology*, 1974, 11, 527-534.

RAY, W. J., & LAMB, S. B. Locus of control and the voluntary control of heart rate. *Psychosomatic Medicine*, 1974, 36, 180-182.

STEPHENS, J. H., HARRIS, A. H., & BRADY, J. V. Large magnitude heart rate changes in subjects instructed to change their heart rate and given exteroceptive feedback. *Psychophysiology*, 1972, 9, 283-285.

Psychological and 33 Physiological Variables Associated with Large Magnitude Voluntary Heart Rate Changes

Joseph H. Stephens, Alan H. Harris, Joseph V. Brady, and John W. Shaffer

ABSTRACT

Forty subjects, given binary and proportional auditory and visual feedback and asked to raise and lower their heart rate on signal, were able to produce increases of up to 46 bpm and decreases of up to 14 bpm, with a mean increase over 5 experimental days of 11 bpm and a decrease of 3 bpm. Increases in both diastolic and systolic blood pressure and increases in skin potential level and number of skin potential responses accompanied voluntary increases in heart rate but not decreases. Subjects with the highest resting heart rate variability and skin potential level were best able to raise their heart rate. Subjects with the highest resting heart rate and highest resting heart rate variability were best able to decrease their heart rate. Subjects with high Ego Strength scores (or low Welsh's Factor A scores) on the MMPI were best able to control their heart rate. The Ego Strength score, resting heart rate, and resting heart rate variability were all significantly intercorrelated. Subjects showed marked individual differences in ability to control heart rate, although there was a significant correlation between ability to raise and ability to lower heart rate.

DESCRIPTORS: Voluntary control, Heart rate, Exteroceptive feedback, Blood pressure, Skin potential, MMPI. (J. H. Stephens)

Blanchard and Young (1973) have reviewed the studies demonstrating changes in human heart rate (HR) obtained by means of feedback and/or reinforcement and have noted that only three studies involving a total of 8 subjects report large magnitude changes of 15 bpm or more. Since this review, Wells (1973) has reported large magnitude HR changes in 6 subjects.

Included in Blanchard and Young's review is our study (Stephens, Harris, & Brady, 1972) in which we reported on 4 subjects who were able to produce large magnitude HR change consequent to a feedback procedure. The procedure employed, however, varied somewhat with each of the 4 subjects. In the present paper we report on 40 subjects, all of whom attempted to raise and lower their HR under a standardized procedure. In addition to describing this procedure which enabled 18 of the 40 subjects to raise their HR an average of more than 10 bpm and 12 subjects to lower their HR an average of more than 4 bpm, we wish to report for this group correlations among 1) ability to raise and lower HR; 2) HR variability; 3) psychological test scores (MMPI); and 4) concomitant blood pressure and skin potential measurements.

Method

Subjects

Eleven female and 29 male subjects ranging in age from 19 to 33 yrs participated in the experiment. Subjects were either university students or hospital personnel. They were recruited through a notice on a university bulletin board and through personal contacts of the experimenters. None of the subjects had any medical disorder, and none was taking medication at the time of the experiment.

Apparatus

Subjects were tested in a reclining position facing a feedback display in a sound attenuated room. All physio-

This research was supported by the Office of Naval Research, Sub-contract No. N0014-70-C-0350.

Address requests for reprints to: Joseph H. Stephens, M.D., The Johns Hopkins Hospital, Baltimore, Maryland 21205.

logical variables were recorded on a Beckman-Offner dynograph in an adjoining room.

Heart beat was detected from electrodes placed on the right arm and left leg. The amplified signal from these electrodes was used to trigger a Beckman Cardiotachometer coupler (Model 9857) and a Schmitt trigger which activated a series of digital counters recording the actual number of beats during different experimental periods. The output signal from the cardiotach channel, which produced a beat-by-beat analog projection of HR, was used to provide discrete feedback of HR to both the subject and the experimenter. The cardiotach signal directed to the experimenter was displayed on a Simpson meter relay (Model 3324). The scale of the metered relay was modified and calibrated to represent 40 bpm at zero deflection and 160 bpm at full-scale deflection. Two adjustable limit pointers contained within the front scale of the metered relay provided variable criterion level controls for both HR raising and lowering procedures. The cardiotach signal provided as feedback to the subject was displayed on a large 20.3 cm illuminated Simpson panel meter (Model 728T). The scale of the subject's feedback meter was also modified and calibrated to represent 40 bpm at zero deflection and 160 bpm at full-scale deflection. A pulsated audio tone synchronized to vary in rate and pitch as a function of the instantaneous HR (increased HR producing a higher pitch and pulsation rate) provided a discrete audible beat-by-beat feedback to the subject. Mounted on a panel directly above the subject's HR feedback meter was an illuminated 3-digit numerical display unit which corresponded to the calibrated criterion setting of the experimenter's adjustable meter pointer. A second panel mounted adjacent to the subject's HR meter provided for the presentation of two different light signals to indicate when program requirements for raising (red) or lowering (green) HR were in effect. In addition, a third light (amber) on the panel was illuminated whenever, and as long as, the subject attained or exceeded the required HR change criterion. A digital display counter on the panel also registered counts (1/sec) corresponding to monetary rewards (½ cent per count) whenever the amber light was illuminated.

Intermittent measurements of blood pressure (BP) were obtained using an automatic cuff and a Roche Arteriosonde approximately every 2 min.

Respiration was measured using a strain gauge tube around the chest.

Skin potential level (SPL) was recorded on one channel of the dynograph through a DC coupled pre-amplifier with a low gain (10 mV/cm). Skin potential responses (SPR) were recorded on a second channel which was AC coupled (3 sec time constant) with a gain of 1 mV/cm. Silver-silver chloride electrodes developed by Ó'Connell and Tursky (1960), were used with Redux electrode jelly. The active electrode was placed on the thenar eminence of the left palm and the reference electrode about 20 cm distant on the dorsal aspect of the left forearm.

Procedure

All subjects participated in 5 weekly experimental sessions lasting 95 min each. Prior to beginning the first session, each subject was interviewed, a medical history was obtained, and the study was explained to the subject in detail. In addition, all subjects completed the MMPI (Dahlstrom & Welsh, 1960) and the 16 Personality Factor Questionnaire (16 PF) (Cattell & Eber, 1957) prior to the first session.

All 5 experimental sessions began with a 15-min baseline period and concluded with a 4-min post-experimental period. Physiological measurements were recorded during the baseline period but not during the 10-min adaptation period which preceded it. Between the baseline and post periods there were 15 periods consisting of: 1) 4 periods during which the red light was on and

during which the subject was instructed to raise his HR; 2) 4 periods during which the green light was on and during which the subject was instructed to decrease his HR; and 3) 7 interval periods separating the raising and lowering periods. Each period of raising was 4 min long and each period of lowering was 8 min long. Interval periods were 4 min long.

The 15-min baseline period served to provide HR averages used in determining criterion values for subsequent "raising" and "lowering" periods during that particular experimental session, increments of 5 to 10 bpm (individually adjusted for each subject) being used in training the "raising" performance and 3 to 5 bpm for establishing "lowering."

After the baseline period, it was determined randomly whether the next period would be a raising or lowering one. Raising and lowering periods were separated by a resting interval and presented according to a random schedule, with never more than 2 of the same in succession. During all experimental sessions, subjects were asked to raise their HR above the criterion number whenever the red light was displayed. When the green light was displayed, subjects were instructed to lower their HR below the criterion number. All subjects were instructed to breathe as normally as possible and to avoid muscle tension or movement during the study. Parts of the procedure are modifications of the one described by Engel and Chism (1967).

During the first experimental day, no feedback was provided and subjects were simply asked to raise or lower their HR when the appropriate signal light was on by "purely mental means without changes in breathing or muscle tension." Furthermore, a flat rate of $7.00 was paid to each subject and there was no additional reward for performance.

On Experimental Day 2, both the meter registering varying HR and the variable tone were presented as proportional feedback. Again, a flat rate of $7.00 was paid and there was no contingency payment, since the amber contingency light was not in operation.

On Experimental Day 3, the amber contingency light was in operation but a flat rate of pay was still in effect. The experimental subject was thus getting no feedback during Experimental Day 1, proportional feedback during Experimental Day 2, and both proportional and binary feedback on Experimental Day 3. The rate of pay during these 3 experimental days was a flat rate, however.

Experimental Days 4 and 5 were identical. They differed from Day 3 only in the fact that the pay was now according to the binary contingency with a guaranteed minimum of $5.00 per session but with the opportunity to increase this amount by being paid ½ cent per sec during the time when the amber light was illuminated. As noted above, the amber light was illuminated during the period when the subject met the criterion as set by the experimenter.

Data Reduction and Analysis

Heart Rate. The cardiotachometer HR was used only for feedback to the subject and for observation by the experimenter during the experiment. Actual HR during each of the various periods, i.e., base, intervals, post, attempted raising, and attempted lowering, was determined from the exact number of beats recorded on the digital counters. HR variability was determined during the 15 min base period at the beginning of each experimental day during which time a count was made of the number of bpm within each 60 sec interval, and the standard deviation of the 15 readings was taken as a measurement of HR variability.

Blood Pressure. All results concerning blood pressure (BP) are based on mean BP readings for the attempted raising periods, the attempted lowering periods, and the

TABLE 1

Mean HR changes of 40 subjects

Days	Base-Interval-Post	Mean HR Changes			
		Change During Attempted Raising	Change During Attempted Lowering	Range During Attempted Raising[a]	Range During Attempted Lowering[a]
1	67.7	+ 6.3	−1.7	− 9 to +29	−12 to +3
2	70.5	+ 9.5	−2.2	−10 to +46	−14 to +2
3	70.6	+12.3	−3.1	− 1 to +37	−11 to +4
4	71.1	+12.7	−2.4	− 1 to +37	− 9 to +4
5	72.5	+13.2	−3.4	− 1 to +47	−14 to +2
Mean of 3, 4, and 5	71.4	+12.7	−3.0	0.0 to +38.3	−8.7 to +2.3
Mean of 1–5	70.5	+10.8	−2.6	−0.4 to +35.2	−8.2 to +2.2

[a]HR in individual subjects recorded only as whole numbers.

base-interval-post (BIP) periods averaged over the last 3 Experimental Days.

Skin Potential. The skin potential (SP) data were analyzed according to the procedure described by Fowles, Watt, Maher, & Grinspoon (1970). The sampling rate for estimation of the slowly changing skin potential level (SPL) was adjusted in accordance with the variability of the record. For the assessment of skin potential responses (SPR), the entire record was inspected and the actual number of responses during any critical period was determined. The criterion for a response was a maximum to minimum difference of 0.3 mV. No attempt was made to exclude responses to the stimuli, i.e., signal lights, during the task. Consequently, the responses during the task may have been spontaneous or in response to the task itself. The unit of SPR was the number of responses/min.

Statistical Analysis. All correlations given in Tables 3 through 5 are based on means of data from Experimental Days 3, 4, and 5. Means and standard deviations for all data were obtained and are available upon request together with the master correlation matrix. Differences between means were tested for significance using the correlated *t* test. The .05 level of statistical significance was adopted.

Results

Heart Rate and Heart Rate Variability

The mean of the base, interval, and post (BIP) periods served as the reference point from which all change scores were calculated. Table 1 shows that during Day 1 when there was no feedback, subjects were nevertheless able to raise their HR an average of 6 bpm and lower their HR nearly 2 bpm. The ability to change HR is seen to increase with experience and an increasing amount of feedback. However, there is little difference between Days 4 and 5 and most of the learning appears to have taken place by Day 3. For this reason, most of our correlations were computed on data which represent mean HR for Days 3, 4, and 5.

It should be noted in Table 1 that HR changes during the attempt to raise range from decreases of 10 bpm to increases of 47 bpm. During the attempt to lower, the changes are less, ranging from a decrease of 14 bpm to an increase of 4 bpm. Throughout this paper all decreases in HR, BP, and SP from the reference BIP are given a negative sign

and this must be taken into account when considering the sign of correlation coefficients.

TABLE 2

Mean HR during days 3, 4, and 5

Subjects	Mean HRs		
	Base-Interval-Post	Change During Attempted Raising	Change During Attempted Lowering
1	51.3	0.0	−1.3
2	72.3	0.0	−6.3
3	86.0	0.3	−1.0
4	74.0	1.7	−0.7
5	80.0	2.7	−2.3
6	66.3	3.0	+0.3
7	70.0	4.0	−2.0
8	68.7	5.0	−4.7
9	80.3	6.3	−3.3
10	73.0	6.7	−1.7
11	67.0	6.7	−2.3
12	91.0	7.0	−5.0
13	68.7	7.3	−2.7
14	60.0	8.0	−1.7
15	67.7	8.0	−1.3
16	55.0	8.7	−0.7
17	76.0	8.7	−3.7
18	62.7	9.0	−3.7
19	77.3	9.0	−2.3
20	56.0	9.3	−1.3
21	70.0	9.7	−2.7
22	74.0	10.0	−2.3
23	68.0	10.3	+1.0
24	81.6	10.3	−1.7
25	61.0	10.7	−4.3
26	64.3	11.7	−1.7
27	63.7	12.0	−1.7
28	62.0	12.0	−4.7
29	84.7	13.0	−8.7
30	67.3	15.3	−7.3
31	71.3	19.7	−2.0
32	70.0	21.0	−5.3
33	67.3	26.0	+2.3
34	78.3	26.7	−5.0
35	75.0	28.0	−3.3
36	80.0	28.3	−3.3
37	96.3	29.7	−7.3
38	70.7	31.7	−6.7
39	82.0	33.3	−4.0
40	68.7	38.3	−3.7

TABLE 3

Correlations between mean HR changes on days 3, 4, and 5 and psychological test scores on 40 subjects

Variables	Correlations				
	MMPI A	HR Variability	HR BIP	HR Change During Attempted Raising	HR Change During Attempted Lowering
MMPI Es	−.77*	.46*	.42*	.32*	−.32*
MMPI A		−.36*	−.25	−.44*	.31*
HR Variability			.44*	.52*	−.55*
HR BIP				.23	−.38*

*p<.05.

Table 2 gives individual HR changes averaged over Days 3, 4, and 5 for each of the 40 subjects arranged in order of increasing ability to raise HR. Subjects were highly consistent in their ability to raise or lower their HR. HR changes during attempted raising on each of the 5 days are highly intercorrelated with the values of r ranging from .53 to .94. Thus, ability to raise the HR on Experimental Day 1 is predictive of ability to raise the HR on the other 4 days. The correlations between HR changes during attempts at raising on Days 3, 4, and 5 have values of r ranging from .86 to .94 which further lends support to our general decision to consider the data of Days 3, 4, and 5 together.

By contrast with attempted raising, HR changes during attempts at lowering on each of the 5 days are less highly correlated and have values of r ranging from .44 to .68. Unlike HR raising, HR changes during attempted lowering on Days 1 and 2 do not accurately predict success at lowering on Days 3, 4, and 5.

The mean base; interval, and post (BIP) HRs during Day 1 and Day 2 are not correlated with any ability to raise or lower HR. However, the mean BIP HR for Days 3, 4, and 5 is positively correlated with an ability to lower HR with an $r = -.38$. (See Table 3. As noted above the negative r represents a positive correlation since HR lowering has a minus sign.) Thus subjects with the highest BIP HR are most able to lower their HR. On the other hand, the ability to raise HR is not in any way related to resting levels of HR. Lest it be thought that some subjects may have learned to increase their HR during BIP in order to increase the criterion level and thus make it easier to decrease HR during lowering periods, the correlation between the slope (trend) of the individual subjects' mean BIP HR on the 5 experimental days and the HR change during attempted lowering on Day 5 was computed. This correlation was found to be −.21 which is not significant. Ability to raise and lower HR are *positively* correlated with $r = -.31$ (see Table 4). Thus subjects able to raise their HR are also the ones most likely to be able to lower their HR.

HR variability measured during the 15-min base period during each experimental day is significantly correlated with both ability to lower and raise HR on that day. The correlation between mean HR variability on Days 3, 4, and 5 and the mean HR change during attempted raising on Days 3, 4, and 5 has an r of .52. The correlation between mean HR variability on Days 3, 4, and 5 and the mean HR change during attempted lowering on Days 3, 4, and 5 has an r of −.55. Thus subjects with the greatest HR variability are those most likely to be able to raise or lower their HR (see Table 3). The positive correla-

TABLE 4

Correlations between mean HR changes and blood pressure changes on days 3, 4, and 5

Variables	Correlations				
	Change During Attempted Raising		Change During Attempted Lowering		
	Diastolic BP	HR	Systolic BP	Diastolic BP	HR
Change During Attempted Raising					
Systolic BP	.82*	.74*	.01	.26	−.16
Diastolic BP		.79*	.05	.35*	−.15
HR			−.08	.03	−.31*
Change During Attempted Lowering					
Systolic BP				.33*	.05
Diastolic BP					.13

*p<.05

tion between HR variability and HR during the BIP period with $r = -.44$ should also be noted.

The Relationship between Heart Rate Changes and Psychological Test Scores

In addition to the standard scales on the MMPI, we also scored this inventory for Welsh's Factor A (Dahlstrom & Welsh, 1960), and Barron's Ego Strength (Es) Scale (Barron, 1956). Welsh's Factor A reflects the largest component of common variance among the basic scales in the MMPI profile and is strongly related to numerous indices of anxiety. The Es Scale has been described as the MMPI scale most consistently related to physiological variables (Roessler, 1973). Welsh's Factor A and the Es Scale are probably measuring a unitary factor in our subjects which is also tapped by Scale Q4 of Cattell's 16 PF. However, although scores on the Es Scale and Factor A are highly correlated ($r = -.77$) in our subjects, Swenson, Pearson, and Osborn (1973) report the r to be only $-.23$ in 50,000 medical patients.

Table 3 demonstrates a correlation between Barron's Es Scale, Welsh's Factor A, and changes in both raising and lowering HR. Thus subjects with the highest ego strength scores and/or lowest anxiety scores are those most likely to be able to raise and lower their HR. Also to be noted is the correlation between HR variability and Barron's Es Scale and Welsh's Factor A. Although not tabulated, Cattell's Factor Q4 is also correlated ($r = -.44$; $p < .05$) with HR change in the same direction as Welsh's Factor A. Contrary to expectations, the Es Scale is positively correlated with HR during the BIP period as it is with HR variability. None of the other scales on the MMPI or 16 PF were significantly correlated with the physiological data.

The Relationship between Heart Rate and Blood Pressure Changes

Table 4 demonstrates a high correlation between changes in blood pressure (BP) and changes in HR during attempted raising. An increase in HR during the period of attempted raising is accompanied by a statistically significant increase in both the systolic and diastolic BP. There is, however, no significant correlation between BP and HR changes during the period of attempted lowering. It was also found that there was a significant positive correlation between mean HR variability and changes in systolic and diastolic BP during attempted raising with r values of .46 and .50 respectively. The mean change in systolic BP during periods of attempted raising HR was $+5.9$ mm, whereas the mean change in diastolic BP during the same period was $+7.4$ mm. Changes in systolic BP during this period ranged from -5 mm to $+26$ mm with changes in diastolic BP ranging from -5 to $+35$ mm. During the period of attempted lowering HR there were mean systolic and diastolic BP increases of approximately 1 mm but these were not statistically significant. During the period of attempted raising HR, the mean systolic BP change correlated with the Es Scale at $r = .34$ and with Welsh's Factor A Scale at $r = .46$. There were no other correlations between the psychological test scales and BP measures. BP readings during the BIP period were not correlated with any other measurements.

Skin Potential and Heart Rate Relationships

Table 5 demonstrates that changes in HR during attempts at raising are positively correlated with basal skin potential levels (SPL) during the BIP period, and with changes in SPL during the raising period, as well as with changes in the number of

TABLE 5
Correlations between mean skin potential and HR changes on days 3, 4, and 5

Variables	Change During Attempted Raising		Change During Attempted Lowering			Base-Interval-Post	
	SPR	HR	SPL	SPR	HR	SPL	SPR
Change During Attempted Raising							
SPL	.42*	.52*	.36*	.33*	−.05	−.02	.13
SPR		.52*	.02	.45*	−.12	.06	.09
HR			.05	.06	−.31*	.38*	.21
Change During Attempted Lowering							
SPL				.44*	.08	.09	.11
SPR					.24	−.22	.28
HR						−.18	−.19
Base-Interval-Post							
SPL							.39*

*$p < .05$

skin potential responses (SPR) per min during the raising period. During the BIP period the mean SPL was 16.3 mV which significantly increased by 3.2 mV during the attempted raising period. During attempted lowering it increased 0.9 mV which was not statistically significant. During attempted raising of HR the SPR increased by 163 percent. There were no significant correlations between these SP measurements and HR measurements during attempted lowering or during the BIP period. In both the attempted raising and lowering periods SPL and SPR changes were correlated positively as were SPL and SPR in the BIP period. Changes in SPL during attempted raising were correlated with changes in SPL during attempted lowering. This was also true for changes in SPR. Thus subjects whose SP level or response changed during attempted raising of HR were also likely to show similar changes when attempting to lower HR. There were no significant correlations between psychological test scores and any of the SP data. Both SPL and SPR during attempted HR raising were correlated with changes in diastolic BP during the same period with significant r values of .44 and .39 respectively. There were no other significant correlations between SP data and BP data. There was also no significant correlation between HR variability and SP data.

Respiration

The respiration tracing was inspected for all 200 experimental sessions, and both rate and amplitude were considered. The data were not quantified because of frequently inadequate tracings and no computer analysis of the data on respiration was performed. However, we were unable to detect any discernible pattern relating respiration to HR changes. Nevertheless, future studies similar to ours should quantify both respiration and EMG for more detailed analysis.

Discussion

Although our study was primarily an attempt to produce large magnitude voluntary HR changes, concomitant measurement of BP, SP, HR variability, and MMPI and 16 PF scores revealed significant correlations, the most important of which are listed as follows:

1. Ability to raise HR is positively correlated with ability to lower HR.
2. Ability to raise HR is correlated negatively with Welsh's Factor A Scale and positively with Barron's Es Scale, resting HR variability, and resting SP level.
3. The ability to lower HR is correlated negatively with Welsh's Factor A Scale, and positively with Barron's Es Scale, resting HR, and HR variability.
4. Increases in HR on demand are accompanied by increases in systolic and diastolic BP and increases in SPL and number of SPRs. There are,

however, no significant BP or SP changes with attempted lowering of HR.
5. Resting HR, resting HR variability, and Barron's Es Scale are all positively correlated.
6. Welsh's Factor A Scale is inversely correlated with resting HR variability although not significantly correlated with resting HR or any SP measurements.

The results of our study confirm the findings of Roessler, Alexander, and Greenfield (1963) who reported that subjects with high ego strength scores as measured by the MMPI showed a trend toward greater physiological responsiveness in HR. Roessler (1973) has also demonstrated high Es Scale subjects to be generally more physiologically responsive even when the effects of trait anxiety are controlled. Our results also are comparable to those of Dykman, Ackerman, Galbrecht, and Reese (1963) who reported that students high on anxiety measures were less reactive in HR than those lower on anxiety measures. Also supported is the finding of Wilson and Dykman (1960) that HR variability is inversely related to anxiety as measured by the MMPI. Our results are in agreement with those reported by Zuckerman, Persky, and Curtis (1968) who found that rated anxiety in patients and controls was not significantly correlated with resting HR or BP. Our results are also in agreement with Stern and Janes (1973) who, in their review of the literature, found that the bulk of evidence indicated no correlation between anxiety levels and either spontaneous activity or basal electrodermal levels. The lack of a significant correlation between changes in SPL or SPR and resting SPL indicates that changes in SP during our experimental sessions were not a function of initial or basal values. This finding is in agreement with that reported by Shapiro and Leiderman (1964).

Most investigators who have studied voluntary control of HR have not also measured BP. However, 25 years ago, Ogden and Shock (1939) described 2 subjects who were able to raise their HR at will. As in our study, the increase was accompanied by an increase in both diastolic and systolic BP.

Shapiro, Schwartz, and Tursky (1972) have, more than any other investigators, studied the interrelationship between HR and BP when either or both are controlled by feedback and reinforcement (see Schwartz, 1972). They have also developed a method for determining BP on each heart cycle and have been able to control BP without changes in HR, and HR without changes in BP, by concurrently placing feedback contingencies on both HR and BP. Nevertheless, our study, which placed feedback contingencies only on HR, does not show a significantly higher correlation between changes in HR and diastolic BP than between changes in HR and systolic BP as reported by Shapiro et al.

Our finding that subjects with a greater HR

variability during the BIP period were better able to increase and decrease HR, like other work in the general area of operant conditioning, suggests that it is easier to increase the frequency of a response already present than to produce a new response.

The finding that increased HR was positively correlated with increased SPL, number of SPRs, and increased systolic and diastolic BP suggests that a generalized activation of the sympathetic nervous system is occurring.

Most significant of all, our data demonstrate under conditions of proportional and binary feedback with monetary contingent reinforcement, many volunteers are able to alter their HR significantly although there are very marked variations in this ability across subjects. This ability also appears correlated with individual differences in psychological and physiological variables. It would seem useful, where possible, for other investigators to measure these variables concomitantly with HR in future biofeedback studies.

REFERENCES

Barron, F. An ego strength scale which predicts response to psychotherapy. In W. G. Dahlstrom & G. S. Welsh (Eds.), *Basic readings on the MMPI in psychology and medicine.* Minneapolis: The University of Minn. Press, 1956. Pp. 226–234.

Blanchard, E. B., & Young, L. D. Self-control of cardiac functioning: A promise as yet unfulfilled. *Psychological Bulletin,* 1973, *79,* 145–163.

Cattell, R. B., & Eber, H. W. *Handbook for the Sixteen Personality Factor Questionnaire.* Champaign, Ill.: Institute for Personality and Ability Testing, 1957.

Dahlstrom, W. G., & Welsh, G. S. *An MMPI Handbook.* Minneapolis: The University of Minn. Press, 1960.

Dykman, R. A., Ackerman, P. T., Galbrecht, C. R., & Reese, W. G. Physiological reactivity to different stressors and methods of evaluation. *Psychosomatic Medicine,* 1963, *25,* 37–59.

Engel, B. T., & Chism, R. A. Operant conditioning of heart rate speeding. *Psychophysiology,* 1967, *3,* 418–426.

Fowles, D. C., Watt, N. R., Maher, B. A., & Grinspoon, L. Autonomic arousal in good and poor premorbid schizophrenics. *British Journal of Social & Clinical Psychology,* 1970, *9,* 135–147.

Ogden, E., & Shock, N. W. Voluntary hypercirculation. *American Journal of Medical Science,* 1939, *198,* 329–342.

O'Connell, D. N., & Tursky, B. Silver-silver chloride sponge electrodes for skin potential recording. *American Journal of Psychology,* 1960, *73,* 302–304.

Roessler, R., Alexander, A. A., & Greenfield, N. S. Ego strength and physiological responsivity. *Archives of General Psychiatry,* 1963, *8,* 142–154.

Roessler, R. Personality, physiology, and performance. *Psychophysiology,* 1973, *10,* 315–327.

Schwartz, G. E. Voluntary control of human cardiovascular integration and differentiation through feedback and reward. *Science,* 1972, *175,* 90–93.

Shapiro, D., & Leiderman, P. H. Studies on the galvanic skin potential level: Some statistical properties. *Journal of Psychosomatic Research,* 1964, *7,* 269–275.

Shapiro, D., Schwartz, G. E., & Tursky, B. Control of diastolic blood pressure in man by feedback and reinforcement. *Psychophysiology,* 1972, *9,* 256–304.

Stephens, J. H., Harris, A. H., & Brady, J. V. Large magnitude heart rate changes in subjects instructed to change their heart rates and given exteroceptive feedback. *Psychophysiology,* 1972, *9,* 283–285.

Stern, J. A., & Janes, C. L. Personality and psychopathology. In W. F. Prokasy & D. C. Raskin (Eds.), *Electrodermal activity in psychological research.* New York: Academic Press, 1973.

Swenson, W. M., Pearson, J. S., & Osborn, D. *An MMPI source book: Basic item, scale and pattern data on 50,000 medical patients.* Minneapolis: The University of Minn. Press, 1973.

Wells, D. T. Large magnitude voluntary heart rate changes. *Psychophysiology,* 1973, *10,* 260–269.

Wilson, J. W., & Dykman, R. A. Background autonomic activity in medical students. *Journal of Comparative & Physiological Psychology,* 1960, *63,* 405–411.

Zuckerman, M., Persky, H., & Curtis, G. G. Relationships among anxiety, depression, hostility, and autonomic variables. *The Journal of Nervous & Mental Disease,* 1968, *146,* 481–487.

Voluntary Control and Reactivity of Human Heart Rate

34

Iris R. Bell and Gary E. Schwartz

ABSTRACT

Factors in human voluntary heart rate control with and without external feedback were studied. Average voluntary heart rate control in the laboratory was comparable to the range of heart rates obtained during accelerative-decelerative 'reactivity' tasks in the laboratory and to heart rates obtained during various situations outside of the laboratory. However, cardiac rate reactivity did not reliably predict voluntary control performance across subjects (Ss). With full instructions, Ss were able to increase but not decrease heart rate relative to resting levels before feedback was provided. With full-scale meter feedback, Ss could both increase and decrease heart rate relative to resting levels. Performance in bidirectional control during feedback remained constant. The ability both to increase and to decrease heart rate transferred to the postfeedback, no-meter condition. Reversing the meaning of the Up and Down cue lights during postfeedback for half of the Ss had no deleterious effect on bidirectional heart rate control. The importance of physiological and situational constraints in bidirectional heart rate control is discussed.

DESCRIPTORS: Heart rate, Bidirectional voluntary control, Reactivity, Out-of-lab pulse rates, Feedback, Instructions, Biological constraints, Patterning.

Previous research has demonstrated that when human subjects are given external feedback and reward for heart rate changes, they can learn to either stabilize (Hnatiow & Lang, 1965; Lang, Stroufe, & Hastings, 1967), increase (Engel & Chism, 1967), or decrease (Engel & Hansen, 1966) their heart rate. Operant bidirectional heart rate control within the same subject has also been reported (Brener & Hothersall, 1966, 1967; Brener, Klein-

man, & Goesling, 1969; Levene, Engel, & Pearson, 1968). However, individual and situational variables affecting bidirectional heart rate control have received little systematic attention.

The study of sources of individual differences in voluntary heart rate control has begun with investigation of the effects of subjective variables such as awareness of cardiac and general autonomic reactivity (Blanchard,

This research was supported by grants to G.E. Schwartz from the Milton Fund and the Spencer Fund of Harvard University, in part by the Advanced Research Projects Agency of the Department of Defense and monitored by the Office of Naval Research under Contract N 00014-70-C-0350 to the San Diego State University Foundation, and by grants to D. Shapiro from the Office of Naval Research, Contract # N 000-14-67-A-0298-0024, and the National Institute of Mental Health grant # MH-08853. The article is based in part on a thesis by I.R. Bell under G.E. Schwartz in fulfillment of the requirements for the A.B. degree from the Department of Biol-

ogy, Harvard University, 1972. The authors express their appreciation to D. Shapiro for his valuable advice and criticisms; to L. Spaiser for constructing the feedback apparatus; and to P. Barker for computer programming the statistical analyses.

The senior author is now at the Sleep Laboratory, Department of Psychiatry, Stanford University Medical Center, Stanford, California 94305.

Address requests for reprints to: Gary E. Schwartz, Ph.D., Department of Psychology and Social Relations, Harvard University, 1544 William James Hall, Cambridge, MA 02138.

Young, & McLeod, 1972; Bergman & Johnson, 1971). However, there is little data on in-laboratory cardiac reactivity *per se* as a predictor of voluntary control performance. Further, although emphasis has been placed on the potential clinical applications of voluntary cardiac control (Engel & Melmon, 1968; Weiss & Engel, 1971; Shapiro & Schwartz, 1972), in-laboratory performance has not typically been compared with individuals' heart rates out-of-the-laboratory (see however, Engel, 1972).

By measuring reactivity of both heart rate and systolic blood pressure during a series of random reinforcement trials, Schwartz (1972) has recently shown that it is possible to predict the relative ease with which subjects can control voluntarily patterns of the two functions (e.g. it is easier for subjects to integrate heart rate and blood pressure—make them both increase or decrease together, than to differentiate them—make them go in opposite directions). In the present experiment, heart rate decelerations and accelerations during Lacey-type 'environmental intake and rejection' tasks (Lacey, Kagan, Lacey, & Moss, 1963) were evaluated as a potential measure of an individual's heart rate 'reactivity' range. It was hypothesized that a brief reactivity test such as this might indicate the potential effectiveness of a lengthier biofeedback procedure for a particular individual. In addition, determining the range of heart rates under different conditions could make it possible to assess natural biological and environmental constraints that influence the degree to which subjects are able to either raise or lower their heart rate (Schwartz, 1972; Schwartz, 1974). As a preliminary step, one purpose of the present study was to place normal subjects' in-laboratory heart rates in the context of out-of-laboratory pulse rates that had been taken in a variety of everyday situations. It was hoped that these data might elucidate why, for example, it is easier to produce large voluntary increases versus decreases in heart rate, relative to "resting" levels (e.g. Headrick, Feather, & Wells, 1971).

Another source of individual differences is subjects' initial, pre-feedback, level of proficiency at heart rate control. Although it has been generally assumed that some feedback training is essential for voluntary control of heart rate, a few reports indicate that subjects can raise and lower heart rate without any external feedback (Bergman & Johnson, 1971, 1972; Brener et al., 1969). There is also indirect evidence that bidirectional control—presumably learned during feedback—transfers to a no-feedback condition (Brener

et al., 1969). However, the Brener group did not compare the degree of control during feedback with that during no-feedback; rather, they measured only the no-feedback performance after various amounts of feedback. The present design followed a sequence of discrete trial blocks from prefeedback to feedback to postfeedback in order to allow evaluation of the effectiveness of feedback training as well as to test transfer of control from one condition to another.

Thus, the present experiment was designed to explore factors in bidirectional voluntary heart rate control before, during, and after continuous, full-scale meter feedback in fully-informed subjects. An individual's reactivity heart rates were expected to provide some indication of subsequent voluntary control performance. The feasibility of subject self-measurement of out-of-the-laboratory pulse rates was studied, and in-laboratory heart rates were considered in the context of a daily range of pulse rates.

Method

Subjects

The subjects (Ss) were 20 healthy male college students, aged 18–25, who were recruited by a general newspaper advertisement for a "psychophysiology study" and paid for their participation.

Apparatus

Electrocardiogram (EKG) standard limb lead II and cardiotachometer output (Lexington Instruments, Inc.) were recorded on a Grass Model 7 polygraph. Hewlett-Packard Redux paste was applied to the two EKG plate electrodes prior to strapping onto the upper right arm and the lower left leg above the ankle. Measures of respiration, digital blood pulse volume, and AC and DC skin potential were also recorded, but not scored.

Feedback was provided by a DC voltmeter which was connected in parallel with the output of the cardiotachometer driver amplifier. The feedback meter was zero-centered at 90 bpm, with a full-scale deflection range of 50–130 bpm. The usefulness of the full-scale meter feedback system without supplemental reinforcement has been demonstrated (Blanchard et al., 1972; Stephens, Harris, & Brady, 1972; Finley, 1970). Trial events were automatically controlled by appropriately programmed solid-state logic modules (Grason-Stadler Series 1200). During trials, the R wave of each cardiac cycle was detected by an electronic switch and automatically counted, Mean heart rate (HR) in beats per trial was displayed on a Hewlett-Packard digital electronic counter driven by the programming equipment. One min trials were used to make the durations comparable to the author's previous research (e.g. Schwartz, 1972).

Procedure

Subjects were seated in a lounge chair in a sound-attenuated, light-controlled room, separated from the apparatus room. Ss were told that the experiment involved performance of a series of tasks requiring mental or physical effort, and that specific instructions would be read immediately prior to each task. During a 15–20 min adaptation period, the electrodes and transducers were attached with a brief explanation of the purpose of each device; and Ss were given a brief rest period while the experimenter (E) brought in the measures on the polygraph.

The experiment consisted of the following sequence of tasks: I. Prestimulus Rest; II. Reactivity; III. Prefeedback Voluntary Control; IV. Feedback Voluntary Control; V. Postfeedback Voluntary Control; VI. Inlaboratory questionnaire; VII. Out-of-laboratory pulse self-measurements and personality questionnaires. Tasks I–V were divided into a series of trials, each 1 min long, with 10–15 sec of rest between trials within a given task. Tasks II–V were organized into blocks of 6 trials that followed the fixed order, RUDRDU (R=Rest; U=Up; D=Down HR). All Ss received the same order of trials to allow intra-individual comparisons to be made. The two orders within each block (order 1=RUD; order 2=RDU) were used as a control for possible habituation effects to either the RUD or the RDU series by itself. The Reactivity tasks were ordered RUDRDU according to the predictions for the separate trials' heart rate effects (Lacey et al., 1963; Campos & Johnson, 1966, 1967; Johnson & Campos, 1967); comparisons between Reactivity and Voluntary Control were thereby facilitated. Prior to Postfeedback, Ss were randomly assigned to one of two groups, Same or Reverse, corresponding to the significance of the cue lights for each group during Postfeedback.

I. Prestimulus Rest consisted of 4 unsignalled trials immediately after the adaptation period. Ss were resting, and no external stimuli were presented.

II. Reactivity established an elicited heart rate response range for each S. Before each Reactivity task, Ss were informed that the experimenter was interested in their "physiological responses" during task performance. In order, the 6 trials were Rest; 'Alphabet'; 'Tones'; Rest; 'Lights'; 'Arithmetic.' The Up HR trials, 'Alphabet' and 'Arithmetic,' were designed to involve both environmental rejection (Lacey et al., 1963) and later verbalization requirements (Campos & Johnson, 1966, 1967; Johnson & Campos, 1967). The Down HR trials, 'Tones' and 'Lights,' were designed to involve environmental intake without a verbalization requirement. Ss were told to relax during all Rest trials.

Reverse Alphabet. In the task, S was told to think the entire alphabet backwards in his head as quickly and as many times as possible. S was asked how many times he had run through the alphabet and at what letter he had stopped at the end of the trial.

Tones. S was instructed to listen to a series of high- (1100 Hz) and low- (330 Hz) pitched tones that occurred for 100 msec, one at a time, in a mixed order determined by a Grason-Stadler sequence counter.

Lights. S was asked to watch a display box of three different colored lights, a blue, a yellow, and a smaller white, flash on and off rapidly, each for 100 msec, one at a time, in a mixed order also determined by the Grason-Stadler sequence counter.

Arithmetic. S was required to perform a complex mental arithmetic subtraction problem in his head, to think each answer silently as it was computed, and to report verbally a final answer only at the end of the trial. Specifically the problem was to subtract the small number "33" repeatedly, starting from the large number "985," without resorting to clever shortcuts.

The Voluntary Control tasks were the first time that the Ss were specifically informed that the experiment involved heart rate control.

The use of a within subject, bidirectional control design suggests the need to establish some baseline criterion from which to judge increases and decreases (Headrick et al., 1971). The Headrick group employed a pre-trial, stimulus-free resting level as their criterion. In this manner, they controlled for the effects of a shifting baseline

during the session. Such a solution is an improvement over the unrevised, prestimulus resting-baseline criterion of other studies. However, an alternative criterion was used in the present experiment in order to control for the stimulus effects of the cue lights themselves. A neutral cue light rest trial was included with each set of Up and Down task trials. Ss were given instructions to refrain from voluntary heart rate control during the neutral trial. The procedure was a test of voluntary control on cue as well as a control for shifting baseline and cue-light stimulus effects.

III. Prefeedback Voluntary Control was a test of the Ss' ability to control heart rate on cue without feedback. Ss were told that one of three different colored cue lights would come on and stay on for the duration of a trial period. The lights were positioned around an inactive meter face on a display box located 3 ft in front of the S. Ss were instructed that blue (B) meant 'increase heart rate'; yellow (Y) meant 'decrease heart rate'; and white (W) meant 'rest and refrain from practicing heart rate control.' The order of the trials was WBYWYB (RUDRDU). Ss were informed that each individual finds his own way of performing the task, and that some Ss do report that their state of mind has an effect on controlling their heart rate. Ss were asked to breathe regularly and to avoid excessive movements during trials. The instructions stated that bonus money would be awarded at the end of the experiment, dependent upon E's assessment of S's "task performance." After the session, Ss were given either 25¢ or 50¢ bonuses contingent upon E's judgment of the degree of bidirectional voluntary control exhibited by S during the experiment.

IV. Feedback Voluntary Control provided meter feedback on a beat-by-beat basis during trials. The Prefeedback instructions were repeated with the additional information about the meter. Ss were told that the meter would light up and pointer be activated only during blue light (Up) and yellow light (Down) trials. During intertrial rest periods and white light (Rest/No practice) trials, the meter would be turned off and the pointer deactivated at the center of the meter. To make the task more personally challenging, Ss were told that heart rate control is a difficult skill to master, but that they should be able to improve upon their current level of skill with concentrated effort. The order of the trials for each feedback block was WBYWYB, and there were 4 blocks of 6 such trials. Thus, Ss received a total of 8 min each of Up, Down, and Rest trials during the Feedback segment.

V. Postfeedback Voluntary Control was a test of transfer of control from the feedback to the no-feedback condition. Ss were instructed that the meter would again be off during all trials and that only the cue lights would be used, as before in the Prefeedback task. All Ss were told that the order of the trials would remain the same as before, i.e., RUDRDU.

It has been suggested that 'voluntary control' of autonomic functions could be partially dependent on the inherent stimulus properties of the external S_D (Katkin & Murray, 1968). In the present experiment, if subjects have learned some 'involuntary' response to the S_D cue light itself, a change in the significance of the cue would be expected to leave subjects continuing to respond as they have previously—in a manner that would now be inappropriate for the cue. On the other hand, subjects would be exhibiting 'voluntary control' if they were able to conform their responses to the altered meaning of the cue lights. Consequently, as an additional variable in the present experiment, Ss were randomly assigned to one of the two cue-light-meaning groups: Half of the Ss (Same group, N=10) were told that the colored cue lights meant the same as they had in the past (B=Up; Y=Down; W=Rest/No practice). The other half of the Ss (Reverse group, N=10) were told that the colored cue lights now meant the opposite from what they had previously meant

(B=Down; Y=Up; W=Rest/No practice). The Same group saw WBYWYB; the Reverse group saw WYBWBY. Thus both groups had the same trial order for Rest, Up, and Down; but the trials were signalled by different colored lights.

VI. In-laboratory Questionnaires were given to assess *S*s' subjective reaction to the experiment in the form of free-response and forced-choice questions on the conscious use of muscular, respiratory, and cognitive maneuvers in heart rate control.

VII. Out-of-laboratory Pulse Self-measurements were completed and returned within 1-4 weeks after the in-lab experiment. Subjects took their own pulses during two consecutive days in a variety of situations, using a structured protocol. The protocol required that the subjects record their heart rate and time of day for the following events: (1) on awakening, before getting out of bed, (2) just after getting out of bed, (3) just before breakfast, (4) just after breakfast, (5) morning walk (including the distance), (6) just before lunch, (7) just after lunch, (8) afternoon walk (including distance), (9) just before dinner, (10) just after dinner, (11) just before retiring—and for the following situations: (1) listening to a lecture, (2) while reading, (3) just before running in place (vigorously for 1 min), (4) just after running in place, (5) just before silently saying the alphabet backwards, (6) just after saying it backwards, (7) just before imagining having had a recent argument (1 min), (8) just after the imagined argument, (9) at the beginning of a period of quiet sitting, (10) after 5 min of sitting quietly.

Analyses

The dependent variable was average heart rate for each 1-min trial. Analysis of variance (ANOVA) was carried out on the prestimulus Rest trials 1–4. Factors for most other ANOVAs were Directions (R vs U) or (R vs D); Blocks (Reactivity; Prefeedback; Feedback Blocks 1–4; Postfeedback); and Orders (RUD vs RDU). Postfeedback comparisons included Lightgroups (Same vs Reverse) and Direction (R vs U) or (R vs D). For purposes of correlation, mean HR values were computed for Prestimulus Rest and for R, U, D in each task of the experiment (i.e. Reactivity; Prefeedback; Feedback; Postfeedback). Out-of-lab pulse rates were averaged across the 2 days of measurement. Matched *t*-tests were performed on the mean (Post-Pre) difference scores of the out-of-lab pulse rates. Difference scores were based on the values of (U−R), (D−R), or (Post−Pre). Except when otherwise indicated, all differences are at least $p<.06$.

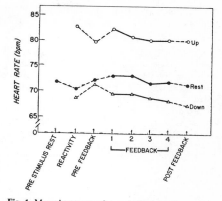

Fig. 1. Mean heart rates for each block of trials (N≐20), A block consisted of 2 Rest (R), 2 Up (U), and 2 Down (D) trials, organized in an RUDRDU order. See text for details.

Results

Unless otherwise specified, *Rest* refers to the *Rest* trials of a specific task and not to *Prestimulus Rest*. Fig. 1 summarizes mean HR for all trial blocks R, U, and D. Table 1 shows frequency distributions of the number of *S*s producing HR increases and decreases (in order of ascending magnitude of HR change in bpm) during the different parts of the experiment.

Reactivity

Reactivity Up HR tasks produced large 12 bpm accelerations above Rest ($F(1/19)=32.698$), with 'Arithmetic' tending to produce a larger increase than 'Alphabet' ($F(1/19)=4.055$). Reactivity Down HR tasks produced small (1 ½ bpm) but significant decelerations relative to Rest ($F(1/19)=4.278$),

TABLE 1

Frequency distributions of number of Ṡs (N =20) producing HR increases and decreases during the different parts of the experiment

Experimental Periods	Number of Ss for 6 HRΔ(bpm) Ranges					
	−8 to −5	−5 to 0	0 to +5	+5 to +10	+10 to +15	+15 to +33
Up-Rest Task						
Reactivity	0	0	5	5	3	7
Prefeedback	0	0	10	4	3	3
Feedback (Blocks I–IV)	0	0	5	9	5	1
Postfeedback	0	2	8	4	1	5
Down-Rest Task						
Reactivity	1	13	5	1	0	0
Prefeedback	2	5	13	0	0	0
Feedback (Blocks I–IV)	3	17	0	0	0	0
Postfeedback	8	10	2	0	0	0

and 'Tones' and 'Lights' decreases did not differ reliably from one another $(F(1/19)=0.157)$.

Prefeedback

In Prefeedback, there was a significant main effect for Directions in the (R vs U) ANOVA, but not in the (R vs D) analysis (respectively, $F(1/19)=32.745$; $F(1/19)=0.428$).

In other words, subjects were able to raise but not lower their heart rate before feedback. The size of the Prefeedback increase was significantly smaller than that of Reactivity block $(F(1/19)=4.659)$, but there was no significant difference in magnitude of the decrease between Reactivity and Prefeedback $(F(1/19)=0.911)$.

Feedback

With feedback, Ss were able both to raise and lower heart rate. ANOVAs showed highly significant main effects for Direction in Feedback Blocks 1–4 $(R,U: F(1/19)=27.313, R,D: F(1/19)=97.400)$. Ss were able to produce decreases in Feedback Block 1 relative to Rest; this decrease being greater than the non-significant decrease observed during Prefeedback $(F(1/19)=12.011)$ (see Table 2).

Postfeedback

After feedback, Ss retained the ability to increase and decrease HR relative to Rest; main effects for Postfeedback Directions were significant $(R,U: F(1/18)=19.629, R,D: F(1/18)=58.177)$.[1] The Blocks (Feedback 4, Postfeedback) by Directions (R,U; R,D) interactions were not significant (respectively, $F(1/18)=0.002; F(1/18)=1.477$), indicating that complete transfer of bidirectional control from the last feedback block to postfeedback did occur. A significant Blocks (Prefeedback, Postfeedback) by Directions (R,D) interaction revealed that Ss could lower their HR after, but not before, feedback training $(F(1/18)=14.750)$. Ss' ability to raise HR was the same before and after feedback $(F(1/18)=0.465)$.[2]

Interestingly, reversing the meaning of the cue lights during Postfeedback had no effect on group performances. There were no significant main effects for Lightgroups. Although the Postfeedback Lightgroups × Directions interaction for (R,U,D) combined

[1]*Df* change here because the between group factor is now included in the ANOVA.

[2]Overall there were few Order effects or Order × Directions interactions and they were not consistent from block to block. It was concluded that order did not have a reliable effect on the magnitude of the increases and decreases which Ss produced within blocks of the voluntary control tasks. There were also no significant differences in rest trials over blocks, indicating a stable baseline.

was significant $(F(2/36)=3.660)$, the differences between groups during Postfeedback had already existed in Feedback Block 4, before group membership had been assigned. In other words the three-way interaction, Lightgroups (Same, Reverse) × Blocks (Feedback Block 4, Postfeedback) × Directions (R,U,D), was not significant $(F(2/36)=0.076)$, indicating that each group had transferred its own specific pattern of HR control from the last feedback block (Block 4) to postfeedback without alteration. Thus, the differences seen during Postfeedback were not a function of the meaning of the cue lights, but rather were due to differences already present during feedback. Since neither Ss nor E knew group assignment until immediately prior to Postfeedback, the group differences could not be attributed to experimenter bias.

Individual and Situational Factors

For Reactivity the magnitudes of the increases were not correlated with those of the decreases $(r=.408)$. (See Table 2.) Moreover the magnitudes of the Reactivity and Voluntary Control increases were not correlated, and the sizes of Reactivity and Voluntary Control decreases were also uncorrelated (see Table 2). Interestingly, the more Ss accelerated during Reactivity Up tasks relative to Rest, the more they decelerated during Postfeedback Down tasks relative to Rest $(r=-.642)$. Overall, however, Reactivity Up HR bracketed all of the Voluntary Control HR Up levels, while only Postfeedback Down HR was lower than the Reactivity Down HR level (Fig. 1). For the three Voluntary Control segments, the sizes of the Prefeedback, Feedback, and Postfeedback were all intercorrelated for increases, but not decreases. Again, within each segment of Voluntary Control, the magnitude of the increases was not correlated with that of the decreases. Thus, in the lab environment, individuals produced a certain range of HRs, but individual HR responses within that range differed from one task situation to another (i.e. Up vs Down or Reactivity vs Voluntary Control).

Out-of-Laboratory Pulse Rates

Fig. 2 presents the out-of-lab mean HRs in bpm. First, to check the reliability of the out-of-lab pulse rates, a number of analyses were performed. A highly consistent correlation between the daily rates reported for each item out-of-the-laboratory was obtained across the 2 days of measurement (median $r=.79$). Difference scores were also correlated comparing the 2 days for (Getting-out-of-bed - Supine awakening), (Post-alphabet - Pre-alphabet), (Post-run - Pre-run), (On retiring - Supine

TABLE 2

Correlation coefficients and significance levels between HR difference scores (up-rest) and (down-rest) and task rest HRs for in-lab data

Tasks:	HR. Diff.:	Correlations							
		React U-R	Prefeed U-R	Feedbk U-R	Postfd U-R	React D-R	Prefeed D-R	Feedbk D-R	Postfd D-R
React	U-R	—	.258	-.089	.174	.408	.277	-.304	-.642*
Prefd	U-R	.258	—	.716*	.650*	-.079	-.257	-.321	-.266
Feed	U-R	-.089	.716**	—	.769**	-.432	-.201	-.319	.069
Postfd	U-R	.174	.650*	.769**	—	-.212	-.269	-.214	.044
React	D-R	.408	-.079	-.432	-.212	—	.083	.297	-.205
Prefd	D-R	.277	-.257	-.201	-.269	.083	—	.004	-.002
Feed	D-R	-.304	-.321	-.319	-.214	.297	.004	—	.267
Postfd	D-R	-.642*	-.266	.069	.044	-.205	-.002	.267	—
Task Rest		.072	-.114	-.116	-.177	.170	.436	-.187	-.149

*p<.01.
**p<.001.

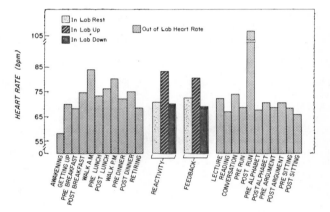

Fig. 2. Mean heart rates out-of-the laboratory compared with those for in-lab Reactivity and Feedback tasks. The in-lab HRs are bracketed by those out-of-the-lab.

awakening), and (Post-sitting - Pre-sitting) (respectively: r=.792, r=.704, r=.877, r=.595, and r=.514). Although the separate difference scores (Post − Pre) for the three daily meals were not correlated across the 2 days, the overall effects of the means in raising HR were reliable; the mean Post-breakfast HR (average of days 1 and 2) was significantly higher than the mean Pre-breakfast HR (t(17)=4.036); the mean Post-lunch was higher than the mean Pre-lunch HR (t(17)=2.978); and the mean Post-dinner was higher than the Pre-dinner HR (t(18)=2.901).[3] There were also reliable differences between Getting-

out-of-bed and Awakening (t(19)=4.574), between Post-alphabet and Pre-alphabet (t(19)=3.174), between Post-run and Pre-run (t(19)=9.814), between On-retiring and Supine awakening (t(19)=3.247), and between Post-sitting and Pre-sitting (t(19)=2.444). The difference scores for the 2 days (post-imagined-argument − Pre-imagined-argument) were not correlated (r=.211), and the mean HR for Post-argument was not significantly higher than that for Pre-argument (t(19)=1.694). Altogether the data suggest that the out-of-lab heart rates can serve as a reliable representation of typical heart rates in the field.

It should be noted that the range of HRs produced by the subjects during Feedback Blocks (1−4) in the laboratory is bracketed, not only by the in-lab Reactivity, R,U,D HRs, but also by the ranges between a

[3]These results also suggest that the Ss were not simply making up the data from day 1 to day 2, since meal effects were *not* correlated across the 2 days, while other tasks such as alphabet showed consistent cross-day results.

number of out-of-lab HRs. For instance, Feedback Rest and Out-of-lab Pre-lunch HRs were at comparable levels (respectively, 72.525 bpm and 72.833 bpm), and they were correlated ($r=.486$). In fact, the mean time of day during which subjects were run in the laboratory (12:40 pm) compares favorably with the mean time of day at which they report eating lunch (12:30 pm). Similarly, Feedback Up (80.987) bpm was close to and correlated with the afternoon walk HR (79.325 bpm) ($r=.450$); Feedback Down (69.081 bpm) was bracketed by and correlated with HR on retiring (67.850 bpm) ($r=.474$).

With the exception of 'Awakening' (while supine in bed) and 'Post-running' (after 1 min running in place), the Feedback R,U,D HRs fall very near the range of HRs that Ss produced in the course of a wide variety of activities at different times of the day.

Also, these data illustrate that resting heart rates in the laboratory are close to the low end of normal heart rates occurring during a typical day. Hence, it is no wonder why decelerations (both elicited by external stimuli and self-generated) are smaller under these conditions than heart rate changes observed for accelerative tasks.

The importance of situational factors in- and out-of-the-lab is implied by the lack of significant correlation between the in-lab Alphabet Reactivity (Alphabet − Rest) difference score and the Out-of-lab Alphabet task (post − Pre) difference score ($r=-.358$).

Since the Alphabet task was also performed during the in-lab Reactivity Up segment, subjects may have been responding less with individual stereotypy to a particular task than with situational stereotypy to the setting in which the task was executed. The Reactivity increase was positively correlated with out-of-the-lab HR difference score for running ($r=.615$). This observation suggests the hypothesis that the physiological mechanisms of the in-lab Reactivity and the out-of-lab Running accelerations were similar. Furthermore, none of the sizes of the Reactivity, Prefeedback, and Feedback decreases was significantly correlated with the magnitude of the deceleration after 5-min of quiet sitting out-of-the-lab (respectively, $r=.091$, $r=.416$, $r=.167$). On the other hand, the more subjects decreased out-of-the-lab HR during quiet sitting, the more they decelerated during Postfeedback ($r=.462$). Perhaps in this latter case, the mechanisms of cardiac deceleration in postfeedback at the end of the experimental session were related to those which function during sitting, an interpretation that is indirectly supported by the lack of correlation be-

tween the feedback and postfeedback decelerations ($r=.267$).

Subjective Reports

Table 3 presents categories of thoughts from a forced-choice list, ranked here by the number of Ss who reported applicability of the categories to Up, Down, Both, or Neither type of voluntary HR control trial. It can be seen that 'excitement,' 'sex,' 'fear,' and 'tension' were used most often during Up trials only; 'relaxation,' 'tranquility,' and 'contentment' were used most often during Down trials only. 'Hunger,' 'Thirst,' and 'future-planning' were not employed during either Up or Down for most of the Ss. Themes of 'sex,' 'violence,' and 'competition' predominated the free-response question about activities and thoughts during Up trials. 'Relaxation' and 'drowsiness' were cited most often in associa-

TABLE 3

Frequency distributions of Ss ($N=20$)[a] reporting use of thought categories during voluntary HR control
Thoughts are partially ranked in descending order of Up-only and ascending order of Down-only frequencies

Thought Categories	Number of Ss Reporting Use		
	Up Only	Down Only	Neither Up Nor Down
Excitement	17	0	1
Sex	17	0	1
Fear	16	0	3
Tension	15	0	1
Tenseness	15	0	3
Anger	11	0	7
Surprise	10	0	9
Switching thoughts	10	0	5
Alertness	7	0	11
Uncertainty	5	0	13
Increased awareness of thoughts	4	0	14
Worry	10	1	6
Reviewing past	9	1	4
Memory of problems	9	1	8
Frustration	8	1	9
Problem-solving	6	1	12
Hunger	2	0	17
Thirst	1	0	18
Love	4	5	8
Future-planning	1	2	16
Restful alertness	1	5	12
Pleasant feeling	1	11	4
Happiness	0	8	10
Day-dreaming	0	11	5
Well-being	0	11	7
Contentment	0	15	4
Relaxation	0	18	1
Tranquility	0	18	1

[a]Frequency distributions for Ss reporting in the categories "both Up and Down" and "bland (no response)" were small and were therefore omitted from the table.

tion with Down trials. Interestingly, none of the thought categories was used during both Up and Down trials by a majority of Ss.

Correlations between the magnitudes of the bidirectional changes and subjective ratings of the extent of muscle and breathing maneuvers were also evaluated. The only significant correlations were between the size of Prefeedback decreases and the reported use of muscle ($r=-.465$), and breathing ($r=-.489$) maneuvers. Nevertheless, for several Ss indirect indications of muscle tension appeared throughout the EKG tracings during the voluntary control Up HR trials (see Burch & Winsor, 1968).

Discussion

These data offer some insights into the interaction between biofeedback, instructional set, and natural physiological and situational constraints in the bidirectional control of heart rate. With full instructions, meter feedback was not necessary for subjects to demonstrate voluntary heart rate increases, and only minimum exposure to feedback was required for subjects to show decreases. Furthermore, over the course of feedback, subjects failed to improve upon their performance.

In a single-session heart rate experiment, the instructional set variable may be equally, if not more important than feedback *per se* (Bergman & Johnson, 1972). Fully-informed subjects are able to draw immediately upon behavioral repertoires which they already associate with high or low heart rates when they enter the laboratory. The clear trends in the subjective reports of cognitive maneuvers along an arousal-relaxation continuum support such a 'behavioral repertoire' hypothesis. Ability to increase heart rate appeared immediately on the first Prefeedback Up trial, and ability to decrease heart rate appeared immediately on the first Feedback Down trial. Apparently, brief exposure to feedback is useful primarily in helping subjects select an effective—albeit previously learned——repertoire for heart rate change (Engel, 1972). One might hypothesize that longer exposure to feedback in a one-session experiment is essential to misinformed or partially-informed subjects who must learn by trial-and-error to call upon a behavioral repertoire to which fully-informed subjects can resort much sooner. In a replication of the present experiment with the addition of an uninformed group, we have verified that a "learning curve" does develop in such subjects (Bell & Schwartz, 1973).

Practice effects might explain the appear-

ance of ability to lower heart rate with feedback. However, the abrupt development of the ability suggests that feedback per se was more important than practice. It could also be hypothesized that looking at the feedback meter itself produced Lacey-type environmental intake decelerations. However, this conclusion is tempered by the observation that subjects were able to transfer 'decrease' ability to Postfeedback, with the meter off and the requirement for environmental intake again absent. Also, the failure of the Reactivity intake tasks, 'Lights' and 'Tones,' to elicit comparable decelerations argues against the strength of environmental intake alone in producing that consistent, and larger, 4 bpm decrease observed with feedback.

It is possible that the lack of immediate external reinforcement or the absence of a constantly-revised criterion hindered the development of learning. On the other hand, the present subjects may simply have reached the situational heart rate limits earlier than they would have with a less informative instructional set. A comparison of revised-criterion and full-scale meter feedback systems with multiple session training is indicated.

The finding that the magnitudes of increases were not correlated with those of decreases supports the hypothesis (Engel, 1972; Engel & Gottlieb, 1970; Lang, 1974) that different physiological mechanisms are responsible for heart rate changes in opposite directions. Also, the general failure of Reactivity heart rates to predict voluntary control performance suggests different mechanisms of physiological response for the two tasks. On the other hand, the fact that the Reactivity tasks closely match the range with which subjects were later able to raise and lower their heart rate under these laboratory conditions (e.g., sitting quietly, motor activity reduced through instructions) illustrates possible general constraints operating on heart rate (Schwartz, 1972; Schwartz, 1974). It would appear that there are different mechanisms (both physiological and cognitive) by which subjects can raise and lower heart rate, but under a given set of conditions, or "state," the average range may be relatively fixed. However, the data suggest that the more similar any 're-activity' task is to a subsequent biofeedback task—particularly with respect to instructions and task demands (e.g., Prefeedback to Feedback in the present study or Random Reinforcement to Contingent Reinforcement in Schwartz, 1972)—the better will be the 'reactivity' prediction of feedback voluntary control. Interestingly, support for this idea also occurs in the out-of-lab pulse rates, where correlations across days for the majority of the tasks are consistently high and significant, while correlations across different tasks within days are almost universally low and non-significant.

The present data illustrate the potential usefulness of out-of-laboratory pulse self-measurement procedures. As noted in Schwartz (1974), although the pulse-taking procedure has problems of possible inaccuracy and falsification of the data, it does have one advantage over other methods in that the pulse rates are all taken when the subjects are in a similar psychophysiological state (attending to pulsations in the artery, sitting still, counting heart beats, etc.). In other words, the recording procedure reduces the number of other activities the subject might be engaged in while taking the measures, hence reducing unwanted variance across situations.

It appears that the pulse rates reported by the present subjects were reliable. In-laboratory heart rates were well within the range of heart rates normally produced during daily activities out-of-the-laboratory. However, the brevity of the testing session and the normality of the in-lab rates relative to the out-of-lab rates suggest that the present subjects were performing within Engel's (1972) "early training stage." A multiple session version of the current experiment would be useful in observing the possible development of the "late training stage" in fully-informed human subjects. The out-of-lab daily cycles in HR levels are a notable reminder of the probable interaction between single-session, in-lab performance and the individual's stage in his daily biological rhythms. Also, they illustrate why decelerations (either self generated or elicited by external stimuli) appear smaller in magnitude than accelerations when resting values are used as baselines, since such baselines generally represent the low values of typical heart rates possible during the average day.[4]

The intermittent observation of muscle tension in the EKG during voluntary control Up trials is consistent with Obrist's views on cardiac-somatic coupling (Obrist, LeGuyader, Howard, Lawler, & Galosy, 1972; Obrist, Webb, Sutterer, & Howard, 1970). Moreover, it has recently been reported that inconspicuous muscle tension is associated with heart rate increases averaging 13 bpm (Belmaker, Proctor, & Feather, 1972). Since the immediate appearance and the large size of the voluntary control increases in the present experiment suggest that muscle tension may have been a concomitant—if not causative—factor during Up HR control for some of the subjects, systematic research monitoring EMG from a number of muscle sites is necessary. The possibility that the muscle tension and the heart rate increases were concomitant by-products of a particular cognitive or affective CNS state cannot be discounted.

Altogether, in light of the present findings, it is hypothesized that the extent and rapidity of learned heart rate control, at least in a single session, is to a large extent determined by (1) the natural ranges of heart rates biologically possible under the physical (and psychological) constraints of the situation, and (2) the instructions given to the subject (directing him to use specific, already available psychophysiological mechanisms in his repertoire). However, this is *not* meant to imply that the nature of the feedback is unimportant, especially when viewed in the context of the other autonomic and somatic responses that may be concurrently changing. Rather it is suggested that feedback may play a particularly important role in determining what specific *patterns* of functions are voluntarily controlled (Schwartz, 1974; Schwartz, in press).

---

[4]It is emphasized that the present data and interpretations concerning HR increases are relevant only to single-session studies. Over the course of a multi-session study, it has been shown that a fully-informed S, given meter feedback, can achieve a HR-range breakthrough into consistently large magnitude accelerations (30–40 bpm), but not into large decelerations (Headrick et al., 1971).

REFERENCES

Bell, I. R., & Schwartz, G. E. Cognitive and somatic mechanisms in voluntary control of heart rate. (Abstract in D. Shapiro, T. X. Barber, L. V. DiCara, J. Kamiya, N. E. Miller, & J. Stoyva (Eds.), *Biofeedback and self control 1972*. Chicago: Aldine, 1973. Pp. 503–504.)

Belmaker, R., Proctor, E., & Feather, B. W. Muscle tension in human operant heart rate conditioning. *Conditional Reflex*, 1972, 7, 97–106.

Bergman, J. S., & Johnson, H. J. Effects of instructional set and autonomic perception on cardiac control. *Psychophysiology*, 1971, 8, 180–190.

Bergman, J. S., & Johnson, H. J. Sources of information which affect training and raising of heart rate. *Psychophysiology*, 1972, 9, 30–39.

Blanchard, E. B., Young, L. D., & McLeod, P. Awareness of heart activity and self-control of heart rate. *Psychophysiology*, 1972, *9*, 63–68.

Brener, J., & Hothersall, D. Heart rate control under conditions of augmented sensory feedback. *Psychophysiology*, 1966, *3*, 23–28.

Brener, J., & Hothersall, D. Paced respiration and heart rate control. *Psychophysiology*, 1967, *4*, 1–6.

Brener, J., Kleinman, R., & Goesling, W. J. The effects of different exposures to augmented sensory feedback on the control of heart rate. *Psychophysiology*, 1969, *5*, 510–516.

Burch, G. E., & Winsor, T. *A primer of electrocardiography*. (5th ed.) Philadelphia: Lea & Febiger, 1968.

Campos, J. J., & Johnson, H. J. The effects of verbalization instructions and visual attention on heart rate and skin conductance. *Psychophysiology*, 1966, *2*, 305–310.

Campos, J. J., & Johnson, H. J. Affect, verbalization, and directional fractionation of autonomic responses. *Psychophysiology*, 1967, *3*, 285–290.

Engel, B. T. Operant conditioning of cardiac function: A status report. *Psychophysiology*, 1972, *9*, 161–177.

Engel, B. T., & Chism, R. A. Operant conditioning of heart rate speeding. *Psychophysiology*, 1967, *3*, 418–426.

Engel, B. T., & Gottlieb, S. H. Differential operant conditioning of heart rate in the restrained monkey. *Journal of Comparative & Physiological Psychology*, 1970, *73*, 217–225.

Engel, B. T., & Hansen, S. P. Operant conditioning of heart rate slowing. *Psychophysiology*, 1966, *3*, 176–188.

Engel, B. T., & Melmon, K. L. Operant conditioning of heart rate in patients with cardiac arrhythmias. *Conditional Reflex*, 1968, *3*, 130. (Abstract)

Finley, W. W. The effect of feedback on the control of cardiac rate. *Journal of Psychology*, 1970, *77*, 43–54.

Headrick, M. W., Feather, B. W., & Wells, D. T. Unidirectional and large magnitude heart rate changes with augmented sensory feedback. *Psychophysiology*, 1971, *8*, 132–142.

Hnatiow, M., & Lang, P. J. Learned stabilization of cardiac rate. *Psychophysiology*, 1965, *1*, 330–336.

Johnson, H. J., & Campos, J. J. The effect of cognitive tasks and verbalization instructions on heart rate and skin conductance. *Psychophysiology*, 1967, *4*, 143–150.

Katkin, E. S., & Murray, E. N. Instrumental conditioning of autonomically mediated behavior: Theoretical and methodological issues. *Psychological Bulletin* 1968, *70*, 52–68.

Lacey, J., Kagan, J., Lacey, B., & Moss, H. The visceral level: Situational determinants and behavioral correlates of autonomic response. In P. Knapp (Ed.), *Expression of the emotions in man*. New York: International Universities Press, Inc., 1963. Pp. 161–196.

Lang, P. J. Learned control of human heart rate in a computer directed environment. In P. A. Obrist, A. H. Black, J. Brener, & L. V. DiCara (Eds.), *Cardiovascular psychophysiology: Response mechanisms, biofeedback and methodology*. Chicago: Aldine, 1974. Pp. 392–405.

Lang, P. J., Sroufe, L. A., & Hastings, J. E. Effects of feedback and instructional set on the control of cardiac-rate variability. *Journal of Experimental Psychology*, 1967, *75*, 425–431.

Levene, H. I., Engel, B. T., & Pearson, J. A. Differential operant conditioning of heart rate. *Psychosomatic Medicine*, 1968, *30*, 837–845.

Obrist, P. A., LeGuyader, D. D., Howard, J. L., Lawler, J. E., & Galosy, R. A. Operant conditioning of heart rate: Somatic correlates. *Psychophysiology*, 1972, *9*, 270. (Abstract)

Obrist, P. A., Webb, R. A., Sutterer, J. R., & Howard, J. L. The cardiac-somatic relationship: Some reformulations. *Psychophysiology*, 1970, *6*, 569–587.

Schwartz, G. E. Voluntary control of human cardiovascular integration and differentiation through feedback and reward. *Science*, 1972, *175*, 90–93.

Schwartz, G. E. Toward a theory of voluntary control of response patterns in the cardiovascular system. In P. A. Obrist, A. H. Black, J. Brener, & L. V. DiCara (Eds.), *Cardiovascular psychophysiology: Response mechanisms, biofeedback and methodology*. Chicago: Aldine, 1974. Pp. 406–440.

Schwartz, G. E. Biofeedback, self regulation, and the patterning of physiological processes. *American Scientist*, in press.

Shapiro, D., & Schwartz, G. E. Biofeedback and visceral learning: Clinical applications. *Seminars in Psychiatry*, 1972, *4*, 171–184.

Stephens, J. H., Harris, A. H., & Brady, J. V. Large magnitude heart rate changes in subjects instructed to change their heart rates and given exteroceptive feedback. *Psychophysiology*, 1972, *9*, 283–285.

Weiss, T., & Engel, B. T. Operant conditioning of heart rate in patients with premature ventricular contractions. *Psychosomatic Medicine*, 1971, *33*, 301–321.

Heart Rate Perception and 35
Heart Rate Control

Richard A. McFarland

ABSTRACT

Twenty-one subjects took the Autonomic Perception Questionnaire (APQ) and later were given another test of ability to perceive heart activity. The second test involved subjects' tracking of their own heart rates (HR). They were then tested for ability to increase and decrease HR from their resting baseline levels. No significant relationships were found between HR control and APQ score. HR decrease success seemed to depend mainly on respiration differences between rest and decrease periods. The subjects who achieved high scores on the heart tracking test increased HR significantly better than did low scorers. This heart perception vs HR increase relationship did not depend upon respiration rate, respiration amplitude, or baseline HR differences between high and low scorers on the tracking test. A low correlation between APQ and tracking score seemed to indicate that the two perception tests measured different attributes of the subjects.

DESCRIPTORS: Heart rate control, Autonomic perception, Respiration rate, Respiration amplitude, Biofeedback.

Several studies have employed the Autonomic Perception Questionnaire, APQ (Mandler, Mandler, & Uviller, 1958), as a measure of subjects' awareness of their Galvanic Skin Responses, GSRs (Greene & Nielson, 1966), or heart rates, HRs (Bergman & Johnson, 1971; Blanchard, Young, & McLeod, 1972). The expected positive relationship between autonomic perception and autonomic control was not obtained in the above studies; however, Stern and Kaplan (1968) found that actors who reported being aware of sweating while imitating emotions were also best able to control their GSRs.

The present experiment attempted to partially clarify the relationship between autonomic awareness and autonomic control by using a more direct measure of cardiac awareness than the opinions of the subjects, namely, a tracking test in which they attempted to shadow their heartbeats. After measuring the abilities of the same subjects to control their HRs, the correlation between their HR control and the direct measure of their abilities to correctly perceive their heart activities was calculated.

Address requests for reprints to: Richard A. McFarland, Ph.D., Department of Psychology, California State University, Fullerton, Fullerton, California 92634.

Since this experimenter wished to measure HR control under as natural conditions as were possible in a laboratory setting, he decided against directly controlling respiration (e.g. by using paced respiration). Instead, he attempted to account for the effects of possible mediators such as respiration rate (Levenson & Strupp, 1973) and respiration amplitude (Sroufe, 1971) by statistically evaluating the relationships between the mediating factors and HR control as well as the relationships between the mediators and scores on the direct heart activity perception (HAP) test and the APQ to determine to what extent heart perception vs heart control relationships were mediation dependent.[1]

---

[1]It is not sufficient simply to say that, if the mediator vs HR control correlations are all non-significant, then the HR perception vs HR control relationship is unmediated. Lack of mediation can be demonstrated only by calculating the ρs for HR control vs HR perception, HR control vs mediator, and mediator vs HR perception, and then using partial correlation techniques as in the present study to determine how much the HR perception vs HR control correlation changes when the influence of the mediator is statistically held constant by partial correlation. If the HR perception vs HR control correlation drops below significance, then mediation must be assumed in spite of the non-significant mediator vs HR control correlation.

Method

Subjects

Twenty-one upper division psychology students, 11 males and 10 females, took the APQ approximately 3 weeks before the HR control test. The total score on the 5 items related to the heart was used as the APQ score of heart awareness.

Apparatus

All physiological measures were recorded with a Beckman R411 Dynograph. When the subjects arrived at the laboratory for the HAP test and the HR control test, they were seated in a comfortable chair in a quiet, although not totally soundproof, room. Two sets of EKG electrodes were attached to the lateral surfaces of the subject's upper arms. The subject's EKG was transmitted to a Beckman 9853A coupler and recorded on one channel of the Dynograph. Leads from the second set of electrodes led to a Beckman 9857 cardiotachometer coupler. The output from the cardiotachometer channel was used to provide feedback to the subject during the experiment by driving the pointer of a Lafayette Instrument Co. 76015 GSR voltmeter. The full 15.24 cm excursion range of the pointer was calibrated to be from 30 bpm to 120 bpm with a center at 75 bpm. Respiration was measured using a Beckman 7001 strain gauge respiration belt securely fastened about the subject's chest and connected to a Beckman 9853A coupler on the Dynograph. Earphones were fitted to the subject's head so that the experimenter could instruct him or her during the experiment.

Procedure

Before the first part of the experiment, the subjects were given the following instructions. "In this part of the experiment, we will try to determine how well you can perceive your heart activity. You will be asked to press a button in rhythm with your heartbeat. To give you some practice, press the button in rhythm with the dial on the meter in front of you. During this practice session only, the dial will move sharply each time your heart beats."

The subject was then given a small button to be pressed with the thumb in rhythm with the oscillation of the voltmeter pointer. The cardiotachometer channel was in the direct mode during this phase so that each heartbeat caused a pointer oscillation. The subject was allowed 30 sec of this HR shadowing practice. The voltmeter was then covered and he was told by the experimenter, "I will now leave the room. Sit quietly while I check the recording. When I tell you over the earphones to begin, begin pressing the button in exact rhythm with your heartbeat as you perceive it. Of course do not feel your pulse, and do not cross your legs during the trials, but simply sit quietly and attend to your heart. Press the button with as few interruptions as possible, although you may occasionally stop briefly if you feel it will help you to perceive your heartbeat better. At the end of each trial I will tell you to rest. There will be 4 two-minute test periods with a one-minute rest period between successive test periods. During rest periods, simply relax and wait for the next command to begin. Do you have any questions?"

During the 4 test periods, each button press caused the event marker on the Dynograph to mark. The absolute difference between the number of button presses and the number of heartbeats emitted by the subject was divided by the number of heartbeats. In order to produce a score that would be larger the better the subject's HR perception, this ratio was subtracted from one to yield the HAP score. Short sections of the record where the subject briefly stopped pressing were discarded and were not included in the above tabulations and calculations.

In the second part of the experiment, the subject was told, "In this part of the experiment you are to try to control your heart rate. When I leave the room, there will be a brief rest period during which you should just relax. When I speak the words, "Increase heart rate," over the earphones (decrease periods came first for alternate subjects), try to raise your HR by as much as possible for the following minute. Watch the meter in front of you to tell how well you are doing. The pointer will move to your right if your HR increases and to the left if it decreases. Do not become discouraged if you do not produce very large movements of the pointer. Even small changes are recorded. Simply do the best you can. At the end of the minute, I will tell you to rest. During the next 30 seconds you are to simply relax. Do not attempt to control your HR, but simply look at that point (a fixation point on the wall opposite the subject), and await the next test period.[2] At the end of the rest period I will tell you to, "Decrease HR," (increase for alternate subjects), and you will then attempt to decrease your HR as much as possible during the next minute. Again, watch the meter to see how well you are doing. This cycle of rest, increase (decrease), rest, decrease (increase) will be repeated ten times. I cannot tell you how to go about increasing or decreasing HR. Each subject seems to have their own method. However, you are not to attempt to change your HR by intentionally changing your breathing rate or depth or by changing your muscle tension. Attempt to control your HR by mental means only. Are there any questions?"

The pointer of the feedback meter was driven by the output of the cardiotachometer channel in the rate mode. Respiration, EKG, and the cardiotachometer output were recorded during all test and rest periods. The HR scores for the three types of periods were obtained by averaging the number of EKG R waves occurring per min during the 10 increase, the 20 rest, and the 10 decrease periods respectively. The respiration rate (RR) score was taken as the number of peak respiration amplitudes occurring per min during the three respective types of periods. Respiration amplitude (RA) was measured as the average height (valley to peak) of the excursion of the recorder pen per respiration cycle during the three respective types of periods. Needless to say, with differences between subjects in tightness of the respiration belt, etc., no absolute measure of RA was possible. However, ratios between the average RAs during rest, increase, and decrease periods were calculated, and these ratios were used as the RA scores for between subjects comparisons.

Results

General Calculations

The following scores were tabulated for each subject: HAP, APQ, Avg HR during rest (also referred to as baseline HR, BHR, since this Avg resting HR was what the increase and decrease scores were compared against), Avg HR during increase periods $-$ BHR = HR increase score, BHR $-$ Avg HR during decrease periods = HR decrease score, Avg RA during increase periods/Avg RA during rest periods = RA inc/rest, Avg RA during rest periods/Avg RA during decrease

---

[2]We do have a little more than the subjects' words that they did not look at the meter during the rest periods, or at least that it made little difference if they did. The last 2 subjects were run with the meter disconnected during rest periods, and these subjects' data were very compatible with those of the other subjects. One of these had the third highest HAP score and the second highest HR increase score. The other ranked seventeenth on the HAP and sixteenth on HR increase.

periods=RA rest/dec, Avg RR during increase periods/Avg RR during rest periods=RR inc/rest, and Avg RR during rest periods/Avg RR during decrease periods=RR rest/dec.

HR Decrease

All 21 subjects were able to decrease their HRs below BHR on decrease trials. The average decrease was 2.84 bpm, and the range was .6 bpm to 7.0 bpm. However, neither the rank order correlation between HR decrease and HAP ($-.22$) nor the HR decrease vs APQ correlation (.23) approached significance.[3] Partial correlations (Kerlanger & Pedhazur, 1973, p. 84) between HAP and HR decrease scores holding BHR, RR rest/dec, and RA rest/dec constant yielded no significant HR perception vs HR control relationships, although the HAP vs HR dec correlation did become positive (.17) when RR and RA influences were partialled out. Therefore, it was concluded that neither HAP nor APQ was significantly related to a subject's ability to decrease HR.

Most of the ability of the subjects to decrease HR was apparently due to statistically significant changes in respiration from rest to decrease periods. The ρ for HR dec vs RA rest/dec=.53 and ρ for HR dec vs RR rest/dec=$-.48$.

HR Increase and HAP

Eleven of the 21 subjects achieved positive HR increase scores. The average increase above BHR was 1.20 bpm with a range of -4.5 to 8.5 bpm. There was a significant HAP vs HR increase correlation (.50). No other measures correlated significantly with the HR increase scores. The ρs for HR inc vs RR inc/rest=.07, HR inc vs RA inc/rest=.28, and HR inc vs BHR=.00.

Partial correlations were carried out between HAP and HR increase holding BHR, RR inc/rest, and RA inc/rest constant. These correlations were .52, .52, and .48 respectively. Therefore, since the HAP vs HR increase correlation remained significant in spite of the statistical removal of the influence of the possible mediating factors, it was concluded that the significant positive HAP vs HR increase correlation was not mediated by BHR artifacts or by differences between high and low HAP subjects in RR or RA maneuvers. Neither can the HR increase difference between the high and low HAP scorers be accounted for by sex differences since there were 5 male and 5 female subjects among both the top 10 and the bottom 10 HAP scorers.

HR Perception (HAP) Learning and HR Increase

To determine to what extent the subjects' ability on the HAP test changed during the 4 2-min HAP

[3]The n for all correlations was 21. Two-tailed tests and the .05 level of significance were used in all tests of hypotheses.

test periods, their HAP scores for the first HAP period were subtracted from their HAP scores in the fourth period. Overall, they improved slightly from the first to the fourth HAP period, $\overline{X}=3.0\%$. More interesting was the fact that the 11 subjects who were later able to increase their HRs averaged a 9.3% increase in HAP score, whereas, the 10 subjects who could not later increase HR averaged a decrease of -4.0% from HAP trial 1 to HAP trial 4. This difference between the two groups was significant, $t(19)=2.29$. Apparently, subjects who learn to perceive heart activity best are also best at increasing HR.

HAP and HR Increase Learning

The HR increase scores (meaning in this case the increase period HR minus the HR in the just preceding rest period) on the first 2 HR increase trials were subtracted from the scores on the last 2 increase trials. Overall, there was a non-significant change in HR increase score over trials, $\overline{X}=-.28$ bpm. There was no significant difference in change over trials in the HR increase scores between the 10 highest and 10 lowest HAP scorers ($\overline{X}$ high=.40 bpm, $\overline{X}$ low=$-.95$ bpm).

HR Increase and APQ

The correlation between APQ score and HR increase score was not significant (.26). Since the partial correlations varied only between .26 and .29, it was concluded that APQ was not significantly related to HR increase ability.

HAP and APQ

HAP scores ranged from .48 to .98, $\overline{X}=.85$. APQ scores ranged from 5 to 50, $\overline{X}=29$. The rank order correlation between HAP scores and APQ scores was positive but small, $p=.13$.

Discussion

The present study attempts to answer two questions. The first question is whether the subjects who claimed by their scores on the APQ to have high ability to perceive their heartbeats would show this superiority over low APQ scorers on a task (HAP test) in which they were asked to directly attend to and track their HRs. The correlation of .13 between APQ and HAP scores indicates that APQ scores have a very low power to predict HAP scores. The present experimenter admits to a bias favoring the HAP as the more valid measure of HR perception for two reasons. First, the HAP is a more direct measure of heart perception than the APQ. Second, Mandler et al. (1958) reported that high APQ scorers overestimated their autonomic reactions which means that high APQ scores do not indicate a high level of accuracy of autonomic perception. Perhaps what the APQ actually measures is the degree to which subjects tend to be concerned or anxious about their heart activity. After all, correlations as high as .50 have been obtained between the

Taylor Manifest Anxiety Scale (Taylor, 1953) and the APQ (Mandler et al., 1958).

The second question concerned the exact relationship between HR perception and HR control. HR decreases were apparently mediated by respiration. However, because circumstances occurred in the present study, perhaps fortuitously, in which HAP vs HR increase relationships were not confounded by BHR artifacts or by RR or RA maneuvers, it was possible to demonstrate an apparently unmediated positive correlation between HR perception and HR increases without compulsory restriction of a subject's breathing.

It is of course still possible that some factor other than those measured, e.g., EMG (electromyogram), could have mediated the HAP vs HR increase relationship. Also, there is the nagging question of whether the baseline HR measured after applying the EKG electrodes is the same as a subject's normal (non-laboratory) baseline HR. Telemetric recording of a subject's HR outside the laboratory might help answer the latter question.

In summary, the two central findings of this paper were (1) A significant positive correlation was found between the direct measure of perception of heart activity and ability to increase HR. (2) This relationship was unmediated by any of the possible confounding factors that were tested since, in each case, the mediator vs HR increase correlation and/or the mediator vs HAP correlation were too small to allow the possible mediator to exert any sizable influence on the HAP vs HR increase relationship. Since the HAP vs HR decrease relationship was also positive (after RA and RR influences had been statistically controlled) all the evidence in the present experiment indicated that the people who have a more correct perception of their heart activity are also best able to control that activity.

The underlying basis of this positive relationship between HR perception and HR control remains to be established. I suspect that it is simply a matter of the high HAP subjects being able to use their superior internal cardiac feedback to supplement the meter feedback and thus more accurately determine what will produce the desired HR changes. A more physiological, and more speculative, guess would be that when there are efficient and/or numerous afferent pathways from an organ like the heart, strong efferent mechanisms to that organ also develop. These are subjects for future research.

One final comment. I have felt somewhat uneasy throughout this paper in referring to HR control vs respiration relationships as mediational while calling HR control vs HAP relationships non-mediational. I feel that the two relationships have at least as many similarities as they do differences. It is helpful to temporarily substitute the term "facilitator" in place of "mediator." As soon as the substitution is made one can see that so called mediators (e.g., respiration) have one very important thing in common with heart perception, namely use of either heart perception or respiration maneuvers facilitates heart control. The main difference between the two facilitators is then only that the one (heart perception) facilitates heart control by acting on the afferent side to provide subjects with the information they need to properly command efferent pathways, whereas, the other facilitator (respiration) is an efferent facilitator, the use of which enables subjects to more efficiently accomplish what the afferent facilitator told them needed to be done. Viewed this way, the present experiment supports the hypothesis that whatever the HAP test measures is an afferent facilitator of HR increases, and that, to be effective, it does not necessarily require the use of the two efferent facilitators, respiration rate and respiration amplitude maneuvers.

REFERENCES

Bergman, J. S., & Johnson, H. J. The effects of instructional set and autonomic perception on cardiac control. *Psychophysiology*, 1971, *8*, 180–190.

Blanchard, E., Young, L., & McLeod, P. Awareness of heart activity and self-control of heart rate. *Psychophysiology*, 1972, *9*, 63–68.

Greene, W. A., & Nielson, T. C. Operant GSR conditioning of high and low autonomic perceivers. *Psychonomic Science*, 1966, *6*, 359–360.

Kerlinger, F. N., & Pedhazur, E. J. *Multiple regression in behavioral research.* New York: Holt, Rinehart and Winston, Inc., 1973.

Levenson, R. W., & Strupp, H. H. Simultaneous feedback and control of heart rate and respiration rate. *Psychophysiology*, 1973, *10*, 200. (Abstract)

Mandler, G., Mandler, J. M., & Uviller, E. Autonomic feedback: The perception of autonomic activity. *Journal of Abnormal & Social Psychology*, 1958, *56*, 367–373.

Stroufe, L. A. Effects of depth and rate of breathing on heart rate and heart rate variability. *Psychophysiology*, 1971, *8*, 648–655.

Stern, R., & Kaplan, N. L. Ability of actors to control their GSRs and express emotions. *Psychophysiology*, 1968, *4*, 294–299.

Taylor, J. A. Personality scale of manifest anxiety. *Journal of Abnormal & Social Psychology*, 1953, *48*, 285–290.

36

Heart Rate Regulation with Success and Failure Signals

Camil Bouchard and John A. Corson

ABSTRACT

The purpose of this study was to examine the effects of success and failure signals on performance of subjects attempting heart rate regulation. Thirty-two experimental subjects formed two major groups, one speeding and the other slowing; half of the subjects in each group were signalled for their successes only, and the other half, for their failures only. The session consisted of three phases: Feedback, No Feedback, and Feedback. The data showed that: subjects receiving success signals increased their heart rate significantly more than those receiving failure signals; subjects receiving failure signals decreased their heart rate significantly more than those receiving success signals; there were no differences between the Feedback and No Feedback phases. The results are discussed in terms of their implications for the understanding of the compatibility between task and signal.

DESCRIPTORS: Positive-negative feedback, Success-failure signals, Biological impact, Strategy identification, Cardiovascular conditioning, Biofeedback.

A considerable body of evidence suggests the presence of differential biological impact of various forms of positive and negative incentive stimuli (Roberts, Note 1). Research with cats (Wenzel, 1961) and with rats (Malcuit, Ducharme, & Belanger, 1968) shows that anticipation of an aversive stimulus is accompanied by HR deceleration and that anticipation of a positive stimulus is accompanied by HR acceleration. At the human level, HR deceleration has also been observed in anticipation of noxious stimulation (Deane, 1969; Obrist, Webb, & Sutterer, 1969; Epstein & Clarke, 1970; Malcuit, 1973). Other observations indicate the presence of HR acceleration during anticipation of a positive stimulus (Doehring & Helmer, 1963; Doehring, Helmer, & Fuller, 1964) or when success was signalled to subjects involved in an avoidance task (Malcuit, 1973).

As pointed out by Schwartz (1974) such differential biological impact of various configurations of stimuli could influence the performance of subjects attempting to regulate bodily processes. The basic objective of the present study is to compare the performance of subjects attempting HR regulation under positive and negative feedback stimuli. More specifically, it was hypothesized, on the basis of the above observations, 1) that the use of positive feedback signals should facilitate HR speeding and interfere with HR slowing; and 2) that the use of negative feedback stimuli should facilitate HR slowing and interfere with HR speeding.

In order to test these hypotheses, subjects were

This work was supported by a grant from the Ministry of Social Affairs of the Province of Quebec (Project # 604-7-859) and by a grant from the Women's Auxiliary Association of the Montreal General Hospital, and was conducted during the period of a research fellowship to the first author from the Ministry of Education of the Province of Quebec. We thank Dr. D. Doehring for his valuable criticisms of the manuscript.

Address requests for reprints to: Dr. John A. Corson, Department of Psychiatry, Dartmouth College, Hanover, New Hampshire 03755.

divided into four groups: HR Increase and Positive Feedback (INC-POS), HR Increase and Negative Feedback (INC-NEG), HR Decrease and Positive Feedback (DEC-POS), and HR Decrease and Negative Feedback (DEC-NEG). Each group was successively exposed to a baseline period and then to Feedback, No Feedback, and Feedback conditions; this series of conditions permitted us to determine whether continuing feedback was necessary for maintenance of performance.

Method

Subjects

Subjects were 32 male volunteer students from McGill and Sir George Williams Universities and Dawson College in Montreal. These subjects were selected after a screening procedure had eliminated those volunteers whose HR was outside a 62 to 78 bpm range (±8 bpm from medical norm, Folkow & Neil, 1971) and those whose sinus arrhythmia was larger than 8 bpm. The first of these screening criteria was applied to ensure easy group matching by creating high homogeneity in starting HR values (Benjamin, 1967); the second was used to eliminate ambiguity in the nature of the feedback given to subjects whose respiratory function had a large effect on HR fluctuations.

Apparatus

The subject was seated in a sound-attenuated booth (I.A.C. Audiometric Testing Room), with the feedback display apparatus placed 2 ft away. Two 12 V lights, one red and the other blue, were adjacent to two counters, one adding (Hengstler, 0 422 364) and the other subtracting (Hengstler, 0 441 364). This feedback display apparatus was mounted on a tripod which permitted adjustment to eye level.

Four physiological measures were recorded: HR, respiration rate (RR), respiration amplitude (RA), and skin conductance level (SCL).

Heart Rate. Beat signals were detected by means of three rectangular nickel-plated electrodes in standard lead II configuration. These signals were transmitted to a tachograph preamplifier (Grass, Model 7 P4D). The output of the preamplifier was fed to two driver amplifiers (Grass, Model 7 DA E). The output, in beats, of the first driver amplifier was sent to the logic circuit binary counters (BRS 200) which controlled the trial and intertrial sequencing. The output, in rate, of the second driver amplifier was sent to a Schmitt Trigger logic module (BRS). This module was adjusted to emit a signal each time the rate was below or above (depending on the polarity) the zero volt reference point of the driver amplifier.

Respiration Rate and Respiration Amplitude. These two measures were obtained by recording the subject's thoracic expansion with a bellows attached around his chest. A strain gauge transducer (Grass, Model PT5A) was connected to the bellows, and the electrical conversion of changes in pressure was fed to a low level DC preamplifier (Grass, Model 7 P1B).

Skin Conductance Level. Two Beckman electrodes (standard size, 650944) were attached to the palmar surface of the subject's index and third fingers on the non-dominant hand. Voltage changes between these two sites were recorded by means of a low-level DC preamplifier (Grass Model 7 P1B). Skin conductance level was obtained by converting the resistance values to reciprocals.

Post-Test Questionnaire. As a preliminary effort to assess possible cognitive and perceptual strategies, a 10-item recognition questionnaire was given at the completion of the experiment. Each of the 10 items was rated by the subjects in terms of its

frequency of use on a 0 ("I did not use it at all") to 5 ("I used it all the time") scale. In addition, the subjects were invited to add any items of their own (a detailed description of this questionnaire is available from the authors).

Procedure

Immediately after the 15-min screening period the subject heard a tape of instructions played on the intercom system. Besides warning him against use of respiratory maneuvers[1] and bodily movements, instructions clearly specified that HR was the physiological function to be regulated and that, depending on the group, success or failure to regulate HR would result in gains or losses of money. In other words, each subject knew whether he would receive success or failure signals, but the required direction of change was not specified until just prior to the first feedback period. When the tape of instructions ended, the experimenter entered the booth and reviewed the instructions with the subject; ambiguous points and procedure-related questions were clarified. Attachment of respiration and skin conductance level measurement accessories followed. Finally the experimenter told the subject that the session was about to start and left the room.

As specified in the instructions the experimental session consisted of 4 different periods: Original Baseline (OB), Feedback 1 (F1), No Feedback (NF), and Feedback 2 (F2). Each period consisted of 8 segments of 60 heart beats' duration (indicated by a red light); each of these segments was separated by intervals of 30 heart beats.

Original Baseline. During the OB period, a blue light, located in front of the subject, flashed in a random sequence. The subject was advised that the flashes were pre-programmed and not related to his HR. He was told that the blue light would flash only during the red light periods. Each subject was asked to count the number of flashes and to report this number at the end of the session. This task forced all subjects to attend to the same stimuli during the baseline period and was designed to prevent this phase from becoming a "relaxation" period. On the completion of the baseline period, the experimenter calculated the mean HR of the last 3 red light periods and set the zero volt reference point of the polygraph driver amplifier at this mean level. The subject was assigned to one of the groups, with the actual group placement being guided by his mean HR in order to obtain matched groups. The subject was only then instructed as to which group he was in (i.e., whether he would be required to increase or decrease HR for the remainder of the session).

Feedback 1 and 2. These periods started respectively 90 sec after the end of the OB period and 90 sec after the NF phase. During each of the 8 trials (red light) the blue light was electronically turned on, for both INC-POS and DEC-POS groups, when a beat-to-beat interval which was in the appropriate direction was detected. The subject was informed that the counter located on top of the blue light would be incremented if the blue light remained on long enough (3 consecutive appropriate beat-to-beat intervals). Each point accumulated on the counter had a value of a half cent.

For both INC-NEG and DEC-NEG groups, the blue light was described as being a signal of failure that had to be avoided or escaped. Three consecutive inappropriate beat-to-beat intervals triggered decrements on the counter located below the blue light. The counter was preset at 1200 ($6.00).

For both speeding groups the performance criterion was increased by 2 bpm on each subsequent trial if the subject had obtained at least 75% of the possible counter increments (INC-

---

[1]If a subject's RR changed by more than 15% during 3 consecutive trials the session was stopped and the subject rejected.

POS) or avoided 75% of the possible counter decrements (INC-NEG). On the other hand, the criterion was decreased by 2 bpm if the subject had failed either to obtain or avoid 25% of the possible increments or decrements. However, in order to avoid giving the subject a false appraisal of his performance, this reduction of the criterion difficulty was not extended below the OB level. The reciprocal procedure was used for subjects belonging to the slowing groups.

Use of this type of shaping procedure involves the risk that the subject might become frustrated and doubtful about the accuracy of the feedback when he experiences increasing difficulty in maintaining the required behavior. In order to minimize this risk the subject was informed that when he was further away from his HR as identified in the OB period, each counter increment (or decrement) would result in a more rapid accumulation (or less rapid loss) of money. For the positive feedback groups, the counter and its electronic accessories were arranged so that for each 2 bpm increase in the degree of difficulty, more points would accumulate at each counter jump. There were four classes of counter jumps: 1-2, 3-4, 5-6, and 7-8 digit increments at a time. This made the functioning of the counter proportional to the degree of difficulty of the task. Reciprocally, since a failure for the negative feedback groups was followed by a loss of points, each deduction was made smaller as the difficulty of the criterion increased.

No Feedback. The NF period followed termination of the F1 phase by 90 sec. This short delay was used to remind the subject that, while he would not receive feedback in the next red light periods, he should continue his attempts at HR regulation. He was reminded that any gains or losses of money recorded in the experimenter's room during those trials would be added to or subtracted from the money counter at the end of the session.

Post-Test Questionnaire. Following the last phase (F2) the subject was asked to complete the questionnaire regarding cognitive and perceptual strategies. After the completion of this questionnaire, he was fully informed of his performance and paid.

Data Conversion

Initial baseline HR for each subject was determined by converting the duration of each of the last 3 blank trials of the OB period to bpm and by averaging these 3 scores. Initial baseline RR was defined as the average length in mm for the last 4 complete respiration cycles of the same blank trials. Finally, initial RA level consisted of the averaged depth in mm of the same 4 complete respiration cycles. Measurement in mm subsequently converted to mV was done from trough to peak periods of the exhalation phase of each respiration cycle. Due to malfunctioning of the apparatus used to record SCL, the data were not usable.

Difference scores for HR, RR, and RA were obtained by subtracting each trial of the subsequent phases from the OB scores. In the statistical analysis of these difference scores, trial 1 of each phase was omitted because it followed very closely upon brief summaries of instructions which were given between the 4 experimental periods.

Results

Initial Baseline Levels

A two-way analysis of variance (Direction (D) × Mode of Feedback (M)) was performed on the average HR, RR, and RA scores of the 3 final blank trials of the OB period. The analysis performed on each of the three physiological variables did not indicate significant differences among groups.

In addition, a separate two-way analysis of variance (D × M) was run on the difference scores obtained by subtracting the HR on the 8th blank baseline trial from that on the second blank baseline trial; this provided an estimation of the effect of the first set of instructions on the HR of the subjects of the various groups during the baseline period. Since no significant differences were found among groups, these results indicate that no differential changes in baseline HR occurred as a result of these instructions.

Difference Scores

Heart Rate. A four-way analysis of variance was run on HR difference scores (D × M × Periods (P) × Trials (T), with repeated measures on P and T). The analysis revealed a significant effect on factor D, $F(1/28)=29.63$, $MS_e=4779.73$.[2] The average HR for both speeding groups was 70.92 bpm as compared to 65.81 bpm for the slowing groups. These scores represented a positive change of 1.72 bpm in the increase direction and a negative change of 3.61 bpm in the decrease direction. A significant difference was also found between the modes of feedback, $F(1/28)=9.78$, $MS_e=1578.16$. Subjects in the positive feedback groups, independently of the direction of change, produced a cardiac acceleration of the order of .59 bpm while a cardiac deceleration of 2.47 bpm was found for subjects in the negative feedback groups. These two main effects indicate a significant differentiation of the effect of positive and negative feedback on HR speeding and slowing (Table 1, Fig. 1). Subjects receiving positive feedback had more success at HR speeding than those being given negative feedback. On the other hand, subjects in the negative feedback condition were better at slowing HR than were those experiencing positive feedback. The numerical difference between INC-POS and INC-NEG groups across the 3 phases was 4.01 bpm favoring the former, while negative feedback helped subjects to decrease their HR 2.11 bpm below the HR of subjects of the DEC-POS group. A significant D × P interaction was also identified, $F(2/56)=5.14$, $MS_e=192.41$; in fact, Fig. 1 shows a gradual slow-

TABLE 1

Mean heart rate (bpm) for original baseline, feedback 1, no feedback, and feedback 2 periods

Groups	Mean Heart Rates			
	Original Baseline	Feedback 1	No Feedback	Feedback 2
INC-POS	70.13	73.56	73.36	74.66
INC-NEG	68.27	68.26	67.40	68.29
DEC-POS	68.77	67.09	66.34	65.22
DEC-NEG	70.07	67.36	65.56	63.33

[2]The .01 rejection region was adopted for all statistical tests.

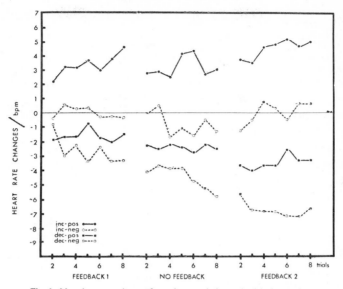

Fig. 1. Mean heart rate changes for each group during each trial of each phase.

ing of HR in both DEC-POS and DEC-NEG groups from the beginning to the end of the session while performance in the INC groups remained stable. A Newman-Keuls test revealed a significant difference between Feedback 1 and 2 periods, $F(3/112)=2.95$ in the slowing direction. It is noteworthy that no significant difference between Feedback and No Feedback phases was observed in any of the groups.

Respiration Rate. No RR differences were found among the four groups in any of the phases. However, the four-way analysis of variance indicated a M × T interaction, $F(6/128)=2.99$, $MS_e=94.16$. This significant interaction suggests that subjects who received negative feedback had a slower RR at the last trial of each phase (14.5 cycles per min) than at the first trial (15.5 cycles per min). No other differences were found relative to this variable.[3]

Respiration Amplitude. The analysis of RA difference scores revealed a significant difference between phases, $F(2/56)=3.21$, $MS_e=.0034$; subjects tended to increase RA during Feedback periods in comparison to the No Feedback period; this phenomenon was most clearly observed with

[3]However, the DEC-POS group showed a tendency to change RR; 3 subjects from this group were rejected during training because they exceeded the criterion of more than 15% RR change during 3 consecutive trials; in other words, 11 subjects who passed the initial screening were tested in order to obtain 8 who did not alter RR beyond the criterion level. There were no subjects in the other groups who altered RR to this extent. Furthermore, an additional DEC-POS group of 8 subjects was tested without use of the 15% rejection criterion and they showed a mean RR change of 51% during Feedback 2.

both speeding groups. However, the four-way analysis of variance did not reveal any significant differences among groups.

Cognitive and Perceptual Strategies. Because of the preliminary nature of the questionnaire (the items used were not mutually exclusive) it was not possible to conduct a formal statistical analysis. However, examination of mean rating scores raises a number of interesting suggestions.

The comparisons of rating scores reveal that the slowing groups used "relaxing thoughts" and "avoided looking at the feedback display" more often than subjects in the speeding groups. On the other hand, subjects in these latter groups used "activating" and "sexual thoughts" more extensively than subjects in the slowing groups. In addition, it appears that the modes of feedback could have influenced the use of two strategies: subjects in the INC-NEG group reported having used "command words" (such as "I have to increase my HR") twice as often as subjects in the DEC-NEG group; this is the opposite pattern to that found with positive feedback. In addition, subjects receiving negative feedback "looked around in a vague way" twice as often as subjects receiving positive feedback.

Frequency of Counter Triggers. As mentioned in the procedure section, each beat in the right or wrong direction (depending on group membership) was signalled to the subject by a blue light; the occurrence of 3 consecutive signalled beats resulted in the counter being triggered in the appropriate direction (the counter triggers were highly salient feedback events).

The frequency of counter triggers was determined for each subject on each trial, and submitted to a four-way analysis of variance ($D \times M \times P \times T$, with repeated measures on P and T). The analysis revealed a significant F for interaction DM, $F(1/28) = 10.79$, $MS_e = 1208.57$. This interaction indicates that subjects in the INC-NEG group received 60% of the possible counter triggers as compared to 43% for the INC-POS group, while subjects in the DEC-NEG group received 40% of the possible feedback signals as compared to 50% for the subjects in the DEC-POS group. As would be expected, these differences in the frequency of counter triggers parallel the data on HR effects shown in Fig. 1. It is worth noting that because of the shaping procedure the percentage of counter triggers was between 40% and 60% for all groups; in other words, even the most successful group (DEC-NEG) continued to experience failure at a fairly high rate.

Discussion

Differential Effects of Positive and Negative Feedback

The results clearly show a relationship between the nature of the feedback signal (success versus failure) and the nature of the task (HR speeding versus HR slowing): HR deceleration is most effectively produced with failure signals and HR acceleration is most effectively produced with success signals. There are various possible explanations for this finding. The most likely explanation appears to be the following: the success and failure signals have different biological impact (activating effects) and therefore differentially influence HR changes in the increase and decrease directions. In other words, one signal might produce a biological change in one direction, thereby aiding that direction of change and hindering or preventing the change in the opposite direction.

The evidence that positive and negative incentive stimuli have different effects on HR was examined in the introduction to this paper. As mentioned, differential HR reactions to positive and negative stimuli have been observed with animals and humans; in the present experiment it could be that those subjects receiving only positive feedback displayed a HR acceleration which helped them to increase HR but hindered their efforts at decreasing HR. Conversely, those subjects receiving only negative feedback may have displayed a cardiac deceleration which would have favored HR decrease but not HR increase.

In these terms the results reveal a compatibility between HR speeding and positive feedback, and HR slowing and negative feedback; they also underline an incompatibility of these tasks and signals when the combination is inverted. These patterns suggest that the results can be understood according to the general notions of preparedness and coun-

terpreparedness (Seligman, 1970). A similar interpretation (in different theoretical terms) can be based upon the work of Bergman and Johnson (1971). These authors have considered the problem of differential effects of various instructions. One could argue that, in the present experiment, the task set by the instructions on the one hand and the effect of the feedback stimuli on the other were divergent for the INC-NEG and DEC-POS groups, and were convergent for the INC-POS and DEC-NEG groups. In this context, the observation that subjects receiving negative feedback signals (which they had to avoid) reported having shifted their attention from the feedback stimuli to other more neutral environmental stimuli ("looking around in a vague way") is of primary importance. One is tempted to suggest that such a perceptual behavior partially isolates subjects from meaningful activating stimuli and thus hinders their efforts to increase HR but helps them to decrease HR. It is worth remembering that Seligman (1970) speculated that the notion of preparedness could be accompanied by such covarying changes in cognitive mechanisms.

In the same vein, the fact that subjects in the negative feedback groups slowed their RR throughout each part of the session is important. This respiratory change may also reflect a behavior which is incompatible with HR speeding, but is compatible with HR slowing. In addition, such respiratory changes may indicate the possibility of concomitant changes in the general activation level; however, because of the technical difficulties in the present study with skin conductance recording, no additional data are available to help clarify this issue.

Differences Between Presence and Absence of Feedback

Of importance in future research and theory is a consideration of the transfer effect; a number of studies have demonstrated the presence of a transfer phenomenon from Feedback to subsequent No Feedback periods (Brener, Kleinman & Goesling, 1969; Sroufe, 1971; Bell & Schwartz, 1972; Lang & Twentyman, 1974; Wells, 1973). Similarly in the present study there was no substantial difference in HR between the Feedback and No Feedback phases. One possible explanation is that the red light indicating the trial periods acquired, by its contiguity to the previous feedback stimuli and by its pairing to specific instructions, a conditioned incentive quality. The maintenance of performance in the No Feedback phase could then be due to the presence of conditioned responses resembling the responses observed in the Feedback phase. However, an alternative explanation should also be considered. Namely, the transfer phenomenon could be due to the ease with which subjects identify the most appropriate strategy(ies) during the initial Feedback condition. Once this identification is accomplished, they would no longer require the presence of feedback. This explanation can be related to Estes' (1971) model of human learning.

These two possible explanations are currently being evaluated in a study in which the order effect of Feedback and No Feedback periods is examined.

REFERENCES

Bell, I. R., & Schwartz, G. E. Cognitive and somatic mechanisms in voluntary control of heart rate. In D. Shapiro, T. X. Barber, L. V. DiCara, J. Kamiya, N. E. Miller, & J. Stoyva (Eds.), *Biofeedback and self control 1972.* Chicago: Aldine Publishing Co., 1973. Pp. 503–504. (Abstract)

Benjamin, L. S. Facts and artifacts in using analysis of covariance to "undo" the law of initial values. *Psychophysiology,* 1967, *4,* 187–206.

Bergman, J. S., & Johnson, H. J. The effects of instructional set and autonomic perception on cardiac control. *Psychophysiology,* 1971, *2,* 180–190.

Brener, J., Kleinman, R. A., & Goesling, W. J. The effects of different exposures to augmented sensory feedback on the control of heart rate. *Psychophysiology,* 1969, *5,* 510–516.

Deane, G. E. Cardiac activity during experimentally induced anxiety. *Psychophysiology,* 1969, *6,* 17–30.

Doehring, D. G., & Helmer, J. E. Psychophysiological responses to variable-interval reinforcement in a human operant situation. *The Psychological Record,* 1963, *13,* 283–292.

Doehring, D. G., Helmer, J. E., & Fuller, E. A. Physiological responses associated with time estimation in a human operant situation. *The Psychological Record,* 1964, *14,* 355–362.

Epstein, S., & Clarke, S. Heart rate and skin conductance during experimentally induced anxiety: Effects of anticipated intensity of noxious stimulation and experience. *Journal of Experimental Psychology,* 1970, *84,* 105–112.

Estes, W. K. Reward in human learning: Theoretical issues and strategic choice points. In R. Glaser (Ed.), *The nature of reinforcement.* New York: Academic Press, 1971. Pp. 16–37.

Folkow, B., & Neil, E. *Circulation.* London: Oxford University Press, 1971.

Lang, P. J., & Twentyman, C. T. Learning to control heart rate: Binary vs analogue feedback. *Psychophysiology,* 1974, *11,* 616–629.

Malcuit, G. Cardiac responses in aversive situations with and without avoidance possibility. *Psychophysiology,* 1973, *10,* 295–305.

Malcuit, G., Ducharme, R., & Belanger, D. Cardiac activity in rats during bar-press avoidance and "freezing" responses. *Psychological Reports,* 1968, *23,* 11–18.

Obrist, P. A., Webb, R. A., & Sutterer, J. R. Heart rate and somatic changes during aversive conditioning and a simple reaction time task. *Psychophysiology,* 1969, *5,* 696–723.

Schwartz, G. E. Toward a theory of voluntary control of response patterns in the cardiovascular system. In P. A. Obrist, A. H. Black, J. Brener, & L. V. DiCara (Eds.), *Cardiovascular psychophysiology: Current issues in response mechanisms, biofeedback and methodology.* Chicago: Aldine Publishing Co., 1974. Pp. 406–440.

Seligman, M. E. P. The generality of the laws of learning. *Psychological Review,* 1970, *77,* 406–418.

Sroufe, L. A. Effects of depth and rate of breathing on heart rate and heart rate variability. *Psychophysiology,* 1971, *8,* 648–655.

Wells, D. T. Large magnitude voluntary heart rate changes. *Psychophysiology,* 1973, *10,* 260–269.

Wenzel, B. M. Changes in heart rate associated with responses based on positive and negative reinforcement. *Journal of Comparative & Physiological Psychology,* 1961, *54,* 638–644.

REFERENCE NOTE

1. Roberts, L. E. *Comparative psychophysiology of the electrodermal and cardiac control systems* (Tech. Rep. No. 53). Hamilton, Ontario: McMaster University, Department of Psychology, 1973.

37

Differential Effects of Heart Rate Modification Training on College Students, Older Males, and Patients with Ischemic Heart Disease

Peter J. Lang, William G. Troyer, Jr.,
Craig T. Twentyman, and Robert J. Gatchel

Seventy male subjects participated in a six session study of feedback-mediated heart rate modification. Three groups of subjects were compared: (1) college students, (2) patients with ischemic heart disease, and (3) healthy males, age-matched to the patients. The groups did not differ in heart rate during rest or in response to a perceptual-motor tracking task. However, the college students produced significantly larger changes in cardiac rate than the other two groups when instructed to modify heart rate (speed or slow) and provided with exteroceptive feedback. The patients showed the poorest overall feedback performance. These differences between groups were greater for speeding than for the slowing task. Relationships were explored between feedback performance and resting heart and respiration rate, drug regime, and personality questionnaires. The results were consistent with the hypothesis that interdependence between psychological stimuli and cardiovascular events is reduced in heart disease.

INTRODUCTION

A variety of investigators have shown that training programs based on visceral

From the University of Wisconsin, Madison.
Dr. Troyer is now at the Abraham Lincoln School of Medicine, Department of Medicine, Chicago, Illinois.
This research was supported in part by grants from the National Institute of Mental Health (MH-10993), the Wisconsin Heart Association, and the University of Wisconsin Graduate School. The computer program for the experimental procedure was written by Michael Falconer who, along with Jean Holland, also assisted with the data analysis.
A part of this research was presented at the meeting of the American Psychosomatic Society, April 1973, in Denver, Colorado.
Address reprint requests to: Peter J. Lang, Ph.D., Department of Psychology, University of Wisconsin, Madison, Wisconsin 53706.
Received for publication December 10, 1974; revision received April 28, 1975.

organ feedback can be used to modify the heart rates of college student subjects (1–5). Furthermore, the success of this work has prompted speculation that such procedures might form the basis for the therapeutic treatment of cardiovascular disease (6,7). Engel and his associates (8,9) have already studied a series of patients with cardiac rate anomolies and explored the use of feedback techniques in reestablishing a more normal rhythm. However, there has as yet been no systematic evaluation of the comparative ability of normal subjects and patients who have been afflicted with heart disease, or even of older nonpatient subjects and the more typical student sample, to perform the basic heart rate modification task. The present study was designed to fill this need.

Reprinted with permission of American Elsevier Publishing Company, Inc. from *Psychosomatic Medicine*, 1975, Vol. 37, 429-446.

The experiment evaluated the performance of three subject groups: (1) young college students, (2) middle-age patients with ischemic heart disease, and (3) non-patients that were matched in age to the heart disease sample. Lang (10) recently proposed that the feedback-based acquisition of visceral control might best be considered an example of skills learning and, furthermore, that variables found to be influential in motor skills acquisition should also be determining factors in visceral learning. It is well known that the efficiency and quality of perceptual-motor performance is reduced with increasing age and disease of the somatic system (11). It was predicted that differences between groups in the present experiment, in trained heart rate control, would be similarly determined.

An accumulating body of evidence (7,5,12) suggests that heart rate speeding and heart rate slowing follow a different pattern of acquisition and are not equally influenced by the traditional learning variables. Thus, performance on speeding and slowing tasks was separately assessed. The experiment was designed to evaluate performance during feedback, transfer of this training to nonfeedback conditions, and, furthermore, to compare the effects of feedback training with the heart rate change prompted by a psychomotor task employing a similar display. The relationships of heart rate change to resting heart rate, changes in respiratory cycle length, and cycle length variability were also examined. Correlational relationships between heart rate performance and six self-report questionnaires were assessed.

METHOD

Subjects

Seventy males, divided into three groups, served as subjects in the experiment. One group was composed of undergraduates at the University of Wisconsin-Madison. Another group consisted of 30 patients with ischemic heart disease, referred by and currently under the care of individual members of the clinical faculty of the University of Wisconsin Medical

School. Twenty-two of these patients had a previous myocardial infarction. Eight of these had a history of anterior chest pain on exertion. Twelve had complained of angina, with no evidence of a previous infarction. Nine subjects had had revascularization surgery. None of the patients was in the convalescent phase postinfarction. All were ambulatory and most were currently active in their vocation. The third group was composed of 20 healthy subjects, age-matched to the patients and free from any known cardiac disease symptoms, contacted through Volunteers for Action. The ages of the patients ranged from 43 to 75, mean 58.0 years, and the age-matched control group from 42 to 71, mean 60.6 years. All subjects were paid $10.00 for their participation and informed of the scientific and potential clinical benefits of the study.

Apparatus

Heart rate and respiration were recorded on a Beckman Type R Dynograph. Heart rate was recorded through Beckman silver-silver chloride electrodes, attached over the lower anterolateral ribs. Two Parks mercury strain gages (3 in. in length), wired in series and taped to the chest and abdomen, recorded respiration. A Beckman A-C coupler with a 1 sec time constant monitored respiration.

A Tektronix RM503 oscilloscope was set so the "R" wave of each EKG interrupted a DEC PDP-12 computer, allowing measurement of each interpulse interval to the nearest 0.004 sec. A Schmitt trigger, connected to the voltage output of the respiration channel, also interrupted the computer and measured each respiration cycle length to the nearest 0.10 sec.

The timing of the experiment, presentation of instructions and feedback, data acquisition and primary data reduction were all accomplished in real-time by the PDP-12. The computer and physiological recording equipment were housed in the room adjacent to the subject room. The subject room was sound shielded from the laboratory and lighted by a low intensity lamp. The subject sat in a semi-reclining chair, facing a DEC VR-12 oscilloscope. The scope was slaved to the computer and the computer presented instructions and feedback displays on the scope face.

Heart Rate Display

Analogue information about the length of R-R intervals was presented in the form of a line sweeping horizontally across the scope from left to right (see Fig. 1). The line was initiated by an R wave and was terminated by the fifth subsequent R wave. At the fifth R wave, a 1 cm vertical marker was briefly illuminated and within microseconds a new line started across the screen. On the oscilloscope display there was also a fixed vertical line, running from the top to the bottom of the screen. The line served as a criterion marker. When the subject was instructed to increase

Fig. 1. The feedback display as presented on the subjects' oscilloscope. The sweep line has terminated beyond the target. The appearance of the word "GOOD" indicates successful heart slowing for this sequence of five interbeat intervals.

his heart rate, his task was to terminate the horizontal line before it crossed the vertical target line. When instructed to slow, the task was to extend the horizontal line as far as possible past the target line. When the subject accomplished the required task the word "GOOD" was briefly illuminated on the screen at the termination of a successful five beat interval. The criterion target line was initially set at the subject's median R-R interval. This was established initially during the 1 min try period at the beginning of the session where the subject was asked to accomplish the speeding or slowing task without the aid of feedback. The target line was subsequently altered automatically to help "shape" the subjects' responses, i.e., if at least two-thirds of all the horizontal lines terminated on one side of the criterion line (either all hits or all misses) during any feedback trial, then a new target line would be set for the subsequent trial. The position of the new criterion line was always midway between the position of the old target line and the place on the screen that represented the subject's median on the last feedback trial. Thus, the shaping schedule made the task somewhat more difficult to achieve for those subjects who were successful and easier for the subjects who were having difficulty.

Tracking Display and Time Estimation

These tasks were included in the design to provide a reference point for evaluating the impact of feedback training on heart rate. It was expected that the unconditioned physiological effects of monitoring a visual display and task involvement would be similar in feedback and tracking. Thus, differences between

these tasks could be attributed to the real effects of training and instructions on heart rate rather than to an artifact of unlearned or previously learned responses to the stimulus context.

The tracking task was visually similar to the display generated by the subject's R-R intervals. The sweep line moved across the screen and terminated at a varying rate, averaging 70 sweeps per minute. However, this display was generated by the computer and the terminations randomly occurred on both sides of the vertical target line. The subject's task was to monitor the lines and press a small microswitch whenever the horizontal line terminated on the designated side of the vertical target line. If the subject pressed within 400 msec after termination, the word "GOOD" was illuminated on the screen. This latency did not press the abilities of the subjects, but did assure attention to the display. Subjects also performed a nondisplay time estimation task. They were instructed to press a microswitch, exactly marking each 10 sec interval over a 1 min period. This estimation task was used as a control procedure for those periods in the heart rate task when subjects were instructed to speed or slow heart rate without the feedback display.

Experimental Design

Each subject came to the laboratory for an introductory session and for six experimental sessions. The initial session for all subjects was used to familiarize them with the laboratory setting, and also to screen the students and age-matched control subjects for cardiac disorder or other medical problems that

TABLE 1. Standard Format across Experimental Sessions and Tasks Associated with Each Time Phase

Time phase	Session	
	Heart rate control	Tracking
1. 3 min	Initial baseline period	Initial baseline period
2. 1 min	Try period *For the next few minutes try to in-* *crease (decrease) your heart rate* *as much as possible*	Time estimation period *Time estimation–Please press the* *button every ten seconds*
3. 3 min	Feedback period *The feedback display will now be pre-* *sented to help increase (decrease)* *your heart rate*	Tracking period *The visual display will now be present-* *ed. Press the button each time* *the moving line falls short of (ex-* *ceeds) the target*
4. 1 min	Transfer period *For this period continue to increase* *(decrease) your heart rate as much as* *possible*	Time estimation period *Time estimation–Please press* *the button every ten seconds*
5. 1 min	Time-out period *Stop working on the heart rate task* *but continue to sit quietly. You will* *receive further instructions shortly*	Time-out period *Stop working for awhile but continue* *to sit quietly. You will receiver further* *instructions shortly*
6. 3 min	Final baseline period *Instructions same as time-out period* *above*	Final baseline period *Instructions same as time-out period* *above*

Note: Periods 3–5 (feedback or tracking, transfer or time estimation, and time-out) were repeated five times in sequence prior to the final baseline period. The feedback and tracking instructions displayed on the oscilloscope screen (shown here in italic type) were presented for 6 sec prior to the 3 min feedback or tracking work period. Instructions for other experimental periods were on continuously during the entire interval.

would prevent them from participating fully in the experiment. At this time questions were answered about the purpose of the study and an explanation was given of how physiological recordings were taken and how the data were stored.

Subjects in both the college sample and the age-matched control group were then randomly assigned to one of the two subgroups, determined by order of subsequent presentation of the tracking and heart rate control sessions. The patients with ischemic heart disease were randomly assigned to one of three experimental groups. The first two patient subgroups were treated the same as those of the college and age-matched samples and were part of the primary experimental design. In this design, one subgroup (N = 10) from each population received three sessions of tracking estimation followed by three sessions of heart rate control. The second subgroup received the sessions in a counterbalanced order with the heart rate control tasks coming first. In each block of three sessions the order of tasks was held constant so that if the task were heart rate control, the first session would be slowing, the second speeding, and the third another slowing session. Similarly, if tracking were the task, the first session would be tracking-right, i.e., pushing the microswitch when the line terminated to

the right of the vertical center line. The next session would be tracking-left, which was followed by another session of tracking-right. These tracking sessions served as a within subject control for the un-conditioned effects of watching the display monitor.

The third, supplementary patient group (N = 10) received six consecutive sessions of heart rate control training, two speeding sessions and four slowing sessions. This group was included to study the effects of longer term instruction and feedback.

Procedure

All sessions followed the same format. Blood pressure was recorded prior to and following each experimental session. The session itself followed a standard format and was controlled by the computer. This format was the same for all groups across all the sessions and can be seen in Table 1. The time of day for each session was kept constant and the six sessions were conducted over a period of 2 to 3 weeks. Subjects came either twice a week or three times a week depending on their schedule.

At the beginning of each session, the subject was seated in a reclining chair. Electrodes and strain gages were applied to the chest and then the experimenter left the room to adjust the polygraph and begin the computer demonstration display. On returning to the subject room the experimenter read a standardized set of instructions which included a reference to the oscilloscope that displayed a tracking demonstration or the analogue display of the subject's median R-R interval, whichever was appropriate for that session. The subject was then informed that the computer would begin the program shortly and was also instructed to relax for the next several minutes until the initial display instructions appeared.

Following each session subjects filled out a short questionnaire which asked about the subject's health, amount of food consumed and amount of exercise in the past 2 hours, etc. After the final session, patient and the older normal subjects filled out a postexperimental questionnaire and the following self-report inventories: the Internal-External (I-E) Scale (13), a Body Perception Questionnaire, the Wilkinson Impulsivity Scale (14), and the Feelings of Inferiority, Muscle Tension and Autonomic Arousal Sub-scales of the Epstein-Fenz Anxiety Inventory (15).

Data Reduction Analysis

The raw heart rate and respiration data were written on magnetic tape at the end of each session by the PDP-12. These data were edited on the computer to eliminate any artifact resulting from missed triggers or equipment failures. For each feedback, transfer, and rest trial block the median and interquartile range for interpulse interval and respiration cycle length were computed.[1] These data were later analyzed by a UNIVAC 1108 computer.

RESULTS

Base Heart Rate and Feedback Performance

Average initial resting heart rates for the primary experimental groups are presented in Table 2. There was a tendency for the age-matched control subjects to have slightly slower base heart rates than the other subjects; however, analysis of variance did not yield a Groups F value that approached significance ($F = 1.67$, $df = 2,54$; $P > 0.15$). Furthermore, there was no significant difference in base heart rate prior to the motor tracking and prior to the heart rate modification tasks ($F < 1$) or was there an initial level difference between training sessions ($F = 1.25$, $df = 2,108$; $P > 0.20$).

---

[1]Median interpulse interval and interquartile range were used in preference to mean interval and standard deviation because the median is less vulnerable than the mean to the effects of a few extreme scores. It is possible for the computer system trigger to stutter and produce occasional spurious long or short beats. While most of these were eliminated through editing, the use of statistics based on median values helps further to insure that such malfunctions will not greatly influence the results.

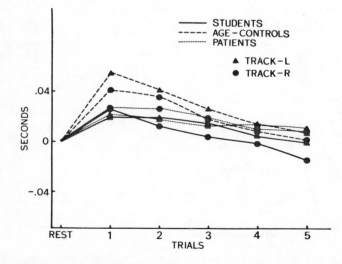

Fig. 2. Change from initial rest in interbeat interval over feedback trials for the two tracking tasks. Change upward from base indicates a decrease in interpulse interval length (an *increase* in heart rate). Data for college students, patients with ischemic heart disease, and their age-matched controls are reported.

TABLE 2.   Heart Rate Expressed in Beats per Minute for Initial Base Periods

	Sessions					
	I		II		III	
	Slow	Track	Speed	Track	Slow	Track
Students	72.85	72.74	70.84	71.36	71.96	72.56
Age-controls	69.99	69.34	68.87	68.93	68.74	65.55
Heart patients	73.02	74.00	71.80	73.20	73.17	72.95

Subjects' heart rates during the tracking and feedback tasks were first analyzed as change in median interpulse interval from each session's initial base heart interval. In Fig. 2 tracking task performance over trials for all groups is presented. The figure displays results for the track-left session and the average of the two track-right sessions. A modest increase in heart rate is apparent on the initial few trials, with a return to baseline toward the end of the session. There was no significant difference in the performance of the three subject groups during the tracking tasks ($F < 1$).

Average performance over trials during the heart rate modification task is presented in Fig. 3. For both speeding and slowing sessions, the students show the best performance, followed closely by the older, healthy subjects. The patients with a history of heart disease profited least from instructions and training, and showed the poorest performance on both heart rate speeding and slowing. This overall impression was confirmed by analysis of variance (Group $F = 5.54$, $df = 2,54$; $P < 0.01$). Planned comparisons of heart rate performance scores were made between the following groups: (1) college students versus age-matched controls and patients and (2) age-matched controls versus patients. In the analysis of overall perfor-

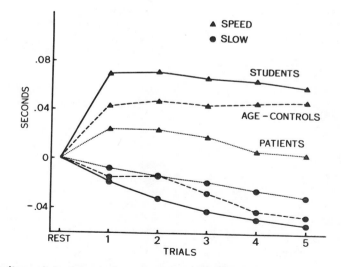

Fig. 3.   Speeding and slowing task changes in interbeat interval over feedback trials. Data from the two slowing sessions are averaged. Separate curves are presented for college students, ischemic heart disease patients, and age-matched controls. An increase in heart rate from 72 to 80 B /M represents a change of 0.08 sec in interpulse interval period.

mance scores (speeding and slowing) for all three sessions, the students clearly showed superior performance relative to the other groups ($F = 6.28, df = 1,57; P < 0.025$). There was also a tendency for the age-matched controls to demonstrate a better performance than the heart disease patients ($F = 2.87, df = 1,57; P < 0.10$). In the analysis of individual training sessions, college students showed a trend towards greater change than the other subjects in the first slowing session ($F = 3.69, df = 1,57; P < 0.10$), but this effect was not present during the second slowing session ($F = 1.27, df = 1,57; P > 0.10$). There was also a tendency for the students to show better performance than the older subjects during the speeding session ($F = 3.02, df = 1,54; P < 0.10$). None of the comparisons between the age-matched controls and patients for the individual sessions approached significance.

Heart rate change during the feedback

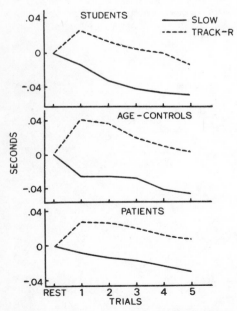

Fig. 4. A comparison of changes in interbeat interval over tracking (right) trials for college students, ischemic heart disease patients, and age-matched controls. Trials are averaged over two slowing sessions.

and tracking tasks as compared separately for each subject group. In Fig. 4, heart interval change over feedback trials is presented as the average of the two slowing sessions (I and III). These data are compared with the heart interval change occasioned by these same subjects during tracking sessions I and III. For all groups, subjects show significantly greater slowing during the feedback task than during tracking for both sessions (students, $F = 13.13$ and 17.38; patients, $F = 19.58$ and 20.35; age-matched controls, $F = 19.77$ and $11.09, df = 1,19$, all P values less than 0.01).

Comparable data for the single speeding session and second tracking session are presented in Fig. 5. As has been found in previous experiments with this method (5,12), college students show faster heart rates when they receive feedback and are instructed to speed than when they visually track a similar but heart unrelated display ($F = 6.38, df = 1,19; P < 0.05$). However, no similar effect is apparent for the patient sample. Analysis of variance confirmed the impression given by Fig. 5. Patients failed to accelerate heart rate with feedback, relative to tracking task changes ($F < 1$). Although the overall difference between tasks was not significant for the age-matched control subjects ($F < 1$), there was not a significant task by trial interaction ($F = 5.11, df = 2,54; P < 0.025$). As can be seen in Fig. 5, speeding task heart rate was faster than tracking heart rate on later trials for the older, healthy subjects.

Instructions and Feedback

Prior to training, all subjects were instructed to attempt to speed and slow heart rate without feedback. While changes in rate were smaller under these conditions than with feedback, some similar group differences were observed. Thus, an analysis of the initial try period (speeding instructions only) yielded a significant Groups effect ($F = 4.34, df = 2,54; P < 0.05$), with college students again showing the greatest speeding performance. This overall impression was confirmed by a

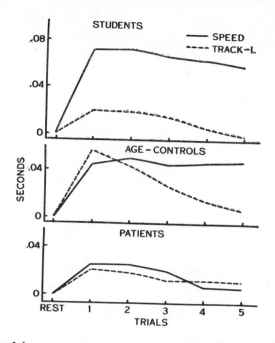

Fig. 5. A comparison of changes in interbeat interval over tracking (left) and feedback speeding trials for college students, ischemic heart disease patients, and age-matched controls.

significant comparison of the students with the other groups for this period ($F = 6.40, df = 1,57; P < 0.025$). However, no try period (instructions-only) group differences were found for heart rate slowing.

To determine if feedback training produced group effects that were independent of those prompted by instructions alone, median interpulse intervals during feedback were analyzed as deviations from the initial try period. No significant difference between groups was found for the speeding session, suggesting that feedback training acted mainly to enhance a degree of instructional control that was already available to the subjects. However, group differences were obtained for the two slowing sessions (Session I, $F = 2.96, df = 2,54; P < 0.10$. Session III, $F = 5.09, df = 2,54; P < 0.01$). Again, it was the college students who showed the best performance. They were able to utilize the feedback more than the older subjects in slowing heart rate beyond the rate achieved with instructions-only.

Transfer of Training

All subjects appeared to sustain heart rate performance changes during the transfer periods relative to their heart rates during the posttracking, time estimation task (task $F = 4.02, df = 2,54; P < 0.05$). However, unlike feedback trials, there was no overall difference between subject groups. Furthermore, analysis of individual groups by sessions showed that the differences between the transfer and time estimation task performance were significant only for the slowing sessions. Thus, no subject group clearly showed significant speeding during the nonfeedback, transfer periods.

Respiration Cycle Length

No group differences in initial base respiration rate were observed ($F = 1.98, df = 2,54; P > 0.10$) nor did groups differ in respiration rate during the try periods that preceded feedback practice, during the

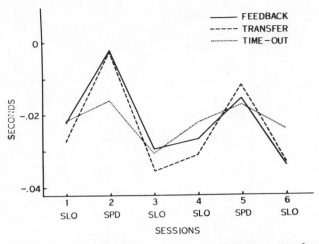

Fig. 6. Changes in average interbeat interval from initial rest over successive sessions for patients receiving extended training. Feedback, transfer, and time-out periods are separately graphed.

speeding or the first slowing session (Fs < 1). However, a significant difference was found during the second slowing session (F = 3.45, df = 2,54; P < 0.05), with college students slowing respiration rate the most, followed by age-matched subjects and then the heart patients. As with the heart rate data, there were no group or session differences in the analysis of respiration during tracking. There was a significant difference between sessions in the analysis of the feedback task (F = 50.29, df = 2,54; P < 0.001)—indicating that respiration rate was relatively faster during the speeding task than during slowing. However, there was no significant difference in respiration cycle length between groups, during either tracking or feedback trials.

Effects of Extended Training

Interpulse interval change over sessions for the extended-training patient group is presented in Fig. 6. Relative to initial base, heart rate was faster during speeding feedback and transfer trials than during the same periods for the slowing sessions (F = 10.89, df = 1,45; P < 0.001). Although the time-out rates tend to be pulled in the di-

rection of that session's feedback instructions, there was no significant difference between sessions for this rest period. There were no speeding-slowing differences for any period in either respiration rate or variability.

It will also be noted in Fig. 6 that these patients did not increase heart rate above their initial base level and, furthermore, that there was no significant improvement over sessions in either speeding or slowing performance (F < 1, df = 3,27; P > 0.20).

Correlational Analysis

Correlations between feedback performance and initial heart rate are presented in Table 3. A close relationship between base average interpulse interval, pulse variability, and performance is apparent for the college students. Thus, college students show greater speeding if they have initially slow, variable heart rates. Furthermore, greater slowing is associated with faster base heart rates for these subjects, as would be predicted by the law of initial values (16). However, very little relationship between base rates and performance is apparent for either older normals or patients.

The failure of base rate to correlate with

TABLE 3. Correlations between Heart Rate Feedback Performance, Base Interbeat Interval (IBI), and Interbeat Interquartile Range (IQR)

		Sessions		
		I (Slow)	II (Speed)	III (Slow)
Students	IBI	−0.41[a]	0.49[b]	−0.55[b]
(N = 20)	IQR	−0.01	0.63[c]	−0.24
Age-controls	IBI	0.14	0.27	−0.01
(N = 20)	IQR	0.16	0.08	0.17
Patients	IBI	−0.09	0.16	−0.06
(N = 30)	IQR	0.35	0.21	0.10

[a] $P < 0.10$.
[b] $P < 0.05$.
[c] $P < 0.005$.

performance for the two older groups is not attributable to a narrower distribution of base values for these subjects. The group standard deviations for median heart period are actually slightly larger for patients and older normal subjects than for college students (0.13, 0.14, 0.11 sec, respectively). However, the failure of the patient group to show a significant relationship between variability and speeding may have been due to the significantly smaller within subject interquartile range (of base heart period) for these subjects (student base IQR = 0.09; age-matched controls, IQR = 0.05; patients IQR = 0.04 sec; $F = 30.79$, $df = 2,54$; $P < 0.001$).

Both the students and older normal subjects showed a negative correlation between respiration cycle length and concur-rent speeding performance (Table 4). No clear relationship between respiration rate and slowing performance was apparent.[2] Patients did not display covariation between heart rate performance and respiration cycle. However, during the base level

---

[2] Blood pressure did not correlate with any of the heart rate base or performance measures or with base respiration. In age-matched subjects, systolic blood pressure was negatively correlated with average respiration period during the first and second slowing sessions ($rs = -0.64$, -0.44; $Ps < 0.002$, < 0.04). Diastolic blood pressure was positively correlated with average respiration period during the speeding session for patients ($r = 0.49$, $P < 0.03$). These results indicate that higher systolic pressure in age-matched subjects was associated with faster respiration during slowing feedback trials and that higher diastolic pressure was associated with slower respiration during the patients' speeding sessions.

TABLE 4. Correlations between Change in Respiration Cycle Length and Heart Rate Feedback Performance

	Sessions		
	I (Slow)	II (Speed)	III (Slow)
Students	0.38	−0.47[a]	−0.01
(N = 20)			
Age-controls	0.21	−0.53[b]	0.04
(N = 20)			
Patients	0.06	0.06	0.19
(N = 30)			

[a] $P < 0.05$.
[b] $P < 0.02$.

TABLE 5.   Correlations between Base Interbeat Interval, Base Respiration Period, and Respiration Period Interquartile Range (IQR)

	Sessions		
	I	II	III
Patients			
Respiration period	0.35[a]	0.43[b]	0.37[b]
Respiration IQR	0.22	0.56[c]	0.41[b]
Age-controls			
Respiration period	−0.20	−0.004	0.12
Respiration IQR	0.23	0.12	0.04
Students			
Respiration period	−0.22	0.04	0.12
Respiration IQR	−0.16	−0.38	−0.22

[a] $P < 0.10$.
[b] $P < 0.05$.
[c] $P < 0.005$.

recording at the beginning of each session, an unusually close relationship between heart period and respiration period was observed for patient subjects (see Table 5): a slower heart rate was strongly associated with a slower and more variable respiration rate. For both groups of nonpatient subjects, there is no such stable relationship between base heart rate and respiration. The correlations for these latter groups all hover around zero, with no more positive than negative values.

Personality and Actuarial Data

Mean personality test scores for the older normals and patients with heart disease are presented in Table 6. The only significant difference between groups was on the Wilkinson Impulsivity Scale. The normal subjects appear nominally more impulsive than the patients on this scale.

None of the six questionnaires administered yielded consistent correlations with heart rate control performance. The highest questionnaire value was obtained for patients, between performance in slowing session III and the I–E scale ($r = 0.40, P < 0.07$). However, resting base heart and respiration period did relate consistently to the I–E scale (see Table 7), particularly for the nonpatient sample. Thus, the more external oriented subjects tended to have relatively slower heart rates and, paradoxically, faster respiration. Slower base heart rates were also associated with high Im-

TABLE 6.   Analysis of Variance Comparing Patients (Primary Sample) with Age-Matched Controls

Scale	Patient means	Age-controls means	df[a]	F ratio	Exact probability
Internal-External	7.00	8.47	(1,31)	1.49	0.23
Body Perception Questionnaire	4.21	3.39	(1,37)	3.04	0.09
Wilkinson Impulsivity Scale	66.72	71.74	(1,37)	4.49	0.04
Epstein-Fenz Anxiety Scale					
Feelings of Inferiority	51.07	49.06	(1,36)	0.28	0.60
Muscle Tension	34.21	36.06	(1,36)	0.00	1.00
Autonomic Arousal	32.48	32.72	(1,36)	0.01	0.93

[a] Changes in df reflect missing data.

TABLE 7. Correlations between the Internal-External Scale Resting Base Heart Period and Respiration Period

	Sessions		
	I	II	III
Patients			
Heart period	⁓0.38	⁓0.33	⁓0.48[a]
Respiration period	0.15	⁓0.15	⁓0.30
Age-controls			
Heart period	0.51[a]	0.52[a]	0.17
Respiration period	⁓0.63[b]	⁓0.66[b]	⁓0.65[b]

[a] $P < 0.05$.
[b] $P < 0.01$.

pulsivity Scale scores for older normals (Session I, $r = 0.53, P < 0.02$; Session II, $r = 0.62, P < 0.005$), as was greater heart period variability (Session I, $r = 0.58, P < 0.001$). None of the anxiety scales were consistently or significantly associated with base heart rate.

Within group correlations with subject age are presented in Table 8. Older patients tended to be less tolerant of delay and more anxious than younger patients. No relationship between age and anxiety was found for nonpatient controls. Within groups, age was not clearly related to heart rate feedback performance. However, the tracking task did yield significant correlations with age. Tracking task heart rate tended to increase more in older subjects in both populations (patients Session II, $r = 0.41, P < 0.07$; age-matched controls Session II, $r = 0.38, P < 0.10$; Session III, $r = 0.50, P < 0.03$).

Drug Effects

The patients who participated in this

study were all under a physician's care, and many were following a drug regimen. In order to analyze for a possible influence of medication on performance, all patient subjects were divided into the following three groups, depending on the known effect of the drug taken on heart rate: (1) no medication or medication with no known effect (e.g., vitamins, Maalox, anticoagulants), $N = 12$; (2) possible effect (e.g., Ornade, Valium, Quinidex), $N = 9$; and (3) definite effect (e.g., Digitoxin, Ismelin, Elavil), $N = 9$. Analysis of variance was used to compare mean performance differences among the three drug groups and the age-matched controls. None of the latter subjects were taking drugs with a confirmed influence on heart rate.

There were no significant differences among the patient drug subgroups in base resting heart rate. However, the group receiving drugs with a known effect on heart rate showed significantly less speeding than did the no-effect group ($F = 4.39, df = 1,19; P < 0.05$). This result is consistent

TABLE 8. Correlations between Subject Age and Questionnaire Scores

	Patients	Age-controls
Wilkinson Impulsivity Scale	0.40[a]	0.09
Epstein-Fenz Anxiety Scale		
Feelings of Inferiority (FI)	0.44[a]	0.08
Muscle Tension (MT)	0.55[b]	−0.01
Autonomic Arousal (AA)	0.59[b]	0.01

[a] $P < 0.05$.
[b] $P < 0.005$.

with the direction of change that would be predicted for this sample. That is to say, six of the nine subjects in the definite effect group were taking medication such as Digitoxin, which would be expected to prompt heart rate decrease or inhibit increasing rates. Again consistent with medication influence, there was a tendency for the definite-drug-effect group to show relatively greater slowing performance than the no-effect patients. However, this only approached significance for subjects' best trial on Session III ($F = 3.51$, $df = 1,19; P < 0.08$). A more reliable drug influence was found for tracking trials. Thus, the no-effect group tended to show a slight increase in heart rate during tracking (as did the age-matched controls); the definite-drug-effect group showed significantly smaller heart rate acceleration than no-effect subjects (tracking Session II, $F = 5.073$, $df = 1,19$, $P < 0.02$; Session III, $F = 4.06$, $df = 1,19; P < 0.04$).

When the no-drug-effect patient subgroup was compared with the age-matched controls, differences similar to those found for the total sample were observed. Thus, age-matched subjects showed significantly more slowing than no-drug-patients on their best trial for Session I ($F = 5.35$, $df = 1,29; P < 0.03$). Differences between groups in speeding were in the direction of better performance for nonpatient subjects, but the best-trial difference was not significant with the reduced sample size ($F = 2.69$, $df = 1,29; P < 0.11$). The biggest effect of drug subgroup was not on heart rate control performance but on resting heart rate variability. Both the no-effect and the definite-effect groups showed less variability than the possible-effect group (Session III, overall $F = 5.975$, $df = 1,19; P < 0.007$). This may reflect the physician's tendency not to give medication to subjects with stable heart rates (the no-effect group), and a concomitant tendency for the drugs to have an anti-arrhythmic consequence in the definite-effect group. As the patients in the possible-effect group were not being treated with powerful heart rate modifiers, their resting variability was

about the same as the nonpatient, age-matched controls.

DISCUSSION

The results of this experiment strongly suggest that the ability to change heart rate in response to instructions and feedback varies significantly with the age and disease state of the subjects. The college students in this study performed similarly to previous samples from this laboratory (5,12); they were able to both increase and decrease heart rate relative to a control task. However, the performance of older men was clearly less efficient than that of students, and ambulatory patients with heart disease showed the poorest performance of the three groups. The deficit appeared on both speeding and slowing tasks. The combined task analysis showed significantly better performance for college students, and a near significant superiority of older normals over the patient sample. When heart rate slowing and speeding tasks were separately compared with tracking sessions, college students showed significant relative acceleration during the speeding task, patients showed no speeding trials heart rate increase, and the older normals had faster speeding task heart rates only on the last few trials of the session. Patients and older normals also increased heart rate less than students in the instructions-only (try) condition. Furthermore, they showed less slowing than college subjects during feedback, relative to the change achieved under the try instruction. In brief, the evidence suggests a hierarchical ordering of heart control ability on feedback tasks, with college students clearly superior to both groups, and the age-matched controls marginally better than the patient subjects.

These results are consistent with the hypothesis that age and disease will prompt a deterioration in ability to instructionally control heart rate and profit from feedback training. Nevertheless, it should be noted that the college and older male sample were drawn from different populations, and thus might differ in ways other than age. It might be conjectured that the reduced performance of the patients was of motivational origins, e.g., they failed to speed heart rate for fear of aggravating their own heart condition. However, no subject expressed this fear. There were no significant differences between patients and controls in subjective report of difficulty in either speeding or slowing. Furthermore, the patients were if anything more concerned about performing well. Both groups similarly rated the training to be of value personally, and the difference was not significant ($t = 0.86, df = 32; P > 0.10$). Finally, the pattern of deficit shown by the patients (relative to college students) was similar to that of the age-matched controls, who were in good health and presumably no more motivated than students to avoid an increment in heart activity.

The correlational data suggest that the poorer performance of the older subjects was attributable in part to differences in cardiovascular lability and perhaps also to special characteristics of the patients' respiratory-cardiovascular dynamics. Thus, college students were significantly more variable in resting heart rate than the patients. Furthermore, as has been previously observed in this laboratory (5,12), lability and base rate were factors contributing to the degree of feedback performance the students achieved (particularly for speeding). These correlations between performance and base measures were absent for the older subjects. This conveys a picture of relative cardiac inflexibility in older subjects (17). They simply had fewer responses available to bring under instructional control.

The patient subjects also showed a unique dependence between respiratory function and heart rate. Under resting conditions these variables were firmly coupled in the heart disease sample, whereas they were essentially unrelated for resting normal subjects. This could reflect the need of damaged cardiac tissue for closer and more rapid oxygenation. Perhaps it indicates damage to collateral, supplying

vessels which force a more rapid respiratory response in cardiac exertion. In any event, the result suggests a reduced influence of psychological control of rate in the face of more immediate, homeostatic needs.

Medication clearly had a significant effect on several base and performance measures. Subjects receiving medication designed to inhibit heart rate increases showed depressed speeding feedback performance and also showed less heart rate increase on the tracking task. As drug administration was allowed to vary freely, it is not clear whether all drug effects were in fact due to medication, or represented differences in the subjects to whom a physician did or did not give a drug. Difference in resting base variability described in the Results section imply the influence of this latter variable. Nevertheless, a comparison of age-matched control subjects and the no-medication-effect patient group yielded a pattern of results similar to that shown by the entire patient sample. This suggests that drugs were not a primary factor in producing the overall impression of poor psychological control of heart rate in ischemic heart disease.

Heart rate control performance did not covary significantly with any of the personality questionnaires. However, the resting physiology of the nonpatient subjects did covary with Rotter's I–E scale and with the Wilkinson Impulsivity Scale. Subjects with slower and more variable heart rates tended to be more externally oriented and more impulsive. This pattern was not found for patients. One is tempted to see this as a further example of the dissociation of psychological control from the cardiovascular system in ischemic patients. Neither group showed covariation between any of the anxiety scales and heart rate. However, considering the effects on life expectancy of ischemic disease, it is not a surprise to find that with increasing age patients become more generally anxious and somewhat less tolerant of delay.

In addition to profiting less than nonpatients from brief heart control training, subjects with ischemic heart disease also failed to show improvement with additional sessions. There were modest transfer effects from feedback to no-feedback conditions. However, in the case of heart rate speeding, it must be pointed out that patients' averages with training never exceeded initial resting levels. It is fair to say that these data do not encourage the broad use of feedback methods as an adjunctive treatment in heart disease. Nevertheless, there are reasons to temper this conclusion. First of all, investigators who have utilized feedback methods in treating arrythmias have used many more sessions than were employed here. Engel and his co-workers (7) describe training programs extending over several weeks with up to 50 sessions. Lang (18) has compared visceral learning to motor skills acquisition, and achieving control over new muscle sequences could easily demand this degree of time and effort. Thus, while patients and older-normals may be less efficient learners than college students, it is quite possible that the former will ultimately respond to long term training. Secondly, the feedback display used here was not optimal for prompting learned speeding. Working in this laboratory, Gatchel (12) recently demonstrated that feedback of every interpulse interval is a superior display compared with the five beat summary display used here. Unfortunately, the Gatchel data were not available at the outset of the present experiment. However, it is reasonable to presume that better performance would have been observed for patients if an analogue display (in which each interbeat interval was represented) had been employed.

Despite considerations of display resolution, drugs, and motivational state, the present data still tend to indicate that patients with heart disease are poor "autonomic athletes." That is to say, they profit little from brief training in gaining intentional control over heart rate. Data from resting conditions, questionnaires, and tracking and feedback performance tasks suggest that disease disrupts the relationship between psychological events and cardiovascular activity. The cardiovascular systems of patients are not finely tuned to psychological demands. This may represent a direct effect of the disease process. With a dramatic disruption of structure, the fine communication between cortical and cardiac systems, hypothesized by theories such as the Laceys' (19), is interdicted. On the other hand, it is possible that individuals who show less covariation between psychological stimuli and the cardiovascular system to begin with are a subset of the population more vulnerable to heart disease. It is usually argued that the vulnerable subject is the one whose cardiovascular system reacts strongly to psychological stress. However, there is an alternative hypothesis with which these data would not be inconsistent (17), i.e., that a cardiovascular system that fails to vary closely with real psychological demands—increasing in response to stress and subsiding rapidly when external and cognitive stimulus conditions change—is functionally less adaptive. Furthermore, a less flexible, psychologically detuned cardiac system may place individuals at risk for cardiovascular illness.

The authors express their thanks to the subjects (patient and nonpatient) whose effort and cooperation were vital to accomplishing this research. The patient subjects were referred primarily by John H. Morledge, M.D., to whom the authors express their gratitude. Thanks are also due to William Rock, M.D., Anthony J. Richtsmeier, M.D., and to the Volunteers for Action who also referred subjects for this research. Kenneth Rosen, M.D., consulted with the authors on drug effects on the cardiovascular system.

REFERENCES

1. Shearn DW: Operant conditioning of heart rate. Science 137:530–531, 1961
2. Shapiro D, Tursky B, Schwartz GE: Differentiation of heart rate and systolic blood pressure in man by operant conditioning. Psychosom Med 32:417–423, 1970
3. Hnatiow M, Lang PJ: Learned stabilization of cardiac rate. Psychophysiology 1:330–336, 1965
4. Brener J, Hothersall D: Heart rate control under conditions of augmented sensory feedback. Psychophysiology 3:23–28, 1966
5. Lang PJ, Twentyman CT: Learning to control heart rate: binary versus analogue feedback. Psychophysiology 11:616–629, 1974
6. Miller NE: Learning of visceral and glandular responses. Science 163:434–445, 1969
7. Engel BT: Operant conditioning of cardiac function: a status report. Psychophysiology 9:161–177, 1972
8. Weiss T, Engel BT: Operant conditioning of heart rate in patients with premature ventricular contractions. Psychosom Med 33:301–321, 1971
9. Bleeker ER, Engel BT: Learned control of ventricular rate in patients with atrial fibrillation. Psychosom Med 35:161–170, 1973
10. Lang PJ: Learned control of human heart rate in a computer directed environment, in Obrist PA, Black AH, Brener J, DiCara LV, Cardiovascular Psychophysiology. Chicago, Aldine, 1974, pp. 392–405
11. Birren JE: Age changes in speed of behavior: its central nature and physiological correlates, in Welford AT, Birren JE, Behavior, Aging, and the Nervous System. Springfield, Ill., Charles C Thomas, 1965, pp. 191–216
12. Gatchel RJ: Frequency of feedback and learned heart rate control. J Exp Psychol 103:274–283, 1974
13. Rotter JB: Generalized expectancies for internal versus external control of reinforcement. Psychol Monogr 80:1–28, 1966
14. Wilkinson HJF: Impulsivity, deliberativeness and time estimation. Unpublished doctoral dissertation. University of Pittsburgh, 1962
15. Fenz WD, Epstein S: Manifest anxiety: unifactoral or multifactoral composition? Percept Mot Skills 20:773–780, 1965
16. Wilder J: Stimulus and Response: The Law of Initial Value. Bristol, England, John Wright & Sons, 1967
17. Troyer WG: Brain-body mechanisms, in Jarvik LF, Blum JE, Eisdorfer C, Intellectual Functioning of the Adult, New York, Springer, 1973
18. Lang PJ: Acquisition of heart rate control: method, theory, and clinical implications, in Fowles DC, Clinical Applications of Psychophysiology. New York, Columbia University Press, in press
19. Lacey JI, Lacey BE: Some autonomic-central nervous system interrelationships, in Black P, Physiological Correlates of Emotion. New York, Academic Press, 1970, pp. 205–227

Evaluation of an 38
Intra-Cardiac Limit of Learned Heart Rate Control

Theodore Weiss and Bernard T. Engel

ABSTRACT

Operant conditioning to increase ventricular heart rate (VHR) was carried out in 3 subjects (Ss) with complete heart block. None of the Ss increased VHR consistently. This finding suggests that operant conditioning of VHR is possible only when the conduction path between atria and ventricles is not interrupted.

DESCRIPTORS: Operant conditioning, Complete heart block, Ventricular heart rate. (T. Weiss)

Previous work (Shearn, 1962; Hnatiow & Lang, 1965; Brener & Hothersall, 1966; Engel & Hansen, 1966; Levene, Engel, & Pearson, 1968) has shown that operant training can lead to the learning of chronotropic control in the intact heart, i.e. at the sino-atrial (SA) node. In addition several studies have demonstrated effects of operant conditioning on atrio-ventricular (AV) conduction. The rate of AV impulse conduction has been modified successfully in rats using both shock avoidance and rewarding electrical brain stimulation (Fields, 1970). In our laboratory, using a similar reinforcement paradigm to that described below, changes in the number of impulses conducted through the AV node in patients with atrial fibrillation have been operantly conditioned (Bleecker & Engel, 1973b), as has the AV conduction pathway of a patient with the Wolff-Parkinson-White syndrome

Supported in part by a Daland Fellowship for Research in Clinical Medicine of the American Philosophical Society (Dr. Weiss).

Address requests for reprints to: Dr. Theodore Weiss, Department of Psychiatry, University of Pennsylvania, Philadelphia, PA 19174.

Portions of this paper were presented at the meeting of the Society for Psychophysiological Research in Galveston, Texas, October 1973.

(Bleecker & Engel, 1973a). In our studies the effects appeared to be mediated by the vagus nerves. We also have employed operant training to effect changes in the frequency of premature ventricular contractions (PVCs) in patients (Weiss & Engel, 1971). In one patient the vagus and in another the cardiac sympathetic nerves appeared to mediate the changes. These results indicated that operant control of ventricular function could occur in the presence of an intact SA or AV node.

Complete heart block (CHB) is a condition in which the heart's atria and ventricles beat with independent, regular rhythms (Friedberg, 1966, pp. 584-616; Cosby & Bilitch, 1972). The atria are activated by the normal cardiac pacemaker in the SA node, and beat at rates of 60 to 80 bpm. The ventricles are activated by a slower pacemaker lying in the intraventricular conduction system. They beat at rates of 30 to 45 bpm. The cause of CHB is anatomic interruption of impulse conduction between atria and ventricles. In long standing CHB this typically consists of fibrosis in the AV node, in the common bundle of His or in the bundle branches (Lev, 1963; Lenegre, 1964). It occurs most commonly in elderly individuals, but also may be congenital or acquired following open heart surgery (Lev,

TABLE 1

Mean ventricular heart rates (VHR) in bpm during control and training portions of sessions
Premature ventricular contraction (PVC) frequency is also shown for S 1

Subjects	Session	VHR			PVC/10 min		
		Control	Training	Δ VHR	Control	Training	Δ PVC
1 (JS)	Baseline (n=1)	39.9	39.3	−0.6	0	0	0
	Training (n=5)	39.2 (37.1–41.5)	39.2 (38.3–40.6)	0	0	4.9(0.3−15.8)	+4.9
2 (CD)	Baseline (n=1)	40.1	39.1	−1.0			
	Training	38.7 (36.8−40.5) (n=7)	38.6(36.4−40.8) (n=16)	−0.1			
3 (JC)	Baseline (n=1)	30.3	30.4	+0.1			
	Training	33.2 (31.6−34.5) (n=6)	32.5 (31.2=33.5) (n=11)	−0.7			

Note. — The range of individual session VHR values for each *S* is shown in parentheses. VHR variance within sessions was small. For example, in a typical training session for *S*2, mean VHR was 39.2 bpm and the standard deviation was 0.84 bpm.

1964; Reemtsma, Delgado, & Creech, 1960).

Thus, CHB appeared to provide a naturally occurring preparation in which to try to define an intra-cardiac limit to learned heart rate control. Could CHB subjects, with interruptions in conduction between the atria and ventricles, learn to control ventricular heart rate (VHR)?

Materials and Methods
Subjects

Three subjects (*S*s) with CHB were studied. Their electrocardiograms (EKGs) showed complete heart block for at least 1 yr prior to training. Comparison with EKGs recorded prior to the development of block indicated that the ventricular pacemaker was in the AV node or His bundle (i.e. above the bundle branches) in *S*s 2 and 3. No earlier tracing was available for *S*1, so his ventricular pacemaker could not be localized definitely. However, it also appeared to be above the bundle branches.[1]

Experimental Design

Laboratory. The *S* lay semi-recumbent in bed in a sound deadened room watching a two light display. One was a green cue light which was on during training when the *S* was to attempt to increase VHR. The second was a white feedback light which was on only when the *S*'s VHR was above his control level. This light was controlled by a special purpose computer in which the output of a cardiotachometer was fed into a Schmitt trigger. Whenever the cardiotachometer output was above the trigger level, the white light turned on.

Each *S* received several training sessions a day. A session began with a 10 min rest period followed by a 10 min control period in which all ventricular heart beats were counted automatically to obtain a control VHR. The light display then was turned on with the trigger level set at that value. One to three training periods each lasting from 1024 to 2048 sec were given in a session; they were separated by 10 min rest periods. *S*s were informed in detail about the contingency controlling the lights. They were asked not to move, alter their breathing pattern, or tense their muscles. During an initial baseline session the *S* simply lay in the bed the prescribed period of time with the feedback lights off.

[1]We wish to thank Dr. John Kastor, Department of Medicine, Section of Cardiology, Hospital of the University of Pennsylvania, for his assistance in analyzing the EKGs.

Pharmacologic and Exercise Studies. Each *S* was tested using the autonomically active drugs isoproterenol (0.5 to 2.0 μg/min), a beta-sympathetic agonist, and atropine (1.0 to 2.0 mg), a vagal blocking agent, administered intravenously. *S*s also were monitored after climbing 2−3 flights of stairs.

Results

Subject 1. JS was a 70 yr old male. Exercise increased his VHR from 38 bpm to 51, in association with frequent PVCs (21/min). (In CHB the regular, infra-atrial pacemaker resumes control without a compensatory pause following the premature beat. This effectively increases VHR.) As soon as PVCs stopped—after 3 min—VHR was at the resting level again. Atrial heart rate (AHR) increased from 70 to 124; it was still elevated (88 bpm) when PVCs stopped. This *S* was unable to produce sustained increases in VHR except during 2 sessions in which he generated large numbers of PVCs (Table 1). However, except by means of PVCs, he did not increase VHR. In the pharmacologic studies isoproterenol increased VHR by about 5 bpm, whereas atropine produced no change (Table 2). Neither agent produced PVCs. Both agents produced large increases in AHR.

TABLE 2

Autonomic drugs: Effects on S's heart rates (bpm) in each condition

Drugs	Subject 1		Subject 2		Subject 3	
	VHR	AHR	VHR	AHR	VHR	AHR
Control	40	78	36	57	35	72
Placebo (2 cc normal saline)	39	77	37	56	35	70
Isoproterenol 1.0 μg/min	40	82	43	81	44	98
1.5	—	—	47	94	46	106
2.0	45	104	—	—	—	—
Atropine 1.0 mg	39	94	—	—	—	—
1.5	—	—	41	86	—	—
2.0	—	—	—	—	35	93

Subject 2. CD was a 22 yr old man whose CHB began shortly after the surgical repair of an atrial septal defect. Exercise produced an increase in VHR from 40 bpm to 46; AHR increased from 73 to 115. This *S* increased VHR in 6 speeding sessions. No PVCs occurred in any sessions. However, he also was unable to produce consistent VHR increases (Table 1). Isoproterenol increased VHR by 11 bpm (Table 2). Atropine also increased VHR by 5 bpm, the only *S* in whom this was the case. Both isoproterenol and atropine increased AHR markedly.

Subject 3. JC was an 80 yr old man. Exercise increased his VHR from 32 bpm to 34; AHR increased from 58 to 88. This *S* failed to increase VHR from the control level in any training session (Table 1). Results of the pharmacologic studies were similar to those in *S* 1. Isoproterenol increased VHR by 11 bpm whereas atropine produced no VHR increase (Table 2). Both led to large magnitude increases in AHR.

Discussion

Exercise and beta-adrenergic stimulation with isoproterenol increased VHR in all subjects. Atropine also increased VHR in subject 2, whose lesion probably was above or near the AV junction (Reemtsma et al., 1960). Despite the capacity of these stimuli to increase VHR, none of the subjects was able to produce consistent, voluntary VHR increases in the laboratory. These findings suggest several possible interpretations. (1) The lack of variability in VHR precluded learning. This explanation seems unlikely since subjects 1 and 2 both increased VHR in some training sessions, albeit through different mechanisms. Yet neither could sustain his behavior. (2) In the cases of subjects 1 and 3 their ages mitigated against learning since it is known that elderly subjects are poor learners (Jerome, 1959, pp. 655–699). This interpretation also seems unlikely since we have been able to train other elderly patients to control heart rate using a similar reinforcement paradigm (Weiss & Engel, 1971; Bleecker & Engel, 1973b). (3) While the nervous system exercises some chronotropic action on the ventricle, this effect is minimal. This interpretation appears most likely, being supported by the physiological studies of Eliakim, Bellet, Tawil, and Muller (1961) and Spear and Moore (1973) in the dog. Previously (Weiss & Engel, 1971) we proposed that one necessary condition for learning heart rate control is the existence of appropriate neural innervation. The present findings are consistent with that concept.

Learned chronotropic control of the ventricle can be mediated at the SA node, at the intact AV node, or in aberrant AV pathways. However, when impulse conduction within or below the AV node has been interrupted—as in the CHB subjects—learned rate control for the lower pacemaker does not appear possible.

REFERENCES

Bleecker, E. R., & Engel, B. T. Learned control of cardiac rate and cardiac conduction pattern in the Wolff-Parkinson-White syndrome. *New England Journal of Medicine*, 1973, *288*, 560–562. (a)

Bleecker, E. R., & Engel, B. T. Learned control of ventricular rate in patients with atrial fibrillation. *Psychosomatic Medicine*, 1973, *35*, 161–175. (b)

Brener, J., & Hothersall, D. Heart rate control under conditions of augmented sensory feedback. *Psychophysiology*, 1966, *3*, 23–28.

Cosby, R. S., & Bilitch, M. *Heart block*. New York: McGraw-Hill Book Co., 1972.

Eliakim, M., Bellet, S., Tawil, W., & Muller, O. Effect of vagal stimulation and acetylcholine on the ventricle *Circulation Research*, 1961, *9*, 1372–1379.

Engel, B. T., & Hansen, S. P. Operant conditioning of heart rate slowing. *Psychophysiology*, 1966, *3*, 176–187.

Fields, C. Instrumental conditioning of the rat cardiac control systems. *Proceedings of the National Academy of Sciences of the United States of America*, 1970, *65*, 293–299.

Friedberg, C. K. *Diseases of the heart*. 3rd ed. Philadelphia and London: W. B. Saunders Co., 1966.

Hnatiow, M., & Lang, P. J. Learned stabilization of heart rate. *Psychophysiology*, 1965, *1*, 330–336.

Jerome, E. A. Age and learning: Experimental studies. In J. E. Birren (Ed.), *Handbook of aging and the individual*. Chicago: University of Chicago Press, 1959. Pp. 655–699.

Lenegre, J. Etiology and pathology of bilateral bundle branch block in relation to complete heart block. *Progress in Cardiovascular Diseases*, 1964, *6*, 409–444.

Lev, M. The normal anatomy of the conduction systems in man and its pathology in atrioventricular block. *Annals of the New York Academy of Sciences*, 1963, *111*, 817–829.

Lev, M. The pathology of complete atrioventricular block. *Progress in Cardiovascular Diseases*, 1964, *6*, 317–326.

Levene, H. I., Engel B. T., & Pearson, J. A. Differential operant conditioning of heart rate. *Psychosomatic Medicine*, 1968, *30*, 837–845.

Reemtsma, K., Delgado, J. P., & Creech, O. Jr. Heart block following intracardiac surgery: Localization of conduction tissue injury. *Journal of Thoracic & Cardiovascular Surgery*, 1960, *39*, 688–693.

Shearn, D. W. Operant conditioning of heart rate. *Science*, 1962, *137*, 530, 531.

Spear, J. F., & Moore, E. N. Influence of brief vagal and stellate nerve stimulation on pacemaker activity and conduction within the atrioventricular conduction system of the dog. *Circulation Research*, 1973, *33*, 27–41.

Weiss, T., & Engel, B. T. Operant conditioning of heart rate in patients with premature ventricular contractions. *Psychosomatic Medicine*, 1971, *33*, 301–321.

Frequency of Feedback 39
and Learned Heart Rate Control
Robert J. Gatchel

The present study investigated the effects of varying frequency of feedback information on learning to accelerate and decelerate heart rate. In the first of two experiments, three feedback frequencies were assessed: information after every heart beat, every 5 beats, and every 10 beats. All feedback groups were compared with a tracking task control group. Results indicated that for speeding sessions, the feedback groups generated faster rates than the tracking group. In addition, there was a significant linear trend across feedback group performance, with Ss receiving continuous feedback (every beat) showing the fastest rates. During slowing sessions, the feedback groups performed better than tracking controls, again supporting a general feedback effect. However, there were no significant trends across feedback groups, suggesting that, unlike speeding, slowing performance is not finely tuned to information input. A second experiment replicated the speeding results, again demonstrating that success at this task varies systematically with frequency of information feedback.

Recent evidence demonstrates that human Ss can learn to change their heart rates when provided with exteroceptive feedback. In much of the initial research, Ss received feedback only about the direction of change relative to a preset criterion heart rate (Brener, Kleinman, & Goesling, 1969; Engel & Hansen, 1966; Shapiro, Tursky, & Schwartz, 1970). This binary feedback procedure was patterned after the operant methods employed in animal research by Miller and colleagues in studies of visceral learning (Miller, 1969). Learned control was conceptualized as the instrumental conditioning of a simple reflexive behavior. However, unlike the dramatic increases and decreases in heart rhythm found in animal research, only modest changes in rate were reported in these studies.

There are data indicating that the binary

[1] This article is based on a dissertation submitted to the Department of Psychology of the University of Wisconsin—Madison in partial fulfillment of the requirements for the PhD. degree. Appreciation is expressed to Peter J. Lang for his valuable contribution and suggestions in all phases of this research. The assistance of Michael Falconer, who wrote the computer program for the experiments, is also gratefully acknowledged. The research was supported in part by grants to Peter J. Lang from the National Institute of Mental Health (MH-10933 and MH-35324) and the Wisconsin Alumni Research Foundation. The experiments were conducted while the author was a National Institute of Mental Health predoctoral fellow (MH-50779).

[2] Requests for reprints should be sent to Robert J. Gatchel, Department of Psychology, University of Texas at Arlington, Arlington, Texas 76019.

feedback used in the above studies of human Ss may have restricted performance. For example, Lang and Twentyman (in press) compared the heart rate control performance of a group of Ss receiving simple binary feedback to that of a group receiving analogue feedback. The latter type of feedback provided information about magnitude, as well as direction of rate change. It was found that the analogue group learned to increase heart rate significantly more than the binary group. Other investigators have also used analogue feedback (see Blanchard & Young, 1973) in training Ss to change heart rhythm. They have reported much greater heart rate acceleration than was previously evidenced in studies using operant techniques with the accompanying binary feedback.

Motor skills learning research also demonstrates that providing analogue response-modulated feedback greatly facilitates the learning of tasks relative to simply providing binary information (Bilodeau & Bilodeau, 1969). Indeed, in agreement with Lang (1974), it is the contention of the present author that learned control of heart rate change is best conceptualized as a complex skills learning task rather than the operant conditioning of a simple reflexive behavior. With this viewpoint, parameters important in human skills learning are assumed relevant to developing self control of cardiac rhythm and maximizing the learning process. One such important parameter shown to significantly affect motor skills performance is frequency of response-modulated feedback (Bilodeau & Bilodeau, 1958). The effect of this variable on learned control of heart rate change was investigated in the present experiments.

The first experiment assessed the heart rate speeding and slowing performance of groups receiving different frequencies of feedback—either information after every beat, or summary information every 5 or every 10 beats. The 1-beat unit is continuous feedback and is the same frequency used in all the earlier analogue heart rate feedback studies. The 5-beat accumulation approximates the length of a respiratory cycle. Tying the feedback unit to this physiological rhythm might be expected to facilitate control learning, since Sroufe

(1971) has shown that respiration can mediate cardiac changes. The 10-beat unit exceeds the rate of occurrence of cardiovascular and related events. It represents a gross summary of performance.

The effects of feedback frequency on transfer of training to nonfeedback conditions were also evaluated. Because feedback was presented via a visual display, a tracking task group was included in this study to control for display monitoring influences on heart rate. The tracking display was generated by a computer rather than S's heart, and a small motor response was called for rather than heart rate change. The second experiment was prompted by the results of the first and served as a cross-validation of the heart rate speeding results. In both experiments, the relationship of respiration rate and variability to learned control was also assessed.

EXPERIMENT I

Method

Subjects. The sample consisted of 40 male undergraduate volunteers from the introductory psychology S pool at the University of Wisconsin—Madison. The Ss received points to be applied to their course grades for participation in this experiment.

Apparatus. Heart rate and respiration rate were recorded on a Beckman dynograph. The respiration transducer consisted of two 3-in.-long mercury strain gauges wired in parallel and taped to the chest and abdomen. Heart rate was recorded through Beckman silver–silver chloride electrodes, attached over the anterolateral lower ribs. An oscilloscope was set so that the r wave of each EKG cycle interrupted a Digital Equipment Co. PDP-12 computer, permitting the measurement of each interpulse interval to the nearest .004 sec. A Schmitt trigger, connected to the voltage output of the dynograph's respiration channel, also interrupted the computer, measuring respiration cycle length in .10-sec. units. The Schmitt trigger was set midway between the average inspiratory peak and expiratory valley, and signaled the computer at the completion of each respiration cycle.

The timing of the experiment, presentation of instructions and feedback, and data acquisition and primary data reduction were all accomplished in real time by the PDP-12. The computer and physiological recording equipment were housed in a room adjacent to S's cubicle. The S's room was sound shielded and illuminated by a low-intensity lamp. The S sat in a semireclined chair, facing a DEC VR-12 oscilloscope. The scope was controlled by the PDP-12, and the computer presented instructions (in alphanumeric form) and feedback displays on the scope face.

Heart rate display. With each of the feedback presentation rates, analogue information about the length of r–r intervals was visually presented in the form of a line sweeping horizontally across the scope from left to right. The line was initiated by an r wave, and was terminated by a specified succeeding wave. At termination, a vertical marker was briefly illuminated, and within microseconds a new line started across the screen. There was a different line sweep speed associated with each of the feedback rates. This kept the display the same in physical size across groups. The display also contained a fixed vertical line, running from top to bottom of the screen, which served as S's target and which appeared continuously on the screen during feedback. If S was requested to speed his heart rate, his task was to terminate the horizontal line before it crossed the target. If his task was slowing, the horizontal line had to extend past the target for a success to be recorded. The word *good* was illuminated on the screen for each success at line sweep termination. An illustration of the display can be found in Lang (1974).

The target line was initially set at S's median r–r interval, established during a 1-min. period, at which time S was asked to perform the desired task (speeding or slowing) without feedback. The target could be altered subsequently, depending on S performance, by a "rule of halves" schedule. This shaping schedule worked in the following manner: If, during a feedback trial, two-thirds of all interpulse intervals fell successfully within the target area, a new target line was set for the next feedback trial. It was set midway between S's previous median and his current median. A similar adjustment to a less difficult target was made for Ss who showed poor performance on a trial (one-third or less of all interpulse intervals falling within the target area).

Tracking display. This was also a moving line display. However, the sweeping line was generated by the computer rather than S's heart. The S's task was to monitor the lines and press a microswitch whenever the line terminated on a designated side of the display target line. The target was positioned in the center of the screen. The word *good* was illuminated on the screen if S's button press occurred within 400 msec. of line termination.

Experimental design. The Ss were randomly assigned to one of the following four experimental groups: (a) 1-beat feedback group, which received information about the length of each r–r interval as it occurred; (b) 5-beat feedback group, which received information about the length of a unit of 5 successive r–r intervals; (c) 10-beat feedback group, which received information about the length of a unit of ten successive r–r intervals; and (d) tracking group, which performed the tracking task on computer generated line sweeps. The line sweep speed for the tracking task was identical to that of the 1-beat feedback group.

Each S came to the laboratory for six separate one-hr. sessions. The initial two sessions for all Ss were tracking task sessions: one session in which the microswitch was to be pressed every time the computer-simulated line sweep terminated to the left of the target line (track-left), and one session of microswitch pressing at right termination of the line (track-right). The two types of tracking task sessions were counterbalanced for order of presentation within each experimental group. These two sessions were for habituation purposes, designed to accustom S to the laboratory and physiological recording. The tracking group Ss also continued tracking during the subsequent four sessions. Each successive block of two sessions consisted of one track-left and one track-right

TABLE 1
STANDARD FORMAT ACROSS EXPERIMENTAL SESSIONS AND TASKS ASSOCIATED WITH EACH TIME PHASE

Time phase	Session	
	Heart rate control	Tracking
1. 3 min.	Initial baseline period	Initial baseline period
2. 1 min.	Try period *For the next few minutes try to increase (decrease) your heart rate as much as possible.*	Time estimation period *Time estimation —Please press the button every ten seconds.*
3. 3 min.	Feedback period *The feedback display will now be presented to help increase (decrease) your heart rate.*	Tracking period *The visual display will now be presented. Press the button each time the moving line falls short of (exceeds) the target.*
4. 1 min.	Transfer period *For this period continue to increase (decrease) your heart rate as much as possible.*	Time estimation period *Time estimation —Please press the button every ten seconds.*
5. 1 min.	Time-out period *Stop working on the heart rate task but continue to sit quietly. You will receive further instructions shortly.*	Time-out period *Stop working for awhile but continue to sit quietly. You will receive further instructions shortly.*
6. 3 min.	Final baseline period Instructions same as time-out period above.	Final baseline period Instructions same as time-out period above.

Note. Periods 3–5 (feedback or tracking, transfer or time estimation, and time out) were repeated five times in sequence prior to the final baseline period. The feedback and tracking instructions displayed on the oscilloscope screen (shown here in italic type) were presented for 6 sec. prior to the 3-min. feedback or tracking work period. Instructions for other experimental periods were on continuously during the entire interval.

session, with order randomly determined. The other groups were administered two heart rate speeding and two slowing sessions, with order randomly determined in session blocks of two.

All sessions followed a standard format that allowed comparisons across groups and sessions. This general format and the tasks associated with each time phase of a session are presented in Table 1.

Procedure. All *S*s were interviewed individually, during which time the broad purpose of the experiment was described. They were also questioned regarding any history of cardiac disorders, medication, and drug usage. The *S*s who were acceptable and willing to participate in the experiment were assigned to one of the experimental groups. The six sessions were conducted over the course of two wk. The time of day was kept constant for each *S*, and times of day were balanced between groups. For each session, *S* was seated in a comfortable chair and electrodes and strain gauges were applied, after which *E* left the room to adjust the polygraph and computer analogue inputs in an adjacent room. The *E* then returned to demonstrate the display and read a standard set of instructions according to session task and experimental group assignment. Experimental control was then turned over to the PDP-12.

Data collection and reduction. Data summaries were printed on the teletype after each experimental session so that a running check could be kept on the operation of the system. However, the data for final analysis were stored on digital tape. This consisted of distributions of interpulse intervals and respiration cycle lengths for each cell of the experimental session (initial base, try period, first feedback, transfer, etc.). These data were later edited on the PDP-12 to eliminate any artifact occasioned by the collection system, and then reduced on a Univac 1108 computer to cell medians and interquartile ranges. These statistics were selected in preference to the mean and standard deviation because they are less influenced by the appearance of a few extreme scores and thus better represent tonic trends.

In the majority of subsequent statistical analyses, the physiological performance measures were transformed beforehand into change scores, calculated for each trial of a session. Change scores were computed for heart rate by subtracting the median r–r interval length of the initial rest period from the median interval length of each subsequent trial. These change scores were made positive if they occurred in the correct direction (e.g., a decrease in r–r interval length from the initial rest for speeding sessions), and negative if they occurred in the opposite direction. In the tracking task, a heart rate increase during track-left sessions and a heart rate decrease during track-right sessions were considered positive scores. Change scores were similarly computed for the respiration rate, respiration cycle length variability, and heart rate variability measures. For the latter two variability measures, an increase in trial variability relative to the initial rest variability was considered a

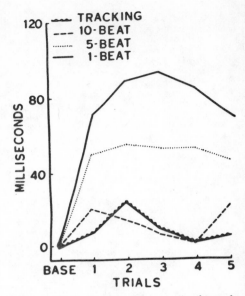

FIGURE 1. Changes in average median interpulse interval length over feedback trials for the tracking group and three feedback groups—Speeding Session 1.

positive score, regardless of the experimental task. These variability measures were scored in this manner so as to parallel heart rate change scoring. This allowed identical statistical analyses to be performed on all physiological measures.

Results

Heart rate speeding sessions. Analysis of variance indicated no significant initial heart rate resting level differences between groups for the speeding sessions.

Mean group feedback trial heart rates for the first speeding session are presented in Figure 1. They are represented as feedback trial changes from the initial rest period. The superiority of the 1-beat group is apparent. The effect is somewhat enhanced in Session 2, with all feedback groups performing better than the tracking group (Figure 2). Analyses of variance confirmed these findings. The feedback change scores yielded a significant main group effect, $F (3, 36) = 3.69$, $p < .025$. Based on results of previous investigations, a planned contrast of group change score means was performed between the tracking control

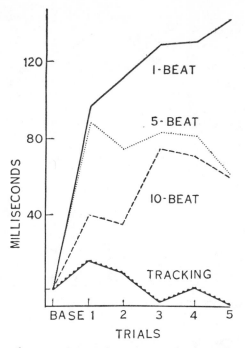

FIGURE 2. Changes in average median interpulse interval length over feedback trials for the tracking group and three feedback groups—Speeding Session 2.

heart rate speeding in the absence of further feedback (transfer trials). Transfer trial change scores across sessions are shown in Figure 3. Analysis of variance indicated a significant main group effect, F (3, 36) = 3.31, $p < .05$, with feedback Ss again being superior to tracking controls, F (1, 36) = 5.17, $p < .05$. Analysis of the three feedback groups indicated a near-significant linear trend across group change score means, F (1, 27) = 3.69, $p < .10$. The session effect was again significant, F (1, 27) = 5.47, $p < .025$, indicating improvement over sessions in transfer performance by all feedback groups.

An analysis of variance was performed to test whether the three feedback groups did better during the feedback trials or during the nonfeedback transfer trials. Results indicated that greater speeding performance was present during the feedback trials, F (1, 27) = 8.11, $p < .01$.

An analysis of respiration rate during feedback and transfer trials revealed no dif-

group and the three combined heart rate feedback groups. This contrast was significant, F (1, 36) = 5.99, $p < .025$, indicating that information feedback produces speeding performance superior to that of tracking controls.

Another analysis of variance, without the tracking group included, was conducted to statistically validate the observable differences between the three feedback groups. A test for trend over the group change score means indicated a significant linear component, F (1, 27) = 4.53, $p < .05$. This trend accounts for nearly 98% of the group variance and indicates that higher rates of feedback produce greater speeding performance. The overall analysis also indicated a significant sessions effect, F (1, 27) = 6.18, $p < .025$, demonstrating that learning took place across sessions for all groups.

These performance differences were also present when Ss were instructed to continue

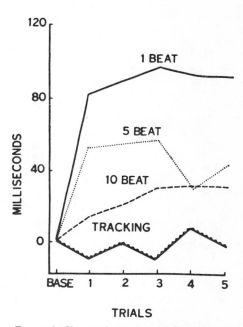

FIGURE 3. Changes in average median interpulse interval length over transfer trials for the tracking group and three feedback groups—Speeding Sessions 1 and 2 combined.

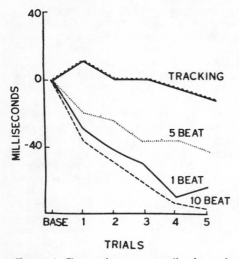

FIGURE 4. Changes in average median interpulse interval length over feedback trials for the tracking group and three feedback groups—Slowing Sessions 1 and 2 combined.

ferences between tracking and combined feedback groups or among the three individual feedback frequencies. Variability in respiration cycle length, however, was significantly greater for combined heart rate feedback groups relative to the tracking group, $F (1, 36) = 6.56, p < .025$. There was no trend across the feedback group change score means. Analysis of transfer trials yielded no major significant results.

Heart rate slowing sessions. Analysis of variance indicated no significant initial heart rate resting level differences between groups for the slowing sessions.

Mean feedback trial change scores across slowing sessions are shown in Figure 4. Analysis of variance yielded a significant main group effect, $F (3, 36) = 3.72, p < .025$. Similar to the speeding task, feedback resulted in performance superior to that of tracking controls, $F (1, 36) = 8.67, p < .01$. Unlike the speeding task, analysis of the feedback groups indicated no significant trend across group means. Thus, as Figure 4 suggests, there are no differences in performance between feedback groups. There was a significant trials effect, $F (4, 108) = 14.65, p < .001$, suggesting a tendency to improve within a session; however, no sig-

nificant improvement was found over sessions.

Transfer trial change scores across sessions are shown in Figure 5. Analysis of variance indicated that, unlike the speeding task, the feedback-trained Ss are not different from tracking controls during transfer trials (no significant group or group contrast effects). Analysis of the feedback-trained groups indicated no trends across group means. Again, there was a significant trials effect, $F (4, 108) = 9.33, p < .001$, but no sessions effect.

Analysis of heart rate variability indicated a group effect, $F (3, 36) = 3.79, p < .05$, with the combined feedback groups showing more increase in variability than tracking controls, $F (1, 36) = 8.39, p < .01$. There was no trend across the feedback group change score means. No effects were present when the transfer trial change scores were analyzed.

Analysis of respiration rate indicated a significant group effect, $F (3, 36) = 3.64, p < .025$. Moreover, the difference between tracking and combined feedback groups was

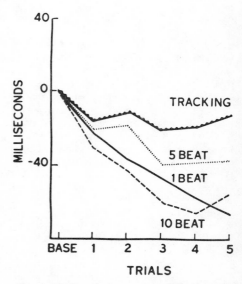

FIGURE 5. Changes in average median interpulse interval length over transfer trials for the tracking group and three feedback groups—Slowing Sessions 1 and 2 combined.

also significant, F (1, 36) = 9.89, p < .005. No trends across feedback group change score means were present. When transfer trial change scores were analyzed, there was again a significant group effect, F (3, 36) = 3.56, p < .025, and a significant difference between tracking and combined feedback groups, F (1, 36) = 9.17, p < .01. Also, similar to the speeding sessions, analysis of variance indicated that respiration cycle variability was greater for the combined feedback groups compared to tracking Ss, F (1, 36) = 4.75, p < .05. There was no trend across feedback group change score means. Analysis of transfer trials yielded no significant results.

EXPERIMENT II

In Experiment I, all Ss performed the tracking task during Sessions 1 and 2. The moving line display for the tracking task had the same sweep speed as the 1-beat feedback display. One can argue that this may have given the 1-beat feedback group an added advantage. They were familiar with the sweep of the moving line, and unlike the 5-beat and 10-beat Ss, they did not have to make the transition to a new display when heart rate training began. The present experiment was designed to control for this possible confounding, as well as to replicate the findings for speeding performance.

Method

Subjects. This sample consisted of 32 male undergraduate volunteers from the introductory psychology S pool at the University of Wisconsin —Madison.

Apparatus and displays. The apparatus and heart rate and tracking displays were identical to those used in the previous experiment.

Experimental design and procedure. Half of the S sample received a tracking task similar to that of Experiment I (1-TR). The other half received a tracking task with line sweep characteristics of the 5-beat display (5-TR). Half of each group was then trained to speed heart rate on a 1-beat feedback display; the other half was trained on a 5-beat feedback display. This yielded four experimental cells, with eight Ss per cell. Each S came to the laboratory for four separate 1-hr sessions. The initial two sessions were tracking task sessions. All Ss then received two heart rate speeding sessions. The procedure was identical to that of Experiment I.

Data collection and reduction. Data were collected and processed in the same manner as Experiment I, and identical statistical analyses were performed.

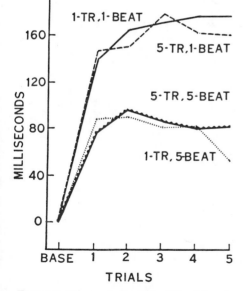

FIGURE 6. Changes in average median interpulse interval length over feedback trials, for the four tracking (TR)–feedback (BEAT) groups—Speeding Sessions 1 and 2 combined.

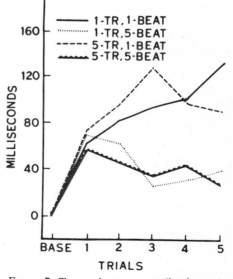

FIGURE 7. Changes in average median interpulse interval length over transfer trials, for the four tracking (TR)–feedback (BEAT) groups—Speeding Sessions 1 and 2 combined.

Results

Heart rate speeding sessions. Analysis of variance indicated no significant initial heart rate resting level differences between groups.

Mean group feedback trial heart rates across sessions are presented in Figure 6. The superiority of the 1-beat feedback groups, regardless of previous type of tracking display, is readily apparent. There was a significant feedback type effect (1-beat vs. 5-beat), $F (1, 28) = 5.99$, $p < .025$, and no significant tracking type (1-TR vs. 5-TR) or interaction effects. There was also a significant sessions effect, $F (1, 28) = 19.27$, $p < .01$, indicating an improvement in performance over sessions.

Transfer trial change scores across sessions are shown in Figure 7. Again, differences between the two feedback groups are apparent. However, analysis of variance indicated only a near-significant feedback type effect, $F (1, 28) = 2.97$, $p < .10$. There was, however, a highly significant sessions effect, $F (1, 28) = 19.32$, $p < .01$.

As in Experiment I, analysis indicated that greater speeding performance was present during feedback trials than during transfer trials, $F (1, 28) = 19.25$, $p < .01$.

Table 2 summarizes the heart rate performance findings of Experiments I and II. Average heart rate changes, in beats per minute, are presented for feedback and transfer periods.

Correlative relationships (Experiments I and II). In both experiments, the relationship of heart rate control performance to various physiological response measures was analyzed. For the speeding data, r_1 refers to the correlation found in Experiment I and r_2 to that found in Experiment II.[3]

In Experiment I, a nonsignificant correlation was found between Ss' average speeding performance and average slowing performance $(r = -.11)$. The correlation between initial heart rate resting level and

---

[3] The physiological response measures used in the correlational analyses are average change scores from the initial rest. Since there were group differences in heart rhythm control performance, heart rate change score averages were transformed to standard scores within each group.

TABLE 2

MEAN HEART RATE CHANGE (IN bpm) FOR FEEDBACK AND TRANSFER PERIODS OVER ALL TRAINING TRIALS AND SESSIONS

Group	Period	
	Feedback	Transfer
Speeding sessions (Experiment I)		
1 beat	10.1	8.8
5 beat	5.5	4.1
10 beat	2.9	2.0
Tracking	.7	−.3
Slowing sessions (Experiment I)		
1 beat	−4.2	−3.8
5 beat	−2.5	−2.5
10 beat	−3.9	−3.3
Tracking	.1	−1.1
Speeding sessions (Experiment II)		
1 beat	17.2	11.9
5 beat	7.9	6.3

average speeding performance during feedback trials was significant, $r_1 = -.47$, $p < .01$, $r_2 = -.52$, $p < .01$: Low resting rate was associated with greater speeding performance. There was also a correlation between initial resting level and average slowing performance during feedback trials, $r = .36$, $p < .10$: High resting rate was associated with greater slowing performance. Heart-rate variability during initial rest was positively correlated with average speeding performance during feedback trials, $r_1 = .48$, $p < .01$; $r_2 = .40$, $p < .05$. This suggests that greater variability in heart rate during rest, which can be viewed as an indicant of cardiac system lability, is associated with greater subsequent speeding performance. This relationship, however, does not hold for slowing performance, $r = .17$, ns.

Average heart rate speeding performance during feedback trials was also found to be positively correlated with average heart rate change during tracking session trials, $r_1 = .32$, $p < .10$; $r_2 = .36$, $p < .05$. This correlation indicates that greater change in heart rate during the tracking task, which can also be viewed as an indicant of system lability, is associated with greater subsequent performance on the speeding task. There was no relationship between slowing performance and this lability measure.

There was a significant correlation between average speeding performance and average respiration rate during feedback trials, $r_1 = -.41$, $p < .05$; $r_2 = -.59$, $p < .01$, i.e., greater speeding performance was associated with faster respiration rate. This was similarly true for transfer trials, $r_1 = -.43$, $p < .05$; $r_2 = -.49$, $p < .01$. For slowing performance during feedback trials, this correlation was in the opposite direction, $r = .30$, $p < .10$, with greater slowing performance associated with slower respiration rate. There was no significant correlation for transfer trials. Respiration cycle length variability was not found to be correlated with any heart rate performance measure for slowing or speeding sessions.

DISCUSSION

The findings of the present investigation clearly demonstrate that success at the heart rate speeding task varies systematically with frequency of information feedback. Continuous analogue feedback (1-beat group) produced the greatest heart rate change. These differences also persisted during transfer trials. In addition, there was a significant tendency for all feedback groups to improve over sessions. The unequivocal cross-validation of these effects in two independent experiments testifies to their stability and to the procedural reliability provided in a computer-directed experiment.

Heart rate slowing trial performance did not parallel speeding performance. Although feedback resulted in performance superior to that of tracking controls, there was no significant trend across feedback groups. The feedback groups, moreover, were not significantly different from tracking controls during transfer trials. In addition, there was no improvement in performance over sessions for either feedback or transfer performance. These data can be taken as evidence that heart rate speeding and heart rate slowing depend on different mechanisms. This possibility had been previously voiced by Engel (1972). It is further reinforced by the very low nonsignificant correlation between speeding and slowing performance found in Experiment I.

The observed differences in speeding and slowing performance are open to two major explanations. First, they could be an effect of initial levels. In this experiment, Ss were well habituated to the laboratory setting with average resting heart rates of about 70 bpm. One can argue that further decreases during slowing sessions would not be large, because of inherent physiological limits of the system. There would thus be a smaller range within which to observe the possible effects of information input rate. However, the nonsignificant correlation between initial resting level and average performance during slowing feedback trials does not greatly substantiate this hypothesis.

A second possible explanation for differential performance effects may be the involvement of a different mechanism in the two tasks. Obrist and his associates (Obrist, Webb, Sutterer, & Howard, 1970) have suggested that cardiovascular events are coupled centrally to somatic events, such that cardiac changes parallel somatic changes in direction and magnitude. They have conducted a number of conditioning and reaction time experiments in which a close coupling of these two events has been demonstrated. A central somatic–cardiac mechanism may be involved in the speeding task, with Ss activating somatic behaviors already in their repertoires in order to increment heart rate.

In support of the above speculation, the results for speeding performance are similar to those for a somatic motor task. That is, higher frequencies of information feedback prompted greater success (Bilodeau & Bilodeau, 1958). The previously reviewed study by Lang and Twentyman (in press), in which analogue feedback produced greater speeding performance than binary feedback, also parallels the results of motor skills research. Moreover, heart rate responding to the tracking motor task in the present study was found to be significantly correlated with subsequent speeding performance but was not correlated with slowing performance. The amount of responding in the tracking task may gauge degree of activation of the central coupling mechanism in individual Ss. It would be predictive of subsequent speeding performance if the coupling mechanism were also involved in this task.

There was also a significant correlation between heart rate variability during initial rest and speeding performance. These results suggest that the degree of system lability is predictive of speeding control acquisition. Related to these findings are a number of studies reporting an association between heart rate activity and motor performance. Connor and Lang (1969) noted that greater cardiac reactance, in the form of large acceleration and secondary deceleration components of the heart rate response curve, was associated with faster reaction times. Lacey and Lacey (1970) have reported similar results. In an earlier study, Lacey and Lacey (1958) also noted a relationship between heart rate activity and motor performance, with high heart rate variability being associated with fast reaction times. Lacey and Lacey have interpreted these data as evidence of a relationship between autonomic activity and cortical excitability, with these two response systems being highly interactive. Indeed, Gellhorn (1964) has argued that autonomic and somatic responses are interactive, as well as parallel to one another, because they are centrally integrated systems. In the heart rate speeding task, certain individuals may learn more than others because their cardiovascular systems are more labile and may activate and be more responsive to the somatic–cardiac coupling mechanism.

In contrast to a central coupling mechanism that may facilitate speeding performance, the mechanism involved in slowing may be more related to true visceral learning. As suggested by Lang and Twentyman (in press), slowing may involve the modification of vagal firing and cardiovascular changes that are relatively independent of central centers controlling somatic activity.

If a central coupling mechanism is more involved in speeding performance, one might well expect respiration to show a close covariation with heart rate in this task. Results, however, offered no conclusive evidence for this possibility. Both the speeding and slowing tasks showed some evidence of respiratory

change associated with performance.[4] Correlational analyses did, however, demonstrate a statistically stronger association between respiration rate and speeding performance relative to that between respiration rate and slowing performance. This held for both feedback and transfer periods. Differences between speeding and slowing may therefore reflect a differential involvement of striate muscular mediators. Unlike slowing, speeding may not involve any new learning of a visceral response. Rather, it may merely reflect the recruitment and tuning of somatic responses, such as respiration and muscle tension, which prompt heart rate acceleration.

Future research investigating the effects of heart rate speeding and slowing training on other cardiovascular and somatic activity should more clearly elucidate whether different innervation mechanisms are involved in the two tasks. In any event, the present study demonstrates striking differences between heart rate speeding and slowing results and highlights the fact that the two tasks are best analyzed as separate human skills.

---

[4] The fact that changes in respiration rate and variability did not directly parallel the heart rate speeding differences may mean that they are not very sensitive measures by which to gauge this physiological system. Sroufe (1971) has shown that respiration depth is a measure that greatly affects both heart rate level and variability. Both respiration depth and muscle tension measures may possibly be more responsive to differences between groups and tasks.

REFERENCES

Bilodeau, E. A., & Bilodeau, I. M. Variable frequency of knowledge of results and the learning of a simple skill. *Journal of Experimental Psychology*, 1958, **55**, 379–383.

Bilodeau, E. A., & Bilodeau, I. M. (Eds.) *Principles of skill acquisition.* New York: Academic Press, 1969.

Blanchard, E. B., & Young, L. B. Self-control of cardiac functioning: A promise as yet unfulfilled. *Psychological Bulletin*, 1973, **3**, 145–163.

Brener, J., Kleinman, R. A., & Goesling, W. T. Effects of different exposures to augmented sensory feedback on the control of heart rate. *Psychophysiology*, 1969, **5**, 510–516.

Connor, W. H., & Lang, P. J. Cortical slow-wave and cardiac rate responses in stimulus orientation and reaction time conditions. *Journal of Experimental Psychology*, 1969, **82**, 310–320.

Engel, B. T. Operant conditioning of cardiac functioning: A status report. *Psychophysiology*, 1972, **9**, 161–177.

Engel, B. T., & Hansen, S. P. Operant conditioning of heart rate speeding. *Psychophysiology*, 1966, **3**, 418–426.

Gellhorn, E. Motion and emotion: The role of proprioception in the physiology and pathology of the emotions. *Psychological Review*, 1964, **71**, 457–472.

Lacey, J. I., & Lacey, B. C. The relationship of resting autonomic activity to motor impulsivity. In H. Soloman, S. Cobb, & W. Penfield (Eds.), *The brain and human behavior.* Baltimore: Williams & Wilkins, 1958.

Lacey, J. I., & Lacey, B. C. Some autonomic-central nervous system interrelationships. In P. Black (Ed.), *Physiological correlates of emotion.* New York: Academic Press, 1970.

Lang, P. J. Learned control of human heart rate in a computer directed environment. In P. Obrist, A. Black, J. Brener, & L. DiCara (Eds.), *Contemporary trends in cardiovascular psychophysiology.* Aldine-Atherton, 1974.

Lang, P. J., & Twentyman, C. T. Learning to control heart rate: Binary vs. analogue feedback. *Psychophysiology,* in press.

Miller, N. E. Learning of visceral and glandular responses. *Science,* 1969, 163, 434–445.

Obrist, P. A., Webb, R. A., Sutterer, J. R., & Howard, J. L. The cardiac-somatic relationship: Some reformulations. *Psychophysiology,* 1970, 6, 569–587.

Shapiro, D., Tursky, D., & Schwartz, G. Differentiation of heart rate and systolic blood pressure in man by operant conditioning. *Psychosomatic Medicine,* 1970, 32, 417–423.

Sroufe, L. A. Effects of depth and rate of breathing on heart rate and heart rate variability. *Psychophysiology,* 1971, 8, 648–655.

Systolic Blood Pressure and Heart Rate Changes During Three Sessions Involving Biofeedback or No Feedback

Steven G. Fey and Ernest Lindholm

ABSTRACT

Two groups of normotensive human subjects of both sexes received contingent feedback for increases or decreases in systolic blood pressure, and two additional groups received random (non-contingent) feedback or no feedback. Subjects in all groups served for three 1-hr sessions separated by intervals of 24 hrs. Reliable decreases in blood pressure, reaching a maximum of 9.5 mm Hg at the end of the third session, were observed in the decrease group. No systematic changes in blood pressure were observed in the increase, random, or no-feedback groups. Heart rate increased or decreased in the groups receiving contingent feedback for increasing or decreasing blood pressure, respectively. It is concluded that contingent feedback is effective in lowering blood pressure and that decreases are augmented by extended training. The covariance of heart rate and blood pressure is discussed with reference to earlier experiments.

DESCRIPTORS: Biofeedback, Blood pressure, Heart rate.

The modification of blood pressure through biofeedback training would appear to be an important area for research since, if large and stable changes can be demonstrated, the technique might be usefully applied to the treatment of essential hypertension. Initial experiments with normotensives have produced encouraging results. Shapiro, Tursky, Gershon, and Stern (1969) trained subjects to increase or decrease systolic blood pressure by providing both auditory and visual feedback as well as a slide of a nude from *Playboy* for changes in the desired direction. During one conditioning session which lasted less than 1 hr, the group

Master's thesis of first author whose present address is Department of Medical Psychology, University of Oregon Medical School, Portland, Oregon 97201. Supported in part by an A.S.U. Faculty Grant-in-Aid Award to the second author. The authors thank Julie Lindholm and Norwood Sisson for valuable advice and assistance.

Address requests for reprints to: Ernest Lindholm, Ph.D., Department of Psychology, Arizona State University, Tempe, Arizona 85281.

reinforced for decreases in blood pressure ("down subjects") showed a steady decrease while the group reinforced for increases in blood pressure ("up subjects") showed a biphasic change (small initial increase, then decrease). During the last 2 trial blocks, the "up" group showed a decrease of 0.6 mm Hg and the "down" group decreased their blood pressure 4.0 mm Hg. Although group differences were not statistically reliable, a significant groups by trials interaction led the authors to conclude that the conditioning procedure had been effective. Heart rate was also monitored, and both groups showed a decline in heart rate over time.

Shapiro, Tursky, and Schwartz (1970a) extended these findings by adding one control group which received non-contingent ("random") feedback and reinforcement. Additionally, the subjects were paid for their participation and received money bonuses for correct performance. In this study, the "up" subjects showed a slight increase in systolic blood pressure (as opposed to the slight decrease in the previous experiment) while the "down" and "random" groups both decreased blood pressure. Again, analysis of variance revealed a groups by trials interaction but no main effects. In a second session, which followed the first after a brief rest, all the subjects were reinforced for lowering blood pressure. All groups showed decreases, and the original "down" group reached the lowest overall level (about 4.5 mm Hg decrease from Session 1 starting baseline). Finally, in comparing the heart rate and blood pressure results, the authors use the absence of a significant three-way interaction (groups by trials by sessions) to argue that heart rate changes were not related to blood pressure changes and hence appeared to be dissociated.

Although the above reported changes were small in magnitude, larger blood pressure decreases have been reported by Brener and Kleinman (1970). Normotensive subjects were told that the biofeedback display (a manometer plus a counter) reflected blood pressure, and that they were to keep the readings as low as possible. A control group was told only to pay attention to the display. Decreases of 10 to 16 mm Hg were observed in the experimental group while the control group showed no consistent changes. Again, both groups showed a decrease in heart rate during the course of the experiment.

This experiment differs from those cited earlier in that it employed continuous feedback, and systolic blood pressure was measured from the index finger rather than the upper arm. Additionally, the primary manipulation was the amount of relevant information given to the experimental and control groups. It is not clear whether these procedural differences can account for the greater blood pressure decreases reported by these authors.

Blanchard and Young (1973) have criticized the approach taken by Shapiro and his co-workers on the grounds that auditory feedback, visual feedback, and rewards in the form of slides of nudes and landscapes as well as money have been confounded. It is thus not clear which event(s) control the behavior. They further criticize the failure of previous experiments to include a no-feedback control group against which the effects of feedback might be more clearly evaluated. We would further point out that only males have been used as subjects in the Shapiro et al. experiments (Brener and Kleinman do not mention the sex of their subjects) and the amount of training on the same task has been limited to less than 1 hr duration.

The present experiment deals with some of these criticisms. The method of recording systolic blood pressure conforms closely to that used by Shapiro and co-workers, but only visual feedback is provided during the trials. In addition to contingent feedback for raising or lowering systolic blood pressure, no-feedback and random feedback control groups are incorporated, responses of both sexes are investigated, and the subjects are given multiple training sessions separated by intervals of 24 hrs.

Method

Subjects

Ten female and 10 male graduate students or friends of graduate students volunteered to serve as subjects. Age ranged from 20 to 43 yrs with a mean of 27.3 yrs. All were normotensive (systolic blood pressure 104 to 127 mm Hg) and none were under a physician's care or taking any form of medication.

The 20 subjects were assigned randomly to four groups with the constraint that males and females were balanced as closely as possible. The four groups were as follows:

Increase Group. Three males and 2 females received contingent feedback for increases in systolic blood pressure.

Decrease Group. Two males and 3 females received contingent feedback for decreases in systolic blood pressure.

Random (non-contingent) Group. Three males and 2 females received feedback on randomly-selected heart beats to produce feedback 50% of the time.

No-feedback Group. Two males and 3 females received the same flashing light pattern as the random group but were told that they were participating in an experiment measuring physiological responses during a vigilance task.

Apparatus

A conventional blood pressure cuff was modified to permit remote inflation and deflation by means of a compressed air cylinder and a low pressure regulator under the control of the experimenter. This system maintained a constant cuff pressure the magnitude of which was changed to an electrical signal by means of a National Semiconductor LX 1600A transducer and continuously monitored on one channel of a Beckman Type 411 Dynograph. The Korotkoff sounds (K-sounds) were detected by placing a Panasonic WM 2056P crystal microphone element over the brachial artery below the cuff. The microphone was held in place with the aid of a lightly wrapped elastic bandage. The electrocardiogram (EKG) was recorded from the two forearms by Grass silver disc electrodes affixed to the skin with Grass electrode paste, and the subjects were grounded by means of a Grass spring clip electrode attached to the ear lobe. The EKG and K-sounds were also continuously monitored on the Dynograph, and the high level outputs of these two channels were fed to Schmitt trigger inputs of a PDP LAB-8 computer. The computer was programmed to note the presence of each R-wave of the EKG and the presence or absence of a K-sound occurring after the R-wave. The presence of the K-sound indicated that the subject's blood pressure on that heart beat was higher than the cuff pressure. Conversely, the absence of the K-sound indicated that the subject's blood pressure was lower than the cuff on that heart beat. The program then either turned on or off the feedback light in front of the subject on a beat-to-beat basis.

Each R-wave was counted and the program disabled the feedback and terminated the trial after 50 heart beats. The number of beats on which the subject's blood pressure was higher than the cuff pressure, and the number of times lower, was printed on the teletype.

The visual feedback display, located directly in front of the subject approximately 61 cm from his or her face, consisted of a 15 watt AC bulb enclosed in a 61 cm square plywood box. The front of the box consisted of a .64 cm thick sheet of translucent white Plexiglass. The visual feedback therefore consisted of a clearly visible but relatively dim and diffuse illumination which had none of the glare or dazzle properties of a naked bulb.

All recording and control equipment was located in one room occupied by the experimenter. The subject occupied a separate room containing only an upholstered chair and the visual feedback display. Necessary air tubing and wires were fed through conduits which connected the two rooms.

Procedure

All subjects came to the laboratory for three recording sessions separated by 24 hr intervals. Each session consisted of 25 trials, each trial being 50 heart beats duration. Each trial was preceded by approximately 5 sec for cuff inflation and stabilization and the end of each trial was marked by a 30 sec intertrial interval (rest period) during which the cuff remained deflated. Prior to the first trial in each session, the subjects were asked to sit quietly for 10 min. This period allowed for potentially heightened physiological reactions to subside. The cuff was then inflated to approximately 180 mm Hg and bled gradually while the pressure was noted at which the first systolic K-sound was detected. The cuff was then re-inflated and held constant at this pressure for 2 or 3 pre-trials to determine the starting (baseline) systolic blood pressure. The baseline blood pressure was defined as the cuff pressure at which K-sounds occurred coincident with 40–60% of the 50 heart beats. As soon as baseline pressure was determined, the subjects were informed that the first trial was beginning. The cuff was then re-inflated to the baseline pressure which ensured that all the subjects had approximately the same probability (40–60%) of receiving feedback on the first trial.

Subsequent to this initial determination, the median systolic pressure was defined as the cuff pressure at which the K-sound occurred coincident with 25–75% of the heart beats. The presence of the K-sound 24% or less of the time indicated that the subject's arterial pressure was at least 2 mm Hg lower than the cuff pressure. Conversely, occurrence of the K-sound 76% or more of the time indicated that the arterial pressure was 2 mm Hg higher than the cuff pressure. For the Increase group, if K-sounds were detected on more than 75% of the 50 heart beats for 2 trials in succession, the task was made more difficult by raising the cuff pressure 2 mm Hg on the next trial. Similarly, for the Decrease group, if K-sounds were absent on more than 75% of the heart beats for 2 trials in succession, the task was made more difficult by lowering the cuff pressure 2 mm Hg. Finally, if successes occurred on less than 25% of the 50 heart beats for 2 trials, the task was made easier by raising the cuff pressure 2 mm Hg for the Decrease group or lowering the cuff pressure a like amount for the Increase group. Systolic blood pressure in the Random and No-feedback groups was simply tracked throughout each trial by inflating the cuff to the pressure at which K-sounds were detected within the 25–75% limits. The general procedure described above for tracking blood pressure closely resembles that described by Shapiro et al. (1970a).

Only visual feedback was provided during trials. However, brief verbal feedback was conveyed to the subjects in the Increase and Decrease groups during the intertrial rest periods. The experimenter said "good" after those trials during which the subject produced the desired response 25–50% of the time, "very good" for 51–75% successes, and "excellent" for successes greater than 75%. The subjects in the Random group received these three levels of verbal feedback in a randomly selected order.

Instructions to Subjects

Following hook-up, each subject was instructed to sit quietly, avoid the movement or tensing of large muscles, and breathe in a regular manner during trials. They were free to shift position

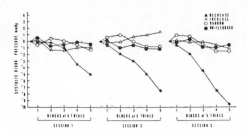

Fig. 1. Systolic blood pressure for the four groups expressed as difference scores. Each point represents the mean of 5 trials and 5 subjects.

and move limbs during the intertrial rest periods. The subjects in the Increase, Decrease, and Random groups were told that the experiment had to do with the control of blood pressure but were not informed as to the direction of the desired change. They were told that the screen would light up if they were successful at controlling their blood pressure, and instructed to keep the screen lighted as much as possible. The subjects in the No-feedback group were told that the experiment had to do with the relationship of blood pressure to vigilance and were instructed to watch the screen carefully and count the number of times the light came on. The subject reported this number to the experimenter at the end of each trial and he responded by saying "O.K." or "that's fine."

Results

Analyses of variance were applied to the data and the .95 level of confidence was adopted as indicating the presence of a reliable difference.

A preliminary analysis of initial blood pressures and heart rates indicated that the four groups did not differ significantly on these measures at the start of each session. Therefore, the data are expressed as difference scores from the starting baseline.

The blood pressure results are summarized in Fig. 1 where systolic blood pressure is plotted as a function of trials. The analysis revealed reliable main effects for groups, $F(3/16)=3.43$, $MS_e=47.33$, trials, $F(4/64)=13.28$, $MS_e=4.54$, and the groups by trials interaction, $F(12/64)=5.61$, $MS_e=4.54$. A Newman-Keuls subsequent test showed that the Decrease group achieved a reliably lower mean blood pressure than the other three groups which did not differ reliably from each other. In the analysis of variance, none of the effects involving sessions was reliable. However, a t-test was performed on the differences between the last trial block of Session 1 and the last trial block of Session 3 for the Decrease group. This result was reliable, $t(4)=2.98$, suggesting that the ability of subjects to reduce blood pressure is augmented, to some extent, by extended training.

The heart rate changes are displayed in Fig. 2. The analysis revealed effects for groups, $F(3/16)=4.17$, $MS_e=20.93$, trials, $F(4/64)=2.55$,

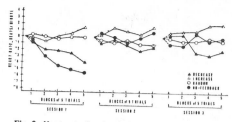

Fig. 2. Heart rate for the four experimental groups expressed as difference scores. Each point represents the mean of 5 trials and 5 subjects.

$MS_e=2.70$, and the groups by trials interaction, $F(12/64)=2.23$, $MS_e=2.70$. A Newman-Keuls subsequent test showed that the Increase blood pressure group achieved a higher mean heart rate than any of the other groups, and the Decrease blood pressure group achieved a lower mean heart rate than any other group excepting the No-feedback group. The No-feedback group achieved a lower mean heart rate than either the Random or Increase blood pressure groups.

Inspection of Fig. 2 suggests that the group differences during Session 1 may have been larger than during the other two Sessions. To explore this, individual analyses of variance were performed for each of the three Sessions. Reliable effects for groups were detected for Session 1, $F(3/16)=3.56$, $MS_e=19.73$, and for Session 3, $F(3/16)=3.34$, $MS_e=21.69$. Newman-Keuls comparisons showed that, for Session 1, the Decrease and No-feedback groups did not differ from each other, but both of these groups achieved lower mean heart rates than either the Increase or Random groups. These latter two groups did not differ from each other. In Session 3, the Increase group achieved a higher mean heart rate than any other group, and the Decrease group achieved a lower mean heart rate than any other group. The two control groups did not differ from each other. From the results of all analyses taken together, and from inspection of Fig. 2, the heart rate results may be summarized as follows: Heart rate tended to remain elevated for the Increase blood pressure group and depressed for the Decrease blood pressure group over the three Sessions. The Random group showed little change, remaining close to baseline. The No-feedback group showed a decrease in heart rate during Session 1 but remained close to baseline thereafter. Thus, the subjects in the No-feedback and Random control groups behaved similarly except during the first Session. We have no explanation for the decreased heart rate observed for the No-feedback group during Session 1.

Since it was our impression from an initial inspection of the data that heart rate and blood pressure change scores tended to covary, correla-

TABLE 1

Spearman rank order correlation coefficients for heart rate and blood pressure for three sessions
Data for block 5 only, 5 subjects per cell

Groups	Correlations		
	Session 1	Session 2	Session 3
Increase	.60	.50	.60
Decrease	.30	.45	.73
Random	.30	.30	.08
No-feedback	.62	.20	.60

tion coefficients were computed using the data from the last trial block for each of the three Sessions. The results, tabulated in Table 1, show that all coefficients are positive. While the number of observations within each cell is too small to permit meaningful statements regarding significance, it nonetheless seems clear that heart rate and blood pressure typically changed in the same direction.

Finally, the heart rate and blood pressure changes for the Increase and Decrease groups across the three Sessions are displayed in Fig. 3. Heart rate and blood pressure both decreased for the Decrease blood pressure group, and heart rate increased for the Increase blood pressure group although these subjects were unsuccessful in raising their blood pressure.

Both males and females served as subjects in the present experiment. The initial blood pressure for females averaged across Groups and Sessions was 108.4 mm Hg and for males, 117.3 mm Hg. This difference was reliable, $F(1/18)=6.73$, $MS_e=27.34$. The initial heart rates for females averaged across Groups and Sessions was 81.3 bpm and 84.7 bpm for the males. This difference was not statistically reliable. Excepting this initial difference in blood pressure, no differences attributable to sex were detected, and both males and females appeared to respond similarly to the experimental manipulations. Using the last trial block

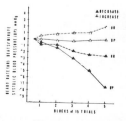

Fig. 3. Heart rate and blood pressure changes for the Groups × Trials Interaction. Only the Increase and Decrease groups are displayed. Each point is the mean of 5 subjects and 15 trials.

of the third session as an example, females in the Decrease group showed an average blood pressure decrease of 10.1 mm Hg while the males decreased 8.9 mm Hg.

Discussion

The present results extend previous findings in several important ways. Considering just the results of the first session in the present experiment, the group given simple visual feedback (plus the one or two words of verbal feedback following each trial) for reductions in systolic blood pressure achieved mean decreases of approximately 5 mm Hg below starting baseline by the end of the session. This is to be compared with decreases of 4 mm Hg and 1.5 mm Hg reported by Shapiro et al. (1969) and Shapiro et al. (1970a), respectively, after approximately the same amount of training. Apparently, simple feedback is as effective as the complex combination of tone and light feedback and reward used by the Shapiro group. Additionally, the present results suggest that multiple sessions, separated by 24 hr intervals, augment subjects' ability to decrease their systolic blood pressure.

No reliable increases in blood pressure were found in the present experiment. Although the Increase group reached a trivial maximum of 1.5 mm Hg above baseline in Session 2, reference to Fig. 3 shows that changes from baseline across all three sessions were negligible. Previous experiments investigating systolic blood pressure increases through contingent feedback (Schwartz, 1972; Shapiro et al., 1970a) have likewise reported changes of only a few mm Hg. It seems quite possible that the response of raising systolic blood pressure is incompatible with the experimental situation in which the subject is placed. That is, sitting quietly in a comfortable chair might be expected to assist subjects in lowering blood pressure, but would make difficult the task of raising blood pressure. Indeed, the subjects in the Increase and Random groups reported feeling tense and anxious. They found the task frustrating since they were not able to keep the feedback light on for any sustained period of time. By contrast, the subjects in the Decrease and No-feedback groups reported feeling relaxed. Interestingly, although the subjects in the Increase group failed to raise their blood pressure, they did raise their heart rates a few bpm during training. This may be a physiological reflection of the psychological tension reported by these subjects. In this regard, the results of the No-feedback group assume particular importance. That is, it could be argued that a "natural" (unconditioned) response to sitting quietly in a comfortable chair is a reduction in blood pressure. For the subjects in the Decrease group, this would trigger the feedback, indicating success at the task. This in turn could promote further relaxation and

further blood pressure decreases, which would be registered as even greater success. However, the subjects in the Increase and Random groups would not receive such fortuitous feedback since unconditioned blood pressure decreases would not increase the probability of feedback for these groups. Thus, they could, conceivably, respond with feelings of anxiety and tension which might prevent or retard further unconditioned blood pressure decreases. This possibility could not be ruled out in previous experiments due to the lack of an appropriate control group. In the present experiment, however, the subjects in the No-feedback group had every reason to believe that they were successful at the task, and they reported no frustration, anxiety or tension. Therefore, if unconditioned systolic blood pressure decreases were to occur as a result of relaxation and feelings of success, decreases should have been observed in the No-feedback group as well as the Decrease group. The fact that the subjects in the No-feedback group showed no systematic blood pressure changes throughout the experiment suggests that the decreases observed in the Decrease group were not due to fortuitous reinforcement. Similarly, the fact that the subjects in the Random group also showed no consistent blood pressure changes suggests that factors such as instructional set and exposure to the experimental environment did not influence systolic blood pressure in this experiment. It appears, therefore, that the decreases were due to the contingent feedback. Further, the failure of the subjects in the Increase group to raise blood pressure might not represent a failure of the biofeedback technique if it is accepted that the response of raising blood pressure is more incompatible with the physical inactivity imposed by the experimental environment than the response of lowering blood pressure.

In the present experiment, heart rate was observed to change in the directions expected for blood pressure. Heart rate increased in the Increase blood pressure condition although these subjects were unsuccessful in raising their blood pressure, and heart rate and blood pressure simultaneously decreased in the Decrease blood pressure condition (see Fig. 3). Previous workers have introduced certain terminology to describe the relationships between heart rate and blood pressure changes. Shapiro and co-workers use the terms "differentiation," "decoupling," and "dissociation" to describe situations in which changes in one variable are statistically reliable while changes in the other are not. This is the case in the Shapiro et al. (1969) experiment where heart rate decreases were observed in the group reinforced for decreases in blood pressure, yet blood pressure and heart rate were considered to be "dissociated" since only the blood pressure decreases were statistically reliable. Schwartz (1972) has defined "differentiation'' as changes of two variables in opposite directions. In one condition in which subjects were trained to simultaneously decrease blood pressure and increase heart rate, both heart rate and blood pressure decreased. Nonetheless, Schwartz concludes that the two variables were "differentiated" since the heart rate decreases were not statistically reliable. Schwartz (1972) has also investigated the degree to which cardiac and blood pressure responses may be "integrated," meaning that the two variables change simultaneously in the same direction. In one integration condition, Schwartz reinforced subjects for simultaneous decreases in heart rate and blood pressure. After 25 of the 35 trials administered in his experiment, blood pressure had decreased about 5 mm Hg and heart rate had decreased about 6 bpm (interpolated from his Fig. 2, bottom left panel). The same number of trials are represented by the end of Session 1 in the present experiment, and reference to Figs. 1 and 2 indicates comparable values of 5 mm Hg for blood pressure and 4 bpm for heart rate for the Decrease blood pressure group. This is an impressively close replication given that the present experiment used subjects of both sexes and employed procedures which differed in many details from those used by Schwartz. Most importantly, feedback in the present experiment was contingent only on blood pressure changes, yet the integration pattern was obtained. Thus, it appears that heart rate and blood pressure tend to simultaneously decrease even in a situation where neither instructional sets nor feedback contingencies are designed to produce simultaneous decreases.

This finding prompted the present authors to re-examine the results of previous experiments in which biofeedback was employed to raise or lower human systolic blood pressure while heart rate was simultaneously monitored. In the experiments by Brener and Kleinman (1970) and Shapiro et al. (1969) as well as the present experiment, decreases in blood pressure were accompanied by decreases in heart rate. (The data of Shapiro et al., 1970a, cannot be evaluated since the direction of heart rate changes are not reported.) Further, heart rate decreases occur in the absence of blood pressure changes (Brener & Kleinman, 1970; Session 1, No-feedback group in present experiment) and during small and transient blood pressure increases (Shapiro et al., 1969). It appears, therefore, that decreases in heart rate are frequently observed in experiments designed to operantly condition blood pressure either up or down. While it could be argued that these heart rate decreases have not always been statistically significant, it can be counterargued that the downward trend is consistent across experiments; further, the absence of statistical significance should never be used to argue for the absence of a relationship, although this was done by Shapiro et al. (1970a, since they use the absence of a significant 3-way interaction to argue that heart rate and blood pressure are dissociated) and Schwartz (1972, since he concludes that heart rate and blood pressure are differentiated because heart rate decreases were not significant while blood pressure decreases were). Finally, when heart rate increases have been reported, they have either been of trivial magnitude (present experiment) or based on a highly selected subset of data (the 5 "best" subjects of Shapiro, Tursky, and Schwartz, 1970b). Similarly, conditioned systolic blood pressure increases are generally unimpressive in magnitude while decreases are more notable. As suggested earlier, increases in heart rate and blood pressure may be relatively difficult to achieve given the physically inactive environment imposed upon the subject and become, therefore, less probable outcomes than decreases or no changes relative to baseline. Additionally, in the present experiment, heart rate and blood pressure were positively correlated (see Table 1). Thus, while inspection of the group means (Figs. 1 and 2) would suggest that blood pressure and heart rate were consistently related only for the Decrease group, the correlations suggest that most subjects, regardless of experimental group, changed their blood pressure and heart rate together. In this regard, the argument for differentiation would be more convincing if, in the experiments purporting to demonstrate differentiation, negative correlations between heart rate and blood pressure had been reported.

The Random and No-feedback control groups in the present experiment showed no consistent blood pressure changes from starting baseline throughout the course of the experiment. By contrast, the random group in the Shapiro et al. (1970a) experiment displayed a decrease in blood pressure over trials. While the reasons for these discrepancies cannot be determined at present, further work with normotensive populations should be encouraged, since this permits inclusion of appropriate control groups and the use of certain manipulations which might not be ethically applied to a clinically hypertensive population. A firm, experimentally derived data base should be developed as rapidly as possible since preliminary results using hypertensive subjects (Benson, Shapiro, Tursky, & Schwartz, 1971; Elder, Ruiz, Deabler, & Dillenkoffer, 1973) suggest that biofeedback techniques, appropriately applied, may be successful in reducing high blood pressure.

REFERENCES

Benson, H., Shapiro, D., Tursky, B., & Schwartz, G. E. Decreased systolic blood pressure through operant conditioning techniques in patients with essential hypertension. *Science*, 1971, *173*, 740–742.

Blanchard, E. B., & Young, L. D. Self-control of cardiac functioning: A promise as yet unfulfilled. *Psychological Bulletin*, 1973, *79*, 145–163.

Brener, J., & Kleinman, R. A. Learned control of decreases in systolic blood pressure. *Nature*, 1970, *226*, 1063–1064.

Elder, S. T., Ruiz, R. Z., Deabler, H. J., & Dillenkoffer, R, L. Instrumental conditioning of diastolic blood pressure in essential hypertensive patients. *Journal of Applied Behavior Analysis*, 1973, *6*, 377–382.

Schwartz, G. E. Voluntary control of human cardiovascular integration and differentiation through feedback and reward. *Science*, 1972, *175*, 90–93.

Shapiro, D., Tursky, B., Gershon, E., & Stern, M. Effects of feedback and reinforcement on the control of human systolic blood pressure. *Science*, 1969, *163*, 588–590.

Shapiro, D., Tursky, B., & Schwartz, G. E. Control of blood pressure in man by operant conditioning. *Circulation Research*, 1970, *26*, Suppl. 1, 27–32. (a)

Shapiro, D., Tursky, B., & Schwartz, G. E. Differentiation of heart rate and systolic blood pressure in man by operant conditioning. *Psychosomatic Medicine*, 1970, *32*, 417–423. (b)

Clinical Applications of 41 Biofeedback: Voluntary Control of Heart Rate, Rhythm, and Blood Pressure

Neal E. Miller

ROLE OF FEEDBACK IN LEARNING VOLUNTARY CONTROL

The novice trying to learn to shoot a basket from the foul line does not have the voluntary control to send the ball swishing through the hoop on the first trial. On the basis of his innate coordinations as refined by previous learning in other situations, he tosses the ball in the general direction of the basket. When he misses, he feels mildly frustrated and is less likely to repeat that set of movements. When he comes nearer, he feels successful and, when he finally sees the ball going through the hoop, that success serves as a reward to make him more likely to repeat the correct set of movements. In this example, seeing where the ball goes is the feedback. Thorndike (1) originally called such feedback *knowledge of results* and showed that it is essential for efficient trial-and-error learning.[1]

If our novice basketball player were blindfolded, so that he did not have the feedback of seeing whether he was succeeding or failing, he could not learn. Within the range of normal spontaneous fluctuations, the typical patient is unable to perceive correctly changes in his blood pressure or heart rate, so that

Research described here from the author's laboratory was supported by Research Grants MH 13189 and MH 19183 from the National Institute of Mental Health and by grants from the Grant Foundation and the Spencer Foundation.

[1] Actually, the foregoing example is somewhat oversimplified because, along with its reward and punishment function, the feedback also can serve a guidance function, with the novice throwing the ball harder when he sees that it has fallen short. However, this is a more sophisticated function that depends on transfer of previous training from similar situations.

he is in a situation analogous to that of the blindfolded basketball player.[2] However, modern instrumentation can give the patient exact moment to moment information on what is happening to his blood pressure or heart rate. This use of instrumentation is analogous to removing the blindfold from the novice who is trying to learn to shoot a basket. The use of instrumentation to provide improved feedback (i.e., knowledge of results) of a biological function has been called *biofeedback*.

SKIN TEMPERATURE AND PERIPHERAL CIRCULATION

In a simple example of biofeedback, the skin temperature of the subject's index finger is measured by a tiny thermistor or thermocouple taped to that finger. The subject is given information about the spontaneous fluctuations in his skin temperature by watching the needle on the meter of an electronic thermometer and/or by listening to the pitch of a tone which goes up as the temperature goes up, and goes down as the temperature goes down. With a well motivated subject who is instructed to try to change his temperature in a specific direction, a movement of the needle in the correct direction indicates success, which serves as a reward, while a movement of the needle in the opposite direction signifies failure, which serves as a punishment. At the same time, the experimenter can reward changes in the correct direction by verbal approval.

Figure 1 illustrates the performance of a subject who has been trained in this way to reduce the temperature of his hand upon command. After the subject had learned, a Doppler effect bloodflow probe was placed over the digital artery of the index finger bearing the thermistor in order to demonstrate the effect of the training on peripheral blood flow. The extreme lefthand part of Figure 1 illustrates the effects of momentary complete occlusion of bloodflow by pressure on the radial and ulnar arteries. The main part of the figure shows that the command, "Cool your hand," produces an immediate marked drop in peripheral circulation and pulse amplitude, followed by a more gradual drop in temperature. As soon as the subject is told to stop, the bloodflow, pulse amplitude and, later, the temperature return to normal. Careful observation of this subject failed to reveal any skeletal responses that could account for the changes in blood flow. A number of other investigators (2, 3) have trained subjects to produce either increases or decreases in skin temperature.

That the control over vasomotor responses can be quite specific is demonstrated by experiments in which the subject is given information on the differ-

---

[2] Even in the case where the patient is able to perceive what is happening (e.g., in paroxysmal tachycardia), he may not make good use of this information; he may not be motivated to try to learn because he is not aware of the possibility of learning. On the other hand, if some patients should learn to control their symptoms, the very fact of control might prevent the phenomenon from coming to the attention of a physician.

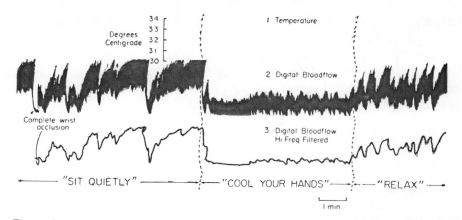

Figure 1. Learned voluntary control over bloodflow and temperature. Temperature is recorded from a thermistor near the tip of the index finger of the right hand, and blood velocity by a Doppler effect probe over the digital artery to that finger. The upper and lower envelopes of the dark band in the center of the record represent the velocities of bloodflow at the peak and trough of the pulse; the width of the band is an indication of pulse amplitude. (Recorded by Lynch, Kohn, and Miller.)

ence between the temperature of the two hands and is required to make the right hand warmer than the left or the left hand warmer than the right. Maslach, Marshall, and Zimbardo (4) and Roberts, Kewman, and Macdonald (5) have ·shown that hypnotized subjects can do this, sometimes changing the temperature of the two hands in different directions. In work that is in progress, Roberts in Minnesota and Lynch, Kohn, and Hama in my laboratory are showing that nonhypnotized subjects can learn to produce a difference between the temperatures of the two hands, first in one direction and then in the opposite one. We even have one subject who can produce such differences between two fingers on one hand. Such specificity of control rules out many factors such as the effects of arousal or of changes in breathing. We have not yet discovered any skeletal responses that can produce such a specific difference, and we hope to rule out such responses still more definitively by recording an electromyogram of the muscles in the hand and the forearm while subjects are producing a difference between two fingers of the same hand.

Because changes in skin temperature can be made so specific, are so easy to measure, and so seemingly benign, we are studying such changes in the hope of finding out more about the laws of cardiovascular learning and of discovering more efficient ways for producing it. We hope to learn the answers to questions such responses still more definitively by recording an electromyogram of the effective than the slightly delayed feedback from changes in temperature? Can learning be facilitated by prior training in muscular relaxation, by instructions to imagine that one finger is warm and the other is cold, or by prior training in correctly identifying small changes in temperature? Will children learn more easily than adults?

In the experiments on temperature, as well as those on other functions to be described subsequently, a few people, like the subject in Figure 1, can learn to produce large changes, but most people produce smaller ones. What is the basis for such large individual differences?

BLOOD PRESSURE

Method of training

In training a subject to change his blood pressure, we use a specially designed servomechanism that controls the pressure in a cuff at slightly above the diastolic level, as determined by the amplitude of the Korotkoff sounds picked up by a microphone over the artery (6). A strain gauge transducer records the pressure in the cuff as an electrical signal which is amplified and recorded on a chart. Whenever the spontaneous fluctuations in blood pressure are large enough in the desired direction, the electrical voltage trips a Schmitt trigger which causes a tone to sound. This tone serves as a signal of success which serves as a reward in the same way as seeing the basketball swish through the hoop.

At first, the criterion for tripping the Schmitt trigger is made very easy so that small spontaneous fluctuations in the right direction will succeed; as the subject learns, the criterion is made progressively more difficult. We have also experimented with giving the patient continuous feedback by allowing him to watch the needle of a meter which records changes in blood pressure.

Direct versus indirect control

Using the foregoing technique, it is not too difficult to train most people to produce modest changes in diastolic blood pressure. However, from a theoretical point of view, there is a question about whether these changes represent direct control over blood pressure or are only indirect effects produced by changes in breathing or muscular tension. In an attempt to settle this question, Pickering, Brucker, and Miller (in preparation) have studied patients with severe paralysis of the skeletal muscles produced by diseases such as polio and muscular dystrophy that leave the autonomic nervous system relatively unaffected. In the light of our earlier results on curarized rats[3] we had hoped that the paralysis might facilitate the learning of blood pressure changes, perhaps by eliminating "noise" induced by indirect effects of skeletal responses. Although this hope was not

---

[3] Early results (7) indicated that rats paralyzed by curare learned changes in heart rate and blood pressure much faster than those not paralyzed, and subsequently transferred these responses from the paralyzed to the nonparalyzed state. Subsequently, there has been a perplexing decline in the visceral learning shown by rats paralyzed by curare (8, 9).

realized, the paralyzed subjects did learn to produce modest changes in diastolic blood pressure averaging 3.7 mm Hg. It was possible to rule out completely changes in respiration as a basis for the changes in blood pressure. Overt activity in other skeletal muscles also could be reasonably ruled out by electromyo: graphic recordings from the few that were spared. However, interestingly enough, when a subject attempted to squeeze a bulb with his completely paralyzed hand, this command to muscles that did not move could produce an increase in both heart rate and blood pressure. In three of the subjects, however, the absence of changes in heart rate during the learned changes in blood pressure contrasted so sharply with the increases in both during attempts to use the paralyzed skeletal muscles that it seems unlikely that they could have been unconsciously using this latter procedure during the learning experiment.

For the theory of learning it is important to determine whether or not changes in visceral responses are produced directly or only indirectly via the mediation of skeletal responses. But for practical applications to either etiology or therapy, the question of mediation is much less important, especially if the skeletal response is reasonably inconspicuous and does not have significant side effects.

Placebo effects

Although one does not have to worry so much about mediation in dealing with therapeutic applications, one does have to be seriously concerned with the possibility of a placebo effect. That such effects can be quite large is indicated by the results in control groups of double-blind studies of the effectiveness of antihypertensive drugs. Thus, with 48 patients who received nothing but placebo medication as control groups in a study by Grenfell, Briggs, and Holland (10), the average decrease in diastolic blood pressure was 12 mm Hg and in systolic blood pressure was 25 mm Hg. Furthermore, such reductions in blood pressure were not produced immediately but occurred progressively during a period of approximately 7 weeks. Thus, in an experiment on learned control of hypertension it would be easy to mistake such a progressive placebo effect for learning. Furthermore, clinical experience plus a study by Shapiro et al. (11) show that the enthusiasm of the physician can contribute to the antihypertensive effect of both placebo and active medication. Thus, a stable baseline before training begins cannot be used to rule out the placebo effect unless both the experimenter and the patients are unaware of when the training begins.

Although placebo effects are a decided nuisance in trying to evaluate the effectiveness of a specific training procedure, they do demonstrate clearly the significance of purely psychologic factors; they are large enough to merit more research than they have received.

Clinical results

One unusual patient, with partial paralysis of both the somatic and sympathetic systems on the left side as a result of brainstem damage from a previous stroke, illustrates the degree of control over diastolic blood pressure that can be learned (12). In order to control for placebo effects and to get a possible benefit from contrasting correct and incorrect responses, this 33-year-old woman was trained to decrease, increase (but never above her original baseline level), and then decrease again her blood pressure during daily practice sessions. At first she was able to change her blood pressure through a range of only approximately 5 mm Hg. As she learned, we required progressively larger changes. In order to measure her control, the mean of diastolic pressure integrated over a 1-min interval was determined. After 10 weeks of ¾-hr training sessions 5 days a week, she had progressed so that she could increase her blood pressure from a baseline average of 76 mm Hg to an average of 94 mm Hg and then reduce it to an average of 65 mm Hg—a range of control totaling 29 mm Hg. It seems unlikely that this increased ability to either raise or lower her blood pressure to the appropriate command could have been a placebo effect. Meanwhile, her baseline blood pressure decreased from 97 mm Hg as an average of 28 readings taken during the month before training to one of 76 mm Hg as an average of 18 readings taken on different days during her 3rd month of training. This overall decrease in baseline readings occurred in spite of the fact that antihypertensive medication was withdrawn during the latter part of training, producing a transient rise in blood pressure.

This patient seemed to be cured because similar decreases were observed on the ward. However, under an unusual combination of emotional stresses, her baseline blood pressure rose, she lost voluntary control, and had to be restored to antihypertensive drugs. After the situational stresses were largely resolved, she returned to training approximately 2.5 years later and has rapidly regained a large measure of voluntary control.

However, the question pointedly raised by this patient is whether or not she merely is using her voluntary control to produce a spuriously low measure in clinical tests while continuing to respond with hypertension to crucial parts of her daily life and thus conceivably misleading her physician about her need for antihypertensive medication. Unfortunately, the only presently available method for continuous recording to answer decisively this crucial question of transfer to daily life involves maintaining a catheter in an artery (13).

Attempts in the author's laboratory to train 27 other patients with essential hypertension to lower their diastolic blood pressures have produced considerably poorer, not really promising, results. Shapiro (14) reports similar lack of encouraging results with diastolic blood pressure. With the more labile systolic pressure, Benson et al. (15) have reported an average decrease of 22 mm Hg during training in five patients with essential hypertension, but this result must be compared with an average placebo effect of 25 mm Hg in the systolic pressure of 48 patients reported by Grenfell, Briggs, and Holland (10). Thus, the practical application of visceral training to the reduction of hypertension awaits the development either of superior methods for selecting the rare patients who can benefit from current techniques or of considerably improved techniques for training. Many plausible ways of improving training remain to be tried. If they succeed, the results must be validated by controls for placebo effects and by tests for transfer to daily life.

CARDIAC ARRHYTHMIAS

The most convincing therapeutic application of biofeedback training to date has been in the treatment of premature ventricular contractions (PVC's). The general method, as described by Weiss and Engel (16), is to record the ECG and to use programming equipment to control an array of lights that instructs patients on what to do and informs them how well they are succeeding. Patients are first trained to alternately speed and slow their heart rates a few beats per minute. This convinces them that they can control their hearts. Then the patients are trained to hold their heart rates within a narrow range. As long as they are within this range a yellow light shines, but a premature beat extinguishes the yellow light and causes a red light to flash because it comes too fast, followed by a green light triggered by the ensuing compensatory pause. Patients learn to identify this sequence as a PVC and to try to prevent it. As learning progresses, they show fewer PVC's while trying to suppress them than during rest periods when they are not. Finally, the feedback is progressively phased out by omitting it on an increasing proportion of trials. This procedure is believed to be important because it helps the patient to identify without aid whether his heart is beating correctly or incorrectly so that he can transfer this practice from the laboratory to his daily life.

Engel and Bleecker (17) report that six of the nine patients trained to date have learned to control their PVC's in the laboratory; the three failures had the most seriously damaged hearts. In clinical tests outside of the laboratory, five patients showed persistence of lowered PVC activity for the considerable number of months for which they were followed up. One had good control 1 year and another 5 years afterwards. In both of these cases, low levels were verified by continuous 10-hr tape recordings taken while patients performed normal daily activities.

Engel and Bleecker (17) also report good results in training three patients to control tachycardia.

Dr. Thomas Pickering is in the process of replicating the foregoing results on PVC's in the author's laboratory. Thus far he has succeeded in training two out of two patients to reduce their PVC's. Figure 2 is a continuous record of one such patient during alternate trials of trying to suppress and trying to produce PVC's. Statistical analyses of the records of this patient and of the other one

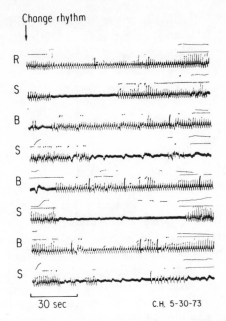

Figure 2. Voluntary control over heart rhythm. Premature ventricular contractions (PVC's) are indicated by large spikes, and normal sinus rhythm by their absence. Line above the ECG indicates skin conductance. R, period of rest; S, patient instructed to suppress PVC's; B, patient instructed to produce bigeminy or, in other words, alternating PVC's and normal beats. Entire figure is from a continuous strip of record.

show that both of them have somehow established definite, but not complete, voluntary control over their PVC's.

The ability of a number of patients from both laboratories to turn their arrhythmias either on or off on command seems unlikely to be a nonspecific placebo effect. This voluntary control may reduce the patient's anxiety, however, and thus have a number of additional effects. The fact that a number of the patients described have been resistant to other forms of therapy further reduces the probability that their improvement was the result of any simple placebo effect. The results on cardiac arrhythmias seem promising enough to merit additional careful attempts at replication by other investigators, and the use of portable ECG tape-recording equipment both before and after treatment in order to secure objective evidence on therapeutic gains in everyday life.

OTHER APPLICATIONS OF INSTRUMENTED FEEDBACK

In moving into a completely new area of application, it is good strategy to do preliminary work first, to be sure that one has an effect before one sets up elaborate time-consuming controls that will be meaningless if there is nothing to control for. Many of the clinical applications of biofeedback are still at the first, preliminary stage. The initial results have been promising enough to warrant moving on to the second stage, that of carefully controlled studies, but we must reserve judgment about any therapeutic effects until these studies are completed. Unfortunately, the interest of the public media, and the claims of those who are trying to make money by selling equipment, have created exaggerated expectations that may lead to premature disillusionment which will interfere with the hard work that is necessary to develop and test therapeutic applications of the new technique of biofeedback.

Headaches

Stoyva and Budzynski (18) have shown that giving tense patients feedback from the electromyographic activity of their muscles can help them to learn to relax, and that for this purpose feedback from the frontalis muscle is superior to that from the forearm. In a clinical application, 75% of 30 patients with tension headaches were improved by being trained to relax their frontalis muscles. With patients suffering from migraine headache, Sargent, Green, and Walters (2) report that 74% of 62 patients definitely benefited from being trained to warm their hands, aided by feedback of information about the temperature of their hands. Because headaches are notoriously subject to placebo effects (19), studies are needed with additional controls (e.g., will clearly diagnosed migraine subjects respond better to training in handwarming than to that in relaxation while clear-cut tension headache patients yield the opposite results?) and with longer-term follow-ups.

EEG rhythms

There is abundant evidence that feedback can be used to train control over certain brain rhythms in the electroencephalogram, for example, the α-wave, and that similar results can be achieved with animals paralyzed by curare (20). Some people trained to produce α-waves offer glowing testimonials of beneficial psychologic effects, but a few report unpleasant effects. While the therapeutic possibilities of such training certainly merit careful investigation, to date there is no carefully controlled evidence for any therapeutic benefits.

Epilepsy

Sterman (21) reports that rewarding four patients for a sensorimotor rhythm (12–14 Hz recorded through the skull above the central part of the cortex) produced a marked decrease in their seizure activity which, after several months, reached the lowest levels in their clinical histories. Kaplan (22; personal communication) failed to secure similar results with three patients, but two new patients rewarded for increasing their dominant frequency within the range of 6–12 Hz, which she believes may have been what was occurring with Sterman's somewhat different filter system, did show definite therapeutic effects. However, she believes that these effects may be attributable to the relaxation that the patients learned rather than to the learning of a specific electroencephalographic rhythm.

Torticollis

Brudny, Grynbaum, and Korein (23) used electromyographic feedback to train nine patients to control their spasmodic torticollis. Feedback from muscle tension was used first to train the patients to decrease progressively the spasm of the contracted muscle and then to increase the contraction in the usually atrophied contralateral muscle. All patients showed some improvement. Three of them were able to control the abnormal positions of their heads for several hours without feedback, and three others have remained symptom-free for from several months to over 1 year. Because these latter three patients had had the symptoms for 3, 10, and 15 years, respectively, and had not responded to previous treatment, it seems unlikely that their marked improvement was attributable to any placebo effect.

CONCLUSIONS

Feedback can be used to help train human subjects to control in one way or another certain functions that previously have been generally considered to be beyond the possibility of learned voluntary control. In preliminary studies, encouraging enough therapeutic results have been secured, especially with cardiac arrhythmias and torticollis, to merit further, more thorough investigation. However, much hard work remains to be done before we can make definitive statements about the therapeutic value of biofeedback training.

LITERATURE CITED

1. Thorndike, E. L. 1932. The Fundamentals of Learning. Teachers College, New York.
2. Sargent, J. D., Green, E. E., and Walters, E. D. 1972. The use of autogenic feedback training in a pilot study of migraine and tension headaches. Headache 12:120.
3. Taub, E. and Emurian, C. E. 1972. Autoregulation of skin temperature using a variable intensity light. Paper presented at Biofeedback Research Society Meeting, Boston.
4. Maslach, C., Marshall, G., and Zimbardo, P. G. 1972. Hypnotic control of peripheral skin temperature: A case report. Psychophysiology 9:600.
5. Roberts, A., Kewman, D. G., and Macdonald, H. 1973. Voluntary control of skin temperature: Unilateral changes using hypnosis and feedback. J. Abnorm. Psychol. 82:163.
6. Miller, N. E., DiCara, L. V., Solomon, H., Weiss, J. M., and Dworkin, B. 1970. Learned modifications of autonomic functions: A review and some new data. Circ. Res. 26/27(suppl. 1):3.
7. Miller, N. E. 1969. Learning of visceral and glandular responses. Science 163:434.
8. Miller, N. E. 1972. Interactions between learned and physical factors in mental illness. Semin. Psychiatr. 4:239.

9. Miller, N. E. and Dworkin, B. R. 1974. Visceral learning: Recent difficulties with curarized rats and significant problems for human research. *In* P. A. Obrist et al. (eds.), Cardiovascular Psychophysiology, pp. 312–331. Aldine, Chicago.

10. Grenfell, R. F., Briggs, A. H., and Holland, W. C. 1963. Antihypertensive drugs evaluated in a controlled double-blind study. South. Med. J. 56:1410.

11. Shapiro, A. P., Myers, T., Reiser, M. F., and Ferris, E. B. 1954. Comparison of blood pressure response to Veriloid and to the doctor. Psychosom. Med. 16:478.

12. Miller, N. E. 1972. Learning of visceral and glandular responses: Postscript. *In* D. Singh and C. T. Morgan (eds.), Current Status of Physiological Psychology: Readings, pp. 245-250. Brooks/Cole, Monterey, Cal.

13. Bevan, A. T., Honour, A. J., and Stott, F. H. 1961. Direct arterial pressure recording in unrestricted man. Clin. Sci. 36:329.

14. Shapiro, D. 1974. Operant-feedback control of human blood pressure: Some clinical issues. *In* P. A. Obrist et al. (eds.), Cardiovascular Psychophysiology, pp. 441–455. Aldine, Chicago.

15. Benson, H., Shapiro, D., Tursky, B., and Schwartz, G. E. 1971. Decreased systolic blood pressure through operant conditioning techniques in patients with essential hypertension. Science 173:740.

16. Weiss, T. and Engel, B. T. 1971. Operant conditioning of heart rate in patients with premature ventricular contractions. Psychosom. Med. 33:301.

17. Engel, B. T. and Bleecker, E. R. 1974. Application of operant conditioning techniques to the control of the cardiac arrhythmias. *In* P. A. Obrist et al. (eds.), Cardiovascular Psychophysiology, pp. 456–476. Aldine, Chicago.

18. Stoyva, J. and Budzynski, T. Cultivated low arousal—An anti-stress response? *In* L. V. DiCara (ed.), Recent Advances in Limbic and Autonomic Nervous System Research. Plenum Press, New York. In press.

19. Shapiro, A. K. 1960. A contribution to a history of the placebo effect. Behav. Sci. 5:109.

20. Miller, N. E. Applications of learning and biofeedback to psychiatry and medicine. *In* A. M. Freedman, H. I, Kaplan, and B. J. Sadock (eds.), Comprehensive Textbook of Psychiatry, pp. 349–365. 2nd Ed. Williams & Wilkins, Baltimore. In press.

21. Sterman, M. B. 1973. Neurophysiological and clinical studies of sensorimotor EEG biofeedback training: Some effects on epilepsy. Semin. Psychiatr. 5:507.

22. Kaplan, B. 1973. EEG biofeedback and epilepsy. Paper presented at 81st Annual Convention of the American Psychological Association, Montreal, 1973.

23. Brudny, J., Grynbaum, B. B., and Korein, J. 1974. Spasmodic torticollis: Treatment by feedback display of EMG—A report of nine cases. Arch. Phys. Med. Rehab. 55:403.

Mailing address: Dr. Neal E. Miller, The Rockefeller University, New York, New York 10021.

The Effects of Muscle Relaxation on Blood Pressure of Essential Hypertensives 42

James E. Shoemaker and Donald L. Tasto

Summary—Muscle relaxation and noncontinuous biofeedback were investigated as potential non-pharmaceutical treatments for essential hypertension. The two procedures were compared to a waiting list control group. Predictions were made regarding the overall treatment effect, sessions within treatment effect, and periods within session effect. The results of this experiment reveal that biofeedback significantly lowers diastolic blood pressure between premeasures and postmeasures. It was also shown that muscle relaxation has a significant effect upon lowering diastolic and systolic blood pressures between premeasures and postmeasures and has a significant effect upon lowering diastolic and systolic blood pressures as subjects progress from the first period of a treatment session to the last period of a treatment session.

Hypertension or high blood pressure is divided into two forms: primary or essential, where the cause is unknown, and secondary, where there is some associated lesion such as chronic nephritis or tumor of the adrenal cortex. The lesion associated with the latter form is presumed to be responsible for the raised blood pressure (Boyd, 1962). On the other hand, any person having an arterial pressure greater than 140/90 and who also has no obvious organic cause for the hypertension is considered to have essential hypertension (Guyton, 1971).

Of importance to the investigation of treatments for essential hypertension, is the fact that an increase in peripheral resistance to blood flow is more closely represented by diastolic rather than systolic pressure (Boyd, 1962; Merrill, 1966; Gantt, 1972). However, in order to comprehensively assess the effects which treatment techniques have on blood pressure, both systolic blood pressure and diastolic blood pressure have been studied.

A combination of operant conditioning and continuous physiological feedback techniques has been used effectively to raise or lower systolic blood pressure in normal subjects (Shapiro et al., 1969; Shapiro et al., 1970; Schwartz et al., 1971), to lower systolic blood pressure in normal subjects (Brener and Kleinman, 1970), to decrease systolic blood pressure variability in normal subjects (Hnatiow, 1971) and to lower systolic blood pressure in hypertensive subjects (Shapiro et al., 1970; Benson et al., 1971). Similarly, Shapiro et al. (1972) have shown that normal male subjects can learn to raise or lower their diastolic blood pressure, and in addition Schwartz (1972) demonstrated that the modifications in blood pressure levels can occur independently of modifications in heart rate.

Reprinted with permission from *Behaviour Research and Therapy*, Vol. 13, 29-43.

With clinical application in mind, a comprehensive questionnaire was administered by Schwartz (1972) in order to assess cognitive activity of the subjects. It was found that the blood pressure decrease–heart rate decrease group tended to check more items associated with relaxation than did the blood pressure increase–heart rate increase group. Schwartz (1972) suggested that '. . . some kind of arousal variable may have been operating. In an earlier study (Shapiro *et al.*, 1969), verbal reports were elicited from subjects after they had undergone treatment. Though inconsistent, reports from some subjects who had undergone reduction in systolic blood pressure revealed that the flashing light which had signaled their reduction probably meant a state of relaxation for them.

The above reports which pertain to relaxation are compatible with Jacobson's conclusion (1939) that there is a general relation between decreases in blood pressure and decreases in muscle activity as shown by the electromyogram. The decreases in muscle activity were brought about by 'progressive relaxation' treatment, however. Jacobson's conclusion (1939) was based upon data gathered from normotensive subjects.

It was the purpose of this experiment to determine whether (1) muscle relaxation and (2) noncontinuous blood pressure feedback are effective in lowering both diastolic and systolic levels of blood pressure in essential hypertensives. Muscle relaxation consists of a technique in which a subject performs certain exercises which facilitate the subject's relaxing. Noncontinuous feedback differs from continuous feedback in that noncontinuous feedback consists of allowing the subject to observe his blood pressure at predesignated intervals, whereas continuous feedback allows the subject to be more or less constantly aware of either his systolic or diastolic blood pressure.

METHOD

Subjects

The subjects were 15 essential hypertensive volunteers who replied to a form letter sent to the faculty and to all state employees at Colorado State University. These letters requested those persons who were experiencing essential hypertension, not secondary hypertension, to apply for the program.

Apparatus

To measure blood pressure, the Narco Bio-System Physiograph Four-A was used to record blood pressure data as attained by the Narco Bio-System Programmed Electrosphygmomanometer PE-300. The PE-300 is a solid state unit which was used in conjunction with an occluding cuff equipped with a microphone. The Physiograph was equipped with millimeter paper and was run at 1 cm/sec during treatment sessions.

A 16 × 24 in. mirror was mounted at an 80° angle over the chart recorder in order that subjects sitting in the upright chair, which was facing the Physiograph, could observe the chart recorder which recorded blood pressures. Relaxation instructions were taped prior to the experiment to be played at a uniform volume on a Cassette Tape Recorder.

The experimental room measured 8 × 10 ft and contained the Physiograph, the Electrosphygmomanometer, a Cassette Tape Recorder, a soft leather recliner, a stool for the experimenter, and a 4 ft table which held the recorder and Electrosphygmomanometer.

To measure blood pressure, the Electrosphygmomanometer was programmed to inflate; deflate the occluding cuff at a fixed rate, 3 mm Hg/sec, and at a fixed time interval of 90 sec. A microphone on the occluding cuff transmitted Korotkoff sounds to the Electrosphygmomanometer which incorporated a transducer/preamplifier. The Electrosphygmomanometer transmitted signals proportional to cuff pressure and amplified Korotkoff sounds to the Physiograph channel amplifier, Ca-200. Finally, the output was recorded on the Physiograph chart recorder.

Prior to measuring blood pressure, the Physiograph and Electrosphygmomanometer were calibrated. One hundred millimeter calibration was obtained by establishing a zero baseline on the millimeter paper. This was accomplished by adjusting amplitude on the channel amplifier at 5.8, and adjustment was also made on the pressure amplitude of the Electrosphygmomanometer for 5.8. Next, the channel amplifier's up-down calibration was set at 0.8 down. The up-down calibration was adjusted in order that the pen followed a zero baseline. After this, amplitude of the Electrosphygmomanometer was set at a constant 8.0 in order that height of Korotkoff sounds would be operationalized. That is, height of amplitude would determine whether or not the initial break on the straight line would be considered diastolic and whether or nor the final break would be considered systolic. The final step in preparation for measurement was adjusting the inflation/deflation rate at a constant for all subjects. The rate was set at 3 mm/sec. and at this rate, one complete cycle at 150 mm pressure could be attained within 1 min 30 sec. Maximum cuff pressure was set at 150 mm pressure for every subject except one whose systolic blood pressure exceeded 150 mm pressure.

Experimental procedure

Premeasurements were taken on every other day at the same time for 3 days. Upon entering the laboratory, subjects were asked to:

> Please sit in the chair for 5 minutes. Lay your arms on the chair rests with your hands opened. I am going to put this cuff (showing occluding cuff) on your upper left arm, and then I will wait until the end of the 5 min before I turn on this machine (showing Electrosphygmomanometer) and take 10 measurements of your blood pressure. Now just relax.

Each subject's premeasure consisted of the lowest diastolic reading recorded during the three different days. The first five initial readings were discarded each day, in order to take account of habituation effects. Since it is generally agreed that the diastolic level is of greater clinical significance than the systolic level (Boyd, 1962; Merrill, 1966; Gantt, 1972), the fifteen subjects were rank ordered by diastolic premeasurement, and then the rank order was divided into five groups. Each subject in each group was randomly assigned to one of three treatments: Relaxation, Biofeedback, or Waiting-List Control.

Subjects in the relaxation treatment entered their first training session, sat, and rested for 5 min in the chair as the Experimenter secured the occluding cuff on the subject's left arm. The subjects were each instructed to:

> Position your arms on the arm rests so that your fingers and thumbs are outstretched and you are in a relaxed position. Sit at rest for 5 min in order for the machine to get an accurate reading of your present blood pressure. At the end of 5 min, the cuff on your left arm will inflate and deflate three times at 90-sec intervals. At the end of these three cycles, a tape recording will give you instructions on muscle relaxation. Listen to the tape recording and follow the instructions given to you at this time. Every 12 min, a 4 min and 30 sec break will be taken in the instruction and your blood pressure will be taken for three cycles. At the termination of instructions, three final readings will be taken. This session should last 1 hr and 20 min.

The cassette recorder was then started, and the experimenter remained in the room in order to start the Physiograph and Electrosphygmomanometer at the appropriate time as well as to observe whether the subject became annoyed by the cuff pressure and desired to terminate the measurements. At the termination of the instructions, three final readings were taken and these were used for computing the diastolic postmeasurement for each treatment session. Subjects in the relaxation treatment underwent six relaxation training sessions.

Three cassettes were prepared prior to the experiment and used during the relaxation training. The tapes provided consistently uniform instructions for each subject undergoing relaxation treatment, and the tapes standardized therapist variables.

Tape 1 was a modification of Jacobson's muscle-tension-relaxation paradigm (1938) as modified by Perkins (1965), and the tape was played for the first two sessions. A $4\frac{1}{2}$ min break was situated at 12 min intervals to allow measurement of blood pressure. Tape 2 consisted of a shortened Perkins modification, and the muscle-tension-relaxation exercises were so suggested as to allow the completion of the exercises after the second 12 min interval. The complete exercise was repeated during the two remaining intervals and this tape was used for sessions three and four. Tape 3 promoted an even quicker completion of the muscle-tension-relaxation exercises. Within each 12 min interval, the complete exercise sequence was suggested. This tape was used for sessions five and six. Sessions for the relaxation training were scheduled on alternate days over a period of 2 weeks. The time schedule for each subject had been established prior to premeasurement so that the subjects' measurements could be taken at the same time of day.

The biofeedback group, upon beginning the first training session, sat and rested for 5 min in the reclining chair as the experimenter secured the occluding cuff on each subject's left arm. The subjects were instructed:

> Position your arms on the arm rests so that your fingers and thumbs are outstretched and you are in a relaxed position. Sit at rest for 5 min in order for the maching to get an accurate reading of your present blood pressure. At the end of 5 min, the cuff on your left arm will inflate and deflate three times at 90-sec intervals. At the end of these three cycles, you will be given the opportunity to observe your blood pressure. You will be able to observe your blood pressure by looking at the mirror which I shall set above the physiograph. In the mirror, you will see the chart recorder of the physiograph and also two lines which will be manipulated by me in order to designate your blood pressure levels. After this initial measurement, you will be given further instructions.

Subsequent to obtaining the initial three measurements, the mirror was placed at an 80 angle to the chart recorder so that the subject who was sitting directly in front of the physiograph, could observe his blood pressure.

A $6\frac{1}{2} \times 9\frac{1}{2} \times \frac{1}{16}$ in. single strength plate of glass had been placed on the chart recorder and now two $8\frac{1}{2} \times 11$ in. plastic overlays with one 11 in. straight line drawn on each, were placed on the plate of glass so that one straight line designated the systolic level of blood pressure and the other straight line served as the demarcation of the diastolic level of blood pressure. The subject could thereby visually observe his diastolic and systolic blood pressure levels. Instructions were then given to the subject:

> As you see in the mirror, the machine is monitoring your blood pressure. The recording pen jumps as your blood flows through the partially closed brachial artery. The peak of your blood pressure is designated by the last jump or blip. This blip is the systolic level of blood pressure. Beyond this point, the artery is closed by the pressure of the air cuff.
>
> During this last phase of the cycle, the cuff deflates and as the artery begins to open, blood begins to jet through to the lower arteries and the systolic level is registered by the blip once again. Pay attention to this phase of the cycle and be particularly aware of the highest and lowest blip by observing the two lines which I manipulate.
>
> You will notice that as the cuff is deflated you will be able to feel the pulsation of your blood against the cuff on your upper arm. The last pulsation will coordinately be registered as the last blip.
>
> In previous experiments, researchers have found that each individual has his own peculiar way of lowering blood pressure. That is, there is some way by which you can get the recorded blips to become lower than the lines I superimpose on the recording paper. (Demonstration is now provided by experimenter.) You see how this sequence is lower than the previous trial's sequence of blips.
>
> No matter what your method of lowering blood pressure is, if it works, follow through with it and continue to lower your blood pressure with the method.

Your blood pressure will be monitored for 12 min, then you will be given a $4\frac{1}{2}$ min break after which you will be given feedback in three more sequences of 12 min of feedback and $4\frac{1}{2}$ min breaks. Keep trying to lower your blood pressure until the time periods have completely elapsed.

The demarcation of systolic and diastolic level, which was provided by the overlays, remained constant after they were matched to each session's premeasure. Upon completion of each session, clarification of the next appointment was made with the subject. Subjects were run on alternate days for a total of six sessions. After six sessions of biofeedback, a final postmeasurement was acquired.

Treatment measures

At the same period of time when premeasurements were obtained on the relaxation and biofeedback groups, premeasurements were also being taken on the control group. On every other day at the same time that the subjects had been premeasured, ten measurements of blood pressure were obtained. The first five measurements were discarded each day, in order to take account of habituation effects. Crucial to the results of this experiment is the fact that the premeasurements consisted of the *lowest* diastolic blood pressure reading of each subject.

Control subjects underwent six sessions. During each session, five measurements were recorded, and those five measurements represented that specific session. Each of the five measurements is classified as a period. Muscle relaxation subjects and biofeedback subjects underwent treatment, and at specific intervals, three measurements were taken. The mean of these three measurements represents the specific period. With five periods in each session, there are five measurements which represent each session. Since the controls were not treated but were used only for base-line measurement, they received five measurements for each session. In each of the treatment groups there were five subjects. The randomized assignment of subjects had insured that subjects were matched among treatment groups on diastolic levels. With five periods in each session and each subject undergoing six sessions, a total of thirty measurements were obtained on each subject.

After participation in the three postmeasurement sessions, arrangements were made with the controls so that they could engage in treatment sessions as had been experienced by the other two experimental groups. Similarly, arrangements were made with the individuals in the two experimental groups so that each person could engage in the treatment process which he had not yet undergone.

RESULTS

Two dependent measures, diastolic and systolic blood pressure, were obtained from each subject for purposes of analysis.

The statistical design consisted of two $3 \times 6 \times 5$ split plot factorial designs representing three treatment conditions, six treatment sessions, and five measurement periods.

The means for systolic and diastolic blood pressures are presented in Tables 1 and 2 respectively. The blood pressure representing each period is the mean of the five subjects from the treatment group. Table 3 summarizes a comparison of the mean differences between pre and post blood pressure measurements. The mean reduction of systolic blood pressure for the relaxation treatment group was 6.8 mm Hg. The biofeedback and control groups increased an average of 0.6 and 1.6 mm respectively. The mean reduction of diastolic blood pressure for the relaxation treatment group was 7.6 mm Hg, and the mean reduction of the biofeedback group was 1.2 mm. The control group increased diastolic blood pressure an average of 1.2 mm.

Table 1. Means of systolic blood pressure for each treatment group across sessions

Treatment	Session 1 Periods					Session 2 Periods					Session 3 Periods						Session 4 Periods						Session 5 Periods					Session 6 Periods				
Control	135	132	133	134	134	134	134	134	134	134	135	134	135	134	134	134	137	137	135	135	136	136	134	135	134	134	133	135	133	133	134	133
Biofeed	135	135	136	136	135	137	135	134	134	135	137	136	136	134	134	134	136	137	134	135	136	136	134	134	134	134	134	135	133	133	133	130
Relax	143	137	135	137	134	141	137	134	134	131	141	136	134	131	130	130	136	135	132	138	141	139	134	131	131	131	131	141	133	132	130	130

Each data point is the mean of five readings which were taken in each period. Each period is represented, therefore, by one data point.

Table 2. Means of diastolic blood pressure for each treatment group across sessions

Treatment	Session 1 Periods					Session 2 Periods					Session 3 Periods					Session 4 Periods						Session 5 Periods					Session 6 Periods				
Controls	93	92	91	92	92	93	92	91	92	92	92	92	91	91	93	93	92	91	92	92	91	91	92	91	91	92	91	91	93
Biofeed	91	91	91	91	91	91	90	90	89	89	91	90	90	89	89	94	91	89	90	91	91	90	90	89	92	91	91	90	89
Relax	92	90	88	87	91	92	88	86	85	84	92	88	87	85	84	92	89	87	86	86	90	85	84	82	82	90	85	82	82	83

Each data point is the mean of five readings which were taken in each period. Each period is represented, therefore, by one data point.

Table 3. Mean differences between pre and post blood pressure measurements

	Treatments		
	Muscle relaxation	Biofeedback	Control
Systolic premeasures	168 128 136 112 138	139 130 127 129 136	130 140 124 133 134
Means for each group	136.4	132.2	132.2
Systolic postmeasures	149 126 129 115 129	142 131 127 127 137	130 141 128 136 134
Means for each group	129.6	132.8	133.8
Mean reduction for each group	6.8	−0.6	−1.6
Diastolic premeasures	98 89 89 88 88	94 90 89 88 88	94 93 89 88 88
Means for each group	90.4	89.8	90.4
Diastolic postmeasures	88 84 80 81 81	91 89 89 86 88	95 94 90 90 89
Means for each group	82.8	88.6	91.6
Mean reduction for each group	7.6	1.2	−1.2

Again it is crucial to note that the premeasurement for each subject consisted of the lowest diastolic reading which was taken during the three premeasurement sessions. Therefore, the mean reductions cited above are statistically conservative.

Table 4. Analysis of variance for the premeasures and postmeasures of systolic blood pressures

Source	SS	df	MS	F	p
T	37.813	2	18.907	0.007	
T by B	21510.920	8	2688.865		
B	16669.920	4	4167.480		

Table 5. Analysis of variance for the premeasures and postmeasures of diastolic blood pressures

Source	SS	df	MS	F	p
T	2223.373	2	1111.687	16.510	<0.001
T by B	538.649	8	67.331		
B	3246.591	4	811.648		

Tables 4 and 5 summarize the analysis of variance results of the systolic and diastolic measures respectively. The significant diastolic results reveal treatment effect and, to isolate the specific effects of treatments, a test of simple effects was utilized. The test of simple main effects is summarized in Table 6. Relaxation and biofeedback treatments were significant ($F = 41.545, df = 4/16, p < 0.00001; F = 3.470, df = 4/16, p < 0.05$) respectively, while the control group did not show a significant reduction in blood pressure between premeasures and postmeasures as indicated by the nonsignificant test for simple main effects.

Table 6. Test of simple main effects for diastolic blood pressure measures

Source	SS	df	MS	F	p
Control group	23.333	4	5.833	0.660	
Biofeedback	122.666	4	30.666	3.470	<0.05
Relaxation	1468.333	4	367.083	41.545	<0.00001
Periods by blocks	141.369	16	8.836		

Tables 7 and 8 summarize the analysis of variance results pertaining to lowering of blood pressures among Sessions 1, 2, 3, 4, 5 and 6. Though the results of both systolic and diastolic analyses were nonsignificant, a linear by linear comparison was performed to investigate whether or not the combined linearity of biofeedback and control groups differed significantly from the relaxation linearity. Figures 1 and 2 illustrate the linear differences, and Tables 7 and 8 include the tests. The significance at the 0.05 level in both

Table 7. Analysis of variance for the systolic blood pressure measures

Source	SS	df	MS	F	p
T	37.813	2	18.907	0.006	
Ss (T)	38180.840	12	3181.737		
D	269.113	5	53.823	2.095	
T by D	244.373	10	24.437	0.951	
$(A_1 + A_2$ vs $A_3)$ by Linear D	146.438	1	146.438	5.700	<0.05
D by Ss (T)	1541.480	60	25.691		
P	1007.276	4	251.819	29.317	<0.000001
T by P	832.231	8	104.029	12.111	<0.000001
$(A_1 + A_2$ vs $A_3)$ by Linear P	680.805	1	680.805	79.260	<0.0001
P by Ss (T)	412.293	48	8.589		
D by P	108.831	20	5.441	1.474	
T by D by P	121.682	40	3.040	0.824	
D by P by Ss (T)	885.787	240	3.691		

Table 8. Analysis of variance for the diastolic blood pressure measures

Source	SS	df	MS	F	p
T	2223.373	2	1111.687	3.524	
SS (T)	3785.340	12	315.437		
D	247.273	5	49.455	2.814	
T by D	196.813	10	19.681	1.120	
$(A_1 + A_2$ vs $A_3)$ by Linear D	130.149	1	130.149	7.407	<0.05
D by Ss (T)	1054.280	60	17.571		
P	682.013	4	170.503	49.956	<0.000001
T by P	379.027	8	47.378	13.881	<0.000001
$(A_1 + A_2$ vs $A_3)$ by Linear P	288.000	1	288.000	84.382	<0.0001
P by Ss (T)	163.827	48	3.413		
D by P	35.827	20	1.791	1.106	
T by D by P	82.653	40	2.066	1.276	
D by P by SS (T)	388.653	240	1.619		

cases means that the slope of the relaxation treatment's linear function is significantly different than the combined linear function of the control and biofeedback treatment groups.

Again, it must be observed that the treatment by session interaction was not insignificant. However, the absence of matching of these particular variables, the downward trend of the relaxation treatment across sessions as contrasted to control and biofeedback groups (these trends represented in Figs. 1 and 2) and finally the statistical test of significant differences among trend components, all contribute to the conclusion that the relaxation treatment group is effecting the lowering of blood pressure of subjects as they progress through sessions.

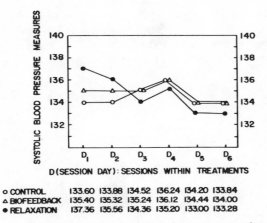

	D₁	D₂	D₃	D₄	D₅	D₆
o CONTROL	133.60	133.88	134.52	136.24	134.20	133.84
△ BIOFEEDBACK	135.40	135.32	135.24	136.12	134.44	134.00
● RELAXATION	137.36	135.56	134.36	135.20	133.00	133.28

Fig. 1. Mean systolic blood pressure measures for each treatment group in each session.

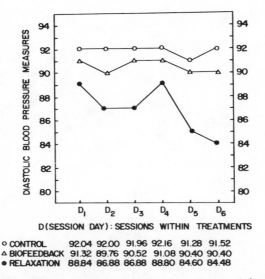

	D₁	D₂	D₃	D₄	D₅	D₆
o CONTROL	92.04	92.00	91.96	92.16	91.28	91.52
△ BIOFEEDBACK	91.32	89.76	90.52	91.08	90.40	90.40
● RELAXATION	88.84	86.88	86.88	88.80	84.60	84.48

Fig. 2. Mean diastolic blood pressure measures for each treatment group in each session.

Another analysis of variance which was part of the $3 \times 6 \times 5$ experimental design, tested whether or not deep muscle relaxation or biofeedback lowered blood pressure significantly across successive periods within treatment sessions. Table 7 summarizes the significant Period effect ($F = 29.317$, $df = 4/48$, $p < 0.000001$) and significant Treatment by Period effect ($F = 12.111$, $df = 8/48$, $p < 0.000001$) of the systolic measures. As in the systolic analysis, the diastolic periods effect and periods by treatment interaction effect were significant (Period: $F = 49.956$, $df = 4/48$, $p < 0.01$; Period by Treatment: $F = 13.881$, $df = 8/48$, $p < 0.000001$). Interpretations of these results are facilitated by Figs. 3 and 4 which include systolic and diastolic measures at each period within sessions.

Of the systolic measures, since both Period and Period by Treatment interaction are significant, it is necessary to determine whether the interaction is due to differences in the linear trend of several of the trends. The interaction of Periods with type of Treatment is illustrated in Fig. 3. It can be seen that the muscle relaxation group, though it was not

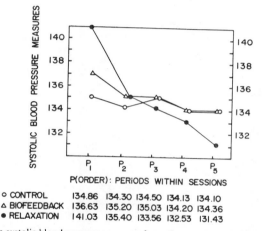

	P_1	P_2	P_3	P_4	P_5
○ CONTROL	134.86	134.30	134.50	134.13	134.10
△ BIOFEEDBACK	136.63	135.20	135.03	134.20	134.36
● RELAXATION	141.03	135.40	133.56	132.53	131.43

Fig. 3. Mean systolic blood pressure measures for each treatment group in each period.

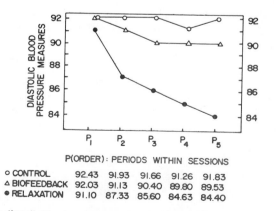

	P_1	P_2	P_3	P_4	P_5
○ CONTROL	92.43	91.93	91.66	91.26	91.83
△ BIOFEEDBACK	92.03	91.13	90.40	89.80	89.53
● RELAXATION	91.10	87.33	85.60	84.63	84.40

Fig. 4. Mean diastolic blood pressure measures for each treatment group in each period.

matched with the other treatment groups, manifests a marked decrease in blood pressures as subjects progress through periods. Systolic blood pressure, as a function of muscle relaxation treatment, decreased an average of 9.6 mm Hg as subjects progressed from period 1 to period 5. Both control and biofeedback groups, however, remain relatively constant throughout periods.

The interaction of Period and Treatment is significant. The question can therefore be asked, 'Is there a difference in the Period linear trend for the three Treatments?' The result from testing the significance of differences in the Period linear trend for control, biofeedback and relaxation groups is shown in Table 7.

Comparing linear trends of the relaxation group and the combined control and biofeedback groups reveals a significant difference ($F = 79.260$, $df = 1/48$, $p < 0.0001$). It is obvious that part of the Period by Treatment interaction is due to differences in the Period linear trend. The sum of squares for the interaction is equal to 832.231; thus the sum of squares due to difference in linear trends, 680.805 accounts for 82 per cent of the period by treatment interaction. This means that 18 per cent of the period by treatment interaction is not accounted for by the linear function.

The 680 sum of squares is the sum of squares accounted for by differences in the relaxation treatment linear trend and the combined linear trend of control and biofeedback treatments. The significance of this difference indicates that the interaction effect may be accounted for by the marked decrease in blood pressure due to relaxation treatment as contrasted to the relatively unchanging blood pressure measures associated with control and biofeedback groups.

Figure 4 depicts the results. The three treatment groups were initially matched as closely as possible. As subjects progressed through periods, the biofeedback and control groups remained relatively undisturbed. The relaxation group, on the other hand, exhibits a lowering of blood pressure as a function of progression through periods. Diastolic blood pressure, as a function of muscle relaxation treatment, decreased an average of 6.7 mm Hg as subjects progressed from period 1 to period 5.

Because the Period and treatment interaction is significant, a test is performed to ascertain whether or not there is a difference in the period linear trend for the three treatments. The result of this test of the significance of differences in the period linear trend for control, biofeedback, and relaxation groups is presented in Table 8.

In contrast the relaxation group linear trend and the combined control and biofeedback linear trend reveals a significant difference ($F = 84.382$, $df = 1/48$, $p < 0.0001$). It is apparent that part of the period by treatment interaction is due to differences in the period linear trend. The sum of squares due to difference in linear trends, 288.000, accounts for 77 per cent of the period by treatment interaction, 379.027 sum of squares. This means that 23 per cent of the period by treatment interaction is not accounted for by the linear function.

The 288 sum of squares is the sum of squares accounted for by differences in the relaxation treatment linear trend and the combined linear trend of control and biofeedback treatments. The significance of this difference indicates that the interaction effect may be accounted for by the drastically decreasing blood pressures brought about by the relaxation treatment as contrasted to the relatively static blood pressure measures associated with control and biofeedback groups.

DISCUSSION

Analyses of the data supported the contention that muscle relaxation training brings about the lowering of systolic and diastolic blood pressure as subjects progress from pretreatment measures to posttreatment measures. Results also support the notion that subjects utilizing biofeedback show, to a lesser degree, a significant reduction in diastolic blood pressure. These biofeedback subjects, however, did not lower systolic blood pressure a significant amount.

One possible explanation for this latter finding is that the biofeedback subjects may have been centering their concentration on the diastolic base. The diastolic line is the final point in each cycle, and subjects seemed to anticipate this final point to the extent of avoiding their full concentration on the systolic line. A subject may be preparing a concentrated effort to lower blood pressure below the diastolic marker; this concentrated effort may be operating to the detriment of the subject's concentrating on the systolic marker.

Another contributing factor which enters into this problem of concentration on more than one measure, is the time element between the diastolic feedback points and the systolic feedback points. The biofeedback sequence exactly duplicated the blood pressure cycle of the subject. The short separation of systolic measures may not allow the subject sufficient time to incorporate his individual lowering technique whereas the greater temporal separation of diastolic measures may allow enough time to prepare a concentrated effort to lower the diastolic blood pressure.

Though two subjects in the biofeedback group lowered their blood pressures at least 6 mm Hg during a treatment session, the remainder of the subjects did not as profitably use the biofeedback. It appears that the continuous feedback used by Schwartz as well as Shapiro and associates offers a viable initial step to self controlled blood pressure reduction. The noncontinuous biofeedback, on the other hand, does not guarantee immediate control over one's blood pressure. Perhaps a successful biofeedback treatment program would incorporate the initial continuous biofeedback followed by noncontinuous biofeedback. By incorporating the initial phase of continuous feedback, the treatment program would insure each subject's mastering the usage of biofeedback. After this mastery stage, independence from the biofeedback could be facilitated by the usage of noncontinuous biofeedback. After mastering discrimination of high and low states of blood pressure, it is hoped that the patient could implement his individualistic method of reducing the high levels of blood pressure.

As the results of the first analysis show, muscle relaxation training significantly reduces diastolic and systolic blood pressure measures. An implication of this result is that patients may be taught muscle relaxation concomitant with biofeedback training resulting in the patient utilizing both in his individualistic method of reducing blood pressure. One subject in the biofeedback group reported that she envisioned serene scenes as she was successfully lowering her blood pressure. The other biofeedback subject who successfully lowered his blood pressure reported his concentrating on relaxing his 'inner organs.' Both idiosyncratic methods worked and there is a common denominator of relaxation in the successful attempts. In addition to teaching muscle relaxation, perhaps a viable treatment program ought to directly encourage mental relaxation.

Another implication was drawn from the analyses. Results obtained from the randomized blocks design were significant in the first analysis. There was a significant difference between premeasurements and postmeasurements. When these same data were viewed from the split-plot factorial perspective, however, the analysis revealed no significant difference between premeasurements and postmeasurements. Utilizing the split-plot factorial essentially meant that the error term, Treatment by Blocks, was replaced by the Treatment by Subjects error term. This latter analysis was not significant which meant that the reduction of blood pressure which was happening in particular blocks was not affecting the subjects generally. Such a result may be explained by the fact that the essential hypertensive subjects can lower their blood pressures to a certain level and not below that level. The subjects who started at highest levels of blood pressure, and were therefore in the highest blood pressure blocks, lowered their blood pressure to the same level as subjects who started at the lower blood pressure blocks.

From observation of the raw data of subjects, this is indeed what is happening. The relaxation subjects all reduced their blood pressures to an acceptable level. The subjects who had begun the experiment in blocks which had lower blood pressure reduced their blood pressures no further than the higher blood pressure blocks. Hence, the greater blood pressure reductions within certain blocks would overshadow the null effects of biofeedback and control. In effect, a significant change among treatment groups could be observed. Statistically, the randomized block design was more efficient because the variation between experimental units within blocks was reduced relative to the variations between blocks. The effort to form homogeneous blocks was well rewarded by the smaller error term and the greater power.

The biofeedback and control group effected little change in blood pressure whereas relaxation brought about clinically significant changes in blood pressure as subjects progressed from session to session. The linear trend comparisons support the contention that the relaxation treatment facilitates lowering of blood pressure as subjects progress from session to session. The analysis of variance on this data, however, does not reveal a significant reduction. This surprising nonsignificance may be accounted for by the lack of matched subjects on the first session mean blood pressures. As can be seen in Figs. 1 and 2, there is a 4 mm spread in the premeasurement matching. Though the linear trend of relaxation is significantly different from the linear trend of biofeedback and control, the premeasurements are so dispersed at the onset of the experiment that the reduction of blood pressure from session to session which is affected by relaxation is not shown as statistically significant.

It is reasonable to speculate that a precise matching on the premeasure session would yield a statistically significant difference among treatment groups. However, to accomplish precise matching on the first session measures would not necessarily mean precise matching is accomplished on initial period matching or even on premeasures for the treatments. In this particular experiment, subjects had been precisely matched on diastolic premeasures taken prior to the experiment although such matching on premeasures did not guarantee precise matching on systolic premeasures, on first session systolic or diastolic measures, or on first period systolic and diastolic measures.

The problem of analysis which has been elucidated in this discussion thus far exists somewhat in the analysis of the final question of this experiment. There was such an overwhelming reduction of blood pressure as subjects progressed from period to period within sessions, however, that the non-matched measurements of the first period did not detract significantly from the overall reductions in blood pressure.

The biofeedback and control groups did not lower blood pressure as subjects progressed from period to period. However, in the relaxation treatment group the systolic mean difference from period 1 to period 5 was 9.6 mm Hg, and the diastolic mean difference was 6.7 mm Hg. These differences are particularly interesting as they show that the unacceptably high blood pressure levels are brought to acceptable blood pressure levels over the course of the relaxation treatment session. These results support the assertion that a subject can reduce his blood pressure in the laboratory setting if the subject utilizes muscle relaxation.

An integration of the test results and the interpretations of the results center upon the effect of relaxation. Relaxation's effect may be explained in part by electromyogram activity which is associated with progressive relaxation. Jacobson (1939) reported a general relationship between decreases in blood pressure and decreases in muscle activity as shown by the electromyogram. One explanation of the decrease in blood pressure is that the muscular relaxation may be changing the equilibrium of the vasodilation and vasoconstriction in the circulatory system so that the imbalance favors vasodilation. The vasodilation, in turn, decreases peripheral resistance, and the decrease in peripheral resistance effects the lowering of blood pressure.

The major implication of this study is that a successful treatment program ought to include training in muscle relaxation. Such training may be bolstered by mastery of biofeedback. It seems that an initial treatment phase would have as its purpose the patient's mastering discrimination of high and low states of blood pressure. The implication here is for further research to investigate combinations of continuous and noncontinuous biofeedback in order to arrive at optimal treatment which would afford discrimination of blood pressure states but independence from biofeedback machinery. Upon mastering independent discrimination of blood pressure state, the patient could utilize the muscle relaxation to lower the high states of blood pressure. Another implication for research emerges as this experiment has shown that subjects can reduce their blood pressure in the laboratory but this experiment has not shown that implementation of the relaxation process in the patient's real environment will effectively lower his blood pressure. In addition, research must be designed to determine whether or not discrimination of blood pressure states is possible in the patient's real environment.

To test treatment efficacy, not only must blood pressure be measured in the subject's real environment, but also follow-up data ought to be acquired over a prolonged period of time in order to test the lasting effect of treatment. To insure that subjects master and retain the muscle relaxation technique, a longer period of treatment may be necessary for certain patients. At the termination of six sessions of treatment, an evaluation of the patient's mastery of muscle relaxation could be made. At this point it would be decided whether or not the patient would be prescribed further sessions of treatment. So too, should follow-up measures indicate that the patient's muscle relaxation technique is ineffective in the patient's real environment, critical examination of the patient technique as well as the environment ought to be undertaken.

Especially relevant to this potential plight is the issue of whether or not external feedback is necessary for the subject's awareness of high blood pressure. If the subject is unaware of high blood pressure when he is in his real environment, it would be imperative to begin investigating the lasting effect of the patient's technique in order to determine a regular schedule for implementing the technique. Perhaps it would be possible for the patient to incorporate the relaxation technique at fixed intervals during the day. The intervals would be determined by empirically finding the length of time which the patient's technique effectively reduces blood pressure.

Another area of investigation which is pertinent to environmental factors involves testing the extent to which the subject can control his environment in order to lower his blood pressure. The patient may gain increasing control over environmental factors which precipitate his high blood pressure, or the patient may in some way adjust to the environmental factors. Muscle relaxation buttresses both these processes, and it would be beneficial to partial out the individual effects of the patient's control and the muscle relaxation process.

With attention being focused upon the pressures impinging upon the patient in his real environment, it will be necessary to acquire follow-up data from the patient's real environment in order to determine whether he can discriminate between high and low states of blood pressure outside of the laboratory and whether he can incorporate a successful technique (e.g., relaxation) for lowering blood pressure in his real environment. The crucial clinical issue is whether or not the patient can take his idiosyncratic means of lowering blood pressure out of the laboratory to his daily living activity. As this issue is addressed, the significance of this thesis is manifest. Relaxation has been shown to be effective as a treatment for lowering the essential hypertensive's high blood pressure. If the relaxation method or a modification of the method can be incorporated into the daily living activity of the essential hypertensive so as to successfully maintain an acceptable level of blood pressure, then this treatment may be used in conjunction with optimal pharmaceutical therapy or, should research indicate the external validity of this laboratory based experiment, as a treatment independent from pharmaceutical therapy.

REFERENCES

BENSON H., SHAPIRO D., TURSKY B. and SCHWARTZ G. E. (1971) Decreased systolic blood pressure through operant conditioning techniques in patients with essential hypertension. *Science* **173**, 740-742.

BOYD W. (1962) *An Introduction to the Study of Disease*. Lea & Febiger, Philadelphia.

BRENER J. and KLEINMAN R. A. (1970) Learned control of decreases in systolic blood pressure. *Nature, Lond.* **226**, 1063–1064.

GANTT C. L. (1972) Drug therapy of essential hypertension. In *Review of Modern Medicine: Hypertension and the Cardiovascular System*. pp. 55–60. Modern Medicine Pubns. Minneapolis.

GUYTON A. C. (1971) *Textbook of Medical Physiology*. Saunders. Philadelphia.

HNATIOW M. (1971) Learned control of heart rate and blood pressure. *Percept. Mot. Skills* **33**, 219–226.

JACOBSON E. (1939) Variation of blood pressure with skeletal muscle tension and relaxation. *Ann. intern. Med.* **12**, 1194–1212.

MERRILL J. P. (1966) Hypertensive vascular disease. In *Principles of Internal Medicine* (Eds. J. V. HARRISON, R. D. ADAMS, I. L. BENNET, W. H. RESNIK, G. W. THORN and M. M. WINTROBE). pp. 702–712. McGraw-Hill. New York.

SCHWARTZ G. E. (1972) Voluntary control of human cardiovascular integration and differentiation through feedback and reward. *Science* **175**, 90–93.

SCHWARTZ G. E., SHAPIRO D. and TURSKY B. (1971) Learned control of cardiovascular integration in man through operant conditioning. *Psychosom. Med.* **33**, 57–62.

SHAPIRO D., SCHWARTZ G. E. and TURSKY B. (1972) Control of diastolic blood pressure in man by feedback and reinforcement. *Psychophysiology* **9**, 296–304.

SHAPIRO D., TURSKY B., GERSHON E. and STERN M. (1969) Effects of feedback and reinforcement on the control of human systolic blood pressure. *Science* **163**, 588–590.

SHAPIRO D., TURSKY B. and SCHWARTZ G. E. (1970) Control of blood pressure in man by operant conditioning. *Circulation Res.* **26**, (Supp. 1: 27–32).

Learned Control of Blood Pressure in Patients with High Blood Pressure

43

Donald A. Kristt and Bernard T. Engel

SUMMARY

Five patients with documented histories of essential hypertension of at least ten years' duration participated in a triphasic study of training to control systolic blood pressure (SBP). Phase 1 was a seven week period during which patients took their BP (systolic and diastolic) at home and mailed these data to us daily. Phase 2 was a three week period during which patients were taught to control SBP using a noninvasive technique: patients were trained to raise, to lower and to alternately lower and raise SBP. Phase 3 was a three month period during which patients again took their BP at home and mailed these data to us daily. Results: (1) all patients learned SBP control: average increase — 15%; average decrease — 11%; (2) during SBP control heart rates, breathing rates, triceps brachii muscle tension and EEG activity did not change; (3) follow-up tests at one and three months showed evidence of retained SBP control; (4) baseline SBP fell from 153 mm Hg during laboratory training to 135 mm Hg at the three month follow-up; (5) phase 3 home BPs fell 18/8 mm Hg from phase 1 levels; (6) at home patients also were able to reduce SBP from 141 mm Hg (average) to 125 mm Hg (average) by means of the lowering technique learned in the laboratory.

Additional Indexing Words:

Biofeedback   Operant conditioning   Essential hypertension

SEVERAL LINES OF EVIDENCE suggest that the central nervous system plays an important role in either the genesis or the maintenance of high blood pressure. Exploration of the human brain has identified numerous areas that mediate blood pressure (BP) changes when electrically stimulated, suggesting that there is an anatomic basis for such a role.[1] Psychological factors also may be reflected in changes in BP[2-5] which some believe to be pathogenetically significant.[5-7] In addition, the current therapeutic ap-

proach to hypertension emphasizes the use of pharmacologic agents that interfere with autonomic control of the cardiovascular system implying some role for the nervous system in maintaining abnormally elevated BP.

Recent investigations also have shown that BP can be brought under voluntary control in the laboratory using operant conditioning techniques.[8-11] This means that a human subject can be taught both to raise and to lower BP to achieve an appropriate level of BP. With regard to individuals with high blood pressure some degree of success has been reported in conditioning lowering of BP.[12-14] Relaxation and meditation techniques also have been applied and show promise for BP lowering.[15-19] Over-all BP control — i.e., lowering and raising — by hypertensive patients has not been explored. The purpose of this report is to show that hypertensive patients can learn to modify their BP using operant conditioning techniques in the

From the Gerontology Research Center (Baltimore), National Institute of Child Health and Human Development, National Institutes of Health and the Baltimore City Hospitals, Baltimore, Maryland.

Dr. Kristt's present address is Johns Hopkins University School of Medicine, 725 N. Wolfe Street, Baltimore, Maryland 21205.

Address for reprints; Bernard T. Engel, Ph.D., Gerontology Research Center, Baltimore City Hospitals, Baltimore, Maryland 21224.

Reprinted by permission of the American Heart Association, Inc. from *Circulation*, 1975, Vol. 51, 370-378.

Table 1

Summary of Medical History

Pt.	Age	Sex	Race	Duration HBP (yrs)	Mean clinic BP (mm Hg)	Pretraining medication (mg)	Cardiac DX	CXR	Other
1	68	M	B	>20	158 / 82	H 25 q.i.d. HY 50 q.d. G 25 t.i.d.	None	Left ventricular prominence; aortic atherosclerosis	Diabetes mellitus
2	46	F	W	>10	166 / 99	HY 50 b.i.d. G 37.5 q.d.	Sinus bradycardia	LV prominence	Malignant hypertension
3	70	F	B	>10	151 / 84	HY 25 q.d. DIG 0.1 q.d.	1° AVB; LVH; CHF	WNL	R CVA-1968; diabetes mellitus
4	49	F	B	>10	146 / 94	HY 50 b.i.d. A 500 t.i.d.	Angina pectoris; CHF	Cardiomegaly	Obesity; intermittent claudication
5	61	F	W	>20	148 / 82	HY 50 b.i.d.	1° AVB; sinus bradycardia	Aortic atherosclerosis; cardiomegaly	Obesity

Abbreviations: HBP = high blood pressure; DX = diagnosis; CXR = chest X-ray; AVB = atrioventricular block; LVH = left ventricular hypertrophy; CHF = congestive heart failure; WNL = normal; CVA = cerebrovascular accident; H = Hydralazine; HY = hydrochlorthiazide; G = guanethadine; A = alpha-methyldopa; DIG = digitoxin.

laboratory, and that such learning will persist throughout a three month follow-up period in the laboratory and in a non-laboratory setting, i.e., the home.

Materials and Methods

Patients

Five volunteer patients were recruited from the Hypertension Clinic of the Baltimore City Hospitals. All five patients had been seen in the clinic for at least ten years prior to study, during which time the diagnosis of high blood pressure of unknown origin was confirmed repeatedly. The principal selection criteria were: 1) willingness to adhere to the experimental protocol; and 2) willingness to consent to hospitalization for the three week training period. The five subjects reported here comprise the total study group for this project. Informed consent was obtained from

each patient. All patients were seen by one investigator (D.K.) in the clinic for at least 6 months prior to referral to the project. The purpose of this delay was to enable the patient to become familiar with his physician so that the novelty of this aspect of the experiment could be minimized. Biographical and pertinent medical information is summarized in table 1.

Experimental Design

This study was arranged in three phases (fig. 1A): Phase 1 was a pretraining assessment period, phase 2 was the laboratory training period, and phase 3 was a posttraining assessment period. Phases 1 and 3 included self-determination of BP by the patients.

Pretraining

At least five weeks prior to hospitalization, patients were taught to record their own BP at home. This they did four

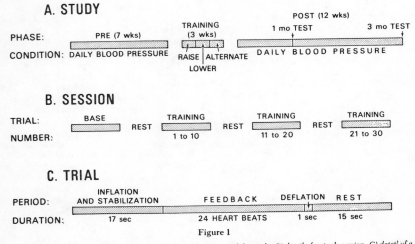

Figure 1

Schematic diagram of experimental design: A) over-all structure of the study; B) detail of a single session; C) detail of a single trial.

times each day until admission. Furthermore, these home BPs were mailed to us daily by the patient. This procedure enabled us to monitor the faithfulness of the patient's adherence to our instructions, and the daily mailing reduced the likelihood that the patient would record spurious values based on data from previous days. Following this pretraining period patients were admitted to the Gerontology Research Center research ward of the Baltimore City Hospitals for 3 weeks. During hospitalization patients were maintained on reduced dosages of their BP drugs to compensate for the improved care and reduced activity during hospitalization.

Laboratory Training

The technique we used to monitor systolic blood pressure (SBP) is a noninvasive procedure first described by Tursky et al.[20] In this method a standard BP cuff is placed around the upper arm and inflated to a fixed pressure where it is maintained for about 30 sec. A microphone is placed over the brachial artery at the distal edge of the cuff and Korotkoff's sounds (KS) are detected. The cuff pressure equals average SBP when 50% of the heart beats are accompanied by KS. When 25% to 75% of the heart beats are accompanied by KS, cuff pressure is within ± 2 mm Hg of average SBP. We used this technique for two purposes: first, to measure SBP as described above; and second, to train patients to control SBP on a beat-to-beat basis as described below.

In the laboratory the patient was recumbent in a hospital bed located in a soundproof room. The experimenter and his equipment were located in an adjacent room. A pair of electrodes were placed on the patient's chest to detect the ECG. A small crystal microphone was placed over the brachial pulse in the antecubital fossa. A standard BP cuff was applied over the microphone. A KS was detected if it occurred between 250 and 500 msec following an R wave of the ECG.

In front of the patient was a vertical array of red, yellow and green cue lights. Illumination of the red light signaled the patient to lower his SBP. The green light indicated SBP raising was expected. The yellow light remained on as long as the patient continued to perform correctly, which meant producing KS during a raising attempt or decreasing KS — i.e., inhibiting their production — during BP lowering. The yellow light, which provided beat-by-beat feedback to the patient of his ability to modify his SBP, served as a reinforcer since keeping it lit was evidence to the patient that he was successfully controlling his SBP. Another source of reinforcement and feedback was a digital meter adjacent to the light panel which gave the patient a cumulative numerical score of his performance; each successful response advanced the meter by two points.

The first week of training was used to teach the patients to raise SBP. During the second week patients were trained to lower SBP. In the third week patients were trained to lower and to raise SBP alternately within a single session. Thus, during this alternating condition, the patients were demonstrating their abilities to control their SBP. There were approximately 14 sessions per week. Patients always were aware of the contingencies which controlled the reinforcement light. They were instructed to modify their BP in accordance with the prevalent experimental conditions. They were never told how to raise or to lower SBP. They were told only that other experiments had shown that it was possible to do so, and that subjects did best when they evolved their own techniques. The subject knew that he could gauge his success on a given trial by noting his cumulative numerical score on the panel meter. In addition, at the end of each session the subject was shown his data and he was told how well or how poorly he had done.

A usual training session (fig. 1B) consisted of a series of pretraining baseline trials and 3 blocks of ten training trials each. A two minute rest period occurred between trial blocks. Training would not begin until the pretraining

baseline SBP was stable — i.e., did not vary more than 2 mm Hg from trial to trial for five consecutive trials. The visual feedback was available only during training trials.

A trial (fig. 1C) consisted of a 17 sec cuff inflation period, a 24 heart beat recording period in which panel lights and the digital meter were functional, and a rapid deflation followed by 15 sec of rest in which cue lights were off. During the rest period the numerical score indicated by the digital meter for that trial remained illuminated. It would reset at the beginning of the next trial. The number of successes per trial and the duration of each trial (i.e., the time for 24 R-R intervals) were recorded by means of digital printout recorders for subsequent analyses.

During each session of each condition (raise, lower, alternate) the criterion was made progressively more difficult depending upon the subject's performance on the preceding trial. For example, if the subject successfully raised his BP on a given trial, the cuff pressure was increased by 2–4 mm Hg on the next trial. If the patient failed to produce between 25% and 75% KS on this trial, the criterion was either not changed or returned to the previous level.

Posttraining

While still in the hospital the patients were taught to use a BP cuff to perform a BP lowering maneuver. The technique required them to make the KS (heard at SBP) disappear while cuff pressure was maintained at the level of SBP. They then determined the new (lower) SBP by slowly releasing the cuff until KS again appeared. Following discharge the patients practiced this technique from 4–30 times each day and made daily records of their performance. In addition, they recorded daily diastolic (DBP) and SBP as they did prior to training for the duration of the three month follow-up period. They returned to the laboratory for a single session test of their ability to alternately raise and lower SBP at the end of the first and third months of follow-up.

Response Measures

During the laboratory phase of the study, in addition to BP and heart rate, we also recorded several other responses. Breathing rate was recorded during two of the alternate sessions. Respiratory excursions were detected by a strain gauge mounted on a belt placed around the chest. Electroencephalograms (EEG) from bilateral occipital placements were recorded during one alternate session; electromyograms (EMG) over the triceps brachii were recorded during one alternate session. The sessions during which breathing rate, EEG and EMG were measured came late in training so that the patient could be expected to evince reliable control of SBP.

Statistical Analyses

Laboratory Training

Statistical analyses were limited to the last four sessions of each training condition since we were interested in stable behavior. There were five baseline trials and 30 training trials during each of these sessions. The baseline value for SBP was that value of SBP which was stable (± 2 mm Hg) over five consecutive trials. Baseline heart rate (HR) was the average for these five trials. Paired consecutive scores during each training session were averaged. Thus, the reduced data sets comprised a matrix of 60 scores (4 sessions × 15 paired consecutive trial scores/session), and a vector of four baseline values for each subject and for each experimental condition. Two measures of performance were derived. First, because the criteria were made progressively more difficult throughout each session, we expected a monotonic change in SBP across the session. To test the significance of this effect we tested the statistical significance of the linear component of trend. This component is arithmetically identical to the regression coefficient. However, since there is no need to make an assumption of linearity (as one would if he

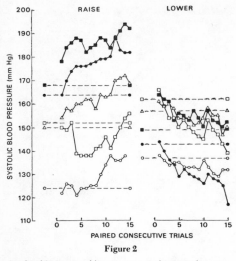

Figure 2

Results of SBP raise and lower training. Each point is the average response during the last four training sessions for that patient. Baseline levels are shown for each patient as a dashed line. Patient 1: ■———■; patient 2: □———□; patient 3: △———△; patient 4: ●———●; patient 5: ○———○.

were fitting a straight line to a set of data), we did not do so. The second measure of performance we used was a count of the number of trials in which the subject's SBP (or HR) exceeded his baseline SBP (or HR) in the appropriate direction. The probability of obtaining a particular frequency was then tested by using a one-tailed (SBP) or two-tailed (HR) test based on the binomial distribution.

Pre and Posttraining

Pre and posttraining BP values were compared within each subject by means of the *t*-test. During the posttraining period the patient not only monitored his BP but also tried to lower it as described previously. Analysis of these data was performed by computing an average difference score for each day, and then performing a *t*-test on the scores.

Results

Laboratory Training

Blood Pressure

All subjects were trained to raise SBP during the first week in the laboratory, and they were trained to lower SBP during the second week. Figure 2 shows the average SBPs produced by the subjects during the last four training sessions of each of these weeks. Table 2 reports the statistical analyses of the lowering and raising data. Trend tests showed that SBP increased across trials reliably for all patients except patient 2. In this patient there was a pattern of substantial fall in SBP (average = 13 mm Hg) early in the session followed by a gradual trial-by-trial raising of SBP (fig. 2). This patient, who had a history of malignant hypertension, noted at one point that "maybe in the back of my mind I really don't want to raise my pressure." During lowering training patient 1 showed a pattern of substantial elevation of SBP early in the session followed by a gradual and significant trial-by-trial lowering of SBP. All other patients modified their SBPs across trials significantly and in the appropriate directions. With the exception of patient 1, analyses of the changes of SBP from baseline showed that those effects paralleled the trend findings (table 2). Thus it may be concluded that all patients showed evidence of being able to lower SBP and four of the five patients were consistently able to raise SBP after these two weeks of training.

During the final week the ability of the patients to control SBP was tested in a series of sessions in which they were required to lower, raise and then lower SBP again. These sessions also consisted of 30 feedback trials, ten in each condition. Figure 3 presents the data for the group. The trend analyses (table 3) showed that: 1) SBP decreased reliably across trials for all patients during the first lowering period; 2) SBP increased reliably across trials for all patients during the raising period; and 3) SBP decreased reliably across trials in three patients during the final lowering period. Ability to alter SBP relative to baseline SBP was variable although all patients were able to modify SBP in one direction at least. Thus, the data from the last week of training indicate that all patients were able to control SBP, some more effectively than others.

Heart Rate, Breathing Rate, EMG and EEG

During each trial we obtained a measure of HR as well as SBP. Despite the changes in SBP which the subjects produced, heart rate did not change systematically with SBP as measured by the coefficient

Table 2

Individual Responses during Training to Raise and to Lower Systolic Blood Pressure

	Raise				Lower			
	Baseline SBP (mm Hg)		Coefficient of linear trend (mm Hg/paired trial)	Percent responses above baseline	Baseline SBP (mm Hg)		Coefficient of linear trend (mm Hg/paired trial)	Percent responses below baseline
Patient	Average	Range			Average	Range		
1	168	154–182	0.6*	100*	149	142–162	−0.9*	27
2	152	142–171	0.4	22	162	150–172	−1.2*	90*
3	150	144–155	0.9*	92*	157	155–162	−0.6*	67*
4	164	149–175	1.1*	92*	143	137–159	−1.2*	92*
5	124	109–134	1.3*	65*	137	124–148	−0.5*	67*
Mean	151.6		0.86	74.2	149.6		−.88	68.6

*P < .01.

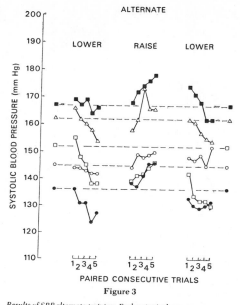

ALTERNATE

LOWER RAISE LOWER

PAIRED CONSECUTIVE TRIALS

Figure 3

Results of SBP alternate training. Each point is the average response during the last four training sessions for that patient. Baseline levels are shown for each patient as a dashed line. See figure 2 for patient identification.

were attending to the cues. Electromyograms of the triceps brachii failed to show observable differences between SBP lowering or raising.

Follow-up

Laboratory

Patients returned to the laboratory after one month and after three months of training. They were tested in a single alternating session on each occasion. Figures 4 and 5 present the SBP data during these sessions in which the patients alternately lowered and raised SBP. Extensive statistical analyses of these data are not warranted since there are too few observations. However, visual inspection of the data suggests the following conclusions. 1) The ability of the patients to control SBP is maintained throughout the observation period. 2) With the exception of patient 3, baseline BP falls from the alternate sessions during the last week of training to the 3 month follow-up sessions. Even in patient 3 baseline SBP during the third month follow-up is slightly less than it was during the laboratory training period. These falls in baseline SBP range from 3 to 18% with an average of 11%. 3) Heart rate (which is not presented in a figure) is similar to that during alternate training. There is little change from baseline and there is no trend across trials as appears in SBP. Thus, these data suggest strongly that the patients were able to retain their abilities to control SBP after one month and after two month intervals during which no formal training procedures occurred.

Home Blood Pressures

Figure 6 and table 6 compare home BP records before and after training for patients 1 to 4. SBP decreased significantly in all four patients. Diastolic pressures also decreased significantly in two of these patients. In patient 5 pretraining home BP determinations are not available. However, her home BP records during the follow-up period showed a decrease in SBP of 14 mm Hg from the first to the last week and a decrease in DBP of 8 mm Hg in the same period.

In addition to merely recording blood pressures at home, the patients also practiced controlling their SBP 4 to 30 times each day during the follow-up

of linear trend (table 4). The only consistent effect seen in the HR data occurred during the raising trials of the first week when HR usually was above baseline.

Table 5 summarizes the data for single sessions of alternate raising and lowering of SBP in which occipital EEG (percent alpha-wave activity per trial) and breathing rate also were recorded in patients 1, 2, 3, 4. There were no noteworthy differences in breathing rate or in the extent of alpha-wave activity between the lowering and raising trials. There was a decline in average alpha activity from baseline to training, however, which suggests that the patients were attending to the feedback light. The absence of sleep spindles further supports the inference that patients

Table 3

Individual Responses during Training to Alternate Systolic Blood Pressure

Patient	Baseline SBP (mm Hg) Average	Range	Lower Coefficient of linear trend (mm Hg/paired trial)	Percent responses below baseline	Raise Coefficient of linear trend (mm Hg/paired trial)	Percent responses above baseline	Lower Coefficient of linear trend (mm Hg/paired trial)	Percent responses below baseline
1	165	146–190	−2.2*	40	2.6*	80*	−2.7*	45
2	151	144–168	−3.9*	80*	1.9**	5	−2.7*	100*
3	162	140–178	−2.8*	55	2.2*	40	−2.2*	70**
4	135	130–149	−2.2*	90*	2.2**	70**	−0.4	95*
5	142	136–164	−0.8*	65**	1.0**	65**	0.8	20
Mean	151.0		−2.38	66.0	1.98	52.0	−1.44	66.0

*P < .01.
**P < .05.

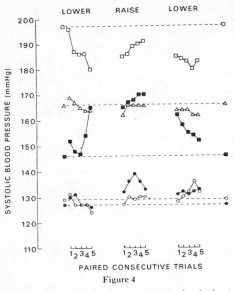

Figure 4

SBP results at one-month follow-up session. Baseline levels are shown as a dashed line. See figure 2 for patient identification.

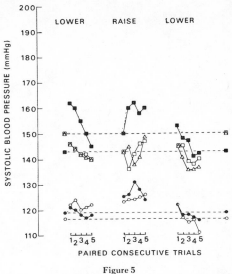

Figure 5

SBP results at three-month follow-up session. Baseline levels are shown as a dashed line. See figure 2 for patient identification.

period. These results also were mailed to the laboratory daily. The mean lowering of SBP that each patient achieved is shown in table 7. The average amount of lowering for all patients was 16 mm Hg. In order to estimate the validity of the home SBP control finding, three of the patients (1, 2 and 3) were tested while in the clinic by a staff physician other than one of us. These results were: patient 1, −5 mm Hg; patient 2, −10 mm Hg; patient 3, −10 mm Hg.

Discussion

The results of this study confirm and substantially extend the findings of Benson et al.[12] that patients with high blood pressure can learn to lower their SBP while in the laboratory. We have shown that these patients not only can be taught to lower pressure but also can be taught to raise pressure and alternately to lower and to raise pressure. Furthermore, the results

Table 4

Individual Heart Rate Responses during Systolic Blood Pressure Training

			Raise				Lower	
	Baseline (beats/min)		Coefficient of linear trend (beats/min/ paired trial)	Percent responses above baseline	Baseline (beats/min)		Coefficient of linear trend (beats/min/ paired trial)	Percent responses below baseline
Patient	Average	Range			Average	Range		
1	57.2	55.5–58.3	−0.1**	83*	58.4	52.3–60.9	−01**	65**
2	50.0	48.5–51.6	−0.2**	73*	45.5	39.6–52.1	0.1	58
3	83.4	77.9–88.0	0.0	81*	81.6	75.8–84.7	0.1*	62
4	68.3	67.3–69.2	0.0	75*	72.7	70.0–76.9	−0.4*	60
5	56.2	47.0–63.0	−0.1	54	49.2	43.4–56.0	0.0	24*
Mean	63.0		−0.08	73.2	61.5		−0.06	53.8

B. Alternate			Lower		Raise		Lower	
	Baseline (beats/min)		Coefficient of linear trend (beats/min/ paired trial)	Percent responses below baseline	Coefficient of linear trend (beats/min/ paired trial)	Percent responses above baseline	Coefficient of linear trend (beats/min/ paired trial)	Percent responses below baseline
Patient	Average	Range						
1	59.9	56.2–63.2	−0.7**	45	0.1	95*	0.0	37
2	47.1	40.4–50.8	−0.2	70**	0.0	25	−0.2	95*
3	70.0	63.9–74.8	0.5**	21	0.4**	35	−0.3	45
4	63.6	60.4–67.7	−0.1	55	0.3	68**	−0.6	42
5	45.2	36.5–52.1	−0.1	50	0.2	55	0.8	25
Mean	57.2		−0.12	48.2	0.20	55.6	−0.06	48.8

*$P < .01$.
**$P < .05$.
(two tailed tests).

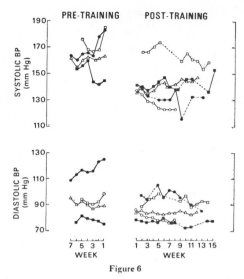

PRE-TRAINING POST-TRAINING

SYSTOLIC BP (mm Hg)

DIASTOLIC BP (mm Hg)

7 5 3 1   1 3 5 7 9 11 13 15
WEEK   WEEK

Figure 6

Home blood pressure records pre and posttraining. Pretraining measurements are not available for patient 5. Dashed lines mean there were no data for that period. See figure 2 for patient identification.

of this study show that the skills learned in the laboratory persist for at least three months.

Our findings also offer some suggestions about the mechanisms of learned SBP control. Heart rates did not undergo changes parallel to those of SBP in the laboratory initially or in either of the follow-up sessions. During training of BP lowering or raising, BP changed gradually and steadily in the 45 min training periods occasionally reaching levels of 40–50 mm Hg above or below baseline, still without alterations in HR.* Moreover, at home the decline in DBP paralleled that for SBP. These findings suggest that our patients may have been controlling SBP by regulating peripheral vascular resistance directly. We plan to try to identify these mechanisms in subsequent studies.

The laboratory findings that brain alpha-wave activity, breathing rate and triceps brachii muscle tension do not change during SBP control periods in

*For example, during the last raising session patient 3 had a maximum change of +53 mm Hg: Baseline SBP = 152, heart rate = 88 beats/min; in trial 4, SBP = 156, heart rate = 90; in trial 16, SBP = 160, heart rate = 90; in trial 24, SBP = 205, heart rate = 87. During the last lowering session patient 2 had a maximum change of −45 mm Hg: Baseline SBP = 161, heart rate = 40; in trial 4, SBP = 138, heart rate = 42; in trial 16, SBP = 127, heart rate = 41; in trial 30, SBP = 116, heart rate = 46.

Table 5

*Systolic Pressure, Heart Rate, Alpha-wave Activity and Breathing Rate during SBP Alternation Sessions**

Patient	Baseline SBP	HR	EEG	Breathing rate	Lower SBP trend	HR trend	EEG	Breathing rate	Raise SBP trend	HR trend	EEG	Breathing rate
1	155	60.0	38	12	−4.3	−0.1	43	11	3.6	0.2	28	12
2	151	64.5	51	12	−1.6	−0.3	27	13	1.7	1.4	40	11
3	145	44.6	48	10	−4.0	0.0	34	10	1.2	0.0	28	11
4	122	65.1	97	14	−0.8	−0.5	86	13	−0.2	−0.6	85	13
Mean	143.2	58.6	58.5	12.0	−2.68	−0.22	47.5	11.8	1.58	0.25	45.2	11.8

*These sessions comprised only one lower and one raise condition.

Abbreviations: SBP (mm Hg); SBP trend (mm Hg/paired consecutive trial); HR (beats/min); HR trend (beats/min/paired consecutive trial); EEG (percentage time alpha-wave activity); breathing rate (breath/min).

Table 6

Comparison of Pre and Posttraining Blood Pressures (mm Hg)

Patient	Pretraining SBP	DBP	Posttraining SBP	DBP	Decline SBP	DBP	% Decline SBP	DBP
1	151	78	142	76	9*	2	5.9	2.6
2	171	93	162	92	9*	1	5.3	1.1
3	160	90	141	83	19*	7*	11.9	7.8
4	168	117	132	97	36*	20*	21.4	17.1
Mean	162.5	94.5	144.2	87.0	18.2	7.5	11.1	7.2

*P < .01.

Table 7

Results of Lowering Practice at Home

Patient	SBP before lowering (mm Hg)	SBP after lowering (mm Hg)	Amount of lowering (mm Hg)
1	138	128	10*
2	170	158	12*
3	141	119	22*
4	129	115	14*
5	126	105	21*
Mean	141	125	15.8

*P < .01.

highly trained subjects is interesting. Since each of these indices has been used as a criterion of relaxation, and since there were no differences between the SBP raise and SBP lower periods, the findings suggest that differential relaxation was not the mechanism by which our patients controlled SBP. These findings are especially relevant since other investigators[15, 17-19] have been training patients with high blood pressure to relax in order to clinically control their BP. Although we wish to emphasize that learning techniques such as we have used, and relaxation techniques such as those just cited are not mutually exclusive, they do seem to be different. At least one of the relaxation methods that has been employed, transcendental meditation, produces decreases in heart rate and increases in EEG alpha-wave activity.[21] As we have just noted, none of these responses corresponded with SBP in our patients. Another point of difference between these two techniques is the return of BP within two weeks to pretraining levels following cessation of four weeks of relaxation therapy.[18] These observations also would support the view that the effect of hospitalization in our study (with decreased patient activity and the increased attention given to the patients) is an unlikely mechanism to account for the prolonged and progressive declines in BP we have reported.

One factor which we believe to be important in the outcome of our study is the home blood pressure recording technique which each of our patients learned. This technique had several effects. From our point of view it enabled us to assess each patient's BP. The requirement that the patient return his results to us daily permitted us to maintain a regular check on

the patient's cooperation, and it reduced the risk that he would enter data on his work sheet without actually taking his BP. From the patient's point of view it afforded him a regular check on his BP so that he could objectively chart his own progress throughout the study. In addition the self-control maneuver which he utilized during the posttraining period gave the patient evidence confirming his ability to regulate his own BP. A similar finding was reported by Benson et al.[19] with patients who practiced meditation throughout a one month follow-up period. In their study patients with borderline high blood pressure who learned to meditate, and who continued to practice meditation, showed a drop of 7/4 mm Hg. It also is interesting to compare these data and the data of the present study with the findings of Brady et al.[18] in which no sustained depressor effect was observed after their patients discontinued relaxation practice.

In three patients (1, 2, 4) the reduced medication schedule that was employed in the hospital has been subsequently maintained. As a result the home posttraining BP records may be understating the magnitude of sustained lowering effects. The most striking example of BP reduction in the face of significant reduction in antihypertensive medications is patient 4. This patient entered training with mean home BP of 168/117 and was being treated with alpha-methyldopa, 500 mg t.i.d., and hydrochlorthiazide 50 mg b.i.d. Clinically her BP had been progressively rising and would have required a change in her medication schedule. Following training her mean home BP was 131/96 and she was taking only 250 mg t.i.d. of the alpha-methyldopa, and the hydrochlorthiazide dosage was unchanged.

Acknowledgment

We wish to acknowledge the assistance of L. R. Baker, M.D., R. Quilter and R. Mathias.

References

1. CHAPMAN WD, LIVINGSTON RB, LIVINGSTON KE, SWEET WH: Possible cortical areas involved in arterial hypertension. Res Publ Assoc Res Nerv Ment Dis 29: 775, 1950
2. BROD J, FENCL V, HEJL Z, JIRKA J: Circulatory changes underlying blood pressure elevation during acute emotional stress (mental arithmetic) in normotensive and hypertensive subjects. Clin Sci 18: 269, 1959
3. JOST H, RUILMAN CJ, HILL TS, GULO JJ: Studies in hypertension II: Central and autonomic nervous system reactions of hypertensive individuals to single physical and psychologic stress situations. J Nerv Ment Dis 115: 152, 1952
4. NESTLE PJ: Blood pressure and catecholamine excretion after mental stress in labile hypertension. Lancet 1: 692, 1969
5. GUTMANN MC, BENSON H: Environmental factors and systemic arterial blood pressure: A review. Medicine 50: 543, 1971
6. SHAPIRO AP: An experimental study of comparative response of blood pressure to different noxious stimuli. J Chronic Dis 13: 293, 1961
7. DAVIES MH: Is high blood pressure a psychosomatic disorder? J Chronic Dis 24: 239, 1971

8. SHAPIRO D, TURSKY B, GERSHON E, STERN M: Effects of feedback and reinforcement on the control of human systolic blood pressure. Science 163: 588, 1969
9. BRENER J, KLEINMAN RA: Learned control of decreases in systolic blood pressure. Nature 226: 1063, 1970
10. SHAPIRO D, SCHWARTZ GE, TURSKY B: Control of diastolic blood pressure in man by feedback and reinforcement. Psychophysiology 9: 296, 1972
11. SHAPIRO D, TURSKY B, SCHWARTZ GE: Control of blood pressure in man by operant conditioning. Circ Res 26 and 27 (suppl I): 1-27, 1970
12. BENSON H, SHAPIRO D, TURSKY B, SCHWARTZ GE: Decreased systolic blood pressure through operant conditioning techniques in patients with essential hypertension. Science 173: 740, 1971
13. ELDER ST, RUIZ ZR, DIABLER HL, DILLENKOFFER RL: Instrumental conditioning of diastolic blood pressure in essential hypertensive patients. J Appl Behav Anal 6: 377, 1973
14. MILLER NE, DiCARA LV, SOLOMON H, WEISS JM, DWORKIN B: Learned modification of autonomic functions: A review and

some new data. Circ Res **26** and **27** (suppl 1): 1-3, 1970

15. BENSON H, ROSNER BA, MARZETTA BR, KLEMCHUK HM: Decreased blood pressure in pharmacologically treated hypertensive patients, who regularly elicited the relaxation response. Lancet **1**: 289, 1974

16. SCHULTZ JH, LUTHE W: Autogenic Therapy, vol 1. New York, Grune & Stratton, 1969

17. PATEL CH: Yoga and bio-feedback in the management of hypertension. Lancet **2**: 1053, 1973

18. BRADY JP, LUBORSKY L, KRON RE: Blood pressure reduction in patients with essential hypertension through metronome-conditioned relaxation: A preliminary report. Behav Ther **5**: 203, 1974

19. BENSON H, ROSNER BA, MARZETTA BR, KLEMCHUK HP: Decreased blood pressure in borderline hypertensive subjects who practiced meditation. J Chron Dis **27**: 163, 1974

20. TURSKY B, SHAPIRO D, SCHWARTZ GE: Automated constant cuff pressure system to measure average systolic and diastolic blood pressure in man. IEEE Trans Biomed Eng **19**: 271, 1972

21. WALLACE RK: Physiological effects of transcendental meditation. Science **167**: 1751, 1970

44

Psychotherapeutic Control of Hypertension

Richard A. Stone and James De Leo

Abstract We conducted a six-month trial to determine the effect of psychologic relaxation on blood pressure. Alterations of peripheral sympathetic-nervous-system activity, as reflected by changes of dopamine-beta-hydroxylase in plasma, were evaluated, and plasma volume and plasma renin activity were measured. Treated patients exhibited significant ($P < 0.05$) reductions of blood pressure when supine and upright, and of plasma dopamine-beta-hydroxylase activity, and furosemide-stimulated renin activity when upright. Blood-pressure changes after six months correlated best with differences in plasma activity of dopamine-beta-hydroxylase with patients supine ($r = 0.54$; $P < 0.05$) and upright ($r = 0.62$; $P < 0.05$). These results suggest that a reduction of peripheral adrenergic activity contributes importantly to the improvement of hypertension observed with this form of therapy. Furthermore, the decrease of furosemide-stimulated plasma renin activity suggests that alterations of the renin-angiotensin system may help lower blood pressure in certain patients. (N Engl J Med 294:80-84, 1976)

P REVIOUS studies have indicated that psychotherapy may ameliorate hypertension. Investigators using a variety of technics, including yoga, Transcendental Meditation, and biofeedback, have observed blood-pressure reductions in many patients.[1-3] Most of these studies report that patients continued drug therapy at reduced dosages, and they do not completely rule out the possibility of increased compliance with prescribed medications. Benson et al. observed a definite reduction of systemic arterial pressure in borderline hypertensive subjects who used meditation and received no drugs.[4] However, the possible contribution of an alteration of dietary salt intake was not eliminated. In the present investigation of a well defined group of hypertensive subjects, we have attempted to determine the affect of a psychologic relaxation technic on blood pressure. The patients received no medications, and possible dietary salt restriction was assessed by the measurement of urinary sodium excretion.

Considerable evidence is accumulating that psychotherapeutic reduction of blood pressure may result from a decrement of neuronal activity.[5-7] The measurement of the enzyme, dopamine-beta-hydroxylase (DβH) in plasma appears to be a useful way to investigate adrenergic function.[8,9] DβH is the enzyme that converts dopamine to norepinephrine within the synaptic vesicles of sympathetic neurons.[10] A neurogenic stimulus is accompanied by the release of norepinephrine through exocytosis and is associated with the simultaneous discharge of the soluble portion of DβH.[11] There is no established pathway of DβH excretion, and the enzyme appears to have a longer metabolic half-life than catecholamines.[12] The proposal of Weinshilboum and Axelrod that plasma DβH activity provides an index of sympathetic-nervous-system function supports the theoretical framework of this study.[9]

Methods

Patients

Nineteen hypertensive patients from the Veterans Administration Hospital of San Diego were studied. None of them had been evaluated or treated previously for elevated blood pressure. Selection was performed arbitrarily by one of us (R.A.S.) who used the criteria of apparent ability to comprehend instructions, motivation, willingness to adhere to the experimental protocol and blood-pressure criteria listed below. Although 15 subjects were hospitalized for selected diagnostic evaluations, all the reported laboratory determinations and blood-pressure measurements were obtained on an outpatient basis. All patients gave their informed written consent, and the Committee on Human Experimentation of the University of California, San Diego, approved the protocol.

From the Division of Nephrology, departments of Medicine, University of California, San Diego, School of Medicine, and Veterans Administration Hospital (address reprint requests to Dr. Stone at the Division of Nephrology, Veterans Administration Hospital, San Diego, CA 92161).

Supported by a grant (HL 18095) from the National Institutes of Health and by the Veterans Administration.

Printed with permission from *The New England Journal of Medicine*, Vol. 294, 80-84, (January 8, 1976).

Diagnostic Procedures

The evaluation of each patient included a complete history and physical examination, multiple determinations of blood pressure (arm-cuff method), measurements of plasma DβH and renin activity (PRA), ^{131}I albumin plasma volume, blood chemical studies including determinations of the blood urea nitrogen concentration and the plasma concentrations of sodium, potassium, chloride, bicarbonate, creatinine, and total protein, a hemogram, a complete urinalysis (including microscopical examination of the urinary sediment), urinary excretion of 17-hydroxycorticosteroids and catecholamines, a roentgenogram of the chest, and an intravenous urogram. In most (15) patients, selective renal arteriography and measurements of PRA in the renal venous effluent from the two kidneys were obtained. The results of all the above studies were normal in all subjects but one (Group 2, Case 5), who exhibited a unilateral atrophic kidney on both the urogram and the arteriogram.

The blood-pressure criterion for entry into the study was a mean arterial pressure (diastolic blood pressure plus one-third pulse pressure) greater than 105 mm Hg (with the subject either supine or upright) during at least 50 per cent of 14 pretreatment determinations. All measurements (arm-cuff method were performed by an independent observer (technician or nurse), who possessed no knowledge of the assigned study groups. Systolic blood pressure was measured by palpation, to fall indicated; diastolic blood pressure represents the disappearance of all Korotkov sounds. Pretreatment and post-treatment (six-month) average blood-pressure and pulse measurements reflect the mean of 14 determinations (seven in the supine and seven in the upright position) over 10 to 14 days between 10 a.m. and 2 p.m.

All patients maintained an unrestricted dietary salt intake documented by urinary sodium excretions of 124 to 235 mEq per 24 hours. Peripheral blood samples were collected in chilled vacuum tubes containing either EDTA (for PRA) or heparin (for DβH). The blood for assay was placed on ice, separated in a refrigerated centrifuge (4°C), and stored at −20°C for subsequent assay. Blood samples for determination of DβH and PRA were obtained between 11 a.m. and noon after four to five hours of upright position and ambulation. Patients were then placed in the supine posture for 45 to 60 minutes, and peripheral venous blood was collected for measurement of DβH, PRA, and protein concentration. Plasma volume was determined while the patients maintained the recumbent position. The patients then received 80 mg of furosemide by mouth, and PRA was measured a third time between 4 and 6 p.m. after four hours of upright position and ambulation.

All patients were followed for a six-month interval. For further analysis, subjects were placed in the following categories (Table 1): Group 1, five controls subjects, who were seen for blood-pressure determinations only once a month throughout the six-month period of observation; and Group 2, 14 patients treated with psychologic relaxation.

Psychologic-Relaxation Technic

All procedures were performed by one of us (J.D.). The subjects attended five 20-minute training sessions and were instruct-

Table 1. Mean Arterial Pressure (MAP) and Plasma-Volume Data before and after Psychologic Relaxation (PR). *

Group	Age (Yr)	MAP¹ (Mm Hg)		Volume/BSA¹ (ML/M²)
		SUPINE	UPRIGHT	
1:	28 ± 3.0			
Before PR		108	111	1380
		± 3	± 3	± 327
After PR:		110	110	1409
		± 3	± 1	± 265
2:	28 ± 1.1			
Before PR		110	112	1796
		± 3	± 2	± 126
After PR		98	100	18/9
		± 3§¶	± 3§¶	± 99

*Data are means ± SEM.
¹Diastolic + 1/3 pulse pressure.
¹Body-surface area (calculated from height & weight).
§ P <0.05 as compared to control patients (by unpaired t-test).
¶ P <0.05 compared to pretreatment (by paired t-test).

ed in a technic based on Buddhist meditation exercises designed to elicit a relaxation response.

They were advised to find a comfortable chair in an area that was relatively quiet and free from distractions. They were then told to loosen tight clothing, sit in an upright position, and relax their muscles.

The subjects were then asked to count their breaths subvocally. The count was to be a continuous arithmetic progression. When distractions occurred, they were told simply to return to counting their breaths.

Finally, the patients were told to repeat the technic twice daily for intervals of 10 to 15 minutes, preferably before breakfast and before retiring.

All patients practiced the technic during the instruction period. Any questions regarding the technic were answered after the exercise.

Chemical Assays

Determinations of PRA were performed with the method of Haber, Koerner, and Page,[13] by means of the radioimmunoassay of angiotensin I generated after incubation at pH 5.5 for one hour at 37°C. Simultaneous blanks were determined at 4°C. Reagents were purchased from New England Nuclear, Boston, Massachusetts. All assays were performed in duplicate, and the values were required to fall within ±15 per cent of the mean. Reproducibility was established by replicate analyses of single plasma samples (20 in number) with "high" and "low" PRA. The inter-assay coefficients of variation (expressed as one standard deviation per mean) was 12 and 14.6 per cent for the "high" and "low" samples respectively. All results are expressed as nanograms of angiotensin I generated per milliliter per hour.

The measurement of plasma DβH activity was performed with the procedure of Nagatsu and Udenfriend.[14] All determinations were done in duplicate on 50-μl aliquots of plasma, and the results were required to fall within ±2 units of the mean. The inter-assay coefficient of variation (for 40 assays) of a single sample was 4.5 per cent. N-ethyl-maleidmide provided an effective way of inactivating endogenous inhibitors as previously described.[15] Results are expressed as International Units (μmoles per minute)/liter of plasma at 37°C, μmoles of octopamine formed (Units per liter). Other blood and urine chemical determinations were performed in the routine hospital laboratories.

Plasma volume was measured in the supine position with the injection of radioiodine labeled serum albumin. The dose was calculated to exceed background count by a factor of four. The isotope was injected intravenously, and plasma samples were obtained at 10 and 20 minutes.

Statistics

Paired and unpaired t-tests were used to determine differences within groups and between groups respectively. Linear regression analysis was performed with standard technics.[16] All values are expressed as the mean ± standard error of the mean (± S.E.M.), unless otherwise stated.

RESULTS

The two groups were similar in age and race. The average age of the five control patients (Group 1) was 28 years (range of 21 to 32 years), and the 14 treatment patients (Group 2) ranged in age from 23 to 36 years (mean of 28 ± 1.1 years). All patients were white; there were only two women, who were both in the treatment group.

The base-line blood pressures were similar in the two groups. Before therapy, mean arterial pressure in the supine and upright positions in Group 2 subjects was 110 ± 3 mm Hg and 112 ± 2 mm Hg respectively. These pressures did not differ (P > 0.05) from those of the control patients (Table 1). The two groups were also similar (P > 0.05) in average systolic and diastolic blood pressures (Fig. 1). After six months of psychologic relaxation measurements of mean arterial pressure in the supine and upright positions in Group 2 were significantly (P < 0.05) less than both their own base-line values and those of the control subjects. Both the systolic and diastolic blood pressures were significantly less (P < 0.05) than their previous pre-

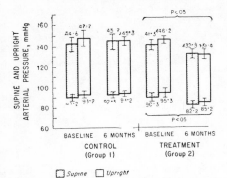

Figure 1. Effect of Psychologic Relaxation on Arterial-Blood Pressure.

Each column represents an average of systolic and diastolic pressures, taken initially and after six months, in the supine and upright positions (expressed as mean ± S.E.M.). The treatment group (Group 2) exhibited significant (P < 0.05) declines of both systolic and diastolic pressures as compared to pretreatment measurements (paired t-test). Treated patients, in both supine and upright positions, also had diastolic and systolic pressures significantly (P < 0.05) less than those of control subjects (by unpaired t-test).

treatment measurements but differed from control patients only in that the diastolic and systolic blood pressures with subjects both upright and supine were lower (P < 0.05, Fig. 1).

Pretreatment measurements of PRA with subjects supine, upright, and furosemide stimulated were similar, (P > 0.05) in both groups (Table 2). Determinations in the supine and upright positions did not differ significantly (P > 0.05) within or between groups at six months. Furosemide-stimulated PRA measurements were significantly less (P < 0.05) than pretreatment values in Group 2 subjects (Table 2).

Pretreatment determinations of plasma DβH activity did not differ (P > 0.05) between the two groups. After six months, patients in the treatment group (Group 2) exhibited an average plasma DβH activity in the upright position of 47 ± 5 Units per liter, which was significantly less (P < 0.05) than both that of the control group and their own base-line measurements (Table 2).

Table 2. Plasma Renin Activity (PRA) and Dopamine Beta-Hydroxylase (DβH) Activity before and after Psychologic Relaxation (PR).*

GROUP	DβH (U/LITER)		PRA (NG OF ANGIOTENSIN I/ML/HR)		
	SUPINE	UPRIGHT	SUPINE	UPRIGHT	FUROSEMIDE STIMULATED
1:					
Before PR	59	61	1.38	3.77	8.6
	±3	±2	±0.3	±1.0	±1.6
After PR	58	61	1.74	4.12	6.3
	±3	±3	±0.6	±0.9	±1.4
2:					
Before PR	51	54	2.76	5.3	8.7
	±5	±6	±1.2	±1.4	±2.2
After PR	47	47	1.98	4.4	7.1
	±5	±5†‡	±0.4	±1.3	±2.3

*All values are means ±SEM.
†P <0.05 as compared to control patients (by unpaired t-test).
‡P <0.05 as compared to pretreatment (by paired t-test).

Base-line radioiodinated plasma-volume measurements (standardized for body-surface area) averaged 1796 ± 126 ml per square meter in Group 2. Volume changes were not significant (P > 0.05, Table 1) in either group.

Plasma protein concentration averaged 7.3 ± .4 g per 100 ml in Group 1 and 7.4 ± 0.6 g per 100 ml in Group 2 before therapy. At six months, Group 1 patients exhibited an average plasma protein concentration of 7.2 ± .5 g per 100 ml, and Group 2 subjects an average of 7.5 ± .4 g per 100 ml. None of these determinations differed (P > 0.05) from the others.

In an attempt to determine the mechanism of blood-pressure alteration, linear-regression analysis was applied to the changes of mean arterial pressure versus the changes of DβH, PRA, and volume determinations (Table 3). Significant correlation was observed for changes of DβH activity in the supine and upright positions in the treatment group and DβH activity in the supine position in the control patients. A significant negative correlation was observed between mean arterial pressure and furosemide-stimulated renin in control subjects, an observation that remains unexplained. Although there was a significant decrement of furosemide-stimulated PRA after treatment, these alterations did not show significant correlation with mean arterial pressure.

DISCUSSION

The present investigation suggests that at least one form of psychologic relaxation is an effective method of therapy for selected young white men with mild or moderate hypertension. Nineteen patients with modest blood-pressure elevation, who had never received antihypertensive therapy, were studied for six months. Fourteen of these subjects (Group 2) were taught a psychologic relaxation exercise, which they were instructed to perform twice a day (morning and evening). This group exhibited a significant reduction of mean arterial pressure, which averaged 12 mm Hg in both the supine and upright positions. As in other investigations,[3,17] there was no significant change of blood pressure in subjects who did not receive any psychotherapeutic instruction. Although interpretation of these findings must be tempered with caution because of the pitfalls of a nonrandomized study, the reduction in the mean arterial pressure of at least 14 mm Hg (range of 14 to 30 mm Hg) in 57 per cent (eight of 14) of patients given psychotherapeutic instruction attests to the efficacy of a rather simple technic.

Although biochemical indexes of peripheral sympathetic-nervous-system activity after psychotherapeutic blood-pressure reduction have not been reported, adrenergic function has been studied in many forms of human hypertension.[18] Chemical measurements of neuronal activity have included the determinations of plasma and urinary catecholamines or metabolites,[19-21] but any potential meaning of these observations had been blunted by the recognition of the concept that urinary and plasma concentrations of catecholamines may be effected by variables other than adrenergic function — i.e., alterations of neuronal reuptake and storage, tissue metabolism, and renal clearance.

We believe that the activity of DβH in plasma may provide a better index of chronic adrenergic activity than assays of catecholamines or metabolites. DβH, a catecholamine-synthesizing enzyme, is released with norepinephrine from the storage granules of sympathetic neurons. There is no known excretion, and no reuptake, and plasma half-life appears to be much longer than that of catecholamines.[12,22] Many animal and human studies support the hypothesis that plasma DβH activity provides a good index of sympathetic-nervous-system activity.[23-25] From the long plasma half-life of DβH[12] and the small amount of soluble enzyme in vesicles in relation to the large circulating pool of DβH, one may propose that DβH activity in plasma will best reflect catecholamine release during a prolonged period.[26-28]

Possible reasons for differing values of plasma DβH activity in human beings have not been established, and some investigators have suggested the DβH in plasma does not represent adrenergic function.[29] Alternative hypotheses include individual variations in plasma enzyme clearance and differences within the storage vesicle of the ratio between soluble DβH and catecholamines.[29] Consequently, one group of investigators has suggested that directional changes of DβH in plasma represent alterations of adrenergic activity better than the determination of absolute amounts of enzyme.[30] Studies in laboratory animals that were not given drugs suggest that enzyme half-life and the ratio of soluble DβH to catecholamines remain constant.[9-12] Previous studies, which indicated individual variability in the relation between enzymatic and immunologic activities,[12] have not been confirmed,[31] and investigations in man continue to suggest that plasma DβH activity is useful as an index of peripheral sympathetic-nervous-system function.[32] However, further human studies will be required to establish the relation of adrenergic function and measurements of DβH activity in plasma.

In the present investigation, plasma DβH activity remained unchanged in control subjects (Group 1), and the stability observed confirms several previous reports of this phenomenon.[15,24,33] On the other hand, there was a significant reduction of plasma DβH activity in treated patients in the upright position. If one analyzes only subjects who exhibited blood-pressure reductions of at least 14 mm Hg, there was a significant decrease of plasma DβH activity in both supine and upright positions. Furthermore, there was a significant correlation of change in mean arterial pressure in both positions with alterations of activities of DβH in plasma in supine and upright positions. The observed relation of changes of DβH and blood pressure suggests that a reduction in peripheral adrenergic activity contributes importantly to the observed amelioration of hypertension with this form of therapy. In addition, these results, in conjunction with previous physiologic studies,[5] support the proposal that changes of DβH in plasma provide an index of alterations of adrenergic function.

Measurements of plasma volume and peripheral venous renin activity were performed in all subjects before and after therapy. No significant alterations of plasma vol-

Table 3. Correlation of Changes in Mean Arterial Pressure (MAP) with Alterations of Renin (PRA), Dopamine-Beta-Hydroxylase (DβH), and Plasma Volume (PV). *

Datum	Group 1		Group 2	
	CORRELATION COEFFICIENT	PROBABILITY	CORRELATION COEFFICIENT	PROBABILITY
Δ Supine MAP (mm Hg):				
Vs Δsupine DβH (U/liter)	0.902	<0.05	0.536	<0.05
Vs Δsupine PRA (ng of angiotensin/ ml/hr)	0.415	NS†	0.264	NS
Vs Δsupine PV (ml/m²)	0.089	NS	0.386	NS
Δ Upright MAP (mm Hg):				
Vs Δupright DβH (U/liter)	0.405	NS	0.615	<0.05
Vs Δupright PRA (ng of angiotensin/ ml/hr)	0.02	NS	0.194	NS
Vs Δfurosemide-stimulated PRA (ng of angiotensin/ ml/hr)	−0.90	<0.05	−0.149	NS

*Standardized for body-surface area.   †No significant correlation.

ume were detected and, therefore, would not provide an explanation for the blood-pressure changes observed. On the other hand, there was a significant decrement of furosemide-stimulated PRA in the treatment group. Since it has been proposed that adrenergic activity influences renin secretory rate,[34] it is attractive to hypothesize that a decrement of sympathetic tone was responsible for the changes of PRA observed. The decrease in PRA is not likely to have been due to changes in blood volume since this measurement did not differ significantly. Furthermore, the decrease of PRA may have contributed to the blood-pressure reduction in certain patients, but the lack of correlation of PRA and mean arterial pressure suggests that a change in the rate of renin release was not the primary mechanism of blood-pressure reduction.

In conclusion, we have demonstrated that at least one psychotherapeutic method can provide improved blood-pressure control in certain patients with mild or moderate hypertension. In addition, we have provided evidence that this blood-pressure reduction is associated with biochemical evidence of reduced peripheral adrenergic activity. We have also detected alterations in the renin angiotensin system that may contribute to the observed amelioration of hypertension in certain patients.

We are indebted to Darrell D. Fanestil, M.D., for advice on the manuscript, to Ms. Rachel Rubin and Mr. James Converse for technical assistance, to Mr. Bryan Tucker for statistical assistance and to Mrs. Linda Brandt for assistance.

REFERENCES

1. Benson H, Rosner BA, Marzetta BR, et al: Decreased blood-pressure in pharmacologically treated hypertensive patients who regularly elicited the relaxation response. Lancet 1:289-291, 1974

2. Kristt DA, Engel BT: Learned control of blood pressure in patients with high blood pressure. Circulation 51:370-378, 1975

3. Patel C: Randomized controlled trial of yoga and biofeedback in management of hypertension. Lancet 2:93-95, 1975

4. Benson H, Rosner BA, Marzetta BR, et al: Decreased blood-pressure in borderline hypertensive subjects who practiced meditation. J Chronic Dis 27:163-169, 1974

5. Wallace RK: Physiological effects of transcendental meditation. Science 167:1751-1754, 1970

6. Henry JP, Stephens PM, Axelrod J, et al: Effect of psychosocial stimulation on the enzymes involved in the biosynthesis and metabo-

lism of noradrenaline and adrenaline. Psychosomat Med 33:227-237, 1971

7. Henry JP, Stephens PM, Santisteban GA: A model of psychosocial hypertension showing reversibility and progression of cardiovascular complications. Circulation Res 36:156-164, 1975

8. Geffen L: Serum dopamine-beta-hydroxylase as an index of sympathetic function. Life Sci 14:1593-1604, 1974

9. Weinshilboum R, Axelrod J: Serum dopamine-beta-hydroxylase activity. Circulation Res 28:307-315, 1971

10. Gewirtz GP, Kopin IJ: Release of dopamine-beta-hydroxylase with norepinephrine during cat splenic nerve stimulation. Nature 277:406-407, 1970

11. Depotter WP, de Schaepdryver AF, Moerman EJ, et al: Evidence for release of vesicle proteins together with nor-adrenaline upon stimulation of the splenic nerve. J Physiol (Lond) 204:102p-104p, 1969

12. Rush RA, Geffen LB: Radioimmunoassay and clearance of circulating dopamine-β-hydroxylase. Circulation Res 31:444-452, 1972

13. Haber E, Koerner T, Page LB: Application of a radioimmunoassay for angiotensin I to the physiologic measurements of plasma renin activity in normal human subjects. J Clin Endocrinol Metab 29:1349-1355, 1969

14. Nagatsu T, Udenfriend S: Photometric assay of dopamine-β-hydroxylase activity in human blood. Clin Chem 18:980-983, 1972

15. Stone RA, Gunnells JC, Robinson RR, et al: Dopamine-beta-hydroxylase in primary and secondary hypertension. Circulation Res: Suppl 1:34 and 35:1-47, 1974

16. Bliss EI: Statistics in Biology. New York, McGraw-Hill Book Company, 1970

17. Patel C: 12-month follow-up of yoga and bio-feedback in the management of hypertension. Lancet 1:62-64, 1975

18. DeQuattro V, Miura Y: Neurogenic factors in human hypertension: mechanism or myth. Am J Med 55:362-378, 1973

19. Nestel PJ, Esler MD: Patterns of catecholamine excretion in urine in hypertension. Circulation Res: Suppl 2: 26 and 27:75-81, 1970

20. Engelman K, Portnoy B, Sjoerdsma A: Plasma catecholamine concentrations in patients with hypertension. Circulation Res 27:Suppl 1:141-146, 1970

21. Louis WJ, Doyle AE, Anavekar S: Plasma norephinephrine levels in essential hypertension. N Engl J Med 288:599-601, 1973

22. Molinoff PB, Brimijoin S, Weinshilboum R, et al: Neurally mediated increase in dopamine-β-hydroxylase activity. Proc Natl Acad Sci USA 66:453-458, 1970

23. Lamprecht F, Williams RB, Kopin IJ: Serum dopamine-beta-hydroxylase during development of immobilization-induced hypertension. Endocrinology 92:953-956, 1973

24. Schanberg S, Stone RA, Kirshner N, et al: Dopamine-beta-hydroxylase: a diagnostic aid in the evaluation of hypertension. Science 183:523-525, 1974

25. Rockson S, Stone RA, Van Der Weyden M, et al: Lesch-Nyhan syndrome: evidence for abnormal adrenergic function. Science 184:934-935, 1974

26. Stone RA, Kirshner N, Reynolds J, et al: Purification and properties of dopamine-β-hydroxylase from human pheochromocytoma. Mol Pharmacol 10:1009-1015, 1974

27. Stone RA, Kirshner N, Gunnells JC, et al: Changes of plasma dopamine-β-hydroxylase activity and other plasma constituents during the cold pressor test. Life Sci 14:1797-1805, 1974

28. Ross SB, Eriksson HE, Hellstrom W: On the fate of dopamine-B-hydroxylase after release from the peripheral sympathetic nerves in the cat. Acta Physiol Scand 92:578-580, 1974

29. Horowitz D, Alexander RW, Lovenberg W, et al: Human serum dopamine-B-hydroxylase: relationship to hypertension and sympathetic activity. Circulation Res 28:594-599, 1973

30. Alexander RW, Gill JR Jr, Yamabe H, et al: Effects of dietary sodium and of acute saline infusion on the interrelationship between dopamine excretion and adrenergic activity in man. J Clin Invest 54:194-200, 1974

31. Rush RA, Thomas PE, Udenfriend S: Measurement of human dopamine-β-hydroxylase in serum by homologous radioimmunoassay. Proc Natl Acad Sci USA 72:750-752, 1975

32. Naftchi EN, Wooten FG, Lowman EW, et al: Relationship between serum dopamine-β-hydroxylase activity, catecholamine metabolism and hemodynamic changes during paroxysmal hypertension in quadriplegia. Circulation Res 35:850-861, 1974

33. Rockson SG, Stone RA, Gunnells JC, et al: Plasma dopamine-β-hydroxylase activity in oral contraceptive hypertension. Circulation 51:916-923, 1975

34. Ganong WF: Biogenic amines, sympathetic nerves, and renin secretion. Fed Proc 32:1782-1784, 1973

Relationship Between Essential Hypertension and Cognitive Functioning: Effects of Biofeedback

Herbert Goldman, Kenneth M. Kleinman, Muriel Y. Snow, Donald R. Bidus, and Bernard Korol

ABSTRACT

Seven male essential hypertensives underwent 9 weekly 2-hr biofeedback training sessions in an attempt to produce decreases in blood pressure. Feedback, contingent upon heart beat by heart beat decreases in systolic pressure, was provided by an automated blood pressure monitoring system. The subjects were administered the Category Test (a subtest of the Halstead-Reitan Neuropsychological Test Battery) both before and after biofeedback training. As controls, 4 male hypertensives underwent 3 weekly sessions in which blood pressure was monitored without feedback being provided. Prior to training, a significant positive correlation was obtained between systolic blood pressure and number of errors made on the Category Test. Biofeedback training produced significant decreases in systolic pressure within sessions and in diastolic pressure between sessions. In the control subjects, no significant changes in pressure were observed. For both systolic and diastolic pressures, significant correlations were obtained between magnitude of decrease during biofeedback training and improvement in Category Test scores subsequent to training.

DESCRIPTORS: Biofeedback, Category Test, Essential hypertension.

Recently, two studies have been reported in which essential hypertensive patients learned to reduce their blood pressure when provided with feedback contingent upon decreases in pressure. Benson, Shapiro, Tursky, and Schwartz (1971) trained 5 patients to decrease systolic pressure from an average of 169.9 mm Hg to 147.3 mm Hg in approximately 5 weeks of consecutive Monday–Friday sessions. Elder, Ruiz, Deabler, and Dillenkoffer (1973) reported decreases in diastolic pressure as great as 25 percent after 4 days of morning and afternoon training sessions. These decreases persisted for at least 1 week following termination of training.

The dangers of prolonged hypertension are usually described in physical terms, i.e., increased incidence of cardiovascular disease and strokes. While comparatively little attention has been directed toward the cognitive or intellectual correlates of high blood pressure, available evidence suggests that hypertension occurs coincidentally with indices of impaired cerebral functioning (Apter, Halstead, & Heimburger, 1951; Goldman, Kleinman, Snow, Bidus, & Korol, 1974; Wilkie & Eisdorfer, 1971; Reitan, 1954).

In the present study, (a) essential hypertensives were tested on both the Wechsler Adult Intelligence Scale (WAIS) and Category Test, a subtest of the Halstead-Reitan Neuropsychological Test Battery; (b) feedback contingent upon decrements in systolic pressure was then presented in an

Supported by Veterans Administration Institutional Research Funds (Medical Research Information Systems No. 0110).

The second author is a Research Consultant, St. Louis VA Hospital; and a member of the faculty in the Department of Psychology, Southern Illinois University, Edwardsville.

Address requests for reprints to: Herbert Goldman, Ph.D., Coordinator, Neuropsychology Laboratory, St. Louis VA Hospital, Jefferson Barracks Division, St. Louis, MO 63125.

attempt to produce decreases in blood pressure; finally, (c) both the WAIS and Category Test were re-administered to determine if the anticipated decreases in pressure resulting from biofeedback training were reflected in improved cognitive functioning. As a control for the effects upon blood pressure of both feedback and habituation to the experimental situation, other hypertensives had their blood pressure monitored without feedback.

The Halstead-Reitan battery is a sensitive indicator of the type of cognitive impairment associated with brain damage (Filskov & Goldstein, 1974; Klove, 1974). The Category Test is the single most sensitive test in the entire battery (Russell, Neuringer, & Goldstein, 1970). Subjects are shown a series of stimuli, each one containing four figures, from which they must choose the "correct" one. Concepts such as size, shape, number, position, brightness, and color determine which choice is correct. The correct concept is changed periodically throughout the series. Feedback (correct or incorrect) is given following each choice. Data consist of the total number of errors made. Patients with brain damage make more errors than normals (Reitan, 1966).

Method

Fourteen male essential hypertensives were given the WAIS and Category Test prior to biofeedback training; 7 of these completed biofeedback training and were retested on the WAIS and Category Test. Three of the 7 were white; 4 were black. Mean age = 53.8 yrs (Range = 35–68); mean number yrs of schooling = 10.0 (Range = 4–13). Mean blood pressure at the beginning of biofeedback training = 167.4/108.6 mm Hg. Seven subjects were unable to complete biofeedback training for various reasons and, as a consequence, were dropped from the study.

Four male essential hypertensives served as controls. These subjects were given the WAIS and Category Test and then underwent sessions of blood pressure monitoring, but without feedback. Two were white, 2 black. Mean age = 51.8 yrs (Range = 38–63); mean number of yrs of education = 9.8 (Range = 8–11). Mean systolic and diastolic pressures at the beginning of the first blood pressure monitoring session = 154.5/98.8 mm Hg.

The subjects were recruited from the St. Louis VA Hospital Outpatient Clinic. Only patients with minimum blood pressure readings of 140/95 mm Hg (taken at least three times with the patient seated) were selected as subjects. Each prospective subject received an EKG, SMA-12 blood profile, complete urinalysis, IVP, chest X-ray, physical and neurological examination, as well as a psychological interview. Only patients showing no signs of pathology on all the above tests were selected as subjects. All subjects remained drug free for the duration of the study.

Both the WAIS and Category Test were administered to all subjects 1 week prior to the beginning of either biofeedback training or blood pressure monitoring.

Biofeedback training was carried out in 9 weekly 2-hr sessions. For the controls, blood pressure monitoring was carried out in 3 weekly 2-hr sessions. At the beginning of each session, 3–5 systolic/diastolic blood pressure readings were taken by auscultation. The mean systolic pressure thus obtained was programmed into the automated blood pressure monitoring

system developed by Shapiro, Tursky, Gershon, and Stern (1969) and commercially available from Lexington Instruments Co., Waltham, Mass. A complete description of the system, along with validation data, may be found in Tursky, Shapiro, and Schwartz (1972).

The system was programmed as a systolic monitor, i.e., it tracked systolic pressure on a trial by trial basis. At the beginning of the first trial, a blood pressure cuff on the subject's left arm was automatically inflated to the previously programmed systolic pressure. Both Korotkoff sounds and the electrocardiogram were continuously monitored during cuff inflation, the former by means of a crystal microphone positioned beneath the cuff and over the brachial artery and the latter by means of electrodes in an EKG Lead II configuration. During the next 30 heart beats, the system sensed the proportion of R-waves not followed by Korotkoff sounds; i.e., when cuff pressure was greater than systolic pressure. The cuff was then deflated for 1 min.

If, on a given trial, the proportion of R-waves not followed by Korotkoff sounds was between .2 and .8, cuff pressure remained constant on the next trial. However, if the proportion was less than .2 or greater than .8, cuff pressure was increased by 4 mm on the next trial in the first case or decreased by 3 mm on the next trial in the second case. Thus, from trial to trial, cuff pressure tracked systolic pressure.

During each trial, feedback was provided to the experimental subjects on a heart beat by heart beat basis. Each R-wave not followed by a Korotkoff sound (indicating a decrease in systolic pressure) resulted in the presentation of both a brief light and moderate intensity tone. From 25–30 trials were given during each training session. The subjects were informed about the nature of their disorder, the purpose of the experiment, how the blood pressure monitoring system worked, and the nature of the feedback contingency. They were instructed to remain as still as possible during periods of cuff inflation; that the greater the frequency of lights and tones they produced, the more they had lowered their blood pressure; and that however they managed to produce lights and tones in the laboratory, they were to practice at home for at least one half hour per day whenever possible.

Control subjects received approximately the same number of trials (without feedback) as the experimental subjects during the 3 weekly monitoring sessions. They were instructed to relax as much as possible both during each monitoring session and at home for at least 30 min per day.

For the experimental subjects, blood pressure data consisted of systolic and diastolic pressures, recorded at the beginning of each training session, as well as systolic pressure recorded during the final trial within each session. Identical data were obtained for the control subjects, except that diastolic pressure was also obtained following the final trial of each monitoring session.

Results

The relationship between blood pressure and Category Test performance in the original sample of 14 subjects has been described elsewhere (Goldman et al., 1974). For the 7 subjects who completed biofeedback training, a significant[1] correlation was obtained between systolic pressure (recorded at the beginning of the initial training session) and number of errors made on the Category Test administered prior to biofeedback training (rho = .75, N = 7).

---

[1]Null hypothesis rejected at .05 level.

In the experimental subjects, diastolic pressure decreased significantly from a mean of 108.6 mm Hg at the beginning of the first session to 93.9 mm Hg at the beginning of the ninth session, $F(6/56)=7.08$, $MS_e=69.67$. It will be recalled that diastolic pressure was recorded only at the beginning of each session. By contrast, the decrease in systolic pressure (from a mean of 167.4 to 161.1 mm Hg) did not reach significance, $F(8/48)=.84$, $MS_e=386.17$.

Neither systolic nor diastolic pressure showed significant between-session changes in the control subjects. Systolic pressure increased from a mean of 154.5 to 157.0 mm Hg, $F(2/6)=.58$, $MS_e=50.40$, while diastolic pressure decreased from a mean of 98.8 to 94.5 mm Hg, $F(2/6)=.95$, $MS_e=40.62$.

Within training sessions, the experimental subjects decreased systolic pressure significantly by an average of 7.0 mm Hg, $F(1/6)=31.76$, $MS_e=49.93$. The control subjects showed a nonsignificant within-session mean decrease in systolic pressure of only 0.7 mm Hg, $F(1/3)=.49$, $MS_e=6.82$. Diastolic pressure showed a nonsignificant mean increase of 0.2 mm Hg, $F(1/3)=.20$, $MS_e=1.82$.

Table 1 shows systolic and diastolic pressures recorded at the beginning of training session 1 (Column 1), systolic pressure recorded on the last trial of session 9 and diastolic pressure taken at the beginning of the ninth session (Column 2), and changes in systolic and diastolic pressures from sessions 1 to 9 (Column 3). Note that 5 of the 7 subjects decreased diastolic pressure to 95 mm Hg or less, the level used to define diastolic hypertension.

The last three columns of Table 1 list subjects' error scores on the Category Test administered both prior to and following biofeedback training.

Following training, 5 of the experimental subjects made fewer errors on the Category Test (Mean decrease = 15.7 errors). Spearman's rho was computed to determine if the magnitude of decrease in systolic or diastolic pressure was positively correlated with the degree of improvement shown in Category Test scores. Rho was significant for both measures (for systolic pressure, rho = .82, N = 7; for diastolic pressure, rho=.78, N=7). It is of interest to note that the 2 subjects (R.D. and J.A.) who showed the smallest decreases in diastolic pressure and *increases* in systolic pressure were the only ones who demonstrated a decrement in performance on the Category Test. As might be expected, a positive correlation was also found between the magnitude of decrease in systolic and diastolic pressure (rho=.92, N=7). Finally, the correlation between pre- and post-training error scores was significant (rho=.75, N=7), thus demonstrating the reliability of the Category Test.

Discussion

The results of this study may be summarized as follows: (a) a significant positive correlation was found between systolic blood pressure (within the hypertensive range) and number of errors made on the Category Test, the latter known to be a clinically useful indicator of cerebral impairment; (b) biofeedback training produced decreases in systolic pressure within training sessions, and decreases in diastolic pressure between sessions; (c) subjects showing the greatest decreases in systolic and diastolic pressures during biofeedback training showed the most improvement on the Category Test administered subsequent to training.

While it is tempting to interpret these results as indicating a direct relationship between blood pressure and cognitive functioning, three methodologi-

TABLE 1

Blood pressure change from training session 1 to training session 9, and Category Test scores prior to and following biofeedback training and the algebraic differences between them

Subject	Blood Pressure			Errors on Category Test		
	First Session Systolic/Diastolic[a]	**Ninth Session S/D**[b]	**Pressure Change S/D**	**Pre-training**	**Post-training**	**Diff.**
I.D.	197/120	183/110	−14/−10	98	81	−17
J.O.	186/120	145/92	−41/−28	119	64	−55
J.A.	165/100	184/95	+19/−5	104	113	+9
R.C.	160/100	164/95	+4/−5	86	97	+11
W.S.	155/120	135/84	−20/−35	39	26	−13
R.A.	167/110	163/98	−4/−12	70	35	−35
J.F.	142/90	139/82	−3/−8	22	12	−10
Mean	167/109	159/94	−8/−15	76.9	61.1	−15.7

[a]Recorded at beginning of training session.
[b]Systolic recorded during final trial; diastolic recorded prior to first trial.

cal shortcomings make such a definitive conclusion premature at this time—the small sample sizes used, differences in the number of sessions given to the control and experimental subjects, and the lack of Category Test scores obtained from the control subjects following a number of monitoring sessions equivalent to the number of biofeedback training sessions given to the experimental subjects.

It is possible, for example, to attribute these results to the single or combined effects of practice on the Category Test, anxiety evoked by the experimental situation, and habituation. Practice effects could have accounted for the improvement in Category Test performance shown by the experimental subjects following biofeedback training, while anxiety effects could have accounted for the observed correlation between systolic pressure and Category Test scores prior to biofeedback training. Higher levels of anxiety would presumably have been reflected in both increased blood pressures and decreased levels of cognitive functioning, thus resulting in a significant correlation. Finally, the obtained correlations between decreases in blood pressure and improvement in Category Test performance could be attributable to the effects of habituation, i.e., the greater the decreases in the subjects' anxiety, the larger the decreases in blood pressure and the more improvement in cognitive functioning would be expected. However, several factors mitigate against interpretation of these results in terms of these variables. Though there are no published reports concerning the effects of practice on the Category Test, in our laboratory we have found performance on this test to be quite stable over time. For example, in an unpublished study, 11 normotensive male subjects very much like those described above (i.e., Mean age = 50.4 yrs; mean number yrs of education = 10.4 yrs) were given the Category Test twice with a 3 month interval between testings (again, an interval similar to that used in the present study). The subjects showed a mean improvement on the second Category Test of only .73 errors. The test-retest reliability of Category Test scores in this sample = .82. Thus, the Category Test is both reliable and subject to minimal practice effects.

As to the effects of anxiety and habituation, increases in the former should have resulted in a generalized increase in arousal which would be reflected in physiological parameters other than blood pressure while the latter process should have been reflected in a generalized decrease in arousal. Mean heart rate (HR), integrated frontalis electromyographic activity (EMG), and basal skin resistance (BSR) were continuously recorded from the experimental subjects during training sessions 1 and 9. None of these measures (recorded prior to the start of biofeedback training during session 1) were significantly correlated (Spearman's rho) either with each other or with Category Test performance prior to biofeedback training. Thus, an interpretation of the observed correlation between systolic blood pressure and Category Test performance in terms of anxiety seems unlikely in view of the lack of generalization of the relationship to other physiological parameters.

With regard to changes in these parameters occurring within or between sessions 1 and 9, neither HR nor EMG showed any significant changes. Only BSR showed a significant increase, and then only between sessions, $F(1/6)=6.82$, $MS_e = 1017.86$. Spearman's rhos indicated that changes in these measures occurring between sessions 1 and 9 were uncorrelated both with each other and with changes in Category Test performance. Thus, the observed decreases in systolic pressure observed within training sessions and in diastolic pressure between sessions were not symptomatic of a generalized decrease in arousal. Likewise, the correlations obtained between changes in blood pressure and Category Test performance were not paralleled by similar relationships with HR, EMG, or BSR. Such findings are difficult to interpret as resulting from the effects of anxiety and habituation.

At this point, it is not possible to explain why only diastolic pressure showed significant between-session decreases when feedback was contingent upon decreases in systolic pressure. Since changes in systolic and diastolic pressures are usually closely related, it can be assumed that the experimental subjects were often reinforced for decreasing diastolic as well as systolic pressure. Perhaps the inherently greater variability of systolic pressure together with the small sample size precluded the obtaining of a significant between-session decrease.

The results of the present study are both suggestive of a relationship between hypertension and reversible cognitive impairment, and are consistent with a growing body of literature indicating that biofeedback training may be of utility in the treatment of essential hypertension. While the precise physiological mechanisms linking blood pressure and cognitive functioning are not yet known, there is evidence that sustained hypertension results in the premature onset of arteriosclerosis, a condition which may well produce impairment in brain function (Guyton, 1961).

The finding of a correlation between magnitude of decrease in blood pressure obtained during biofeedback training and degree of improvement in Category Test performance implies, but does not prove, that biofeedback training produced effects upon blood pressure which persisted beyond the laboratory setting. Future research must directly address the question of the generalization of the effects of biofeedback training upon blood pressure.

REFERENCES

Apter, N., Halstead, W., & Heimburger, R. Impaired cerebral functions in essential hypertension. *American Journal of Psychiatry*, 1951, *107*, 808–813.

Benson, H., Shapiro, D., Tursky, B., & Schwartz, G. Decreased systolic blood pressure through operant conditioning techniques in patients with essential hypertension. *Science*, 1971, *173*, 740–742.

Elder, S., Ruiz, Z., Deabler, H., & Dillenkoffer, R. Instrumental conditioning of diastolic blood pressure in essential hypertensive patients. *Journal of Applied Behavior Analysis*, 1973, *6*, 377–382.

Filskov, S., & Goldstein, S. Diagnostic validity of the Halstead-Reitan Neuropsychological Battery. *Journal of Consulting & Clinical Psychology*, 1974, *42*, 382–388.

Goldman, H., Kleinman, K., Snow, M., Bidus, D., & Korol, B. Correlation of diastolic blood pressure and cognitive dysfunction in essential hypertension. *Diseases of the Nervous System*, 1974, *35*, 571–572.

Guyton, A. *Textbook of medical physiology*, Philadelphia: W. B. Saunders Company, 1961. Pp. 430–431.

Klove, H. Validation studies in adult clinical neuropsychology. In R. Reitan & L. Davison (Eds.), *Clinical neuropsychology: Current status and applications.* Washington: Winston-Wiley, 1974. Pp. 211–235.

Reitan, R. Intellectual and affective changes in essential hypertension. *American Journal of Psychiatry*, 1954, *110*, 817–828.

Reitan, R. A research program on the psychological effects of brain lesions in human beings. In N. R. Ellis (Ed.), *International review of research in mental retardation.* Vol. 1. New York: Academic Press, 1966. Pp. 153–218.

Russell, E., Neuringer, C., & Goldstein, G. *Assessment of brain damage: A neuropsychological key approach.* New York: Wiley-Interscience, 1970. Pp. 8–9.

Shapiro, D., Tursky, B., Gershon, E., & Stern, M. Effects of feedback and reinforcement on the control of human systolic pressure. *Science*, 1969, *163*, 588–590.

Tursky, B., Shapiro, D., & Schwartz, G. Automated constant cuff pressure system to measure average systolic and diastolic blood pressure in man. *IEEE Transactions on Bio-medical Engineering*, 1972, *33*, 301–321.

Wilkie, F., & Eisdorfer, C. Intelligence and blood pressure in the aged. *Science*, 1971, *172*, 959–962.

Instrumental Blood Pressure Conditioning in Out-Patient Hypertensives

S. Thomas Elder and Nancy K. Eustis

Now that the efficacy of instrumental conditioning of blood pressure in several specialized situations has been established experimentally (Benson *et al.*, 1971; Brener and Kleinman, 1970; Schwartz, 1972; Schwartz, Shapiro and Tursky, 1971; Shapiro, Schwartz and Tursky, 1971; Shapiro *et al.* 1969; Shapiro, Tursky and Schwartz, 1970; Elder *et al.*, 1973) there is the matter of assessing the effectiveness of instrumental conditioning in a routine clinical application over an extended period. This is an important question since the effective management of essential hypertension must center around a procedure which can be employed easily on an out-patient basis and which the patient may eventually administer to himself. Therefore, the purpose of this study was to see if essential hypertension could be lowered by the use of instrumental conditioning on an out-patient basis without a concurrent effort to alter the patient's normal environment (e.g. eating and sleeping habits, daily activity schedule, and medication regimen).

METHOD

Subjects

Subjects (Ss) were drawn from both student and non-student populations. All reported they had been previously diagnosed as (essential) hypertensive by their family physicians, and no attempt was made to verify the diagnosis. No limitations as to sex, age, race or medication were set; volunteer patients were admitted to the study as they became available. A descriptive summary of the 22 participants is compiled in Table 1. There were 14 males and 8 females; the mean age was 50.23 with a range of 23–80 yr, and 20 of the Ss were on medication for hypertension.

Apparatus

The apparatus consisted of a standard E & M Physiograph Six equipped with a model PE-100 Programmable Electro-Sphygmomanometer. With this system, it was possible to obtain an indirect measure of systolic and diastolic blood pressure displayed by a strip chart recorder. An aluminum panel containing high intensity red and green lamps was located on a small table about 1.5 m directly in front of the S.

Procedure

Informed consent was obtained at the outset and each S was asked to advise his physician that he was participating in the study. The next step consisted of setting up a fairly regular schedule for the S to attend conditioning sessions. Initially, the last four patients were subjected to daily (massed) rather than distributed (spaced) training sessions. Other than the rate at which training sessions were scheduled, there was no difference in procedure between the massed (N = 4) and spaced (N = 19) groups. In the case of spaced training, treatment sessions were distributed as follows: twice a week for 2 weeks, once a week for 2 weeks, two sessions spaced 2 weeks apart, and a final session 1 month later. Spaced training sessions were thus distributed over an 80-day period.

Upon arrival for Session 2, the S was directed to urinate and then was asked to have a seat nearby until he or she was called. Ten to twenty min later, he or she was invited into the laboratory and seated in an upholstered reclining chair facing the signal panel of the apparatus. The cuff was secured

Reprinted with permission from *Behaviour Research and Therapy*, 1975, Vol. 13, 185–188.

to the upper left arm which rested on the arm of the chair and care was taken to position the crystal microphone directly over the brachial artery. Next, his or her blood pressure was measured automatically every minute for a total of ten successive determinations. No training procedures were introduced at this time, and the mean of these readings was taken as the patient's *basal* systolic and diastolic blood pressure, respectively.

Two min later, the first 10 training trials were given, making a total of 20 trials for the session. All sessions thereafter were composed of 20 trials each, with a 2-min rest interval between the first and the last halves. In view of the data reported by Elder, Leftwich and Wilkerson (1974), reinforcement/feedback was always contingent on diastolic rather than systolic pressure changes.

Generally, the training procedure conformed to that designated as strategy III in the Elder *et al.* experiment; more specifically, positive stimulus feedback (a green light) followed reductions in diastolic blood pressure, and negative stimulus feedback (a red light) accompanied trials during which blood pressure increased or no change occurred. In addition, verbal reinforcement was provided once during the first and second halves of each session in the form of "That's good!" or "You just got a green light, keep up the good work!" in close temporal contiguity with the presentation of the green exteroceptive stimulus. The instructions to the *S* at this point consisted simply of telling him that the aim was to teach him to lower his blood pressure, and that whenever the green light appeared it meant he had been successful and the red light signified he had not.

Actually, *Ss* received a green light whenever their pressure dropped below basal, and a red light whenever their pressure increased or showed no change. This was done in order that no *S* would receive a green light for a blood pressure higher than the original basal pressure or the initial blood pressure at the start of the session.

RESULTS

To provide within-sessions as well as between-sessions comparisons, two means were determined for each session: the first, Mean A, was obtained from the scores generated over trials 1-10; the second,

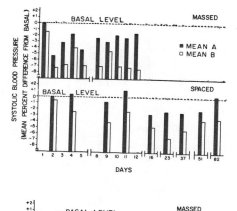

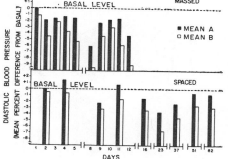

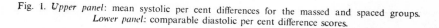

Fig. 1. *Upper panel*: mean systolic per cent differences for the massed and spaced groups. *Lower panel*: comparable diastolic per cent difference scores.

Mean B, was based on scores from trials 11–20. Then the differences between each of these means and the S's basal pressure were determined and expressed as a percentage of the S's basal pressure.

Mean per cent difference scores were prepared from the systolic and diastolic data for both the massed- and the distributed-practice groups. The systolic data are displayed in the upper half, and the concomitant diastolic data are plotted in the lower half, of Fig. 1. The black bars represent average performance for the first half of the session, Mean A; the white bars represent average performance for the last half of each session, Mean B. By comparing adjacent black and white bars, it can be seen that in every instance a within-sessions decrement in blood pressure was observed. Mann–Whitney U-tests between systolic and diastolic Means A and B of the massed sample gave $U = 11$ ($p < 0.01$), and for the comparison of diastolic Means A and B, $U = 19$ ($p < 0.01$). Similarly, statistical comparisons resulted in $U = 6$ ($p < 0.001$) for the spaced group systolic Means A and B, and $U = 17$ ($p < 0.01$) for the diastolic Means A and B. Inspection of the A and B means between groups revealed that the massed group showed a decrement in both systolic and diastolic pressure over ten training sessions, whereas the spaced group showed a systolic pressure decrement in six of the eight sessions, with a similar reduction in diastolic pressure in seven of the eight sessions.

In three of four cases, statistical comparisons between the two groups showed the massed group performed significantly better than the Ss in the spaced training condition (Mann–Whitney comparisons of the systolic Means A yielded $U = 21.5$, $p < 0.05$; of systolic Means B, $U = 15$, $p < 0.02$; of diastolic Means A, $U = 27$, N.S. at the 0.05 level; of diastolic Means B, $U = 24$, $p < 0.05$). In the case of the group which received distributed practice, a follow-up examination was conducted 30 days after the last training session, and these data appear in Fig. 1 as Means A and B on Day 82. Although the systolic pressure showed a return toward basal level, the mean diastolic pressure tended to remain at the levels obtained during the final training session (Day 51).

Since the spaced sample consisted of 11 males and 7 females, a statistical comparison in search of a sex difference in performance was carried out. Comparison of systolic Means A and B failed to show significant differences. Similar comparisons of diastolic Means A and B (see lower half of Fig. 2) revealed a reliable superiority in favor of the female group (Mann–Whitney comparison of Means A: $U = 20.5$, $p < 0.05$; of Means B: $U = 11$, $p < 0.01$).

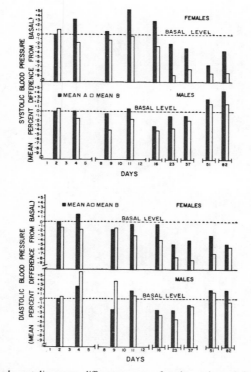

Fig. 2 *Upper panel*: systolic mean difference scores for the male and female sub-samples. *Lower panel*: comparable diastolic difference scores.

DISCUSSION

In general, these data are in agreement with the earlier reports by Miller, Shapiro *et al.*, and Elder *et al.* that essential hypertensive patients can be trained through instrumental conditioning to lower their own blood pressure. Moreover, it was observed that massed training was superior to spaced practice and within the spaced group the females learned the instrumental response somewhat better than the males. A similar female vs male performance comparison within the massed sample was not warranted by sample size and available data.

In general, the results of this study were not as dramatic as the earlier data from the Elder *et al.* experiment. Both studies yielded positive results, but only in the first case did the data satisfy Blanchard and Young's (1973) criterion of at least a 20 per cent change in response before clinical significance has been achieved. A few of the Ss were able to reduce their blood pressure by as much as 20 per cent (see, for example, Ss 9 and 20 in Table 1), but these instances were rare and not typical of either the massed or spaced sample.

There are several plausible reasons why the out-patients in this study did not show a reduction directly comparable to that by the hospitalized patients in the previous study. First, 20 of the 22 patients in this study were on medication, while all of the subjects in the Elder *et al.* experiment were free of medication for hypertension. It is reasonable to assume that anti-hypertensive agents such as reserpine and α-methyl-dopa interfere with instrumental acquisition of autonomic responses in several ways, including the direct or indirect blockage of neural transmission in circuits essential to the development of conditioning. There are some data which indicate that this may be the case (e.g., Elder and McLean, 1974).

Another, and perhaps more important, difference between the two studies was the fact that patients in the hospital sample were admitted to the study only after a thorough examination and appropriate laboratory tests failed to show evidence of secondary hypertension. In contrast, no such preliminary systematic examination and tests were possible in the present study: all patients reported they had been diagnosed as essential hypertensives. Nevertheless, several of the out-patients who volunteered for this study had long histories of hypertension; some of these and undoubtedly some of the others did not fit the criteria for a diagnosis of essential or primary hypertension (Pickering, 1968, 1970). Although it may be likely that instrumentally conditioned reductions in arterial pressure may be possible in cases of secondary hypertension, theoretical considerations suggest that the best results are to be found in patients whose arterial pressure has been elevated by primary rather than secondary sources.

An additional difference between the two studies centers about the fact that Ss in the first study were hospitalized whereas those in the present study were not. There are many data in the learning literature which show that strong drives contribute to the strength of an instrumentally conditioned response. It may be that hospitalization generates a stronger drive to acquire self-control of blood pressure than exists among out-patients. In the first case, Ss' life styles were interrupted completely: in the present study, they were unaffected except for the fact that most patients were taking orally administered anti-hypertensive medication. Stronger drive levels among the out-patient sample may have led to far greater pressure decrements than were observed in this instance.

Finally, the two studies were different in that patients in the first had little opportunity for interpolated activity between sessions, whereas those in this study went about their regular daily routines without interruption. Retroactive interference from interpolated activity may therefore account, perhaps in part, for the superiority of the massed over the spaced samples in the present case, as well as the superiority

Table 1. Description summary of volunteer out-patient sample

S#	Age	Sex	Medication	Basal Pressure Sys	Basal Pressure Dias	Last Training Session Sys	Last Training Session Dias
1	64	F	Reserpine	139	85.5	118	76.1
2	59	M	Aldomet, Diuril	106.7	73.0	127.0	79.0
3	47	M	Valium	165.5	102.7	159.7	98.8
4	52	F	Dyazide	126.0	81.0	116.0	80.2
5	64	M	Esamil	170.0	88.0	157.8	83.4
6	35	M	Alduril	248.5	123.5	204.5	124.0
7	58	M	Raudixn	141.0	89.5	154.1	90.5
8	47	M	Aldolin	123.0	96.0	121.2	92.2
9	80	F	Yes*	175.0	69.5	149.1	57.5
10	80	M	Kerlex	146.5	72.5	153.4	78.5
11	66	F	Salutisen, Becotin	130.5	72.5	122.7	68.3
12	58	F	Diuril	155.0	101.0	138.0	88.1
13	48	F	Alduril	164.1	95.3	159.9	105.1
14	57	M	No	145.5	82.9	147.2	87.9
15	62	F	Diuril	129.7	70.5	117.1	67.2
16	23	M	Meprobamate	124.1	75.9	126.1	67.7
17	24	M	Yes*	141.7	83.1	149.9	79.3
18	28	M	Yes*	123.8	82.2	115.1	77.0
19	29	F	Rauzid	107.3	81.8	114.0	82.9
20	53	M	Hydropress	189.3	93.6	148.7	76.1
21	40	M	Hydropress	133.1	77.4	118.9	70.6
22	31	M	Yes*	141.2	82.1	135.9	73.6

*Form of medication not known

of the Elder *et al.* sample over both groups used in the study. Irrespective of theoretical considerations and explanations, it is clear that instrumental regulation of essential hypertension is more effective with hospitalized than out-patient populations. Even so, these data provide additional support for the idea that essential hypertension can be regulated through instrumental conditioning of the blood pressure response even on an out-patient basis, and that a subject's relative degree of success is statistically predictable.

Department of Psychology,   S. THOMAS ELDER
University of New Orleans,   NANCY K. EUSTIS
New Orleans, La. 70122, U.S.A.

REFERENCES

BENSON H., SHAPIRO D., TURSKY B. and SCHWARTZ G. (1971) Decreased systolic pressure through operant conditioning techniques in patients with essential hypertension. *Science* 173, 740–742.
BLANCHARD E. B. and YOUNG L. D. (1973) Self-control of cardiac functioning: a promise as yet unfulfilled. *Psychol. Bull.* 79, 145–163.
BRENER J. and KLEINMAN R. A. (1970) Learned control of decreases in systolic blood pressure. *Nature* 226, 1063–1064.
ELDER S. T., LEFTWICH D. A. and WILKERSON L. (1974) The role of systolic versus diastolic contingent feedback in blood pressure conditioning. *Psychol. Rec.* (in press).
ELDER S. T. and McLEAN J. H. (1974) Motor and visceral learning in rats injected with varying amounts of reserpine. Paper read at American Psychological Association meeting, New Orleans.
ELDER S. T., RUIZ Z. R., DEABLER H. L. and DILLENKOFFER R. L. (1973) Instrumental conditioning of diastolic blood pressure in essential hypertensive patients. *J. appl. Behav. Anal.* 6, 377–382.
KIMMEL H. D. (1967) Instrumental conditioning of autonomically mediated behavior. *Psychol. Bull.* 67, 337–345.
MILLER N. E. (1969) Learning visceral and glandular responses. *Science* 163, 434–445.
MILLER N. E. (1970) personal communication.
MILLER N. E., DiCARA L. V., SOLOMON H., WEISS J. M. and DWORKIN B. (1970) Learned modifications of autonomic functions: a review and some new data. *Circulat. Res.* 26 and 27, Suppl. I.
PICKERING R. T. (1968) *High Blood Pressure.* Grune and Stratton, New York.
PICKERING R. T. (1970) *Hypertension: Causes, Consequences, and Management.* Churchill, London.
SCHWARTZ G. E. (1972) Voluntary control of human cardiovascular interaction and differentiation through feedback and reward. *Science* 175, 90–93.
SCHWARTZ G. E., SHAPIRO D. and TURSKY B. (1971) Learned control of cardiovascular interaction in man through operant conditioning. *Psychosom. Med.* 33, 57–62.
SHAPIRO D., SCHWARTZ G. E. and TURSKY B. (1972) Control of diastolic blood pressure in man by feedback and reinforcement. *Psychophysiology* 9, 296–304.
SHAPIRO D., TURSKY B., GERSON E. and STERN M. (1969) Effects of feedback and reinforcement on the control of human systolic blood pressure. *Science* 163, 588–589.
SHAPIRO D., TURSKY B. and SCHWARTZ G. E. (1970) Differentiation of heart rate and blood pressure in man by operant conditioning. *Psychosom. Med.* 32, 417–423.

A Simple Feedback 47
System for the Treatment of
Elevated Blood Pressure

Edward B. Blanchard, Larry D. Young, and
Mary Ruth Haynes

A relatively simple, open-loop feedback system for use in teaching patients with elevated blood pressure to lower their blood pressure is described. It is based on once per minute determinations of blood pressure which are read by the experimenter and then presented to the patient by closed circuit television. The procedure is reliable and trouble free. Four single subject design experiments are described in which the elevated systolic blood pressures of four patients suffering from essential hypertension or borderline hypertension were lowered to the normal range. Decrease in blood pressure ranged from 9 to 55 millimeters of mercury. Control conditions in each experiment indicate that the feedback procedure was responsible for the lowering of blood pressure.

Hypertension represents a major health problem (Pickering, 1968). In fact, the Framingham studies have shown that even small increments in elevated blood pressure increase the risk of other types of heart disease. The traditional treatments for elevated blood pressure have included changes in diet and chemotherapy. Recently, a possible alternative treatment mode has emerged in the form of teaching hypertensive patients to control their own blood pressure through biofeedback or other self control techniques. To date, four studies have been reported in which such patients were treated with a biofeedback technique (Benson, Shapiro, Tursky & Schwartz, 1971; Elder, Ruiz, Deabler, & Dillenkoffer, 1973; Miller, 1972; Schwartz & Shapiro, 1973). Unfortunately, as noted by

This research was supported in part by a grant from the National Heart and Lung Institute, 1RO1HL14906. Requests for reprints should be addressed to: Edward B. Blanchard, Psychiatry Department, University of Mississippi Medical Center, Jackson, Mississippi 39216. Graphs of session by session data for each subject are also available upon request.

Reprinted with permission from *Behavior Therapy*, 1975, Vol. 6, No. 2, 241-245.

Brady, Luborsky & Kron (1974), and by Blanchard & Young (1974), all of the studies cited above suffer from one or more faults which preclude drawing definite conclusions about the efficacy of biofeedback treatment of hypertension.

Moreover, most of the feedback systems described to date are relatively complex (Benson, *et al.*, 1971; Miller, 1972; Brener & Kleinman, 1970; Tursky, Shapiro & Schwartz, 1972) and require highly skilled personnel to maintain their operation[1] thus, they are possibly beyond the scope of many less well equipped laboratories. This paper describes a relatively inexpensive, simple, openloop feedback system, based on closed circuit television, which can be used to teach subjects to control their blood pressure and the results of four preliminary experiments of blood pressure self-control designed to confirm the efficacy of the feedback system in patients with elevated blood pressure.

METHOD

Apparatus

Blood pressure was recorded automatically in a relatively standard fashion using (1) a Narco Bio-Systems automatic cuff pump and sphygnomanometer with a microphone for detecting Korotkoff sounds and (2) a Grass 7P8 preamplifier with a Grass Model 7 Polygraph to record the cuff pressure and the Korotkoff sounds. The latter were recorded on the same channel and superimposed on the cuff pressure recording. With this apparatus it was possible to make a determination of blood pressure once every minute.

The novel feature of this study, the feedback system, consisted of a Sony television camera which was permanently focused on a piece of graph paper such that the graphical display completely filled the screen of a television monitor connected to the camera. The television monitor, located in the experimental chamber, was in easy view of the subject; its display constituted the visual feedback of blood pressure.

During feedback conditions the subject's systolic blood pressure was read from the polygraph record by the experimenter as the pressure at which a Korotkoff microphonic was first recorded. The scale of the paper permitted an accuracy of reading within 2.5 mm Hg. Immediately after reading the blood pressure value, the experimenter graphed it as a point. The subject thus received feedback of his blood pressure on a minute-to-minute basis and also had the complete history of his blood pressure during the session available to him throughout the session.

An example of what the subject saw is given in Fig. 1. The top line represented the baseline blood pressure for that session. The two lower lines were values 5 and 10 mm Hg below that value, respectively.

Procedure

All subjects were comfortably seated in a recliner in an air-conditioned, sound attenuated room. Facing them, approximately 8 ft away, was an 18 in. television screen. The blood pressure cuff was connected to the upper left arm and the microphone situated over the brachial artery. Each subject was informed that the experiment was designed to see how well he could learn to control his blood pressure through mental means. They were asked to alter neither their respiration pattern nor their level of muscle tension. Subjects were continually monitored on closed circuit television to detect the latter.

---

[1] Personal communication, D. Shapiro, 1972.

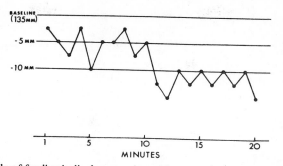

FIG. 1. Example of feedback display seen by subject on television screen. Top line represents sessions baseline blood pressure; two lower lines are 5 and 10 mm Hg below baseline pressure, respectively. No numerical values appear on subject's display.

Each session lasted 40 min. The first 20 min were devoted to allowing the subject to relax and become adapted. During the second 20 min, the experimental trial, various experimental conditions were introduced. Two different experimental conditions were used: *Baseline* in which the subject was asked to attend to ongoing commercial television programs and *Feedback* during which the subject was asked to try to reduce his blood pressure using the feedback display. Viewing of commercial television (usually soap operas or game shows) was used as a control since it was felt subjects would be more likely to attend to this meaningful material than to a random plotting of points, but would not be unduly aroused by it.

Sessions were daily for the most part. Different numbers of sessions were run because different subjects were available for different lengths of time (Table 1).

Subjects

The two hospitalized patients were seen while on a VA psychiatric ward but were referred because of their elevated blood pressure. Medication was held constant during the study.

RESULTS

A systolic blood pressure, averaged over the entire 20 min trial, was calculated for each subject for each session. The feedback condition consistently led to decreases in systolic blood pressure with mean de-

TABLE 1
EXPERIMENTAL RESULTS FOR FOUR SUBJECTS

Subject desig- nation	Demographic data				Average blood pressure for various conditions (mm Hg)					
	Age	Sex	Status	Drugs	Baseline	Feedback	Baseline	Feedback	Follow-up	
									Time	Pressure
S1	50	Male	Hospitalized	5 mg diazepam t.i.d.	149.0 (4)[a]	122.3 (5)	134.3 (3)	—	—	—
S2	25	Male	Outpatient	—	144.0 (4)	135.0 (9)	142.3 (3)	—	—	—
S3	39	Female	Outpatient	—	181.7 (4)	130.3 (9)	146.3 (4)	126.0 (4)	1 wk	129
S4	43	Male	Hospitalized	5 mg diazepam t.i.d.	141.7 (4)	123.0 (8)	124.0 (8)	117.0 (4)	2 wk	125

[a] Numbers in parentheses indicate number of sessions each subject was run in that condition.

creases ranging from 9 to 55 mm Hg (Table 1). The return to Baseline conditions to complete the experimental analysis led to cessation of improvement in all subjects. Reintroduction of Feedback in two cases (S3 and S4) led to further decrease in systolic blood pressure. Follow-up data for two subjects, of an admittedly short duration, revealed some maintenance of the decreases in blood pressure.

Reliability Data

Since this procedure is subject to experimenter error or bias, the reliability of the reading of the polygraph record "on-line" was checked in two ways. For five of the feedback sessions, at the completion of the session, a second experimenter read the polygraph record and separately recorded her readings. Perfect agreement was obtained for 86 of the 100 readings and agreement within 2.5 mm Hg, the limits of accuracy, was obtained in 96 of the 100 readings.

The second check on reliability was to have the same experimenter who read the record "on-line" re-read it several days after the session, for 5 sessions. Perfect agreement was obtained for 75 of the 100 readings and agreement within 2.5 mm of mercury was obtained in 92 of the 100 readings. Time checks on the two experimenters over 100 feedback points revealed that it required an average of 4.1 sec (SD = 0.92) from the time the value appeared on the polygraph until it was plotted for the subject.

DISCUSSION

It is not possible to separate the relative contributions of the various aspects of the treatment package; Subjects received *instructions* to lower their blood pressure and thus may have had different expectations than during baseline phases; and they received *feedback* of their blood pressure; and they possibly tried to *relax* as a strategy for lowering their blood pressure. Brady *et al.* (1974) have shown that relaxation training can have substantial effects. Furthermore, these results should be interpreted somewhat cautiously since (1) no data on generalization of decreases in blood pressure outside of the laboratory were obtained and (2) only minimal follow-up data, as an indication of stability over time, were obtained. In any event, these results, obtained with a simple feedback system, which is relatively maintenance-free and easy to install are comparable to those reported elsewhere in the biofeedback literature.

REFERENCES

BENSON, H., SHAPIRO, D., TURSKY, B., & SCHWARTZ, G. Decreased systolic blood pres
sure through operant conditioning techniques in patients with essential hypertension.
Science, 1971, **173**, 740–742.

BLANCHARD, E. B., & YOUNG, L. D. Clinical applications of biofeedback: A review of evidence. *Archives of General Psychiatry*, 1974, **30**, 573–589.

BRADY, J. P., LUBORSKY, L., & KRON, R. E. Blood pressure reduction in patients with essential hypertension through metronome-conditioned relaxation: A preliminary report.
Behavior Therapy, 1974, **5**, 203–209.

BRENER, J., & KLEINMAN, R. A. Learned control of decreases in systolic blood pressure.
Nature (London), 1970, **226**, 1063–1064.

ELDER, S. T., RUIZ, Z. R., DEABLER, H. S., & DILLENKOFFER, R. L. Decreased systolic
blood pressure through operant conditioning techniques in patients with essential hypertension. *Journal of Applied Behavior Analysis*, 1973, **6**, 377–382.

MILLER, N. E. Postscript. In D. Singh & Morgan, C. T. (Eds.), *Current status of physiological psychology: Readings*. Monterey: Brooks/Cole, 1972. Pp. 245–250.

PICKERING, G. W. *High Blood Pressure* (2nd ed.). New York: Grune and Stratton, 1968.

SCHWARTZ, G. E., & SHAPIRO, D. Biofeedback and essential hypertension: Current findings and theoretical concerns. In L. Birk (Ed.), *Biofeedback: Behavioral Medicine*.
New York: Grune and Stratton, 1973. Pp. 133–143.

TURSKY, B., SHAPIRO, D., & SCHWARTZ, G. E. Automated constant cuff pressure system
to measure average systolic and diastolic blood pressure in man. *IEEE Translations
Biomedical Engineering*, 1972, **19**, 271–276.

VIII

EPILEPSY

Reduction of Seizures and 48 Normalization of the EEG in a Severe Epileptic Following Sensorimotor Biofeedback Training: Preliminary Study

William W. Finley, Hoyt A. Smith, and Murray D. Etherton

Sensorimotor rhythm (SMR) biofeedback training was attempted in a 13-year-old male with frequent epileptic seizures. Prior to training the subject was averaging almost eight clinical seizures an hour. The SMR filter was tuned sharply to 12 ± 1 Hz. Feedback was conducted over approximately six months and continues to the present. In that time the subject's percentage of SMR increased from about 10%, prior to training, to 65% after the 34th training session. Correspondingly, his rate of clinical seizures decreased by a factor of 10 and a significant reduction in percentage of epileptiform discharges was noted. Beginning with trial 35, the subject was provided feedback of epileptiform activity in combination with 12 Hz activity. The combined effect of these two treatment variables was to reduce the trial-to-trial variance in the dependent variables of interest.

1. Introduction

Since Kamiya (1962, 1969) first determined that human subjects could be trained to discriminate and control their own EEG activity, operant conditioning or biofeedback control of central and autonomic nervous system functions has been demonstrated by numerous investigators. An obvious and attractive use for operant conditioning (biofeedback training) of EEG activity would be the suppression of epileptic seizures. By conditioning a patient to suppress the electrical brain pattern associated with the attack, or by conditioning the patient to generate an EEG rhythm incompatible with the seizure pattern, it may be possible to reduce the incidence of seizures. So far, the most promising results have been attained with the latter approach. Sterman and Friar (1972) reported suppression of seizures in an epileptic following operant conditioning of the sensorimotor EEG rhythm. The sensorimotor rhythm (SMR) was first recognized as a distinct EEG rhythm by Sterman and

*Address for correspondence: William W. Finley, Department of Psychophysiological Studies, Children's Medical Center, P.O. Box 7352, Tulsa, Oklahoma 74135, U.S.A.

Reprinted with permission from *Biological Psychology*, 1975, Vol. 2, No. 3, 189-203.

Wyrwicka (1967). Working with the cat, Sterman found a rhythm of 12–14 Hz localized over the sensorimotor cortex, maximal in amplitude and duration only during those periods when the animal was observed to be in a somewhat rigid and motionless posture. Through operant conditioning procedures the animals were encouraged to produce high amplitude, long duration SMR by rewarding them with milk whenever SMR was detected electronically through high 'Q' filters.

The impetus for operant conditioning of the SMR in epileptics came from an EEG and behavioral study conducted by Sterman, LoPresti and Fairchild (1969) on monomethylhydrazine toxicity in the cat. As subjects, Sterman used the same cats he had previously used in operant conditioning of SMR and other EEG rhythms. The most interesting finding of the monomethylhydrazine study was a significant delay of convulsions occurring only in those animals with prior SMR training. All of the other animals immediately succumbed to highly devastating and lethal seizures.

In consideration of these findings, Sterman and Friar (1972) trained a 23-year-old epileptic female to produce the SMR. Prior to training, her attacks, *grand mal* type, occurred irregularly at a rate of about two per month. Within one month of SMR training onset a noticeable decline in the patient's rate of seizures was evident. The following months brought almost a total cessation of reported seizures.

Since the Sterman and Friar study, a number of other investigators have attempted to replicate Sterman's findings. Most notably, Kaplan (1973) employed a PDP-12 computer, programmed to function as a variable band pass filter in an attempt to train two epileptics to generate SMR EEG activity. Unfortunately, an increase in SMR could not be detected in any of her subjects. However, biofeedback training of 9 Hz central mu (which may have included other EEG rhythms) resulted in a reduction of seizure incidence in two of her three subjects. There was no change in production of mu activity. Therefore, she conservatively interpreted her results showing seizure rate reduction as being caused by inadvertently training the subjects to function at a lower level of arousal. Kaplan's inability to replicate Sterman's findings may be due to her use of a digital filter. At the 81st Annual American Psychological Association meeting in Montreal, Quebec, Kaplan conceded that her digital filter may have been too 'strict' or 'critical' in terms of what it would accept as an SMR burst. On the other hand, Sterman's initial filter may have been too liberal in terms of the frequency range which would be passed as SMR. Moreover, both the 'Twin T' band pass filter and the digital filter 'ring' to high voltage spikes often seen in the EEG of epileptic patients. What this means in terms of operant conditioning or biofeedback of SMR is that using a typical band pass or digital filter, one may inadvertently operantly condition an epileptic patient to produce epileptogenic or other high voltage synchronous activity. Although not described in the Sterman and Friar (1972) study,

Sterman did utilize amplitude discrimination circuitry which served to protect the filter from 'ringing' to epileptogenic spikes[1].

In view of the difficulty of Kaplan (1973) in replicating Sterman and Friar's findings of SMR induced seizure suppression, and the question of what other EEG frequencies may have been passed by Sterman's filter, an attempt was made to replicate Sterman and Friar's findings with an extremely 'sharp' very critical 'Twin T' band pass filter, equipped with clipping circuitry.

2. Method

2.1. Patient history

The subject was a 13-year-old white male with a history of convulsive disorder dating back to febrile convulsions noted at the age of 2. By the age of 4 his seizures had been diagnosed as '*petit mal* type' with 3/sec spike-wave discharges noted on the EEG. These seizures were poorly controlled by various medications. A definite worsening of the seizures was noted at the age of 7 when he began to fall with each seizure. With these attacks the subject suddenly loses consciousness and muscle tone. If standing, he falls to the floor where he remains flaccid from 20 sec to 30 min. The average duration of these attacks is approximately 30 sec. His attacks are occasionally associated peripherally with bilateral epileptic myoclonus. His eyes may be observed to roll upwards under partially closed eyelids. At the end of the seizure his return to full awareness is usually very rapid. These attacks have continued to the present time. Prior to onset of the study, he was averaging around 75 falling-type seizures for every 10 hr of wakefulness. The high rate of observed seizures had been proven refractory to all previous therapeutic efforts by neurologists working in his behalf. The onset of one of his seizures is shown in fig. 1.

The trace shown in fig. 1 was recorded just prior to initiation of his SMR training in July 1973. As best as can be determined, at the time of this writing, his attacks may be classified as a prolonged atonic seizure disorder (Gastaut and Broughton, 1972). The subject's medical history is replete with many changes in his dosage levels and medication. Several months prior to initiation of the research described he was placed on Valium, 30 mg, t.i.d., and Phenobarbital, 60 mg, t.i.d. Since he seemed to derive the greatest therapeutic benefit from these two medications he has been maintained on these throughout his study participation. Due to the long standing severity of the subject's seizures his parents have always been extremely careful in making certain their son received the prescribed medication at the proper time. Therefore the question of drug therapy compliance has not been a problem with this subject. Gas–liquid chromatography testings have revealed normal amounts of anticonvulsant medication in the subject's blood serum.

---

[1] In subsequent work reported by Sterman (Sterman, Macdonald and Stone, 1974) these discriminatory circuits are described.

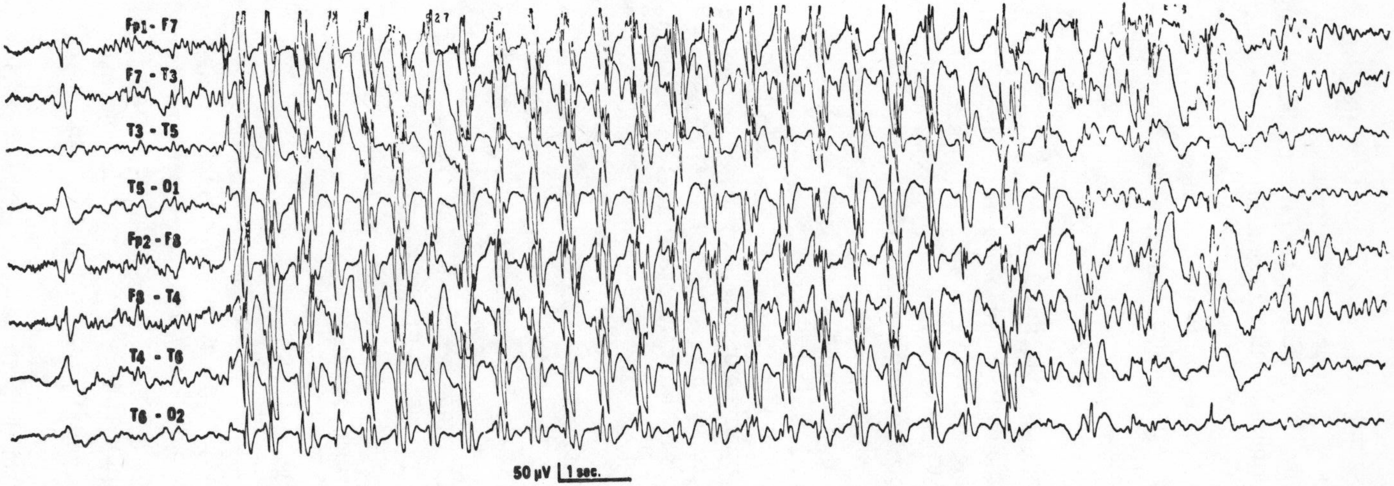

Fig. 1. Onset of atonic seizure in subject D.Y. prior to feedback training.

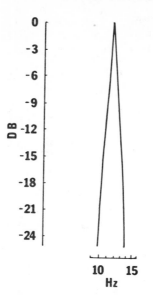

Fig. 2. Frequency–response curve for the sensorimotor rhythm filter. Peak frequency was set at 12 Hz. Clipping circuitry at the filter input accounts for the extreme 'sharpness' of the frequency–response curve. According to the curve an 11 Hz signal would have to achieve a voltage approximately ten times that of the peak frequency in order to activate the feedback apparatus.

2.2. *Apparatus*

The active electrode for EEG biofeedback was placed intermediate between positions C_3 and F_3 (International 10–20 system) and was referred to A_2. The amplified EEG signal was taken from the Grass model 8A5A amplifier from J_7 to the input of two adjustable 'Twin T' band pass filters tuned to 12 ± 1 Hz and 5.5 ± 1.5 Hz. The skirts of the 12 Hz (SMR) filter are quite steep (due to the fact that the input to the filter is clipped) with slopes ranging from 76 to 188 dB/octave. The frequency–response curve of the 12 Hz filter is shown in fig. 2. From J_7, the signal is again amplified, then clipped, and finally sent to the 12 Hz notch filter. Due to the clipping circuitry only signals of 60 µV or less were passed unclipped to the filter. In man the SMR is thought to range between 5 and 15 µV although normative figures have yet to be reported. Most of the time it is not visible in the 'raw EEG'. Fig. 3(a) shows the raw EEG trace in channel 1 with the amplified (gain in channel 2 at peak frequency is 2.4 times greater than in channel 1) SMR frequency appearing in channel 2. A short burst of 12 Hz activity is visible in the unfiltered EEG of channel 1. The position of the 12 Hz state relay is charted in channel 3. The 12 Hz state relay and feedback apparatus were activated by 12 Hz activity equal to or greater than 5 µV. A voltage of 5 µV was chosen for reinforcement because: (1) the patient showed 5 µV, 12 Hz bursts about 10% of the time prior to training; and (2) evidence presented by Sterman indicates that the

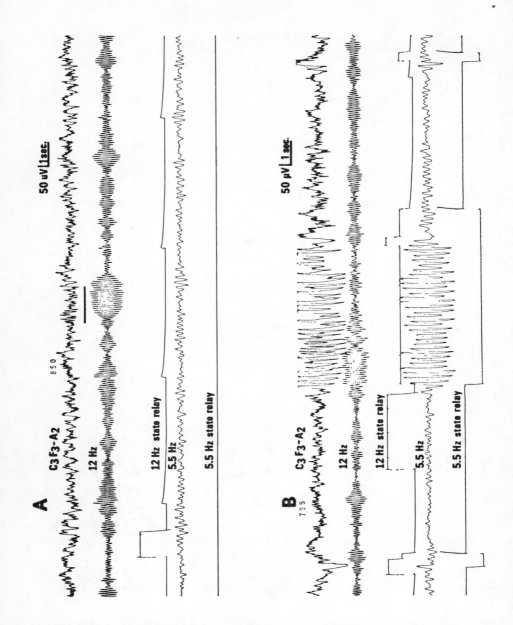

Fig. 3. (a) Training record for 12 Hz feedback. A well-defined burst of 12 Hz activity is underlined in channel 1. The gain in channel 2 is 2.4 times that of channel 1 at 12 Hz. The 12 Hz (SMR) state relay is on when the trace pen of channel 3 is deflected down. The off position is shown when the 12 Hz disappears for at least 0.5 sec causing the state relay pen of channel 3 to be deflected up. (b) Training record showing the occurrence of 5.5 ± 1.5 Hz (epileptiform) discharge occurring simultaneously with a burst of 12 Hz activity shown in channel 2. Note that the position of the 12 Hz state relay pen is intermediate between on and off.

epileptic patient should benefit from reinforcement of 'high voltage' SMR activity. Thus, as high a voltage as possible for this particular patient was selected for reinforcement.

The 5.5 ± 1.5 Hz filter skirts roll off at 20 dB/octave. The purpose of this filter was to monitor the occurrence of epileptiform discharges (spikes, spike-waves, or high voltage slow wave activity) throughout the study and interrupt 12 Hz feedback whenever epileptiform activity passed through or, as in the case of spikes, 'rang' the filter.

When the designated parameters for SMR passed through the 12 Hz filter, the signal was then rectified to operate the state relay which in turn operated the subject's feedback apparatus. The position of the state relay was recorded simultaneously on the oscillograph of the EEG. A flow chart for the feedback system is shown in fig. 4. Examination of the chart reveals that an epileptiform discharge passing through the 5.5 Hz filter would, if occurring in conjunction with 12 Hz activity, interrupt or shut off SMR feedback to the subject. On the oscillograph, this would be observed as a deflection of the SMR state relay pen to a position intermediate between the on and off position. Such a situation may be seen in fig. 3(b). The percentage of time the 12 Hz and 5.5 Hz state relays were on was determined on-line from three General Controls counters. A reading was taken for every 100 sec epoch during resting baselines and feedback training.

Visual feedback in the form of a blue light and an auditory signal, a 1500 Hz 65 dB (ref. 0.0002 dyn/cm²) tone, were activated by the 12 Hz state relay when it moved to the on position. The subject was rewarded for 12 Hz production by receiving one point for every 5 sec of 12 Hz activity he accumulated.

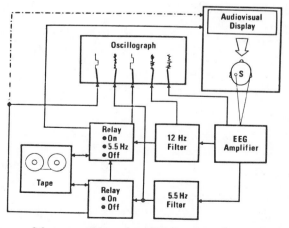

Fig. 4. Flow diagram of the external loop from EEG to feedback display and reinforcement apparatus. The broken line running from the 5.5 Hz state relay to the audiovisual display depicts the loop used to inform the subject of the occurrence of epileptiform activity beginning on trial 35.

A 'beat the clock' game was introduced to encourage him to 'work harder' to produce more SMR. The object of the game was to accumulate a certain number of points before the time on a clock (Gra Lab Universal Timer, model 171) in front of him elapsed. If the subject 'beat the clock' he was immediately rewarded with anywhere from $1.00 to $3.00, depending on the amount offered for that game. Biofeedback training was initiated in July 1973. The subject received 1 hr of feedback training three times a week (Monday, Wednesday and Friday, 10–11 a.m.) from that time to the present. The only exception to this procedure occurred in the first week of October 1973 (trials 29, 30 and 31) when tape recordings of previous training sessions were used to activate the feedback apparatus. Thus, the subject received noncontingent reinforcement or false feedback.

Beginning 15 October 1973 (trial 35) the subject was provided with feedback of his epileptiform activity via the dashed loop shown in the flow chart of fig. 4. Consequently, detection of a spike and/or wave discharge interrupted 12 Hz feedback to the patient and turned on a red light located just above the blue (12 Hz feedback) light. The subject was instructed to attempt to turn off the red light whenever it occurred as he could not accumulate points or win money as long as the red light was illuminated. Consequently, beginning with trial 35, the combination of two treatment effects was being evaluated. In effect, this produced a deliberate confounding of two independent variables.

3. Results

Figure 5 shows the subject's seizure rate per hour, observed in the early evening by his parents at home, across training trials as a function of the percentage of SMR (12 ± 1 Hz) overall. The term 'overall' refers to an average of his percentage of SMR for pre- and postfeedback 5 min baselines and during the actual 12 Hz operant conditioning session. The plots for seizure rate per hour, observed at home, were averaged over two to three evening observations so as to derive three estimates of the patient's seizure activity per week. It should be noted that the parents are extremely reliable, very accurate observers of their son's seizures.

3.1. EEG correlates

The results are reported separately for trials 1–34 and 35–80, since in effect there are two different treatment conditions. During trials 1–34, the subject was provided feedback only of his 12 Hz SMR activity. Beginning with trial 35 the subject was also provided feedback of epileptiform activity by means of a red light. The results for seizure rate per hour (home), shown in the middle graph of fig. 5, and the percentage of SMR (overall) were correlated using the Pearson r. For trials 1–34, $r = -0.42$ ($p < 0.025$); trials 35–80, $r = 0.14$ (NS); trials 1–80, $r = -0.54$ ($p < 0.0005$). Thus, across all trials, as the percentage of SMR increased, the seizure rate per hour decreased.

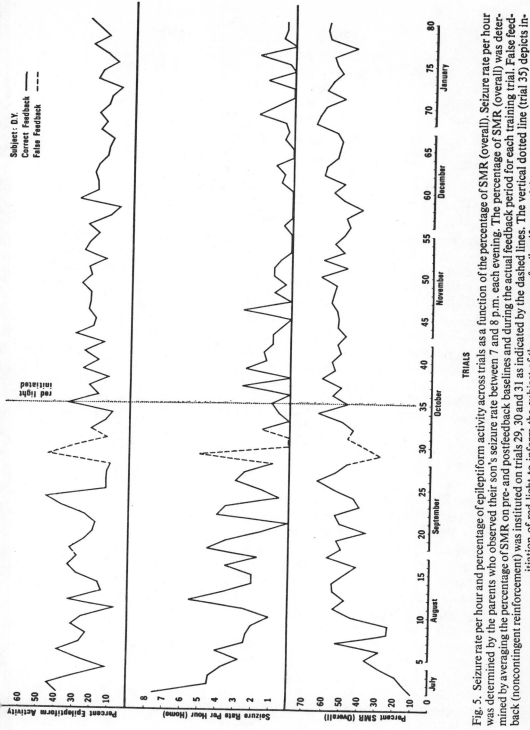

Fig. 5. Seizure rate per hour and percentage of epileptiform activity across trials as a function of the percentage of SMR (overall). Seizure rate per hour was determined by the parents who observed their son's seizure rate between 7 and 8 p.m. each evening. The percentage of SMR (overall) was determined by averaging the percentage of SMR on pre- and postfeedback baselines and during the actual feedback period for each training trial. False feedback (noncontingent reinforcement) was instituted on trials 29, 30 and 31 as indicated by the dashed lines. The vertical dotted line (trial 35) depicts initiation of red light to inform the subject of the occurrence of epileptiform activity.

Table 1.

Correlations of SMR (12 Hz) activity during baseline and
feedback periods with seizure rate per hour (home observations)
and epileptiform activity*.

Variables	Seizure rate/hr (home)	Epileptiform activity
SMR prefeedback baseline	−0.43	−0.46
SMR feedback	−0.52	−0.52
SMR postfeedback baseline	−0.45	−0.54

*All Pearson r correlations statistically significant ($p < 0.0005$; df = 78).

The relationship of pre- and postfeedback SMR, as well as SMR during the feedback training, with seizure rate per hour (home) for trials 1–80 is shown in table 1. It is apparent from the correlations shown in table 1 that SMR activity is negatively correlated with seizure activity at home, not only during the feedback training sessions, but during the resting, baseline periods as well.

Seizure rate per hour (home) was then correlated with trials so as to determine if a progressive linear trend exists towards seizure reduction. A significant negative correlation would show that as trials increase (in number) frequency of clinical seizures decrease. For trials 1–34, $r = -0.54$ ($p < 0.01$); trials 35–80, $r = -0.21$ (NS); trials 1–80, $r = -0.65$ ($p < 0.0005$). Hence, the subject showed a significant tendency at home for seizure rate per hour to decrease with trials. A positive correlation of SMR activity with trials would reflect improvement. For trials 1–34, $r = 0.57$ ($p < 0.01$); trials 35–80, $r = 0.29$ ($p < 0.025$); trials 1–80, $r = 0.64$ ($p < 0.0005$). The observed positive correlation of the percentage of SMR with trials reflects that the subject was improving in his ability to generate 12 Hz activity. A correlation of seizures per hour observed by the subject's parents at home was then performed with seizures observed and recorded during SMR feedback training in the laboratory. A significant correlation of 0.50 ($p < 0.0005$) was found over the $6\frac{1}{2}$ months of training, which suggests that the subject's parents' observational skills were modestly reliable. That the correlation was not higher is undoubtedly due to the fact that the time of day was different; training EEGs being obtained in the late morning and parents' observation during early evening. In an earlier effort to check on the parents' reliability at observing seizures, they were found over a period of 1 hr to agree perfectly (100% agreement) with number of seizures recorded on the EEG. A check on number of EEG recorded seizures with SMR activity revealed a significant negative correlation of −0.50 ($p < 0.0005$) over the 80 trials. A significant reduction in EEG recorded seizures was also noted over the 80 trials ($r = -0.54$, $p < 0.0005$). A significant reduction in EEG recorded seizures was already apparent by trial 34 ($r = -0.41$, $p < 0.01$).

The percentage of SMR (overall) was next correlated with the percentage of epileptiform activity (5.5 ± 1.5 Hz filter), excluding all clinical seizures. The percentage of epileptiform activity is shown in the top graph of fig. 5. For trials 1–34, $r = -0.53$ ($p < 0.01$); trials 35–80, $r = -0.23$ (NS); trials 1–80, $r = -0.54$ ($p < 0.0005$). Table 1 gives the correlations for pre- and postfeedback SMR and feedback SMR with epileptiform activity. Collectively, these results show that as the percentage of SMR increased, the percentage of epileptiform activity decreased. The observed negative relationship between SMR and epileptiform activity was sustained even in the absence of feedback during the resting pre- and postfeedback baseline periods. When the percentage of SMR (overall) was correlated with trials 1–80, holding epileptiform discharges statistically constant, and excluding clinical seizures, a significant partial correlation of 0.56 ($t = 5.94$, df $= 77$, $p < 0.0005$) was found. During trials 1–34, where the greatest rate of improvement occurred, a significant partial correlation of 0.43 ($t = 2.66$, df $= 31$, $p < 0.01$) was apparent. Therefore, one cannot argue that the percentage of SMR increased over trials only because epileptiform discharges were decreasing.

The correlation of epileptiform discharges with trials 1–34 was $r = -0.47$ ($p < 0.01$); trials 35–80, $r = -0.39$ ($p < 0.005$); trials 1–80, $r = -0.39$ ($p < 0.0005$). That the subject's epileptiform activity showed a decrement across trials reflects an improvement in his EEG with training.

3.2. Epileptiform feedback

Inspection of fig. 5 reveals an apparent reduction in trial-to-trial variation of the three variables (SMR, seizure rate and epileptiform activity) occurring at about the time epileptiform activity feedback by red light was initiated. The means and variances of SMR (12 Hz) feedback only, and SMR plus epileptiform activity feedback, are provided in table 2. The F_{max} test revealed statistically significant reductions in variance for all three variables over trials 35–80, compared with trials 1–34. For seizure rate per hour it is apparent that a major

Table 2.

Means and variances of SMR (12 Hz) feedback only (trials 1–34) and SMR plus epileptiform activity feedback (trials 35–80).

	SMR (overall)		Seizures per hour (home)		Epileptiform activity	
	trials		trials		trials	
	1–34	35–80	1–34	35–80	1–34	35–80
$\bar{X}$	42.45	55.22	2.65	0.67	24.67	19.40
S^2	193.94	31.07	3.12	0.58	125.37	37.79
F_{max}	6.24		5.39		3.32	
p	< 0.01		< 0.01		< 0.01	

reason for reduction of variance was that the seizure rate had reached zero per hour on several of the observation periods that the parents had made at home.

3.3. False feedback

On trials 29, 30 and 31 (see fig. 5) noncontingent or false feedback was introduced in place of correct or contingent feedback. Within one day the subject's rate of seizures increased to five per hour. The observed increase in rate of seizures continued for two consecutive days. The subject and his family were unaware of the change in procedure, although they were quite aware of the seizure increase. The increase in seizure rate was preceded by a decrease in the 12 Hz percentage as seen in fig. 5 (dashed lines). The observed effect, although anticipated due to the noncontingent reinforcement, is well within the range of normal fluctuation. Therefore one cannot be certain whether the observed change was merely coincidental. Unexpectedly the subject's SMR percentage began to climb on trials 30 and 31. This was accompanied by an almost complete cessation of the patient's seizures over the next four days (two trials). Reinstitution of contingent or correct feedback resulted in a slight initial decrease in the percentage of SMR followed by a sharp increase on trials 33 and 34. The patient's rate of seizures per hour has remained at a very low level at the time of writing. No further efforts at sham feedback control were made due to concern for the patient.

4. Discussion

The results of this study represent a successful attempt to replicate the findings of Sterman (Sterman and Friar, 1972; Sterman, 1973; Sterman, Macdonald and Stone, 1974). Since the subject was reinforced only for the production of 11–13 Hz, it is probable that the therapeutic effect is due to enhancement of SMR activity. However, these findings do not preclude the possibility that biofeedback training of other EEG frequencies would effect similar therapeutic results. Although Sterman and Friar (1972) presented evidence for the acquisition of SMR within three separate training sessions, the findings of this investigation are the first to show an acquisition curve for SMR across training trials. Of greatest importance is the demonstration of an acquisition curve for seizure rate per hour which is almost a mirror-image of the curve for 12 Hz. A similar relationship with 12 Hz was also found for epileptiform discharges. These results allow us to make at least one important inference about the functional significance of the reinforced pattern of electrical activity. Specifically, these results are consistent with the hypothesis that the 12 Hz is related to processes involved in the inhibition of epileptogenic activity.

Assuming an epileptic seizure represents a massive neural excitatory discharge, it appears that the technique of biofeedback of 12 Hz provides a non-pharmacological tool for altering the balance of excitation–inhibition within the epileptic brain. Precisely how the brain learns or acquires inhibitory activity is of course not known. Acquisition of 12 Hz is, however, quite evident, not only from the acquisition curve seen across trials, but also in that elevated 12 Hz percentage levels are sustained beyond the actual feedback period.

Even when the subject had not experienced actual feedback for as long as 36–60 hr the prefeedback 12 Hz was still negatively correlated with epileptiform and clinical seizure activity. Such a finding may be interpreted as showing that the therapeutic effects do extend beyond the period of 12 Hz feedback training. Correspondingly, the higher the percentage levels of 12 Hz during the feedback and postfeedback baseline conditions, the lower were the subject's rate of seizures at home over the next 36–60 hr intertrial interval. Thus, feedback and postfeedback baseline 12 Hz percentage levels are, to a limited degree, predictive of seizure frequency for our subject. Whether the percentage of 12 Hz is correlated with future seizure'activity in the untrained patient remains to be determined.

Because 12 Hz activity was elevated and seizure activity reduced during the pre- and postfeedback baseline periods, it does not seem likely that attentive factors could be held accountable for inhibiting seizure activity. During the pre- and postfeedback 5 min baseline periods the subject was relatively inattentive and at rest. During the baseline recordings the EEG was closely watched in order to ensure that the subject remained in a state of relaxed wakefulness. Therefore it appears improbable that the subject's epileptic activity was being inhibited merely by sensory stimulation as has been shown in animal models of Guerrero-Figueroa, Barros and DeBalbian Verster (1963).

The introduction of the red light, which informed the subject of his epileptiform activity, is not unlike the attempts by Stevens (Stevens, 1960; Stevens, Milstein and Dodds, 1967) to condition endogenous spike discharges in man. Stevens et al. (1967) have been unable to demonstrate any decrease in the incidence of spontaneous spike or spike-wave activity or effect on seizure rate following the conditioning sessions. In this investigation the red light was not accompanied by an electric shock or other physically aversive stimulus. However, due to the logic circuitry, the subject could not turn on the tone and blue light, indicative of 12 Hz activity, in the presence of the red light. Thus, the subject could not accumulate points during illumination of the red light, making it more difficult to 'beat-the-clock' and win money. Although introduction of the red light in combination with 12 Hz feedback did not appear to cause any further substantial reduction in epileptiform or seizure activity, the combined effect did seem to be associated with a reduction in the trial-to-trial variations of epileptiform, seizure and percentage of 12 Hz activity. It is difficult to be certain, given only one subject, that epileptiform feedback produced the observed change in all three variables. A 'ceiling-effect' might also account for the reduction in variation. As already mentioned in the results section, trial-to-trial variation of seizure rate per hour (home) is, at least in part, due to the attainment of zero seizures per hour.

Clearly, more patients must be trained with the combined feedback procedure before any conclusions can be drawn.

Almost from the very beginnings of the biofeedback movement, clinical applications have been sought for this novel research tool. Even before the term 'biofeedback' was introduced and the technique became almost faddish, feedback procedures were used by physical therapists to restore voluntary control in weak, injured and paralytic muscles by re-establishing functionally certain neural pathways. More recently, new clinical applications have been sought in the field of psychosomatics. Progress in biofeedback application has been claimed for disorders such as essential hypertension, cardiac arrhythmias, tension headaches, and migraine headaches. Now it appears that epilepsy may be added to this growing list. Whether or not all epileptics may experience therapeutic benefits from SMR training remains to be determined. Certainly, not all epileptics are helped by the usual anticonvulsant medications. In the present study, our subject's seizures had never been controlled despite repeated medication changes and readjustments. Problems of drug compliance were not encountered with our subject. The observed reduction in the subject's abnormal slow-wave activity and in polyspike discharges points to the fact that EEG changes were observed in the direction of normalization. Perhaps SMR biofeedback training may find future application in the treatment of an abnormal EEG *per se*.

The findings of this investigation are, of course, limited by a number of methodological inadequacies, foremost of which is that data on only one subject are reported. Other limitations are also apparent. Of the many dependent variables examined, perhaps the most important was number of seizures per hour. The parents' observations of their son's seizure frequency are considered to be quite reliable. However, these observations are 'time-locked' to a particular hour of the day. Furthermore, the subject was very much aware that he was being closely observed. For these reasons extensive monitoring of the EEG through radio telemetry would be highly desirable. Future investigations should also attempt to perform serial power spectral analyses of the subject's EEG both in and out of the biofeedback training condition.

A problem central to the use of SMR feedback in the human is that this rhythm, although clearly defined in cats by Sterman and Wyrwicka (1967), has not been adequately identified in humans; in particular its relationship to mu (9 Hz) has not been described. The location and frequency characteristics of SMR have much in common with mu activity and also are similar to faster alpha rhythm components as well. Thus another possibility is that alpha rhythm feedback from the central areas of the human cortex may be of therapeutic benefit to the epileptic patient.

Just how much improvement can be expected to occur as a result of SMR training is not known. Our subject is still severely handicapped by his epilepsy. Yet, as of this writing, 20 May 1974, his percentage of 12 Hz, SMR activity continues to increase while his seizure rate and EEG tracings continue to show improvement. On 25 October 1973 our subject's parents observed for the first time in six years two seizures in which the subject maintained his posture while standing and did not fall. Since then, additional non-falling seizures have been observed. Thus, a reasonable goal of biofeedback therapy for this subject would be to reduce the incidence of his falling seizures.

It is important to emphasize the possibility that the results reported may be highly idiosyncratic to the individual who served as the subject of the present investigation. Hence, caution should be exercised in the interpretation and generalization of these findings. However, notwithstanding, it can be concluded that the results of two separate studies with a total of five independent cases all indicate that biofeedback training of 11–14 Hz activity may lead to a reduction of epileptic seizure activity. The findings of this single case study showed that the frequency of the subject's seizures varied inversely with his percentage of biofeedback induced SMR activity. Furthermore, the subject showed similar improvement in his EEG since the percentage of epileptiform activity decreased as the number of SMR training trials and the percentage of SMR increased.

Although the basis for these effects cannot be specified at this time, it seems probable that functional changes associated with the voluntary enhancement of the SMR were taking place within the central nervous system.

References

Gastaut, H. and Broughton, R. (1972). *Epileptic seizures.* Charles C. Thomas: Springfield, Illinois.

Guerro-Figueroa, R., Barros, A. and DeBalbian Verster, F. (1963). Some inhibitory effects of attentive factors on experimental epilepsy. *Epilepsia,* **4,** 225–240.

Kamiya, J. (1962). *Conditioned discrimination of the EEG alpha rhythm in humans.* Abstract of paper presented at the Western Psychological Association.

Kamiya, J. (1969). Operant control of the EEG alpha rhythm and some of its reported effects on consciousness. In: Tart, C. T. (Ed.) *Altered States of Consciousness.* Wiley: New York, 507–517.

Kaplan, B. J. (1973). *EEG biofeedback and epilepsy.* Unpublished doctoral dissertation, Brandeis University.

Sterman, M. B. (1973). Neurophysiologic and clinical studies of sensorimotor EEG biofeedback training: some effects on epilepsy. In: Birk, L. (Ed.) *Seminars in Psychiatry.* Grune and Stratton, **5,** 507–525.

Sterman, M. B. and Friar, L. (1972). Suppression of seizures in an epileptic following sensorimotor EEG feedback training. *Electroencephalography Clinical Neurophysiology,* **33,** 89–95.

Sterman, M. B., LoPresti, R. W. and Fairchild, M. D. (1969). *Electroencephalographic and behavioral studies of monomethylhydrazine toxicity in the cat.* Technical Report AMRL-TR-69-3, Air Force Systems Command, Wright-Patterson Air Force Base, Ohio.

Sterman, M. B., Macdonald, L. R. and Stone, R. K. (1974). Biofeedback training of the sensorimotor EEG rhythm in man: effects on epilepsy. *Epilepsia,* in press.

Sterman, M. B. and Wyrwicka, W. (1967). EEG correlates of sleep: evidence for separate forebrain substrates. *Brain Research,* **6,** 143–163.

Stevens, J. R. (1960). Electroencephalographic studies of conditioned cerebral response in epileptic subjects. *Electroencephalography Clinical Neurophysiology,* **12,** 431–444.

Stevens, J. R., Milstein, V. M. and Dodds, S. A. (1967). Endogenous spike discharges as conditioned stimuli in man. *Electroencephalography Clinical Neurophysiology,* **23,** 57–66.

Biofeedback in Epileptics: Equivocal Relationship of Reinforced EEG Frequency to Seizure Reduction

Bonnie J. Kaplan

INTRODUCTION

In 1963 Brazier described a 13- to 14-Hz EEG rhythm recorded from sensorimotor cortex in cats. When operantly conditioned, this sensorimotor rhythm (SMR) was accompanied by behavioral immobility and correlated with increased resistance to seizure-inducing compounds (Roth et al., 1967; Wyrwicka and Sterman, 1968; Sterman et al., 1969). The altered seizure threshold in SMR-trained cats caused Sterman and his colleagues to consider the potential application of such training in human epileptics, and they have since used the biofeedback techniq: e to reinforce 12- to 14-Hz activity in four patients (Sterman and Friar, 1972; Sterman et al., 1974).[1]

Although all four patients have experienced a reduction in seizure incidence which the researchers have attributed to EEG biofeedback, the reported evidence for a change

in 12- to 14-Hz activity is less compelling than the evidence of clinical improvement. Without a correlated change in the EEG, it is difficult to make inferences about the cause of seizure reduction. Observation of cat SMR is relatively easy because it is a dominant rhythm, but detection of 12- to 14-Hz activity in humans is complicated by the presence of other activity such as alpha. An increase in 12- to 14-Hz activity could be demonstrated convincingly with objective evidence such as a significant increase in the energy in that range of the EEG or an increase in the percentage of time that activity is present, but the data reported by Sterman et al. (1974) have not been subjected to such statistical analysis.

Another problem is that the functional correlate of SMR in humans is not clear. Although Sterman and his colleagues initially believed that cat SMR was the analog of human central mu (also called wicket rhythm or *rhythme en arceau*; Gastaut, 1952; Gastaut, et al., 1952), they now believe that 12- to 14-Hz activity in humans exists as a unique, low-amplitude rhythm recorded by scalp electrodes from Rolandic cortex. In addition, whereas the lower frequency $(9 \pm 2$ Hz) central mu blocks to contralateral movement, it is said that human SMR does not (Sterman et al., 1974). The problem is confounded further by the work of Finley (1974) in which successful biofeedback training of Rolandic activity referred to as SMR was correlated with a

*Present address: Neuropsychology Laboratory, Veterans Administration Hospital, West Haven, Connecticut 06516, and Department of Neurology, Yale University School of Medicine, New Haven, Connecticut 06510.

Key words: *Epilepsy — EEG — Biofeedback*

[1] Subsequent references in this paper will use the term "SMR" to refer only to the 12- to 14-Hz rhythm in cats.

Reprinted with permission from *Epilepsia*, 1975, Vol. 16, 477-485.

decrease in seizure incidence in one patient; however, this trained rhythm did block to contralateral fist-clenching (Finley, *personal communication*). Because of the apparent confusion with respect to the nature of the EEG activity being trained and the difficulty in drawing conclusions about the cause of the reported improvements in seizure rates, the present experiments were designed as a further test of the efficacy of biofeedback techniques in seizure control.

Experiment 1 was a replication of the Sterman and Friar study (1972): subjects were given biofeedback training of 12- to 14-Hz EEG activity recorded from the Rolandic area. This attempt differed from Sterman and Friar's study in two ways: (1) a combination analog and digital method of filtering was used to reduce the possibility of accidentally reinforcing irrelevant EEG signals; (2) a method of quantifying power in the 12- to 14-Hz band was developed in order to provide an objective measure of EEG change.

Experiment 2 used the methods of Experiment 1 except that the EEG frequency range selected was 6 to 12 Hz, so that the dominant Rolandic activity was reinforced for each of the patients. The rationale for training on this frequency range (hereafter referred to as dominant central activity) was based on several factors. Some of the early spectra showed an unexplained increase in power in lower frequencies (Sterman, 1972), so Experiment 2 was designed to determine whether intentional training of such activity might reduce seizures. In addition, training a frequency range known to occur during normal, interictal periods provided a test of the possibility that training on any nonseizure EEG activity would help to normalize the EEG. Finally, although none of the three patients in Experiment 2 had a clear mu-shaped rhythm, it was appealing to train a frequency range which would encompass synchronous activity in the approximate range predicted for central mu, particularly since several additional researchers have recently interpreted mu to be the human analog of feline SMR (Rougeul et al., 1972; Lanoir, 1973).

METHOD

Scalp EEGs from the Rolandic area of the right hemisphere were recorded on a six-channel Grass Model V polygraph, and simultaneously on a Hewlett-Packard FM tape recorder. Electrode placement in Experiment 1

was referential (1 cm posterior to C4 referred to A1). Although Experiment 2 began with the same placement, it was later changed to a bipolar recording (from C4 to about 2 cm anterior to P4) which was thought to maximize the recorded amplitude of central mu. The signal was prefiltered by an analog filter (Krohn Hite, 24 db/octave rolloff) and was subsequently passed to a PDP-12 computer programmed to function as a digital filter based on peak and trough detection. Both filters set to the identical bandpass (approximately 12 to 14 Hz in Experiment 1 and 6 to 12 Hz in Experiment 2). As shown in the frequency response curves (see insets in Figs. 1 and 3), the digital portion of this system allowed a rapid transition from maximum response to absolutely zero response without the rolloff characteristics and tails typical of analog filters.

When the appropriate EEG frequency occurred, the PDP-12 triggered a relay-controlled feedback device (e.g., a tone, music, colored lights, television, tape recorder, or slide projector) which was chosen according to the preference of each patient. Patients were told that the feedback signals represented EEG activity and that they should try to increase the amount of feedback. Feedback was given in an 8 × 9 foot audiometric chamber where the patient sat in a reclining chair. The sessions, which occurred approximately three times per week, consisted of 2 min of eyes closed baseline (EC), 2 min of eyes open baseline (EO), 30 min of feedback training (FB), and a repeat of EC and EO baselines.

The patients chosen were adults under age 35, with seizures which were uncontrolled by anticonvulsant medication; clinical data are summarized in Table 1. Although four patients participated in the study, the total N was five because one patient (SM) participated in both experiments, which ran consecutively. Clinical EEGs (assessed by a clinical electroencephalographer) and serum levels of barbiturates and diphenylhydantoin were determined prior to biofeedback and periodically during the course of the study.

RESULTS

Three measures of biofeedback efficacy were used: clinical evaluation of EEGs, daily seizure incidence as reported by the patient, and EEG power spectral analysis. Power spectra were computed by the OLFFT1 program (DECUS Library No. 12-63), averaging samples of 4-sec

TABLE 1. *Summary of clinical data and seizure rates*

Patient data		Patient		
	JS	SM	AS	MD
Age and sex	21, F	30, F	29, M	20, F
Most frequent type of seizure	grand mal	akinetic	petit mal	psychomotor
Seizure history (years)	14	21	12	6
Medications	diphenylhydantoin (300 mg) phenobarbital (300 mg) ethosuximide (750 mg) acetazolamide (750 mg)	diphenylhydantoin (250 mg, 300 mg, 300 mg) phenobarbital (97.2 mg, 97.2 mg, 97.2 mg) primidone (875 mg, 750 mg, 125 mg) diazepam (0 mg, 0 mg, 20 mg)	diphenylhydantoin (300 mg) phenobarbital (100 mg) primidone (500 mg)	diazepam (15 mg) mephobarbital (100 mg) carbamazepine (400 mg) acetazolamide (750 mg)
Average seizure frequency				
Prior to biofeedback	2.3/month (25)a	12/day (18) estimate	12/day (14) estimate	3.5/day (51)
During Experiment 1	1.8/month (20)	13.4/day (14)	b	2.5/day (26)
During Experiment 2	b	7.9/day (20)	2.8/day (27) [3.7/day (7)]c	b
After termination of study	3/month (10)	6.0/day (8)	0.01/day (36) [0.1/day (36)]	1.9/day (60)

Three dosage levels are listed for SM; see text for explanation.
aNumber in parentheses = number of weeks from which average is calculated.
bDid not participate.
cNumbers in brackets refer to "little" seizures; see text.

epochs selected from the first and second halves of the sessions of tape-recorded EEG. Since power in the total range calculated by this program (0 to 31.75 Hz, hereafter referred to as "total power") exhibited much day-to-day variation, an index of relative power was derived by dividing power in the experimental range (12-14 Hz in Experiment 1 or 6-12 Hz in Experiment 2) by the total power. This ratio provided a measure of power in the relevant frequency range which was less sensitive to day-to-day fluctuations.

Power spectra were computed for EEG epochs sampled and averaged under three conditions: (1) baseline EC, (2) baseline EO, and (3) during FB. The results from the EC and EO conditions paralleled the FB data; the one exception (for patient MD) will be discussed. Two-tailed t-tests were used to determine whether changes in power spectra were significant; all differences reported as reliable met the criterion of $p \leqslant 0.05$.

Experiment 1:

There were no changes in the clinical EEGs or seizure rates which could be attributed to biofeedback training of 12- to 14-Hz activity. JS: There were no changes in the clinical EEGs, in seizure incidence, or in 12- to 14-Hz activity for JS. The relative amount of 12- to 14-Hz activity remained constant at about 3% of the total power (Fig. 1).

SM: There were no changes in SM's clinical EEGs or in the relative amount of 12- to 14-Hz activity (about 4% of total power; Fig. 2). SM was the only patient in the study whose medications were changed during the course of the study; they were changed once during each experiment for clinical reasons. The change in seizure rate can more reasonably be attributed to the medication change than to the feedback training.

Experiment 2:

Changes seen in seizure rates were not correlated with any learning in the 6- to 12-Hz range of the EEG; consequently, improved clinical conditions could not be attributed to EEG biofeedback.

SM: The medication change which occurred during this experiment was followed by an improvement in seizure rate (Fig. 3). No changes occurred in her clinical EEG or in her dominant central activity.

AS: There were no changes in his clinical EEGs or power spectra (Fig. 4). Three months after the study began, AS began to discriminate between "big" and "little" petit mal seizures. Although the latter were very difficult to detect, he made an effort to quantify them. The incidence of "big" seizures decreased from a prefeedback baseline of approximately 12 per day to an average of fewer than one per day. Decreases in the smaller absences were also

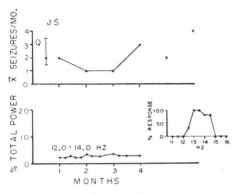

FIG. 1. Seizure incidence and power in the 12-14 Hz range for JS. Q = the median and interquartile range of seizures for 25 weeks preceding Experiment 1. X indicates the number of seizures for 2 months after termination of the study. Inset represents response of filtering system when set for 12-14 Hz range.

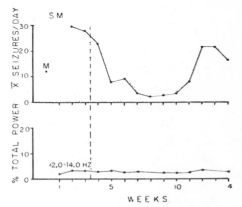

FIG. 2. Seizure incidence and power in the 12-14 Hz range for SM during Experiment 1. Dashed vertical line represents medication change. M = estimated mean number of seizures per day for 18 weeks preceding Experiment 1.

reported (Table 1 and Fig. 4). Because his clinical condition improved over the course of the study, even though there was no correlated change in the EEG, laboratory sessions were ended gradually. For 9 months he had one session of laboratory training approximately every 2 weeks. In addition he has been using a portable machine (Cyborg Corporation, Model J131 EEG machine) at home since April 1973 (week 20 in Fig. 4). Although laboratory sessions have now ended, he continues to use the portable machine on the average of twice a week. His interictal EEG is normal; the use of the portable equipment therefore poses no danger of accidentally reinforcing paroxysmal activity.

MD: There was one change in the experimental situation which was correlated with a change in power distribution in MD's spectra (Fig. 5). After a few weeks of the usual training situation (with eyes open), it was decided that she would be more relaxed sitting with her eyes closed in the dark. From that point on, her feedback consisted of taped music of her own selection (the volume of which was diminished in the absence of 6- to 12-Hz activity), and the power of her dominant central activity increased significantly. Since the amount of 6- to 12-Hz activity during FB increased only into the region of EC (as illustrated in Fig. 5) and did not surpass it, the change probably reflects normal habituation, particularly increased alpha due to closing her eyes.

In addition to the change in power spectra,

MD experienced a decrease in seizures. For the year immediately preceding biofeedback training, she had an average of 3.5 seizures per day. This incidence dropped to fewer than one per day for the last 6 weeks of laboratory training sessions. MD has also developed the ability to detect the beginning of a seizure occasionally (an aura which she cannot verbalize) and is sometimes able to block it. She reports that she was not able to block seizures prior to the biofeedback experience. Finally, MD's clinical EEG changed. Whereas hyperventilation previously activated paroxysmal discharge, after 4 months of biofeedback training this no longer occurred.

Follow-up treatment for MD did not include the use of a portable unit since she has occasional interictal spike-slow wave discharges which might be reinforced accidentally. Instead, she is working with a tape recording of deep muscle relaxation exercises (Jacobson, 1938).

DISCUSSION

The data of Experiment 1 are clear: biofeedback training in two epileptics resulted in no clinical improvement, no change in the proportion of 12- to 14-Hz activity present in the power spectra, and no change in the clinical EEGs. This may mean that in these two

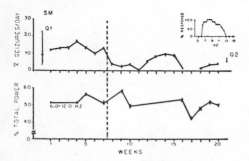

FIG. 3. Seizure incidence and power in the 6-12 Hz range for SM during Experiment 2. Dashed vertical line represents medication change. Q1 = median and interquartile range for the 14 weeks of Experiment 1. Q2 = median and interquartile range for 8 weeks after termination of Experiment 2. Inset shows response of filtering system when set for 6- to 12-Hz range.

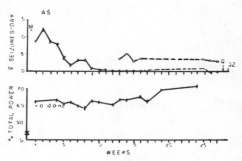

FIG. 4. Seizure incidence and power in the 6-12 Hz range for AS. Dashed horizontal line indicates data not available. ●———● = incidence of "big" seizures; ○———○ = incidence of "little" seizures (see text). M = estimated mean number of seizures per day for 14 weeks preceding Experiment 2. Q1 = median and interquartile range for 28 weeks of bimonthly followup laboratory sessions. Q2 = median and interquartile range for 9 weeks after termination of all laboratory sessions.

particular patients no such rhythm could be trained, or it may mean that there is no distinct, trainable human Rolandic rhythm in the 12- to 14-Hz range. A recent attempt to train 12- to 14-Hz activity in three normal subjects was also unsuccessful (Kuhlman, 1974). Because central mu may be the human analog of SMR, Kuhlman also trained the mu rhythm in three normal subjects. In all three subjects, training resulted in a significant increase in central mu.

Interpretation of Experiment 2 is difficult because of the lack of correlation among the three dependent variables. No significant changes in 6- to 12-Hz activity occurred which could be attributed to biofeedback training. The only clinical EEG change was MD's decreased response to hyperventilation, which her neurologist interprets to be a reflection of developmental changes. Decreases in seizure incidence occurred for AS and MD which could not be attributed to medication changes, and MD reports a new ability to block some of her seizures. These changes in seizure incidence were not accompanied by any detectable changes in the EEG which could be attributed to biofeedback training.

A possible explanation for the decreased seizure rates is that during the research, patient compliance in taking prescribed medications improved. This interpretation is not appropriate here because all serum levels were within therapeutic range (10 to 25 μg/ml for barbiturates; 11 to 21 μg/ml for diphenylhydantoin).

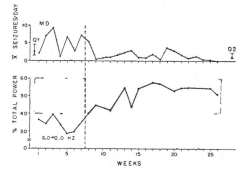

FIG. 5. Seizure incidence and power in the 6-12 Hz range for MD. Dashed vertical line indicates change in experimental condition (see text). Shaded area represents interquartile range of EC condition. Q1 = median and interquartile range for 51 weeks preceding Experiment 2. Q2 = median and interquartile range for 60 weeks after termination of study.

Another possible explanation for the apparent clinical improvement is suggested by the well-recognized difficulty in obtaining accurate seizure reports. It is possible that the patients may have denied some seizures, motivated by their desire to get well and to "please" the experimenter. The accuracy of seizure reports is partly a function of the type of seizure experienced. MD's seizures are quite apparent to her, easily reported, and verified by friends and family. JS and SM have very obvious seizures and their records received continual verification from family. AS's reports may be less accurate than those of the other patients; his absences are sometimes difficult to detect and he lives alone, thus precluding family verification.

Other variables which can be responsible for changes in seizure activity are usually grouped under the rubric of "placebo effect." The biofeedback setting with its impressive array of electronic instrumentation and intensive interaction with the experimenter may provide an excellent background for the maximization of placebo effects. In order to sort out the effects of EEG biofeedback from placebo effects, a true extinction period would require continuing to provide the biofeedback setting, but switching to random or noncontingent reinforcement. The extinction period used by Sterman and his colleagues confounded these variables by terminating the patients' visits to the laboratory (Sterman et al., 1974). An appropriate extinction period was impossible in the present research. AS's use of the portable unit and MD's relaxation exercises would have had to end; the explanation for suspending these home activities would have been very difficult to provide. The only true extinction period used to date appears to be Finley's (*personal communication*) in which noncontingent reinforcement was provided in the feedback setting without the knowledge of the patient or his family. In this one patient, extinction was said to result in that the EEG rhythm previously reinforced decreased in amount and seizure activity increased.

It is this author's view that if a clinical change is to be attributed to the training of a physiological variable, some statistically significant change in that variable should be apparent. If such a demonstration is not possible, the issue of causality remains an open question. The results of the present work must be interpreted in light of the lack of change in the EEG activity being trained, and this same problem of demonstrating a correlated EEG change applies to the work of Sterman and his colleagues.

The most reasonable explanation for the improved clinical condition of AS and MD is that they learned to function at a lower level of arousal. Both AS and MD experience elevated seizure rates during stress. MD, for instance, often experiences psychomotor seizures when talking or worrying about school work. Both AS and MD spontaneously reported that the biofeedback situation has provided them with a new skill of relaxing. For AS the biofeedback situation is one of relaxed but focused attention. MD felt that general relaxation increased as she learned to sit quietly in a dark room several times a week. Therefore, it seems likely that AS and MD learned some relaxation techniques which are responsible for their improved clinical condition. However, it should be emphasized that although relaxation techniques are known to be beneficial for certain patients (Lennox, 1960), sensory stimulation has been just as helpful for others (Ounsted et al., 1966).

cortex rolandique, était accompagné d'une diminution de la fréquence des crises chez quatre sujets épileptiques (Sterman et al., 1974). Un tel "biofeedback training" des activités à 12-14 Hz effectué chez deux sujets épileptiques est resté sans effet sur les EEG, le nombre des crises et la proportion des spectres de puissance de l'EEG pour les fréquences intéressées par l'apprentissage. Ensuite, le même traitement a été appliqué aux activités rolandiques à 6-12 Hz chez trois épileptiques. Chez deux sujets, les crises ont diminué sans changement du traitement. Puisqu'on n'a pas trouvé d'apprentissage pour l'activité à 6-12 Hz cette diminution des crises ne peut pas être attribuée au biofeedback EEG. On suggère qu'à travers la situation de biofeedback on a réalisé chez ces deux patients une nouvelle forme de relaxation. En tenant compte d'une part de l'absence de modifications EEG statistiquement valables après le biofeedback EEG et d'autre part du nombre réduit de sujets jusqu'à maintenant entraînés, il semble raisonnable d'avoir une attitude réservée tant qu'on ne pourra pas établir un rapport de causalité entre cette méthode et les variations de la fréquence des crises.

(C. A. Tassinari, *Marseilles*)

SUMMARY

It has been reported that biofeedback training of 12- to 14-Hz activity recorded over Rolandic cortex was accompanied by a reduction in seizure incidence in four human epileptics (Sterman et al., 1974). Biofeedback training of 12- to 14-Hz activity was provided for two epileptics and had no effect on clinical EEGs, seizure incidence, or proportion of EEG spectral power in the frequency range being trained. Subsequently, biofeedback training of 6- to 12-Hz Rolandic activity was provided for three epileptics. Two patients experienced reductions in seizure not accompanied by medication changes. Since no learning of 6- to 12-Hz activity was detected, the changes in seizure incidence are not attributed to EEG biofeedback. It is suggested that the experience in the feedback setting provided these two patients with new techniques of relaxation. In view of the lack of statistical evidence of EEG changes following EEG biofeedback and the small number of patients trained to date, it appears wise to maintain a cautious attitude until the issue of causality is clear.

RÉSUMÉ

On a rapporté que le "biofeedback training" des activités à 12-14 Hz enregistrées sur le

RESUMEN

Se ha publicado que el entrenamiento de la bioretroalimentación (biofeedback) de la actividad de 12-14 Hz registrada en la corteza rolándica, se acompañaba de una reducción de la incidencia de ataques en cuatro enfermos epilépticos (Sterman y col., 1974). El entrenamiento de la retroalimentación biológica de la actividad de 12-14 Hz se realizó en dos epilépticos sin que se produjeran modificaciones en los EEGs, incidencia de ataques o en la proporción del espectro del EEG en los márgenes de la frecuencia sometida a entrenamiento. Seguidamente el entrenamiento por biofeedback de la actividad rolándica de 12-14 Hz se realizó en tres enfermos epilépticos. En dos enfermos, sin modificar la medicación, los ataques disminuyeron en número. Puesto que no se detectó aprendizaje de la actividad de 6-12 Hz, la reducción de la incidencia de ataques no se atribuyó a la bioretroalimentación electroencefalográfica. Como sugerencia se propone que en estos dos enfermos la técnica de bioretroalimentación proporcionó nuevos procedimientos de relajación. En vista de la falta de evidencia estadística de alteraciones electroencefalográficas tras la bioretroalimentación del EEG y el reducido número de enfermos entrenados hasta la fecha, parece lógico mantener una actitud cautelosa hasta que se aclare el tema de causalidad.

(A. Portera Sanchez, *Madrid*)

ZUSAMMENFASSUNG

Es ist berichtet worden, dass ein Biofeedback-Training von 12-14 Hz-Aktivität über dem Rolandi'schen Cortex bei 4 anfallskranken Patienten mit einer Reduktion der Anfallshäufigkeit einherging (Sterman u.a., 1974). Ein Biofeedback-Training der 12-14 Hz-Aktivität wurde bei 2 Anfallskranken durchgeführt und zeigte keine Auswirkungen auf das klinische EEG, die Anfallshäufigkeit oder den Anteil des trainierten Frequenzbereichs am Powerspektrum des EEG. Daraufhin wurde ein Biofeedback-Training mit 6-12 Hz-Aktivität über der Rolandi'schen Region bei 3 Anfallskranken durchgeführt, Bei 2 Patienten wurden die Anfälle reduziert ohne dass die Medikation geändert worden war. Da ein Lerneffekt der 6-12 Hz-Aktivität nicht entdeckt wurde, kann die Veränderung der Anfallshäufigkeit nicht dem EEG-Biofeedback zugeschrieben werden. Es wird vermutet, dass die Erfahrungen dieser beiden Patienten mit der Feedback-Methode ihnen neue Möglichkeiten der Entspannung vermittelten. Angesichts fehlender statistisch nachgewiesener Veränderungen im EEG nach Biofeedback und der kleinen Anzahl von Patienten, die bis heute trainiert wurde, scheint es angebracht, zurückhaltend zu sein, bis die kausalen Zusammmenhänge klar sind.

(D. Scheffner, *Heidelberg*)

ACKNOWLEDGMENTS

The author wants to acknowledge the clinical advice of Dr. G. Gascon and the general assistance of Dr. T. Mulholland and Messrs. D. Goodman, R. Boudrot, and P. Eberlin.

REFERENCES

Brazier MAB. The problem of periodicity in the electroencephalogram: Studies in the cat. *Electroencephalogr Clin Neurophysiol* 15:287-298, 1963.

Chase MH and Harper RM. Somatomotor and visceromotor correlates of operantly conditioned 12-14 c/sec sensorimotor cortical activity. *Electroencephalogr Clin Neurophysiol* 31:85-92, 1971.

Finley WW. Reduction of seizures and normalization of the EEG in a severe epileptic following sensorimotor biofeedback training. *Proceedings of the Biofeedback Research Society Meeting*, Colorado Springs, Colorado, 1974.

Gastaut H. Etude électrocorticographique de la réactivité des rythmes rolandiques. *Rev Neurol* 87:176-182, 1952.

Gastaut H, Terzian H and Gastaut Y. Etude d'une activité électroencéphalographique méconneu: "Le rythme rolandique en arceau." *Marseille Méd* 89:296-310, 1952.

Howe RC and Sterman MB. Cortical-subcortical EEG correlates of suppressed motor behavior during sleep and waking in the cat. *Electroencephalogr Clin Neurophysiol* 32:681-695, 1972.

Jacobson E. *Progressive Relaxation*. University of Chicago Press, Chicago, Illinois, 1938.

Kuhlman WN. Topography and long term feedback training of sensorimotor area EEG activity in normal human subjects. *Proceedings of the Biofeedback Research Society Meeting*, Colorado Springs, Colorado, 1974.

Lanoir J. Cortical rhythms during intermediate sleep stages in the chronically implanted unrestrained cat. *Rev EEG Neurophysiol (Paris)* 3:46-53, 1973.

Lennox WG. *Epilepsy and Related Disorders:* Volume One. Little, Brown, Boston, 1960, 574 pp.

Ounsted C, Lee D and Hutt SJ. Electroencephalographic and clinical changes in an epileptic child during repeated photic stimulation. *Electroencephalogr Clin Neurophysiol* 21:388-391, 1966.

Roth SR, Sterman MB and Clemente CD. Comparison of EEG correlates of reinforcement, internal inhibition, and sleep. *Electroencephalogr Clin Neurophysiol* 23:509-520, 1967.

Rougeul A, Letalle A and Corvisier J. Activité rhythmique du cortex somesthésique primaire en relation avec l'immobilité chez le chat libre éveillé. *Electroencephalogr Clin Neurophysiol* 33:23-39, 1972.

Sterman MB. Studies of EEG biofeedback training in man and cats. *Highlights of 17th Annual Conference: VA Cooperative Studies in Mental Health and Behavioral Sciences*, 1972, pp 50-60.

Sterman MB and Friar L. Suppression of seizures in an epileptic following sensorimotor EEG feedback training. *Electroencephalogr Clin Neurophysiol* 33:89-95, 1972.

Sterman MB, LoPresti RW and Fairchild MD. *Electroencephalographic and Behavioral Studies of Monomethyl Hydrazine Toxicity in the Cat*. Technical Report AMRL-TR-69-3, Air Systems Command, Wright-Patterson Air Force Base, Ohio, 1969.

Sterman MB, Macdonald LR and Stone RK. Biofeedback training of the sensorimotor electroencephalogram rhythm in man: Effects on epilepsy. *Epilepsia* 15:395-416, 1974.

Wyrwicka W and Sterman MB. Instrumental conditioning of sensorimotor cortex EEG spindles in the waking cat. *Physiol Behav* 3:703-707, 1968.

50

Comments on "Biofeedback in Epileptics: Equivocal Relationship of Reinforced EEG Frequency to Seizure Reduction" by Bonnie J. Kaplan

Henri Gastaut

I am surprised to see the notion of subjective probability gradually replace calculation of probabilities in my field, the field of clinical neurophysiology. In other words, I am surprised to see neurophysiological solutions estimated rather than calculated by rigorous criteria and with a view to logical coherence. It is true that problems may by their nature not be amenable to logical processing; they may lie not in the fields of physics and psychology but in those singularly less precise ones of paraphysics and parapsychology.

I will take as an example the study of various types of Yoga meditation. This study was undertaken using the methods of: *electroencephalography*, studied by half a dozen teams whose only common finding was an increase in the incidence and amplitude of the alpha rhythm; *polygraphic recording* by two or three teams, who observed a diminution in muscular tension and slowing in respiratory rhythm; *basal metabolism*, measured by two main teams, who found opposite results — the one finding oxygen consumption to be diminished, the other finding no diminution.

These findings should have lead to the conclusion that Yoga meditation, at least that studied in this way, represents nothing other than a state of physical and mental relaxation corresponding to a slight hypnagogic state with accentuation of the alpha rhythm similar to that in the initial subphase of going to sleep, for which I, 15 years ago, suggested the designation

IA1. This conclusion, however, was not drawn. On the contrary, a strict relation was thought to exist between the alpha rhythm and meditation, to the point that biofeedback training was later used to reinforce the alpha rhythm artificially and to create in this way a certain mental state, the "alpha state," which eminent psychologists have defined as "internal serenity," "lucid detachment," or "appeasement of the spirit." This causal relation presumed on the basis of subjective probability has as much chance of being true as of being false!

Nonetheless the uncertain validity of the method has not prevented exploitation. Small industries sell to the general public apparatuses to enhance the alpha rhythm and have thus launched the craze of electronic Yoga. Certain centers of "biofeedback training" undertake to treat patients with epilepsy by teaching them to produce good alpha rhythm entirely devoid of paroxysms of spikes or of spike-waves. I find that this is exaggerated and I said as much in my inaugural address at the 8th International Congress of Electroencephalography and Clinical Neurophysiology, where I expressed indignation that the emblem of electroencephalography, the alpha rhythm, is used to exploit people (Gastaut, 1974).

But it is not only the alpha rhythm which has been put to use. For some years a sensorimotor rhythm has been invoked, recorded over the sensory-motor cortex of cat and the Rolandic region of man, which appears

Reprinted with permission from *Epilepsia*, 1975, Vol. 16, 487-488.

only in the absence of any movement. Concluding that the rhythm was related to an inhibitory thalamocortical discharge, Sterman and Friar (1972) proposed that this rhythm be enhanced by "biofeedback training" to increase inhibition in epileptic patients and to reduce EEG paroxysms and clinical seizures. They reported, first in one patient, then in four, and finally in five patients, a close relation between the sensorimotor rhythm and diminution in seizures.

I find these conclusions premature and I feel duty-bound to say so because it was I who discovered the somatomotor rhythm in man (rhythm en arceau or mu-rhythm, Gastaut 1952; Gastaut et al., 1952) and suggested that it represents "inhibition of sensory and motor representation at the level of Rolandic cortex." (Gastaut et al., 1964, 1965). Therefore I believe Dr. Kaplan's study has great importance since i

makes clear the equivocal nature of the relation between EEG activity reinforced by biofeedback training and other associated manifestations. The author is to be commended when she concludes her article as follows: "In view of the lack of statistical evidence of EEG changes following EEG biofeedback and the small number of patients trained to date, it appears wise to maintain a cautious attitude until the issue of causality is clear." That opinion accords with mine as expressed in my article on biofeedback training which will appear in the *Bordas Dictionary of Psychology*, which ends thus: "The conclusion to draw from all these facts is not to condemn out of hand training by biological retroaction in man, but rather to wait until its value, even its existence, has been demonstrated before proposing that it be used."

REFERENCES

Gastaut H. Etude électrocorticographique de la réactivité des rythmes rolandiques. *Rev Neurol* 87:176-182, 1952.

Gastaut H. Du rythme de Berger au culte alpha et à la culture alpha. Conférence inaugurale au VIIIème Congrès International d'Electro-encéphalographie et de Neurophysiologie Clinique, Marseille, September, 1973. *Rev EEG Neurophysiol.* 4:5-20, 1974.

Gastaut H, Broughton R, Regis H, Naquet R, and Gastaut Y. Quelques données nouvelles à propos du rythme mu. *Rev Neurol,* 111:331-332, 1964.

Gastaut H, Naquet R, and Gastaut Y. A study of the mu rhythm in subjects lacking one or more limbs. *Electroencephalogr Clin Neurophysiol.* 18:720-721, 1965.

Gastaut H, Terzian H, and Gastaut Y. Etude d'une activité électroencéphalographique méconnue: "Le rythme rolandique en arceau." *Marseille médical* 89:296-310, 1952.

Sterman M B and Friar L. Suppression of seizures in an epileptic following sensorimotor EEG feedback training. *Electroencephalogr Clin Neurophysiol* 33:89-95, 1972.

51

Reply to Professor Gastaut's Comments on "Biofeedback in Epileptics"

Bonnie J. Kaplan

I want to thank Professor Gastaut for his thoughtful comments, and to express my essential agreement that the area of biofeedback has at times been prone to exaggerated claims and to the substitution of subjective interpretation for data. These problems have had the undesirable effects of (1) misleading the public, (2) causing some responsible investigators to avoid pursuing any research using the biofeedback method, and (3) causing some biofeedback investigators to search for other labels (e.g., "sensory feedback," "information feedback") to describe their work, in order to avoid the unfortunate connotations which have come to be associated with the very word "biofeedback."

I do feel, however, that it would be regrettable to discourage the entire field of research on the basis of the inadequacies of some studies, or on the basis of equivocal results such as those which I have reported. The value of the biofeedback technique as a non-pharmacological method of therapy has been demonstrated convincingly in areas such as EMG feedback for the rehabilitation of muscle groups. If the value of the technique has not been demonstrated convincingly in the area

of EEG feedback, then perhaps what is lacking is careful research by additional responsible scientists. The data from animal models are promising: biofeedback training of neuronal activity in monkeys (Wyler, Fetz, and Ward, *Exp Neurol.* 44:113-125, 1974) and in cats (Sterman, LoPresti, and Fairchild, *Tech. Rep. AMRL-TR-69-3*, Wright-Patterson AFB, 1969) has been correlated with decreased seizure activity. In the animal work the exact electrical activity which was correlated with altered seizures was specifiable. While there are no known adverse effects of EEG biofeedback training, the procedure is by no means trivial; it requires tremendous amounts of time for both patient and experimenter. Until (and if) we have adequate research to demonstrate that the clinical improvement reported from the various laboratories is due to EEG biofeedback and no other factors, and until (and if) we can specify the neuronal activity which is responsible for decreasing seizures, we should follow Professor Gastaut's advice of waiting before proposing the widespread clinical application of the method.

Bonnie J. Kaplan, Ph.D.

Reprinted with permission from *Epilepsia*, 1975, Vol. 16, 488-489.

Firing Patterns of Epileptic and Normal Neurons in the Chronic Alumina Focus in Undrugged Monkeys During Different Behavioral States

52

Allen R. Wyler, Eberhard E. Fetz, and Arthur A. Ward, Jr.

SUMMARY

This communication summarizes data from a series of experiments on the activity of single units in chronic epileptogenic alumina foci in precentral cortex of undrugged monkeys. The foci contained a mixture of normal and epileptic cells, which differed consistently in their spontaneous firing patterns under various behavioral conditions, and in their responses to electrical stimulation: (1) during restful waking the spontaneous activity of normal precentral cells rarely exhibited intervals less than 10 msec, whereas the activity of epileptic cells included high frequency bursts with intervals less than 5 msec. The percentage of total activity in bursts was defined as the 'burst index'; (2) responses evoked antidromically by pyramidal tract stimulation and orthodromically by stimulation of center median of thalamus consisted of single action potentials in normal cells and bursts in epileptic cells; the probability of evoking a burst in epileptic cells was proportional to the burst index; (3) bidirectional operant conditioning of firing rates was most readily successful in normal cells and appeared to be increasingly difficult in epileptic cells in proportion to their burst index and (4) during sleep, epileptic cells fired in longer and higher frequency bursts than normal cells.

To the extent that both types of cells receive similar inputs, these observations suggest that many epileptic cells in the alumina focus are intrinsically hyperexcitable, viz. they respond abnormally to normal inputs rather than responding normally to abnormally intense inputs. These hyperexcitable neurons may drive other cells in the focus, but activity of both may be operantly controlled.

INTRODUCTION

Experimental models of epileptic processes are essential for scientific investiga-

Reprinted with permission from *Brain Research*, 1975, Vol. 98, 1-20.

tion of neural mechanisms underlying epileptogenesis and their possible control. Such models fall into two broad classes, usually termed 'acute' and 'chronic'. Acute models of epilepsy generate patterns of neural hyperactivity, resembling interictal and/or ictal episodes, relatively quickly after application of a drug (penicillin, strychnine, Metrazol, etc.) or a stimulus (electrical, freezing, etc.), and typically complete their natural histories within minutes or hours. The experimental popularity of acute models can be attributed in part to the convenience of rapid onset, control of dosage, and intensity of neural response. Although such models may mimic some naturally occurring, acute epileptic phenomena, the degree to which acute convulsants accurately represent naturally occurring chronic human epilepsy remains debatable; moreover, concordance with the human disease is often further compromised by the use of anesthetic and/or paralyzing agents[14], and acute surgical procedures which preclude observation under normal behavioral conditions. The electrophysiological properties of various acute models have recently been reviewed elsewhere[2,4] and are not the subject of this review.

The second class of epileptic models, namely chronic, involves application of agents which results in a more gradual evolution of an epileptogenic focus which generates interictal and ictal patterns for longer times. Of these, the model generally acknowledged to most closely resemble chronic focal epilepsy in humans is that produced by application of aluminum hydroxide to neocortex of the rhesus monkey[15, 25,26]. Monkey alumina and human foci are remarkably similar with respect to ictal and interictal EEG patterns, natural history of ictal episodes, and patterns of single unit activity[7,12,15,25,26]. Therefore, the electrophysiological properties of cells in alumina focus would be of considerable relevance to understanding natural epileptogenic mechanisms. Furthermore, the behavioral control of neuronal activity in chronic foci can be investigated in trained animals; besides providing important data on modification of epileptic activity, such studies would have important implications for the learned control of human epilepsy.

Activity of single cells in chronic alumina foci was first recorded extracellularly in anesthetized monkeys by Schmidt et al.[21,27] and from undrugged monkeys by Sypert and Ward[24]; both groups found many cells in the focus which fired in high-frequency bursts during interictal periods and became tonically active or inactive during propagated seizures. A remarkably stereotyped burst pattern, the 'long-first-interval' burst, which characterized some cells in the alumina focus was first documented by Calvin, Sypert and Ward[8]. Since this stereotyped burst pattern is not readily explained in terms of normal synaptic or circuit mechanisms, and is never seen in normal cortex, it would seem to provide important clues to the nature of hyperactivity in these cells. Intracellular recordings have been obtained from alumina foci, despite technical difficulties presented by the gliotic scar[3,13,19,20]; these studies have confirmed the presence of unstructured and structured burst patterns, (often coincident with augmented depolarization shifts[19]) but have failed to elucidate the mechanism of the long-first-interval burst.

In a recent series of studies we have documented the firing patterns of cells in the alumina focus under a variety of natural behavioral conditions and have investigated the degree to which monkeys could learn to control the activity of these cells. This review summarizes these separately reported observations on the interictal behavior of normal and epileptic neurons in the alumina focus during waking, sleep, operant conditioning of unit activity[11,28-33] and in response to antidromic and orthodromic stimulation[30,32]. This report is not intended to review data obtained from acute foci nor extensively review non-behavioral acute experiments on alumina foci, since such data does not address the present issue of this report, namely the activity of single cells recorded from chronic epileptic foci in alert, undrugged monkeys under different natural behavioral conditions.

METHODS

Eight *Macaca mulatta* monkeys were rendered epileptic by subpial alumina gel injections in sensorimotor cortex using the modified Kopeloff method[16] recently reviewed by Ward[26]. All monkeys developed EEG correlates of focal epilepsy and 7 who underwent 24-h seizure monitoring developed documented focal motor and/or generalized seizures.

Between 3 and 9 months following the development of seizures, all monkeys were implanted with a chronic recording mount and a bipolar pyramidal tract stimulating electrode. In addition, 5 monkeys had silver ball epidural EEG electrodes permanently placed peripheral to the focus, and two of these had bipolar stimulating electrodes in the ipsilateral nucleus center median (CM) of thalamus. These procedures have been described in more detail in previous reports[10,11,28-33]. The animals were then trained to bidirectionally control the activity of normal single precentral units by differentially reinforcing high or low firing rates[11,29]. Except for the anesthesia of surgery, these monkeys received no other medication.

Terminology

Because similar terms are used in slightly different contexts in the literature, the terms used in this report will be defined as follows:

(1) *Bursts* are considered the hallmark of abnormal (pathologic) single unit activity and consist of consecutive action potentials (AP) with interspike intervals shorter than 5 msec. Normal precentral units may exhibit high frequency firing under certain conditions, *e.g.* sleep, active movements or operant conditioning of high rates, but intervals rarely become shorter than 5 msec. As discussed elsewhere[24] bursts produced by electrode injury are distinguished from epileptic bursts by being more variable in duration, being a function of electrode position and being less stable over prolonged periods. Epileptic bursts encountered in the alumina focus can be further classified as follows:

(a) *Stereotyped bursts* have a repeatable sequence of short interspike intervals; thus, if successive stereotyped bursts are aligned along their first AP in a dot raster, the remaining APs of each burst are also aligned with little variance.

(b) *Structured bursts* have a repeatable timing sequence of successive interspike intervals, including a relatively long interval. The most frequently encountered

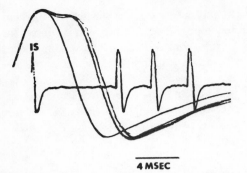

4 MSEC

Fig. 1. Spontaneous long-first-interval burst recorded in alumina focus. Superimposed fast (1 msec) sweeps of individual action potentials comprising the long-first-interval bursts of the slower sweep. All action potentials occurring in the afterbursts had a 'compound' waveform whereas initial spikes and single spikes during normal activity had 'simple' action potentials. The second portion of the compound AP's corresponded to the wave form of simple AP's. The early and late portions of the compound AP varied independently as a function of electrode depth[30]. Peak-to-peak AP's were 1.5 mV (negativity upwards). The time bar at the bottom calibrates the slower sweep.

example is the *long-first-interval (LFI) burst*, which is initiated by a single AP called the initial spike followed by a relatively long interspike interval (4–12 msec), in turn followed by a higher frequency stereotyped burst, called the *afterburst*. (Fig. 1.)

(c) *Unstructured bursts* have no repeatable timing sequence from one burst to the next.

(2) *Burst index.* For an isolated unit the burst index is the per cent ratio of APs occurring in bursts to total APs within a 15-sec epoch. The burst index was determined by an on-line PDP8/e computer programmed to identify a burst on the basis of consecutive interspike intervals less than 5 msec. Thus, a normal precentral unit with all interspike intervals greater than 5 msec would have a burst index of 0.0, whereas a unit exhibiting only high frequency bursts would have a burst index of 100.

(3) *Pyramidal tract (PT)* neuron: a neuron which responds to each of 3 pyramidal tract stimuli at 500 pulses/sec with an invariant latency (usually less than 1.2 msec).

(4) Several types of *behavioral schedules* were used during operant conditioning sessions: *DRH*, differential reinforcement of high rates of unit activity; *DRO*, differential reinforcement of zero unit activity; *DRR*, differential reinforcement of regular activity (low burst index) and *DRB*, differential reinforcement of bursting activity (high burst index); S^Δ, an extinction or 'time out' period with no reinforcement. *Bidirectional conditioning* means that increases *and* decreases in a response were successively conditioned in the same session.

RESULTS

This report comprises observations on more than 300 distinctly isolated neurons of which over 200 were subjected to bidirectional operant conditioning; more than

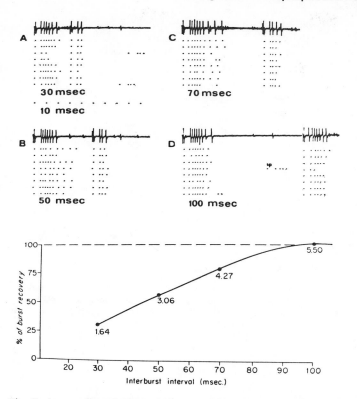

Fig. 2. Attenuation of antidromically evoked bursts as inverse function of preceding interburst interval. Top: long-first-interval bursts evoked by pairs of pyramidal tract shocks separated by specified intervals. A: 30 msec; B: 50 msec; C: 70 msec and D: 100 msec. (sp = spontaneous burst occurring between evoked bursts.) Bottom: mean duration of second burst as per cent of maximum, plotted as function of interburst interval. (Fom ref. 30.)

half of all the units were pyramidal tract neurons. Neurons were characterized as normal or epileptic if their burst index was lower or greater than 10 respectively. This criterion was quite reliable because normal precentral neurons rarely had interspike intervals shorter than 5 msec, even under conditions which generated shortest inter-spike intervals, such as DRH periods (Figs. 3 and 4) or slow wave sleep (SWS) (Fig. 6). Thus, all neurons with burst indices greater than 10 could reliably be considered to be epileptic. Epileptic neurons were further subdivided into two groups: group 1 epileptic neurons had a high burst index (generally greater than 60) whose variance during quiet wakefulness was low (typically less than ± 10). This variance was documented during periods when the animal was not moving, but alert by behavioral and EEG criteria. Group 2 epileptic neurons had lower and more variable burst indices (variance greater than ± 10); although the burst index of a group 2 neuron could temporarily exceed that of a group 1 neuron, this was never sustained. Of the total population of recorded cells, slightly less than 50% were epileptic as judged by these criteria.

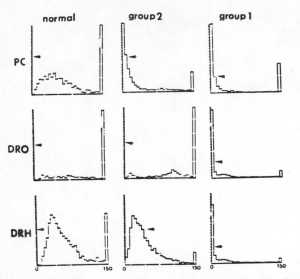

Fig. 3. Representative interspike interval histograms of activity from normal, group 1 and group 2 neurons recorded in the cortical focus of one monkey. Samples were taken during preconditioning period (PC), differential reinforcement of high rates (DRH), and differential reinforcement of zero activity (DRO). Examples of activity from which histograms were compiled are shown in Fig. 4. Bin width is 5 msec; the last bin contains all interspike intervals greater than 145 msec. Arrows indicate 1000 counts. (From ref. 29.)

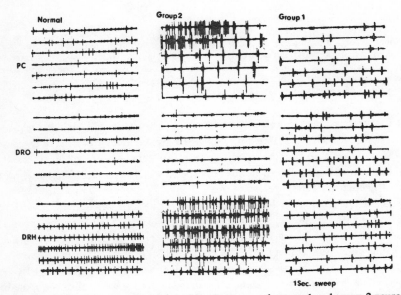

Fig. 4. Representative examples of unit activity from normal, group 1 and group 2 neurons from the same epileptic focus. Continuous sample of activity is shown in consecutive sweeps; samples were taken in different behavioral periods of operant conditioning sessions illustrated in Fig. 5. Because of slow sweep (1 sec), the single AP's comprising the high-frequency epileptic bursts of the group 1 and group 2 neurons are not resolved. (From ref. 29.)

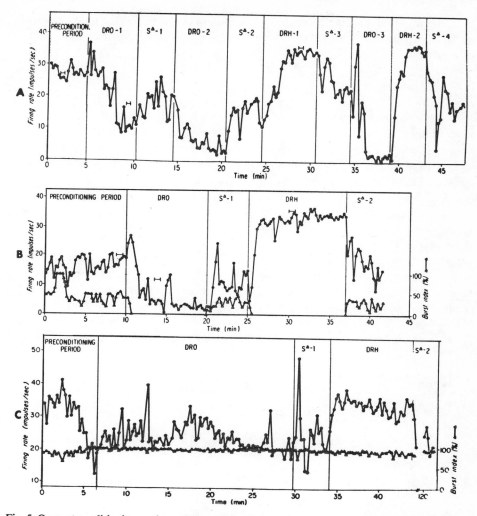

Fig. 5. Operant conditioning sessions with normal, group 1 and group 2 epileptic neurons in alumina focus of same monkey. Graphs plot average firing rate (scale at left) and burst index (scale at right) in successive 15-sec intervals. Firing rates of a normal neuron (A) were bidirectionally controlled, most convincingly in DRO-3 and DRH-2. Firing rates of a group 2 epileptic neuron (B) were also bidirectionally controlled, and burst index went to zero during both behavioral periods. Firing rates of a group 1 epileptic neuron (C) were not convincingly modified and burst index remained high and constant under all conditions. (From ref. 29.)

All cells which demonstrated the long-first-interval burst pattern were pyramidal tract (PT) neurons, and conversely long-first-interval bursts were never recorded from non-PT neurons. Since this structured burst pattern appears to be restricted to only pyramidal tract neurons, the following discussion will distinguish two main classifications of epileptic neurons: PT and non-PT neurons.

Before discussing the behavior of epileptic neurons within the alumina focus, we will describe the behavior of normal neurons recorded from the same cortical substrate.

I. Normal neurons in epileptic cortex

Cells exhibiting normal firing patterns were usually recorded in the same electrode tracks in which abnormal, bursting units were also encountered. These normal cells fired in regular patterns characteristic of neurons recorded from homologous regions of normal cortex. The majority responded to some form of peripheral stimulation, usually passive movement of contralateral joints. Normal units were often observed to fire single action potentials synchronously with bursts of a simultaneously-monitored neighboring epileptic unit, particularly when the monkey was either inattentive or asleep. When the monkey was alerted, or actively moving, such synchronous unit firing was often dissociated[29]. Interspike intervals were typically greater than 10 msec and these cells often fired in relation to spontaneous movements. During EEG events such as spindles, spikes, and K complexes, such units fired in high-frequency clusters of APs, but the firing frequency attained during such clusters was generally lower than that characteristic of epileptic cells (Figs. 6 and 7) [9,18,22,23,28]. In contrast to epileptic neurons, normal PT units responded with a single AP to a pyramidal tract stimulus. Normal neurons (both PT and non-PT) also re-

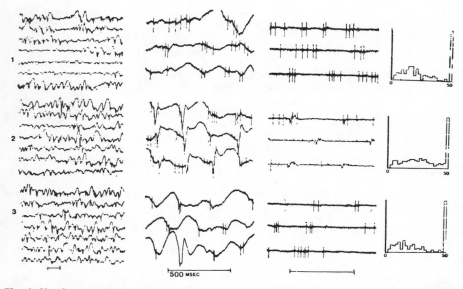

Fig. 6. Simultaneous EEG and unit activity of a normal non-PT neuron recorded in an epileptic focus during stages 1–3 sleep (rows 1–3 respectively). Left column taken at slow sweep, whereas the next column is at faster sweep. (Time bars calibrate 500 msec.) The third column shows the unit activity, with the high pass filter at 300 Hz. The right column shows interspike interval histograms of the unit activity. (From ref. 28.)

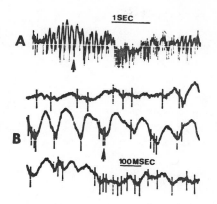

Fig. 7. Unit activity of a normal PT neuron recorded in epileptic cortex during a sleep spindle. Sweep A shows same activity as in 3 consecutive faster sweeps in B (negativity downwards). Arrows identify the same point in sweeps A and B. Note that the high-frequency unit activity during the peaks of the spindles does not approach the firing frequency or structure of epileptic bursts. (From ref. 28.)

sponded to a single center median (CM) stimulus with a single AP[32]. Repetitive stimuli to center median at frequencies from 1–10 hz evoked EEG recruiting responses with concomitant single unit activity consisting of variable latency, waxing–waning clusters of APs, but interspike intervals in such clustered APs were never less than 5 msec (ref. 32). After these monkeys demonstrated proficiency at operant control of normal cells, we found no normal pyramidal tract neurons that were not easily bidirectionally controlled (for example see Fig. 5); this fact allowed us to use normal PT cells as controls for behavioral variables in subsequent operant conditioning sessions of epileptic cells. Of the normal non-PT cells 98 % were easily bidirectionally conditioned.

In summary, normal PT and non-PT cells recorded from the alumina foci responded to pyramidal tract stimulation, center median stimulation, slow wave sleep, and bidirectional operant conditioning like neurons recorded from homologous regions of normal cortex.

II. Highly epileptic cells (Group 1)

Cells in the alumina focus were designated as highly epileptic, or 'Group 1' if they fired predominantly in high-frequency bursts (mean burst index greater than 60), and exhibited relatively little variance in burst index during quiet wakefulness. Since PT and non-PT group 1 cells differed consistently in burst structure and other characteristics these two types of cells are best discussed separately.

A. Pyramidal tract cells

Group 1 PT neurons fired predominantly in structured long-first-interval (LFI) bursts during periods of *quiet wakefulness*. For a given cell, these bursts recurred with remarkably repeatable sequence of spikes, with the mean duration of the long-first-interval often being close to an interger multiple of the first afterburst interval[11,30]. Some units exhibited first intervals with a bimodal distribution and a few showed an exceedingly invariant first interval[8,11,30]. In many cells the initial spike of the LFI burst had a 'simple' waveform, identical to single APs which occurred between bursts during regular firing; in contrast, the afterburst APs were typically larger and longer, often clearly compounded of two portions, suggesting multiple sites of spike initiation (Fig. 1 and ref. 30). PT stimulation evoked a simple antidromic AP, which usually formed the initial spike of a complete LFI burst, which was structurally similar to spontaneous LFI bursts. The fact that juxtathreshold intensity PT shocks evoked either a complete LFI burst or no response at all suggests that the afterbursts are generated within the cell consequent to the initial spike and do not depend on synchronous activation of neighboring cells. A second antidromic spike could also be timed to invade the cell during the long-first-intervals, indicating that the cell was not in cathodal block during this interval[30] (this conclusion has recently been substantiated by intracellular recordings from LFI bursting neurons in monkey cortex reported by Reynolds *et al.*[20]). The number of spikes per burst was relatively constant for a given cell, except when the preceding interburst interval was less than 100 msec, in which case the afterburst was shortened. This graded recovery of the burst generating mechanism was observed for both spontaneous and antidromically evoked LFI bursts (Fig. 2)[11,30,32].

Stimulation of center median nucleus of the thalamus orthodromically evoked a burst similar in timing to the afterburst of the LFI burst (Fig. 8); in two cells the CM stimulus occasionally evoked a complete LFI burst.

In *operant conditioning sessions*, the firing rates of group 1 PT cells could, in general, be more readily increased during DRH periods than decreased during DRO periods. Usually the mean burst index remained steady during conditioned

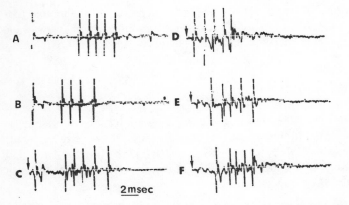

Fig. 8. Long-first-interval bursts of a group 1 PT cell, spontaneously occurring in A and B, and antidromically evoked in C. (Arrows indicate stimuli.) Sweeps D–F show variable latency response to thalamic stimuli; these orthodromically evoked bursts are similar in timing to the afterbursts of spontaneous and antidromically evoked afterbursts. Action potential amplitudes were 1 mV. (From ref. 32.)

rate changes; that is, mean firing rates changed without altering the relative proportion of bursts. However, during transient increases in firing rate, bursts often recurred rapidly enough to be attenuated. We also noted that after transient suppression of unit rates on DRO, the initial activity following the pause was invariably a burst. This suggests an inverse relation between firing rate and the probability of burst activity. When the monkey was reinforced for suppressing the burst index, on a schedule which differentially reinforced regular activity (DRR), he could change the firing patterns from bursting modes to regular firing patterns[11]. However, the drop in burst index was associated with a rise in total firing rate such that a decreasing interburst interval ultimately resulted in complete attenuation of the afterburst. This would suggest that the change in pattern was mediated by a net increase in synaptic drive[11].

During *sleep*, the structure of the burst changed such that afterburst interspike intervals approached their minimal duration of less than 2 msec, while the first interval became considerably shorter and extremely variable (Fig. 9). Occasionally the sleep bursts also were characterized by long second or long third intervals (Fig. 10)[28]. Although the total duration of the burst did not increase, the number of APs per burst increased by 100% or more. In all instances, the burst structure reverted to its original form when the monkey was awakened. During the transition into sleep, the mean interburst intervals tended to become slightly longer and less variable than during wakefulness (Fig. 10).

In summary, group 1 epileptic PT neurons fired abnormally with a high proportion of LFI bursts during all behavioral conditions; their response to pyramidal tract and center median stimulation was usually a burst, in contrast to single AP

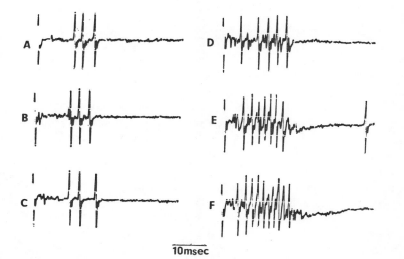

10msec

Fig. 9. Comparison of burst structure of an epileptic PT neuron occurring during quiet wakefulness (A–C) and stage 2 sleep (D–F). Although the total burst duration did not increase, the number of AP's per burst approximately doubled during sleep. (From ref. 28.)

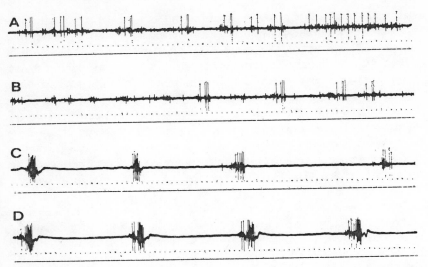

Fig. 10. Activity of a group 1 PT neuron during 4 behavioral states: A: during active wakefulness, with initiation of movement of the contralateral arm at end of sweep. B: during quiet wakefulness, in absence of overt movements. C: during early stage 2 sleep. D: during sleep spindle. Action potential was 0.9 mV, and timing markers calibrate 10 msec intervals. During sleep, the background units fired synchronously with the epileptic unit. (From ref. 28.)

evoked in normal PT cells from the same sites. During operant conditioning sessions, monkeys were able to successfully increase firing rates, but did not consistently succeed in suppressing activity, especially burst activity. (Fig. 5.) During sleep the burst activity was intensified and the burst index increased.

B. Non-pyramidal tract neurons

Group 1 non-PT epileptic neurons fired primarily with a mixture of stereo typed and unstructured bursts. Cells with higher burst indices tended to have a greater proportion of stereotyped bursts. By definition, PT stimulation did not elicit a short invariant latency antidromic response; however, several units responded to pyramidal tract stimulation with a burst structurally similar to spontaneously occurring bursts (Fig. 11). The brief but variable latencies of some of these responses (1.4 msec), suggests that these bursts were evoked orthodromically, via axon collaterals of neighboring pyramidal tract neurons. Single center median stimuli also evoked bursts similar in structure to spontaneous bursts (Fig. 11).

In *operant conditioning* sessions, the group 1 non-PT neurons were not successfully bidirectionally conditioned; in contrast to PT neurons, their rates were not significantly increased by reinforcement of high rates of activity. Although some cells demonstrated appropriate changes in the occurrence of interburst unit activity, such activity was such a small proportion of total activity that significant firing rate changes were not achieved[29].

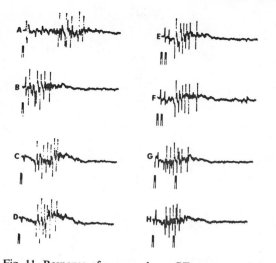

Fig. 11. Response of a group 1 non-PT neuron to thalamic and pyramidal tract stimulation. All sweeps triggered from stimulus marker. Sweeps A and B demonstrate variable latency response to thalamic stimulation. Sweeps C and D show the same cell's response to pyramidal tract stimulation. Response to paired thalamic stimuli separated by 2 msec in E and F and 10 msec in G and H. Action potentials were 600 μV. (From ref. 32.)

During *sleep*, the total burst duration increased (Fig. 12), but interspike intervals within the burst did not decrease significantly since, during wakefulness, they already approximated maximal firing rates of 500 per sec. During all periods of synchronized sleep, the interburst intervals were approximately 250 msec, only slightly longer than the average interburst interval seen during wakefulness. Moreover, these bursts recurred regularly, independently of EEG events such as spindles, K complexes or sharp waves.

In summary, group 1 non-PT neurons fired predominantly in structured and unstructured bursts, both spontaneously and in response to orthodromic stimuli (center median); they appeared more difficult to condition than other types of cells and exhibited prolonged bursts during all stages of sleep.

III. Moderately epileptic (Group 2) cells

The alumina focus also contained a large proportion of cells whose firing patterns were intermediate between normal and highly epileptic cells. These 'moderately epileptic' or 'Group 2' cells were characterized by a highly variable burst index, whose mean value was usually below 60. The bursts of most PT and all non-PT group 2 cells were unstructured bursts, with the exception of a few PT cells which exhibited LFI bursts. With this distinction in mind, the following observations applied to both PT and non-PT group 2 cells.

During *quiet wakefulness* firing patterns of group 2 cells by definition contained a smaller and more variable proportion of bursts than group 1 cells. The nature of

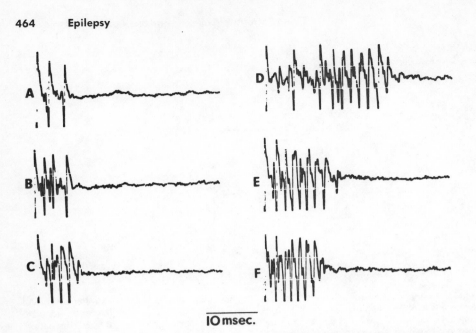

IO msec.

Fig. 12. Comparison of burst structure of a group 1 non-PT neuron during wakefulness and stage 2 sleep. Sweeps A–C show 3 spontaneous bursts during wakefulness; sweeps D–F show bursts recorded during stage 2 sleep. Peak-to-peak AP amplitude was 0.5 mV. (From ref. 28.)

the response evoked by electrical stimulation — either orthodromically from CM or antidromically from PT — tended to be similar to the spontaneous firing pattern at the time of stimulation. Thus, when the cell was firing in bursts, the evoked response tended to be a burst; when the cell was firing regularly, the evoked response tended to be a single AP. The probability of evoking a burst was proportional to the burst index at the time of stimulation and the duration of cell inactivity which immediately preceded stimulation: *i.e.*, the longer the duration between preceding activity and the stimulus, the higher the probability that the evoked activity (antidromic or orthodromic) would be a burst. Thus, the fluctuating propensity of group 2 cells to fire in bursts applied to both spontaneous and electrically evoked activity.

During *operant conditioning* sessions, experienced monkeys were successful in bidirectionally controlling firing rates of virtually all group 2 cells[29]; that is, they could increase firing rates on DRH and decrease them on DRO. Some group 2 cells with extremely variable burst indices occasionally showed complete suppression of burst activity during conditioning periods, regardless of whether the schedule reinforced high or low firing rates (Fig. 5B). This suggests that increased arousal or attention may reduce the conditions for bursting in group 2 cells.

During *sleep*, the burst index of all group 2 cells increased markedly[28]. Cells with higher waking burst index often fired exclusively in high-frequency bursts during sleep; those with lower waking burst index also increased their burst index, but not always to 100%. During sleep the bursts typically contained decreased interspike intervals, sometimes doubling the number of action potentials. Sleep bursts of group 2 cells were significantly higher in frequency than sleep-related clusters of APs from normal cells and often became indistinguishable from those of group 1 cells. Waking the monkey immediately reduced the burst index of group 2 cells.

In summary, group 2 cells fired with a moderate and highly variable proportion of unstructured bursts during quiet waking; responded to electrical stimulation with bursts or single spikes, depending on the spontaneous pattern at the time of stimulation; were readily bidirectionally conditioned and during sleep exhibited bursts of higher frequency firing than normal cells.

Effects of recording and conditioning on cell types and seizures

The relative proportion of normal and group 1 and 2 epileptic cells varied as a function of both location relative to the site of alumina injection and over time. Several millimeters from the injection site most cells were normal and the proportion of epileptic cells was highest near the focus defined by EEG spiking. A systematic mapping of cell types with respect to the injection site remains to be done to quantify this relation. The proportion of cell types also showed some variation for electrode tracks made at contiguous sites on separate days. However, such proportions became more repeatable when pooled over 5 day periods. In several animals the relative number of epileptic cells encountered was found to decrease systematically over several weeks of recording and conditioning[33]; these animals also experienced fewer seizures during recording and conditioning days and were generally successful in controlling firing rates of cells in operant conditioning sessions. In contrast, other monkeys who were exposed to similar recording and conditioning procedures had a constant and high proportion of epileptic cells; these animals did not succeed in controlling firing rates of units and experienced no reduction in seizures. As discussed elsewhere[33], a number of variables may be involved in these differences, including differences in the severity of the focus.

DISCUSSION

These observations suggest a number of conclusions concerning the nature of the pathological processes in the chronic epileptic focus and their possible behavioral manipulation. The precentral alumina focus clearly contains a spectrum of cell types, from normal cells, whose spontaneous and evoked responses resemble those observed in normal cortex, to highly epileptic cells whose predominant firing pattern under the same conditions consists of high frequency bursts.

Data pooled from several animals would indicate that for those regions of cortex in the immediate periphery (1–2 mm) of the injection sites the relative percentage of neurons is approximately: group 1, 10%; group 2, 40%; and normal neurons 50%. These approximations need clearer quantification since we do not know what variables in the preparation of the animal might influence these data.

For epileptic cells the proportion of cell activity occurring in bursts (burst index) ranges from low and variable (group 2 epileptic cells) to high and invariant (group 1 epileptic cells). The propensity of epileptic cells to respond with a burst to conditions which produced single action potentials in normal cells was consistently observed over a wide range of behavioral situations. Thus, the responses evoked antidromically by pyramidal tract stimulation and orthodromically by thalamic stimulation tended to be bursts for epileptic cells and single spikes for normal cells. The degree to which burst responses were evoked by stimulation was directly proportional to the cell's burst index at the time of stimulation. Thus, the higher the burst index, the more consistently the cell exhibited a burst response to antidromic or orthodromic stimulation. Furthermore, during sleep, the same differences between normal and epileptic neurons were maintained; events such as sleep spindles associated with a doublet or triplet firing in normal neurons were correlated with exaggerated bursts in epileptic neurons.

These data bear on the classic debate of whether bursting neurons in epileptogenic cortex are intrinsically hyperexcitable or are simply normal cells responding to an abnormally intense synaptic input. Thus, there are two contrasting views of the epileptic focus: (1) the focus is maintained by a group of intrinsically bursting 'epileptic' or 'pacemaker' neurons[19,25,27] or (2) the focus is perpetuated by a group interaction within an 'epileptic aggregate'[1,4,5,17] of individually normal cells, synchronized perhaps by subcortical centers like thalamus. A common argument against the concept of intrinsically hyperexcitable neurons is the lack of evidence that such neurons respond in a hyperexcitable fashion to stimulation which would evoke normal responses in a normal neuron. Assuming that the normal and epileptic cells recorded at the same cortical sites in our studies received similar synaptic input, the fact that the latter responded with bursts would suggest an intrinsic hyperexcitability. Although burst responses to stimulation of pyramidal tract or thalamus could have been due to activation of a population of neurons converging on the epileptic cell, the same should apply to adjacent normal neurons. If both types of cells receive similar input, the fact that normal neurons responded with single spikes suggests that burst responses of epileptic cells reflect intrinsic hyperexcitability.

The highly structured long-first-interval burst pattern found in many group 1 cells further supports the concept of intrinsic hyperexcitability. It is difficult to account for the length and invariance of the long interval on the basis of reverberating circuits, which would involve two synapses. The fact that LFI bursts were antidromically evoked in all-or-none fashion by juxtathreshold PT stimuli strongly implicates intrinsic pathology. Moreover such structured burst patterns have been evoked from single cells in alumina gel foci by slight local mechanical and metabolic cellular injury[31]. It should be noted that LFI bursts have never been seen as part of injury patterns in normal cortex. In any case this data gives supportive evidence that such extremely structured burst patterns may be produced by damage to single cells in the alumina focus and probably does not involve extensive neuronal circuits. Calvin[6] has hypothesized that a normal neuron may be driven into bursting firing mode by biasing 2% of its synaptic input towards membrane excitation. One could argue that the epileptic units we observed were bursting in response to massive synchronized synaptic input. Although this may explain the labile, unstructured bursts of the very weak group 2 epileptic neurons it is an unlikely explanation for the sustained, stereotyped bursts of group 1 units.

Although the above data clearly demonstrate that within the experimental alumina epileptic focus one may find pyramidal tract neurons whose spontaneous and evoked activity is pathologic, this data is not as conclusive for those cells classified as non-PT neurons. This latter group of neurons may comprise a heterogeneous population, some of which could be considered 'interneurons'. Steriade and co-workers[22,23] have recently reported data on a group of precentral neurons which they consider interneurons. Such cells had the following characteristics in normal cortex: (1) their 'normal' firing patterns were high frequency bursts, which by our criteria would be epileptic; (2) the majority responded orthodromically (monosynaptically) with a short latency burst to pyramidal tract stimulation; (3) such cells also responded orthodromically (slightly longer latencies) to VL stimulation with a burst; (4) duration of spontaneous bursts increased during sleep (5) their average firing rates changed with alerting and (6) during wakefulness the ability to evoke firing from these cells by pyramidal tract or VL stimulation decreased, but when evoked, their latencies were somewhat shorter. The above data is quite compatable with some of the group 1 non-PT neurons we considered 'epileptic' in that a few such cells had burst responses orthodromically evoked by pyramidal tract and CM stimulation, lengthened their bursts during sleep, stabilized their firing rates during alerting (see Fig. 4 in ref. 29), and had, on the average, smaller amplitude APs than the PT cells. If some of our group 1 non-PT cells were in fact interneurons, this might account for the inability to operantly control their firing patterns and the stability of their 'burst indices'. Although the above may exclude a few group 1 non-PT cells as being 'epileptic' it does not adequately explain the behavior of all the non-PT cells which demonstrated burst firing. Moreover, it now places more importance on the elucidation of mechanisms responsible for pathologic behavior of those cells clearly identified as pyramidal tract neurons: cells whose firing patterns during undrugged, behavioral conditions in normal cortex are clearly defined.

The hypothesis that normal cells may be synaptically driven to high frequency firing may be particularly relevant to understanding the rapid spread of epileptiform activity during propagated seizures, as well as explaining the continued high-frequency bursts characteristic of certain neurons during interictal periods. When epileptic neurons produce an ictal event, they presumably recruit surrounding neuronal activity into synchronous firing until a 'critical mass' is reached, at which point clinical manifestations of the propagation of the pathological cellular activity become apparent. We postulate that the group 1 epileptic neurons are relatively autonomous and act as 'pacemakers' to the focus, and that the group 2 epileptic neurons may represent the potential 'critical mass' available for rapid enlargement of the focus. Once this 'critical mass' has been activated, additional normal neurons may be recruited to produce the ictal event.

Ultimately, extracellular recordings cannot unequivocally resolve the issue of whether the primary pathology responsible for hyperexcitable single cell behavior is due to a hyperexcitable postsynaptic membrane or a hyperintense synaptic input, although the above evidence suggests the former alternative for group 1 cells. The intracellular records of Prince and Futamachi[19] in alumina focus showed mixtures of normal and augmented synaptic potentials, and patterns of single spikes and bursts similar to those characteristic of our group 2 cells. Prince and Futamachi concluded that their observations were consistent with an abnormal synaptic input to cells that otherwise appeared normal. A direct test of intrinsic membrane hyperexcitability by intracellular current injection remains to be done for cells in the chronic alumina focus; such tests in the acute penicillin focus have failed to reveal any membrane pathology.

Although the mechanism by which the epileptic cells become hyperexcitable remains to be elucidated it appears that the bursts of group 1 PT neurons (LFI cells) are probably autonomously sustained, and thereby qualifies such cells as intrinsically hyperexcitable neurons. The concept of 'epileptic' or 'pacemaker' neurons[25] does not necessarily imply complete autonomy, nor does it exclude the possibility of synchronizing influences in a population of cells. Indeed the fact that the epileptic cells could be orthodromically activated and their firing rates modified during operant conditioning sessions confirms the existence of some synaptic input. The ease with which firing rates of cells could be operantly conditioned appeared to be inversely related to their burst index. Thus, an experienced monkey could be trained relatively quickly to bidirectionally control the firing rate of most normal and group 2 cells. In contrast, firing rates of group 1 cells appeared more difficult to operantly condition; rate increases in LFI cells could be more readily produced than decreases[11,29]. However, these findings should be interpreted with caution, since successful operant conditioning depends critically on numerous behavioral variables, particularly the amount of training. Thus, the fact that most group 1 cells were encountered in initial operant conditioning sessions[33] could perhaps partially account for the greater difficulty in conditioning them. The fact that firing rates of some group 1 PT cells with burst indices of 80–95% could be conditioned and the burst index decreased[11] suggests a degree of synaptic control over even highly epileptic cells. Whether this control over 'pacemaker' as well as recruited cells can become therapeutically significant remains an intriguing clinical challenge.

It should be reiterated that these results and hypotheses may only be applicable to alumina gel foci, and are not necessarily related to mechanisms operative in acute foci. Since all the patterns of burst firing (including long-first-interval bursts) recorded from alumina foci in monkey have also been documented in human foci[7], the data reported here may well be relevant to understanding mechanisms operating in human foci.

ACKNOWLEDGEMENTS

This work was supported by U.S. Public Health Service Grants NS-05211 and NS-04053 and NINDS Teacher–Investigator Award NS-11,027 (E. Fetz). Dr. Fetz is also associated with the Department of Physiology and Biophysics and Regional Primate Research Center.

REFERENCES

1 AJMONE-MARSAN, C., Electrographic aspects of 'epileptic' neuronal aggregates, *Epilepsia (Amst.)*, 2 (1961) 22–28.

2 AJMONE-MARSAN, C., Acute effects of topical epileptogenic agents. In H. H. JASPER, A. A. WARD, JR. AND A. POPE (Eds.), *Basic Mechanisms of the Epilepsies*, Little Brown, Boston, Mass., 1969, pp. 259–319.

3 ATKINSON, J. R., AND WARD, A. A., JR., Intracellular studies of cortical neurons in chronic epileptogenic foci in the monkey, *Exp. Neurol.*, 10 (1964) 285–295.

4 AYALA, G. F., DICHTER, M., GUMNIT, R. J., MATSUMOTO, H., AND SPENDER, W. A., Genesis of epileptic interictal spikes. New knowledge of cortical feedback systems suggests a neurophysiological explanation of brief paroxysms. *Brain Research*, 52 (1973) 1–17.

5 AYALA, G. F., MATSUMOTO, H., AND GUMNIT, R. J., Excitability changes and inhibitory mechanisms in neocortical neurons during seizures, *J. Neurophysiol.*, 33 (1970) 73–85.

6 CALVIN, W. H., Synaptic potential summation and repetitive firing mechanisms: input–output theory for the recruitment of neurons into epileptic bursting firing patterns. *Brain Research*, 39 (1972) 71–94.

7 CALVIN, W. H., OJEMANN, G. A., AND WARD, A. A., JR., Human cortical neurons in epileptogenic foci: comparison of interictal firing patterns to those of 'epileptic' neurons in monkeys, *Electroenceph. clin. Neurophysiol.*, 34 (1973) 337–351.

8 CALVIN, W. H., SYPERT, G. W., AND WARD, A. A., JR., Structured timing patterns within bursts from epileptic neurons in undrugged monkey cortex, *Exp. Neurol.*, 21 (1968) 535–549.

9 EVARTS, E. V., Temporal patterns of discharge of pyramidal tract neurons during sleep and waking in the monkey, *J. Neurophysiol.*, 27 (1964) 152–171.

10 FETZ, E. E., AND BAKER, M. A., Operantly conditioned patterns of precentral unit activity and correlated responses in adjacent cells and contralateral muscles, *J. Neurophysiol.*, 36 (1973) 179–294.

11 FETZ, E. E., AND WYLER, A. R., Operantly conditioning firing patterns of epileptic neurons in the monkey motor cortex, *Exp. Neurol.*, 40 (1973) 587–607.

12 GIBBS, E. L., AND GIBBS, F. A., Diagnostic and localizing value of electroencephalographic studies in sleep, *Res. Publ. ass. nerv. ment. Dis.*, 26 (1949) 366–376.

13 GLOTZNER, F. L., FETZ, E. E., AND WARD, A. A., JR., Neuronal activity in the chronic and acute epileptogenic focus, *Exp. Neurol.*, 42 (1974) 503–578.

14 HALPERN, L. M., AND BLACK, R. G., Flaxedil (gallamine triethiodide): evidence for central action, *Science*, 155 (1967) 1685–1687.

15 JASPER, H. H., Application of experimental models to human epilepsy. In D. P. PURPURA, J. K. PENRY, D. TOWER, D. M. WOODBURY AND R. WALTER (Eds.), *Experimental Models of Epilepsy*, Raven Press, New York, 1972, pp. 585–602.

16 KOPELOFF, L. M., DHUSID, J. C., AND KOPELOFF, N., Chronic experimental epilepsy in *Macaca mulatta*, *Neurology (Minneap.)*, 4 (1954) 218–227.

17 MATSUMOTO, H., AYALA, G. F., AND GUMNIT, R. J., Neuronal behavior and triggering mechanisms in cortical epileptic focus, *J. Neurophysiol.*, 32 (1969) 688–703.

18 POMPEIANO, O., Sleep mechanisms. In H. H. JASPER, A. A. WARD, JR. AND A. POPE (Eds.), *Basic Mechanisms of the Epilepsies*, Little, Brown, Boston, Mass., 1969, pp. 453–467.

19 PRINCE, D. A., AND FUTAMACHI, K. J., Intracellular recordings from chronic epileptogenic foci in the monkey, *Electroenceph. clin. Neurophysiol.*, 29 (1970) 496–510.

20 REYNOLDS, A. F., JR., OJEMANN, G. A., AND WARD, A. A., JR., Intracellular recordings during focal hypothermia and alumina experimental foci, *Exp. Neurol.*, 46 (1975) 583–604.

21 SCHMIDT, R. P., THOMAS, L. B., AND WARD, A. A., JR., The hyperexcitable neuron. Microelectrode studies of chronic epileptic foci in monkeys, *J. Neurophysiol.*, 27 (1959) 285–297.

22 STERIADE, M., AND DESCHENES, M., Inhibitory processes and interneuronal apparatus in motor cortex during sleep and waking. II. Recurrent and afferent inhibition of pyramidal tract neurons, *J. Neurophysiol.*, 37 (1974) 1093–1113.

23 STERIADE, M., DESCHENES, M., AND OAKSON, G., Inhibitory processes and interneuronal apparatus in motor cortex during sleep and waking. I. Background firing and responsiveness of pyramidal tract neurons and interneurons, *J. Neurophysiol.*, 37 (1974) 1065–1092.

24 SYPERT, G. W., AND WARD, A. A., JR., The hyperexcitable neuron: microelectrode studies of the chronic epileptic focus in the intact, awake monkey, *Exp. Neurol.*, 19 (1967) 104–114.

25 WARD, A. A., JR., The epileptic neuron. In H. H. JASPER, A. A. WARD, JR. AND A. POPE (Eds.), *Basic Mechanisms of the Epilepsies*, Little, Brown, Boston, Mass., 1969, pp. 263–298.

26 WARD, A. A., JR., Topical convulsant metals. In D. P. PURPURA, J. K. PENRY, D. TOWER, D. M. WOODBURY AND R. WALTER (Eds.). *Experimental Models of Epilepsy*, Raven Press, New York, 1972, pp. 13–36.

27 WARD, A. A., JR., AND SCHMIDT, R. F., Some properties of single epileptic neurons, *Arch. Neurol. (Chic.)*, 5 (1961) 308–313.

28 WYLER, A. R., Epileptic neurons during sleep and wakefulness, *Exp. Neurol.*, 42 (1974) 593–608.

29 WYLER, A. R., AND FETZ, E. E., Behavioral control of firing patterns of normal and abnormal neurons in chronic epileptic cortex, *Exp. Neurol.*, 42 (1974) 448–464.

30 WYLER, A. R., FETZ, E. E., AND WARD, A. A., JR., Spontaneous firing patterns of epileptic neurons in the monkey motor cortex, *Exp. Neurol.*, 40 (1973) 567–585.

31 WYLER, A. R., FETZ, E. E., AND WARD, A. A., JR., Injury-induced long-first-interval bursts in cortical neurons, *Exp. Neurol.*, 41 (1973) 773–776.

32 WYLER, A. R., FETZ, E. E., AND WARD, A. A., JR., Antidromic and orthodromic activation of epileptic neurons in neocortex of awake monkey, *Exp. Neurol.*, 43 (1974) 59–74.

33 WYLER, A. R., FETZ, E. E., AND WARD, A. A., JR., Effects of operantly conditioning epileptic unit activity on seizure frequencies and electrophysiology of neocortical experimental foci, *Exp. Neurol.*, 44 (1974) 113–125.

IX

BIOFEEDBACK IN REHABILITATION

Sensory Feedback Therapy as a Modality of Treatment in Central Nervous Systems Disorders of Voluntary Movement

53

Joseph Brudny, Julius Korein, Lucie Levidow, Bruce B. Grynbaum, Abraham Lieberman, and Lawrence W. Friedmann

Article abstract

Sensory feedback therapy may significantly improve the function of neurologic patients with disorders of voluntary movement, including torticollis, dystonia, and hemiparetic-spastic disorders of varied etiology. Thirty-six consecutively selected patients were studied, most of whom had received conventional therapy for up to 25 years with limited or no improvement. The patients learned volitional control of the functionally defective muscle group by means of audiovisual displays of integrated myoelectric activity from the monitored muscles. As volitional control of motor activity was achieved, the exteroceptive feedback was gradually withdrawn. Thirty-two of the patients responded with varying degrees of improvement ranging from functional "recovery" to symptomatic relief within 8 to 12 weeks. Apparently, a significant number of patients with disrupted internal feedback loops can incorporate the learned movement pattern by using those components of neuromuscular system that are still functionally available.

L imitations of conventional methods in rehabilitation of neurologic patients are well documented.[1,2] The use of learning techniques variously described as operant conditioning,[3] instrumental learning,[4] and "sensory feedback therapy" have been studied more extensively in the past decade. The physiologic bases of these techniques have been discussed in terms of sensory motor integration[5,6] and plasticity of the central nervous system.[7,8] The current study was initiated in 1971 as a practical clinical attempt to use audiovisual sensory feedback from muscle to treat disorders of voluntary movement that were not significantly benefited by other forms of therapy. The group studied included patients with torticollis, dystonia, and hemiparesis or quadriparesis with spasticity and/or weakness related to a variety of etiologies.

Initially, the techniques employed various trial-and-error methods, but these subsequently evolved into a prospective study with a well-developed protocol. The present report deals with the authors' findings during this period.

Patient population. The patient population (see table 1) was selected primarily on the basis of lack of response to conventional forms of therapy. The group included 2 patients with quadriparesis caused by spinal cord injury, 13 patients with hemiparesis, 13 patients with torticollis, 5 patients with dystonia, and 3 patients with facial spasms. All patients had their illness for at least nine months, with no further improvement using conventional forms of therapy, except for 4 who were treated early in

From the Departments of Rehabilitation Medicine and Neurology, New York University Medical Center, Bellevue Hospital Center, and ICD Rehabilitation and Research Center, New York City.

Supported in part by ICD Sensory Feedback Therapy Unit grant, NYU Medical Center Neurology Research Fund, SRS Rehabilitation, Research and Training Center (Medical) 16-P-56801/2-13.

Received for publication May 7, 1974.

Dr. Brudny's address is Department of Rehabilitation Medicine, Bellevue Hospital Center, First Ave. and 27th Street, New York, NY 10016.

Table 1. Patient population

Quadriparesis	2
Hemiparesis	13
Torticollis	13
Dystonia*	5
Facial spasms	3
Total	36

*Although the primary problem in these patients was dystonia, four of the five were being treated for the torticollis component of their disease (see table 4).

the study. All patients had some component of volitional motor activity present, which could not be utilized in any meaningful manner.

The patients' ability and motivation to cooperate and understand instructions were essential for the therapy. The presence of aphasia, organic mental syndrome, or mental deficiency that impaired patients' ability to follow instructions were reasons for exclusion from the study. The age of the patients ranged from 13 to 68 years. The duration of their illness was 9 months to 25 years, with the exception of 4 patients with hemiparesis. Each of these patients was independently evaluated by a physiatrist and a neurologist before acceptance into the study.

Method. Several modifications of the electromyograph (EMG), designed to detect, amplify, rectify, integrate, and display the myoelectric potential were used in this study. The transducers were skin electrodes. The integration technique provided quantification of changing EMG signal levels continuously. This change was reflected in both visual and auditory displays. The visual display provided information by means of a dial pointer on a calibrated scale, or oscilloscopic display of two-dimensional changes of the electric potentials (amplitude and rate), or digital readout of integrated muscle potential measured in microvolt-seconds. The auditory display provided rising and falling intensity of sound or a changing click rate. All these displays are proportional to the integrated EMG activity, over a selected time period.

We found that little time was needed for the patients to understand the relationship between muscle contraction or relaxation and the corresponding changes in the audiovisual display. A brief demonstration of technique often was carried out on a normal muscle in order for the patients to understand the concept. Therapy was directed toward two major goals: volitional decrease of spasm in spastic or spasmodic muscles and volitional increase of contraction and strength of the atrophied and/or paretic muscles. The therapeutic goals were achieved in a step-by-step fashion with a set of controls allowing for gradual change in the gain loop of the sensory feedback, thus demanding progressively better performance from the patient. The reward for performance was the achievement of voluntary control, confirmed directly and often by mirror viewing.

The therapeutic sessions usually were scheduled three times a week and lasted a half-hour, on the average. When a patient could volitionally change abnormal activity, usually after one to three sessions, and could maintain such control over several sessions, including functional improvement of the preexisting deficit, gradual withdrawal of feedback was instituted by decreasing the number and duration of reinforcement sessions.

Initially, photographs and occasionally motion pictures were taken before and after treatments. Currently all patients are videotaped prior to their entry into the study to demonstrate the degree of their functional impairment or movement disorders. In addition, a base line of physiologic parameters including electroencephalogram, EMG, and integrated EMG activity of the involved and contralateral muscles are recorded and taped with quantification of the integrated EMG expressed in microvolt-seconds. The measures are obtained with muscles relaxed (at rest) and during maximal activity (voluntary or involuntary).

After treatment, repeat videotapings, as well as physiologic parameters are recorded for comparison. Some of these techniques are described elsewhere.[9-11] A functional scale of activity of daily living also was developed for comparing the effects of therapy.

Results. The results were evaluated in terms of the patients' ability to modify their longstanding motor disorders, first with feedback, then when feedback was withdrawn. For example, in patients with hemiparesis, gains were measured in terms of upper extremity function: (1) relief of spasms with no functional component, (2) assistive function of the extremity, and (3) actual prehension. In patients with spasmodic disorders like torticollis, results were considered in terms of duration of the patients' ability to maintain a neutral neck position, first with feedback and then when feedback was withdrawn. Changes of the EMG and integrated EMG activity of the involved muscles before and after therapy also were noted.

In the two patients with injuries of the spinal cord at the C-5,C-6 level, there was total paralysis of lower extremities, and the upper extremities had some minimal degree of nonfunctional movement for up to three years. Improvement occured in both patients and is exemplified by the following case report.

Case 1. This patient is a 28-year-old electrician with a fracture dislocation of C-5,C-6 vertebrae, resulting in paraplegia and marked weakness of both upper extremities. The patient had a laminectomy with limited improvement. For three years he received conventional physical therapy and was treated for multiple decubiti. He was a total care patient.

Sensory feedback therapy was initiated with two specific goals: relaxation of the right spastic biceps and pronation of the forearm for use of a wrist-driven splint.   Within two weeks the patient achieved both goals, step by step. The same progress took place concurrently in the left arm without sensory feedback therapy. Two years later, the patient has retained these functions and can feed and groom himself, type, and drive an electric wheelchair.

The results using sensory feedback therapy in the patients with hemiparesis is illustrated in table 2. Note that four of these patients were studied prior to nine months after onset of their illness, and in two of these, no changes occurred. By current criteria these four would be excluded since spontaneous improvement is probable during this period. Three examples are presented:

Case 2. The patient is an 18-year-old high school girl who has a left spastic hemiparesis observed from the age of one. Previous treatment included right cryothalamectomy with some improvement. She also had several release and reconstruction procedures on both upper and lower extremities. Sensory feedback therapy was tried for relief of painful, constant, "dystonic'' contractions of the left peroneal muscle group that failed to respond to use of cast and brace.

Within two weeks she achieved voluntary control of her lower extremity, was free of pain, and discarded the brace. Subsequently, treatment to relieve her spastic clenched hand was started. This hand never had been used in any functional manner. Within six weeks of sensory feedback therapy she learned to control opening her left hand and later used her hands to cut meat, tie her shoelaces, and cook.

Case 3. This is a 57-year-old sculptor who had a cerebrovascular episode two years ago that resulted in aphasia and right hemiplegia. The patient gradually recovered except for marked somatosensory and kinesthetic disturbance of his right hand. He had no functional use of his right hand, which was continuously showing ''athetoid-like'' involuntary move-

ment. With sensory feedback therapy, he learned to control the involuntary movements. He began to use the right hand for meaningful functions, such as drawing and painting, within four weeks.

He still undergoes therapy.

Case 4. This patient is a 45-year-old truck driver with right hemiplegia secondary to cerebral hemorrhage. Nine months of conventional therapy failed to restore any meaningful voluntary motion in the fairly flaccid right upper extremity, which revealed atrophied muscles. A right Hoffmann's sign was present and deep tendon reflexes were increased. Four weeks of sensory feedback therapy resulted in the return of meaningful functional control of the entire extremity, including prehension. There also was considerable restoration of muscle bulk in the previously atrophied muscles of the shoulder and arm. These results were retained after eight months of follow-up.

Table 2. Patients with hemiparesis

Patient	Age and sex	Etiology	Duration of illness (years)	Upper extremity disability	Duration of therapy (weeks)	Results
1	21 F	Thrombosis	1	R spastic	12	+ +
2	19 M	Embolism	1	L spastic	8	+ +
3	24 F	Thrombosis	1	L spastic	8	+
4	68 M	Thrombosis	3 months*	R flaccid	2	0
5	45 M	Hemorrhage	9 months	L flaccid	6	+ + +
6	57 M	Thrombosis	1.5	R sensory loss athetosis	4	+ + +
7	44 M	Hemorrhage	3 months*	R spastic	6	+ +
8	16 F	Embolism	1	L spastic	6	+ + +
9	48 M	Thrombosis	6 months*	R spastic	6	+ +
10	50 F	Hemorrhage	3	L spastic	8	+ +
11	13 M	Hemiatrophy	1	L spastic	6	+ +
12	65 M	Meningioma, postoperative	3 months*	R spastic	4	0
13	18 F	Cerebral palsy	17	L spastic athetosis	4	+ + +

0   No change
+   Spasticity control

+ +   Assistive capacity
+ + + Prehension

*Treated early in the study prior to nine months' duration of illness.
Note: illustrative case reports Nos. 2, 3, and 4 in the text are Nos. 13, 6, and 5, respectively, in this table.

surgical procedures performed were cryothalamectomy and direct section of muscles. Psychotherapy had been attempted in eight of the patients.

Prior to sensory feedback therapy none of the patients could maintain voluntary neutral neck position for longer than a few minutes while seated. After 8 to 12 weeks of sensory feedback therapy, all the patients, with feedback, could maintain head position in neutral state for the duration of the session with minor fluctuations; without feedback, nine could maintain the neutral head position for significant periods (table 3). Quantitative EMG studies are reported elsewhere.[9] A smaller number could maintain head position with normal restitution for hours to

The next group of patients consists of those with primary torticollis (table 3). Of the 13 patients with torticollis, most had gone through a large variety of treatments. Medications used included diazepam, haloperidol, levodopa, and amantadine hydrochloride, while

months. Three patients clearly required feedback of some form to maintain normal head position, and reinforcement was required in at least three patients thus far, but the longest follow-up has been only two years. A case report of one of the best results is presented.

Case 5. This patient is a 55-year-old assembly worker who had had spasmodic torticollis for three years.   He could not work during this period. His chin and face were virtually fixed to the right, with hypertrophy of the left sternocleidomastoid and right trapezius muscles. He occasionally was able to turn his head to neutral position by touching his left chin with his finger.

After eight weeks of sensory feedback therapy, he learned voluntary control of his neck muscles, regaining and maintaining neutral neck position. Treatment included learning both relaxation of the hypertrophied muscle and strengthening of the opposite, relatively atrophied muscle. The resulting improvement has lasted for approximately two years without feedback.

Table 3. Patients with torticollis

Patient	Age and sex	Duration of illness (years)	Maintenance of neutral head position before therapy	Maintenance of neutral head position without feedback after 8-12 weeks of therapy	Current therapy
1	55 M	3	0	Months*	Reinforcement
2	48 M	10	0	Months*	Reinforcement
3	31 M	1	0	Hours	Discontinued
4	58 M	15	Minutes	Months*	Discontinued
5	54 F	13	Minutes	Hours	Reinforcement
6	41 M	13	0	5-10 Minutes	Discontinued
7	41 F	1	0	Hours	Discontinued
8	33 M	9 months	0	2-5 Minutes	Discontinued
9	54 F	15	0	Hours	In treatment
10	52 F	6	Minutes	Hours	In treatment
11	61 M	25	0	Hours	In treatment
12	62 M	3	0	30 Minutes	In treatment
13	48 F	3	0	2-5 minutes	

*Occasional spasmodic episodes occurred at times in relation to emotional stress or fatigue.

Note: after 8 to 12 weeks of sensory feedback therapy, all patients could maintain neutral head position for the duration of the session, approximately 30 minutes, when continuous sensory feedback was present. Case report No. 5 in the text is patient No. 1 in this table. In the last column, "reinforcement" indicates occasional periodic half-hour sessions of therapy separately by months; "discontinued" refers to patients in whom therapy was stopped; "in treatment" indicates patients who are continuing weekly treatment after the 8 to 12-week initial set of sessions in an attempt to achieve further improvement or secondary goals.

Occasional sessions for reinforcement were useful. The patient has been back to work during this period.

Since in each case only a primary goal was set for the patient, for example, ability to read or to sit with head straight, many of these patients will require further treatment for secondary goals.

In the five cases with dystonia (see table 4) results were less satisfactory. Three of these patients already had had cryothalamectomy and one patient clearly had no response and was considering surgery. The following case report is an example of good response to therapy.

Case 6. This is an 18-year-old boy with dystonia musculorum deformans that began at the age of eight years. He underwent cryothalamectomy twice on the left and once on the right side with remarkable improvement.

The only residual deficit has been recurrent and recently painful spasms of the left ankle plantar flexors, with inversion of the foot. After six weeks of therapy he learned to control the spasms while ambulating. This was done with feedback first and then without feedback, for increasingly longer periods of time. He is still undergoing therapy.

In a patient with blepharospasm the technique was unsuccessful, but in two patients with hemifacial spasms, voluntary decrease in frequency and duration of spasm was achieved to the point that the patients could control the spasms and return to work.

Discussion and conclusion. Although the results of early stages of our study appear promising and at times dramatic, the mechanism of sensory feedback therapy is not clear and future studies will require further serious, cautious, and statistically significant evaluations. The prelimi-

Table 4. Patients with dystonia

Patient	Age and sex	Duration of illness (years)	Family history	Prior treatment	Results	Current problem	Maintenance of neutral head position with feedback after 8-12 weeks	Maintenance restitution of normal head position without feedback after 8-12 weeks
1	20 M	14	?	*Surgery, drug therapy	Transient improvement	Torticollis	30 minutes	2-5 minutes
2	33 F	3	+	Drug therapy	No change	Torticollis	5-10 minutes	2-5 minutes
3	22 F	10	+	*Surgery, drug therapy	Improvement	Torticollis	30 minutes	Hours
4	13 M	9	+	Drug therapy	No change	Torticollis	* 0	0
5	18 M	10	+	*Surgery, drug therapy	Marked improvement	Left lower extremity dystonia	30 minutes†	Days†

*Cryothalamectomy.
†Maintenance of normal foot position.

Note: Illustrative case report No. 6 in the text is patient No. 5 in the table.

nary results indicate that sensory feedback therapy, especially in chronic resistant poststroke cases, should be explored further. Work paralleling ours is going on in this country[12] and abroad[13] and it is our hope that other investigators will also undertake such research.

At present this brief discussion of the study and its results will be confined to the major conclusion from our observations that with this technique the transfer of motor control from indirect exteroceptive feedback to direct, internal feedback is possible. In the nomenclature of Taub and Berman[14] the auditory and visual displays of integrated EMG activity can be considered as indirect feedback of motor performance in contrast to direct feedback derived from movements and related to proprioception and vision.

In normal subjects studied by other investigators, such indirect EMG feedback was used by means of operant conditioning, and resulted in control of single motor units; such control was retained eventually by the subjects when feedback was withdrawn.[15,16] In deafferented monkeys, previously thought to be incapable of purposive limb movement,[17,18] indirect feedback resulted in restoration of volitional movements in the deafferented limbs.[14]

In our patients, despite a varied etiology and different levels of anatomic interruption (in the central nervous system) of the normally closed loop sensory motor interaction,[19] the response to indirect sensory feedback was relatively uniform. In the early stages of therapy most patients were able volitionally to change the displays of EMG activity rather promptly. In the subsequent stages of therapy, when spatial displacement resulted from an increasingly larger degree of volitional change of the functional activity of the muscle, direct feedback by observation of the moving limb or mirror viewing of the altered position seemed to enhance the effects of ongoing indirect auditory feedback. If the final stages of therapy were reached, the control of movement was maintained when all external feedback was eliminated.

The patients who could control the previously defective motor act at this point, even without visual feedback,

apparently were able to use the functionally available components of the nervous system for developing new learned movement patterns, or modifying preexisting ones, or both. The retention of such learned motor control for the follow-up period of up to two years indicates that these learned movement patterns can become incorporated into the system of patterned volitional movements.[20]

Limitations of the technique are evident and always should be explained to the patient. This caution is important since one of the possible complications noted was depression, if the patient's expectations were greater than the results achieved.

Further investigations under controlled circumstances are required to determine whether the results obtained are specific to sensory feedback therapy,[21,22] and if so, to determine more precisely the characteristic of motor performance, learning and retention curves, the most appropriate time for reinforcement in different types of disorders, and an appropriate rationale for initiating therapy.

From our experience it seems that certain patients may always require external feedback for some degree of motor control, and current technology may be applied to develop portable EMG feedback units. We feel that this area of clinical research is of great promise in rehabilitation of neurologic patients, especially since this technique does not involve surgical or drug therapy.

Addendum. Since the completion of this report, 17 additional patients have been entered into the ICD Sensory Feedback Therapy Research Program. These include 12 patients with torticollis, two patients with dystonia, and three patients with hemiparetic syndromes. Thus far the results of sensory feedback therapy with these patients conform to those reported in this study.

Acknowledgments

We wish to acknowledge the efforts and criticisms of Mr. Marvin Welsinger, Mr. Geoffrey Frankel. and Dr. Sidney Weinstein.

REFERENCES

1. Taft LT, Delagi EF, Wilkfe OL, et al: Critique of rehabilitative technics in treatment of cerebral palsy. Arch Phys Med Rehabil 43:238-43. 1962
2. Herman R: Neuromotor Control Systems — A Study of Physiological and Theoretical Concepts Leading to Therapeutic Application. Department of Rehabilitation Medicine. School of Medicine, Philadelphia. Final report. 23P-551 15/3-03. December 1971
3. Skinner BF: The Behavior of Organisms New York, Appleton-Century Crofts, 1938
4. Miller NE: Learning of visceral and glandular responses. Science 163:434-445, 1969
5. Anokhin PK: Cybernetics and integrative activity of the brain. In: The Handbook of Contemporary Soviet Psychology. New York, Basic Book Inc., 1969
6. Connolly K: Intersensory Integration and motor impairment. In: Mechanisms of Motor Development. New York, Academic Press, 1970
7. Luria AR: Higher Cortical Functions in Man. New York, Basic Books, Inc., 1966
8. Bach-y-Rita P: Brain Mechanism In Sensory Substitution, New York. Academic Press, 1972
9. Brudny J, Grynbaum BB, Koreln J: New therapeutic modality for treatment of spasmodic torticollis. (Abstr) Arch Phys Med Rehabil 54:575, 1973 (Article in press)
10. Korein J, Maccario M, Carmona A, et al: Operant conditioning In subjects with normal and abnormal EEG activity. (Abstr) Neurology (Minneap) 21:395, 1971
11. Korein J, Levidow L, Brudny J: Self-regulation of EEG and EMG activity using bio feedback as a therapeutic tool. (Abstr) EEG Clin Neurophysiol 36:222, 1974
12. Johnson HE, Garton WH: Muscle re-education in hemiplegia by use of electromyographic device. Arch Phys Med Rehabil 54:320-322, 1973
13. Miller NE: Personal communication from Institute of Experimental Medicine, Academy of Medical Sciences of the U.S.S.R. In Freedman AM, Kaplan HI, Sadock BJ (Editors): Comprehensive Textbook of Psychiatry. Ed 2. Baltimore, The Williams & Wilkins Company, 1974 (in press)
14. Taub E, Berman AJ: Movement and learning in the absence of sensory feedback. In Freedman SJ (Editor): The Neurophysiology of Spatially Oriented Behavior. Homeward, Ill., Dorsey Press, 1966, pp 173-192
15. Basmajian JV: Methods in training the conscious control of motor units. Arch Phys Med Rehabil 48:12-19, 1967
16. Basmajian JV: Muscles Alive, Baltimore, The Williams & Wilkens Company, 1967
17. Lassek AM: Inactivation of voluntary motor function following rhizotomy. J Neuropathol Exp Neurol 12:83-97, 1953
18. Twitchell TE: Sensory factors in purposive movement. J Neurophysiol 17:239-252, 1954
19. Smith KV: Cybernetic theory and analysis of learning. In Bilodeau E (Editor): Acquisition of Motor Skill, New York, Academic Press, 1966
20. Paillard J: The Patterning of Skilled Movements. In Field J, Magoun HW, Hall VE (Editors): Handbook of Physiology. Washington, D.C., American Physiological Society, 1960, vol 3, section 1, pp 1679-1708
21. Stroebel CF, Glueck BC: Biofeedback treatment in medicine and psychiatry: An ultimate placebo? In Birk L (Editor): Biofeedback: Behavioral Medicine. New York, Grune & Stratton, Inc., 1973
22. Cleeland CS: Behavioral technics in the modification of spasmodic torticollis. Neurology (Minneap) 23:1241-1247, 1973

Assessment of an Audio-Visual Feedback Device Used in Motor Training

C. G. Kukulka and J. V. Basmajian

INTRODUCTION

The use of audio and visual feedback for training of conscious control of single motor units (SMU) has stimulated interest in its practical applications in physical medicine. The new discipline of biofeedback promises to further both our understanding of the learning processes involved and the improvement of therapeutic techniques used in rehabilitation of the physically disabled. Although occasional publications on electromyographic biofeedback have appeared from the 1920's to 1950's (1, 2, 3, 4), direct efforts to exploit it were not initiated until the early 1960's. Thus, the early work of Basmajian and his colleagues first led to specific training methods (5, 6); with expanding usage, increasing standardization of the basic techniques has been inevitable (7, 8). It is now well known that subjects can consciously maintain activity of and change the frequency of individual motor units (i.e., motoneurons) while the rest of the musculature remains silent (6, 9, 10, 11). Furthermore, as a normal subject continues the isolation of a single unit, a progressive inhibition of neighboring units occurs (12). This fine control can be maintained even when distracting movements of the ipsilateral extremity, contralateral extremity, and head are performed (13); it is even possible during repetitive electrical stimulation of the muscle's nerve supply (14). The application of

[1] From the Emory University Regional Rehabilitation Research and Training Center, Atlanta, Georgia.

Received for publication August 30, 1974.

[2] Director, Emory University Regional Rehabilitation Research and Training Center, % Georgia Mental Health Institute, 1256 Briarcliff Road, N.E., Atlanta, Georgia 30306 (address for reprints).

The authors are indebted to Mr. James Perry, Mr. James Hudson, Mr. Harold Clifford, and Mrs. E. Regenos for valuable technical and computer assistance.

cold to the overlying skin causes excessive firing of an isolated SMU (15), while induced ischemia results in increased difficulty in recalling and maintaining SMU activity (16).

The influence of this research on the practical application of biofeedback has led to a gradual development of therapeutic techniques (17). As early as 1960, Marinacci and Horande presented various case histories and discussed the effectiveness of the display of the EMG to patients in restoring function for seven different neuromuscular conditions (18). Encouraging results were later presented by Andrews who trained stroke patients to flex and extend the involved elbow (19), while more recently Johnson and Garton described a biofeedback training procedure using a portable unit for reeducation of the involved tibialis anterior in stroke patients (20). Increasing interest has developed in the techniques of muscle relaxation. Budzynski et al. (21) developed a device which utilizes EMG activity for inducing deep muscle relaxation and applied it to relieving tension headaches (22). More recently, Wickramasekera observed marked decrease in frequency and intensity of tension headaches along with decreased EMG activity of the frontalis muscle following three weeks of EMG feedback training (23). Additional relaxation studies have indicated decreased levels of gastrocnemius activity in cerebral palsy (24), reduced spasm frequency of neck muscles in spasmodic torticollis (25), and decreased neck muscle activity resulting from neck trauma (26).

With the continual advancements in medical technology, the development of integrated circuitry, and the increasing understanding of man's neuromuscular system, medical and engineering personnel have begun to concentrate on the use of conscious motor-unit control to control myoelectric orthoses and prostheses. Simard and Ladd have developed training procedures (27) and the description of the levels of motor unit control in thalidomide children (28) and quadriplegic patients (29). Trombly has described a "myoelectric torque motor unit" that was tested effectively with C4-C5 quadriplegic patients (30); and recently, Harris et al. have described improvements in postural stability and control of voluntary motions in cerebral palsy children equipped with electronic sensory aids (31).

These recent advances in biofeedback research have prompted a group at Emory University to develop a miniaturized EMG biofeedback device, the Mini-Trainer.[3] Electronically, the device consists of 1) a differential amplifier for detection of muscle activity, 2) a high-pass filter for filtering 60 Hz interference, 3) a rectifier for inverting negative deflections to positive, 4) an integrator to determine the average of the positive deflections, 5) a level detector to read the amount of activity from the integrator, 6) a light-emitting diode for visual feedback, and 7) a multivibrator for audio feedback. Muscle activity is detected by two $\frac{1}{4}''$ diameter cylindrical electrodes applied with electrode paste to the overlying skin surface of the muscle (fig. 1). A dial on the underside of the trainer allows for variation in the threshold level for activation.

The purpose of this study was two-fold: 1) to develop a practical training pro-

[3] The Basmajian-Emory Muscle Trainer is available from: Bio-Feedback Technology, Inc., 10592 Trask Avenue, Garden Grove, California 92643.

gram for using a portable audio-visual EMG feedback device, and 2) to assess the functioning of this device in regard to a) variations in the threshold for activation of the trainer, b) the occurrence of possible patterns of muscular activity when subjects attempted to activate the trainer, and c) changes in active range of motion after training with the device. All subjects were trained to abduct the big toe of the right foot because the abductor hallucis is one of the few skeletal muscles normal subjects have difficulty controlling (32, 33).

MATERIALS AND METHODS

Selection of subjects

Thirteen adult volunteers between the ages of 21 and 45 years of age, with no history of pathology affecting normal motor control, participated in this study.

Instrumentation

Mini-trainer on-off activation, separate EMG records from intramuscular electrodes through regular amplifiers, and the range of motion from a special device were stored on a Thermionic recorder.[4] Reduction of data was conducted on a PDP 8/I computer. Minor adaptations of the regular model Mini-trainer were made for the study. The trainer was coupled to the tape recorder so that whenever the trainer was activated, a square wave was recorded. A protractor-type dial was devised to allow for standardization of the Mini-trainer's variable threshold levels (fig. 1). An electrogoniometer was designed so that range-of-motion recordings for the great toe could be made simultaneous with recordings of EMG activity and trainer activation (fig. 1).

Experimental set-up

The subject lay in a semi-reclining position with the right foot secured in the electrogoniometer. Bipolar fine-wire electrodes were inserted into the middle of the belly of abductor hallucis of the right foot. A dual source-follower and ground electrode were placed approximately 2 cm anterior and 2 cm posterior-inferior respectively to the medial malleolus. This allowed ample room for placement of the mini-trainer pick-up electrodes (fig. 1).

Minimum trainer threshold

Whenever the threshold of the mini-trainer is turned to its lowest setting, artifactive feedback signals are emitted by simple contact with the subject's skin. Therefore this artifact was eliminated first. With the subject at rest, the trainer was applied over various points of the muscle belly; the threshold was gradually increased until skin contact no longer activated the trainer. This setting was recorded as the minimum trainer threshold.

---

[4] Thermionics Products (Electronics) Ltd. Hythe-Southampton, England, sold and serviced by Edwin Industries Corporation, 11933 Tech Road, Silver Spring, Maryland 20904.

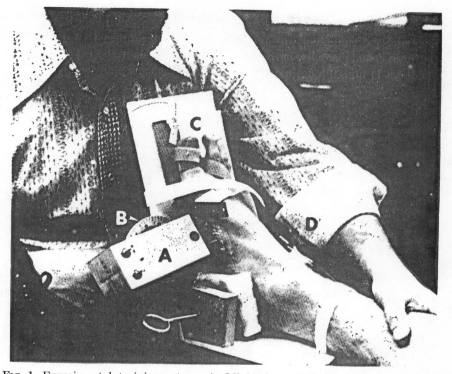

FIG. 1. Experimental training set-up. A, Minitrainer applied to skin over abductor hallucis with bipolar electrodes; B, Protractor added to regular instrument for establishing threshold values; C, ROM electrogoniometer with the visible dial for instant readings; D, Spring connectors to which bipolar fine-wire electrodes (invisible here) are attached for independent intramuscular EMG recordings of the muscle.

Pre-test

The subject was familiarized with the audio and visual responses, and was informed he would be asked to produce a steady feedback response by consciously activating the device, by visible abduction of the big toe without resistance or by both responses simultaneously.

Maximum isometric contractions against resistance were made under the 3 feedback conditions to provide the data reducing devices with a reference. Recordings were made for each 5-second trial.

Tests

Three feedback conditions were presented: no feedback, audio feedback, and visual feedback. The order of presentation was randomized prior to testing of the subjects. At the beginning of each experiment, the subject was assigned an order of presentation and this order was maintained throughout his training.

1. Maximum Range of Motion

Maximum range of motion recordings were made under the 3 feedback conditions. The subject was asked to abduct the big toe as far as possible and range of motion was noted as well as recording of muscular activity from the fine-wire electrodes. *Minimum range of motion* was specified as 3° less than maximum initial motion.

2. Initial Threshold Level

Initial threshold level was determined by having the subject abduct the big toe and concentrate on activating the trainer set at the minimum trainer threshold. Five-unit increments of the threshold were made and the subject was asked to activate the trainer at each level. At the threshold where the subject could not activate the trainer for more than 2 seconds, a 5-second EMG recording was made. Determination of this duration was made by viewing the trainer output on a storage oscilloscope and estimating the duration the trainer was activated. Following the first recording, the threshold was decreased to the level prior to failure and increments of 1 unit were made. At the failure level, a final 5-second EMG recording was made. This procedure was repeated with the second type of feedback. The lowest threshold of the two feedbacks was considered the initial threshold.

3. Dual Control Testing

Dual control testing was determined by the subject's ability to both maintain steady feedback and abduct the toe through a set range of motion. Four conditions were presented:
   a. Minimal range of motion, minimum trainer threshold
   b. Minimal range of motion, initial threshold
   c. Initial maximum range of motion, minimum threshold
   d. Initial maximum range of motion, initial threshold

The four conditions were grouped into Group 1 (a, b) and Group 2 (c, d). The order of performance of each group was alternated from subject to subject. Each feedback condition was tested with 2-minute rest periods.

Training

Each subject underwent two training sessions during the experiment. The type of feedback used in the first session was randomly chosen; the second training session utilized the alternative feedback. In this way, no one type of feedback was continuously used first. The subject was first required to concentrate on gradually producing increased muscle activity as the threshold of the trainer was increased. Once the subject displayed proficiency in producing feedback and an inability to increase the threshold level, emphasis was shifted to using his newly developed muscle activity to create more motion. Figure 2 is a diagram of the training and in-training testing procedure used in one training session. Beginning with random selection of the feedback and proceeding clockwise, one can follow the progression of the training session as described below.

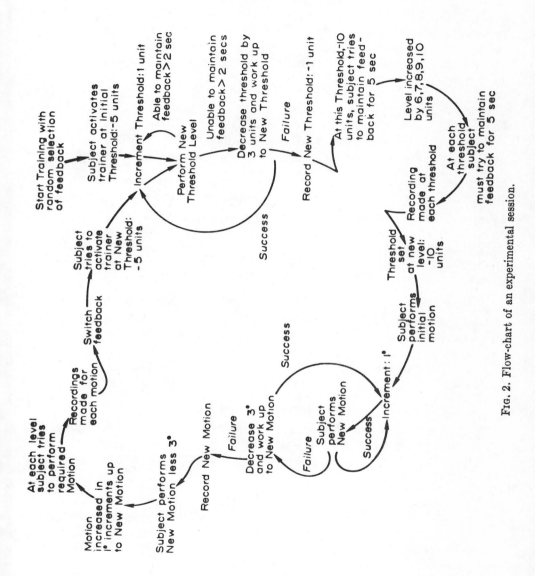

FIG. 2. Flow-chart of an experimental session.

1. Training to Increase the Threshold

Training to increase the threshold was begun at 5 units below the initial threshold. The subject was asked to maintain steady feedback as increments of 1 were made. At the failure level, the threshold was decreased 2 or 3 units and repetitions performed for reinforcing the feedback response. When a level was reached which the subject was unable to surpass in 3 or 4 trials, training was stopped, time for training and threshold were noted, and the subject rested for 2 minutes.

2. In-Training Test of Threshold

In-training test of threshold was begun with the subject maintaining the feedback at 10 units below threshold determined during training. The level was increased by 6, 7, 8, 9 and 10 units; 5-second recordings of trainer activity, muscular activity, and range of motion were made followed by a 2-minute rest period.

3. Training to Increase Range of Motion

Training to increase range of motion was begun by having the subject abduct to the initial range of motion. Increments of 1° were made with repeats at various levels for reinforcement of the feedback. At the level where range of motion remained unchanged for 3–4 trials, the motion and time for training were noted and the subject was asked to rest for 2 minutes. Threshold was set and maintained at 10 units below the level determined during previous threshold training.

4. In-Training Test for Range of Motion Increase

In-training test for range of motion increase was conducted by first having the subject abduct to 3° below the motion determined in training. Increments of 1°, 2°, and 3° were made. Five-second recordings were made at each level. The subject was asked to rest for 2 minutes. Threshold was set and maintained at 10 units below the level determined during previous threshold training.

5. Repeat Procedures

Procedures 2 to 4 were repeated with the second feedback. For beginning threshold and range of motion training, the newly determined levels for each were used in place of initial levels. In this manner, both variables were progressively increased.

Post-test

1. Using the procedures described for the pre-test, final measurements were made of maximum isometric contraction, range of motion, and threshold.

2. Dual control testing was conducted as in the pre-test, but with 9 conditions presented:
   a. Minimal range of motion, minimum trainer threshold;
   b. Minimal range of motion, initial threshold;
   c. Minimal range of motion, final threshold;
   d. Initial range of motion, minimum trainer threshold;
   e. Initial range of motion, initial threshold;

TABLE 1

Maximum motion, motion maintained for longest duration, and the duration each was held during 5 second trials, initially and finally

Subject	Maximum motion (degrees)		Duration held (seconds)		Motion of longest duration (degrees)		Duration held (seconds)	
	Initial (degrees)	Final (degrees)	Initial (seconds)	Final (seconds)	Initial (degrees)	Final (degrees)	Initial (seconds)	Final (seconds)
L.S.	7	9	.1	1.0	3	7	1.5	1.7
W.B.	23	22	.9	.2	22	21	2.3	1.7
N.K.	1	3	2.5	2.0	1	1	2.5	3.0
J.K.	6	7	.9	2.4	2	7	3.1	2.4
B.L.	18	27	3.0	.1	18	25	3.0	2.5
V.G.	13	19	.3	1.8	12	19	2.3	1.8
J.B.	18	20	.6	.3	17	19	2.1	1.5
J.W.	9	11	.1	1.4	8	10	1.6	3.0
J.S.	5	1	.4	3.0	4	1	1.8	3.0
T.W.	7	15	.2	.8	4	14	2.8	3.0
A.F.	6	8	.4	.4	1	7	1.5	2.3
L.M.	17	22	.1	1.7	15	22	1.1	1.7
V.L.	6	8	.8	2.8	2	8	1.7	2.8

f. Initial range of motion, final threshold;
g. Final range of motion, minimum trainer threshold;
h. Final range of motion, initial threshold; and
i. Final range of motion, final threshold.

The 9 conditions were grouped into Group 1 (a, b, c), and Group 2 (d, e, f), and Group 3 (g, h, i). The order of performance of each group was randomized for each subject.

Analysis of data

Independent EMG, range of motion, and Mini-trainer activation data were reduced on a PDP 8/I computer. The EMG was sampled at a rate of 1000 Hz and integrated over an interval of 0.1 seconds for 5.0 second trials. Range of motion and Mini-trainer activation were sampled at the end of every 0.1 second interval. Print-out of range of motion was in degrees, and for Mini-trainer, a "0" represented off and a "1" represented on. The range of motion values were interpreted in two ways: 1) maximum motion obtained in a five-second trial, and 2) motion maintained for the longest duration in a five-second trial.

RESULTS

Most subjects felt that with concentrated thinking about the position the toe should be in, they were better able to complete the motion required. Several of the subjects also expressed a preference to a rhythmical cadence of commands for turning on the trainer, and then resting. When this cadence was broken, threshold levels often had to be lowered for reinforcement. All subjects stated that they

TABLE 2

Increase in maximum motion and motion of longest duration with corresponding decrease in duration maintained

Subject	Change in maximum motion (degrees)	Change in duration maintained (seconds)	Change in motion of longest duration (degrees)	Change in duration maintained (seconds)
L.S.	+4	+0.9	+2	+0.2
W.B.	−1	−0.7	−1	−0.6
N.K.	0	−0.5	+2	+0.5
J.K.	+5	+1.5	+1	−0.7
B.L.	+7	−2.9	+9	−0.5
V.G.	+7	+1.5	+6	−0.5
J.B.	+2	−0.3	+2	−0.6
J.W.	+2	+1.3	+2	+1.4
J.S.	−3	+2.6	−4	+1.2
T.W.	+10	+0.6	+8	+0.2
A.F.	+6	0.0	+2	+0.8
L.M.	+7	+1.6	+5	+0.6
V.L.	+6	+2.0	+2	+1.1

experienced fatigue during training. Two-minute rest periods were given between each test and frequently during training to combat this occurrence. During training, each subject experienced at least one muscle cramp. Two to three minute rest periods with gentle massage alleviated this problem and training could resume.

Table 1 summarizes the range of motion (ROM) values with the corresponding durations that each were held for initial and final trials. For maximum motion, 11 of 13 subjects displayed increases ($\overline{X}$ gain $= 3.73° \pm 2.78°$, S.D.; Range 1° to 9°), while for motion maintained for the longest duration, 10 subjects increased and 1 remained the same ($\overline{X} = 5.27° \pm 3.0°$; Range 0° to 10°). N = 11 for both groups. When increases for each of these motions were compared for each subject, an increase or decrease in one coincided with a similar change in the other. No consistent pattern could be found (table 2). The time each motion was maintained throughout a five-second trial was compared initially and finally for each subject. It was thought that an increase in these motions might also show an increase in the time they were maintained. In table 2, it is seen that in most instances motion increases also displayed increases in the duration for which they were maintained, but that this was not consistent for all subjects.

The values for maximum motion and motion of longest duration were categorized as to the corresponding feedback used. Initially, 4 of 13 subjects obtained greatest motions with feedback, while finally, 8 of 13 subjects obtained greatest motions with feedback (table 3). When ROM values were gathered initially and finally, 3 trials were always performed with a random order of presentation of the 2 feedbacks and no feedback. Using the two ROM values, initial and final comparisons were made regarding the sequence of these trials. Initially, maximum ROMs were observed in the 1st and 3rd trials (6 subjects for each trial) while 1 subject produced greatest motion in the 2nd trial. Finally, maximum ROMs

TABLE 3

Occurrence of maximum motion and motion of longest duration

Subject	Initial		Final	
	Feedback	Order	Feedback	Order
L.S.	None	1	Visual	2
W.B.	None	1	None	3
N.K.	Audio	3	Audio	3
J.K.	Audio	1	Visual	3
B.L.	None	2	Visual	3
V.G.	None	3	Audio	1
J.B.	None	3	None	3
J.W.	None	1	Audio	3
J.S.	None	3	None	3
T.W.	Audio	3	Audio	3
A.F.	None	1	Audio	3
L.M.	None	1	None	1
V.L.	Visual	3	None	1

TABLE 4

Correct responses for initial and final dual control tests

Subject	Initial test				Final test			
	Motion accuracy		Feedback accuracy		Motion accuracy		Feedback accuracy	
	Audio	Visual	Audio	Visual	Audio	Visual	Audio	Visual
L.S.	3	4	2	4	8	3	2	7
W.B.	4	4	2	2	6	8	3	3
N.K.	4	4	3	4	6	6	9	7
J.K.	4	3	2	2	8	8	7	8
B.L	4	4	4	3	8	9	3	6
V.G.	4	4	2	3	9	9	7	5
J.B.	4	4	2	2	9	9	4	5
J.W.	4	4	4	2	8	8	8	9
J.S.	4	4	4	0	7	7	5	5
T.W.	4	4	2	2	8	9	3	2
A.F.	1	2	2	4	0	2	7	6
L.M.	4	4	0	0	8	9	5	4
V.L.	1	1	4	4	4	3	8	7
Total correct responses	45	46	33	32	89	90	71	74
Maximum possible correct responses	52	52	52	52	117	117	117	117

TABLE 5

Correct responses for each trial of final dual control test

	Minimal motion	Initial maximum motion	Final maximum motion
Audio			
Minimum trainer threshold	12–12	12–11	6–12
Initial threshold	11–3	11–10	9–8
Final threshold	11–3	10–7	7–5
Visual			
Minimum trainer threshold	13–12	10–13	7–13
Initial threshold	11–5	10–10	9–7
Final threshold	12–3	10–5	8–4

were observed in the 3rd trial (9 subjects) with 3 subjects and 1 subject producing greatest motions on the 1st and 2nd trials respectively (table 3).

In the dual control tests, the subjects were tested for their ability to simultaneously produce a set ROM and also activate the feedback for at least two seconds of a five second trial. The correct responses for each subject, together with total scores are presented in table 4. In the initial test, four combinations of two ROMs (minimal and initial maximum) and two thresholds (minimum trainer and initial) were presented. The final test required three ROMs (minimal, initial maximum, and final maximum) and three thresholds (minimum trainer, initial, and final) for a total of nine combinations.

The number of subjects with correct responses for ROM and feedback production for each trial of the final test are presented in table 5. The first value is the number of subjects that produced the required motion and the second value the number of subjects that produced the required feedback. Although the majority of subjects felt that the audio feedback was easier to activate and offered more incentive, the accuracy for producing the feedback and desired motion was similar with both types of feedback. In regard to production of feedback, accuracy decreased as threshold increased with the poorest accuracy at final threshold levels. ROM production displayed a slight decrease in accuracy as the motion increased with only slight changes as the thresholds were increased (table 5).

Another aspect of EMG output which we wished to investigate was whether a repeatable pattern was evident when a subject was asked to activate the trainer. The in-training threshold tests were designed so that six threshold levels of graduated difficulty were presented to the subject who was asked to activate the trainer for five-second trials with no rest between trials. Each integrated EMG value for the first 0.5 seconds of trainer activation was represented as a per cent of maximum contraction, and each of these values was plotted against its corresponding time value. This was done for the six thresholds with both audio and visual feedback. When analyzed in this graphic manner, no particular pattern emerged. All subjects displayed a random fluctuation of EMG activity once the feedback was produced. An example of this is presented in figure 3.

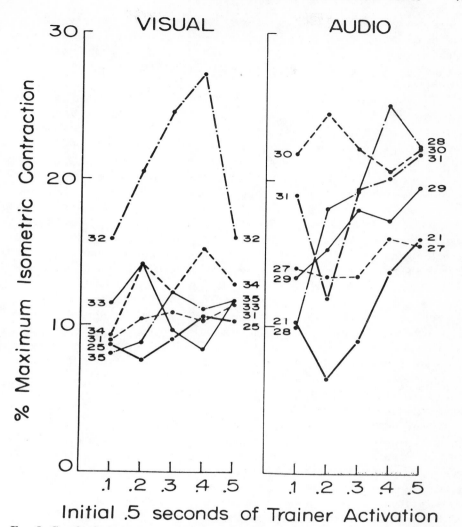

FIG. 3. Graph of per cent of maximum isometric contraction *vs.* initial 0.5 sec of trainer activation (subject L.S.). The numbers preceding and following each line designate the threshold level at which the trainer was set for that trial.

DISCUSSION

Our results in training normal subjects clearly indicate the effectiveness of the biofeedback training protocol used, and encourage its application in a clinical setting. This effectiveness may be attributed to three important factors:

1. The performances of each of the two tasks (ROM and feedback production) were separated so that all emphasis was given to one task at a time. The need for this was first made evident in pilot studies where all subjects expressed difficulty

in concentration when asked to perform both tasks simultaneously. The dual control tests used supported this assumption. As greater demands were made, proficiency in simultaneous task performance eroded even though each subject had met criteria for all ROM and threshold levels when previously asked to perform them separately.

2. Continual adjustments for feedback and ROM reinforcement were built in for when a subject's proficiency dropped off. By cluing a subject to his correct responses through biofeedback, positive reinforcement was continually ongoing. All subjects described a certain "positive feeling" on performing a task successfully; they describe a range of sensations involving tension, position, and rhythm, as well as unexplainable feelings. The continual adjustments were, therefore, made to maximize this "positive feeling" and hence encourage a high proficiency.

3. Progressive increasing of the threshold requirements was necessary to ensure improvement in the subject's ROM abilities. Our flow-chart for an experimental session depicts the training session as a smooth moving cycle allowing for transition from one task to the next, incorporating the previous improvements to further the subject's overall proficiency in the immediate task he is performing.

With these factors in mind, we feel that in using a biofeedback device to improve a subject's ROM capabilities: 1) emphasis must first be placed on making the subject aware of the activity of his muscle through his ability to produce feedback; 2) the muscle activity must be increased by increasing the demands for feedback production (increase threshold); 3) positive re-enforcement must be maintained by continual adjustment of the threshold level; and 4) the newly-acquired muscle activity must be used to perform a greater ROM.

The feasibility of monitoring both maximum range and duration of motion is more remote in a clinical setting than in a study such as this, but the implication of the two motions bears directly on the clinician's evaluation and the setting of criteria for a patient's performance. In working towards increasing ROM, not only is it important for a patient to perform as great a motion as possible, but also to display a repeatability and/or consistency in performing the motion. Using the motion maintained for the longest duration as the criterion for consistency, the closer this motion comes to maximum motion, the more one would suspect a qualitative training effect—and this is what did occur in this study.

More basic research is needed to further delineate the factors involved in voluntary control of skeletal muscles using biofeedback. For example, we believe that both an order effect and the type of feedback we used influenced our results to some degree. With a larger sample population, a statistical evaluation could be made for clarification. Two subjects showed a decrease in ROM at the end of training; perhaps the effect of fatigue on these subjects may have contributed to the poorer outcome. Greater control over the time allowed for training might reveal the factors involved. One subject (W.B.) displayed the greatest initial ROM, but his ROM decreased by 1° in the final test. A subject's proficiency in performing a task before training could have some bearing on his overall ability to increase his proficiency. This could be significant in the selection of normal subjects in biofeedback training studies.

The results of this investigation have encouraged us to use the Mini-Trainer in a clinical setting. Following the training design presented here, experimentation is now being conducted for: 1) re-education of tibialis anterior in patients who have suffered a cerebrovascular accident and have residual footdrop, and 2) early finger joint mobilization following lacerations of long flexor tendons in the hand.

SUMMARY

A miniature biofeedback device, the Basmajian-Emory Muscle Trainer, has been developed at the Emory University School of Medicine. A training and testing protocol was designed for using this device in the training of precise voluntary control of individual skeletal muscles. Thirteen normal subjects were trained to abduct the big toe of the right foot, eleven of whom displayed increases in maximum motion. Use of a biofeedback device to improve a subject's ROM capabilities requires consideration of four factors: (1) initial emphasis must be on making the subject aware of his muscle activity, (2) the muscle activity must be increased, (3) the positive re-enforcement of feedback must be continual, and (4) the newly acquired muscle activity must be used to perform a greater ROM. The results of this study encourage the use of the Mini-Trainer in a clinical setting.

REFERENCES

1. Adrian, E. D., and Bronk, D. W. The discharge of impulses in motor nerve fibres. Part II. The frequency of discharge in reflex and voluntary contractions. J. Physiol., *67:* 119–151, 1929.
2. Smith, O. C. Action potentials from single motor units in voluntary contraction. Amer. J. Physiol., *108:*629–638, 1934.
3. Gilson, A. S., and Mills, W. B. Activities of single motor units in man during slight voluntary efforts. Amer. J. Physiol., *133:*658–669, 1941.
4. Harrison, V. F., and Mortensen, O. A. Identification and voluntary control of single motor unit activity in the tibialis anterior muscle. Anat. Rec., *144:*109–116, 1962.
5. Basmajian, J. V. Control and training of individual motor units. Science, *141:*440–441, 1963.
6. Basmajian, J. V., Baeza, M., and Fabrigar, C. Conscious control and training of individual spinal motor neurons in normal human subjects. J. New Drugs, *5:*78–85, 1965.
7. Basmajian, J. V., and Samson, J. Standardization of methods in single motor unit training. Amer. J. Phys. Med., *52:*250–256, 1973.
8. Basmajian, J. V. Control of individual motor units. A guide and preliminary reading for prospective subjects in single motor unit training experiments. Amer. J. Phys. Med., *52:*257–260, 1973.
9. Simard, T. G., and Basmajian, J. V. Methods in training the conscious control of motor units. Arch. Phys. Med., *48:*12–19, 1967.
10. Lloyd, A. J., and Leibrecht, B. C. Conditioning of a single motor unit. J. Exper. Psychol., *88:*391–395, 1971.
11. Leibrecht, B. C., Lloyd, A. J., and Pounder S. Auditory feedback and conditioning of the single motor unit. Psychophysiology, *10:*1–7, 1973.
12. Smith, Jr., H. C., Basmajian, J. V., and Vanderstoep, S. F. Inhibition of neighboring motoneurons in conscious control of single spinal motoneurons. Science, *183:*975–976, 1974.

13. Basmajian, J. V., and Simard, T. G. Effects of distracting movement on the control of trained motor units. Amer. J. Phys. Med., 46:1427–1449, 1967.
14. Scully, H. E., and Basmajian, J. V. Effect of nerve stimulation on trained motor unit control. Arch. Phys. Med., 50:32–33, 1969.
15. Clendenin, M. A., and Szumski, A. J. Influence of cutaneous ice application on single motor units in humans. Phys. Ther., 51:166–175, 1971.
16. Simard, T. G., Basmajian, J. V., and Janda, V. Effects of ischemia on trained motor units. Amer. J. Phys. Med., 47:64–71, 1968.
17. Schaefer, S., and Engel. R. R. Operant control of autonomic function: biofeedback bibliography. Percep. and Motor Skills, 36:863–875, 1973.
18. Marinacci, A. A., and Horande M. Electromyogram in neuromuscular re-education. Bull. Los Angeles Neurol. Soc., 25: 57–71, 1960.
19. Andrews J. M. Neuromuscular re-education of hemiplegia with aid of electromyograph. Arch. Phys. Med., 45: 530–532, 1964.
20. Johnson, H. E., and Garton, W. H. Muscle re-education in hemiplegia by use of electromyographic device. Arch. Phys. Med., 54:320–322, 1973.
21. Budzynski, T. H., and Stoyva, J. M. An instrument for producing deep muscle relaxation by means of analog information feedback. J. Appl. Behav. Anal., 2:231–237, 1969.
22. Budzynski, T. H., Stoyva, J. M., and Adler, C. Feedback-induced muscle relaxation: application to tension headache. J. Behav. Ther. Exper. Psychiat., 1:205–211, 1970.
23. Wickramasekera, I. The application of verbal instructions and EMG feedback training for the management of tension headache: a preliminary study. Headache, 13:74–76, 1973.
24. Amato, A., Hermsmeyer, C. A., and Kleinman, K. M. Use of electromyographic feedback to increase inhibitory control of spastic muscles. Phys. Ther. 53:1063–1066, 1973.
25. Cleeland, C. S. Behavioral techniques in the modification of spasmodic torticollis. Neurology, 23:1241–1247, 1973.
26. Jacobs, A., and Fenton, G. S. Visual feedback of myo-electric output to train muscle relaxation in normal persons and patients with neck injuries. Arch. Phys. Med., 50: 34–39, 1969.
27. Simard, T. G., and Ladd, H. W. Pre-orthotic training. An electromyographic study in normal adults. Amer. J. Phys. Med., 48:301–312, 1969.
28. Simard, T. G., and Ladd, H. W. Conscious control of motor units with thalidomide children: an electromyographic study. Devel. Med. Child Neurol., 11:743–748, 1969.
29. Simard, T. G., and Ladd, H. W. Differential control of muscle segments by quadriplegic patients: an electromyographic procedural investigation. Arch. Phys. Med., 52:447–452, 1971.
30. Trombly, C. Myoelectric control of orthotic devices for the severely paralyzed. Amer. J. Occup. Ther. 22:385–389, 1968.
31. Harris, F. A., Spelman, F. A., and Hymer, J. W. Electronic sensory aids as treatment for cerebral-palsied children. Inapproprioception: Part II. Phys. Ther., 54: 354–365, 1974.
32. Iida, M., and Basmajian, J. V. Electromyography of hallux valgus. Clinical Orthoped. and Related Res., 101:220–224, 1974.
33. Robison, M. E., Doudlah, A. M., and Waterland, J. C. The influence of vision on the performance of a motor act. Amer. J. Occup. Ther., 19:202–204, 1965.

A Preliminary Report on Biofeedback Training for Early Finger Joint Mobilization

55

C. G. Kukulka, D. Mike Brown, and J. V. Basmajian

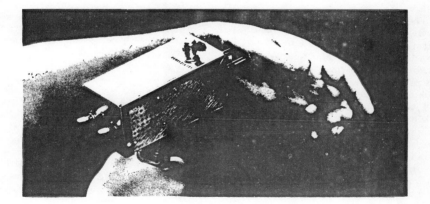

Using a newly developed, small, portable EMG biofeedback device for facilitating training, restoration of finger function after surgical repair of tendons was quickly achieved in three patients. Their case reports are discussed and are offered to encourage wider use of biofeedback in the therapy of such patients.

C.G. Kukulka, B.S., R.P.T., D. Mike Brown, O.T.R., and J.V. Basmajian, M.D., F.A.C.A., Director, are with Emory University Regional Rehabilitation Research and Training Center, and Grady Memorial Hospital, Atlanta, Georgia.

Figure 1 Experimental model of Basmajian-Emory Muscle Trainer being applied to thenar muscles. This greatly miniaturized EMG equipment, used with surface electrodes, is self-contained (battery-operated) and capable of eliciting minimal EMG activity. A red light and a buzzer are activated when the EMG reaches a threshold set by the sensitivity dial

In recent publications[1,2] the use of a miniaturized EMG biofeedback muscle trainer (Figure 1) and a training protocol were reported together with the encouraging results obtained in training hemiparetic patients to dorsiflex the foot. The application of biofeedback in rehabilitation medicine depends upon the visual and/or auditory monitoring of muscular contractions. Both patients and therapists receive immediate objective assessment of the functioning of the muscles; they can then work together on either recruiting or inhibiting the activity.[3] Electromyographic biofeedback grew out of early work on the training of single motor units.[3] Subjects given visual and acoustic feedback of their electromyography were trained to consciously control the activity of their spinal motor neurons with amazing accuracy and facility. An accelerated interest has grown up in the past decade in the use of EMG biofeedback for training patients with neurological disabilities.

Feedback training has been used successfully to restore function in various neuromuscular disorders[4] and upper extremity paresis of stroke patients.[5] Muscle relaxation can be facilitated with techniques developed for relieving tension headaches,[6,7] reducing neck muscle spasm in spasmodic torticollis[8,9] and neck trauma,[10] relaxing gastrocnemius activity,[11] improving postural stability and voluntary control[12] in cerebral palsy, and decreasing uncontrolled peroneus longus activity during knee extension.[13]

Early digital mobilization following lacerations and surgical repair of the long flexor tendons in the hand appears to be an additional application of the device. Postoperative rehabilitative techniques are based on the concept of stressing scar tissue in an effort to accelerate or induce remodeling of the scar to form more favorable adhesions that will permit tendon gliding.[14] The usefulness and adaptability of the device to aid in early mobilization therefore has significance. Case reports of three patients who benefited from a biofeedback training program are given and point the way in which a biofeedback trainer may be used effectively.

Training Procedure

The patients received therapy three times a week for three weeks. Each session was begun with 15 minutes of whirlpool bath at 36°C followed immediately by 20 minutes of exercise under the supervision of a therapist. Only active motions were performed during the first week, progressing to active-assistive motion the second week, and gentle stretching the third week. Twenty minutes of biofeedback training followed each therapy session. The Mini-Trainer was used taking into consideration the four factors described previously;[1,2] in brief, these are: (a) inducing patient awareness of muscle activity through the instant electromyographic feedback using both a visual and an acoustical signal; (b) increasing the muscle activity; (c) positively reinforcing correct responses; and (d) using the newly acquired activity to create greater motions.

The primary emphasis in using the feedback device was to facilitate the long flexor muscles to the fingers. Two surface electrodes were placed over the belly of the flexor digitorum superficialis and the trainer threshold level was adjusted in accordance with the patient's performance. Various exercises were performed with the forearm both pronated and supinated. Initially, isometric contractions were performed in varying finger and wrist positions. Mass flexions of the fingers were then performed, first without regard to wrist position, and then with the wrist in a functional position. The patients progressed to grasping built-up dowel rods of various sizes while activating the trainer and then to making isolated proximal interphalangeal (PIP) motions. Isolated flexion of the distal interphalangeal (DIP) joint was also attempted; but, because of the deep position of the flexor profundus, feedback from the superficialis had to be used. Active ranges of motion (ROM) of the joints were measured upon the command "make a fist."

Case Reports

Patient 1: *History.* A 48-year-old woman sustained lacerations of the flexor digitorum superficialis and profundus tendons through the crease of the metacarpophalangeal (MP) joints—the "no man's land"—in the left ring and little fingers. One week later, delayed primary surgical repairs were performed on the tendons to the ring finger with implantation of a silastic rod in the little finger. Twenty-two days after surgery the surgical bandages were removed and therapy for the ring finger was started the following day.

Results. Initial active ROM readings of the

ring finger were: MP joint, 0-68°; PIP, 35-50°; and DIP, 5-22°.

Following training, active ROM became normal in the MP joint; 10-100° in the PIP; and 0-30° in the DIP. She was now able to touch the distal palmar crease with the tip of the ring finger.

Patient 2: *History.* A 42-year-old man suffered a laceration to the flexor digitorum superficialis and profundus tendons of the index, long, and ring fingers of the right hand. Also, the radial anterolateral volar digital nerve to the index finger was severed. The site of laceration was at the level of the distal palmar crease. Ten days later a delayed primary anastomosis of tendons and nerve was performed. Approximately three and one half weeks post-surgery, therapy was begun.

Results. Initial active ROM readings were:

Finger	MP	PIP	DIP
Index	15-58°	32-43°	10-10°
Long	10-54°	27-33°	10-10°
Ring	18-57°	32-38°	10-12°

Following training, active, ROM became:

Index	Normal	11-88°	0-24°
Long	Normal	12-86°	0-24°
Ring	Normal	9-87°	0-26°

Patient 3: *History.* A 44-year-old man sustained lacerations to the flexor pollicis longus and flexor digitorum superficialis of the index finger at the distal wrist crease. Eleven days later a delayed primary repair was performed on the involved tendons. Three and one half weeks post-surgery, therapy was begun.

Results. Initial active ROM reading for the thumb MP joint was 10-38° and IP was 21-21°; for the index MP joint it was 11-40°; PIP, 43-48°; and DIP joint, 9-17°.

Following training, active ROM became normal for both MP joints. The ROM of the thumb IP became 4-38°; that of the index PIP, 6-77°; and DIP, 0-74°.

Summary

Three patients had severe lacerations of various extrinsic flexor tendons of the hand in areas once considered moderate to poor post-surgical recovery regions. Three weeks of range of motion exercise coupled with biofeedback training resulted in the return of good joint motion. The favorable results displayed by these patients has encouraged the use of biofeedback training in early finger joint mobilization at the Hand Rehabilitation Center, Grady Memorial Hospital, Atlanta, Georgia.

Acknowledgments

We thank Dr. L.O. Vasconez, Chief of the Hand Clinic, Division of Plastic Surgery, Grady Memorial Hospital, for referring the patients and for his continued interest and support of the biofeedback research project. This work was supported in part by Grant No. 16-P-56808/4-10 from the Social and Rehabilitation Service, Department of Health, Education, and Welfare.

REFERENCES

1. Kukulka CG, Basmajian JV: An assessment of an audiovisual feedback device for use in motor training, *Am J Phys Med 54:* August, 1975
2. Basmajian JV, Kukulka CG, Narayan MC, Takebe K: Biofeedback treatment of foot-drop after strokes compared with standard rehabilitation techniques, Part I. Effects on voluntary control and strength, *Arch Phys Med, 56:* 231-236, 1975
3. Basmajian JV: *Muscles Alive: Their Functions Revealed by Electromyography,* 3rd edition, Baltimore, Williams & Wilkins, 1974
4. Marinacci AA, Horande M: Electromyogram in neuromuscular re-education. *Bull Los Angeles Neurol Soc,* 25: 57-71, 1960
5. Andrews JM: Neuromusclar re-education of hemiplegia with aid of electromyograph. *Arch Phys Med,* 45: 530-532, 1964
6. Budzinski TH, Stoyva JM, Adler C: Feedback-induced muscle relaxation: Application to tension headache. *J Behav Ther Exper Psychiatry,* 1: 205-211, 1970
7. Wickramasekera I: The application of verbal instructions and EMG feedback training for the management of tension

headache: A preliminary study. *Headache,* 13: 75-76, 1973
8. Cleeland CS: Behavioral techniques in the modification of spasmodic torticollis. *Neurology,* 23: 1241-1247, 1973
9. Brudny J, Grynbaum BB, Korein J: Spasmodic torticollis: treatment by feedback display of EMG. *Arch Phys Med,* 55: 403-408, 1974
10. Jacobs A, Felton GS: Visual feedback of myo-electric output to train muscle relaxation in normal persons and patients with neck injuries. *Arch Phys Med,* 50: 34-39, 1969
11. Amato A, Hermsmeyer CA, Kleinman KM: Use of electromyographic feedback to increase inhibitory control of spastic muscles. *Phys Ther,* 53: 1063-1066, 1973
12. Harris FA, Spelman FA, Hymer JW: Electronic sensory aids as treatment for cerebral-palsied children. Inapproprioception: Part II. *Phys Ther,* 54: 354-365, 1974
13. Swaan D, van Wieringen PCW, Fokkema SD: Auditory electromyographic feedback therapy to inhibit undesired motor activity. *Arch Phys Med,* 55: 251-254, 1974
14. Peacock EE, Jr, Madden JW, and Trier WC: Postoperative recovery of flexor tendon function. *Am J Surg,* 122: 688-692, 1971

Biofeedback Treatment of Foot-Drop After Stroke Compared with Standard Rehabilitation Technique: Effects on Voluntary Control and Strength

56

J. V. Basmajian, C. G. Kukulka, M. G. Narayan, and K. Takebe

• The effectiveness of biofeedback training was compared to conventional physical therapy training in 20 adult hemiparetic patients with chronic foot-drop. They were randomly placed into two groups of ten patients each: the first group treated over five weeks with therapeutic exercise and the second group treated over five weeks with therapeutic exercise plus biofeedback training. In the second group receiving the biofeedback training the increase in both strength and range of motion was approximately twice as great as in the first group. The improvement displayed by even the first group of patients suggests that a potential for functional improvement exists that is often unexploited. The addition of biofeedback facilitates the process. Four patients in the biofeedback group achieved and retained conscious control of dorsiflexion; three of them are now able to walk without the use of their short leg brace.

The explosive growth of biofeedback includes its application in rehabilitation medicine—especially with electromyography (EMG). With visual and/or auditory monitoring of muscular contractions, both patient and therapist receive immediate objective assessment of the functioning of the muscles; then both can work on either recruiting or inhibiting the activity. In some early studies, EMG feedback was used for restoring function in various neuromuscular disorders[1] and upper extremity paresis of stroke patients.[2] A great deal of interest has been generated in the area of muscle relaxation, with techniques developed for relieving tension headaches,[3,4] reducing neck muscle spasm in spasmodic torticollis[5,6] and neck trauma,[7] relaxing gastrocnemius activity[8] and improving postural stability and voluntary control[9] in cerebral palsy, and decreasing uncontrolled peroneus longus activity during knee extension.[10] Efforts to harness single motor unit activity for control of myoelectric orthoses and prostheses[11,12] have dwindled in the recent years, yet the potential in this area should not be underestimated.

In a previous study[13] we developed a training protocol for using a miniature portable audiovisual EMG feedback device (Basmajian-Emory Muscle Trainer, Biofeedback Technology, Inc, Garden Grove, CA). Our successful training of normal subjects to control the relatively "uncontrollable" abductor hallucis led to the present study of the effectiveness of biofeedback training of hemiparetic patients to dorsiflex the foot compared with the effectiveness of standard exercise therapy.

Theoretical advantages in using a small portable biofeedback unit might be threefold: (1) *Increased body image*—Patients afflicted with hemiparesis often express the belief that the muscles on their affected side are "dead"; through the use of biofeedback, they should realize that these muscles are indeed alive and that some level of voluntary control is possible, sometimes a dramatic level. (2) *Improved muscle training* —Conventionally, after all attempts at muscle re-education have failed, correction of foot-drop is obtained by applying a short leg brace; biofeedback provides an additional modality for muscle training and possibly avoids the use of braces. (3) *Improved self-treatment*—The portability of the device permits supplementary self-treatment which can be learned easily from a trained clinician.

The purpose of this study was to test the effectiveness of biofeedback training compared to conventional physical therapy training in the treatment of paralytic foot-drop. Tibialis anterior muscle was selected because of its primary function as the chief ankle dorsiflexor. The parameters investigated were strength of dorsiflexion, active range of motion (ROM) and functional improvement in walking.

From the Regional Rehabilitation Research and Training Center, Emory University, Atlanta.
This study was supported in part by Grant No. 16-P-56808/4-10 from the Social and Rehabilitation Service, Department of Health, Education and Welfare.
Submitted for publication August 13, 1974.

Fig 1—Experimental arrangement.

Materials and Methods

Subjects

Twenty adult volunteers (ten men, ten women) between 30 and 63 years of age (mean, 50.7) participated in this study (table 1). All subjects were selected according to a protocol that called for the following criteria: (1) a cerebrovascular accident at least three months before; (2) residual foot dorsiflexion paresis; (3) a minimum passive dorsiflexion from complete plantarflexion to neutral position (90°); (4) ability to ambulate with or without a cane and/or short leg brace; and (5) no receptive aphasia.

Training Sessions

The subjects were randomly divided into two groups. Group 1 consisted of ten subjects who received 40 minutes of therapeutic exercise. Group 2 consisted of ten subjects who received 20 minutes of therapeutic exercise plus 20 minutes of biofeedback training using a miniature muscle trainer.

Therapeutic exercise sessions were always conducted by the same therapist. All subjects received treatment three times a week for five weeks.

Instrumentation

A spring dynamometer strength-measuring device was designed for dorsiflexion recordings. To minimize procedural error for the two testing sessions of each subject, flexion of the knee was maintained at 30° and the chain length between foot pad and spring was kept constant (fig 1).

Patient Evaluation

Prior to the first treatment session of each patient, a neurological examination was performed to assess motor performance and sensory impairments. A functional analysis of gait was made and graded according to the quality of dorsiflexion (table 2). Because more than six months had elapsed since the stroke for most of the subjects, their neurological status was considered stabilized, in spite of individual differences in functional abilities.

The starting point for beginning treatment was based on the particular recovery stage of the patient. Three basic recovery stages were defined thus:

Stage 1—Patient is able voluntarily to move the entire limb in partial flexion and extension-synergy patterns while supine, but displays no voluntary isolated control of any joints. (Treatment was initiated using these synergy patterns with graded resistance to facilitate individual joint motions.)

Stage 2—Patient displays strong synergy patterns through complete ROM with ability to partially isolate knee and hip motions and slight ankle motions in certain positions. (Treatment was initiated with reinforcement of dorsiflexion in the positions in which the patient performed well, gradually working to the more difficult ones.)

Stage 3—Patient is able to voluntarily control all joint motions but with increased difficulty from proximal to distal joints; when increased resistance is applied to mass movements, synergy patterns predominate; ankle dorsiflexion can be performed in most positions, but persistent foot-drop occurs during walking. (Treatment was initiated with the patient performing ankle dorsiflexion in various body positions and simultaneously with varying hip and knee motions.)

Testing Procedure

Each subject was tested by an investigator other than the therapist two days before and two days after training. The subject was placed in a semireclining position with the knee maintained in 30° flexion. Each recording session was conducted in four steps. Only steps 1 and 2 are reported here—muscle strength and ROM measurements. Steps 3 and 4, consisting of bilateral nerve conduction velocity measurements of the peroneal nerves and complex stroboscopic and conventional gait analyses, will be given in subsequent papers.

Step 1—Muscle strength was recorded with the use of the spring-dynamometer apparatus. The subject's foot was secured to the foot-pad by taping, and he was instructed to

Table 1: Characteristics of Group 1 and Group 2 Patients

Group 1, 10 patients (physical therapy only)					Group 2, 10 patients (physical therapy and biofeedback)				
Case no.	Age, yr	Sex	Duration, mo	Recovery stage	Case no.	Age, yr	Sex	Duration, mo	Recovery stage
1	62	F	36	1	11	48	F	24	1
2	58	F	12	2	12	53	M	4	2
3	37	F	20	2	13	60	M	65	2
4	47	F	50	2	14	52	F	27	2
5	56	M	36	2	15	52	M	12	2
6	63	M	120	3	16	38	F	5	1
7	44	F	4	1	17	62	M	10	2
8	47	M	21	2	18	30	M	48	3
9	47	M	120	3	19	45	M	6	3
10	45	F	28	3	20	58	F	24	3
Average									
	50.6		44.7			50.8		22.5	

Table 2: Description of Grading System for Gait Evaluation

0—No dorsiflexion: complete foot drop; constant toe dragging.

1—Trace dorsiflexion: primarily reflexive in flexion synergy; constant toe dragging.

2—Poor dorsiflexion: continues to drag toes during swing through; occasionally, entire sole down in early stance (foot flat).

3—Fair dorsiflexion: occasional heel-toe gait pattern; most frequently, entire sole down in early stance.

4—Good dorsiflexion: good heel-toe gait pattern; when patient tires, reverts to toe drag and/or foot flat.

5—Normal heel-toe gait pattern.

dorsiflex the foot as far as possible. Five-second readings were made five times with 30-second rest periods between readings.

Step 2—Active ROM measurements were made with the subject in the sitting position. Goniometric measurements for each subject were conducted by the same investigator at each testing session. Three measurements were made of the subject's active motion and the greatest was considered maximum for that day.

TREATMENT REGIME

All 20 patients progressed through a general treatment regime of exercise and gait training always given by the same physical therapist (C.G.K.). Primary emphasis during exercise was consistently on facilitating ankle dorsiflexion. The various body and limb positions in which each patient performed well were noted and progression was gradually attempted to encompass as many positions as possible. Standard gait training was initiated by practicing swing-through of the affected leg, progressing to walking in the parallel bars, walking with a four-pronged cane, and where possible, walking with a straight cane. All gait training was performed without a short leg brace.

Biofeedback treatment followed the manner described in the basic study,[13] but with more frequent rest periods. In brief, this consists of: (a) making the subject aware of his muscle activity through his ability to produce feedback; (b) having the subject increase this muscle activity by increasing the demands for feedback production (increased mini-trainer threshold); (c) positively reinforcing the subject by continually adjusting the threshold level; and (d) shifting the final emphasis to using the newly acquired muscle activity to perform a greater ROM.

All patients used audio and visual feedback for equal periods during each session. Training was done with the patient seated in a comfortable chair and with the knee in varying positions.

FOLLOW-UP EXAMINATION

Follow-up examinations were conducted 4 to 16 weeks after completion of training. These consisted of a gross measurement of each patient's ability to actively dorsiflex the foot and an assessment of the gait pattern based on our grading system for gait analysis (table 2).

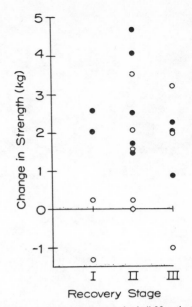

Fig 2—Graph of changes in strength of all 20 patients on the basis of recovery stage. Open circles, group 1 patients; filled circles, group 2 patients.

Results

Both groups of patients showed changes in ROM and strength of dorsiflexion after training (table 3). In group 2 (patients receiving both treatments) the increase in both categories was approximately twice as great as that in group 1.

The influence, if any, of the recovery stage and duration of hemiparesis on the changes in strength and ROM was investigated to ascertain why such large discrepancies existed between the two training groups (figs 2 and 3). For all three stages, the average increase in strength of group 2 patients was always greater, with a lessening in the difference between the two groups from stage 1 through stage 3. Group 2 patients in stages 1 and 2 displayed marked increases in ROM (fig 3) while group 1 patients had their greatest increases in stage 3 (table 4).

Interpretation of the possible influence of the duration of the hemiparesis was more difficult because of its wide range, but some clarification appears on looking at the durations of one year or less, those between one and three years, and those greater than three years. Among patients who had hemiparesis for one year or less, group 2 patients all displayed greater strength increases; among those between one and three years' duration, only one patient in group 1 recorded a greater increase than the three patients in group 2. There were five patients in whom the duration exceeded three years; of these, the three patients in group 1 displayed a wide variability in strength changes while the two patients in group 2 both showed moderate improvement. Taken as a

Table 3: Changes in Range of Motion and Strength for Group 1 and Group 2 Patients After Training

	Group 1. 10 patients (physical therapy only)			Group 2. 10 patients (physical therapy and biofeedback)	
Case no.	Motion, degrees	Strength, kg	Case no.	Motion, degrees	Strength, kg
1	—2	—1.30	11	20	2.60
2	15	0.25	12	7	4.10
3	12	1.60	13	—4	1.50
4	21	3.55	14	14	2.55
5	4	0.00	15	26	1.75
6	2	2.00	16	17	2.05
7	—3	0.25	17	2	4.70
8	11	2.10	18	16	2.05
9	—3	—1.00	19	5	0.90
10	0	3.25	20	5	2.30
Average	5.7	1.07		10.8	2.45

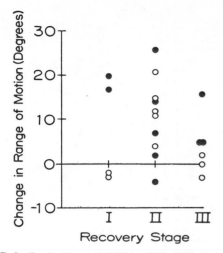

Fig 3—Graph of changes in ROM for all 20 patients on the basis of recovery stage. Open circles, group 1 patients; filled circles, group 2 patients.

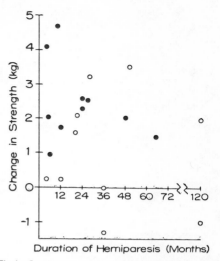

Fig 4—Graph of changes in strength of all 20 patients on the basis of duration of hemiparesis. Open circles, group 1 patients; filled circles, group 2 patients.

whole, the relationships of ROM changes to the duration of hemiparesis in the two groups does not show as clear a separation (fig 5).

A more functional analysis of the change in gait pattern, based on the grading system for gait evaluation (table 1), shows that the most noted improvements were displayed by cases 17, 18 and 19 of group 2, each of whom had constant toe drag prior to treatment (table 5). These patients all achieved consciously controlled dorsiflexion sufficient to produce a more normal heel-toe gait pattern. Cases 17 and 19 had worn short leg braces prior to training and were able to walk well without them following training.

The follow-up examination of cases 17 and 19 (four months and one month after final treatment, respectively) revealed no regression. On some days when they felt tired and needed to walk long distances, they resumed using their braces because they felt more secure. At follow-up (three months after training) case 13 of group 2, who had been hemiparetic for five years and had not shown much improvement immediately following training (from grade 1 to grade 2), was walking with high-top shoes and without his brace. He said that the treatments gave him more confidence, and our reevaluation of his gait showed an improvement to grade 3. The remaining patients in group 2 maintained the same gait pattern as they had achieved by the end of training.

In group 1, cases 4 and 6 displayed good gait improvements by the end of the training period (table 5), but they were not able to consistently repeat their performance. These patients started at a lower level of performance (grade 1) than those previously discussed (cases 17, 18 and 19). Although each could consciously dorsiflex the foot when initiating walking, their performance readily deteriorated, requiring them to stop, rest for a brief interval, think of the motion, and then resume walking. At follow-up, all group 1 patients who were evaluated displayed no further change in their gait patterns.

Discussion

The greater increases in strength and ROM of the patients who received combined conventional therapy and biofeedback training, strongly support the effectiveness of biofeedback therapy. Although the sample sizes available when the total groups are subdivided according to recovery stage and duration of the hemiparesis are small and inconclusive, some general remarks can be made. The greatest and some of the least increases were made for both strength and ROM in the patients with hemiparesis for one year or less. Also, there are good increases around the two-year and four-year periods with some poor performances interspersed throughout this range, leading us

Table 4: Average Change of ROM and Strength of Group 1 and Group 2 Patients With Consideration of the Recovery Stage

Group	Recovery stage 1			Recovery stage 2			Recovery stage 3		
	No. of patients	Strength, kg	ROM, degrees	No. of patients	Strength, kg	ROM, degrees	No. of patients	Strength, kg	ROM, degrees
1 (physical therapy)	2	—0.53	—2.50	5	1.50	12.60	3	1.42	—0.33
2 (physical therapy biofeedback)	2	2.83	18.50	5	2.92	9.00	3	1.75	8.67

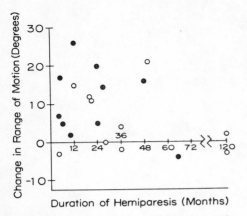

Fig 5—Graph of changes in ROM of all 20 patients on the basis of the duration of the hemiparesis. Open circles, group 1 patients; filled circles, group 2 patients.

to question at what point in the recovery of a stroke victim does his neurological status become completely stabilized so that no further recovery is possible. In group 1, two patients who had had hemiparesis for ten years actually displayed the extremes in performance—one doing exceptionally well and the other, poorly. We would emphasize the apparent potential that exists for many hemiparetic patients. Although the overall response of group 2 was much better, some good strength and ROM increases were displayed by individuals receiving physical therapy only. Two patients in this group (cases 4 and 6) started at grade 1 and achieved a two-step increase in performance. These grade increases are similar to those in the biofeedback-trained patients (cases 17, 18 and 19) although they started at a higher level (grade 2).

With regard to the influence of recovery stage, stage 2 appears to include patients with the most improvement, but the very small sample sizes of the other two stages prevent firm conclusions.

The use of strength and ROM measurements to assess training effects would be meaningless without an overall improvement in the gait pattern. This improvement in our patients emphasizes the effectiveness of biofeedback training. The quantitative improvements of the biofeedback group were impressive, but the startling results were in the four patients who could control dorsiflexion for prolonged periods of time in their activities of daily living. The two group 1 patients who were trained to achieve active dorsiflexion had a low level of endurance and an inconsistent repeatability of performance. The contrast between the long endurance and accurate repeatability of the four patients who had started at grades 2 or 3, and the two group 1 patients who started at grade 1 suggests that the initial performance level may be an important factor in the training.

The use of audio and visual feedback had a strong and immediate reenforcing effect on the patient's response to performing a prescribed task. Individual motivation was continually maintained with the immediate feedback. Swaan, van Wieringen and Fokkema,[10] in reporting good results using biofeedback training, have called for more research in describing the variables involved in training. The results of our investigation are promising, yet certain questions require clarification, primarily the effects of sample population characteristics. Much larger groups of patients need to be treated and data analyzed in regard to patient age, duration of illness, and residual deficits. The effects of these variables could significantly influence the results of such investigations.

The continuing development of biofeedback training techniques offers much promise for its use as an added modality in the treatment of physically handicapped individuals. The results presented here lend a favorable outlook to its use in stroke rehabilitation. We believe that biofeedback can play an important role as an adjunct to regular therapy sessions in which facilitation and/or inhibition of muscle activity is desired.

Acknowledgment: We are indebted to the staff in physical and occupational therapy at Grady Memorial Hospital and to James Perry, James Hudson and Eleanor Regenos for technical assistance.

ADDRESS REPRINT REQUESTS TO:
J. V. Basmajian, M.D.
Georgia Mental Health Institute
1256 Briarcliff Road, N.E.
Atlanta, GA 30306

Table 5: Gait Analysis (Dorsiflexion Control During Gait)

Case no.	Group 1 (physical therapy only)			Time,* wks	Case no.	Group 2 (physical therapy and biofeedback)			Time,* wks
	Start of training	End of training	Follow-up			Start of training	End of training	Follow-up	
1	0	1	1	4	11	0	1	1	16
2	0	1	1	4	12	1	2	2	16
3	1	1	1	15	13	1	2	3	12
4	1	3	3	5	14	1	2	2	9
5	1	2	2	4	15	1	2	2	9
6	1	3	3	4	16	1	2	2	6
7	1	1			17	2	4	4	16
8	2	3	3	16	18	2	4		
9	2	2	2	4	19	2	4	4	6
10	3	3			20	3	4	4	8

*Time in weeks since end of training.

References

1. Marinacci AA, Horande M: Electromyogram in neuro-muscular re-education. Bull Los Angeles Neurol Soc 25:57-71, 1960

2. Andrews JM: Neuromuscular re-education of hemi-plegic with aid of electromyograph. Arch Phys Med Rehabil 45:530-532, 1964

3. Budzynski T, Stoyva J, Adler C: Feedback-induced muscle relaxation: application to tension headache. J Behav Ther Exper Psychiat 1:205-211, 1970

4. Wickramasekera I: Application of verbal instructions and EMG feedback training to the management of tension headache: preliminary observation. Headache 13:74-76, 1973

5. Cleeland CS: Behavioral technics in modification of spasmodic torticollis. Neurology (Minneap) 23:1241-1247, 1973

6. Brudny J, Grynbaum BB, Korein J: Spasmodic torti-collis: treatment by feedback display of EMG. Arch Phys Med Rehabil 55:403-408, 1974

7. Jacobs A, Felton GS: Visual feedback of myoelectric output to facilitate muscle relaxation in normal per-sons and patients with neck injuries. Arch Phys Med Rehabil 50:34-39, 1969

8. Amato A, Hermsmeyer CA, Kleinman KM: Use of electromyographic feedback to increase inhibitory con-trol of spastic muscles. Phys Ther 53:1063-1066, 1973

9. Harris FA, Spelman FA, Hymer JW: Electronic sensory aids as treatment for cerebral-palsied children: inap-proprioception: part II. Phys Ther 54:354-365, 1974

10. Swaan D, van Wieringen PCW, Fokkema SD: Auditory electromyographic feedback therapy to inhibit unde-sired motor activity. Arch Phys Med Rehabil 55:251-254, 1974

11. Simard TG, Ladd HW: Pre-orthotic training: Elec-tromyographic study in normal adults. Am J Phys Med 48:301-312, 1969

12. Trombly CA: Myoelectric control of orthotic devices: for severely paralyzed. Am J Occup Ther 22:385-389, 1968

13. Kukulka CG, Basmajian JV: Assessment of an audio-visual feedback device for use in motor training. Am J Phys Med (Baltimore) (in press)

X

OTHER APPLICATIONS OF BIOFEEDBACK AND OPERANT CONDITIONING

Voluntary Control of Penile Tumescence

57

Raymond C. Rosen, David Shapiro, and Gary E. Schwartz

This study investigated the voluntary control of penile tumescence in the absence of external erotic stimulation. Twelve experimental subjects were given analogue visual feedback and monetary rewards for increases in penile diameter as measured by a strain gauge. Twelve control subjects were given no analogue feedback and noncontingent rewards but the same instructions to maximize erections. While both groups were capable of voluntary penile tumescence, significantly improved performance was observed in the experimental group. Two distinct psychophysiological patterns of voluntary penile tumescence were observed. A "tension" pattern was associated with marked heart rate acceleration, irregular respiration, and variable penile response. A "relaxation" pattern was associated with stable heart rate, regular respiration, and smooth tumescence curves. In using these procedures for the treatment of sexual dysfunctions, it is suggested that feedback and reward be given for a combined pattern of sexual and autonomic responses.

INTRODUCTION

In a previous study [1] elicited penile tumescence was shown to be susceptible to suppression by instrumental conditioning. A red light was presented to normal male volunteers whenever their erection exceeded a criterion increase, and in this way they learned to significantly inhibit tumescence over the course of three experimental sessions.

Simple instructions to enhance or inhibit erection have also been found to affect penile tumescence in the presence or absence of erotic stimuli [2,3]. It seems that subjects who are readily able to conjure up sexual images or fantasies are able to utilize these images to "voluntarily" control the engorgement of the penile *corpora*. Such a finding is consistent with research indicating effects of conscious thought processes on other physiological variables [4].

Although the above studies provide strong evidence for some degree of instrumental or voluntary control of erec-

From the Department of Psychiatry, CMDNJ-Rutgers Medical School, Piscataway, N.J. 08854.

David Shapiro, PhD, is from UCLA.

Gary E. Schwartz, PhD, is from Harvard University.

This research was supported in part by funds from NIMH Research Grant MH-08853 and Office of Naval Research Contract N00014-67-A-0298-0024, NR 101-052.

Address reprint requests to: Raymond C. Rosen, PhD, Department of Psychiatry, CMDNJ-Rutgers Medical School, Piscataway, N.J. 08854.

Received for publication August 13, 1974; final revision received June 12, 1975.

tion, several experimental questions are indicated: (1) Do feedback and reward enhance control of erection in the *absence* of erotic stimulation? (2) Can feedback and reward be shown to provide greater control than instructions alone in the facilitation of erection? (3) To the extent that voluntary control of tumescence can be developed, what psychophysiological mechanisms are involved?

The present study was designed to investigate the voluntary control of erection in the absence of external erotic stimulation. An attempt was made to evaluate the extent to which feedback and reward procedures enhance such control. Moreover, by concurrently monitoring cardiovascular and respiratory changes, specific physiological mechanisms of control were examined.

METHOD

The research was conducted in the Psychophysiology Laboratories of Harvard Medical School at the Massachusetts Mental Health Center. Penile tumescence was monitored and recorded following the same procedure as in the previous study (1). Other physiological responses recorded were beat to beat changes in heart rate by means of a Lexington Instruments cardiotachometer, and respiration by means of a strain-gauge belt. In order to provide analogue visual feedback for penile tumescence increments, a small,orange light located directly in front of the subject was programmed for light intensity changes proportional to increases in penile diameter. In addition, two other signal lights were utilized: a bright, white light signaled a bonus of 25 cents each time the subject reached criterion for that trial,and a blue light indicated the end of the trial.

The subjects were 24 paid volunteers without any history of sexual dysfunction. All subjects received a thorough preexperimental briefing session in order to explain the general purpose of the study, and to obtain informed consent. Subjects who appeared anxious about the procedures were excluded. After subjects were comfortably seated in the sound- and temperature-controlled experimental room, the physiological recording apparatus was attached and the experiment began.

Following a preexperimental adaptation period, each subject received two 20 min experimental sessions. In order to maximize the control of tumescence, a shaping procedure was employed. On the first trial, the white bonus light was presented to experimental subjects who showed a penile diameter increase of at least 1.5 mm. After each successful trial,

the criterion was raised by 0.5 mm penile diameter. Each trial was programmed to continue until the subject attained the criterion for that trial, or 100 sec had elapsed. A variable intertrial interval of 20–40 sec was employed, with the contingency that the subject's penile volume had to be returned to baseline level before the next trial was begun.

The 12 subjects in the control group received similar experimental instructions and procedures except that the orange analogue light remained constant, and bonuses were programmed noncontingently. Yoked bonuses ensured a comparable incentive level for control subjects. These subjects therefore received the same duration and order of trials as well as payment for the experiment, but were unassisted by the analogue feedback and contingent rewards. In the previous study (1) the feedback light had produced suppression of response and therefore it was unnecessary in this experiment to control for the eliciting effects of the feedback stimulus.

All subjects were instructed to maximize erections in the presence of the orange light, without any overt bodily movement. Questionnaires were administered after each session, and all subjects were debriefed after the second experimental session.

RESULTS

Penile tumescence was scored by measuring the strain-gauge diameter increase from the beginning to the end of each trial. Figure 1 indicates that the shaping procedure was effective in that progressively larger penile diameters were obtained on each successive trial. An analysis of variance performed on these data show that the trials effect was significant ($p < 0.001$), as was the groups × trials interaction ($p < 0.05$). The

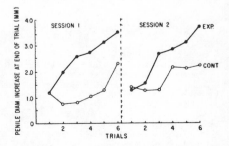

Fig. 1.   Mean penile diameter increase over six trials in the two experimental sessions. The 12 subjects receiving feedback and reward are indicated by the solid circles, and the controls by the open circles.

TABLE 1.   Mean Percent Criterion (Rewarded) Responses per Session.

MEAN % CRITERION (REWARDED) RESPONSES/SESSION

	Session 1	Session 2
EXP.	65.4	71.58
CONT.	29.1	41

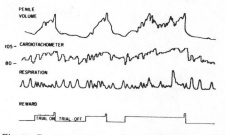

Fig. 2. Representative portion of a sample polygraph record. This record illustrates the "tension" pattern of response: irregular tumescence, heart rate increase, and irregular respiration.

significant interaction effect indicates that the experimental group benefited more from the repeated trials than the control group. Another measure of effectiveness of the procedures is the percentage of trials in each session that the subject successfully attained the criterion for that trial. The group means for this result are presented in Table 1.

A major purpose of this study was to develop some notions concerning the psychophysiological mechanisms of tumescence control through the analysis of associated cardiovascular and respiratory changes. In reviewing the cardiotachometer and respiration data, two different patterns of response are clearly apparent. Figures 2 and 3 show sample polygraph records of these patterns. The response configuration in Fig. 2 is indicative of a "tension" pattern, involving marked heart rate acceleration, irregular respiration, and more variable penile response during tumescence. The "relaxation" pattern, indicated in Fig. 3, consists of regular cardiotachometer and respiration records, as well as smooth, regular penile tumescence curves. It should be noted that all tumescence responses indicated in these two figures 'were criterion responses (i.e., earned the subject a bonus), but that different psychophysiological patterns were employed.

The magnitude of heart rate changes associated with the "tension" pattern is indicated in Fig. 4. A Fabritek Signal Averager was used to average the subject's cardiotachometer response over a series of successive tumescence responses. In order to select records that represented the two characteristic patterns of response, four independent raters rated all tumescence

responses. All raters judged the penile tumescence responses of subjects #09 and #05 to be "relaxed," and those of subjects #04 and #07 to be "tense." The raters were unaware of the associated heart rate or respiratory changes, but based their ratings entirely on the regularity of the tumescence records. The heart rate differences between "relaxed" and "tense" responses is clearly evident in the figure.

DISCUSSION

The data presented confirm the hypothesis that voluntary control of penile tumescence is possible in the absence of external erotic stimulation. While both groups in this experiment were able to produce erections on cue, the addition of analogue feedback and reward produced significantly greater improvement over the course of the two training sessions.

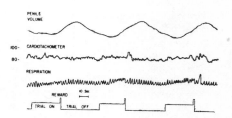

Fig. 3. Sample polygraph record illustrating the "relaxation" pattern of smoother tumescence changes, steady heart rate and regular respiration.

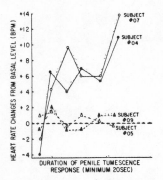

DURATION OF PENILE TUMESCENCE
RESPONSE (MINIMUM 20SEC)

Fig. 4. Heart rate averaged over tumescence responses for four subjects. Subjects #07 and
#04 had irregular tumescence records, while
subjects #09 and #05 were judged to have
"relaxed" tumescence responses.

Moreover, the cardiotachometer and respiratory data suggest two distinct patterns of psychophysiological mediation:
tension and relaxation.

In interpreting this result it is important
to bear in mind the nature of the experimental demands. Subjects were placed in a
somewhat stressful situation (attachment
of electrodes and transducers in an isolated experimental chamber) and required
to produce erections on cue in order to
earn bonuses. Some subjects may have
reacted to this situation in a manner
analogous to the "performance demand"
situation described by Masters and Johnson (5). Although these subjects were able
to achieve some degree of penile tumescence, it is apparent from their polygraph
records (Figs. 2 and 3) that they were unable to remain calm and relaxed in the
process. One might even speculate that
this pattern of autonomic response is a
likely precursor to premature ejaculation.
Although it is not clear what causes some
subjects to become tense in this situation
while others remain relaxed, review of the
postsession questionnaires indicates that
the relaxed subjects seemed to feel generally more positive about the experience.

While this study was conducted with
normal volunteers in an artificial laboratory situation, certain clinical inferences
can be drawn from the results. Feedback

and reward procedures appear to facilitate
voluntary control of penile tumescence,
and one case study in the literature (6)
describes the use of such procedures in the
treatment of a homosexual. However, the
different autonomic patterns obtained in
this study suggest an important limitation
on the clinical use of feedback and reward.
It is likely that the individual with an erec-
tile disorder would be especially anxious
concerning this response, and would
therefore produce a tension-like pattern of
response, which might compound the
problem. A possible solution might lie in
feedback and reward for an integrated pattern of autonomic responses (7).

SUMMARY

This study was conducted in order to
investigate the possible voluntary control
of penile tumescence in the absence of external erotic stimulation. To the extent that
tumescence is psychogenically as well as
reflexogenically mediated, the use of feedback and reward are indicated for the enhancement of voluntary control.

Twenty-four normal male volunteers
were divided into two groups. In the experimental group, subjects were provided
with analogue feedback in the form of a
variable intensity orange light for increases in penile tumescence. Subjects
also earned a bonus each time tumescence
exceeded a predetermined criterion in accordance with a shaping procedure. Control subjects received no analogue feedback and noncontingent rewards. Two 20
min experimental sessions were used for
all subjects, and postsession questionnaires were completed after each session.

Results indicated that while both
groups were capable of voluntary control
of tumescence, the feedback and reward
procedures significantly improved performance over trials. This study also attempted to assess the psychophysiological
mechanisms involved in voluntary penile
control. Heart rate and respiration data in
this regard suggest two distinct patterns of
response: tension and relaxation. The
artificial demands of the experiment may

well have contributed to the tension pattern observed in certain subjects.

The different psychophysiological patterns of response suggest a cautious extrapolation of these procedures to the clinical situation. While biofeedback procedures may be useful in the treatment of psychogenic potency disorders, it might be necessary to utilize a *pattern* of autonomic response, rather than penile tumescence alone.

REFERENCES

1. Rosen RC: Suppression of penile tumescence by instrumental conditioning. Psychosom Med 35:509–514, 1973
2. Laws DR, Rubin HB: Instructional control of an autonomic sexual response. Appl Behav Anal 2:93–99, 1969
3. Henson DE, Rubin HB: Voluntary control of eroticism. Appl Behav Anal 4:37–44, 1971
4. Schwartz GE: Cardiac responses to self induced thoughts. Psychophysiology 8:462–467, 1971
5. Masters WH, Johnson VE: Human Sexual Inadequacy. Boston, Little Brown, 1970
6. Quinn JT, Harbisan JJ, McAllister H: An attempt to shape human penile responses. Behav Res Ther 8:213–216, 1970
7. Schwartz GE: Voluntary control of human cardiovascular integration and differentiation through feedback and reward. Science 175:90–93, 1972

Modification of Human Acid Secretion with Operant-Conditioning Procedures

58

William E. Whitehead, Pierre F. Renault, and Israel Goldiamond

In an attempt to control gastric acid secretion with operant-conditioning techniques, four normal women were given visual feedback on gastric pH plus money reinforcers. When money was made dependent on increased secretion in a differential-reinforcement-of-high-rates schedule, the rate of secretion of three of the four subjects increased to three times baseline. When money was then made dependent on decreased secretion in a differential-reinforcement-of-other-behaviors schedule, the rate of secretion of these three subjects returned to baseline levels. Heart rate, respiratory frequency, abdominal electromyographic activity, and stomach motility (measured by the electrogastrogram method) were not consistently correlated with acid secretion across subjects, although individual subjects showed substantial correlations between acid secretion and one or more other physiological response.

DESCRIPTORS: gastric acid secretion, operant conditioning of gastric acid secretion, gastric pH, biofeedback, differential reinforcement of high rate to increase gastric acid secretion, DRO to reduce gastric acid secretion, visceral learning

A variety of autonomic responses have been modified with operant-conditioning procedures (Miller, 1969; Shapiro and Schwartz, 1972). Miller (1969) and others have called attention to the possible value of these techniques in the

[1]Based on a dissertation submitted by the first author in partial fulfillment of the requirements for a Ph.D. degree at the University of Chicago. Support for this research came from National Institutes of Mental Health grant MH-19979, from State of Illinois grant 302-12, from Food and Drug Administration grant FDA 72-42, and from funds provided by the Department of Psychology, University of Chicago. The first author was supported by an N.I.M.H. Predoctoral Fellowship. We thank Ms. Barbara Klein for typing the manuscript. Reprints may be obtained from William E. Whitehead, Department of Psychiatry, University of Cincinnati College of Medicine, Cincinnati, Ohio 45267.

treatment of psychophysiologic disorders. Successful clinical applications have included elimination of ruminative vomiting (Lang and Melamed, 1969), reduction in cardiac arrhythmias (Weiss and Engel, 1971), and reduction of blood pressure in essential hypertension (Benson, Shapiro, Tursky, and Schwartz, 1971; Elder, Ruiz, Deabler, and Dillenkoffer, 1973).

Welgan (1974) reported an attempt to condition by operant means increased gastric pH in duodenal ulcer patients. Gastric secretions were continuously aspirated and pH was measured outside the body. Subjects served in a single session, and 15-min periods of visual and auditory feedback alternated with 15-min periods of rest. Group data were generally consistent with the hypothesis that feedback plus instructions reduced gastric acidity, but did not provide definitive support for this hypothesis. In an earlier study, Gorman and Kamiya (1972) measured pH within the stomach during three sessions, in which instructions to increase pH alternated with instructions to decrease pH, accompanied by auditory feedback. Group data demonstrated a significant difference between increase and decrease conditions.

Technical problems and the equivocal nature of some of these data underscore the need for additional studies. The technical difficulties include the absence of immediate feedback in Welgan's (1974) study and the nonlinear relation of intragastric pH to acid secretion in Gorman and Kamiya's (1972) study. Continuously aspirating from a stomach tube introduces relatively long delays between secretion and measurement, especially as the tube tends to clog when the stomach is empty. Although measuring pH within the stomach is more immediate, it may be less valid as a measure of acid secretion for the following reasons: acid is secreted at a constant concentration (Cummins, 1973), but the contribution of a given amount of acid secretion to intragastric pH is determined by the volume of fluid already in the stomach. Moreover, pH is logarithmically related to acid concentration, so that a change from pH3 to pH2 reflects 10 times as much difference in acid concentration as a change from pH4 to pH3 (Gambescia, Krawiec, Desiderio, and Polish, 1967).

The current investigation overcame these difficulties. Intragastric pH was used to provide immediate feedback and reinforcement to the subjects; in order to measure more validly acid secretion, the contents of the stomach were repeatedly neutralized to pH7. Titration to this endpoint rendered the measurement of acid secretion independent of volume changes, since the amount of sodium biocarbonate required was taken as the dependent measure of acid secretion.

METHOD

Subjects

Four female volunteers (ages 21 to 28 yr), with no history or symptoms of gastrointestinal pathology, were paid $10 for each baseline session and a varying amount that depended on performance but that averaged about $10 for each conditioning session. Additional payment of up to $200 was available for finishing the study (approximately five months) without missing more than four sessions.

Apparatus

Subjects swallowed a plastic tube (Figure 1) containing a pH electrode (Beckman 39042) and two smaller tubes, one used to inject sodium bicarbonate into the stomach and the other to inject water if the side holes became clogged with mucus. The electrode tip was enclosed in a plastic cuff (8 mm outside diameter) to prevent it from becoming engulfed in the stomach lining. The reference for the pH electrode was a fiber junction electrode with its tip immersed in

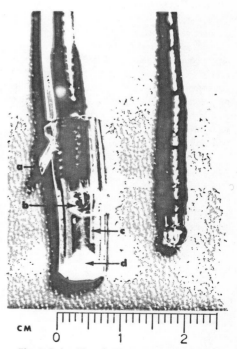

Fig. 1. Left, pH probe. Letter a, polyethelene tube used to infuse sodium bicarbonate into stomach (cut off flush with cuff in practice); b, hole in cuff to allow stomach contents to contact pH electrode; c, polyethelene tube used to wash out cuff with water; d, plug in end of cuff to facilitate washing outside holes. Right, pH electrode without cuff.

a pan of saturated potassium chloride solution in which the subject held one hand (Rovelstad, Owen, and Magath, 1952).

The pH electrode was connected to a high-impedance amplifier whose output was recorded on a polygraph. Standard buffer solutions were used to calibrate the system. The output of the polygraph amplifier drove a volt meter that provided visual feedback to the subject and drove an electronic circuit that closed a relay whenever pH decreased by a predetermined amount.

Subjects faced a display panel with a counter that accumulated reinforcements, a white light that flashed whenever the counter advanced, and red and green stimulus lights. During conditioning sessions, a meter on the panel showed relative changes in intragastric pH.

Method of Measuring Acid Secretion

Sodium bicarbonate (1 Normal) was injected to neutralize the stomach contents to pH7. Gastric acid secretion then caused pH to decrease at a rate that depended on the rate of acid secretion, and subjects received reinforcement for appropriate small changes in the rate of pH decrease. Each time stomach pH fell to 2, additional sodium bicarbonate was injected to titrate the pH back to 7. The amount of sodium bicarbonate required repeatedly to neutralize the stomach contents, expressed as miliequivalents (mEq) per minute, was the dependent measure of acid secretion.

Occasionally, recorded pH showed large, rapid fluctuations, indicating that the pH electrode was not in contact with fluid, or recorded pH failed to show any change for much longer than would be expected for that subject (as judged by the experimenter), indicating the electrode tip was clogged with mucus or engulfed in the gastric mucosa. When either occurred, 10 to 20 cc of water was injected into the cuff. If this failed to correct the problem, the tube containing the pH electrode was raised or lowered slightly. Amount of water injected into the stomach and number of times electrode position was adjusted were recorded.

A control experiment was conducted to compare the technique of titrating acid secretion in the stomach to the more traditional technique of aspirating and titrating outside the body. Two 1-hr observations of basal secretion and two 1-hr observations of histalog-stimulated secretion (0.5 mg intramuscular) for each method were compared in three subjects. Data are given in Table I. Rate of secretion varied as much between measurements taken with the same method as it did between different methods, and one method did not give results systematically different from the other. This held both for basal secretion (low rate of secretion) and histalog-stimulated secretion (high rate of secretion).

Experimental Design

The number of baseline sessions ranged from five to 13, depending on the stability of basal secretion from session to session. After baseline, increased acid secretion was reinforced until acid secretion rose above baseline levels for several consecutive sessions. Decreased acid secretion was then reinforced.

Increase training consisted of a differential-reinforcement-of-high-rates (DRH) schedule in which reinforcement was presented only if intragastric pH decreased by a specified amount (0.1 pH unit typically) within a 10-sec trial. If this

Table 1

Comparison of pH Method and Aspiration Method of Measuring Gastric Acid Secretion

Subject	Session	Basal mEq/hr		Histalog mEq/hr	
		pH method	Aspiration	pH method	Aspiration
B.W.	Initial Study	6.27	4.37	25.73	21.68
	Replication	3.07	4.65	36.70	27.64
C.D.	Initial Study	1.20	0.91	11.00	14.60
	Replication	9.80	1.87	28.00	13.50
R.R.	Initial Study	3.90	3.52	18.20	25.21
	Replication	4.50	2.75	22.60	7.64

criterion was not met within 10 sec, pH had to decrease by this amount within the next 10-sec trial. If the criterion was met in less than 10 sec, the reinforcement counter advanced and a new trial started immediately.

Decrease training consisted of a differential-reinforcement-of-other-behavior (DRO) schedule in which reinforcement was presented only if a criterion interval of time passed with no decrease in pH. A 2-sec interval was used at the beginning of training, and was gradually increased to 5 sec.

The subject was told before each session what the contingency of reinforcement was and how much money each successful trial was worth. Size of the reinforcer was varied from session to session (one to three cents) depending on the contingency and on past performance. The aim was to make expected earnings equal to $10 per session.

Before the experiment, subjects were taught to swallow a stomach tube during three or more 1-hr sessions that served to habituate any unconditioned effects of swallowing a tube. Sessions occurred at least 8 hr after the subject's last meal to avoid any stimulation of acid secretion by food. Subjects' stomachs were emptied by hand aspiration at the beginning of each session; if food was present, the session was not conducted. Sessions were held at the same time each day to avoid variations in acid secretion attributable to the circadian rhythm of acid secretion (Moore and Englert, 1970). Subjects lay in bed on their left side during sessions to reduce gastric emptying. Sessions lasted 105 min. The experimenter stood in an adjacent room out of the subject's sight.

Controls for Mediation

Abdominal muscle EMG (electromyographic) activity and respiration were recorded in three subjects to evaluate the most likely sources of skeletal muscle mediation. To assess the extent of possible cognitive mediation of acid secretion, one subject was instructed (a) to think about food, (b) to think about whatever she liked that she believed would increase acid secretion, and (c) to look at pictures of prepared food while acid secretion was measured. This occurred before training.

Gastric acid secretion might have been stimulated by putting too much water into the stomach and distending it (Sugawara, Isaza, Curt, and Woodward, 1970). To assess whether this could account for observed changes in acid secretion, the correlation of amount of water added with acid secretion was calculated. The tactile stimulation involved in adjusting the position of the pH electrode might also have stimulated acid secretion. This was assessed by calculating the correlation of movements of the pH electrode with acid secretion.

To determine whether the observed changes in acid secretion were part of a generalized autonomic arousal, the correlations of acid secretion with heart rate and gastric motility, as measured by the electrogastrogram (Russell and Stern, 1967), were calculated. The electrogastrogram measures slow electrical potentials generated by the stomach, which can be recorded from a skin surface electrode over the antrum.

RESULTS

The data for each subject are reported separately below because each subject was treated as a separate experiment and procedures were varied from subject to subject.

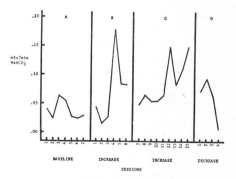

Fig. 2. Subject C.D. A, baseline; B, initial increase (DRH) training with no stimulus light during trials; C, subsequent DRH training with red stimulus light on during trials; D, decrease (DRO) training with green stimulus light on during trials. Ordinate is average rate of sodium bicarbonate infusion required repeatedly to neutralize gastric secretions.

Subject C.D.

The baseline rate of secretion, depicted in Section A of Figure 2, averaged 0.0373 mEq/min (range: 0.0240 to 0.0629). There was no tendency for the rate of secretion to increase or decrease systematically across baseline sessions, suggesting that any unconditioned effects of swallowing a tube had habituated by the time baseline sessions began.

The effects of reinforcing secretion on a DRH schedule are depicted in Section B of Figure 1. The rate of secretion was unchanged for the first three sessions, but increased abruptly in the fourth session and remained well above baseline in the fifth and sixth sessions.

Beginning with the seventh session of increased training, a red stimulus light was introduced during 10-sec trial periods. The effect of this change (Section C of Figure 1) was to decrease secretion to near-baseline levels for five sessions. The rate of secretion then increased well above baseline and remained high. For the last four sessions of increase training, the average rate (0.1225 mEq/min) was more than three times the baseline average.

Section D of Figure 1 shows the effects of switching to a DRO schedule that made reinforcement contingent on decreased acid secretion. By the fourth session, the rate of secretion was practically nil (0.0066 mEq/min).

Following the third increase-training session, gastric motility, amount of water injected, and number of times the electrode position was

adjusted were recorded. Only amount of water added was positively correlated with acid secretion ($r = 0.386$). The multiple correlation of all three measures with acid secretion was 0.4274.

Instructions to increase acid secretion by thinking about food, given before conditioning, had no effect. However, instructions to look at pictures of prepared food were associated with increased secretion in two sessions (0.0910 and 0.1280 mEq/min) but not in a third (0.0223 mEq/min). Instructions to think about whatever the subject believed might increase acid secretion produced no change. These instruction conditions were given at the end of the baseline period.

Subject P.S.

Figure 3 shows no tendency for the rate of secretion to increase or decrease systematically across baseline sessions. The mean rate was 0.0531 mEq/min (range: 0.0196 to 0.0941).

Introduction of the DRH schedule produced no apparent effect for seven sessions. The rate of secretion then increased gradually to values well above baseline. A period of 11 days intervened between Sessions 13 and 14, but this interruption did not affect the measures taken upon return. The average rate for increase Sessions 8 to 21 was 0.1762 mEq/min, more than three times the baseline average.

During two control sessions, gastric secretions were aspirated and titrated outside the body to provide validity checks on the conditioned in-

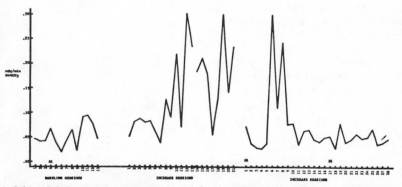

Fig. 3. Subject P.S. Baseline, increase (DRH), and decrease (DRO) training. Eleven days separate increase Sessions 13 and 14. M denotes first session following start of menstrual flow. Ordinate is average rate of sodium bicarbonate required repeatedly to neutralize gastric secretions.

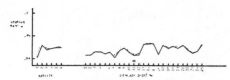

Fig. 4. Subject C.C. Baseline and increase (DRH) training sessions with 15-min timeouts at beginning and end of session. Timeouts not included in data represented. M denotes first session following start of menstrual flow. Ordinate is average rate of sodium bicarbonate infusion required repeatedly to neutralize gastric secretions.

creases in secretion. Feedback was not available, but conditions were otherwise similar to DRH training sessions. These sessions occurred between DRH (increase) Sessions 14 and 15 and between 15 and 16 in Figure 3. Values of 0.0839 and 0.1226 mEq/min, both well above baseline, were obtained for these aspiration sessions.

Institution of the DRO (decrease) schedule, shown in Figure 3, was associated with a return to baseline levels during five sessions. This was followed by an abrupt increase. The rate of secretion returned again to baseline but did not fall consistently below baseline.

Analysis of the other measures recorded indicated that across all sessions, amount of water added to the stomach was highly correlated with acid secretion (0.451), as were respiratory rate (0.391) and number of times the position of

the electrode was adjusted (0.396). The multiple correlation coefficient of these variables plus motility and EMG with acid secretion was 0.5498. Heart rate correlated 0.444 and gastric motility correlated 0.127 with amount of acid secreted.

Subject C.C.

The average baseline rate, shown in Figure 4, was 0.0193 mEq/min (range: 0.0013 to 0.0280). For the first 25 sessions of increase training, a 15-min timeout period was scheduled at the beginning and end of each session in an attempt to establish control over differential rates of secretion in the same session. This procedure did not increase secretion within 25 sessions. Moreover, secretion was not higher during the DRH portion of these sessions than during timeout periods.

By contrast, the two subjects previously described had increased acid secretion substantially within 10 sessions when the DRH contingency had been in effect during the entire session. For these reasons, the timeouts were eliminated.

Reinforcing acid secretion for the whole session was not immediately effective, as shown in Figure 5. However, sessions in which the rate of secretion was above the baseline range of variability became increasingly frequent, and for the last six sessions of increase training, the rate of secretion was 0.0629 mEq/min, which was more than three times the baseline average.

Seven sessions of decrease training followed. The DRO contingency was in effect for the whole session. By the fifth session, rate of secretion had returned to baseline but not below.

At about the time this subject began decrease training, a preliminary analysis of the data indicated that amount of water added to the stomach was consistently correlated with acid secretion across subjects. These correlations suggested that changes in acid secretion might have been produced by varying the distension of the stomach with water. To evaluate this possibility, the average amount of water added during the last several days of increase training was computed for Subject C.C., and an equivalent amount of water was added each day of decrease training. This resulted in an average of 3.35 ml/min of water added during the last seven increase

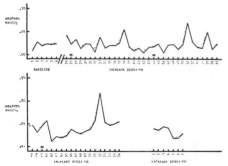

Fig. 5. Subject C.C. Baseline, increase (DRH) training without timeouts, and decrease (DRO) training without timeouts. M denotes first session following start of menstrual flow. Ordinate is average rate of sodium bicarbonate infusion required repeatedly to neutralize gastric secretions.

training sessions *versus* 3.31 ml/min in the seven decrease sessions. These essentially equal amounts of water added were associated with average rates of acid secretion of 0.0519 mEq/min and 0.0277 mEq/min, respectively. Thus, changes in acid secretion associated with the two contingencies of reinforcement appeared to be independent of amount of water added by the experimenter. (This analysis was based on the middle 75 min of each 105-min session.)

Of the possible mediating variables measured, only amount of water added and gastric motility were positively correlated with acid secretion (0.435 and 0.226 respectively). The multiple correlation of these plus respiration, abdominal EMG, and movements of the electrode was 0.4549. Heart rate correlated −0.065 with acid secretion.

Subject B.S.

The baseline average, shown in Figure 6, was 0.0741 mEq/min (range: 0.0642 to 0.0918). There was no apparent tendency for the rate of secretion to increase across baseline sessions. However, during a session in which the effects of colored stimulus lights were being evaluated, a baseline measurement period was introduced, and this was associated with a rate of secretion well above baseline (Section B of Figure 6).

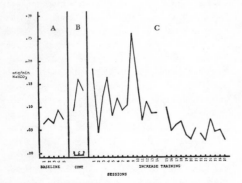

Fig. 6. Subject B.S. A, baseline sessions; B, effects of stimulus lights in one session; C, increase (DRH) training sessions. In Section B, point R is red light, point G is green light, point B is baseline. Data represented in sections A and C do not include first and last 15 min of each session. Ordinate is average rate of sodium bicarbonate infusion required repeatedly to neutralize gastric secretions. See text for details.

This may have been due either to incomplete habituation or to the residual effects of gastric irritation observed in this subject before this session.

During the first 21 sessions of increase training, depicted in Section C of Figure 6, the DRH contingency was preceded and followed by 15-min timeout periods. For the first few DRH sessions, the rate of secretion was high and quite variable. Gradually, however, rate of secretion declined until the average was lower than the initial baseline. The timeout periods were then eliminated (Sessions 22 to 27), but rate of secretion continued to decline. Thus, for this subject, the DRH schedule did not acquire control over increased acid secretion.

Further analysis of the data suggested that an alternative response might have come under the control of the reinforcement contingencies, namely, rapid gastric emptying. This would produce a high frequency of reinforcement with no increase in acid secretion because a larger change in pH is produced by the same amount of acid secretion when the volume of the stomach contents is reduced.

Support for this possibility comes from an analysis of the amount of sodium bicarbonate required to neutralize gastric pH to 5 once it had fallen to pH 2. The amount of bicarbonate required should decrease as the volume of the stomach contents decreases. In fact, the average amount of bicarbonate required was found to be significantly less ($p < 0.01$) during the last five conditioning sessions (0.190 mEq) compared to the five baseline sessions (0.599 mEq), despite the fact that significantly ($p < 0.01$) more water was added during the last five conditioning sessions. Gastric motility also tended to be greater at the end of conditioning than during baseline, but this difference was not significant.

Discrimination Training

For Subject C.D., an attempt was made to establish stimulus control over differential rates of acid secretion. The procedures used included (a) unsystematic alternation between the DRH and DRO schedules with a distinctive stimulus light associated with each for 12 sessions, (b) systematic alternation between the DRO schedule and timeout periods with a cue light for the

DRO schedule during 15 sessions, and (c) systematic alternation between DRH and DRO schedules with distinctive stimulus lights associated with each during 21 sessions. None of these procedures was effective.

DISCUSSION

Results of this investigation indicate that human gastric secretion can be brought under the control of visual feedback that is related to monetary reward. Three of four subjects increased their fasting rate of secretion to three times baseline values when acid secretion was reinforced on a DRH schedule. For all three, acid secretion returned to baseline or below when the reinforcement contingency was changed to DRO. For one subject, rate of secretion did not increase in response to the DRH schedule. It was suggested that an alternative response came under control, namely, rapid emptying of the stomach.

The DRO schedule did not reliably reduce acid secretion below baseline. This raises the possibility that the DRO contingency may have been ineffective and that decreased secretion may represent extinction. However, data from Subject P.S., showing that an 11-day interruption in the sequence of DRH sessions resulted in no diminution, show that the DRO schedule was more effective than simple lack of exposure to the experimental procedures. The DRO schedule reduced secretion within one to five sessions.

Because the DRO contingency was apparently effective in reducing high rates of secretion in normals, it may prove effective for duodenal ulcer patients, in whom acid secretion is also greater than normal. Analogous differences in the response of hypertensive patients and normals to relaxation training have been reported (Tasto and Shoemaker, 1973). Relaxation training significantly reduced blood pressure in hypertensive patients but not in normals.

Maintenance of learned changes after training is also important to assessing the clinical value of these techniques. Maintenance was not systematically evaluated in this study, although data from one subject suggest that learned increases were maintained for at least 11 days. Animal studies indicate that learned changes in

heart rate are maintained for at least three months without intervening practice (DiCara and Miller, 1968).

Differences between subjects in the time required to establish control over acid secretion appeared to be related to the conditioning procedures used. In the first two subjects, acid secretion was reinforced throughout each session, and substantial increases were produced within 10 DRH conditioning sessions. The remaining two subjects were initially tested with 15-min timeouts at the beginning and end of DRH sessions, and no increase in acid secretion was observed within 25 to 27 DRH sessions. When one of these latter subjects was switched to reinforcement throughout the session, her rate of secretion eventually increased. The inference that changing contingencies within a session was responsible for these differences in outcome is supported by the data for Subject C.D. In this subject, rapid control was established over both increases and decreases when the appropriate contingencies were presented in separate sessions; however, when both contingencies were presented in the same session, control could not be established.

Analysis of the correlation of gastric acid secretion with gastric motility, striate muscle activity, respiratory frequency, amount of water injected into the stomach, and number of times the position of the electrode in the stomach was adjusted revealed substantial correlations in some subjects. However, only amount of water added was consistently and positively correlated with acid secretion across subjects, and a control study in one subject indicated that amount of water added could not account for the observed changes in secretion. Multiple correlation coefficients of all these variables with acid secretion ranged from 0.4274 to 0.5498 in individual subjects. The existence of these high correlations should not be interpreted to mean that the operant contingencies were not governing acid secretion, as is clearly shown by the relationship between procedures and outcomes obtained. It is possible that subjects working for monetary reinforcement bring into play a variety of physiological and other mechanisms that help produce and maintain the response required for the reinforcer to be delivered. Whether there are individual differences in the mechanisms employed, and whether the amount or nature of their contribution changes as consequential control is established, are interesting questions that cannot be answered by these data.

Analysis of the correlations between acid secretion and heart rate (range: −0.065 to 0.444) and between acid secretion and motility (range: −0.010 to 0.226) suggested that the observed changes in acid secretion were relatively specific and could not be attributed to a generalized change in vagal tonus.

Tests of the potential for cognitive mediation proved inconclusive. However, no subject reported using a strategy involving cognitive mediation. One subject reported that rapid shallow breathing increased acid secretion, but the low correlation between respiratory frequency and acid secretion did not support this hypothesis.

These results are in agreement with the reports of Gorman and Kamiya (1972) and Welgan (1974) in indicating that gastric secretion can be brought under consequential control. These results differ from the reports cited in failing to show control over differential rates of secretion within the same session.

The finding that rate of human gastric acid secretion can be modified with operant-conditioning procedures suggests that such procedures may be useful in the treatment of hypersecretion associated with duodenal ulcer.

REFERENCES

Benson, H., Shapiro, D., Tursky, B., and Schwartz, G. E. Decreased systolic blood pressure through operant conditioning techniques in patients with essential hypertension. *Science*, 1971, **173**, 740-742.

Cummins, A. J. Applied anatomy and physiology of the stomach. In H. L. Bockus (Ed.), *Gastroenterology*, vol. I. Philadelphia: W. B. Saunders Co., 1963. Pp. 265-288.

DiCara, L. V. and Miller, N. E. Long term retention of instrumentally learned heart-rate changes in curarized rats. *Communications in Behavioral Biology*, Part A, 1968, **2**, 19-23.

Elder, S. T., Ruiz, Z. R., Deabler, H. L., and Dillenkoffer, R. L. Instrumental conditioning of diastolic blood pressure in essential hypertensive patients. *Journal of Applied Behavior Analysis*, 1973, **6**, 377-382.

Gambescia, J., Krawiec, J., Desiderio, V., and Polish, E. Gastric pH in situ with multiple electrodes. In C. M. Thompson, D. Berkowitz, and E. Polish (Eds.), *The stomach*. New York: Grune & Stratton, 1967. Pp. 197-203.

Gorman, P. J. and Kamiya, J. *Biofeedback training of stomach pH*. Paper presented at the Western Psychological Association Meeting, San Francisco, 1972.

Lang, P. J. and Melamed, B. G. Case report: Avoidance conditioning of an infant with chronic ruminative vomiting. *Journal of Abnormal Psychology*, 1969, **74**, 1-8.

Miller, N. E. Learning of visceral and glandular responses. *Science*, 1969, **163**, 434-445.

Moore, J. G. and Englert, E., Jr. Circadian rhythm of gastric acid secretion in man. *Nature*, 1970, **226**, 1261-1262.

Rovelstad, R. A., Owen, Jr., C. A., and Magath, T. B. Factors influencing the continuous recording of in situ pH of gastric and duodenal contents. *Gastroenterology*, 1952, **20**, 609-624.

Russell, R. W. and Stern, R. M. Gastric motility: the electrogastrogram. In P. H. Venables and I. Martin (Eds.), *A manual of psychophysiological methods*. New York: John Wiley & Sons, 1967. Pp. 219-243.

Shapiro, D. and Schwartz, G. E. Biofeedback and visceral learning: clinical applications. *Seminars in Psychiatry*, 1972, **4**, 171-184.

Sugawara, K., Isaza, J., Curt, J. R., and Woodward, E. R. Distension of the pyloric antrum as a stimulus for gastrin release. *Archives of Surgery*, 1970, **100**, 201-204.

Tasto, D. L. and Shoemaker, J. E. *The effects of muscle relaxation on blood pressure for essential hypertensives and normotensives*. Paper presented at Association for Advancement of Behavior Therapy Meeting, Miami, 1973.

Weiss, T. and Engel, B. T. Operant conditioning of heart rate in patients with premature ventricular contractions. *Psychosomatic Medicine*, 1971, **33**, 301-321.

Welgan, P. R. Learned control of gastric acid secretions in ulcer patients. *Psychosomatic Medicine*, 1974, **36**, 411-419.

A Biofeedback Treatment 59 for Stuttering

Richard Hanna, Franz Wilfling, and Brent McNeill

Auditory feedback of laryngeal muscle tension was found to reduce stuttering dramatically in an exploratory study of a single patient. Amplitude of EMG signals was similarly reduced. Apparently, the therapeutic effect of biofeedback cannot be attributed to masking, distraction, or suggestion.

Feedback of electromyographic activity (EMG) has recently been used to treat several disorders that involve muscle tension. Hardyck, Petrinovitch, and Ellsworth (1966) eliminated subvocalization in students with reading problems by providing them with auditory feedback of laryngeal muscle activity. Jacobs and Felton (1969) used visual EMG feedback to induce relaxation in neck-injured patients. Several patients suffering from tension headaches have benefited from auditory feedback of frontalis muscle activity (Budzynski et al., 1973). Netsell and Cleeland (1973) reduced lip hypertonia in a parkinsonian patient by means of EMG feedback, and Cleeland (1973) also applied this paradigm to the modification of spasmodic torticollis. A general review of the current state of EMG feedback is provided by Basmajian (1972).

Encouraged by the ease with which subjects achieved positive results in the above studies, we have begun to investigate the feasibility of feedback training for stutterers. Many researchers are of the opinion that the stuttering block is accompanied by a spasm of the laryngeal muscles (Van Riper, 1971; Schwartz, 1974). Our own preliminary investigations have revealed that EMG spikes from the throat differentiate periods of stuttering from periods of normal speech. Thus, if feedback training will allow a stutterer to reduce his laryngeal muscle tension, it may also reduce his stuttering.

Reprinted with permission from *Journal of Speech and Hearing Disorders*, 1975, Vol. 40, No. 2, 270-273.

METHOD

John was a 19-year-old student with a 10-year history of stuttering. Although the frequency and duration of his blocks varied with the situation, he was consistently a severe stutterer. John had received several types of speech therapy without apparent benefit. His disfluencies were accompanied by obvious throat and facial tension.

Two surface EMG electrodes were attached 2 cm bilateral to the body center line, approximately 1 cm superior to the thyroid prominence. A ground electrode was attached to the left wrist. The patient sat in a padded armchair in a soundproof room, accompanied by one of the authors, while a technician in an adjacent room recorded integrated EMG data on a Beckman-type R411 polygraph. Head movement did not appear to produce EMG artifacts.

Cards from the Thematic Apperception Test (TAT) were used as stimuli for speech. The patient's task was to speak for three minutes about the situation portrayed on each card. After a baseline period of nine minutes of speech, auditory feedback was presented through a speaker at the patient's side. The feedback consisted of a tone that increased in frequency in proportion to the amplitude of the EMG signal. It was explained to the patient that the tone reflected tension in his speech muscles: the greater the tension, the higher the pitch of the tone. His task was to produce a low-frequency tone as often as possible. The biofeedback effect was demonstrated by having the patient swallow several times. He practiced tensing and relaxing his throat without speaking until, after one and one-half minutes, he was able to play the tone like a musical instrument. Next, the patient practiced saying his name, address, and similar information several times, noting changes in the pitch of the tone as he blocked on these words. Within two and one-half minutes, he was able to chat without stuttering severely and without greatly increasing the frequency of the tone. After this very brief practice period, John resumed the TAT task but with the biofeedback apparatus in operation. He was told that the feedback would be turned on and off intermittently while he spoke. The practice session was followed by four talking periods that lasted nine minutes each. Biofeedback was presented for the first and third periods but not for the second and fourth.

John returned for a second biofeedback session six days later. This session was similar to the first one except that John was surreptitiously given false feedback during one nine-minute condition. This was accomplished by "wiring up" another subject in an adjacent room and presenting this person's feedback to John, ostensibly as his own.

RESULTS AND DISCUSSION

Tape recordings of both sessions were analyzed in one-minute segments (Figures 1 and 2). The dependent measure was the percentage of syllables stuttered, a stutter being defined as any unusual prolongation, hesitation, or

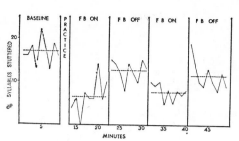

Figure 1. Percentage of syllables stuttered during baseline, feedback, and no feedback periods of the first experimental session.

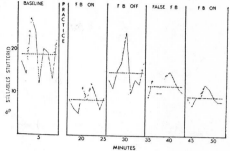

Figure 2. Percentage of syllables stuttered during baseline, feedback, no feedback, and false feedback periods of the second experimental session.

repetition of a syllable. Recorded stutters were counted on two separate days, and the data were averaged.

Stuttering was reduced to less than 50% of baseline during the two biofeedback conditions in each session. The general decline in stuttering over each session probably reflects the familiar adaptation effect (Van Riper, 1971) plus some carry-over of the biofeedback effect. These two effects are difficult to separate and probably tended to obscure differences between "off" and "on" conditions. Nevertheless, an on-off reversal is clearly evident.

As anticipated, the false feedback condition in the second session produced a slight decrease in stuttering relative to no feedback. In effect, the patient was essentially receiving random signals to relax his speech musculature. The fact that false feedback was substantially less effective than genuine feedback indicates that the results cannot be explained in terms of distraction, masking, or suggestion. Moreover, during the false feedback condition, the patient kept complaining that "this thing isn't adjusted right," which suggests that he had indeed acquired an awareness of his laryngeal muscle activity.

Speech rate data are presented in Table 1. These slow rates largely reflect John's difficulty in finding things to say about the TAT cards. It is clear that John spoke faster during biofeedback periods, although to some extent this faster rate could be attributed to increased fluency. It can be tentatively concluded that biofeedback does not operate simply by slowing the stutterer's rate of speech.

TABLE 1. Speech rate in syllables per minute.

Session 1		Session 2	
Baseline	47.1	Baseline	44.0
F B off	55.8	F B off	44.7
F B on	57.1	F B on	55.7
		False F B	52.0

TABLE 2. Mean number of EMG spikes per 100 syllables per minute.

Session 1		Session 2	
Baseline	24.2	Baseline	25.6
F B on	17.4	F B on	16.0
F B off	22.3	F B off	22.7
F B on	17.6	False F B	19.9
F B off	20.6	F B on	15.3

EMG data are presented in Table 2. The EMG record was scored for spikes associated with pen trace deflections greater than 1 cm. In this case, 1 cm corresponded to an action potential of 0.1 mv. Spikes attributable to yawning were not counted. These data follow the same trends that are evident in Figures 1 and 2, although differences between conditions are not so dramatic. Clearly, however, these data provide additional evidence that laryngeal tension and stuttering are intimately related and that by reducing the former, the latter may be similarly affected.

Biofeedback as a treatment for stuttering deserves to be investigated with heterogenous groups of stutterers in the context of an intensive treatment program emphasizing transfer and maintenance of fluency. Although this treatment requires relatively sophisticated instrumentation, it is conceivable that after sufficient training, a stutterer could learn to attend to somesthetic cues of laryngeal tension in the absence of biofeedback equipment. Indeed, this has been demonstrated in other biofeedback applications. Perhaps biofeedback is the technique ". . . that will prevent or eliminate the core disruptions of the motor sequences that perhaps comprise the heart of the (stuttering) problem" (Van Riper, 1973, p. 203).

ACKNOWLEDGMENT

The authors wish to express their thanks to Robert D. Hare for the use of his laboratory, which was funded by the Medical Research Council of Canada. Reprints may be obtained from R. Hanna, Department of Psychology, University of British Columbia, Vancouver, B.C., Canada V6T 1W5.

REFERENCES

BASMAJIAN, J. V., Electromyography comes of age. *Science,* **176,** 603-609 (1972).

BUDZYNSKI, T. H., STOYVA, J. M., ADLER, C. S., and MULLANEY, D. J., EMG biofeedback and tension headache: A controlled outcome study. *Psychosom. Med.,* **35**:6, 484-496 (1973).

CLEELAND, C. S., Behaviour technics in the modification of spasmodic torticollis. *Neurology, (Minneap.)* **23,** 1241-1247 (1973).

HARDYCK, C. D., PETRINOVICH, L. F., and ELLSWORTH, D. W., Feedback of speech muscle activity during silent reading: Rapid extinction. *Science,* **15,** 1467-1468 (1966).

JACOBS, A., and FELTON, G. S., Visual feedback of myoelectric output to facilitate muscle relaxation in normal persons and patients with neck injuries. *Arch. phys. Med. Rehab.*, **30,** 34-39 (1969).

NETSELL, R., and CLEELAND, C. S., Modification of lip hypertonia in dysarthria using EMG feedback. *J. Speech Hearing Dis.*, **38,** 131-140 (1973).

SCHWARTZ, M. F., The core of the stuttering block. *J. Speech Hearing Dis.*, **39,** 169-171 (1974).

VAN RIPER, C., *The Nature Of Stuttering*. Englewood Cliffs, N.J.: Prentice-Hall (1971).

VAN RIPER, C., *The Treatment of Stuttering*. Englewood Cliffs, N.J.: Prentice-Hall (1973).

60

On Voluntary Ocular Accommodation

Robert R. Provine and Jay M. Enoch

Young observers were challenged to induce a marked monocular accommodative response to a relatively weak accommodative stimulus by placing a -9 diopter contact lens on the eye. At first, observers could not produce the desired response, but with training, three of four subjects achieved criterion. Both a voluntary accommodative response and a response to an adequate accommodative stimulus were apparently involved. The voluntary component of the response could be demonstrated by having the observers repeat the task in total darkness.

Accommodation is a change in the curvature and thickness of the crystalline lens which is made in order to bring light from near objects into focus on the retina. At this time we have limited understanding of the nature of the adequate stimulus for accommodation (Campbell & Westheimer, 1959) and the extent to which the response is innate (reflexive) or learned (Fincham, 1951; Heath, 1956; Campbell, 1959; Borish, 1970; Toates, 1972). It is therefore desirable to better understand the conditions under which accommodation may be induced.

In the present study, we examine the capacity of an observer to voluntarily induce positive accommodation in the absence of an adequate stimulus or in the presence of a markedly blurred stimulus. The blurred stimulus may approximate a nonstructured visual field (Whiteside, 1952; Westheimer, 1957; Fincham, 1962). We trained normal young observers to accommodate objects at infinity while wearing a -90 diopter (D) contact lens. This task had to be learned because observers had little prior experience with such a large step in accommodative demand in the absence of auxiliary distance cues and in the presence of a poor quality image. After the observers mastered this task, they were tested for their ability to induce accommodation in darkness in the absence of any visual stimulus.

The work on which this paper is based was conducted at the Washington University School of Medicine, St. Louis, Missouri. This work was supported in part by National Eye Institute Research Grant No. 7-R01-EY-01418-01. Reprint requests should be addressed to: Jay M. Enoch, Department of Ophthalmology, University of Florida College of Medicine, Gainesville, Florida 32610.

METHOD

The subjects were four females between 16 and 18 years of age. All were emmetropic or manifested low hyperopia and had at least a 10 D accommodative amplitude. The right eye was used in all experiments; the left eye was patched. Initially, the subjects viewed a monocularly presented stimulus pattern which consisted of two horizontal rectangles of light (each measuring $2°12'$ x $1°50'$ and separated by $44'$ measured at the entrance pupil of the eye). A small fixation point was centered between the two rectangles. The field was focused at infinity by the optical system, that is, the target array was located at the focal point of a field lens. The system was a classical Badal optometer (Ogle, 1961) incorporated in a Stiles-Crawford (S-C) apparatus (Enoch & Hope, 1972) that was modified for S-C peak finding determinations (Blank, Provine, & Enoch, 1975). The S-C apparatus was used to present the target array. (Once the accommodative task described in this report was mastered, we sought to determine the effect of marked accommodation on photopic receptor orientation as estimated by the Stiles-Crawford effect.) The stimulus was red-orange (Wratten 23A filter over a 6-V 15-A tungsten source), and the luminance level of the rectangles measured in the plane of the entrance pupil of the eye was 2.6 log mL. The stimulus yielded a photopic response without producing glare. The two exit pupils of the instrument which were projected into the plane of the entrance pupil of the eye were 0.3 mm in diam. The two traces of the rectangles in the field stop were separated by 2 mm in the entrance pupil. These traces were polarized 90° relative to each other. The fixation point was not polarized and therefore served as a Scheiner's disk target (e.g., Borish, 1970) aperture (two 0.3-mm-diam apertures separated by 2 mm). Centuries ago, Father Scheiner devised a most sensitive system for measuring when an object is in focus on the retina. He allowed light from a single object to pass two small apertures in the pupil. When the object in space is focused on the retina, the two light beams fuse to form a single image. Any other focal plane results in a double image with the beams either crossed or uncrossed.

The subject's eye and pupil were visualized by means of infrared (IR) light sources (tungsten bulbs with IR bandpass filters) and a RCA 6914A infrared image converter unit which were part of the S-C test apparatus (Enoch & Hope, 1972). The latter apparatus also had a bite bar and forehead press, which permitted the positioning of the observer's entrance pupil with x, y, z controls.

For the experiment, subjects were fitted with a single -9 D soft (flexible, hydrophilic) contact lens (Bausch and Lomb, Inc., Soflens) and placed in the Stiles-Crawford test device (Enoch & Hope, 1972) which presented the previously described target at infinity (Blank, Provine, & Enoch, 1975). Observers could focus the target by exerting an amount of positive accommodation equivalent to the negative power induced by the contact lens. Subjects were asked to accommodate on the target to the best of their ability for 4-6 sec and then to relax. Subsequent trials were begun after a 20-30-sec rest period or when the observers signaled readiness. Subjects received feedback concerning their performance in two ways: they could judge their own success in sharpening the test target and making the fixation spot single (Scheiner's disk-type stimulus, Borish, 1970), and in addition they received trial-by-trial comments from the experimenter, who estimated accommodative performance by observing the degree of the pupil contraction of the subject.[1] Subjects' pupils were visualized by means of the IR image converter. After each accommodative trial, the subjects were asked to estimate their performance on a 1-4 graded scale, after which the experimenter commented on the degree of associated pupillary constriction.

RESULTS AND DISCUSSION

The stimulus array provided a relatively weak accommodative stimulus even when not blurred (few structural details in the field, near monochromatic light in a dark field, very small aperture dimensions). At first, none of the observers could accommodate on the target when a -9 D contact lens was placed on the eye. If a -0.5 D contact lens was substituted, no difficulty was encountered in clearing the target. Therefore, the variable involving the contact lens could be eliminated. Since the subjects had difficulty focusing the test stimulus while wearing the -9 D lens, we investigated the problem of inducing the desired accommodative response.

As a first step in training accommodation, subjects were given experience in monocularly viewing objects held at about 10 cm from their right eyes. They were told to concentrate on what they experienced when they made the effort to focus upon such near objects. The subjects practiced the accommodation task daily between weekly experimental sessions. They were especially instructed to observe near objects, such as a pencil point held about 10 cm from the eye, and to notice how the background blurred when the pencil point was in focus. Subjects were then asked to attempt to blur the background in the same manner without the pencil point being in view.

These introductory training routines complemented test sessions using the Stiles-Crawford apparatus (Enoch & Hope, 1972). When observers attempted to perform the assigned accommodative task in the apparatus, there was usually a great expenditure of effort. There was often an observable trembling of the head and body which necessitated continuous careful positioning of the eye by means of x, y, z controls located on the Stiles-Crawford apparatus. There was a tendency to stare during maximum accommodative effort, hence problems of lid effects on lens curvature were not significant. Lenses centered well. Brief periods of concentrated effort were used because of the considerable discomfort to observers and because lens drying tended to degrade image quality.

Observer performance during early trials was poor and erratic; entrance pupil contraction[1] ranged from 0% to 20% of initial diameter (approximately 7-8 mm) as estimated in reference to a precision reticule scale in the infrared image converter viewing system (the reticule was marked in 0.25-mm steps). Only one of four subjects made progress toward mastering the task during the first test session. During the second test period a week later (the third week of the experiment), this subject was able to sharpen the target and frequently effected a 50% reduction in her pupil diameter (25% of initial pupil area). At this time, the subject became increasingly accurate in estimating her own performance at the task. There was a 1-3-sec latency between the time when an accommodative effort was initiated and when maximum pupil constriction was noted. A similar course of events was followed by two of the three remaining subjects who eventually mastered the accommodation task during the next one to two test sessions. Once improvement in performance began, the observers rapidly learned the task. Subjects were considered to have mastered the task when they reported clearing the test target (a subjective criterion) and when they showed at least a 40%-60% reduction of pupil diameter (an externally observable criterion). It was difficult for the subjects to hold the fixation point single when they cleared the target (Scheiner's disk effect, e.g., see Borish, 1970). When the fixation point was single, the target was properly focused on the retina.[2]

Experienced observers mentioned that the accommodation task required somewhat less effort after mastery was achieved. However, the task remained strenuous even after months of weekly 2-h experimental sessions. Subjects often reported "eye strain," headaches, dizziness, and in one case, nausea, while performing the task, and these forms of discomfort occasionally persisted for several hours.

Evidence concerning the strategies used in solving the accommodation problem was obtained by means of oral and written reports provided by the subjects. Although all subjects reported that the key to the problem was found in concentrating on the task and in imagining they were looking at a near object,[3] it is not clear why all subjects had low initial success rates, since this was reported as their consistent strategy from the beginning. Learning to "concentrate on," or "attend to," the difficult task was apparently an important factor. During early experimental sessions, any room noise or comment by the experimenter would seriously disrupt an ongoing effort. Experienced observers were less distractable. Observers' reports of attentional shifts or loss of concentration were often correlated with observed pupillary events. For example, a great deal of pupillary oscillation was often correlated with subjects' reports that they were unable to maintain attention.

Feedback appeared to play a varied, but important, role in learning the accommodative task. During early test trials, observers' estimates of their own performance were poorly correlated with data on pupil size. Verbal reports from inexperienced observers suggested that they equated their accommodative performance with the degree of physical effort expended on the task. This was evidently a poor criterion. However, during the period of rapid improvement in response, experimenter feedback was reported to be valuable. When subjects learned to induce sufficient accommodation amplitude to clear the target, they had another more immediate and accurate source of feedback concerning their performance. The amount of blur would be reduced and the fixation point would become less double as the required accommodative response was approximated.

Three of the subjects who were able to reduce pupil diameter by approximately 40%-60% during accommodation would apparently induce more than 9 D of accommodation in their initial response to the stimulus. This is suggested by their report that they overshot the endpoint in the test apparatus and had to come back to clear the stimulus. The experimenter often noted correlated pupillary oscillation in such cases, i.e., the pupil would constrict to some maximum value, then dilate slightly. The finding of such oscillation in the accommodative response suggests that while the induction and direction of the primary response were apparently voluntary, the establishment of the accommodative endpoint was mediated by stimulus properties. That the initial part of the response was most probably voluntary was evidenced by the finding that two experienced subjects who were asked to induce comparable accommodation in total darkness were able to reduce pupil diameter 40%-60%, as estimated by the experimenter using the infrared viewer. This indicates that subjects can be trained to utilize internal performance criteria and are not dependent upon visual feedback for the initiation and/or short-term maintenance of an accommodative response.[4]

The observation that the subjects can reliably learn to accommodate for objects while wearing the -9 D lens further indicates that marked accommodation can be induced and maintained in situations which are freed from cues of apparent object distance. Although this fact has been known by clinicians and is used in their tests of positive and negative relative accommodation (e.g., Borish, 1970), these latter tests are not ordinarily performed using dioptic steps anywhere as great as the approximately 9 D step used in this study.

Several investigators have previously demonstrated the presence of voluntary accommodation in a variety of tasks (Carr & Allen, 1906; Sisson, 1938; Mark, 1962; Cornsweet & Crane, 1973). However, none of the earlier studies attempted to produce as great an induced response as the one we describe. We showed that observers can be trained to induce nearly their entire accommodative amplitude. Furthermore, we were able to demonstrate the voluntary nature of the learned accommodative task by having observers produce it in total darkness.

Accommodation obviously involves a complex response mechanism. In this study, we posed a very difficult viewing task for the observers. On the basis of their performance, we infer the presence of a combined voluntary response coupled with a response to a relatively weak but adequate visual stimulus. We make this inference because the visual stimulus alone was not sufficient to induce the appropriate response. Therefore, some factor had to be learned and a similar response, once learned, could be elicited in total darkness on command. If this position is valid, then comparable but less extreme accommodative tasks may be learned in everyday experience. By extension, one may inquire as to the role of experience in the development of the initial accommodative response (Haynes, White, & Held, 1965). Further, one may ask what effect the physical symptoms evidenced in attempts to accommodate have in specific clinical cases (Marg, 1951). This seems to be a most fertile ground for further investigative effort.

REFERENCES

BLANK, K., PROVINE, R., & ENOCH, J. Shift in the peak of the photopic Stiles-Crawford effect with marked accomodation. *Vision Research*, 1975, in press.

BORISH, I. *Clinical refraction* (3rd ed.). Chicago: Professional Press, 1970.

CAMPBELL, F. W. The accommodation response of the human eye. *British Journal of Physiological Optics*, 1959, **16**, 188-203.

CAMPBELL, F. W., & WESTHEIMER, G. Factors influencing accommodation responses of the human eye. *Journal of the Optical Society of America*, 1959, **49**, 563-571.

CARR, H., & ALLEN, J. A study of certain relations of accommodation and convergence to the judgement of the third dimension. *Psychological Review*, 1906, **13**, 258-275.

CORNSWEET, T. N., & CRANE, H. D. Training the visual accommodative system. *Vision Research*, 1973, **13**, 713-715.

ENOCH, J. M., & HOPE, G. M. An analysis of retinal receptor orientation. III. Results of initial psychophysical tests. *Investigative Ophthalmology*, 1972, **11**, 765-782.

FINCHAM, E. F. The accommodation reflex and its stimulus. *British Journal of Ophthalmology*, 1951, **35**, 381-393.

FINCHAM, E. F. Accommodation and convergence in the absence of retinal images. *Vision Research*, 1962, **1**, 425-440.

HAYNES, H., WHITE, B. L., & HELD, R. Visual accommodation in human infants. *Science*, 1965, **148**, 428-530.

HEATH, G. Components of accommodation. *American Journal of Optometry*, 1956, **33**, 569-579.

MARG, E. An investigation of voluntary as distinguished from reflex accommodation. *American Journal of Optometry*, 1951, **28**, 347-356.

MARK, H. On the accuracy of accommodation. *British Journal of Ophthalmology*, 1962, **46**, 742-744.

OGLE, K. *Optics*. Springfield, Illinois: Thomas, 1961. P. 235.

SISSON, E. D. Voluntary control of accommodation. *Journal of General Psychology*, 1938, **18**, 195-198.

TOATES, F. M. Accommodation function of the human eye. *Physiological Review*, 1972, **52**, 828-871.

WESTHEIMER, G. Accommodation measurements in empty visual field. *Journal of the Optical Society of America*, 1957, **47**, 714-718.

WHITESIDE, T. Accommodation of the human eye in a bright and empty visual field. *Journal of Physiology* (London), 1952, **118**, 65 p.

NOTES

1. It is well established that pupil contraction accompanies accommodation (e.g., Borish, 1970).

2. An observer's subjective reports of his ability to accommodate to the test stimulus has been objectively verified. In a separate exercise, a young male subject who was successful in inducing marked accommodation was retinoscoped during a trial external to the apparatus. He was found to be accommodating within 0.5 diopter of the experimental demand (Blank, Provine, & Enoch, 1975) when requested to reproduce the experimental task (—9 D contact lens with infinity fixation).

3. In contrast, the two observers used by Cornsweet and Crane (1973) found that imagining an object moving toward or away from them was not helpful in learning the accommodative response.

4. It is perhaps relevant that Cornsweet and Crane (1973) have noted that there is a high degree of intertask transfer in voluntary accommodation tasks.

Biofeedback and Reinforcement to Increase Heterosexual Arousal in Homosexuals

61

David H. Barlow, W. Stewart Agras, Gene G. Abel, Edward B. Blanchard, and Larry D. Young

Relatively few procedures exist for developing heterosexual arousal in the treatment of sexual deviation (Barlow, 1973) although several recent studies suggest this is a necessary component of treatment (Feldman and MacCulloch, 1971; Bancroft, 1970; Barlow, 1974).

In recent years, biofeedback techniques have been applied to many types of disorders (Blanchard and Young, 1974). Basic to biofeedback technology is the notion that providing a person with feedback (or immediate information) of a bioelectric response enables him to learn (gain) self-control of that response. These responses traditionally have been considered involuntary and include heart rate (Scott et al., 1973a), blood pressure (Benson et al., 1971), stomach acid pH (Welgan, 1972), and electroencephalographic activity (Sterman, 1972). In the present experiments, biofeedback and its attendant technology was applied to the problem of generating heterosexual arousal in homosexual males.

Frequently, in biofeedback research, reinforcement has been used in addition to feedback in attempting to teach self-control of a response. In fact, an alternate way of conceptualizing and describing the biofeedback research is in terms of operant conditioning (e.g., Weiss and Engel, 1971; Scott et al., 1973b). In one sense, however, feedback and reinforcement are inextricably confounded: the delivery or non-delivery of a reinforcer provides the S with information about the rightness or wrongness of his response and hence, binary feedback about it. Likewise, if feedback or knowledge of whether the response has reached a criterion level or not is effective in leading to a change in the response, then feedback functions as a reinforcer. Reinforcement, however, may be viewed as providing both information about the response (feedback) plus an incentive to change it in the desired direction in addition to any incentive provided by successful performance of a task. Thus, if one provides Ss with a separate, functionally defined reinforcer in such a way that no additional information about the response is conveyed, it becomes possible to detect additive effects of reinforcement over feedback effects. Such was the second purpose of this study.

Several recent analogue experiments with volunteers have reported success in modifying erections through feedback and or reinforcement. Price (1973) found that heterosexual volunteers who received analogue visual feedback as well as binary feedback, provided by a colored light once the needle had passed a pre-set criterion, showed a shorter latency to peak erection and maintained criterion erection longer than a control group receiving no feedback. Both groups were listening to erotic audio tapes. Rosen (1973) demonstrated significant suppression of tumescence in a group of heterosexual volunteers provided with response contingent signal lights. A group receiving non-contingent feedback did not show this effect. In a technical paper, Laws and Pawlowski (1973) have suggested audio feedback of tumescence as a treatment for deficits in sexual arousal. In the clinic, Harbison, Quinn and McAllister (1970), in an uncontrolled case study, reported increasing heterosexual responsiveness in homosexuals through reinforcement of erection. In one of their homosexual patients they were able, over a long series of trials, to increase erection to a heterosexual stimulus (female slide) through rewarding progressively larger responses with sips of iced lime after the patient was water deprived. In addition

* This research was supplied in part by Research Grant MH-20258 from the National Institute of Mental Health and by United States Public Health Service Clinical Research Center Grant MO1 RR00626.

to the reinforcement, this S was given feedback, of sorts, in that a light was flashed for each successful trial. A second homosexual patient was similarly rewarded for maintaining progressively longer and clearer fantasies of heterosexual behavior. Since other treatments were also applied and no experimental analysis was performed, it is not possible to evaluate the effectiveness of the procedure.

In the present experiment the separate effects of feedback and reinforcement to increase heterosexual arousal in homosexuals was experimentally evaluated using single case experimental design methodology (Barlow and Hersen, 1973). Since each experiment was somewhat different in design and purpose, each will be described separately.

METHOD

Subjects

The first S was a 15-yr-old male who had engaged in homosexual behavior for 4 yr after being seduced by an uncle. Typically he would visit a homosexual meeting place in town once a week or more where he would be 'picked up' by older men. He was referred after being apprehended while engaging in sexual behavior with a 50-yr-old man. Although no legal charges were pressed, he reported a strong desire to change his pattern of sexual arousal. He was particularly bothered by frequent 'uncontrollable' erections which occurred each time he saw an attractive older male. Although he had no prior heterosexual behavior or heterosexual masturbatory fantasies, he reported that occasionally he found girls attractive.

The second subject was a 21-yr-old male with an 11-yr history of homosexual masturbatory fantasies. Homosexual behavior began 6 months prior to referral and averaged one contact a week with partners whom he would meet in local bars. He had seen several professionals before referral and was initially ambivalent about changing his sexual preferences. He was advised to visit a local gay counseling center but returned several months later requesting a change in sexual preferences. Although he had dated several girls he did not find the dates enjoyable since he was afraid that the girls might make sexual demands on him.

The third subject was a 15-yr-old male who was referred after homosexual behavior had become 'uncontrollable'. He reported a 5-year history of homosexual behavior which had increased to a frequency of one or more times per day in the last year. A more serious problem, however, was unsolicited and indiscriminate sexual propositions to most boys and men with whom he came in contact. This behavior made it extremely difficult to remain in his community and he was referred to our treatment center when he requested a change in his sexual preferences and relief from his 'sexual compulsion'. The S reported no heterosexual contacts.

Measures

Penile circumference. Measures of penile circumference changes were recorded by a mechanical strain gauge (Barlow *et al.* 1970) using a Grass Model 7 polygraph and a 7P1 DC Preamplifier. Before the experiment began the S was instructed to put the strain gauge in place and report flaccidity of his penis. After detumescence was visually confirmed, the subject was instructed to manipulate himself to a full erection and inform the experimenter so that this might also be visually confirmed. The magnitude of pen deflection corresponding to a full erection was obtained by comparison of the polygraph recordings under these two conditions. All penile responses throughout the entire experiment were expressed as a percentage of full erection. Polygraph recordings of the circumference of a full erection were checked approximately every 2 weeks and did not vary appreciably for any subject.

Experimental treatment and generalization probe sessions were conducted on alternate days, with the exception of weekends, and in different rooms. Generalization probe sessions were conducted in the following manner: from a large collection of slides, selected by each S on the basis of 'attractiveness' to him, three male and three female slides were chosen each day for use in the generalization probe sessions. During these sessions the examiner waited until a 30-sec period with no pen deflection had transpired before presenting a slide. This level of penile circumference served as a baseline for that session. The six slides were then projected on a screen in front of the subject in random order for 2 min each. The interval between slides was 30 sec or a return of the penile response to baseline values, whichever was longer. Subjects were instructed not to manipulate their penis since this produced marked movement artifacts on the polygraph recording. (For a more detailed discussion of penile measurement procedures see Barlow *et al.*, 1970). The responses to the three male and three female slides were averaged to yield measures of both homosexual and heterosexual arousal for each generalization probe session. One of these three female slides was then selected by the subject for use during the treatment sessions.

Procedure

Baseline. Prior to the begininning of the treatment sessions, baseline levels of both homosexual and heterosexual arousal, as measured by penile circumference changes were determined during six generalization probe sessions.

Feedback. To provide analogue feedback to subjects in the treatment sessions, the output from the J6 terminal of the 7P1 DC Preamplifier was displayed visually by means of a voltmeter placed on a table approximately two meters from the S, who was seated in a comfortable chair. The S, voltmeter, and projection screen were in a separate room from the polygraph. For each S the voltmeter was adjusted so that extreme left and right positions of the needle on the scale represented a flaccid or erect penis respectively. All Ss reported the voltmeter scale and movement of the needle was clearly visible. They were further instructed to try to become aroused and to use the visual feedback to assist them. They were told that through closely monitoring their arousal it would be possible to learn to become aroused to females and that this procedure had helped other patients with similar problems. At each change of phases a brief description of the modification was given with instructions to continue trying to become aroused. These 'treatment' sessions consisted of six 2-min presentations of the one female slide the S had chosen. There was a minimum of 30 sec between slide presentations for any increment in penile circumference to subside to baseline levels. The mean increase in penile circumference to these six presentations was computed and represented the S's heterosexual arousal for that particular session.

No feedback. The sessions in the NFB condition differed from those of the preceeding phase only in that the FB meter was not connected to the polygraph (S was informed that this modification was part of treatment and should enable him to continue improving his heterosexual arousal). This condition provided for each S a simple control for the effects of exposure to erotic heterosexual stimuli. Previous work in our lab (Herman, Barlow and Agras, in press) had demonstrated that in some circumstances such exposure is itself a sufficient condition for increased heterosexual arousal and, therefore, must be evaluated as a source of any observed changes.

These three phases, baseline, feedback, no feedback, just mentioned were common to all Ss. For S1 the fourth condition was a second series of FB trials and Condition 5 was a return to baseline conditions to complete the experimental analysis. Both S2 and S3, however, participated in further FB conditions to which were added various reinforcement procedures. These will be discussed for S2 and S3 individually.

Subject 2. Following Baseline, FB, and NFB conditions, S2 received a second series of FB trials. Condition 5 consisted of the addition of contingent monetary (25c) and verbal reinforcement to FB. This S and the following S were told that a 'conflict' remained between their desire to learn heterosexual arousal and their homosexual tendencies and at this time it would help them to overcome their conflict if they received money as they increased their heterosexual arousal. They were instructed that this was a routine alteration in treatment at this time but they were not informed of the explicit contingencies. A shaping procedure was employed with the following criterion for reinforcement. The first response was reinforced, the response of the second trial was reinforced if it equalled or surpassed the response of Trial 1, the criterion for Trial 3 was the mean of Trials 1 and 2, and the criterion for all successive trials was the median of the preceding three trials or the previous criterion, whichever was greater. In the final phase of the experiment for S2, all procedures of the preceding condition (No. 5) were held constant with the exception that the monetary reinforcement was increased from 25c to $1.00 per criterion response.

Subject 3. The fourth condition for S3 consisted of the addition of contingent verbal and contingent monetary (25¢) reinforcement to FB for each criterion response. Initially a criterion for reinforcement employing 'mean' instead of median was employed. After three sessions this initial schedule appeared to be too sensitive to single large responses (thereby straining the schedule) and was abandoned in favor of the median criteria described for S2. This median criterion was then utilized for a complete six-session phase.

In Condition 5, FB and Noncontingent Reinforcement , S3 was informed at the conclusion of each experimental session that, "You had a good session today and you earned 75c." In the sixth condition, S3 continued to receive money non-contingently at the end of each FB session but emission of a criterion level response was immediately followed by verbal reinforcement from the experimenter. Finally, all monetary reinforcement was eliminated from the seventh condition and S3 received only FB plus Contingent Verbal Reinforcement.

RESULTS

Figure 1 presents the average erection emitted by S1 to the six presentations of the heterosexual slide in treatment sessions and the average response to both male and female slides during the generalization probe sessions. Results are presented in blocks of two sessions.

The within-session data demonstrate a progressive increase in heterosexual arousal throughout treatment with heterosexual arousal climbing to 80 per cent before dropping somewhat during the last two sessions. In general, this increase continued regardless of the presence or absence of feedback. In the generalization probe sessions, heterosexual arousal again showed a gradual but clinically substantial increase throughout treatment with regard to experimental conditions. That is, presence or absence of feedback seemingly had no effect on the observed increase which reached 80 per cent of full erection. Homosexual arousal was variable but remained at approximately 50 per cent of full erection across experimental conditions. This S also reported increased heterosexual arousal during the experiment. At follow-up immediately following the experiment (see Fig. 1) and at 2 and 6 months he reported the gains were maintained and he was now dating girls quite regularly.

Figure 2 presents the average erection emitted by S2 in treatment sessions and average responses to both male and female stimuli in the generalization probe sessions. Again, results are presented in blocks of two sessions.

Heterosexual arousal within sessions remained low with no substantial change throughout initial feedback and no feedback sessions. The addition of reinforcement contingencies (25c) proved ineffective but increasing the magnitude of reinforcement to $1.00 produced the first increase in heterosexual arousal (to 40 per cent) within treatment. Unfortunately this effect could not be tested through a withdrawal and reinstatement of the reinforcement since the S was forced to drop out of the experiment. Generalization probe sessions revealed, however, that the increase in heterosexual arousal during the last reinforcement phase did not generalize to the probe sessions in which heterosexual arousal remained low throughout the experiment. Homosexual arousal gradually declined during the probe sessions from approximately 40 per cent to below 20 per cent. Interestingly, the S reported consistent increases in heterosexual arousal and decreases in homosexual arousal throughout the experiment. Despite these reports he had not engaged in any heterosexual behavior by the end of the experiment although

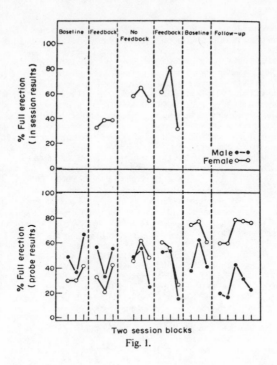

Fig. 1.

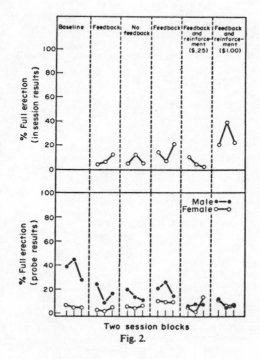

Fig. 2.

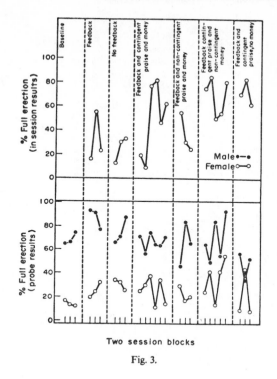

Fig. 3.

heterosexual masturbatory fantasies had increased slightly. Homosexual masturbatory fantasies had declined somewhat although homosexual behavior remained relatively stable.

Figure 3 presents the average erection generated by S3 to the heterosexual stimulus in the treatment sessions and average responses to male and female stimuli in the generalization probe sessions. Once again, results are presented in blocks of two sessions.

The within-session data show little change in arousal during feedback or no feedback. There is a marked increase in heterosexual arousal to a high of 80 per cent with the introduction of the combination of contingent, social, and monetary reinforcement. Delivering reinforcement non-contingently led to a consistent decrease in arousal, to a low of 25 per cent. During the next two phases contingent praise was seemingly isolated as the reinforcing event since heterosexual arousal returned to a high of 80 per cent and remained there despite the fact that money was delivered non-contingently (Phase 6) or not at all (Phase 7).

However, these within-session increases in arousal did not generalize to the probe sessions. There was a slight increase in heterosexual arousal with the start of treatment, from 15 per cent to approximately 30 per cent, but despite some variability heterosexual arousal remained at approximately 30 per cent throughout the experiment. Homosexual arousal stayed consistently high until the final phases when it decreased slightly. This S also reported consistent increases in heterosexual arousal and decreases in homosexual arousal but demonstrated no change in sexual behavior.

DISCUSSION

These data fail to confirm the effectiveness of biofeedback to increase heterosexual arousal. In two cases (S2 and S3) biofeedback of penile erection had no effect either within treatment sessions or in generalization probe sessions. In a third subject (S1), clinically significant increases were noted but these increases continued despite withdrawal of feedback, suggesting that feedback was not responsible for the observed gains. Although it is not clear what therapeutic factors produced these increases, one possibility is continued exposure to heterosexual stimuli which was demonstrated in another experiment to produce increases in heterosexual arousal (Herman et al., in press). In any case, these data reaffirm the dangers of drawing conclusions on mechanisms of therapeutic action from uncontrolled case studies without experimental manipulations to isolate effective therapeutic ingredients. It is entirely possible, for example, that an 'exposure' effect or some other therapeutic variable was responsible for the successes in the Harbison et al. (1970), study rather than the feedback and reinforcement contingencies.

Unlike feedback, there is some evidence that reinforcement contingencies can produce increases in heterosexual arousal. When the magnitude of reinforcement was sufficient in $S2$, an increase was noted but this was not confirmed by a reversal. For $S3$, however, a combination of social and monetary reinforcement was sufficient to produce increases within sessions and this effect was confirmed by drops in arousal after. withdrawal of the contingencies despite the presence of feedback. Later phases seemed to isolate praise as the effective reinforcer in this patient's case. However, the effects were weak and clinically insignificant since no generalization of these increases was noted in the probe sessions.

In general, then, there is no evidence from these data that biofeedback or reinforcement is an effective treatment for producing clinically significant increases in heterosexual arousal. These results also underline, once again, the difficulties in relying on self-report as an indicator of progress. The first subject reported increases in heterosexual arousal which were confirmed by changes in penile responding to heterosexual stimuli. This subject, in turn, reported a reasonable heterosexual adjustment which was confirmed by relatives. The second and third subjects also reported increases in heterosexual arousal which were not confirmed by objective measures. In these subjects there was no behavioral evidence of heterosexual adjustment. This discrepancy between self-report and progress objectively measured is well known (e.g. Barlow et al., 1972; Lang, 1968) and requires constant vigilance on the part of clinical researchers.

Department of Psychiatry and Human Behavior,
University of Mississppi Medical Center,
2500 North State Street, Jackson,
Mississippi 39216, U.S.A.

DAVID H. BARLOW*
W. STEWART AGRAS†
GENE G. ABEL
EDWARD B. BLANCHARD
LARRY D. YOUNG‡

* Author to whom reprint requests should be directed.
† Dr. Agras is now at Stanford University.
‡ Mr. Young is now at Harvard University.

REFERENCES

BARLOW D. H. (1973) Increasing heterosexual responsiveness in the treatment of sexual deviation: A review of the clinical and experimental evidence. *Behav. Therapy* **4**, 655–761.
BARLOW D. H. (1974) The treatment of sexual deviation: Towards a comprehensive behavioral approach. In *Innovative Treatment Methods in Psychopathology* (Eds. K. S. CALHOUN, H. E. ADAMS and K. M. MITCHELL). Wiley, New York.
BARLOW D. H., BECKER R., LEITENBERG H. and AGRAS W. S. (1970) A mechanical strain gauge for recording penile circumference change. *J. appl. Behav. Anal.* **3**, 73–76.
BARLOW D. H. and HERSEN M. (1973) Single case experimental designs: Uses in applied clinical research. *Archs gen. Psychiat.* **29**, 319–325.
BANCROFT J. H. J. (1970) A comparative study of aversion and desensitization in the treatment of homosexuality. In *Behavior Therapy in the 1970's* (Eds. L. E. BURNS and J. L. WORSLEY). Wright, Bristol.
BENSON H., SHAPIRO D., TURSKY B., and SCHWARTZ G. E. (1971) Decreased systolic blood pressure through operant conditioning techniques in patients with essential hypertension. *Science* **173**, 740–742.
BLANCHARD E. B. and YOUNG L. D. (1974) Clinical applications of biofeedback training: A review of evidence. *Arch. gen. Psychiat.* **30**, 573–589.
FELDMAN M. P. and MacCULLOCH M. J. (1971) *Homosexual Behavior: Theory and Assessment.* Pergamon Press, Oxford.
HARBISON J., QUINN J. and McALLISTER H. (1970) The positive conditioning of heterosexual behavior. Paper presented to conference on Behavior Modification, Dublin.
HERMAN S. H., BARLOW D. H. and AGRAS W. S. (in press) An experimental analysis of exposure to 'explicit' heterosexual stimuli as an effective variable in changing arousal patterns of homosexuals. *Behav. Res. & Therapy.*
LANG D. J. (1968) Fear reduction and fear behavior: Problems in treating a construct. In *Research in Psychotherapy* (Ed. J. M. SHLIEU). Vol. III. American Psychological Association, Washington D.C.
LAWS D. R. and PAWLOWSKI A. V. (1973) The application of a multi-purpose biofeedback device to penile plethysmography. *J. Behav. Ther. & exp. Psychiat.* **4**, 339–343.
PRICE K. P. (1973) Feedback effects on penile tumescence. Paper presented by *Annual Convention of Eastern Psychological Association.*
ROSEN R. C. (1973) Suppression of penile tumescence by instrumental conditioning. *Psychosom. Med.* **35**, 509–514.
SCOTT R. W., BLANCHARD E. B., EDMUNSON E. D. and YOUNG L. D. (1973a) A shaping procedure for heart-rate control in chronic tachycardia. *Percept. Mot. Skills* **37**, 327–338.

SCOTT R. W., PETERS R. D., GILLESPIE W. J., BLANCHARD E. B., EDMUNSON E. D. and YOUNG L. D. (1973b) The use of shaping and reinforcement in the operant acceleration and deceleration of heart rate. *Behav. Res. & Therapy* **11**, 179–185.

STERMAN M. B. (1973) Neurophysiological and clinical studies of sensorimotor EEG biofeedback training: Some effects of epilepsy. In *Biofeedback: Behavioral Medicine* (Ed. L. Birk), Grune & Stratton, New York.

WEISS T. AND ENGEL B. T. (1971) Operant conditioning of heart rate in patients with premature ventricular contractions. *Psychophysiol.* **8**, 263–264.

WELGAN P. (1972) Instrument control of gastric acid secretions in ulcer patients. Unpublished doctoral dissertation. Doc. No. 72–18, 755. University Microfilms, Ann Arbor, Michigan.

Behaviorally Conditioned 62
Immunosuppression
Robert Ader and Nicholas Cohen

An illness-induced taste aversion was conditioned in rats by pairing saccharin with cyclophosphamide, an immunosuppressive agent. Three days after conditioning, all animals were injected with sheep erythrocytes. Hemagglutinating antibody titers measured 6 days after antigen administration were high in placebo-treated rats. High titers were also observed in nonconditioned animals and in conditioned animals that were not subsequently exposed to saccharin. No agglutinating antibody was detected in conditioned animals treated with cyclophosphamide at the time of antigen administration. Conditioned animals exposed to saccharin at the time of or following the injection of antigen were significantly immunosuppressed. An illness-induced taste aversion was also conditioned using LiCl, a nonimmunosuppressive agent. In this instance, however, there was no attenuation of hemagglutinating antibody titers in response to injection with antigen.

INTRODUCTION

The hypothesis that immunosuppression might be behaviorally conditioned was invoked to explain certain incidental observations made in a study of illness-induced taste aversion (1). In the illness-induced taste aversion paradigm (2–4) an animal is given a distinctively flavored drinking solution such as saccharin, which is followed by a toxic agent capable of eliciting temporary gastrointestinal upset. Lithium chloride, apomorphine, and cyclophosphamide are but a few of the toxins that are effective in inducing a taste aversion after a single trial in which the toxin (the unconditioned stimulus or US) is paired with a novel drinking solution (the conditioned stimulus or CS). By pairing different volumes of a preferred saccharin solution with a single intraperitoneal (ip) injection of 50 mg/kg cyclophosphamide (CY), rats acquired an aversion to the saccharin solution; the magnitude of the reduction in saccharin

From the Departments of Psychiatry and Microbiology, University of Rochester School of Medicine and Dentistry, Rochester, New York 14642.

Presented at the Annual Meeting, American Psychosomatic Society, March 23, 1975, New Orleans.

This research was supported by Grants K5-MH-06318 to RA and K4-AI-70736 and 9R01-HDA1-07901 to NC from the United States Public Health Service and by funds generously provided by Mr. Arthur M. Lowenthal of Rochester, New York.

Address reprint requests to: Dr. Robert Ader, Department of Psychiatry, University of Rochester Medical Center, 300 Crittenden Blvd., Rochester, New York 14642.

Received for publication November 27, 1974; revision received February 14, 1975.

intake and the resistance to extinction of this aversion were directly related to the volume of saccharin consumed on the day of conditioning. It was also observed that some of the cyclophosphamide-treated animals died and that mortality rate tended to vary directly with the volume of saccharin originally consumed.

In order to account for this observation, it was hypothesized that the pairing of a neutral stimulus (saccharin) with cyclophosphamide, an immunosuppressive agent (5), resulted in the conditioning of immunosuppression. If the conditioned animals that were exposed to saccharin every 2 days over a period of 2 months responded to this conditioned stimulus by becoming immunologically impaired, they would have been more vulnerable to the superimposition of latent pathogens that may have existed in the environment.

We report here our initial documentation of behaviorally conditioned immunosuppression.

METHODS

Ninety-six male Charles River (CD) rats, approximately 3 months old, were individually caged under a 12 hr light-dark cycle (light from 5 AM to 5 PM) and provided with food and water ad libitum. During a period of adaptation the daily provision of tap water was slowly reduced until all animals were provided

with and consumed their total daily allotment during a single 15 min period (between 9 and 10 AM). This regimen was maintained throughout the experiment. The first 5 days under this regimen provided data on the baseline intake of water under these conditions.

On the day of conditioning (Day 0), animals were randomly distributed into conditioned, nonconditioned, and placebo groups. Conditioned animals received a 0.1% saccharin chloride solution of tap water during their 15 min drinking period and 30 min later were given ip injections of CY (50 mg/kg in a volume of 1.5 ml/kg).[1] Nonconditioned animals were, as usual, provided with plain tap water and 30 min after drinking were similarly injected with CY. Placebo animals received plain water and ip injections of an equal volume of vehicle (distilled water). On the following two days all animals were provided with plain water during their 15 min drinking period.

Three days after conditioning all animals were injected ip with antigen, 2 ml/kg of a 1% thrice washed suspension of sheep red blood cells (SRBC; approximately 3×10^8 cells/ml). Thirty minutes later randomly selected subgroups of conditioned and nonconditioned animals were provided with saccharin or plain water and/or received ip injections of CY or saline according to the treatment schedule outlined in Table 1.

One group of conditioned animals received a single drinking bottle containing the saccharin solution and drinking was followed by a saline injection; these animals constituted an experimental group. Two additional groups of conditioned animals received plain water; one of these groups was subsequently injected with CY (in order to define the unconditioned response produced by the immunosup-

---

[1]Cyclophosphamide was generoulsy supplied by the Mead Johnson Research Center, Evansville, Indiana.

TABLE 1. Experimental Treatments

Group	Day 0		Subgroup	N	Day 3		Day 6	
	Drnk. Soln.	Inj.			Drnk. Soln.	Inj.	Drnk. Soln.	Inj.
Conditioned (N= 67)	Saach.	CY	CS$_1$	11	Sacch	Sal	H$_2$O	—
				9	H$_2$O	—	Sacch	Sal
			CS$_0$	10	H$_2$O	Sal	H$_2$O	—
				9	H$_2$O	—	H$_2$O	Sal
			US	10	H$_2$O	CY	H$_2$O	—
				9	H$_2$O	—	H$_2$O	CY
			CS$_2$	9	Sacch	Sal	Saach	—
Nonconditioned (N=19)	H$_2$O	CY	NC	10	Sacch	Sal	H$_2$O	—
				9	H$_2$O	—	Sacch	Sal
Placebo (N=10)	H$_2$O	Placebo	P	10	H$_2$O	—	H$_2$O	—

pressive drug) while the second received saline (as a control for taste aversion conditioning, per se). Following antigen administration a nonconditioned group was provided with saccharin and injected with saline. These animals provided a control for the effects of saccharin consumption and the ip injections. Placebo animals remained unmanipulated and received plain water during the 15 min drinking period. On Day 6 of the experiment, conditioned and nonconditioned animals that had received antigen but had not been manipulated on Day 3 were first treated as described for Day 3, i.e., one conditioned group received the saccharin drinking solution, one conditioned group received water and CY, and one conditioned group received neither saccharin nor CY; a nonconditioned group also received saccharin. In addition, there was one experimental sample of conditioned animals that was provided with saccharin on Days 3 and 6. All animals remained unmanipulated on Days 7 and 8. Throughout this period the volume of plain water or saccharin consumed was measured daily.

On Day 9 (6 days after injection with SRBC), all animals were sacrificed. Trunk blood was collected in heparinized tubes for subsequent analysis of plasma

corticosterone (8) and in nonheparinized tubes for the collection of sera to be used in the hemagglutinating antibody assay. Serum from each rat was heat inactivated (56°C for 30 min) and divided into aliquots some of which were stored at -70°C and others of which were refrigerated and assayed for hemagglutinating antibody activity withn 24 hr of collection. Antibody titrations were performed according to standard procedures in microtiter trays and hemagglutination was assessed under the microscope. Titers were recorded as reciprocals of the end-point dilutions expressed as powers of the base 2.

The provision of plain water or saccharin and the injections of CY or placebo were conducted from coded data sheets. Similarly, antibody titrations and plasma corticosterone determinations were conducted without knowledge of the group to which an animal belonged.

RESULTS AND DISCUSSION

Cyclophosphamide treatment administered 30 min after the ingestion of a novel saccharin drinking solution resulted in an aversion to the saccharin solution (Fig 1). Conditioned animals provided with saccharin on Day 3, on Day 6, or on Days 3 and 6 showed a reduced intake of the distinctively flavored solution on those days.

With regard to antibody responses, the following pattern of results was predicted. Sera from placebo-treated animals were expected to be relatively high titered. Nonconditioned animals, although subsequently presented with a saccharin drinking solution, were also expected to show high antibody levels. However, it was anticipated that the titers of sera from nonconditioned animals might be somewhat lower than those of placebo animals as a result of the CY administered 3 days before injection with SRBS (6,7). Sera from conditioned animals that were given antigen but never again exposed to either saccharin or CY were expected to have antibody titers equivalent to those of unconditioned animals. Conditioned animals that were given a second injection of CY, an unconditioned stimulus for immunosuppression, were expected to show a minimum antibody response to SRBC. The critical groups for testing the hypothesis that immunosuppression can be behaviorally conditioned were the conditioned animals

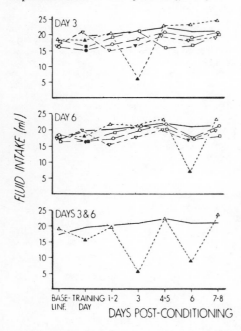

Fig. 1. Mean intake of plain water (open symbols) and saccharin (filled symbols) for placebo (——) and nonconditioned (▼) animals, and conditioned animals that received saccharin (△), cyclophosphamide (□), or neither (○) on Day 3, Day 6, or Days 3 and 6. As a point of reference, the placebo-treated animals are shown in each panel.

that were given one or two exposures to saccharin, the conditioned stimulus, following exposure to SRBC. Evidence in support of the hypothesis would be provided by an attenuation of the antibody response in these animals.

Antibody titers from the several groups are shown in Fig. 2. Conditioned animals exposed to saccharin on Day 3 or Day 6 did not differ and were combined to form a single conditioned group (group CS) that received only one exposure to the conditioned stimulus, saccharin. Similarly, the conditioned animals that remained unmanipulated (group CS_0), the conditioned groups treated with CY on Day 3 or 6 (group US), and the nonconditioned animals given saccharin on Day 3 or 6 (group NC) were combined into single groups.

The results were as we had predicted. Placebo-treated animals showed the highest antibody titers. Conditioned animals

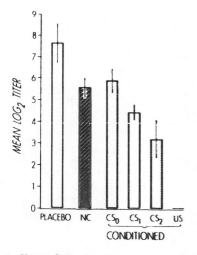

Fig. 2. Hemagglutination titers (means ± SE) obtained 6 days after ip injection of antigen (SRBC). NC = nonconditioned animals provided with saccharin on Day 3 or Day 6; CS_0 = conditioned animals that did not receive saccharin following antigen treatment; CS_1 = conditioned animals given one exposure to saccharin on Day 3 or Day 6; CS_2 = conditioned animals exposed to saccharin on Days 3 and 6; US = conditioned animals injected with cyclophosphamide following treatment with antigen.

that received neither saccharin nor CY and nonconditioned animals that were subsequently exposed to saccharin after antigen treatment showed similar hemagglutination titers that were also relatively high, although significantly lower than the titers of immune sera from placebo animals in the case of both unconditioned $(t = 2.07, P < 0.05)$ and conditioned $(t = 1.71, P < 0.10)$ animals.[2] As expected, the hemagglutination tests revealed that administration of CY after SRBC caused complete immunosuppression. Conditioned animals that experience a single exposure to saccharin following antigen treatment (group CS_1) showed an antibody response that was significantly lower than that of placebo as well as nonconditioned animals $(t = 1.96, P < 0.05)$ and conditioned animals that were not exposed to saccharin $(t = 2.14, P < 0.05)$. The conditioned animals that experience two exposures to saccharin also showed an attentuated antibody response that was significantly below all other groups with the exception of the conditioned animals that received only one exposure to the conditioned stimulus.

Relative to placebo-treated animals, the reduction in hemagglutinating antibody titers shown by nonconditioned animals (group NC) and conditioned animals that were not given either saccharin or CY after antigen treatment (group CS_0) is most simply explained as resulting from some residual effect of CY administered on the day of conditioning (3 days prior to injection with SRBC) (9). These groups, then, become the relevant control condition against which to assess the antibody responses of the conditioned animals exposed to saccharin following antigen treatment. This latter condition did not result in complete suppression of the immune response, but conditioned animals exposed to saccharin did show a

---

[2]The significance levels reported in the text are based on two-tailed t-tests. Based on the specific differences that were predicted, however, it would be appropriate to report one-tailed probabilities and the reader may wish to interpret the results in this light.

significant attentuation of the antibody response relative to these control groups. The attentuation would not appear to have resulted from saccharin, per se, since a comparable exposure to saccharin in association with and following antigen treatment was experienced by the nonconditioned animals for whom saccharin was not a conditioned stimulus. Also, behavioral conditioning, per se, did not result in antibody titers that differed from those of nonconditioned animals. The results, then, support the notion that the association of saccharin with CY enabled saccharin to elicit a conditioned immunosuppressive response.

The present study yielded little additional data that would be of direct importance in suggesting an explanation for this phenomenon. There were no differences among the several groups in body weight measured prior to the adaptation period, on the day before conditioning, or at the time that animals were sacrificed. Also, in conditioned animals exposed to saccharin there were nonsignificant correlations ranging from -0.34 to 0.16 between hemagglutination titer and volume of saccharin consumed. The correlation between plasma corticosterone level sampled at the time that animals were sacrificed and antibody titer was virtually zero, and there were no group differences in steroid levels at this time.

Consistent with the known immunosuppressive properties of adrenocortical steroids and despite the failure to observe differences in plasma corticosterone levels *at the time of sacrifice*, it could be postulated that the attentuated antibody response observed in conditioned animals is a reflection of a nonspecific "stress" response to the conditioning procedures, or, perhaps, of a behaviorally conditioned elevation in steroid level in response to saccharin. Further support for such an explanation might be derived from the relationship between immune processes and physical and socioenvironmental "stress" or emotional responses (11–19) which, presumably, act through the hypothalamus, and from the several

studies (e.g., 20,21) that suggest that hypothalamic lesions may influence some immune responses.

In order to evaluate the possibility that an elevation in adrenocortical steroids was responsible for the attentuation of antibody titers in conditioned animals, a second study used lithium chloride instead of cyclophosphamide as the US in inducing a taste aversion. Whereas lithium chloride also produces noxious gastrointestinal effects, it is not immunosuppressive. In this study, antigen was injected 5 days after conditioning, and the population of conditioned animals that was subsequently provided with the saccharin drinking solution (Group CS, $N = 10$) was exposed to the CS three times: at the time of injection with SRBC, and 2 and 4 days later. As in the first experiment, all animals were sacrificed 6 days after treatment with antigen.

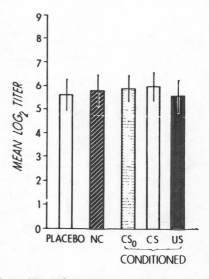

Fig. 3. Hemagglutination titers (means ± SE) obtained 6 days after ip injection of SRBC in animals conditioned with LiCl as the US. NC = nonconditioned animals; CS_0 = conditioned animals that did not receive saccharin following antigen treatment; CS = conditioned animals given three exposures to saccharin; US = conditioned animals injected with LiCl following treatment with antigen.

The association of LiCl with saccharin was effective in inducing an aversion to the saccharin solution. Conditioned animals showed a 66% reduction in consumption of the saccharin solution on the initial test day relative to the intake measured on the day of conditioning. This corresponds closely to the 61%–68% reductions shown by animals conditioned with cyclophosphamide. Antibody titers for the conditioned animals and for the several control groups are shown in Fig. 3. As indicated by the high titers found in animals injected with LiCl at the time of injection with SRBC, LiCl is not an unconditioned stimulus for suppression of the immune response. Although conditioning was effective in inducing an avoidance of the CS solution, antibody titers were similar in all groups.

It is not unreasonable to assume that an elevation in steroid levels might accompany the conditioning of a taste aversion. Nevertheless, the present data provide no support for the hypothesis that such an elevation in steroid levels could have been solely responsible for the attentuated immune response that was observed when conditioned animals were exposed to a CS previously associated with the administration of an immunosuppressive agent. The probability of an interaction between the magnitude and /or duration of an elevation in steroid level and the residual effects of cyclophosphamide, however, remains as a viable hypothesis.

The present results suggest, again, that there may be an intimate and virtually unexplored relationship between the central nervous system and immunologic processes and that the application of behavioral conditioning techniques provides a means for studying this relationship in the intact animal. Confirmation of the capacity of behavioral conditioning procedures to suppress (or elicit) immune responses would raise innumerable issues regarding the normal operation and modifiability of the immune system in particular and the mediation of individual differences in the body's natural armamentarium for adaptation and survival in general. Such data also suggest a mechanism that may be involved in the complex pathogenesis of psychosomatic disease and bear eloquent witness to the principle of a very basic integration of biologic and psychologic function.

SUMMARY

The present study was designed to examine the possibility that behavioral conditioning techniques could be used to modify immune processes.

An illness-induced taste aversion was conditioned in rats by pairing saccharin (CS) with cyclophosphamide (CY), an immunosuppressive agent (US). Three days after conditioning, animals received ip injections of SRBC; 30 min later, subgroups of conditioned animals were (a) supplied with the CS solution, (b) provided with water but injected with the US, or (c) given neither CS nor US. A nonconditioned group was provided with the saccharin drinking solution, and a placebo group was injected with antigen but was otherwise unmanipulated.

The association of saccharin and CY was effective in inducing an aversion to the CS when it was presented 3 days after conditioning (at the time of antigen administration). Hemagglutinating antibody titers measured 6 days after injection of SRBC were high in placebo-treated rats. Relatively high titers were also observed in nonconditioned animals and in conditioned animals that were not subsequently exposed to the CS. No agglutinating antibody was detected in conditioned animals treated with CY at the time of antigen administration. In contrast, conditioned animals exposed to the CS when injected with SRBC (and /or 3 days later in additional samples of conditioned animals) were significantly immunosuppressed.

Similar procedures were used in a second experiment in which LiCl, a nonimmunosuppressive agent, was used as the US. While LiCl was effective in inducing a taste aversion, conditioned animals showed no attentuation of hemagglutinating antibody titers.

The results are interpreted as providing evidence for behaviorally conditioned immunosuppression. Further, it is suggested that this phenomenon is not mediated directly by nonspecific elevations in adrenocortical steroids that may be presumed to accompany an illness-induced taste aversion.

The authors acknowledge with gratitude the technical assistance of Elsje Schotman, Sumico Nagai, Darbbie Mahany, and Betty Rizen.

REFERENCES

1. Ader R: Letter to the editor. Psychosom Med 36:183–184, 1974
2. Garcia J, Ervin RF, Koelling RA: Learning with prolonged delay of reinforcement. Psychon Sci 5:121–122, 1966
3. Garcia J, Kimmeldorf R, Koelling R: Conditioned aversion to saccharin resulting from exposure to gamma radiation. Science 122:157–158, 1955
4. Garcia J, McGowan BK, Ervin RF, Koelling RA: Cues: Their relative effectiveness as a function of the reinforcer. Science 160:794–795, 1968
5. Gershwin ME, Goetzl EJ, Steinberg AD: Cyclophosphamide: Use in practice. Ann Intern Med 80:531–540, 1974
6. Santos GW, Owens HA, Jr: A comparison of selected cytotoxic agents on the primary agglutinin response in rats injected with sheep erythrocytes. Bull Johns Hopkins Hosp 114:384–401, 1964
7. Makinodan T, Santos GW, Quinn RP: Immunosuppressive drugs. Pharmacol Rev 22:198–247, 1970
8. Friedman SB, Ader R, Grota LJ, Larson T: Plasma corticosterone response to parameters of electric shock stimulation in the rat. Psychosom Med 29:323–329, 1967
9. Miller TE, North JDK: Host response in urinary tract infections. Kidney Int 5:179–185, 1974
10. Zurier RB, Weissman G: Anti-immunologic and anti-inflammatory effects of steroid therapy. Med Clin North Am 57:1295–1307, 1973
11. Brayton AR Brain PF: Studies on the effects of differential housing on some measures of disease resistance in male and female laboratory mice. J Endocrinol 61:xlviii–xlix, 1974
12. Fessel WJ: Mental stress, blood proteins, and the hypothalamus. Arch Gen Psychiatry 7:427–435, 1962
13. Gisler RH: Stress and the hormonal regulation of the immune response in mice. Psychother Psychosom 23:197–208, 1974
14. Hamilton DR: Immunosuppressive effects of predator induced stress in mice with acquired immunity to Hymenolepsis nana. J Psychosom Res 18:143–153, 1974
15. Hill OW, Greer WE, Felsenfeld O: Psychological stress, early response to foreign protein, and blood cortisol in vervets. Psychosom Med 29:279–283, 1967
16. Solomon GF, Amkraut AA, Kasper P: Immunity, emotions and stress. Psychother Psychosom 23:209–217, 1974
17. Solomon GF, Moos RH: Emotions, immunity, and disease. Arch Gen Psychiatry 11:657–674, 1964
18. Vessey SH: Effects of grouping on levels of circulating antibodies in mice. Proc Soc Exp Biol Med 115:252–255, 1964
19. Wistar R, Hildemann WH: Effect of stress on skin transplantation immunity in mice. Science 131:159–160, 1960
20. Korneva EA, Kahl LM: Effect of destruction of hypothalamic areas on immunogenesis. Fed Proc 23:T88–T92, 1964

Food-Reinforced Inhibition 63
of Conditioned Salivation in Dogs
M. M. Shapiro and Dennis L. Herendeen

Twelve dogs salivated to a tone that was followed by food, but not to a noise for which there was an added response dependency. The noise was followed by food if and only if they did not salivate. The addition of this response dependency vitiated the classically conditioned response to the noise. A yoked-control group of 6 dogs receiving the same sequences of stimuli and food salivated to both the tone and noise stimuli.

The historically separate development of instrumental learning (Thorndike, 1898) and classical conditioning (Pavlov, 1910) indirectly corroborated the earlier philosophical distinction between voluntary and reflexive behaviors. Consequently, the responses of the autonomic nervous system were relegated to modifiability exclusively through classical conditioning (Hilgard & Marquis, 1940; Keller & Schoenfeld, 1950).

The validity of this prescription was questioned by several researchers. Kimmel and Hill (1960) modified the galvanic skin response, Shearn (1962) the heart rate, and Shapiro (1962) salivation, all with response-dependent reinforcement. Miller and his associates (Miller, 1969) attempted to systematically investigate the phenomenon using much more sophisticated control procedures.

Sheffield (1965), meanwhile, posed a somewhat different question. Instead of asking whether an autonomic response could be modified through response-dependent reinforcement, Sheffield asked whether the addition of a response dependency would modify classical conditioning. Sheffield attempted, unsuccessfully, to train 4 dogs to inhibit salivation in order to obtain food that was preceded by a "conditioned" stimulus. This failure appeared to conflict with the other above mentioned results until Miller (1972) questioned the replicability of the previous work by him and his associates. The problem was once again open.

The present experiment is a direct test of the hypothesis that autonomic responses can be modified by response-dependent reinforcement. However, the experiment was originally designed to pursue the technique proposed by Sheffield (1965), which has the equally compelling implication that classical conditioning may be overridden by a re-

[1] This research was supported in part by Grant No. HD-01333 from the National Institutes of Health to the first author. Portions of this paper were presented at the meeting of the Western Psychological Association, San Francisco, April 1971.
[2] Requests for reprints should be sent to M. M. Shapiro, Department of Psychology, Emory University, Atlanta, Georgia 30322.

sponse dependency. The basic procedure of the present experiment was a within-subject design in which one stimulus was always followed by food and another stimulus was followed by food if and only if the dog did not salivate to the stimulus. Within a classical conditioning conceptualization, the experiment consisted of presenting each subject with 2 conditioned stimuli, one reinforced on 100% of the trials and the other reinforced on less than 100% of the trials; previous research (Sadler, 1968) had shown that dogs salivated equally and indiscriminately to 2 stimuli even when one of the stimuli was followed by food on as few as 50% of the trials.

Viewed as classical conditioning, the experimenter's addition of a response dependency should be irrelevant. As long as the probability of the conditioned stimulus being followed by the unconditioned stimulus was high, the interstimulus intervals appropriate, the stimulus characteristics salient for the species, and the animals alert and healthy, "these stimuli necessarily result in the formation of a new connection . . . [Pavlov, 1927]." The procedure guaranteed the fulfillment of these requirements; the auditory stimuli, the salivary response, and subjects employed in this experiment were literally the classic case. Furthermore, the within-subject design provided a test of the conditionability of each subject. As a further precaution, a separate control group was run with 100% and partial reinforcement but without the response dependency.

If the experimental animals regularly salivated to the classical conditioned stimulus and regularly failed to salivate to the other stimulus, the food regularly followed both stimuli. The salivary response to both stimuli was reinforced, but a salivary conditioned response was acquired to only one of the stimuli. Not only would an instrumental response dependency have modified an autonomic response, but the acquisition of a classically conditioned response would have been nullified.

Method

Subjects

Subjects were 18 mongrel dogs.

Apparatus and Procedure

The experiment consisted of 30 days of training, 12 trials per day. A conditioned stimulus consisted of the 80-db. 10-sec. presentation of either a white noise or a 1,600-Hz. tone. If a food unconditioned stimulus was scheduled, the conditioned stimulus remained on for the additional 2 sec. during which food was presented. All subjects received the same treatment during the 5 days of the first phase of the experiment; each day there were 12 trials of the tone, terminating with the delivery of 8 gm. of food. The trials were presented with a mean intertrial interval of 8.5 min.

All animals were surgically prepared between the third and fourth days of training. A polyethylene tube was inserted into the left parotid salivary duct, brought under the dog's skin and out the dorsal surface of the neck. The salivary response was recorded by connecting the polyethylene tube to a glass tube, .93-cm. in diameter, containing approximately 100 ml. of a 90% water and 10% alcohol solution. The lower end of the glass tube was connected to a drop-counting device located 1.5 m. below the level of the chamber top. Each drop of saliva delivered a pulse to a printout counter. The surgical and recording techniques have been described previously in detail (Shapiro & Miller, 1965).

In the second phase of the experiment, the dogs were divided into 3 groups and trained to discriminate between 2 stimuli for 20 days. The tone was presented for 6 trials per day for all groups and was always terminated with food, thereby continuing the conditioning procedure of the first phase. For 2 groups, the noise was presented on the other 6 trials for 10 sec., but was terminated with food if and only if the subject did not salivate; if 2 or more drops occurred, no food followed the 10-sec. noise. (Drops formed on the end of a hypodermic needle and were recorded when the drop became large enough (.01 ml.) to fall. Since partially formed drops were present at the onset of stimuli, the first drop recorded represented salivation >0 and ≤ 1, the second drop recorded represented salivation >1 and ≤ 2, etc. Therefore, the error of measurement was $+1$ and a response of 2 drops constituted the smallest definable response criterion.) The trials were presented in an unsystematic order with a mean intertrial interval of 8.5 min. One of the 2 groups received response feedback by the chamber lights flashing for 30 msec. as a drop of saliva was recorded; the other group received no response feedback. (It was considered possible that the response dependency would be effective only with external response feedback.) A third group was trained under a procedure in which the tone was always terminated with food but the noise was terminated with food on a yoked-control schedule. Each animal of this group was yoked to a specific animal in the no-feedback group on a one-to-one basis. Each control animal was presented with the exact same sequence of conditioned and unconditioned stimuli as his counterpart in the experimental group, thereby mimicking the stimulus contingencies and eliminating the response dependency.

A third phase of the experiment consisted of 5 days on which the noise was presented on each of 12 trials, terminating with food if and only if the experimental animals did not salivate during the conditioned stimulus. The procedure in the third phase was identical to the procedure in the second

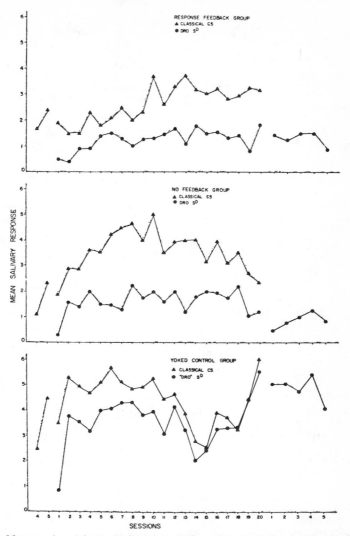

FIGURE 1. Mean number of drops of salivary responding to the classically conditioned stimulus (CS) and the discriminative stimulus for the differential reinforcement of other behavior (DRO S^D) for all 3 groups during Days 4–5 of classical conditioning, all 20 days of discrimination training between classical conditioning and DRO, and all 5 days of subsequent DRO training.

phase in all respects except for the inclusion of additional noise trials and exclusion of tone trials.

RESULTS

The mean salivary response to the 2 stimuli in Phases 1, 2, and 3 are shown in Figure 1. The tone that always terminated with food is called the classically conditioned stimulus, classical CS, and the noise that terminated with food if the animal did not respond is called the discriminative stimulus for the differential reinforcement of other behavior, DRO S^D. The graphs for the 2 experimental groups clearly reflect the formation of conditioned responses to the tone, classical CS and not to the noise, DRO S^D. Conditioning to the noise was not

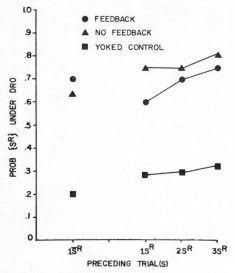

FIGURE 2. Probability of reinforcement (S^R) following 1 nonreinforcement (S̄^R) and 1, 2, or 3 reinforcements (S^R) for all 3 groups during the last 5 days of training with 12 trials of differential reinforcement of other behavior (DRO).

obtained for the experimental groups in spite of the fact that the noise terminated with food on approximately 60%–80% of the trials. An analysis of variance for all days or for the last 5 days of Phase 2 showed a significant difference in responding to the 2 stimuli ($F = 153.50$, $df = 1/95$, $p < .01$; $F = 144.54$, $df = 1/20$, $p < .01$, respectively) for the no-feedback group. An analysis of variance for the yoked-control group in Phase 2 also showed a significant difference in responding to the 2 stimuli over all days ($F = 69.47$, $df = 1/95$, $p < .01$), but this difference disappeared by the last 5 days ($F = 4.06$, $df = 1/20$, $p > .05$). The yoked-control group ultimately formed conditioned responses to both stimuli, although the group had precisely the same stimulus presentations as the no-feedback group. The failure of the noise to elicit a conditioned salivary response in the 2 experimental groups is obviously not attributable to subject characteristics or stimuli and their temporal characteristics, but must be the result of the supposedly irrelevant response dependency.

The difference between the experimental groups and the control group was maintained in Phase 3 ($F = 211.40$, $df = 1/16$, $p < .01$). The results from Phase 3 may also be seen

in Figure 2. The graph shows the mean probability of not responding following a nonreinforced trial (1S̄^R), a reinforced trial (1S^R), 2 reinforced trials (2S^R), or 3 food-reinforced trials (3S^R). The probability of not responding is, of course, the probability of obtaining a reinforcement under the DRO schedule for the 2 experimental groups. For the yoked-control group, the probability of not responding is what the probability of reinforcement would have been if they had been on a DRO schedule. The results show that the probability of the experimental animals responding was approximately equal to the complement of the probability of the yoked-control animals responding. That is, the experimental animals failed to exhibit a conditioned salivary response with the same frequency with which the control animals exhibited a conditioned salivary response.

DISCUSSION

Two conclusions may be drawn from the results of this experiment. First, the presentation of appropriate conditioned and unconditioned stimuli does not necessarily result in the acquisition of the classically conditioned response. Second, autonomic responses are modifiable through an instrumental procedure of response-dependent reinforcement. A more general conclusion is that neither the effects of stimulus-dependent reinforcement nor the effects of response-dependent reinforcement are restricted to either skeletal or autonomic responses. It is difficult to conceive of a response dependency that also does not provide a stimulus contingency; reinforcement is dependent upon the response, but specific stimuli may precede the reinforcement (Shapiro, 1960).

It is equally difficult to conceive of a stimulus dependency that also does not provide a response contingency; reinforcement is dependent upon the stimulus, but any particular response does or does not temporally intervene between the stimuli. Coexistent response contingencies and stimulus contingencies both affect behavior. Classically conditioned responses alter the saliency of the ensuing reinforcing stimulus, and instrumentally conditioned responses alter the conditional probabilities of the reinforcing stimulus. Experiments are generally designed to investigate stimulus dependencies or response dependencies, but stimulus contingencies and response contingencies are both present. The reinforcement dependencies specify the potential relationships of events to reinforcement; the reinforcement contingencies are the actual relationships of events to reinforcement.

Empirical laws of learning relate to contingencies not dependencies. There are 2 types of reinforcement dependencies that can be specified by an experimenter, not 2 types of learning.

REFERENCES

Hilgard, E. R., & Marguis, D. G. *Conditioning and learning.* New York: Appleton-Century-Crofts, 1940.

Keller, F. S., & Schoenfeld, W. N. *Principles of psychology.* New York: Appleton-Century-Crofts, 1950.

Kimmel, H. D., & Hill, F. A. Operant conditioning of the GSR. *Psychological Reports*, 1960, 7, 555–562.

Miller, N. E. Learning of visceral and glandular responses. *Science*, 1969, 163, 434–445.

Miller, N. E. Experiments on psychosomatic interactions. Paper presented at the meeting of the Eastern Psychological Association, Boston, April 1972.

Pavlov, I. P. Conditioned reflexes: An investigation of the physiological activity of the cerebral cortex. (Trans. by G. V. Anrep) London: Oxford University Press, 1927.

Pavlov, I. P. *The work of the digestive glands.* (2nd ed.) (Trans. by W. H. Thompson) London: Charles Griffin, 1910.

Sadler, E. W. A within- and between-subjects comparison of partial reinforcement in classical salivary conditioning. *Journal of Comparative and Physiological Psychology*, 1968, 66, 695–698.

Shapiro, M. M. Respondent salivary conditioning during operant lever pressing in dogs. *Science*, 1960, 132, 619–620.

Shapiro, M. M. Mediation between instrumental and consummatory responses. Paper presented at the meeting of the American Psychological Association, St. Louis, September 1962.

Shapiro, M. M., & Miller, T. M. On the relationship between conditioned and discriminative stimuli and between instrumental and consummatory responses. In W. Prokasy (Ed.), *Classical conditioning, A symposium.* New York: Appleton-Century-Crofts, 1965.

Shearn, D. W. Operant conditioning of heart rate. *Science*, 1962, 137, 530–531.

Sheffield, F. D. Relation between classical and instrumental learning. In W. Prokasy (Ed.), *Classical conditioning, A symposium.* New York: Appleton-Century-Crofts, 1965.

Thorndike, E. L. Animal intelligence. An experimental study of the associative processes in animals. *Psychological Monographs*, 1898, 2(4, Whole No. 8).

XI

BIOFEEDBACK INSTRUMENTS

Of Bread, Circuses, and Alpha Machines 64

Robert L. Schwitzgebel and John D. Rugh

A few years ago, an undergraduate was brought by his roommate to the college counseling center where one of the present writers was working as a trainee. The student was agitated, repeated apparently meaningless words, and showed common signs of an acute schizophrenic reaction. Part of the conversation, as best as it can now be recalled, went as follows:

Counselor: Have you been eating OK?
Student: Harvard Union [name of a dining hall].
Counselor: No, have you been to all the meals?
Student: [No answer].
Roommate: He's missed some.
Counselor: How many?
Roommate: Lunch, and I don't know about breakfast for sure—I don't think he got dressed in time.
Counselor: Why no lunch?
Roommate: [Long pause, glances at troubled friend] They wouldn't let him in.
Counselor: What?!
Roommate: [Confidingly] He ate his meal tickets.

People who confuse symbols with their referents, or secondary reinforcers with primary ones, are likely to be headed for trouble. Semanticist Alfred

This study was supported in part by National Institute of Mental Health Research Grant MH20315 to Robert L. Schwitzgebel.

We hope that readers will appreciate the risk and openness of all cooperating equipment suppliers who submitted devices for public inspection, particularly lower priced items that may not be representative of their product line. The authors wish especially to acknowledge the assistance of Allan Armstrong in testing the devices and of Erich Pfeiffer in technical and editorial matters.

Requests for reprints should be sent to John Rugh, Department of Psychology, Claremont Graduate School, Claremont, California 91711.

Korzybski popularized the distinction between the map and the territory. Psychology, as an academic and professional enterprise, measures productivity principally by words rather than by experience. Hence psychology seems to value an original hypothesis or an elegant theory more than it values a practical tool that can alter experience. A job applicant, for example, will probably be asked about publications but not about patents (even though 8%–34% of psychology faculty members, depending on professional orientation, find the journals "very dull" and are "very dissatisfied" with editorial policy—Lipsey, 1974).

The *basic commodities* of psychology are behaviors, perceptions, and emotions—not theories, hypotheses, statistics, paradigms, and models that are the linguistic conveniences used by professionals. The *marketable symbols* are degrees, titles, licenses, and publications. Students are expected to manipulate words with considerable proficiency but are asked only rarely to demonstrate a similar proficiency in changing emotions and behavior of people in life situations. Psychology, as a social endeavor, is obligated to benefit people—to reduce violence, addictions, phobias, suicides, divorce; to increase cooperation, tolerance, learning, happiness, etc. Taxpayers, clients, and donors are sufficiently tolerant or naive to allow considerable sloppiness, faking, and error, but eventually an enterprise designed only for amusement and enrichment of psychologists will be repudiated. David McClelland once publicly suggested, not entirely facetiously, that a PhD degree ought to be granted to anyone who could prove by acceptable methods that he or she had "cured" three people.

Degrees and licenses are useful symbolic inventions, similar to money or maps. However, their value (beyond the paper they are printed on, as a commodity) is determined by social convention. Sooner or later the symbols of help must be backed up by tangible and experienced benefits (i.e., by primary reinforcers like bread and circuses). The confusion of symbol and thing has possibly contributed to the ironic situation of psychology PhDs desperately looking for work, while surrounded by problems and opportunities in everyday affairs.

The worth of psychology is best measured by the skill of its practitioners in manipulating palpable material assemblages from which environments are formed that can predictably alter individual human behavior, perception, and emotion. In our opinion, *the immediate task of persons interested in increasing psychological wealth is to stop manipulating verbal symbols and get on with careful manipulation and observation of the material world.*

Brooks (1965), Kranzberg (1968), Price (1965), and others have argued that historical evidence does not generally support the assumption that practical technology "grows out of" scientific theoretical endeavors. Technology is not necessarily "applied science." The discontinuity of theory and practice in psychology, despite frequent claims to the contrary by practitioners, has been noted by Breger and McGaugh (1965), Franks (1966), and London (1972). London has forcefully argued for practical instrumentation:

What is important, at this juncture, is the development of systematic practice and of a technology to sustain it. My thesis is that, in the long run, scientific understanding will derive from them. . . . New equipment, new drugs, new gimmickry and gadgetry should now be the basis for systematically developing new methods of behavior modification and for streamlining the established techniques with controlled experimental testing. Instead of looking for new principles, or justifying worn-out ones, we should look for new applications: What could we do to treat such-and-such if we had such-and-such machinery? What would be required to build it? To test it? And then, finally, to determine what it means? (p. 918)

Some Precedents

Much of the work of B. F. Skinner (1970), who reported that he "was always building things" (p. 2), follows the strategy just suggested. He is credited with inventing the bar-press apparatus, cumulative recorder, verbal summator, air crib, and updated versions of the teaching machine. However, the most widely used apparatus of demonstrated value is the bed pad for enuretics generally credited to Mowrer and Mowrer (1938). In a now-classic paper, they described their use of a battery-operated device of their own construction.

A subsequent survey of the literature by the Mowrers revealed that a German pediatrician, M. Pfaundler, had reported in 1904 his practice of equipping beds in a hospital children's ward with an electric bell to signal nurses when a child needed changing. He was surprised to observe that often no wetting at all occurred after a month's use and, in some cases, there was immediate inhibition. The inconvenience of the apparatus, which required 20–30 cc of urine to activate and which resulted in subsequent oxidation of the metal screens, might account for its lack of use.

Francis Galton was among the most distinguished early psychotechnicians. In a paper entitled "Measurement of Character," he concluded:

An ordinary generalization is nothing more than a muddle of vague memories of inexact observations. It is an easy vice to generalize. We want lists of facts, every one of which may be separately verified, valued and revalued, and the whole accurately summed. It is the statistics of each man's conduct in small every-day affairs, that will probably be found to give the simplest and most precise measure of his character. (Galton, 1884, p. 185)

His own attempts to do this included fastening spring gauges to chair legs at a dinner table to measure the "inclination" of one person to another; surreptitiously sounding a variable-pitch whistle while at the zoo or after passing an interesting-looking person to see if the individual would orient to the sound; attaching the elastic air bag of a pneumocardiograph under his coat while delivering a lecture; estimating the dullness of a sermon by noting the number of "fidgets" of members of the congregation; inventing a pocket-sized counter; and standardizing fingerprint identification (Pearson, 1914).

From beginnings such as these, behavior instrumentation has expanded to include at least a dozen different types of apparatus (e.g., electrosleep machines, toilet-training devices, antistuttering and antisnoring devices, timers, token dispensers, aversive conditioning apparatus). A survey of such devices has been published elsewhere (Schwitzgebel & Schwitzgebel, 1973).

In the past decade, traditional Pavlovian conditioning of the autonomic nervous system has been supplemented by operant-feedback methods. Long-term practical benefits of feedback may be demonstrated eventually in the treatment of hypertension, cardiac arrhythmias, low back pain, neuromuscular impairment, phobias, tension headache, and so forth (Shapiro & Schwartz, 1972); but most popular attention has been focused on the possibility of altering emotional or mental states by brain wave monitoring (Kamiya, 1969; Nowlis & Kamiya, 1970). Alpha rhythms, with frequencies between 7.5 and 13 Hz, are reportedly associated with relaxed awareness, such as produced during meditation (Brown, 1969; Wenger & Bagchi, 1961). Small engineer-psychologist-entrepreneur teams sprang up to meet a "public demand for alpha devices." This is the first and, as is noted later, perhaps the last widespread, citizen-level psychotechnology industry.

While there has been no obvious harm to the vast majority of users of biofeedback devices, some individual exceptions might be found. Potential risks might include the development of psychophysical anomalies, temporal or spatial disorientation, disruption of conventional work or sleep patterns, raising false hopes for improved emotional or social life, embarrassment or invasion of privacy (e.g., "lie detectors"), and economic loss. Potential personal and social benefit should be weighed against such potential harms. Comprehensive assessment, however, is a very complex undertaking. As a beginning effort, the present authors evaluated the most consumer-relevant parameters of popular-priced electroencephalogram (EEG) feedback devices.

Evaluation of Alpha Devices

The basic method of brain wave feedback is simple. Its adequate accomplishment is difficult. Biopotentials (small fractions of a volt) in the brain are correlated with mental activity. These signals are amplified and then filtered so that a specified magnitude and frequency of brain wave will trigger a tone or light. Complications arise from the fact that the magnitude of brain wave signals measured on the scalp is only 10–100 millionths of a volt, that there often exist high levels of external interference such as noise from 60-Hz power lines, and that the forehead or scalp has a typically high impedance. Conventional, laboratory-quality oscillographs cost several thousand dollars, so what does a person get by mail order for a few hundred dollars? This is what we investigated.

In January 1974, as an independently funded research project, we contacted all known United States suppliers ($N = 23$) who sold one or more EEG feedback devices. Of a total of 49 devices, we attempted to acquire by loan or by purchase one "popular-priced" device (arbitrarily defined as under $250) from each manufacturer. This totaled 16 devices. The company was informed that they would have an opportunity to question test results of their own apparatus prior to publication. Three devices were unavailable from the manufacturers and are not included in the sample. In some cases these devices were obtained by other means and were tested; however, the results are not reported here, out of courtesy to the manufacturer. Each device was subjected to a routine series of

test procedures during which 48 different characteristics were examined. Of these characteristics, only those that met the following three criteria are included in this report: (a) the characteristic has parameters that a user may consider important when purchasing or using a device; (b) testing revealed that the devices differed with respect to the parameter—that is, there would be no value in reporting an invariant characteristic; and (c) the test procedures used to examine the parameter were able to be developed sufficiently to yield quantifiable and reasonably objective results.

With respect to several of the parameters reported here, there appears to be no generally accepted standard. For example, there is no objectively ideal filter bandwidth. This characteristic varies widely among devices and may considerably alter the effectiveness of the device as a training tool. Certainly it makes the results of different investigators difficult to compare. The research necessary to evaluate the therapeutic efficacy of certain EEG feedback apparatus characteristics simply has not been done.

The results of the evaluations are summarized in Table 1. Device evaluations are applicable only to the models indicated. Readers are urged to contact the supplier regarding any recent changes in price, accessories, etc.

Many of the parameters presented in Table 1 are self-explanatory. However, others may not be familiar to the general reader or may need clarification for technical reasons. These parameters are briefly described or qualified as follows:

Electrode-scalp impedance: a measure of the unit's electrode-scalp interface resistance. The measure was made by applying two of the electrodes as per manufacturer's instructions to the forehead, three inches apart. Electrode impedance was measured after 10 minutes by recording the voltage drop across the two electrodes connected in series with a 1-MΩ resistor and a battery-powered 9-Hz signal generator with a 1-V rms sine wave output.

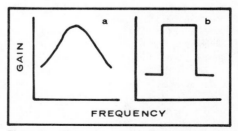

Figure 2. Illustrative frequency response curves for analog (a) and digital (b) filters.

TABLE 1 : COMPARATIVE TEST DATA

Supplier	Device/price	Weight (g)	Size (cm)	Electrode-scalp impedance (ohm)	Input impedance (ohm)	Minimum detectable signal (μV p − p)	Filter	Filter bandwidth (3 decibel points, Hz)	Alpha filter center frequency (Hz)
Alpha Metrics	Model S/$105	147	10 × 5 × 3	5.2K	110K	3	A	9.7	9
Aquarius	Alphaphone/$80	276	4 × 10 × 7	24K	1M	2	A	16.5	14
Autogenic Systems Inc.	Model 70/$495[a]	2,200	11 × 32 × 14	10K	>1M	1	Adj, D	Adj	Adj
Biofeedback Instruments	Model M102/$143	896	16 × 2 × 5	5.2K	10K	8	Adj, A	.9	Adj
Bio-Logic Devices	Model BF-21/$50	168	11 × 7 × 3	2K	60K	6	A	2.7	11.7
BioScan Corporation	Alphascan 400/$225	1,500	20 × 11 × 16	9.6K	>2M	7	Adj, D	Adj	Adj
Cyborg Corporation	Model T-131/$175	392	10 × 4 × 15	3.9K	280K	9	A	9	7.8
Extended Digital Alpha Kit	Alpha kit/$60	336	14 × 5 × 9	2K	5M	3	Adj, A	5.7	11
Inner Space Electronics	Model 7000/$70	280	10 × 5 × 8	13K	200K	5	A	4.2	10
J&J Enterprises	EEP-4/$69	252	11 × 8 × 8	5.8K	200K	3	A	7.6	11
Medlab	Alpha 100A/$97	504	15 × 13 × 6	4.9K	170K	5	A	7.5	10.5
M.O.E.	Biocouple 301/$98	812	18 × 17 × 8	1.9K	20K	5	Adj, D	Adj	Adj
Psionics	ETC 102/$200	280	16 × 11 × 5	8.6K	500	6	A	7.5	10

Note. Addresses of all companies are listed in the Buyer's Guide, this issue.
  Abbreviations are: D = digital. A = analog. Adj = adjustable. Sgl = single-ended. Dif = differential. LED = light-emitting diode.
  Although every precaution has been taken to assure the accuracy of the data, performance can vary from unit to unit.
  No warranty for the safety, effectiveness, or performance of listed devices is implied, or liability assumed, by the National Institute of Mental Health, the publisher, or the testing facility and its employees.
  [a] Price increase from $245 to $495 occurred after testing was completed.

Input impedance: a measure of the device's input amplifier characteristics. A high input impedance is desirable to reduce output amplitude error caused by variation in electrode-scalp impedance. The error can be greatly minimized if input impedance is at least 10 times greater than the electrode-scalp impedance.

Minimum detectable signal (μVp-p): the smallest input signal at 9 Hz which will produce a detectable feedback signal. In general, alpha EEG waves are greater than 10 μV; thus units having minimum detectable signals *less than* 10 μV would probably function properly in most applications.

Filter (analog/digital): Analog filters are typified by an inverted-U frequency response curve; digital filters are typified by very sharp cutoff points with relatively constant gain over the band-pass range (see Figure 2). The center frequency or cutoff points of some devices are adjustable. Table 1 indicates devices with this capacity.

Filter bandwidth (3 decibel points): a measure of the device's selectivity. This indicates how broad a spectrum of input frequencies the filter will respond to. Note that some devices have an adjustable bandwidth.

Input (differential or single ended): A differential input amplifier has two active electrodes and one ground electrode. In general, the differential amplifier is less sensitive to environmental electrical noise because it rejects those signals that are common to the two active electrodes (common mode signal) and amplifies only the difference signal occurring between the two active electrodes (differential mode signal). The ability of the differential amplifier to reject common mode noise and amplify the differential signal should be provided in the manufacturer's specifications, usually in the form of a ratio. This common mode rejection ratio (CMRR) is the ratio of the amplifier's common mode gain to the amplifier's differential mode gain. The higher the ratio, the better.[1] Single-

ON ALPHA-WAVE FEEDBACK DEVICES

Input	60-Hz suppression (decibel)	EEG gain control	Calibrated threshold control	Feedback volume control	Expected battery life (hours)	Type of feedback	Potted circuit	Preamplifier output jack	Auxiliary equipment output jack	Warranty (years)	Special features
Sgl	−64	Yes	No	No	500	FM	Yes	Yes	Yes	½	Long battery life; small size; broadband filter
Dif	−19	Yes	No	No	12	AM FM	No	No	No	5	Small size; broadband filter; six accessory options
Dif	−72	Yes	Yes	Yes	23	AM FM	Yes	Yes	Yes	5	Present-time alpha meter; white noise feedback "spectrum modulation"; electrode and battery test; sleep alarm
Sgl	−53	Yes	No	No	62	AM	No	No	No	1	Includes GSR and EKG feedback; electrode test
Sgl	−35	No	No	Yes	130	FM	No	No	No	1	Selectable alpha and theta filter
Dif	−40	No	Yes	Yes	24	Tone burst	No	Yes	Yes	2	Digital upper frequency cutoff control; LED visual feedback mode
Dif	−31	No	Yes	No	36	Tone burst	No	No	No	1	LED visual feedback mode; training course for alpha
Dif	−44	Yes	No	Yes	15	AM FM	No	No	No	?	Kit not recommended for beginners; three filter ranges; several feedback modes; integrator
Sgl	−53	Yes	No	Yes	200	Tone burst	No	Yes	Yes	¼	Internal speaker
Sgl	−28	Yes	No	Yes	80	AM	Yes	No	Yes	1	White noise feedback; optional mounted headphones
Dif	−73	No	Yes	No	48	AM	No	Yes	Yes	1	Internal speaker; electrode and battery test
Dif	−119	No	Yes	Yes	10	Tone burst	No	Yes	Yes	5	LED visual feedback; built-in frequency calibrator
Dif	−33	Yes	No	No	11	Tone burst	No	No	Yes	1	Included package of saltines ("Zen soda crackers") as a philosophical irony

ended amplifiers have two electrodes and must depend on heavy filtering to reduce unwanted environmental noise.

60-Hz suppression (decibel): a measure of a particular filter's ability to suppress 60-Hz differential signals. The figure was calculated by subtracting the unit's gain (decibel) at 60 Hz from the unit's gain at 9 Hz. Note that this measure is not an indication of the unit's common mode rejection characteristics but is a measure of the unit's filter characteristics. In general, devices with greater suppression will be less subject to 60-Hz noise.

[1] CMRR figures are not provided here. In order to obtain the CMRR, measures must be made between the input amplifier network and the filter. This cannot be done on potted circuits, nor was the ratio supplied by many of the manufacturers.

Expected battery life: This figure was calculated from the manufacturer's discharge curves for the 2UG (9-V transistor battery) for a cutoff point of 1.2 V per cell (and 7.2 V for the battery). The figures are for continuous use, assuming a constant feedback signal at a temperature of 70° F. The actual battery life that can be expected is higher than the listed value because devices of this type are normally used intermittently. Some units were also found to operate satisfactorily below the cutoff point of 7.2 V. Battery life can be extended substantially by using alkaline-type batteries.

Type of feedback: All units were equipped with an output jack for audio feedback with headphones. The nature of the feedback signal was classified according to the following categories:

1. *AM*. An audible tone or white noise (carrier) is amplitude modulated by the amplified EEG signal. The amplitude of the EEG signal

is indicated by the tone's loudness. Frequency is indicated by the frequency of the changes in tone loudness.

2. *FM.* An audio frequency tone or white noise is frequency modulated by the amplified EEG signal. The frequency of the EEG signal is indicated by the frequency of changes in the tone's center frequency. The amplitude of the EEG signal is indicated by the amount of frequency deviation of the tone.

3. *FM–AM.* An audio frequency tone or white noise is both frequency and amplitude modulated by the amplified EEG signal.

4. *Tone burst.* A tone burst or clicking noise is heard when an EEG signal is present and exceeds a preset value. The repetition rate of the tone burst may indicate the EEG's frequency. Amplitude information is not directly indicated on the signal.

Potted circuit: A potted circuit is one in which the electronic components and circuit board are encapsulated in plastic. Although potting provides protection from environmental influences, repair of the circuit is difficult or impossible.

There is the possibility that devices supplied to us by the manufacturer were specially prepared or prechecked. Therefore, we conducted spot reliability checks by comparing the device sent to us with the same model in private use. The fundamental reason that "doctoring" is not a serious problem in evaluation, however, is that almost all deficiencies lie in basic design errors rather than poor quality control.

State of the Art

An examination of the data in Table 1 suggests that there is little uniformity among manufacturers with respect to the optimal value of many device characteristics. For example, filter bandwidth was found to vary from 16.5 to .9 Hz, and alpha-filter center frequency was found to vary from 7.8 to 14.0 Hz. *The wide variation found in device characteristics makes the results of different investigators difficult to compare.*

Even after ideal functional characteristics are generally agreed upon, commercial devices do not necessarily reflect this consensus. It has been established, for example, that the input impedance of bioelectric amplifiers should be at least 10 times greater than the source impedance and preferably much higher (Geddes, 1972; Roman & Lamb, 1962). Source impedance—which varies according to several factors such as the type of electrode, type of electrode jelly, and subject preparation technique—was found to average about 5,000 Ω in

our tested devices. One device, however, had an input impedance as low as 500 Ω.

Unfortunately, manufacturers do not always provide advertising literature indicating many of their products' specifications, which makes an intelligent selection of a device very difficult. Of the 13 manufacturers listed in Table 1, 5 did not provide information in their advertising literature regarding input impedance, and 6 did not provide information on their alpha-filter center frequency. Prospective purchasers would be wise to ask manufacturers to supply this and other relevant data prior to purchase. At minimum, clinicians and researchers should know the characteristics of the particular apparatus they are using and clearly indicate these in the apparatus sections of published reports.

No single device will perform ideally in all applications. Producing and marketing a diverse-function, high-quality product at a popular price is a very demanding endeavor. Each device is likely to have unique characteristics that make it well suited in some situations but limited or unusable in others. For example, users who anticipate employing a device in an electrically noisy environment would do well to select a device with good 60-Hz suppression (−60 decibels) and a differential input with a high common mode rejection ratio. Another application may require long usage periods, and the purchaser would do well to select a device with a long battery life. Expected battery life of tested devices ranged from 10 to 500 hours. Research applications generally require a device with high input impedance (> 1 MΩ), adjustable filters, and outputs for auxiliary recording equipment.

Clearly, there have been some abuses such as excessive claims and poorly designed apparatus in the marketing of alpha devices. Further, the Food and Drug Administration has taken the position that the safety and effectiveness of biofeedback apparatuses have not been established and that the labeling of some of these apparatuses may therefore be inadequate (Davis, Note 1). Bills pending before Congress would permit the Food and Drug Administration to regulate devices in a manner similar to drugs, including the establishment of a category of "prescription devices." One supplier who has been routinely requiring medical authorization following legal action by the government reported no serious decrement in sales (Toomim, Note 2). Whether this would hold on an industry-wide basis is unknown. Apparently, a much more serious threat to small manufacturers is the likely requirement of "preclearance" wherein safety and efficacy may need to be demonstrated by "sufficient well-controlled investigations, including clinical investigations where appropriate, by experts qualified by scientific training and experience . . ." (Committee on Labor and Public Welfare, 1973, p. 42).

As inventors working in a nonverbal medium, developers of biofeedback apparatus can add "materially" to human psychological wealth. But there is still a large pool of inventive talent in our society generally unaware of common psychological methodologies such as contingency management or behavior mapping. Here are numerous opportunities for creative instrumentation. No central clearinghouse exists where inventors, manufacturers, psychologists, engineers, and public consumers can exchange information of interest (e.g., patents, product test reports, do-it-yourself projects, supplier lists, used equipment exchange, summaries of state and federal regulations). Such an organiza-

tion would certainly deal with words and images—but only as the necessary "metaphysics" of psychological hardware. What the early Psychological Corporation did for psychological testing needs to be done now for instrumentation.

The skillful composition of human environments is not limited to, but certainly involves, machines to alter light, sound, and material. As our material environment becomes more responsive to individual wishes, the traditional dichotomy of dream and reality will diminish. Lecture, novels, and theories may be gradually supplemented by programmable flow patterns of tactile and visual sensation. In a decade or so, a new craft may evolve that will use certain skills of chemists, electronic engineers, film makers, computer scientists, physiologists, architects, applied physicists, and some adventuresome psychologists who do not confuse a meal ticket with a sensuous feast.

REFERENCE NOTES

1. Davis, J. B. (Director, Division of Scientific Review, Office of Medical Devices, Food and Drug Administra-

tion). Personal communication, January 9, 1974.
2. Toomim, H. Personal communication, June 3, 1974.

REFERENCES

Breger, L., & McGaugh, J. L. Critique and reformation of "learning theory" approaches to psychotherapy and neurosis. *Psychological Bulletin*, 1965, *63*, 338–358.

Brooks, H. The interaction of science and technology: Another view. In A. W. Warner, D. Morse, & A. S. Eichner (Eds.), *The impact of science on technology.* New York: Columbia University Press, 1965.

Brown, B. B. *Awareness of EEG-subjective activity relationships detected within a closed feedback system.* Sepulveda, Calif.: Experiential Physiology Laboratory, Veterans Administration Hospital, 1969 (Mimeo). (In R. L. Schwitzgebel & R. K. Schwitzgebel [Eds.], *Psychotechnology: Electronic control of mind and behavior.* New York: Holt, Rinehart & Winston, 1973.)

Committee on Labor and Public Welfare, Subcommittee on Health, United States Senate. *Medical devices amendments.* Washington, D.C.: U.S. Government Printing Office, 1973.

Franks, C. M. Clinical application of conditioning and other behavioral techniques: Conceptual and professional considerations. *Conditional Reflex*, 1966, *1*, 36–50.

Galton, F. Measurement of character. In R. L. Schwitzgebel & R. K. Schwitzgebel (Eds.), *Psychotechnology: Electronic control of mind and behavior.* New York: Holt, Rinehart & Winston, 1973. (Reprinted from *Fortnightly Review*, 1884, *42*, 179–185.)

Geddes, L. A. *Electrodes and the measurement of bioelectric events.* New York: Wiley, 1972.

Kamiya, J. Operant control of the EEG alpha rhythm and some of its reported affects on consciousness. In C. T. Tart (Ed.), *Altered states of consciousness: A book of readings.* New York: Wiley, 1969.

Kranzberg, M. The disunity of science-technology. *American Scientist*, 1968, *56*, 21–34.

Lipsey, M. W. A survey of graduate students and faculty in psychology. *American Psychologist*, 1974, *29*, 541–553.

London, P. The end of ideology in behavior modification. *American Psychologist*, 1972, *27*, 913–918.

Mowrer, O. H., & Mowrer, W. M. Enuresis—A method for its study and treatment. *The American Journal of Orthopsychiatry*, 1938, *8*, 436–459.

Nowlis, D. P., & Kamiya, J. The control of electroencephalographic alpha rhythms through auditory feedback and the associated mental activity. *Psychophysiology*, 1970, *6*, 476–485.

Pearson, K. *Life and letters of Francis Galton* (4 vols.). Cambridge, England: Cambridge University Press, 1914.

Price, D. J. DeS. Is technology historically independent of science? A study in statistical historiography. *Technology and Culture*, 1965, *6*, 553–567.

Roman, J., & Lamb, L. Electrocardiography in flight. *Aerospace Medicine*, 1962, *33*, 527–544.

Schwitzgebel, R. L., & Schwitzgebel, R. K. (Eds.). *Psychotechnology: Electronic control of mind and behavior.* New York: Holt, Rinehart & Winston, 1973.

Shapiro, D., & Schwartz, G. E. Biofeedback and visceral learning: Clinical applications. *Seminars in Psychiatry*, 1972, *4*, 171–184.

Skinner, B. F. An autobiography. In P. B. Dews (Ed.), *Festschrift for B. F. Skinner*. New York: Appleton-Century-Crofts, 1970.

Wenger, M., & Bagchi, B. Studies of autonomic function in practitioners of Yoga in India. *Behavioral Science*, 1961, *6*, 312–323.

Biofeedback Instrumentation: Soldering Closed the Loop

65

David A. Paskewitz

I ran across the statement very recently in the book of Theophrastus On Inspiration that many men have believed and put their belief on record, that when gouty pains in the hips are most severe they are relieved if a fluteplayer plays soothing measures. That snake-bites are cured by the music of the flute, when played skillfully and melodiously, is also stated in a book of Democritus, entitled On Deadly Infections, in which he shows that the music of the flute is medicine for many ills that flesh is heir to. So very close is the connection between the bodies and the minds of men, and therefore, between physical and mental ailments and their remedies.

Aulus Gellius (c. 160 A.D.)

Biofeedback derives its name from a combination of biology and feedback, the latter concept a familiar one in the fields of engineering and control theory. The biofeedback idea is a simple one: Knowledge of the dynamic status of biological systems will enable voluntary control of such systems. Typically, some physiological variable is sensed through electrodes, amplified, filtered, processed, and displayed to the subject, placing that subject in a feedback loop with the equipment forming a significant information path within the total system. Subjects may be human or infrahuman, but this article deals exclusively with human biofeedback instrumentation. Many of the same techniques and instruments are suitable for either application.

Requests for reprints should be sent to David A. Paskewitz, Department of Psychiatry, University of Maryland Medical School, Baltimore, Maryland 21201.

In spite of the fact that some physiological variables, for instance, respiration or heart rate, can be sensed without electronic assistance, many cannot, and the development of biofeedback has been closely linked to instrumentation from the beginning. The earliest instrumentation grew out of standard psychophysiological apparatus such as polygraphs, operational amplifiers, logic modules, and the like. The standard biomedical polygraph or clinical electroencephalograph (EEG) machine remains the instrument of choice for most basic researchers in the field. Likewise, the variables processed and returned to the subject have tended to be those already under study by psychophysiologists, many of whom can be included among the biofeedback researchers. Much of the processing and display of information is still accomplished in unique, one-of-a-kind arrays of equipment. There are two other classes of biofeedback instruments, however, that are closely tied to recent advances in electronic technology.

For the clinical researcher or the clinician applying biofeedback techniques to patients, the bulky polygraph or EEG machine with its ink-writing galvanometers and paper drive is considered neither necessary nor desirable. The clinician tends to place more emphasis on appearance, reliability, and ease of operation than does the basic research investigator, whose equipment is often physically separated from the subject and may be calibrated prior to each session. A considerable number of clinically oriented systems and devices have become available to meet the needs of practitioners. (Most of these are listed in the Buyer's Guide of this issue.)

Another class of instruments is designed for the private use of individuals, as a home practice adjunct to some therapy, or by those with an interest in exploring self-awareness, meditation, psychic phenomena, etc. The prime consideration with these instruments is frequently cost, with ease of use a secondary consideration. Often the reliability and accuracy of the instruments are given far too little attention.

In all three categories, but most particularly in the latter two, recent electronic progress in the area of inexpensive, sophisticated linear and digital integrated circuits has made possible designs that only a few years ago would have been awkward and prohibitively expensive for the average clinician, let alone a private individual. High-quality operational amplifiers are selling for less than 50¢ each, making possible highly selective filters, sensitive precision rectifiers, accurate integrators, and quiet input amplifiers at low cost. For less than $5 each, and sometimes less than $1, it is possible to purchase timers, signal generators, voltage-controlled oscillators, decade counters, monostable multivibrators, digital displays, or accurate, short-circuit-proof power supply regulators. (Several sources for these components appear in the Buyer's Guide.) In the area of clinical instruments these advances have resulted in instruments that are not only inexpensive but versatile and sophisticated as well. Personal home-use units would be all but impractical without integrated circuits, both in cost and complexity.

Another recent advance with impact primarily on biofeedback research is the growing availability of inexpensive ($4,000–$20,000) small-to-medium-scale minicomputers operating in a real-time environment. Even small computers with minimal complements of memory can be used to process data and present feedback information according to some contingency if equipped with analog-to-digital conversion, a clock, and some digital or relay output. It is not inconceivable that the increasing appearance of so-called "microcomputers," with 8- or 12-bit processors and memory on a single board for well under $1,000, may lead to extensive use of digital signal processing in complex biofeedback situations. A number of investigators have already used computers in biofeedback research (Beatty, 1971; Legewie & Probst, 1969; Vaitl & Kenkmann, 1972). Some advantages to the processing of data by real-time computer systems, apart from the inherent storage and summation capabilities, are the relative ease of realizing dynamic alterations in the criteria for presenting the feedback information, the ability to present random proportions of false feedback information, or the ease of combining several variables to form complex contingencies or information displays.

Biofeedback instrumentation has focused most heavily on three measures: the electroencephalogram, the electromyogram, and skin temperature, with lesser emphasis on heart rhythm, galvanic skin response (GSR), and blood pressure. With the exception of skin temperature and blood pressure, which employ special sensors, measurement of these variables requires electrode contact with the subject. Three types of electrodes are commonly used: sponge, metal, and "pellet" electrodes. Electrodes are usually offered by the manufacturers of biofeedback devices. In most cases the choice of electrodes involves factors of cost and ease of use over considerations such as nonpolarizability or electrode resistance, although such considerations can be of great importance, particularly in a research setting. Silver–silver chloride "pellet" electrodes are probably the best general choice.

EEG Biofeedback

Biofeedback of EEG signals has primarily involved recognizing the EEG alpha rhythm (8–13 Hz) and informing the subject of its presence, although some research has focused on beta (15–30 Hz), theta (4–8 Hz), or sensorimotor (about 14 Hz) rhythms as well. Alpha rhythm feedback achieved popularity through the work of Kamiya (1968, 1969), Brown (1970, 1971), and others (Hart, 1968; Nowlis & Kamiya, 1970), who reported that positive changes in subjective mood were related to increases in alpha activity through biofeedback. Recent evidence, however, has called into doubt many of the assumptions underlying these relationships (Beatty, 1972; Lynch & Paskewitz, 1971; Paskewitz & Orne, 1973; Walsh, 1974), and there has been little evidence of the clinical efficacy of alpha feedback procedures (Blanchard & Young, 1974).

The typical situation involves placing the subject or patient in a comfortable position, attaching scalp electrodes for the EEG and perhaps earphones for the feedback signal, and telling the person to attempt to increase the amount of feedback tone. Subjects are usually told that they are increasing their alpha activity and something about the presumed relationship between alpha activity and relaxation, peace of mind, or pleasant state. Sometimes subjects are told nothing, are misled, or are given a feedback signal for a lack of activity as an experimental control. Similar procedures are involved in training for other brain rhythms. The first requirement in providing biofeedback is to amplify the small (3–300-μV) surface EEG signals to a level sufficient for further analysis. Since the signals of interest are buried in high amounts of radio-frequency interference, line-frequency interference (60 Hz), muscle artifacts, and other unwanted signals, any feedback instrument must possess a differential amplifier at the input with high common mode rejection. This characteristic means that only voltages representing differences between the two inputs are amplified, while voltages common to both electrodes, between the electrodes and ground, for instance, are amplified minimally. To maintain high common mode rejection, electrode resistances should be kept as low as possible. Many amplifiers also contain notch filters to remove 60-Hz interference from the signals. Second, the amplifier should not introduce significant noise into the signal and should be relatively free from input offset and blocking effects. If a dc voltage difference exists between two electrodes, this difference, if amplified along with a varying signal voltage perhaps one-thousandth that amplitude, would result in an output so large that it would drive a recording pen off scale and the small signal would be totally lost. For this reason, EEG amplifiers are almost always ac coupled, using capacitors to pass only the varying component of the input signal. If, as is often the case, particularly when low-frequency signals are of interest, these capacitors are made large, then large signals at the input, artifact, for instance, can charge these capacitors such that the resulting off-scale output may continue for several seconds before usable signals are available again. Some designs limit the amount of blocking automatically. Another feature of a good input amplifier is high-input impedance, which simply means that the amplifier does not offer low enough resistance to the voltage source to load it down. A final feature of the input amplifier, shared by the remainder of the biofeedback system, is that it should not be electrically dangerous to the subject, that is, it should be shockproof. Most instruments, with the exception of standard biomedical recorders and EEG machines, use batteries to power the amplifiers and often the entire system. Such systems usually employ optical coupling techniques or similar high-quality isolation schemes between the battery-operated device and any line-powered instrumentation. These precautions assure that the equipment cannot be a source of line current to the subject even if a component should fail.

In the area of brain wave biofeedback, filtering and detection circuits that allow only the frequencies of interest to provide feedback to the subject fall into two broad categories, analog and digital. Analog circuits deal with the signal as it comes from the amplifier, separating signals by their amplitude and frequency. Digital circuits, on the other hand, change the signal into a binary representation, for instance, either above or below zero, and then distinguish frequencies by measuring times between changes in binary state. Analog filters are primarily of the active type, employing frequency-dependent components in the feedback path of an operational amplifier. Such filters usually exhibit Butterworth characteristics, that is, they are reasonably flat within the passband and roll off at the corners of the band anywhere from 6 to 48 decibels per octave. The higher the roll-off, the greater the tendency of a filter to "ring," or to be affected by sharp, transient inputs that temporarily cause the filter to emit an output near the center of the passband. Too low a roll-off, however, can lead to the filter passing relatively unattenuated, high-amplitude activity outside the range of frequencies specified. A reasonable compromise appears to be a 24-decibel-per-octave response (4 pole). Most stand-alone filters, as well as many analog filters built into integrated units, allow independent adjustment of both the upper- and lower-corner frequencies, allowing the user to choose the width of the passband as well as its center frequency. Other filters only allow adjustment of center frequency, with a fixed relationship between center frequency and bandwidth; many less expensive models only switch preset bands or allow only one fixed band. (Sources for some stand-alone and component filters are listed in the Buyer's Guide.)

The detection of significant activity within the passband of an analog filter is usually accomplished through integration and level detection (Boudrot, 1972; Pasquali, 1969). Absolute value or precision full-wave rectifier circuits take the signal from the filter, invert the negative half of the waves, and pass the signal on to an integrator that smooths the ripple from the signal. The charge and discharge time constants of the integrator must be sufficiently long to remove the ripple, but not so long as to constitute a significant delay in detecting activity or its cessation. The decision as to whether significant activity is occurring within the passband is generally made by level-detection circuitry. Such a circuit frequently has an adjustable threshold control to allow the user to set the amount of activity within the band that is necessary for the level to be exceeded and the circuit to change to the "on" state. This "on" state is then used to gate on a feedback signal and the timers used for duration or percentage time measures.

An alternative to simple percentage time measurement is the use of a resetting integrator or voltage-controlled oscillator. In this case the greater the amplitude of activity through the filter, the greater the number of resets or the higher the oscillator frequency. Not only can the frequency be used as a feedback signal to the subject, but the number of resets or cycles during some time period becomes a measure of the amplitude of activity within the band of interest.

The alternative approach to analog filtering is digital filtering in the time domain. Such discrimination can present the user with essentially step-function cutoffs at the band edges, but does so at the loss of amplitude information. Such information can be preserved, but not through the filter. Two basic time-related techniques are used: pulse-width discrimination and time-to-amplitude conversion. In pulse-width discrimination, the analog signal, sometimes prefiltered, is fed into a zero-crossing detector that changes states when the signal crosses from positive to negative and changes back again when the signal recrosses the zero baseline. An adjustable threshold can control the minimum amplitude necessary to initiate detection of the crossing and, therefore, pulse-width discrimination. Assuming a reasonably approximate sine wave input, the length of time in one and then the other state is the wave period, the reciprocal of the frequency $(1/f)$. Either this full-wave period or the half-wave period, the length of time in one of the two states, may be tested to determine if the frequency of which it is the reciprocal falls within the passband selected. If the period is too short, the frequency is too high; if it is too long, the frequency is too low. Starting monostable multivibrators of the band-limit-period lengths at the beginning of the tested period, and gating their outputs with the duration in an appropriate way, yields an output pulse for each wave of a frequency within the passband of the filter. A retriggerable monostable or other continuity circuit can maintain a signal between output pulses for feedback gating or percentage-time measurement purposes (Paskewitz, 1971).

Time-to-amplitude conversion also detects the baseline zero crossing, but it begins to charge a capacitor when the crossing occurs and charges it until the end of the wave period. The charge is then dumped, and a peak-sampling circuit captures the amplitude of the differentiated signal as it resets. A window comparator looks at the peak amplitude and produces an output if the amplitude falls between preset limits. Since the charge on the capacitor, and hence the amplitude of the peak, is a function of the length of time it is allowed to charge, these amplitude limits will define the frequency limits of the filter. Any number of window comparators may, of course, be employed to perform detection of selected frequency bands or a complete spectral analysis (Rouse, 1974).

Since signals of large amplitude such as movement artifact can cause filter ringing in units employing analog filters, some circuits contain artifact detectors that prevent the feedback signal from occurring during periods of such artifact. While artifact is readily apparent on a chart recording, and can at least be discounted, artifact detection circuits become of greater importance in equipment designed to be used without chart recordings.

Feedback stimuli that are presented to the subject to provide information concerning the presence of alpha activity have been varied. Visual stimuli of both on–off and continuous brightness changes have been employed, as have hue changes. Auditory stimuli have ranged from white noise to pure tones that vary in pitch, loudness, or presence–absence and that may warble with brain waves as well. No studies have clearly documented the efficacy of one form over another, although subjects may have definite preferences for one or another type.

Electromyogram Biofeedback

The measurement of muscle activity through the electromyogram (EMG) has been one of the most active areas in biofeedback research. Although EMG feedback has been used for a number of years, its use has surged upward with the popularity of the biofeedback movement. Blanchard and Young (1974) distinguished four uses of EMG biofeedback in clinical practice. The first is in retraining muscles in paralyzed patients, and a second use involves training to eliminate subvocalization in reading, situations where EMG biofeedback seems to be of some utility. A third use is in teaching patients relaxation in the face of general or specific anxieties. The results in this context are, at best, unclear. Likewise, the fourth use of EMG biofeedback, treatment of tension headache through EMG relaxation training, does not allow a clear picture of the role of the biofeedback itself, even though the results of the total treatment package appear effective (Blanchard & Young, 1974; Budzynski, Stoyva, Adler, & Mullaney, 1973).

In EMG training the subject is fitted with electrodes usually placed on the forehead in the region of the *frontalis* muscle (except in the case of muscle retraining or subvocalization elimination). After relaxing, the subject is asked to lower his or her muscle activity as much as possible, using the feedback signal as a guide.

Instrumentation in this area begins with input amplifier considerations similar to those outlined for EEG recordings, that is, low-noise, high-gain amplifiers with high common mode rejection and high input impedance, that are battery operated and that usually contain a 60-Hz notch filter. Additional filtering is carried out to remove frequencies below 80–100 Hz, primarily EEG and heart interference. High-frequency cutoffs above 250–350 Hz may also be employed. The EMG activity, consisting of a large number of random firings from the portion of muscle under the electrodes, is usually smoothed by integration. As with EEG devices, the choice of integrator time constants can affect the quality of the signal considerably. A short time constant causes the integral to follow rapid changes in EMG amplitude, almost down to the level of individual motor unit firings. Such a signal, while reflecting instantaneous level, may confuse the subject by changing spontaneously, seemingly without the subject meaning to change it. A long time constant, on the other hand, yields changes based only on the gross general level of activity under the electrodes and may change too slowly to reflect attempted changes on the part of the subject. (Many of the instruments listed in the Buyer's Guide allow the user to adjust the time constant, either continuously or in discrete steps.)

Some instruments provide a readout of the averaged EMG. This readout may take the form of an analog meter (often with two or more scales for high- and lower-level signals) or may be a digital display. The latter is usually achieved by allowing the averaged EMG to control a resetting integrator or voltage-controlled oscillator and counting the frequency of reset or oscillation for some fixed period of time. This method of display has the advantage of providing quantifiable data for research purposes, particularly if the frequency is calibrated in some absolute scale like microvolts per second.

Feedback information to the subject usually takes the form of a tone, where the pitch of the tone follows the integrated EMG level. The relationship between the change in EMG level and the change in pitch of the tone is usually adjustable according to the wishes of the user. There may also be a minimum threshold below which changes in EMG are not reflected in the tone. Another popular form of auditory feedback consists of sharp clicks, the rate of which reflects the averaged EMG level. Sometimes different-colored lights are used to inform the subject whether he is doing well, poorly, or otherwise.

Temperature Biofeedback

Skin temperature biofeedback has been suggested as an effective treatment for migraine headaches (Sargent, Green, & Walters, 1973) or for Raynaud Syndrome (Surwit, 1973). In either case, warming the extremities is said to control the symptoms. Clinical evidence concerning the effectiveness of such feedback has not been particularly convincing (Blanchard & Young, 1974).

The biofeedback of skin temperature is accomplished through the use of a small, temperature-sensitive thermistor bead, taped to the skin wherever desired. The size of this bead determines, in large part, the rapidity with which the instrument responds. This thermal lag inherent in the sensor eliminates the need to average the signal, necessary in most other feedback modalities. The resistance of the bead changes with its temperature, but not in an entirely linear fashion. For this reason, a correction for nonlinearity is almost always built into the circuit. Some instruments have provision for more than one sensor bead and may allow for the determination of temperature difference between the two sensors. These can be placed at two different locations, the forehead and forearm, for instance, in cases of migraine treatment. Readout of the temperature may be accomplished by an analog meter or by a digital display. Most instruments have some provision for reading both absolute temperature of the site and relative temperature, which simply involves expanding the readout scale so that changes of a fraction of a degree result in large changes of the display. Most instruments provide for an auditory feedback mode, either clicks, tone bursts, or a continuous tone that reflects the changes in temperature. Some instruments may have light displays that show levels or direction of change as well. For personal use or general clinical situations the absolute accuracy of the instrument may not be of particular importance. However, research needs dictate that both accuracy and linearity be as high as possible. Full-scale sensitivity of one tenth a degree is hardly useful if drift, noise, or other shortcomings create greater than one-degree error.

Heart Rate Biofeedback

Biofeedback of the electrocardiogram (EKG) has, with few exceptions, focused on alterations in heart rate. Much of the work in heart rate biofeedback has been pursued as basic research into the parameters of voluntary control of autonomic functions (Brener & Hothersall, 1966; Schwartz,

Shapiro, & Tursky, 1971), although the primary clinical applications have been in the area of cardiac arrhythmias (Weiss & Engel, 1971). Most instrumentation in this area is built for the specific requirements of a given researcher. Basic EKG amplifier needs parallel those for EEG and EMG activity, although the stronger EKG signal requires somewhat less amplification than those signals. Following amplification the next requirement is detection of the R-wave of ventricular depolarization. Most often, simple Schmitt trigger-level detectors are used for this purpose, although these can often suffer from problems associated with baseline shifts, muscle artifacts, and variations in R-wave amplitude. Several suggestions have been advanced to help overcome these problems (James, Paul, & Wessel, 1972). Following detection some form of cardiotachometer (heart rate meter) is used to display the beat-to-beat rate represented by the period of time between each beat and the immediately preceding one. These instruments are available from the manufacturers of biomedical chart recorders and polygraphs. Some investigators have added circuits to average several beats and to inform the subject of the direction of change of the average, often with the aid of light displays. The most rudimentary instruments may merely click or chirp with each R-wave, although subjects usually have difficulty judging rate change from such information.

Galvanic Skin Response Biofeedback

Almost all galvanic skin response (GSR) biofeedback has been experimentally rather than clinically oriented (Crider, Shapiro, & Tursky, 1966; Kimmel & Hill, 1960). Instruments designed to enable biofeedback of the GSR are perhaps the least expensive of biofeedback instruments (see the Buyer's Guide) since they do not require the input amplifiers necessary to measure the EEG, EMG, or EKG signals, and frequently they do not possess the degree of accuracy necessary for useful temperature measurement. The typical circuit places the subject electrodes in one arm of a resistance bridge. A voltage is applied to this bridge, and the output of the bridge is usually amplified for further use. The best circuits are either constant voltage or constant current designs, which hold one or the other parameter constant across the subject for changes in subject resistance. Inexpensive designs may hold neither parameter constant, rendering these instruments unsuitable for research purposes. Many devices allow a selection of ac or dc coupling of the signal (a feature that allows the user

to monitor either the absolute level of skin resistance, along with transient changes, when dc coupled or only transient changes with ac coupling). Readouts typically include either a meter, a voltage-controlled oscillator, or both.

Blood Pressure Biofeedback

Blood pressure biofeedback in human subjects is aimed toward a reduction of hypertension and is almost always accomplished through indirect measurement using a standard inflatable cuff (Shapiro, Tursky, Gershon, & Stern, 1969; Tursky, Shapiro, & Schwartz, 1972). The cuff is commonly placed on the upper arm and a microphone placed distal to the cuff. The cuff is inflated to a pressure as close as possible to systolic pressure. Under these circumstances the presence of a Korotkoff sound at the sensor indicates that the systolic pressure at that particular heart beat was sufficient to overcome cuff pressure. The absence of the sound, conversely, means a systolic pressure lower than cuff pressure. The presence or absence of these sounds may be directly indicated to the subject if the cuff pressure is kept constant for a given period of time, resulting in beat-by-beat feedback. Logic circuits may be employed to determine automatically the point at which 50% of the heart beats result in Korotkoff sounds, the systolic pressure. Cuff pressure may be raised or lowered to follow the general trend of systolic pressure.

General Comments

For anyone interested in acquiring biofeedback instrumentation, several considerations should be resolved. The personal use of biofeedback devices is probably a matter of deciding if the features and reliability of available devices warrant the cost involved. Alternatively, individuals with some electronic sophistication may choose to build their own devices of modest performance, following circuits published in electronics magazines (Lutus, 1974; Waite, 1973). For the professional, the choices depend on the intended use of the instrument. If the device is used primarily for teaching biofeedback principles to groups, the user may wish to consider one of the several compatible component systems that have input amplifiers, filters, integrators, level detectors, oscillators, audio amplifiers, and the like with uncommitted inputs and outputs that can be interconnected in a variety of ways to demonstrate biofeedback techniques. (Sources of such systems are listed in the Buyer's Guide.) Those who foresee their work as restricted to clinical applications, and who do not anticipate quantifying activity for a particular measure, will probably be satisfied with one of the commercially available instruments designed for clinical settings. If a clinician's needs include quantification (a probable need if he or she engages in clinical research that demonstrates performance levels on the part of patients), then the clinician will want to consider either the more sophisticated commercial equipment or a specially designed collection of instruments that meet these particular circumstances, since the clinician with research interests will be dissatisfied with a clinical instrument that lacks a means of quantifying the physiological data. The clinical user of biofeedback equipment is also likely to be dissatisfied with the performance of devices intended for personal use, unless these devices are being considered for home use by particular patients.

Those professionals whose interests lie primarily in biofeedback research will doubtless continue to develop unique collections of equipment specific to their needs, especially in light of the close ties between biofeedback research and electronic technology and the need for both versatility and accuracy. Such arrays will probably give way to computer control and analysis in some situations. With either hardware or computer systems, the researcher must, unless he or she is electronically sophisticated and/or skilled in computer programming, rely on technical assistance. The availability of such assistance may be a major factor in determining research direction. Alternatively, the less technically sophisticated researcher may wish to consider one of the better clinical research devices with custom modifications or consult with manufacturers regarding custom arrays of equipment or special instruments. In any case, the availability of a wide range of devices of varying quality, price, sophistication, and application makes it likely that most problems in biofeedback will continue to be conceptual and behavioral rather than technological in nature.

REFERENCES

Beatty, J. Effects of initial alpha wave abundance and operant training procedures on occipital alpha and beta wave activity. *Psychonomic Science*, 1971, *23*, 197–199.

Beatty, J. Similar effects of feedback signals and instructional information on EEG activity. *Physiology and Behavior*, 1972, *9*, 151–154.

Blanchard, E. B., & Young, L. D. Clinical applications of biofeedback training: A review of evidence. *Archives of General Psychiatry*, 1974, *30*, 573–589.

Boudrot, R. An alpha detection and feedback control system. *Psychophysiology*, 1972, *9*, 461–466.

Brener, J. M., & Hothersall, D. Heart rate control under conditions of augmented sensory feedback. *Psychophysiology*, 1966, *3*, 23–28.

Brown, B. B. Recognition of aspects of consciousness through association with EEG alpha activity represented by a light signal. *Psychophysiology*, 1970, *6*, 442–452.

Brown, B. B. Awareness of EEG-subjective activity relationships detected within a closed feedback system. *Psychophysiology*, 1970, 7, 451–464.

Budzynski, T. H., Stoyva, J. M., Adler, C. S., & Mullaney, D. J. EMG biofeedback and tension headache: A controlled outcome study. *Psychosomatic Medicine*, 1973, *35*, 484–496.

Crider, A. B., Shapiro, D., & Tursky, B. Reinforcement of spontaneous electrodermal activity. *Journal of Comparative and Physiological Psychology*, 1966, *61*, 20–27.

Hart, J. T. Autocontrol of EEG alpha. *Psychophysiology*, 1968, *4*, 506. (Abstract)

James, G. W., Paul, M. H., & Wessel, H. U. Precision digital heart rate meter. *Journal of Applied Physiology*, 1972, *32*, 718–723.

Kamiya, J. Conscious control of brain waves. *Psychology Today*, April 1968, pp. 57–60.

Kamiya, J. Operant control of the EEG alpha rhythm and some of its reported effects on consciousness. In C. Tart (Ed.), *Altered states of consciousness: A book of readings*. New York: Wiley, 1969.

Kimmel, H. D., & Hill, F. A. Operant conditioning of the GSR. *Psychological Reports*, 1960, *7*, 555–562.

Legewie, H., & Probst, W. On-line analysis of the EEG with a small computer (period-amplitude analysis). *Electroencephalography and Clinical Neurophysiology*, 1969, *27*, 533–535.

Lutus, P. Simplified biofeedback circuit detects alpha-wave activity. *Electronic Design*, 1974, *22*(12), 154.

Lynch, J. J., & Paskewitz, D: A. On the mechanisms of the feedback control of human brain wave activity. *The Journal of Nervous and Mental Disease*, 1971, *153*, 205–217.

Nowlis, D. P., & Kamiya, J. The control of electroencephalographic alpha rhythms through auditory feedback and the associated mental activity. *Psychophysiology*, 1970, *6*, 476–484.

Paskewitz, D. A. A hybrid circuit to indicate the presence of alpha activity. *Psychophysiology*, 1971, *8*, 107–112.

Paskewitz, D. A., & Orne, M. T. Visual effects on alpha feedback training. *Science*, 1973, *181*, 360–363.

Pasquali, E. A relay controlled by alpha rhythm. *Psychophysiology*, 1969, *6*, 207–208.

Rouse, L. O. Some instrumentation and methodology for EEG biofeedback. *Proceedings of the Biofeedback Research Society Annual Meeting*, 1974, p. 109.

Sargent, J. D., Green, E. E., & Walters, E. D. Preliminary report on the use of autogenic feedback training in the treatment of migraine and tension headaches. *Psychosomatic Medicine*, 1973, *35*, 129–135.

Schwartz, G. E., Shapiro, D., & Tursky, B. Learned control of cardiovascular integration in man through operant conditioning. *Psychosomatic Medicine*, 1971, *33*, 57–62.

Shapiro, D., Tursky, B., Gershon, E., & Stern, M. Effects of feedback and reinforcement on the control of human systolic blood pressure. *Science*, 1969, *163*, 588–589.

Surwit, R. S. Biofeedback: A possible treatment for Raynaud's disease. In L. Birk (Ed.), *Biofeedback: Behavioral medicine*. New York: Grune & Stratton, 1973.

Tursky, B., Shapiro, D., & Schwartz, G. E. Automated constant cuff pressure system to measure average systolic and diastolic blood pressure in man. *IEEE Transactions on Bio-medical Engineering*, 1972, *19*, 271–276.

Vaitl, D., & Kenkmann, H-J. Stabilisation der Pulsfrequenz durch visuelle Rückmeldung. *Zeitschrift für Klinische Psychologie*, 1972, *1*, 251–271.

Waite, M. Build an alpha brain wave feedback monitor. *Popular Electronics*, January 1973, *3*, 40–45.

Walsh, D. H. Interactive effects of alpha feedback and instructional set on subjective state. *Psychophysiology*, 1974, *11*, 428–435.

Weiss, T., & Engel, B. T. Operant conditioning of heart rate in patients with premature ventricular contractions. *Psychosomatic Medicine*, 1971, *33*, 301–321.

Buying Biofeedback 66

Daniel A. Girdano

Until recently, it was believed that the autonomic nervous system, programmed by nature to respond to physical needs and instincts, was not significantly influenced by the higher voluntary cortex. Recent neurophysiological information along with the resurgence of yoga, meditation, and the general desire to alter one's state of consciousness has led to the conclusion that one can, in fact, control consciousness and influence some basic autonomic functions of the body. Thousands are trying to learn such control. Some of these seekers of altered states have been successful, but others have become frustrated, using hit-and-miss techniques haphazardly obtained from friends, lectures, and magazine articles. The search for a passive shortcut to nirvana via "mechanical gurus" has helped to make learning to control one's state of consciousness a big business. Peruse the advertisement section in any of the popular scientific journals and you will find a myriad of psychophysiological instruments and techniques for sale: electromyograph biofeedback, electroencephalograph biofeedback, alpha/theta brainwave monitors, galvanic skin response monitors, thermal trainers, plethysmo-monitors, dream recall machines, along with meditation, ESP techniques, biorhythms and Kirlian photography kits. To add to the confusion, one finds advertisements for instruments ranging in price from $29.95 to $10,000 on the same page. It is difficult for the reader to know whether the increased expenditure necessary to obtain the more expensive model buys needed sophistication or fancy woodgrain luxury. Those confused novitiates should not feel left out, for at recent A.M.A. and A.P.A. conventions physicians, psychiatrists and psychologists alike ordered up a variety of electronic junk. However, one can substantially cut his losses by knowing a little bit about electronics and some basics about the psychophysiological parameter to be measured or trained.

Reprinted with permission of the author.

Knowledge of the psychophysiological system to be trained is essential in the decision concerning which equipment to purchase. Biofeedback systems involve the sensing of bioelectrical signals being emitted by the body and the subsequent or giving back of those signals in a form which is familiar or recognizable by the senses we have learned to perceive--mainly sight and sound. The body constantly communicates its activities and most of us have learned to key into the more obvious feelings, sounds, and outward signs of mind-body interaction such as hunger pangs, diarrhea, and constipation as indicators of gastrointestinal status.

Departure from the obvious, readable signs of mind-body inter-action (such as brain waves, smooth muscle action, blood pressure, skin temperature) demands progressively more sophistication in signal-receiving, modulation, and feedback. If gross muscle ten-sion is the parameter for study, less electronic sophistication is necessary than for the detection of one-tenth of a degree digital temperature change. Because of the endless range of psychophysiological parameters to be studied, there can be some leeway in equipment, but to match a delicate parameter with a crude machine is like trying to eat crab legs with a claw hammer. The difference in instruments runs the gamut from home trainers to highly selective research equipment.

BIOFEEDBACK INSTRUMENTS

Biofeedback equipment can be classified as (1) home trainers, which are relatively inexpensive and virtually worthless ($99.95-$250.00), (2) clinical trainers, which are useful and fairly ac-curate, but limited in versatility ($500-$1,000), and (3) research units which are amazing, but expensive ($1,000-$10,000).

THE HOME TRAINERS

Tension Reducers. The instruments in this class are fraught with drawbacks. They lack sensitivity, accuracy, and filtering capaci-ty. One generally does not need an instrument to distinguish the difference between 10 and 50 microvolts (the energy output of a relaxed versus a contracted muscle). What is needed is an instru-ment which can distinguish a resting muscle from a relaxed muscle, a variation of between 1 and 10 microvolts. Most home trainers are not sensitive enough to sense such low voltage changes nor are they sophisticated enough to filter out environmental or instru-ment noise. Likewise, the "time in loop" or delay between energy output and feedback is so long that it is difficult to determine what feeling or movement caused the change in feedback sound.

Instant Zen. The most popular feedback system is the alpha/theta brainwave instrument which roughly resembles an EEG. The popularity of yoga and meditation has increased the interest in these instru-ments as an adjunct to meditation or as an alternate training method. Again, the lack of sensitivity and filtering capacity allows for false signals to trigger the feedback sound. There are

numerous reports of individuals who, simply by moving or focusing
the eyes trigger the feedback and think they are meditating because
their alpha trainers are sounding off. False feedback can be produced by improper placement of electrodes, improper technique or
preparing the placement site, inability of the instrument to filter
out muscle twitches, eye movement, swallowing movements, heart
beats, or electrical noise.

Yet the alpha faddists gain in popularity as they attribute the
learning of mind control, intuition, accelerated healing, control
of pain, increase in I.Q., improved sleep, even the loss of weight
to those little 8-12 Hz brainwaves. There is nothing mystical or
magical about alpha. Alpha is a slow synchronized wave, common
to the normal EEG. Everyone has it--when you close your eyes,
bursts of alpha appear. It is more difficult to willfully stay
in alpha for any length of time than to produce it in spurts, but
individuals can be trained to do so. Monitoring summated brain
waves merely indicates the general level of brain activity. For
example, in the beta state (often referred to as non-alpha and
characterized by low, fast waves) the brain is usually working
faster and is involved in more analytical thinking than when one
is in alpha. That does not say anything about the quality of
thinking or about right or wrong analysis, it just indicates that
the brain is more active. Certainly not all thinking activity is
stressful. One may be in a beta state, thinking, problem solving,
feeling challenged, but not threatened, and be quite relaxed.
However, while beta does not necessarily mean arousal, arousal
almost always occurs during beta; and conversely, one seldom
encounters physiological arousal during alpha. Reducing arousal
or inducing tranquility yields many obvious benefits, but there
is little evidence to support most of the popular fad claims
made for alpha.

It is well to remember that frequency of brain waves is only
one-dimension--another is amplitude of the wave or energy output.
Recent evidence suggests that the brain activity which generates
60-microvolt alpha. Most trainers are set to trigger feedback
at only one energy output level and cannot be adjusted. If the
instrument is set too high, the user may be in alpha, but getting
no feedback; thus confusing and retarding learning. If set too
low, learning may likewise be hampered.

Safety. In the testimony given before the recent Congressional
hearings which investigated the safety of medical devices, it was
emphasized that, to date, there exists no documentation evidenc-
ing harm resulting from the use of a biofeedback instrument.
Nevertheless, it is fortunate that most inexpensive home trainers
are battery operated, as electrostatic (or Faraday) shields which
protect the user from electric shock are not mandatory in the
United States.

Policing safety and effectiveness of manufactured products is a
difficult task as is evidenced by the attempt to control ver-the-
counter drugs. It seems more feasible to focus on the promotion
and advertising of such instruments, as few of them can live up to

promotional claims. And while the systems are not harmful, they are a diversion of time and money and constitute a consumer health problem.

RESEARCH EQUIPMENT

Research equipment is expensive, but the $5,000 to $10,000 investment buys sophistication and capacities not found in the home trainers or clinical training models. It buys sensitivity, diverse forms of feedback, data acquisition, instant response, and programmable logic.

Whether sensing the muscle potentials of a paraplegic who has very few, if any, motor units, or in the training of deep neuromuscular relaxation, one is concerned with energy in the 1 to 5 microvolt range. The instrument also needs to sense changes of one microvolt so that the feedback signal will change with such minute energy changes. A good research unit needs to accurately sense a 0.5 microvolt signal and have less than one microvolt of instrument noise.

The increased expenditure should also buy stimulus synthesis. A good research training instrument should have the capability of delivering several types of feedback because what turns one person on may be annoying to another. Simple meter or tone feedback may be applicable in some situations, but in others an experimenter may need lights, numerical readouts, variable tone, tone off and on, or a compound stimuli synthesis of lights and sound together. In many systems external sources of sound such as stereo music can be used as feedback.

Essential to any research effort is data acquisition which is available only on expensive units--EMG energy in microvolt/seconds, time in alpha, exact temperature in tenths or hundredths of degrees, heart rate, blood pressure--just to mention a few possibilities. Most newer instruments are now bypassing the time-consuming polygraph and record such information in a digital format, which is ready to be plugged into stastical formulae. If one is really hurting for places to spend money, the digital data can be plugged directly into a computer.

Another important feature of research equipment is speed in loop. A drawback to many clinical and home trainers is that they have slow or delayed feedback. Without accurate and instant tracking of the physical event, one is not completely sure which feeling or movement elicited the feedback response. This not only slows learning, but confuses stimulus-response research. The better instruments work at 0.1 megahertz.

One final consideration which one may think a luxury (until challenging instrument flexibility in various experimental applications) is programmable logic. Timing, gating, shaping signals, adjusting time constants, and detecting levels allows for great versatility of experimental design.

CLINICAL TRAINERS

The clinical trainers might be classified as the "in-betweens." They lie between the home trainers and research units in price, sensitivity, versatility and overall quality. Most systems are sensitive enough to measure minute fluctuations in energy, but are inferior to research units in noise immunity and filtering capacity. They can accurately sense the energy of resting muscles and are adequate for most training procedures. The feedback loop leaves a little to be desired, but is usually sufficient for most applications of relaxation training. Clinical trainers are not made for data collection, an item which is not necessary for training. Likewise, they lack versatility in types of feedback, which may limit use in certain situations.

An important factor is that these trainers are used by technicians trained in the placement and application of electrodes, thus eliminating a common source of error. When used for the purpose for which they were designed by qualified personnel with knowledge of limitations, such systems can be an adequate compromise, especially when money and portability are important factors.

SUMMARY

Biofeedback can be considered one of the most significant biomedical advancements of our times. Although used in the practice of medicine, biofeedback must be considered as an educational tool, giving information which can aid one in the learning of self control. Often such control can eliminate the cause of exacerbation of a physical condition which may lead to disease. Biofeedback is not as practical as meditation or autosensory neuromuscular relaxation, but it is more efficient and is exact enough for research. As always, the faddist, the instant seekers and fastbuck promoters are finding ways to misuse and to bilk. Likewise, many serious educators and researchers with little money and experience are having difficulty in buying and using biofeedback. My advice to these consumers is to:

1. Do some homework. Match up system specifications with desired application. Check specifications for gain, sensitivity, input impedence, feedback control and versatility, noise immunity, sensitivity (especially minimum signal detectable), calibration, and filter band with 60 hertz rejection. Some units even have built-in electrode testing capabilities.

2. Do comparison shopping. There are many good systems available at competitive prices. It is possible to buy more system than one needs, but most often buying versatility allows for expansion of application as knowledge of possibilities is enhanced. An article by Robert L. Schwitzgebel and John D. Rugh, "Biofeedback Apparatus: List of Suppliers," *Behavior Therapy* 1975, pp. 6238-6240, may be of some assistance.

3. Read the research or clinical reports as to what instruments are being used, and communicate with those individuals doing the type of work in which you are interested.

4. As always, be leery of advertising claims, even those with scientific footnotes. Be concerned with warranties and unless your staff includes an electrical engineer, check the instruction manual for clarity and ease of application. Likewise, check the company's track record for standing behind its product.

5. Do not be afraid to use the technical sales staff of a company or feel obligated by such assistance. Most reputable companies are willing to spend time educating for, in the long run, knowledge of equipment will sell good equipment.

NAME INDEX

Ackerman, P. T, 308
Adler, C., 103, 137
Adrian, E. D., 270
Akutsu, K., 55
Alexander, A. B., 211, 308
Allison, J., 54
Anand, B. K., 52, 56
Armington, J. C., 261
Arnold, M. B., 4
Axelrod, J., 402

Bagchi, B. K., 52, 53
Balshan, I., 208
Banquet, J. P., 65
Barber, T. X., 13, 126, 128, 129, 190
Barnes, R. H., 175
Basmajian, J. V., 13, 44, 45, 480, 521
Beatty, J., 264
Bell, I., 27
Benson, H., 28, 69, 75, 78, 95, 218, 372, 398, 402, 407
Bergman, J. S., 298
Bernstein, D. A., 176
Birk, L., 237
Birren, J. E., 255
Bishop, G. H., 255
Blanchard, E. B., 211, 237, 298, 303, 361, 415, 418
Bleecher, E. R., 373
Boddy, J., 255, 260
Bolles, R. C., 4
Borkovec, T. D., 176
Brady, J. P., 418, 420
Brazier, M.A.B., 440
Breger, L., 552
Brener, J., 14, 298, 311, 361, 365
Bridger, A. A., 138
Briggs, A. H., 371

Brod, J., 95
Bromfeld, E., 26
Brooks, H., 552
Brown, B.B., 240
Brudny, J., 376
Budzynski, T. H., 134, 137, 178, 179, 180, 183, 195, 202, 218, 375, 481

Calverly, D. S., 126, 129
Carrington, P., 71
Cleaves, C., 202
Cleeland, C. S., 269, 521
Connor, W. H., 357
Crider, A., 3
Curtis, G. C., 308

Dahlstrom, W. G., 143
Das, N. N., 52, 53, 54
Davidson, R. J., 26
Deibler, W. P., 264, 365, 407
Dewan, E. M., 247
DiCara, L., 40, 134, 229
Dillenkoffer, R. L., 365, 407
Dykman, R. A., 308

Ehrisman, W. J., 175
Ekman, P. W., 23
Elder, S. T., 365, 407, 415
Ellsworth, D. W., 521
Ellsworth, P., 23
Emurian, C., 282, 286
Engel, B. T., 330, 344, 357, 373
Engstrom, D., 244
Ephron, H. S., 71

Fairchild, M. D., 426
Feldman, S. E., 5
Felton, G. S., 521

Fetz, E. E., 41
Fichtler, H., 176
Finley, W. W., 440
Finnochio, D. V., 41
Fisher, C., 126
Fleishman, E. Z., 14
Fokkema, S. D., 502
Fowles, D. C., 305
Fox, R. S., 7
Franks, C. M., 552
French, C. A., 211
Friar, L., 425, 441
Friesen, V., 23

Galbrecht, C. R., 308
Gale, A., 270
Galin, D., 233
Galton, F., 552
Gannon, L., 148
Garton, W. H., 481
Gastaut, H., 52, 53, 54
Gatchel, R., 344
Gelder, M. G., 190
Gellhorn, E., 358
Germana, J., 14
Gershon, E., 360
Goldstein, I. B., 191
Goleman, D. J., 29
Goodman, N. J., 211
Gorman, P. J., 511, 520
Goyeche, J.R.M., 55
Graham, D. T., 22
Granda, A. M., 261
Gray, S. J., 5
Green, A. M., 190, 218
Green, E. E., 135, 190, 218, 288, 375
Greenburg, A., 264
Greenfield, N. S., 308
Grenfell, R. F., 371
Grinker, R. R., 4
Grinspoon, L., 305
Grynbaum, B. B., 376

Hahn, K. W., 190
Hamma, H., 282
Harbison, J., 529
Hardyck, C. D., 521
Hart, J., 243
Hartley, J., 244
Headrick, M. W., 301, 312
Hilgard, E. R., 107
Hill, F. A., 543
Hill, R., 58
Hinkle, J. E., 175
Holland, W. C., 371
Horande, M., 481

Izard, C. E., 23, 31

Jacobs, A., 521

Jacobson, E., 176, 190, 212, 218, 379, 390
Janes, C. L., 308
James, W., 4, 31
Jasper, H. H., 255
Johnson, H. J., 298
Johnson, V. E., 510
Jones, R. C., 261
Johnson, H. E., 481

Kamiya, J., 13, 134, 240, 269, 425, 511, 520
Kaplan, B., 375, 426
Kaplan, N., 320
Kasamatsu, A., 52, 55
Katkin, E. S., 3, 4, 22
Katz, J., 126
Kewman, D. G., 281, 369
Kimmel, E., 58
Kimmel, H. D., 22, 543
Kleinman, R. A., 361, 365
Kohn, S., 282
Korein, J., 376
Korzybski, A., 551
Krakaner, L. J., 5
Kranzberg, M., 552
Kron, R., 418
Kruglanski, A., 242
Kuhlman, W. N., 445

Lacey, B. C., 358
Lacey, J. L., 358
Ladd, H. W., 481
Lang, P. J., 14, 298, 350, 351, 357
Laws, D. R., 529
Lazarus, A. A., 30
Lehmann, D., 56
Lehrer, P. M., 190
Levenson, R. W., 298
Lief, H. I., 7
Loder, M. H., 190
London, P., 552
LoPresti, R. W., 426
Love, W. A., 190
Lubin, A., 261, 264
Luborsky, L., 418
Luderman, P. H., 308
Luthe, W. L., 61, 167, 218
Lynch, J. J., 230
Lynch, W. C., 282

MacDonald, H., 281, 369
Maer, F., 26
Maher, B. A., 305
Marinacci, A. A., 481
Marshall, G., 281, 369
Marston, A. R., 5
Maslach, C., 281, 286, 369
Mason, J. W., 4
Masters, W. H., 510
Mathews, A. M., 190
McAllister, H., 529

McClelland, D., 551
McGaugh, J. L., 552
McKenzie, R., 175
Melzack, R., 163
Mendelsohn, G. A., 9
Menzies, R., 122
Meyer, R. G., 190
Miller, N., 13, 40, 74, 134, 281, 282, 286, 349,
    370, 415, 543
Moeller, T. A., 190
Montgomery, W., 175
Mornell, L. K., 260
Mowrer, O. H., 552
Mowrer, W. M., 552
Mulholland, T., 247
Mullaney, D. J., 183
Murphy, G., 190
Murray, E. N., 3, 4, 22

Nachmansohn, M., 126
Naranjo, C., 56
Newman, R., 126, 130
Neyers, M. A., 28
Nowlis, D. P., 240, 269

Obrist, P. A., 271, 357
O'Hanlon, J. F., 264
Orme-Johnson, D. W., 54
Orne, M. T., 243, 270, 274-275
Ornstein, R., 233
Otis, L., 68

Paskewitz, D. A., 230, 243, 270, 274-275
Pawlowski, A. V., 529
Penfield, W., 70
Peper, E., 247
Persky, H., 308
Petrinovitch, L. F., 521
Pfaundler, M., 552
Plotkin, W. B., 247
Price, D. J., 552
Price, K. P., 529

Quinn, J., 529

Rahe, R. H., 5
Ramsey, C. S., 5
Ray, W. J., 298
Reese, W. G., 308
Regestein, Q. R., 270
Riddick, C., 190
Roberts, A. H., 281, 282, 289, 369
Roessler, R., 287, 308
Rosen, R. C., 529
Rubinstein, R., 126
Ruiz, R. Z., 365, 407

Sargent, J. D., 135, 288, 375
Schmidt, R. R., 452
Schultz, J. H., 167, 218, 221

Schwartz, G., 3, 6, 19, 26, 27, 28, 29, 53, 54,
    134, 135, 218, 318, 324, 360, 365, 379, 407
Selye, H., 4, 5, 75
Shaines, N., 143
Shapiro, D., 13, 17, 308, 360, 364, 372, 407, 415
Shapiro, G., 134, 135
Shapiro, M. M., 543
Shearn, D. W., 543
Sheffield, F. D., 543
Shnidman, S., 3
Shor, R. E., 106
Shroetter, K., 126
Simard, T. G., 481
Skinner, B. F., 552
Spiegel, H., 138, 143
Spiegel, J. P., 4
Sprague, L. Y., 163
Sroufe, L. A., 350
Sterman, M. B., 375, 425, 426, 428, 429, 440,
    441
Stern, J. A., 308
Stern, M., 360
Stern, R., 320
Sternbach, R. A., 148
Stoyva, J., 13, 127, 130, 134, 137, 183, 195, 202,
    218, 375
Strayer, F., 269
Strupp, H. H., 298
Sugi, Y., 55
Surwillo, W. W., 254, 255, 259, 260
Swaan, D., 502
Sypert, G. W., 452

Tasto, D. L., 175
Taub, E., 282, 286
Thorndike, E. L., 367
Trombly, C., 481
Tursky, B., 19, 360, 407
Twentyman, C., 250, 298, 357

Ullman, M., 117

van Wieringen, P.C.W., 502
Villarreal, R., 5

Wallace, R. K., 28, 53, 54, 60, 78, 80, 218
Walters, E. D., 135, 190, 218, 288, 375
Ward, A. A., 452
Watt, N. R., 305
Wegner, M. A., 52, 53
Weil, A., 118
Weiner, B., 4, 6
Weinshilboum, R., 402
Weiss, J. M., 229
Weiss, T., 373
Weisz, A. Z., 163
Weitzenhoffer, A., 122
Welgan, P. R., 512, 513
Welsh, G. S., 143
Wickramesekera, I., 175, 481

Williams, H. L., 261
Wilson, A. F., 78
Wilson, J. W., 308
Witkin, H. A., 129, 130
Wolberg, L. R., 122
Wolpe, J., 9, 61, 195, 218, 221
Wyrwicka, W., 426

Young, L. D., 211, 237, 303, 415, 418, 361
Younger, J., 81

Zimbardo, P. G., 281, 369
Zimmerman, R. R., 176
Zuckerman, M., 308

SUBJECT INDEX

Age regression, 102, 104
  under hypnosis, 111
Agglutinating antibody, 539-542
Alpha enhancement
  and use in migraine headache experiment,
    137-143
Alpha rhythm, 448
Alpha state, 150, 154-155
  in pain experiment, 160-163
  and stress, 59
Alpha waves, 375
  blood pressure, 339
  and heart rate, 20-21
  left sensory motor area, 28
  and migraine headaches, 72
  and seizures, 444
  and transcendental meditation, 53
  and yoga, 52
  and Zen, 56
Alpha wave devices, 552-556
Alpha-theta wave device, 567-568
Analog filter, 554
Anesthesia effect
  under hypnosis, 102, 104
Animal
  cat, sensorimotor rhythm, 426, 440
  monkey, 450
  physiological control, 228
  rats, and taste aversion, 536-542
Anxiety, 8, 9, 191, 192, 201, 218, 222
  "direct action", 8, 9
  Freudian, 7
  palliative, 8, 9
  transactional language, 6
  self regulation, 8, 9
Apparatus
  in alpha/age experiment, 256
  in alpha enhancement, 238

in alpha/light experiment, 271
in blood pressure experiment, 379-380, 412,
  418
and EEG experiment, 20
in epilepsy study, 429-432, 441
in expectations experiment, 243-244
in gastric acid secretion study, 511-512
in headache experiment, 183-184, 191, 196
in heart rate experiment, 299, 303-304, 311,
  325, 331-332, 350-351, 355, 361
in hypnosis experiment, 118
in hypnotic suggestibility experiment, 283
in motor training experiment, 482
in migraine headache experiment, 137-138
in occipital alpha experiment, 247-248
in ocular accommodation experiment, 526
in pain experiment, 150
in penile tumescence experiment, 504, 530
in relaxation experiment, 203, 212-213, 219
in salivation experiment, 544
in skin temperature experiment, 283-284, 289-
  290
in sleep deprivation experiment, 264
in stuttering experiment, 522
in voluntary movement experiment, 474
in visceral response experiment, 166
Arrhythmias
  atrial fibrillation, 45
  complete heart block (CHB), 346-348
  premature ventricular contraction, 346-348,
    373-374
  tachycardia, 373-374
Asthma, 201
Atrio-ventricular conduction, 346-348
Artifact, and alpha wave activity, 242-245
Auditory hallucination under hypnosis, 103-105
Autogenic training, 202, 288-292
Autonomic control patterns, 26

Autonomic nervous system
　　systolic, 15-18
　　diastolic, 19
　　EEG, 20-21
Autonomic Perception Questionnaire, 320-323
Autonomic response, 14

Barber Suggestibility Scale, 119
Barton's Ego Strength Scale, 307
Basal skin resistance, and blood pressure, 410
Basmajian-Emory Muscle Trainer, 481, 493,
　　495-496, 498
Behavior modification, 5-6
Biofeedback clinics, 212
Blindness, and hypnosis, 117
Blood circulation, and skin temperature, 368-
　　370
Blood pressure, 5, 218
　　changing, 370-373
　　and heart rate, 15-18, 19, 304-305, 307, 311,
　　　339
　　placebo effect, 371
　　systolic, 15-18
　　and transcendental meditation, 54
　　and yoga, 53
　　and Zen, 55
Blood pressure biofeedback device, 563
Blushing, 228
Brain
　　cortical activity, 27-28
　　hemispheric asymmetry, 25-26
　　wave frequency changes, 254-261

Cardiac arrhythmias. See Arrhythmias
Cardiac control rate, 14-15
Cerebral functioning, 407
　　and blood pressure, 408-410
Cerebral palsy, 496
Christian Science, 136
Cognitive mechanisms, 22-23
Cognition, heart rate and blood pressure, 27
Coping
　　and adrenal hormone levels, 7
　　and humor, 7
　　various procedures, 8
Cortical activity
　　in monkeys, 41
　　see also, Neuron, monkey
Curare. See Drugs, curare
Curarization, in rats, 370

Delta waves, 60
Dopamine-beta-hydroxylase, and blood
　　pressure, 402-405
Drugs
　　action on cardiac anomalies, 347-348
　　and heart rate, 341
Drugs (specific)
　　alpha-methyldopa, 400
　　apomorphine, 536
　　clonidine, 93

curare, 22, 40, 74-75, 281
cyclophosphamide, 536-542
lithium chloride, 536
methlydopa, 93
Metrazol, 452
monomethylhydrozine, 426
phenobarbital, 427
penicillin, 452
reserpine, 415-416
strychnine, 452
Valium, 427
Duodenal ulcer, 512
Dystonia, 473

Electrocardiagram, 323
Electroencephalogram feedback devices, 552-
　　556, 558, 559-561
Electroencephalogram (EEG), 127, 166, 375,
　　448-449
　　and alpha activity, 43, 44, 244-245, 250
　　and blood pressure, 395, 396-397
　　and epilepsy, 426, 432-435, 441
　　and heart rate control, 20-21
　　and hemispheric asymmetry, 25-26
　　and meditation, 28, 53, 54, 68, 246
　　in monkeys, 452
　　from occipital region, 20
　　in pain experiment, 150, 154, 159-160, 162
　　in relaxation experiment, 203
　　in sleepwalking, 107-108
　　and yoga, 52
　　and Zen, 55
Electrode placement, 260
Electrode-scalp impedance, 554
Electrogastrogram, 515
Electromyogram (EMG), 190-193, 323, 474
　　and biofeedback training, 219-222
　　and blood pressure, 395, 396-397, 410
　　facial muscle, 23-25
　　frontalis, 183-188
　　and gastric acid secretion, 515
　　and headaches, 481
　　and heart rate control, 318
　　laryngeal muscle, 521-524
　　movement and skin temperature, 286
　　neuromuscular disorders, 498
　　and relaxation, 218-222
　　and skin temperature, 369
　　and torticollis, 376
EMG biofeedback device, 551-552
Exercise and cardiac anomalies, 348
Emotion, 4-7
Epilepsy, 375-376
Eye
　　movement, 270-277
　　pupil contraction, 526-528
Eye-Roll Hand Levitation Method, 137-138

Facial muscle, 23-25
Facial spasms, 473, 478

Feedback
  AM, 556
  AM-FM, 556
  analogue, 350, 357
  auditory, 176, 180, 219, 230, 231-233, 238-
    240, 257, 264, 266, 282, 289-290, 303,
    304, 312, 360, 365, 431, 499-500
  binary, 15, 349-350
  false, 266, 269
  FM, 556
  positive-negative, 324-329
  random, 360, 365
  and tension headaches, 175
  tone burst, 556
  visual, 219, 309, 360, 365, 395, 413, 499-500
  visceral organ, 331, 336-337
Feedback techniques and heart rate control,
    297-301
Filter bandwidth, 554

Galvanic skin response (GSR), 60, 320-323
  and alpha, 323
  and asthma, 87-88
  and transcendental meditation, 65, 68
GSR biofeedback device, 563
General adaptation syndrome, 4-5

Harvard Group Scale of Hypnotic
    Susceptibility, 118, 119, 120, 121, 282,
    283
Headache, 201, 496
  EMG training, 211
  migraine, 72, 73-74, 288-289, 375
  tension, 375
Heart rate, 168-169, 170, 218
  in animals, 229
  and curarization in rats, 40
  and blood pressure, 410
  and motor activity, 358
  and penile tumescence, 504, 510
  and tonal stimulus, 43-44
Heart rate biofeedback device, 562
Hemiparesis, 473, 474-476, 500
His bundles, 346
Homosexuals and heterosexual arousal, 529-
    534
Hypertension
  essential, 412-416
  and meditation, 69
Hypnosis, 39, 281-282
  dream content, 126-132
Hypnosis Induction Profile, 134, 137-143
Hypnotic suggestibility and alpha activity, 244

Input, 554-555
Input impedance, 554
Insomnia, 201
Instruments, 552-557

Jacobson-Wolpe cognitive training, 219-222

Knowledge of results, 367
Korotkoff sounds, 370, 395, 408

Langley Porter Neuropsychiatric Institute, 230
Laryngeal muscle spasm, 521
Leukemia, 7
Light and alpha wave activity, 243

Maharishi Mahesh Yogi, 53
Mantra, 69-70
Masochism, 68
Mattson's Anxiety Scale, 205
McGill Pain Questionnaire, 147
McReynold's Anxiety Behavior Checklist, 202
Meditation, 28-30, 228, 393
  and blood pressure, 393
  transcendental, 28
  Zen, 29
Method
  procedure
    in alpha/age experiment, 255-256
    in alpha enhancement experiment, 238,
      248, 252
    in alpha/light experiment, 271-272
    in asthma experiment, 84
    in blood pressure experiment, 362, 380-
      382, 394-396, 403, 408, 412-413, 418-419
    in epilepsy experiment, 441
    in expectation experiment, 243-244
    in foot drop study, 499-500
    in gastric acid secretion study, 514-515
    in headache experiment, 138-139, 176, 184,
      190-191, 196-197
    in heart rate experiment, 299, 311-313, 320,
      325-326, 332-334, 342
    in heart rate change experiment, 304
    in hypnosis experiment, 118, 283-284
    in immunosuppression experiment, 537-
      538
    in motor training experiment, 482-487
    in ocular accommodation experiment, 526-
      527
    in pain experiment, 150-155
    in penile tumescence experiment, 503, 530-
      531
    in relaxation experiment, 203, 213, 219-220
    in salivation experiment, 544-545
    in skin temperature experiment, 282-284,
      290-291
    in sleep deprivation experiment, 264
    in visceral response experiment, 166-168
  subjects
    in alpha/age experiment, 255
    in alpha enhancement experiment, 238, 252
    in alpha/light experiment, 271
    in asthma experiment, 84
    in blood pressure experiment, 15, 379, 394,
      402, 408, 412, 419
    in epilepsy experiment, 427-429, 441, 453
    in expectation experiment, 243

in finger flexion study, 496-497
in foot drop study, 499
in gastric acid secretion study, 511
in headache experiment, 136-137, 176, 183, 190, 196
in heart rate experiment, 299, 303, 311, 320, 325, 331, 347, 350, 351-352, 355, 361, 362
in hypertension experiment, 91
in hypnosis experiment, 118, 282
in immunosuppression experiment, 537
in motor training experiment, 482
in occipital alpha experiment, 247
in ocular accommodation experiment, 526
in pain experiment, 149
in penile tumescence study, 503, 530
in relaxation experiment, 202, 212, 219
in salivation experiment, 544
in skin temperature experiment, 282, 283, 239
in sleep deprivation experiment, 264
in stuttering experiment, 522
in visceral response experiment, 166
in voluntary movement experiment, 474-479
Minnesota Multiphasic Personality Inventory, 60, 61, 137-143, 286
Mooney Problem Checklist, 204, 206
Muscle activity
and blood pressure, 390-391
Muscle rigidity
under hypnosis, 100
Muscle (specific)
abductor hallucis, 482, 498
depressor, 24, 25
facial, 23-25
flexor digitorum superficialis, 496-497
flexor pallicis longus, 496-497
frontalis, 24, 25, 203, 208, 212, 215, 375
laryngeal, 521-524
masseter, 24, 25
tibialis anterior, 498
triceps brachii, 399
Muscular changes
and heart rate control, 30'
Muscular dystrophy, 370
Music and EEG, 26

Neuron, monkey
epileptic, 463-68
normal, 453, 458-459, 467-468
pyramidal tract cells, 454, 462-463, 465-468
Neuropsychology, 31
Non-rapid eye movement, 127-129, 131
Nowicki Strickland Locus of Control Scale, 176, 180

Oxygen consumption, and Zen, 56

Pain control 109-110

Pain Rating Index, 152, 155-158
Palmar skin resistance
and transcendental meditation, 54
and yoga, 52
and Zen, 55
Paralysis, 370-373
Peripheral blood flow, 228
Penile tumescence, 529-534
Polio, 370
Placebo, and hypertension, 94
Placebo effect
and alpha waves, 252
and blood pressure, 371
and headaches, 375
and hypnosis, 136
and pain, 158, 162
and paralysis, 372
and seizures, 445
Placebo group, in immunosuppression experiment, 536-541
Plasma corticosterone, 539-540
Plasma renin activity, and blood pressure, 403-405
Procedure. *See* Method, procedure
Psychoendocrinology, 5
and leukemia, 7
Psychology, 4
Psychopathology, and alpha rhythms, 60
Psychophysiology of Zen, 29
Psychotic episodes, 72
Pulmonary function, in asthma, 85
Pulse rates, 314-316

Rapid eye movement, 80
and dream recall, 127-129, 131
Raynaud's disease, 289
Reading, 211
Rehabilitation, 498-502
Relaxation, 148
and blood pressure, 17, 94, 393
and heart rate, 17
and hypnosis, 103, 105, 112
and penile tumescence, 510-511
Respiration, 169, 170
and blood pressure, 395-397
and heart rate, 30, 308, 327, 337-338, 354, 356-357
and penile tumescence, 510
and transcendental meditation, 54
and yoga, 52-53
and Zen, 55
Respiratory changes and heart rate control, 301
Results
in alpha/age experiment, 256
in alpha experience experiment, 239, 248-249, 252
in alpha/light experiment, 272-275
in blood pressure experiment, 382-388, 396-398, 403-404, 408, 413-414, 419-420

in epilepsy experiment, 432-436, 441-444, 454-465
in gastric acid secretion study, 515-519
in headache experiment, 139-141, 191-192, 197-198
in heart rate experiment, 299-300, 305-308, 321-322, 334-336, 347, 352-355, 356, 363-364
in motor training experiment, 487-491
in ocular accommodation experiment, 527
in pain experiment, 155-160
in penile tumescence study, 503-504, 531-534
in relaxation experiment, 204, 213-215, 220-221
in salivation experiment, 545
in skin temperature experiment, 284-286, 292-293
in sleep deprivation experiment, 265-267
in stuttering experiment, 522-523
in voluntary movement experiment, 474
Rolandic cortex, 440-441, 446, 449

Saccharin, 531-537
Schizophrenia, 72
Seasickness, 10
Seizures, 427
Sensorimotor rhythm, 425-439
Single motor units, 484, 496
Sino-atrial node, 346-348
Skin
    electrical activity, 43
    blister formation, 123
    see also, Galvanic skin response, palmar skin resistance
Skin conductance, 325
Skin potential, 305-308
Skin temperature, 369, 370
Skin temperature biofeedback device, 562
Sleep, and alpha rhythm, 229
Sleepwalking, 107-109
Spielberger State Anxiety Inventory, 265
Spinal cord injury, 473
Stress Without Distress, 5
Stress
    and avoidance, 9-10
    immunosuppression, 539-549
Subjects. *See* Method, subjects

Subvocalization, 521

Taste aversion, 536-542
Taylor Manifest Anxiety Scale, 323
Tellegen Absorption Scale, 282-283
Temperature
    change and blister formation, 120
    finger, 169
Thematic Apperception Test, 522-523
Tension reducing devices, 567
Thermal imagery, 289
Theta waves, 233, 264
    and blood pressure, 95
    and mantras, 59, 69
Torticollis, 376, 473, 477-479, 496
Transcendental meditation, 53-54
    and asthma, 83-88
    cardiovascular activity, 54
    electrocortical activity, 53
    electrodermal activity, 54
    as psychiatric treatment, 59-76
    and respiration, 54

Ventricular heart rate, 347-348
Vision, and alpha, 230, 247-251

Wechsler Adult Intelligence Scale and Category Test, 407-410
Welsh's factor A, 307
Wicket rhythm, 440
Wilkinson Addition Test, 265
Wilkinson Impulsivity Scale, 340, 343
Williams Word Memory, 265
Wolff-Parkinson-White syndrome, 346

Yoga, 51-53, 448
    electrocortical activity, 52
    electrodermal activity, 52
    respiration, 52
    cardiovascular activity, 53
Yogi, 52-53

Zen, 54-56
    electrocortical activity, 55
    electrodermal activity, 55
    respiration, 55
    cardiovascular response, 55